REAL ESTATE TRANSFER, FINANCE, AND DEVELOPMENT

CASES AND MATERIALS

Tenth Edition

■ ■ ■

Ann M. Burkhart

Curtis Bradbury Kellar Professor of Law
Distinguished University Teaching Professor
University of Minnesota

R. Wilson Freyermuth

John D. Lawson Professor of Law and
Curators' Distinguished Teaching Professor
University of Missouri

Christopher K. Odinet

Professor of Law and
Michael and Brenda Sandler Fellow in Corporate Law
University of Iowa College of Law

Grant S. Nelson

William H. Rehnquist Professor of Law Emeritus
Pepperdine University

Dale A. Whitman

James E. Campbell Missouri Endowed Professor of Law Emeritus
University of Missouri

AMERICAN CASEBOOK SERIES®

WEST
ACADEMIC
PUBLISHING

American Casebook Series is a trademark registered in the U.S. Patent and Trademark Office.

COPYRIGHT © 1976, 1981, 1987, 1992 WEST PUBLISHING CO.
© West, a Thomson business, 1998, 2003, 2006
© 2009 Thomson Reuters
© 2015 LEG, Inc. d/b/a West Academic
© 2021 LEG, Inc. d/b/a West Academic
    444 Cedar Street, Suite 700
    St. Paul, MN 55101
    1-877-888-1330

West, West Academic Publishing, and West Academic are trademarks of West Publishing Corporation, used under license.

Printed in the United States of America

ISBN: 978-1-68467-681-1

To
Chris, Shari, and Dub
and with special thanks to Grant and Dale

PREFACE

This is the Tenth Edition of a book on which Grant Nelson and Dale Whitman began collaborating almost 50 years ago. Notably, this is also the first edition during that period on which they have not actively participated in the editorial process.

The contributions that Grant Nelson and Dale Whitman have made to the field of mortgage law and mortgage law scholarship are immeasurable. The most notable contribution, of course, is the magisterial Restatement (Third) of Property—Mortgages, on which they served as Reporters. A quarter-century after its promulgation in 1997, the Restatement of Mortgages continues to inform and teach students, lawyers, and judges as they encounter the intricacies and nuances of mortgage law. While we would have loved to have had Grant and Dale participate in this edition— they are outstanding scholars and teachers, but they've been even better colleagues!—they understandably have chosen to spend their considerable energies enjoying the pleasures of retirement and grandchildren. Along with all practitioners, scholars, and teachers of real estate transactions and finance, we owe them an enormous debt. We hope that our stewardship of their work is a suitable installment payment on that debt.

Six years have passed since the publication of the Ninth Edition in 2015. At the time, we were emerging from the mortgage crisis precipitated by the Great Recession that began in 2007–08. Residential and commercial real estate values were stabilizing and increasing from the dramatic declines experienced during the Great Recession. Fannie Mae and Freddie Mac were once again earning substantial profits, though they remained in federal conservatorship (and remain so today), as political consensus regarding the government's proper role in the residential mortgage market remained elusive (and still remains elusive). Commercial mortgaged-backed securities (CMBS) issuances had resumed—not reaching the levels seen just prior to the Great Recession, but nearing $100 billion a year. American homeownership rates, which during the Great Recession dropped below 65% for the first time since the mid-1990s, were beginning to creep back up. As we approached 2020, and the homeownership rate reached 68.5%, many were hopeful we were getting back to normal again.

And then there was COVID-19. The economic disruption associated with the pandemic is in many respects as profound, if not more so, than the disruption of the Great Recession, because the pandemic essentially brought certain sectors of our economy to a near-halt. Mortgage defaults on shopping center properties have skyrocketed, as tenants faced with pandemic-related operational restrictions cannot pay their rents. Mortgage defaults on hotel properties have increased significantly as personal and business travel has plunged during lockdowns. Residential mortgage defaults have increased significantly as borrowers—many of whom lost jobs or income due to the pandemic, and some who are still unemployed—find themselves unable to make their full monthly payments. Executive orders and legislation adopted as a response to COVID have resulted in temporary moratoria against tenant evictions and mortgage foreclosures. These measures were certainly intended to "kick the can down the road" while the country has struggled to get the pandemic under control. But eventually the piper must be paid. As COVID-related moratoria expire, both the residential and commercial markets will experience another wave of modification requests. We may see yet another foreclosure crisis if borrowers, lenders, and servicers cannot restructure debts in a fashion that enables borrowers to save their homes and commercial projects. For this reason, the legal rules underlying our mortgage system—those governing the transfer of land; those governing the creation, transfer, modification, and enforcement of mortgage loans; and those governing the priority of conflicting liens—remain of enduring importance.

We are very pleased to welcome a new co-editor on the Tenth Edition: Professor Christopher K. Odinet of the University of Iowa College of Law. Chris is the author of the recent Cambridge University Press book *Foreclosed: Mortgage Servicing and the Hidden Architecture of Homeownership in America*. He is a prolific young scholar in commercial and consumer finance, with a special emphasis on mortgage lending and financial technology.

Despite the incorporation of much new material, the order of coverage and basic organization of this edition remain similar to previous editions. Thus, teachers who have used the book in the past should find the transition to this edition easy. Because there is far more here than can be used in a single law school course, a few comments about ways law teachers can employ the book may be helpful. Chapters Three through Seven, which deal with basic mortgage law concepts, can form the basis for a 3-credit course in "Real Estate Finance." Alternatively, Chapters One (Contracts for the Sale of Land) and Two (Deeds and Titles) could form the basis of a short "Property II" course for students whose first-year Property class did not cover conveyancing. Or, portions of Chapters One and Two can be added to the material in Chapters Three through Seven to support a three-credit or four-credit "Real Estate Transactions" course. The materials in Chapters Eight through Ten, which cover government regulation of the mortgage market and real estate development (both in traditional subdivisions and modern common interest communities), can be covered in a separate "Real Estate Development" course, or can be selectively added to the basic mortgage material in Chapters Three through Seven.

In this edition, we have streamlined and eliminated some materials included in previous editions. For example, this edition has eliminated the material formerly included in Chapter Eleven of prior editions (material on investment concepts, ground leasing, and mezzanine financing), as well as the extensive excerpt on wraparound financing included in Chapter Seven of prior editions. With the assistance of West, we gathered information from teachers using the book in making editorial decisions for this edition. None of the faculty who responded reported that they were using that material in their respective course configurations. If you have previously used any of those materials and wish to continue to do so, we are happy to provide an electronic copy of those materials on request for you to share with your class.

There are three other books, all available through West Academic Publishing, that both students and teachers (especially those teaching this material for the first time) may find useful. Nelson, Whitman, Burkhart, and Freyermuth's treatise, Real Estate Finance Law, now in its sixth edition, closely parallels the organization of the mortgages material in this casebook. It is available in both a student edition and a two-volume practitioner's edition. The practitioner's edition includes more complete coverage of subrogation and marshaling, as well as more extensive material on the financing of condominium and planned communities. It also includes an extensive collection of commercial forms that is not found in the student edition. Land Transactions and Finance (Fifth Edition), a book in West's "Black Letter" series, is more succinct and less costly but follows an order of presentation similar to that of the treatise and functions as an effective study companion to this casebook.

Finally, the Restatement (Third) of Property—Mortgages (1997) provides an authoritative discussion of most important mortgage law topics in a traditional restatement format. The Restatement's comments, illustrations, tables, and Reporters' Notes are exhaustive; it is an essential resource for both the beginning and experienced teacher of mortgage law.

We have edited the cases liberally to focus on the significant property and mortgage law issues. Ellipses denote omissions in the text of the cases, but we have not indicated omissions of footnotes or omission of mere citatons. Where footnotes are retained, they keep their original superscript numbers. Each of the notes following the cases begins with an italicized topic heading to guide the reader in studying them.

We are most appreciative of all those whose work we have built on here: the judges, clerks, and lawyers who contributed to the judicial opinions we have reprinted, and the countless people with whom we have discussed the concepts of real estate law with which this book deals. These include our prior students, research assistants, faculty colleagues, practicing lawyers, and members of The American Law Institute, the

American College of Real Estate Lawyers, the American College of Mortgage Attorneys, the American College of Commercial Finance Lawyers, and the Section of Real Property, Trust and Estate Law of the American Bar Association. We are also each grateful to our families, and especially our spouses, for their enduring support and patient understanding during the hours we spent in preparing this edition.

As in the last edition, we renew a special word of thanks to two departed colleagues: the late Professor Roger Bernhardt of Golden Gate University and the late Professor Patrick Randolph of the University of Missouri-Kansas City. Each worked tirelessly to analyze new developments in property and mortgage law and to engage other scholars and lawyers in debating these developments. Each of them helped clarify our thinking and formulate strategies for teaching the concepts in this book. We miss them greatly.

And, of course, a final word of thanks to Grant Nelson and Dale Whitman. The credit is theirs. Any errors are ours.

ANN M. BURKHART
R. WILSON FREYERMUTH
CHRISTOPHER K. ODINET

June 2021

SUMMARY OF CONTENTS

PART 3. REAL ESTATE DEVELOPMENT

TABLE OF CONTENTS

PART 2. REAL ESTATE FINANCE

PART 3. REAL ESTATE DEVELOPMENT

TABLE OF CASES

The principal cases are in bold type.

REAL ESTATE TRANSFER, FINANCE, AND DEVELOPMENT

CASES AND MATERIALS

Tenth Edition

PART 1

THE TRANSFER OF OWNERSHIP

∎ ∎ ∎

CHAPTER ONE

CONTRACTS FOR THE SALE OF LAND

■ ■ ■

The first two chapters of this book deal with the processes through which persons buy and sell real estate. Although there are many possible variations, even the simplest of realty transfers usually takes place through a series of well-defined steps: (1) the execution of a contract of sale; (2) inspections of the property and examination of the seller's title by the buyer; (3) the arranging of financing by the buyer, if needed; (4) the closing or "settlement"; (5) the recording of the deed and any mortgage or other security instrument that the buyer has executed; and (6) the issuance of title insurance. The first three steps are the subject of Chapter One. Chapter Two will cover the latter three steps.

A. REAL ESTATE BROKERS

A large proportion of all real estate on the market is "listed" with real estate brokers. The listing process involves the execution by the seller of a contract appointing the broker to be the seller's agent in obtaining a buyer. If the broker is successful (and the definition of "success" may be a matter of dispute, as we will see below), the seller must pay the broker a commission, usually computed as a percentage of the actual sales price. A typical listing contract, prepared by the Nebraska Real Estate Commission for optional use by real estate agents in that state, is reproduced below.[1] The footnotes are not part of the listing contract, but are provided to aid your understanding of the contract.

**THIS IS A LEGALLY BINDING AGREEMENT.
IF NOT UNDERSTOOD, SEEK LEGAL ADVICE.**

This agreement has been prepared by the Nebraska Real Estate Commission as a sample form of an exclusive listing agreement between a broker and a seller. Some provisions of this agreement may not apply to your particular transaction. This agreement may be modified to a non-exclusive listing agreement or to add, or delete paragraphs so long as such modifications do not conflict with the requirements of Neb. Rev. Stat. §§ 76–2401 to 76– 2430, the Nebraska Real Estate License Act, and any rules and

---

[1] The form is updated from time to time and is available on the Commission's web site, www.nrec.ne.gov/pdf/forms/RIGHT2SL.pdf.

regulations promulgated pursuant to such act. This document is not intended to convey legal advice. If you have any legal questions regarding this document, you should consult an attorney.

Commission rates and contract terms are not regulated by law and are subject to negotiation between the real estate broker and the seller.

EXCLUSIVE RIGHT-TO-SELL LISTING AGREEMENT

This Exclusive Right-to-Sell Listing Agreement ("Agreement") is made and entered into by and among _____ ("Seller" or "Owner") and _____, whose address for purposes of this Agreement is _____ ("Broker") for the purposes and under the terms set forth below, with Seller's specific Limited Agent[2] with such Broker being _____ [insert name of affiliated licensee(s)] and such other affiliated licensees of Broker[3] as may be assigned by Broker in writing. The affiliated licensee(s) named in this paragraph and the Seller's Limited Agents who may be appointed by the Broker are collectively referred to in this Agreement as "Seller's Limited Agent". All responsibilities and duties of Broker shall also be the responsibilities and duties of the Seller's Limited Agent. The parties acknowledge that Seller has been provided with and signed (or acknowledged electronic receipt of) a written copy of the current brokerage agency disclosure outlining the types of real estate services offered by Broker as approved by the Nebraska Real Estate Commission.

1. **Purpose of Agreement**. The purpose of this Agreement is to engage the efforts of Broker to accomplish the sale of the real property legally described as: _____
also known as _____
                    (Street Address)   (City)   (State)
together with any items of personal property conveyed pursuant to Paragraph 5 (collectively referred to as the "Property").

2. **Effect of this Agreement**. By contracting with Broker, Seller agrees to conduct all negotiations for the sale of the Property through Seller's Limited Agent and to refer to Seller's Limited Agent all inquiries received in any form from any source during the term of this Agreement.[4]

---

[2] The agents are "limited" in the sense that they are required to perform only specific duties. Those duties are spelled out in Neb. Stat. § 76–2417, and are repeated in Paragraph 23 of this listing contract.

[3] This is a reference to other salespeople who operate out of the broker's office and under the broker's supervision.

[4] Suppose Seller breaches this agreement by secretly negotiating with a prospective buyer unknown to Broker, and later enters into a contract with that buyer during the "carryover" period after the listing agreement expires (you will see this carryover provision in ¶ 10(e). In such a

3. The Listing Period. This Agreement shall begin _____, 20___ and shall continue through _____, 20___ (this period of time is referred to as the "Listing Period").

4. Price and Terms. The offering price for the Property shall be $_____ on the following terms: _____.

5. Price to Include. The price for the Property shall include all attached fixtures, except: _____.

The following personal property is also included: _____.

6. Title. Seller represents to Broker that title to the Property is solely in Seller's name. Seller shall deliver to Broker, upon request, copies of all relevant title materials. Seller represents that there are no known encroachments affecting this Property, except (If none, state "None"): _____.

Seller agrees to convey marketable title by warranty deed or _____.

If the Property has been or will be assessed for local improvements installed, under construction or ordered by public authority at the time of signing a Purchase Agreement, Seller will be responsible for payment of same.

Broker may terminate this Agreement upon written notice to Seller that title is not satisfactory to Broker.

7. Evidence of Title. Seller agrees to convey a marketable title to buyer, evidenced by a policy of title insurance or an abstract certified to date.

8. Possession. Possession of the Property shall be delivered to buyer on _____.

9. Property Condition Disclosure Statement; Indemnification. Seller represents to the Broker solely for the purposes of this Agreement that Seller has completed or will promptly complete the Seller Property Condition Disclosure Statement as required by Nebraska law fully and accurately to the best of the Seller's knowledge. Seller further states that all oral representations made to Seller's Limited Agent are accurate. Seller's Limited Agent shall not list the Property until the Seller Property Condition Disclosure Statement is complete.

Seller agrees to indemnify and hold harmless Broker and any subagents (collectively, the "Listing Company"), from any claim that may be made against the Listing Company by reason of the Seller having breached the terms of this Section 9. The Listing Company agrees to indemnify

---

situation, Seller will be liable to Broker for a commission based on the sale. International Network, Inc. v. Woodard, 405 P.3d 424 (Colo.Ct.App.2017).

and hold harmless Seller from any claim that may be made against Seller by reason of the Listing Company having breached the terms of this Section 9.

10. Compensation of Broker. In consideration of services to be performed by Seller's Limited Agent, Seller agrees to pay Broker a commission[5] of _____, payable upon the happening of any of the following:

(a) If during the term of this Agreement, Seller, Broker or any other person:

     (1) sells the Property; or

     (2) finds a buyer who is ready, willing and able to purchase the Property at the above price and terms or for any other price and terms to which Seller agrees to accept; or

     (3) finds a buyer who is granted an option to purchase or enters into a lease with option to purchase and the option is subsequently exercised; or

(b) If this Agreement is revoked or materially breached by Seller; or

(c) If Broker is prevented in closing the sale of this Property by existing claims, liens, judgments, or suits pending against the Property, or Seller thereof; or

(d) If Broker is unreasonably hindered by Seller in the showing of or attempting to sell the Property; or,

(e) If within [180][6] days after the expiration of this Agreement, Seller sells the Property to any person found during the term of this Agreement, or due to Broker's efforts or advertising under this Agreement, unless this Property is listed with another licensed broker after the expiration of this Agreement, in which case no compensation shall be paid.

11. Limitation on Broker's Compensation. Broker may accept compensation when Broker or affiliated licensee (other than Seller's Limited Agent) is serving as a Buyer's Agent. In all other cases, Broker shall not accept compensation from the Buyer, the Buyer's agent, or any entity participating in or providing services for the sale without written agreement of Seller.

12. Cooperating with Other Brokers. Broker may accept the assistance and cooperation of other brokers who will be acting as

---

[5] The commission is usually expressed as a percentage of the selling price. Under Nebraska law, as in many states, there is nothing to prevent the parties from agreeing to a flat-fee commission or computing the commission on some other basis.

[6] The 180-day figure is not in the contract form, but is probably representative of the time period that is usually filled in this blank.

subagents of the Seller or as agents for a buyer. If Broker participates in a local multiple listing service Broker shall submit the Property to such listing service. Seller authorizes Broker to compensate from the amount described in paragraph 10: ( ) Seller's subagent; ( ) buyer's agent; ( ) agents acting for both the buyer and the Seller-dual agents.[7]

13. Forfeiture of Earnest Money. In the event of forfeiture of the earnest money made by a prospective buyer, the monies received, after expenses incurred by Broker, shall be divided between Broker and Seller, one-half thereof to Broker, but not to exceed the commission agreed upon herein, and the balance to Seller.

14. Cost of Services. Broker shall bear all expenses incurred by Broker, if any, to market the Property and to compensate cooperating brokers, if any. Broker will not obtain or order any products or services to be paid by Seller unless Seller agrees in writing. Broker shall not be obligated to advance funds for the benefit of Seller.

15. Maintenance of the Property. Seller agrees to maintain until delivery of possession, the heating, air conditioning, water heater, sewer, plumbing and electrical systems and any built-in appliances in good and reasonable working condition. Seller further agrees to hold Broker harmless from any and all causes of action, loss, damage, or expense Broker may be subjected to arising in connection with this section. Seller also agrees that Broker shall not be responsible for maintenance of the Property.

16. Nondiscrimination. Pursuant to Neb. Rev. Stat. § 76–2417, Broker and its licensees and subagents shall perform their duties in accordance with all applicable federal, state and local laws, rules and regulations and ordinances, including fair housing and civil rights statutes and regulations.

17. Escrow Closing. Seller agrees that the closing of any sale of the Property made by Broker may be handled by an escrow agent and authorizes Broker to transfer all earnest monies, down payments and other trust funds to the escrow agent along with documents and other items received by Broker related to the sale. The cost of the escrow closing shall be paid by Seller or as negotiated with the Buyer in the purchase agreement.

18. Smoke and Carbon Monoxide Detectors. Seller agrees to install at Seller's expense any smoke and/or carbon monoxide detectors required by law.

19. Lead Based Paint. If the Property is residential real property and was constructed prior to 1978, Seller shall provide a lead-based paint

---

[7] Often all three blanks are checked, so that other agents can receive a split of the commission whether they technically represent the seller, the buyer, or both.

disclosure form to buyer in accordance with 42 U.S.C. § 4852d and attach it to this Agreement.

20. Sanitary Improvement District. If the Property is located within a Sanitary Improvement District ("SID") within the State of Nebraska, Seller shall provide the Broker with the most recent SID statement to be provided to any potential buyer as required by Neb. Rev. Stat. § 31–727.03.

21. New Construction. If the Property consists of new construction, Seller represents that the Property will comply with all applicable laws, rules, regulations, ordinances and codes as of the date the certificate of occupancy is issued.

22. Advertising; "Lock Box". Seller gives permission to Broker to advertise the Property in any lawful way, except as follows: _____.

Seller gives permission to Broker to use a "lock box."

23. Duties and Responsibilities of Seller's Limited Agent. Seller's Limited Agent shall have the following duties and obligations:

(a) To perform the terms of this Agreement;

(b) To exercise reasonable skill and care for Seller;

(c) To promote the interest of Seller with the utmost good faith, loyalty and fidelity including:

(1) Seeking the price and terms which are acceptable to Seller except that Seller's Limited Agent shall not be obligated to seek additional offers to purchase the Property while the Property is subject to a contract for sale;

(2) Presenting all written offers to and from Seller in a timely manner regardless of whether the Property is subject to a contract for sale;

(3) Disclosing in writing to Seller all adverse material facts actually known by Seller's Limited Agent; and

(4) Advising Seller to obtain expert advice as to material matters of that which Seller's Limited Agent knows but the specifics of which are beyond the expertise of Seller's Limited Agent;

(d) To account in a timely manner for all money and property received;

(e) To comply with the requirements of agency relationships as defined in Neb. Rev. Stat. §§ 76–2401 through 76–2430, the Nebraska Real Estate License Act,[8] and any rules or regulations promulgated pursuant to such sections or act; and

---

[8] The main burden of these provisions is disclosure of the agency relationship to the parties to the sale.

(f)   To comply with all applicable federal, state, and local laws, rules, regulations, and ordinances, including fair housing and civil rights statutes and regulations.

24. <u>Confidential Information</u>. Seller's Limited Agent, even if acting as a Limited Dual Agent, shall not disclose any confidential information about Seller, without Seller's written permission, unless disclosure is required by statute, rule, or regulation, or failure to disclose the information would constitute fraudulent misrepresentation.

25. <u>Adverse Material Facts</u>. Seller's Limited Agent, even if acting as a Limited Dual Agent, is required to disclose adverse material facts to any prospective buyer. Adverse material facts may include, but are not limited to, any environmental hazards affecting the Property which are required by law to be disclosed, physical condition of the Property, any material defects in the Property, any material defects in the title to the Property, or any material limitation on Seller's ability to perform under the terms of the contract.

26. <u>Modification of this Listing Contract</u>. No modification of this Agreement shall be valid, unless made in writing and signed by the Seller and Broker.

27. <u>Brokerage Services Only</u>. Seller acknowledges that Broker is acting as a real estate broker only and not as an attorney, tax advisor, lender, appraiser, surveyor, structural engineer, property inspector, consultant, or other professional service advisor. **Seller is hereby advised to seek such other professional advice as may be important to Seller.**

28. <u>Release of Information</u>. Seller authorizes Broker to obtain any information relating to utility expenses and all pertinent information regarding the present mortgage(s) or Deed(s) of Trust on the Property including existing balance, interest rate, monthly payment, balance in escrow account and pay off amount. Seller authorizes the dissemination of sales information including selling price and terms after closing of the transaction.

29. <u>Entire Agreement</u>. This Agreement constitutes the entire agreement between the Seller and the Broker and any prior negotiations or agreements, whether oral or written, are not valid unless set forth herein.

30. <u>Copies of Agreement</u>. This Agreement may be executed in any number of counterparts, each of which shall be deemed to be an original and all of which together shall comprise but a single instrument. Seller acknowledges receipt of a copy signed by the Broker or Broker's affiliated licensee.

---

31. **Additional Provisions**. _____.

Dated this ____ day of _____, 20___.

[Block for names, addresses, e-mail addresses, and signatures omitted]

NOTES AND QUESTIONS

1.   *The broker's authority*. What, exactly, does the broker have legal authority to do? Is it merely to show, advertise, and market the property, or to enter into an actual contract of sale? The usual view is that only the former authority is contemplated, and the broker cannot force the sale to take place if the seller refuses to go forward (although the seller may nonetheless be liable for the commission). See Forbis v. Honeycutt, 301 N.C. 699, 273 S.E.2d 240 (1981); Davito v. Blakely, 96 Ill. App. 2d 196, 238 N.E.2d 410 (1968); cf. Ward v. Mattuschek, 134 Mont. 307, 330 P.2d 971 (1958). See also Diversified Devel. & Inv., Inc. v. Heil, 119 N.M. 290, 889 P.2d 1212 (1995) (broker did not have "apparent authority" to grant extension of time for exercise of option). If the language of the listing agreement is specific enough, it may give the broker a "power of attorney" to enter into a sales contract and consummate the sale. If the seller intends to grant a power of attorney to the broker, the agreement must state this in clear, unmistakable fashion. See, e.g., Roskwitalski v. Reiss, 338 Pa. Super. 85, 487 A.2d 864 (1985) (language purporting to give agent "the sole and exclusive right to sell said property" gave broker no power to form a contract with buyer).

2.   *Must the listing agreement be in writing?* The Statute of Frauds in nearly all states requires listing agreements to be written. See, e.g., Bishop v. Hansen, 105 Wash. App. 116, 19 P.3d 448 (2001); Westside Estate Agency, Inc. v. Randall, 6 Cal.App.5th 317, 211 Cal.Rptr.3d 119 (2016) (lack of written agreement precluded broker's claim for commission on sale of $46 million residence). New York is a notable exception. N.Y. Gen. Oblig. Law § 5–701(10); Miranda v. Aliotta, 41 Misc.3d 71, 980 N.Y.S.2d 236 (Sup.Ct.2013) (oral agreement did not specify commission rate, but broker held entitled to a reasonable commission). Still, it is wise to use a writing even in New York. An oral listing may comply with the Statute of Frauds if another written document (such as the contract of sale) sufficiently describes it. See C. Porter Vaughn, Inc. v. Dilorenzo, 689 S.E.2d 656 (Va.2010).

3.   *Types of listings*. The three common types of listings are described in Real Estate Listing Service, Inc. v. Connecticut Real Estate Comm'n, 179 Conn. 128, 425 A.2d 581 (1979):

> Those categories are: the open listing, under which the property owner agrees to pay to the listing broker a commission if that broker effects the sale of the property but retains the right to sell the property himself as well as the right to procure the services of any other broker in the sale of the property; the exclusive agency listing, which is for a time certain and authorizes only one broker to sell the property but permits the property owner to sell the property himself

[Handwritten margin notes:] Broker authority is to show, market, not enter sale unless given "POA"

[Handwritten margin notes:] SoF requires a writing, except New York. Another written doc. may satisfy SoF.

listings:
× open
× exclusive agency
× exclusive right to sell.

without incurring a commission; . . . and the exclusive right to sell listing, under which the sale of the property during the contract period, no matter by whom negotiated, obligates the property owner to pay a commission to the listing broker.

Which type of listing arises under the Nebraska Real Estate Commission form reproduced on page 3? Nearly all residential properties are listed on an "exclusive right to sell" basis. Can you explain why?

4. *The relationship of commissions to selling price.* The standard rationale for basing real estate commissions on selling prices is that, because higher prices will result in larger commissions, agents have an incentive to obtain the highest possible prices for their clients, the sellers. Economists Steven D. Levitt and Chad Syverson have questioned this relationship. They noted that in a Chicago suburb, properties owned by real estate agents personally tended to remain on the market longer and sell for higher prices than properties owned by clients of agents:

> Real estate agents have a better sense than others of the best price a home can command. But when they work for others, they don't have the financial incentive to pursue it. Most home sales generate a 6 percent commission, split between the brokerage firms representing the buyer and seller. The agent generally receives half of the firm's draw, or 1.5 percent of the sale. So if a home sells for $500,000, the agent personally receives $7,500. Not bad for what may be just a few days of work. If the agent works for an additional week and urges the seller to hold out for $515,000, that's an extra $15,000 for the seller, but only an extra $225 for the agent. Because every additional dollar throws only a penny and a half into the pocket of the agent, the economists reason, the agent may push clients to accept lowball offers.

Daniel Gross, Why a Real Estate Agent May Skip the Extra Mile, N.Y. Times, Feb. 20, 2005.

5. *Multiple listing services.* In addition to a listing agreement, the seller and the broker also will prepare a form containing detailed information about the house or other property (e.g., area, number of rooms and baths, heating system, sewer system, appliances, and existing financing). This information will find its way into the publication of the multiple listing service (the "MLS"), which is operated by a local board of realtors, where all member brokers and their salespeople will see it. This information often includes one or more photographs of the property. Multiple listing services now maintain this information in an on-line database rather than a printed book.

listing agreement + form w/ detailed info on property which hits MLS

Traditionally, access to the multiple listing service was essential to the successful marketing of the property. The listing broker's main function was to provide such access, because nonbrokers and nonmembers of the local board of realtors could not list property directly with the MLS. Member of the local MLS generally felt that they had every right to exclude listings by nonmembers or agents they considered marginal. Are there antitrust problems with this attitude? Most courts have found no antitrust violation in restricting access to the MLS to members of the local board of realtors. See, e.g., Wells Real Estate, Inc. v. Greater Lowell Bd. of Realtors, 850 F.2d 803 (1st Cir.1988); Supermarket of Homes, Inc. v. San Fernando Valley Board of Realtors, 786 F.2d 1400 (9th Cir.1986). But see Thompson v. Metropolitan Multi-List, Inc., 934 F.2d 1566 (11th Cir.1991) (local MLS could not demand its members be affiliated with National Association of Realtors).

6. *Minimum service laws.* About half of U.S. states have enacted a "minimum service" statute. Their purpose is to require that real estate brokers provide a full panoply of services, and thus to prevent the operation of "fee for service" brokers who offer each service individually, with a separate charge for each. Traditional real estate agents have been strong advocates for these statutes. The Antitrust Division of the U.S. Department of Justice has condemned such laws, noting that they diminish consumer choice and raise the cost of selling a house. In a 2008 press release, it commented as follows:

> Fee-for-service brokers "unbundle" the package of real estate services typically offered by traditional full-service real estate brokers and charge a fixed or hourly fee for specific services, such as listing the house in the MLS, negotiating or closing contracts, and pricing the home. These brokerage models enable consumers to save thousands of dollars by allowing them to purchase only those services they want.

> Why would some consumers use a fee-for-service broker? Most consumers want to make as much money as possible on the sale of their home and spend no more than necessary when purchasing a home. In many cases, the standard broker's commission can offset a portion of the equity value that has been building up in a seller's home or push the price of a home beyond a buyer's purchasing power. Consumers who want to perform some of the steps involved in selling a home can reap significant financial savings by purchasing only those real estate brokerage services they actually want. . . .

> Although many consumers do want to buy all the services these provisions require a broker to provide, other consumers prefer to save money by performing some services themselves. . . .

> Do minimum service laws result in better service for consumers? Minimum service laws do not ensure quality. They merely require that real estate brokers provide—and consumers purchase—more services. State policymakers concerned with ensuring quality real estate brokerage services can help in other ways—by fostering

competition among real estate brokers and by enforcing existing state licensing, continuing education, and disciplinary rules.

See Muller, Encouraging Price Competition among New Jersey's Residential Real Estate Brokers: Reforms to Promote the Growth of Alternative Brokerages and Reduce Transaction Costs, 39 Seton Hall L. Rev. 665 (2009).

7. *The evolution of real estate sales in the internet era.* Beginning in the late 1990s, some brokers began to create "virtual office websites" or VOWs (such as eRealty and zipRealty) using MLS data. These sites enabled an interested buyer to register and obtain access to MLS data via the internet. This created efficiencies for both brokers and buyers—buyers could readily find information on properties that matched the buyer's interests without having to have an agent act as a gatekeeper, and brokers did not have to spend as much time reviewing the MLS to identify properties that met the buyer's criteria and interest. But virtual office websites prompted concern among traditional brokers that large brokers might leave MLSs and provide listings directly to customers via the internet. In 2003, the National Association of Realtors (NAR) adopted a policy that permitted listing brokers to opt out of allowing their listings to be provided to a prospective buyer through a VOW. In 2005, the DOJ sued to block the policy, alleging that it was anti-competitive, suppressed technological innovation, and discouraged competition on price and quality. In 2008, the DOJ and the NAR settled the lawsuit by a ten-year consent decree under which NAR-affiliated MLSs agreed not to discriminate against the use of VOWs to deliver brokerage services.

2008 DOJ/NAR settlement

Following the consent decree, creativity in the marketing of real estate by internet exploded. This has included the development of "hybrid" brokerages like Redfin (which more easily facilitates fee-for-service transactions), "portal" sites like Zillow and Trulia (which do not provide brokerage services but aggregate real estate information, and make money from advertisements from brokers and other real estate service providers), and "iBuyers" like Opendoor (which buys homes directly from sellers based on a pricing algorithm and then uses the MLS to resell the homes). See James S. Bradbury, Comment, Revenge of the Realtors: The Procompetitive Case for Consolidating Multiple Listing Services, 90 U.Colo.L.Rev. 267 (2019).

Nevertheless, the consent decree did not eliminate all turf battles between traditional realtors and internet entrepreneurs. For example, consider American Home Realty Network, Inc., which operated an online service called NeighborCity.com (intended to connect prospective buyers with agents representing only buyers). NeighborCity.com included pictures and textual descriptions obtained from MLS databases by "data scraping" rather than by consent. Several MLSs obtained injunctions preventing NeighborCity.com from publishing photographs (and in some cases, textual descriptions) on the ground that the information was protected by copyright and its publication by NeighborCity.com constituted copyright infringement. See, e.g., Metropolitan Regional Information Systems, Inc. v. American Home Realty Network, Inc., 722 F.3d 591 (4th Cir.2013); Regional Multiple Listing Serv. of Minn., Inc. v.

American Home Realty Network, Inc., 960 F.Supp.2d 958 (D.Minn.2013). See also Kathyrn S. Robinson, Comment, Providing Copyright Protection to Real Estate Listings: Protecting Brokers, Sellers, and Consumers, 15 J. Marshall Rev.Intell.Prop.L. 318 (2016). Could an MLS simply refuse to license its information to unaffiliated internet sites, or would that present antitrust problems?

DRAKE V. HOSLEY

Supreme Court of Alaska, 1986
713 P.2d 1203

MOORE, JUSTICE. This is an appeal from a summary judgment granted in favor of Charles Hosley, entitling him to a real estate broker's commission under a contract with the seller. The superior court concluded that Hosley had fulfilled the terms of a written agreement with the seller by finding a buyer who entered into a contract to purchase in accord with the seller's terms. We affirm.

On March 5, 1984, Paul Drake signed an exclusive listing agreement with The Charles Hosley Company, Realtors (hereafter "Hosley"). The agreement authorized Hosley to act as Drake's agent until March 30, 1984, to sell some land Drake owned in North Pole, Alaska. The agreement provided for payment of a ten percent commission if, during the period of the listing agreement, (1) Hosley located a buyer "willing and able to purchase at the terms set by the seller," or (2) the seller entered into a "binding sale" during the term set by the seller.

Hosley found a group of three buyers, Robert Goldsmith, Dwayne Hofschulte and David Hystrom (hereafter "buyers"), who were interested in the property. On March 23, 1984, Drake signed a purchase and sale agreement, entitled "earnest money receipt," in which he agreed to sell the land to the buyers at a specified price and terms. The buyers also signed the agreement. It provided that closing would occur "within 10 days of clear title" and "ASAP, 1984." A typed addendum stated that Drake agreed to pay Hosley a commission of ten percent of the price paid for the property. Both Drake and Hosley signed the addendum.

On April 3, 1984, Hosley received a preliminary commitment for title insurance. The title report listed a judgment in favor of Drake's ex-wife as the sole encumbrance on the title. The next day Hosley called Drake's attorney, Tom Wickwire, to ask about the judgment. Wickwire stated that the judgment would be paid with the cash received at closing.

Two or three days later, attorney Wickwire called Hosley and stated that his client (Drake) wanted the sale closed by April 11. Wickwire explained that he had negotiated a discounted settlement with Drake's ex-wife that required payment by April 11. Wickwire claims that Hosley agreed to close by April 11. Hosley disagrees, and claims that he merely stated that he would try to close as quickly as possible.

extension of judgment

When Hosley became concerned that the buyers would not be able to close on April 11, he telephoned the attorney for Drake's ex-wife and learned that the April 11 deadline for payment of the judgment had been extended until the end of the month.

April 11

On April 11, Wickwire called Hosley to set up the closing. Hosley told Wickwire that the buyers could not close that day because they did not have the money and would not have it before May 1. Wickwire indicated that he would advise Drake to call off the sale because the buyers had refused to perform. Wickwire mailed a letter to Hosley, dated April 11, stating that Drake's offer to sell was withdrawn. Hosley received the letter on approximately April 18. On April 12, Drake sold his property through another broker to different buyers.

April 12

downpayment

On April 12, Hosley went to Wickwire's office to close the sale and submitted checks from the buyers totaling $33,000 for the down payment. Wickwire refused the checks, stating that another buyer already had purchased the property.

Hosley filed a complaint, alleging he had fulfilled the terms of the exclusive listing agreement and was entitled to payment of a commission. The parties filed cross-motions for summary judgment. The trial court granted Hosley's motion and denied Drake's. Drake appeals.

I.   . . .

exclusive listing

Alaska Statute § 08.88.361 provides that "[a] commission is earned when the real estate broker fulfills the terms of a written personal services contract." The exclusive listing agreement between Drake, as seller, and Hosley, as broker, provided that a ten percent commission would be paid to Hosley if one of three conditions occurred:

a) if a property is sold or a *binding sale or lease agreement is entered into by Seller* during the term set by seller; or

b) if during the term of this Agreement [Hosley] *finds a buyer willing and able to purchase* at the terms set by Seller; or

carryover c) if a buyer located by [Hosley] enters into a binding sale or lease agreement within 120 days after the expiration of this Agreement. (Emphasis added.)

It is undisputed that during the term of the agreement, Hosley found a group of three buyers, and that Drake entered into a purchase and sale agreement ("earnest money receipt") with the buyers. The earnest money agreement signed by Drake stated: "I hereby approve and accept the above sale for said price and on said terms and conditions and agree to consummate the same as stated." A typed addendum to the earnest money agreement provided: "Seller agrees to pay a Realtors' commission in the amount of 10% of price to be paid by partial assignment of the deed of trust at the rate of $1,000/month."

On the basis of these facts, the trial court concluded that Hosley had performed the terms of his agreement with Drake. The court found that, within the terms of the listing agreement, Hosley located a group of buyers who entered into a binding sale agreement with Drake. The court ruled that Hosley therefore was entitled to his commission.

Drake's argument

Drake invites this court to adopt the reasoning of *Ellsworth Dobbs, Inc. v. Johnson*, 50 N.J. 528, 236 A.2d 843 (1967), and hold that a real estate broker does not earn a commission unless the contract of sale is performed.

The traditional rule followed by a majority of jurisdictions is that a broker is entitled to a commission when he produces a buyer ready, willing and able to purchase the property on the seller's terms, even if the sale is not completed. Sowash v. Garrett, 630 P.2d 8, 12 (Alaska 1981). See generally Annot., 12 A.L.R. 4th 1083 (1982). The rationale for concluding that a potential purchaser is deemed "willing and able" the instant the purchaser signs a contract with the seller is explained in *Kopf v. Milam*, 60 Cal. 2d 600, 35 Cal. Rptr. 614, 617, 387 P.2d 390, 393 (1963):

> When a vendor enters a valid unconditional contract of sale with a purchaser procured by a broker, the purchaser's acceptability is conclusively presumed because the vendor is estopped to deny the qualifications of a purchaser with whom he is willing to contract.

Dobbs reasoning

Drake suggests that the rule of *Dobbs* is better reasoned because it emphasizes that a broker has not produced a ready, willing and able buyer if the buyer refuses or is unable to perform at closing. Dobbs, 236 A.2d at 853. In a practical world the true test of a willing buyer is not met at the time a purchase agreement is signed, but at the time of closing of title. Id. Since the broker's duty to the owner is to produce a buyer who is financially able to pay the purchase price, it is reasonable to allow the owner to accept the buyer and enter into a sales contract without becoming liable for a broker's commission unless the sale is consummated. Id.

The *Dobbs* court also noted that when an owner of property lists it for sale with a broker, the owner usually expects that money for payment of a commission will come from the sale proceeds. Id. at 854. For these reasons, the *Dobbs* court concluded that:

> public policy requires the courts to read into every brokerage agreement or contract of sale a requirement that barring default by the seller, commissions shall not be deemed earned against him unless the contract of sale is performed.

Id. at 857.

We find such reasoning persuasive. We also note that several jurisdictions recently have adopted the *Dobbs* rule, or modified versions of it. See Annot., 12 A.L.R. 4th 1083, 1088, 1094–1103 (1982). However, adoption of the rule does not assist Drake in this case. The *Dobbs* court specifically held that "in the *absence of default by the seller,* the broker's right to commission . . . comes into existence only when his buyer performs in accordance with the contract of sale." Dobbs, 236 A.2d at 855 (emphasis added). A broker still is entitled to a commission if "improper or frustrating conduct" by the owner prevents title from passing. Id. at 853.

[margin note: Dobbs Rule isn't relevant here]

Drake claims that there is a genuine issue of fact regarding whether the buyer or seller refused to perform. In particular he argues that there is a material factual dispute "whether Hosley, acting for the buyers, first agreed with Wickwire to close the sale on April 11, 1984, then . . . refused to close on that day . . . ." Drake is correct that the existence of an agreement is disputed. However, there is no genuine issue as to whether Hosley was acting for the buyers. Other than a bare allegation in Drake's pleadings, the record is devoid of any evidence that Hosley was representing the buyers. Hence, the buyers could not be bound whether or not an agreement to expedite closing was made by Hosley and Wickwire.

[margin note: Hosley wasn't an agent of buyers]

Drake points to the fact that Hosley told Drake's attorney that the buyers could not close on April 11 because they did not have the money. The fact that Hosley communicated a message from the buyers does not make him their agent. Further, the affidavit of Drake's attorney, Wickwire, does not state that Hosley ever claimed or intimated that he was acting in any role other than as Drake's broker.

In short, Drake failed to make any showing that Hosley was the buyers' agent and had authority to modify their contract. In the absence of such evidence, any agreement between Drake's attorney and Drake's broker could not modify the contractual obligations of the buyers. Since Hosley's right to a commission does not turn on whether he and Drake's attorney agreed to expedite closing, the disputed agreement was not a material fact that would preclude summary judgment.

Under the terms of the earnest money agreement, the buyers were required to close within ten days after evidence of clear title was furnished. Hosley stated that he received a report from the title insurance company on April 3. The report carried a typist's date of April 2. We agree with the trial court that the buyers met the terms of the earnest money agreement by submitting checks for the down payment to Drake's agent on April 12— which was within ten days of either the April 2 or April 3 date. Thus, it was not the buyers who prevented the sale from going through. . . .

To summarize, Hosley found a group of buyers who were willing and able to perform in accord with the terms set by the seller, but they were prevented from doing so by the seller's frustrating conduct. The buyers

[margin note: Summary]

tried to perform by tendering checks for the down payment "within 10 days of clear title," as required by the earnest money agreement. The sale did not take place because the seller, Drake, sold the property to a third party during the ten-day closing period. Thus, even under the *Dobbs* rule, Hosley is entitled to his commission.

The judgment in favor of Hosley is AFFIRMED.

NOTES AND QUESTIONS

1. *Is the commission owed if no closing occurs?* The common law rule recognizing the broker's claim for the commission despite the buyer's failure to close is still alive and well, despite the inroads of cases like *Dobbs*. See, e.g., Ash Park, LLC v. Alexander & Bishop, Ltd., 363 Wis.2d 699, 866 N.W.2d 679 (2015); Fairbourn Commercial, Inc. v. American Housing Partners, Inc., 94 P.3d 292 (Utah 2004). The court in *Fairbourn Commercial* refused to adopt the *Dobbs* rule, concluding that "absent a contractual provision conditioning a broker's commission on a buyer's performance, '[t]he broker is not an insurer of the subsequent performance of the contract.'" 94 P.3d at 294 (quoting Bushnell Real Estate, Inc. v. Nielson, 672 P.2d 746, 751 (Utah 1983)). Is this explanation satisfactory?

If the *Dobbs* rule applies and the agent cannot collect a commission from the seller, can the agent recover from the breaching buyer who refuses to close? See Bailey v. Montgomery, 31 Ark. App. 1, 786 S.W.2d 594 (1990) (rejecting such a claim on the ground that the agent, whose listing agreement was with the sellers, had no contractual relationship with the buyers). Could language obligating the buyers on these facts be inserted into the contract of sale? Bear in mind, too, that the agent may well have the right to share any earnest money retained by the seller if the buyer breaches the sales contract. See ¶ 13 of the Nebraska listing agreement, supra.

2. *Modifying the listing agreement.* As *Drake v. Hosley* makes clear, the broker and the seller are free to contract out of the "ready, willing, and able" rule. Review ¶ 10(a)(2) of the Nebraska listing form. Does it entitle the agent to a commission if the buyer signs a contract of purchase but later backs out of it? If you were the seller and your jurisdiction had not adopted the *Dobbs* rule, how would you modify the contract form to ensure that you would not have to pay a commission unless an actual closing of the sale occurred?

Modifying a listing agreement to condition the seller's obligation for a commission appropriately can be harder than it looks. Consider the following examples:

(a) Seller and Broker modify the listing agreement by adding a sentence that says "Broker's commission will be paid from sale proceeds at closing." Seller and Buyer enter into a contract, but Buyer refuses to close. Is Broker entitled to a commission? Compare Arvida Realty Sales, Inc. v. William R. Tinnerman & Co., 536 So. 2d 1041 (Fla.Ct.App.1988) and Chamberlain v. Porter, 562 A.2d 675 (Me.1989) (no) with Fairbourn Commercial, Inc. v.

American Housing Partners, Inc., supra note 1, and Realty Assocs. of Sedona v. Valley Nat'l Bank of Az., 153 Ariz. 514, 738 P.2d 1121 (Ct.App.1986) (yes).

(b)   Seller and Broker modify the listing agreement by adding a sentence that says "Broker's commission is payable only as, if, and when title passes, except for willful default on the part of the Seller." Broker obtains a written offer from a buyer at the listing price demanded by Seller, but Seller rejects it and refuses to enter into a contract. Has the broker earned a commission? See Graff v. Billet, 477 N.E.2d 212 (N.Y.1984) (in effect holding the "willful default" exception referred only to willful default by seller under a binding contract of sale, not willful refusal to enter into a contract in the first place). Two judges dissented from the holding in *Graff*, stating that "[p]ermitting the seller unilaterally to defeat the broker's right to a commission by withholding his signature from a perfectly acceptable contract of sale contravenes the fundamental proposition . . . that a party cannot take advantage of a failure of a condition precedent caused by his own conduct." In what ways does the language of the Nebraska listing agreement address this problem? In particular, how would the language of ¶ 4 of that agreement (depending on how the parties filled in the blank) affect this situation? See, e.g., RealPro, Inc. v. Smith Residual Co., LLC, 138 Cal.Rptr.3d 255 (Ct.App.2012).

(c)   Broker identifies a buyer that is willing to pay $20,000 more than Seller's asking price, but only if Seller provides financing. Seller and the buyer then enter into an installment land contract at the agreed price, with Seller agreeing to receive payment in monthly installments over 20 years. The buyer takes possession but then defaults after three months. Under the Nebraska listing agreement, would Broker be entitled to a commission based on the full price? If you were representing the Seller, how might you modify the listing agreement to condition the Seller's commission obligation in the event a buyer defaults on installment payments? See Ferrara v. Firsching, 91 Nev. 254, 533 P.2d 1351 (1975). In particular, what changes might you make to ¶ 4 and ¶ 10? [Note that a similar situation can arise if the listing agreement was for a lease, and the broker finds a tenant who enters into a lease but later defaults on the rent. See, e.g., Hildebrandt v. Anderson, 180 Or. App. 192, 42 P.3d 355 (2002).]

3.   *Licensing.* All U.S. states license and regulate the real estate brokers. Typically there are two classes of licensees: brokers and salespersons. The salesperson is the entry level license, requiring no prior experience and the passage of a fairly simple exam. The broker's license is harder to obtain, requiring prior experience as a salesperson and a more difficult exam. The functional differences are that salespersons can work only under the supervision of a broker, and any commissions must be paid to the broker (who will then divide them with salespersons as appropriate). See Maclay v. Idaho Real Estate Comm'n, 300 P.3d 616 (Idaho 2012).

Acting as a broker without a license is forbidden, and may result in denial of any claim for a commission. See, e.g., Woischke v. Stursberg & Fine, Inc., 906 N.W.2d 586 (Minn.Ct.App.2018), vacated on procedural grounds, 920 N.W.2d 419; Amirkhanian v. Berniker, 147 A.D.3d 475, 47 N.Y.S.3d 22 (2017);

Ga. Code Ann. § 43–40–24. In some states licensed attorneys may act as brokers, although they usually may not supervise other salespersons. However, the attorney who occupies such a dual role is in a tricky position; duties of confidentiality as a lawyer may well conflict with duties of disclosure as a broker (as discussed further in the notes below).

4. *Conflicts of interest.* Unless agreed to by all parties after full disclosure, conflicts of interest by a broker can give rise to private liability as well as public discipline from the state licensing body. The agent who causes loss to the principal by virtue of the conflict may lose the commission and be subjected to a judgment for damages. See, e.g., Meerdink v. Krieger, 15 Wash. App. 540, 550 P.2d 42 (1976).

The conflict of interest problem is remarkably pervasive, mainly because of the operation of multiple listing services. Suppose Broker #1 obtains a listing on B's house. Broker #2 sees the listing on the MLS and knows just the customer who would like to buy it. Broker #2 writes an offer, her customer signs it, and Broker #2 transmits the offer to Broker #1 for submission to the seller. If the seller accepts the offer and the sale closes, Broker #1 and Broker #2 will divide the commission according to the bylaws or rules of the MLS or local custom; splits of 50–50 or 60–40 are common. On these facts, it is clear that Broker #1 is the seller's agent, but whose agent is Broker #2? Her commission is being paid by the seller, but she spends most of her time and effort with the buyer, and it is in that direction that her real loyalties probably lie. For example, if we could overhear all of her conversations, we would be much more likely to hear her say to the buyer, "I'll see if I can get the seller to come down $1,000," than to say to the seller, "I'll see if I can get the buyer to come up $1,000."

Is this a violation of Broker #2's fiduciary duty? If so, should that duty be redefined? Traditionally, the selling agent is considered a subagent of the listing agent, and hence an agent of the seller. Does any language in the Nebraska listing agreement bear on the issue? See generally Brown & Grohman, Real Estate Brokers: Shouldering New Burdens, Probate & Property, May/June 1997, at 14; Black, Proposed Alternatives to Traditional Real Property Agency: Restructuring the Brokerage Relationship, 22 Real Est. L.J. 201 (1994).

5. *Agency disclosure requirements.* In a large number of states, statutes or regulations now require real estate brokers to disclose in writing whether they represent the buyer or seller. In the absence of a specific disclosure, many consumers are unaware of the traditional principle that the selling agent is a subagent of the seller. A 1983 Federal Trade Commission survey concluded that 72 percent of buyers believed that the selling brokers who helped them find property were representing them rather than the sellers. See Federal Trade Commission, The Residential Real Estate Brokerage Industry: A Staff Report by the Los Angeles Regional Office 69 (1983). Do you think that the buyers in *Drake* believed that Hosley was representing them? Does the typical buyer know or care whom the agent represents? Does it really matter? See

Brown, Grohman, & Valcarcel, Real Estate Brokerage: Recent Changes in Relationships and a Proposed Cure, 29 Creighton L. Rev. 25 (1995).

6.   *Buyers' brokers.* If a broker is representing the buyer, how is the broker compensated? Obviously most buyers are not eager to pay these brokers direct commissions; they assume that a "full" commission is already built into the price of the house and will be paid by the seller. In most cases, listing brokers concede that it is appropriate to split their commissions with selling brokers who represent buyers. [Can you explain why?] Hence, the buyer is not "out of pocket" for the buyer's agent's commission.

What happens if, after signing a contract to purchase, the buyer backs out of the transaction and no closing occurs? Under the *Dobbs* rule, the seller will owe no commission, so there is nothing to split with the buyer's broker. Can the buyer's broker recover her or his split (say, 3 percent of the contract price) from the buyer directly? See Hamilton v. Hopkins, 834 So. 2d 695 (Miss. 2003) (buyer's broker entitled to commission from breaching buyer). Of course, the sale may not close for reasons other than a breach by the buyer. Perhaps the seller is unable to satisfy some of the contract's conditions, thus allowing the buyer to terminate the contract. Is the buyer's broker entitled to a commission, to be paid by the buyer? A typical buyer's broker agency agreement will say something like this:

> COMPENSATION. Broker's compensation is earned when, during the term of this agreement, Buyer contracts to acquire real property as specified in this agreement. Buyer will be responsible for paying Broker $_____ or ___% of the total purchase price, but will be credited with any amount Broker receives from a seller or a real estate licensee who is working with a seller.

Under this clause, if there is no "amount" received from the seller or the listing broker (because the closing never occurs), the buyer seems to be left with full liability for the commission. Moreover, the commission is earned, according to this clause, when the buyer "contracts to acquire real property," whether the contract is ever performed or not. See, e.g., RC Royal Dev. & Realty Corp. v. Standard Pacific Corp., 177 Cal.App.4th 1410, 100 Cal.Rptr.3d 115 (2009) (brokerage agreement provided buyer would owe commission if the buyer acquired a "beneficial interest in the property"; buyer subsequently entered into contract that buyer later refused to close due to seller's failure to obtain timely certificate of occupancy as required by contract; buyer held liable for commission because contract gave buyer a beneficial interest even though buyer never acquired legal title).

The similarity to the *Dobbs* issue is obvious, and suggests that a buyer would be well-advised to protect against the risk of being liable for a commission to a buyer's broker if no closing occurs. Can you craft language that would modify the "Compensation" clause reproduced above to do so? Would adding a sentence providing that "Broker's compensation will be paid at the time of closing" be sufficient?

7. *Other forms of representation.* It is theoretically possible for a broker to represent both the buyer and the seller quite explicitly. A number of states now expressly allow dual agency by statute or regulation.

> [D]ual agency was, and is, perilous because it requires identical loyalties to parties with different, often opposite, wishes and needs. The dual agent must not violate the duty of loyalty to one party by fulfilling the duty of loyalty to the other. Brokers who inadvertently became dual agents have little chance of avoiding a breach of their duties. In particular, a dual agent must disclose the existence of the dual agency to both principals.

Brown & Grohman, supra note 4. The need for disclosure (and the risk of liability if it is not provided) should be obvious. See, e.g., Brown v. FSR Brokerage, Inc., 62 Cal.App.4th 766, 72 Cal.Rptr.2d 828 (1998) (broker was a dual agent but failed to disclose that fact to seller; agent told buyer that he thought he could "talk down" the seller's price, and then proceeded to do so; dual agency was disclosed to seller only after sale closed; agent held liable to seller for damages on account of the failure to disclose).

Another novel form of representation now authorized in a number of states is the "transaction broker" or "nonagent broker." This person does not represent either party to the exclusion of the other, but has a duty to facilitate the transaction for both sides. Both dual agents and transaction brokers have a duty of evenhandedness toward the parties, and cannot disclose confidential information obtained from either party to the other. Beyond this duty of even-handedness, however, there are many uncertainties in the scope of duties of such brokers. Sieverling, The Changing Face of the Real Estate Professional: Keeping Pace, 63 Mo. L. Rev. 581 (1998); Mariea, Transaction Brokerage Enters the Playing Field for Real Estate Brokers and Licensees, J. Mo. Bar, July/Aug. 1999, at 196; Miller, You Can't Serve Two Masters. Unless You're a Realtor, 76 Bench & Bar of Minn. (April 2019), at 26. Despite the duty of evenhandedness, dual agents and transaction brokers continue to be paid as a percentage of the selling price, which gives them an economic incentive to maximize the price and thereby favor the seller. See Wilson, Nonagent Brokerage: Real Estate Agents Missing in Action, 52 Okla. L. Rev. 85 (1999). Is this incentive tolerable because the broker also has an incentive to make the sale happen as quickly as possible (which might tend to favor buyers)?

8. *Duty to disclose material facts.* A broker has a duty to disclose to a buyer material defects known to the broker but unknown to and unobservable by the buyer, even if the broker is only representing the seller. Cases holding the broker liable for affirmative statements that turn out to be false (even though the broker did not realize it at the time) are quite common. See, e.g., Shaffer v. Earl Thacker Co., 6 Haw.App. 188, 716 P.2d 163 (1986). So are cases finding liability where the broker was silent in the face of actual knowledge of a material fact concerning the property. See, e.g., Strawn v. Canuso, 140 N.J. 43, 657 A.2d 420 (failure to disclose existence of nearby toxic waste dump); Hermansen v. Tasulis, 48 P.3d 235 (Utah 2002) (failure to disclose unstable

soil). It is unlikely that a broker can escape this sort of liability by an exculpatory clause in the sale contract. See Syvrud v. Today Real Estate, Inc., 858 So.2d 1125 (Fla.Ct.App.2003).

But does the broker have a duty to investigate the condition of the property (and then to disclose whatever material defects that investigation reveals)? In Easton v. Strassburger, 152 Cal. App. 3d 90, 199 Cal. Rptr. 383 (1984), California extended such a duty in a case where a home had suffered several hundred thousand dollars in damage in an earthslide. The agent did not disclose this fact to the buyer, but there was no direct evidence that the agent knew it. The court held the agent liable for damages anyway, holding that the agent had a duty "to conduct a reasonably competent and diligent inspection" and "to disclose to prospective purchasers all facts materially affecting the value or desirability of the property that such an investigation would reveal."

duty to investigate

California real estate brokers were understandably exercised about *Easton.* In response to their lobbying efforts, the California legislature enacted a statute to "codify and make precise" the holding of *Easton* and to clarify the scope of the duties that it imposes with respect to "residential real property comprising one to four dwelling units." Cal. Civ. Code § 2079. The required duty of care is "the degree of care that a reasonably prudent real estate licensee would exercise" and "is measured by the degree of knowledge through education, experience, and examination, required to obtain a license." Id. § 2079.2. The inspection need not include areas that are normally inaccessible. Id. § 2079.3. The statute does not relieve the buyer of "the duty to exercise reasonable care to protect himself or herself, including those facts which are known to or within the diligent attention and observation of the buyer or a prospective buyer." Id. § 2079.5. The statute also requires the buyer to bring any action for nondisclosure within two years of the date of purchase. Id. § 2079.4.

How do these provisions assist brokers? Is the California approach a reasonable accommodation of the rights of purchasers and brokers? Where does it leave the buyer of nonresidential property? By contrast to *Easton,* courts outside California generally have not held brokers liable for silence regarding defects of which they had no actual knowledge, but that could have been discovered by inspection. See Blackmon v. First Real Estate Corp., 529 So. 2d 955 (Ala. 1988); Harkala v. Wildwood Realty, Inc., 200 Ill. App. 3d 447, 146 Ill. Dec. 232, 558 N.E.2d 195 (1990); Teter v. Old Colony Co., 190 W. Va. 711, 441 S.E.2d 728 (1994).

9.   *What must be disclosed?* In some cases, the duty to disclose may extend beyond facts about the physical property itself. This may include information about the broker's potential conflicts of interest or financial information about the client's ability to perform. See, e.g., Silverman v. Pitterman, 574 So. 2d 275 (Fla.Ct.App.1991) (divorcing couple listed house with broker who, unknown to wife, had a romantic relationship with the husband's divorce lawyer; wife's complaint against broker stated claim for

breach of fiduciary duty); Holmes v. Summer, 188, Cal.App.4th 1510, 116 Cal.Rptr.3d 419 (2010) (broker knew that property was subject to multiple mortgages that exceeded the sale price by nearly $400,000, and that seller could not deliver clear title unless existing mortgage lenders would agree to a "short sale" and release their liens without receiving full payment; court held broker should have known these facts made it likely that the seller would breach the sale contract of sale, and thus had a duty to disclose these facts to the buyer before the buyer signed the contract); Lombardo v. Albu, 199 Ariz. 97, 14 P.3d 288 (2000) (buyer's broker held liable to seller for nondisclosure of known adverse financial information about buyer that resulted in buyer being unable to qualify for financing and therefore failing to close). However, courts in many states have refused to require the broker to disclose information that the buyer could have learned through exercising reasonable care, such as by a review of public records. For example, a broker likely need not disclose that a violent criminal or sex offender lives next door if the buyer could have discovered that information through a public offender registry. See, e.g., Troja v. Pleatman, 65 N.E.3d 809 (Ohio Ct.App.2016). [Query: Consider the *Holmes* case in the previous paragraph. The mortgages in that case were discoverable on the land records where buyer could have found them in a title search; why didn't that excuse the broker's nondisclosure?]

In addition, the broker is not liable if the buyer misconstrues true information that the broker provides. In Saffie v. Schmeling, 224 Cal.App.4th 563, 168 Cal.Rptr.3d 766 (2014), the broker told the buyer in a 2006 transaction that the land had been certified as "buildable" under geological regulations, and provided the buyer with a 1986 report of the geologist so stating. The buyer assumed that the report was still valid, but the applicable regulations had changed and the land could no longer be built on. The court found that everything the broker said was true, and that the broker was not responsible for the buyer's mistaken assumptions. Would the same result have followed if the broker had been acting as a buyer's broker?

B. THE STATUTE OF FRAUDS AND PART PERFORMANCE

In most transactions, there is usually a rather detailed written agreement of sale, often filled in on a printed form. Considerable time—30 to 90 days or more—commonly passes between the contract's execution and its performance at the "closing," when the seller receives the purchase price and the buyer receives legal title by a deed. Why the delay, and why the need for a detailed contract? Two reasons stand out:

1. Buyer wants to be certain that Seller really owns the property, and that Seller title is "good" or "clear" or "marketable." This determination takes time and money, and Buyer does not want to go to the trouble unless she is confident that Seller is obligated to complete the sale at the agreed price.

2.   Buyer needs to borrow part (usually most) of the money needed to buy the property. Obtaining a loan involves time, trouble, and some expense. Moreover, most institutional lenders will not even consider Buyer's application for a loan unless she has a signed contract of purchase.

These are the two most pervasive reasons a contract and an "executory period" are needed. You may be able to think of many more. Here are a few possibilities:

3.   Buyer needs time to sell her previous house or terminate her existing lease and to arrange to move her personal effects.

4.   Seller needs time to find another home and to arrange to buy or rent it.

5.   Buyer is concerned about the physical condition of the house—the roof, plumbing, furnace, foundation, etc.—and wants an expert to inspect them and report to her before Buyer is unconditionally obligated to complete the purchase.

law of vendor and purchaser

The standard contract doctrines—offer, acceptance, consideration, and so forth—apply equally to real estate contracts. But real estate sales contracts have a number of unique features that justify separate treatment in a property or real estate course. These features are often termed the law of "vendor and purchaser."

Types of contracts. It is important to recognize that there are two quite different types of contracts that sellers and buyers might use for very different purposes. The first type, described above and explored in some depth in this chapter, is usually termed a "short-term," "earnest-money," "deposit receipt," "binder," or "marketing" contract. Its function is to permit the parties to prepare for the transfer of title by making the arrangements described above. It usually provides for the closing—the delivery of a deed and the payment of the purchase price—to occur within a few weeks or months after the contract is signed. Usually, the buyer takes possession on the closing date. The buyer will typically give the seller some "earnest money"—anywhere from a few hundred dollars to as much as 10% of the purchase price or more—at the time the contract is signed. If the seller is to accept something other than cash for part of the purchase price, such as the buyer's promissory note secured by a mortgage, the contract will mention this fact, but the note and mortgage themselves will be separate documents, usually signed at or just prior to the closing.

#1

#2

The second type of sales contract is often called a "real estate installment contract," or (especially in the Midwest) a "contract for deed." It contemplates that the buyer will go into possession immediately on execution of the contract, make installment payments to the seller on a regular basis (say, monthly) over a long time period (say, ten to forty years), and finally receive a deed when the last installment is paid. The seller is financing the purchase and the contract is being used much like a mortgage, to secure the buyer's obligation to pay the installments as they come due under the contract. See Nelson, The Contract for Deed as a Mortgage: The Case for the Restatement Approach, 1998 B.Y.U. L. Rev. 1111. This type of contract presents different problems than the earnest-money contract. It is, in effect, a "mortgage substitute," and we will address it further in Chapter Three. Unfortunately, courts sometimes cite cases dealing with one type of real estate sales contract in attempting to resolve litigation dealing with the other type. The results are sometimes satisfactory and sometimes disastrously confusing. Be careful not to fall into this trap.

The requirement of a writing. All states have enacted a statute of frauds, which requires that transfers of land—and contracts for such transfers—must be in writing to be enforceable. See, e.g., Mo.Rev.Stat. § 432.010. As such, the overwhelming majority of real estate sales contracts are in writing, especially if a broker is involved. In fact, in most residential transactions where one or both parties are working with a broker, the parties will use a preprinted form contract provided by the broker and typically drafted by the local or state brokers' association. [The broker does not want the deal to "fall through," and knows there will be more pressure on the parties (both legally and psychologically) to complete the transaction if the contract is written.] Most of these contracts are several pages in length and cover a variety of "standard" issues. The following form is representative, if a bit simplified.

Contract for the Purchase and Sale of Real Estate (Single-family Residence)

THIS CONTRACT, made and entered into this _____ day of _____, 20___ by and between _____ ("the Seller") and _____ ("the Buyer").

WITNESSETH: For and in consideration of the mutual obligations of the parties hereto, the Seller hereby agrees to sell and convey unto the Buyer and the Buyer agrees to purchase from Seller, upon the terms and conditions hereinafter set forth, the following described real estate situated in the County of _____, State of _____, to wit:

[INSERT LEGAL DESCRIPTION HERE]

[LIST ANY PERSONAL PROPERTY TO BE INCLUDED WITH THE REAL ESTATE.]

PRICE. The price for said property shall be $_____, to be paid by Buyer as follows: $_____ at the time of the execution and delivery of this contract, the receipt of which is hereby acknowledged by the Seller, and which is deposited with the Seller, as earnest money, and as a part of the purchase price and consideration for this agreement; and by delivery to Seller of the remaining balance of the purchase price, if any, in cash or by certified check.

In the event of a material breach of this contract by the Buyer, the Seller may retain the earnest money deposit as liquidated damages for the Buyer's breach, or in the alternative may waive the right to liquidated damages and obtain such other remedies as are available in law or equity.

TITLE QUALITY. Title shall be marketable of record, subject to existing street and utility easements, the lien of the current year's property taxes and any special assessments, zoning ordinances and codes, and covenants, conditions, or restrictions (CC & Rs) that do not materially affect the value of the property for use as a residence.

TITLE APPROVAL. Seller shall, within ten days after the execution of this contract, obtain and forward to Buyer a preliminary title report on the property issued by a title insurance company doing business in _____. Within ten days after receipt of that report, Buyer will notify Seller in writing of any objections to matters shown thereon which, in Buyer's opinion, make title unmarketable as defined above. Seller shall within five days of receipt of such objections notify Buyer whether Seller elects to (1) terminate the contract at that time and refund Buyer's earnest money deposit, or (2) attempt to cure the title matters to which Buyer has objected. If Seller elects to attempt to cure such title matters, Seller shall effect such cure before the date of closing. In the event of Seller's failure to effect such cure within that time, Buyer may elect (1) to terminate the contract and receive a return of Buyer's earnest money deposit, or (2) to complete the purchase with an abatement of the purchase price in an amount equivalent to the reduction in value of the property resulting from the title defects objected to.

TITLE INSURANCE. Seller will provide Buyer at closing or immediately after closing with an ALTA owner's policy of title insurance, showing marketable title in Buyers subject only to the matters mentioned above.

FINANCING. The Buyer's obligation to purchase the property under this contract is conditioned upon the Buyer's obtaining of a [conventional] [FHA] [VA] mortgage loan in the amount of $_____ payable over a period of not less than ___ years and bearing interest at a rate of not more than ___ percent and ___ origination fee (points) payable by the Buyer. Said loan shall carry ❏ a fixed interest rate ❏ an adjustable interest rate which adjusts on a _____-year basis. The Buyer agrees to use reasonable efforts to obtain such a loan. In the event Buyer is unable to obtain a commitment from an institutional lender in

_____ County for such a loan by _____, 20___, Buyer, at Buyer's option, may terminate this contract by notice to Seller on or before that date, and Buyer's earnest money deposit shall immediately be refunded. If Seller is given no notice by the stated date of Buyer's inability to obtain a loan commitment, this condition shall be deemed satisfied.

SELLER DISCLOSURE and BUYER'S INSPECTION. With seven days after acceptance of this contract, Seller will complete and submit to the Buyer the Seller's Disclosure Form attached to this contract. Buyer may, at Buyer's expense, obtain such inspections, engineering reports, and other analyses of the property as Buyer shall deem desirable. In the event any information in the Seller's Disclosure Form, or any inspection or report obtained by Buyer, shall disclose conditions unacceptable to Buyer, Buyer shall notify Seller within 21 days after acceptance of this contract of Buyer's objection to such conditions, together with a copy of any inspection or report obtained by Buyer disclosing those conditions. Any objection shall be made in good faith and shall specify the specific condition or conditions objected to. Seller shall notify Buyer within five days after receipt of such objections whether Seller elects (1) to terminate the contract at that time and refund Buyer's earnest money deposit, or (2) to cure, at Seller's expense, the conditions to which Buyer has objected. If Seller elects to attempt to cure such conditions, Seller shall be obligated to effect such cure before the date of closing.

Buyer shall indemnify and hold Seller harmless from any liability, costs (including reasonable attorneys' fees), liens, and damages to Seller or other occupants of the property arising from Buyer's inspections, studies, and analyses of the property, and the entry onto the property of Buyer or persons employed or contracted by Buyer. Following each entry on the property by such persons, Buyer shall leave the property in substantially the same condition as it was in prior to the entry and inspection.

[ALTERNATIVE 1] SELLER WARRANTIES. Seller warrants that: (a) Seller has received no claim or notice of any building or zoning violation concerning the property which has not or will not be remedied prior to closing; (b) there is, to the best of Seller's knowledge, no action pending by any governmental authority to take the property by power of eminent domain; (c) all obligations against the property including taxes, assessments, liens and other encumbrances of any nature shall be paid or brought current on or before closing; and (d) the plumbing, heating, air conditioning and ventilating systems, electrical system, and appliances shall be in satisfactory working condition, and there will be no leaks on the roof or basement, at the time of closing.

[ALTERNATIVE 2] NO WARRANTIES BY SELLER. Buyer acknowledges that, with the exception of the Seller's Disclosure Form attached to this contract, neither Seller nor any agent or broker has made any representations, guaranties, warranties, or covenants of any kind, express or implied, relative to the property, its use or value, or the transaction contemplated by this contract, including without limitation the condition or quality of the property or the improvements on it, compliance with zoning ordinances, building or housing codes, or compliance with other federal, state, or local law. Buyer agrees to take the property "as is," and subject to all faults and conditions existing thereon.

RISK OF LOSS. All risk of loss or damage to the property shall be borne by the Seller until closing. In the event there is loss or damage to the property between the date of this contract and the date of closing, by reason of fire, vandalism, flood, earthquake, or acts of God, and the cost to repair such damage shall exceed ten percent (10%) of the purchase price of the property, Buyer may, at Buyer's option, either proceed with this transaction if Seller agrees in writing to repair or replace damaged property before the date of closing, or declare this Agreement null and void and receive a refund of Buyer's earnest money deposit. If damage to property is less than ten percent (10%) of the purchase price and Seller agrees in writing to repair or replace and does actually repair and replace damaged property prior to the agreed closing date (or such additional time period as the parties may mutually agree upon), this transaction shall proceed as agreed; but if Seller fails so to agree in writing, Buyer may declare this Agreement null and void and receive a refund of Buyer's earnest money deposit.

ADJUSTMENTS AT CLOSING. At the date of closing property taxes and special assessments for the current year shall be prorated between Buyer and Seller. Seller will pay the cost of the owner's policy of title insurance and any applicable transfer tax. Buyer will pay the cost of recording the deed and the deed of trust, and will pay all costs associated with Buyer's mortgage loan applications and financing. The escrow or closing fee and all other expenses of sale shall be shared equally by Buyer and Seller.

CLOSING. Closing shall occur, and legal title shall pass by warranty deed to Buyer on the ___ day of _____, 20___ at 2 o'clock pm or at such other time and place as the parties may mutually agree. Time is of the essence in all provisions of this contract.

POSSESSION. Possession shall be delivered to the Buyer at the time of closing.

REAL ESTATE COMMISSIONS. The Buyer and Seller hereby represent to one another that neither has contracted for representation by any real estate broker in connection with this sale, and each will indemnify and hold harmless the other from any liability for any real estate commission for which he or she has contracted in connection with this sale.

COMPLETE AGREEMENT. This contract constitutes the entire agreement between Buyer and Seller with regard to the property, and supersedes and replaces all prior discussions, negotiations, and agreements between them, whether written or oral.

IN WITNESS WHEREOF, the Buyer has executed this agreement on the day and year first above written and acknowledges receipt of one copy of this contract.

[EXPIRATION OF OFFER (to be used if this is an offer to purchase)]. The Buyer's offer to purchase as set forth herein shall automatically expire on the _____ day of _____ at 12:00 noon if not accepted by Seller or withdrawn by Buyer prior to that time.

_____
Buyer
Date_____ Time_____
Seller hereby accepts the foregoing offer.

_____
Seller
Date_____ Time_____

Forms such as this can prove valuable to unsophisticated buyers and sellers, as the forms often provide somewhat balanced rules to address potential issues (such as the risk of casualty loss during the gap period, the risk of title defects, and the remedies available following breach) that unsophisticated parties may not have otherwise known to address in their agreement. This may be doubly important given that in many states, neither the seller nor the buyer in a residential transaction will consult a lawyer before signing the contract. Buyers and sellers often do not want to incur the additional costs associated with legal fees, and brokers sometimes worry that having a lawyer review the form may diminish the likelihood that the parties will actually execute the contract—either because a lawyer may suggest changes that would be unacceptable to the other party, or because the buyer may find a different and more desirable property while their lawyer is reviewing the form.

Many brokers are thorough and careful in assisting the parties to complete and execute the sale contract, but this does not always happen. Sometimes a broker may be in a hurry to have the parties sign the sales contract before the buyer or the seller has second thoughts about the terms of the deal. Sometimes a key term of the deal is sufficiently complex that the parties cannot describe it clearly (and a responsible broker will be reluctant to help the parties "wordsmith" because that could constitute the unauthorized practice of law). When no broker or lawyer is involved, contracts are often sketchier and sloppier. There may be no writing at all, or someone who should sign the sales contract may fail to do so, or a key term may be left blank. How do you suppose this dynamic contributed to the dispute reflected in the following case?

JOHNSTON V. CURTIS

Court of Appeals of Arkansas, 2000
70 Ark. App. 195, 16 S.W.3d 283

oral agreement
+
partial performance
= no SoF

BIRD, JUDGE. Appellants Gerald Johnston and Bebe Dare Johnston bring this appeal from the Circuit Court of Lonoke County contending that the court erred in finding that the parties orally modified a written real estate contract and that their nonperformance of the contract was not excused. . . . We affirm the decision of the trial court . . . .

On October 9, 1997, the parties entered into a written real estate contract, whereby the Curtises offered to sell and the Johnstons agreed to buy a house in Cabot for $114,000. A real estate agent was not involved. Under the terms of the contract, the transaction was subject to the Johnstons obtaining a home loan of $102,600, which was 90 percent of the purchase price. Specifically, the contract provided that the Johnstons' obligation was subject to:

> The Buyer's ability to obtain a loan secured by the property in an amount no less than $102,600, with Jan Turbeville at Arkansas Fidelity Mortgage Co., payable over a period of not less than ____ Years, with interest not to exceed ____% per annum.

Deanna Curtis testified that after the Johnstons told her and her husband that they had been pre-approved for their loan, the Curtises purchased a home in Searcy, and they moved out of the home in Cabot after they signed the contract with the Johnstons. However, because the house appraised for only $110,000, the mortgage company denied the loan to the Johnstons. Thereafter, the parties entered into an oral agreement whereby the Johnstons agreed to buy and the Curtises agreed to sell the house for $110,000. On November 3, 1997, after the lease on the Johnstons' home in Hot Springs expired but before the parties closed on the house in Cabot, the Johnstons paid the Curtises $500, took "early possession" of, and moved into, the home in Cabot. Deanna Curtis testified that she and her husband allowed the Johnstons to move into the home before closing only after they had made "some kind of a show of good faith." The Johnstons tendered a check for $500 to the Curtises for the Curtises to hold until closing.

Jan Turbeville, a mortgage loan originator, testified that she had a difficult time obtaining a loan for the Johnstons, but that a loan for ninety percent of the purchase price was finally approved at the reduced price of

$110,000, and the transaction was set for closing on November 17. She testified that when the loan was approved, the Johnstons were informed of the terms. She also testified that one of the terms of the loan was that Bebe Dare Johnston's name would not be on the title of the home, but that the title of the home would be in Gerald Johnston's name only. She also testified that during the initial meeting that she had with the Johnstons, Gerald Johnston did not put any parameters on the type of financing that he would accept. In addition, she testified that he accepted the terms of the final loan for which he was approved. She stated that had Gerald Johnston not approved the terms of the loan, she would have neither set a closing date nor ordered any of the documents needed for closing.

Deanna Curtis testified that the parties were to close on the house on November 17, but that they were informed that day that the Johnstons had refused to close. Thereafter, the Curtises demanded that the Johnstons vacate the premise. The Curtises then listed the home with a realtor and sold the property in March 1998 for $100,000. Deanna Curtis testified that after deducting the six-percent commission, they received $94,000, less closing costs.

[handwritten margin note: Refusal to close / Sold 100k]

Gerald Johnston testified that the parties had entered into a real estate contract, but stated that the terms of the agreement were that he purchase the home for $110,000 if he could obtain a loan at an acceptable rate of interest and acceptable closing costs. He stated that he had been led to believe by a mortgage lender that the interest rate would be between nine and ten percent. However, he admitted that the written real estate contract did not state that the offer was contingent upon obtaining a loan with an interest rate between nine and ten percent. Johnston testified that he and his wife were originally set to close on the house on November 8 or 9, and that they showed up at the office to close, but that the papers were not ready. He said that he was told on November 17 that the closing would take place that afternoon, but at that time the mortgage company did not know the amount of the closing costs or the interest rate. He said that someone by the name of Brown called him later that afternoon and told him the interest rate and the amount of the closing costs and that they were beyond what he had discussed. Gerald Johnston told Brown that he and his wife were not interested. He said that he was quoted an interest rate of 10.75%, but that it was too high and that he was only interested in purchasing the house if he would obtain an acceptable interest rate. Gerald Johnston also stated that he was never informed, until the trial, that his wife was not going to be named on the deed, and he said that he would not have purchased the home without her name being included on the deed. He denied that Turbeville had several conversations with him concerning the transaction. Gerald Johnston stated that the $500 check he wrote to the Curtises when they moved into the home was not earnest money, but was given to cover any damages that they might cause to the home. He stated

[handwritten margin note: "500 not earnest $"]

that he stopped payment on the check because the Curtises were not acting in good faith.

The trial court found that the parties had orally modified their agreement to reduce the price from $114,000 to $110,000, but subject to all the other terms of the original contract, that the oral modification to the contract was not subject to the requirements of the statute of frauds, and that the Johnstons had breached the contract by their failure to close. Damages were awarded to the Curtises in the amount of $10,000, representing the difference between the modified contract price and the amount for which the Curtises later sold the house to someone else.

For appellants' first point on appeal, they argue that the court erred in finding that the parties had orally modified the written contract and that the oral modification was not barred by the statute of frauds. Appellants argue that there was not a meeting of the minds between the parties because they had not agreed on an acceptable loan amount, interest rate or closing costs. In the alternative, they argue that even if an oral contract existed, it violated the statute of frauds.

A meeting of the minds, or what is more commonly known as an objective indicator of agreement, see Fort Smith Serv. Fin. Corp. v. Parrish, 302 Ark. 299, 789 S.W.2d 723 (1990), does not depend upon the subjective understanding of the parties, but instead requires only objective manifestations of mutual assent for the formation of a contract. Hagans v. Haines, 64 Ark. App. 158, 984 S.W.2d 41 (1998). The meeting of the minds is essential to the formation of a contract and is determined by the expressed or manifested intention of the parties. Id. The question of whether a contract has been made must be determined from a consideration of the parties' expressed or manifested intention determined from a consideration of their words and acts. Id.

The Johnstons argue that the oral contract between the parties provided that they would purchase the home for $110,000 if they were given an acceptable interest rate and closing costs. After a consideration of the parties' words and acts, it is clear that the contract was modified from $114,000 to $110,000. Through their testimony, both parties admit that they changed the terms of the agreement from the purchase prices of $114,000 to $110,000. They also state that those were the only terms changed. The original real estate contract was silent as to what would constitute an acceptable rate of interest or acceptable closing costs. In addition, Turbeville testified that the Johnstons did not discuss with her what interest rate or amount of closing costs would be acceptable to them.

The Curtises argue that the statute of frauds is an affirmative defense and that the Johnstons are barred from arguing it as a defense because they did not specifically plead such in their answer. While it is true that the statute of frauds is an affirmative defense, see Ark. R. Civ. P. 8, the

answer didn't plead SoF however court amended pleadings to proof court in this case amended the pleadings to conform to the proof. Arkansas Rule of Civil Procedure 15(b) states, "When issues not raised by the pleadings are tried by express or implied consent of the parties, they shall be treated in all respects as if they had been raised in the pleadings." In the case at bar, after the Curtises presented their case, the Johnstons made a motion to dismiss the case, the court denied the motion, stating that the pleadings were amended to conform to the proof, and it considered the issues of the applicability of the statute of frauds. Therefore, even though it was not raised in the Johnstons' answer, this court can address the defense of the statute of frauds.

A contract for the sale of land comes within the statute of frauds and must be in writing to be enforceable. Ark. Code Ann. § 4–59–101 (Repl. 1996). A material modification of a contract comes within the statute of frauds and must be in writing in order to be valid and binding. Shumpert v. Arko Telephone Communications Inc., 318 Ark. 840, 888 S.W.2d 646 (1994). Such a contract cannot be modified in essential parts by parol agreement so as to be valid against a plea of invalidity under the statute of frauds. Id. See also Arkmo Lumber Co. v. Cantrell, 159 Ark. 445, 252 S.W. 901 (1923); J.W. Davis v. Patel, 32 Ark. App. 1, 794 S.W.2d 158 (1990). The court found that the statute of frauds did not apply in this case because a written agreement may be modified by an oral agreement. We disagree, but we affirm the court because, even though the trial court applied the wrong reason, it reached the correct result. Van Camp v. Van Camp, 333 Ark. 320, 969 S.W.2d 184 (1998).

In the case at bar, the statute of frauds is not applicable because of the Johnstons' part performance of the contract. In order to remove an oral agreement from the statute of frauds, it is necessary to prove both the making of the oral agreement and its part performance by clear and convincing evidence. Langston v. Langston, 3 Ark. App. 286, 625 S.W.2d 554 (1981). A requirement that the evidence be clear and convincing does not mean that the evidence be uncontradicted. Freeman v. Freeman, 20 Ark. App. 12, 722 S.W.2d 877 (1987). Partial performance of a contract by payment of a part of the purchase price and placing a buyer in possession of land pursuant to an agreement of sale and purchase is sufficient to take the contract out of the statute of frauds. Sossamon v. Davis, 271 Ark. 156, 607 S.W.2d 405 (1980). In the case at bar, the parties orally modified the contract by changing the purchase price from $114,000 to $110,000. The Johnstons admit that they took possession of the home, and they admit to tendering a check to the Curtises for $500. In addition, Deanna Curtis testified that when the Johnstons requested to take possession of the home prior to closing, she and her husband asked the Johnstons to show their good faith by tendering the check for $500 before they allowed the Johnstons to take early possession of the home. The Johnstons' acts of taking possession of the property and paying a portion of the purchase price are sufficient to take the oral modification to the contract out of the statute of frauds.

For appellants' second point on appeal, they argue that the court erred in not finding that the contract between the parties was subject to conditions precedent that appellants obtain acceptable financing and acceptable closing costs. In addition, they argue that because Mrs. Johnston's name was not going to appear on the deed, another condition of their contract was not satisfied. They contend that because all of these conditions precedent were not satisfied, their failure to perform was excused.

Whether a provision of a contract amounts to a condition precedent is generally dependent on what the parties intended, as adduced from the contract itself. *Stacy v. Williams*, 38 Ark. App. 192, 834 S.W.2d 156 (1992). When the terms of a written contract are ambiguous and susceptible to more than one interpretation, extrinsic evidence is permitted to establish the intent of the parties and the meaning of the contract then becomes a question of fact. Id. Furthermore, evidence of a parol agreement that a written agreement is being delivered conditionally constitutes an exception to the parol evidence rule. Id.

[handwritten margin note: Stacy: irrelevant case]

For this argument, the Johnstons rely on *Stacy v. Williams*, supra. However, that case is distinguishable from the one at bar because in *Stacy*, the parties made obtaining financing a condition precedent to the contract, and the appellees were never approved for any financing. In the case at bar, the Johnstons were approved for financing, but refused to close because they found the rate and the closing costs unacceptable. However, the original contract stated only that the Johnstons would receive a loan for $102,600, which was ninety percent of the purchase price. Although the contract form that the parties used contained a blank space where a limitation on the interest rate of their loan could have been inserted, it was left blank. The contract contained no mention of any limitation in the amount of the closing costs.

The Johnstons also argue that they should be excused from performing the contract because Mrs. Johnston's name was not going to be on the deed. However, the Johnstons did not become aware of that fact until the day of the trial, more than a year after they refused to perform the contract. They cannot rely on a fact of which they were unaware at the time of their breach as an excuse for their failure to perform. See *Barbara Oil Co. v. Patrick Petroleum Co.*, 1 Kan. App. 2d 437, 566 P.2d 389 (1977). . . .

NOTES AND QUESTIONS

1. *What sort of writing is required?* The court in *Johnston* says that "[a] contract for the sale of land comes within the statute of frauds and must be in writing to be enforceable." But that is not quite accurate; the parties' written

agreement did not specify the exact or maximum possible interest rate for the Johnston's financing, yet the court enforced the agreement anyway.

The Arkansas Statute of Frauds, which is entirely typical, states:

> Unless the agreement, promise, or contract, *or some memorandum or note thereof*, upon which an action is brought is made in writing and signed by the party to be charged therewith, or signed by some other person properly authorized by the person sought to be charged, no action shall be brought to charge any . . . person upon any contract for the sale of lands, tenements, or hereditaments, or any interest in or concerning them. [Ark. Code Ann. § 4–59–101]

Thus, putting the full agreement in writing via a printed form is only one way of satisfying the statute's demands. Any "memorandum" that contains the essential terms of the agreement (just what terms are "essential" is discussed further in note 3) and is properly signed will do. The writing will suffice even though:

- it is entirely handwritten. See, e.g., Aguado v. Franco, 2019 WL 117860 (Cal.Ct.App.2019).

- it is a letter, a check, or some other type of document not drawn for the purpose of memorializing the contract. See Collins v. Morris, 122 Md.App. 764, 716 A.2d 384 (1998) (will executed by vendor); Putt v. City of Corinth, 579 So.2d 534 (Miss.1991) (minutes of city utilities commission); Hines v. Tripp, 263 N.C. 470, 139 S.E.2d 545 (1965) (exchange of letters); Timberlake v. Heflin, 180 W.Va. 644, 379 S.E.2d 149 (1989) (complaint filed in divorce action); Richardson v. Schaub, 796 P.2d 1304 (Wyo.1990) (financial statement filed with Department of HUD).

- it consists of several related documents in which the court can collectively find the necessary elements. See Rohlfing v. Tomorrow Realty & Auction Co., 528 So. 2d 463 (1988); Pee Dee Oil Co. v. Quality Oil Co., 80 N.C.App. 219, 341 S.E.2d 113 (1986).

- it has been destroyed prior to trial, or is otherwise unavailable for introduction into evidence, if there is credible proof that it once existed. See Reed v. Hess, 239 Kan. 46, 716 P.2d 555 (1986); Brawley v. Brawley, 87 N.C.App. 545, 361 S.E.2d 759 (1987).

- it was written long after the contract was formed.

- it was not delivered to the party seeking to enforce it, e.g., D'Angelo v. Schultz, 306 Or. 504, 760 P.2d 866 (1988), or the party seeking to enforce it did not know it existed until after the litigation arose, e.g., Smith v. McClam, 289 S.C. 452, 346 S.E.2d 720 (1986).

Courts also apply the signature requirement with flexibility. A handwritten signature clearly suffices, but any written mark placed by the party to signify the party's assent is sufficient (even the proverbial 'X'). See, e.g., Hessenthaler v. Farzin, 388 Pa. Super. 37, 564 A.2d 990 (1989) (mailgram). Cf. Durham v. Harbin, 530 So.2d 208 (Ala.1988) (printed letterhead and typed name of seller do not suffice as a "signature" unless the seller placed or used them "for the purpose of authenticating the writing as binding on him"). If the contract is for the sale of full title to co-owned property, all of the co-owners must sign. If only one signs, to what extent is the agreement enforceable? See, e.g., Johnson v. Cook, 167 S.W.3d 258 (Mo.Ct.App.2005); Bayview Loan Servicing, LLC v. White, 134 A.D.3d 755, 24 N.Y.S.3d 310 (2015). What if the owners are spouses holding as tenants by the entirety? See, e.g., Carpenter v. Crespo, 161 A.D.3d 934, 78 N.Y.S.3d 165 (2018).

Consider whether a sufficient memorandum exists in the following case. Lumley was a tenant farmer of Kapusta's land. Kapusta lived in another state and wished to sell the land. Kapusta called Lumley and asked if Lumley wanted to buy the land; Lumley said that she would get an appraisal. She went to Bank, which issued a report that valued the land at $526,000, but which stated "[t]his evaluation is not an appraisal." Based on Bank's valuation, Lumley sent Kapusta a cashier's check for $526,000, deeds to be executed by Kapusta, and a note stating "[t]he purchase of all the property is contingent on all documents being signed, notarized, and returned the same day as signed." Kapusta endorsed and deposited the check in her bank account and signed the deeds, but did not return them to Lumley; instead, Kapusta telephoned Lumley and stated that she wanted an official appraisal of the property. When no formal appraisal followed, Kapusta returned the money to Lumley. Can Lumley successfully argue that the check (which Kapusta endorsed and deposited) and the signed deeds collectively satisfied the Statute? See Lumley v. Kapusta, 878 N.W.2d 65 (N.D.2016).

2. *Electronic communication.* In 2000, Congress enacted the Electronic Records in Global and National Commerce Act ("E-Sign"), which makes a major and preemptive modification of the state statutes of frauds. E-Sign provides:

> Notwithstanding any statute, regulation, or other rule of law . . . with respect to any transaction in or affecting interstate or foreign commerce—
>
> (1) a signature, contract, or other record relating to such transaction may not be denied legal effect, validity, or enforceability solely because it is in electronic form; and
>
> (2) a contract relating to such transaction may not be denied legal effect, validity, or enforceability solely because an electronic signature or electronic record was used in its formation. [15 U.S.C. § 7001]

An "electronic signature" means any electronic sound, symbol, or process, attached to or logically associated with a contract or other record and executed or adopted by a person with the intent to sign the record. 15 U.S.C. § 7006(5).

Similar language appears in the Uniform Electronic Transactions Act (UETA), enacted in 48 states. Under E-Sign and UETA, it is perfectly clear that an enforceable contract of sale can result from an exchange of faxes, texts, or e-mails. See McClare v. Rocha, 86 A.3d 22 (Me.2014).

3. *What must the writing contain?* As *Johnston* demonstrates, the Statute of Frauds does not require the writing to include the entire agreement, but only its "essential" terms. This means identification of the parties and a description of the land to be sold, along with words indicating that a sale is intended. The price is also essential. Most courts require that it be stated explicitly, though courts have enforced agreements for the price to be set by an appraisal process. See, e.g., MacThompson Realty, Inc. v. City of Nashua, 993 A.2d 773 (N.H. 2010). Cf. Pettigrew v. Collins, 539 S.E.2d 214 (Ga.Ct.App. 2000) (contract that provided for sale for "appraised value" without specifying a method of appraisal held ambiguous and unenforceable). If the buyer is paying part of the price in installments, a court may find the writing insufficient if it does not spell out the details of payment. See Trotter v. Allen, 285 Ala. 521, 234 So.2d 287 (1970); de Vaux v. Westwood Baptist Church, 953 So.2d 677 (Fla.Ct.App.2007). Courts usually will assume that the price is to be paid in cash if there is no contrary statement. See, e.g., Busching v. Griffin, 465 So.2d 1037 (Miss.1985).

The writing must identify the land with reasonable certainty. If the written description is ambiguous, courts will usually admit extrinsic evidence as to the precise boundaries intended to be covered, e.g., Prezioso v. Aerts, 858 N.W.2d 386 (Wis.2014), though some courts will admit only extrinsic evidence that clarifies a written description and not evidence supplying a description not found in the writing. For example, suppose that Seller and Buyer enter a writing that describes the property as "5 acres land adjoining property owned by Buyer and this being formerly land of Seller located on north side of Highway 223. This 5 acres to be surveyed at earliest possible time at which time plat will be attached and serve as further description on property." Seller owns only one parcel of land adjoining the property of Buyer, but that parcel is 100 acres in size. Is the description sufficient to satisfy the Statute of Frauds? Should the court consider extrinsic evidence to clarify the parameters of the intended parcel? Should it matter whether the requisite survey was done? See Cousar v. Shepherd-Will, Inc., 387 S.E.2d 723 (S.C.Ct.App.1990); see also Calvary Temple Assembly of God v. Lossman, 557 N.E.2d 1309 (Ill.Ct.App.1990) ("residence which [Harvey] occupies on the subject property" held insufficient description).

The "best practice" is to include a formal legal description by metes and bounds or by reference to a recorded map or subdivision plat. This would clearly be sufficient to permit a surveyor to locate the boundaries of the parcel on the ground. Suppose, however, that a party uses only a street address (e.g., "125 Pine Street"). Most courts find street addresses to be adequate if the city and state are given and there is no ambiguity. See, e.g., Park West Village, Inc. v. Avise, 714 P.2d 1137, 1141 (Utah 1986); French v. Bank of New York Mellon, 729 F.3d 17 (1st Cir. 2013). What if the writing did not include the city and state, but the seller owns only one parcel of real estate bearing an address of 125 Pine Street? See, e.g., Maccioni v. Guzman, 145 A.D.2d 415, 535 N.Y.S.2d 96 (1988); Seabaugh v. Sailer, 679 S.W.2d 924 (Mo.Ct.App.1984) ("my farm" sufficient description where seller owned only one farm); Moudy v. Manning, 82 S.W.3d 726 (Tex.Ct.App.2002).

The use of street addresses is not a good practice, because they are often quite ambiguous as land descriptors. See, e.g., Boyer v. Sinclair & Rush, Inc., 67 S.W.3d 627 (Mo.Ct.App. 2002) (contract contained a single street address but also described two parcels of land known by two addresses); Maryland State Housing Co. v. Fish, 208 Md. 331, 118 A.2d 491 (1955) (property was a double house on a single parcel of land, known by two distinct street addresses). Some courts are quite strict, refusing to enforce vague land descriptions. See Calvary Temple Assembly of God v. Lossman, 200 Ill. App. 3d 102, 146 Ill. Dec. 122, 557 N.E.2d 1309 (1990) ("the residence which [purchaser] occupies on the subject property" held to be an insufficient description because it was unclear how much land or other structures around the home were to be included); Cousar v. Shepherd-Will, Inc., 300 S.C. 366, 387 S.E.2d 723 (App. 1990) ("5 acres land adjoining property owned by the purchaser" held unenforceable). Washington and Idaho are perhaps the most strict jurisdictions in the nation, requiring an accurate and complete legal description, and rejecting entirely the use of street addresses. See Ray v. Frasure, 200 P.3d 1174 (Idaho 2009); Home Realty Lynnwood, Inc. v. Walsh, 189 P.3d 253 (Wash.Ct.App.2008). Is there any point to requiring such hyperprecision? If so, what?

A reference to a county tax map or an existing survey (even one that has not been recorded) may well suffice; see Nguyen v. Yovan, 317 S.W.3d 261 (Tex.Ct.App. 2009). But a description by reference to a survey will not suffice if the survey has not been completed when the contract is signed; Min Quin Shao v. Corley, 95 So.3d 14 (Ala.Ct.Civ.App.2012).

Among the items that need *not* be included in the writing are the date and place of closing, provisions for apportionment of property taxes, and a statement as to the type of deed to be delivered. Courts will supply these "nonessential" terms by implication (or "gap filling") See, e.g., Kane v. McDermott, 191 Ill.App.3d 212, 138 Ill.Dec. 541, 547 N.E.2d 708 (1989). For example, courts will assume that the closing is to occur "within a reasonable time" if the writing contains no agreed date. See Guel v. Bullock, 127 Ill.App.3d 36, 82 Ill.Dec. 264, 468 N.E.2d 811 (1984). Likewise, the writing need not include an acknowledgment before a notary public, and the signatures of witnesses; absent a statute specifically requiring them, these are not necessary for the formation of a valid land sale contract.

gap fillers

4.   *Who must sign?* The English version of the Statute of Frauds and most American versions require a signature by the "party to be charged"—i.e., the person who is resisting enforcement of the agreement (usually the defendant). See, e.g., Ark. Code Ann. § 4–59–101, supra note 1. However, in a few states, the signature must be that of "the vendor." This statutory language

seems to suggest that in such states a vendor could simply make up her own writing, sign it, and enforce the contract against the purchaser. However, case law in those states usually requires evidence that the signed writing was in some way delivered to, accepted by, or otherwise acknowledged by the purchaser. See Schwinn v. Griffith, 303 N.W.2d 258 (Minn.1981).

5. *Modifications and rescissions.* An oral modification of a contract of sale falls within the Statute of Frauds and must be supported by a writing. By contrast, an oral rescission falls outside the Statute and can be enforced. See Sabot v. Rykowsky, 363 N.W.2d 550 (N.D.1985). Is this distinction sensible? Are modifications more likely to be falsely invented by a party than rescissions? An oral modification is simply ignored by the courts, leaving the original contract in effect. Still, part performance of the contract as modified may take the modification out of the Statute of Frauds and make it binding, as in *Johnston.*

Should courts permit an oral modification if it covers a "nonessential" term? See Garcia v. Karam, 154 Tex. 240, 276 S.W.2d 255 (1955). For example, oral modifications of the agreement's provisions governing time of performance are often upheld. See, e.g., Johnson v. Sellers, 798 N.W.2d 690 (S.D. 2011); Tiedemann v. Cozine, 297 N. J. Super. 579, 688 A.2d 1056 (1997). This is often justified on a reliance theory. If V orally tells P, "Don't worry about closing on time; I'll give you an extra two weeks," and P in fact delays getting ready to close for two additional weeks, it is almost irresistible for a court to recognize the validity of the modification and allow P to enforce the contract despite P's late tender of performance.

6. *Can an admission substitute for the writing?* Suppose there is no writing that evidences the parties' agreement, but the defendant admits in pleadings, depositions, or on the witness stand that there was an oral agreement. Can the defendant still avoid its enforcement by raising the Statute of Frauds as a defense? The traditional answer was yes, but a number of courts have expressed discomfort with that position. See Anchorage-Hynning & Co. v. Moringiello, 697 F.2d 356 (D.C.Cir.1983); Kolodziej v. Kolodziej, 54 A.D.2d 228, 388 N.Y.S.2d 447 (1976); Powell v. City of Newton, 703 S.E.2d 723 (N.C.2010). Does a reversal of the traditional rule create an undesirable incentive for perjury? See Nix v. Wick, 66 So.3d 209 (Ala.2010); Stevens, Ethics and the Statute of Frauds, 37 Cornell L. Q. 355 (1952).

7. *The part performance doctrine.* As *Johnson* illustrates, the doctrine of part performance may allow enforcement of an oral agreement.[9] What acts by the buyer are necessary to comprise part performance sufficient to justify enforcement? The three most often mentioned by the courts are (1) payment of part (or all) of the purchase price; (2) the buyer's going into possession of the

---

[9] Part performance is *not* a substitute for the agreement itself, the formation of which must still be proven, even though it is oral. See Lumley v. Kapusta, 878 N.W.2d 65 (N.D.2016) (would-be seller's deposit of buyer's check could not constitute part performance where buyer failed to prove that seller and buyer ever agreed on the price); Kiernan v. Creech, 268 P.3d 312 (Alaska 2012). Often, as the *Johnston* court noted, courts hold that proof of the existence of a contract must be by "clear and convincing" evidence.

realty; and (3) the making of substantial improvements. The first two factors were present in *Johnston*. The courts require these factors in various combinations. Most courts demand that two or all three factors must be present. Nearly all courts agree that partial payment alone is not sufficient. See Tikvah Realty, LLC v. Schwartz, 43 A.D.3d 909, 841 N.Y.S.2d 616 (2007); Zappa v. Basden, 188 Ga.App. 472, 373 S.E.2d 246 (1988). If improvements are used as a factor, presumably they must actually make the property more valuable. See Johnson v. Cook, 167 S.W.3d 258 (Mo.Ct.App.2005) (rejecting part performance due to "improvements" that actually "devalued the land and caused damage that cannot be repaired"). Is "part performance" an apt name for the doctrine? Which of the factors can fairly be termed "performance" of the agreement?

There are two traditional theoretical justifications for part performance. The first theory is based on estoppel or reliance, and is articulated in Section 129 of the Restatement (Second) of Contracts:

> A contract for the transfer of an interest in land may be specifically enforced notwithstanding failure to comply with the Statute of Frauds if it is established that the party seeking enforcement, in reasonable reliance on the contract and on the continuing assent of the party against whom enforcement is sought, has so changed his position that injustice can be avoided only by specific enforcement.

Note that the Restatement language is not limited to the "big three" acts— payment, possession, and improvements—but suggests that a broader range of actions could constitute "reasonable reliance." For example, suppose the purchaser gives up her previous business location and terminates her lease in reliance on the oral agreement. See Payne v. Mill Race Inn, 152 Ill.App.3d 269, 105 Ill.Dec. 324, 504 N.E.2d 193 (1987). Can you think of other acts by a buyer that would satisfy the Restatement test? What about acts by a seller? Courts that follow this broader view sometimes call the doctrine "promissory estoppel" rather than "part performance." See, e.g., Jacobson v. Gulbransen, 623 N.W.2d 84 (S.D.2001).

[handwritten margin note: restatement looser]

The other theoretical justification grows out of the idea that the Statute of Frauds serves an evidentiary role; we demand a writing because it is otherwise too easy for one of the parties to invent a contract where none existed. If this is the Statute's role (is it?), then alternative types of evidence, such as the buyer's acts of part performance, ought to be equally satisfactory proof of the agreement's existence if they are strong and unequivocal enough. Consider Justice Cardozo's famous statement of this view:

[handwritten margin note: if SoF is purely evidentiary]

> Not every act of part performance will move a court of equity, though legal remedies are inadequate, to enforce an oral agreement affecting rights in land. There must be performance "unequivocally referable" to the agreement, performance which alone and without the aid of words of promise is unintelligible or at least extraordinary unless as an incident of ownership, assured, if not existing. An act which admits of explanation without reference to the alleged oral contract

> or a contract of the same general nature and purpose is not, in general, admitted to constitute a part performance.

Burns v. McCormick, 233 N.Y. 230, 135 N.E. 273 (1922). See also Winecellar Farm, Inc. v. Hibbard, 27 A.3d 777 (N.H.2011) (holding payments made by a putative purchaser could be explained as rent under a lease rather than under a contract or sale); Martin v. Scholl, 678 P.2d 274 (Utah 1983) (putative buyer's 30 years of work as a ranch foreman were not sufficiently referable to a contract of purchase). Cardozo's position cannot be taken literally; one could almost always explain acts of part performance plausibly on noncontract grounds (e.g., that the "buyer" was merely a tenant). Courts rarely apply the "unequivocal referability" that strictly. See Sutton v. Warner, 12 Cal.App.4th 415, 15 Cal.Rptr.2d 632 (1993); Collins v. Morris, 122 Md.App. 764, 716 A.2d 384 (1998).

Some courts clearly emphasize either the reliance-estoppel theory or the evidentiary theory, but there are plenty of opinions that mix the two theories or seem to apply both together. See, e.g., Blackwell v. Mahmood, 992 A.2d 1219 (Conn.Ct.App.2010). Should a court demand "unequivocal referability" if it adopts the fraud-estoppel theory? Should it demand proof of significant harm to the purchaser if it adopts the evidentiary theory?

Most plaintiffs who rely on part performance are buyers. Is there any reason not to let a *seller* assert the doctrine? Under the Restatement, a seller can also assert the doctrine of part performance. See Restatement (Second of Contracts § 197 cmt. e . Is it sufficient for the seller to assert part performance by demonstrating the buyer's actions, or should the seller be required to show his *own* acts of "part performance"? Should the answer depend on the court's theoretical rationale for part performance? Logically, under the evidentiary theory, once the evidence is presented either party should be able to use it. By contrast, under the reliance theory, only the party who engages in the acts of reliance should be in a position to use them to enforce the agreement. Compare Pearson v. Gardner, 202 Mich. 360, 168 N.W. 485 (1918), with Palumbo v. James, 266 Mass. 1, 164 N.E. 466 (1929).

8.   *Letters of intent.* In commercial transactions, the parties often execute a "letter of intent" before they actually execute a written purchase and sale agreement. The letter of intent functions as a precursor to a later agreement, setting the stage for further negotiation as to certain details. As Judge Easterbrook explained, the letter of intent "allows parties to approach agreement in stages, without fear that by reaching a preliminary understanding they have bargained away their privilege to disagree on the specifics." Empro Mfg. Co. v. Ball-Co Mfg., Inc., 870 F.2d 423 (7th Cir.1989).

Sometimes, a letter of intent does not always lead to a full written contract. Because the letter of intent often identifies the parties, the property, and the price, the party disappointed when the deal "falls through" may attempt to enforce the letter of intent as a sufficient memorandum that satisfies the Statute of Frauds. For this reason, letters of intent customarily include explicit statements disclaiming that the letter of intent creates any binding obligation. The following language is representative:

> Notwithstanding the above, it is agreed that neither party to the proposed transaction discussed in this Letter of Intent will be under any legal obligation with respect to the proposed transaction unless and until a formal written purchase and sale agreement has been executed and delivered by all parties to be bound thereby.

If the letter of intent is truly nonbinding, does it serve any useful purpose? If so, what might that purpose be?

Suppose that Seller and Buyer execute such a letter of intent on March 1. For the next four months, the parties negotiate over the terms of a written purchase and sale agreement; their respective lawyers ultimately agree on the final terms, but no formal agreement is ever signed. Seller ends up selling the land to a different buyer. On what theory or theories, if any, could Buyer argue that Seller had an enforceable obligation with respect to the transaction?

9. *Rethinking the Statute of Frauds.* Consider the following critique of the Statute of Frauds:

> Because the statute of frauds is satisfied by a memorandum that contains only a sketchy reference to the agreement it memorializes, compliance with the statute actually does little to prevent fraud, perjury, or misrecollection. Moreover, there are many reasons for putting an agreement in writing that are independent of the statute of frauds. These reasons include: (1) Written agreements are more certain than oral ones; (2) they are not as open to misinterpretation; (3) only written agreements can take advantage of certain other statutes and legal rules, such as the parol evidence rule and the recordation and registry laws; (4) the discipline of a writing requires the parties to think through their agreement in more detail than they might otherwise; and (5) the ceremony of a writing encourages the parties to take their understanding seriously, thus increasing the likelihood of voluntary performance. These reasons are compelling enough that parties likely would use written agreements even if no statute of frauds existed. [Michael Braunstein, *Remedy, Reason, and the Statute of Frauds: A Critical Economic Analysis*, 1989 Utah L.Rev. 383, 385–86.]

Does this argument justify repeal of the statute? Or are there countervailing policy considerations justifying relatively strict compliance with the statute? Go back to the *Johnston* case. When the parties entered the initial October 1997 transaction, no real estate agent represented either party, and the Johnstons do not appear to have had any legal advice. In that context, do you think the Johnstons fully understood the potential consequences of not filling in the blank for the maximum permissible interest rate—either at the time they signed the writing or when they later orally agreed to the reduced price?

Do you think they believed the interest rate was a "nonessential" term? Do you believe the court reached the "correct" result?

C. REMEDIES AND REAL ESTATE CONTRACTS

The two most widely employed remedies for the breach of a real estate sale contract are the legal remedy of damages and the equitable remedy of specific performance.[10] An award of damages usually contemplates that the seller will keep the property or sell it to someone else. An order of specific performance, by contrast, means that the seller must convey the property to the buyer, who in turn must pay the agreed price. As a general principle, both the buyer and seller may seek either of these remedies if the other party breaches.

In the absence of contrary agreement, the nonbreaching party can recover its "consequential," "incidental," or "out-of-pocket" damages incurred due to the breach, as long as such damages were foreseeable. The nonbreaching party can also recover "expectation" or "loss of bargain" damages, traditionally measured by the difference between the contract price and the market value of the land on the date of the breach. Under this measure, a nonbreaching seller will recover no expectation damages if the property's value exceeds the contract price, and a nonbreaching buyer will recover no expectation damages if the property is worth less than the contract price. See Kuish v. Smith, 181 Cal.App.4th 1419, 105 Cal.Rptr.3d 475 (2010). As the following case illustrates, sometimes calculating the appropriate "loss of bargain" can be a challenge.

DONOVAN V. BACHSTADT
Supreme Court of New Jersey, 1982
91 N.J. 434, 453 A.2d 160

[Editors' Note: Bachstadt contracted to sell real estate to the Donovans for $58,900. The contract provided that Bachstadt would finance $44,000 by way of a purchase money mortgage, helping the Donovans avoid the need for bank financing (which at the time was available only at very high interest rates). Under applicable usury statutes, the purchase money mortgage could not have borne an interest rate exceeding 10.5%. When it became apparent that Bachstadt did not have and could not obtain marketable title to the property, the Donovans sued Bachstadt for breach of the contract, seeking compensatory and punitive damages. While the case was pending, the Donovans bought another home and obtained a mortgage loan bearing a 13.25% interest rate. Bachstadt's breach was undisputed, so the trial was limited to damages. Bachstadt argued that

---

[10] Rescission also is available, although nonbreaching parties do not request it frequently. See, e.g., Greenstreet v. Fairchild, 313 S.W.3d 163 (Mo.Ct.App.2010) (allowing buyers to rescind a long-term installment contract because sellers persistently breached it by trespassing on the property).

because the breach was a failure of seller's title, the Donovans were limited by the common law to rescission of the contract and recovery of their deposit. The Donovans instead sought both consequential damages (their title search and survey costs) and loss-of-bargain damages measured by the difference in interest costs between the 10.5% interest rate in the contract and the 13.25% interest rate on the loan they had to take out to buy a different home. The trial court awarded the Donovans the costs for title search and survey, but denied any recovery for the interest rate differential, holding that the contract was for the sale of the property and the financing "was only incidental" to the sale. The Appellate Division reversed, holding that N.J.S.A. § 2A:29–1 allowed a nonbreaching party to recover consequential damages even where the seller's breach was due to a defective title, and remanded to the trial court for a hearing as to damages.]

SCHREIBER, J. . . . The initial inquiry is whether plaintiffs are entitled to compensatory damages. We had occasion recently to discuss the measure of damages available when a seller breaches an executory contract for the sale of real property. St. Pius X House of Retreats v. Diocese of Camden, 88 N.J. 571, 582–87, 443 A.2d 1052 (1982). We noted that New Jersey follows the English rule, which generally limits a buyer's recovery to the return of his deposit unless the seller wilfully refuses to convey or is guilty of fraud or deceit. The traditional formulation of the English rule has been expressed by T. Cyprian Williams, an English barrister, as follows:

> Where the breach of contract is occasioned by the vendor's inability, without his own fault, to show a good title, the purchaser is entitled to recover as damages his deposit, if any, with interest, and his expenses incurred in connection with the agreement, but not more than nominal damages for the loss of his bargain. T.C. Williams, The Contract of Sale of Land 128 (1930).

In *St. Pius*, we found no need to reexamine the English rule, though we raised the question whether the American rule that permits a buyer to obtain benefit of the bargain damages irrespective of the nature of the reasons for the seller's default might not be more desirable.

We also referred in *St. Pius* to N.J.S.A. 2A:29–1, which provides:

> When any person shall contract to sell real estate and shall not be able to perform such contract because of a defect in the title to the real estate, the person with whom such contract was made . . . may, in a civil action, recover from the vendor, not only the deposit money, with interest and costs, but also the reasonable expenses of examining the title and making a survey of the property, unless the contract shall provide otherwise. This section shall not preclude the recovery by the purchaser from the vendor of any other damages to which he may be entitled.

This statute modified the common law rule to enable a buyer to recover the reasonable expenses of examining the title and making a survey of the property in addition to the deposit, unless the contract provided otherwise.... [In 1951,] the last sentence was modified to read "This section shall not preclude the recovery by the purchaser from the vendor of any other damage to which he may be entitled by law."... There is nothing in the statute that prevents the Court from adopting the American rule and awarding loss of the benefit of the bargain damages....

We are satisfied that the American rule is preferable. The English principle developed because of the uncertainties of title due to the complexity of the rules governing title to land during the eighteenth and nineteenth centuries. Oakley, Pecuniary Compensation for Failure to Complete a Contract for the Sale of Land, 39 Cambridge L.J. 58, 69 (1980). At that time the only evidence of title was contained in deeds that were, in a phrase attributed to Lord Westbury, "difficult to read, disgusting to touch, and impossible to understand." The reason for the English principle that creates an exception to the law governing damages for breaches of executory contracts for the sale of property is no longer valid, and the exception should be eliminated. *Cessante ratione legis, cessat et ipsa lex* (the reason for a law ceasing, the law itself ceases). See Fox v. Snow, 6 N. J. 12, 14, 22–23, 76 A.2d 877 (1950) (Vanderbilt, C. J., dissenting). Indeed, in England the rule has been modified by placing the burden of proof on the vendor to establish that he has done everything within his power to carry out the contract. Malhotra v. Choudhury, [1978] 3 W.L.R. 825; [1979] 1 All E.R. 186 (C.A.).

Whether titles are clear may be ascertained by record searches. See N. J. S. A. § 46:21–1; Jones, The New Jersey Recording Act—A Study of its Policy, 12 Rutgers L. Rev. 328, 329–30 (1957). Moreover, limitation periods may be applicable. See N.J.S.A. § 2A:14–30; 13A N.J. Practice (Lieberman, Abstracts and Titles) § 1643 at 140 (3d ed. 1966). Thus, it is standard practice for title examiners to search the back title for 60 years and until a warranty deed is found in the chain of title. Palamarg Realty Co. v. Rehac & Piatkowski, 80 N.J. 446, 460, 404 A.2d 21 (1979). Further, the parties may insert appropriate provisions in their agreements protecting them from title defects so that to a very large extent sellers may control the measure of redress.

There is no sound basis why benefit of the bargain damages should not be awarded whether the subject matter of the contract is realty or personalty. Serious losses should not be borne by the vendee of real estate to the benefit of the defaulting vendor. This is particularly so when an installment purchase contract is involved that extends over a period of years during which the vendee makes substantial payments upon the principal, as well as extensive improvements to the property....

We are satisfied that a buyer should be permitted to recover benefit of the bargain damages when the seller breaches an executory contract to convey real property. Here the defendant agreed to convey marketable title. He made that bargained-for promise and breached it and is responsible to the plaintiff for the damages occasioned thereby. The next question is how to compute those compensatory damages. . . .

[margin note: ✻✻ how to compute]

The specific elements to be applied in any given case of a seller's breach of an executory agreement to sell realty may vary in order to achieve the broad purposes of reparations; some items, however, will almost invariably exist. Thus, the purchaser will usually be entitled to the return of the amount paid on the purchase price with interest thereon. Costs and expenses incurred in connection with the proposed acquisition, such as for the title search and survey, would fall in the same category. The traditional test is the difference between the market price of the property at the time of the breach and the contract price. Ganger v. Moffett, 8 N.J. 73, 79, 83 A.2d 769 (1951); King v. Ruckman, 24 N. J. Eq. 298 (Ch.), aff'd, 24 N.J. Eq. 556 (E. & A. 1873). See cases cited in Annotation, Measure of Recovery by Vendee Under Executory Contract for Purchase of Real Property Where Vendor is Unable to Convey, 48 A. L. R. 12, 15–17 (1927). Under this standard, the buyer who had taken possession before title passed would be entitled to recover for improvements he made that increased the value of the property. Sabaugh v. Schrieber, 87 Ind. App. 588, 162 N.E. 248 (1928).

[margin note: MKT price @ breach – contract price ——— traditional]

The difference between market and contract price may not be suitable in all situations. Thus, where a buyer had in turn contracted to sell the realty, it is reasonable to measure his damages in terms of the actual lost profit. See Bonhard v. Gindin, 104 N.J.L. 599, 142 A. 52 (E. & A. 1928) (awarding the consideration paid, search fees, taxes and assessments paid, and lost profits from a sale to a third person); see also Giumarra v. Harrington Heights, 33 N. J. Super. 178, 109 A.2d 695 (App. Div. 1954) (awarding contract buyer of realty lost profits in action against contract buyer's assignee). What the proper elements of damage are depend upon the particular circumstances surrounding the transaction, especially the terms, conditions and nature of the agreement.

The plaintiffs here assert that their damages are equivalent to the difference in interest costs incurred by them in purchasing a different home at another location. This claim assumes that the financial provision of the contract concerning the purchase money mortgage that the defendant agreed to accept was independent and divisible from the purchase of the land and house. The defendant contends that he did not agree to loan these funds in connection with the purchase of some other property, but that this provision was incidental to the sale of the house. Neither position is entirely sound. This financing was an integral part of the transaction. It can be neither ignored nor viewed as an isolated element.

The relationship of the financing to the purchase of a home has changed in recent years. As interest rates rose and the availability of first mortgage funds was sharply reduced, potential homeowners, though desirous of purchasing homes, found financing difficult to obtain. The seller's acceptance of a purchase money mortgage became an important factor in effecting a sale. See Rand, Home Resale Market: Pattern Shift, N.Y. Times, March 22, 1981, § 11, at 18, col. 3. In evaluating a contract such a financial arrangement could play an important part in determining price. The rise in interest rates, the expense of mortgage credit and the availability of funds has rendered traditional methods of financing acquisition of homes impractical. Walleser, The Changing Complexion of Home Mortgage Financing in America, 31 Drake L. Rev. 1, 2 (1981). Favorable vendor financing could lead to increased market value. Only then might a buyer be able to purchase. Iezman, Alternative Mortgage Instruments: Their Effect on Residential Financing, Real Est. L.J. 3, 4 (1981). The importance of a seller's purchase money mortgage to the overall agreement to convey property was recognized in *King v. Ruckman*, 24 N.J. Eq. 298 (Ch.), aff'd, 24 N.J. Eq. 556 (E. & A. 1873). The seller agreed to convey certain property and to accept as part of the purchase price a purchase money mortgage with 6% interest payable in five annual installments. The seller refused to convey. The buyer obtained a final decree for specific performance including the purchase money mortgage. The Chancery Court's view of the mortgage confirmed by the Court of Errors and Appeals on review was:

> The benefit accruing to the purchaser from having time for the payment of the bulk of the principal, and of the rate agreed on for interest, is apparent. It is a material ingredient of the bargain, as much so in reality, though not in degree, as the price, and cannot be withheld from the purchaser in this case by the willful misconduct of the vendor, for the sole benefit of the vendor himself. 24 N.J. Eq. at 303.

The interest rate is not sufficiently discrete to calculate damages in terms of it alone under these circumstances.

In some circumstances, interest rate differentials are an appropriate measure of damages. Where the buyer has obtained specific performance, but because of the delay has incurred higher mortgage rates, then his loss clearly should include the higher financing cost. *Godwin v. Lindbert*, 101 Mich. App. 754, 300 N.W.2d 514 (1980), is illustrative. The buyers lost their commitment for a mortgage with an interest rate of 8¾ when the seller refused to convey. The buyers succeeded in obtaining specific performance but were compelled to borrow funds at 11½. They were awarded the difference reduced to present value. See also Reis v. Sparks, 547 F.2d 236 (4th Cir. 1976). Moreover, we are not unmindful of the possibility that a buyer might demonstrate that a lending institution's commitment to advance the funds initially at a certain interest rate was due to the buyer's financial condition. The particular realty might well be a secondary and incidental consideration for the loan. Therefore, an interest differential occasioned by the seller's default might be a proper factor in fixing damages where the buyer shortly thereafter purchased another property financed at a higher interest rate.

This is not such a situation. The defendant's motive was to sell a house and not to lend money. In measuring the plaintiffs' loss there should be a determination of the fair market value of the property and house that could be acquired with a purchase money mortgage in the principal amount of $44,000 at an interest rate of 10½ (no appeal was taken from the judgment of reformation) for a 30-year term. The valuation should be at the time the defendant failed to comply with the judgment of specific performance. The plaintiffs would be entitled to the difference between $58,900 and that fair market value. If the fair market value was not more than the contract price, the plaintiffs would not have established any damage ascribable to the loss of the bargain. They are also entitled to their expenditures for the survey, search, and counsel fees for services rendered in preparation of the aborted closing. The plaintiffs have hitherto received the return of the deposit.

NOTES AND QUESTIONS

1. *The English rule.* The English rule, which limits the purchaser to restitutionary recovery when the seller's title is defective but the seller has acted in good faith, is followed in about half the American jurisdictions (absent explicit contrary agreement). It does not apply, however, if the seller breaches the contract, even in good faith, for reasons unrelated to the title. See Beard v. S/E Joint Venture, 321 Md. 126, 581 A.2d 1275 (1990). Are you persuaded by *Donovan's* conclusion that the American rule is superior? Do you agree with the court's conclusion that the New Jersey statute allows the court to award expectation damages?

2. *Damages resulting from higher interest rate.* The final paragraph in *Donovan* seems to say that the court will not allow the buyers any damages to account for the higher interest rate they obtained in buying another house. Perhaps the court was concerned that while market conditions and the Donovans' creditworthiness justified an interest rate of 13.25% (the rate they received), the usury statute prevented Bachstadt from charging the Donovans more than 10.5%—and that holding Bachstadt liable for damages when the law prevented him from charging a true "market" interest rate is inequitable.

But the court goes on to say that the Donovans may recover damages measured by the difference between the contract price and the fair market value—and that in calculating the latter amount, the trial court should determine "the fair market value of the property and house that could be acquired with a purchase money mortgage in the principal amount of $44,000 at an interest rate of 10½%." Is this value greater than the value of the house with no financing attached to it? It seems obvious that it is. The Donovans surely would not have been willing to pay as much for the house with no accompanying financing, given the much higher interest rates prevailing in the market at the time. How would you calculate the added amount they would be willing to pay for the favorable financing? Does factoring that into the determination of the house's fair market value add the equivalent amount to their damages?

3.   *Date and measurement of valuation.* The traditional rule for loss of bargain damages measures the property's market value as of the date of the breach. But when the buyer breaches, the seller often puts the property back on the market and may have to wait for months or even years before another buyer is found. In a declining market (like the one experienced following the market crash that began in 2007), the ultimate resale price may be much lower than the value on the date of the breach. If the seller has continued to make a diligent effort to resell, should the actual resale price be the relevant value for purposes of computing damages? The court so held in Kuhn v. Spatial Design, Inc., 585 A.2d 967 (N.J.Super.Ct.1991) (following the rule for sales of goods found in U.C.C. Article 2). Contra Jones v. Lee, 971 P.2d 858 (N.M.Ct.App.1998). Courts frequently seem to assume that the resale price is good evidence (perhaps the "best" or only available evidence) of market value, and often use it without much discussion of the matter. See White v. Farrell, 964 N.Y.S.2d 467, 987 N.E.2d 244 (2013) ("the resale price, in a particular case, may be very strong evidence of fair market value at the time of the breach").

When the seller breaches and the buyer seeks damages, the buyer may argue that the court should value the property as of the time of trial in the damages action rather than at the date of the breach. In a rising market, the buyer can argue that, but for seller's breach, buyer would have owned property worth much more by the time of trial, and hence that the breach damaged the purchaser that much more. See, e.g., Reese v. Wong, 93 Cal.App.4th 51, 112 Cal.Rptr.2d 669 (2001) (expressing sympathy to the argument, but rejecting it because a statute mandated the standard date-of-breach valuation).

A further reason why courts may prefer to rely on the actual resale price as the relevant measure of value is that otherwise the court must act on the basis of appraisal testimony, which can be notoriously imprecise. For example, in Askari v. R & R Land Co., 179 Cal.App. 3d 1101, 225 Cal.Rptr. 285 (1986), the appraisers for the two parties were $400,000 apart in their estimates of value as of the trial date—an amount that was 32 percent of the original contract price of $1.25 million. Such variations in appraisals are not unusual and scarcely build one's confidence in the measurement of damages.

4.   *Incidental and consequential damages of the buyer.* As Donovan illustrates, a nonbreaching buyer can recover amounts spent for title examination and survey costs; such expenses are plainly foreseeable. Can a nonbreaching buyer recover the following expenditures as part of a consequential damages award?

(a)   Airfare for travel to negotiate and execute the contract which the seller subsequently breached? See Fountain v. Mojo, 687 P.2d 496 (Colo.Ct.App.1984).

(b)   Additional rent, taxes, mortgage interest, and other carrying costs incurred by the buyer at her present home while she locates and purchases substitute property?

(c)   Loss of favorable financing from a bank that is no longer available due to an increase in market interest rates? See Wall v. Pate, 104 N.M. 1, 715 P.2d 449 (1986).

(d)   The cost of leasing temporary quarters elsewhere, including rent, advertising for a place to lease, and the expense of moving to the leased premises? See Ruble v. Reich, 259 Neb. 658, 611 N.W.2d 844 (2000) (allowing buyers to recover rent they paid for temporary quarters, but deducting the amount of property taxes and interest they would have paid after closing if the sale had closed on time, and that they saved by renting instead).

(e)   Profits lost by the buyer, either from business operations to be conducted on the property or from plans to renovate the property and resell it? See Greenwich S.F., LLC v. Wong, 190 Cal.App.4th 739,118 Cal.Rptr.3d 531 (2010) (evidence of lost profits was too uncertain and speculative). Cf. Hoang v. Hewitt Ave. Assocs., LLC, 936 A.2d 915 (Md.Ct.App.2007) (purchaser's 25-year track record of building and marketing homes in the area made its claim for lost profits reasonably certain).

If these items are recoverable as damages, should they (or any of them) be offset by the fact that the buyer still has the purchase money, and may have earned interest on it (if it was to have been paid in cash) or has saved the interest which she would have paid on the money (if she intended to borrow it)?

5.   *Seller's consequential damages.* Now consider the types of consequential damages that a seller might properly recover. Should they include the following?

(a)   Carrying costs of the property until it is resold (assuming continuing reasonable efforts to resell)? Such costs might include property taxes, insurance, utilities, maintenance, and interest on existing mortgage loans. See Mueller v. Johnson, 60 Wash.App. 683, 806 P.2d 256 (1991); Ner Tamid Congregation of North Town v. Krivoruchko, 660 F.Supp.2d 927 (N.D.Ill.2009) (approving recovery of these items). But other courts refuse such claims. See DiScipio v. Sullivan, 30 A.D.3d 677, 816 N.Y.S.2d 578 (2006); Quigley v. Jones, 334 S.E.2d 664 (Ga.1985). One court put it this way: "Allowing such damages to be recovered . . . could incent the seller to hold the property indefinitely while waiting for market conditions to change, or for a purchaser willing to pay a specific price, because the seller knows his breaching buyer is responsible for all costs the seller is incurring by continuing to own the property." Goldman v. Olmstead, 414 S.W.3d 346, 352 (Tex.Ct.App.2013). Do you agree?

(b)   Interest income the seller expected to earn on the purchase price, or on purchase-money mortgage financing he was obligated under the contract to provide to the purchaser? See Askari v. R & R Land Co., 179 Cal.App.3d 1101, 225 Cal.Rptr. 285 (1986) (approving recovery of lost interest on purchase-money financing); Van Moorlehem v. Brown Realty Co., 747 F.2d 992 (10th Cir.1984) (denying recovery for interest seller expected to earn on cash purchase price).

(c)   The cost of a second real estate broker's commission on the resale, if the seller was obliged to pay a commission on the first sale even though it did not close? Compare Mueller v. Johnson, 60 Wash.App. 683, 806 P.2d 256 (1991) (approving recovery of resale expense) with Johnston v. Curtis, 70 Ark.App. 195, 16 S.W.3d 283 (2000) (rejecting such recovery). Other resale expenses (e.g., advertising) presumably would be treated similarly.

What about the use value of the property during the period the seller is attempting to resell? If the seller in fact rents the property to a tenant during the interim, it seems obvious that the rent collected should offset the seller's claim for incidental and consequential damages. Should a similar result follow, with an offset for fair rental value, if the seller continues to use the land himself? Suppose the seller does not in fact use the property, but it remains available and adaptable to the seller's use?

SCHWINDER V. AUSTIN BANK OF CHICAGO
Illinois Court of Appeals, 2004
348 Ill.App.3d 461, 809 N.E.2d 180, 284 Ill.Dec. 58

JUSTICE GORDON delivered the opinion of the court. . . . The record and testimony in this case reveal that on June 21, 2000, plaintiffs, Thomas F. Schwinder and Susan L. Londay, tendered an offer to purchase a condominium unit located at 3117 South Benson, in Chicago, Illinois, which was owned by defendants, Austin Bank of Chicago, trustee under trust agreement dated February 24, 1978, known as trust No. 5861 (hereinafter Trustee), and Marian Baginski. As the sole beneficiary of this land trust, Baginski was thus authorized to convey the title to plaintiffs.

On July 5, 2000, Baginski accepted the offer from plaintiffs to purchase the condominium unit. The purchase contract between the parties was a form real estate contract prepared by Baginski's attorney and utilized for all real estate transactions in the Bridgeport Crossing Condominium complex in which the condominium unit was located. . . .

[Baginski failed to tender a deed on the agreed closing date because he was in the process of obtaining a divorce and was uncertain whether the court in the divorce action would require him to make some particular disposition of the condominium unit. He signed an agreement permitting the buyers to move in without a closing, upon their promise to pay a fee of $1,500 per month "until such time as Seller is able to close on the sale of the property." After the divorce court approved the sale of the condominium, and despite repeated efforts by the buyers to get Baginski to schedule a closing of the sale, he refused to do so. The buyers then brought this action for specific performance of the contract. The court reviewed the terms of the original contract and the agreement for possession which modified the contract, concluded that the contract as modified was valid and enforceable, and granted the buyers specific performance.]

Finding the purchase contract valid and enforceable, we must now consider whether the grant of specific performance was proper in this case. The principle underlying the specific performance remedy is to grant equitable relief where the damage remedy at law is inadequate. See Geist v. Lehmann, 19 Ill. App. 3d 557, 561, 312 N.E.2d 42, 46 (1974). At the time this branch of equity jurisdiction was evolving in England, the presumed uniqueness of land, as well as its importance to the social order, led to the conclusion that damages at law could never be adequate to compensate for the breach of a contract to transfer an interest in land. Hence, specific performance became a fixed remedy in this class of transactions. See 11 S. Williston on Contracts § 1418A (3d ed.1968); 5 Corbin on Contracts § 1143 (1964).

"Two distinct elements enter into the application of [specific performance]: first, the extent to which the evidentiary function of the statutory formalities is fulfilled by the conduct of the parties; second, the reliance of the promisee, providing a compelling substantive basis for relief in addition to the expectations created by the promise." Restatement (Second) of Contracts § 129, comm. b, at 322 (1981). The evidentiary element can be satisfied by a meticulous examination of the evidence and realistic appraisal of the probabilities on the part of the trier of fact; commonly summarized in a standard that calls upon the trier of fact to be satisfied by "clear and convincing evidence. Restatement (Second) of Contracts § 129, comm. b, at 322 (1981). The substantive element requires consideration of the adequacy of the remedy of restitution. Restatement (Second) of Contracts § 129, comm. b, at 322 (1981).

Illinois courts have long held that where the parties have fairly and understandingly entered into a valid contract for the sale of real property, specific performance of the contract is a matter of right and equity will enforce it, absent circumstances of oppression and fraud. Giannini v. First National Bank of Des Plaines, 136 Ill. App. 3d 971, 981, 91 Ill. Dec. 438, 483 N.E.2d 924, 933 (1985). Contracts to devise or convey real estate are enforced by specific performance on the ground that the law cannot "do perfect justice." Giannini, 136 Ill. App. 3d at 981, 91 Ill. Dec. 438, 483 N.

E.2d at 933; Hagen v. Anderson, 317 Ill. 173, 177, 147 N.E. 791, 793 (1925). Generally, a party will be entitled to specific performance of a contract for conveyances of real estate only upon establishing either that the party has performed according to the terms of the contract or that the party was ready, willing and able to perform but was prevented, and thus excused from doing so by the acts or conduct of the other party. *Omni Partners*, 246 Ill. App. 3d at 63, 185 Ill. Dec. 657, 614 N.E.2d at 1346; Tantillo v. Janus, 87 Ill. App. 3d 231, 234, 42 Ill. Dec. 291, 408 N.E.2d 1000, 1003 (1980).

Specific performance is a matter of sound judicial discretion controlled by established principles of equity and exercised upon a consideration of all the facts and circumstances of a particular case. *Omni Partners*, 246 Ill. App. 3d at 62, 185 Ill. Dec. 657, 614 N.E.2d at 1345; Djomlija v. Urban, 107 Ill. App. 3d 960, 967, 63 Ill. Dec. 627, 438 N.E.2d 558, 563 (1982). In this regard, the trial court should balance the equities between the parties. Hild v. Avland Development Co., 46 Ill. App. 3d 173, 179, 4 Ill. Dec. 672, 360 N.E.2d 785, 790 (1977). Accordingly, a court using its equitable powers may refuse to grant specific performance where the remedy would cause a peculiar hardship or inequitable result. . . .

In applying the requirements needed for specific performance, first, we must set forth that both plaintiffs and defendants freely and understandingly entered into a purchase contract for the sale of the condominium unit. There is no question from the facts in this case that there was no fraud or oppression by either party upon the other at the time of execution of the purchase contract. In fact, defendants note multiple times in their brief that both parties fully understood the purchase contract before they executed it.

Next we must turn to whether a condominium is the proper subject of specific performance. Although neither of the parties contends that specific performance cannot be granted when dealing with a condominium unit, the question of uniqueness is an issue of concern for courts. On one side is the argument that condominium units are real estate, per se unique and thus entitled to a remedy in equity. See *Giannini*, 136 Ill. App. 3d at 981, 91 Ill. Dec. 438, 483 N.E.2d at 933–34. On the other side is the argument that a condominium unit is but one of thousands with the same layout, typically in the same building, and therefore are only entitled to remedies at law. See Centex Homes Corp. v. Boag, 128 N.J. Super. 385, 389, 320 A.2d 194, 196 (1974). However, using either argument, there is no question that the condominium unit in this case is unique. *Giannini*, 136 Ill. App. 3d at 980–81, 91 Ill. Dec. 438, 483 N.E.2d at 932–33 (although there has been debate over whether condominium units are unique and thus are the proper subject of specific performance, this court held that condominiums are "real property" for the purposes of specific performance); but see *Centex Homes*, 128 N.J. Super. at 389, 320 A.2d at 196 (finding that except upon a showing of unusual circumstances or a change in the vendor's position, such as where the vendee has entered into possession, the vendor's damages are usually measurable, his remedy at law is adequate and there is no jurisdictional basis for equitable relief). The condominium unit in this case is obviously unique under the *Giannini* argument, and it meets the exact exception making it unique under the *Centex Homes* argument. *Giannini*, 136 Ill. App. 3d at 980–82, 91 Ill. Dec. 438, 483 N.E.2d at 932–34; *Centex Homes*, 128 N.J. Super. at 389, 320 A.2d at 196. The condominium unit was not sold as a sample; it was substantially upgraded to plaintiffs' specifications. Furthermore, plaintiffs themselves have made improvements to the condominium unit. Lastly, and most importantly, the condominium unit in this case has been plaintiffs' home for the past two years. The uniqueness of this condominium unit to the plaintiffs makes it an unquestionably proper subject for specific performance and makes the remedy at law inadequate.

Finding that a remedy at law was inadequate, the trial court found, and we agree, that it would be inequitable to deny specific performance in this case. The above-enumerated facts bear this out. Notably, plaintiffs paid the earnest money to defendants, took possession of the condominium unit, withdrew their 401(k) for a down payment, obtained mortgage commitment papers and made substantial improvements to the condominium unit. It would be inequitable for the court to allow plaintiffs to bear all the loss they suffered and move them out of their home when they complied with all of the terms of the agreement.

Furthermore, at all times during the pendency of the sales contract, plaintiffs were ready, willing and able to perform but were prevented, and thus excused, from doing so by Baginski's refusal to schedule a closing date. Plaintiffs were ready with a mortgage approval and a down payment in hand to close on the condominium unit the very instant Baginski assigned a closing date. However, Baginski repeatedly refused to schedule the closing date, and thus, plaintiffs never consummated the sale of the condominium unit.

Based on the foregoing, the trial court's determination to grant specific performance of the purchase contract was proper in this case. . . .

NOTES AND QUESTIONS

1. *Specific performance for the nonbreaching buyer.* The *Schwinder* case provides the customary judicial statements that an award of specific performance is discretionary with the court and is appropriate where the nonbreaching party's legal remedy (damages) would be inadequate. *Schwinder* is also typical in its suggestion that damages are rarely an adequate remedy for breach of a real estate sale contract by the buyer, and that specific performance is thus available as a matter of right. Other decisions state a position that is nearly as broad. See, e.g., Friendship Manor, Inc. v. Greiman, 581 A.2d 893 (N.J.Super.Ct.App.Div.1990) ("There is a virtual presumption,

because of the uniqueness of land and the consequent inadequacy of monetary damages, that specific performance is the buyer's appropriate remedy for the vendor's breach of the contract to convey."). In an action by the buyer, specific performance seems easy to justify; the buyer gets the very land it contracted to buy, and no other parcel would be exactly the same. Given that, is there a point to requiring the nonbreaching buyer to put forward evidence that damages would be inadequate?

2.   *Specific performance for the nonbreaching seller.* A presumptive award of specific performance for the nonbreaching seller seems conceptually harder to justify, because the seller would simply receiving money. As one court stated in a dispute over the buyer's breach of a $1.775 million home sale contract:

> [E]ven assuming that each and every parcel of land, house, apartment, condominium, etc., is, in fact, "unique," there is nothing "unique" about cash, or more specifically, the cash of potential purchasers. . . . Sellers could have sold the Property to other purchasers for a price comparable to that in the Contract (or more) if they had listed the Property for sale after the Buyers notified the Sellers of their (the Buyers') intent to terminate the Contract. Then, the Sellers could have kept the proceeds of the sale and the $40,000 in earnest money paid by the Buyers. One of the Sellers even admitted in her deposition that, around the time the Buyers backed out of the Contract, if someone other than the Buyers had given her a check for $1,775,000 to purchase the Property, that would have been satisfactory to her.

> Further, it is undisputed that the Sellers did not make any changes to the Property to accommodate these specific Buyers that caused the Sellers to incur additional expenses or that made the Property less attractive to other potential purchasers. Simply put, there was nothing "unique" about the Buyers in this case that would support an order requiring these specific Buyers to purchase the Property. Thus, we reject the assertion that, simply because real property is generally considered to be "unique," the Sellers in this case were automatically entitled to specific performance of the Contract.

Sexton v. Sewell, 351 Ga.App. 273, 830 S.E.2d 605 (2019); see also *Centex Homes, Inc. v. Boag,* discussed in *Schwinder* (rejecting view that mutuality of remedy justifies specific performance for nonbreaching seller as a matter of right). A few other cases have also cast doubt on the usual assumption that a vendor may have specific performance as a matter of course. See Seabaugh v. Keele, 775 S.W.2d 205 (Mo.Ct.App.1989); Wolf v. Anderson, 334 N.W.2d 212 (N.D.1983); Perron v. Hale, 701 P.2d 198 (Idaho 1985); People's United Bank, NA v. Alana Provencale, Inc., 189 A.3d 71 (Vt.2018) (denying specific performance to seller that made no evidentiary showing as to why damages would be inadequate).

Do you agree? Real estate is notoriously illiquid. In a slow market, it may take the nonbreaching seller many months or even years to resell the property.

Because damages are measured on the date of breach, if the purchaser breaches, the vendor is left with the task of disposing of the land. This forces the vendor to pay the holding costs of the property for an unknown period and to take the risk that a falling market will result in an ultimate sale at a price well below the market value on the date of breach. Resale of the property may be further delayed by the existence of the old contract, which clouds the title until the matter has been resolved by settlement or a court decision. All of these are risks that the vendor thought she or he had gotten rid of under the original contract of sale. A decree of specific performance will put them back on the purchaser, where they belong.

Dale A. Whitman, Ann M. Burkhart, R. Wilson Freyermuth & Troy A. Rule, The Law of Property § 10.5, at 631 (4th ed.2019). Does this concern justify the behavior of most courts, who tend to award specific performance to the nonbreaching seller as a matter of right? Would this concern apply with equal force if the seller is the developer of a brand new 500-unit condominium project, and the seller had the closed the sales of four other units with identical floor plans during the same week in which the buyer breached? See *Centex Homes*, 320 A.2d at 196 (developer's legal remedy was adequate; specific performance denied).

3.   *Grounds for denial of specific performance*. There are a variety of situations in which courts have denied specific performance and relegated the plaintiff to other remedies. These include:

(a)   Because specific performance is an equitable remedy, it will be refused if it would produce unjust or unconscionable results, as the court in *Schwinder* indicated. See 6A Powell, Real Property, ¶ 930; Kilarjian v. Vastola, 877 A.2d 372 (N.J. Ch. Div. 2004) (specific performance for buyer denied where seller wished to remain in her home because of severely deteriorating health); Dergo v. Kollias, 567 N.W.2d 443 (Iowa Ct.App.1997) (specific performance denied where purchaser failed to disclose identity of "true buyer" for whom purchaser was acting).

(b)   If the vendor has resold the land to a good faith purchaser for value, the court will not grant specific performance. See UFG, LLC v. Southwest Corp., 848 N.E.2d 353 (Ind.Ct.App.2006). But a subsequent purchaser who takes with notice of the previous contract takes subject to the equitable rights created by it, and must give up the land if the original purchaser obtains an order of specific performance. Wilde v. O'Leary, 374 N. J. Super. 582, 866 A.2d 205 (2005).

(c)   A court will deny specific performance if performance would be impossible. For example, specific performance will be denied if the seller's title is defective and the buyer refuses to waive the defect. See Anderson v. Onsager, 455 N.W.2d 885 (Wis. 1990). Suppose the buyer asserts that she is incapable of paying the purchase price, and thus that her performance is impossible. Should the court refuse an award of specific performance to the seller on this ground? In Ash Park, LLC v. Alexander & Bishop, Ltd., 783 N.W.2d 294 (Wis. 2010), the buyers planned to build a shopping center on the land, but their intended primary tenant refused to enter into a lease. The buyers argued that this made their performance of the contract impossible, but the court was unpersuaded and ordered specific performance. [Query: What happens if the court awards specific performance but the buyer does not have the money to close?]

(d) If the purchaser was buying the land for the purpose of immediate resale at a profit, some courts have denied specific performance to the buyer on the ground that the land's supposed uniqueness was of no real consequence to the buyer given the plan to resell. See Watkins v. Paul, 95 Idaho 499, 511 P.2d 781 (1973). Cf. Chan v. Smider, 31 Wash. App. 730, 644 P.2d 727 (1982). Does the buyer's mere profit motive justify denial of specific performance? See Brenner, Specific Performance of Contracts for the Sale of Land Purchased for Resale or Investment, 24 McGill L. J. 513 (1978).

4.   *Specific performance with abatement of the price.* If the seller does not own all the property covered by the contract, the purchaser may desire, and can generally obtain, specific performance with an abatement of the price to reflect the shortage in the land. See, e.g., Burk v. Hefley, 32 Ark.App. 133, 798 S.W.2d 109 (1990); Ewing v. Bissell, 105 Nev. 488, 777 P.2d 1320 (1989). The same principle is applied if the seller contracts to sell the entire parcel but owns only a fractional undivided interest in it. See Chastain v. Schomburg, 258 Ga. 218, 367 S.E.2d 230 (1988).

5.   *Specific performance plus damages?* If the court orders specific performance, the nonbreaching party can also recover forseeable consequential damages. See, e.g., Houston v. Willis, 24 So.3d 412, 420 (Miss.Ct.App.2009) (awarding damages to seller for mortgage payments, insurance, and taxes buyer should have been paying during the period of delay); Godwin v. Lindbert, 300 N.W.2d 514 (Mich.Ct.App.1980) (awarding damages to buyer for higher cost of mortgage funds due to interest rate increase during period of seller's nonperformance); Woliansky v. Miller, 704 P.2d 811 (Ariz.Ct.App.1985) (buyer allowed damages for deterioration to improvements during five-year delay in seller's performance). Suppose Seller breaches a contract for the sale of undeveloped land on which Buyer planned to build a home. After two years of litigation, Buyer obtains specific performance and Seller delivers a deed; Buyer also seeks $15,000 in damages, claiming that construction costs had increased by this amount during the two-year delay. Should the court allow Buyer to recover this amount? See, e.g., Bravo v. Buelow, 168 Cal.App.3d 208, 214 Cal.Rptr. 65 (1985). See also Garland, Purchaser's Interest Rate Increase: Caveat Venditor, 27 N.Y.L.S. L. Rev. 745 (1982); Dale A. Whitman, Ann M.

Burkhart, R. Wilson Freyermuth & Troy A. Rule, The Law of Property § 10.5 nn. 219–22 (4th ed. 2019).

    6.   *The vendee's lien and the vendor's lien.* If the seller breaches but refuses to return the purchaser's earnest money, some states give the purchaser a "vendee's lien" on the property to secure recovery of the deposit. See Sparks v. Charles Wayne Group, 568 So.2d 512 (Fla.Ct.App.1990) (buyer may file a notice of lis pendens in support of vendee's lien). Unless the contract is recorded (which is unlikely), if the seller conveys the land to a good faith purchaser for value without notice of the prior contract, that purchaser will take the land free of the vendee's lien. See State Sav. & Loan Ass'n v. Kauaian Dev. Co., 50 Haw. 540, 445 P.2d 109 (1968). Cf. In re Pearl, 40 B.R. 860 (Bankr.D.N.J.1984).

    If the buyer breaches after the seller has transferred title to her (not a very common situation), the seller has a "vendor's lien" (perhaps more aptly a "grantor's lien") in most states to secure payment to the grantor of the remaining purchase price. See, e.g., Bolen v. Bolen, 169 S.W.3d 59 (Ky.Ct.App.2005). Again, however, a further transfer by the purchaser to a good faith purchaser for value will defeat the lien. See Union Bank, N.A. v. North Idaho Resorts, LLC, 399 P.3d 907 (Idaho 2017); Cooksey v. Sinder, 682 S.W.2d 252 (Tex.1984).

    The vendee's lien is an aid to rescission and restitution, whereas the vendor's lien is an aid to specific enforcement of the contract. In both cases a personal "deficiency" judgment is available if the foreclosure of the lien does not produce sufficient funds to pay the plaintiff fully. See Quintana v. Anthony, 109 Idaho 977, 712 P.2d 678 (Ct.App.1985).

"Earnest money" and liquidated damages. The buyer nearly always makes an earnest money deposit when submitting an offer to buy real estate. If the seller accepts the offer, the seller may hold the earnest money directly, or it may be held until the closing by the broker or the seller's attorney. [Which would you prefer as a buyer? As a broker?] Customs with respect to the size of an earnest money deposit vary widely. In the Northeastern states, deposits are very substantial—typically 10 percent of the total price (and sometimes more). In the South and West it is often much smaller, and may be as little as a few hundred dollars, especially in lower-priced tract subdivisions. The amount is a matter of negotiation, and typically plays an important role in the determination of the seller's remedies if the buyer breaches. Often, the contract will provide a clause allowing the seller to retain the deposit as liquidated damages if the buyer breaches. An illustrative clause, taken from the sales contract form reprinted earlier in Section B of this chapter, reads as follows:

    In the event of a material breach of this contract by the Buyer, the
    Seller may retain the earnest money deposit as liquidated

damages for the Buyer's breach, or in the alternative may waive the right to liquidated damages and obtain such other remedies as are available in law or equity.

If the buyer breaches, of course, the amount of the deposit could end up being much smaller or much greater than the seller's actual economic loss due to the breach. Thus, liquidated damages clauses tend to raise two common questions which the following materials explore. First, does including a liquidated damages clause preclude the seller from asserting alternate remedies (such as suing for actual damages if the seller's actual loss exceeds the deposit)? Second, must the seller return any of the deposit if it exceeds the seller's actual loss?

RAVENSTAR, LLC v. ONE SKI HILL PLACE, LLC
Supreme Court of Colorado, 2017
401 P.3d 552

CHIEF JUSTICE RICE delivered the Opinion of the Court. This case requires us to determine whether a liquidated damages clause in a contract is invalid because the contract gives the non-breaching party the option to choose between liquidated damages and actual damages. We hold that such an option does not invalidate the clause and instead parties are free to contract for a damages provision that allows a non-breaching party to elect between liquidated damages and actual damages. However, such an option must be exclusive, meaning a party who elects to pursue one of the available remedies may not also pursue the alternative remedy set forth in the contract. Therefore, under the facts of this case, we conclude that the liquidated damages clause in the contracts at issue is enforceable.

In 2008, Petitioners, five Colorado companies, entered into separate contracts (the "Agreements") to buy to-be-built condominium units from Respondent, developer One Ski Hill Place, LLC ("OSHP"). Petitioners paid earnest money and construction deposits of fifteen percent of the purchase price of each unit. But Petitioners were unable to obtain financing and failed to close by the agreed-upon 2010 deadline, thereby breaching the Agreements.

Each Agreement contains an identical provision governing default (the "Damages Provision"), which provided, in sum, that if a purchaser of a unit defaulted, then OSHP had the option to retain all or some of the paid deposits as liquidated damages or, alternatively, to pursue actual damages and apply the deposits toward that award. The Damages Provision in full stated:

> If Purchaser defaults in the performance of any obligation under this Agreement . . . Seller shall have the right to terminate this Agreement and shall be entitled *to retain all or a portion of the Earnest Money and Construction Deposit . . . as liquidated*

[margin note: I → Can contract to elect between 2 damages, but must be exclusive.]

damages ("Seller's Liquidated Damages"). *Alternatively and in lieu of* Seller's Liquidated Damages, Seller may elect to terminate this Agreement and recover its actual damages resulting from Purchaser's default calculated in accordance with Colorado law, in which case Seller may seek an award of such actual damages and may retain an amount equal to the Earnest Money and Construction Deposit and apply such funds toward satisfaction of any such award. If Seller elects to seek actual damages, Seller must provide Purchaser with written notice of such election within 30 days after the end of Purchaser's cure period, and if Seller fails to provide such notice, then Seller will only be entitled to Seller's Liquidated Damages. (Emphasis added.)

After Petitioners defaulted and breached the Agreements, OSHP chose to keep the full deposits as liquidated damages. Petitioners then filed this case against OSHP, seeking the return of their deposits.

OSHP filed a motion for summary judgment. In response, Petitioners contended that the Damages Provision in the Agreements was unenforceable because the Provision gave OSHP the option to choose liquidated damages or actual damages. Therefore, Petitioners argued, the parties did not mutually intend to liquidate damages, as Colorado law requires. The trial court rejected this argument, ruling that the parties mutually intended to liquidate damages as a matter of law. Nonetheless, the trial court denied summary judgment to OSHP because disputed issues of material fact remained as to whether the amount of liquidated damages was reasonable and whether actual damages would have been difficult to ascertain, both requirements of an enforceable liquidated damages provision.

Petitioners then stipulated that the amount of liquidated damages was reasonable and that actual damages were difficult to ascertain, thereby resolving the remaining disputed issues of fact. The trial court entered judgment in favor of OSHP, and Petitioners appealed. A division of the court of appeals affirmed the trial court's judgment and orders and held that the "mere presence of an option to elect between liquidated damages and actual damages does not render the liquidated damages clause unenforceable." Specifically, the division concluded that optional liquidated damages clauses do not necessarily operate as a penalty, nor did the clause here operate as a penalty under the facts of this case. We granted certiorari. . . .

A liquidated damages provision is valid and enforceable if three [*valid if*] elements are met: (1) "the parties intended to liquidate damages"; (2) "the amount of liquidated damages, when viewed as of the time the contract was made, was a reasonable estimate of the presumed actual damages that the breach would cause"; and (3) "when viewed again as of the date of the contract, it was difficult to ascertain the amount of actual damages that would result from a breach." *Klinger v. Adams Cty. Sch. Dist. No. 50*, 130 P.3d 1027, 1034 (Colo. 2006) (*quoting Rohauer v. Little*, 736 P.2d 403, 410 (Colo. 1987)). If any one of the elements is not met, the provision is an invalid penalty. *Id.* A penalty differs from a liquidated damages clause because "a penalty is designed to punish for a breach of contract[,] whereas liquidated damages are intended as fair compensation for the breach." 25A C.J.S. Damages § 200 (2016).

"liquidated damages are intended as fair comp. for breach."

Here, the parties stipulated that the second and third elements of the test were satisfied. Thus, the only contested element is whether the parties intended to liquidate damages. The presence of a liquidated damages provision "itself is evidence of the parties' intention to liquidate damages in advance." *Oldis v. Grosse-Rhode*, 35 Colo.App. 46, 528 P.2d 944, 947 (1974); *see also O'Hara Grp. Denver, Ltd. v. Marcor Hous. Sys., Inc.*, 197 Colo. 530, 595 P.2d 679, 683 (1979) (holding that "on the basis of the contracts," the parties intended to liquidate damages). But we have never determined whether the presence of an alternative damages remedy negates the required intent to liquidate damages and therefore invalidates a liquidated damages clause. The parties cite to a number of court of appeals cases to support their respective positions, however, none of the cited cases is on point. Instead, we turn to existing Colorado law on freedom of contract and apply this framework to the case before us. . . .

[T]he very notion of a contract includes the enforceability of mutually bargained-for duties and risks. *See Town of Alma v. AZCO Constr., Inc.*, 10 P.3d 1256, 1264 (Colo. 2000) ("Contract law is intended to enforce the expectancy interests created by the parties' promises so that they can allocate risks and costs during their bargaining."). And "[a]n essential corollary of the concept of bargained-for duties is bargained-for liabilities for failure to perform them. Important to the vitality of contract is the capacity voluntarily to define the consequences of the breach of a duty before assuming the duty." *Isler v. Tex. Oil & Gas Corp.*, 749 F.2d 22, 23 (10th Cir. 1984).

Applying these principles, we conclude that the parties here were free to bargain for liquidated damages as a sole and exclusive remedy, but they did not, and instead bargained for the risk allocation memorialized in the Damages Provision currently in the Agreements. Striking the option to liquidate damages in the Damages Provision, like Petitioners encourage, would be antithetical to the principles of freedom of contract and would require us to restructure the contract, which we are reluctant to do. *See Roberts v. Adams*, 47 P.3d 690, 694 (Colo. App. 2001) ("The court's duty is to interpret and enforce contracts as written, not to rewrite or restructure them.").

Intent to liquidate can't be conflated with intent to liquidate as sole remedy

The freedom to contract for the alternative damages remedies of liquidated damages and actual damages does not negate the parties' intent to liquidate damages. All that this court requires is that "the parties intended to liquidate damages." *Klinger*, 130 P.3d at 1034. An intent to liquidate damages should not be conflated with an intent to liquidate damages as the sole and exclusive remedy. The parties must only mutually intend to make liquidated damages one of the available remedies that the non-breaching party could pursue. So long as the parties mutually intend the stipulated sum to be the agreed-upon measure of damages if the non-breaching party elects liquidated damages, the mutual intent element of Klinger is satisfied. Therefore, the mere presence of an option to seek either liquidated damages or actual damages does not render the liquidated damages clause invalid as a matter of law.

However, such an option must be exclusive. In other words, a provision that allows a non-breaching party to pursue liquidated or actual damages must only allow the non-breaching party to pursue one of those options. If the non-breaching party elects to pursue the liquidated damages set forth in the contract, it may not in addition pursue the alternative actual damages remedy set forth therein. Otherwise, an election to pursue liquidated damages would function as an invalid penalty.

Here, by providing in the Agreements that OSHP "shall be entitled to retain all or a portion of the Earnest Money and Construction Deposit . . . as liquidated damages," the parties clearly mutually intended both that liquidated damages be one of the available remedies OSHP could pursue and that the stipulated sum (i.e., the Earnest Money and Construction Deposit) be the agreed-upon measure of damages if OSHP elected to pursue liquidated damages. Therefore, the liquidated damages clause of the Damages Provision before us is enforceable, meaning OSHP properly retained Petitioners' full deposits.

In support of their position that the option to choose between actual damages and liquidated damages renders a liquidated damages clause unenforceable by negating the intent element of the liquidated damages test, the Petitioners point to a variety of out-of-state cases. Notably, they point to *Lefemine v. Baron*, 573 So.2d 326, 329 (Fla. 1991), in which the Florida Supreme Court held that such an option "indicates an intent to penalize the defaulting buyer and negates the intent to liquidate damages in the event of a breach." They also reference *Grossinger Motorcorp, Inc. v. American National Bank & Trust Co.*, 240 Ill.App.3d 737, 180 Ill.Dec. 824, 607 N.E.2d 1337, 1346 (1992), where the Illinois Appellate Court held that "[o]n its face, the optional nature of the liquidated damages clause shows that the parties never intended to establish a specific sum to constitute damages in the event of a breach." There, the court reasoned that "if such an optional provision were enforceable, it would be invoked only as a penalty when the liquidated damages exceeded the actual damages." *Id.*,

180 Ill.Dec. 824, 607 N.E.2d at 1347. Both courts then struck the optional liquidated damages clause and allowed the non-breaching parties to recover only actual damages resulting from the breach. . . .

However, we do not find the reasoning of such courts persuasive. These courts have assumed that the non-breaching party would choose the remedy of liquidated damages only when actual damages are lower than the stipulated sum and thereby inferred "an intent to penalize the defaulting buyer." *See Lefemine*, 573 So.2d at 329. However, a non-breaching party might instead reasonably choose to retain liquidated damages even though actual damages may be higher for two primary reasons.

First, whereas actual damages must be proved, liquidated damages offer certainty. Here, for example, at the time OSHP had to elect between remedies, the ultimate actual damages were difficult to ascertain because the real estate being sold was a condominium unit in a yet-to-be-constructed building. Thus, electing liquidated damages provided certainty of relief that may not have otherwise been available. Second, the non-breaching party may prefer to forgo the possibility of lengthy and costly litigation involved in seeking actual damages. This is particularly true where, as here, the liquidated damages consist of money already paid to the seller. Because, at the time of breach, the non-breaching party may not know its actual damages without engaging in time-consuming and expensive fact and expert discovery, electing liquidated damages avoids this time and cost expenditure.

Instead, we agree with other jurisdictions that have found no issue with the presence of an option for both liquidated and actual damages in a contract. For example, we find more persuasive the reasoning of courts such as the Washington Court of Appeals which enforced a contractual clause that permitted liquidated damages as one of multiple alternate remedies, including actual damages, on the ground that the right to pursue any of the remedies was specifically reserved in the contract. *Noble v. Ogborn*, 43 Wash.App. 387, 717 P.2d 285, 286 (1986); *see also, Sampson v. McAdoo*, 47 Md.App. 602, 425 A.2d 1, 3 (Md. Ct. Spec. App. 1981); *G.H. Swope Bldg. Corp. v. Horton*, 207 Tenn. 114, 338 S.W.2d 566, 568 (1960); *Sheffield v. Paul T. Stone, Inc.*, 98 F.2d 250, 252 (D.C. Cir. 1938). . . . Ultimately, this line of cases better comports with our well-established precedent regarding freedom of contract. Accordingly, we are unpersuaded by the Petitioners' claim that reasoning from other jurisdictions should change our conclusion today.

For the foregoing reasons, we affirm the judgment of the court of appeals.

SAN FRANCISCO DISTRIBUTION CENTER, LLC V. STONEMASON PARTNERS, LP

District Court of Appeal of Florida, Third District, 2014
183 So.3d 391

EMAS, J. . . . In January 2012, San Francisco Distribution entered into a contract with Stonemason to buy a commercial property in Miami Beach for $5,250,000.00. The effective date of the contract was January 16, 2012, and San Francisco Distribution was required to close within forty-five days of the effective date. Under the terms of the contract, San Francisco Distribution was required to pay a total deposit amount of $400,000, to be held in escrow by Wells Fargo. The contract provided that in the event of a default by San Francisco Distribution:

> Seller (Stonemason) may either (1) retain all deposit(s) paid or agreed to be paid by Buyer as agreed upon liquidated damages, as consideration for the execution of this Contract, and in full settlement of any claims, upon which this Contract will terminate or (2) seek specific performance. If Seller retains the deposit, Seller will pay the Listing and Cooperating Brokers named in Paragraph 12 fifty percent of all forfeited deposits retained by Seller (to be split equally among the Brokers) up to the full amount of the brokerage fee.

San Francisco Distribution's broker was Thomas Martino, who also served as the closing agent. When San Francisco Distribution failed to close, Stonemason demanded the $400,000 deposit amount as liquidated damages per the contract, but was told by Martino that the deposit had been returned to San Francisco Distribution. Accordingly, Stonemason filed suit against San Francisco Distribution and Martino. The complaint alleged several counts against San Francisco Distribution, all of which were dismissed by the court with the exception of a breach of contract count.

In its amended answer to the complaint, San Francisco Distribution admitted that the contract did not close but asserted, in its affirmative defenses, that Stonemason was not entitled to the $400,000 deposit because it had subsequently sold the property to another buyer for $200,000 more than the San Francisco Distribution contract price, and that therefore, Stonemason suffered no damages.[3] In addition, San Francisco Distribution asserted that because the liquidated damages clause of the contract was unreasonable and unrelated to actual damages suffered by Stonemason, it was unconscionable and void and also was an unenforceable penalty clause because it provided the alternative remedy of specific performance.

---

[3] The contract with the new buyer was not executed until May 30, 2012, after the lawsuit had already been filed. The sale closed on August 8, 2012 for a purchase price of $5,450,000.00.

Stonemason moved for summary judgment against San Francisco Distribution on the breach of contract claim. After a hearing, the trial court granted Stonemason's motion for summary judgment and entered final judgment against San Francisco Distribution in the amount of $400,000 plus interest, attorney's fees and costs. This appeal followed . . . .

In *Hyman v. Cohen*, 73 So.2d 393, 398 (Fla.1954), the Florida Supreme Court discussed the difference between a forfeiture provision (e.g., liquidated damages) and an unenforceable penalty provision. The Court held that where the contracting parties actually intend to liquidate their damages, the provision is valid, but where it is clear the parties' real intention is to induce performance under the contract, the provision is unenforceable. *Id.*

The Supreme Court established a test to determine when a liquidated damages provision will be found enforceable, and when it should be found unenforceable as a penalty clause. First, in order to uphold the provision, "the damages consequent upon a breach must not be readily ascertainable."[5] *Lefemine [v. Baron]*, 573 So.2d [326,] at 328. "Second, the sum stipulated to be forfeited must not be so grossly disproportionate to any damages that might reasonably be expected to follow from a breach as to show that the parties could have intended only to induce full performance, rather than to liquidate their damages." *Id.*

San Francisco Distribution . . . contends that the amount of liquidated damages is unconscionable, in light of the fact that Stonemason ultimately sold the property to a subsequent buyer for more than the original contract price, and therefore suffered no damages. . . .

San Francisco Distribution's no-damages argument rests on the premise that a subsequent buyer paid $5.45 million, $200,000 more than the original contract price. While perhaps superficially appealing, such an argument looks solely at the ultimate sales price, ignoring the contractual provision itself and other aspects of potential damages consequent to a buyer's breach. Such a determination would invite speculation in assessing what a certain piece of real property might be worth weeks, months or even years after a contract is signed. *See Hutchison v. Tompkins*, 259 So.2d 129, 132 (Fla.1972) (observing that the "land sale market in Florida fluctuates from year to year and season to season, and it is generally impossible to say at the time a contract for sale is drawn what vendor's loss (if any) will be should the contract be breached by purchaser's failure to close"); *Valenti v. Coral Reef Shopping Center*, 316 So.2d 589, 592 (Fla. 3d DCA 1975) (same, citing *Hutchison*, 259 So.2d at 129).[6] Further speculation would

---

[5] The determination to be made is whether damages were readily ascertainable at the time of the contract, not whether damages were readily ascertainable at the time of the breach. *See Valenti v. Coral Reef Shopping Ctr.*, 316 So.2d 589, 592 (Fla. 3d DCA 1975) . . . .

[6] San Francisco Distribution continued to assert on appeal that the damages were readily ascertainable at the time of the breach, ignoring the fact that, as held in *Hutchison* and *Valenti*,

follow regarding the nature and extent of a seller's loss of other potential buyers during the period of time when the property was taken off the market during the pendency of the original transaction.[7]

In *Hot Developers, Inc. v. Willow Lake Estates, Inc.*, 950 So.2d 537 (Fla. 4th DCA 2007), on nearly identical facts, our sister court affirmed summary judgment on behalf of a seller seeking to keep the deposit under a forfeiture clause even though the seller sold the property to a subsequent buyer for $100,000 more than the defaulting buyer agreed to pay under the contract. In *Bradley v. Sanchez*, 943 So.2d 218 (Fla. 3d DCA 2006), the buyers contracted to purchase a home from seller for $10,500,000.00. The contract contained a liquidated damages clause in the amount of the total deposit—$510,000. When the buyers defaulted on the contract, seller sought to retain the deposit as liquidated damages. Summary judgment in favor of the seller was upheld and the liquidated damages amount of the deposit was found to be reasonable, despite the buyers' argument that the seller had since sold the property to another buyer for $10,400,000.00 (an amount which, when combined with the $510,000 deposit, exceeded by $410,000 the original purchase price of $10,500,000).

We hold that the liquidated damages clause at issue in this case is not a "penalty clause" but rather, an enforceable liquidated damages clause which gave the seller an option, upon buyer's breach, between enforcing the contract by specific performance or by forfeiture of the deposit as liquidated damages. We further hold that neither the amount of the deposit, as a percentage of the purchase price, nor the sale to a subsequent buyer in an amount that exceeded the original contract price, rendered the clause unenforceable. . . .

NOTES AND QUESTIONS

1.   *When does the presence of a liquidated damages clause bar other remedies?* Unless the contract explicitly provides otherwise, the seller can seek specific performance in lieu of liquidated damages; an agreement by the seller to liquidate *damages* does not imply an agreement to limit an *equitable* remedy. The *Stonemason* court so held (in a portion of the opinion not included above); see also Orr v. Goodwin, 953 A.2d 1190 (N.H.2008); Conner v. Auburn Partners, L.L.C., 852 So.2d 755 (Ala.Ct.App.2002). Cf. Gulf City Body & Trailer Works, Inc. v. Phoenix Props. Trust, Inc., 531 So.2d 870 (Ala.1988) (specific performance denied where contract explicitly made liquidated damages seller's sole remedy).

---

the relevant timeframe for this determination is the time of the contract. *See also, Bradley v. Sanchez*, 943 So.2d 218 (Fla. 3d DCA 2006).

[7]   San Francisco Distribution's argument also overlooks the seller's carrying costs during this timeframe, and the fact that, under the terms of the contract at issue, 50 percent of the forfeited deposit was to be distributed in equal amounts to the brokers involved in the transaction.

Where a liquidated damages clause makes clear that it is the seller's sole damages remedy (like the clause in *Stonemason*), the clause clearly precludes the seller from asserting a claim for actual damages. But what if the clause provides the seller with the "option" of either liquidated damages or actual damages, such as the one in *Ravenstar*? In this situation, the *Ravenstar* opinion is consistent with significant authority that the vendor may elect either actual damages or the liquidated sum (or that, if the clause provides retention of the deposit is optional with the vendor, the seller can make the election after the breach has occurred). See, e.g., Frasier v. Schauweker, 915 S.W.2d 601 (Tex.Ct.App.1996); Hoelscher v. Schenewerk, 804 S.W.2d 828 (Mo.Ct.App.1991); Alexsey v. Kelly, 205 A.D.2d 649, 614 N.Y.S.2d 734 (1994). By contrast, some courts hold that such an "optional" clause is not really a liquidated damage clause at all, but is inherently a penalty clause and thus unenforceable. See Catholic Charities of Archdiocese of Chicago v. Thorpe, 741 N.E.2d 651 (Ill.Ct.App.2000) (holding that such a clause is an attempt by the vendor "to have his cake and eat it too."); see also Real Estate World, Inc. v. Southeastern Land Fund, Inc., 227 S.E.2d 340 (Ga.1976); Lefemine v. Baron, 573 So.2d 326 (Fla.1991).

Are you persuaded by the court's reasoning in *Ravenstar*? Should the size of the deposit make a difference? In *Lefemine* (one of the cases rejected by *Ravenstar*), the buyer's deposit was $38,500 (10% of the sale price). But as noted earlier, deposits can vary dramatically by custom and practice. For example, suppose that Buyer made a deposit of $1,000 pursuant to a contract to buy Seller's home for $385,000. Is $1,000 a meaningful amount for a seller to agree to accept in lieu of actual damages?

Even if the mere presence of an "optional" clause like the one in *Ravenstar* does not bar the seller from seeking actual damages, the manner in which the seller exercises its rights under the clause may have that effect. For example, in Orr v. Goodwin, 953 A.2d 1190 (N.H.2008), the contract stated that on buyer default, "the amount of the deposit may, at the option of Seller, become the property of the Seller as reasonable." When the buyer breached the $1.02 million contract, the seller retained the $25,000 deposit. The seller had no further communication with the buyer during the ensuing 18 months, before then bringing a lawsuit for actual damages claimed to have been suffered beyond the deposit amount. The court concluded that the seller had made an election to take the deposit as liquidated damages and thus could no longer recover actual damages. Thus, a seller that wishes to preserve its right to seek actual damages should at a minimum clearly communicate this intent to the buyer at the time of breach, and most likely should make an immediate refund of the deposit. See, e.g., McKeon v. Crump, 53 P.3d 494 (Utah App.2002) (seller's retention of deposit was election of remedy); Heflin v. Brackelsberg, 374 S.W.3d 755 (Ark.2010) (whether retention of deposit by sellers for one year was election of remedies was material issue of fact); Sampson v. McAdoo, 47 Md.App. 602, 425 A.2d 1 (1981) (to preserve its ability to recover actual damages, seller must make affirmative election to forgo deposit, without waiting to see whether liquidated or actual damages would be greater).

2. *Evaluating the "reasonableness" of the deposit as liquidated damages.* The court in *Stonemason* articulates a "prospective" approach to evaluating whether the deposit is reasonable (enforceable) or a "penalty" (unenforceable). Under this approach, the court evaluates the reasonableness of the amount as of the time the contract is entered into rather than the date of breach. See also Fuqua Constr. Co. v. Pillar Dev., Inc., 667 S.E.2d 633 (Ga.Ct.App.2008); Kelly v. Marx, 705 N.E.2d 1114 (Mass.1999); Guiliano v. Cleo, Inc., 995 S.W.2d 88 (Tenn.1999); Watson v. Ingram, 881 P.2d 247 (Wash.1994). Courts tend to uphold the retention of even substantial deposits (i.e., 10% or more) as prospectively reasonable. See, e.g., U.S. v. Ponnapula, 246 F.3d 576 (6th Cir.2001) (15%); Leeber v. Deltona Corp., 546 A.2d 452 (Me.1988) (Florida law) (15%); Siegel v. Levy Organization Dev. Co., Inc., 538 N.E.2d 715 (Ill.Ct.App.1989) (20%); Wallace Real Estate Inv., Inc. v. Groves, 881 P.2d 1010 (Wash.1994) (17%). Not only can sellers incur substantial consequential damages (e.g., legal fees, carrying costs of continued ownership, and possible liability for a brokerage commission on the transaction despite the breach due to the "ready, willing, and able" rule), but as we saw during the market downturn post-2007, land values can drop (even by 10% or more) very quickly during periods of market upheaval.

Still, some courts have expressed discomfort with a purely prospective approach—particularly in cases where the buyer made a significant deposit and the property's market value increased prior to the buyer's breach so that the seller suffered little or no actual loss. In this situation, an estimate of damages that seemed reasonable when made may turn out to be a gross exaggeration of the seller's actual damages. The Restatement (Second) of Contracts § 356(1) (1981) suggests that the liquidated amount must be reasonable "in the light of the anticipated or *actual* loss caused by the breach" (emphasis added), and a significant number of recent decisions have refused to allow retention of the deposit as liquidated damages where it would result in a substantial windfall to the seller based on actual loss at the time of the breach. See, e.g., Hershey v. Simpson, 725 P.2d 196, 200 (Idaho Ct.App.1986); Orr v. Goodwin, 953 A.2d 1190 (N.H.2008) (liquidated amount must be reasonable both as of the date of contracting and the date of breach); Mason v. Fakhimi, 865 P.2d 333 (Nev.1993) (liquidated amount must be reasonable as compared to actual damages suffered, but holding amount that was three times seller's actual damages was not unduly disproportionate). The cases are somewhat evenly divided; the appendix to the majority opinion in Kelly v. Marx, 694 N.E.2d 869 (Mass.Ct.App.1998) listed 22 states that determine reasonableness only as of the date of the contract, and 20 states that also require reasonableness at the date of the breach.

A few courts that purport to evaluate reasonableness at the time of contracting nevertheless take the view that the seller may not retain the deposit if the seller suffers no damages at all. See Stabenau v. Cairelli, 577 A.2d 1130 (Conn.Ct.App.1990); Shanghai Invst. Co. v. Alteka Co., 993 P.2d 516 (Haw.2000) (proof of actual damages required to justify retention of $5 million deposit on a $35 million purchase), overruled on other grounds, Blair v. Ing, 31

P.3d 184 (Haw.2001). Section 356 of the Restatement (Second) of Contracts appears to support this position, but there is not much support for it in the cases. See Restatement (Second) of Contracts § 356, cmt. B illus. 4; Note, "Keep the Change!": A Critique of the No Actual Injury Defense to Liquidated Damages, 65 Wash.L.Rev. 977 (1990).

From an economic viewpoint, a liquidated damages provision is a form of insurance which the buyer purchases from the seller. The buyer says, in effect, "If I fail to perform this contract, I realize that I may be liable for actual damages. Whether those damages will be large or small is impossible to predict, because they will depend on future changes in market values that are inherently uncertain. Because I'm averse to that sort of risk, I would prefer to fix in advance a sum that I will have to pay if I breach. Whether your actual damages are high, low, or nonexistent, I will pay the agreed amount instead." If the liquidated amount is fairly bargained between the parties, it presumably represents a result that both of them prefer when they contract. Hence, any court decision that overrides this outcome will have the effect of undermining the bargaining process, giving one party a windfall for which he or she did not bargain, and producing a result that is economically inefficient. As one court put it, "[t]he negotiated liquidated damages sum represents the parties' best estimate of the value of the breach and permits the parties to allocate and incorporate these risks in their negotiations." Watson v. Ingram, 881 P.2d 247 (Wash.1994). This perspective is certainly more consistent with the traditional view that a court should only evaluate the *prospective* reasonableness of the clause, at the time of contracting.

Can one push the analogy even further and argue that the court should simply enforce the deposit clause, regardless of the amount, if the court concludes that the clause was the result of fair negotiation between the parties? See Rea, Efficiency Implications of Penalties and Liquidated Damages, 13 J. Legal Stud. 147 (1984). To some extent, this is what courts have done in New York, as reflected in Uzan v. 845 UN Ltd. Partn., 10 A.D.3d 230, 778 N.Y.S.2d 171 (2004). In *Uzan*, two Turkish billionaires contracted to buy two penthouse apartments in New York's Trump Tower for a price of $32 million. The 9/11 attacks occurred a few weeks before the scheduled closing, and the buyers refused to close; at the time, buyers had deposited $8 million, or 25% of the purchase price. The contract provided that if the buyers defaulted, seller "shall have the right to retain, as and for liquidated damages, the Down payment and any interest earned on the Down payment." The buyers sued to recover the deposit, attacking the clause as an unreasonable and invalid liquidation of damages. The court allowed the seller to retain the deposit, holding that the reasonableness of the deposit amount did not matter. In doing so, the court distinguished between "liquidated damages clauses [which] have traditionally been subject to judicial oversight to confirm that the stipulated damages bear a reasonable proportion to the probable loss caused by the breach" and "real estate down payments" which it held could be refunded only upon "a showing of disparity of bargaining power between the parties, duress, fraud, illegality or mutual mistake." *Uzan*, 10 A.D.3d at 237,

778 N.Y.S.2d at 176. Is the court's conclusion appropriate given the language of the contract (which stated that the seller had the right to retain the deposit "as and for liquidated damages")?

3.   *Statutory reforms.* Several states have adopted statutes setting a presumptively valid level of liquidated damages as a percentage of the sales price. These statutes typically apply only to sales of single-family residences. For example, California's statute provides a safe harbor that allows the seller to retain a deposit of up to 3% of the sale price if the buyer breaches. A seller can take a larger deposit, but can only retain the larger amount if the seller demonstrates that the liquidated amount is valid under the common law rules discussed in Note 2, supra. See Cal.Civ.Code § 1675; see also Wash.Rev.Code § 64.04 (5% of sales price).

4.   *Can the seller attack the validity of the liquidated damages clause?* Typically, it is the breaching buyer that challenges the enforceability of a liquidated damages clause. But sometimes, a seller that has taken a minimal deposit—but then suffered actual damages from buyer's breach that exceeded the deposit amount—will attempt to argue that the clause was an invalid liquidation of damages. The seller almost always loses these cases, see, e.g., Orr v. Goodwin, 953 A.2d 1190 (N.H.2008); City of Kinston v. Suddreth, 146 S.E.2d 660 (N.C.1966); Mahoney v. Tingley, 529 P.2d 1068 (Wash.1975). Nevertheless, the argument occasionally works. See Community Dev. Serv., Inc. v. Replacement Parts Mfg., Inc., 679 S.W.2d 721 (Tex.Ct.App.1984).

5.   *Limitations on the buyer's remedies.* In several cases involving sales of new condominium units, courts have dealt with contracts that gave the developer the usual right to retain the purchaser's earnest money deposit as liquidated damages, or to assert other legal or equitable remedies. But these contracts were unusual in that they limited the buyer's remedy—in the event of a breach by the developer, the buyer was limited to termination of the contract and refund of the deposit (i.e., rescission and restitution).

In a condominium development, sales contracts are often signed before construction of the project commences. As a result, the executory period of the contracts can be quite lengthy. The obvious purpose of this sort of clause is to permit the developer, if the units' values rise during construction, to cancel the original contracts and sell to other buyers at higher prices. Such clauses have aroused considerable disfavor in the Florida courts. Consider the following language from Ocean Dunes of Hutchinson Island Dev. Corp. v. Colangelo, 463 So. 2d 437 (Fla. App. 1985):

> There is no question that parties to a contract may agree to limit their respective remedies and that those remedies need not be the same. Jay Vee Realty Corp. v. Jaymar Acres, Inc., 436 So. 2d 1053 (Fla. 4th DCA 1983); Wright & Seaton v. Prescott, 420 So. 2d 623 (Fla. 4th DCA 1982). Such contractual provisions, however, must be reasonable to be enforced. . . . There is nothing reasonable about the foregoing default provisions. In this contract, the seller's obligations are wholly illusory, while the buyers' are quite real. The developer

can opt to sell the unit to any new buyer willing to pay a higher price than the existing contract price, or even fail to show title to be vested in the developer as required by paragraph 5 of the Agreement, with absolutely no harmful consequences; the developer must only return the buyer's *own* money. A return of one's own money hardly constitutes damages in any meaningful sense. It is especially unconscionable in this case in light of the buyers' deprivation of the use of their money for several years.

If the seller's obligations are illusory, as the *Ocean Dunes* court held, what is the result? Traditionally, courts held that if one party had no meaningful obligation, the contract was unenforceable by either party for lack of consideration. But increasingly in modern times, the courts are likely to restructure such contracts to make the obligation meaningful. See I Farnsworth, Contracts § 2.13 (1990). That is what the court did in *Ocean Dunes*. It imposed a duty on the part of the seller to grant specific performance, despite that contract's disclaimer of that remedy. See also Embree v. Bank of New York Mellon, 2013 WL 6384776 (D.N.H. 2013), where the court concluded that the limitation to a return of earnest money should be enforced only if the vendor's breach was unintentional.

D. TIME OF PERFORMANCE AND TENDER

Closings of real estate sales often occur later than the parties originally agreed. There are many reasons; many things can go wrong or need to be resolved. Often the real estate broker or brokers, who have an obvious interest in getting the deal closed, will work energetically at solving the problems. But when the closing does not occur by the agreed time, several facts take on critical importance. Did the original contract make "time of the essence?" If it did not, has one of the parties properly made "time of the essence" unilaterally? If time is not "of the essence," how far beyond the agreed closing date is the late party permitted to perform? Has one party tendered performance of the contract so as to place the other in breach?

As the agreed closing date approaches, it is common to have a flurry of communications, some of which may lack precision and clarity. The following case is illustrative.

MILLER V. ALMQUIST

New York Supreme Court, Appellate Division, 1998
241 A.D.2d 181, 671 N.Y.S.2d 746

TOM, JUSTICE. This case arises out of a proposed sale of a cooperative unit between next door neighbors. The plaintiff-buyers live in Apartment 4S at 150 East 69th Street in Manhattan. The defendant-sellers lived in Apartment 4T (the "Premises"). The buyers anticipated buying the sellers' apartment with the goal of consolidating the two apartments into a single living unit for their growing family.

On February 25, 1997, the parties entered into a contract of sale for the Premises at a purchase price of $545,000 to be paid in cash. The contract provided for a 10% down payment and contained no financing contingency clause. However, the buyers did not represent that they would not seek financing, and they did apply for a loan. The contract specified a closing date of April 1, 1997, but did not specify that time was of the essence. At the time of contract, the buyers paid a down payment of $54,500 to be held in escrow by the sellers' attorney. The contract further provided that in the event the buyers defaulted, the sellers would be permitted to terminate the contract and the buyers would forfeit their down payment.

The cooperative Board of Directors approved the sale on March 25, 1997, six days prior to the scheduled closing date. Thereafter, the buyers experienced delays arising from loan clearance and documentation. By letter dated March 31, 1997, the buyers' attorney sought an adjournment of the closing until April 16, 1997, subject to the availability of the cooperative's transfer agent. As a consequence, neither party appeared on April 1st. By responsive letter dated April 2, 1997, the sellers' attorney agreed to the adjournment, but claimed that time was now of the essence.

On April 14, 1997, the buyers' attorney contacted the lender to arrange for apportionment of the proceeds for the April 16th closing. For the first time, the lender's attorney asked how certain tax liens[11] would be resolved. The buyers' attorney contacted his client, who indicated that the liens had been satisfied years ago, but that they could not immediately locate canceled checks evidencing satisfaction of the liens. The lender required proof of payment by the next morning, April 15th, indicating that otherwise the April 16th closing would have to be adjourned pending receipt of proof. The buyers received a faxed copy of the satisfaction of lien from the New York State Department of Taxation and Finance. This documentation had been sent to the buyers' office at 5:22 PM on April 14th, followed by written confirmation dated April 15th. The clients provided the documentation to their attorney, who then provided it to the lender enclosed with a letter faxed to the lender's attorney at 11:24 AM on April 15th. This evidence of satisfaction was acceptable to the lender. However, a closing could not be scheduled with the lender at this time for the following day due to the delay in obtaining the satisfaction. The lender indicated that it was available to close on April 18th.

Also on April 15th, several communications went back and forth between the buyers and sellers. Initially, the buyers' attorney contacted

---

[11] Editors' Note: These were apparently liens for state income taxes owed by the buyers, which might have had priority over the new mortgage if they were not satisfied prior to or at the closing.

the sellers' attorney, and indicated that the buyers' lender had just informed the buyers about the results of the lien search. This was followed by a faxed letter at 5:58 PM to the sellers' attorney confirming a prior conversation that the buyers could not attend the closing scheduled for the next day. This letter also confirmed the buyers' willingness to pay the sellers $300 per day for maintenance and opportunity cost, which counsel characterized as being well in excess of that calculated by the sellers' attorney. The buyers' attorney initially indicated that the buyers would be able to close in seven days, and asked for a response.

The buyers did not appear on April 16, 1997 for the scheduled closing. By certified mail dated April 16, 1997, the sellers' attorney informed the buyers' attorney that as a consequence of the buyers' failure to appear that day, and the prior declaration that time was of the essence, the buyers were in default and the down payment would be delivered to the sellers. By faxed letter dated April 16, 1997, at 12:58 PM, the buyers' attorney now sought to confirm the assurance given in a prior conversation that the buyers were now ready, willing and able to close on April 18, 1997, again subject to the availability of the cooperative's transfer agent. By letter faxed at 5:26 PM on April 16, 1997, the buyers' attorney confirmed a conversation with the sellers' attorney that the sellers would not appear on April 18th and had declined to agree to any other date. By letter faxed and hand delivered on April 18th, the buyers' attorney informed the sellers' attorney that a closing date was reserved for April 23, 1997 since this was the first available date for the cooperative's transfer agent. This letter also advised the sellers that the time of the essence clause had not been contemplated in the contract and constituted only a unilateral declaration by the sellers' attorney. By a second letter that day, faxed at 5:01 PM, the buyers' attorney again confirmed that his clients were ready, willing and able to close on April 23rd, but that the sellers had stated an unwillingness to attend. By letter dated April 21, 1997, the buyers' attorney rejected the default notice and again confirmed his clients' willingness to close; the letter demanded that the down payment remain escrowed. The same letter also indicated that the buyers had been willing to make several concessions to keep the deal alive, that the sellers had suffered no prejudice, and that the sellers' attorney would be acting in bad faith if the closing did not take place. By an April 22, 1997 letter, the sellers' attorney then contacted the transfer agent to cancel the April 23, 1997 reservation. The buyers warrant that they appeared for closing on April 23, 1997 with all necessary documentation and a check for $490,000.

The buyers commenced this action on or about April 27, 1997, seeking to enjoin the sellers from terminating the contract, from implementing a forfeiture of the down payment and from contracting to sell the apartment to any other party. The sellers cross-moved for summary judgment dismissing the complaint on the basis that the contract already had been terminated, after which the buyers also sought summary judgment. By order and judgment entered June 5, 1997, the [trial court], noting the absence of a financing contingency clause and finding that the sellers had made time of the essence, granted the sellers' cross-motion for summary judgment dismissing the complaint. Plaintiffs-buyers appeal and we now reverse. . . .

When a contract for sale of real property does not specify that time is of the essence, either party is entitled to a reasonable adjournment of the closing date. In granting an adjournment, the other party may unilaterally impose a condition that time be of the essence as to the rescheduled date. The effectiveness of this condition, though, is contingent on the specificity of the notice and on the reasonableness of the time period. The notice in this case was sufficiently clear and unequivocal. The question is whether it afforded the buyers a reasonable time to close. What constitutes a reasonable time to close depends on the facts and circumstances of the particular case. Among the factors to be considered are the nature and object of the contract, the previous conduct of the parties, the presence or absence of good faith, the experience of the parties and the possibility of hardship or prejudice to either one, as well as the specific number of days provided for the performance. Reasonableness in this case turns on whether the post-notice time period provided a reasonable time period in which to close especially when the time of the essence provision was unilaterally made by the sellers after the buyers had selected a very short adjourned closing date.

We initially note that the time period from the initial scheduled closing date of April 1st to the time when the buyers were ready, willing and able to close was very short. From the receipt of the time of the essence letter dated April 2, 1997 to the April 15th request for an adjournment was a matter of days, and this entire period was only six weeks after the contract was signed. The very brevity of the additional adjournment—two days for the buyers' purposes—supports the conclusion that the few days initially allowed were not reasonably sufficient to achieve the buyers' purpose. Parenthetically, although the buyers requested 15 days for the initial adjournment, they reasonably could have requested a longer period. Insofar as time was not of the essence for the contract's law date, and in the absence of discernible prejudice, the sellers could not have rejected a moderately longer adjournment period. A moderately longer adjournment period, as it turns out, would have avoided the very problem that arose in this case. The delay was occasioned only by the usual sort of documentation glitch that is not uncommon in residential closings. If the sellers had extended the usual courtesies under these circumstances, there is every indication that the buyers, after the very minor adjournment sought, would have presented a check for the entire purchase price, and neighbors could have parted as friends.

The previous conduct of the parties, as well as the time periods involved, does not reveal extensive delays or acts of bad faith on behalf of the buyers. The buyers' attorney explained the delay and communicated regularly with the sellers' counsel; his explanation, which is a reasonable one, is well documented in the record. By April 14th, counsel knew that the financing was already approved; he was calling in regard to apportioning the check. The delay was merely to finalize the documentation required in connection with the lender's lien search and to reschedule for those parties appearing in a representative capacity. Hence, the sellers were assured that the sale would close in the immediate future.

The evidence in this case clearly shows that the buyers were not experienced in the real estate field. They suffered hardship as a result of their inability to close under the facts and circumstances of this case. They sought to acquire the next door apartment to break through so as to make adequate room for their growing family, which included two young children (ages two and four years old), and the wife's mentally retarded sister, whom they expected to move in with them. Because of the short delay, the buyers have lost not only their opportunity to purchase the adjacent apartment, but also their $54,500 deposit. Conversely, the sellers have failed to show how the delay of a few days would have prejudiced them, since they would have received the all-cash deal they had bargained for, as well as several thousand dollars in expenses dating back to April 1, 1997. It is undisputed that the sellers subsequently sold the premises to a third party at a higher sale price.

Taking all of these factors into consideration, we cannot conclude that the time allotted in the time of the essence letter in response to a short adjourned closing date chosen by the buyers was reasonable so as to inflexibly bind the buyers to an April 16th closing date. . . .

In the various cases claimed by the sellers to support their position, there were significant warnings during the course of unreasonable delays that the delays had to end. The time periods allowed in tandem with the conduct of the parties factored into the determination whether the time to which the delaying party would be held was unreasonable. By sharp contrast, it was unreasonable under the unusual circumstances of the present case for the sellers, having unilaterally declared time to be of the essence, to have held the buyers to the very limited time period in issue, especially since time had not been made of the essence when the buyers had selected the date only days before. Under the present circumstances, in which only a single adjournment had been sought during a two-week period, it would be unreasonable to inflexibly hold the buyers to that date on the basis that the buyers had made the initial selection. . . .

NOTES AND QUESTIONS

1. *The significance of time being "essential."* Courts often state that time is always of the essence at law, but time is not of the essence in equity unless the contract itself or the surrounding circumstances dictate otherwise. See, e.g., Hamilton v. Bradford, 502 F.Supp. 822 (S.D.Miss.1980); JPMorgan Chase Bank, N.A. v. Cam, 161 A.3d 650 (Conn.Ct.App.2017); 2 Am.L.Prop. § 11.45 (1952). But what does this glib statement mean about the precise position of a late-performing party where time is not "of the essence"?

If time is not "of the essence," the party who is late but who tenders performance within a reasonable time after the agreed closing date may enforce the contract by specific performance. See, e.g., Marioni v. 94 Broadway, Inc., 866 A.2d 208 (N.J.Super.Ct.App.Div. 2005); Parker v. Byrne, 996 A.2d 627 (R.I.2010). In *Miller v. Almquist*, the buyers could have obtained specific performance if they had wanted it. Likewise, *Miller* illustrates that the party who is reasonably late can rescind and recover her earnest money if the other side later refuses to perform. While the party who is late in tendering performance may obtain specific performance, that party has also committed a breach (although a nonmaterial one) and is thus liable for consequential damages caused by the delay. See, e.g., Richardson v. Van Dolah, 429 F.2d 912 (9th Cir. 1970); McPherson v. Dauenhauer, 69 P.3d 733 (Or.2003); 15 Williston, Contracts § 46:1 (4th ed. 2018 update). Only the damages resulting from the delay per se should be recoverable, and in many cases the net amount will be quite small. For example, if the seller delays in conveying an apartment building, the buyer will have lost the rental income for that period, but also will have avoided the property taxes, insurance, maintenance expenses and mortgage interest that accrued during the same period. The buyers' offer to pay $300 per day for the delay in closing in the *Miller* case was an apparent recognition of their duty to pay these interim damages.

What is more uncertain is whether the late-performing party is limited to specific performance or may also recover damages if the other party repudiates the contract. Limited case authority allows the late-performing party to obtain damages as well as equitable remedies. See Davis v. Lacy, 121 F.Supp. 246 (E.D.Ky.1954); Tanenbaum v. Sears, Roebuck & Co., 401 A.2d 809 (Pa.Super.Ct.1979); Restatement (Second) of Contracts § 242, illus. 4 & 5 (1981). We think the supposed distinction between law and equity in this area is simply a red herring.

By contrast, if the contract affirmatively makes "time of the essence," the consequences for the late-performing party dramatically change. The delay is treated as a material breach, and the other party's duty of performance is discharged. Consequently, the other party is entitled to rescission, damages, or (if that party is the seller) retention of the buyer's earnest money if the usual common law tests are met. See Thor Props., LLC v. Willspring Holdings LLC, 118 A.D.3d 505, 988 N.Y.S.2d 47 (2014); Lewis v. Muchmore, 26 S.W.3d 632 (Tenn.Ct.App.2000); ULTA § 2–302(b). Even a very slight delay is sufficient to discharge the innocent party. See, e.g., Miceli v. Dierberg, 773 S.W.2d 154

(Mo.Ct.App.1989) (delay of 3½ hours); Doctorman v. Schroeder, 114 A. 810 (N.J.1921) (delay of 30 minutes where contract fixed a specific hour for closing). If time is of the essence, there is no "good faith" duty to give the late party a time extension. See Lafayette Place Assocs. v. Boston Redev. Auth., 694 N.E.2d 820 (Mass.1998). If the sales contract sets a date but not an hour, tender at any reasonable time on that date is sufficient. See Elm Land Co., Inc. v. Glasser, 174 A.2d 233 (N.J.Super.Ct.App.Div.1961).

2.   *How much delay is unreasonable?* Even if time is not of the essence, an *unreasonable* delay will put the late party in material breach and deny the late party enforcement of the contract. See Ronne v. Ronne, 568 P.2d 1021 (Alaska 1977) (one month delay reasonable); E. Shepherdstown Developers, Inc. v. J. Russell Fritts, Inc., 183 W. Va. 691, 398 S.E.2d 517 (1990) (three year delay unreasonable); ULTA § 2–302(e). One of the champion cases is Krotz v. Sattler, 586 N.W.2d 336 (Iowa 1998), finding a ten-year delay reasonable! As a rule of thumb, the courts routinely find delays of 30 to 90 days to be reasonable. Can you explain why the delay sought by the buyers in *Miller* was reasonable?

3.   *Circumstances making time essential.* Merely stating a precise date and time for the closing in the sales contract will not make time essential. A further statement (e.g., "Time is of the essence in the performance of this contract") is necessary. But even if the contract contains no such statement, courts may consider time of the essence due to special circumstances, such as rapidly fluctuating values or evidence that one of the parties was particularly concerned with an on-time performance and the other party was aware of this fact. See Gunn v. Heggins, 964 So.2d 586, 593 (Miss.Ct.App.2007); Woodhull Corp. v. Saibaba Corp., 234 Ga.App. 707, 507 S.E.2d 493 (1998); 3A Corbin, Contracts § 716 (1960).

4.   *Unilateral notice making time essential.* As the *Miller* case illustrates, even if time was not originally of the essence, either party can unilaterally make it so by giving the other notice to that effect and by fixing a date for performance that is a reasonable time beyond the date of the notice. According to the New York view, the notice must "clearly and distinctly set a new date and time for closing," and inform the other party that "[he] would be considered in default if [he] did not perform by a given date;" see Latora v. Ferreira, 102 A.D.3d 838, 958 N.Y.S.2d 727 (2013). If we assume that the sellers' April 2 letter in *Miller* was faxed to the buyers, it made time of the essence and gave the buyers 14 days to close. What factors made this allowance of time unreasonable? Cf. In re 1111 Myrtle Ave. Group LLC, 575 B.R. 567 (Bankr.S.D.N.Y.2017) (notice period of 13 days found reasonable under the circumstances); Spellane v. Natarajan, 169 A.D.3d 1406, 93 N.Y.S.3d 489 (2019) (notice period of 8 days reasonable where allowed by specific language of contract).

Once such notice is given, it binds both parties. Does the recognition of such unilateral notices (which probably need not be in writing) violate the underlying principle of the Statute of Frauds? Does their recognition give one party alone the right to modify the contract? See Whitman, Burkhart, Freyermuth & Rule, The Law of Property § 10.9 (4th ed.2019).

5. *Waiver of timely performance.* Even if time is of the essence, either party can waive the other's duty to perform strictly on time. For example, the seller may call the buyer and say, "I know you've been having trouble getting your financing arranged, but don't worry about being ready to close next Friday (the date fixed in the contract). I'll work with you on this." See, e.g., Livas v. Kodrick, 143 Ill.App.3d 1097, 98 Ill.Dec. 85, 493 N.E.2d 1106 (1986); Dellicarri v. Hirschfeld, 210 A.D. 584, 619 N.Y.S.2d 816 (1994). A waiver also may be inferred from the circumstances, without a formal statement. See Marioni v. 94 Broadway, Inc., 374 N.J. Super. 588, 866 A.2d 208 (2005) (waiver found when parties continued to negotiate about a closing date after time set for closing had elapsed); Quirk v. Schenk, 34 Mass.App.Ct. 931, 612 N.E.2d 1194 (1993) (waiver inferred from party's readily giving multiple extensions). Contra Miami Child's World, Inc. v. City of Miami Beach, 688 So.2d 942 (1997) (multiple extensions do not amount to a waiver).

After giving a waiver, a party may reinstate a "time is of the essence" requirement but must, as in *Miller*, give a reasonable time for the other party to prepare to close. See Tarlow v. Kelly, 158 Or.App. 7, 970 P.2d 688 (1999). The parties also may enter into a formal extension of time, but provide that (the new) time remains essential. See Enclave, Inc. v. Resolution Trust Corp., 986 F.2d 131 (5th Cir.1993).

6. *When tender is excused.* Ordinarily the obligations of the seller (to tender a deed conveying marketable title) and of the buyer (to tender the unpaid balance of the purchase price) are concurrent conditions. Neither party can regard the other as in breach, or sue for breach, without first tendering her or his own performance. Radkiewicz v. Radkiewicz, 353 Ill.App.3d 251, 288 Ill.Dec. 723, 818 N.E.2d 411 (2004) (seller who never tendered deed cannot forfeit earnest money deposited by buyer); Steinberg v. Linzer, 27 A.D. 3d 450, 812 N.Y.S.2d 565 (2006) (buyer who never tendered purchase price cannot recover her earnest money unless seller's title is incurably defective). A "tender" is defined as an offer to perform immediately, coupled with the ability to carry out the offer. Some courts say that the party tendering must actually have the necessary documents (the deed, the check, etc.) in hand and offer to deliver them, conditioned of course on the other party's performance. See Miller v. Johnson, 125 N.M. 175, 958 P.2d 745 (Ct.App.1998). A formal offer of tender by a party may be excused, however, when:

(a) the other party has anticipatorily repudiated the contract. See, e.g., Princes Point LLC v. Muss Dev. L.L.C., 138 A.D.3d 112, 24 N.Y.S.3d 292 (2016).

(b) even without a repudiation, it is apparent that the other party will not perform, or is obstructing the attempted tender. See Bourke v. Webb, 627 S.E.2d 454 (Ga.Ct.App.2006) (purchasers not required to tender, where time was of the essence and seller had not completed construction of the house on time).

(c)   the other party's performance has become impossible (e.g., the seller's title is incurably defective). See Kessler v. Tortoise Dev., Inc., 134 Idaho 264, 1 P.3d 292 (2000); Martocci v. Schneider, 119 A.D.3d 746, 990 N.Y.S.2d 240 (2014). Cf. Esplendido Apartments v. Olsson, 144 Ariz. 355, 697 P.2d 1105 (Ct.App.1984) (seller's title defects were no excuse for buyer's failure to tender where buyer was unaware of defects).

7.   *Mutual failure to tender*. If time is not of the essence and neither party tenders on the agreed date, neither is in breach; the closing is automatically extended until one sets a date and notifies the other. Again, the notice must be given a reasonable period prior to the date established as the new closing date. See Fisher v. Applebaum, 947 A.2d 248 (R.I.2008); Limpus v. Armstrong, 3 Mass.App.Ct. 19, 322 N.E.2d 187 (1975). A remarkable example is Barber v. Fox, 36 Mass. App. Ct. 525, 632 N.E.2d 1246 (1994), in which a party to an intrafamily sale of land demanded (and got an order of) performance nearly 20 years after the contract date; no earlier demand had ever been made!

But suppose time *is* essential and neither party tenders on the date fixed for closing. There is a good deal of authority for the view that both parties are discharged on the ground that it is impossible to make a tender of substantial performance after that date has passed. See, e.g., Gunn v. Heggins, 964 So.2d 586 (Miss.Ct.App.2007); Pittman v. Canham, 2 Cal.App.4th 556, 3 Cal.Rptr.2d 340 (1992) ("When is a contract no longer a contract? When [time is of the essence,] it contains concurrent conditions and neither party tenders timely performance. Unlike love or taxes, concurrent conditions do not last forever."). Still, if both parties act as if the contract is still in force (e.g., by continuing efforts to prepare for a closing) despite the delay, a court might consider their behavior as evidence of a mutual intent to waive the "time is of the essence" clause and keep the sales contract intact. See Galdjie v. Darwish, 113 Cal.App.4th 1331, 7 Cal.Rptr.3d 178 (2004).

E.   TITLE TO BE CONVEYED

In this section we consider whether a buyer of real estate can justifiably refuse to complete the purchase because the buyer is dissatisfied with the quality of the seller's title. Note that we have not yet investigated the mechanics of title search and examination—the process through which the buyer learns what the quality of the seller's title is. A thorough discussion of that topic will come in the next chapter. For present purposes, it is enough to say that there are two main methods that buyers employ to ascertain the quality of the seller's title, depending on the conditions and customs of the locality. One method (the older of the two) is to obtain a written attorney's opinion as to the seller's title.[12] The second method (in

---

[12]   The attorney may base that opinion on a personal search of the official public records in the county courthouse, or may instead review an *abstract*, which is a copy or summary of the instruments filed in the courthouse, but prepared and sold by a privately owned abstract company.

more common use today) is to obtain a title report, sometimes called a "commitment" or "binder" from a title insurance company. The company may base its report on a search of its own internal records (called a "title plant") or, less commonly, a search of the public records. The report is not proof that the seller has title in a literal sense; it is merely a statement that the company is willing to issue a policy of insurance that the land's title is as stated in the report. In turn, if the company issues a policy of insurance based on the report after closing, the company is thus liable to indemnify the insured buyer if the buyer suffers a loss due to any title defect not disclosed in the policy. As a practical matter, buyers treat the title report as stating the results of a title search. There is little doubt that attorneys' opinions of title are gradually fading from use (except with respect to oil, gas, and mining interests), and that title insurance is becoming increasingly widespread.

Unless the contract provides otherwise, the law infers that the seller's title will be marketable—and if it is not, the buyer's obligation to perform will be excused. The following materials explore when a seller has "marketable" title, what defects defeat marketability, and the issues involved in negotiating provisions of the contract governing the seller's title obligation.

HAISFIELD V. LAPE
Virginia Supreme Court, 2002
264 Va. 632, 570 S.E.2d 794

Opinion by JUSTICE DONALD W. LEMONS. In this consolidated appeal, we consider whether a "line-of-sight" or "view" easement renders title to the property at issue unmarketable, thereby justifying the buyers' refusal to close the transaction. . . .

On February 14, 2000, Audrey Lea Haisfield and Laurel Ridge, LLC (collectively, "Haisfield") entered into a land sale contract ("Purchase Agreement") with Kenneth R. Lape, Trustee of the Kenneth R. Lape living trust and Barbara Gsand Lape, Trustee of the Barbara Gsand Lape living trust (collectively, the "Lapes"). The Purchase Agreement was for the sale of approximately 99 acres in Albemarle County owned by the Lapes and referred to as Laurel Ridge Farm ("Laurel Ridge"). Laurel Ridge was once part of a larger piece of land that encompassed approximately 148 acres owned by the Lapes known as Oakmont Farm. In 1994, the Lapes conveyed approximately 48 acres ("Oakmont") of Oakmont Farm to Dr. Hamilton Moses, III and Alexandra G. Moses (the "Moseses"). At the time of the Purchase Agreement, Oakmont Farm was two separate parcels: Oakmont, owned by the Moseses and Laurel Ridge, owned by the Lapes.

Personal search is most common in the South and along the Atlantic seaboard, especially outside major urban areas; abstracts are more commonly used in rural areas of the Midwest and West.

The Purchase Agreement required Haisfield to deposit $50,000 with McLean Faulconer, Inc., a real estate firm, as an earnest money deposit to be held in escrow. Further, the Purchase Agreement provided that "[s]hould Purchaser default and/or breach this [Purchase Agreement], the Seller shall be entitled to retain the earnest money deposit of $50,000.00 as liquidated damages in lieu of all other remedies provided at law or in equity against the Purchaser."

A closing date of June 30, 2000 was set. On June 29, 2000, through an agent, Haisfield notified the Lapes that the chain of title to Laurel Ridge contained a restrictive covenant that rendered title to the property unmarketable. The line-of-sight easement, discovered by Haisfield just prior to closing, was found in the 1994 deed conveying Oakmont to the Moseses from the Lapes. In part, the Oakmont deed contained the following covenant:

> [F]or a period of thirty (30) years from the date of this deed [May 3, 1994], no building shall be built on the current Albemarle County Tax Map Parcel 111–5A [Laurel Ridge] . . . which may be visible from the main residence (Oakmont) located on the property conveyed by this deed.

Haisfield gave the Lapes 60 days pursuant to Paragraph 14 of the Purchase Agreement to cure the defect created by the Moseses' line-of-sight easement. Further, she maintained that she was justified in refusing to close the transaction and was entitled to the return of her $50,000 earnest money deposit if the defect was not cured. Paragraph 14 states the following:

> At settlement Seller shall convey the Property to the Purchaser by a general warranty deed containing English covenants of title, free of all encumbrances, tenancies, and liens (for taxes and otherwise), but subject to such restrictive covenants and utility easements of record which do not materially and adversely affect the use of the Property for residential purposes or render the title unmarketable. . . . If the examination reveals a title defect of a character that can be remedied by legal action or otherwise within a reasonable time, Seller, at its expense, shall promptly take such action as is necessary to cure such defect. If the defect is not cured within 60 days after Seller receives notice of the defect, then Purchaser shall have the right to (1) terminate this Contract, in which event the Deposit shall be returned to Purchaser, and Purchaser and Seller shall have no further obligations hereunder[.] . . .

The Lapes disagreed that the line-of-sight easement rendered title to Laurel Ridge unmarketable, and efforts between the parties to reach a settlement in the matter were unsuccessful.

Consequently, on July 28, 2000, the Lapes filed a motion for judgment claiming that Haisfield breached the Purchase Agreement and claiming the $50,000 earnest money deposit plus interest as liquidated damages for the breach. Subsequently, Haisfield filed a grounds of defense and counterclaims against the Lapes maintaining that the Lapes failed to deliver marketable title and asking the court to return to her the $50,000 earnest money deposit.

... [T]he trial court held that the line-of-sight easement did not materially or adversely affect the use of the Laurel Ridge property for residential purposes nor did it render title unmarketable under the terms of the Purchase Agreement. . . .

The plain language of Paragraph 14 of the Purchase Agreement requires the seller to convey the property by a general warranty deed containing English covenants of title free of all encumbrances but subject to such restrictive covenants and utility easements of record "which do not materially and adversely affect the use of the Property for residential purposes or render the title unmarketable." In this appeal, we are only concerned with the marketability of title. In the interpretation of this provision of the Purchase Agreement, we are guided by an oft-cited principle of contract interpretation:

> Words that the parties used are normally given their usual, ordinary, and popular meaning. No word or clause in the contract will be treated as meaningless if a reasonable meaning can be given to it, and there is a presumption that the parties have not used words needlessly.

D.C. McClain, Inc. v. Arlington County, 249 Va. 131, 135–36, 452 S.E.2d 659, 662 (1995).

The plain meaning of Paragraph 14 is that, if a particular restrictive covenant or utility easement does render the title unmarketable, the seller will have failed to perform in accordance with its terms unless the defect is remedied within a reasonable time. While it is true that Paragraph 14 of the Purchase Agreement operates as a waiver of objection to certain easements or restrictive covenants, a restrictive covenant that renders title unmarketable is not one of them. If the line-of-sight easement constitutes a restrictive covenant that renders title unmarketable, and the defect is not removed within a reasonable time, Haisfield is entitled to terminate the contract without penalty.

In *Madbeth, Inc. v. Weade*, 204 Va. 199, 202, 129 S.E.2d 667, 669–70 (1963), we stated:

> A marketable title is one which is free from liens or encumbrances; one which discloses no serious defects and is dependent for its validity upon no doubtful questions of law or fact; one which will

not expose the purchaser to the hazard of litigation or embarrass him in the peaceable enjoyment of the land; one which a reasonably well-informed and prudent person, acting upon business principles and with full knowledge of the facts and their legal significance, would be willing to accept, with the assurance that he, in turn, could sell or mortgage the property at its fair value.

However, not all liens and encumbrances render a title unmarketable. In *Sachs v. Owings*, 121 Va. 162, 170, 92 S.E. 997, 1000 (1917), we held that:

> A vendee cannot elect to rescind and treat the contract as rescinded on the ground that the title is not a marketable title because there are encumbrances on the land purchased, if they are of such character and amount that he can apply the unpaid purchase money to the removal of the encumbrances. This can be done where the amount of the encumbrance is definite, does not exceed the unpaid purchase money due, is presently payable (as was the case with the delinquent tax lien in the instant case), and its existence is not a matter of doubt or dispute, or the situation is not such with respect thereto as to expose the vendee to litigation on the subject.

which encumbrances don't break marketability

See also Davis v. Beury, 134 Va. 322, 338, 114 S.E. 773, 777 (1922).

In this case, the amount of the encumbrance is not definite, such as a tax lien or judgment lien. The line-of-sight easement acts as a building restriction upon the property, much like the building restrictions found to render title unmarketable in *Scott v. Albemarle Horse Show Ass'n*, 128 Va. 517, 104 S.E. 842 (1920). In *Scott*, we agreed with the purchaser's assertion that the building restrictions in the tendered deed were not in compliance with the terms of the contract and rendered title unmarketable. Id. at 529–30, 104 S.E. at 846. Finally, the line-of-sight easement in this case is not an "open, visible, physical [e]ncumbrance of the property [that] must have been taken into consideration in fixing the price of the property. . . ." Riner v. Lester, 121 Va. 563, 572, 93 S.E. 594, 597 (1917). In *Riner*, we stated that:

> where the circumstances and the conduct of the parties show that the existence of an open, visible, physical [e]ncumbrance of the property must have been taken into consideration in fixing the price of the property, the purchaser can neither refuse to complete the purchase nor require an abatement of the [purchase] price. [Id.]

another way title can be rendered unmarketable

The line-of-sight easement in this case is clearly an encumbrance upon the property restricting its use in such a manner as to render the title unmarketable. The existence of the easement is not an open, visible, physical encumbrance of the property that might have been considered in the establishment of a purchase price. The existence of a restrictive covenant that renders title to the property unmarketable is not excepted under the provisions of Paragraph 14 of the Purchase Agreement. Under these circumstances, Haisfield was not in breach of the Purchase Agreement by refusing to close the transaction.[13] The trial court erred in holding that Haisfield was in breach and ordering the payment of $50,000 in liquidated damages plus interest. . . .

NOTES AND QUESTIONS

1. *The implied covenant of marketable title.* In *Haisfield*, the contract of sale expressly provided that title must be marketable. Even in the absence of such an express statement, every contract for the sale of real estate is deemed to contain an implied covenant that title will be "marketable" unless the parties agree otherwise. See, e.g., Wallach v. Riverside Bank, 206 N.Y. 434, 100 N.E. 50 (1912); Osswald v. Osswald, 703 N.W.2d 383 (Wis.Ct.App. 2005); Conklin v. Davi, 388 A.2d 598, 600 (N.J.1978).

2. *Defects making title unmarketable.* There is a large body of lore dealing with the question of whether a particular problem relating to land involves *title* or renders title unmarketable. The results of this sort of litigation are not entirely predictable, so the list below should be taken only as a general guide to the issue.

(a) *Encumbrances.* Courts usually treat the traditional types of real estate encumbrances (leases, covenants, mineral reservations, mortgages, easements, and liens) as matters affecting title. If the contract of sale does not expressly provide that the purchaser will take subject to them, such interests render title unmarketable. See Hastings v. Gay, 55 Mass.App.Ct. 157, 770 N.E.2d 11 (2002) (mortgage, lease and lien); Turner v. Taylor, 268 Wis.2d 628, 673 N.W.2d 716 (2003) (easement). This fact emphasizes the need for careful contract drafting. Too frequently the contract fails to list existing encumbrances (which exist in some measure on almost every parcel of real estate) or merely contains a general statement such as "subject to all encumbrances of record." Either approach can be highly dangerous, the former to the seller and latter to the buyer. For example, in Stevenson v. Baum, 65 Cal.App.4th 159, 75 Cal.Rptr.2d 904 (1998), the buyer of a mobile home park agreed in the contract to take "subject to easements of record." It turned out that there was an oil company pipeline easement, and that the oil company had the right to force removal of several mobile homes if necessary to get access to its pipeline. Because of the sales contract language, the buyer was "stuck" with this burden.

---

[13] Editors' Note: Haisfield only wanted to rescind the contract and get her deposit back. Suppose that land prices in the area had increased, and Haisfield had sought loss of bargain damages instead. As noted earlier in Part C, under the English rule about half of the states deny such damages if the seller acted in good faith. Query: do you think the Lapes' conduct met the "good faith" standard here?

In many cases, of course, both parties are fully aware of an existing encumbrance, and the buyer is perfectly willing to take subject to it. If the contract makes no mention of a certain encumbrance, but there is proof that the buyer knew of it when she signed the contract, can the buyer later object to it on title marketability grounds? The *Haisfield* court seemed to think not. But other courts have usually held that the buyer's knowledge of an encumbrance did not waive the right to object to it as making title unmarketable. See, e.g., Create 21 Chuo, Inc. v. Southwest Slopes, Inc., 918 P.2d 1168 (Haw.Ct.App.1996); 325 Schermerhorn, LLC v. Nevins Realty Corp., 23 Misc.3d 1109(A), 886 N.Y.S.2d 69 N.Y. (2009), aff'd, 76 A.D.3d 625, 906 N.Y.S.2d 339 (2010).

(b) *Visible or beneficial encumbrances.* In the same vein, courts sometimes hold that an easement does not make the title unmarketable if it is obviously visible and is beneficial to the land. A typical example would be a power line easement for electrical distribution along the boundary line of a residential lot. Compare Ford v. White, 179 Or. 490, 172 P.2d 822 (1946) (visible power line easement; title held to be marketable) with Atlas Realty of East Meadow, Inc. v. Ostrofsky, 56 Misc.2d 787, 289 N.Y.S.2d 784 (1967) (2.5 foot easement for visible wires and poles; title not marketable). Open and visible public road easements do not render title unmarketable. See Whitman v. Larson, 172 A.D.2d 968, 568 N.Y.S.2d 485 (1991); Egeter v. West & North Props., 92 Or.App. 118, 758 P.2d 361 (1988) (if road is not open and visible, title is unmarketable).

(c) *Access.* Courts usually hold that a complete lack of access to a public road makes title unmarketable, presumably on the theory that it would subject the buyer to the risk of a suit to establish an easement of necessity. See Regan v. Lanze, 40 N.Y.2d 475, 387 N.Y.S.2d 79, 354 N.E.2d 818 (1976); Hinton Hardwoods, Inc. v. Cumberland Scrap Processors Transp., LLC, 2008 WL 5429569 (Ky.Ct.App.2008). But the access, to be legally sufficient, need not be particularly convenient or direct. See Kirkwall Corp. v. Sessa, 39 A.D.2d 185, 333 N.Y.S.2d 108 (1972), rev'd on other grounds, 48 N.Y.2d 709, 422 N.Y.S.2d 368, 397 N.E.2d 1172 (1979).

(d) *Encroachments.* Courts usually hold that an encroachment (a structure built by a neighboring property owner which overlaps the property boundary) renders title unmarketable. See, e.g., Azat v. Farruggio, 162 Md.App. 539, 875 A.2d 778 (2005). The same is true if a structure built by the owner of the property in question extends onto adjoining land. See Sydelman v. Marici, 56 A.D.2d 866, 392 N.Y.S.2d 333 (1977); Klavens v. Siegel, 256 Md. 476, 260 A.2d 637 (1970). The encroachment need not be a permanent structure.

(e) *Title by adverse possession.* If the seller's title is based exclusively on adverse possession, most courts hold that the title is not marketable, although it may be perfectly valid. The difficulty is that a lawsuit might require detailed factual proof of the existence and nature of the seller's acts of possession, which is an unreasonable risk to impose on the purchaser. See Tri-State Hotel Co. v.

Sphinx Inv. Co., 212 Kan. 234, 510 P.2d 1223 (1973). Cf. Conklin v. Davi, 76 N. J. 468, 388 A.2d 598 (1978) (buyer not entitled to rescission if seller could prove acquisition of title by adverse possession). [Query: How could the buyer draft the contract to avoid the result in *Conklin*?] The same principle is applied to other nondocumented methods of acquiring land, such as accretion of soil to land abutting a river. See Gaines v. Dillard, 545 S.W.2d 845 (Tex.Ct.Civ.App.1976).

(f) *Ordinance violations.* A variety of local zoning, environmental, and other land use ordinances may affect an owner's ability to use the real estate. Traditionally, courts have held that the mere existence of such ordinances does not render title unmarketable. See, e.g., Haw River Land & Timber Co., Inc. v. Lawyers Title Ins. Corp., 152 F.3d 275 (4th Cir.1998) (ordinance prohibiting cutting timber). As the court explained in Gloucester Landing Assocs. v. Gloucester Redev. Auth., 802 N.E.2d 1046 (Mass.Ct.App.2004) (citations omitted):

> The fact that the Property turned out to be far less valuable because [the state] refused to issue the [waterways] license does not render the title unmarketable. "There is a difference between economic lack of marketability, which concerns conditions that affect the use of land, and title marketability, which relates to defects affecting legally recognized rights and incidents of ownership." Thus, "[a]n individual can hold clear title to a parcel of land, although the same parcel is valueless or considered economically unmarketable because of some restriction or regulation on its use."

Some courts have concluded that *existing* structures or conditions that are in violation of zoning or other land use ordinances do make title unmarketable. See Radovanov v. Land Title Co. of Am. Inc., 189 Ill.App.3d 433, 545 N.E.2d 351 (1989) (pending suit for violation of housing code); Lohmeyer v. Bower, 227 P.2d 102 (Kan.1951) (violation of city setback ordinance); Allison Dunham, Effect on Title of Violation of Building Covenants and Zoning Ordinances, 27 Rocky Mt. L. Rev. 255 (1955). But the weight of modern authority holds that such violations do not affect marketability. See, e.g., Cone v. Stranahan, 44 A.D.3d 1145, 843 N.Y.S.2d 717 (2007) (violation of wetlands regulation); Fernandes v. Jamron, 9 A.D.3d 379, 780 N.Y.S.2d 164 (2004) (lapse of subdivision approval); Elysian Invst. Group v. Stewart Title Guaranty Co., 105 Cal.App.4th 315, 129 Cal.Rptr.2d 372 (2002) (recorded notice of building code violations).

(g) *Hazardous waste.* While the presence of illegal hazardous waste on the property may affect its marketability in an economic sense, it does not render title unmarketable. See Humphries v. Ables, 789 N.E.2d 1025 (Ind.Ct.App.2003) (contaminated soil).[14]

---

[14] In some states, hazardous waste statutes affirmatively require the seller to disclose the land's status in the contract; in these states, nondisclosure may permit the buyer to rescind even if the violation would not have rendered title unmarketable. See Johnson Machinery Co. v.

Under the law of many states, a lien (or even a "superlien," having a priority superior to all other interests) can be imposed on the property to reimburse the government for the cost of environmental cleanup. If the government has already imposed such a lien and it remains unsatisfied, title is obviously unmarketable. But if the lien is merely a possibility at the time of the sale (e.g., because contamination is present), and not yet a reality, title will probably be considered marketable. See, e.g., South Shore Bank v. Stewart Title Guar. Co., 688 F.Supp. 803 (D.Mass.1988), aff'd, 867 F.2d 607 (1st Cir.1988); Chicago Title Ins. Co. v. Kumar, 24 Mass.App.Ct. 53, 506 N.E.2d 154, 156–57 (1987); Lick Mill Creek Apts. v. Chicago Title Ins. Co., 231 Cal.App.3d 1654, 283 Cal.Rptr. 231 (1991).

For this reason, anyone purchasing land previously used for commercial, industrial, or agricultural purposes should have a qualified engineer or consultant conduct an environmental assessment of the land. Even though federal environmental laws do not impose a "superlien" on the contaminated property, such laws may create a duty of cleanup on the current owner of a hazardous waste site (even though that owner may not have caused the contamination and had no knowledge of it at the time of purchase). See Comprehensive Environmental Response, Compensation and Liability Act of 1980 (CERCLA), § 107(a), 42 U.S.C. § 9607(a); New York v. Shore Realty Corp., 759 F.2d 1032 (2d Cir.1985). There is an "innocent landowner" exemption in CERCLA, but its requirements are difficult to meet. See, e.g., U.S. v. Serafini, 706 F. Supp. 346 (M.D.Pa.1988).

(h) *Violations of covenants.* Even if the buyer has agreed to take title subject to restrictive covenants, she may still claim that the title is unmarketable if there is an existing violation of those covenants. The cases on this point are divided. See Coons v. Carstensen, 15 Mass.App.Ct. 431, 446 N.E.2d 114 (1983); Camp v. Commonwealth Land Title Ins. Co., 787 F.2d 1258 (8th Cir.1986).

(i) *Title links not of record.* Suppose one of the deeds in the seller's chain of title was never recorded (although it exists and is in the seller's possession). Is seller's title marketable? In general, the "muniments of title" (i.e., the documents that comprise the links in the chain) need not be recorded unless the contract provides for "marketable title of record." See Lucas v. Ind. Sch. Dist. No. 284, 433 N.W.2d 94 (Minn.1988). But if there is an actual break in the chain of title—i.e., a deed that is not only unrecorded but missing—seller's title is unmarketable. See Ferrara v. Walters, 919 So.2d 876 (Miss.2005).

(j) *Unreasonable risk of litigation.* If the property's title is currently being contested in litigation, the title is obviously unmarketable. Muniz v. Crystal Lake Project, LLC, 947 So.2d 464 (Fla.Ct.App.2006). Similarly, if one of the matters discussed in the prior notes presents an unreasonable risk of litigation, then the title is unmarketable. But an alleged defect which is not reasonably debatable or a threat of baseless litigation does not render title

---

Manville Sales Corp., 590 A.2d 1206 (N.J.Super.Ct.1991) (contract failed to disclose state land's prior use as sanitary landfill).

unmarketable. See *Stewart Title Guaranty Co. v. Greenlands Realty, L.L.C.*, 58 F.Supp.2d 360 (D.N.J.1999). Thus, the presence of a racially restrictive covenant in a deed in the seller's chain of title does not render title unmarketable since the Fair Housing Act makes such a covenant legally unenforceable. Likewise, as noted above, the threat of litigation concerning nontitle aspects of the land does not make title unmarketable. See *Humphries v. Ables*, 789 N.E.2d 1025 (Ind.Ct.App.2003) (possibility of litigation over hazardous waste contamination).

3. *Notice to the vendor of title defects.* The buyer is expected to examine the title before the closing and delivery of the deed. If the buyer finds a basis for objection to the quality of the title, she must notify the seller and give a fair opportunity for the seller to cure the defect unless the defect is by its nature incurable. This means that the buyer cannot give notice to the seller a day or two prior to the date of closing; if that happens, the seller will receive an extension of the closing date to have a reasonable chance to cure the defect, even if time is of the essence. See *Pederson v. McGuire*, 333 N.W.2d 823 (S.D.1983); *Chin v. Zoet*, 418 N.W.2d 191 (Minn.Ct.App.1988); III Am.L.Prop. § 11.51 (1952). Upon receiving notice of the title defect, the seller has a duty to make a reasonable (or "good faith") effort to cure the defect unless a cure would be impossible. See *Snowdon Farms v. Jones*, 8 Neb.App. 599, 599 N.W.2d 845 (1999); *Johnson v. Lambros*, 143 Idaho 468, 147 P.3d 100 (2006); *Harris v. Hosten*, 17 Misc.3d 1123, 351 N.Y.S.2d 69 (2007). Typically, the contract of sale will provide a date by which the buyer must give notice of any defect (as in the sample form in Section B on page 26).

4. *Time of title marketability.* Unless the contract provides otherwise, the seller's title need not be marketable until the closing date. See, e.g., *Wright v. Bryan*, 226 Va. 557, 311 S.E.2d 776 (1984). This means that the buyer cannot place the seller in breach for unmarketable title until the closing date (again, unless the contract provides otherwise). Indeed, at the time of the contract, the seller need not have title at all, as long as it appears possible for the seller to obtain it by the closing date.

This rule is probably unobjectionable in short-term earnest money contracts, but it gives rise to more serious problems with long-term installment contracts. Under an installment contract, the purchaser may make payments for many years with no assurance that the vendor will be able to cure the title problem by the time the last payment is made and the vendor delivers a deed. Some cases give the purchaser under such a contract an immediate right of rescission if the vendor is unable to provide reasonable assurances that it can effect a cure. See *Leavitt v. Blohm*, 11 Utah 2d 220, 357 P.2d 190 (1960).

5. *Satisfying liens at closing.* As *Haisfield* indicates, if the property is subject to a mortgage or other lien, the seller can usually discharge that lien with the proceeds of the sale. If this can be done, the buyer cannot object to the mortgage or lien as making title unmarketable because it will be paid off and extinguished by the time title passes to the buyer. There is ancient contrary authority, but such a strict approach is entirely unrealistic; courts today treat

the seller's title as marketable if it will become so at the closing. See, e.g., New York Prop. Holding Corp. v. Rosa, 26 A.D.3d 186, 809 N.Y.S.2d 34, 35 (2006); Lone Star Dev. Corp. v. Miller, 564 F.2d 921 (10th Cir.1977); see generally III Am.L.Prop. § 11.49 (1952).

Of course, this approach does not always work. If the aggregate balance owing on the liens on the property exceeds the net proceeds of sale, there are only two ways to clear the liens. One is for the seller to pay them using additional cash—money that the seller may not have or want to part with. The other is to persuade the holders of one or more of the liens to release them for a payment of less than the full amount owing (sometimes called a "short sale"). If neither solution is available, the seller will be in breach of the sales contract due to the remaining liens unless the buyer agrees to waive the problem and take title subject to the remaining liens in exchange for a reduced sale price.

6.   *Bringing the title examination "down" to the closing date.* Even though the buyer will have obtained a title examination or title report several days or weeks prior to the closing, the buyer understandably will not wish to tender the cash purchase price unless she can first check the public records immediately prior to accepting delivery of and recording the deed. If this is not done, the buyer may later discover that a last-minute title defect (e.g., a judgment lien against the seller) has arisen, thereby impairing the buyer's title. This scenario actually happened in Prochaska v. Midwest Title Guarantee Co., 85 Wash.App. 256, 932 P.2d 172 (1997) (judgment lien recorded against seller nine minutes before the buyer's deed was recorded; title company did not discover judgment lien; buyer held to have taken property subject to the lien). While the court later vacated the opinion (presumably following a settlement), 950 P.2d 497 (Wash.Ct.App.1997), the opinion seems correct.

In fact, it is impractical for the buyer to do an updated title search personally in the final moments prior to the closing. In most transactions, the buyer who obtains a policy of title insurance relies upon the title insurer to do so. A more complete discussion of the role of title insurance in the closing appears in Chapter Two.

7.   *"Insurable" title.* Sometimes, a contract will require the seller to deliver title that is "insurable," e.g., "Buyer agrees to accept a title such as any reputable title company, subject to the exceptions in this contract provided, would approve and insure." E.g., Patten of New York Corp. v. Geoffrion, 193 A.D.2d 1007, 598 N.Y.S.2d 355 (1993). Such language is actually a bit sloppy, because it does not identify the particular title insurance policy form, and some policy forms contain standard exclusions that might seriously disadvantage the purchaser. [We discuss title insurance in greater detail in Chapter Two.]

Nevertheless, the concept of "insurable title" can add considerable flexibility to the transaction. Suppose that a title investigation reveals a fairly minor defect. For example, suppose that home is in a neighborhood with a 50-year old restrictive covenant that requires cedar shake roofs, but every home in the neighborhood is in violation because every owner installed an asphalt shingled roof more than 25 years ago, and the homeowners association long ago resolved not to enforce the covenant. There may be a question as to whether the title is marketable (is it?), but the seller can probably persuade a title insurer to "insure over" the defect (i.e., to refrain from showing the defect as an exception to the policy's coverage). The insurer may do so if it concludes that there is no serious risk that the covenant would be enforced in the future. Using the "insurable title" standard in such a case may allow a transaction to proceed that might otherwise falter. [Of course, the contract could provide that title will be both marketable and insurable. See Nelson v. Anderson, 676 N.E.2d 735 (Ill.Ct.App.1997).]

It is clear that "insurable" is a lower standard than "marketable," as it is possible that a title company will be willing to "insure over" a defect that would make the title unmarketable. A buyer might hesitate to agree to accept a title that was insurable but not marketable, as the buyer might anticipate difficulty getting another title company to insure that title when the buyer attempts to resell the property at a later time. If the buyer has bargained for a marketable title, the court will not force him or her to accept one that is insurable but not marketable; see Nelson v. Anderson, 676 N.E.2d 735 (Ill.Ct.App.1997); U.S. Bank v. Smith, 7 Misc.3d 1005(A), 801 N.Y.S.2d 243 (2005).

8. *Merger of title covenants.* A well-known doctrine termed "merger" holds that if the buyer has a legitimate basis to object to the seller's title, the buyer must raise the objection prior to accepting delivery of the deed. Unless the sale contract provides otherwise, once the buyer accepts the deed, the buyer is deemed to be satisfied with the quality of the title received, so far as the contract is concerned. The seller's title obligation "merges" into the deed, and any future objection based on a title defect must be based on a breach of the covenants of title contained in the deed itself. See Donchi, Inc. v. Robdol, LLC, 640 S.E.2d 719 (Ga.Ct.App.2007); Dansie v. Hi-Country Estates Homeowners Ass'n, 987 P.2d 30 (Utah 1999). Thus, the buyer cannot rescind the sale based on unmarketability of the seller's title after accepting the deed; the only remedy for breach of a deed's covenants of title is damages. See III Am.L.Prop. § 11.65 (1952). [We address deed covenants of title further in Chapter Two.] Courts will occasionally refuse to apply the merger doctrine in cases of fraud or mutual mistake. See, e.g., Czarobski v. Lata, 862 N.E.2d 1039 (Ill.Ct.App.2007), aff'd, 882 N.E.2d 536 (Ill.2008) (mutual mistake regarding property tax assessment).

The doctrine of merger does not apply to most nontitle matters, such as warranties or covenants in the sales contract regarding the physical condition of the property. See Campbell v. Rawls, 381 So.2d 744 (Fla.Ct.App.1980) (warranty that air conditioning system would be in working order); Williams v. Runion, 173 Ga.App. 54, 325 S.E.2d 441 (1984) (builder's warranty of quality on new house). See also Bruggeman v. Jerry's Enters., Inc., 583 N.W.2d 299 (Minn.Ct.App.1998) (merger doctrine did not prevent seller from enforcing repurchase option contained in contract of sale).

9. *Type of deed to be delivered.* The implied covenant of marketable title says nothing about the nature of the deed the seller must tender to the buyer

at closing. In a well-drafted sales contract, the parties will specify the type of deed to be delivered. A deed may contain a broad range of covenants of title, a more limited range, or none at all (a "quitclaim" deed). These distinctions are covered in Chapter Two. But any deed, whether it contains covenants of title or not, will transfer whatever title the grantor has. Thus, there is no logical basis to assume that a covenant in the contract calling for marketable title necessarily implies that seller will deliver a warranty deed. See Department of Public Works & Bldgs. v. Halls, 35 Ill.2d 283, 220 N.E.2d 167 (1966); Lininger v. Black Hills Greyhound Racing Ass'n, 82 S.D. 507, 149 N.W.2d 413 (1967). Similarly, a contract clause providing that the seller will deliver a quitclaim deed does not logically negate the implied covenant that title will be marketable. See, e.g., Wallach v. Riverside Bank, 206 N.Y. 434, 100 N.E. 50 (1912).

F. EQUITABLE CONVERSION

Even if the time between execution and performance of a real estate sale contract (the "executory period") is brief, many events can occur during that period that raise legal questions, particularly where the contract did not anticipate these events. For example:

- Seller dies, leaving a will that gives Seller's real estate to A and Seller's personal property to B. If Buyer completes the purchase, who gets the purchase money, A or B?

- Creditor obtains a judgment against Seller. Does Creditor have a lien against the land?

- The state imposes a tax on the land. Who is liable for the tax, Seller or Buyer?

- The owner of the land has the ability to vote in an election (such as an election to establish a public utility district or a homeowners association board election). Who has the right to vote: Seller or Buyer?

- The home is destroyed in a fire. Who bears the risk of loss: Seller or Buyer?

Where the parties' contract does not address these matters specifically, the law's traditional method of dealing with them is to employ a doctrine called *equitable conversion*. In brief, this doctrine holds that "equitable" title passes to the buyer as soon as the parties form an enforceable contract to sell real estate—even though "legal" title will remain with the seller until the closing and the delivery of a deed to the purchaser.

The situations where courts have used equitable conversion doctrine fall in two basic categories. The first involves a *characterization* issue: during the executory period, should we characterize a given party (either the seller or the buyer) as owning a *real* property or a *personal* property interest? These cases require that the court label each party's interest as either real estate or as personal property. The second typically involves a *risk* issue: if a casualty occurs that jeopardizes the property's value or usefulness, which party must absorb the risk or sustain the loss? Must the buyer complete the purchase despite the loss, or may the buyer rescind (or at least insist on reduction of the price)? Risk questions can take a variety of forms. Some risks are physical (such as fire, earthquake, flood, or frost damage to crops). Other risks flow from changes in the land's legal status: an amendment to a zoning ordinance, a new building code requiring the retrofitting of existing structures, or a taking of the property by eminent domain. The parties may agree expressly in the contract as to how to allocate these risks, but they sometimes fail to do so. In those cases, the law must supply some presumptive rule to allocate the risk, and courts often use the doctrine of equitable conversion to do so.

As you read *Grant v. Kahn* and the materials that follow, consider whether the underlying issue involves *characterization* or *risk*. Is equitable conversion a suitable way of resolving the issue?

GRANT V. KAHN

Maryland Court of Appeals, 2011
198 Md. App. 421, 18 A.3d 91

WOODWARD, J. . . . [On May 29, 2007, Kareem Grant contracted to purchase a house in Wheaton, Maryland from Jeffrey Ganz for $320,000. The contract contained the following provision:

> This contract is contingent on Buyer obtaining approval for loan(s) to purchase the Property (the "Financing Contingency"). This contract is contingent until 9 p.m. 45 Days after Date of Ratification ("Financing Deadline") upon Buyer Delivering Notice to Seller on the Regional Form #100 removing this Financing Contingency.

Grant never provided Ganz with Regional Form #100, indicating that he had obtained a loan approval and was removing the contingency. He apparently did in fact obtain a suitable loan because on July 31, 2007, Grant and Ganz closed on the sale of the property.

At the time of closing, Grant did not realize that a short time earlier, on July 20, the Kahns had obtained a money judgment against Ganz for about $172,000. About eight months after the closing, on March 27, 2008, the Kahns asked the circuit court to issue a Writ of Execution directing the sheriff to levy upon the property. Grant then filed a motion to release the property from the levy. In Maryland, as in most states, a judgment becomes a lien on the real property of the judgment debtor. In some states, the lien attaches only when the judgment or some record of it is recorded in the real property records, but this is not necessary in Maryland; the lien takes effect as soon as the judgment is entered in the court's docket records.]

Grant argues that the doctrine of equitable conversion prevented the judgment against Ganz from attaching to the property. Specifically, Grant contends that, under the doctrine of equitable conversion, on May 29, 2007, when Grant and Ganz entered into the contract of sale, Grant became the equitable owner of the property and Ganz held only bare legal title. According to Grant, because a judgment creditor's lien cannot attach to bare legal title, the judgment against Ganz could not attach to the property after the execution of the contract of sale. Grant rejects the theory that the financing contingency in the contract of sale prevented the doctrine of equitable conversion from applying, because Grant could have waived the contingency and sought specific performance. Additionally, Grant contends that language in this Court's opinion in *Chambers v. Cardinal*, 177 Md. App. 418, 935 A.2d 502 (2007), which is contrary to his position, is merely dicta. Lastly, Grant submits that sound public policy supports a determination that equitable conversion occurred despite the financing contingency, because to hold otherwise would expose buyers who commonly rely on such contingencies to significant risks "associated with the seller's creditworthiness or lack thereof."

The Kahns counter that the circuit court was correct in its determination that the doctrine of equitable conversion was not applicable under the circumstances of the instant case. According to the Kahns, "[t]he ability of a buyer to specifically enforce a contract for realty is the lynchpin upon which rests the determination of whether equitable conversion has occurred." The Kahns contend that Grant could not have obtained specific performance of the contract of sale, because "specific performance requires that all contingencies and conditions precedent be satisfied by the party demanding the same." Here, according to the Kahns, the financing contingency remained unsatisfied and unremoved at the time that the confessed judgment was entered against Ganz, and thus equitable conversion had not occurred to prevent the judgment from attaching to the property. The Kahns also assert that Grant could not waive the financing contingency, because such contingency benefitted both Ganz, as seller, and Grant, as buyer. Finally, the Kahns contend that sound public policy supports affirming the circuit court, because fault lies with the title company that failed to bring the title examination up-to-date prior to closing. The Kahns conclude that a contrary holding would allow judgment debtors to shelter property from liens by entering into nonbinding contracts of sale. . . .

"Equitable conversion . . . is a theoretical change of property from realty to personalty, or vice versa, in order that the intention of the parties, in the case of a contract of sale, or the directions of the testator, in the case of directions in a will, may be given effect." Coe v. Hays, 328 Md. 350, 358,

614 A.2d 576 (1992). "The doctrine of equitable conversion and, more particularly, by contract, is well-established in Maryland." DeShields v. Broadwater, 338 Md. 422, 437, 659 A.2d 300 (1995). Our courts have routinely cited Thompson on Real Property's treatment of the topic:

> The legal cliché, that equity treats that as being done which should be done, is the basis of the theory of equitable conversion. Hence, when the vendee contracts to buy and the vendor to sell, though legal title has not yet passed, in equity the vendee becomes owner of the land, the vendor of the purchase money.

11 Thompson on Real Property § 96.06(a) (David A. Thomas ed., 2002 & Supp. 2008) (footnote omitted). See DeShields, 338 Md. at 437; Coe, 328 Md. at 358, 614 A.2d 576; Himmighoefer v. Medallion Industr., Inc., 302 Md. 270, 278, 487 A.2d 282 (1985).

Speaking for the Court of Appeals in *Watson v. Watson*, 304 Md. 48, 61, 497 A.2d 794 (1985), Judge Lawrence Rodowsky wrote:

> The doctrine of equitable conversion by contract rests on the maxim that equity considers as done that which ought to be done. Hence, an equitable conversion will place equitable title in the purchaser only if the contract is one under which the vendor would be subject to a decree for specific performance. As explained by Chief Judge Jeremiah Townley Chase for the Court in *Hampson v. Edelen*, [2 H. & J. 64, 66 (1807)],
>
> > [a] contract for land, bona fide made for a valuable consideration, vests the equitable interest in the vendee from the time of the execution of the contract, although the money is not paid at that time. When the money is paid according to the terms of the contract, the vendee is entitled to a conveyance, and to a decree in Chancery for a specific execution of the contract, if such conveyance is refused.
>
> The commentators are in accord that equitable conversion by contract takes place only if the contract is specifically enforceable.

Judge Rodowsky went on to discuss the legal effect of a judgment entered against a vendor after the contract has been made:

> One result of the doctrine is that a *judgment entered against the vendor after the contract has been made does not become a lien on the realty*. A vendor's judgment creditor may not execute on the realty because the vendor, sometimes described as trustee for the purchaser, has a right to the balance of the purchase money but has no beneficial interest in the property. Equitable title is superior to a later judgment lien.

Watson, 304 Md. at 60, 497 A.2d 794 (emphasis added); accord, Caltrider v. Caples, 160 Md. 392, 396, 153 A. 445 (1931) (stating that " '[a] judgment obtained by a third person against the vendor, mesne the making [of] the contract and the payment of the money, cannot defeat or impair the equitable interest thus acquired, nor is it a lien on the land to affect the right of such cestui que trust.' ") (quoting Hampson, 2 H. & J. at 66)).

In *Himmighoefer*, the Court of Appeals elaborated on this aspect of the doctrine:

> It is a general rule that the holder of an equitable title or interest in property, by virtue of an unrecorded contract of sale, has a claim superior to that of a creditor obtaining judgment subsequent to the execution of the contract. . . . The effect of such a contract is to vest the equitable ownership of the property in the vendee, subject to the vendor's lien for unpaid purchase money, and to leave only the legal title in the vendor pending the fulfillment of the contract and the formal conveyance of the estate. The right of the vendee to have the title conveyed upon full compliance with the contract of purchase is not impaired by the fact that the vendor, subsequently to the execution of the contract, incurred a debt upon which judgment was recovered. A judgment creditor stands in the place of his debtor, and he can only take the property of his debtor subject to the equitable charges to which it is liable in the hands of the debtor at the time of the rendition of the judgment.

302 Md. at 279, 487 A.2d 282 (emphasis added) (citations and quotations omitted) (quoting Stebbins-Anderson Co. v. Bolton, 208 Md. 183, 187–88, 117 A.2d 908 (1955)).

"[I]t is elementary that either party to a contract may waive any of the provisions made for his benefit." Twining v. Nat'l Mortg. Corp., 268 Md. 549, 555, 302 A.2d 604 (1973). " '[A]lthough a party may waive a provision included in a contract for that party's sole benefit, a party cannot waive a contractual requirement that benefits both sides to the transaction.' " Cattail Assoc., Inc. v. Sass, 170 Md. App. 474, 500, 907 A.2d 828 (2006) (quoting Citadel Equity Fund Ltd. v. Aquila, Inc., 371 F. Supp. 2d 510, 520 (S.D.N.Y. 2005)). "Accordingly, the application of the doctrine of waiver when one party seeks to enforce a contract . . . ordinarily requires a determination whether the condition was inserted in the contract solely for the benefit of the party seeking to enforce the contract despite its nonoccurrence." Id. (quoting 25 Samuel Williston, A Treatise on the Law of Contracts § 39:24 (Richard A. Lord ed., 4th ed.1992, Supp. 2006)). . . .

In the instant case, there is no question that the parties entered into a valid contract for Grant to purchase the property from Ganz and that the judgment lien against Ganz was entered after the execution of the contract but before settlement thereon. The central issue is whether the financing contingency in the contract of sale prevented equitable conversion from occurring at the time that the contract was made. Specifically, we need to decide whether the financing contingency prevented specific enforcement of the contract by Grant, which thereby would have precluded equitable conversion. See *Watson*, 304 Md. at 61, 497 A.2d 794 (stating that "[t]he commentators are in accord that equitable conversion takes place only if the contract is specifically enforceable.").[3]

Our review of the financing contingency in the contract indicates that it unquestionably benefitted Grant by making the contract contingent on his ability to secure the necessary financing. On the other hand, the financing contingency gave Ganz only the power, after the initial 45 day period, to impose a time limit for Grant to either remove the contingency or let the contract terminate, without liability. Therefore, the financing contingency benefitted only Grant, and because Grant could waive the contingency at any time, the contract was specifically enforceable by Grant.

In addition, according to the financing contingency, from May 29, 2007 to July 13, 2007 (the 45 day period following the date of the contract ratification), the contract was "contingent on [Grant] obtaining approval for [a] loan[] to purchase the [p]roperty." Grant did not exercise that option, and the contract was not terminated by him. After 9 p.m. on July 13, 2007 (the "deadline" for providing Ganz notice by Form #100 removing the financing contingency), the contingency, by its express terms, continued unless it was satisfied. After passage of the deadline, Ganz had the option to give notice to Grant that the contract would become void if Grant failed to deliver Form #100 within three days. Ganz did not exercise this option, and the contract continued to be in effect.

Instead, on July 31, 2007, Grant and Ganz met for settlement on the property, and Grant tendered the full amount of the purchase price. At that time Ganz had no option or discretion under the contract not to convey the property to Grant. Thus, if Ganz had refused such conveyance, specific performance of the contract was available to Grant. See Watson, 304 Md. at 61, 497 A.2d 794 (stating that "[w]hen the money is paid according to the terms of the contract, the vendee is entitled to a conveyance, and to a decree in Chancery for a specific execution of the contract, if such conveyance is refused").

We conclude that the financing contingency consisted of conditions subsequent. Neither party took advantage of the conditions permitting

---

[3] Although not raised by Grant, the Court of Appeals in *Caltrider v. Caples*, 160 Md. 392, 397–98, 153 A. 445 (1931), rejected the judgment creditor's argument that the contract of sale was not specifically enforceable, holding that the judgment creditor had no standing to raise that argument. The Court reasoned that the judgment creditor acquired no more rights than those retained by the vendor/judgment debtor, and the vendor had obviated the necessity of deciding the question of specific performance by carrying out the agreement. *Id.*

termination of the contract, so that the contract continued in effect. Therefore, the financing contingency did not prevent the occurrence of equitable conversion at the time of the execution of the contract. Accordingly, on July 24, 2007, when the circuit court entered a confessed judgment against Ganz, equitable title to the property was held by Grant, and the judgment could not attach as a lien on the property. Grant's claim of equitable title was superior to that of the Kahns as judgment creditors. The circuit court erred in coming to a contrary conclusion. . . .

Finally, Grant claims that "sound public policy" dictates that the decision of the circuit court be reversed. Grant reasons that the trial court's decision "endangers the free transferability of residential real property" by exposing buyers to significant risks associated with sellers who have "poor credit histories or financial difficulties." The Kahns counter that a reversal of the circuit court's decision "would implicitly allow judgment debtors to remove their real estate assets from the grasp of their judgment creditors by entering into non-binding contracts of sale which can be unilaterally nullified by their putative purchasers simply by giving notice." We agree with Grant.

Under the Kahns' theory, a buyer entering into a contract of sale with a financing contingency would be exposed to the risk of judgment liens entered against the seller after the execution of the contract. These liens could affect the sale itself where, for example, the total of all liens or encumbrances on the property exceed the purchase price, and the judgment creditor challenges the sufficiency of the purchase price. Such uncertainty, in our view, would adversely affect the free transferability of real property. The Kahns' concern over a debtor using a pretextual sale to avoid the anticipated lien of a judgment creditor is addressed by the doctrine of equitable conversion. Equitable conversion requires a "contract for land, bona fide made for a valuable consideration." *Watson*, 304 Md. at 61, 497 A.2d 794; see Birckner v. Tilch, 179 Md. 314, 323, 18 A.2d 222 (stating that "[i]n order to work a conversion, the contract must be valid and binding"), cert. denied, 314 U.S. 635, 62 S.Ct. 68, 86 L.Ed. 509 (1941). Therefore, we conclude that sound public policy supports the application of the doctrine of equitable conversion to the case sub judice.

NOTES AND QUESTIONS

1.   *Two types of contracts.* The contract of sale in *Grant* was a short-term "earnest money" contract. The buyer under these contracts typically makes no installment payments—just a single payment of the balance of the price on the closing date—and ordinarily does not take possession until the closing date. By contrast, the buyer under a long-term installment contract (called in some states a "contract for deed") takes possession of the land shortly after the contract is signed, makes payments (monthly, quarterly, or annually) for a number of years, and receives a deed only when the final installment is paid.

Courts have applied equitable conversion without much distinction to both types of contracts. But it is much easier to visualize the buyer as an "owner of real estate" in the long-term installment contract case because the buyer has possession and is making payments that are similar to the payments that would be due under a mortgage loan. For example, consider Akers v. Butler, 476 S.W.3d 183 (Ark.Ct.App.2015), in which the Butlers purchased a lot in Forest Ridge Estates from the developer on a contract for deed. When the Butlers signed the contract and took possession, the developer had not yet recorded any restrictive covenants on the land; six months later, the developer recorded restrictive covenants purporting to cover the entire neighborhood (including the Butlers' lot). Years later, several neighbors sued the Butlers for violating the covenants by renting out the barn for commercial uses; the Butlers argued that the covenant was not enforceable against them because they purchased "ownership" of the land before the covenants were recorded. Should equitable conversion apply here? Why or why not?

Even in short term earnest money contracts, should the buyer's rights in the real estate be considered sufficient to regard the buyer as an equitable owner?

2. *Acceptance of equitable conversion.* Equitable conversion is widely, but not universally, accepted by American courts. One article cites 32 jurisdictions as having adopted the doctrine in some context or other. Nock, Strait & Weaver, Equitable Conversion in Washington: The Doctrine That Dares Not Speak Its Name, 1 U.Puget Sound L.Rev. 121 (1977). For historical background on the doctrine, see Harlan Stone, Equitable Conversion by Contract, 13 Colum.L.Rev. 369 (1913); C.C. Langdell, A Brief Survey of Equity Jurisdiction, 1 Harv.L.Rev. 355 (1887).

3. *Necessity of a contract.* Conversion occurs only if there is a contract that equity would specifically enforce. There is no equitable conversion if, at the relevant time, there is only an unaccepted offer or an unexercised option. See Riddle v. Elk Creek Salers, Ltd., 52 S.W.3d 644 (Mo.Ct.App.2001). Likewise, if the contract has expired at the relevant time, conversion does not occur. Lewis v. Muchmore, 26 S.W.3d 632 (Tenn.Ct.App.2000). But if an enforceable contract exists at the time in question, courts in characterization cases have held conversion occurred, even if the contract is later rescinded, abandoned, or never enforced. See III Am. L. Prop. § 11.23 (1952); Frietze v. Frietze, 78 N.M. 676, 437 P.2d 137 (1968) (contract was in force at time of purchaser's death, and equitable conversion governed passage of his title, even though contract was never performed).

4. *When conversion is inapplicable.* Courts occasionally have developed "exceptions" to equitable conversion, perhaps manipulating them to avoid results they consider unfair. For example, equitable conversion will not occur if the vendor's title is unmarketable as of the date that conversion is in issue. See Bleckley v. Langston, 112 Ga.App. 63, 143 S.E.2d 671 (1965) (risk of loss case); Coe v. Hays, 328 Md. 350, 614 A.2d 576 (1992) (characterization case). This exception is consistent with the rule in note 3 that equitable conversion

can occur only if there is a contract that equity would specifically enforce. As *Grant* suggests, some courts hold that there is no conversion until all conditions precedent to the transfer of legal title have been fulfilled. See, e.g., Sanford v. Breidenbach, 173 N.E.2d 702 (Ohio Ct.App. 1960) (sellers failed to provide required septic easement).

5.   *Judgment liens*. The issue in *Grant* was whether equitable conversion changes the seller's interest during the executory period from realty into personalty, and therefore prevents a judgment against the seller from creating a lien against the land. The case law on this point is split. Compare Bank of Hawaii v. Horwoth, 787 P.2d 674 (Haw.1990) and SMS Fin., LLC v. CBC Fin. Corp., 417 P.3d 70 (Utah 2017) (applying equitable conversion; no judgment lien on the land) with Bedortha v. Sunridge Land Co., 822 P.2d 694 (Or.1991) and Schleuter Co. v. Sevigny, 546 N.W.2d 309 (S.D.1997) (rejecting equitable conversion and holding judgment lien attached). See generally Whitman, Burkhart, Freyermuth & Rule, The Law of Property § 10.13 (4th ed. 2019).

Does the Maryland court's rationale in *Grant* for refusing to recognize the judgment lien make any sense? What about the countervailing public policy that a person's interest in land should be accessible to that person's creditors in payment of legitimate debts? If the lien is "docketed" (i.e., entered into the court's records) during a short-term earnest money contract's executory period, title company or attorney will normally find it prior to the closing in bringing the title search "down to date" (note 6, page 100). A competent title searcher will identify the lien, and either the seller will pay it off from the proceeds of the sale or (if the proceeds are insufficient and the seller has no other funds to pay it) the sale will be rescinded and the buyer's earnest money refunded. Thus, a judgment lien against the seller is really no different than any other lien that might attach to the property during the executory period. How can the *Grant* court assert that the buyer is exposed to significant risks in this situation?

If the sales contract is a long-term installment contract, the attachment of a judgment lien to the vendor's interest presents a more significant problem. The purchaser may be unaware of the lien and may continue to make payments on the contract price, possibly ending up paying more than the encumbered property is worth. Of course, the purchaser could procure another title search before making each payment, but this would be ludicrously burdensome and costly. See the Utah court's discussion of this issue in Cannefax v. Clement, 818 P,2d 546 (Utah 1991).

What about a judgment lien that is docketed against the *buyer* during the executory period of the sales contract? Here, equitable conversion is very widely applied to make the judgment a lien on the buyer's interest. See Fulton v. Duro, 687 P.2d 1367 (Idaho Ct.App.1984); Hannah v. Martinson, 232 Mont. 469, 758 P.2d 276 (1988); Farmers State Bank v. Slaubaugh, 366 N.W.2d 804 (N.D.1985); Butler v. Wilkinson, 740 P.2d 1244 (Utah 1987).

6.   *Death of a contracting party*. The death of a contracting party during the executory period is the most-commonly discussed equitable conversion

characterization issue. If a court concludes that equitable conversion occurred at the time of the seller's death, the seller's interest descends as personal property to his legatees or, if seller died intestate, to his statutory next-of-kin. If it is the buyer who dies, her interest descends as realty to her devisees or, if she died intestate, to her statutory heirs.

In the case of the seller's death, this means that "bare" legal title descends to the devisees or heirs, who have a duty to convey it to the buyer at the closing. See Mackiewicz v. J.J. & Assoc., 245 Neb. 568, 514 N.W.2d 613 (1994). The deceased seller's personal property legatees or next-of-kin will receive the purchase price, and the devisees or heirs who were forced to convey away the legal title to the real estate receive nothing. See In re Estate of Line, 122 Ohio App.3d 387, 701 N.E.2d 1028 (1997). In the case of the buyer's death, the buyer's devisees or heirs will be entitled to delivery of the deed at the closing, but the purchase price will be paid out of the personal property estate of the deceased buyer—and thus will reduce the assets going to the purchaser's personal property legatees or heirs. See Timberlake v. Heflin, 379 S.E.2d 149 (W.Va.1989); III Am.L.Prop. § 11.26–.27 (1952).

Equitable conversion is usually unimportant if the decedent died intestate, because modern intestacy statutes commonly make the same person or group of persons heirs of the real property and next-of-kin takers of the personal property of the intestate decedent. The issue is more critical if the decedent left a will that designates different individuals as devisees and legatees. For example, suppose the decedent was the buyer, and her will provides, "I leave all my personal property to John and all my real property to Mary." Is it plausible to suppose the decedent intended Mary to get the land and John to suffer the payment of the price out of the personal property he would have received?[15] Does it matter whether the will was executed before or after the contract? Whether the will mentions the specific land in question? Would it be more "equitable" for Mary to take the land, but subject to the "vendor's lien" for the unpaid price, so that Mary would have to pay the remainder of the purchase price to keep the land?

Similar concerns can arise in the event of the seller's death. Suppose the seller's will leaves his personal property to John and his real estate to Mary. If the seller executed the will at a time when the land in question was already under contract, and especially if that land was the only real estate the seller owned, how likely is it that the seller intended the contract to cut Mary out of receiving the financial benefits of the real estate contract? Yet this is the result

---

[15] The real problem here is the so-called "doctrine of exoneration," which requires the decedent's debts—even contractual debts secured by a real estate sales contract—to be paid out of the decedent's personal property estate. The doctrine of exoneration is plainly weakening in the United States. Increasingly, courts hold that property subject to a mortgage, for example, will pass pursuant to a decedent's will with the mortgage still encumbering it, rather than requiring the mortgage to be paid off from the personal property estate, unless the testator's will expressly requires exoneration. See In re Estate of Vincent, 98 S.W.3d 146 (Tenn.2003) (testator's statement in will, that executor was to pay his "just debts" was not specific enough to require exoneration of mortgage debt on land). The Uniform Probate Code abolishes exoneration with respect to mortgages, although it makes no reference to exoneration of an obligation to pay the purchase price of land pursuant to a real estate sales contract. UPC § 2–609.

under the doctrine of equitable conversion. See Father Flanagan's Boys' Home v. Graybill, 178 Neb. 79, 132 N.W.2d 304 (1964). If the will predates the contract, cutting Mary out seems easier to accept as a result; arguably, the seller would have expected that would be the result of entering the contract. See In re Estate of Pickett, 879 So.2d 467 (Miss.Ct.App.2004).

Given the inherent ambiguities involved in these characterization situations, a few states have changed the foregoing rules by statute. See, e.g., Rowe v. Newman, 290 Ala. 289, 276 So.2d 412 (1972). If you were a state legislator, would you adopt a statutory rule to address these characterization issues? Or would you prefer to allow the courts discretion to continue to apply the doctrine of equitable conversion (or not) on a case by case basis?

7.   *Risk of loss.* When property is damaged during the executory period, applying equitable conversion imposes the loss on the buyer (as the equitable "owner" of the land). Unless the contract provides otherwise, the buyer would be subject to a decree of specific performance, forcing the buyer to pay the full price even though the real estate's value is diminished by the loss. Which party had possession of the property at the time of the loss is said to be irrelevant. See 6A Powell, Real Property ¶ 933 (1979). Consider whether this result fulfills the following policy objectives:

- Is it consistent with the probable expectation of the parties?

- Does it place the risk on the party best able to protect against the risk?

- Does it place the risk on the party best situated to insure against the risk?

See generally Fineberg, Risk of Loss in Executory Contracts for the Sale of Real Property, 14 Colum. J.L. & Soc. Prob. 453 (1979). Applying the doctrine of equitable conversion in a casualty loss situation usually fails all three of these objectives. [Can you explain why?] But whatever its merits (or lack thereof), many courts have applied it in "risk of loss" cases. See, e.g., Continental Ins. Co. v. Brown, 630 F.Supp. 302 (W.D.Va.1986); Ambrose v. Harrison Mut. Ins. Ass'n, 206 N.W.2d 683 (Iowa 1973); Bleckley v. Langston, 112 Ga.App. 63, 143 S.E.2d 671 (1965).

It is clear, however, that the parties can modify this risk allocation as they wish in the sales contract. See, e.g., Holscher v. James, 124 Idaho 443, 860 P.2d 646 (1993); Noor v. Centreville Bank, 996 A.2d 927 (Md.Ct.App.2010). Printed form contracts (such as the one in Section B, page 26) routinely place the risk of loss on the seller until the closing, or perhaps until the buyer takes possession (in the rare case where buyer takes possession prior to closing). As a result, litigated cases today usually involve the relatively rare situations where the sales contract is silent on the risk of loss issue.

The previous discussion presumes that the loss in question is not the fault of either party. Even if the contract imposes the risk of loss on the seller, the buyer is nevertheless legally responsible if the buyer negligently or intentionally starts a fire that damages the premises. See Voorde Poorte v.

Evans, 66 Wash.App. 358, 832 P.2d 105 (1992). Likewise, even if equitable conversion would otherwise impose the risk on the buyer, the seller will bear the loss for damage caused by the seller's own fault. See Sposit v. Navratil, 72 Ohio App.3d 493, 595 N.E.2d 467 (1991) (seller negligent in allowing water pipes to freeze prior to closing).

8. *The minority view: risk remains on the vendor.* A few courts have refused to follow equitable conversion in risk of loss cases; they usually place the risk on the seller until legal title or possession is transferred, and permit the buyer to rescind in the event of a loss or (at the buyer's option) to get specific performance with an abatement of the price to account for the land's reduced value. See Libman v. Levenson, 236 Mass. 221, 128 N.E. 13 (1920); Anderson v. Yaworski, 120 Conn. 390, 181 A. 205 (1935); Lampesis v. Travelers Ins. Co., 101 N.H. 323, 143 A.2d 104 (1958); Skelly Oil Co. v. Ashmore, 365 S.W.2d 582, 588 (Mo.1963).

Perhaps the most sensible approach is represented by Brush Grocery Kart, Inc. v. Sure Fine Market, Inc., 47 P.3d 680 (Colo.2002). The court held that equitable conversion would impose the risk of loss on the purchaser only in cases where the purchaser had taken possession of the property at the time of the loss. This result is similar to that reached by the Uniform Vendor and Purchaser Risk Act, discussed in Note 11 infra. See also Alley v. McLain's Inc. Lumber & Constr., 182 S.W.3d 312 (Tenn.Ct.App.2005) (where purchaser had timber cut on the property, person cutting timber might be shielded from liability to vendor by equitable conversion doctrine, but only if purchaser was entitled to possession at the time timber was cut).

9. *Types of losses.* Although the losses that equitable conversion imposes on the purchaser are usually the result of fire, flood, wind, or other physical hazards, the risk of change in the property's *legal* status is sometimes allocated to the purchaser in the same way. The following situations are illustrative:

(a) *Zoning change.* See, e.g., Mohave County v. Mohave-Kingman Estates, Inc., 120 Ariz. 417, 586 P.2d 978 (1978); J.C. Penney Co. v. Koff, 345 So. 2d 732 (Fla.Ct.App.1977); cf. Clay v. Landreth, 187 Va. 169, 45 S.E.2d 875 (1948) (contract will not be enforced if zoning change has made property unusable for purchaser's intended purpose).

(b) *Building code change.* See Cox v. Supreme Sav. & Loan Ass'n, 126 Ill.App.2d 293, 262 N.E.2d 74 (1970).

(c) *Eminent domain action.* See Arko Enters., Inc. v. Wood, 185 So. 2d 734 (Fla.Ct.App.1966); Annot., 27 A.L.R.3d 572 (1969).

(d) *Liability for the cost of cleanup of hazardous waste.* United States v. Capital Tax Corp., 545 F.3d 525 (7th Cir.2008).

10. *Loss from title defects.* Suppose the event that occurs during the executory period of the sales contract and causes a loss also is a title defect, such as the imposition by the city of a lien for a sewer improvement assessment. Should this event be treated as a breach of the covenant of

marketable title (imposing the risk on the seller) or handled under equitable conversion (imposing the risk on the purchaser)? See Byrne v. Kanig, 231 Pa.Super. 531, 332 A.2d 472 (1974). The eminent domain cases raise a similar issue (although the courts do not always recognize it), because a pending eminent domain action is a defect in marketable title. See III Am.L.Prop. § 11.49 n.52 (1952).

11. *The Uniform Vendor and Purchaser Risk Act (UVPRA)*. Eleven states have adopted the UVPRA, which changes the impact of equitable conversion on the risk of certain types of losses. UVPRA § 1 provides:

> Any contract hereafter made in this State for the purchase and sale of realty shall be interpreted as including an agreement that the parties shall have the following rights and duties, unless the contract expressly provides otherwise:
>
> (a) If, when neither the legal title nor the possession of the subject matter of the contract has been transferred, all or a material part thereof is destroyed without fault of the purchaser or is taken by eminent domain, the vendor cannot enforce the contract, and the purchaser is entitled to recover any portion of the price that he has paid;
>
> (b) If, when either the legal title or the possession of the subject matter of the contract has been transferred, all or any part thereof is destroyed without fault of the vendor or is taken by eminent domain, the purchaser is not thereby relieved from a duty to pay the price, nor is he entitled to recover any portion thereof that he has paid.

UVPRA's background is discussed in Frank Lacy, The Uniform Vendor and Purchaser Risk Act and the Need for a Law—Revision Commission in Oregon, 36 Or.L.Rev. 106 (1957). See also Whitman, Burkhart, Freyermuth & Rule, The Law of Property § 10.13 (4th ed.2019). Based on the language of the UVPRA, consider the following questions:

- What sorts of losses are covered? What about the "legal" losses mentioned in Notes 9 and 10 above?

- How much is a "material part" of the property? If the property is a house worth $150,000, what about damage of $100? $1,000? $10,000? See National Factors, Inc. v. Winslow, 52 Misc.2d 194, 274 N.Y.S.2d 400 (1966).

- If the damage is less than "material," the purchaser has no right under UVPRA to rescind. But can the purchaser insist on an abatement of price in the amount of the damage?

- If the damage is "material," the buyer may rescind. Can the buyer specifically enforce the contract with an abatement of the price? See Lucenti v. Cayuga Apts., Inc., 59 A.D.2d 438, 400 N.Y.S.2d 194 (1977).

- What does it mean for "possession" to be "transferred"? Has possession been transferred if the buyer, at the time of the loss, has the legal right to possession but has not actually gone into occupancy yet? See Unger v. Nunda Township Rural Fire Protection Dist., 135 Ill.App.3d 758, 90 Ill.Dec. 416, 482 N.E.2d 123 (1985).

- Suppose the sales contract says that the buyer will accept the property "as is." Does that language shift the risk of casualty loss to the buyer? Redner v. New York, 53 Misc.2d 148, 278 N.Y.S.2d 51 (1967).

In a state without UVPRA, it is obviously crucial to have a contract clause covering the risk of loss issue. How should such a clause be worded? Is it sufficient to say "Risk of loss shall be on the vendor until legal title is transferred"? Should the clause track the language of the Act? See M. Friedman, Contracts and Conveyances of Real Property 382 (3d ed.1975). As a legal drafting skills exercise, try your hand at writing a sales contract clause that deals clearly with all of the issues raised in this set of Notes.

NOTE ON THE IMPACT OF CASUALTY INSURANCE

The seller usually has a casualty insurance policy in force because the seller usually has owned and/or occupied the property for some time before putting it on the market. The buyer usually applies for a new casualty insurance policy to take effect on the date of closing. Thus, there is a lack of correspondence between the insurance coverage and the risk of loss, especially if the buyer has the risk of loss under the doctrine of equitable conversion or an express contractual provision.

Casualty insurance is a personal contract between the insurer and the insured. Thus, the insurer is not obligated to pay the proceeds to anyone except the insured under the policy. But to let the seller keep the insurance proceeds—and, at the same time, enforce the contract of sale for the full purchase price—would obviously result in the unjust enrichment of the seller. [You can imagine a seller in these circumstances saying, "This is one of the best fires I ever had!"]

To avoid this unjust enrichment, many courts require the seller to pay or credit the insurance proceeds to the buyer, up to the full purchase price. Gilles v. Sprout, 293 Minn. 53, 196 N.W.2d 612 (1972); Hillard v. Franklin, 41 S.W.3d 106 (Tenn.Ct.App.2000). Courts sometimes say that the seller holds the insurance proceeds in "constructive trust" for the buyer, but this means simply that the buyer is credited with them. See, e.g., New Hampshire Ins. Co. v. Vetter, 326 N.W.2d 723 (S.D.1982); Fellmer v. Gruber, 261 N.W.2d 173 (Iowa 1978); Chapline v. North Am. Acceptance Corp., 25 Ariz.App. 465, 544 P.2d 682 (1976). New York courts have refused to credit the buyer with the insurance proceeds in all cases, but has allowed a credit if the buyer was obligated to pay and did pay the premiums. See Raplee v. Piper, 3 N.Y.2d 179, 164 N.Y.S.2d 732, 143 N.E.2d 919 (1957); accord, Wilson v. Fireman's Ins. Co., 269 N.W.2d

170 (Mich.1978). See generally Allen Fineberg, Risk of Loss in Executory Contracts for the Sale of Real Property, 14 Colum.J.L. & Soc.Prob. 453, 476 (1979); James Fischer, The Presence of Insurance and the Legal Allocation of Risk, 2 Conn.Ins.L.J. 1, 27 n.107 (1996); Annot., Rights of Vendor and Purchaser, as Between Themselves, in Insurance Proceeds, 64 A.L.R.2d 1402 (1959).

Suppose the buyer willingly pays the full price despite the fire or other damage (perhaps because the buyer planned to demolish the structure anyway), and makes no claim to the insurance proceeds. Can the insurer refuse to pay the seller's claim on grounds that; (1) insurance is a contract of indemnity and the seller has suffered no loss to be indemnified, or (2) the seller, having contracted to sell the property, no longer had an insurable interest in it at the time of the loss? Compare Wolf v. Home Ins. Co., 100 N.J. Super. 27, 241 A.2d 28 (1968) (seller can collect) with Westfall v. Am. States Ins. Co., 43 Ohio App.2d 176, 334 N.E.2d 523 (1974) (seller had no insurable interest). Does payment of the insurance proceeds in such a situation give the vendor an unjustifiable windfall? See Banks McDowell, Insurable Interest in Property Revisited, 17 Cap.U.L.Rev. 165 (1988).

Suppose instead that it is the buyer who carries the insurance, is named as insured, and has the risk of loss. Obviously, in the event of a casualty loss the purchaser is entitled to claim the insurance proceeds. If the risk is on the seller, however, the buyer arguably has no loss and no insurable interest. As a result, the buyer's insurer in this situation may entirely avoid payment under the policy. See Sanford v. Breidenbach, 111 Ohio App. 474, 173 N.E.2d 702 (1960).

In general, the seller has no right to the insurance proceeds when the buyer is the insured under the policy. But if the sales contract specified that the buyer was to carry insurance, the courts often infer that the parties intended for the seller to have the benefit of the policy, up to the outstanding balance on the contract, and permit the seller to claim it. See Nevada Refining Co. v. Newton, 88 Nev. 333, 497 P.2d 887 (1972); Marbach v. Gnadl, 73 Ill.App.2d 303, 219 N.E.2d 572 (1966). Cf. Phillips v. Bacon, 245 Ga. 814, 267 S.E.2d 249 (1980). This right of the seller is even more clear if the purchaser expressly promised to carry casualty insurance on the property for the seller's benefit. See Rosario-Paolo, Inc. v. C & M Pizza Restaurant, Inc., 84 N.Y.2d 379, 618 N.Y.S.2d 766, 643 N.E.2d 85 (1994).

G. THE CONDITION OF THE PROPERTY

The buyer customarily enters into a transaction expecting the land and improvements will meet the buyer's expectations, both in terms of their physical condition generally and their compliance with certain legal standards (such as zoning or building codes). Yet the law traditionally applied the *caveat emptor* principle to the purchase of land. Under this principle, the seller of land had no liability for defective conditions, except in cases where (a) the seller made an express warranty that the premises were free of defects, or (b) the seller committed fraud by affirmatively misrepresenting the condition of the premises. Thus, the seller's mere silence concerning defects was not actionable unless the seller engaged in other conduct, such as active concealment efforts, that made the silence misleading. See, e.g., Swiedler v. Ferguson, 393 S.E.2d 456 (Ga.Ct.App. 1990). Likewise, absent an express warranty, builders of structures traditionally had no contractual liability for construction defects.

The traditional approach presumed that the buyer of real estate was fully capable of evaluating the physical condition of the premises and whether that condition met both the buyer's expectations of quality and applicable legal requirements. Is this presumption justified? In recent years, while not rejecting *caveat emptor* altogether, courts have shown an increasing willingness to question its application, at least in the context of certain residential real estate sale transactions.

JENSEN V. BAILEY
Florida Court of Appeals, 2011
276 So. 3d 980

WALLACE, JUDGE. Eric Jensen and Joyce Jensen appeal a final judgment awarding damages against them and in favor of Cynthia Bailey on her claim for the Jensens' failure to disclose material defects in their residence to Mrs. Bailey under *Johnson v. Davis,* 480 So. 2d 625 (Fla.1985). Because the circuit court found that the Jensens had no knowledge of the defects but improperly found the Jensens liable to Mrs. Bailey under a "should have known" standard, we reverse the final judgment.

In June 2005, the Jensens entered into a contract with Gene Bailey and Cynthia Bailey for the sale and purchase of the Jensens' residence in St. Petersburg. Before the parties signed the contract, the Jensens filled out a property disclosure statement for the Baileys' review. One of the questions on the disclosure statement asked whether the sellers were aware "of any improvements or additions to the property, whether by you or by others, that have been constructed in violation of building codes or without necessary permits?" In response to this question, the Jensens checked the "NO" box. The parties closed the sale in July 2005, and the Baileys took possession of the property.

Approximately two years later, the Baileys filed an action for damages against the Jensens. In their complaint, the Baileys alleged claims for breach of contract, nondisclosure of material defects in the residence under Johnson, and fraudulent concealment. The Jensens filed an answer denying the material allegations of the complaint and raised affirmative defenses. Mr. Bailey died while the action was pending in the circuit court, and Mrs. Bailey continued the action as the sole plaintiff.

After a bench trial that lasted two days, the circuit court entered a detailed verdict in favor of Mrs. Bailey on her nondisclosure claim under *Johnson*. In the verdict, the circuit court ruled, in pertinent part, as follows:

> At trial two main categories of problems emerged. One was the alleged defective sanitary sewer which caused reoccurring backups into the home. The other was a trio of unpermitted changes in the home which were discovered to be not in conformity with building codes and would thus require reconstruction.

> After careful consideration the court finds the evidence insufficient to support [Mrs. Bailey's] claims regarding the sewer system. On the other hand, the evidence was that ... the [Jensens] had substantial remodeling work done in their master bath, their kitchen, and in the bedroom by the installation of French doors. It was uncontroverted that these three jobs required proper permits. The evidence supports the conclusion that neither the [Jensens] nor those who they hired obtained the permits. Expert testimony indicated that the work was not properly done, did not conform to the codes applicable when done, and would require reconstruction in full conformity with newer, more stringent codes.

> There was no evidence that the [Jensens] actually knew about the failure to obtain permits or the improper work. They, like perhaps many trusting people, relied upon the individuals or companies they hired to do the work legally and in a proper fashion.

> These facts presented a difficult question regarding the extent to which Florida law will protect a buyer in a residential real estate transaction from material defects which are not actually known to the seller but should have been known by them. As a practical matter, homeowners have a responsibility to obtain proper permits and generally can find no protection from their failure to do so because they merely relied on someone else to do so. Since such permits are required, it does not seem an unreasonable conclusion that the homeowner is likewise expected to know whether the permits were actually issued and posted for the construction. These logical assumptions appear to be the foundation for the questions presented to sellers in the typical real property disclosure forms. That is, the owner is expected to know about these important matters with regard to their property because they are in a position to need to know.

The circuit court concluded "that the proofs support a *Johnson v. Davis* claim [that] the [Jensens] should have known about the absence of permits and reported same in the disclosure statement. As a result [, Mrs. Bailey is] entitled to relief." Based on the verdict, the circuit court entered a final judgment in favor of Mrs. Bailey and against the Jensens for $33,370 in damages, plus $13,787.31 in prejudgment interest. The Jensens' appeal followed, and Mrs. Bailey filed a cross-appeal. . . .

This case requires us to decide whether liability under the rule in *Johnson* may be based on a finding of the seller's constructive knowledge of an undisclosed material defect instead of his or her actual knowledge. We conclude that to hold the seller liable under *Johnson*, the buyer must prove the seller's actual knowledge of an undisclosed material defect. . . .

actual knowledge of undisclosed material defect

A nondisclosure claim under *Johnson* has four elements: (1) the seller of a home must have knowledge of a defect in the property, (2) the defect must materially affect the value of the property, (3) the defect must be not readily observable and must be unknown to the buyer, and (4) the buyer must establish that the seller failed to disclose the defect to the buyer. 480 So. 2d at 629. Here, we address the first element, the seller's knowledge of a defect in the property.

Notably, the only consideration pertinent to the seller's state of mind under *Johnson* is knowledge of a defect materially affecting the value of the property at the time the seller enters into the contract with the buyer. *Billian v. Mobil Corp.*, 710 So. 2d 984, 988 (Fla. 4th DCA 1998). As the Fourth District has explained:

> *Johnson* does not specify any state of mind element with regard to the act of non-disclosure for the cause of action it identifies. . . . Significantly, *Johnson* casts the cause of action in terms of "duty," a concept drawn from the law of negligence. If the facts of a case give rise to a duty to disclose under *Johnson,* the seller's state of mind motivating the failure to disclose is immaterial; the forgetful or unsophisticated seller is just as liable as the knowing dissembler.

Id. Thus the critical issue under the first element of liability under *Johnson* is the seller's knowledge, not his or her intent. The question raised by this case is whether anything less than actual knowledge is sufficient to satisfy the first element.

The late Chief Justice Joseph Boyd dissented in *Johnson*, and he raised this question in his dissent. Chief Justice Boyd expressed his fear that the majority's holding in *Johnson* would lead to "making the seller a guarantor of the good condition of the property" and thus "significantly burden the alienability of property." 480 So. 2d at 631 (Boyd, C.J., dissenting). He predicted that the courts would ultimately construe *Johnson*'s requirement of actual knowledge to permit a finding of liability based on constructive knowledge:

Johnson dissent

> The trend will proceed somewhat as follows. At first, the cause of action will require proof of actual knowledge of the undisclosed defect on the part of the seller. But in many cases the courts will allow it to be shown by circumstantial evidence. Then a rule of constructive knowledge will develop based on the reasoning that if the seller did not know of the defect, he should have known about it before attempting to sell the property. Thus the burden of inspection will shift from the buyer to the seller. Ultimately the courts will be in the position of imposing implied warranties and guaranties on all sellers of real property.

Id. This case proves that Chief Justice Boyd's fear about the eventual effect of the majority's holding in *Johnson* was not completely unjustified. Here, the circuit court found the Jensens liable to Mrs. Bailey in the absence of proof of their actual knowledge of the asserted material defects based on a "should have known" standard.

However, this court has consistently reversed judgments in favor of the buyer for nondisclosure under *Johnson* in the absence of proof of the seller's actual knowledge of the defect. *See Brown v. Carter*, 13 So.3d 111, 113–14 (Fla. 2d DCA 2009); *Spitale v. Smith*, 721 So. 2d 341, 345 (Fla. 2d DCA 1998); *Slitor v. Elias*, 544 So. 2d 255, 258–59 (Fla. 2d DCA 1989). In *Slitor*, we said:

> *Johnson* does not convert a seller of a house into a guarantor of the condition of the house. As we have said, to prove a cause of action under *Johnson*, a buyer of a house must prove the seller's knowledge of a defect which materially affected the value of the house. While knowledge in this regard can be proven by circumstantial evidence, it must nevertheless be proven by competent, sufficient evidence which, as we have explained, did not exist here.

Id. (citation omitted). Other Florida courts have recognized that liability for nondisclosure under *Johnson* requires proof of the seller's actual knowledge of the defect. *See Billian*, 710 So. 2d at 988 ("*Johnson* creates a duty to disclose where a seller knows of certain facts under circumstances giving rise to the duty"); *Haskell Co. v. Lane Co.*, 612 So. 2d 669, 674 (Fla. 1st DCA 1993) (quoting Slitor, 544 So. 2d at 258, for the proposition that "*Johnson* does not convert a seller of a house into a guarantor of the condition of the house").

In reaching a contrary conclusion, the circuit court relied on two cases, *Nystrom v. Cabada*, 652 So. 2d 1266 (Fla. 2d DCA 1995), and *Revitz v. Terrell*, 572 So. 2d 996 (Fla. 3d DCA 1990). The circuit court concluded that each of these cases supported the use of a "should have known" liability standard for nondisclosure claims under *Johnson*. We read these cases differently.

In the *Nystrom* case, Mr. Nystrom, acting as his own contractor, had **Nystrom** constructed the residence in question and had occupied it for one year before selling it. 652 So. 2d at 1267. Although Mr. Nystrom was not a licensed contractor, he had extensive experience in the construction industry and had performed all of the carpentry work in the house. *Id.* at 1268. After the buyer moved into the house, she discovered that it had numerous structural defects. *Id.* at 1267. An engineering firm issued a report concluding that the house "was a 'hazardous building' in regard to high-wind resistance." *Id.* In the buyer's action against Mr. and Mrs. Nystrom, the trial court ruled in favor of the buyer. *Id.* at 1268.

On appeal, this court affirmed the trial court's finding of liability in favor of the buyer. *Id.* In upholding the trial court's determination of the Nystroms' liability, this court said:

> Since the serious structural defects which the experts found to exist all arose from the carpentry, the record supports the finding that Mr. Nystrom *knew or should have known* of these defects and had a duty to disclose them to [the buyer] under *Johnson v. Davis*, 480 So.2d 625 (Fla. 1985).

Id. at 1268 (emphasis added).

To be sure, the *Nystrom* court used the questionable "should have **Circumstantial** known" language in stating its conclusion in favor of the buyer on the **≠** liability issue. However, the facts in *Nystrom* showed that Mr. Nystrom, **should've** who had extensive experience in construction, built the residence, **known** performed all of the carpentry work, and lived in the residence for one year before selling it to the buyer. The problems in the house resulted directly from the defective carpentry that Mr. Nystrom personally performed. It follows that Mr. Nystrom certainly had to know about the serious defects in the home because he had built it and lived in it before selling it to the buyer. Under these circumstances, the *Nystrom* court's use of the phrase "should have known" is a convenient or shorthand way to express the conclusion that the buyer established Mr. Nystroms' actual knowledge of the defects in the property through circumstantial evidence. *Nystrom* does not support using a "should have known" standard to find the Jensens liable for nondisclosure under *Johnson* on the very different facts in this case.

Revitz, the other case relied upon by the circuit court, involved a failure **Revitz** by the sellers' real estate agent to disclose to the buyer defects in a residence relating to building code violations and the availability of low-cost flood insurance for the property. 572 So. 2d at 996–97. The trial court ruled in favor of the sellers based on a finding that the undisclosed defects were not material as a matter of law. Id. at 998. On appeal, the Third District found that the trial court had used an incorrect test in determining that the undisclosed items were immaterial. Id. at 998–99. For this reason, the Third District reversed the final judgment for the sellers and remanded the case to the trial court for further proceedings. *Id.* at 999.

In *Revitz,* the trial court did not make any findings concerning the real estate agent's knowledge of the undisclosed defects. *Id.* at 998 n. 6. Referring to the undisclosed problems, the Third District said that "[a]ssuming that the seller[s'] agent knew, or reasonably should have known, . . . there was a duty to disclose that fact to the buyer." *Id.* at 998. The Third District emphasized the evidence in the record tending to establish that the sellers' agent must have known of the undisclosed defects. *Id.* at 998 n. 6. The emphasis in the opinion on this evidence suggests that the *Revitz* court, like the *Nystrom* court, was using the phrase "should have known" as a shorthand reference to circumstantial evidence establishing the agent's actual knowledge. However, this question need not detain us. As the Third District said in its opinion, the basis for the reversal of the final judgment was "the trial court's misinterpretation of Florida law" on the issue of whether the undisclosed defects were material. *Id.* It follows that the Third District's discussion of the agent's knowledge of the undisclosed defects was dicta. Accordingly, *Revitz* does not support the circuit court's decision to base a determination of the Jensens' liability on a "should have known" standard. Furthermore, the circuit court was obligated to follow this court's decisions in *Brown, Spitale,* and *Slitor,* which require proof of the seller's actual knowledge of the defect to establish liability under *Johnson.* . . .

NOTES AND QUESTIONS

1.   *Types of real estate.* The court in *Jensen* couched its ruling in terms of houses or residences. Doubtless most cases that arise do indeed deal with houses, but there is no reason that the principle of fraudulent concealment need be limited in that way. In *Johnson v. Davis,* the original 1985 Florida Supreme Court decision establishing the duty of disclosure in Florida, the court noted, "This duty is equally applicable to all forms of real property, new and used." But there are contextual differences in the marketing and sale of residential and nonresidential real estate. First, it is much less probable that a seller will fill out a lengthy disclosure questionnaire for nonresidential property. Such disclosure forms are quite common in residential transactions, especially sales in which one or both parties is working with a broker. Second, there is a much greater probability that the contract of sale for a nonresidential property will contain an "as is" clause, or perhaps a much more extensive clause disclaiming any duty on the seller's part to disclose or warrant anything regarding the property's condition. The following notes explore the extent to which such clause will be effective in barring the seller's liability.

2.   *Imputed knowledge of the seller.* Do you agree that it is unjust to charge a seller with liability for failure to disclose based on imputed knowledge—i.e., that the seller ought to have known, or had a duty to know, of the defect? See also Anderson v. Kriser, 266 P.3d 819 (Utah 2011) (only actual

knowledge will give rise to liability); Cook's Pest Control, Inc. v. Rebar, 28 So. 3d 716 (Ala.2009) (same).

3.　*"Latent" defects and "reasonable" reliance.* The nondisclosure cases make clear that the buyer's reliance on the seller's nondisclosure must be reasonable. Obviously, the buyer cannot reasonably object that the seller failed to disclose a visible hole in the roof. As *Jensen* puts it, "the defect must be not readily observable and must be unknown to the buyer." But what does it mean that the defect must be "not readily observable"? A defect in a home's roof may not be evident to an unsophisticated buyer, but might be obvious to a home inspector with significant contracting experience. Should a court treat such a defect as "readily observable"? Many courts have answered this question with an emphatic yes. See, e.g., Jackowski v. Borcheit, 209 P.3d 514, 522 (Wash.Ct.App.2009) ("[i]n a fraudulent concealment claim, the plaintiff must prove the defect would not have been disclosed by a careful, reasonable inspection by the purchaser"). A decision like *Jackowski* effectively imposes an expectation that a reasonable buyer will obtain a professional inspection. As a policy matter, is this expectation appropriate? Why or why not?

Courts have also tended to treat a buyer's reliance as unreasonable when the buyer could have ascertained the relevant facts from a review of accessible public records. See, e.g., Khindri v. Getty Petroleum Mktg., Inc., 33 Misc.3d 1208(A) (N.Y.Sup.Ct.2011) (seller did not disclose pending public hearing on road-widening, which would have prevented buyer's use of land as a gas station; "justifiable reliance does not exist when plaintiff has failed to inspect public records, meaning that such party had the means to discover the true nature of the transaction entered into by the exercise of ordinary intelligence and failed to make use of such means"); Troja v. Pleatman, 65 N.E.3d 809 (Ohio Ct.App.2016) (no duty to disclose neighbor had criminal record of violent crimes where that information was publicly accessible).

4.　*Active concealment and other "markers" of seller risk.* A stronger case for liability exists where the seller has taken active steps to hide a material defect. See, e.g., Van Deusen v. Snead, 441 S.E.2d 207 (Va.1994) (seller put new mortar over foundation cracks to conceal them); Andreychak v. Lent, 607 A.2d 1346 (N.J.Super.Ct. 1992) (seller of house with defective septic system had falsely obtained city certification of system, which buyers relied upon); George v. Lumbrazo, 184 A.D.2d 1050, 584 N.Y.S.2d 704 (1992) (seller paneled over wall to conceal cracks). Additional factors that tend to increase the probability of seller liability include the following:

- the property is a personal residence, purchased by an unsophisticated person.

- the defect is dangerous to health or safety. See, e.g., Roberts v. C & S Sovran Credit Corp., 621 So.2d 1294 (Ala.1993) (seller could be liable for defective septic system as a "specific defect" that affects "health or safety").

- the seller personally created the defect, or previously attempted to repair it and failed to do so. See Anderson v. Harper, 622 A.2d 319 (Pa.Super.Ct.1993) (sellers had ineffectively attempted to repair septic system).

- the seller gave reassurances to the buyer about the quality of the improvements (e.g., "You have nothing to worry about so far as the roof is concerned."), or signed a sales disclosure form that did not disclose known defects. See Santiago v. Tanaka, 366 P.3d 612 (Haw.2016) (seller had duty to disclose complete information regarding sewer charges where partial statements were misleading); Hays v. Wise, 19 N.E.3d 358 (Ind.Ct.App.2014); Brewer v. Brothers, 611 N.E.2d 492 (Ohio Ct.App.1992). If the seller knows the statement to be false, the buyer may have a claim for affirmative misrepresentation. See, e.g., TIAA Global Invsts., LLC v. One Astoria Square LLC, 127 A.D.3d 75, 7 N.Y.S.3d 1 (2015); McNulty v. Chip, 116 A.3d 173 (R.I.2015). Even if the seller believes the statement to be true, the buyer may have a claim for rescission based on mutual mistake. See Harding v. Willie, 458 N.W.2d 612 (Iowa Ct.App.1990).

5. *Implied warranties on existing housing.* You will see when you read the next case that the courts have created implied warranties of quality in the sale of a *new* house by a builder-vendor. The courts have consistently refused to imply similar warranties in the sale of *existing* houses by ordinary consumers to one another. See Everts v. Parkinson, 555 S.E.2d 667 (N.C.Ct.App.2001). Thus, buyers of existing housing are limited to claims based on: (1) affirmative fraudulent misrepresentations; (2) nondisclosure claims under a *Johnson v. Davis*-type standard; and (3) any express warranties or contractual covenants that the seller may have given in the sales contract.

6. *"Psychologically impacted" housing.* Much debate has occurred regarding "psychologically impacted" real estate; i.e., land as to which some past event has made the land undesirable to prospective purchasers. For example, in Reed v. King, 145 Cal.App.3d 261, 193 Cal.Rptr. 130 (1983), the buyer learned after closing that the home she had bought had been the site of a multiple murder ten years earlier. The court held that the buyer had the opportunity to establish at trial that this was a material fact (in the sense that it had a significant effect on market value); if she could do so, she could obtain rescission and damages for nondisclosure under California law. In another notorious case, Stambovsky v. Ackley, 169 A.D.2d 254, 572 N.Y.S.2d 672 (1991), the New York courts held that the seller of a home had a duty to disclose to an out-of-town buyer that the home was "haunted" where the seller had "deliberately fostered" that belief to local citizens for a decade prior to the home's sale. Other forms of past criminal activity may have even more significant effects than ghosts. For example, if a prior owner had used the home for dealing drugs or operating a house of prostitution, a buyer might be quite disturbed if old customers continued to return. [A relative of one of the authors once purchased a house in the latter category, and subsequently had a number

of very interesting conversations with former "clients" who did not know the property had changed hands and uses.] Are these prior activities "material facts" that must be disclosed to the buyer?

Some courts have rejected the whole notion of "psychologically impacted" houses. In Milliken v. Jacono, 96 A.3d 997 (Pa.2014), the court exonerated the sellers for nondisclosure that a grisly murder-suicide had occurred in the house 14 months before the sellers placed it on the market, concluding that this was not a "material defect." The court commented:

> The implications of holding that non-disclosure of psychological stigma can form the basis of a common law claim for fraud or negligent misrepresentation . . . are palpable, and the varieties of traumatizing events that could occur on a property are endless. Efforts to define those that would warrant mandatory disclosure would be a Sisyphean task. One cannot quantify the psychological impact of different genres of murder, or suicide—does a bloodless death by poisoning or overdose create a less significant "defect" than a bloody one from a stabbing or shooting? How would one treat other violent crimes such as rape, assault, home invasion, or child abuse? What if the killings were elsewhere, but the sadistic serial killer lived there? What if satanic rituals were performed in the house?

> It is safe to assume all of the above are events a majority of the population would find disturbing, and a certain percentage of the population may not want to live in a house where any such event has occurred. However, this does not make the events defects in the structure itself. The occurrence of a tragic event inside a house does not affect the quality of the real estate, which is what seller disclosure duties are intended to address.

Is this argument persuasive? Note that many states have adopted statutes that preclude seller liability for nondisclosure of various forms of "psychological impact." The real estate brokerage industry has pressed aggressively for such statutes. Idaho Code § 55–2801, is typical:

> "[P]sychologically impacted" means the effect of certain circumstances surrounding real property which include, but are not limited to, the fact or suspicion that real property might be or is impacted as a result of facts or suspicions including, but not limited to the following:

> > (1) That an occupant or prior occupant of the real property is or was at any time suspected of being infected or has been infected with a disease which has been determined by medical evidence to be highly unlikely to be transmitted through the occupancy of a dwelling place;

> > (2) That the real property was at any time suspected of being the site of suicide, homicide or the commission of a felony which

had no effect on the physical condition of the property or its environment or the structures located thereon; or

(3) That a registered or suspected sex offender occupied or resides near the property.

See also Shelley Ross Saxer, "Am I My Brother's Keeper?": Requiring Landowner Disclosure of the Presence of Sex Offenders and Other Criminal Activity, 80 Neb.L.Rev. 522 (2001); Williams, Stigmatized Property Law, 85 Mich.B.J. 34 (Feb.2006); Fisk, Stigma Damages in Construction Defect Litigation: Feared by Defendants, Championed by Plaintiffs, Awarded by (Almost) No Courts—What Gives?, 53 Drake L.Rev. 1029 (2005).

7. *Disclosure and the Fair Housing Act.* Many of these psychologically impacted land statutes first arose during the early days of public awareness of HIV/AIDS. Courts have held persons with AIDS have a "handicap" within the meaning of the Fair Housing Act. See, e.g., Ryan v. Ramsey, 936 F.Supp. 417 (S.D.Tex.1996); Baxter v. City of Belleville, 720 F.Supp. 720 (S.D.Ill.1989). One section of the Fair Housing Act provides that it is unlawful "[t]o make, print, or publish . . . any notice, statement, or advertisement, with respect to the sale or rental of a dwelling that indicates any preference, limitation, or discrimination based on race, color, religion, sex, handicap, familial status or national origin, or an intention to make any such preference, limitation, or discrimination." 42 U.S.C. § 3604(c). Suppose a seller with AIDS is selling a home, and the state has no "psychologically impacted land" statute. If you were advising the seller's broker, would you advise the broker to disclose that the seller has AIDS? Would making that disclosure violate § 3604(c) of the Fair Housing Act? See generally Note, Secrets Worth Keeping: Toward a Principled Basis for Stigmatized Property Disclosure Statements, 58 UCLA L.Rev. 281 (2010).

8. *Off-site conditions.* To what extent may the seller's duty of disclosure extend to off-site conditions—matters located elsewhere but affecting the property's surroundings or neighborhood? In Strawn v. Canuso, 657 A.2d 420 (N.J.1995), the New Jersey Supreme Court held a subdivision developer liable for failing to disclose to its customers the existence of a hazardous waste dump site located within a half-mile from some of the houses. Should a disclosure duty extend to such conditions? Why or why not?

"Psychologically impacted land" statutes typically do not cover all possible concerns of sellers and their agents, particularly with respect to off-site conditions. For example, suppose you are selling your house, and the house next door is a licensed group home for mentally handicapped persons. Must you disclose this fact to prospective purchasers? Would disclosure violate § 3604(c) of the Fair Housing Act? What if home next door is a halfway house for recovering alcoholics or recently released felons? What if it is a private home, but the owner is an avowed white nationalist and the prospective buyer is an African-American?

9. *Disclaiming the duty to disclose.* Can a seller avoid liability for failure to disclose defects by expressly disclaiming the duty in the sales contract? Sellers sometimes attempt to do so through "as is" clauses (e.g., "Buyer purchases the property 'as is' and seller has no duty to disclose information concerning the property") and/or "non-reliance" clauses ("Buyer has not relied on any statements or representations of Seller regarding the property or its condition").

The cases are reasonably clear that a specific disclaimer identifying the specific type of defect in question will be effective. See, e.g., Rice v. Patterson Realtors, 857 P.2d 71 (Okla.1993) ("Buyer accepts the flood and water risk attendant to the Property"); Slack v. James, 614 S.E.2d 636 (non-reliance clause identifying specific statements effective to bar claims related to those statements). With respect to more "generic" clauses (e.g., "Buyer takes the property 'as is' "), the picture is more mixed. Many recent cases refuse to give effect to "as is" clauses. See, e.g., TIAA Global Invsts., LLC v. One Astoria Square LLC, 127 A.D.3d 75, 7 N.Y.S.3d 1 (2015); McNulty v. Chip, 116 A.3d 173 (R.I.2015). By contrast, the court enforced a fairly elaborate, well-drafted "as is" clause in Alires v. McGehee, 85 P.3d 1191 (Kan.2004). If an "as is" clause may not relieve the seller from an affirmative duty of disclosure, why would a seller bother to include such a clause in the sales contract?

10. *Statutory disclosure requirements.* Many states have now adopted statutes requiring home sellers to disclose specific information to their purchasers. A typical example is Md. Code Real Prop. § 10–702, which applies to sellers of existing (not newly constructed) one-to-four family homes. On or before the date a contract of sale is signed, the seller must either give a disclaimer of all warranties and representations, or a disclosure of any defects of which the seller has knowledge in a "laundry list" of the house's systems and features. The purchaser can rescind the sales contract if the required statement is not given, but cannot rescind on the basis of the information disclosed in the statement. The principal proponent of these statutes has been the real estate brokerage industry, which has been (understandably) worried about a broker's liability for failure to disclose material facts. The Maryland statute provides that brokers have a duty to inform buyers and sellers of their rights and obligations under the statute; a broker who does so "shall have no further duties under this section to the parties to a residential real estate transaction; and is not liable to any party to a residential real estate transaction for a violation of this section." California, Illinois, and Rhode Island have adopted similar statutes. Cal.Civ.Code § 1102 et seq.; Ill.Stat.Ch. 765 § 77/1 et seq.; R.I.Gen.L. § 5–20.8–1 et seq.

Some jurisdictions expressly permit rescission for noncompliance with the requirements of a disclosure statement statute. See, e.g., Little v. Stogner, 592 S.E.2d 5 (N.C.Ct.App.2004) (rescission is sole remedy). Other statutes provide, either directly or by judicial construction, for the recovery of damages by the buyer for a false disclosure. See, e.g., Iadanza v. Mather, 820 F.Supp. 1371 (D. Utah 1993); Hays v. Wise, 19 N.E.3d 358 (Ind.Ct.App.2014). Perhaps surprisingly, several courts have granted damages in such cases even when the buyer had actual knowledge of the falsity of the disclosure. See, e.g., Woods v. Pence, 708 N.E.2d 563 (Ill.Ct.App.1999); Bohm v. DMA Partnership, 607 N.W.2d 212 (Neb.Ct.App.2000). [Of course, that knowledge might be reflected in the price the buyer agreed to pay, and to that extent would reduce the damages the buyer could recover.] By contrast, some statutory forms disclaim that the disclosure forms a part of the parties' contract. See, e.g., Brasier v. Sparks, 17 Cal.App.4th 1756, 22 Cal.Rptr.2d 1 (1993) (no liability where disclosure statement expressly recited that "it is not a warranty of any kind by the sellers . . . and is not intended to be part of any contract between the buyer and seller"). What is such a disclosure actually worth? One answer is illustrated by *Jensen*—a seller who checks "no" or "no knowledge" when the seller in fact knows of the defect provides documentary proof of his or her concealment, which provides key evidence necessary to establish a fraudulent misrepresentation and concealment claim.

New York's disclosure statute allows a seller to opt out of all disclosure obligations by crediting the buyer with $500 toward the price. If this is done, the seller can be held liable only for common law fraud, not fraudulent concealment. See Bishop v. Graziano, 10 Misc.3d 342, 804 N.Y.S.2d 236 (Dist.Ct.2005). Is $500 sufficient compensation for the rights protected by the duty of disclosure?

We now turn to an additional theory of seller liability, usually termed an "implied warranty." This theory generally is limited to new residences where the seller is a builder-vendor. It also may apply where extensive repairs, renovations or improvements have been made to an existing home by a contractor. Although applicable to a more narrow category of real estate, this theory may allow recovery on the basis of much less stringent proof by the buyer. The overwhelming majority of U.S. jurisdictions have adopted some form of this implied warranty.

SPEIGHT V. WALTERS DEVELOPMENT CO., LTD.

Supreme Court of Iowa, 2008
744 N.W.2d 108

LARSON, JUSTICE. The plaintiffs, Robert and Beverly Speight, appeal from a summary judgment entered against them in their suit for breach of implied warranty of workmanlike construction against the builder of their home. The court of appeals affirmed. Both the district court and the court of appeals expressly declined to recognize an implied warranty claim in favor of third-party purchasers, deferring for such a decision to this court. We now extend our common law of implied warranty to cover such parties and therefore vacate the decision of the court of appeals, reverse the judgment of the district court, and remand for further proceedings.

The Speights are the present owners of a home in Clive, Iowa, which was custom-built in 1995 by the defendant, Walters Development Company, Ltd. It was built for use by the original buyers, named Roche. The Roches sold the home to people named Rogers, who in turn sold it to the Speights on August 1, 2000. Sometime after purchasing the home, the Speights noticed water damage and mold. A building inspector determined that the damage was the result of a defectively constructed roof and defective rain gutters. Nothing in the record indicates that any of the owners between the original builder and the Speights had actual or imputed knowledge of these defects.

The Speights filed suit against Walters on May 23, 2005, alleging a breach of implied warranty of workmanlike construction and general negligence in construction of the home. Both the Speights and Walters moved for summary judgment raising the issue of whether the Speights, as remote purchasers, could pursue a claim for breach of an implied warranty of workmanlike construction. Walters also raised the issue of whether the plaintiffs' claim for breach of implied warranty was barred by Iowa Code section 614.1(4) (2005), the applicable statute of limitations. The district court concluded that, under the present state of the law, the Speights could not maintain an implied warranty claim and, in any event, such claim would be barred by the statute of limitations. . . .

The implied warranty of workmanlike construction is a judicially created doctrine implemented to protect an innocent home buyer by holding the experienced builder accountable for the quality of construction. See 17 Richard A. Lord, Williston on Contracts § 50:30 (4th ed. 2007) [hereinafter Lord]. Home buyers are generally in an inferior position when purchasing a home from a builder-vendor because of the buyer's lack of expertise in quality home construction and the fact that many defects in construction are latent. These defects, even if the home were inspected by a professional, would not be discoverable. See Sean M. O'Brien, Note, Caveat Venditor: A Case for Granting Subsequent Purchasers a Cause of Action Against Builder-Vendors for Latent Defects in the Home, 20 J. Corp. L. 525, 529 (Spring 1995).

The implied warranty of workmanlike construction addresses the inequities between the buyer and the builder-vendor by requiring that a building be constructed "in a reasonably good and workmanlike manner and . . . be reasonably fit for the intended purpose." *Kirk v. Ridgway*, 373 N.W.2d 491, 492 (Iowa 1985). In *Kirk* this court applied the doctrine of implied warranty of workmanlike construction to the sale of a home by the builder to the first owner. In doing so, we noted that interest in consumer protection had increased, and the complexity of homes had increased, making it difficult for a buyer to discover defects in the construction. In *Kirk* we rejected the application of the doctrine of caveat emptor under which "it has been observed, courts considered purchasing as a game of chance." *Id.* at 493 (citing Roberts, *The Case of the Unwary Home Buyer: The Housing Merchant Did It*, 52 Cornell L.Q. 835, 836 (1967)). We noted that home buyers are ill-equipped to discover defects in homes, which are increasingly complex, and therefore must rely on the skill and judgment of the vendor.

In *Kirk* we held that, in order to sustain a claim that a builder-vendor has breached the implied warranty of workmanlike construction, the buyer must show:

(1) [t]hat the house was constructed to be occupied by the [buyer] as a home;

(2) that the house was purchased from a builder-vendor, who had constructed it for the purpose of sale;

(3) that when sold, the house was not reasonably fit for its intended purpose or had not been constructed in a good and workmanlike manner;

(4) that, at the time of purchase, the buyer was unaware of the defect and had no reasonable means of discovering it; and

(5) that by reason of the defective condition the buyer suffered damages.

Id. at 496; see also *Flom v. Stahly*, 569 N.W.2d 135, 142 (Iowa 1997).

In *Kirk* we defined a "builder" as

a general building contractor who controls and directs the construction of a building, has ultimate responsibility for completion of the whole contract and for putting the structure into permanent form thus, necessarily excluding merchants, material men, artisans, laborers, subcontractors, and employees of a general contractor.

373 N.W.2d at 496 (quoting *Jeanguneat v. Jackie Hames Constr. Co.*, 576 P.2d 761, 762 (Okla. 1978)).

The plaintiffs ask this court to take the cause of action recognized in *Kirk* one step further by applying it to the case of a subsequent purchaser. Jurisdictions outside of Iowa are split on this issue.

Many jurisdictions do not permit subsequent purchasers to recover for a breach of the implied warranty of workmanlike construction.[1] This holding stems from the lack of a contractual relationship between the subsequent purchaser and the builder-vendor. Michael A. DiSabatino, J.D.,

---

[1] [Editors' Note: The court cited decisions from Alabama, California, Colorado, Connecticut, Delaware, Florida, Georgia, Kansas, Kentucky, Minnesota, Missouri, New York, South Dakota, Tennessee, Utah, and Wisconsin. Pennsylvania adopted this approach in 2014. We have omitted the court's string citation in the interest of brevity.]

Annotation, Liability of Builder of Residence for Latent Defects Therein as Running to Subsequent Purchasers from Original Vendee, 10 A.L.R. 4th 385, 388 (1981) [hereinafter DiSabatino]. The implied warranty of workmanlike construction is contractual in nature, and because privity is traditionally required in order to maintain a contract action, some courts have concluded that the lack of privity between the subsequent purchaser and the builder-vendor prevents the subsequent purchaser's implied-warranty claim. O'Brien, 20 J. Corp. L. at 537; see also Mary Dee Pridgen, Consumer Protection and the Law § 18:19 (2006) [hereinafter Pridgen] (discussing the holding in *Crowder v. Vandendeale,* 564 S.W.2d 879, 881 (Mo. 1978)); 2 James Acret, Construction Law Digests § 14:12 (2007) [hereinafter Acret] ("The implied warranty of habitability arises out of a contract between the builder and the initial buyer. There is no hint in the case law that it arises out of the general duty to build a reasonably fit house, by reason of which the builder would be liable to remote purchasers, that is, the general public, having no privity with it." (discussing the holding in *Foxcroft Townhome Owners Ass'n v. Hoffman Rosner Corp.,* 96 Ill. 2d 150, 70 Ill. Dec. 251, 449 N.E.2d 125 (Ill. 1983)). Further, because there is a lack of privity between the subsequent purchaser and the builder-vendor, there is no reliance by the subsequent purchaser on any representations made by the builder-vendor regarding the quality of construction. See Pridgen, § 18:19. Finally, some courts have concluded that the justifications for eliminating the privity requirement in products liability cases do not exist in the sale of real estate. See DiSabatino, 10 A.L.R. 4th at 397–98 ("The court reasoned that a house which is not the product of a mass marketing scheme or which is not designed as a temporary dwelling differs from the usual item to which the principles of strict liability have generally been applied, in that it is not an item which generally changes owners or occupants frequently." (discussing *Coburn v. Lenox Homes, Inc.,* 173 Conn. 567, 378 A.2d 599 (Conn.1977)).

Other jurisdictions do permit subsequent purchasers to recover for a breach of the implied warranty of workmanlike construction.[2] The purpose of the implied warranty of workmanlike construction is to ensure that innocent home buyers are protected from latent defects. This principle is "equally applicable to subsequent purchasers" who are in no better position to discover those defects than the original purchaser. Acret, § 14:12 (discussing and quoting the holding in *Lempke v. Dagenais,* 130 N.H. 782, 547 A.2d 290 (N.H. 1988)); see also Pridgen, § 18:19 ("The purpose of a warranty is to protect innocent purchasers and hold builders accountable for their work. With that object in mind, any reasoning which would arbitrarily interpose a first buyer as an obstruction to someone equally as

---

[2] [Editors' Note: The court cited decisions from Arizona, Arkansas, Idaho, Illinois, Indiana, Louisiana, Maine, Mississippi, Nebraska, New Hampshire, New Jersey, North Carolina, Ohio, Oklahoma, Rhode Island, South Carolina, Texas, West Virginia, and Wyoming. Again, we have omitted the court's string citation in the interest of brevity.]

Policy Justifications for IWWC Same for Subsequent

Y

deserving of recovery is incomprehensible." (quoting *Moxley v. Laramie Builders, Inc.*, 600 P.2d 733, 736 (Wyo. 1979))). Thus, the public policy justifications for eliminating the doctrine of caveat emptor for original purchasers of new homes similarly support allowing subsequent purchasers to recover on a theory of a breach of the implied warranty of workmanlike construction. See O'Brien, 20 J. Corp. L. at 531–32 ("[B]y definition, latent defects are not discoverable by reasonable inspection. Thus, home buyers are left with the choice of relying on a builder-vendor's expertise, or not buying a home at all. As one court stated, "[t]o apply the rule of caveat emptor to an inexperienced buyer, and in favor of a builder-vendor who is daily engaged in the business of building and selling houses is manifestly a denial of justice." Further, the purpose of the implied warranty of workmanlike construction is to ensure the home "will be fit for habitation, a matter that depends upon the quality of the dwelling delivered not the status of the buyer." Pridgen, § 18:19.

The lack of privity between the subsequent purchaser and the builder-vendor is not an impediment, in these jurisdictions, to allowing a subsequent purchaser to recover on an implied-warranty claim. Though the implied warranty of workmanlike construction "has roots in the execution of the contract for sale," it exists independently of the contract by its very nature. O'Brien, 20 J. Corp. L. at 538 (citations omitted). Additionally, requiring privity to sue for a breach of an implied warranty has been disfavored in products liability cases in some jurisdictions. Many jurisdictions find similar justifications for extinguishing the privity requirement in the purchase of a home. See O'Brien, § 50:30 ("[T]he builder was in the same position as a manufacturer who sells an article which, if defective, will be imminently dangerous to persons who come in contact with it, 'and liability is not limited to those with whom the manufacturer contracts.'" (quoting *Leigh v. Wadsworth*, 361 P.2d 849 (Okla.1961))). From a practical perspective, these jurisdictions note that many latent defects "are often not discoverable for some time after completion of the house. By the time the defects come to light, the original purchasers may have sold the home. For that reason, subsequent purchasers need protection for faulty construction." Pridgen, § 18:19. Additionally, the reality is that our society is increasingly mobile, and as a result, a home's ownership is likely to change hands a number of times. See O'Brien, 20 J. Corp. L. at 526 (noting that, at the time the note was written, "[n]early four million single-family used homes [were] sold in the United States every year"). A blanket rule prohibiting subsequent purchasers from recovering for a breach of the implied warranty of workmanlike construction would do injustice to those who purchase a home from a previous buyer shortly after the home was constructed when the subsequent purchaser later discovers that the home was defectively constructed. Finally, one author posits that the doctrine of assignment allows for the transfer to the subsequent purchaser of the original purchaser's right to sue for breach of the implied warranty of workmanlike construction. *Id.* at 538–40.

We believe that Iowa law should follow the modern trend allowing a subsequent purchaser to recover against a builder-vendor for a breach of the implied warranty of workmanlike construction. As in many jurisdictions, this court has eliminated the privity requirement in products liability cases raising a breach of implied warranty claim. *See State Farm Mut. Auto. Ins. Co. v. Anderson-Weber, Inc.,* 252 Iowa 1289, 110 N.W.2d 449, 456 (Iowa 1961). As the court discussed in *State Farm,* the privity requirement was eliminated in other jurisdictions to "ameliorate the harsh doctrine of caveat emptor," and because "the [implied warranty] obligations on the part of the seller were imposed by operation of law, and did not depend for their existence upon express agreement of the parties," privity was not necessary. *Id.* at 454 (quoting *Henningsen v. Bloomfield Motors, Inc.,* 32 N.J. 358, 161 A.2d 69 (N.J. 1960)). The same is true in a case such as the present one in which a home buyer raises an implied warranty claim. Further, the implied warranty of workmanlike construction is a judicial creation and does not, in itself, arise from the language of any contract between the builder-vendor and the original purchaser. Thus, it is not extinguished upon the original purchaser's sale of the home to a subsequent purchaser. The builder-vendor warrants that the home was constructed in a workmanlike manner, not that it is fit for any particular purpose the original owner intended. As such, there is no contractual justification for limiting recovery to the original purchaser.

Additionally, the public policy justifications supporting our decision to recede from the doctrine of caveat emptor in the sale of new homes by builder-vendors equally apply to the sale of used homes to subsequent purchasers. As discussed above, latent defects are, by definition, undiscoverable by reasonable inspection. Thus, the subsequent purchaser is in no better position to discover those defects than the original purchaser. It is inequitable to allow an original purchaser to recover while, simultaneously, prohibiting a subsequent purchaser from recovering for latent defects in homes that are the same age.

Walters contends that allowing the recovery the Speights seek would lead to increased costs for builders, increased claims, and increased home prices. However, builder-vendors are currently required to build a home in a good and workmanlike manner. The implied warranty of workmanlike construction reasonably puts the risk of shoddy construction on the builder-vendor. The builder-vendor's risk is not increased by allowing subsequent purchasers to recover for the same latent defects for which an original purchaser could recover. As discussed more fully below, the statute of limitations and statute of repose are the same for original purchasers and subsequent purchasers, thus eliminating any increased time period within which a builder-vendor is subject to suit.

Walters argues that allowing subsequent purchasers to recover for a breach of the implied warranty of workmanlike construction would subject builder-vendors to unlimited liability; however, we are not persuaded. Iowa Code section 614.1(11) provides a safety net—a statute of repose for potential plaintiffs seeking to recover for breach of an implied warranty on an improvement to real property. A statute of repose works to "terminate[ ] any right of action after a specified time has elapsed, regardless of whether or not there has as yet been an injury." *Bob McKiness Excavating & Grading, Inc. v. Morton*, 507 N.W.2d 405, 408 (Iowa 1993) (quoting *Hanson v. Williams County*, 389 N.W.2d 319, 321 (N.D. 1986)). Section 614.1(11) applies to an action for breach of the implied warranty of workmanlike construction in the purchase of a building. *See id.* at 409. That section provides:

> An action arising out of the unsafe or defective condition of an improvement to real property based on tort and implied warranty . . . and founded on injury to property, real or personal, or injury to the person or wrongful death, shall not be brought more than fifteen years after the date on which occurred the act or omission of the defendant alleged in the action to have been the cause of the injury or death.

Pursuant to section 614.1(11), the period of repose begins to run on the date of the act or omission causing the injury. In cases involving the construction of a building, such as this home, that period begins upon completion of the construction of the building. *See Bob McKiness Excavating & Grading, Inc.*, 507 N.W.2d at 409. As a result, builder-vendors are not liable on an implied warranty claim after the statute of repose has run, regardless of who owns the home. In summary, we adopt what we view to be the emerging and better view that subsequent purchasers may recover for breach of implied warranty of workmanlike construction against a builder-vendor as recognized in *Kirk* for first-party purchasers. Subsequent purchasers, of course, may not be afforded greater rights of recovery than the original purchasers.

The defendant contends that, even if we recognize a cause of action under these circumstances, it would be barred by the statute of limitations under Iowa Code section 614.1(4). The district court and the court of appeals agreed and concluded that this suit was time barred. We disagree. Under Iowa Code section 614.1:

> Actions may be brought within the times herein limited, respectively, *after their causes accrue,* and not afterwards, except when otherwise specially declared: . . .
>
> 4.   *Unwritten contracts—injuries to property—fraud—other actions.* Those founded on unwritten contracts, those brought for injuries to property, or for relief on the ground of fraud in

cases heretofore solely cognizable in a court of chancery, and all other actions not otherwise provided for in this respect, within five years. . . . (Emphasis added).

when accrued

The question in this case is when the plaintiffs' cause of action accrued. The defendant argues, and the district court held, that the cause of action accrued in 1995, when the house was sold by the defendant to the original purchasers. The Speights filed this suit in 2005, which was well beyond the five-year statute of limitations, according to the defendant. The defendant's time-bar argument relies on Iowa Code section 554.2725(2), under which all actions for breach of implied warranty accrue at the time of delivery, not at the time the damage is discovered. The Speights counter that their claim is not based on the sale of goods and, therefore, section 554.2725(2), which is part of the Uniform Commercial Code (UCC), does not apply. We agree with the Speights' position. Article 2 of the UCC applies only to transactions involving the sale of goods. Iowa Code § 554.2102. Goods are "all things . . . which are movable at the time of identification to the contract for sale." *Id.* § 554.2105(1). Clearly, the construction of a home is not a transaction for the sale of goods to which the UCC applies. Therefore, the limitation provided in section 554.2725(2) does not apply to cases such as the present one. We made that clear in *Brown v. Ellison*, 304 N.W.2d 197 (Iowa 1981), in which we distinguished cases involving breach of implied warranties of workmanship from those under the UCC.

> We hold that the discovery rule is applicable to cases arising from express and implied warranties. This holding, of course, does not apply to situations in which statutes expressly provide that a cause of action accrues when the breach occurs, regardless of the aggrieved party's lack of knowledge of the breach. See, e.g., Iowa Uniform Commercial Code, § 554.2725. . . . The trial court was, therefore, correct in applying the discovery rule.

Brown, 304 N.W.2d at 201.

We reject the defendant's argument that the plaintiffs' cause of action accrued in 1995 when the house was originally sold. Under the discovery rule, a cause of action does not accrue until the injured party has actual or imputed knowledge of the facts that would support a cause of action. We have said:

> Knowledge is imputed to a claimant when he gains information sufficient to alert a reasonable person of the need to investigate. As of that date he is on inquiry notice of all facts that would have been disclosed by a reasonably diligent investigation.

Perkins v. HEA of Iowa, Inc., 651 N.W.2d 40, 44 (Iowa 2002). The Speights' suit was filed on May 23, 2005, which was within five years of their purchase of the home. It cannot, therefore, be credibly argued that the plaintiffs had knowledge—either actual or imputed—of the defect more than five years before their suit was filed because they did not even own the property at that time.

We adopt and apply the doctrine of implied warranty of workmanlike construction to subsequent, as well as initial, purchasers. We conclude as a matter of law that the plaintiffs could not have gained actual or imputed knowledge of the defect in their home more than five years prior to commencing this action, and their suit is therefore not time-barred under Iowa Code section 614.1(4). We vacate the decision of the court of appeals, reverse the judgment of the district court, and remand for further proceedings.

NOTES AND QUESTIONS

1. *Severity of defects.* Few if any new houses are perfectly constructed. How serious must the defects be to breach the implied warranty? The cases present a wide range of answers. Recall from *Speight* that in Iowa the standard is that the house must be constructed "in a reasonably good and workmanlike manner and . . . be reasonably fit for the intended purpose." This is a relatively pro-buyer standard, and could cover a wide range of possible defects, such as the defective roof and rain gutters involved in *Speight*. See Deisch v. Jay, 790 P.2d 1273 (Wyo.1990) (builder liable for "minor construction defects causing temporary injury"—in this case, a damp basement that caused articles stored there to become moldy); Roper v. Spring Lake Dev. Co., 789 P.2d 483 (Colo.Ct.App.1990) (foul odor in garage, apparently caused by sour drywall, dead animals in the soil, or a nearby gas line).

Other courts are less pro-buyer and require much more serious defects. See, e.g., Stuart v. Coldwell Banker Commercial Group, Inc., 745 P.2d 1284, 1290 (Wash.1987) (warranty breached only by structural defects that "profoundly compromise" the dwelling); Samuelson v. A.A. Quality Constr., Inc., 749 P.2d 73 (Mont.1988) (warranty "limited to defects which are so substantial as reasonably to preclude the use of the dwelling as a residence"). The extremely narrow view of the warranty taken by the Washington Supreme Court in *Stuart* was widely criticized. See Hansen v. Residential Dev., Ltd., 128 Wash. App. 1066 (2005) (not reported in P.2d).

After *Speight*, the Iowa Supreme Court later held that the implied warranty did not apply to the sale of a lot with no dwelling, holding that a buyer that was a for-profit developer did not require the protection of a judicially-imposed warranty, regardless of the work performed by seller to make the lot buildable. Rosauer Corp. v. Sapp Dev., L.L.C., 856 N.W.2d 906 (Iowa 2014). Would the same result logically follow if the buyer was a consumer purchasing the lot as the site of a future retirement home?

Suppose the buyer purchases an existing townhome and contracts with a builder for a "gut renovation" (one that preserves the building's exterior/facade but involves a gutting and reconstruction of the interior). Should the implied warranty apply? See, e.g., 116 Waverly Place LLC v. Spruce 116 Waverly LLC,

2019 WL 495716 (N.Y.Sup.Ct.2019) (no; warranty applies only to "new" homes).

2. *Time limitations on actions.* If the courts overcome the privity problem and permit remote grantees to sue the builder or contractor, the period of potential liability (on average) can last for a much longer time than under the older cases that required direct privity. [Can you explain why?] One way to limit this liability is to require that the suit be brought within a "reasonable time." Several courts have imposed such a limitation. See, e.g., Bankston v. Pulaski County Sch. Dist., 665 S.W.2d 859 (Ark.1984); Redarowicz v. Ohlendorf, 441 N.E.2d 324 (Ill.1982). But from whose viewpoint is "reasonableness" to be judged? Suppose a home is sold for the fifth time, 20 years after it was built, to an owner who immediately notices the defect and files a lawsuit against the original builder?

In response to lobbying efforts by the construction and remodeling industries, many states have responded to the issue of time limitations on claims against builders and contractors by enacting special statutes of repose. Statutes of limitation usually are construed as incorporating the "discovery rule," meaning that their time periods do not begin to run until the injury was or should have been discovered. See, e.g., Haidar v. Nortey Foundation Designs, Inc., 239 S.W.3d 924 (Tex.Ct.App.2007). By contrast, a statute of repose fixes a time period (usually commencing from the date construction is completed or the house is sold) after which claims are cut off, irrespective of discovery. See Alsenz v. Twin Lakes Village, Inc., 843 P.2d 834 (Nev.1992); N.C.Gen.Stat. § 1–50(a)(5)(f) (establishing six-year statute of repose from "the later of the specific last act or omission or substantial completion"). Note that a statute of repose and a statute of limitations can operate side by side. See, e.g., Gomez v. David A. Williams Realty & Constr., Inc., 740 N.W.2d 775 (Minn.Ct.App.2007) (2-year statute of limitations, 10-year statute of repose).

Even a statute of repose is not always a safe harbor for a builder. In Pfeifer v. City of Bellingham, 772 P.2d 1018 (Wash.1989), a plaintiff was injured in a fire in a condominium project that was allegedly built improperly. She sued the builder, not for the defects per se, but for the tort of intentionally concealing a known and dangerous condition. The court held that the statute of repose did not bar this sort of tort action. See also Boghossian v. Ferland Corp., 600 A.2d 288 (R.I.1991) (statute of repose that expressly barred "tort actions" did not cut off action against builder that sounded in contract).

3. *Does a specific express warranty disclaim an implied warranty?* Given the rule that a disclaimer of the implied warranty must appear in "clear and unambiguous language," should a court find that a specific written warranty with a one-year term supplants the implied warranty? Several courts have refused to do so. See Graham Constr. Co. v. Earl, 208 S.W.3d 106 (Ark.2005); Bridges v. Ferrell, 685 P.2d 409 (Okla.Ct.App.1984).

4. *Drafting effective disclaimers.* There is general agreement that an express disclaimer can negate the implied warranty. As the Hawaii Supreme

Court explained in Association of Apt. Owners of Newtown Meadows v. Venture 15, Inc., 167 P.3d 225 (Haw.2007):

> [T]he burden on [the builder] to establish that it disclaimed the implied warranty of habitability is "very high," . . . and such disclaimers are strictly construed against the defendant; see also Tusch Enters. v. Coffin, 113 Idaho 37, 740 P.2d 1022, 1030 (1987) (observing that "[t]he majority of states permit a disclaimer of an implied warranty of habitability, but the disclaimer must be clear and unambiguous and such disclaimers are strictly construed against the [defendant].")

Id. at 256, 167 P.3d at 249. See Board of Managers v. Wilmette Partners, 760 N.E.2d 976 (Ill.2001), where the disclaimer wasn't specific enough. As legal counsel for builders and contractors become increasingly sophisticated at drafting effective disclaimers, will there be a gradual erosion of the protections that the courts have provided to consumers in the form of an implied warranty? Writing an effective disclaimer is difficult but not impossible. See Hicks v. Superior Court, 8 Cal.Rptr.3d 703 (Ct.App.2004); Jones v. Centex Homes, 939 N.E.2d 1294 (Ohio Ct.App.2010); Mattingly v. Palmer Ridge Homes LLC, 238 P.3d 505 (Wash.Ct.App.2010) (all finding disclaimers to be effective).

Suppose that the original purchaser of the home makes an effective disclaimer of the implied warranty, but later resells the home to Buyer, who is unaware of that disclaimer. Should the implied warranty extend to Buyer? See, e.g., Fattah v. Bim, 31 N.E.3d 922 (Ill.Ct.App.2015) (yes; disclaimer ineffective against remote buyer), rev'd, 52 N.E.3d 332 (Ill.2017) (implied warranty does not extend to remote buyer after original purchaser waived warranty).

5.   *Notice and opportunity to repair statutes.* In some states, such as California, construction defect litigation reached what builders considered to be epidemic proportions. In an attempt to stem the tide, approximately 30 states adopted "NOR" (short for "notice and opportunity to repair") statutes in the 1990s and 2000s. These NOR Statutes require property owners to put builders on notice of construction defect claims and give them an opportunity to cure the defects. Such statutes, which have been vigorously supported by the National Association of Home Builders and other builder groups, usually prohibit the filing of a suit until some fixed time (e.g., 60 days) after the builder is given notice, and they require the builder to respond to the notice either by disputing it, inspecting the property, or making a cash offer of settlement. See Standard Pacific Corp. v. Superior Court, 98 Cal.Rptr.3d 295 (Ct.App.2009) (homeowners must give builder notice and opportunity to cure, as a prerequisite to filing suit, unless builder has failed to provide proper documentation); Hoch, The Kansas Residential Construction Defect Act: A Schematic Blueprint for Repairs, 74 J. Kan. Bar Assn. 20 (Mar.2005).

6.   *Nonresidential real estate.* Should the implied warranty be extended to nonresidential properties as well? Is the average landlord or small business owner better able to protect himself or herself than the average home buyer? A few courts have extended the protection to commercial properties. See, e.g.,

Hayden Bus. Ctr. Condo. Ass'n v. Pegasus Dev. Corp., 105 P.3d 157 (Ariz.Ct.App.2005) (business center condominiums); Pollard v. Saxe & Yolles Dev. Co., 12 Cal.3d 374, 115 Cal.Rptr. 648, 525 P.2d 88 (1974) (apartment buildings); Hodgson v. Chin, 403 A.2d 942 (N.J.Super.Ct.1979) (stores purchased for business use). But see Dawson Indus., Inc. v. Godley Constr. Co. Inc., 224 S.E.2d 266 (N.C.Ct.App.1976) (refusing to apply the warranty to commercial property); Tomcho, Commercial Real Estate Buyer Beware: Sellers May Have the Right to Remain Silent, 70 S.Cal.L.Rev. 1571 (1997). Only a handful of the NOR statutes apply to nonresidential construction.

H. CONDITIONS IN CONTRACTS

The provisions of a contract for the sale of real estate may contain covenants, conditions, or both. For present purposes, it is highly important to distinguish among them, although this is a matter that the laypersons who usually prepare such contracts often forget or ignore.

A covenant, of course, is a promise. One who enters into it is obligated to perform, and one who fails to do so may be subject to a suit for breach, with such remedies as damages, specific performance, and rescission potentially available to the nonbreaching party.

A condition, on the other hand, is not a promise at all. Instead, it is merely a statement that a party's obligation to perform some covenant is dependent upon the happening of a specified event or occurrence. For example, V may covenant with P to sell his house to P, but may add the condition that he is obligated to do so only if it does not rain on the following Tuesday. This particular condition is rather unusual and probably has little utility, but it does illustrate that conditions may involve events that no one promises will occur, and indeed that may be entirely outside the control of the parties.

A particular statement in a sales contract can be both a covenant and a condition. For example, consider the clauses concerning V's delivery of the deed transferring marketable title and P's payment of the purchase price at the closing. These are obviously covenants because each party is promising to perform and will be liable for breach for failure to do so. But such clauses also are conditions; as we have already seen, they are usually construed to be concurrent conditions. As a result, neither party is obligated to perform until the other tenders the promised performance.

Not all conditions in a sales contract are concurrent. By its terms or context within the body of the sales contract, a particular condition may be a *precedent* one—which means that it stands on its own, and that the other party's duty to perform certain covenants under the contract depends on that condition being fulfilled first. Prudent buyers of real estate understandably try to protect themselves with various conditions precedent, so that they can rescind the contract and receive a refund of their deposit under certain circumstances. Perhaps the most common condition precedent is the buyer's obtaining a commitment of satisfactory financing to complete the purchase. Obviously, the buyer does not want to be bound to complete the deal if the buyer cannot borrow the needed funds on satisfactory terms. Other common conditions precedent might relate to the buyer's sale of other real estate; the successful procurement of a zoning change; the obtaining of an appraisal valuing the property at or above the agreed purchase price; satisfactory completion of an inspection of the physical condition of the improvements; satisfactory completion of other tests related to the property (e.g., tests for soil strength or water percolation, or a satisfactory environmental report); or obtaining of an easement to benefit the buyer's use of the land.

The seller can also use conditions to protect its interest. For example, if the seller is to provide financing for part of the purchase price, the seller may condition this duty on the receipt of a credit report and financial statement from the purchaser that meet certain standards.

The use of conditions is not the only way for the buyer to handle the problem of hoped-for (but as yet unassured) future events such as obtaining financing or procuring a zoning change. One alternative is the use of an option to purchase the property in the future. Under this method, the optionor (the seller-to-be) grants to the optionee (the buyer-to-be) an irrevocable offer to sell the property, usually at a fixed price for a specific period of time. The optionee pays consideration for the optionor's promise to leave the offer open for the time specified. This promise becomes contractually binding, and the offer itself becomes irrevocable. The optionee can decide for herself (after making the necessary investigations and inquiries) whether to exercise the option and buy the property (or not). The holder of the option right "exercises" the option by accepting the offer to buy the real estate. If the optionee decides not to purchase, she merely lets the option lapse without any further liability.

One potential advantage of using an option is that it is unnecessary for the buyer to spell out in advance all of the conditions precedent that must be satisfied before the purchaser must buy the real estate. It is entirely up to the buyer whether to exercise the option right. The disadvantage of the option method is that one generally must pay for an option, and the buyer loses the money paid for the option if it lapses without exercise. Options are not common in single-family residence transactions, but are a common method for the acquisition of land for the development of subdivisions or for commercial development. See Temkin, Too Much Good Faith in Real Estate Purchase Agreements? Give Me an Option, 34 Kan. L. Rev. 43 (1985).

Drafting of conditions. Effective drafting of conditions is of paramount importance. Financing clauses in real estate sales contracts often are stated in incredibly loose language, such as "Subject to the buyer's obtaining suitable financing" or the like. Forgetting for the moment about the question of what sort of financing will be "suitable," what do the words "subject to" mean? Do they impose a condition, a covenant, or both? More specifically, do they excuse a party (and if so, which party?) from performance if financing is not obtained? Do they impose on a party (again, which party?) an obligation to seek financing? Another favorite word of lay drafters in the financing clause context is "contingent," as in "this contract is contingent on obtaining financing." The same questions apply.

Moreover, do not assume that preprinted form contracts are models of professional drafting; many of them are simply dreadful. Phrases like "subject to" and "contingent on" are vague and can easily provoke litigation. Although many lawyers, judges, and real estate agents may use these phrases, you should not. If your client desires a condition precedent, call it a condition—and be thoughtful and intentional about the way you draft it.

Call it what it is — a condition.

Recall that the point of the financing condition is that if the purchaser is unable to obtain the described financing, the purchaser can rescind the contract and have the earnest money deposit refunded. See Saulcy Land Co. v. Jones, 983 P.2d 1200 (Wyo. 1999). Although conditions concerning financing usually are inserted for entirely legitimate reasons, they may become a pretext for one or both parties to attempt to rescind the sales contract for reasons that have nothing to do with financing.

SOUTHPORT CONGREGATIONAL CHURCH— UNITED CHURCH OF CHRIST V. HADLEY

Supreme Court of Connecticut, 2016
320 Conn. 103, 128 A.3d 478

ROBINSON, J. . . . On September 22, 2010, the decedent [Albert Hadley] executed a will specifically devising the property, which is located at 504 Pequot Avenue in Southport, to [Southport Congregational Church]. One and one-half years later, on March 21, 2012, the decedent contracted to sell the property to Winn. The sales contract, which was the standard form real estate contract provided by the Fairfield County Bar Association, contained a mortgage contingency clause stating: "This [a]greement is contingent upon BUYER obtaining a written commitment for a loan. . . . [If] BUYER is unable to obtain a written commitment for such a loan . . . and if BUYER so notifies SELLER or SELLER'S attorney, in writing, at or before 5:00 p.m., on April 16, 2012, then this [a]greement shall be null and void. . . . If SELLER or SELLER's attorney does not receive such written notice . . . this [a]greement shall remain in full force and effect." The decedent waived specific performance as a remedy under the contract and agreed to retain Winn's down payment as liquidated damages in the event of Winn's default. By letter . . . dated March 6, 2012, the decedent pledged to donate the proceeds from the sale to Cheekwood [Botanical Garden and Museum

So, if no loan, can back out.

death before contingency period

e.c.

of Art]. The decedent died on March 30, 2012, nine days after signing the contract and before Winn had obtained financing or the mortgage contingency period had expired. . . .

[In the process of administering Hadley's estate, the trial court ultimately ordered the property to be sold, rejecting the church's argument that the church's consent to the sale was necessary because the church was a specific devisee under Hadley's will. In these proceedings, Cheekwood filed a claim to the proceeds from the sale, arguing that Hadley's interest in the property terminated when he signed the contract under the doctrine of equitable conversion, leaving him with only an interest in the expected proceeds from the sale (which he had then assigned to Cheekwood by the March 6, 2012 letter). By contrast, the church asserted that equitable conversion did not apply because the contract's mortgage contingency clause was unfulfilled and unexpired at the time of the defendant's death, such that Hadley retained his interest in the property and that this interest passed to the church at his death. The trial court resolved these arguments in favor of Cheekwood and against the church. The intermediate appellate court reversed.]

On appeal, Cheekwood contends that the mortgage contingency clause did not preclude the equitable conversion of title because the parties intended for the contract to be fully enforceable at signing, subject only to the possible termination within a specified period by Winn if she could not obtain financing. In response, the church argues that the clause was an unsatisfied condition precedent to the contract and, thus, the contract was not yet enforceable and title could not have passed to Winn. We agree with Cheekwood that the mortgage contingency clause did not preclude the application of equitable conversion, and that equitable title passed to Winn at the execution of the contract. . . .

[T]he doctrine of equitable conversion does not apply when the seller's duty to convey title is subject to a condition precedent.[12] "A condition precedent is a fact or event which the parties intend must exist or take place before there is a right to performance." Lach v. Cahill, 138 Conn. 418, 421, 85 A.2d 481 (1951). When the seller's duty to convey title is conditional, and does not arise at execution, the buyer cannot immediately

---

[12] We recognize that the modern trend in contract law is to abandon the distinction between conditions precedent and conditions subsequent. Nevertheless, our state's case law has previously recognized a difference between conditions precedent and conditions subsequent. See Seymour Trust Co. v. Sullivan, 152 Conn. 282, 286, 206 A.2d 420 (1964) (parties "forfeit[ed] their rights . . . by operation of a condition subsequent expressly provided for in the contract"); Dolak v. Sullivan, 145 Conn. 497, 503, 144 A.2d 312 (1958) ("obligations under [contract] were subject to extinguishment, in whole or in part, upon the happening of a condition subsequent"); Westmoreland v. General Accident Fire & Life Assurance Corp., 144 Conn. 265, 272, 129 A.2d 623 (1957) (The contract "does not contemplate that [a condition] is a condition precedent to cancellation. If such adjustment is not a condition precedent, it certainly is not a condition subsequent. . . ."); Detels v. Detels, 79 Conn.App. 467, 473, 830 A.2d 381 (2003) ("the parties may have created a condition subsequent that would operate to discharge the plaintiff from his obligation").

enforce the contract. Under such circumstances, it cannot be said that the parties intended for title to pass to the buyer at signing. *See* Parker v. Averett, 114 Ga.App. 401, 402, 151 S.E.2d 475 (1966); Noor v. Centreville Bank, [193 Md.App. 160, 167–68, 996 A.2d 928 (2010). "[E]quity can hardly regard that as presently done which the parties . . . have agreed shall be done only in the future." Anderson v. Yaworski, [120 Conn. 390, 393, 181 A. 205 (1935)]. . . .

If, however, the duty under the contract arises immediately at execution, subject to a condition subsequent, equitable conversion may apply. A condition subsequent creates a situation in which "an existing right is cut off by the nonperformance of the condition. . . ." Bulkley v. Norwich & Westerly Railway Co., 81 Conn. 284, 287, 70 A. 1021 (1908). Conditions subsequent do not delay the seller's duty to convey title. See Grant v. Kahn, 198 Md.App. 421, 431–34, 18 A.3d 91 (2011). Because the contract takes full force and effect at execution, and the buyer immediately gains the right to enforce the contract against the seller, nothing prevents title from passing to the buyer at signing.

For instance, in *Grant v. Kahn, supra,* 198 Md.App. at 432, 18 A.3d 91, the Maryland Court of Special Appeals held that a mortgage contingency "consist[ing] of conditions subsequent" did not prevent title from passing to the buyer at execution of a contract. The court noted that: (1) the buyer could specifically enforce the contract against the seller; (2) the contingency benefited the buyer, who could remove it at any time; and (3) the seller had no discretion not to convey the property at closing. *Id.,* at 431–32, 18 A.3d 91. "Neither party took advantage of the conditions permitting termination of the contract, so . . . the contract continued in effect." *Id.* The court added, "there is no rule providing that the existence of *any* contingency acts to prevent equitable conversion." (Emphasis in original.) *Id.,* at 434, 18 A.3d 91.

The Texas Court of Appeals similarly held in *Parson v. Wolfe,* 676 S.W.2d 689, 692 (Tex.App.1984), that equitable conversion applied despite a mortgage contingency clause when the seller died prior to closing. The court rejected the notion that the clause was a condition precedent to the contract, noting that the clause was "intended as a measure of the time that was reasonable for the buyer's performance, and not as a condition that, if unfulfilled, would bar specific performance." *Id.*

Thus, the relevant inquiry in the present case is whether the parties intended for the mortgage contingency clause to be a condition precedent to the decedent's duty to convey title. The proper interpretation of the clause requires us to determine the intent of the parties. . . .

We conclude that the parties did not intend for the mortgage contingency clause to be a condition precedent to the decedent's duty to convey title. The unambiguous language of the clause . . . plainly and unambiguously denotes the parties' intention for the sale to proceed as planned unless Winn notified the decedent that she could not obtain financing within twenty-one days.

Two phrases in the mortgage contingency clause, in particular, support this conclusion. First, the clause states that if Winn did not notify the decedent of her inability to obtain financing within twenty-one days, the contract would "remain in full force and effect." (Emphasis added.) If the contract was not already in effect, the use of the word "remain" would be inappropriate. Second, if Winn notifies the decedent that she is unable to obtain financing, the contract "shall be null and void. . . ." There would be no need to "void" or "nullify" anything if the contractual duty had not yet arisen. Although the contract was "contingent upon BUYER obtaining a written commitment for a loan," read in complete context, this clause limits only Winn's duty to purchase the property, rather than the contract in general.

We have previously interpreted several mortgage contingency clauses and determined them to be conditions precedent to the contract, but none of those cases involved a possible application of equitable conversion, and they do not control the present case. See Loda v. H.K. Sargeant & Associates, Inc., 188 Conn. 69, 77–78, 448 A.2d 812 (1982); Luttinger v. Rosen, 164 Conn. 45, 47–48, 316 A.2d 757 (1972). The mortgage contingency clauses in those cases were conditions precedent only to the buyer's duty to purchase the property. In the context of equitable conversion, the crux of our inquiry is whether the seller's duty to convey title was contingent, since equitable conversion, at its core, depends on whether title passed to the buyer at signing. We did not decide in our previous cases whether the seller's duty to convey title was conditional.

The present case more closely resembles *Grant* and *Parson*, in which the Maryland and Texas courts squarely addressed the effect of a mortgage contingency clause on the application of equitable conversion. As in those cases, the mortgage contingency clause in this case benefited the buyer, who could waive it at any time and specifically enforce the contract against the seller. The facts of this case are similar to those in *Parson*, in which the seller died prior to closing, and the court held that the parties did not intend for the clause to delay the seller's duty to convey title. The mortgage contingency clause is also similar to that in *Grant*, wherein the buyer could terminate the contract if he could not obtain financing within a specified period. Although the clause in the present case differs slightly from that in *Grant*, those differences more strongly evidence the parties' intent for title to pass to Winn at signing. The contingency period in *Grant* continued indefinitely in the absence of action by the parties. In contrast, the contingency period in this case expired within twenty-one days, after which the contract "remain[ed] in full force and effect." Additionally, in *Grant*, the seller could terminate the contract upon notice to the buyer, which voided the contract in three days unless the buyer removed the contingency. In the present case, the decedent never had any discretion not to proceed with the sale. . . .

Finally, looking more broadly to the parties' intent, the decedent's goal to redirect his bequest from the church to Cheekwood is evident. In deciding whether to apply equitable conversion, we must give due consideration to the " 'presumed intention of the owner' "; United States v. O'Dell, [247 F.3d 655, 684 (6th Cir.2001)] and "the result to be accomplished." United States v. 74.05 Acres of Land, [428 F.Supp.2d 57, 62 (D.Conn.2006)]. The decedent's letter to the president of Cheekwood stated: "I hereby wish to memorialize and confirm my pledge to donate the proceeds from the sale of my . . . house . . . to . . . Cheekwood. . . . [I]f I have not given such proceeds to Cheekwood during my lifetime, my estate shall be obligated to give such proceeds to Cheekwood. . . . I understand that Cheekwood is relying on this pledge and, accordingly, I intend this pledge to be enforceable against and binding upon my estate, any provisions in my [w]ill to the contrary notwithstanding." Betty Ann Hadley also attested to the decedent's intent to redirect his bequest from the church to Cheekwood. Her affidavit states that the decedent "declared that he was redirecting the gift in his [w]ill from [the church] to Cheekwood." The affidavit continues to state the following: "He discussed this bequest many times over the weeks prior to signing it and he had several conversations with his attorney . . . about this change in his original will. It was his clear intention that the proceeds from the . . . home be given to Cheekwood as he had already been very generous to the [church] and he stated in my presence that he intended to give this gift to [Cheekwood] instead of the [church]." Because the core of the doctrine of equitable conversion is the parties' intent, these statements further support the application of equitable conversion to this case. . . .

The decedent in the present case "took every step necessary" on his part to effect a sale of the property to Winn. Moreover, his intent to sell the property and benefit Cheekwood is evident from the record, despite the fact that he died before the mortgage contingency period in the contract had expired or been waived by Winn. Equitable conversion nonetheless occurred, and this fact should not prevent the sale from closing as the parties intended. . . .

NOTES AND QUESTIONS

1. *Conditions precedent and subsequent.* The *Hadley* court draws a distinction between a condition precedent (where a contractual duty to perform arises only when the condition is satisfied) and a condition subsequent (where a contractual duty to perform arises when the contract was executed, but may be discharged if the condition occurs). Perillo, Contracts § 11.7 (5th ed.2014). The court treated the financing condition as a condition subsequent, holding

that Hadley was bound immediately and was discharged only if the buyer (Winn) did not give timely notice of an inability to obtain financing. Because Winn never provided such notice, Hadley remained bound (and thus, the court reasoned, seller had a duty to perform that justified applying equitable conversion).

In truth, most contingency provisions in modern real estate sale contracts are meant to (and generally do) operate as conditions precedent. Consider, for example, the financing contingency in the form contract in Section B on pages 27–28. It states that the Buyer's obligation to perform is conditioned on the Buyer obtaining financing which meets the specified terms. If Buyer does not obtain that financing, Buyer can "terminate" the contract and recover the deposit by giving timely notice to Seller; if Buyer does not give timely notice, then the condition is "deemed satisfied"—and Buyer thus becomes bound to purchase the property *at that point*. Do you think that the parties in *Hadley* understood or believed that their financing contingency was in any meaningful way different from the one in the form contract on pages 27–28?

As the *Hadley* court acknowledged, the trend in modern contract law is to no longer distinguish between conditions precedent and subsequent. The Restatement (Second) of Contracts discards the term "condition subsequent." It takes the approach that if an event must occur before performance is due (i.e., what is described above as a condition precedent), the event is a "condition." Restatement (Second) of Contracts § 224 (1981). An event that enables one party to discharge an already existing obligation is not a "condition" under the Restatement (Second). As the drafters explain:

> Occasionally, although the language of an agreement says that if an event does not occur a duty is "extinguished," "discharged," or "terminated," it can be seen from the circumstances that the event must ordinarily occur before performance of the duty can be expected. When a court concludes that, for this reason, performance is not to become due unless the event occurs, the event is, in spite of the language, a condition . . . . [Id. cmt. e]

2. *Rethinking* Hadley: *for whose benefit does a condition exist, and who can choose to waive it?* Perhaps a more helpful way to think about the problem in *Hadley* is to consider which party was the intended beneficiary of the financing contingency. A typical financing contingency operates to benefit the buyer, and most courts interpret such clauses as benefiting the buyer.[16] See, e.g., Crabby's, Inc. v. Hamilton, 244 S.W.3d 209 (Mo.Ct.App.2008). When a condition benefits one party, that party can choose to waive the benefit of the condition, perform anyway, and enforce the contract. Thus, if the financing

---

16 Suppose that the buyer plans to borrow 80% of the purchase price from a bank, and seller is going to agree to accept an installment note from buyer for the other 20% of the purchase price. In this situation, the seller has a legitimate concern about the nature of the buyer's bank financing; if the buyer's monthly payments to the bank are too high, the buyer may be more likely to default on installment payments to the seller. In this situation, a financing condition could certainly benefit the seller as well as the buyer. See, e.g., Fleischer v. McCarver, 691 S.W.2d 930 (Mo.Ct.App.1985).

condition benefits only the buyer, the buyer can choose to waive it and enforce the contract, even if the seller objects. See, e.g., Watson v. Gerace, 175 Fed.Appx. 528 (3d Cir.2006); Virginia Oak Venture, LLC v. Fought, 448 S.W.3d 179 (Tex.Ct.App.2014); see also Garnot v. LaDue, 45 A.D.3d 1080, 845 N.Y.S.2d 555 (2007) (buyer could waive property inspection condition). By contrast, if a condition benefits both parties, one party cannot act unilaterally to waive it and insist on performance over the other party's objection. See, e.g., Pelligreen v. Wood, 111 S.W.3d 446 (Mo.Ct.App.2003) (condition benefited seller, so buyer could not waive it); Arata v. Shefco, Ltd., 330 P.3d 115 (Utah Ct.App.2014).

The financing condition in the form contract on pages 27–28 is explicit. It benefits the buyer—termination can occur only "at Buyer's option." Thus, the seller under such a form could not use the buyer's inability to obtain financing as a basis to withhold performance. Now go back to the condition in *Hadley*. Do you think that language is materially different? It certainly benefits Winn as a buyer; is there anything about the language that suggests the parties also intended the condition to benefit Hadley as seller? Some courts have held that if the contract provides that failure of a condition makes the contract "null and void," the condition benefits both parties and one party cannot waive it. See, e.g., Ormond Realty v. Ninnis, 491 A.2d 169 (Pa.Super.Ct.1985). *Hadley* takes this view; do you agree? If Hadley truly meant for the condition to benefit him too (such that he could have refused to perform if Winn had not obtained timely financing), how should he have drafted the condition differently?

3. *"Obtaining" financing.* It is one thing for a borrower to obtain a loan commitment from a lender, and it is a different thing for the buyer to obtain the loan itself. Lenders commonly use language in their loan commitments that allow them to cancel if, prior to funding, the borrower's financial condition or employment status adversely changes. If the borrower cannot actually obtain the money, having once gotten a loan commitment is pretty cold comfort. But unless the financing condition expressly provides that it is met only by the actual funding of the loan, courts usually find that a financing condition is satisfied by the issuance of a loan commitment, even if it is later withdrawn. See, e.g., Malus v. Hager, 712 A.2d 238 (N.J.Super.Ct.1998); Bruyere v. Jade Realty Corp., 375 A.2d 600 (N.H.1977). The buyer in this unfortunate situation usually will forfeit his or her earnest money deposit (typically pursuant to a liquidated damages clause in the sales contract).

Compare the result in Aubin v. Miller, 781 A.2d 396 (Conn.Ct.App.2001). In *Aubin*, the buyer lost his job shortly after he applied for the loan. The contract was "conditioned on the Purchaser being able to obtain a mortgage loan"—not merely a commitment for a loan. The court allowed the buyer to rescind the contract and to recover the earnest money. In fairness, which party do you think should bear the risk that the buyer will become uncreditworthy after obtaining a loan commitment? Does your answer depend on whether you represent the buyer or the seller?

Seller financing not required per se

4. *Institutional financing vs. seller financing.* Suppose that a contract conditions Buyer's obligation on Buyer's obtaining "a commitment for a loan at an interest rate not to exceed 6%." Buyer applies to several banks, but the best interest rate that Buyer can obtain is 7%. Seller then offers to finance the Buyer's purchase by taking an installment note for the purchase price, with the note to bear a 6% interest rate. Is the condition satisfied such that Seller can compel the Buyer to accept the Seller-provided financing and complete the purchase? Many courts have held that unless the contract clearly obligates a buyer to accept seller financing, an offer of seller financing would not satisfy the condition. See, e.g., Proctor v. Holden, 540 A.2d 133 (Md.Ct.Spec.App. 1988); Woods v. Austin, 347 So.2d 897 (La.Ct.App.1977); Gardner v. Padro, 517 N.E.2d 1131 (Ill.Ct.App.1987). Why not? Why should a court presume that a financing condition contemplated institutional financing? See Raushenbush, Problems and Practices with Financing Conditions in Real Estate Purchase Contracts, 1963 Wis.L.Rev. 566, 576.

5. *Buyer's good faith obligation to seek financing.* Suppose again that a contract conditions Buyer's obligation to purchase land on Buyer's obtaining "a commitment for a loan at an interest rate not to exceed 6%." Buyer never bothers to apply for a loan and thus never receives a commitment. In this situation, Buyer cannot invoke the condition and refuse to perform; courts uniformly hold that a buyer (the only party that can apply for financing) has a duty to make good faith efforts to obtain financing. See, e.g., McCoy v. Brown, 24 A.3d 597 (Conn.Ct.App.2011); Noles-Frye Realty (Nai Latter & Blum) v. Dixon, 246 So.3d 603 (La.Ct.App.2018). The court must imply some duty of good faith on the buyer in this context, or the buyer's obligation to purchase would be illusory.

The contract form on pages 27–28 obligates the Buyer to "use reasonable efforts" to obtain a loan. Would the Buyer satisfy this standard if it filed one loan application? Two? Three? Perhaps not surprisingly, results vary. See Whitman, Burkhart, Freyermuth & Rule, The Law of Property § 10.11, at 658 (4th ed.2019) (collecting cases). What if the Buyer filed only one, but the Buyer's credit was so poor that no other institution would have approved the loan? See Stevens v. Cliffs at Princeville Assocs., 684 P.2d 965 (Haw.1984). Is "reasonable efforts" sufficient, or should one or both parties seek a more explicit standard?

I. INTRODUCTION TO MORTGAGE FINANCING

It is fairly rare for a buyer of real estate to pay cash. In most transactions, a buyer must obtain financing from some source to complete the purchase. Although financing can take a wide variety of forms, it is usually one or a combination of the following:

- a loan from a third-party lender (e.g., a bank) to the buyer;

- the "taking over" by the buyer of the payments on an existing loan that the seller or some former owner obtained from a third-party lender; and

- financing provided by the seller, usually in the form of a deferral of receipt of some portion of the purchase price.

In each of the above cases, the buyer's obligation to repay is generally represented by a promissory note requiring monthly or other regular installment payments. Because real estate is an excellent form of security for a loan, most financing extended to enable the purchase of realty is secured by that same realty, commonly by means of an instrument known as a mortgage (or, where permitted by state statute, a deed of trust). A mortgage involves a transfer by a debtor-mortgagor to a creditor-mortgagee of a real estate interest, as security for the performance of an obligation (normally, the payment of a debt evidenced by a promissory note). If the debtor defaults on the note, the mortgagee can have the real estate sold and the proceeds applied toward payment of the debt through a process known as foreclosure.

Of course, not all mortgages are related to acquiring real property. An owner of real estate may borrow money to start a new business or to send a child to college, and may give a mortgage to secure repayment of the loan. In American law, the characterization of a mortgage as "purchase money" in nature (i.e., the money was borrowed to enable the borrower to buy the property) has important consequences with respect to its priority as against competing liens, and in some states with respect to the ability of the lender to obtain a "deficiency judgment" if the borrower defaults and a foreclosure sale does not bring a price sufficient to repay the debt.

Today, most mortgages are "amortized" (repaid) over a substantial number of years. Until the 1930s, most mortgages were of the "balloon-note" type. Typically these were short-term mortgages for three to five years, with borrowers only making interest payments until the loan came due. At that point, if the borrower had not saved enough to pay the entire principal, the borrower had to ask the lender to renew the loan or to attempt to refinance the balance due with another lender. During the Great Depression of the 1930s, many lenders were forced to demand full payment and to foreclose on properties when mortgagors could not pay off their balloon mortgages. With the encouragement of Congress and the Federal Housing Administration, lenders during this period developed the amortized mortgage loan, which allows mortgagors to repay loans over many years by making monthly principal and interest payments. Prior to default, no large lump sum of principal ever comes due on the typical amortized mortgage loan, because the regular monthly payments are sufficient to cover the repayment of both full principal and all interest over the term of the loan.

[handwritten margin notes:] Promissory note represents obligation to repay

mortgage — transfer of real estate interest as security for performance of obligation (usu. payment of debt evidenced by prom. note)

Because the level monthly payment, fully amortized loan is so common in modern real estate financing, its characteristics are important to grasp. The monthly payment is set so that only a portion (though it is a relatively large portion in the early years) is needed to cover the interest that has accrued since the last preceding payment. The remainder of each monthly payment is applied to reduce the outstanding principal balance of the loan. Thus, the interest that accrues in each month will be less than the interest for the preceding month because interest is being computed on a continually declining principal amount.

For example, suppose a borrower signs a promissory note to repay $100,000 over a period of thirty years, with interest at the rate of 6% per annum. The loan is made on January 1, 2021, with level repayment installments to be made monthly by the borrower. Thus, the first monthly payment will be due February 1, 2021. Interest alone at the end of that first month would be $100,000 times 1/2 of 1% (the monthly equivalent of 6% per annum), or $500. Consultation of a standard table of mortgage payments reveals that the full payment due (including both interest and amortization of the principal) is $599.55. The amortization schedule below shows the effect of the borrower's first payment and the next few payments that follow it.

Amortization Schedule
($100,000 loan @ 6% for 30 years)

Payment Date		Period	Total Payment	Interest Payment	Principal Payment	Remaining Balance
February	2021	1	599.55	500.00	99.55	99,900.45
March	2021	2	599.55	499.50	100.05	99,800.00
April	2021	3	599.55	499.00	100.55	99,699.85
May	2021	4	599.55	498.50	101.05	99,598.80
June	2021	5	599.55	497.99	101.56	99,497.24
July	2021	6	599.55	497.49	102.06	99,395.18
August	2021	7	599.55	496.98	102.57	99,292.61
September	2021	8	599.55	496.46	103.09	99,189.52
October	2021	9	599.55	495.95	103.06	99,085.92
November	2021	10	599.55	495.43	104.12	98,981.79
December	2021	11	599.55	494.91	104.64	98,877.15

The last payment, which would be made at the end of the 360th month of the loan on January 1, 2051, will be approximately the amount necessary to discharge entirely the small sum still remaining on the principal balance. Of course, filling in the schedule above for a full 360 months is a tedious process unless you use a computer, but if you did so you would see that the amount we originally specified as the monthly payment, $599.55, is precisely the amount necessary to amortize the loan's balance fully over a 30-year period.

The amount of the regular monthly payments necessary to amortize a loan over a given period of time depends on several factors: (1) the frequency of payments (usually monthly for mortgage loans); (2) the term or period of repayments; (3) the interest rate; and (4) the amount borrowed. The table below shows the monthly payments for each one thousand dollars borrowed at various interest rates and terms. You can apply the table to any principal amount simply by multiplying the factor shown by the number of thousands of dollars borrowed.

Monthly Payment Factors (per $1,000 of debt) (rounded)
Term of Loan

Interest Rate	20 years	30 years	40 years
3%	5.55	4.22	3.58
4%	6.06	4.77	4.18
5%	6.60	5.37	4.82
6%	7.16	5.99	5.50
7%	7.75	6.65	6.21
8%	8.36	7.34	6.95
9%	9.00	8.05	7.71
10%	9.65	8.78	8.49
11%	10.32	9.52	8.28
12%	11.01	10.29	10.08
13%	11.72	11.06	10.90
14%	12.44	11.85	11.71
15%	13.17	12.64	12.53

Several observations can be made about the level payment, fully amortized loan. The principal balance declines quite slowly during the early years. After five years of regular payments on the loan in the foregoing example, the principal would be reduced to $92,920, a reduction of only $7,080.

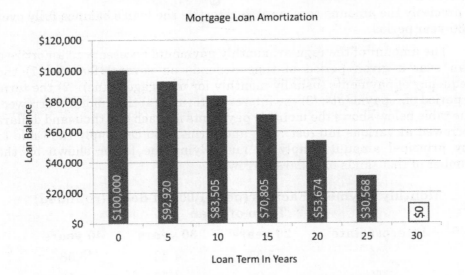

As noted above, each monthly payment is partly allocated to interest and partly to principal. These allocations change over time; in the early years the bulk of each payment is applied toward interest, as the amortization schedule above shows. In later years, more and more of each payment is applied to principal. The graph below shows these changes.

The effect of higher interest rates on the payment can be quite startling. In our example, an interest rate of 7% (rather than the 6% we assumed) would raise the monthly payment by $65, to $665. These figures suggest something of the adverse impact high interest rates can have on the demand for housing. Lengthening the loan term can reduce the monthly payments, but beyond about 30 or 40 years, the impact is not very great. In our example (with a 6% interest rate), increasing the maturity from 30 to 40 years would lower monthly payments by only $50, to $550. Further increases in maturity would bring the monthly payments somewhat closer to $500 per month, the interest-only level (which forms a "floor" below which payments could not go no matter how long the loan term).

The level payment, fully amortized loan is very widely used in single family home financing, and quite commonly employed with commercial and industrial property as well. Beginning in the late 1970s, both federal and state regulators of lending institutions began to permit lenders to use other "innovative" loan repayment formats on home loans. For example, adjustable rate mortgages (ARMs) permit modification of the interest rate during the life of the loan (with concomitant changes in maturity or monthly payment).

Principal amortization is in a sense a form of forced savings. Some households might prefer to minimize, or even eliminate entirely, the amortization component. The lender, however, generally will prefer a relatively more rapid reduction in principal because the loan is seen as a safer investment if the borrower is accumulating equity in the property. During the first half of the 2000s, "interest only" mortgages—i.e., with no portion of the monthly payments allocated to the amortization of principal—once again became fairly common because sharp increases in housing prices in some areas of the United States made it difficult for home buyers to afford the payments on fully amortizing mortgage loans. As in the Great Depression, beginning in 2008 these loans indeed proved riskier, and went into default more often, than fully amortizing loans.

When interest rates are falling or have stabilized at low levels, buyers prefer to finance most home sales with new mortgage loans from institutional lenders such as banks, savings associations, and mortgage companies. When interest rates are rising or have stabilized at high levels, buyers and sellers are more willing to seek alternative or "creative" financing techniques. The variations on these alternative financing methods are virtually endless, but the following list suggests the major ways in which home sales can be financed. Many of these techniques assume that the seller is willing to defer the receipt of all or part of the sale price.

- *All cash sale.* Buyer pays all cash to seller. Buyer may have cash from savings, from gifts from relatives, or by borrowing under a new mortgage loan from an institutional lender.

- *Assumption or taking subject to existing mortgage.* Buyer "takes over" the seller's existing mortgage loan and pays cash equal to the difference between the sales price of the property and the principal balance that remains on the existing loan. The buyer may "take over" the loan either by signing an "assumption agreement" (which makes her personally liable on the mortgage debt), or merely by taking "subject to" the mortgage without any express promise to pay the mortgage debt. In the latter case, the buyer is not personally liable for the repayment of the remaining debt, but will still have a powerful economic incentive to repay the mortgage loan in full (to avoid foreclosure and the possible loss of the buyer's cash investment in the property).

- *Seller financing.* Buyer enters into a mortgage loan or an installment contract with seller for all or a large portion of the total purchase price. This is the only debt obligation involved in the transaction. The loan will bear interest and require regular installments payments that are similar to an institutional loan. The seller treats the obligation as an investment. This technique is feasible only if the seller does not need to receive the full amount of the sale price in cash immediately upon the sale of the property.

- *Combination of assumption/subject to and seller financing.* In this combination, the buyer "takes over" the seller's existing mortgage financing, but cannot raise enough cash to pay the entire difference between the sale price and the loan balance. The buyer gives the seller a promissory note secured by a second mortgage on the real estate for part of this difference, thereby reducing the cash demanded of the buyer to a manageable level.

- *Wrap-around financing.* In a "wraparound" financing arrangement, the transaction between the buyer and the seller is structured as seller financing. The seller, however, has a preexisting mortgage loan on the property (usually in the form of an institutional mortgage loan), and does not pay off this preexisting mortgage at the time of the transfer to the buyer. Instead, the seller continues to make payments on the "underlying" institutional loan while the buyer makes payments to the seller on the new (or "wraparound") loan. The interest rate on the wraparound loan often is higher than on the preexisting mortgage loan, resulting in a tidy profit for the seller. From the seller's viewpoint, one of the advantages of the wraparound arrangement over an assumption/subject to financing arrangement is that the seller will not be caught unaware of a default on the preexisting first mortgage because the payments on it are made directly by the seller rather than by the buyer.

Note that any loan assumption, taking subject to a preexisting mortgage, or "wraparound" of the preexisting institutional mortgage will be problematic if the preexisting mortgage agreement contains an enforceable due-on-sale clause. Such a clause permits the lender to demand an immediate payoff of the loan if the real estate is transferred. In most cases, a due-on-sale clause is indeed enforceable in an arm's length sale transaction. If the lender chooses to enforce the due-on-sale clause, the parties' contract of sale may be frustrated if the buyer is unable to obtain financing sufficient to pay off the preexisting mortgage debt. [We return to the due-on-sale clause and its implications in Chapter Five.]

NOTE ON THE FORECLOSURE PROCESS: HISTORY AND MODERN APPROACHES

Mortgage foreclosures. When a mortgage loan goes into default, the mortgagee normally has the right to "accelerate," which has the effect of making the entire debt due and payable. The mortgagee may, under some circumstances, simply decide to proceed against the mortgagor personally in a personal action to recover the debt, and forgo reliance on the mortgage security. Usually, however, the mortgagee will choose (and in some states will be required by law) to foreclose the mortgage first. Although methods of foreclosure vary, under most circumstances there will be a sale of the mortgaged premises. The proceeds of the sale will be used to pay off the mortgage debt and the surplus (if any) will go to any subordinate lienholders and the mortgagor. If the sale does not yield enough to cover the debt, the mortgagee will usually be able to obtain a personal judgment for the deficiency against the mortgagor.

Where more than one mortgage exists on the same property, questions of priority become paramount. Suppose, for example, the mortgagor gave a $65,000 long-term first mortgage to a savings association on Blackacre, which then was worth $75,000. Assume that after paying the mortgage down to about $60,000, the mortgagor borrows $12,000 from another lender and gives that lender a mortgage to secure the $12,000 debt. This is a second mortgage. Suppose that the first mortgage is foreclosed. What will the purchaser at the foreclosure sale get and what will she pay for it? Here it is important to remember one of the basic functions of foreclosure—to put the foreclosure sale purchaser in the shoes of the mortgagor as of the time of execution of the mortgage being foreclosed. Thus, the purchaser will obtain a title that is free and clear of all mortgages or other liens junior or subordinate to the mortgage being foreclosed. Accordingly, a sale purchaser, assuming that the market value of Blackacre free and clear of liens is still $75,000, will be willing to pay at most $75,000. For this she will get title free of the second mortgage. In other words, any junior liens are wiped out. If, however, the sale brings more than the $60,000 first mortgage debt, the second mortgagee should normally have a claim to the surplus superior to that of the mortgagor.

Suppose, instead, that the first mortgage is not in default but that the second mortgage is—and that the second mortgagee forecloses. What will the sale purchaser get and what will she pay for it? Again, the sale will put the purchaser in the shoes of the mortgagor as of the time the mortgage being foreclosed was executed. Thus a purchaser will obtain fee title to Blackacre, but subject to the first mortgage. In other words, the foreclosure of a junior mortgage normally will not affect the status of a senior mortgage on the property. Therefore, in calculating what a purchaser will bid, she will at the very least subtract from the market value of Blackacre free and clear of liens the amount due on the first mortgage. Thus, assuming that this market value is still $75,000, the most the purchaser should bid is $15,000 (the fair market value less the amount due on the senior lien). Although the sale purchaser will not usually be personally liable on the first mortgage debt, if she does not pay it off she runs the risk that the first mortgage will be foreclosed and that she will lose her title to Blackacre.

The impact of English history. An understanding of the modern real estate mortgage requires a limited consideration of its historical antecedents. Although the mortgage has its roots in both Roman law and in early Anglo-Saxon England, the most significant developments for our purposes are the English common law mortgage and the effects on that mortgage of the subsequent intervention of English equity courts. These developments substantially influenced the substance of American mortgage law and are responsible for much of its terminology.

Although the common law mortgage as it developed in the 14th and 15th centuries varied, in form it was a conveyance of fee simple ownership, but expressly on condition subsequent. For example, assume B loaned A $1,000. A would convey Blackacre to B and his heirs, but on the condition that, if A repaid the $1,000 to B on a specified day, A would have the right to reenter and terminate B's estate. There were several important attributes to this transaction. B, the mortgagee, received legal title to the land and the normal incidents of that title. Perhaps the most striking and important feature of this mortgage was that the grantee, having legal title from the outset, got the incidents of that title even though unnecessary or even antagonistic to the sole purpose of the conveyance (which was security for the grantor's repayment). The most significant of these incidents was possession. Originally, the mortgagee used possession and the right to collect rents and profits as a method to get a return on the loan, as the taking of any interest was then usurious and unlawful. Later the custom developed to leave the mortgagor in possession, although the mortgagee nevertheless retained the right to obtain possession. If the lender did obtain possession, the lender was required to account to the mortgagee for any rents and profits collected (i.e., to apply them against the mortgage debt).

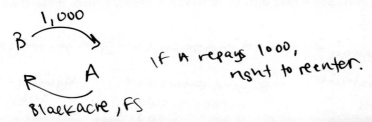

The condition with provision for reentry was gradually displaced by a covenant by the mortgagee to reconvey upon full performance by the mortgagor. This covenant had a double operation. It was effective at law as a condition, and also was a promise which equity would enforce specifically. Its development apparently coincided with that of the equity of redemption referred to below, and its popularity was based on the practical advantages to the mortgagor of getting back its interest by a reconveyance, instead of by reentry. Regardless of which form was used, if the mortgagor failed to perform on the day set, the mortgagee's estate became absolute.

This common law mortgage was especially harsh on the mortgagor. The payment date was called the law day. Under the common law, if for any reason the payment was not made on that day, the mortgagor forfeited all interest in Blackacre. This was an absolute rule. It applied even if the mortgagor could not find the mortgagee to make the payment. Time was strictly of the essence.

The intervention of equity. The excesses and harshness of the common law mortgage inevitably yielded to the moderating influence of English Chancery. Initially, equity intervened to aid the mortgagor who had failed promptly to perform on law day where the mortgagor could establish traditional equitable grounds for relief such as fraud, accident, misrepresentation, or duress. In other words, even though the mortgagee's rights at law were absolute, the mortgagor who had the financial capability to tender the amount due and owing could get the property back after law day so long as he or she could fit within the grounds described above. However, by the 17th century, the granting of such relief by equity became much more routine so that the mortgagor was able, as a matter of course and right, to redeem the land from the mortgagee by tendering the principal and interest within a reasonable time after law day. It was no longer necessary to establish any more specific equitable grounds for relief. This right to tardy redemption was referred to as the mortgagor's equity of redemption and became recognized as an equitable estate in land.

[margin note: reasonable time to pay]

The mortgagor's right to tardy redemption obviously created a substantial problem for the mortgagee. Even though the mortgagor had defaulted, the mortgagee could never be reasonably sure that the mortgagor would not sue in equity to redeem. The mortgagee obviously needed to be relieved at some point of the threat of redemption. Thus, this same period saw the concurrent development in equity of the mortgagee's right to foreclosure. When the mortgagor failed to pay on law day or to bring a suit to redeem, at the request of the mortgagee in a bill setting forth the details of the mortgage and default, equity would order the mortgagor to pay the debt, interest and costs within a fixed period. Failure to comply with the decree meant that the mortgagor's right to redeem was forever barred. This type of foreclosure, which is little used today, is known as strict foreclosure because the land is forfeited to the mortgagee no matter what its value in relation to the original mortgage debt (no sale of the land is involved).

[margin note: balanced by right to foreclose]

Whatever the original reasons for the chancellor's interventions, clearly the later equity view was that the mortgagee's interest was only security. Law courts recognized this, just as clearly as equity courts did, but law courts felt powerless to alter the design of the legal device chosen by the parties to achieve their purpose. To the law courts, because the parties had seen fit to have the entire legal title given as security (not absolutely, as the mortgagor could get it back by paying on a certain day), that was that. No such limitations were felt by the courts of equity, which felt free to superimpose upon the legal device various restrictions or additions so as to give to the mortgagee only that protection in regard to the property which was necessary or desirable for the protection of the security. What this protection should be inevitably would be a compound of conflicting economic interests, contradictory social ideals, business expediency, feelings of "fairness" in the particular case, and attempts (justifiable or otherwise) at logical consistency with other legal rules, plus other miscellaneous considerations.

In developing this view of the mortgage as a security transaction the equitable theory of the nature and incidents of the mortgagor's interest in the property before default underwent considerable change. For one thing, the term "equity of redemption," which had previously and appropriately been applied to the mortgagor's right to get back the property after default, was applied somewhat inappropriately to this entirely distinct equitable ownership before default. This, however, is merely a matter of nomenclature. But the analytical nature of the interest itself was the subject of serious and important inquiry and decision.

At first the mortgagor's interest was looked upon as a purely in personam right against the mortgagee, but soon it was perceived to be in rem, and finally was regarded as an equitable estate, a conception conforming to both popular and legal notions. For example, it could be cut into lesser estates; it had to be conveyed by a formal conveyance with formal limitations; it descended on to the heirs of the mortgagor; it could be devised, mortgaged, or entailed; and it prevailed against heirs, purchasers, and other successors of the mortgagee. In other words, it came to be treated, for all practical purposes, as ownership of the land—subject, of course, to the mortgage.

The American development. While strict foreclosure is actually used in a few states and is theoretically available in some special situations in others, the major method of foreclosure in the United States today involves a public sale of the premises. There are two main types of sale foreclosure used in the United States today. The most common type is judicial foreclosure where a public sale results after a full judicial proceeding in which all interested persons must be made parties. In many states this is the sole method of foreclosure. It is time-consuming and costly. The other method of foreclosure is by power of sale. Under this method, after varying types and degrees of notice to the parties, the property is sold at a public sale, either by some public official such as a sheriff, by the mortgagee, or by some other third party. No judicial proceeding is required in a power of sale foreclosure. It is available only where both the mortgage instrument and a state statute authorize it.

equity of redemption

It is important to remember that as a general proposition, the mortgagor cannot lose his or her equity of redemption (or equity of tardy redemption, as it is sometimes called) unless there has been a valid foreclosure of the mortgage. In other words, even though the mortgage is in substantial default, normally no agreement of the parties in the mortgage, or contemporaneous with it, can cut off a recalcitrant mortgagor's rights in the mortgaged property without the mortgagee resorting to foreclosure. This concept, which will be considered in greater detail later, is sometimes referred to as the *prohibition against clogging the mortgagor's equity of redemption.*

Suppose, however, that there has been a valid foreclosure and that the mortgagor's equity of redemption has been cut off. About 20 states, by a variety of legislative methods, have created something called *statutory redemption.* This type of redemption becomes available *only* when the equity of redemption has been effectively cut off by a valid foreclosure. Statutory redemption, as we will see later, varies widely from state to state. In general, however, these statutes permit the mortgagor, and sometimes junior lienors or the holders of other subordinate interests, to redeem for some fixed period after the sale. The time periods vary from as short as a few months in some states to as long as 18 months or more in a few others. The statutory right of redemption was created, in part, to afford the mortgagor or other person entitled to exercise the right additional time to refinance and save the property, but mainly to put pressure on the mortgagee to bid the value of the property at the foreclosure sale, at least up to the amount of the mortgage debt. To enforce this purpose the redemption amount is usually the *foreclosure sale price* and *not the mortgage debt.* A secondary purpose of these statutes in some states is to allow an additional period of possession to a hard-pressed mortgagor. It is important to remember that statutory redemption normally begins *only* after foreclosure has validly terminated the mortgagor's equity of redemption.

The deed of trust as a mortgage variant. In many states the deed of trust represents the most commonly used mortgage instrument. This device normally involves a conveyance of the realty to a third person (often the lender's lawyer, employee, or subsidiary corporation) in trust to hold as security for the payment of the debt to the lender-noteholder whose role is analogous to that of the mortgagee. Deeds of trust will almost always contain a power of sale in the trustee to be exercised after a default at the request of the lender-noteholder. Such a deed of trust is essentially similar to a mortgage with a power of sale. Indeed, in some states the same statutes regulating foreclosure of power of sale mortgages are applicable to deeds of trust as well. In other states, mortgages are required to be foreclosed by judicial process, and only the deed of trust can employ a power of sale. Other differences may also exist in a particular state; for example, deficiency judgments or post-sale redemption may be treated differently with deeds of trust than with mortgages.

CHAPTER TWO

DEEDS AND TITLES

■ ■ ■

A. DEEDS

Even though a contract of sale creates an "equitable title" in the purchaser under the doctrine of equitable conversion, the parties to a real estate contract always understand that if the contract is performed as agreed, the seller will deliver a deed to the buyer. Delivery of the deed will transfer legal title, and it is that sort of transfer that is the subject of this chapter.

Although deeds are the most common mode of conveying legal title, they are not the only way. Transfer of title to real property can occur at death by will, Laymon v. Minnesota Premier Props., LLC, 903 N.W.2d 6 (Minn.Ct.App. 2017), or by intestate succession. Transfer can also occur by court decree or, in the case of government land, by legislative act. Although technically not transfers, such events as adverse possession and death of a joint tenant have much the same effect. But the delivery of deeds surpasses all of these other ways of transferring title in frequency and importance, and in cases involving negotiated sales of real property the delivery of a deed is nearly always the object of the parties' agreement.

1. HISTORY OF THE DEED

PATTON AND PALOMAR ON LAND TITLES
§ 3, at 4–7 (3d ed. 2002)

History of English System of Conveyancing. We do not know the origin of the practice of transferring title to real estate by a written instrument. It may have been in existence and quite highly developed at the very dawn of written history. It appears to have passed from one predominating civilization to the next till it reached the Roman era, and from the latter into the legal systems of continental Europe. But Roman law did not, directly at least, exercise any appreciable influence on English land law. Instead, therefore, of finding transfers of title in England made from the time of the Roman occupation by the execution and delivery of a deed, we find that possession was the only evidence of title and that proof of a transfer of title existed solely in the memory of witnesses present at the time when the change of possession occurred. As to estates for years, a transfer of title was effected by a mere entry of the new owner, but in the case of freehold estates the change had to be in the form of a symbolic ceremony known as livery of seisin. This was a ceremony consisting of a symbolic delivery of the corporeal possession of land by the grantor, or "feoffor," as he was called, to the grantee, or "feoffee." The parties, with their witnesses, went upon the land, and the feoffor gave to the feoffee a stick, twig, piece of turf, or a handful of earth taken from the land. Sometimes a ring, cross, knife, or anything else, was handed over as a token of the delivery. As a further part of the ceremony, the feoffor used proper and technical words to show his intent to transfer the land to the feoffee and to establish or limit the estate or interest in the land that the feoffor intended the feoffee to have. The words "I give" (Latin, "do") were the proper words to use for the conveyance, while the words "to him" (i.e., the feoffee) "and his heirs," or "to him and the heirs of his body," designated the limitation, either as a fee simple or a fee tail. A distinction was made between livery in deed and livery in law. The former arose when the livery of seisin took place on the land itself; the latter when the parties were not actually on the land, as when the transfer was made in sight of the premises, but without an actual entry on them. In the latter case, the feoffor, pointing out the land, bade the feoffee enter and take possession of it. Should the feoffee do so within the lifetime of the parties, the feoffment was valid in law. Livery of seisin also required an abjuration of the land by the donor, or feoffor; that is, he had to vacate the land, leaving the feoffee in possession. No writing was necessary to give evidence of livery of seisin, although writings became customary in very early times.

In later times, however, livery of seisin usually was accompanied by a written deed, especially when the limitations of the estate granted were numerous. The deed, however, was only evidence of title, and not a conveyance itself. The use of a writing remained optional with the parties and was not legally required until the passage in 1677 of the Statute of Frauds. Only incorporeal interests and future estates could be transferred by a deed alone, since they were not capable of livery of seisin due to the absence of the element of possession. The instrument used was called a deed of grant, which resulted in the common law distinction between things that "lie in livery" and those that "lie in grant." In the case of freehold estates in corporeal real property, the deed that the Statute of Frauds required did not operate to transfer the title and livery of seisin remained essential in England, theoretically at least, until dispensed with by the Real Property Act of 1845, § 3. Nevertheless, the enactment of the Statute of Uses in 1535 had practically that effect in that it brought into almost universal use modes of alienation that did not require the symbolic ceremony. The Statute of Uses directly permitted (1) a contract in the form of a covenant to stand seized of property for the benefit of a beneficiary related to the covenantor by blood or marriage, and (2) a contract, or deed, of bargain and sale of lands "whereby the bargainor for some pecuniary consideration bargains and sells, that is, contracts to convey, the land to the bargainee; and becomes by such bargain, a trustee for, or seised to the use of, the bargainee." The statute executed the contract in both cases and, thus, the purchaser acquired the seisin and possession of the land as though there had been a livery of seisin.

But, because the Statute of Uses enabled a landowner by a mere contract of sale to vest the title in another without livery of seisin or other publicity, the same parliament passed a companion act for the express purpose of preventing clandestine conveyances. This was the Statute of Enrollments. It made a deed of bargain and sale of a freehold interest void unless within six months it was enrolled in a court of record at Westminster, or in certain other public offices. These two statutes were part of a plan to provide a general scheme for the transfer of title by deed and for the recording or registration of land conveyances. Because of the landholding aristocracy's propensity to withdraw the details of their family settlements and domestic arrangements from the public eye, however, their conveyancers welcomed the first part of the plan and set themselves to work to frustrate the second. The common-law deed of "lease and release" had previously been somewhat used to effect a transfer of title without the formal livery of seisin. It now was brought into general use to effect a conveyance that would not be within the Statute of Enrollments. . . . All the conveyancer had to do was to have the owner execute a lease (usually in the form of a bargain and sale deed of an estate for one year), followed at once by a release of the reversion to the lessee. This cumbersome use of two instruments for every transfer continued in England until the fictitious lease was abolished in 1841. Four years later, the Real Property Act was passed, making a simple deed of grant sufficient to convey all estates.

NOTE ON DEEDS IN MODERN AMERICAN REAL ESTATE PRACTICE

As the following materials reflect, American law has largely discarded the significance of the forms of deeds used historically in England. Here, a simple deed need contain only the following written elements: identification of the grantor and grantee, a description of the land being conveyed, some words indicating that title is to pass (such as "hereby conveys title" or the like), and the grantor's signature. A writing is necessary in every state under the Statute of Frauds. [*Simple deed requirements*]

Nonetheless, use of the old English terms often persists, even though the terms no longer carry their historic meaning. You will soon see a good example: a Washington statute authorizes the use of a "bargain and sale" deed, Wash. Rev. Code § 64.04.040, even though the meaning of the term "bargain and sale" (referring to a deed in the form of a contract of sale that was "executed" by the Statute of Uses) has long been lost. Another example is the word "grant," which is very often used as a term of conveyance in American deeds. It originated in England as referring to a conveyance of a nonpossessory interest, such as a future interest or an easement. But today it has entirely lost that connotation, and may be used to pass any interest in land, possessory or nonpossessory.

Modern deeds often contain covenants of title by which the grantor assures the grantee that he or she has title to pass. A deed that contains a broad statement of such covenants is usually called a "general warranty deed." Sometimes the grantor is willing to covenant that the grantor personally has done nothing to impair the title, but is unwilling to assure that previous owners have not done so. Such a deed, warranting only against the acts of the grantor, is often termed a "special warranty deed." Finally, a deed that contains no covenants of title at all is usually in the form of a "quitclaim" deed, under which the grantor will typically "remise, release, and quitclaim" the described land to the grantee. Once again, we see a "repurposing" of an ancient term: the "release" portion of an old deed of "lease and release."

Sometimes the old English deed terminology has been adapted by modern statutes as a way of automatically importing certain warranties of title into deeds. For example, the Washington statute mentioned above has the effect of imposing a "special warranty" if the deed uses the term "bargains and sells." Likewise, in California the use of the word "grant" will make the deed a special warranty deed. Cal. Civ. Code § 1113. In Missouri, the words "grant, bargain and sell" will make the deed a general warranty deed. Mo. Rev. Stat. § 442.420. There are many other examples around the country.

None of this is to say that the historic deed forms used in England would not work in the United States in their original contexts. Because most states treat the Statute of Uses as having been received at the inception of statehood, there is every reason to expect that a "covenant to stand seized" or a "bargain and sale" deed in the traditional English form would be given effect. See, e.g., Brevard County v. Ramsey, 658 So.2d 1190 (Fla.App.1995). Likewise, there is nothing today that would prevent a grantor from using the "lease and release" technique to convey a fee simple estate. But it is hard to imagine why anyone would bother to go through these contortions when the simple statement that "A hereby grants to B the following described land" will do the job perfectly well.

BALE V. ALLISON
Court of Appeals of Washington, 2013
294 P.3d 789

LAU, J. Robert E. Fletcher used a quitclaim deed to gift his Winthrop cabin to his nephews, John and Robert G. Fletcher. John and Robert appeal the trial court's determination that the failure to recite consideration invalidated the deed. We conclude the deed is valid because it met all statutory requirements and no recital is required to effectively gift real property. Accordingly, we reverse the judgment awarding title to Denny and Allen Bale. . . .

Bob Fletcher owned a parcel of real property including a cabin in Winthrop, Washington. John and Robert Fletcher were Bob's nephews. Starting around 1960, Bob took his nephews to visit the cabin two or three times a year. John and Robert's father (Bob's brother) died in 1964 when the boys were young, so Bob "took [them] under his wing." Bob lived with John and Robert for two years and married their mother (Bob's brother's widow) in 1968. That marriage lasted only two years. Until 1971, John continued visiting the cabin property two or three times a year.

J+R nephews

Bob married Edna Fletcher in 1971. Denny and Allen Bale ("the Bales") are Edna's adult sons from a previous marriage. When Bob and Edna married, the cabin on the Winthrop property was a small, rustic Forest Service cabin that lacked indoor plumbing and running water.

Bales are adopted sons?

Bob and Edna were married 28 years. During that time, the Bales made numerous improvements to the Winthrop property . . . . They also contributed furnishings and appliances to the cabin. They "provided the time and labor, and materials and payments necessary for these extensive renovations, improvements, and maintenance in reliance on their understanding that they would own the Winthrop property after [Bob] died." John and Robert stopped visiting the cabin during Bob and Edna's marriage because Edna did not "appreciate" them.

Edna died in 1999 and Bob again invited John and Robert to visit the cabin. John visited the property a couple times a year. He did maintenance work each time: "I did as much as I had to do to maintain the property while I was there and leave it like it was better than it was when I got there, just like [Bob] always told everyone to do." About a year and a half after Edna died, Bob married Garry Allison.

Bob executed a will in October 2003 in which he made three bequests: (1) to his stepsons, "Dennis Bale and [Allen] Bale, I give my property in Winthrop, WA, share and share alike"; (2) $2,000 to his adopted daughter; and (3) the rest, residue, and remainder of his estate to Garry Allison. In devising the Winthrop property to the Bales, Bob indicated his desire that they allow Garry Allison, John, and Robert to use the property for their enjoyment " 'at the discretion of Dennis Bale and [Allen] Bale.' "

Bob was diagnosed with terminal lung cancer in the fall 2008. John testified that after the diagnosis, Bob invited him and Robert over for lunch. Garry Allison was also present at the lunch. John and Robert both testified that Bob told them at that time, "I want you boys to have the cabin." John found a preprinted quitclaim deed online and filled it out. John and Robert then took Bob to Bank of America to get the deed notarized. Bob signed the deed, and the notary acknowledged his signature. John recorded the deed in Okanogan County on December 19, 2008.

post Fall 2008, quitclaim to J+R

The deed "conveys and quitclaims" the cabin property to John and Robert. The spaces after "in consideration of" and "quit claims to" are blank. Handwritten at the top of the deed after "Grantee" are the names "Robert Gary Fletcher" and "John Franklin Fletcher" and "Robert Ernest Fletcher" after the word "Grantor." In the preprinted real estate excise tax affidavit (REETA) and supplemental statement, under the heading "Gifts without consideration," Bob checked the box indicating, "There is no debt on the property; Grantor (seller) has not received any consideration towards equity. No tax is due." Also handwritten after "Reason for exemption" is "gift, w/no debt." The REETA also lists Bob as grantor and John and Robert as grantees. The Okanogan County treasurer stamped the REETA "Not Subject to Excise Tax."

Bob died in April 2009 and Garry Allison was named personal representative under the 2003 will. After Bob's death, John amended the previously recorded quitclaim deed by adding "for love and affection" and also wrote in his name and Robert's name in the "quit claim to" blank.[2] John also prepared a new REETA to include considerable personal property in and around the cabin. Garry Allison signed the REETA in her capacity as personal representative of Bob's estate. John rerecorded the quitclaim deed on June 26, 2009.

When the Bales learned that Bob quitclaimed the Winthrop property to John and Robert, they filed a "complaint for specific performance, damages and further equitable relief" against John, Robert, and Garry Allison, requesting that the Winthrop property be transferred from John and Robert to them. They alleged numerous claims, including breach of oral contract, breach of implied contract, promissory estoppel, undue influence, and tortious interference.

Garry Allison moved for summary judgment on all claims. The court granted summary judgment dismissal on the undue influence, tortious interference, and promissory estoppel claims but denied summary judgment on the oral and implied contract issues. The trial evidence related primarily to the Bales' oral contract to devise claim.

The court entered a judgment awarding clear title to the Bales and entered written findings and conclusions. Regarding the quitclaim deed, the court's conclusions of law state:

> 1.   The quit claim deed executed by [Bob] in December 2008 lacks specific and necessary terms to effectively transfer title. The quit claim deed is incomplete and fails to state what consideration, if any, was given for the deed. There were blanks

---

[2]   When asked why he altered the language, John testified that in February 2009, he had discussed the deed with an attorney friend. The friend advised him to rerecord the deed because the original deed failed to recite consideration. John asked the friend "if it was standard to correct verbiage on a quitclaim and rerecord it, and she said yes, we do it all the time." John decided to rerecord the deed and did so in June 2009, two months after Bob died.

left as to whom the property was conveyed. Because of the fatal defects as to consideration, the quit claim deed is ineffective and did not transfer title to John and Robert G. Fletcher.

2.   The quit claim deed executed by [Bob] in December 2008 does not meet the fundamental statutory requirements for a "good and sufficient conveyance, release and quitclaim to the grantee[s]" pursuant to RCW 64.04.050, and therefore, is ineffective to transfer the Winthrop property to John and Robert G. Fletcher.

3.   Because [Bob] is deceased and died testate, the December 2008 quit claim deed cannot be reformed by the personal representative, and the post-death alterations to the December 2008 deed are improper and of no legal effect.

The court concluded that given the deed's invalidity, Bob's October 2003 will controlled distribution of his estate and the property passed to the Bales.

The court rejected the Bales' oral contract to devise and implied contract claims. . . . The court ordered John and Robert to transfer all rights and title to the Winthrop property to the Bales under a quitclaim deed.

John and Robert appeal the trial court's conclusion that the quitclaim deed was invalid for failure to recite consideration. The Bales cross appeal the court's conclusion that they failed to establish an oral contract to devise. . . .

John and Robert contend the trial court erred in ruling that "fatal defects as to consideration" rendered the quitclaim deed ineffective. They argue that transfer of real property intended as a gift requires no recital of consideration under Washington law.

Construction of deeds is a matter of law. *Niemann v. Vaughn Cmty. Church,* 154 Wash.2d 365, 374, 113 P.3d 463 (2005). Whether the trial court properly determined the legal consequences of the deed's failure to recite consideration is subject to de novo review. The goal of deed construction is to effectuate the parties' intent. *Niemann,* 154 Wash.2d at 374, 113 P.3d 463. "In other words, 'it is a factual question to determine the intent of the parties' with the court then 'apply[ing] the rules of law to determine the legal consequences of that intent.' " *Niemann,* 154 Wash.2d at 374–75, 113 P.3d 463 (alteration in original) (quoting *Veach v. Culp,* 92 Wash.2d 570, 573, 599 P.2d 526 (1979)).

Real property conveyances, including gifts, must be accomplished by deed. RCW 64.04.010; *Oman v. Yates,* 70 Wash.2d 181, 185–86, 422 P.2d 489 (1967) (gifts in general); *Holohan v. Melville,* 41 Wash.2d 380, 385, 249 P.2d 777 (1952) (gift of real property). "Every deed shall be in writing, signed by the party bound thereby, and acknowledged by the party before *written signed by party handed notarized legal description of property* [handwritten margin note]

some person authorized . . . to take acknowledgment of deeds." RCW 64.04.020. Deeds also require a complete legal description of the property conveyed. *Berg v. Ting*, 125 Wash.2d 544, 551, 886 P.2d 564 (1995).

Washington courts have affirmed both real property gifts and gifts without consideration. *See Kessler v. Kessler,* 55 Wash.2d 598, 600, 349 P.2d 224 (1960) ("It was not against public policy, under the facts of this case, for the competent and grateful mother to have executed a deed of gift to her son of her residence property."); *Stringfellow v. Stringfellow,* 53 Wash.2d 639, 641, 335 P.2d 825 (1959) (father gifted stocks to son by "caus[ing] the issuance of the stock certificate in the son's name" no consideration recited); *State v. Superior Court of Snohomish County,* 165 Wash. 648, 650, 5 P.2d 1037 (1931) (parents could have deeded their home to their daughter "without any consideration at all," but never made that argument). The real estate tax regulation WAC 458–61A–201(1) treats a gift of real property as a nontaxable event. It provides:

> Generally, a gift of real property is not a sale, and is not subject to the real estate excise tax. *A gift of real property is a transfer for which there is no consideration given in return for granting an interest in the property.* If consideration is given in return for the interest granted, then the transfer is not a gift, but a sale, and it is subject to the real estate excise tax to the extent of the consideration received. (Emphasis added.)

Bob used a quitclaim deed to gift the Winthrop property to John and Robert without any recital of consideration. RCW 64.04.050 provides a sample quitclaim deed form containing a blank for consideration:

Quitclaim deeds *may* be in substance in the following form:

> The grantor (here insert the name or names and place of residence), *for and in consideration of (here insert consideration)* conveys and quitclaims to (here insert grantee's name or names) all interest in the following described real estate (here insert description), situated in the county of . . ., state of Washington. Dated this . . . day of . . ., 19 . . .

> Every deed in substance in the above form, when otherwise duly executed, shall be deemed and held a good and sufficient conveyance, release and quitclaim to the grantee, his or her heirs and assigns in fee of all the then existing legal and equitable rights of the grantor in the premises therein described, but shall not extend to the after acquired title unless words are added expressing such intention. (Emphasis added.)

*operative
words*

↓   ↘

convey

quitclaim

In *Newport Yacht Basin Ass'n of Condominium Owners v. Supreme Northwest, Inc.*, 168 Wash.App. 56, 277 P.3d 18 (2012), we explained that "a quitclaim deed need not precisely match the form described in RCW 64.04.050 in order to convey fee title." *Newport Yacht,* 168 Wash.App. at 67, 277 P.3d 18. We further explained that "the operative words of a quitclaim deed are 'conveys and quitclaims.'" *Newport Yacht,* 168 Wash.App. at 67, 277 P.3d 18 (quoting 18 William B. Stoebuck & John W. Weaver, *Washington Practice: Real Estate: Transactions* § 14.2, at 116 (2d ed. 2004)).

In *Newport Yacht,* we discussed consideration in the context of quitclaim deeds:

> As our Supreme Court has long recognized, "[g]enerally speaking, inadequacy of price is not sufficient, standing by itself, to authorize a court of equity to set aside a deed." *Downing v. State,* 9 Wash.2d 685, 688, 115 P.2d 972 (1941). Only where the inadequacy of consideration for conveyance of realty is so great as to shock the conscience may a court invoke its equitable power to set aside the conveyance. *Downing,* 9 Wash.2d at 688, 115 P.2d 972; *see also Binder v. Binder,* 50 Wash.2d 142, 150, 309 P.2d 1050 (1957). *However, quitclaim deeds are commonly used in transactions that are not the result of a sale for value.* 17 Stoebuck & Weaver, *supra,* § 7.2, at 472. *Such instruments are "used in donative transactions, in which, despite the recital of consideration in the deed, no actual consideration passes except perhaps love and affection."* 17 Stoebuck & Weaver, *supra,* § 7.2, at 472. Similarly, quitclaim deeds are often used "to clear title, to correct errors in prior deeds, and to adjust disputed boundaries between adjoining landowners." 17 Stoebuck & Weaver, *supra,* § 7.2, at 472. In such circumstances, "the common practice in Washington . . . to recite consideration of 'ten dollars and other good and valuable consideration' is sufficient to support a conveyance by deed." 17 *Stoebuck & Weaver, supra,* § 7.7, at 483.

Newport Yacht, 168 Wash.App. at 82–83, 277 P.3d 18 (emphasis added).

No Washington case addresses whether a quitclaim deed must recite consideration when the grantor intends to convey real property as a gift. Professors Stoebuck and Weaver address this question in their authoritative real property treatise:

> The Washington statute that gives the general form of a deed, RCWA 64.04.020, does not say that the deed must recite consideration. However, the statutes that set out the three statutory forms all say, "for and in consideration of (here insert consideration)." Two questions arise: Must consideration in fact be given? Must a Washington deed recite consideration?

Washington authority on the question is not as clear as might be wished, but *the Supreme Court of Washington does seem to have adopted the rule that a deed is valid without valuable consideration.* In other words, land may be conveyed by deed as a gift. The gift cases involve gifts between close relatives, such as spouses or parent to child, but gifts should be possible between non-relatives, though perhaps more subject to being set aside on grounds of fraud or some related equitable ground than are gifts to close relatives. Gift deeds have been upheld between wife and husband and between parent and child. Dictum in two other gift cases that a gift may be supported by "consideration" in the form of love and affection or of past consideration is confusing, since a true gift need not be supported by any form of consideration. When some consideration is given, it need not be in an "adequate" amount; *i.e.,* mere inadequacy of consideration is not ground to set aside a deed. Thus, the common practice in Washington, as in other states, to recite consideration of "ten dollars and other good and valuable consideration" is sufficient to support a conveyance by deed. However, the lack of consideration or inadequacy of consideration, along with other suspicious circumstances, may give grounds to set a deed aside for fraud or upon some related equitable theory. That subject will be discussed later in this chapter.

A deceptively simple question in Washington is, what is the correct form of deed to make a gift? In the gift cases reported in the preceding paragraph, or in any Washington appellate decision that can be found, the courts either did not quote the language of a gift deed or described a deed that recited nominal consideration. *The problem is that Washington lawyers habitually use one of the three special statutory deed forms, and, as previously noted, those forms all call for at least a recital of consideration.* A common practice is to use one of the statutory forms, usually the quitclaim deed form, so that the grantor will not "donate" warranties as well as title, and to recite as consideration the rote phrase, "ten dollars and other good and valuable consideration," or the phrase, "ten dollars, love and affection, and other good and valuable consideration." Aside from the fact that the deed contains a false recital, this works, but on its face, the deed is subject to a small amount of the excise tax imposed on real estate sales by RCWA Chapter 82.45. To get around that slight embarrassment, some Washington lawyers insert a recital, a sort of "P.S.," in some convenient blank space in the deed, reciting that the deed is one of gift, and no consideration of money value actually passed. Since no excise tax is due on gifts, this moves the county treasurer to stamp the deed "No Tax Due," but it compounds the falsity of the previous recital of consideration. Cautious draftsmen, who tend to be fussy about such details, may wonder if there is a better, truer way to draft a gift deed.

It should be possible to rely upon the general deed statute, RCWA 64.04.020, and to draft a deed that meets the three essentials, in writing, signed by the grantor, and acknowledged, without any recital of consideration, since the statute does not require it. In fact, such deeds are used to grant easements in Washington, and easements, being "interests" in land, are just as much within the deed statutes as are conveyances in fee simple. Of course the deed needs to name the grantor and grantee, describe the land, and contain appropriate words of conveyance. The general deed statute does not give words of conveyance, and the draftsman wants to avoid using the words of any of the three special deed forms; so, the word "conveys" or the phrase "grants and conveys" might be used. Assuming the donor does not want to make warranties, it would be well to add a disclaimer of warranties, to avoid any argument that the grantor intended one of the special statutory forms. The following is a form of deed that should be sufficient to make a gift of a fee simple estate in Washington:

> Grantors, John Doe and Jane Doe, husband and wife, hereby grant and convey as a gift, without warranties, to Richard Roe and Mary Roe, husband and wife, the following described real estate in fee simple absolute: (legal description), situated in the County of _____, State of Washington.

> Dated this _____ day of _____, 20____.

17 *Stoebuck & Weaver* § 7.7, at 482–84 (footnotes omitted).

The Bales rely exclusively on RCW 64.04.050, quoted above, to argue that the December 2008 quitclaim deed was ineffective because it was "devoid of any statement of consideration." The Bales do not dispute that Bob intended to gift the real property to John and Robert. They cite no statute or case authority requiring a deed to recite consideration when the grantor intends to convey the real property as a gift. *See State v. Logan,* 102 Wash.App. 907, 911 n. 1, 10 P.3d 504 (2000) (" 'Where no authorities are cited in support of a proposition, the court is not required to search out authorities, but may assume that counsel, after diligent search, has found none.' ") (quoting *DeHeer v. Seattle Post-Intelligencer,* 60 Wash.2d 122, 126, 372 P.2d 193 (1962)). The Bales' reliance on RCW 64.04.050 is questionable because the statute's use of the term "may" is permissive, not mandatory. Nor do they challenge Professors Stoebuck and Weaver's analysis discussed above. For the reasons discussed above, we hold no recital of consideration is required to effectively gift real property. The trial court erred when it

[handwritten margin note: don't dispute intended gift]

[handwritten margin note: no recital of consideration needed to effectively gift real prop]

concluded the deed's invalidity premised on the recital of consideration omission.

The Bales also claim the deed's invalidity because "the notary failed to enter in her acknowledgment the identity of the person appearing before her." They offer no additional argument on this issue and cite no authority supporting their claim that this omission invalidated the deed, and we can decline to address it. *See Palmer v. Jensen*, 81 Wash.App. 148, 153, 913 P.2d 413 (1996) ("Passing treatment of an issue or lack of reasoned argument is insufficient to merit judicial consideration."). Even if we consider this argument, it fails.[6] Review of the disputed deed shows that the grantor's and grantees' names appear on the document. Bob signed and dated the deed. The notary's signature appears directly beneath Bob's signature. The deed contains a blank in the certification: "I certify that I know or have satisfactory evidence that ____, the person(s) who appeared before me. . . ." Despite this omission, it is clear that the notary acknowledged Bob's signature because he was the only person who signed the deed. The notary's uncontroverted trial testimony supports this conclusion.[7]

[The court also concluded that the Bales had not presented sufficient evidence of an oral contract by Bob to devise the cabin to them.]

NOTES

1.   *Consideration.* The modern cases generally agree with *Bale* that a deed is not a contract, and that no consideration is necessary to the validity of a deed. See, e.g., Celtic Corp. v. Tinnea, 254 S.W.3d 137 (Mo. App. 2008); Estate of Dykes v. Estate of Williams, 864 So. 2d 926 (Miss. 2003); Cox v. Cox, 138 Idaho 881, 71 P.3d 1028 (2003); Chase Fed. Sav. & Loan Ass'n v. Schreiber, 479 So. 2d 90 (Fla. 1985). Nevertheless, one still finds opinions purporting to set aside deeds for lack of consideration. See, e.g., Voccola v. Forte, 139 A.3d 404 (R.I. 2016); West America Housing Corp. v. Pearson, 171 P.3d 539 (Wyo. 2007). Almost invariably in these cases, however, there is some element of fraud, deceit, or mistake in the transaction, and not merely the absence of consideration. In re Estate of Bontkowski, 337 Ill. App. 3d 72, 785 N.E.2d 126 (2003) ("If, however, a person has been induced to part with a thing of value for little or no consideration, equity will seize upon the slightest circumstance

---

[6]   Given our decision, we need not address the Bales' argument that John and Robert knew the deed was defective when they attempted to rerecord it after Bob's death. We also need not address whether the attempted alteration cured the allegedly defective deed. Regardless, John and Robert do not argue that the rerecorded deed cured any alleged error. They argue that the original December 2008 deed was valid as written and recorded

[7]   To the extent the Bales also argue that the failure to enter the grantees' names in the middle part of the deed results in invalidity, the above reasoning applies. Again, the Bales cite no authority for their argument that such an omission invalidates the deed. And as discussed above, the deed elsewhere makes clear that John and Robert are the grantees. We construe the deed to give effect to the grantor's intent. *Zunino*, 140 Wash.App. at 222, 165 P.3d 57.

of oppression, fraud, or duress for the purpose of administering justice in the case at hand").

2. *Modifying a deed after delivery.* Note that neither the Fletchers nor the court gave any weight to the alteration and re-recording of the deed after its delivery. That's correct; changes made to a deed by its grantee after its delivery are of no legal consequence. See Julian v. Peterson, 966 P.2d 878 (Utah App. 1998) (adding the name of an additional grantee after delivery of deed was ineffective); Lee v. Lee, 97 Cal. Rptr. 3d 516 (Cal.App. 2009) (similar).

However, courts will sometimes allow the *grantor* to make changes to the deed and redeliver it, and if the changes do not conflict with the original grant, they will be given effect. For example, if the original deed contained a typographical error in the legal description, the grantor can correct the description and redeliver the deed. See Green v. Crane, 386 S.E.2d 757 (N.C.App. 1990). Texas has allowed correction of an improper acreage description, an inaccurate metes and bounds description, and a defective description of the grantor's capacity, but not a correction adding to the originally-described land. Myrad Props., Inc. v. LaSalle Bank N.A., 300 S.W.3d 746 (Tex. 2009). In all events, it is obvious that such a "correction" signed only by the grantor cannot deprive the grantee of the rights granted by the original deed. See Hilterbrand v. Carter, 27 P.3d 1086 (Or. App. 2001).

2. REQUIREMENTS FOR A DEED

The minimum requirements for a valid written deed are determined by state statutes and can vary by jurisdiction. The Washington state statute below provides a useful model to study.

Revised Code of Washington

64.04.020. Requisites of a Deed. Every deed shall be in writing, signed by the party bound thereby, and acknowledged by the party before some person authorized by this act to take acknowledgments of deeds.

64.04.030. Warranty Deed—Form and Effect. Warranty deeds for the conveyance of land may be substantially in the following form, without express covenants:

> The grantor (here insert the name or names and place of residence) for and in consideration of (here insert consideration) in hand paid, conveys and warrants to (here insert the grantee's name or names) the following described real estate (here insert description), situated in the county of _____, state of Washington. Dated this _____ day of _____, (year)___.

Every deed in substance in the above form, when otherwise duly executed, shall be deemed and held a conveyance in fee simple to the grantee, his or her heirs and assigns, with covenants on the part of the grantor: (1) That at the time of the making and delivery of such deed he or she was lawfully seized of an indefeasible estate in fee simple, in and to the premises therein described, and had good right and full power to convey the same; (2) that the same were then free from all encumbrances; and (3) that he or she warrants to the grantee, his or her heirs and assigns, the quiet and peaceable possession of such premises, and will defend the title thereto against all persons who may lawfully claim the same, and such covenants shall be obligatory upon any grantor, his or her heirs and personal representatives, as fully and with like effect as if written at full length in such deed.

64.04.040. Bargain and Sale Deed—Form and Effect. Bargain and sale deeds for the conveyance of land may be substantially in the following form, without express covenants:

> The grantor (here insert name or names and place of residence), for and in consideration of (here insert consideration) in hand paid, bargains, sells and conveys to (here insert the grantee's name or names) the following described real estate (here insert description) situated in the county of _____, state of Washington. Dated this _____ day of _____, (year)___.

Every deed in substance in the above form when otherwise duly executed shall convey to the grantee, his or her heirs or assigns an estate of inheritance in fee simple, and shall be adjudged an express covenant to the grantee, his or her heirs or assigns, to wit: That the grantor was seized of an indefeasible estate in fee simple, free from encumbrances, done or suffered from the grantor, except the rents and services that may be reserved, and also for quiet enjoyment against the grantor, his or her heirs and assigns, unless limited by express words contained in such deed; and the grantee, his or her heirs, executors, administrators and assigns may recover in any action for breaches as if such covenants were expressly inserted.

NOTES AND QUESTIONS

1. *Multiple deeds to the same land.* Laypersons often have the misconception that there is only a single piece of paper that is the "official" deed to a given parcel of land. The truth is otherwise; anyone (whether the owner or not) may make up and sign as many deeds to a parcel as he or she wishes. Of course, once one of those deeds is signed by the owner of the land and delivered to a grantee, the grantor no longer has title. Any deed that the grantor might subsequently give to another grantee will convey nothing (we will assume for now that the first deed was recorded—more about this later in the chapter), and will have no legal significance apart from possibly subjecting the grantor to liability on any covenants of title expressed in the later deed.[1]

---

[1] Indeed, there is no inherent legal wrong in A executing and delivering a deed to land in which A owns no interest. In fact, if any reader would like a deed to the Space Needle in Seattle (or any other piece of valuable real estate except our houses—be as choosy as you wish), you may simply write to one of the authors and we will be happy to send you one! Needless to say, the deed

A common related misconception is that "the" deed is passed down from one owner to another in succession indefinitely. What actually occurs is that each owner, as he or she makes a sale or gift of the property, prepares and executes a brand-new deed and delivers it to the grantee. Assuming that the deed from the previous transfer was recorded (so that one can obtain a copy of it from the courthouse if a dispute about its existence or content arises), it is irrelevant whether that prior deed is even in existence any longer. People commonly retain deeds by which they have acquired land in their files or safety-deposit boxes, but except in very rare cases (e.g., the need to have them examined to detect a forgery), continued possession of the deed has no significance.

2. *Using old terminology in new ways.* Many states have statutes that incorporate certain specific covenants of title into a deed if the deed uses specified "magic" words. The Washington statutes reproduced above illustrate that phrases which originated in medieval deeds continue to be used in the United States, but are often given new and different meanings and are employed in ways the old English lawyers would have thought wholly inappropriate. Can you see the difference between a "warranty deed" and a "bargain and sale deed" in Washington? That difference is purely a product of the Washington legislature's creative definitions, and has nothing to do with the ways the same terms were used at common law.

3. *The writing requirement.* The application of the Statute of Frauds to conveyances (as distinct from contracts of sale or brokerage listing agreements already studied) requires further explanation.

(a) *Exceptions.* Many states except certain types of conveyances, such as those of interests having a duration of one year or less. The point of such an exemption is to legitimize short-term oral leases.

Perhaps surprisingly, there is some authority that an oral gift of land is effective if the donee takes possession and engages in other acts of detrimental reliance. The principle involved is not well-defined, but seems to be analogous to the doctrine of "part performance" of land sale contracts. See Troxel v. Bishop, 201 S.W.3d 290 (Tex. App. 2006); Lynch v. Lynch, 239 Iowa 1245, 34 N.W.2d 485 (1948); Patrick McFadden, Oral Transfers of Land in Illinois, 1988 U. Ill. L. Rev. 667. But see Restatement (Second) of Property: Donative Transfers § 31.4 (rejecting this view).

(b) *Signatures.* Ordinarily, only the grantor must sign the deed. Even if the deed contains covenants that will bind the grantee, the grantee need not sign; the grantee's acceptance of the deed is regarded as sufficient evidence of assent.[2]

---

we send you will be a quitclaim deed, containing no covenants of title, and because we do not own the Space Needle, the deed will in fact convey nothing at all to you. We will use a quitclaim deed so that you cannot hold us liable for damages when you determine that you failed to acquire any title to the Space Needle through the deed.

[2] A deed signed only by the grantor was known in England as a *deed poll.* A deed that the grantee also signed was known as a *deed of indenture,* a term apparently derived from the practice

(c) *Acknowledgment.* Most Statutes of Frauds (unlike Washington's statute) do not require acknowledgment by a notary or other officer for validity of the deed. In a few states, acknowledgment is required; see, e.g., Fla. Stat. § 689.04 (warranty deeds); Ariz. Rev. Stat. § 33–401; Neb. Rev. Stat. § 76–211. In most states, then, an unacknowledged deed that is nevertheless executed and delivered is perfectly valid as between the grantor and the grantee. See, e.g., Central Mortg. Co. v. Seye, 100 N.E.3d 969 (Ohio Ct. App. 2017) (mortgage valid between the parties despite failure to include acknowledgment of mortgagor's signature).

However, acknowledgment is almost uniformly required for *recordation* in the public records. If a deed has not been properly acknowledged, the recording officer will (or at least should) refuse to accept the deed for recording. Thus, while the grantee of an unacknowledged deed may have title, the grantee could not record evidence of that title (and would thus be at risk of having that title extinguished if the grantor later conveyed the same land to a good faith purchaser for value). We return to discuss recording and the recording acts later in this chapter.

4. *Elements of a deed.* The essential components of a deed are few: it must identify the grantor(s) and grantee(s), identify the land being conveyed, contain some words indicating title is to pass (so-called "words of grant"), and be signed by the grantor(s). In a few states acknowledgment or witnesses are necessary.

Now refer to the modern deed reprinted on the next page, and see if you can find and interpret the following items:

(a) The grantor's name and signature.

(b) The grantees' names and an indication of the manner in which they are taking title. (Washington is a community property state.)

(c) The recitation of consideration. As you saw in *Bale v. Allison*, in most states neither the actual payment of consideration nor its recitation are necessary to the validity of the deed. Still, the recitation remains common—a historical artifact, left over from the post-Statute of Uses era when covenants to stand and bargain and sale deeds were used.

---

of having the grantee sign on a portion of the paper, which would then be cut off with a wavy or zig-zag cut (thus, "indented") and retained by the grantor as a sort of receipt, with the grantee receiving the portion the grantor had signed.

(d) The description of the real estate, here accomplished by reference to a previously recorded subdivision plat.

(e) A statement of "exclusions"—matters to which the fee simple title will be subject. The main purpose of this statement is not to inform the grantee of the nature of the exceptions (the statement comes too late in the due diligence process and is too broadly worded for that), but to preclude the grantor from becoming liable based on a breach of deed covenants of title as a result of the existence of the matters mentioned as exclusions. The buyer should already have learned about these exclusions from a title report, title commitment, attorney's opinion, or the like, and will have satisfied herself (if she is well-advised) that they are acceptable.

(f)   Language indicating an intent to make a conveyance—or "words of grant." A variety of words have been held sufficient by various courts, including alienate, assign, assure, convey, enfeoff, give, quitclaim, set over, and transfer. But sometimes a grantor will use words that simply do not indicate an intent to transfer anything. Such a deed is ineffective. See Raley v. Raley, 121 Miss. 555, 83 So. 740 (1920) (the words "warrant and defend" are not words of grant and convey nothing).

The words of grant in the Washington deed also trigger the warranties of title described in the Washington statutes set out above. We will investigate deed warranties in general later in this chapter, but you should be able to understand from the statutory language the basic notion behind the two types of warranties.

Note that the deed does not contain any statement about the duration of the estate being transferred. You will recall that at common law, the words "and her heirs" were necessary to give the grantee a fee simple. Today, however, virtually every state presumes that a fee simple is intended unless contrary language appears; hence, no specific statement of the estate's duration is required.

In states that continue to use more archaic deed forms, it is common to include a "habendum" clause (from the Latin "habendum et tendendum"—"to have and to hold"), which states the quality of the estate, especially if it is less than a fee simple. For example, language indicating a life estate might read, "To have and to hold for his life only."

(g)   The date. Although a date is not essential, see, e.g., Federal Nat'l Mortg. Ass'n v. Buhl, 186 Conn. App. 743, 201 A.3d 485 (2018) (absence of date did not render deed invalid), it is usually included. The critical date is not the date of execution of the deed, but rather the date of delivery (because delivery is when the deed "speaks"). Nevertheless, the execution date is the one normally inserted in the deed itself.

(h)   The notary public's certificate of acknowledgment.

(i)   The stamp of the public official (in Washington known as the auditor, but in most states, the county recorder) indicating that the deed has been officially recorded.

(j)   The auditor's stamp indicating that the recording fee (here, $32.00) has been paid.

(k) Stamps indicating the payment of the transfer taxes. Washington state charges a graduated percent of the sale price (starting at 1.1% and increasing to 3% on sales over $3 million in price), and Snohomish County an additional 0.5 percent, for a total of $3,360 on a house selling for $210,000. Washington is a rather expensive place to transfer land! At least 37 states impose a real estate transfer tax.

5. *Does the deed convey an estate or something less?* A deed is presumed to convey a fee simple absolute estate (assuming the grantor has one to convey) unless the deed expresses a contrary intent. But drafters of deeds sometimes insert language that leaves the reader uncertain as to whether something less than a fee simple estate is intended, and if so, exactly what is being conveyed. For example, a conveyance of "a strip of land for a right of way" or "a right of way over a strip of land" may be thought to grant only an easement and not an estate. See Severns v. Union Pac. R.R. Co., 125 Cal. Rptr. 2d 100 (Cal.App. 2002); Little Miami, Inc. v. Wisecup, 13 Ohio App. 3d 239, 468 N.E.2d 935 (1984). There are hundreds of such cases, mostly dating from the late 19th and early 20th centuries, when agents for railroads acquired land interests for tracks, and were often careless or imprecise in describing the nature of the interests they obtained. The outcomes of the cases are variable and hard to predict; they turn on the precise language used in the deed.

The issue has become important for several reasons. One is that in the late 20th and early 21st centuries, railroads have allowed communication companies to install fiber optic lines along their tracks. This is perfectly permissible if the railroad has a fee simple estate, but may violate the rights of the underlying landowner if the railroad has only an easement. Another reason is that an easement may be terminated by abandonment, while a fee simple estate cannot. See Union Pac. R. Co. v. Ameriton Props. Inc., 448 S.W.3d 671 (Tex. Ct. App. 2014); Kershaw Sunnyside Ranches, Inc. v. Yakima Interurban Lines Ass'n, 126 P.3d 16 (Wash. 2006).

Even a reference to an "easement" or "license" may be subject to reinterpretation if a court feels the word does not describe the legal result the parties desired. See Ouellette v. Butler, 125 N.H. 184, 480 A.2d 76 (1984) (grant of "license" interpreted to create easement). Good drafting thus requires careful and unambiguous expression of the parties' intentions.

6. *Exceptions and reservations.* Another problem arises from the use of "exceptions" and "reservations" in deeds. In theory, an "exception" is a holding back of some previously existing interest in or portion of the land, while a "reservation" creates and leaves with the grantor a newly formed interest in the land. Thus, it would be proper for a grantor conveying title to all of Blackacre but the south fifty feet of the parcel to "except the south fifty feet"; by contrast, a grantor conveying fee simple title to Blackacre but wishing to retain a life estate would properly "reserve a life estate." In practice the two terms are used almost interchangeably, and the distinction between them has little significance. See O'Brien v. Village Land Co., 794 P.2d 246 (Colo. 1990).

However, careless use of the terms can have disastrous consequences. For example, suppose that Cook owned Parcel A (a 130-acre parcel) and Parcel B (a 450-acre parcel) and held a road easement over adjoining property for access to the parcels. Cook first subdivided Parcel A and sold the lots, delivering deeds that "excepted" validly existing easements. When Cook later tried to subdivide Parcel B and allow lot buyers in Parcel B to cross the road running through Parcel A, buyers of the Parcel A lots sued to block use of the road to benefit Parcel B, on the ground that Cook did not "reserve" title to the road so as to grant easements in the road to the buyers of Parcel A. What result? See, e.g., Cook v. Nissimov, 580 S.W.3d 745 (Tex. Ct. App. 2019).

A common law rule states that a deed may not create an interest in a *third party* by way of an exception or reservation; such clauses may operate only in favor of the grantor. [Of course, the grantor could then transfer the interest, so reserved or excepted, to another party by a second deed.] See Shirley v. Shirley, 259 Va. 513, 525 S.E.2d 274 (2000). This rule is so obviously artificial and apt to defeat intention that many modern cases have refused to follow it; see Simpson v. Kistler Inv. Co., 713 P.2d 751 (Wyo. 1986); Malloy v. Boettcher, 334 N.W.2d 8 (N.D. 1983), Note, 60 N.D. L. Rev. 317 (1984). See also Peters v. Smolian, 49 Misc.3d 408, 12 N.Y.S.3d 824 (2015) (right of first refusal not invalid under "stranger to the deed" rule). But the wise drafter will avoid the problem.

7.   *The need for an existing grantee.* A deed that conveys a present (as distinct from a future) interest must have an ascertainable grantee—i.e., a living person or an existing juridical entity, such as a corporation, partnership, trust, or governmental unit. See, e.g., In re Estate of Savich, 671 N.W.2d 746 (Minn. Ct. App. 2003) (deed purportedly delivered to grandmother after her death was void). Thus courts often hold deeds void if the grantee is a corporation or other entity that has not yet been formed or that has been dissolved. See, e.g., Stone v. Jetmar Props., LLC, 733 N.W.2d 480 (Minn. Ct. App. 2007) (deed to LLC not yet formed is void); Haney's Chapel United Methodist Church v. United Methodist Church, 716 So. 2d 1156 (Ala. 1998) (deed to "this community for a Union Church" is void); Piedmont & Western Inv. Corp. v. Carnes-Miller Gear Co., 96 N.C. App. 105, 384 S.E.2d 687 (1989) (deed to dissolved corporation is void); Myers v. Francis, 548 So. 2d 833 (Fla. Ct. App. 1989) (deed that fails to name a grantee is void). See also Morris v. Off-Piste Capital LLC, 418 P.3d 66 (Utah Ct. App. 2018) (while attempted conveyance to nonexistent entity void, misnaming of corporate grantee will not defeat validity of deed if extrinsic evidence enables court to ascertain intended grantee).

Trusts are a little different. A deed to a trustee is valid even though the trust has not yet been formed, because the trustee can hold title in her or his individual capacity until the trust is created. Luna v. Brownell, 185 Cal. App. 4th 668, 110 Cal. Rptr. 3d 573 (2010).

8.   *Returning title by handing deed back?* A grantee will sometimes hand a deed back to the grantor with the intent of reconveying title to the land to

the grantor. But this doesn't work; no reconveyance results. See Stockwell v. Stockwell, 790 N.W.2d 52 (S.D. 2010); see also Ward v. Ward, 874 N.E.2d 433 (Mass. App. Ct. 2007) (grantor cannot revoke deed after delivering it). Delivering a deed is like squeezing toothpaste out of a tube; you can't put it back in again!

B. LAND DESCRIPTIONS

BROWN, BOUNDARY CONTROL AND LEGAL PRINCIPLES
4–5 (2d ed. 1969)

Land is fixed in place. If it is to be divided among various people, it must be marked by monuments, or directions must be given explaining how it can be monumented relative to existing monuments. The earliest land holdings were wholly dependent upon found or set monuments. But monuments and marks on the earth's surface are subject to destruction or movement by intentional or unintentional means: trees die, wooden stakes rot, rivers change their course, and ploughs remove stakes. Certainty of monumented boundary lines may be destroyed with the destruction of the monuments marking them. To cope with the problem of replacing lost monuments, especially in the Nile Valley of Egypt where frequent floods destroyed many land markers, man devised measuring methods that would enable him to reset new monuments reasonably close to the spot occupied by the old monuments. Measurements start from some definite point, a monument, and go a fixed distance in a given direction. By relating numerous monuments to one another by measurements, a lost monument can be replaced by distance and direction from other monuments.

Land ownerships have shape, size, and location. The shape and size of a parcel of land may be defined without the aid of monuments, such as a square, a parallelogram, a circle, or an irregular parcel, by bearings and distances. But the place where the particular shape is located is related to a fixed monument on the face of the earth. Even latitude and longitude are fixed by two monuments (or datums): a spot in Greenwich, England and the poles of the earth. All the advancements in land location technique have not eliminated the monument as the ultimate means by which land is controlled.

In the early days in the United States *free surveys* often existed. A surveyor could start at any point, survey a selected quantity of land, monument, and describe it. He was not limited by previous ownerships or previous surveys. Today practically all boundary surveys are dependent partly or wholly upon monuments or points previously established on the earth. If a new parcel is described, it is related to existing boundaries, which in turn are related somehow to a fixed monument. If a new parcel is established by survey, it is done by measurements from fixed monuments. Monuments are the backbone in relation to which land is located.

From early Colonial times down to the present, various systems have been adopted to describe real property relative to monuments, said systems being dependent upon either local laws, common laws, state laws, Colonial laws, or Federal laws. Townships, ranges, and sections of land as first defined by the Continental Congress and later enacted into Federal law represent the most widespread system used to mark and describe land within the United States.

The government survey system referenced by Brown originated with a committee headed by Thomas Jefferson, an experienced surveyor. The committee recommended the system to the Continental Congress, which adopted it on April 26, 1785. Most of the land added to the United States subsequent to that time has been surveyed under the system. The map on the next page shows the modern coverage of the system, and also illustrates the network of Base Lines and Principal Meridians which it superimposes on the nation. The Principal Meridian lines run North-South and the Base Lines run East-West. Spaced out parallel to the Base Line, and running East-West, are lines dividing the land into "Townships." As the diagram below shows, the second Township south of the Base Line would be called "Township 2 South." Each township has a side about 6 miles in length. Similarly, the North-South lines running parallel to the Principal Meridian divide the land into "Ranges"; the third Range West of the Principal Meridian would be called "Range 3 West." Note carefully that the term "Township" has a double meaning here; it refers both to the distance north or south of the Base Line, and also to the individual square parcel of land, six miles on a side, which is identified by stating both a Township and a Range number, as in "Township 2 South, Range 3 West."

Each Township (using the latter meaning of the term) is further subdivided into 36 "Sections," each about one mile square. Note the numbering system, which begins in the Northeast corner of the Section and continually loops back and forth, winding up with Section 36 in the Southeast corner. Each Section may be further divided as the owners or their surveyors desire into quarters, quarter-quarters, and so on. On the diagram you should be able to pick out the land which would be described as "The Southeast quarter of the Northwest quarter of Section 14, Township 2 South, Range 3 West, San Bernardino Base and Meridian." It is useful to know that a Section contains approximately 640 acres, a quarter-section 160 acres, and a quarter-quarter-section 40 acres. Thus, while the expression "plowing the South 40" is not quite legally explicit, you can see its origin.

GENERALIZED DIAGRAM OF THE RECTANGULAR SYSTEM OF SURVEYS

Township Grid

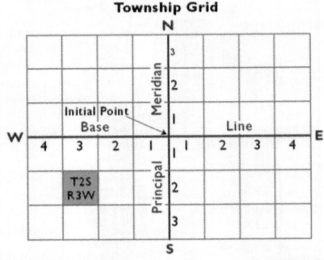

Township 2 South, Range 3 West

Section 14

For more detailed information on the government survey system, its history, and its modern operation, see Robillard & Wilson, Evidence and Procedures for Boundary Location (6th ed. 2011).

If land in a government survey state is being broken into smaller parcels for agricultural use, the fractional-section method of description illustrated above may be quite satisfactory. However, if land is to be developed for urban uses, such as businesses, homes, and apartments, the parcels are likely to be so small and/or so irregularly-shaped that they cannot be described satisfactorily as fractions of sections. Two other methods therefore come into common usage for urban property (and for rural property in states without the government survey system.) One is the recorded subdivision plat; the other, older and somewhat diminishing in use, but still very important, is the "metes and bounds" description. Both of these methods often use the government survey system as an initial starting point or framework; indeed, descriptions which rely to some degree on all three methods are quite common.

A subdivision plat is a map, generally prepared by an engineer or surveyor at the request of the landowner, which meets certain publicly-promulgated standards for format and accuracy, and which is filed as a permanent record in the appropriate government office, usually that of the county recorder. The plat must usually be approved by the governing body of the local government (e.g., the city council or the county commission) before the recorder will accept it for filing, and that approval is usually conditioned on compliance with a "subdivision ordinance" which imposes various technical standards (street width, lot size, installation of curb and gutter, etc.) and may compel dedication to the local government of streets, utility easements, and even school sites. See J. Juergensmeyer, T. Roberts, P. Salkin & R. Rowberry, Land Use Planning and Development Regulation Law, ch. 7 (4th ed. 2018).

A subdivision plat may include hundreds of lots, or only two or three. It will normally show a reference to some preexisting monument or to an element of the government survey system, such as a section corner. Once the plat has been officially filed, it can form the basis for legal descriptions of individual lots; the description need not go "behind" the plat or recite the underlying monument references, so the description of a lot can be very brief: "Lot 3, Block K, Ridgefield Acres Subdivision, as shown in Plat Book D, page 23, Official Records of Orange County." Nearly all modern single-family residential developments are built on land covered by platted subdivisions, and they are fairly common with commercial property (such as shopping centers) as well.

The other major type of land description is "metes and bounds." It involves a written description of the property's boundaries, usually by a series of "calls," each of which states the location of an individual boundary line. Of course, the point of beginning of the calls must be monumented somehow. This may be done by direct reference to a monument. Alternatively, the metes and bounds description may lie within (and make reference to) a lot in a platted subdivision or a section in the government survey system.

BROWN, BOUNDARY CONTROL AND LEGAL PRINCIPLES
14–15 (2d ed. 1969)

Direction of Travel. True metes and bounds descriptions and many quasi-metes and bounds descriptions have a direction of travel. A bearing may be stated in either of two directions on a map or plat but only one can be used in a written perimeter description. In the figure below, starting at the point of beginning, the direction of travel is to the southeast, making the first written bearing in the description S 45°00′E, not N 45°00′ W. Because the relationship of one line to another is shown by the plotting of the lines in the figure below, it is immaterial whether the bearing on the plat is written S 45°00′E or N 45°00′W.

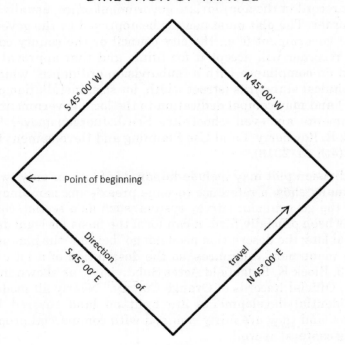

DIRECTION OF TRAVEL

Monuments. Monuments are classified as either *natural, artificial, record,* or *legal.* Naturally occurring monuments such as rivers, lakes, oceans, bays, sloughs, cliffs, trees, hills, and large boulders are permanent objects found on the land as they were placed by nature and are usually considered controlling over *artificial monuments* (man-made) such as iron stakes, wooden stakes, rock mounds, stones, and wooden fences, but, if the writings clearly indicate a contrary intent, especially where the lines of a survey are called for, the control might be reversed. Some man-made monuments, because of the certainty of location, visibility, stability, and permanence, are considered equal in rank to natural monuments. In this classification would fall sidewalks, street paving, curbs, wells, canals, concrete buildings, and concrete fences.

NOTES

1. *Units of measurement.* The following table, published by the National Bureau of Standards, may help you deal with the various units of length sometimes used in legal descriptions.

Units	Inches	Links	Feet	Yards	Rods	Chains	Miles	Meters
1 inch	1	0.126 263	0.083 333 3	0.027 777 8	0.005 050	0.001 262	0.000 015 783	0.025 400.05
1 link	7.92	1	0.66	0.22	0.04	0.01	0.000 125	0.201 168 4
1 foot	12	1.515 152	1	0.333 333	0.060 606	0.015 151	0.000 189 394	0.304 800 6
1 yard	36	4.545.45	3	1	0.181 818	0.045 454	0.000 568 182	0.914 401 8
1 rod	198	25	16.5	5.5	1	0.25	0.003 125	5.029 210
1 chain	792	100	66	22	4	1	0.0125	20.116 84
1 mile	63 360	8 000	5 280	1 760	320	80	1	1 609.347 2
1 meter	39.37	4.970 960	3.280 833	1.093 611 1	0.198 838	0.049 710	0.000 621 370	1

2. *Conflicts and ambiguities in land descriptions.* It is not unusual for a description of land in a deed (or a contract of sale) to contain conflicting information. The courts have established a descending list of priorities to resolve such conflicts. The usual order of this list (with items higher on the list controlling, and having priority over, items lower on the list) is as follows:

- Natural monuments (trees, streams, rocks, etc.)
- Artificial monuments (buildings, curbs, etc.)
- Courses (directions in relation to true North)
- Distances (feet, chains, rods, etc.)
- Quantity (e.g., acres)

Perhaps the best explanation for this list is that matters higher on the list are easier for people to locate or estimate with the naked eye than matters lower down. Thus, it is easier to locate a tree than to estimate a course (direction), which in turn is easier to estimate than the acreage of a plot of land.

Do not assume that, because natural monuments are given the highest priority, it is desirable to use them whenever possible. Quite the contrary is true. Suppose you were searching a title and got back to a deed that made a reference to "the big white rock beside Perkins Creek." Unfortunately, the creek is now in a concrete culvert and the rock is long gone, removed to make room for the construction of a shopping center. Because natural monuments are impermanent, it may be impossible to locate them when someone needs them in the future.

3. *Sketching a metes and bounds description.* As a lawyer, you should not attempt to fulfill the role of a surveyor or engineer (unless, of course, you have actually been trained to do so). But you can and should examine legal descriptions with a critical eye. In most cases, you can sketch a metes and bounds description by hand and see if it makes sense. Here's a real one to try:

A 1.1608 acre tract of land more or less, in the northwest quarter of the southwest quarter of Section 34, Block Y, Arnold and Barrett

Survey, Hutchinson County, Texas, said tract being more particularly described as follows:

Beginning at a ½″ iron rebar marking the southwest corner of said tract, being S. 89 degrees 55′ 08″ E. a distance of 852.31 feet from a 5/8 inch rod marking the southwest corner of the said northeast quarter of the southwest quarter of Section 34;

A Thence S. 89 degrees 55′ 08″ E. along the south line of said northeast quarter of the southwest quarter of Section 34 a distance of 224.94 feet.

B Thence N. 13 degrees 52′ 47″ W. a distance of 270.96 feet;

Thence S. 89 degrees 52′ 00″ W. a distance of 160 feet;

Thence S. 0 degrees 00′ 47″ E. a distance of 262.37 feet to a point of beginning.

If your sketch is correct, the resulting land parcel should look like the diagram appearing below. It is easy for transcription errors to creep into metes and bounds descriptions as they are copied from one document to another. Your sketch may well reveal such an error, particularly if the error is a fairly gross one (such as substituting "east" for "west" or the like).

Modern surveyors and engineers use computer programs to prepare such drawings. The program will also determine whether the description "closes"—i.e., whether the termination of the final "call" returns to the point of beginning. [If it does not, the description contains an error.] If you discover an error, don't try to correct it yourself; get the assistance of an engineer or surveyor.

4.   *Omissions and errors in property descriptions.* If a deed lacks any legal description at the time the grantor executes and delivers it, the deed is a nullity and conveys no legal title to the grantee, as the deed lacks a subject matter on which it can operate. See, e.g., West v. Witschner, 428 S.W.2d 538 (Mo. 1968). This sometimes happens when the drafter uses a deed form and inserts into the blank for the legal description the words "See attached Exhibit A"—intending to attach the legal description as an exhibit—but then forgets to attach the description prior to execution and delivery. See, e.g., Maurice v. Maurice, 131 A.D.3d 454, 15 N.Y.S.3d 133 (2015). When such an omission occurs, the grantee does not have the implied authority to fill in a description of the property. Thus, a deed that lacks any property description is void unless the grantor has given the grantee express authority to fill in the correct legal

description, or unless the grantor later takes action sufficient to ratify the deed. See, e.g., Reserve Petroleum Co. v. Hodge, 147 Tex. 115, 213 S.W.2d 456 (1948).

More frequently, the description simply contains an error—numbers in a distance call in a metes-and-bounds legal description get reversed, the wrong section is identified in a government survey description, or a lot or block number is misidentified as compared to the recorded plat. An error will not render a deed or other instrument of conveyance a nullity unless a court, pursuing an inquiry based on the words contained in the description and relevant extrinsic evidence, cannot identify the property to the exclusion of other properties. If a surveyor can locate the boundaries of the land from the description and words of reference contained in the deed, the description is sufficient. See, e.g., Ault v. Holden, 44 P.3d 781 (Utah 2002) (while distance identified in final call of metes-and-bounds description was not sufficient for legal description to close, description was valid because surveyor was able to extrapolate boundary based on description's statement that property included "approximately 17 acres"); Reverse Mortgage Solutions, Inc. v. Rahman, 415 Ill.Dec. 374, 82 N.E.3d 578 (Ct. App. 2017) (omission of three lines from legal description did not defeat sufficiency of deed where recorded deed by which grantor acquired property contained correct description). See also JPMorgan Chase Bank, N.A. v. Zhan Hua Cao, 160 A.D.3d 821, 76 N.Y.S.3d 82 (2018); In re Thompson, 799 S.E.2d 658 (N.C. Ct. App. 2017); In re Ivy, 604 B.R. 540 (Bankr. W.D. Ark. 2019). If there is a material mistake as to the identity or boundaries of the property that would otherwise defeat the sufficiency of the property description, a court may exercise its equitable authority to grant reformation in appropriate cases.

Under the weight of authority, a description by reference to a street address or a parcel number (such as a tax parcel number) can be a sufficient description if the court can determine the boundary either from the face of the deed itself or by reference to extrinsic evidence to which the deed refers. See, e.g., Bayview Loan Servicing, LLC v. Newell, 231 So.3d 588 (Fla. Ct. App. 2017); Bank of America, N.A. v. Schmitt, 823 S.E.2d 396 (N.C. Ct. App. 2018); In re Wenzel, 554 B.R. 861 (Bankr. W.D. Wis. 2016). Cf. MTC Financial Inc. v. California Dept. of Tax & Fee Admin., 41 Cal. App. 5th 742, 254 Cal. Rptr. 3d 485 (2019) (parcel number not sufficient to cure absence of precise legal description where no other extrinsic proof offered to establish boundary of land intended to be covered by mortgage). Decisions in Washington and Idaho (and the occasional decision in other states) have taken a contrary view and have concluded that a deed containing only a street address or tax parcel number does not satisfy the state's Statute of Frauds, reasoning that the precise boundary of the land that the grantor intended to transfer cannot be identified without resort to extrinsic proof. See, e.g., In re Dolven, 549 B.R. 386 (Bankr. D. Idaho 2016); Key Design Inc. v. Moser, 138 Wash.2d 875, 983 P.2d 653 (1999).

C. DELIVERY AND ESCROWS

1. DELIVERY AND TESTAMENTARY TRANSFER

The expression "signed, sealed, and delivered" once applied quite literally to deeds. As we have already seen, the grantor's signature is still required. Traditionally, a deed also had to be "sealed" to be valid. A seal was traditionally a blob of wax into which an impression of the grantor's ring or other insignia had been pressed. Later, it became permissible to simply write the word "seal" or the letters "l.s." (for *locus sigilium*, the place of the seal) beside the grantor's signature. In most states, the necessity of a seal has now been abolished. See III Am. L. of Prop. § 12.58 (1952). The requirement still appears in a few statutes, but in most states, "curative" statutes would operate to validate a deed that had been executed without the proper seal. But see Game Place, L.L.C. v. Fredericksburg 35, LLC, 813 S.E.2d 312 (Va. 2018) (invalidating a long-term lease that was not executed under seal, and concluding that the defect was not cured by state's curative statute).

Delivery continues to be a crucial requirement, and one that is frequently litigated. As between the parties, it is delivery that makes the deed operative; a deed which has not been delivered is entirely void. An undelivered deed (purloined by the grantee, for example) can be recorded and would appear from the records to be perfectly valid. The cheating grantee might then purport to make a further conveyance to a bona fide purchaser. But even if this occurs, the purchaser gets no title. See Lange v. Wyoming Nat'l Bank of Casper, 706 P.2d 659 (Wyo. 1985).

A valid delivery requires the coincident presence of two factors: an intent by the grantor to pass title immediately, and some act or behavior on the grantor's part to evidence that intent. The act is usually the manual handing over of the deed to the grantee, but any act which sufficiently evidences the requisite intent will do. Occasionally a court may even say that no act at all is necessary if the intent is sufficiently clear, but the standard doctrine is that both the intent and the act must exist. See Johnson v. Johnson, 760 S.E.2d 618 (Ga. Ct. App. 2014) (without an act of delivery, no title could pass).

Delivery is seldom an issue in the context of real estate sales (as distinguished from gifts) because the sales transaction generally is supervised by an attorney, escrow agent, title insurance company, or other professional who understands the delivery requirement. Problems tend to arise in intra-family transfers and most often, it seems, when the grantor is contemplating his or her own death.

BLANCETT V. BLANCETT

Supreme Court of New Mexico, 2004
136 N.M. 573, 102 P.3d 640

CHÁVEZ, JUSTICE. . . . This case concerns the delivery of two deeds executed by Richard Blancett, a 79 year old rancher in San Juan County. One of the deeds reserved a life estate in Richard and conveyed to [Richard's son, Linn Blancett,] a remainder in the surface estate of much of Richard's property. The other reserved a life estate in Richard and conveyed a remainder in the mineral estate of the same property to both Linn and his brother Ed. In 1993 Richard physically delivered the two deeds ("the 1993 deeds") to Linn's wife. Although Richard had some difficulty reading, he nevertheless understood the deeds, though apparently he failed to notice that the property described encompassed more land than he in fact owned. Richard testified that he had the deeds drafted solely as a "stop gap estate planning tool" until he could prepare more formal estate documents, and he indicated to Linn that he intended the delivery to be a conditional rather than an immediate conveyance. Specifically, Richard testified that he told Linn not to record the deeds unless Richard died or did something "crazy" before creating formal estate planning documents. While Linn disputes the context of this discussion and claims that the statement was made in jest, the trial judge found Richard's version to be credible and deemed Richard's statement to be an oral condition that precluded legal delivery of the deeds.

In addition to his statements to Linn around the time of conveyance, Richard testified that four years following delivery of the deeds, with Linn's knowledge, he began an extensive process of formal estate planning, including drafting a will and limited family partnership agreement, which disposed of some of the same property covered by the 1993 deeds. Richard testified that during that time he continued to believe that he owned the property at issue in the deeds. Linn did not record the 1993 deeds for over eight years, until after Richard executed his estate documents, which conveyed to Linn less property than did the deeds.

In 2001, Richard filed a complaint to nullify the 1993 deeds, claiming that because he expressly conditioned the conveyance, the physical transfer to Linn did not constitute legal delivery. . . . After finding that Richard orally conditioned the delivery of the deeds and did not intend a present conveyance, the trial court entered an order nullifying and rescinding the deeds. . . .

An effective legal delivery of a deed requires (1) intent by the grantor to make a present transfer and (2) a transfer of dominion and control. *Den Gar Enters. v. Romero*, 94 N.M. 425, 428 29, 611 P.2d 1119, 1122–23 (Ct.App.1980). It is well settled in New Mexico that a grantor's intent is central and may be determined from words, actions or surrounding circumstances during, preceding or following the execution of a deed. *Id.;* *Waters v. Blocksom*, 57 N.M. 368, 370, 258 P.2d 1135, 1136 (1953); *Martinez v. Martinez*, 101 N.M. 88, 91, 678 P.2d 1163, 1166 (1984).

Here, both parties concede that a grantee's possession of a validly executed deed ordinarily raises a presumption of legal delivery, which a grantor may rebut with evidence negating his or her intent to make a present transfer. *See Waters*, 57 N.M. at 371, 258 P.2d at 1138; *Vigil v. Sandoval*, 106 N.M. 233, 236, 741 P.2d 836, 839 (Ct.App.1987). Linn urges us, however, to hold that when a grantor physically delivers a deed to a grantee and no conditions of delivery appear on the face of the deed, the presumption becomes irrebuttable. Under such a rule, derived from common law, any oral conditions made by the grantor become void and legal delivery is absolute, regardless of the grantor's intent. See *Ritchie v. Davis*, 26 Wis.2d 636, 133 N.W.2d 312, 317 (1965) (holding that a grantor may not make a delivery in escrow or upon condition to a grantee); 11 Thompson on Real Property § 94.06(g)(2) (David A. Thomas ed., 2d ed.2002); Robert G. Natelson, Modern Law of Deeds to Real Property § 17.7 (1992).

The rule that Linn advocates stands in direct contrast to our established case law on deed delivery, which requires a threshold showing of a grantor's intent to irrevocably transfer title. *See Den Gar*, 94 N.M. at 428–29, 611 P.2d at 1122 23; *Waters*, 57 N.M. at 370, 258 P.2d at 1136; *Martinez*, 101 N.M. at 91, 678 P.2d at 1166. While Linn attempts to distinguish the above cases because they did not involve oral instructions by the grantor not to record until a future occurrence, the distinction Linn draws is inapposite. In *Den Gar*, for instance, the court upheld the trial court's finding that physical delivery to the grantee was ineffective because the grantor lacked the requisite intent to make a present transfer of title. Linn argues that *Den Gar* turned not on the grantor's intent to deliver but on the fact that the grantor had already issued a conflicting deed to his mother. The court's holding, however, clearly rested on the grantor's lack of present intent to divest himself of title in the second deed. *Id.* at 428–29, 611 P.2d at 1122–23 (considering evidence of grantor's earlier transfer to his mother, in addition to grantor's words and actions at, prior, and subsequent to delivery, and concluding that the grantor did not intend to convey the title to the subject property).

Similarly, *Waters* upheld a lower court's ruling that the grantor lacked the necessary intent to deliver a deed to his brother, the grantee, by considering extrinsic evidence such as the grantee's insistence that he would not record the deed during the grantor's lifetime. 57 N.M. at 368, 371–72, 258 P.2d at 1135, 1137–38. In summarily attributing the court's holding to the fact that the deed was found in the grantor's possession after his death, Linn overlooks the fact that possession was only one of the many factors the court examined in concluding the grantor lacked intent to make an irrevocable transfer when he passed the deed to the grantee.

Further, in *Martinez*, this Court expressly rejected the theory that there can be no conditional delivery to a grantee unless the conditions are expressed in the deed itself. 101 N.M. at 90, 678 P.2d at 1165. There the purchaser in a real estate contract argued that the deed was legally delivered when his parents, the sellers, handed it to him to deliver to a mortgagee to hold in escrow until the mortgage had been fully paid. This Court upheld the lower court's findings that the parents' statements made the delivery conditional and prevented legal delivery. *Id.* at 91, 678 P.2d at 1166. Linn argues that the holding in *Martinez* is consistent with a rule against conditional deliveries of deeds because the parents gave the deed to their son "to transmit to a depositary to hold in escrow," rather than to the grantee to hold with conditions. However, the *Martinez* court in fact relied on the same reasoning we reiterate today: a grantor's intent is controlling, regardless of whether a deed is physically transferred to a grantee. *Id.* at 90–91, 678 P.2d at 1165–66; *see also Nosker v. W. Farm Bureau Mut. Ins. Co.*, 81 N.M. 300, 301–02, 466 P.2d 866, 867–68 (1970) (holding that the fact that certain contract conditions had to be met before title could pass precluded an effective transfer, even though deed had been manually delivered). . . .

Consistent with *Martinez* and the above cases, we hold that there may be no legal delivery of a deed without intent to make a present transfer. Nonetheless, while we reject a per se rule against conditional deliveries of deeds, we hold that physical delivery of a deed to a grantee creates a presumption of legal delivery, which a grantor may then rebut with evidence that he or she lacked intent to make a present transfer. In doing so, we acknowledge the important policy concerns that Linn cites—protecting third party purchasers and creditors, and lending certainty and stability to land titles—and believe they will be adequately served by using the rule as a burden shifting device.

In support of our approach, we note that other jurisdictions that apply the common law rule seem to do so for the purpose of shifting the burden of proof regarding a grantor's intent to irrevocably deliver a deed. In most of the cases cited by Linn, even when a grantor physically delivered a deed that was unconditional on its face, the grantor was nonetheless able to offer evidence to rebut the presumption of intent to make a present transfer. *See, e.g., Walls v. Click*, 209 W.Va. 627, 550 S.E.2d 605, 612 (2001) (acknowledging that delivery requires both transfer and intent to make a present transfer, and determining that the surrounding circumstances were insufficient to rebut—and in fact supported—the grantor's prima facie proof of intent to irrevocably transfer by physically delivering the deed to grantee); *State ex rel. Pai v. Thom*, 58 Haw. 8, 563 P.2d 982, 987 88 (1977) (noting that delivery to the grantee was absolute, but then considering evidence of the surrounding circumstances to evaluate whether grantor indeed intended to make a present transfer).

This burden shifting approach, rather than a per se rule of preclusion, accommodates New Mexico's strong interest in honoring parties' intent in land transactions, a policy that finds support in modern property jurisprudence. At the same time, providing grantees the benefit of such a presumption, and requiring grantors in cases such as this to present evidence of a lack of intent in order to avoid summary judgment, may help to provide certainty and stability in land transactions—policies that Petitioner cites in favor of the common law rule. . . .

We agree with the Court of Appeals that the trial court's determination that Richard lacked the intent necessary for legal delivery was supported by substantial evidence. Specifically, the record shows that (1) Richard told Linn not to record the 1993 deeds unless Richard died without a will or did something "crazy"; (2) Richard testified as to his lack of intent to make a present transfer; (3) Richard offered evidence that he subsequently conducted formal real estate planning, including executing a will and family limited partnership, that were inconsistent with the terms in the 1993 deeds; and (4) Linn did not record the deeds for eight years, until he learned that he stood to receive less property than the deeds had provided.

Linn disputes the admissibility of much of this evidence. Specifically, he argues that Richard's subsequent estate planning is legally irrelevant to Richard's intent at the time of delivery. We are not persuaded that the evidence offered was irrelevant. *See Rothrock v. Rothrock*, 104 S.W.3d 135, 138 (Tex.Ct.App.2003) (noting the question of delivery is controlled by the grantor's intent and is answered by all the circumstances "preceding, attending and following . . . execution"). In *Rothrock*, the court excluded evidence of the grantor's subsequent behavior because under Texas law and the facts of that case, such evidence was relevant to whether the grantor had changed his mind after delivery, rather than bearing on what his intent had been at the time of delivery. We see no inconsistency between the court's reasoning in *Rothrock* and New Mexico cases on delivery. *See, e.g.*, *Den Gar*, 94 N.M. at 429, 611 P.2d at 1123 (considering evidence that grantee did not record the deed until at least a year after physical conveyance as relevant to parties' intent and understanding at the time of conveyance).

Further, Linn argues that other "documentary" evidence, which he claims may be equally evaluated by the fact finder and appellate courts, contradicts the evidence offered by Richard. For example, he points to language in a lease that Richard executed to Linn following the 1993 deeds that referred to Richard's "life estate" in the same property described in the deeds, arguing that this demonstrated Richard's belief that his delivery of the deeds had been complete. However, the trial court did not find the language in the lease to bear on Richard's intent in conveying the earlier deeds, and we leave such weighing of evidence to the fact finder.

Because we find substantial evidence to support the lower court's determination that Richard lacked the intent to make a present conveyance, we affirm.

NOTES AND QUESTIONS

1. *Physical delivery.* The physical act of delivery often is subordinated to the issue of the grantor's intent. For example, if the grantor clearly has the requisite intent, but is physically incapacitated, gestures or nods can be an adequate delivery. See Arwe v. White, 117 N.H. 1025, 381 A.2d 737 (1977). In Barker v. Nelson, 306 Ark. 204, 812 S.W.2d 477 (1991), the grantor showed the deed to the grantees and gave them photocopies of it, but kept the original. Nevertheless, the court found a delivery.

By contrast, as *Blancett* illustrates, the mere fact that a deed had been handed over does not always establish delivery because the requisite intent on the part of the grantor may be lacking. For example, there is no delivery if the deed is merely handed to the grantee so that she can inspect it, or for some other temporary purpose. See Everett v. Everett, 912 So.2d 151 (Miss. Ct. App. 2005). Similarly, if the grantor announces that he intends to remain on the land, or if he in fact remains on it after handing over the deed, or if other circumstances indicate lack of intent to make an immediate transfer, the courts may find lack of delivery. See, e.g., In re Estate of Plance, 644 Pa. 232, 175 A.3d 249 (2017); Cusick v. Meyer, 124 Or. App. 515, 863 P.2d 486 (1993); Den-Gar Enters. v. Romero, 94 N.M. 425, 611 P.2d 1119 (Ct. App. 1980); Avery v. Lillie, 260 Iowa 10, 148 N.W.2d 474 (1967).

2. *Recordation of the deed.* Courts widely hold that a recorded deed is presumed to have been delivered. See In re Estate of Hardy, 910 So.2d 1052 (Miss. 2005). While a few decisions indicate that the presumption arises only if the grantor records the deed, in most states it applies regardless of which party records. See Rausch v. Devine, 80 P.3d 733 (Alaska 2003). A few states make this presumption conclusive. See Mass. Gen. Laws Ann., ch. 183, § 5; Mattox v. Mattox, 777 So.2d 1041 (Fla. Ct. App. 2001) (recording is delivery *per se* in the absence of fraud on the grantor). In most states, however, the presumption is rebuttable. See, e.g., Hoefer v. Musser, 417 S.W.3d 330 (Mo. Ct. App. 2013); Estate of Skvorak v. Security Union Title Ins. Co., 140 Idaho 16, 89 P.3d 856 (2004). From the standpoint of title examination, the conclusive presumption is very comforting. Title searchers dislike having to worry about whether a recorded deed was validly delivered or not, because an undelivered deed is void.

If recording raises a rebuttable presumption of delivery, what sort of evidence will rebut the presumption? The cases are varied and unpredictable. Courts sometimes hold that delivery has occurred even though the grantor retained the recorded deed itself, see LeMehaute v. LeMehaute, 585 S.W.2d

276 (Mo. Ct. App. 1979), or retained possession of the land, see Hartley v. Stibor, 96 Idaho 157, 525 P.2d 352 (1974). Adding to the uncertainty, the doctrines relating to grantor retention of the deed or of possession also are sometimes stated as presumptions, leading to cases that devolve into battles over presumptions and burdens of proof.

Finally, bear in mind that although recording may help prove that a delivery has occurred, recording is not essential to the validity of any deed, and it is clear that a delivery can occur without recording, See Johannes v. Idol, 181 P.3d 574 (Kan. Ct. App. 2008); Nationstar Mortg. LLC v. O'Malley, 415 P.3d 1022 (N.M. Ct. App. 2018). Nevertheless, many laypeople mistakenly believe that the recording of the deed is necessary for a conveyance of title to occur. To what extent, if any, might this explain the result in *Blancett*?

3.   *Acceptance.* Most courts agree that acceptance of the delivery by the grantee is an essential element in the conveyance of title. Of course, acceptance is rarely an issue because the grantee ordinarily is happy to receive the land. Most courts say that acceptance is presumed, at least if the deed is beneficial to the grantee. See Collins v. Columbia Gas Transmission Corp., 188 W. Va. 460, 425 S.E.2d 136 (1992). But if acceptance of the land would be burdensome, the presumption does not apply. See Messer v. Laurel Hill Assocs., 93 N.C. App. 439, 378 S.E.2d 220 (1989). Even if the presumption applies, the grantee can overcome the presumption by expressly declining to accept the deed if she does not want it. See State v. Thomason, 845 N.W.2d 640 (S.D. 2014); Hood v. Hood, 384 A.2d 706 (Me. 1978).

4.   *Deeds conveying future interests.* For an effective delivery, the grantor must intend for the deed to be operative immediately upon delivery and acceptance. But the deed itself need not pass title to a present possessory estate; it may convey a future interest instead. Thus, the courts distinguish the following two scenarios:

- Grantor signs a deed which purports to grant fee simple title and hands it to Grantee, stating, "This grant is yours, but it does not take effect until next January 1." The deed is wholly ineffective.

- Grantor signs a deed which, by its terms, states that Grantor will remain in possession until next January 1, at which time Grantee is to have possession. Such language creates a springing executory interest in Grantee. If Grantor hands the deed to Grantee, the deed is valid, and Grantee immediately becomes the owner of that executory interest.

Will the second scenario work even if the grantor also reserves in the deed itself a power to revoke the future interest? Compare Tennant v. John Tennant Memorial Home, 167 Cal. 570, 140 P. 242 (1914) and St. Louis County Nat'l Bank v. Fielder, 364 Mo. 207, 260 S.W.2d 483 (1953) (holding that it will) with Butler v. Sherwood, 196 A.D. 603, 188 N.Y.S. 242 (1921) (retention of power to revoke prevented inter vivos transfer to grantee).

Frequently the grantor wishes to make an *ambulatory* disposition of the property—one that is not finalized until death, and that can be revoked so long as the grantor remains alive. Of course, the traditional instrument to accomplish this is a will. But the delay and cost associated with the will probate process may discourage some persons from making a will. There are other alternatives, such as joint tenancies and inter vivos trusts, that the grantor can use to make an ambulatory disposition of real property without the necessity of probate. But can the grantor simply use a deed?

WIGGILL V. CHENEY
Supreme Court of Utah, 1979
597 P.2d 1351

MAUGHAN, JUSTICE. This case involves the disposition of certain real property located in Weber County, State of Utah. The judgment before us invalidated a Warranty Deed, because of no valid delivery. We affirm. . . .

The material facts are undisputed. Specifically, on the 25th day of June, 1958, Lillian W. Cheney signed a deed to certain real property located in the city of Ogden, Utah, wherein the defendant, Flora Cheney, was named grantee. Thereafter Lillian Cheney placed this deed in a sealed envelope and deposited it in a safety deposit box in the names of herself and the plaintiff, Francis E. Wiggill. Following the deposition of the deed, Lillian Cheney advised plaintiff his name was on the safety deposit box and instructed plaintiff that upon her death, he was to go to the bank where he would be granted access to the safety deposit box and its contents. Lillian Cheney further instructed, "in that box is an envelope addressed to all those concerned. All you have to do is give them that envelope and that's all." At all times prior to her death, Lillian Cheney was in possession of a key to the safety deposit box and had sole and complete control over it. Plaintiff was never given the key to the safety deposit box.

Following the death of Lillian Cheney, plaintiff, after gaining access to the safety deposit box, delivered the deed contained therein to Flora Cheney, the named grantee.

The sole issue presented here on appeal is whether or not the acts of plaintiff constitute a delivery of the deed such as will render it enforceable as a valid conveyance.

The rule is well settled that a deed, to be operative as a transfer of the ownership of land, or an interest or estate therein, must be delivered. It was equally settled in this and the vast majority of jurisdictions that a valid delivery of a deed requires it pass beyond the control or domain of the grantor. The requisite relinquishment of control or dominion over the deed may be established, notwithstanding the fact the deed is in possession of the grantor at her death, by proof of facts which tend to show delivery had been made with the intention to pass title and to explain the grantor's subsequent possession. However, in order for a delivery effectively to transfer title, the grantor must part with possession of the deed or the right to retain it.

The evidence presented in the present case establishes Lillian Cheney remained in sole possession and control of the deed in question until her death. Because no actual delivery of the deed occurred prior to the death of the grantor, the subsequent manual delivery of the deed by plaintiff to defendant conveyed no title to the property described therein, or any part thereof, or any of its contents.

NOTES AND QUESTIONS

1.   *No delivery if the grantor's intent is testamentary.* Lillian obviously wanted the real estate to pass to Flora on Lillian's death. Why should the law stand in the way of that result? The answer lies in the law's extensive formality requirements for a valid will; at least two witnesses must sign in the presence of the testator and each other. This requirement serves an important anti-fraud purpose; almost invariably, when the authenticity of a will is disputed, the testator is dead and cannot testify to her intent.

Could the deed in *Wiggill* be upheld as a will? There are two obvious problems. First, it does not "read" like a will—on its face, it appears to convey title to the property immediately and not at Lillian's death. Second, it did not have the signatures of two witnesses as required under the will statute.

Could the deed be upheld on an agency theory? After Lillian died, the plaintiff (executor of Lillian's estate) handed the deed to Flora. Was the plaintiff acting as Lillian's agent, consummating the transaction by delivery? Does the fact that Lillian was dead prevent this argument? Cf. Womack v. Stegner, 293 S.W.2d 124 (Tex. Civ. App. 1956) (where grantor delivered deed with grantee's name left blank, but authorized the person receiving delivery to fill in any name he wished, the agency was irrevocable and could be exercised after the grantor died).

2.   *What actions evidence an intent to make a present delivery?* Suppose Lillian had given Flora a key to the safe-deposit box during Lillian's lifetime. Would this have effected delivery? See, e.g., Estate of Dittus, 497 N.W.2d 415 (N.D. 1993) (no delivery; delivery of one of two keys "is inconclusive, without other evidence, of intent to presently transfer title"). What if the safe-deposit box had been rented in the joint names of Lillian and Flora, and that both had keys from the outset? Would Lillian's placing the deed in the box constitute delivery? See Moseley v. Zieg, 180 Neb. 810, 146 N.W.2d 72 (1966) (finding no delivery on similar facts). By contrast, what if Lillian had, during her life, placed the box exclusively in Flora's name? See Estate of Blettell v. Snider, 114 Or. App. 162, 834 P.2d 505 (1992) (finding delivery occurred).

3.   *Oral reservation of a life estate.* Suppose the grantor hands the deed to the grantee directly, but simultaneously makes an oral statement that it is to be effective only on the grantor's death, and that the grantor will keep the

DEEDS AND TITLES

land during his life. As we have already suggested, such conduct is often taken as evidence that the grantor does not intend a *present* transfer of any interest, and thus that nothing passes at all. See, e.g., Broomfield v. Broomfield, 242 Ark. 355, 413 S.W.2d 657 (1967). By contrast, it is perfectly clear that the grantor can reserve a life estate *in the deed itself*, and make a valid delivery that will convey title subject to the retained estate. See, e.g., Farina v. Bastianich, 116 A.D.3d 546, 984 N.Y.S.2d 46 (2014); Lanford v. Cornett, 415 P.2d 984 (Okla. 1966).

4. *Death escrow.* A common variant is the handing of the deed by the grantor to a third party, with instructions to give it to the grantee on the grantor's death. This arrangement is sometimes termed a "death escrow" and perhaps surprisingly, it can work. The courts have had a good deal of difficulty deciding which delivery (to the third party, or to the grantee) is the one that really counts—but when they select the latter, they usually say that it "relates back" to the date of the former; see Pipes v. Sevier, 694 S.W.2d 918 (Mo. Ct. App. 1985). [Otherwise, the courts are put in the awkward position of sustaining a delivery by a dead grantor.] The death escrow is an apparent exception to the usual rule (which we will study presently) that for a "true" escrow with relation-back effect to exist, there must be an underlying contract of sale.

The death escrow will be ineffective if the grantor reserves the right to revoke the deed (whether he exercises that right or not), because such a power would indicate an intent not to make a present transfer. See Albrecht v. Brais, 324 Ill. App. 3d 188, 754 N.E.2d 396 (2001); Rausch v. Devine, 80 P.3d 733 (Alaska 2003); III Am. L. Prop. § 12.67 (1952). Of course, if the third party is a trusted friend of the grantor, and if the grantee is not told about the deed, the grantor has a practical power to revoke whether it is stated explicitly or not. But that fact will not stand in the way of the validity of the arrangement. See Vasquez v. Vasquez, 973 S.W.2d 330 (Tex. Ct. App. 1998).

The usual judicial interpretation of the death escrow is that the grantor has the right to possess the land for the remainder of his life, despite the fact that the language of the deed itself does not expressly reserve a life estate, and that the grantee immediately obtains title subject to the retained life estate. See Garrett v. Garrett, 302 P.3d 1061 (Idaho 2013); Herman v. Mortensen, 72 Cal. App. 2d 413, 164 P.2d 551 (1945); Ferrell v. Stinson, 233 Iowa 1331, 11 N.W.2d 701 (1943). How can this result be explained? Why didn't the court in *Wiggill* treat Lillian's actions as creating a death escrow?

Do not confuse the death escrow cases with the cases described in Note 3, where the grantor orally imposes a condition but manually hands the deed to the grantee directly. Likewise, do not confuse the death escrow cases with cases where the grantor makes an unconditional delivery to a person who is the agent of the grantee. There is no doubt that a delivery to the grantee's agent (for example, the grantee's attorney) is effective. See DiMaio v. Musso, 2000 Pa. Super 326, 762 A.2d 363 (2000). Even a delivery to the grantor's own attorney can suffice if the attorney is also instructed to record the deed. See Caruso v. Parkos, 637 N.W.2d 351 (Neb. 2002).

5.   *"Beneficiary deeds" or "transfer on death" deeds.* The desire of people to leave their land to others at death without making a will or a trust is obvious from the materials above. Why not let them do it? That is precisely the purpose of the "beneficiary" or "transfer on death" (TOD) deed. At this writing, over twenty U.S. jurisdictions have authorized TOD deeds.

A TOD deed is executed and recorded during the lifetime of the grantor, but (by its express terms) it becomes effective only at the grantor's death. Until that time, the deed creates no interest of any kind, present or future, in the grantee. The grantor can revoke the deed at any time before death, typically by recording a notice of revocation or by deeding the property to someone else prior to death. See, e.g., Sheils v. Wright, 51 Kan. App. 2d 814, 357 P.3d 294 (2015). If the deed is not revoked, it will pass whatever interest the grantor holds in the property at the time of death, subject to any mortgages, liens, or other encumbrances imposed on the property during the grantor's life.

Assume that Utah had enacted a TOD deed statute at the time of the actions in *Wiggill*. Would it still make sense for a court to hold, as in *Wiggill*, that Lillian's deed is void because her intent is testamentary? Or does the existence of the TOD statute signal that the policy underlying the Statute of Wills, with its accompanying formalities, is no longer important enough to demand strict adherence?

2.   DEFECTIVE DEEDS

If there is a legal defect in the drafting, execution, or delivery of a deed, we need to consider what legal consequences will ensue. If the error is simply a mistake or inadvertence, equity will reform the deed at the instance of one of the parties. If the defect is very minor, such as the omission of a seal or an acknowledgment (in the few states that require them for validity), it is often possible to find a "curative act" passed by the legislature which restores such deeds to full validity, either as soon as the deed is recorded or after the passage of a few years. In some circumstances, a minor mistake will have no impact whatsoever on the validity of the deed. See, e.g., Samuels v. Garlick, 49 N.E.3d 1116 (Ind. Ct. App. 2016) (mortgage was valid to cover mortgagors' land, even though it mistakenly described more land than mortgagors actually owned).

Our concern here is with defects that are more substantial, including such matters as the grantor's incapacity and the grantee's fraud or forgery. Here there are two possible classifications: the deed may be either *void* or *voidable.* In either case, if the grantee has not made a further conveyance, a court will set aside the deed if the grantor requests. The distinction between a void deed and a voidable deed becomes critical if the grantee has subsequently transferred the land to a bona fide purchaser (BFP) who has paid value and has taken title from the grantee without notice of the defect.

If the court treats the defect as rendering the deed void, even the BFP will have no title. If, however, the deed is merely voidable, then the title will be unassailable in the hands of the BFP.[3]

Of all the categories of defects in deeds, perhaps the one as to which the law is clearest is forgery—a false signature, or an addition, deletion, or alteration to the essential language of the deed after it is signed. Such a deed is void, and unavailing even in the hands of a BFP who has no notice of the forgery. See Zurstrassen v. Stonier, 786 So. 2d 65 (Fla. Ct. App. 2001); Northlake Dev. L.L.C. v. BankPlus, 60 So. 3d 792 (Miss. 2011); Scott D. Erler, D.D.S. Profit Sharing Plan v. Creative Fin. & Investments, L.L.C., 203 P.3d 744 (Mont. 2009) (forged deed void, but could be ratified by purported grantor); Shvartser v. Lekser, 308 F. Supp.3d 260 (D.D.C. 2018) (deed of trust executed under forged power of attorney void); Faison v. Lewis, 25 N.Y.3d 220, 32 N.E.3d 400 (2015) (subsequent mortgage given by grantee of forged deed likewise void); Nationstar Mortg., LLC v. Fuller, 182 A.D.3d 531, 122 N.Y.S.3d 628 (2020) (recording of forged instrument does not transform it into document capable of establishing a valid property interest).[4]

Sometimes, the grantee procures the delivery of a deed that bears the grantor's authentic signature, but through fraud. In this situation, the effect of the deed will depend on the type of fraud. One type, often called "fraud in the inducement," involves misrepresentations which persuade the grantor to sign the deed, such as the tender of a worthless check or false statements about the grantee's financial position. In such cases courts nearly always hold the deed voidable, not void. See Malcom v. Wilson, 534 So. 2d 241 (Ala. 1988) (grantee induced grantor to sign deed by falsely asserting that she was pregnant with his child and by threatening him with legal action and bodily harm).

By contrast, the fraud may consist of a false statement to the grantor about the nature of the instrument itself (e.g., telling the grantor it is a letter rather than a deed), or an act such as slipping a deed in among other

---

[3] If the grantor continues to possess the land, the grantor's very presence will serve as notice to future buyers; one who fails to make inquiry of the person in possession will generally be held to have whatever knowledge a reasonable inquiry would have produced. Hence, it is nearly impossible for a subsequent purchaser to become a BFP in such circumstances. See, e.g., Houston v. Mentelos, 318 So.2d 427 (Fla. Ct. App. 1975); Stevens v. American Sav. Inst., Inc., 289 Or. 349, 613 P.2d 1057 (1980).

[4] The same principle is true when someone prepares and records a forged mortgage release—the release is void and the mortgagee's lien continues to be effective, even as against a BFP. See, e.g., 1601 Bay LLC v. Wilmington Sav. Fund Society, FSB, 282 So.3d 1027 (Fla. Ct. App. 2019); Zimmer v. Fryer, 190 La. 814, 183 So. 166 (1938); Life Ins. Co. v. Cates, 193 N.C. 456, 137 S.E. 324 (1927). Strangely (and wrongly), the occasional decision has protected the BFP in this situation. See, e.g., Schiavon v. Arnaudo Bros., 84 Cal. App. 4th 374, 100 Cal. Rptr. 2d 801 (2000); Bank of New York v. Langman, 986 N.E.2d 749 (Ill. Ct. App. 2013). Some courts have held that the BFP will be protected if the mortgagee had reason to know of the fraudulent release but failed to take action before the BFP acquired its interest. See, e.g., Sunrise Sav. & Loan Ass'n v. Giannetti, 524 So.2d 697 (Fla. Ct. App. 1988).

innocuous papers which the grantor is signing. Such behavior is sometimes called "fraud in the execution" or "fraud in the factum." Here the cases diverge, with some holding the deed void, especially if the grantor is old, illiterate, disabled, confused, or has reason to place particular reliance on the trustworthiness of the grantee. See Silva v. Napier, 528 S.W.3d 297 (Ark. Ct. App. 2017); Tafolla v. Tafolla, 2011 WL 1466472 (Cal. Ct. App. 2011); Valle v. Washington Mut. Bank, 2009 WL 1919392 (Cal. Ct. App. 2009); Houston v. Mentelos, 318 So. 2d 427 (Fla. Ct. App. 1975); Hoffer v. Crawford, 65 N.W.2d 625 (N.D. 1954). Such cases seem to the courts to be tantamount to forgery. But if the grantor is competent and alert, and deals with the grantee at arm's length, the court is more likely to paste the "voidable" label on the deed, protecting the later BFP. The court may even call the grantor negligent for his failure to examine closely the documents he signed. Compare Dines v. Ultimo, 532 So. 2d 1131 (Fla. Ct. App. 1988) (grantors were told they were signing credit references; conveyance valid in hands of a BFP) with Fronning v. Blume, 429 N.W.2d 310 (Minn. Ct. App. 1988) (grantors were told they were signing a description of their farm; conveyance held void).

Finally, there are cases in which the grantor knows that the instrument is a deed, but its contents or details are falsely represented to him by the grantee. Here, the usual result is like that of fraud in the inducement, and the deed is merely voidable, even if the grantor is illiterate or feeble. See Jenkins v. Maint., Inc., 76 N.C. App. 110, 332 S.E.2d 90 (1985); McCoy v. Love, 382 So. 2d 647 (Fla. 1979).

Lack of delivery is the other defect which traditionally makes a deed absolutely void. But here too, the desire of the courts to protect the BFP is sometimes irrepressible. For example, in Webb v. Stewart, 255 Or. 523, 469 P.2d 609 (1970), the grantor handed the deed to the grantee to place in escrow; the escrow company was expected to deliver the deed later when the grantee paid for the land. Instead, the grantee took the deed to the courthouse and recorded it, and then gave a mortgage on it. The court thought the deed should be deemed voidable rather than void. Ultimately, it made no difference in the outcome because the mortgagee had constructive notice of the grantor's continued interest from his possession of the property and hence was held not to be a BFP without notice of the deed's defect.

Numerous other types of defects are fairly uniformly held to make deeds merely voidable. These include the incompetency or incapacity of the grantor (unless it is a matter of public record), duress or undue influence exercised by the grantee, and infancy. See, e.g., Matter of LeBovici, 171 Misc. 2d 604, 655 N.Y.S.2d 305 (1997); First Interstate Bank v. First Wyoming Bank, 762 P.2d 379 (Wyo. 1988). Contra: Scott v. Nelson, 820 So. 2d 23 (Miss. Ct. App. 2002) (deed by grantor who was incompetent and under conservatorship held void); James B. Nutter & Co. v. Black, 225 Md.

App. 1, 123 A.3d 535 (2015) (mortgage signed by disabled borrower without consent of record guardian held void). See also Borries v. Goshen Mortg., LLC, 219 So.3d 593 (Miss. Ct. App. 2017) (original deed of trust was not void for lack of named beneficiary where it was later corrected to identify beneficiary, but original did not give constructive notice for priority purposes). All in all, the courts seem to be drifting toward an increasingly pro-BFP position. Is there anything wrong with that? Should the rule simply be that any recorded deed is conclusively presumed good if necessary to protect a BFP? Or should forgery be the sole exception to such a rule?

3.   ESCROW CLOSINGS

An *escrow* may be used to effect the closing of a real estate sale and the delivery of a deed. Literally, an escrow is a delivery of a deed by the grantor to an independent third party with instructions that it be delivered to the grantee following the occurrence of certain stated conditions. The deed is "made out" to the grantee, not the escrow agent. The conditions may be as complex as the grantor desires, but the most common is the payment to the escrow agent by the grantee of the remainder of the cash purchase price. The escrow agent is usually responsible for disbursing the funds thus deposited in an appropriate manner—i.e., by paying off and discharging any existing mortgages and other encumbrances to which the buyer is not taking subject, by sending checks to the title insurer, surveyor, property inspector, and other providers of ancillary services in connection with the transfer (including the escrow agent's own fee), and finally by remitting the balance of the funds to the seller.

There is no legal requirement that any real estate transaction be closed through escrow, and in some areas of the nation escrows are almost unheard of. They are widely used in larger urban areas throughout much of the country, and are virtually universal for property sales in the West Coast and Mountain West states.

The escrow concept is useful in several respects. First, it places a person or entity with considerable expertise in the role of computing the flows of funds, assembling and recording the necessary documents, and performing the other mechanical (but rather complex) functions necessary to complete a real estate sale. Of course, other entities such as lawyers and lenders could do this as well, and do so in many areas. But the escrow has further advantages. It avoids the inconvenience of a face-to-face closing, in which all of the parties must gather in the same room to "pass the papers." When an escrow is used, the documents and checks may be signed by the parties at any convenient time and left with the escrow agent. Then on the designated closing date, once all conditions are satisfied, the agent "closes" the escrow simply by recording the conveyances.

The escrow device provides an easy method of making sure that the seller's title remains clear down to the very moment of closing, because the escrow agent can perform a "down-date" of the title search just before recording, and can refrain from closing if the search reveals a recently recorded adverse conveyance. In jurisdictions that do not use escrows, there is often a gap of a few days or a week between the time of the title search and the closing. Sometimes lawyers in these jurisdictions deal with the problem by actually closing in or near the courthouse, and doing a title down-date immediately before or after the closing, but this can be inconvenient as well.

Finally, if the legal prerequisites are met, the escrow has a "relation back" feature. The ultimate delivery to the grantee by the escrow agent is usually deemed to relate back to the date the grantor placed the deed in escrow. Particularly in cases of the grantor's intervening incompetence or death, "relation back" makes the delivery valid. In jurisdictions which do not use escrows, such events are not necessarily fatal to the transaction, but they can bog the grantee down in a search for the grantor's heirs or devisees (if the grantor has died) or the appointment of a guardian or conservator (if the grantor has become incompetent). Escrow makes these efforts unnecessary.

Despite these advantages, escrows are a mixed blessing. On the West Coast, where "independent" escrow companies (having no other connection with the transaction) are commonly used, the cost of the escrow company's services can be very substantial. Plainly the use of independent escrow agents can contribute to high overall settlement costs. It is probably more efficient to use an entity already involved in the transaction, such as the lending institution which is providing the financing or the title insurer.

It is common, and certainly a desirable practice, for the parties to submit written escrow instructions to the escrow agent. They may each submit their own, or may both sign the same set of instructions. It is important, of course, that there be no conflict between the instructions of the buyer and the seller, and no conflict between the escrow instructions and the contract of sale.

NOTES AND QUESTIONS

1. *Additional readings.* The best treatment of escrows (although now somewhat dated and oriented toward Illinois law) is Mann, Escrows—Their Use and Value, 1949 U. Ill. L. F. 398. See also Segal, Working With Escrow Agreements, Prac. Real Est. Law., Vol. 16, No. 1, at 35 (2000); Note, Escrow Agreements, 8 Miami L.Q. 75 (1953); Note, Survey of Escrow—A Legal Adolescent, 8 Ark. L. Rev. 164 (1954).

2. *Attorneys as escrow agents.* The escrow agent must be a third party, and not one of the parties to the transaction itself. There seems to be no legal

objection in most jurisdictions to an attorney for one or both of the parties serving as the escrowee. See Fisk v. Peoples Liberty Bank & Trust Co., 570 S.W.2d 657 (Ky. Ct. App. 1978). But see Patel v. Gannaway, 726 F.2d 382 (8th Cir. 1984) (court cautioned lawyers about the ethical risks of serving as an escrowee while at the same time representing one of the parties as an attorney). Do you think this is a good practice? Can you envision situations where there is an irreconcilable conflict between the duty of fairness to both parties that an escrow agent is expected to fulfill and the attorney's professional responsibilities in the representation of her or his client?

3. *Requirements and characteristics of a "true" escrow.* To have a "true" escrow (the significance of which will be discussed below), there are at least two additional requirements. First, the grantor, when depositing the deed with the escrow agent, must not reserve any power to recall it. See Malcolm v. Tate, 125 Or. 419, 267 P. 527 (1928); Loubat v. Kipp & Young, 9 Fla. 60 (1860). Second, the parties must have entered into an enforceable contract of sale. See Merry v. County Bd. of Educ., 264 Ala. 411, 87 So. 2d 821 (1956); Johnson v. Wallden, 342 Ill. 201, 173 N.E. 790 (1930); Jozefowicz v. Leickem, 174 Wis. 475, 182 N.W. 729 (1921).

If a "true" escrow exists, the most important result is that the second delivery (to the grantee) will relate back in time to the first delivery (to the escrowee), and hence will be valid irrespective of the grantor's intervening death or incompetence. See, e.g., Donnelly v. Robinson, 406 S.W.2d 595 (Mo. 1966); Morris v. Clark, 100 Utah 252, 112 P.2d 153 (1941). This "relation back" is obviously fictitious, and will not inevitably apply in all situations. Its purpose is to prevent injustice and effectuate the intention of the parties. See Clodfelter v. Van Fossan, 394 Ill. 29, 67 N.E.2d 182 (1946); Mann, supra note 1, at 413.

In addition, a "true" escrow puts the deed beyond the grantor's control pending the second delivery. The grantor has no right to withdraw it from the escrow, and if he or she purports to give a second deed to another grantee who has notice of the escrow, that deed will pass nothing. See Chaffin v. Harpham, 166 Ark. 578, 266 S.W. 685 (1924); DeBoer v. Oakbrook Home Ass'n, Inc., 218 Neb. 813, 359 N.W.2d 768 (1984). This insulation of the grantor from the deed applies only so long as the underlying sales contract remains enforceable. If the underlying sales contract is terminated by agreement or breached by the purchaser, the grantor can then get the deed back.

If the purported escrow is not a "true" escrow, there is no relation back; the grantor may reclaim the deed from the escrow at any time prior to the second delivery, presumably whether any express right to do so has been reserved or not. Nonetheless, the escrow is not void, and if the grantor remains alive and competent, and makes no attempt to withdraw the deed, there is no reason why the second delivery should not constitute a valid transfer of title.

It is plausible that relation back should not apply if the grantor has a power to recall the deed; on those facts, we cannot really be certain that the grantor intended to go through with the transfer until it actually occurred. But the justification for the requirement that there be an underlying enforceable contract is more questionable. Would any policy be disserved if even pure gifts via escrow, with no contract of sale at all, were allowed to relate back? [Indeed, they are in the limited context of the death escrow, discussed earlier in this section.] See Ralph Aigler, Is a Contract Necessary to Create an Effective Escrow?, 16 Mich. L. Rev. 569 (1918) (criticizing the contract requirement).

4.   *Escrow instructions and the Statute of Frauds.* Somewhat ironically, the very presence of an escrow may make a contract enforceable. If the contract was oral, the written escrow instructions may supply the requisite memorandum of the parties' agreement so as to satisfy the Statute of Frauds. See Wood Bldg. Corp. v. Griffitts, 164 Cal. App. 2d 559, 330 P.2d 847 (1958). The Statute of Frauds does not apply to the escrow instructions themselves, because they do not constitute a contract for the sale of realty. Thus, they are enforceable though oral; see Lewis v. Shawnee State Bank, 226 Kan. 41, 596 P.2d 116 (1979); Young v. Bishop, 88 Ariz. 140, 353 P.2d 1017 (1960). Moreover, the courts are fairly lenient in supplying omitted terms or correcting confusing instructions, even if there is a writing. See, e.g., Animalfeeds Int'l Inc. v. Banco Espirito Santo e Comercial de Lisboa, 101 Misc. 2d 379, 420 N.Y.S.2d 954 (1979); Shaheen v. American Title Ins. Co., 120 Ariz. 505, 586 P.2d 1317 (Ct. App. 1978) (escrowee had authority to disburse sale proceeds to seller, although instructions did not so state). Of course, the best practice is to prepare careful, thorough written instructions.

Yet written escrow instructions can also pose problems. Suppose there is a conflict between the original contract and the instructions; which should prevail? If the contract did not make time of the essence, but the escrow instructions do, what is the result? Should lawyers advise incorporating the contract by reference into the instructions, or combining both into a single document?

5.   *When does title pass?* The very essence of an escrow is that the "closing" (i.e., the second delivery) cannot occur until various conditions have been met. Suppose they have been met, but the escrow agent has not yet recorded the deed or manually delivered it to the grantee. Has legal title passed? The question might be important if, for example, a creditor of the grantor attempts to attach the property at that point. See Lowry v. C.I.R., 171 F. App'x 6 (9th Cir. 2006); Matter of Berkley Multi-Units, Inc., 69 B.R. 638 (Bankr. M.D. Fla. 1987); and Sturgill v. Indus. Painting Corp., 82 Nev. 61, 410 P.2d 759 (1966) (all holding title passes when the last condition occurs, irrespective of recording or physical delivery). But see TDNI Props., LLC v. Saratoga Glen Builders, LLC, 80 A.D.3d 852, 914 N.Y.S.2d 746 (2011) and Roberts v. Osburn, 589 P.2d 985 (Kan. Ct. App. 1979) (title passes only when escrow agent delivers deed). Does the doctrine of relation back make this point irrelevant?

6.   *Duties of escrow agents.* An escrow agent occupies a fiduciary position with respect to the parties, and is liable for negligence or breach of instructions. See, e.g., Banville v. Schmidt, 37 Cal. App. 3d 92, 112 Cal. Rptr. 126 (1974)

(negligence); Miller v. Craig, 27 Ariz. App. 789, 558 P.2d 984 (1976) (failure to follow instructions). Cf. Jafari v. F.D.I.C., 2 F.Supp.3d 1125 (S.D.Cal. 2014) (no duty owed to third party who expected to receive proceeds of escrow).

Closer questions arise when the escrow agent fails to disclose to one of the parties information it obtains from the other party, or from its general business dealings. See Karen Jacobsen, California Escrow Agents: A Duty to Disclose Known Fraud?, 17 Pac. L. J. 309 (1985). This issue is most common when the escrowee is also a title insurance company and has particular knowledge of title problems with the property, but has not been specifically instructed to investigate the title or write an insurance policy on it. See, e.g., Axley v. Transamerica Title Ins. Co., 88 Cal. App. 3d 1, 151 Cal. Rptr. 570 (1978) (no duty to warn seller that she was undersecured by deeds of trust); Shaheen v. American Title Ins. Co., 120 Ariz. 505, 586 P.2d 1317 (App. 1978) (no duty to inform party of title defects, where no title insurance purchased); Gordon v. New Mexico Title Co., 77 N.M. 217, 421 P.2d 433 (1966) (no duty to investigate presence of unfiled mechanic's liens).

There is significant authority that an escrow agent who discovers fraud, or facts which suggest fraud, by one party has a duty to disclose them to the other party. See Mark Props. v. Nat'l Title Co., 116 Nev. 1158, 14 P.3d 507 (2000); Manley v. Ticor Title Ins. Co., 168 Ariz. 568, 816 P.2d 225 (1991); Sargeant & Hill, Recent Developments in Title Insurance Law, 36 Tort & Ins. L.J. 605 (2001). Do you think escrow agents should be forced into the "traffic cop" mode by the courts?

Suppose the escrowee purports (in the printed instructions) to exculpate itself from liability for negligence or failure to follow instructions. A California court held such an attempt ineffective in Akin v. Business Title Corp., 264 Cal. App. 2d 153, 70 Cal. Rptr. 287 (1968). Should this result follow if the escrowee is not generally in the escrow business, and is merely serving as an accommodation to the parties?

7. *Risk of loss from an escrow agent's default.* If an escrow agent absconds with the funds and is unavailable for suit, who stands the loss? The usual answer depends on whether title has passed or not. If it has, the money belongs to the seller, who must stand the loss; if title has not passed, it was the buyer's money that was stolen. See, e.g., In re Brown, 28 Fed. Appx. 725 (9th Cir. 2002) (Washington law); Bixby Ranch Co. v. United States, 35 Fed. Cl. 674 (1996); Flores, A Comparison of the Rules and Rationales for Allocating Risks Arising in Realty Sales Using Executory Sale Contracts and Escrows, 59 Mo. L. Rev. 307 (1994). Here is a situation in which the time of passage of title, discussed in note 5, clearly matters! The same rule usually applies to closings handled by attorneys or others which are not technically escrows, but which raise the same problems when the closing agent decamps with the dollars. See, e.g., Lawyers Title Ins. Corp. v. Edmar Constr. Co., Inc., 294 A.2d 865 (D.C.

1972). Does this insistence in placing all of the loss on one party or the other make sense? After all, the crook was really employed by both parties.[5]

If title insurance is being issued in connection with the escrow, the title insurer may provide a "closing protection letter" to the insured, in effect promising to indemnify the insured if the escrow holder embezzles funds. See, e.g., GE Capital Mortg. Servs., Inc. v. Privetera, 346 N.J. Super. 424, 788 A.2d 324 (App. Div. 2002) (holding that such a letter did not protect the holder of a prior mortgage, who was not being insured by the title company).

8.   *Wrongful delivery by escrow agents.* Suppose the escrow conditions have not yet been fulfilled, but the grantee somehow obtains the deed from the escrowee—e.g., by theft, fraud, or bribery. Everyone would agree that the grantee cannot claim title, for there is no intent on the part of the grantor to make a delivery yet. See Allen v. Allen Title Co., 77 N.M. 796, 427 P.2d 673 (1967). But if the grantee nevertheless records the deed and immediately resells to a bona fide purchaser, who will prevail as between the BFP and the grantor? From the BFP's viewpoint the title appears perfect (assuming the grantor is not in possession of the land). Is the grantor equally innocent? To put the question slightly differently, is the purported transfer void or voidable? The prevailing view (from which there is considerable dissent, both scholarly and judicial) is that the deed is void, just as in the case of an undelivered deed stolen directly from the grantor. See, e.g., Miguel v. Belzeski, 797 F. Supp. 636 (N.D. Ill. 1992) (Illinois law); Clevenger v. Moore, 126 Okla. 246, 259 P. 219, 54 A.L.R. 1237 (1927); Watts v. Archer, 252 Iowa 592, 107 N.W.2d 549 (1961). The contrary cases are collected in Am. Jur. 2d Escrow § 34 (2014). Certainly, if the grantor later ratifies the wrongful delivery, or fails to act in a timely fashion after learning of it, a court may properly protect the BFP.

D.   TITLE COVENANTS IN DEEDS

With this section we begin our consideration of *title assurance*—the set of mechanisms that buyers of land use to: (1) learn in advance whether their sellers have and can convey the quality of title they claim; and (2) obtain recovery if the title, after the transfer, turns out not to be as represented. This section addresses the deed covenant, which is a statement in (or a legal inference from) the deed itself that gives the grantee contractual rights against the grantor if the title is not as promised. In subsequent sections we will examine three other mechanisms: (1) the recording system; (2) the Torrens or title registration system; and (3) title insurance.

---

[5]   Where the escrow or closing agent is a lawyer for one of the parties, the normal loss allocation rule mentioned above might not be followed. In Johnson v. Schultz, 691 S.E.2d 701 (N.C. 2010), the attorney embezzled the sale proceeds after the closing occurred. The court noted that the custom in North Carolina was for the attorney to represent the buyer, even though he might also prepare a deed or perform other services for the seller as well. The court also thought the buyer was in a better position than the seller to protect against the lawyer's default by obtaining a closing protection letter from the title insurance company. Hence, the court imposed the loss on the buyer.

Of the title assurance mechanisms in use in the United States, the deed covenant is the crudest and least effective. It provides the grantee with no information regarding the grantor's title except that which the grantee or his or her attorney may bring to bear through other mechanisms of title investigation. While a deed covenant nominally allocates to the grantor responsibility for the risk of undisclosed and unexcepted title defects, the disappointed grantee only has a claim against the grantor for damages for breach of the covenant—a claim for which the grantee may ultimately obtain only an uncollectible judgment.

For these reasons, few buyers of real estate today rely exclusively on deed covenants for title assurance. But most deeds delivered in sale transactions do contain covenants of title, and suits on them do continue to be brought and litigated. This often occurs when the grantee has obtained title insurance; if the title insurer pays the insured grantee for the loss the grantee suffers due to a title defect, the title insurer becomes subrogated to the grantee's rights and may then sue the grantor on the deed covenant. See Kelly v. National Attorneys Title Assurance Fund, 955 N.E.2d 224 (Ind. Ct. App. 2011).

Of course, a deed may contain no covenants of title at all. Such a deed is termed a "quitclaim" deed, and no covenants of title are implied in it. As the Texas Supreme Court explained:

> Quitclaim deeds are commonly used to convey "interests of an unknown extent or claims having a dubious basis." A quitclaim deed conveys upon its face doubts about the grantor's interest; any buyer is necessarily put on inquiry as to those doubts. Thus, a quitclaim deed *without warranty of title* cannot be a warranty (or "misrepresentation") of title.

Geodyne Energy Income Production Partn. I-E v. Newton Corp., 161 S.W.3d 482, 487 (Tex. 2005) (emphasis in original). Note carefully that a quitclaim deed is just as effective as a warranty deed in actually transferring *whatever title the grantor has*. The only distinction between warranty deeds and quitclaim deeds lies in the remedies (or lack of remedies) the grantee has if the title fails; there is no difference in the quality of the title conveyed.

Instead of a quitclaim, which contains no covenants of title, the grantor may include some covenants. American law generally recognizes six distinct types of title covenants in deeds. A "full warranty" deed (something of a misnomer, because the term "warranty" is also the name of one of the six specific covenants) will include all six. In some states, it is customary to spell out each warranty in detail on the face of the deed, but in many jurisdictions there are statutes that impose certain deed covenants whenever specific words (like "grant," "convey and warrant," or the like) are used in a deed.

The first three of the six possible covenants are usually termed "present" covenants, because they can be breached (if at all) only at the moment the deed is delivered. These are:

Covenant of seisin. "Seisin" is a now-obsolete medieval term that represented the concept of legal possession in law. Hence, the covenant of seisin is a promise by the grantor that he or she owns and is in possession of the land, although not necessarily free of encumbrances. See Estate of Patterson v. Palmetto Bank, 646 S.E.2d 885 (S.C. Ct. App. 2007). A few states treat it as a covenant that the grantor possesses the land, whether or not by legal right, but this is a minority view. The distinction is important if the land is transferred while an adverse possessor or holdover tenant is in possession. Compare Boatmen's Nat'l Bank v. Dandy, 804 S.W.2d 783 (Mo. Ct. App. 1990) (deed covenants of title are not violated by presence of an adverse possessor) with Double L. Props., Inc. v. Crandall, 51 Wash. App. 149, 751 P.2d 1208 (1988) (presence of adverse possessor breaches covenant of seisin).

Right to convey. This covenant usually overlaps with the covenant of seisin, but not always. For example, a grantor who is attorney in fact for the owner of the land under a valid power of attorney would have the right to convey, but would not have seisin.

Covenant against encumbrances. This is a promise that title is passing free of mortgages, liens, easements, future interests in others, covenants running with the land, or similar interests. Note that in many cases, the grantee is aware of and intends to take the real estate "subject to" some encumbrances. The careful lawyer who prepares a deed for a grantor containing this covenant will list on the face of the deed, as "subject to" exceptions to the covenant, those encumbrances that the grantee has agreed to accept, and hence that cannot be a basis for a later suit on this covenant.

The next three types of covenants are usually termed "future" covenants, because they are by definition breached only when an *eviction* of the grantee occurs, and this may occur some time after the delivery of the deed itself.

Warranty and *quiet enjoyment*. In substance, these two covenants are identical. They amount to a promise by the grantor to compensate the grantee for the loss if the title turns out to be defective or subject to an encumbrance, and the grantee thereby suffers an eviction.

Further assurances. This is a promise by the grantor to execute such further documents as may be necessary to perfect the grantee's title at a future date. For example, if the grantor did not have title at the time he made the original deed to the grantee, but later obtained title, the grantor could be compelled to execute a further deed to the grantee. The covenant is enforceable in equity by a decree of specific performance. It will also prevent the grantor from later claiming title against the grantee by adverse possession. See Carrozza v. Carrozza, 944 A.2d 161 (R.I. 2008).

Most of the covenants above are nicely summarized in Lloyd v. Estate of Robbins, 997 A.2d 733 (Me. 2010). Whether the distinctions among them are useful or serve sound policy is debatable. See Levin, Warranties of Title—A Modest Proposal, 29 Vill. L. Rev. 649 (1984). Nevertheless, the distinctions continue to be relevant, as demonstrated by the explanatory material below and the *Brown v. Lober* case. For further discussion, see Whitman, Burkhart, Freyermuth & Rule, The Law of Property § 11.13 (4d ed. 2019); 6A Powell, Real Property ¶ 904ff (1979); III Am. L. Prop. § 12.124ff (1952).

A grantor may limit the coverage of the title covenants through specific language. In a general warranty deed, the grantor covenants not only against interests held by persons claiming through the grantor, but also interests created by the grantor's predecessors in title. By contrast, some grantors may choose to deliver only a "special warranty deed" or a "limited warranty deed," under which the grantor warrants only against interests held by persons claiming through the grantor.[6] Thus, if the grantor's predecessor granted a mortgage on the land that has not been satisfied, the existence of that mortgage would (if not excepted in the deed) breach the covenant against encumbrances if the grantor had delivered a general warranty deed, but not if the grantor had delivered a special warranty deed.

It is useful at this point to compare a deed's title covenants with the covenant of marketable title (discussed in Chapter One) that is implied in contracts for the sale of land. The most obvious point of similarity is that both concern *title*. In general, the same sorts of title defects that might breach the contractual covenant will be breaches of the deed covenants as well—failures of title, encumbrances, and so on. Courts are split, however, as to whether the presence of known or visible easements will violate a covenant against encumbrances in a deed. Compare Marathon Builders, Inc. v. Polinger, 263 Md. 410, 283 A.2d 617 (1971) with Gill Grain Co. v. Poos, 707 S.W.2d 434 (Mo. Ct. App. 1986). For other types of title defects, the grantee's knowledge at the time the deed is delivered is probably irrelevant. See Midfirst Bank v. Abney, 850 N.E.2d 373 (Ill. Ct. App. 2006) ("The fact that a purchaser may have actual knowledge of an encumbrance does not relieve the vendor of his liability upon the covenants contained in

---

[6] Under a special warranty deed, questions can arise about whether the title defect in question was created by the grantor or arose during the grantor's ownership. For example, if the grantor engaged in conduct that reduced the size of the land parcel under the doctrine of boundary by acquiescence, is the grantor liable? Compare Egli v. Troy, 602 N.W.2d 329 (Iowa 1999) (yes) with Mason v. Loveless, 24 P.3d 997 (Utah Ct. App. 2001) (no). See also Greenberg v. Sutter, 173 Misc. 2d 774, 661 N.Y.S.2d 933 (1997) (grantor who permitted an adverse possessor to acquire a portion of her land would violate subsequent special warranty deed, even though she had no actual knowledge of the adverse possession).

his deed. Such knowledge on the part of the purchaser does not operate as a release or discharge of a covenant.").

As discussed in Chapter One, a few courts have held that the implied covenant of marketable title in a sales contract can be breached by violations of zoning or other public ordinances that do not themselves affect title. By contrast, courts usually hold that such violations do not violate deed covenants of title. See Arnell v. Salt Lake County Bd. of Adjustment, 112 P.3d 1214 (Utah Ct. App. 2005); Barnett v. Decatur, 261 Ga. 205, 403 S.E.2d 46 (1991). But see War Eagle, Inc. v. Belair, 694 S.E.2d 497 (N.C. Ct. App. 2010) (existing zoning violation breached covenant against encumbrances). Likewise, the presence of illegal hazardous waste on the land is not a breach of a deed covenant against encumbrances, unless the condition has actually triggered the assertion of a lien for cleanup expenses by a federal or state agency. See Cameron v. Martin Marietta Corp., 729 F. Supp. 1529 (E.D.N.C. 1990).

There are other important differences between the contractual covenant of marketable title and deed covenants of title. One is the available remedy. If a buyer of land discovers prior to closing that title is unmarketable, the buyer has a right to rescind. Under a deed covenant, damages are usually the only remedy unless the covenant of further assurances can be used to compel a further conveyance that will perfect the title; rescission of the transaction generally is not available to the grantee. Another difference lies in the standard of quality that the title must meet. Under the implied covenant of marketable title in a sales contract, the title must be not only good, but marketable as well, meaning that it must not be subject to an unreasonable risk of litigation. There is no such requirement in the context of deed covenants, where a title that is good in fact will suffice despite the possibility that numerous questions could reasonably be raised or litigated about it. For example, in Fong v. Batton, 214 So. 2d 649 (Fla. Ct. App. 1968), there was a gap in the public records in the grantor's chain of title. Such a condition would probably make title unmarketable, but the court held that it did not constitute a breach of the covenant of seisin, because the grantee had received actual title notwithstanding the record gap.

Present vs. future covenants. The distinction between the present and future deed covenants is important for several reasons. One is the application of the statute of limitations. A breach of the present covenants occurs, if at all, at the time the deed is delivered. Consequently, the statute of limitations for a claimed breach of a present covenant commences running at the moment of delivery. See Lloyd v. Estate of Robbins, 997 A.2d 773 (R.I. 2010). Often, the grantee is typically unaware of the title defect, and may not learn of it until some months or years later—at which point the statute of limitations may bar her claim for breach of the present covenant. Thus, a deed containing only present covenants gives a highly ephemeral form of protection. Fortunately, this problem does not exist with a future covenant because the statute of limitations for a future covenant runs only from the date of an eviction resulting from the breach—and one can hardly be evicted without knowing about it.

Real estate lawyers say that the future covenants "run with the land," whereas the present covenants do not. What does it mean for a covenant to "run with the land"? To illustrate, suppose A deeds land to B by a general warranty deed containing all six covenants. B subsequently conveys the land to C (whether with or without title covenants), and C then discovers a title defect that predated the original conveyance by A. May C recover against A? So far as the present covenants are concerned, the breach occurred when the A-B deed was delivered. Unless B expressly assigned to C the cause of action that B has against A based on the breach of a present deed covenant, according to the weight of authority C has no claim against A based on the present covenants; the present covenants in the A-B deed do not "run" to the more remote grantee C. A few courts have circumvented this difficulty by the simple expedient of holding the B-C deed to constitute an implied assignment to C of B's cause of action against A. See III Am. L. Prop. § 12.127 (1952). With respect to the future covenants, C's position is much brighter, for they are uniformly held to run with the land, and hence to permit the more remote grantee C to recover directly from A. See, e.g., Holmes Dev., LLC v. Cook, 48 P.3d 895 (Utah 2002); Bridges v. Heimburger, 360 So. 2d 929 (Miss. 1978).

Because a future deed covenant can be breached only by an eviction, it becomes important to know what sorts of occurrences will amount to an eviction. If the holder of the paramount title asserts it directly and forcibly, as by "throwing out" the grantee by force, no one would doubt that an "eviction" has occurred. But this is a rare circumstance.

BROWN V. LOBER

Supreme Court of Illinois, 1979
75 Ill.2d 547, 27 Ill. Dec. 780, 389 N.E.2d 1188

[Plaintiffs purchased the land in question in 1957, receiving a deed containing covenants of seisin, right to convey, against encumbrances, warranty, and quiet enjoyment. In 1974, they negotiated the sale of the coal rights to the land to Consolidated Coal Company for $6,000. The coal company later discovered that a prior owner had reserved a two-thirds interest in the coal rights, and that the plaintiffs had only one-third. The plaintiffs sold that one-third interest to the coal company for $2,000, and then filed this action against the estate of their grantor, claiming a breach of the covenants of title in the deed and seeking $4,000 in damages. The court held that the plaintiffs' action on the present covenants was barred by the jurisdiction's 10-year statute of limitations and that no breach of the future covenants had yet occurred. Plaintiffs appealed.]

This court has stated on numerous occasions that, in contrast to the covenant of seisin, the covenant of warranty or quiet enjoyment is prospective in nature and is breached only when there is an actual or constructive eviction of the covenantee by the paramount titleholder.

The cases are also replete with statements to the effect that the mere existence of paramount title in one other than the covenantee is not sufficient to constitute a breach of the covenant of warranty or quiet enjoyment: "[T]here must be a union of acts of disturbance and lawful title, to constitute a breach of the covenant for quiet enjoyment, or warranty . . . . ." *Barry v. Guild*, 126 Ill. 439, 446, 18 N.E. 759, 761 (1888). "[T]here is a general concurrence that something more than the mere existence of a paramount title is necessary to constitute a breach of the covenant of warranty." *Scott v. Kirkendall*, 88 Ill. 465, 467 (1878). "A mere want of title is no breach of this covenant. There must not only be a want of title, but there must be an ouster under a paramount title." *Moore v. Vail*, 17 Ill. 185, 189 (1855).

The question is whether plaintiffs have alleged facts sufficient to constitute a constructive eviction. They argue that if a covenantee fails in his effort to sell an interest in land because he discovers that he does not own what his warranty deed purported to convey, he has suffered a constructive eviction and is thereby entitled to bring an action against his grantor for breach of the covenant of quiet enjoyment. We think that the decision of this court in *Scott v. Kirkendall*, 88 Ill. 465 (1878), is controlling on this issue and compels us to reject plaintiffs' argument.

In *Scott*, an action was brought for breach of the covenant of warranty by a grantee who discovered that other parties had paramount title to the land in question. The land was vacant and unoccupied at all relevant times. This court, in rejecting the grantee's claim that there was a breach of the covenant of quiet enjoyment, quoted the earlier decision in *Moore v. Vail*, 17 Ill. 185, 191 (1855):

> Until that time, (the taking possession by the owner of the paramount title,) he might peaceably have entered upon and enjoyed the premises, without resistance or molestation, which was all his grantors covenanted he should do. They did not guarantee to him a perfect title, but the possession and enjoyment of the premises. 88 Ill. 465, 468.

Relying on this language in *Moore,* the *Scott* court concluded:

> We do not see but what this fully decides the present case against the appellant. It holds that the mere existence of a paramount title does not constitute a breach of the covenant. That is all there is here. There has been no assertion of the adverse title. The land has always been vacant. Appellant could at any time have taken peaceable possession of it. He has in no way been prevented or

hindered from the enjoyment of the possession by anyone having a better right. It was but the possession and enjoyment of the premises which was assured to him, and there has been no disturbance or interference in that respect. True, there is a superior title in another, but appellant has never felt "its pressure upon him." 88 Ill. 465, 468–69.

Admittedly, *Scott* dealt with surface rights while the case before us concerns subsurface mineral rights. We are, nevertheless, convinced that the reasoning employed in *Scott* is applicable to the present case. While plaintiffs went into possession of the surface area, they cannot be said to have possessed the subsurface minerals. "Possession of the surface does not carry possession of the minerals. To possess the mineral estate, one must undertake the actual removal thereof from the ground or do such other act as will apprise the community that such interest is in the exclusive use and enjoyment of the claiming party." *Failoni v. Chicago & North Western Ry. Co.*, 30 Ill. 2d 258, 262, 195 N.E.2d 619, 622 (1964).

Since no one has, as yet, undertaken to remove the coal or otherwise manifested a clear intent to exclusively "possess" the mineral estate, it must be concluded that the subsurface estate is "vacant." As in *Scott,* plaintiffs "could at any time have taken peaceable possession of it. [They have] in no way been prevented or hindered from the enjoyment of the possession by anyone having a better right." 88 Ill. 465, 468. Accordingly, until such time as one holding paramount title interferes with plaintiffs' right of possession (e.g., by beginning to mine the coal), there can be no constructive eviction and, therefore, no breach of the covenant of quiet enjoyment.

What plaintiffs are apparently attempting to do on this appeal is to extend the protection afforded by the covenant of quiet enjoyment. However, we decline to expand the historical scope of this covenant to provide a remedy where another of the covenants of title is so clearly applicable. . . .

The covenant of seisin, unquestionably, was breached when the Bosts delivered the deed to plaintiffs, and plaintiffs then had a cause of action. However, despite the fact that it was a matter of public record that there was a reservation of a two-thirds interest in the mineral rights in the earlier deed, plaintiffs failed to bring an action for breach of the covenant of seisin within the 10-year period following delivery of the deed. The likely explanation is that plaintiffs had not secured a title opinion at the time they purchased the property, and the subsequent examiners for the lenders were not concerned with the mineral rights. Plaintiffs' oversight, however, does not justify us in overruling earlier decisions in order to recognize an otherwise premature cause of action. The mere fact that plaintiffs' original contract with Consolidated had to be modified due to their discovery that paramount title to two-thirds of the subsurface minerals belonged to another is not sufficient to constitute the constructive eviction necessary to a breach of the covenant of quiet enjoyment. . . .

NOTES AND QUESTIONS

1. *What constitutes eviction?* The mere fact that a grantee believes someone else has better title will not constitute an eviction. See Green Harbour Homeowners Ass'n, Inc. v. Ermiger, 72 A.D.3d 1186, 898 N.Y.S.2d 302 (2010). However, the following acts by the holder of paramount title have been held to constitute an eviction (sometimes termed a "constructive eviction") of the grantee, and thus to breach the future covenants:

(a) When the grantee takes the deed, the paramount titleholder is already in possession of the land or has constructed encroachments on it. Riddle v. Udouj, 267 S.W.3d 586 (Ark. 2007).

(b) The paramount titleholder obtains a decree of specific performance, ejectment, or other order giving him possession or confirming his title to the land. Foley v. Smith, 14 Wash. App. 285, 539 P.2d 874 (1975).

(c) The paramount titleholder orders the grantee off the land and threatens litigation against her. McCleary v. Bratton, 307 S.W.2d 722 (Mo. Ct. App. 1957).

(d) The grantee buys the paramount title to avoid being evicted by its holder. Greenwood v. Robbins, 108 N.J. Eq. 122, 154 A. 333 (1931).

(e) The grantee surrenders her claim to the holder of the paramount title and moves off the land. Solares v. Solares, 232 S.W.3d 873 (Tex. App. 2007); Brewster v. Hines, 185 S.E.2d 513 (W.Va. 1971).

(f) The grantee is sued by the person with paramount title, and enters into a reasonable settlement of the suit in which the grantee is left with only a part of the land originally granted by the deed in question. Garcia v. Herrera, 125 N.M. 199, 959 P.2d 533 (1998).

(g) The paramount title holder physically interferes with the possession of the grantee. See, e.g., Jackson v. Smith, 80 S.W.3d 443 (Ark. 2010) (paramount title holder cut off electricity to grantee).

Incidentally, if the government is the holder of the paramount title, that fact alone will comprise an eviction, and no further action by the government is necessary. See Cover v. McAden, 112 S.E. 817 (N.C. 1922); Seldon v. Dudley E. Jones Co., 74 Ark. 348, 85 S.W. 778 (1905).

2. *Limits on recovery.* There is nearly universal agreement that the recovery by the grantee under a deed's covenants of title cannot exceed the consideration received by the covenantor-grantor, plus interest. See Bedard v. Martin, 100 P.3d 584 (Colo. Ct. App. 2004); Annot., 100 A.L.R. 1194 (1937). Some courts instead limit the covenantor's liability to the value of the land at

the time of delivery, with the purchase price received by the grantor taken as evidence of the land's value. See, e.g., Bridges v. Heimburger, 360 So.2d 929 (Miss. 1978). If the land has risen in value, or the grantee has made improvements, this can result in the grantee's bearing a substantial share of the total loss, particularly if there is a total failure of title. The limitation has been criticized. See Jon Groetzinger, Breach of the Warranty Covenants in Deeds and the Allowable Measure of Damages, 17 N.H. Bar J. 1 (1975). An occasional court decision and a few statutes remove the limitation and permit recovery based on the current land value. See Bridwell v. Gruner, 212 Ark. 992, 209 S.W.2d 441 (1948); 6A Powell, Real Property ¶ 908 n. 24 (1979).

The limitation on recovery to the amount the grantor received applies equally to all of the covenants. For example, if the property turns out to have been encumbered by a mortgage with a balance greater than the price the grantor received for the land, the grantor's liability on the covenant against encumbrances is limited to the purchase price. See, e.g., Forrer v. Sather, 595 P.2d 1306 (Utah 1979).

3.   *What did the grantor receive?* In some cases the "consideration received" by the grantor is not so easy to measure. If the land was transferred in exchange for other land, what is the amount of the consideration? See Maxwell v. Redd, 209 Kan. 264, 496 P.2d 1320 (1972). Or suppose the land was transferred as a gift, with no consideration or only a nominal amount? Does this preclude recovery entirely? See Ragsdale v. Ragsdale, 172 S.W.2d 381 (Tex. Civ. App. 1943) (no recovery).

4.   *Measuring damages.* Damages for a breach of the covenant against encumbrances are equal to the amount required to remove the encumbrance, if this is possible, and otherwise the diminution the encumbrance causes to the value of the land. See Yonkers City Post No. 1666, VFW v. Josanth Realty Corp., 67 N.Y.2d 1029, 503 N.Y.S.2d 321, 494 N.E.2d 452 (1986). In Ellison v. F. Murray Parker Builders, Inc., 573 S.W.2d 161 (Tenn. Ct. App. 1978), the grantees bought their house by warranty deed for $46,500. A few years later they contracted to sell it for $59,500. However, a title examination disclosed that a previously unknown sewer easement ran under the house. They did not remove the easement, but instead reduced the selling price by $3,000, to $56,500, and completed the sale. They then brought an action against their grantor for breach of the covenant against encumbrances. An expert appraiser testified that the easement reduced the land's value by $6,700 as of the date the plaintiffs bought it. What should their recovery be: (1) the $6,700 reduction in value? (2) the $3,000 reduction in the actual selling price? (3) Zero, on the ground that, notwithstanding the encumbrance, they still sold the property for much more than they had paid? The court opted for the first figure; do you agree?

5.   *Limitation to actual loss.* The damages that a grantee-covenantee recovers must be related to her actual outlay or loss. Thus, if there is an encumbrance but the grantee does not clear it or pay it off, and it causes her no physical inconvenience, her recovery on the covenant will be merely

nominal. See In re Meehan's Estate, 30 Wis. 2d 428, 141 N.W.2d 218 (1966). Similarly, if the grantee is able to persuade the holder of the outstanding encumbrance or paramount title to deed or release it to her without cost, she has only nominal damages. See, e.g., Creason v. Peterson, 24 Utah 2d 305, 470 P.2d 403 (1970).

6. *Defending the grantee's title: interest, costs and attorneys' fees.* Under the covenants of warranty and quiet enjoyment, the grantee can "tender" the defense of title to the grantor, who then has the obligation to defend against the claim of the putative paramount titleholder. See, e.g., Erickson v. Chase, 231 P.3d 1261 (Wash. Ct. App. 2010); Coco v. Jaskunas, 986 A.2d 531 (N.H. 2009). In Edmonson v. Popchoi, 256 P.3d 1223 (Wash. 2011), the court held that this meant an active, good faith defense, and not merely a "quickie" settlement, followed by the payment of damages to the grantee. If the grantor fails to accept the obligation to defend the title, the grantor becomes liable for the court costs and (usually) the attorneys' fees expended by the grantee in negotiating or litigating in good faith against the person claiming paramount title. See Dionne v. LeClerc, 896 A.2d 923 (Me. 2006); Creason v. Peterson, 470 P.2d 403 (Utah 1970). Some courts will allow recovery of these expenses even if the grantee does not first demand that the grantor defend the title. In addition, the grantee usually can obtain interest on her recovery, at least if she was deprived of the use or profits of the land by the acts of the paramount titleholder.

Suppose the grantee litigates the title against a putative paramount titleholder and *wins.* Has the grantee, by winning, thereby established that there was no title defect, and thus that the covenantor is not liable to her for anything, either damages or attorney fees? This is the usual view! See Nunes v. Meadowbrook Dev. Co., 24 A.3d 539 (R.I. 2011); Stumhoffer v. Perales, 459 S.W.3d 158 (Tex. Ct. App. 2015); Sanpete Am., LLC v. Willardsen, 269 P.3d 118 (Utah 2011); Black v. Patel, 594 S.E.2d 162 (S.C. 2004). Given the costs associated with her title defense, is such a result the ultimate "Catch-22" for the winning grantee?

7. *After-acquired title.* Covenants in deeds are of importance in the operation of the doctrine known as "after-acquired title" or "estoppel by deed." Suppose A purports to convey land to B by general warranty deed, but at the time A really has no title at all. Obviously, B gets nothing (except a claim against A on the covenants of title). Later, however, A acquires the title from the true owner. The doctrine of after-acquired title holds that the title then inures instantly and automatically to B. See Mack Oil Co. v. Garvin, 39 P.3d 775 (Okla. 2001); 6A Powell, Real Property ¶ 937 (1979).[7] This result can be justified in terms of estoppel. If A has given B covenants of title, the grantor A

---

[7] The operation of the doctrine is not limited to deeds. For example, a mortgage containing covenants of title that is given by A (who has no title) to B will become effective if A later obtains title to the land. See, e.g., Kebreau v. Bayview Loan Servicing, LLC, 225 So.3d 255 (Fla. Ct. App. 2017); Rabo Agrifinance, Inc. v. Terra XXI, Ltd., 336 P.3d 972 (N.M. Ct. App. 2014); RNT Holdings, LLC v. United Gen. Title Ins. Co., 230 Cal. App.4th 1289, 179 Cal. Rptr.3d 175 (2014); Guess v. Gathings, 728 So.2d 1038 (La. Ct. App. 1999).

ought to be estopped to deny, when A later acquires title, that the title has passed to B. Under this reasoning, a quitclaim deed ordinarily will not cause the doctrine to operate, unless it also contains some specific representation by A that he has the title (and quitclaims commonly do not). See Carkuff v. Balmer, 795 N.W.2d 303 (N.D. 2011); Kennedy Oil v. Lance Oil & Gas Co., Inc., 126 P.3d 875 (Wyo. 2006); Sorenson v. Wright, 268 N.W.2d 203 (Iowa 1978).

Estoppel by deed situations can raise a number of hard questions. Can the grantee seek damages for breach of the title covenant rather than claiming after-acquired title? Must the grantee show actual detrimental reliance as in ordinary estoppel cases? See, e.g., Shedden v. Anadarko E. & P. Co., L.P., 635 Pa. 381, 136 A.3d 485 (2016) (no). For discussion of these and other matters, see Whitman, Burkhart, Freyermuth & Rule, The Law of Property § 11.5 (4th ed. 2019).

Estoppel by deed can cause serious problems for title examiners, for the deed that contains the covenants and therefore creates the estoppel is obviously out of time sequence in the chain of title, and hence may be very hard to locate in the public records. Moreover, if the party who is relying on the doctrine is not a bona fide purchaser, his or her interest may be defeated by the operation of the recording acts. See F.D.I.C. v. Taylor, 267 P.3d 949 (Utah Ct. App. 2011). These and other problems encountered by title searchers are addressed in the next section.

E. TITLE ASSURANCE METHODS

1. INTRODUCTION

In this section we treat the central issue in the transfer of real estate: proof of title. Obviously, no responsible person wants to advance very much cash (or credit) toward the purchase of land without being certain that the purported seller really owns it or otherwise has the right to convey it. Even if individual buyers might sometimes be fairly casual in this respect, they usually find that they must borrow some or all of the purchase price, and their institutional lenders (who usually insist on a mortgage or other security interest in the real estate being purchased) are not casual at all. Nobody wants a mortgage on the proverbial Brooklyn Bridge!

How does one find out whether the person who claims to own land really owns it?[8] Most laypeople would answer by saying that one must "search the title," but laypeople rarely understand what a "title search" involves. It is widely understood that the county court house (or other local government depository) contains some records, and that a search is made by using those records. But many people probably assume that the "search"

---

[8]   The simplest answer, of course, is to ask the seller. But the seller might be mistaken or crooked, and our study of covenants of title in the previous section should have convinced you that recoveries on such covenants are problematic at best. What buyers need is an independent source of title information.

is simply a matter of going to the proper officials in the courthouse and *asking* them who owns the land in question. In other words, the notion is widespread that someone in local government somehow keeps track of the ownership of each parcel of land, and has the duty of answering the public's questions about title.[9]

For the most part in the United States, local governments take no active role in determining the state of the title to land, but instead merely act as passive depositories for the instruments affecting title that people choose to "record" by having them copied by the relevant public official. To one who wishes to know the state of the title to a parcel, the local government (typically, at the county level) says not "We will tell you who owns it," but rather "Here are all of the deeds, mortgages, liens, and other documents that have been left with us. You are welcome to look through them and draw your own conclusions about the title." If the searcher reaches erroneous conclusions about the title after examining the documents on file, that is the searcher's problem. The county simply is not liable unless its employees have made a mechanical or clerical error in copying or indexing the papers.[10]

In most American jurisdictions, recording is done at the county level, but there are exceptions. In Hawaii and Alaska recording is administered by the state. In several New England states, towns rather than counties operate recording systems. Connecticut, for example, has about 170 recording offices. The recording function may be carried out by the clerk of the local trial court, the county clerk, or by a separate official known as the "county recorder," the "register of deeds," or the like. All told, there are about 3,600 recording jurisdictions in the country. There is a nice summary of the systems in Hone, Land and Property Research in the United States 184 (1997).

"Well," you may say, "if I must look at all of these musty old documents and then decide for myself who has the title, can I at least be certain that all of the legally relevant documents are here?" The answer is "not

---

[9] If we were concerned with motor vehicles instead of land, that concept would be generally accurate. In most states there is some statewide authority (e.g., a Department of Motor Vehicles) that can provide computerized and virtually instantaneous data about the ownership of a particular car or truck. There is a similar (though considerably more complex) system for land in nine states, but it is used in only a handful of localities. It is called the Torrens or title registration system, and we will take a brief look at it later in this section. But it is not a popular approach.

[10] In some states the responsible official can be held liable for negligence. See, e.g., Badger v. Benfield, 337 S.E.2d 596 (N.C. Ct. App. 1985) (clerk is liable if negligence is the proximate cause of plaintiff's injury). Cf. Antonis v. Liberati, 821 A.2d 666 (Pa. Commw. Ct. 2003) (clerk held immune from liability for negligence for incorrectly indexing a mortgage). In most states, recording officials are required by law to be bonded, but the bond is often for a limited amount, usually considerably less than the value of the average parcel of real estate. Recovery against the local government itself may be barred by sovereign immunity, and courts obviously will be reluctant to levy large personal judgments against public officials or employees. For all of these reasons, negligence suits against recorders often result in an inadequate recovery. We will address later the question of who, as between the party recording the instrument and the party searching for it, will prevail as to the title when the recorder has made an error.

entirely." Someone holding a prior claim may have failed to record the deed evidencing that claim. As we will see in the next section, this possibility may not matter to you as a potential buyer, because the state's recording act may protect you against that prior claim based on the claimant's failure to record.

Unfortunately, recording acts only protect against certain types of adverse claims. There are other types of adverse claims to the title that are entirely outside the coverage of the recording system—and thus might have full validity even though a title searcher, despite meticulous examination, cannot find a trace of them in the courthouse. Such adverse claims include claims that do not arise out of or appear in a written instrument, such as adverse possession, prescriptive easements, implied easements, and oral boundary line agreements. The searcher has another problem: a deed in the records that appears to be valid on its face may be subject to a variety of defects. For example, a deed might have been forged, may have a defective acknowledgment, or may never have been validly delivered to its grantee. A deed may have been given by a grantor who was without capacity or have been executed by an attorney in fact whose power of attorney had been revoked. The recorder's office makes no representation that the instruments it preserves are correct, and in many cases one cannot detect such defects by examining the document itself. Some defects may make the deed void whereas others make it only voidable. Even in the later case, where a good faith purchaser might prevail, the purchaser may be forced to litigate to prove the superiority of her title, hardly an attractive prospect.

Even if none of these technical problems arise, it is all too easy for a searcher to make a mistake. In theory, one can construct a complete title history of any parcel back to the original conveyance from the sovereign, but in many situations, this is impractically burdensome, and searches are often limited to periods of 30 to 60 years. Of course, this is a calculated risk because earlier defects in the title could exist. Even within the period searched, a searcher might miss an entry, misread a document, or misplace a sheet of notes. These kinds of mistakes may result in liability for damages if the searcher is a lawyer or an abstractor, but damages are sometimes hard to collect, and in any event are a poor substitute for the land itself.

Professor Ted Fiflis, after surveying all of the problems we have just described, listed nineteen specific ways in which a title search in the public records might produce erroneous results. Fiflis, Land Transfer Improvement: The Basic Facts and Two Hypotheses for Reform, 38 U. Colo. L. Rev. 431, 453–54 (1966). See also R. Lynwood Straw, Off-Record Risks for Bona Fide Purchasers of Interests in Real Property, 72 Dick. L. Rev. 35 (1967); Stroup, The Unreliable Record Title, 60 N.D. L. Rev. 203 (1984). Other writers have arrived at different numbers, but the point is clear: a search of the records, even if diligently made, still leaves a buyer or mortgagee of the land open to serious title risks.

At this point you may be ready to throw up your hands and exclaim that you want no part of such a defective system of title assurance. You will probably take little comfort in the assertion that these "unfindable" adverse claims crop up rather infrequently. After all, the fact that the chances are one in a thousand is pretty cold comfort if *your* client happens to be the one who "wins" the adverse claim lottery. The truth is that our system is defective, and that if one looks only at the formal legal structure one would probably conclude that in modern, mobile society it presents unacceptable risks. For precisely that reason, an unofficial, privately owned system of title assurance, called "title insurance," has arisen to absorb and spread most of the risks that the public records system presents. In terms of speed, accuracy, and effective risk-spreading it is quite successful, although it operates in a market environment that involves little price competition and thus may impose excessive costs on consumers.[11] Further, the very existence of the private title insurance industry has made reform of the public records system more difficult, because the title insurers are antagonistic to institutional changes which would render their own services obsolete or in less demand.

But we are ahead of our story. Before we study reform of the existing system or the efforts of private industry to supplement it, we need to understand how the current system operates.

2.   RECORDING ACTS

In addition to providing a repository for title documents (and a method for searching those documents, to which we will turn shortly), the recording system provides a mechanism for establishing priorities among conflicting claims. For example, suppose that O, the owner of Blueacre, delivers A a deed to Blueacre on Monday. Then, two days later, O delivers B a deed to the same property. Who owns Blueacre?

Under the common law rule, the answer is simple. Conflicting claims of title are decided under the "first in time, first in right" principle, which would give A's claim priority over B's. Once O conveyed Blueacre to A, O no longer had title to Blueacre and thus could not subsequently transfer title to Blueacre to B. [This is an example of the maxim *nemo dat quod non habet* (or "no one can give what she does not have.")] But how would B know that O no longer had title to Blueacre? Even the most thorough investigation would not necessarily reveal the prior conveyance to A. In such a situation, it seems inequitable to penalize B, particularly if he paid

---

[11] On the economics of the title insurance industry, see Owen, Kickbacks, Specialization, Price Fixing, and Efficiency in Residential Real Estate Markets, 29 Stan. L. Rev. 931 (1977); Whitman, Home Transfer Costs: An Economic and Legal Analysis, 62 Geo. L. J. 1311 (1974).

valuable consideration to O based upon a reasonable belief that O had good title to convey.

The recording system eliminates many of the risks posed by the common law rule. Each state has a mechanism through which purchasers like A can record their deeds, thereby providing notice of the transaction to potential subsequent purchasers like B (who can search those records before buying to identify prior claims). Conversely, if A fails to record, a recording act may protect a subsequent purchaser like B by giving them priority. In essence, a recording act creates a statutory estoppel rule in favor of a bona fide purchaser (such as B). If A fails to record her deed and thereby put B on constructive notice (or record notice) of A's prior claim, the recording statute estops A from asserting the common law's prior-in-time rule to establish a superior title claim to B. The result is that B becomes the owner of the land—even though, technically, O had no title to convey to B! As a result, A risks losing her interest in Blueacre if she fails to record her deed promptly.

Types of recording acts. There are three basic types of recording acts in the United States. One is a "pure race" statute, which is in effect only in three states;[12] North Carolina's statute provides an example:

> No (i) conveyance of land, or (ii) contract to convey, or (iii) option to convey, or (iv) lease of land for more than three years shall be valid to pass any property interest as against lien creditors or purchasers for a valuable consideration from the donor, bargainor or lessor but from the time of registration thereof in the county where the land lies . . . [N.C. Gen. Stat. § 47–18(a).]

Under a pure race statute, if one grantor purports to sell land to two different grantees, the grantee who records her deed first will prevail over the other grantee in a title dispute—even if the grantee who records first has actual knowledge of the other grantee's claim!

> *Problem 1.* O, owner of Blueacre in fee simple absolute, conveys Blueacre to A. A does not record his deed. O subsequently conveys Blueacre to B, who pays valuable consideration, with full knowledge of A's unrecorded deed. B promptly records her deed. Under a pure race statute, A's failure to record his deed renders that deed ineffective against B. B's knowledge of A's unrecorded deed is irrelevant. B now owns Blueacre.

> *Problem 2.* O, owner of Blueacre in fee simple absolute, conveys Blueacre to A. A does not record his deed. O subsequently conveys Blueacre to B, who pays valuable consideration, without

---

[12] These states are Delaware, Louisiana, and North Carolina. A few other states have specialized race-type statutes that apply to specific types of conveyances. These include, for example, Arkansas (mortgages), Ohio (mortgages and oil and gas leases), and Pennsylvania (mortgages except for purchase money).

knowledge of A's unrecorded deed. A then records his deed shortly
before B records her deed. Under a pure race statute, A owns
Blueacre. B cannot claim the benefit of the recording statute
because she failed to record her deed prior to A's recording.

Before we move forward, take special note of two key points that are
critical for a proper understanding of how a recording statute applies:

- A deed does not have to be recorded to be effective against the
  grantor of the deed. In Problem 1, O's conveyance to A was
  valid even though A had not recorded the deed. If the later
  transfer to B had not arisen, O could not have recovered
  possession of Blueacre based upon A's failure to record.[13]

- In applying a recording statute, you should always ask
  whether the later purchaser may claim the benefit of the
  recording act's protection. In Problem 2, for example, it is
  tempting to say that A's title is valid because A was first to
  record—and thus that A qualifies for the protection of the
  recording statute. But remember that A's claim was already
  prior in time to B's claim—thus, A prevails under the common
  law first-in-time rule *unless B can successfully assert the
  benefit of the recording act.* In Problem 2, A prevails because
  A was first in time and, by recording, prevented B (the
  subsequent purchaser) from qualifying for the protection of
  the recording act.

By contrast, most American states have adopted recording acts that
protect subsequent purchasers only if they are "good faith" or "bona fide"
purchasers for value—i.e., only if they do not have notice of a prior
unrecorded claim. Because recording acts function as statutory estoppel
rules, incorporating a "notice" principle makes some sense conceptually. If
a later purchaser knows or should know of another party's prior unrecorded
deed, how can that purchaser have *reasonably* relied on the absence of that
deed in the public records—and thus why should the law elevate the later
purchaser in priority over the prior purchaser?

Approximately half of the states have adopted a "pure notice"
recording act, such as Iowa:

An instrument affecting real estate is of no validity against
subsequent purchasers for a valuable consideration, without
notice, or against the state or any of its political subdivisions

---

[13] At first, this seems inconsistent with the language of the quoted "pure race" recording act,
which appears to say the conveyance is not valid until it is recorded. But notice the language
carefully: "[no] conveyance of land . . . shall be valid to pass any property interest *as against* . . .
purchasers for a valuable consideration . . . but from the time of registration thereof." In other
words, lack of compliance with the recording act affects the validity of A's claim against future
third party purchasers, but not against the grantor O.

during and after condemnation proceedings against the real estate, unless the instrument is filed and recorded in the county in which the real estate is located. . . . [Iowa Code § 558.41(1)]

Under a pure notice statute, the second grantee will prevail over the first if she gave value without actual knowledge or other reason to know of the first grantee's claim—without regard to the order in which the two competing claims are recorded.

> *Problem 3.* O, owner of Blueacre in fee simple absolute, conveys Blueacre to A. A does not record his deed. O subsequently conveys Blueacre to B, who pays valuable consideration, without knowledge of A's deed. Under a pure notice statute, A's failure to record his deed renders that deed ineffective against B. B owns Blueacre.

> *Problem 4.* O, owner of Blueacre in fee simple absolute, conveys Blueacre to A. A does not record his deed. O subsequently conveys Blueacre to B, who pays valuable consideration, with full knowledge of A's unrecorded deed. Under a pure notice statute, A's deed remains effective against B, despite A's failure to record, because B has actual notice of A's prior claim. A owns Blueacre.

> *Problem 5.* O, owner of Blueacre in fee simple absolute, conveys Blueacre to A, who timely records. O subsequently conveys to B, who pays valuable consideration and does not know about A's prior claim. Under a pure notice statute, A's timely recording gave B constructive (or record) notice of A's claim. A owns Blueacre.

The remaining states have adopted "race-notice" recording acts, such as California's statute:

> Every conveyance of real property or an estate for years therein, other than a lease for a term not exceeding one year, is void as against any subsequent purchaser or mortgagee of the same property, or any part thereof, in good faith and for a valuable consideration, whose conveyance is first duly recorded. . . . [Cal. Civ. Code § 1214.]

Under a race-notice statute, the second grantee will prevail over the first only if (1) the second grantee has no knowledge or reason to know of the first grantee's claim and (2) the second grantee records her deed before the first grantee records.

> *Problem 6.* O, owner of Blueacre in fee simple absolute, conveys Blueacre to A. A does not record his deed. O subsequently conveys Blueacre to B, who pays valuable consideration, without knowledge of A's deed. B records her deed. Under a race-notice statute, B qualifies for the protection of the recording act, and thus A's prior deed is ineffective against B. B owns Blueacre.

Problem 7. O, owner of Blueacre in fee simple absolute, conveys Blueacre to A. A does not record his deed. O subsequently conveys Blueacre to B, who pays valuable consideration, with full knowledge of A's unrecorded deed. B records her deed. Under a race-notice statute, B does not qualify for the protection of the recording act because she knew of A's prior claim. Thus, A's deed remains effective against B despite A's failure to record it. A owns Blueacre.

Problem 8. O, owner of Blueacre in fee simple absolute, conveys Blueacre to A. A does not record his deed. O subsequently conveys Blueacre to B, who pays valuable consideration, without knowledge of A's unrecorded deed. B does not record her deed. Subsequently, A finally records his deed. Under a race-notice statute, B does not qualify for the protection of the recording statute because B did not record prior to A's recording. Thus, A's deed remains effective against B. A owns Blueacre.

NOTES AND QUESTIONS

1. *Recording acts and their justifications.* Can you articulate the ostensible rationale behind each type of recording act? What are the benefits and shortcomings of each? In a dispute involving the interpretation of Colorado's recording act, the Colorado Court of Appeals construed the Colorado recording act as a "pure-notice" act rather than a "race-notice" act:

> [A] pure notice statute serves to protect subsequent purchasers, allowing them to rely on the record title as it exists at the time of their purchase. The danger of a race-notice statute is that a prior interest holder who has failed to record may cut off the claim of a subsequent purchaser who relied on the record at the time of his closing but has not yet had time to record his own instrument. Characterizing the statute as a pure notice statute rather than a race-notice statute will encourage purchasers to record their interests as soon as acquired. [Fees-Krey, Inc. v. Page, 42 Colo. App. 8, 12, 591 P.2d 1339, 1343 (1978).]

Do you agree? For competing views, see generally 6A Powell, The Law of Real Property ¶ 905[1] (rev. ed. 1992); Taylor Mattis, Recording Acts: Anachronistic Reliance, 25 Real Prop., Prob. & Tr. J. 17 (1990); Francis S. Philbrick, Limits of Record Search and Therefore of Notice (pt. 1), 93 U. Pa. L. Rev. 125 (1944).

Bear in mind that, under all three types of recording statutes, A always will prevail over a subsequent purchaser if A records immediately. To illustrate, consider the facts of Prochaska v. Midwest Title Guarantee Co., 85 Wash. App. 256, 932 P.2d 172 (1997). A plaintiff who had obtained a judgment against the property owner recorded a certified copy of the judgment at 10:05 am. [Recording the judgment made it operative as a lien against the owner's real estate located in the county where the judgment was rendered.] Nine minutes later, at 10:14 am, the deed by which the owner was selling his property was recorded by the buyers' escrow company. The court correctly held that because the judgment was recorded first (though not by much), it had priority over the deed under Washington's race-notice statute. As a result, the title received by the buyers was subject to the judgment lien. The buyers had title insurance (fortunately) and their title company ended up having to pay off the lien. The title company argued that it could not have found the judgment in its search—the judgment had not yet been indexed by the recorder's staff, and it was probably lying in an "in-box" waiting to be processed. The court took the view that indexing the judgment was not part of "recording" it, and that once the judgment had been accepted and date-and-time stamped by the recorder of deeds, it was considered to be "recorded." Perhaps the title company should have thumbed through the documents in the in-box! In jurisdictions with large recording volumes, however, this approach might be completely impractical, resulting in a risk that the title insurance company must simply bear as a cost of doing business.

2. *Interests "outside" the recording act.* By their terms, recording acts usually exclude short-term leases (typically those for less than one to three years, depending on the state), which are not required to be in writing pursuant to the Statute of Frauds. Consequently, a short-term tenant need not record the lease to protect herself against a future transfer of the property by her landlord to a later purchaser. In most cases, the tenant's possession would give notice to the purchaser in any event, but the rule described above operates even if the tenant is not in possession.

With this exception, virtually all interests in land *that are evidenced by a writing* are within the recording acts.[14] Specifically, there is no doubt today that express easements, restrictive covenants, contracts of sale, and even options to sell[15] are covered; one who takes any of these interests can best protect her interest by recording. By contrast, documents that do not create or transfer interests in land are often held to be nonrecordable; the records, after all, are not a public bulletin board. For example, if a purchaser under an installment land contract (which is otherwise generally recordable) cannot record it because the vendor's signature was not acknowledged, she may try to record a "notice of interest" or an affidavit of ownership instead. Such a paper is not a conveyance, and may be held technically unrecordable;[16] still, as a

---

[14] See 6A Powell, Real Property ¶ 914 (1979). Interests in land owned by the Federal government cannot be defeated by operation of state recording acts, and conveyances by the Federal government (and many states) need not be recorded to be protected from a subsequent BFP. See III Am. L. Prop. § 17.8 (1952).

[15] Because an option to buy land provides the optionee with a specifically enforceable right, the optionee has an equitable interest in the land. For this reason, it is highly desirable that options be recordable, and most cases have held that they are. See, e.g., Strong v. Clark, 56 Wash. 2d 230, 352 P.2d 183 (1960).

[16] Coggins v. Mimms, 373 So. 2d 964 (Fla. Ct. App. 1979); Ward v. Superior Court, 55 Cal. App. 4th 60, 63 Cal. Rptr. 2d 731 (1997) (homeowners' association may not record document asserting that homeowner is in violation of association covenants). If the instrument is legally unrecordable but is in fact placed in the records, it gives no constructive notice to those who should have searched for it but failed to do so. See, e.g., In re Ryan, 851 F.2d 502 (1st Cir. 1988); Phipps

practical matter, the recorder may accept it, and future searchers will probably find it.

More serious difficulties arise with interests that are not created by or evidenced in a written document.[17] The classic example is title by adverse possession, which arises by operation of law; there is no instrument to be recorded! Thus, it is entirely possible for the adverse possessor to complete possession for the statutory period, then vacate the land (so that his presence will no longer warn a buyer of his title), and yet prevail over a subsequent BFP from the record owner. Mugaas v. Smith, 33 Wash. 2d 429, 206 P.2d 332, 9 A.L.R. 2d 846 (1949).

The same sort of problem can occur with prescriptive easements, implied easements and easements by estoppel (irrevocable licenses). Here, the cases are mixed. Some hold that a subsequent purchaser takes subject to such interests even though no evidence of them appears in the records. See In re Boston Regional Medical Center, Inc., 240 B.R. 813 (Bankr. D. Mass.1999) (BFP takes subject to prescriptive easement). By contrast, the Restatement (Third) of Property—Servitudes takes the position that prescriptive and implied easements are subject to being extinguished under the recording act,[18] and some recent decisions agree. See, e.g., Tiller v. Hinton, 19 Ohio St. 3d 66, 482 N.E.2d 946 (1985) (holding that an implied easement is based on an "equitable right to reform the grant" and that such an equitable right is not enforceble against a BFP for value). Of course, some such easements will involve visible use of which a subsequent purchaser would have inquiry notice in any event. Cf. Otero v. Pacheco, 94 N.M. 524, 612 P.2d 1335 (Ct. App. 1980) (purchasers took subject to easement for buried sewer line discoverable by inspection or inquiry),

A similar problem is raised by mechanic's liens. Persons who supply labor or materials for a building project, but do not receive payment, are permitted to file claims of lien on the real property, and ultimately to have it sold to raise the necessary funds to pay their claims. Title search difficulties arise because the claimant generally is given some amount of time after *completion* of the work to file the claim in the public records. Once filed, the priority of the lien

---

v. CW Leasing, 186 Ariz. 397, 923 P.2d 863 (Ct. App. 1996). It may, however, give actual notice to those who actually find and read it in a record search. See Annot., 3 A.L.R. 2d 589 (1949).

[17] Marital rights provide an example. Common law dower and curtesy and some of their modern statutory counterparts apply not solely to land owned at the decedent's death, but to all land owned during the marriage. Yet there is no practical way that a title searcher can tell whether a former owner of the land was married or not. Most courts today would protect subsequent BFPs for value from such dower and curtesy claims. E.g., Petta v. Host, 115 N.E.2d 881 (Ill. 1953). Bankruptcy presents another example. The property of a bankrupt is automatically transferred to the trustee in bankruptcy. There is no deed representing this transfer, and therefore nothing to record in the county records (although the federal court having jurisdiction of the case will reflect the matter in its docket records).

[18] Restatement (Third) of Property—Servitudes § 7.14 (2000). While making such interests generally subject to extinguishment, the Restatement provided exceptions for appurtenant interests where "extinguishment of the benefit would result in depriving the dominant estate of rights of way for access or utilities necessary to reasonable enjoyment of the land" and for interests discoverable "by reasonable inspection or inquiry."

relates back in time, under many statutes, to the date the particular work or the entire project *commenced*. Consequently, one who purchases the land between these two dates (the beginning of the work or project and the end of the lien filing period) cannot be certain of taking title free of such liens. The problem is particularly acute when the work has been fairly minor in nature, so that the buyer of the property may not even realize that it has been done. The relation-back feature of a mechanic's lien is obviously very attractive to lien claimants, whose claims otherwise would be cut off by a transfer of the property to a BFP, but it also tends to render the public records less reliable.

Additional title search problems are raised by claims, judgment liens or other encumbrances that are allowed to be (and normally are) recorded in places other than the county recorder's office. The nature of these items varies from state to state, but the following are typical: (1) real property tax liens recorded in the county treasurer or tax collector's office; (2) assessment liens for street, sewer, and other improvements in various city offices; (3) wills in the office of the clerk of the probate or other relevant court;[19] (4) judgment liens in the office of the municipal, district, county or state clerk of court; (5) bankruptcies and federal condemnations in the office of the federal bankruptcy or district court clerk; and (6) zoning or other land use information (technically not an aspect of title, but equally important to real estate purchasers) in a city or county zoning administrator's office. This list is merely illustrative, and in some localities a buyer must check many more sources of information. One compilation for Cleveland, Ohio, listed 76 types of records in 16 different public offices that might contain land title data. See Johnstone & Hopson, Lawyers and Their Work 274–75 (1967). This is surely an extreme example, but the point is that a searcher may spend a great deal of time and effort in a very inefficient process!

3. *Simultaneous recording.* In First Bank v. East West Bank, 199 Cal. App. 4th 1309, 132 Cal. Rptr. 3d 267 (2011), an owner executed and delivered two conflicting mortgages on his property to two different lenders, neither of which knew of the other. Both mortgages were recorded, by two different title companies, on the same day. Because of California's practice of allowing title companies to present documents for recording before the opening of business hours, both mortgages were time-stamped at exactly 8:00 am on the same day. For legal purposes, both mortgages were recorded simultaneously—so which had priority? The court held that neither one was a "subsequent" conveyance and thus concluded that the two mortgages had equal priority. The court's analysis is flawed; can you explain why? Suppose that the owner had granted both mortgages the previous day, with the First Bank loan closing at 10:00 a.m. and the East West Bank loan closing at 12 noon. On what basis would you argue that First Bank's mortgage has first priority?

4. *Damages for the prior-in-time claimant who loses?* Consider the scenario in Problem 3 on page 215. Would A have a basis to recover damages

---

[19] Although a will obviously effects a transfer, most states' recording acts do not cover wills; instead, the records of the probate court in which the will was proved constitute public notice of its existence and contents. See III Am. L. Prop. § 17.8 (1952).

against O for the loss A suffers because B prevails under the recording act? In one sense, A brought the loss on himself by failing to record in a timely manner. But in another sense, A would have suffered no loss if O had not made a subsequent conveyance of land that O no longer owned. Should O thus be liable to A? Several cases suggest that such liability should indeed arise, although on a variety of theories. See, e.g., Bardwell v. White, 762 So. 2d 778 (Miss. Ct. App. 2000) (breach of duty of good faith and fair dealing); Jones v. Garden Park Homes Corp., 393 S.W.2d 501 (Mo. 1965) (recovery in tort); Patterson v. Bryant, 216 N.C. 550, 5 S.E.2d 849 (1939) (restitution to avoid unjust enrichment).

3.   BONA FIDE PURCHASERS

Except under a pure-race statute, the only subsequent purchasers who are protected by the recording acts against prior unrecorded conveyances are bona fide purchasers. Having the status of a BFP encompasses two elements: paying value and lacking notice of the prior conveyance. There is a good deal of legal lore on each of these elements.

Value. Paying value is a requirement that obviously excludes mere donees. See, e.g., Gregg v. Link, 774 S.W.2d 174 (Tenn. Ct. App. 1988) (prior unrecorded deed to first donee took precedence over later recorded deed to second donee); Fritz v. Mazurek, 156 Conn. 555, 244 A.2d 368 (1968); Bagwell v. Henson, 124 Ga. App. 92, 183 S.E.2d 485 (1971).[20] The recipient of the land must give up something in return. Most courts require more than nominal or "grossly inadequate" consideration, but do not necessarily demand that the price paid be comparable to the land's fair value. Because nearly all of the statutes, either explicitly or by judicial interpretation, protect subsequent mortgage creditors as well as purchasers, a lender who advances a loan and takes a mortgage or deed of trust as security has given "value," even though the lender expects that the loan will be fully repaid.

A common problem arises if a creditor takes a mortgage or other security interest in land to secure a preexisting debt. For example, a bank may make an unsecured loan and later ask the debtor to grant it a mortgage as security. Unless the bank somehow changes its position detrimentally in return for the mortgage (e.g., by granting an extension of time for repayment), the majority view is that the bank has not given value under the recording acts, and its mortgage will be subordinate to any prior unrecorded conveyances the debtor has made of the land. Gabel v. Drewrys Ltd., U.S.A., Inc., 68 So. 2d 372 (Fla. 1953); Annot., 39 A.L.R. 2d 1088

---

[20] By contrast, because Colorado's recording statute, Colo. Rev. Stat. § 38–35–109(1), protects "any person with any kind of rights" in the property, Colorado's courts have interpreted it to protect donees. See Eastwood v. Shedd, 166 Colo. 136, 442 P.2d 423 (1968).

(1955).[21] The notion, then, is that the "value" ought to be paid contemporaneously or subsequent to the conveyance.[22]

The timing of the payment of "value" can be critical. To be a BFP, one must have no notice of the prior unrecorded instrument at the time the value is paid. This is simple enough when the buyer pays cash at closing, but is more complicated with an installment contract sale. Suppose the buyer begins making monthly payments, but only learns of the prior unrecorded conveyance after paying half of the total price. Some sort of *pro tanto* protection seems in order; the most common method of accomplishing it is to give the buyer a lien on the real estate for the amount she paid before getting notice of the prior transferee's rights. See, e.g., Westpark, Inc. v. Seaton Land Co., 225 Md. 433, 171 A.2d 736 (1961). Should the buyer also get a lien for any improvements she has made? Should the buyer simply be permitted to complete her payments as per the contract, except with the payments accruing after she receives notice being made to the holder of the unrecorded title? See 5 Tiffany, Real Property § 1305 n. 41 (3d ed.1939) (describing cases taking this position).

Finally, consider the plight of the judgment creditor whose defendant-debtor has made unrecorded transfers of his real estate. The creditor, relying on the records, may assume that the debtor has substantial assets. He retains legal counsel, pays court costs and witness fees, obtains a judgment, and then discovers that the unrecorded deeds have left the defendant without assets. Can the creditor claim the protection of the recording acts? The typical answer is no, on the ground that the judgment creditor has not paid any contemporaneous "value" for his judgment lien (i.e., the judgment creditor is not a "reliance" creditor). See Faust Corp. v. Harris, 467 P.3d 710 (Okla. 2019); Wallin v. Wallin, 800 S.E.2d 617 (Ga. Ct. App. 2017); ABN AMRO Mortg. Group, Inc. v. American Residential Serv., LLC, 845 N.E.2d 209 (Ind. Ct. App. 2006); In re Brosnahan, 312 B.R. 220 (Bankr. W.D.N.Y. 2004); Texas American Bank/Levelland v. Resendez, 706 S.W.2d 343 (Tex. Ct. App. 1986); IV Am. L. Prop. § 17.10 n. 24, § 17.29 (1952); Note, Status of Judgment Creditors Under the Recording Acts, 32 Notre Dame L. Rev. 471 (1957).[23] By contrast, if a property is subject to a

---

[21] Conceptually, the same is true of a mechanic's lien claimant who originally performed work without taking any interest in the land as security, and who gives up no further value in return for the lien when it arises. See Stout v. Lye, 103 U.S. (13 Otto) 66, 26 L.Ed. 428 (1880). In many cases, however, the "relation back" feature of the mechanic's liens provides the lien claimant with greater priority than the claimant would gain through the recording act.

[22] Compare the case of the creditor who previously made an unsecured loan, and who later takes a deed of the land in satisfaction of the debt. This situation is different, for here the creditor has incurred a clear legal detriment—it has deemed the debt satisfied, given up its claim against the debtor, and thus should be deemed to have given value. See IV Am. L. Prop. § 17.10 n. 29 (1952) (collecting cases). Cf. Wight v. Chandler, 264 F.2d 249 (10th Cir. 1959).

[23] In a few states, courts have held that an unrecorded mortgage is subordinate to a subsequent judgment lien, either because the state's recording statute explicitly so provides or because the state's courts have interpreted the statute accordingly. See, e.g., Atkins North Am., Inc. v. Tallahassee MH Parks, LLC, 277 So.3d 1156 (Fla. Ct. App. 2019); Golub v. Kirk-Scott, Ltd.,

recorded judgment lien and the judgment creditor executes the lien through a foreclosure sale, a BFP who purchases the property at the execution sale before the prior conveyances are recorded will be protected. See IV Am. L. Prop. § 17.30 (1952); Valley Nat'l Bank v. Avco Dev. Co., 14 Ariz. App. 56, 480 P.2d 671 (1971). Does this distinction make sense? Suppose the judgment creditor is the BFP at the execution sale; should the creditor be protected?

Lack of notice. The second aspect of BFP status is lack of notice of the prior unrecorded conveyance. Thus, it is necessary to consider what sorts of notice might be imputed to a purchaser of real estate to deprive the purchaser of BFP status:

- *Actual knowledge* of the prior conveyance (such as through an express statement or direct observation) obviously constitutes notice. Rumors or gossip in the community usually are not sufficient, but if the buyer has heard some apparently reliable information about an adverse claim, she is expected to make a reasonable investigation of it.[24] See Beins v. Oden, 843 A.2d 147 (Md. Ct. App. 2004); 6A Powell, Real Property ¶ 916 n. 11 (1979); Annot., 109 A.L.R. 746 (1937); Caruso v. Parkos, 262 Neb. 961, 637 N.W.2d 351 (2002) (subsequent purchaser was not a BFP, where he learned of prior deed from conversations with family members). Information given to the purchaser's attorney will also suffice if a reasonable person would further investigate it. See First Alabama Bank of Huntsville v. Key, 394 So. 2d 67 (Ala. Civ. App. 1981).

- *Constructive record notice* clearly constitutes notice of a prior conveyance. Generally speaking, the recording of an instrument affecting title to land provides subsequent purchasers with constructive notice of its contents. The fact that a subsequent purchaser did not search the records and did not discover the prior claim on the record is irrelevant.

- *Constructive inquiry notice* can also constitute notice of a prior unrecorded conveyance. This occurs where the purchaser does not actually know of information suggestive

---

157 Idaho 966, 342 P.3d 893 (2015); Schleuter Co. v. Sevigny, 564 N.W.2d 309 (S.D. 1997); Solans v. McMenimen, 951 N.E.2d 999 (Mass. Ct. App. 2011); McDuff Estate v. Kost, 158 A. 373 (R.I. 1932).

24 Investigation requires that the purchaser must make an inquiry of the adverse claimant himself (if the claimant can be identified and located by reasonable effort). It is not enough for the purchaser to inquire of the seller, who in this context is in effect presumed to be a crook. Note carefully that the purchaser will be deemed to have whatever knowledge a proper and reasonable investigation would have turned up, whether she in fact makes any investigation or not. Courts sometimes describe this imputation of knowledge to the purchaser as a form of "constructive" notice or "inquiry" notice.

of an adverse claim, but where the court imputes to the purchaser notice of information that would have been revealed in a reasonable investigation (if the purchaser had bothered to conduct one). The classic example occurs where the holder of an unrecorded claim of title is in physical possession of the land. If B is purchasing Blueacre from O in the belief that O owns it based on O's apparent record title, but A (who in fact holds a prior unrecorded deed from O) is in physical possession of Blueacre; A's possession should be a "red flag" that a reasonable buyer in B's position would investigate further. Courts typically will impute to B in this situation whatever information a prudent investigation of A would reveal (in this example, that investigation would almost certainly reveal A's prior unrecorded deed).

NOTES AND QUESTIONS

1. *Who has notice of a recorded instrument?* The public records are sometimes said to be notice of their contents to "all the world," but this is an overstatement; the public records give no notice to people who have no thought of buying any interest in the land in question, and who consequently have no reason to search the records. For example, a construction contractor who damaged a telephone company's underground cable was held not to have had constructive notice of the cable's existence despite the fact that the company had a recorded easement for it. See Mountain States Tel. & Tel. Co. v. Kelton, 79 Ariz. 126, 285 P.2d 168 (1955).[25]

The public records *are* notice to subsequent purchasers, but even this statement is tempered by the concept of reasonableness. Suppose installment contract purchaser B (whose crooked vendor O has made a prior unrecorded deed to A) agrees to pay for the land in monthly installments over ten years. A, the grantee of the prior deed, records it after B has made installment payments for two years. Does A's recording automatically constitute record notice to B and prevent B from thereafter claiming the status of a BFP? The answer should be no, as this would require B to search the title before each monthly payment (an unjustifiable burden). In this situation, B will not be held to have notice of A's deed until some actual information concerning it reaches B. See, e.g., Dame v. Mileski, 80 Wyo. 156, 340 P.2d 205 (1959); Giorgi v. Pioneer Title Ins. Co., 85 Nev. 319, 454 P.2d 104 (1969).

2. *Other public records that give constructive notice.* The types of public records that give notice to purchasers are not limited to those in the county recorder's office. Other documents, such as property tax and assessment

---

[25] In most states today, a state statute or regulation other than the recording act creates a "dig safely" mechanism that enables owners and their contractors to call to have underground utilities located prior to digging. Owners or contractors who dig without complying with this process and who thus damage underground utilities can be held liable, but this duty (and the breach of that duty) arise under that separate statute, not by virtue of the recording act.

records and the docket records of the clerk of court, also are deemed to be constructive notice of adverse claims. See, e.g., Emigrant Bank v. Drimmer, 171 A.D.3d 1132, 99 N.Y.S.3d 79 (2019) (genuine issue of fact regarding whether examination of tax records would have revealed unrecorded mortgage precluded summary judgment for buyer under recording act). The court records that give constructive notice are not limited to judgments (which give rise to a liens on the defendant's real estate). Indeed, the very filing of a lawsuit in which the land's title is in question gives notice to a subsequent purchaser under the doctrine of *lis pendens*.[26] Thus, a purchaser of the land would take title subject to an adverse claim ultimately established in that litigation. Today, many states have statutory provisions for the filing of a "notice of lis pendens" in the county recorder's office, where a title searcher is much more likely to find it. But these statutes do not usually preempt fully the common law notion that the pendency of a suit involving land title is itself notice. See Chrysler Corp. v. Fedders Corp., 670 F.2d 1316 (3d Cir. 1982); IV Am. L. Prop. § 17.11. Consequently, court records always must be searched. For a comparison of common law and statutory lis pendens procedures, see Kelly v. Perry, 111 Ariz. 382, 531 P.2d 139 (1975), and Ravitch v. Stollman Poultry Farms, Inc., 162 Conn. 26, 291 A.2d 213 (1971).

By contrast, records maintained only in zoning and planning offices usually do not give constructive notice of adverse interests created thereby. See Story Bed & Breakfast v. Brown County Area, 794 N.E.2d 519 (Ind. Ct. App. 2003) (covenants filed only with county planning office); Ioannou v. Southold Town Planning Bd., 304 A.D.2d 578, 758 N.Y.S.2d 358 (2003) (same); First American Title Ins. Co. v. J.B. Ranch, Inc., 966 P.2d 834 (Utah 1998) (map filed only in county clerk's office); Island Venture Assocs. v. New Jersey Dept. of Envt'l Protection, 359 N.J. Super. 391, 820 A.2d 88 (App. Div. 2003) (restrictive covenant filed only with state environmental agency).

3.   *Inquiry notice from possession.* Courts almost universally follow the rule that a purchaser of land is deemed to have inquiry notice of facts that an inspection of the land and inquiry of persons in possession would disclose. See, e.g., Nampa Highway Dist. No. 1 v. Knight, 462 P.3d 137 (Idaho 2020); Mazza v. Realty Quest Brokerage Corp., 185 Misc. 2d 162, 712 N.Y.S.2d 288 (Civ. Ct. 2000); In re Crowder, 225 B.R. 794 (Bankr. D.N.M. 1998). But see Madison v. Gordon, 39 S.W.3d 604 (Tex. 2001) (possession by unrecorded titleholder of one apartment in a four-plex gave no constructive notice of possessor's unrecorded title where possessor appeared to be merely an ordinary tenant).

Trouble arises in determining what constitutes possession and what sorts of facts would lead a reasonable buyer to make further inquiry. For example, if the possession of the land is consistent with the record title (e.g., the grantor and his or her family are residing there), no inquiry is necessary. See, e.g.,

---

[26] Although a judgment will give rise to a lien on real property without regard to the nature of the litigation that produced the judgment, lis pendens based on the pendency of litigation requires that the litigation involve title to the land in question. See Central St. Matthew United Church of Christ v. Atkins, 264 So.3d 1243 (La. Ct. App. 2019) (cancellation of lis pendens notice proper where litigation did not address title to property).

Diamond v. Wasserman, 8 A.D.2d 623, 185 N.Y.S.2d 411 (1959) (possession by husband of home titled in wife's name did not give constructive notice of husband's alleged unrecorded interest to buyer from wife, since husband's possession was "consistent with the title of the apparent owner of record"). However, the cases tend to be highly fact-dependent, and thus a prudent purchaser should inquire of the possessor in any event. See, e.g., Yancey v. Harris, 234 Ga. 320, 216 S.E.2d 83 (1975) (buyer held to have notice of mother-in-law's unrecorded interest in home titled in son-in-law's name, where mother-in-law was sole occupant of the home); Tompkins County Trust Co. v. Talandis, 176 Misc. 2d 632, 673 N.Y.S.2d 301 (1998) (possession by record owner's ex-wife gave notice of her rights under unrecorded separation agreement); Martinez v. Affordable Housing Network, Inc., 123 P.3d 1201 (Colo. 2005) (continued possession of former owner under unrecorded lease with option to repurchase gave constructive notice of owner's rights to subsequent buyer). See generally IV Am. L. Prop. § 17.13 (1952); Comment, Grantor's Possession as Constructive Notice, 34 Miss. L. J. 325 (1963).

Suppose the property is a commercial store, and the tenant under an unrecorded lease puts a sign on the front of the building advertising his name and business. Here, a purchaser is surely expected to go inside and ask the tenant about the tenant's rights. The sign is not essential; it is possession by the tenant that does the trick. See, e.g., Apex Fin. Corp. v. Garza, 155 S.W.3d 230 (Tex. Ct. App. 2004); Grand Island Hotel Corp. v. Second Island Dev. Co., 191 Neb. 98, 214 N.W.2d 253 (1974); New Freedom Corp. v. Brown, 260 Md. 383, 272 A.2d 401 (1971).[27]

There also are many cases in which the facts are more ambiguous, and it is hard to predict the results. This is especially true where the holder of the unrecorded interest makes only sporadic or limited use of the property, such as camping or vacationing, running grazing stock, cutting timber, or parking motor vehicles. Compare Bradford v. Kimbrough, 485 So. 2d 1114 (Ala. 1986) with White v. Boggs, 455 So. 2d 820 (Ala. 1984). See IV Am. L. Prop. § 17.15 (1952). If the owner of the unrecorded interest places a sign on the property giving his name and address or telephone number, its presence will probably give inquiry notice to prospective purchasers even if his personal possession is dubious or weak. See, e.g., Chaffin v. Solomon, 255 Or. 141, 465 P.2d 217 (1970); Wineberg v. Moore, 194 F. Supp. 12 (N.D. Cal.1961), aff'd, 349 F.2d 685 (9th Cir. 1965).

    4.   *Inquiry notice from deed references.* A recorded instrument can sometimes refer to or describe a prior unrecorded one. For example, suppose a deed in the chain of title to Blackacre recites that the title is being transferred "subject to an easement previously granted to J.A. Jones for an irrigation ditch over the westerly ten feet." Suppose further that a deed really did grant an easement to J.A. Jones, but that deed was never recorded. Would a purchaser of Blackacre have inquiry notice of the easement? Under the traditional view,

---

[27] Incidentally, if the buyer does inquire of the party in possession, and the latter falsely denies his own interest in the land, the possessor will be estopped to assert that interest later. See Losey v. Simpson, 11 N.J. Eq. 246 (1856).

the reference to Jones's unrecorded easement in the later recorded deed will give a later purchaser notice of the easement if inquiry of Jones would have revealed the true nature of Jones's rights (assuming that Jones could be located by reasonable effort). See 14 Powell on Real Property § 82.02; Clancy v. Recker, 455 Pa. 452, 316 A.2d 898 (1974); Harper v. Paradise, 233 Ga. 194, 210 S.E.2d 710 (1974). See also Donald J. Kochan & James Charles Smith, When Inquiring Minds Ought to Know . . ., Prob. & Prop. 57–63 (Jul./Aug. 2017) (noting that in deciding the scope of the duty to inquire, courts tend to look at the precise language of the instrument in question and the actions a reasonable purchaser would take in response).

The traditional rule is obviously burdensome to title examiners, and several states have abolished it by statute. See, e.g., Colo. Rev. Stat. § 38–35–108 (when a recorded document "contains a recitation of or reference to some other instrument purporting to affect title to said real property, such recitation or reference shall bind only the parties to the instrument and shall not be notice to any other person whatsoever unless the instrument mentioned or referred to in the recital is [recorded]"); Mass. Gen. Laws Ann. ch. 184, § 25; Neb. Rev. Stat. §§ 76–275.04. Should other states adopt similar statutory provisions?

5.   *Does a quitclaim deed impart inquiry notice?* There is older authority that one who takes a quitclaim deed cannot be a BFP, because the form of deed itself indicates that the grantor is uncertain of his own title. Courts in a few states continue to express this view. See, e.g., Wells Fargo Bank, N.A. v. Sky Vista Homeowners Ass'n, 2017 WL 1364583 (D. Nev. 2017) ("a grantor's refusal to issue standard warranties of title puts a reasonable and prudent person on inquiry notice of any competing interests"). But this view makes no sense as a policy matter. There are plenty of good reasons for certain grantors to use a quitclaim deed, and having a quitclaim deed in one's chain of title should not by itself prevent a purchaser from qualifying for the protection of the recording statute. The better view, and the recent weight of authority, is that a grantee under a quitclaim deed may qualify as a BFP if the grantee is otherwise without notice of an adverse claim. See, e.g., Martinez v. Affordable Hous. Network, Inc., 123 P.3d 1201, 1207–08 (Colo. 2005) ("Colorado has rejected the now-disfavored notion that a quitclaim deed is enough, in itself, to put a purchaser on notice of a defect in title."); Sabo v. Horvath, 559 P.2d 1038 (Alaska 1976); 11 Thompson on Real Property § 92.09(c)(3)(C); Note, Deeds—Quitclaim Grantee as a Bona Fide Purchaser, 28 Ore. L. Rev. 258 (1949). Nevertheless, a rapid succession of transactions involving quitclaim deeds may be suspicious enough to trigger inquiry notice of an unrecorded interest. See, e.g., *Martinez*, supra (back-to-back quitclaim deeds should have raised suspicion in ultimate grantee's mind, and inquiry of possessor would have revealed possessor's unrecorded option); Schwalm v. Deanhardt, 21 Kan. App. 2d 667, 906 P.2d 167 (1995) (buyer's mortgagee held to have inquiry notice of seller/grantor's prior unrecorded mortgage, where buyer acquired title by quitclaim deed and granted mortgage on the same day).

6.   *Improperly recorded deeds and "curative acts."* Suppose a deed is recorded in error, in that sense that it was defectively acknowledged, no recording fee or tax was paid, or in some other fashion it failed to meet the requirements for proper recording. Nevertheless, the deed may contain accurate and highly important information about the title. In this situation, should the deed impart constructive notice of its contents to subsequent purchasers?

To demonstrate the point using an example that has produced a great deal of recent litigation, suppose that O (the owner of Blackacre) grants a mortgage to Bank. The mortgage is notarized, but not properly; O did not appear before the notary in person as the state acknowledgment statute requires. Being improperly acknowledged, the mortgage is not eligible to be recorded, and the recorder should reject it. Nevertheless, Bank presents the mortgage for recording and the recorder (unaware of the problem) accepts the mortgage and records it. Several months later, O purports to deed Blackacre to P (without having paid off the mortgage to Bank); P does not conduct a title search and does not know of Bank's mortgage. Under the traditional rule, if it is established that the mortgage was improperly notarized, P would not have constructive notice of Bank's mortgage—even though a simple title search would have revealed it! The ostensible justification for this approach is that the mortgage was not entitled to be present in the records in the first place. See IV Am. L. Prop. §§ 17.27, 17.31 n. 16 (1952); In re Crim, 81 S.W.3d 764 (Tenn. 2002); In re Phelps, 341 B.R. 848 (Bankr. W.D. Ky. 2006); Allen v. Allen, 86 Mass. App. Ct. 295, 16 N.E.3d 1078 (2014). Under this view, P would take title to Blackacre free of Bank's mortgage lien!

Perhaps it makes sense to treat such a document as unrecorded if the defect in the acknowledgement is patent (i.e., obvious on its face and thus apparent to anyone seeing it). See, e.g., *Allen*, supra (missing name); Metropolitan Nat'l Bank v. United States, 901 F.2d 1297 (5th Cir. 1990) (notary's conflict of interest apparent on face of mortgage). But as applied to a latent defect, this approach is dubious as a policy matter, as it compromises the reliability of the public records. A subsequent purchaser who conducts the most scrupulous due diligence will not ascertain that a document in its chain of title was improperly acknowledged where that defect is latent. If the grantor of a defectively acknowledged deed has a legal basis to invalidate it, but fails to take action to do so, the grantor should be estopped from taking such action once a subsequent good faith purchaser for value has intervened. The better view, and the trend in recent decisions, is that the recording of an defectively acknowledged instrument will still provide constructive notice of its contents if the defect is latent. See, e.g., Hildebrandt v. Hildebrandt, 683 P.2d 1288 (Kan. Ct. App. 1984); In re Spencer, 354 B.R. 758 (Bankr. D.S.C. 2006). Under this approach, P would take title to Blackacre subject to Bank's unsatisfied mortgage.

Two other factors could influence the effectiveness of an improperly acknowledged deed. First, in 42 states, legislatures have enacted "curative statutes" providing that either immediately upon recording or after the passage of some number of years, deeds or other instruments lacking seals, acknowledgments, or other technical requirements are nevertheless deemed to have been properly recorded. See In re Messer, 50 N.E.3d 495 (Ohio Ct. App. 2016) (discussing Ohio statute). Such statutes remove uncertainty from a title examiner's life, but they also raise a more fundamental question: is acknowledgement of the signature(s) on the deed by a notary public really necessary? Acknowledgment is supposed to be a protection against forgery, but because of the casual way in which many notaries approach their duties, it is not a very effective protection. The Uniform Simplification of Land Transfers Act (USLTA) would have abolished the acknowledgment requirement altogether, USLTA § 2–301(b), but it was not enacted in any state.

The second factor is the possibility that a title searcher sees the improperly acknowledged instrument on the record (even if it should not have been recorded), reads it, and thus obtains actual knowledge of the prior claim. If a title searcher in fact finds and reads the document, he or she will gain actual knowledge, and hence will be held to have notice of whatever information it provides, and may well be under a duty to make further reasonable inquiries based on that information. See Chandler v. Cameron, 229 N.C. 62, 47 S.E.2d 528 (1948); 6A Powell, Real Property ¶ 914 n. 3; 5 Tiffany, Real Property § 1264 n. 65 (3d ed. 1939); Annot., 59 A.L.R. 2d 1299, 1318 (1958).

4.   SEARCHING A TITLE

With the foregoing basic knowledge of recording acts and the public records system, we are now ready to discuss how titles are searched. If you practice law in the Northeastern United States, there is a good chance that you will use this information directly in your practice. In other areas of the country, abstract or title insurance companies perform most searches, but an understanding of the process is still very helpful to real estate attorneys. For a good description of abstract companies and their work, see Ford v. Guarantee Abstract & Title Co., 220 Kan. 244, 553 P.2d 254 (1976).

All privately held land titles (except those derived from accretion or adverse possession) can be traced back through a chain of owners to some original conveyance from a sovereign, typically the federal government or a state. Set forth below is a hypothetical chain of title that we can use as the basis for illustration of title search problems. You may wish to sketch it out on a separate piece of paper so you can keep it before you as you read the remainder of this section.

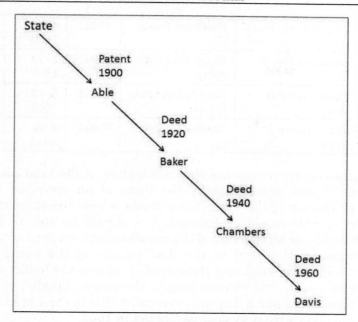

The patent is merely a grant of title by the state. The present owner of the land is Davis, and we will assume that he proposes to sell it to your client, who has asked you to search and examine the title. When you receive this assignment, you know nothing about the prior title history of the land; you are merely told its legal description (Lot 4, Block G, Suburban Acres) and the fact that Donald Davis presently claims to own it.

How will you proceed? The answer depends on the type of indexing system used by the recorder's office in your jurisdiction. From the title searcher's viewpoint, indexing by tract or parcel is by far the better method. This approach allocates a separate page or set of pages in the index books to each parcel of land, or perhaps to each tract (such as a quarter-quarter section), even though it might contain several parcels. As each instrument is brought into the courthouse for recordation, an entry is made on the appropriate page for each parcel affected by the instrument. A brief example is set forth below.

Parcel Index Lot 3, Block L. Eastlawn Estates Subdivision					
Type of Instrm't	Grantors, etc.	Grantees, etc.	Doc. No.	Date Files	Book & Page
(Note: for prior instruments, see SE1/4 of NW1/4, T4N,R2E.)					
Subdiv. Plat	Eastlawn Devel. Co.	————	45872	9–15 1949	34–17 Plat Bk
Deed of Trust	Eastlawn Devel. Co.	Fourth State Bank	47339	10–10 1949	117–667

Reconv.	Fourth State Bank	Eastlawn Devel. Co.	48960	5–12 1950	119–88
Deed	Eastlawn Devel. Co.	Shaw, Harry & Betty	48961	5–12 1950	119–89
Deed of Trust	Shaw, Harry & Betty	Last Federal Sav. & Loan	48962	5–12 1950	119–90
Lis Pen	Shaw, Harry & Betty	Gotcha, George	53964	8–30 1952	124–733

This illustration represents the title history of the land commencing at the time it was subdivided by the filing of an approved plat. The reference at the top of the illustration shows where the same land's pre-subdivision records would be indexed. You should be able to follow the imposition and later satisfaction of the construction loan deed of trust given by the developer, the deed to the first owners of the house that the developer built on the land, and their deed of trust to the lender who made the loan with which first owners bought the house. Finally, you can see that they apparently had a dispute concerning title to their land, and were sued in connection with it by George Gotcha in 1952.

With a tract index, the construction by the title examiner of a chain of title is relatively easy because all of the relevant information is together on a single page or pages. Of course, it may be necessary to consult other records in other offices (e.g., for wills, intestacies, judgments, property taxes, etc.), but in most cases the chain of title can be determined without much trouble. The title examiner must then pull the books from the shelves, or check the microfilm or computer-scanned copies, and examine the actual copies of the instruments themselves to see if they appear to be regular and indeed affect the land in question. The references in the last column on the right in the index book tell the searcher the exact book and page number where each document will be found. If any prior owner has made an "adverse conveyance"—one that impairs the present quality of the title or makes it unmarketable—this fact will be very easy to see. For example, a lis pendens would be considered such an adverse conveyance unless it had been removed later or a statute of limitations had cut it off.

The tract index is very convenient for title searchers, but it does require a reasonable amount of skill on the part of the recording office personnel, who must read every instrument with some care to determine what land it affects, and properly index it, perhaps under multiple parcels. This is not difficult when the legal description is based on a recorded subdivision plat as in our illustration, but it can be formidable with descriptions based on natural monuments (e.g., "to the old white oak tree").

Perhaps for this reason, only a few American states provide in their recording statutes for the maintenance of tract or parcel indexes.[28]

In the great majority of states, the only official indexes available to title searchers in the courthouse are "name" or "grantor-grantee" indexes—those based on the names of the parties to a given instrument. A name index is easier to construct and maintain, but much more difficult to search than a tract index. The overall advantages of the tract index are attested by the fact that virtually every privately owned set of title records ("title plant") in the nation employs tract indexing.

For many years there was little pressure from any organized group—recorders, lawyers, title companies, or the public—for reform of the traditional name index system. In recent years, however, a movement has taken root, with the encouragement of a few progressive county recorders and of Fannie Mae and Freddie Mac (the two principal federally sponsored secondary market purchasers of mortgage loans), to develop and implement computer-based tract indexing systems.[29] The organization most actively involved in this movement is the Property Records Industry Association (PRIA). The Uniform Real Property Electronic Recording Act (URPERA), endorsed by PRIA, has been promulgated the Uniform Law Commission and authorizes recorders to accept electronic filings. URPERA, promulgated in 2005, has now been adopted in 35 jurisdictions.

Such filings can be indexed and therefore searched by any item of information—names, tract, type of document, date, or other relevant information. To service this new demand, a number of commercial firms are providing software (and as needed, hardware) to permit recorders to accept electronic documents, record them in a quasi-automated fashion, and make them searchable by members of the public and the title insurance industry via the Internet. A fair number of recorders' offices, usually in populous counties, have already made this shift, and others are seriously considering it. Thus, it seems possible that within a few years, a truly modern system of public land title records will be available in much of the United States (though with all of the legal limitations of the recording system still intact, of course).

Suppose you are not fortunate enough to practice in a state with an official tract index. (Ironically, in those states few lawyers perform

---

[28] See generally Note, The Tract and Grantor-Grantee Indices, 47 Iowa L. Rev. 481 (1962). The USLTA mandates a tract index, but it has not been adopted by any state legislature. See § 6–207. The USLTA also contains an interesting and apparently unprecedented feature requiring those who present instruments for recordation to supply "information fixing the location sufficiently to enable the recording officer to determine where in the geographic index the document is to be indexed." USLTA § 2–302(a)(4).

[29] See Whitman, Digital Recording of Real Estate Documents, 32 John Marshall L. Rev. 227 (1999). Recorders are authorized (but not required) to accept electronic documents for recording by the Uniform Electronic Transactions Act (UETA) § 17–19, promulgated in 1999 and adopted in every state except Illinois and New York.

searches in the public records.) Instead, you find that you must search in the name indexes in your courthouse. How can you construct a chain of title to the land your client wishes to buy from Davis? There are dual sets of name indexes; one set is arranged alphabetically by the name of the grantee(s) to each instrument, and the other alphabetically by the name of the grantor(s). You will begin your work in the grantee index, which might take a form like this:

| Grantee Index   Year 1960 | | | | | | |
| Grantee's Names beginning with   Da | | | | | | |
Type of Instrm't	Grantee's Name	Grantor's Name	Doc. No.	Date Filed	Book & Page	Brief Legal Description
Release of Easm't	Davis, Abner	Voltzman Elect. Power Co.	2243	5-22 1960	344-221	Lt. 14, Block B Ridge Estates
Mech's Lien	Damion Plumbing & Heating	Fish, Frederick	4322	8-16 1960	346-132	E ½ of SE ¼ Sec. 22, R2E T3N
Deed	Davis, Donald	Chambers, Elaine	2089	8-19 1960	346-367	Lot 4, Block G Suburban Acres
Lease	Dalton's Men's Wear	Watson Real Estate, Inc.	4531	8-28 1960	346-451	Lots 3-4, Brown's Addition No. 2

There are several interesting features of the grantee index page above. The grantees' names are not in exact alphabetical order, because they are entered on the page (this one is labeled "Da") as they come into the office for recordation. In some sophisticated offices, a computer program may be used to resort and reprint the pages periodically in accurate alphabetical order. Note that all entries are during the year 1960. In large urban counties, a new set of index books is generally made up each year. If this were not done, the books would soon become so large as to be physically unmanageable. In rural counties with few transactions, the indexes might be allowed to accumulate over five or even ten years before a new set is begun.

Now, to search Donald Davis's title, we must begin by looking for his name in the grantee index, because if Davis owns the land he must have been a grantee under a deed at some point in time. Unless we can get a copy of Davis's deed from him or he tells us when he acquired the land, we will not know which one of the grantee books to check, so we must start with the present year and work our way backwards, looking for Davis's name as a grantee. When we finally get to 1960 and read the page reproduced above, we will find him. Scanning across to the "Brief Legal Description" column will verify that the entry does in fact affect the land we are searching. Unfortunately, in some states there is no such column, and we would have to look up in the actual record books each deed that is indexed with Davis as a grantee to see what land it covers. If Davis had bought a good deal of real estate in the county, this could become exceedingly tedious. Even where the indexes carry this column, there may be a serious but rarely litigated question as to whether a title searcher can safely rely upon it. As a practical matter, however, searchers obviously do so.

We must now look for the next link (going backward in time) in the chain of title. We do so by looking for Elaine Chambers's name in the grantee index, because the entry that we found under Davis's name told us that Chambers was Davis's grantor. We assume that Chambers received title to the land prior to the time she deeded it to Davis (although this need not always be true under the doctrine of estoppel by deed), and begin looking for her name as a grantee in 1960. Searching back year by year, we will find her as a grantee from Baker in 1940. We then search for Baker as a grantee, and so on, until we come back to the original patent from the state in 1900.

We now have a complete chain of title to the land, but that is only the first of three major steps in searching the record title. The second step involves determining whether any one of the owners we have identified has made any adverse conveyances. Suppose, for example, that Able (who obtained the land in 1900) granted an easement to Zoller in 1910. You might wish to pencil in such a grant on the diagram of the chain of title. We would certainly want to advise our client that the easement exists. How can we discover such conveyances? We must use the other set of name indexes, those arranged alphabetically by the name of the grantor. A part of a typical page might look as follows:

Grantor Index   Year <u>1960</u>
Grantor's Names beginning with   <u>Aa through Ac</u>

Type of Instrm't	Grantor's Name	Grantor's Name	Doc. No.	Date Filed	Book & Page	Brief Legal Description
Mortg.	Ackerman, Alan	Third Nat'l Bank	2276	1-14 1910	22-889	Pt. of N ½ Sec. 5 R3E T6S
Grant of Easement	Abie, Abner	Zoller, Charles	2298	2-21 1910	22-970	Lot 4, Block G Suburban Acres
Assign. of Mtg.	Abbott Mortgage Co.	Philadelphia Soc. for Savings	2375	4-12 1910	23-29	Lot 18, Summit Ridge Add'n
Release of Mtg.	Abbott Mortgage Co.	Weller, Frank Martha	2418	7-7 1910	23-445	S ½ of NE 1/4 Sec. 12, R3E T5S

We will begin with Able's name.[30] Able acquired the land in 1900 and deeded it away to Baker in 1920. Therefore, we will look for any conveyances with Able as a grantor during that period. (We will discuss later whether a title searcher also needs to look under Able's name prior to 1900 or after 1920). Again, we check the records year by year, this time in the grantor index. The page reprinted above shows that in 1910 Able was a grantor to Zoller of an easement. Unless we subsequently find a release of the easement by Zoller (which we can find by looking in the grantor index under his name), we must conclude that the easement still exists and report it to our client as affecting the current state of the title. Of course, some off-record circumstances, such as a stone wall that has blocked the path of the easement for 30 years, might convince us that despite the records the easement is no longer viable but has been terminated by prescription.

We must check the grantor index in a similar fashion for Baker, Chambers, and Davis to see if any of them made adverse conveyances. We are very likely to find, for example, that one or more of them gave mortgages or deeds of trust on the land. We must then use the grantor index to trace any further transfers or releases of these interests to determine whether they still affect the title today. We might even discover that Baker was a crook, and gave a deed to some person outside our chain of title (say, Zobell), in 1930. Zobell, in turn, might have started a chain of further conveyances leading down to a present owner who would claim title as against Davis.

---

[30] Why not begin with the state itself? It is surely possible that the state land office inadvertently issued two patents on the same land. If our chain of title derives from the second, then it presumably has no validity at all. In some states, the recording acts or other statutes specifically treat state patents in the same manner as other deeds. Thus, if the first patent were unrecorded in the county records, the second one would prevail in the hands of a BFP. See 2 Patton, Titles § 296 (2d ed. 1957) (listing 16 states with such statutes); Meacham v. Stewart, 19 Or. 285, 24 P. 241 (1890). In other jurisdictions there is no applicable statute, and the records of the state land office are sufficient to sustain the first patent even against a BFP holder of the second. See, e.g., United States v. Buras, 332 F. Supp. 1017 (E.D. La. 1970), rev'd, 458 F.2d 346 (5th Cir. 1972); Moran v. Palmer, 13 Mich. 367 (1865). In these states, a careful title searcher ought to review the records in the land office to make certain that no earlier patent covers the land in question. The same is true of federal patents because state recording statutes cannot divest them. Patton, supra; Lomax v. Pickering, 173 U.S. 26, 19 S.Ct. 416, 43 L.Ed. 601 (1899); Sayward v. Thompson, 11 Wash. 706, 40 P. 379 (1895); 8A Thompson, Real Property § 4348 (1963). Even though the records of the United States patent offices are constructive notice to subsequent purchasers, and many states would probably take the same position with respect to state-issued patents, it is doubtful that many title searchers attempt to check for duplicate or overlapping patents. On federal patent procedures generally, see III Am. L. Prop. § 12.20 (1952).

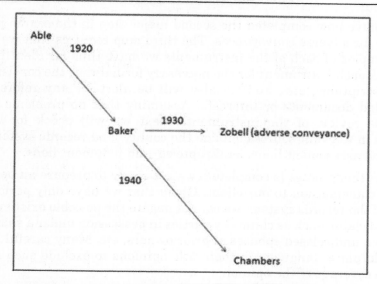

If the deed from Baker to Zobell is recorded, it (and persons claiming under it) would have priority over the chain of title we have discovered from Baker through Chambers to Davis, and Davis would own nothing. Fortunately, because the deed to Zobell was recorded, we will be able to find it by our normal search process, and thus can warn our client not to buy the land from Davis. On the other hand, if the deed from Baker to Zobell is not recorded, then we would need only to show that Chambers, Davis, or our own client was a BFP in order to cut off Zobell by operation of the recording acts. Incidentally, if Chambers, for example, were a BFP, then Davis (and our client) could take the land safely even though they were aware of the unrecorded adverse conveyance to Zobell. This is so because of the so-called "shelter rule," which says that once title has come into the hands of a BFP who is protected by the recording acts, the BFP can pass that protection on to grantees even if they have notice of the prior adverse conveyance. See Wachovia Bank, N.A. v. Swenton, 133 A.D.3d 846, 20 N.Y.S.3d 405 (2015); Hendricks v. Lake, 12 Wash. App. 15, 528 P.2d 491 (1974); IV Am. L. Prop. § 17.11 nn. 18–20 (1952); 3 Pomeroy, Equity Jurisprudence 55–57 (5th ed. 1941). The one exception is that if title is transferred back to one who had previously held it with notice of the adverse conveyance before it was "cleansed" by the BFP, he will not be protected. Thus, one cannot "clean up" one's own title merely by running it through a BFP. See Rose v. Knapp, 153 Cal. App. 2d 379, 314 P.2d 812 (1957). If the shelter rule did not exist and the news of Baker's adverse conveyance to Zobell became common knowledge in the community after Baker's conveyance to Chambers, Chambers might find that she owned the land but could not as a practical matter sell it to anyone, because no one else could qualify as a BFP without notice of the adverse conveyance.

We have now completed the second major step in the search process, checking for adverse conveyances. The third step requires that we look at the full copies of each of the instruments we have thus far identified. We will check each instrument for the necessary formalities, the consistency of legal descriptions, etc., and we also will be alert for any references to unrecorded documents or interests. Assuming that no problems emerge from this review of the instruments, next we will check for adverse interests in relevant sources outside the county land records system, such as tax and assessment liens, bankruptcies, and judgment liens.

Once this process is completed, we are ready to prepare an opinion of title for transmission to our client. Given that we have only performed a search of the records system, we cannot negate the possible existence of an off-record claim, such as claims by parties in possession under a short-term oral lease, undisclosed spouses of prior owners, etc. Many careful lawyers use "boilerplate" language in their title opinions to exclude such matters from the coverage of the opinion.

Note that in our title search we assumed that the names of the various prior owners are unambiguous and readily found in the indexes. But this is not always the case. One Connecticut lawyer gave the following examples to the authors:

> In the Town of New Milford, Connecticut, all documents which appear to concern a religious organization are indexed under "C" for "Church" even if the word "church" doesn't appear in the name (e.g., First Lutheran Society). Likewise, in New Milford all Federal agencies are indexed under "U" for "United States of America" (a deed from "John Smith, Secretary of Housing and Urban Development" will be indexed under "U" as "United States of America—HUD." In the Town of Farmington for many years, all documents pertaining to financial institutions were indexed under "B" for "Bank" (e.g., Society for Savings).

Obviously, as with politics, never forget that all recording systems are local!

Computerized alphabetization of the indexes may not help, and may actually make things worse. The Connecticut lawyer mentioned above referred to a case in which "The property owner is X. Y. Z. Corporation, Inc., and I didn't find the $20,000,000.00 mortgage because it was indexed 5 pages away under XYZ Corp." Searching titles is not for out-of-towners or the faint of heart!

NOTES AND QUESTIONS

1.   *The "misindexed" deed.* Suppose that the recorder accepts a properly executed and delivered deed for recording, and places a copy of it into the official record books, but then makes an error in indexing the deed. For

example, suppose that the grantee's last name is "Britt" but that the recorder misspells the grantee's name when entering the deed into the indexes and thus wrongly indexes the deed in the name indexes under the last name "Tritt."[31] [If the county has a tract index, the misspelling of the grantee's name would be a harmless error as long as the deed is still indexed on the appropriate tract page, but misindexing could still occur if the recorder placed the deed on the wrong tract page.]

A misindexed deed is virtually worthless to a title searcher because the indexes are essential to the title search process. The task of finding a recorded but misindexed deed is the proverbial task of finding a needle in a haystack. [Can you explain why?] The traditional rule was that a misindexed deed gave constructive notice to subsequent purchasers (even though such purchasers had little chance of finding it). See, e.g., Miller v. Simonson, 140 Idaho 287, 92 P.3d 537 (2004); Anderson v. North Florida Production Credit Ass'n., 642 So.2d 88 (Fla. Ct. App. 1994); In re Harris, 183 B.R. 657 (D.D.C. 1995). One might defend this approach on the theory that the person that recorded the deed should not be held accountable for the recorder's error.

Of course, the person that recorded the deed knows that she did so, and is thus in a position to "double-check" to make sure that the recorder indexed it properly so that subsequent purchasers have the ability to find it in a title search. By contrast, the subsequent purchaser without knowledge of the prior misindexed deed is most unlikely to discover the problem. By virtue of this realization, one might argue that the person that recorded the deed is in the position of "cheaper cost avoider" and thus the deed should not be deemed to give constructive notice unless it is also properly indexed. A number of recent decisions treat misindexed instruments as failing to give constructive notice. See Hudson City Sav. Bank v. 59 Sands Point, LLC, 162 A.D.3d 644, 79 N.Y.S.3d 60 (2018); Dyer v. Martinez, 147 Cal. App. 4th 1240, 54 Cal. Rptr. 3d 907 (2007); Coco v. Ranalletta, 189 Misc. 2d 535, 733 N.Y.S.2d 849 (2001); Keybank Nat'l Ass'n v. NBD Bank, 699 N.E.2d 322 (Ind. Ct. App. 1998); Hanson v. Zoller, 187 N.W.2d 47 (N.D. 1971); Mortensen v. Lingo, 13 Alaska 419, 99 F. Supp. 585 (1951).

In First Citizens Nat'l Bank v. Sherwood, 817 A.2d 501 (Pa. Super. Ct. 2003), the court took an intermediate position, holding that although a misindexed document ordinarily would not give constructive notice, it might do so if a computerized search facility provided by the recorder allowed full text searches of the recorded documents. Can you explain why such a search mechanism would overcome the misindexing error?

---

[31] This is an example of the kind of recording error that will disappear as recording offices ultimately shift toward universal electronic recording. In counties that have fully adopted e-recording, the indexes may be generated automatically by the recorder's software system using the names reflected in the electronic deed. Under such an approach, if the parties have spelled the names of the grantor and grantee correctly, misindexing could not occur. Where the recorder has to manually input and produce indexes, however, human error produces the occasional misindexing.

2.   *The misspelled deed*. Suppose that a deed or mortgage misspells the grantor's last name. For example, suppose that a mortgage granted to First Bank identifies the borrower as "John Bolen" even though the borrower's correct legal name is "John Bolan." First Bank records the mortgage. If the land is later sold to a purchaser who has no knowledge of First Bank's mortgage, does that purchaser take with constructive notice of the mortgage, or can the purchaser argue that the recording of the mortgage under the incorrect name failed to give constructive notice of First Bank's mortgage?

Under the *idem sonans* doctrine, a mistake or misspelling of a name would not necessarily defeat the ability of a recorded instrument to provide constructive notice, at least where the correct name and the misspelled name sound similar. Applying this notion here, First Bank might argue that if the purchaser searched under "sound-alike" spellings, the purchaser would have located First Bank's mortgage. The weight of recent authority, however, would reject the doctrine in this situation. See, e.g., National Packaging Corp. v. Belmont, 47 Ohio App.3d 86, 547 N.E.2d 373 (1988) (notice of judgment lien that misspelled judgment debtor's name did not give constructive notice to subsequent purchaser of land). Is it too burdensome too expect the purchaser to search under plausible alternative spellings? By contrast, is it too burdensome to expect the grantee to confirm that the grantor's name is spelled correctly prior to recording?

Would the misspelling of an owner's first name on an instrument defeat the ability of subsequent purchasers to locate the instrument? Why or why not? See, e.g., United States v. Z Invst. Props., LLC, 921 F.3d 696 (7th Cir. 2019) (omission of single letter from debtor's first name did not invalidate federal tax lien on debtor's property).

3.   *Name changes*. Suppose that Chris Jackson owns Blueacre in fee simple absolute. He borrows $300,000 from First Bank, granting First Bank a mortgage on Blueacre which is timely recorded. Two years later, Jackson legally changes his name to Mahmoud Abdul-Rauf after he converts to Islam, but nothing is recorded in the land records indicating the name change. Another year later, using his now-legal name, Mahmoud Abdul-Rauf conveys Blueacre to Buyer, who pays value and has no actual knowledge of First Bank's mortgage (which remains unsatisfied). When Jackson defaults, First Bank begins a foreclosure proceeding; Buyer argues that Buyer took title free of First Bank's mortgage. What result? Should First Bank have to correct the records following Jackson's name change to maintain the recorded status of its mortgage? Why or why not?

5.   CHAIN OF TITLE PROBLEMS

There are certain types of adverse conveyances that are difficult or impossible to find, even though they are in fact recorded. Your teacher may want you to go over them in detail, and may assign additional reading for that purpose. We will merely summarize them below.

The wild deed. A wild deed is one that is not properly connected to the chain of title because a predecessor has failed to record his or her deed. For example, suppose that O purchased Blueacre (an undeveloped parcel) in 2000 as an investment. In 2005, O conveyed Blueacre to A, but A failed to record. In 2010, A conveyed Blueacre to B, and B recorded his deed (but does not take possession). Finally, in 2020, O conveys Blueacre to C, who pays value and has no knowledge of B's prior claim. Does B's deed—which does appear in the public records—give constructive notice of B's prior claim to C? The answer is no. Because A never recorded, there is a "missing link" in B's chain of title. Searching via name indexes, C will never be able to locate B's prior claim because B's deed is "wild." Courts have uniformly ruled that a wild deed does not give constructive notice. See, e.g., Board of Educ. of City of Minneapolis v. Hughes, 118 Minn. 404, 136 N.W. 1095 (1912); In re Nowlin, 558 B.R. 907 (Bankr. C.D. Cal. 2016). Would the wild deed be a problem if the jurisdiction has a tract index?

The late-recorded deed. Suppose that O, the owner of Blueacre, grants an easement over Blueacre to X in 2010. X fails to record the deed immediately. In 2015, O then deeds Blueacre to Y. In 2016, X belatedly records the easement. Then, in 2021, Y deeds Blueacre to Z, who pays value and takes possession without knowledge of X's easement. X then tries to assert the right to use the easement against Z. Is Z a BFP, or did Z take title with constructive notice of X's easement (which did appear on the record in 2021 when Z purchased Blueacre)?

If the jurisdiction has a tract index, Z will have constructive notice of X's easement, which Z would find on the appropriate tract page (even if it was recorded out of sequence). But in a jurisdiction that has only name indexes, you should see the problem for Z. A search of the grantor index for adverse conveyances under O's name will reveal no conveyances by O until the 2015 deed to Y. At that point, a searcher in Z's position is likely to stop looking in the grantor index under O's name, and instead will begin searching under Y's name. If so, Z would never find X's easement (and would wrongly conclude that no easement existed). Z would only find X's easement if Z kept searching under O's name for adverse conveyances even after 2015.

Should a title searcher like Z be expected to look for the adverse conveyance not only during the period each previous owner had title, but also thereafter—potentially down to the present time? Such a search is not impossible to do, but it adds greatly to the title searcher's burden. Nearly half of the cases on this point treat the adverse conveyance as if it were unrecorded, thereby sparing title searchers additional work. See, e.g., Rolling "R" Constr., Inc. v. Dodd, 477 So.2d 330 (Ala. 1985). By contrast, others would hold that X's recorded easement did give constructive notice to Z, even though it was recorded out of sequence. See, e.g., Angle v. Slayton, 102 N.M. 521, 697 P.2d 940 (1985). Who was in the better position to have avoided this problem: X (by timely recording) or Z (by extending his title search)?

The early-recorded deed. You may think an "early-recorded deed" is a typographical error—how can a deed be recorded before it is effective? But under the doctrine of after-acquired title, this is exactly what can happen. For example, suppose that in 2000, O has no title to Blueacre at all, but executes and delivers a warranty deed purporting to convey Blueacre to X (who timely records). In 2015, O actually obtains a deed from the legal owner of Blueacre (through a legitimate chain of title), and records that deed. Under the doctrine of estoppel by deed, O's title immediately inures to X. But now suppose that O in 2020 purports to convey Blueacre by deed to Y, who pays value and has no knowledge of X's prior claim of title. Does X's "too early recorded" deed give constructive notice of X's prior claim to Y? Again, you should be able to see the problem. In searching for adverse conveyances by O, Y is likely to begin searching in the grantor index under O starting in 2015 (which is when O actually acquired title and recorded). Searching forward, Y will find no adverse conveyances; Y would discover the adverse conveyance to X only if Y searched the indexes for adverse conveyances by O prior to 2015. But Y is unlikely to search backwards; it may not occur to Y that O might have purported to deed the land to someone else years before O obtained title to it!

By contrast to the "too late recorded" problem, most courts have held that the too-early-recorded deed does not provide constructive of its contents to subsequent purchasers. See, e.g., Sabo v. Horvath, 559 P.2d 1038 (Alaska 1976); Deutsche Bank Nat'l Trust Co. v. Arrington, 772 S.E.2d 571 (Va. 2015); Wells Fargo Bank, N.A. v. Simpson, 36 N.E.3d 266 (Ill. Ct. App. 2015). Who was in the better position to have avoided this problem: X (by recording in the proper sequence), or Y (by extending her search)? Will this problem arise if the county maintains a tract index?

The deed for one parcel encumbers another parcel. Suppose that a former owner, O, held two adjacent lots and sold one while retaining the other. The deed contained a covenant that neither lot would ever be used except for a single-family residence. Now suppose your client, X, has agreed to buy the lot that O retained, and you are searching its title. The retained lot is encumbered by the single-family residence covenant, but how can you discover that fact? The covenant encumbering the retained lot is contained in a recorded deed, but it is in the deed for a *different lot* than the lot for which you are searching. *If* the grantor index in your county includes a "brief description" column, and *if* the recorder's office personnel indicated in that column that the deed for the first lot affected both lots, you can easily find the covenant that encumbers the title to the lot you are searching. If either of these facts is not true, you will find the encumbrance on the retained lot only by reading in detail *every* deed the former owner ever recorded. Note that if the former owner was a real estate developer, that might be a very large number of deeds!

About half of the cases considering this problem save the title searcher the extra work; they would treat the encumbrance on the retained lot as not having been recorded within the chain of title to the retained lot (and thus as not imparting constructive notice of the restriction to X).[32] See, e.g., Witter v. Taggart, 78 N.Y.2d 234, 573 N.Y.S.2d 146, 577 N.E.2d 338 (1991); Huntington Nat'l Bank v. R Kids Count Learning Center, LLC, 97 N.E.3d 1228 (Ohio Ct. App. 2017). By contrast, other courts have held that the deed with the covenant is recorded within the chain of title and thus would give constructive notice of the covenant to X. See, e.g., Guillette v. Daly Dry Wall, Inc., 367 Mass. 355, 325 N.E.2d 572 (1975).

In many areas of the nation, particularly in the Midwest and on the West Coast, there is little search activity in the typical recorder's office. Instead, most title searches are conducted in private "title plants" owned by abstract or title insurance companies. Because these title plants are invariably arranged on a tract index basis, these chain of title problems are, for the most part, of no practical importance in such areas. How should a court deal with a chain of title issue in a state where few searchers will ever encounter it in practice? And what of the importance of reform of the public records, by computerization and tract indexing, in such states? See Hale, Real Property E-Conveyances and E-Recordings: The Solution or Cause of Mortgage Fraud, 5 Okla. J.L. & Tech. 1 (2009) (noting capacity of systems to allow for full-text searching of documents to eliminate chain of title problems).

6.   MARKETABLE TITLE ACTS

As described previously, a complete title search would trace the chain of title back to a grant from the original owner, and would involve searches for adverse conveyances by all prior owners in the chain of title. In many states, this would require a search covering 150 years or more. Not only are such searches expensive to conduct, but in most cases the likelihood of an "ancient" title defect is remote.

Some state bar associations have attempted to streamline the search process through the development of so-called "title standards." Title standards allow attorneys who examine titles to pass certain minor or trivial title defects without being concerned that some later attorney will attack the title as unmarketable on the same grounds. Title standards commonly provide a standard search period, see, e.g., Ga. Title Standard 2.1 ("A record title search covering a period of 50 years or more is considered sufficient to determine marketability[.]"), and may also provide

---

[32]   Under this approach, how should the covenant have been created in a way that would have obviated this problem?

suggested procedures for curing certain common defects. These standards do not have the force of law, however, except to the extent that:

- they are adopted by a state's legislature, see Neb. Rev. Stat. § 76–557 (in examining title, "it shall not be considered negligence for a registered abstracter or an attorney to follow the Title Standards promulgated by the Nebraska State Bar Association"); or

- the parties to a contract of sale explicitly incorporate such standards into the title provisions in their contract, see., e.g., Youngblut v. Wilson, 294 NW.2d 813 (Iowa 1980).

For a useful (if now dated) survey of state title examination standards, see Kraettli Q. Epperson & Kevin A. Sullivan, Title Examination Standards: A Status Report, 4 Prob. & Prop. 16 (Sept./Oct. 1990).

Because the title standards do not have the force of law, a prospective buyer of Blackacre who limits their title search to 50 years might not discover that in a document recorded 60 years earlier, the owner of Blackacre created an easement, restrictive covenant, or reversionary interest affecting title to Blackacre. The buyer might thus proceed with the purchase and may unknowingly take subject to this "ancient" interest. The question thus arises: if we truly want to streamline the title search process, should the owner of such an "ancient" interest have to re-record some evidence of that interest periodically in order to maintain its validity?

Twenty states have adopted a "marketable record title" statute designed to streamline the search process in this manner. These statutes assist the searcher by limiting the historic scope of a title search to a "root deed" or "root of title" identified by reference to a period of time defined by the statute (ranging from 20 years in North Dakota to 50 years in Indiana). These statutes require a person who claims an interest in land by virtue of an "ancient" instrument (one that was created longer ago than the statutory search period) to record a notice sufficient under the statute to preserve that interest, so that the interest appears in writing within the shortened chain of title. If the person fails to do so, the statute extinguishes that interest.

For example, imagine that in 1930, B (then-owner of Blackacre) granted and recorded an easement that burdened Blackacre for the benefit of the adjoining parcel, Whiteacre. In 1960, B conveyed Blackacre to C by a recorded deed that made no mention of the easement. In 1975, C conveyed Blackacre to X by a recorded deed that again made no mention of the easement. Then, in 2020, X contracts to sell Blackacre to Y. There is no visible evidence that an easement exists over Blackacre, Y has no knowledge of the easement's existence, and the easement's existence is not mentioned in any deed in the chain of title to Blackacre since the easement was recorded in 1930. Absent a marketable title statute, the current owner of Whiteacre could continue to enforce the easement (absent evidence sufficient to establish its abandonment or termination in some other manner). Under a marketable title statute with a 50-year search period, however, Y does not have to search any further back in the records than the 1960 B-to-C deed (the last deed in the otherwise-complete chain of title as of 1970, 50 years prior to the 2020 X-to-Y contract). Because no evidence of the easement appears in that deed or any subsequent deed in the chain of title, the easement is extinguished. See generally Basye, Clearing Land Titles, Ch. 5 (3d ed. 2014); Barnett, Marketable Title Acts—Panacea or Pandemonium, 53 Cornell L. Rev. 45 (1967); Swenson, Utah Marketable Title Act, 8 Utah L. Rev. 200 (1963). Marketable title acts are found in California, Connecticut, Florida, Illinois, Indiana, Iowa, Kansas, Kentucky (applicable only to possibilities of reverter and rights of entry); Michigan, Minnesota, Nebraska, North Carolina, North Dakota, Ohio, Oklahoma, South Dakota, Utah, Vermont, Wisconsin, and Wyoming.[33]

Unfortunately, the existing marketable title acts contain a number of exceptions for interests that are permitted to survive despite the fact they are mentioned only in documents predating the root of title. These include rights of the United States government (which state law has no power to cut off, of course), rights of state and local governments, visible easements, roads or highways, utility or railroad easements, mineral rights, and so on. The exceptions are usually the result of political pressures brought by lobbyists for the groups or industries affected; they obviously make the acts much less effective in reducing search periods, because they make stopping at the root of title more risky. See, e.g., Note, Property Law—North Carolina's Marketable Title Act—Will the Exceptions Swallow the Rule?, 52 N.C.L. Rev. 211 (1973).

Marketable title acts were given a considerable boost by the development of a model act by Lewis Simes and Clarence Taylor at the University of Michigan in 1960. See Simes, A Handbook for More Efficient Conveyancing (U. Mich. L. School 1960). Half of the existing marketable title acts have been passed since that time. Most marketable title acts are found in Midwestern states where title searches commonly are performed by abstract companies who work in their own private tract-indexed title plants. But two New England states, Connecticut (1967) and Vermont (1969), and two Southern states, North Carolina (1973) and Florida (1963), have passed marketable title acts. Tract indexes are not widely used in these four states, a fact that makes it possible for two or more chains of

[33] The New York statute barring possibilities of reverter and rights of entry was held unconstitutional as a taking of property in Board of Education of Central School District No. 1 v. Miles, 15 N.Y.2d 364, 259 N.Y.S.2d 129, 207 N.E.2d 181 (1965). All other state decisions have upheld the constitutionality of marketable title statutes. See, e.g., Miami v. St. Joe Paper Co., 364 So.2d 438 (Fla. 1978); Presbytery of Southeast Iowa v. Harris, 226 N.W.2d 232 (Iowa 1975); Wichelman v. Messner, 83 N.W.2d 800 (Minn. 1957); Hiddleston v. Nebraska Jewish Educ. Soc., 186 Neb. 786, 186 N.W.2d 904 (1971); Pinkney v. Southwick Invsts., L.L.C., 2005 WL 1926507 (Ohio Ct. App. 2005).

title to exist simultaneously—each of which is apparently valid under the language of the marketable title statute. This could easily occur if a purported grantor 50 or more years ago gave two deeds of the same land to two grantees. Even a forged deed can be a valid root of title. See Marshall v. Hollywood, Inc., 236 So. 2d 114 (Fla. 1970). Conflicting chains of title may also arise when (i) a grantor executes a wild deed, e.g., Esterholdt v. PacifiCorp., 301 P.3d 1086 (Wyo. 2013); (ii) when the legal description in a deed to one parcel of land overlaps with the legal description contained in a prior deed, e.g., Lehmann v. Cocoanut Bayou Ass'n, 157 So.2d 289 (Fla. Ct. App. 2014); or (iii) when an invalid sale occurs, e.g., Mobbs v. City of Lehigh, 655 P.2d 547 (Okla. 1982) (void tax deed created chain of title for purposes of marketable title act). A tract index would almost certainly disclose this problem to a title searcher, but a name index system in a marketable title act state might not.

Moreover, one might argue that marketable title acts operate unfairly on persons whose rights in land are old, but are still perfectly valid and valuable. See, e.g., Gray v. Treder, 204 A.3d 1117 (Vt. 2018) (marketable title statute terminated implied easement of necessity which was not marked by visible use); H & F Land, Inc. v. Panama City-Bay County Airport, 736 So. 2d 1167 (Fla. 1999) (same). Contra: Canali v. Satre, 688 N.E.2d 351 (Ill. Ct. App. 1997). Should such persons be put to the trouble of re-recording their documents every few decades? What about the owners in a 60-year old homeowners association; should they have to re-record their CC&Rs periodically to prevent them from being extinguished? What about those who own numerous interests in the land of others, such as mining or utility companies?

7. THE TORRENS SYSTEM FOR TITLE REGISTRATION

Even a modern, computerized, tract-indexed recording system aided by marketable title and curative acts still leaves much to be desired. Two main defects are noteworthy. First, such a system does not directly inform anyone what the state of the title actually is for a parcel of land. The current records system presents a mass of old documents and lets the searcher determine the state of the title, with all of the potential for error that such a process implies. Second, determining title by a search of the records allows the existence of a large number of "off-record" interests that cannot be found but nonetheless may affect the title. Some of these adverse claims might be identified by inspection of the land or other means, but many cannot be discovered with any reasonable degree of effort.

Is there a better system, one that will solve these problems without introducing others that are equally objectionable? The solution adopted by most other nations is the "Torrens" or title registration system. It was originally developed in 1858 in Australia by Sir Robert Torrens, who modeled it on the English system of maintenance of title records for ships.

The Torrens system spread throughout Australia, New Zealand, and other members of the British commonwealth, and is now in widespread use in the United Kingdom itself. See C. Dent Bostick, Land Title Registration: An English Solution to an American Problem, 63 Ind. L.J. 55 (1988). By 2004, all of England and Wales was covered by the registration system and about four-fifths of the land was actually registered. See Elizabeth Cooke & Pamela O'Connor, Purchaser Liability to Third Parties in the English Land Registration System: A Comparative Perspective, 120 Law Q. Rev. 640, 651 (2004). Similar title registration systems are widely used today in other countries.

The fundamental principle of the Torrens system is that government ought to be more than a mere custodian of the records of title. Rather, the government should take the next logical step of certifying the condition or state of the title to interested parties. We take this idea for granted with motor vehicles in the United States, but as applied to land titles it is a radical departure from accustomed methods. Interest in the Torrens system blossomed in the United States around the turn of the 20th century, and about 20 states adopted statutes authorizing it.[34] But the system's weaknesses as implemented, and the strong opposition of lawyers and title insurers, have combined to give the Torrens system only a tiny footprint in the U.S.[35]

In the American version of the Torrens system, registration is completely voluntary and usually quite costly. The owner brings what is in substance a quiet title action before a court or a quasi-judicial tribunal. Doing so might be expected to cost thousands of dollars.[36] Notice is sent to all persons having apparent claims to the land, and a hearing is held. If the registrant's title appears sound, the court orders the land registered. A certificate of title is created and held in the registration office, and a duplicate copy may be given to the owner. The certificate amounts to a

[34] The United States statutes are described in Patton, Evolution of Legislation on Proof of Title to Land, 30 Wash. L. Rev. 224 (1956); 6A Powell, Real Property ¶ 919ff (1979); Shick & Plotkin, Torrens in the United States (1978). The latter book's authors were employed as consultants to the title insurance industry, historically a vigorous foe of the Torrens system; the book might fairly be described as a "hatchet job" on Torrens. The English approach is compared to the U.S. system in Bostick, Land Title Registration: An English Solution to an American Problem, 63 Ind. L. J. 55 (1988).

[35] The Torrens system is used extensively in only four states. The areas of largest use in the United States are: (1) Hennepin County, Minnesota (Minneapolis), with 40 percent to 45 percent of the parcels registered under the system; (2) Cook County, Illinois, with about one-third of the land registered; (3) the Southern District Registry of Middlesex County, Massachusetts (Cambridge) with about 20 percent of the land registered; and (4) Hawaii, with about 45 percent of the land registered. The system is legislatively authorized today in Colorado, Georgia, Hawaii, Massachusetts, Minnesota, North Carolina, Ohio, Virginia, and Washington, but in several of those states activity under it is virtually nonexistent. The system was repealed, with respect to new registrations, effective in 1997, in both New York and Illinois, although existing registrations in those states continue to be effective.

[36] By contrast, a buyer of land will typically be able to obtain an acceptable owner's policy of title insurance for an amount that is less (and often significantly less) than the cost of prosecuting a quiet title action.

governmental certification that the registered owner is indeed the owner of the land, and that his or her title is not subject to any claims or encumbrances other than those shown as "memorials" on the certificate.

From that point forward, all title transactions affecting the land must be memorialized on the registry's official copy of the certificate of title or they will not be binding. Memorials may be added (e.g., if the owner gives a neighbor an easement) or deleted (e.g., if the owner satisfies a mortgage). If the owner transfers the fee title, a new certificate is made up, carrying over the memorials that represent interests still in effect and discarding those that have become obsolete. Thus, anyone can determine the state of the title by simply looking at the official copy of the certificate in the registry, and by then examining the underlying documents referred to in the current memorials on the certificate. These documents are retained by the registry. No historical search of the title is ever required, for only the current certificate and the instruments memorialized on it are relevant.[37]

Once a parcel is registered, transfers are very inexpensive and (if the system is well administered) quick and easy. But the initial cost of title registration has been a serious detriment, because most landowners have little interest in spending a large sum today so that future owners will be able to consummate transfers cheaply. Two additional problems have impeded the expansion of the Torrens system. One is the fact that existing American Torrens systems (much like marketable title acts) have numerous statutory exceptions to their coverage, so that the certificate is not really the complete statement of the title that users might desire. In addition to federal government claims (which are beyond the power of the states to bring under the system), common exceptions are made for persons in possession, mineral claims, observable easements, public roads, and so on—generally the same sorts of exceptions found in the marketable title acts, and for the same basic reasons. Compare Tetrault v. Bruscoe, 398 Mass. 454, 497 N.E.2d 275 (1986) (prescriptive easement does not affect registered land unless it is noted on certificate of title) with Henmi Apartments, Inc. v. Sawyer, 3 Haw. App. 555, 655 P.2d 881 (1982) (valid implied easement can arise upon registered land).

The other major impediment to the expansion of Torrens relates to the registry's liability if its administrators make a mistake. Recall that the certificate is conclusive as to the fee title it displays. Consequently, an error by registration officials might result in a mortgage or easement being cut

[37] An interesting and largely unresolved question is whether a person holding a certificate of title is bound by conveyances of prior interests that are not memorialized on the certificate, but of which the holder has actual notice. In In re Collier, 726 N.W.2d 799 (Minn. 2007), the Minnesota Supreme Court noted that a holder of a certificate, by the terms of the statute, had to be in "good faith" to be protected by the Torrens act. Hence, the court concluded that although a holder would not be subject to the doctrine of constructive notice, one who had *actual* notice of a prior but unmemorialized interest would be subject to it. The Supreme Court of Canada agreed with this view in United Trust Co. v. Dominion Stores Ltd., [1977] 2 S.C.R. 915.

off, or even the vesting of title in a person who had no right to it. The American Torrens systems all include funds out of which persons who lose their interests by such errors can be compensated, but the funds often are absurdly small in comparison to the potential liability, and in general the full faith and credit of the state or county does not back the Torrens system registry.[38]

For all of these reasons, it is not hard to see why the Torrens system of title registration has not been an astounding success in the United States. Its future has seemed dim, and reforming the predominant recording system seems a more fruitful endeavor. See McCormack, Torrens and Recording: Land Title Assurance in the Computer Age, 18 Wm. Mitchell L. Rev. 61 (1992). If there is any remaining hope for renewed interest in Torrens in the U.S., it lies in the efforts of entrepreneurs to incorporate blockchain technology in real property records and documentation. The ability of blockchain to maximize efficiencies in real estate transactions (i.e., to fully "tokenize" real estate ownership claims or to eliminate the need for title insurance as an intermediary) would effectively seem to require title registration.

F. TITLE INSURANCE

Title insurance is the predominant method of assuring real estate titles in the United States today. An exclusively American invention, title insurance attempts to solve the problems we have discussed in connection with the recording system. In substance, a title insurance policy is the insurer's promise that, if the title is not in the condition described by the policy on its effective date, the insurer will attempt to fix the problem or will indemnify the insured for resulting loss.

There are two kinds of title insurance policies: those insuring the interests of lenders (i.e., "loan" policies, which essentially insure the validity and expected priority of the lender's mortgage lien) and those insuring the interests of owners (i.e., "owner's" policies). It is lenders and secondary market mortgage investors who have made title insurance the important force in real estate conveyancing that it is today. The secondary market, in which financial institutions (e.g., life insurance companies, banks, and federally chartered corporations such as Fannie Mae and Freddie Mac) and mortgage securitizers buy mortgages from local lenders, has been particularly insistent on title insurance. This is a reasonable insistence, because an investor who is acquiring mortgages from many states and localities is understandably reluctant to rely on the opinions and malpractice insurance policies of numerous local lawyers whose

---

[38] For example, in Gill v. Johnson, 21 Cal. App. 2d 649, 69 P.2d 1016 (1937), a plaintiff against the California state fund was held entitled to a $48,000 judgment. Unfortunately, this completely exhausted the fund's meager resources and left it $8000 in debt! New registrations under the California law virtually ceased after this decision, and the statute was repealed in 1955.

qualifications and experience are hard to judge and police. Title insurance provides a standardized, fungible nationwide means of title assurance, and thus is a far more attractive option.

Nearly all title insurers obtain title searches and examinations before issuing policies. In some states this is legally mandated, and it is generally considered foolish to do otherwise. The search may be done by a local lawyer who is approved by the title company. In this setting, the title company is paid only a "risk premium", because it is not required to perform the title search and the attorney is separately compensated by the client for the title examination work. In other areas or among other companies, the insurer's own employees may perform title searches, either in the company's private title plant or in the public records. Under this method, the company generally charges an "all-inclusive" premium to the insured that covers both the search costs and the appropriate risk premium. The "approved attorney" approach is predominant in the East and the Midwest, especially outside major cities. The "all-inclusive" approach is widely used in the West and in major cities throughout the rest of the United States.

Under the "all-inclusive" method, the company or its agent usually issues a "preliminary report" or "binder" that shows the matters disclosed by its search, which will be listed as exceptions in the policy. The purchaser treats this report much like a lawyer's title opinion based on a record search.

For the reasons mentioned above, the vast majority of lenders now insist on the issuance of a lender's policy whenever a new mortgage loan is made. It is the nearly universal custom that the borrower must pay the premium for this policy. An owner's policy (usually, but not always obtained) may be paid for by the buyer of the property (commonly in the East) or by the seller (commonly in the West). As we will see below, there are often significant differences between the coverage of lender's and owner's policies, with the former usually having fewer exceptions and thus absorbing a broader range of risks.

Virtually all title insurance underwriters and many agents and abstractors are members of the American Land Title Association (ALTA), a trade association headquartered in Washington, D.C. For many years ALTA has promulgated title insurance policy forms that are very widely used throughout the United States. The form below is standard ALTA owner's policy form. We have summarized or omitted some of the "conditions" in the form for the sake of brevity.

OWNER'S POLICY OF TITLE INSURANCE

Issued by

BLANK TITLE INSURANCE COMPANY

Adopted by the American Land Title Association June 17, 2006

Any notice of claim and any other notice or statement in writing required to be given to the Company under this Policy must be given to the Company at the address shown in Section 18 of the Conditions.

COVERED RISKS

SUBJECT TO THE EXCLUSIONS FROM COVERAGE, THE EXCEPTIONS FROM COVERAGE CONTAINED IN SCHEDULE B, AND THE CONDITIONS, BLANK TITLE INSURANCE COMPANY, a Blank corporation (the "Company") insures, as of Date of Policy and, to the extent stated in Covered Risks 9 and 10, after Date of Policy, against loss or damage, not exceeding the Amount of Insurance, sustained or incurred by the Insured by reason of:

1. Title being vested other than as stated in Schedule A.

2. Any defect in or lien or encumbrance on the Title. This Covered Risk includes but is not limited to insurance against loss from

    (a) A defect in the Title caused by

    (i) forgery, fraud, undue influence, duress, incompetency, incapacity, or impersonation;

    (ii) failure of any person or Entity to have authorized a transfer or conveyance;

    (iii) a document affecting Title not properly created, executed, witnessed, sealed, acknowledged, notarized, or delivered;

    (iv) failure to perform those acts necessary to create a document by electronic means authorized by law;

    (v) a document executed under a falsified, expired, or otherwise invalid power of attorney;

    (vi) a document not properly filed, recorded, or indexed in the Public Records including failure to perform those acts by electronic means authorized by law; or

    (vii) a defective judicial or administrative proceeding.

    (b) The lien of real estate taxes or assessments imposed on the Title by a governmental authority due or payable, but unpaid.

    (c) Any encroachment, encumbrance, violation, variation, or adverse circumstance affecting the Title that would be disclosed by an accurate and complete land survey of the Land. The term "encroachment" includes encroachments of existing improvements located on the Land onto adjoining land, and encroachments onto the Land of existing improvements located on adjoining land.

3.   Unmarketable Title.

4.   No right of access to and from the Land.

5.   The violation or enforcement of any law, ordinance, permit, or governmental regulation (including those relating to building and zoning) restricting, regulating, prohibiting, or relating to

(a) the occupancy, use, or enjoyment of the Land;

(b) the character, dimensions, or location of any improvement erected on the Land;

(c) the subdivision of land; or

(d) environmental protection

if a notice, describing any part of the Land, is recorded in the Public Records setting forth the violation or intention to enforce, but only to the extent of the violation or enforcement referred to in that notice.

6.   An enforcement action based on the exercise of a governmental police power not covered by Covered Risk 5 if a notice of the enforcement action, describing any part of the Land, is recorded in the Public Records, but only to the extent of the enforcement referred to in that notice.

7.   The exercise of the rights of eminent domain if a notice of the exercise, describing any part of the Land, is recorded in the Public Records.

8.   Any taking by a governmental body that has occurred and is binding on the rights of a purchaser for value without Knowledge.

9.   Title being vested other than as stated in Schedule A or being defective

(a) as a result of the avoidance in whole or in part, or from a court order providing an alternative remedy, of a transfer of all or any part of the title to or any interest in the Land occurring prior to the transaction vesting Title as shown in Schedule A because that prior transfer constituted a fraudulent or preferential transfer under federal bankruptcy, state insolvency, or similar creditors' rights laws; or

(b) because the instrument of transfer vesting Title as shown in Schedule A constitutes a preferential transfer under federal bankruptcy, state insolvency, or similar creditors' rights laws by reason of the failure of its recording in the Public Records

    (i)   to be timely, or

    (ii)   to impart notice of its existence to a purchaser for value or to a judgment or lien creditor.

10. Any defect in or lien or encumbrance on the Title or other matter included in Covered Risks 1 through 9 that has been created or attached or has been filed or recorded in the Public Records subsequent to Date of Policy and prior to the recording of the deed or other instrument of transfer in the Public Records that vests Title as shown in Schedule A.

The Company will also pay the costs, attorneys' fees, and expenses incurred in defense of any matter insured against by this Policy, but only to the extent provided in the Conditions.

BLANK TITLE INSURANCE COMPANY

BY: _____ PRESIDENT

BY: _____ SECRETARY

EXCLUSIONS FROM COVERAGE

The following matters are expressly excluded from the coverage of this policy, and the Company will not pay loss or damage, costs, attorneys' fees, or expenses that arise by reason of:

1. (a) Any law, ordinance, permit, or governmental regulation (including those relating to building and zoning) restricting, regulating, prohibiting, or relating to

    (i)   the occupancy, use, or enjoyment of the Land;

    (ii)   the character, dimensions, or location of any improvement erected on the Land;

    (iii) the subdivision of land; or

    (iv) environmental protection;

or the effect of any violation of these laws, ordinances, or governmental regulations. This Exclusion 1(a) does not modify or limit the coverage provided under Covered Risk 5.

(b) Any governmental police power. This Exclusion 1(b) does not modify or limit the coverage provided under Covered Risk 6.

2. Rights of eminent domain. This Exclusion does not modify or limit the coverage provided under Covered Risk 7 or 8.

3.   Defects, liens, encumbrances, adverse claims, or other matters

(a) created, suffered, assumed, or agreed to by the Insured Claimant;

(b) not Known to the Company, not recorded in the Public Records at Date of Policy, but Known to the Insured Claimant and not disclosed in writing to the Company by the Insured Claimant prior to the date the Insured Claimant became an Insured under this policy;

(c) resulting in no loss or damage to the Insured Claimant;

(d) attaching or created subsequent to Date of Policy (however, this does not modify or limit the coverage provided under Covered Risk 9 and 10); or

(e) resulting in loss or damage that would not have been sustained if the Insured Claimant had paid value for the Title.

4.   Any claim, by reason of the operation of federal bankruptcy, state insolvency, or similar creditors' rights laws, that the transaction vesting the Title as shown in Schedule A, is

(a) a fraudulent conveyance or fraudulent transfer;[39] or

(b) a preferential transfer for any reason not stated in Covered Risk 9 of this policy.

5.   Any lien on the Title for real estate taxes or assessments imposed by governmental authority and created or attaching between Date of Policy and the date of recording of the deed or other instrument of transfer in the Public Records that vests Title as shown in Schedule A.

SCHEDULE A

Name and Address of Title Insurance Company: _____

[File No.:_____] Policy No.: _____

Address Reference: _____

Amount of Insurance: $ _____ [Premium: $ _____]

Date of Policy: _____ [at a.m./p.m.]

1.   Name of Insured:

2.   The estate or interest in the Land that is insured by this policy is:

---

39   See, e.g., Banner Bank v. First Am. Title Ins. Co., 916 F.3d 1323 (10th Cir. 2019) (receiver's action to invalidate deed of trust as fraudulent conveyance excluded from coverage under mortgagee's loan policy).

3.   Title is vested in:

4.   The Land referred to in this policy is described as follows: [Editors' Note: legal description is inserted here.]

SCHEDULE B
EXCEPTIONS FROM COVERAGE

This policy does not insure against loss or damage, and the Company will not pay costs, attorneys' fees, or expenses that arise by reason of:

1.   [Policy may include regional exceptions if so desired by the issuing Company.]

2.   [Variable exceptions such as taxes, easements, CC&Rs, etc., shown here]

CONDITIONS

1.   DEFINITION OF TERMS

The following terms when used in this policy mean:

(a) "Amount of Insurance": The amount stated in Schedule A, as may be increased or decreased by endorsement to this policy, increased by Section 8(b), or decreased by Sections 10 and 11 of these Conditions.

(b) "Date of Policy": The date designated as "Date of Policy" in Schedule A.

(c) "Entity": A corporation, partnership, trust, limited liability company, or other similar legal entity.

(d) "Insured": The Insured named in Schedule A.

(i)   the term "Insured" also includes

(A) successors to the Title of the Insured by operation of law as distinguished from purchase, including heirs, devisees, survivors, personal representatives, or next of kin;

(B) successors to an Insured by dissolution, merger, consolidation, distribution, or reorganization;

(C) successors to an Insured by its conversion to another kind of Entity;

(D) a grantee of an Insured under a deed delivered without payment of actual valuable consideration conveying the Title

(1) if the stock, shares, memberships, or other equity interests of the grantee are wholly-owned by the named Insured,

(2) if the grantee wholly owns the named Insured,

(3) if the grantee is wholly-owned by an affiliated Entity of the named Insured, provided the affiliated Entity and the named Insured are both wholly-owned by the same person or Entity, or

(4) if the grantee is a trustee or beneficiary of a trust created by a written instrument established by the Insured named in Schedule A for estate planning purposes.

(ii) with regard to (A), (B), (C), and (D) reserving, however, all rights and defenses as to any successor that the Company would have had against any predecessor Insured.

(e) "Insured Claimant": An Insured claiming loss or damage.

(f) "Knowledge" or "Known": Actual knowledge, not constructive knowledge or notice that may be imputed to an Insured by reason of the Public Records or any other records that impart constructive notice of matters affecting the Title.

(g) "Land": The land described in Schedule A, and affixed improvements that by law constitute real property. The term "Land" does not include any property beyond the lines of the area described in Schedule A, nor any right, title, interest, estate, or easement in abutting streets, roads, avenues, alleys, lanes, ways, or waterways, but this does not modify or limit the extent that a right of access to and from the Land is insured by this policy.

(h) "Mortgage": Mortgage, deed of trust, trust deed, or other security instrument, including one evidenced by electronic means authorized by law.

(i) "Public Records": Records established under state statutes at Date of Policy for the purpose of imparting constructive notice of matters relating to real property to purchasers for value and without Knowledge. With respect to Covered Risk 5(d), "Public Records" shall also include environmental protection liens filed in the records of the clerk of the United States District Court for the district where the Land is located.

(j) "Title": The estate or interest described in Schedule A.

(k) "Unmarketable Title": Title affected by an alleged or apparent matter that would permit a prospective purchaser or lessee of the Title or lender on the Title to be released from the obligation to purchase, lease, or lend if there is a contractual condition requiring the delivery of marketable title.

2. CONTINUATION OF INSURANCE

The coverage of this policy shall continue in force as of Date of Policy in favor of an Insured, but only so long as the Insured retains an estate or interest in the Land, or holds an obligation secured by a purchase money Mortgage given by a purchaser from the Insured, or only so long as the Insured shall have liability by reason of warranties in any transfer or conveyance of the Title. This policy shall not continue in force in favor of any purchaser from the Insured of either (i) an estate or interest in the Land, or (ii) an obligation secured by a purchase money Mortgage given to the Insured.

3. NOTICE OF CLAIM TO BE GIVEN BY INSURED CLAIMANT

The Insured shall notify the Company promptly in writing (i) in case of any litigation as set forth in Section 5(a) of these Conditions, (ii) in case Knowledge shall come to an Insured hereunder of any claim of title or interest that is adverse to the Title, as insured, and that might cause loss or damage for which the Company may be liable by virtue of this policy, or (iii) if the Title, as insured, is rejected as Unmarketable Title. If the Company is prejudiced by the failure of the Insured Claimant to provide prompt notice, the Company's liability to the Insured Claimant under the policy shall be reduced to the extent of the prejudice.

4. PROOF OF LOSS [Editors' Note: Company may require insured to provide a written proof of loss.]

5. DEFENSE AND PROSECUTION OF ACTIONS [Editors' Note: Company must provide a defense of the insured in litigation in which a third party asserts a claim covered by the policy. Company may also institute an action to establish the insured's title or prevent or reduce loss to the insured.]

6. DUTY OF INSURED CLAIMANT TO COOPERATE [Editors' Note: Insured must cooperate with Company's efforts in defending insured's title.][40]

7. OPTIONS TO PAY OR OTHERWISE SETTLE CLAIMS; TERMINATION OF LIABILITY [Editors' Note: Company has

---

[40] See, e.g., Pike v. Conestoga Title Ins. Co., 44 N.E.3d 787 (Ind. Ct. App. 2015) (homeowners precluded from recovering under owner's policy for loss of home at tax sale where they received two tax sale notices but did not notify the insurer until after sale occurred and tax deed had been delivered).

option to settle claim with insured or with third parties other than insured.]

8. DETERMINATION AND EXTENT OF LIABILITY

This policy is a contract of indemnity against actual monetary loss or damage sustained or incurred by the Insured Claimant who has suffered loss or damage by reason of matters insured against by this policy.

(a) The extent of liability of the Company for loss or damage under this policy shall not exceed the lesser of

    (i)   the Amount of Insurance; or

    (ii) the difference between the value of the Title as insured and the value of the Title subject to the risk insured against by this policy.

(b) If the Company pursues its rights under Section 5 of these Conditions and is unsuccessful in establishing the Title, as insured,

    (i)   the Amount of Insurance shall be increased by 10%, and

    (ii) the Insured Claimant shall have the right to have the loss or damage determined either as of the date the claim was made by the Insured Claimant or as of the date it is settled and paid.

(c) In addition to the extent of liability under (a) and (b), the Company will also pay those costs, attorneys' fees, and expenses incurred in accordance with Sections 5 and 7 of these Conditions.

9. LIMITATION OF LIABILITY

(a) If the Company establishes the Title, or removes the alleged defect, lien, or encumbrance, or cures the lack of a right of access to or from the Land, or cures the claim of Unmarketable Title, all as insured, in a reasonably diligent manner by any method, including litigation and the completion of any appeals, it shall have fully performed its obligations with respect to that matter and shall not be liable for any loss or damage caused to the Insured.

(b) In the event of any litigation, including litigation by the Company or with the Company's consent, the Company shall have no liability for loss or damage until there has been a final determination by a court of competent jurisdiction, and disposition of all appeals, adverse to the Title, as insured.

(c) The Company shall not be liable for loss or damage to the Insured for liability voluntarily assumed by the Insured in settling any claim or suit without the prior written consent of the Company.

10. REDUCTION OF INSURANCE; REDUCTION OR TERMINATION OF LIABILITY

All payments under this policy, except payments made for costs, attorneys' fees, and expenses, shall reduce the Amount of Insurance by the amount of the payment.

11. LIABILITY NONCUMULATIVE

The Amount of Insurance shall be reduced by any amount the Company pays under any policy insuring a Mortgage to which exception is taken in Schedule B or to which the Insured has agreed, assumed, or taken subject, or which is executed by an Insured after Date of Policy and which is a charge or lien on the Title, and the amount so paid shall be deemed a payment to the Insured under this policy.

12. PAYMENT OF LOSS . . .

13. RIGHTS OF RECOVERY UPON PAYMENT OR SETTLEMENT [Editors' Note: If Company pays a claim, it is subrogated to the rights of the insured against other parties.]

14. ARBITRATION . . .

15. LIABILITY LIMITED TO THIS POLICY; POLICY ENTIRE CONTRACT

(a) This policy together with all endorsements, if any, attached to it by the Company is the entire policy and contract between the Insured and the Company. In interpreting any provision of this policy, this policy shall be construed as a whole.

(b) Any claim of loss or damage that arises out of the status of the Title or by any action asserting such claim shall be restricted to this policy.

(c) Any amendment of or endorsement to this policy must be in writing and authenticated by an authorized person, or expressly incorporated by Schedule A of this policy.

(d) Each endorsement to this policy issued at any time is made a part of this policy and is subject to all of its terms and provisions. Except as the endorsement expressly states, it does not (i) modify any of the terms and provisions of the policy, (ii) modify any prior endorsement, (iii) extend the Date of Policy, or (iv) increase the Amount of Insurance.

16. SEVERABILITY . . .

17. CHOICE OF LAW; FORUM . . .

18. NOTICES, WHERE SENT . . .

The "Variable Exceptions" listed in Schedule B of the policy are, in essence, the outstanding interests in the land held by others as disclosed by the title search. Typical of such claims would be existing mortgages (in an owner's policy) or prior mortgages (in a lender's policy), utility easements, applicable covenants, the lien of the current year's property taxes if they have not been paid, and so on. In most cases the company will have issued a preliminary title report or binder prior to the issuance of the policy itself. The preliminary title report will indicate the matters that the company expects to show as "Exceptions" on Schedule B of the policy based on the results of its title search. Sometimes the title insurance company can be persuaded that one or more of these matters is so old or so unlikely to be asserted that the company can safely "insure over" it, dropping it from Schedule B. In some areas, the title company may charge an additional premium (to cover the added risk) when they do so.

Although the standard owner's policy reproduced above is very widely used, there are many variations in policy forms. For example, in 2013 ALTA updated an enhanced homeowner's policy, which is available only for one-to-four family residences. It provides many types of coverage not available under the policy printed above, including failure of a prior owner to obtain a proper building permit or subdivision approval, violations of restrictive covenants, damage from mineral extraction, inconsistencies between the map attached to the policy and the public records, and lack of both pedestrian and vehicular access. Remarkably, the enhanced homeowner's policy also covers certain events occurring *after* the policy is issued—a form of protection completely foreign to traditional title insurance. These events include forged documents, construction of encroaching structures, adverse possession, prescriptive easements, and enforcement of zoning ordinances that require removal of structures or prevent use of the land as a single-family residence. In addition, the enhanced homeowner's policy applies an automatic percentage increase to the original policy amount (10 percent per year) for each of the first five years after the policy is issued. This automatic coverage increase helps to cover increases in the value of the property. Moreover, the enhanced policy automatically covers a spouse who acquires the property pursuant to a divorce, inheriting heirs, related family trusts and their beneficiaries. None of these parties is covered by the standard policy.

In contrast, title insurance companies in some states commonly use policies prepared by state trade associations or customized by individual companies that provide *less* coverage than the standard ALTA owner's policy. Among the types of coverage that may be missing from these policies are rights of access, encroachments and boundary discrepancies, unfiled mechanic's liens, and unrecorded easements, liens, or other encumbrances. Such limited-coverage policies usually fail to insure marketability of the title as well. Of course, these variations in coverage are reflected in the premium charged for the policy, with the enhanced homeowner's policy costing more (perhaps 20 percent more than the standard policy) and the limited-coverage policy costing less. In addition to providing greater coverage, issuance of an ALTA policy usually requires a physical inspection of the property, and perhaps a survey, whereas a limited-coverage policy may not.

Loan policies. Loan policies differ from owners' policies in that the insuring language at the beginning of the policy is generally broader in scope. For example, the standard ALTA loan policy, adopted June 17, 2006, tracks the general coverage of the owner's policy reprinted above, but adds the following items:

9.   The invalidity or unenforceability of the lien of the Insured Mortgage upon the Title. This Covered Risk includes but is not limited to insurance against loss from any of the following impairing the lien of the Insured Mortgage

> (a)   forgery, fraud, undue influence, duress, incompetency, incapacity, or impersonation;

> (b)   failure of any person or Entity to have authorized a transfer or conveyance;

> (c)   the Insured Mortgage not being properly created, executed, witnessed, sealed, acknowledged, notarized, or delivered;

> (d)   failure to perform those acts necessary to create a document by electronic means authorized by law;

> (e)   a document executed under a falsified, expired, or otherwise invalid power of attorney;

> (f)   a document not properly filed, recorded, or indexed in the Public Records including failure to perform those acts by electronic means authorized by law; or

> (g)   a defective judicial or administrative proceeding.

10.   The lack of priority of the lien of the Insured Mortgage upon the Title over any other lien or encumbrance.

11.   The lack of priority of the lien of the Insured Mortgage upon the Title

> (a)   as security for each and every advance of proceeds of the loan secured by the Insured Mortgage over any statutory lien for services, labor, or material arising from construction of an improvement or work related to the Land when the improvement or work is either

(i)   contracted for or commenced on or before Date of Policy; or

(ii) contracted for, commenced, or continued after Date of Policy if the construction is financed, in whole or in part, by proceeds of the loan secured by the Insured Mortgage that the Insured has advanced or is obligated on Date of Policy to advance; and

(b) over the lien of any assessments for street improvements under construction or completed at Date of Policy.

12. The invalidity or unenforceability of any assignment of the Insured Mortgage, provided the assignment is shown in Schedule A, or the failure of the assignment shown in Schedule A to vest title to the Insured Mortgage in the named Insured assignee free and clear of all liens.

13. The invalidity, unenforceability, lack of priority, or avoidance of the lien of the Insured Mortgage upon the Title

(a) resulting from the avoidance in whole or in part, or from a court order providing an alternative remedy, of any transfer of all or any part of the title to or any interest in the Land occurring prior to the transaction creating the lien of the Insured Mortgage because that prior transfer constituted a fraudulent or preferential transfer under federal bankruptcy, state insolvency, or similar creditors' rights laws; or

(b) because the Insured Mortgage constitutes a preferential transfer under federal bankruptcy, state insolvency, or similar creditors' rights laws by reason of the failure of its recording in the Public Records

(i)   to be timely, or

(ii) to impart notice of its existence to a purchaser for value or to a judgment or lien creditor.

14. Any defect in or lien or encumbrance on the Title or other matter included in Covered Risks 1 through 13 that has been created or attached or has been filed or recorded in the Public Records subsequent to Date of Policy and prior to the recording of the Insured Mortgage in the Public Records.

Loan policies, unlike owners' policies, are generally assignable. Thus, a secondary market purchaser of the mortgage gets the benefit of the original loan policy. If the mortgagee purchases at a foreclosure sale of the mortgage, the policy's protection continues (although only for the amount of the previous mortgage loan).[41] Although loan policies are very useful to mortgagees, they do not solve all possible problems. A loan policy will not, for example, protect against the eventuality that the debt itself is unenforceable because the promissory note was a forgery, because the lender failed to disburse the loan funds to the mortgagor, or because the note was not delivered to an assignee of the mortgage. See Lawyers Title Ins. Co. v. Novastar Mortg., Inc., 862 So.2d 793 (Fla. Ct. App. 2003).

NOTES AND QUESTIONS

1. *Additional readings.* Two excellent treatises on the subject of title insurance are D. Barlow Burke, Law of Title Insurance (1986) and Joyce D. Palomar, Title Insurance Law (2020). For a highly useful compendium of information on title insurance, including discussion of coverage and claims procedures with sample policy forms, see James L. Gosdin, Title Insurance: A Comprehensive Overview (Am. Bar Ass'n, 4th ed. 2016).

2. *Practice of law?* Consider the policy forms reproduced above. Is the issuance of a commitment for title insurance really a legal opinion as to the state of the title, and thus the unauthorized practice of law? See In re Paplauskas, 228 A.3d 43 (R.I. 2020); Joyce D. Palomar, Title Insurance Law §§ 13:7 to 13:9 (2020); Payne, Title Insurance and the Unauthorized Practice of Law Controversy, 53 Minn. L. Rev. 423 (1969).

3. *Must the insurer do a search?* Must the company represent that it has searched the title? Some states have statutes so requiring. See, e.g., Fla. Stat. § 627.7845; N.J. Stat. § 17:46–B9; N.C. Gen. Stat. § 58–2–132; Ariz. Rev. Stat. § 20–1567(A). In a state with no statute, is there any remedy (beyond a claim on the policy itself if a defect arises) for the title company's failure to search? See Note, Title Insurance: The Duty to Search, 71 Yale L.J. 1161 (1962).

Several courts have held that the title company may be liable as an abstractor for a negligent (or, presumably, nonexistent) search, irrespective of the language of the policy. See, e.g., Bank of California v. First Am. Title Ins. Co., 826 P.2d 1126 (Alaska 1992); Garton v. Title Ins. & Trust Co., 106 Cal. App. 3d 365, 165 Cal. Rptr. 449 (1980); U.S. Bank, N.A. v. Integrity Land Title Corp., 929 N.E.2d 742 (Ind. 2010); 100 Invst. Ltd. Partn. v. Columbia Town Center Title Co., 430 Md. 197, 60 A.3d 1 (2013) (local title company liable for negligent search, but exculpation clause precluded negligence claim against title insurance underwriter); Tess v. Lawyers Title Ins. Corp., 251 Neb. 501, 557 N.W.2d 696 (1997). Cf. Focus Inv. Assocs. v. American Title Ins. Co., 992 F.2d 1231 (1st Cir.1993) (no liability for negligence where title company did not issue a preliminary report to insured). There are also several cases finding no tort liability. See Davis, More Than They Bargained For: Are Title Insurance Companies Liable in Tort for Undisclosed Title Defects?, 45 Cath.

---

[41] If a third party buys land at a foreclosure sale, however, the third-party buyer does not obtain the benefit of the lender's loan policy. See, e.g., Hovannisian v. First Am. Title Ins. Co., 14 Cal. App.5th 420, 221 Cal. Rptr.3d 883 (2017). Such a buyer would have to obtain its own owner's policy.

U. L. Rev. 71 (1995); Palomar, Title Insurance Companies' Liability for Failure to Search Title and Disclose Record Title, 20 Creighton L. Rev. 455 (1987).

Why would a plaintiff prefer to rely on a negligence theory rather than a claim or suit on the title insurance policy itself? Several reasons may exist:

(a) The period provided in the policy for filing a claim (often 90 days) may have expired.

(b) The insured may wish to claim consequential or punitive damages that are permitted in tort, but not in contract. See, e.g., Red Lobster Inns of America, Inc. v. Lawyers Title Ins. Corp., 492 F. Supp. 933 (E.D. Ark. 1980).

(c) An outstanding title interest was not shown on the preliminary title report, and hence the insured was not warned of its existence, but it was shown as a Schedule B exception when the policy itself was issued. See Heyd v. Chicago Title Ins. Co., 218 Neb. 296, 354 N.W.2d 154 (1984); Garton v. Title Ins. & Trust Co., 106 Cal. App. 3d 365, 165 Cal. Rptr. 449 (1980); Shotwell v. Transamerica Title Ins. Co., 16 Wash. App. 627, 558 P.2d 1359 (1976).

(d) The party making the claim was not insured, but nonetheless relied on the policy. For example, in Barrington Reinsurance Ltd., LLC v. Fidelity Nat'l Title Ins. Co., 143 N.M. 31, 172 P.3d 168 (N.M. Ct. App. 2007), the title company issued a policy to A. Shortly thereafter, A sold the property to B, and the title company advised B not to bother getting a new title policy since the old one was still quite fresh. The court held that under the circumstances it was entirely foreseeable that B would rely on the policy, and held the insurer liable.

(e) The insured's economic loss due to the title defect exceeds the policy limit. See, e.g., Heyd v. Chicago Title Ins. Co., 218 Neb. 296, 354 N.W.2d 154 (1984); Dreiblebiss Title Co., Inc. v. MorEquity, Inc., 861 N.E.2d 1218 (Ind. Ct. App. 2007) (policy limit restricts amount insurer must pay in performing its contract, but does not limit damages recoverable for breach of contract to search and report title accurately).

Look again at Paragraph 15 of the Conditions in the owner's policy form. Should this language make it impossible to assert a claim based on negligence that is not covered by the policy language, or in an amount that exceeds the policy limit?

4. *Must the insurer cure the title defects?* Does the policy impose an affirmative duty on the title company to cure title defects that come to light, or may the company merely wait until a loss is sustained and then compensate the insured? Policy language usually purports to give the insurer the choice on this point, but there is a judicial authority that the insurer must actually attempt to cure the alleged defeat and clear the title if it is feasible to do so. See Stewart Title Guar. Co. v. West, 110 Md. App. 114, 676 A.2d 953 (1996);

Shada v. Title & Trust Co., 457 So. 2d 553 (Fla. Ct. App. 1984); Summonte v. First Am. Title Ins. Co., 180 N.J. Super. 605, 436 A.2d 110 (1981).

5. *What sorts of claims are covered?* Consider whether the ALTA owner's policy, supra, covers the insured against the following items (assume that none of these items are mentioned in Schedule B of the policy):

(a) A mechanic's lien, filed by a plumber who has worked on the property before the sale of the property and the issuance of the policy, but whose lien is not filed until after the sale occurs. By statute, the lien's priority "relates back" to the date the work was commenced.

(b) A set of restrictive covenants limiting the use of the property to single-family dwellings only.

(c) A reservation of oil and gas rights, made by the grantor of a deed 100 years ago.

(d) Lack of delivery of a deed in the chain of title for the insured property.

(e) A dower right or other marital property claim by the (until now undisclosed) wife of a former owner.

(f) A claim against the insured owner, made by a grantee of a deed from that owner based on a warranty in the deed. See Stewart Title Guar. Co. v. Lunt Land Corp., 162 Tex. 435, 347 S.W.2d 584 (1961).

(g) A zoning ordinance that prevents the most economical use of the property (although the current use does not violate the ordinance).

(h) Failure of the subdivider who developed the property to obtain the necessary local government approvals for the subdivision. See Hocking v. Title Ins. & Trust Co., 37 Cal. 2d 644, 234 P.2d 625 (1951).

(i) An easement that runs along one side of the property for storm drainage purposes. The ditch was visible to the insured when he or she inspected the property before purchasing it. Cf. Jones v. Grow Inv. & Mortg. Co., 11 Utah 2d 326, 358 P.2d 909 (1961).

(j) An easement for a buried pipeline running across the property. The pipeline is recorded, but it is not visible from the surface. See Guarantee Abstract & Title Ins. Co. v. St. Paul Fire & Marine Ins. Co., 216 So. 2d 255 (Fla. Ct. App. 1968).

6. *Claims against title insurers.* Title insurance is quite different than most other insurance products. Title companies that operate by the "all-inclusive" method spend a great deal of money in *loss avoidance*—i.e., in searching titles to identify existing encumbrances and defects, so that these items can be excluded from the coverage of the insurance policies to be written. For this reason, the operating expenses of title insurers constitute a much higher percentage of their total operating revenue, roughly 90 percent, than is the case with other insurance products. Likewise, because the efforts of title insurers at loss avoidance are generally successful, title insurers spend a much

lower percentage (under 8 percent on average) of their operating revenue on loss payments and loss adjustment expense (litigation and negotiation costs) than other types of insurers. See Joyce D. Palomar, Title Insurance Law § 1.15 (2020).

What are the main types of losses title companies experience? Among the important ones are the following:

- Mechanic's liens
- Plant search errors
- Examination and opinion errors
- Forgeries
- Property taxes

Mechanic's liens are a particular problem for title insurers. A mechanic's lien can be filed by a contractor or materials seller who supplies labor or materials to improvements on a parcel of real estate and is not paid. Typically the claim or notice of lien must be recorded in the public records within a fixed period (usually, six to 12 months, depending on the jurisdiction). The difficulty arises from the fact that the lien's priority date then "relates back," commonly to the date that work on the project commenced. If some other party buys the property or accepts a mortgage on it between the time work commenced and the time the notice of lien is recorded, she or he may be "stuck" with the lien despite the fact that no search in the public records could have disclosed it. This is, of course, an outrageously bad system—unless you happen to be a contractor or materials supplier, in which case you consider it eminently reasonable.

Many title insurance companies refuse to insure against unfiled mechanic's liens, or insure against them only for an extra premium, due to their "unfindable" nature. Mechanic's lien claims often result from cost overruns and developer insolvencies in commercial or residential construction projects. These insolvency situations tend to occur during periods when interest rates are high and construction costs are rising rapidly. As a result, title insurance claims arising from mechanic's liens tend to be cyclical, following national economic trends.

7. *Owners and loan policies.* Suppose that Smith is buying a home and financing a portion of the purchase price with a $200,000 mortgage loan from First Bank. First Bank requires a loan policy of title insurance. When Smith sees a copy of the loan policy commitment issued to First Bank, and sees that it does not contain any unacceptable title matters on Schedule B, Smith decides to go ahead and close without obtaining a separate owner's policy, reasoning "The title seems acceptable and, if it isn't and I suffer a title loss, the insurer will pay off the mortgage." Can you explain why Smith's reasoning is faulty and Smith should obtain an owner's policy? Suppose that two years later, Smith discovers that his grantor was an imposter and Smith is evicted by the

rightful landowner. The insurer will pay off the balance of First Bank's mortgage loan; what will happen next?

G. SETTLEMENT

1. OVERVIEW OF SETTLEMENT PROCEDURES

Once the title has been examined, financing arranged, and other necessary conditions satisfied and investigations completed, the buyer and seller will exchange a deed converging title for the purchase price in a process called "closing" or "settlement." Settlement procedures are straightforward, although somewhat complex. Usually a designated "closing agent"—who may be an attorney, a title insurance company, an escrow company, or (less commonly) a real estate broker or mortgage lender—will handle the settlement process. The closing agent's tasks may include the following:

1. Reviewing the preliminary title report to determine what liens or encumbrances exist on the property, and then inquiring of their holders (e.g., existing lending institutions) the exact amount that will be necessary to pay them off as of the closing date.

2. Obtaining executed copies of the deed, the new note and mortgage or other security device if any, and a multitude of other forms and documents, including written and recordable satisfactions of mortgages or liens that will be paid off at the closing.

3. Obtaining funds from the buyer and the new lender.

4. Arranging for or verifying completion of some miscellaneous ancillary services, such as surveys, pest inspections, etc.

5. Computing the necessary proration adjustments between buyer, seller, and old and new lienholders for such matters as property taxes, insurance, and local assessments.

6. Seeing that appropriate documents are recorded and mailed to the persons entitled to receive a copy of them.

7. Disbursing funds to the providers of ancillary services, to taxing authorities if any, and to the seller and prior lienholders who are being paid off.

There is great national variation in the filling of the roles of title examiner and closing agent. Along most of the East Coast (with exceptions in New York City and Washington, D.C.) attorneys commonly do both jobs; in fact, they frequently do the actual searches in the public records, although the more sophisticated members of the bar employ lay assistants or independent contractors for this phase of their work. In the Mountain West, the West Coast, and Texas, the examination of titles is generally done by private title insurance companies, often in their own private title plants. In these areas of the United States, the closing agent is usually an "escrow agent"—a private corporation (sometimes affiliated with a title company or lending institution) set up to receive and disburse documents and funds in real estate transactions.

In rural areas of the Midwest, title assurance was traditionally in the form of an "abstract," a book or sheaf of documents that summarized or set forth in full each instrument in the public records relating to the land in question. Abstracts were prepared by specialized "abstract companies." They were usually passed down from one owner to the next, and were updated with each transfer, thus saving a great deal of time and duplication that would be necessary if a complete record search had to be made each time land was sold. Under the Midwestern practice, the abstract was typically examined by an attorney, who provided his or her opinion of the title to the new lender and the buyer. The attorney might also handle the closing function. Today, in urban areas of the Midwest the use of abstracts has now largely been supplanted by "all-inclusive" title insurance.

Would consumers be better off if attorneys were more involved in the real estate sale and settlement process? Consider In re Opinion No. 26 of Committee on Unauthorized Practice of Law, 139 N.J. 323, 654 A.2d 1344 (1995), in which the New Jersey Supreme Court approved the practice commonly followed in South Jersey, where brokers and title insurance companies handle virtually all aspects of home sales with no attorney representing either party. Although the court felt that having lawyers represent both sides of the sale was wise and desirable, it noted:

> The record fails to demonstrate that the public interest has been disserved by the South Jersey practice over the many years it has been in existence. While the risks of non-representation are many and serious, the record contains little proof of actual damage to either buyer or seller. Moreover, the record does not contain proof that, in the aggregate, the damage that has occurred in South Jersey exceeds that experienced elsewhere. In this case, the absence of proof is particularly impressive, for the dispute between the realtors and the bar is of long duration, with the parties and their counsel singularly able and highly motivated to supply such proof as may exist. The South Jersey practice also appears to save money. For the record demonstrates what is obvious, that sellers and buyers without counsel save counsel fees.

2.　REAL ESTATE SETTLEMENT PROCEDURES ACT

Congressional concern with the high costs of settlement services and with allegedly abusive practices in the settlement industry resulted in the enactment of the Real Estate Settlement Procedures Act, 12 U.S.C. § 2601 et seq. (RESPA). RESPA has been amended substantially by Congress several times since its original enactment in 1974. Following the Dodd-Frank Act, administration of RESPA now rests with the Consumer Financial Protection Bureau.

RESPA's basic thesis is that if consumers are given advance information about settlement services and costs, they will shop more vigorously and will bargain down prices to competitive levels. Section 5 of RESPA requires lending institutions to give to loan applicants, within three days of the borrower's loan application, a "Loan Estimate" which provides an estimate of the various closing costs the borrower is likely to incur. This estimate comes on a standardized form (to facilitate comparison shopping), and requires the lender to distinguish the estimated costs for services for which the buyer can't "shop" for a better price (where the lender mandates a certain provider) and those for which the buyer can "shop" for a better price. Given that this information is provided *after* the loan application has been made, do you think that this information has much impact on shopping behavior or prices? If accurately prepared, the Loan Estimate does inform borrowers well in advance of the closing date of the amount of cash they must bring to the closing so that they are unlikely to arrive without sufficient funds to close.

At the closing, RESPA § 4 requires the closing agent to use a standard settlement statement called the "Closing Disclosure." This form likewise tracks the structure of the Loan Estimate, thus allowing the borrower to compare the estimated costs (as shown on the Loan Estimate) with the actual closing costs. If the actual closing costs exceed the estimated costs by more than the permitted "tolerances," the lender violates RESPA unless the excess charges are refunded within 30 days.[42]

Because of the limited size of the pages in this book, it isn't feasible to reprint the Loan Estimate or the Closing Disclosure in legible form here. Both are available in blank and filled-in versions on the CFPB's web site, along with compliance guides, and links to the rule itself. See https://www.consumerfinance.gov/compliance/compliance-resources/mortgage-resources/tila-respa-integrated-disclosures/. We recommend that you download the forms and become familiar with them.

Kickbacks, referral fees, and fee-splitting. Perhaps the most controversial aspect of RESPA is Section 8, which prohibits referral fees

---

[42] The permitted tolerances vary depending on the type of expense. For example, there is zero tolerance for a lender's loan origination fee. By contrast, a 10% tolerance is allowed for other costs, such as title insurance or appraisal costs.

and fee-splitting among providers of settlement services, except to the extent that the fee is for the reasonable value of services actually performed. The core language of Section 8 is set forth below:

> § 8(a).   No person shall give and no person shall accept any fee, kickback, or thing of value pursuant to any agreement or understanding ... that business incident to or a part of a real estate settlement service involving a federally related mortgage loan shall be referred to any person.

> § 8(b).   No person shall give and no person shall accept any portion, split, or percentage of any charge made or received for the rendering of a real estate settlement service in connection with a transaction involving a federally related mortgage loan other than for services actually performed.

Both civil penalties (statutory damages of three times the amount paid for the service) and criminal penalties are provided for violations. Referral fees were very widespread prior to the enactment of RESPA, and there is no doubt that their frequency has declined. Today, they are much more likely to take the form of free services, trips, information, food and beverages, tickets to concerts and sporting events, office space, and so on, rather than in the form of cash.

Most of the entities that formerly were involved in paying referral fees, such as title insurers, were pleased with the passage of Section 8 of RESPA. Yet there is by no means universal agreement that Section 8's prohibition on referral fees is a good thing, even if it is effectively enforced. See Owen, Kickbacks, Specialization, Price Fixing, and Efficiency in Residential Real Estate Markets, 29 Stan. L. Rev. 931 (1977), arguing that because real estate brokers are more price-competitive than title insurers, the "monopoly profits" earned by the latter are more likely to filter down to consumers (in the form of lower brokerage commissions) if the title insurers are permitted to pay referral fees to brokers. If this is so (and it appears to be), the referral fee prohibition in RESPA is counterproductive.

After the passage of Section 8 of RESPA, a number of real estate brokers, attorneys, and lenders attempted to circumvent it by establishing or purchasing title insurance companies of their own. This practice, known as "controlled business," permits an attorney or broker (for example) who is a part owner of a title company to refer customers to the title company and to recover the profits in the form of dividends or partnership distributions rather than illegal referral fees. The major title insurance underwriters consider this referral of controlled business highly objectionable, because it allows new or "upstart" title companies, particularly those controlled by large real estate brokers, to divert business away from older and more established title insurance companies.

In 1983, Congress attempted to resolve the "controlled business" issue by an amendment to RESPA. It permits the referral of business to a controlled entity if:

(a) a timely disclosure of the relationship is made to the consumer,

(b) an estimate is given of the charges generally made by the controlled entity,

(c) the consumer is not required to use the controlled entity, and

(d) the referring entity receives nothing of value for the referral except a return on its ownership interest.

Do you suppose these restrictions have inhibited the referral of business to controlled entities?

NOTES AND QUESTIONS

1. *Expansion of RESPA's scope.* In 1992, Congress amended RESPA again, expanding its coverage from traditional first lien home purchase loan transactions to include refinancings and subordinate lien transactions (e.g., "home equity" and "home improvement" loans) as well. The statutory amendment also made it clear that the making of a mortgage loan was itself a "real estate settlement service" subject to RESPA. The original statute was unclear on this point.

2. *Fees to attorneys.* Because attorneys act as agents for title insurance underwriters in many areas of the country, there has been concern that an attorney might receive a fee from a title company that purported to compensate for the attorney's work as agent, but that would in fact constitute payment for referring business to the title company. If the latter were shown, it would, of course, violate Section 8 of RESPA. In a 1992 regulation, HUD attempted to deal with this issue by providing that "for an attorney of the buyer or seller to receive compensation as a title agent, the attorney must perform core title agent services (for which liability arises) separate from attorney services, including the evaluation of the title search to determine the insurability of the title, the clearance of underwriting objections, the actual issuance of the policy or policies on behalf of the title insurance company, and, where customary, issuance of the title commitment, and the conducting of the title search and closing." 57 Fed. Reg. 49600 (Nov., 2, 1992). Does it strike you as odd that a federal agency would need to adopt a regulation to prevent lawyers from profiting by referring their clients' business to title companies?

3. *What is "fee-splitting"?* Section 8 of RESPA prohibits the payment or receipt of a division of fees or charges made for a settlement service, other than for services actually performed. This rule against fee-splitting was asserted by the plaintiff-borrower in Mercado v. Calumet Federal Sav. & Loan Ass'n, 763 F.2d 269 (7th Cir. 1985). The case involved a lender who, without clear authority in the mortgage documents, demanded that an existing borrower

refinance at a higher interest rate and with payment of various new loan charges. The court held that, because there was no third party with whom the asserted borrower's fees were being split, Section 8 was not violated. RESPA, the Seventh Circuit noted, is not a "general mortgage loan antifraud provision." It left the plaintiff to her state court remedies based on the contract documents.

The question of "mark-ups" by lenders or other settlement service providers has been controversial. For example, suppose the lender pays a recording fee of $25, but charges the borrower $50 for it. Is this illegal "fee-splitting"? In Freeman v. Quicken Loans, Inc., 566 U.S. 624 (2012), the United States Supreme Court held, in a unanimous opinion, that Section 8(b) of RESPA does not prevent the retention of an unearned fee by a single settlement-service provider. See also Clements v. LSI Title Agency, Inc., 779 F.3d 1269 (11th Cir. 2015). Rather, Section 8(b) applies only when a fee is divided among two or more persons. *Quicken Loans* rejected HUD's Policy Statement 2001–1, 66 Fed. Reg. 53052 (2001), which took the position that mark-ups and unearned fees violate Section 8(b) of RESPA.

4.   *Requiring use of a specific title insurer.* Section 9 of RESPA prohibits sellers of real estate from requiring buyers to purchase title insurance from any particular company. One might think this sort of rule is so clear-cut that no one would think of violating it, but in Weisberg v. Toll Brothers, Inc., 617 F. Supp. 539 (E.D. Pa. 1985) the court approved a $265,000 settlement in a class action under Section 9 brought by 334 home buyers in Bucks County, Pennsylvania against 17 defendant builders. Each of the class members was awarded approximately 105 percent of the amount he or she originally spent on the title insurance, despite the court's observation that the violation of RESPA had in fact cost them nothing, because the title companies to which they were directed by the builders charged virtually the same rates as all other title companies in the area!

Note that there is no similar rule prohibiting lawyers or lenders from requiring the use of a particular title company, although if they do so, and if they also have a financial interest in the title company, they will have to provide the "controlled business" disclosure statement described in the text.

PART 2

REAL ESTATE FINANCE

■ ■ ■

CHAPTER THREE

THE USE OF MORTGAGE SUBSTITUTES

■ ■ ■

A. THE ABSOLUTE DEED, THE CONDITIONAL SALE, AND RELATED TRANSACTIONS

This chapter addresses financing devices which attempt to circumvent the mortgagor's equity of redemption and other substantive mortgage law protections. Perhaps the most transparent such device is the "contemporaneous option," i.e., a provision in a mortgage granting the mortgagee an option to acquire the mortgaged premises, typically at a price equal to the unpaid balance of the mortgage debt at the time of exercise. Traditionally, courts have treated such an option as an invalid "clog" on the equity of redemption. See, e.g., In re First Phoenix-Weston, LLC, 575 B.R. 828 (Bankr.W.D.Wis.2017). The language of the court in Humble Oil & Refining Co. v. Doerr, 123 N.J.Super. 530, 303 A.2d 898 (1973), reflects this pervasive "anti-clogging" rule:

> For centuries it has been the rule that a mortgagor's equity of redemption cannot be clogged and that he cannot, as a part of the original mortgage transaction, cut off or surrender his right to redeem. Any agreement which does so is void and unenforceable as against public policy. A classic statement of the rule appears in 4 Pomeroy, Equity Jurisprudence (5th ed. 1941), § 1193 at 568 et seq.:

>> § 1193. *Once a Mortgage, Always a Mortgage; Collateral Agreements and Agreements Clogging the Equity of Redemption.*—In general, all persons able to contract are permitted to determine and control their own legal relations by any agreements which are not illegal, or opposed to good morals or to public policy; but the mortgage forms a market exception to this principle. The doctrine has been firmly established from an early day that when the character of a mortgage has attached at the commencement of the transaction, so that the instrument, whatever be its form, is regarded in equity as a mortgage, that character of mortgage must and will always continue. If the instrument is in its essence a mortgage, the parties cannot by any stipulations, however express and positive, render it anything but a mortgage, or deprive it of the essential attributes belonging

to a mortgage in equity. The debtor or mortgagor cannot, in the inception of the instrument, as a part of or collateral to its execution, in any manner deprive himself of his equitable right to come in after a default in paying the money at the stipulated time, and to pay the debt and interest, and thereby to redeem the land from the lien and encumbrance of the mortgage; the equitable right of redemption, after a default is preserved, remains in full force, and will be protected and enforced by a court of equity, no matter what stipulations the parties may have made in the original transaction purporting to cut off this right. . . .

As a part of the doctrine it is well settled that an option to buy the property for a fixed sum cannot be taken contemporaneously by the mortgagee. . . .

So strong is the policy behind the rule that it is applied to hold such options absolutely void and unenforceable regardless of whether there is actual oppression in the specific case. In 1904, in the leading case of Samuel v. Jarrah Timber and Wood Paving Corp., [(1904) A.C. 323], the question of whether it should continue to be so applied was squarely presented to the House of Lords for reconsideration and possible change. The House affirmed the Court of Appeals and held that an option to purchase for a fixed sum taken by a mortgagee as a part of the original transaction was void as a clog on the equity of redemption regardless of fairness. Although it acknowledged that the rule might be used as a 'means of evading a fair bargain come to between persons dealing at arms' length and negotiating on equal terms,' it nevertheless concluded that, in view of the long line of precedents applying the doctrine as a fixed rule without deviation, there should be no change therefrom. Noting that the virtue of such a fixed rule is that it serves 'to obviate the necessity of inquiry and investigation in cases where suspicion may be probable and proof difficult,' Lord Macnaghten said:

Having regard to the state of authorities binding on the Court of Appeals, if not this House, it seems to me that they could not have come to any other conclusion, although the transaction was a fair bargain between men of business without any trace or suspicion of oppression, surprise or circumvention. [(1904) A.C. 323, 325]

NOTES

1. *Is the clogging doctrine justified in the option context?* Is it sound policy to hold any contemporaneous option "absolutely void and unenforceable

regardless of whether there is actual oppression in the specific case"? Consider the following analysis of this question:

> An overly dogmatic approach to such options may . . . unduly discourage the flow of capital to a variety of socially useful projects. For example, the prospect of being able to share in the success of a corporate mortgagor may very well induce a mortgagee to consider use of a variety of techniques that afford the mortgage lender the opportunity to acquire equity ownership in the mortgagor's real estate. In this connection, corporate mortgagors commonly grant their lenders warrants to purchase their stock. Conceivably a rigid application of the clogging principle could render such warrants unenforceable because they enable a mortgage lender to acquire an interest in the mortgaged corporate assets without having to resort to foreclosure. Even assuming that a court would be reluctant to apply the anti-clogging concept where the mortgagee acquires such an indirect interest in the mortgaged assets, it is not difficult to envisage its application in a variety of other settings where a mortgage lender is encouraged to provide capital by the prospect of sharing more directly in any future success of mortgagor. For example, suppose that part of the inducement to a mortgage lender to provide long term financing for several of borrower's shopping center developments is the prospect of being able later to acquire one or more of those projects or at least a significant interest in them, should the projects prove successful. A strict application of the anti-clogging doctrine could frustrate the use of options in such situations even though the lender's primary motivation is to share in the mortgagor's success rather than to avoid foreclosure when the mortgagor's venture proves to be a failure. . . .
>
> Thus, it seems preferable to reject the inflexible position that all mortgagee attempts to enforce such options are invalid in favor of an approach which validates them unless their enforceability is expressly tied to mortgagor default. Such an approach recognizes that the essence of the equity of redemption is the right of the mortgagor in default to insist that she be deprived of the mortgaged real estate only by a foreclosure process that tests its value at a public sale.

Nelson, Whitman, Burkhart & Freyermuth, Real Estate Finance Law 42–43 (6th ed.2015).* There are several decisions upholding the enforceability of options against clogging attacks, finding that the option in question was not being used to circumvent foreclosure. See, e.g., MacArthur v. North Palm Beach Utils., Inc., 202 So.2d 181 (Fla.1967); Blackwell Ford, Inc. v. Calhoun, 219 Mich.App. 203, 555 N.W.2d 856 (1996). For further consideration of this problem, see John C. Murray, Clogging Revisited, 33 Real Prop.Prob. & Tr. J. 279 (1998); James D. Cooper-Hill & Joseph J. Slama, The Convertible

---

* Reprinted with permission of LEG, Inc. d/b/a West Academic.

Mortgage: Can It Be Separated from the Clogging Rule?, 27 S.Tex.L.Rev. 407 (1986).

Several states have enacted legislation limiting the impact of the clogging rule in the option-mortgage context. New York specifies that an option to acquire an equity or other ownership in property granted to a mortgagee simultaneously, or in connection with, a mortgage is not "unenforceable" so long as its exercise "is not dependent upon the occurrence of a default" in the mortgage transaction and the mortgage obligation is $2.5 million or more. N.Y.Gen.Oblig. Law § 5–334 (1985). California and Virginia have similar statutes (without a monetary limitation) which apply to mortgages on all property other than residential real estate containing four or fewer units. Cal.Civ.Code § 2906; Va. Code Ann. § 55.1–315(B)(2). Under the Restatement such an option is normally enforceable "unless its effectiveness is expressly dependent on mortgagor default." Restatement (Third) of Property (Mortgages) § 3.1(c) (1997).

2. *The deed in escrow as a clog.* Sometimes, in conjunction with the execution of a "traditional" mortgage, the mortgagor will also deliver to mortgagee or an escrow agent a deed to the mortgaged real estate. The understanding is that if the mortgagor timely repays the debt, the deed will be returned to the mortgagor; however, in the event of default, the mortgagee or escrow agent can record the deed as a substitute for foreclosing the mortgage. Such a deed is a clog on the equity of redemption and is invalid. See, e.g., C. Phillip Johnson Full Gospel Ministries, Inc. v. Investors Fin. Servs., LLC., 418 Md. 86, 12 A.3d 1207 (2011); In re Greene, 2007 WL 1309047 (Bankr. E.D. Va. 2007); Panagouleas Interiors, Inc. v. Silent Partner Group, Inc., 2002 WL 441409 (Ohio Ct.App.2002); Oakland Hills Dev. Corp. v. Lueders Drainage Dist., 212 Mich.App. 284, 537 N.W.2d 258 (1995); Vitvitsky v. Heim, 52 A.D.3d 1103, 860 N.Y.S.2d 305 (2008); Basile v. Erhal Holding Corp., 148 A.D.2d 484, 538 N.Y.S.2d 831 (1989); Marple v. Wyoming Prod. Credit Ass'n, 750 P.2d 1315 (Wyo.1988); Nelson, Whitman, Burkhart & Freyermuth, Real Estate Finance Law § 3.1 (6th ed.2015); John C. Murray, Mortgage Workouts: Deeds in Escrow, 41 Real Prop.Prob. & Tr.J. 185, 187–189 (2006).

3. *Subsequent conveyances as clogs.* The "anti-clogging" doctrine does not apply generally to transactions that are *subsequent* to the execution of the mortgage. For example, courts routinely uphold the "deed in lieu of foreclosure," which amounts to a conveyance of the equity of redemption to the mortgagee when the mortgagor is in default and facing threatened foreclosure. See C. Phillip Johnson Full Gospel Ministries, Inc. v. Investors Fin. Servs., LLC., 418 Md. 86, 12 A.3d 1207 (2011) ("After a mortgagor defaults on a note, she may legitimately contract with the noteholder to execute a conveyance, in exchange for adequate consideration, so long as there is no overreaching."); Nelson, Whitman, Burkhart & Freyermuth, Real Estate Finance Law § 3.3 (6th ed.2015). Nevertheless, this type of "subsequent" transaction can receive close judicial scrutiny for a variety of other reasons which we examine in detail later in this volume. See Chapter Five, Section D, infra; In re Greene, 2007 WL 1309047 (Bankr.E.D.Va.2007).

Should subsequent *executory* agreements between mortgagor and mortgagee be similarly shielded from the clogging principle? Suppose that after mortgagor goes into default, the parties negotiate an agreement whereby mortgagor delivers a quitclaim deed to the mortgaged real estate. The parties agree that if the debt is paid off within six months, the deed is to be returned to the mortgagor, but if the mortgagor fails to do so, the mortgagee can record the deed. Suppose further that the mortgagor does not pay off the debt within the six month period and mortgagee records the deed. If mortgagor later tenders to mortgagee the full amount of the mortgage debt, will such a redemption attempt be effective? For the view that "the policy supporting the rule against clogging in contemporaneous agreements also has force where a subsequent transaction provides for a future waiver of mortgagor's redemption rights," see Restatement (Third) of Property (Mortgages) § 3.1, cmt. f and illus. 15 (1997); Patmos Fifth Real Estate, Inc. v. Mazl Bldg., LLC, 124 A.D.3d 422, 2 N.Y.S.3d 83 (2015). Do you agree? See Nelson, Whitman, Burkhart & Freyermuth, Real Estate Finance Law § 3.3 (6th ed.2015). For a contrary view, see In re First Union Baptist Church of Bronx, 2018 WL 770401 (S.D.N.Y.2018) (holding executory deed in lieu enforceable as a "complex, multi-faceted agreement on a number of terms and . . . the product of extensive arms-length negotiations" which "offered far more than a mortgage or lien on property"); Rothschild Reserve Int'l, Inc. v. Silver, 830 So.2d 224 (Fla.Ct.App.2002); Ringling Joint Venture II v. Huntington Nat'l Bank, 595 So.2d 180 (Fla.Ct.App.1992) (upholding deed, but noting that such agreements "should be carefully scrutinized to assure that they do not violate the favored right of redemption.").

4. *Mezzanine financing, Article 9 security interests in the borrower entity, and clogging.* In a mezzanine loan, the lender has the borrower grant the lender a U.C.C. Article 9 security interest in the entity (typically a partnership or an LLC) that owns the real estate. The real estate is often also subject to a conventional mortgage loan. The "mezz" lender may be a different entity than the mortgage lender, and in such cases the two lenders will generally enter into an intercreditor agreement, with the mezz lender taking a subordinate position.

Suppose that a single lender takes both a mortgage lien on the real estate and an Article 9 security interest in the borrowing entity. In effect, this arrangement gives the lender a choice of remedies in the event of borrower default: (a) foreclose the mortgage on the real estate, or (b) conduct an Article 9 foreclosure sale of the ownership rights in the borrowing entity. This may be particularly appealing to the lender in states that do not authorize nonjudicial foreclosures of mortgage liens. In such states, a contested real estate foreclosure may be a drawn-out and expensive process, while an Article 9 sale of the ownership entity can be accomplished very quickly and without judicial supervision.

However, if the lender exercises its Article 9 sale rights, a serious question arises: is such a sale an invalid clog on the equity of redemption of the mortgage? The answer is not clear. In one sense, the borrowing entity still retains the right to redeem the real estate from the mortgage lien by paying off the mortgage debt, as no foreclosure of the mortgage has taken place. Nevertheless, if the lender acquires the ownership entity at the Article 9 sale, the lender effectively acquires the real estate (keep in mind that the majority of commercial real estate ownership entities are single-asset entities, owning no property other than the one parcel of real estate), and in doing so cuts off the borrower's right to redeem the land from the mortgage in practical terms. Viewed in this way, the Article 9 sale looks a great deal like a clog on the equity of redemption.

In HH Cincinnati Textile L.P. v. Acres Capital Servicing LLC, 2018 WL 3056919 (N.Y.Sup.Ct.2018), the lender held both a mortgage and a mezz loan interest in the borrower entity. The borrower sought to enjoin an Article 9 sale of the borrower on the ground that it would be a clog on the equity of redemption. The court refused to issue an injunction and allowed the Article 9 sale to proceed. The court reasoned that (1) the borrower would not be irreparably injured by the sale because it could be fully compensated by money damages if the sale were later held invalid; (2) the borrower had a right of redemption under U.C.C. § 9–623 until the Article 9 sale of the borrower entity occurs; and (3) the borrower had the ability to take part in the bidding process at the Article 9 sale. Some viewed this result as authority for the view that taking and enforcing an Article 9 security interest in the borrower entity is not an invalid clog on the borrower's equity of redemption in the real estate.

The court's reference to redemption rights under U.C.C. § 9–623 is technically correct, but probably not very meaningful; under U.C.C. § 9–612, the lender can schedule an Article 9 foreclosure sale of the ownership of the borrower entity after only 10 days' notice to the borrower. Few borrowers could arrange alternative financing to redeem within such a short period of time. Further, in a June 2020 opinion in the same case, HH Mark Twain LP v. Acres Capital Servicing LLC, 2020 WL 2857649 (N.Y.Sup.Ct.2020), the court asserted that its 2018 opinion was not a ruling on the merits of the clogging claim, which was still available for the court to consider. So the issue remains unclear. If you were the mezz lender, would you schedule an Article 9 foreclosure sale of the borrower entity on only 10 days' notice? Why might you instead choose to schedule the sale using a longer notice period more comparable to the one that might be required for foreclosure of a mortgage? See generally Martin A. Schwartz, Legal Magic: Turning Real Property Foreclosures into Uniform Commercial Code Sales, 94 Fla. Bar J. 39 (May/June 2020).

5.   The "absolute deed." If one cannot effectively shortcut the need to foreclose by taking a deed along with the mortgage, can one accomplish the same goal by dispensing with the mortgage entirely and merely taking a deed? The material that immediately follows deals with this and related questions.

ROGER A. CUNNINGHAM & SAUL TISCHLER, DISGUISED REAL ESTATE SECURITY TRANSACTIONS AS MORTGAGES IN SUBSTANCE

26 Rutgers L.Rev. 1, 1–4, 6–7 (1972)*

Ever since the English Chancellors regularly began to allow redemption of mortgages after default, creditors have sought ways to have real property serve as security free from any right in the debtor to redeem. As one writer put it, "[T]he big idea is to find a form of a transaction that will have the practical effect of security, yet will be held not to be a security but to belong to a wholly different jural species and so be held immune from security law."

Creditors may use two devices to create real property security without appearing to enter into a security transaction. A creditor may require his debtor to grant him land by absolute deed, under oral agreement or tacit understanding that he will reconvey only if the debtor pays the debt when due. Alternatively, a creditor may obtain from his debtor an absolute deed to real property and execute to his debtor some sort of written agreement (almost invariably withheld from public record) to reconvey the property to the debtor upon receiving payment of the debt. The written agreement to reconvey may take the form of an option to repurchase, an unconditional contract obligating the grantee to reconvey and the grantor to repurchase, or a lease back to the grantor with an option to repurchase at or before the end of the lease term. Some such options or contracts provide for the deposit in escrow of a deed of reconveyance.

The use of an absolute deed to secure a debt, with or without a written collateral agreement for reconveyance upon satisfaction, is designed to eliminate the "grantor's" equity of redemption and the necessity of foreclosure if the debtor defaults. The written instrument, whether option to repurchase, contract to reconvey, or other arrangement, usually contains provisions making time "of the essence" and forfeiting the grantor's right in case he fails to exercise the option or tender payment under the contract within the time limited.

Besides avoiding the expense and delay involved in foreclosure, the creditor often expects to gain other advantages by securing his interest with an absolute deed rather than a regular mortgage. These other advantages include the right to possession of the land prior to default, the right to possession of chattels severed from the land by the debtor or third parties, preventing the debtor from encumbering the land with further mortgages or judgment liens, and the possibility of enlarging the creditor's security interest to cover future advances to the debtor without the execution of a new security instrument. . . .

* Reprinted with permission of Rutgers University, The State University of New Jersey, West Publishing Co. and the authors.

It is important to keep in mind that the crucial question is *not* whether the parties to a deed absolute on its face intended to create the relation of mortgagor and mortgagee, but whether they intended the deed to stand as security for a debt. Where the parties cast their transaction in the form of an absolute conveyance instead of a mortgage, they do *not* intend to create the relation of mortgagor and mortgagee. Thus, the real issue is whether the circumstances are such as to justify treating the transaction as a mortgage in substance though the parties did not so intend. If the purpose of a conveyance was security, it will be treated as a mortgage even though the parties may have agreed or understood that the debtor should have no right to redeem. The right to redeem after default is an inseparable incident of the mortgage relationship and, as with ordinary mortgages, the parties cannot contract against its exercise where their relationship is in substance that of mortgagor and mortgagee.

BOUFFARD V. BEFESE, LLC

Supreme Court of New York, Appellate Division, 2013
111 A.D.3d 866, 976 N.Y.S.2d 510

. . . In 1993, Riccardo Tedesco owned property in Ossining (hereinafter the property). In 1993 or 1994, Jerry Bouffard purchased the property and held it on Tedesco's behalf because Tedesco was facing foreclosure. Bouffard financed this purchase with a mortgage in the sum of approximately $209,000.

In 2004, Tedesco wanted to borrow money to finance a business venture. Since he was unable to obtain conventional financing, Tedesco approached Rego DiPietro, who referred Tedesco to Jeff Reback, a "hard money lender." Acting through his uncle, David Reback, Jeff Reback, on behalf of his company JR Factors, Inc., agreed to lend Tedesco $175,000 in return for a mortgage on the subject property. In May 2004, Bouffard and Tedesco appeared at David Reback's office and Bouffard executed the loan documents creating the mortgage. Tedesco did not repay the principal of this loan.

In August 2004, Tedesco determined that he needed an additional $200,000 to invest in his business venture. He again approached Rego DiPietro, who again contacted Jeff Reback. However, because he estimated that the subject property was worth only approximately $500,000 and was already encumbered by approximately $385,000 in debt, Jeff Reback was unwilling to extend further mortgage-based financing. Instead, acting through David Reback and Rego DiPietro, Jeff Reback proposed that another company he owned, Befese, LLC (hereinafter Befese), would purchase the property for $200,000, take the deed to the property, and enter into an option agreement permitting Bouffard and Tedesco to repurchase the property within 90 days at an option price of $220,000. At trial, Jeff Reback admitted that he offered these terms because he wished to avoid the foreclosure process if Tedesco defaulted on the loan. Tedesco accepted these terms and, on August 4, 2004, Bouffard attended a closing at David Reback's office and signed both the deed and the option agreement. Befese accepted the deed, but did not record it at that time and did not take physical control of the property. Tedesco and Bouffard failed to repurchase the property within the 90-day option period or during two subsequent extensions which Jeff Reback offered in exchange for an increased option payment. Befese never commenced a foreclosure action relating to the subject property.

In September 2005, Befese sold the subject property to Francisco Ippoliti. Ippoliti, who intended to develop the property, then entered into a partnership with Rego DiPietro's son, Frank DiPietro. However, on December 5, 2005, Ippoliti conveyed the deed from himself to himself and Frank DiPietro, and, on the same day, Ippoliti and Frank Dipietro conveyed the deed to Hawkes Crossing, LLC (hereinafter Hawkes Crossing). Hawkes Crossing was an entity controlled by James Zappi. Zappi owned property adjoining the property and had previously negotiated with Tedesco and Rego DiPietro about acquiring the property so that he could develop the two parcels together.

In 2006, Bouffard, Tedesco, and a third plaintiff commenced this action seeking, inter alia, to set aside the August 2004 deed. Hawkes Crossing, which was not named as a defendant, intervened to protect its title to the property. . . .

After a nonjury trial, the Supreme Court concluded, among other things, that the August 2004 deed was not intended as a conveyance, but was instead intended to act as a mortgage security for the $200,000 loan. Based upon the terms of the option agreement, the court determined that the loan was usurious and void pursuant to Banking Law § 14–a and General Obligations Law § 5–501. The court declared, inter alia, that the deed is null and void, and that Bouffard held title to the property, subject to certain lien interests of other parties. The court also dismissed Hawkes Crossing's cross claims against Ippoliti and Frank DiPietro, finding that, while Ippoliti and Frank DiPietro had reason to question whether they could transfer good title to Hawkes Crossing, Zappi also had reason to question whether Ippoliti and Frank DiPietro could convey good title and should have conducted further investigation prior to closing. Hawkes Crossing appeals from the court's determination that the deed was null and void and the court's dismissal of its cross claims.

Real Property Law § 320 provides, in pertinent part, that a "deed conveying real property, which, by any other written instrument, appears to be intended only as a security in the nature of a mortgage, although an absolute conveyance in terms, must be considered a mortgage" (Real Property Law § 320; see People v. Gass, 206 NY 609, 616 [1912]; DeMaio v.

Capozello, 74 A.D.3d 864, 865 [2010]; *Henley v. Foreclosure Sales, Inc.,* 39 A.D.3d 470 [2007]; *Leonia Bank v. Kouri,* 3 A.D.3d 213, 217 [2004]; *Basile v. Erhal Holding Corp.,* 148 A.D.2d 484, 485 [1989]). In determining whether a deed was intended as security, " 'examination may be made not only of the deed and a written agreement executed at the same time, but also [of] oral testimony bearing on the intent of the parties and to a consideration [of] the surrounding circumstances and acts of the parties' " (*Henley v. Foreclosure Sales, Inc.,* 39 A.D.3d at 470, quoting *Corcillo v. Martut, Inc.,* 58 A.D.2d 617, 618 [1977]). Thus, " 'a court of equity will treat a deed, absolute in form, as a mortgage, when it is executed as a security for a loan of money. That court looks beyond the terms of the instrument to the real transaction; and when that is shown to be one of security, and not of sale, it will give effect to the actual contract of the parties' " (*Basile v. Erhal Holding Corp.,* 148 A.D.2d at 485, quoting *Peugh v. Davis,* 96 US 332, 336 [1877]).

Here, the factual and credibility determinations of the trial court, which acted as the factfinder in this case, were warranted by the facts. The testimony established that, notwithstanding its form, the August 2004 transaction was, in substance, a mortgage loan. As the court noted, Jeff Reback candidly admitted that he was willing to lend Tedesco more money, but only if the transaction was structured in such a way that, if Tedesco defaulted, he could avoid the foreclosure process and simply take the property. In addition, it was uncontroverted that Befese made no attempt to exercise control over the property until Tedesco had defaulted not only on the original "option agreement," but also on its two extensions.

This Court considered similar facts in *Booth v. Landau* (103 A.D.2d 733, 734 [1984]). In that case, the defendants simultaneously executed both a one-year option allowing the plaintiff's attorney to repurchase the property at a substantially higher price and a one-year lease in favor of the plaintiff's husband. Based upon those facts, this Court determined that the deed was intended as security for a loan within the meaning of Real Property Law § 320 and should be considered a mortgage. Similarly, in *Basile v. Erhal Holding Corp.* (148 A.D.2d at 484), the plaintiff executed a mortgage to the defendant in the sum of $101,202.59, along with a "deed in lieu of foreclosure," which the defendant agreed not to record as long as the plaintiff fulfilled her obligations under the mortgage. This Court again found that, under those circumstances, the deed in lieu of foreclosure was intended as security for the plaintiff's debt to the defendant. Here, too, the Supreme Court correctly applied the principle that, "[w]here a deed has been given as security, it cannot be turned into a conditional sale by way of an agreement to reconvey" (*Leonia Bank v. Kouri,* 3 A.D.3d at 217, citing *Mooney v. Byrne,* 163 N.Y. 86, 96 [1900]).

Since the August 2004 transaction was a mortgage loan, the Supreme Court correctly concluded that Befese could have obtained good title only by foreclosing on the subject property in the same manner as any other mortgagee (*see Leonia Bank v. Kouri*, 3 A.D.3d at 217–218). However, even if Befese had attempted to do so, such a proceeding would have been unavailing, as the loan was plainly usurious and, therefore, unenforceable (*see O'Donovan v. Galinski*, 62 A.D.3d 769, 769–770 [2009]; *Abir v. Malky, Inc.*, 59 A.D.3d 646, 649 [2009]).

The maximum rate of interest permitted by law is, in general, 16% annually (*see* General Obligations Law § 5–501; Banking Law § 14–a[1]; *O'Donovan v. Galinski*, 62 A.D.3d at 769; *Abir v. Malky, Inc.*, 59 A.D.3d at 649). "In determining whether a transaction is usurious, the law looks not to its form, but its substance, or real character" (*O'Donovan v. Galinski*, 62 A.D.3d at 769 [internal quotation marks omitted]). "Whether a transaction constitutes a cover for usury is a question of fact" and, "[w]hen determining whether a transaction constitutes a usurious loan it must be considered in its totality and judged by its real character, rather than by the name, color, or form which the parties have seen fit to give it" (*Abir v. Malky, Inc.*, 59 A.D.3d at 649 [internal quotation marks omitted]). To constitute usury, " '[i]t must appear that the real purpose of the transaction was, on the one side, to lend money at usurious interest reserved in some form by the contract and, on the other side, to borrow upon the usurious terms' " (*id.*, quoting *Donatelli v. Siskind*, 170 A.D.2d 433, 434 [1991]). "A usurious contract is void and relieves the plaintiff of the obligation to repay principal and interest thereon" (*Abir v. Malky, Inc.*, 59 A.D.3d at 649).

Here, the undisputed evidence established that the gross amount of the August 2004 loan was $200,000. The option payment of $20,000 represents 10% of the gross loan proceeds over 90 days and, thus, something in excess of 40% annually, or approximately 2½ times the statutory maximum of 16% (*see* General Obligations Law § 5–501; Banking Law § 14–a[1]; *O'Donovan v. Galinski*, 62 A.D.3d at 769; *Abir v. Malky, Inc.*, 59 A.D.3d at 649). Thus, this transaction was plainly usurious.

Based on the foregoing, Hawkes Crossing's contention that it acquired good title from Ippoliti and Frank DiPietro is without merit. Real Property Law § 245 provides that a "greater estate or interest does not pass by any grant or conveyance, than the grantor possessed or could lawfully convey, at the time of the delivery of the deed." Thus, "conveyances of land to which the grantors had no title convey no interest to the grantees" (*O'Brien v. Town of Huntington*, 66 A.D.3d 160, 167 [2009]). Likewise, "[i]f a document purportedly conveying a property interest is void, it conveys nothing, and a subsequent bona fide purchaser or bona fide encumbrancer for value receives nothing" (*ABN AMRO Mtge. Group, Inc. v. Stephens*, 91 A.D.3d 801, 803 [2012]; *see Solar Line, Universal Great Bhd., Inc. v. Prado*, 100 A.D.3d 862, 863 [2012]; *First Natl. Bank of Nev. v. Williams*, 74 A.D.3d 740, 742 [2010]; *Ameriquest Mtge. Co. v. Gaffney*, 41 A.D.3d 750, 751 [2007]).

While Hawkes Crossing is correct that Real Property Law §§ 266 and 291 protect the title of a bona fide purchaser for value who lacks knowledge of fraud by the grantor or affecting the grantor's title (*see* Real Property Law §§ 266, 291; *Panther Mtn. Water Park, Inc. v. County of Essex*, 40 A.D.3d 1336, 1338 [2007]; *Fischer v. Sadov Realty Corp.*, 34 A.D.3d 630, 631 [2006]), these sections do not protect Hawkes Crossing's purported interest in the subject property. As discussed above, the deed conveying the property to Befese is void as a consequence of the usurious loan underlying the August 2004 transaction (*see Abir v. Malky, Inc.*, 59 A.D.3d at 649). Consequently, the subsequent transfers from Befese to Ippoliti, Ippoliti to Ippoliti and Frank DiPietro, and Ippoliti and Frank DiPietro to Hawkes Crossing did not enjoy the protection provided by Real Property Law § 266 (*see Solar Line, Universal Great Bhd., Inc. v. Prado*, 100 A.D.3d at 863). Since the August 2004 transaction was a usurious mortgage and, therefore, void, all further attempted transfers of interest in the subject property are a nullity. Accordingly, the Supreme Court correctly concluded that Bouffard held title to the subject property and that Hawkes Crossing held no interest in it. . . .

NOTES

1. *Difference between absolute deed and conditional sale*. The *Bouffard* case involves two different "suspect" transactions. In the first, Tedesco (who was facing foreclosure) deeded the property to Bouffard, who agreed to hold it on Tedesco's behalf. This is what courts often call an *"absolute deed"* transaction. On the face of things, it appears that Tedesco has "sold" the real estate to Bouffard. However, if Bouffard had thereafter tried to argue that this deed had conveyed him outright title, Tedesco could have presented extrinsic evidence to establish that the deed (although absolute on its face) nevertheless created only a mortgage, i.e., that the parties intended to use title to the property as security for Tedesco's obligation to repay Bouffard for advancing the amount needed for Tedesco to avoid losing the property at foreclosure.

In the second, Bouffard and Tedesco (who then needed additional financing) deeded the property to Befese, LLC, which paid Bouffard and Tedesco $200,000 and granted them an option to repurchase the property within 90 days at a price of $220,000. This transaction is what courts often call a *"conditional sale"* transaction. Here, it was clear that Bouffard and Tedesco had the right to reacquire the real estate if they complied with the terms of the option. Because the option had expired, however, they prevailed only by establishing that the deed was intended to serve as security for a loan or obligation they owed to Befese and thus should be treated as a mortgage.

There is a third type of transaction that is less complex and merits brief mention. In this transaction, the deed is also accompanied by a second written document, but unlike in *Bouffard*, that document does not purport to give the grantor an option to purchase the property, but instead *makes it clear* that the deed was intended to serve as security for a debt. For example, suppose this second writing is a letter from grantee to grantor that states "if you pay off the $5,000 you owe me with 10 percent interest by the end of next year, I will reconvey the real estate to you." Here the court will treat the deed and the letter together as a mortgage; the letter simply provides the "defeasance" language found in a typical mortgage. See, e.g., BMBT, LLC v. Miller, 322 P.3d 1172 (Utah App.2014); Leona Bank v. Kouri, 3 A.D.3d 213, 772 N.Y.S.2d 251 (2004).

2.   *Parol evidence rule and Statute of Frauds.* At this point, you might wonder why attempting to recharacterize an absolute deed or conditional sale does not run afoul of both the parol evidence rule and the Statute of Frauds. The former normally bars extrinsic evidence that would vary the terms of a written document executed with the intent that it embody the complete agreement of the parties; the latter requires that the transfer of interests in land normally be in writing. Courts usually do not permit either the parol evidence rule or the Statute of Frauds to prevent an attempt to establish that an absolute deed or conditional sale was intended as security. Why not? See, e.g., Nelson, Whitman, Burkhart & Freyermuth, Real Estate Finance Law § 3.15 (6th ed.2015); Restatement (Third) of Property (Mortgages) § 3.2, cmts. c & d (1997); Newell v. Newell, 254 So.3d 878 (Ala.2017).

3.   *Relevant factors.* As *Bouffard* indicates, in determining whether an absolute deed or conditional sale should be treated as a mortgage, courts look to the totality of the circumstances surrounding the transaction, including the language in the deed, any contemporaneous written agreement, any oral testimony bearing on the intent of the parties, and other surrounding circumstances and acts of the parties. These other circumstances may include a significant disparity between the value received by the grantee and the actual value of the property, the grantee's continued possession, the grantee's continuing duty to maintain the property and/or pay real estate taxes, the grantee's financial distress (including the prospect of imminent foreclosure), and disparity in sophistication or bargaining power between the grantor and grantee. See, e.g., Zaman v. Felton, 219 N.J. 199, 98 A.3d 503 (2014).

Although no one factor is usually dispositive, most courts require that there be an obligation or debt owed to the grantee and that the conveyance was intended as security for that obligation. However, significant confusion exists concerning the nature and form of that obligation or debt. More specifically, there is disagreement as to whether the grantor must be personally liable for its payment. Some decisions require that "a specific debt" be due "from mortgagor to mortgagee" or that "there must be a right of the grantee to demand and enforce his debt and the obligation of the grantor to pay." See Hall v. Livesay, 473 So.2d 493 (Ala.1985); Toulouse v. Chilili Coop. Ass'n, 108 N.M. 220, 770 P.2d 542 (App.1989). Such language strongly suggests that the grantor must be personally liable on the underlying debt or obligation. An extreme version of this approach may require the production of a promissory note or at least some written evidence of the debt or obligation.

Other jurisdictions are much less demanding in this regard. For these courts, the terms "debt" or "obligation" seem to encompass the mere "expectation or assumption" on the part of the parties that a repayment of the consideration will occur and do not require a formal personal obligation of the grantor to repay. According to the Eleventh Circuit, requiring a personal obligation

> overlooks the fact that numerous secured real estate loan transactions are nonrecourse loans. Express creation of a recourse obligation—or the absence thereof—is undoubtedly an important fact to consider, but it cannot be the determinative factor. Instead, a court must look at the intent of the parties in light of *all* the circumstances surrounding the transaction.

In re Cox, 493 F.3d 1336 (11th Cir.2007). See also Hatchett v. W2X, INC., 993 N.E.2d 944, 960–61 (Ill.Ct.App.2013) ("While a debt relationship is essential to establish and equitable mortgage, direct evidence is not necessary to prove the relationship and no particular *type* of evidence is required."). Moreover, courts have imputed the existence of a debt or obligation where there is evidence the parties intended a loan transaction and other factors suggest a mortgagor-mortgagee relationship. See Johnson v. Cherry, 726 S.W.2d 4 (Tex.1987).

Consider, in this regard, the approach of Restatement (Third) of Property (Mortgages) §§ 3.2, 3.3 (1997):

§ 3.2   The Absolute Deed Intended as Security*

(a) Parol evidence is admissible to establish that a deed purporting to be an absolute conveyance of real estate was intended to serve as security for an obligation, and should therefore be deemed a mortgage. The obligation may have been created prior to or contemporaneous with the conveyance and need not be the personal liability of any person.

(b) Intent that the deed serve as security must be proved by clear and convincing evidence. Such intent may be inferred from the totality of the circumstances, including the following factors:

(1) Statements of the parties;

(2) The presence of a substantial disparity between the value received by the grantor and the fair market value of the real estate at the time of the conveyance;

(3) The fact that the grantor retained possession of the real estate;

(4) The fact that the grantor continued to pay real estate taxes;

(5) The fact that grantor made post-conveyance improvements to the real estate; and

---

(6)   The nature of the parties and their relationship prior to and after the conveyance.

(c)   Where, in addition to the deed referred to in subsection (a) of this section, a separate writing exists indicating that the deed was intended to serve as security for an obligation, parol evidence is admissible to establish that the writings constitute a single security transaction.

§ 3.3   The Conditional Sale Intended as Security

(a)   Parol evidence is admissible to establish that a deed purporting to be an absolute conveyance of real estate accompanied by a written agreement conferring on the grantor a right to purchase the real estate, was intended to serve as a security for an obligation, and should therefore be deemed a mortgage. The obligation may have been created prior to or contemporaneous with the conveyance and need not be the personal liability of any person.

(b)   [Subsection (b) is identical to § 3.2(b) except that it includes, as an additional factor, the "terms on which the grantor may purchase the real estate."]

How would you evaluate the second transaction in *Bouffard* under Restatement § 3.3? Do you agree with the court's decision to recharacterize the transaction as an equitable mortgage? Why or why not?

4.   *Burden of proof.* Should the same burden of proof apply in both absolute deed and conditional sale settings? While a "clear and convincing" standard is the norm in absolute deed situations, it has been less broadly required in the conditional sale context. Many courts follow a "preponderance of the evidence" standard in the latter situation. These courts reason that because the written documents in the conditional sale establish on their face that the grantor has the right to regain title to the real estate, permitting grantor to establish that the transaction was intended as security does not contradict the written documentation to the same degree as in the absolute deed setting. Restatement (Third) of Property (Mortgages) § 3.3, cmt. b (1997) ("The grantee's expectations arguably are disturbed to a much lesser extent where a formal agreement expressly provides for grantor's reacquisition of the real estate than where grantee is compelled to part with title that he or she may well have assumed to be indefeasible."). Nevertheless, in the conditional sale situation, the use of extrinsic evidence not only contradicts the deed to the grantee but also contravenes a second written document as well. Should it thus be more difficult to justify the use of extrinsic evidence in the conditional sale, or at least justify the application of the same standard to both types of transaction? See id. § 3.3, cmt. b; Nelson, Whitman, Burkhart & Freyermuth, Real Estate Finance Law § 3.18 (6th ed.2015).

5.   *Dangers in use of an absolute deed or conditional sale.* While most courts permit the grantor to establish by extrinsic evidence that the deed was intended to secure a debt, there is always the possibility that the grantor will be unable to sustain the heavy burden of producing clear and convincing

evidence of that intent. In that event, the grantor loses its interest in the land. Moreover, the grantor also runs the risk that if the grantee (mortgagee) records the conveyance, the grantee may in turn sell the land to a bona fide purchaser, who will take title free of the grantor's interest in the land. See, e.g., Finstad v. Gord, 844 N.W.2d 913 (N.D.2014) (court refused to recharacterize absolute deed as equitable mortgage as against claim of subsequent bona fide purchaser). Why did the court in *Bouffard* refuse to protect Befese as a bona fide purchaser? In most states, the grantor will be protected if he or she remains in possession because this will constitute constructive notice of the grantor's claim to any potential purchaser. See, e.g., Martinez v. Affordable Housing Network, Inc., 123 P.3d 1201 (Colo.2005).

Use of an absolute deed or conditional sale may sometimes disadvantage the grantee. Suppose the grantee is willing to concede that the transaction was actually a mortgage. The essential terms may be difficult to establish; can the grantee-mortgagee's right to accelerate be established by parol testimony? Even more important is the absence of a power of sale in the documents, at least in jurisdictions that allow nonjudicial foreclosure. In all likelihood, if the court recharacterizes the deed as a mortgage, judicial foreclosure will be necessary because of the lack of a power of sale. See Nelson, Whitman, Burkhart & Freyermuth, Real Estate Finance Law § 3.9 (6th ed.2015).

6.   *Other reasons for using an absolute deed as security.* The *Bouffard* case demonstrates another reason why parties sometimes attempt to "hide" the true nature of their transaction. Befese wanted to avoid the consequences of usury law, which capped the permissible interest rate at 16%, by having the transaction appear not to be a loan but a sale/repurchase. In other cases, an income tax motive may be present; the grantee may wish to mask the difference between the sale price and the repurchase price as a capital gain rather than as ordinary interest income. See Nelson, Whitman, Burkhart & Freyermuth, Real Estate Finance Law § 3.17 (6th ed.2015).

DOWNS V. ZIEGLER

Court of Appeals of Arizona, Division 1, 1970
13 Ariz.App. 387, 477 P.2d 261

HAIRE, JUDGE. Plaintiffs Claude and Mary Downs, commenced an action to foreclose a real estate mortgage and to hold Albert Ziegler, the mortgagor, and three doctors alleged to have subsequently agreed to pay the mortgage, liable for any deficiency remaining after the foreclosure sale of the mortgaged property. The case was tried to the court sitting without a jury, and the court entered judgment for plaintiffs on the issue of foreclosing the subject mortgage, and for the defendant doctors on the issue of their liability for any resulting deficiency. Plaintiffs appealed from that judgment.

The facts necessary for a determination of this appeal are as follows: Defendant Ziegler was in the construction business, having built and owned four apartment buildings. One of the apartments was built on land conveyed to Ziegler by the plaintiffs. Ziegler paid for this land by giving the plaintiffs an installment promissory note in the sum of $75,000.00, secured by a mortgage on the land. Some two years after the purchase of the land Ziegler encountered financial difficulties. At that time Ziegler was unable to meet his financial obligations, including a $30,000.00 promissory note for a personal loan from the Continental National Bank. One of the bank's officers contacted his own brother, Dr. Howland (one of the defendant doctors), and advised him of Ziegler's situation, suggesting that he, in association with two other doctors (Drs. Zemer and Sadler), undertake a refinancing of the property owned by Ziegler. The plan was that the doctors would collectively make available their credit so that $21,000.00 could be obtained to prevent foreclosure on the property, and also that they would guarantee payment of Ziegler's obligation to the bank in the sum of $30,000.00.

The arrangement was consummated under an agreement dated April 15, 1965, pursuant to which Ziegler agreed to convey to the doctors his interest in the mortgaged parcel here involved, in exchange for the doctors' agreement to advance funds to bring current the various secured indebtednesses against the property, and to guarantee payment of Ziegler's promissory note to the bank in the amount of $30,000.00. The agreement also provided for the "assumption of payment [by the doctors] of the balance due and owing . . . on any obligations secured by mortgages of record with respect to . . ." the property here involved. The agreement further provided that Ziegler could "repurchase" the property before the expiration of a year by paying to the doctors an amount calculated to reimburse the doctors for their expenditures, plus $10,000.00. In conjunction with this agreement the deeds were executed for the different properties involved, none of which purported to bind the doctors to pay Ziegler's debts, but transferred title "subject to" enumerated encumbrances.

Defendant Ziegler cross-claimed against the defendant doctors, seeking judgment against them for any deficiency which might be rendered against him in favor of the plaintiffs. In turn, the doctors cross-claimed against the defendant Continental National Bank alleging fraud and deceit on the part of the bank in inducing them to enter into the agreement of April 15, 1965. The trial court severed the doctors' cross-claim against the bank for trial at a later time.

At the trial the court admitted, over plaintiffs' objection, extrinsic evidence which tended to show that the April 15, 1965 agreement was in reality a mortgage rather than a contract of sale.

The principal issues raised on appeal are (1) whether the trial court properly admitted extrinsic evidence to show that the agreement of April 15, 1965 was actually a mortgage; (2) if extrinsic evidence was admissible, whether that evidence was sufficient to support the trial court's determination that the agreement was a mortgage rather than an agreement of sale; and (3) whether the trial court erred in admitting into evidence certain requests for admissions made by Ziegler and the bank. Collateral issues are raised in addition to these and will be considered elsewhere in this opinion.

There is no dispute between the parties that if the subject agreement be construed as an agreement of sale, then the defendant doctors would be personally liable for the payment of the mortgages here involved. There is additionally no assertion that the doctors would be liable for those sums if the court properly found a mortgage, and indeed the contrary has been affirmed by the appellants in their reply brief, acknowledging therein that a first mortgagee, absent consideration for the alleged assumption of liability in the second mortgage, cannot recover from a second mortgagee. See, e.g., Garnsey v. Rogers, 47 N.Y. 233, 7 Am.Rep. 440 (1872); Savings Bank of Southern California v. Thornton, 112 Cal. 255, 44 P. 466 (1896); and G. Osborne, Mortgages § 266 (2d ed. 1970). Further, no claim has been made that there was consideration given for the assumption of liability in the agreement if properly held to constitute a second mortgage. Indeed, the dispute between the parties has not touched upon the *effect* of the trial court's finding of a mortgage, but has centered on the propriety of making such a finding in light of an instrument purporting on its face to be an agreement of sale.

In addition to the assumption language previously quoted, the agreement states:

> "8.   Nothing herein contained shall be construed to involve a loan from Buyers to Sellers or to create the relationship of mortgagors and mortgagees between the parties hereto, it being understood and agreed between Buyers and Sellers that the transaction provided for are a sale and a conveyance of real property and option for a valuable consideration to purchase real property under specified conditions and on specified terms."

Although there is case authority in other jurisdictions that if an agreement for reconveyance expressly recites that the transaction is not a mortgage such a recital is conclusive of the matter, it has also been held that such a recital is not conclusive, and that a deed intended as security for a debt will be found a mortgage *no matter how strong* the language of the deed or of any accompanying instrument. 59 C.J.S. Mortgages § 27b at 64 (1949). We believe that the provisions of A.R.S. § 33–702 are pertinent to the decision of this question in Arizona. That statute provides:

> "Every transfer of an interest in property, other than in trust, made only as a security for the performance of another act, is a mortgage, except a transfer of personal property accompanied by

an actual change of possession, which is deemed a pledge. *The fact that a transfer was made subject to defeasance on a condition, may, for the purpose of showing that the transfer is a mortgage, be proved except against a subsequent purchaser or encumbrancer for value and without notice, notwithstanding that the fact does not appear by the terms of the instrument.*" (Emphasis supplied).

Additionally, there is abundant Arizona case authority holding that parol evidence is admissible to show that a conveyance absolute on its face was intended as a mortgage even though the instrument was knowingly cast in the form of a conveyance, and that the true nature of the transaction is a question of intention to be inferred from all the facts and circumstances surrounding the transaction. See Merryweather v. Pendleton, 90 Ariz. 219, 367 P.2d 251 (1961); Britz v. Kinsvater, 87 Ariz. 385, 351 P.2d 986 (1960); Charter Gas Engine Co. v. Entrekin, 30 Ariz. 341, 246 P. 1038 (1926); and Coffin v. Green, 21 Ariz. 54, 185 P. 361 (1919). We therefore hold that in this case the trial court properly admitted extrinsic evidence for the purpose of showing that the parties intended an arrangement to secure the repayment of the defendant doctors rather than a sale. However, this extrinsic evidence must be clear and convincing in order to show that a deed absolute and a separate option to repurchase together constitute a mortgage. Merryweather v. Pendleton, supra, 90 Ariz. at 223, 224, 367 P.2d at 253. In the case under consideration, we are of the opinion that the defendant doctors sustained this burden.

Our Supreme Court has said that:

> "Whether a transaction ostensibly a conditional sale is in fact an equitable mortgage or pledge depends ultimately upon the intent of the parties. Where, as in this case, the parties' testimony as to their intentions is wholly contradictory, such intentions must be determined from and in light of all the circumstances surrounding the transaction." (Merryweather v. Pendleton, supra, 90 Ariz. at 226, 367 P.2d at 255).

Of primary importance in Arizona in determining whether a transaction was intended to be a security device, i.e., a mortgage, or an absolute conveyance is the presence of a subsisting obligation. Our Supreme Court has drawn a firm distinction between a deed of conveyance coupled with an option to purchase, from which there cannot be inferred from the surrounding facts an intended obligation to repay, and a security device through which the sum paid was actually intended as a loan. Merryweather v. Pendleton, supra; and Charter Gas Engine Co. v. Entrekin, supra. This indeed is the prevailing rule. See 59 C.J.S. Mortgages § 28 (1949). Certain criteria which have been considered by the courts in determining whether a security device was intended have been succinctly enumerated in Merryweather, supra. These criteria are:

"(1) the prior negotiations of the parties, to discern if such negotiations contemplated a mere security for a debt; (2) the distress of the maker; (3) the fact that the amount advanced was about the amount that the 'grantor' needed to pay an existing indebtedness; (4) the amount of the consideration paid in comparison to the actual value of the property in question; (5) a contemporaneous agreement to repurchase; and (6) the acts of the parties in relation to each other, i.e., whether their acts are ordinarily indicative of a vendor-purchaser relationship or that of a mortgagor and mortgagee." (90 Ariz. at 239, 367 P.2d at 264).

The parol testimony is without contradiction that in their negotiations the parties contemplated security for the repayment of funds advanced by the doctors. The presence of other facts surrounding the agreement also furnish sufficient support in the record to find a mortgage. It is undisputed that at the time of the agreement, Ziegler was in severe financial distress, being threatened with foreclosures. The defendant doctors, further, guaranteed Ziegler's note to the bank in the amount of $30,000.00, which was about to be recalled, and the additional obligations undertaken by the doctors were for the amounts required to make current mortgage payments. In addition to these facts, there is uncontradicted testimony in the record that the doctors never as much as inspected the premises, never took possession of or occupied the same, and never collected any rents accruing therefrom. These surrounding facts are more consistent with a mortgagor-mortgagee relationship than with a seller-buyer relationship, and together with the doctors' testimony as to intent, furnish ample support for the trial court's conclusions. . . .

The judgment of the trial court is affirmed.

NOTES

1. *Assumptions of liability by junior mortgagees.* The key to understanding the *Downs* case lies in the paragraph of the opinion that cites *Garnsey v. Rogers*. The court there refers to the old rule that holds that, if a junior mortgagee enters into an assumption agreement, promising to pay a senior mortgage debt, the "first mortgagee, absent consideration for the alleged assumption of liability in the second mortgage, cannot recover from a second mortgagee." The doctors argued that (1) their deed should be recharacterized as a mortgage; (2) hence, it was a junior mortgage, subordinate to the Downs mortgage; (3) Downs had given them no consideration for their assumption agreement; (4) and therefore Downs could not enforce the assumption agreement against them by recovering a deficiency from them. If the court had refused to recharacterize the deed as a mortgage, this line of defense by the doctors would have fallen apart, since it is perfectly clear that when a grantee of a deed assumes a preexisting mortgage, the mortgagee can directly enforce the assumption agreement.

The underlying rule is silly, although apparently Downs did not attack it on the merits. Why should an assumption agreement by a grantee be enforceable by the mortgagee (irrespective of whether the mortgagee gave consideration for it), while an assumption agreement by a junior mortgagee cannot be enforced unless the mortgagee gave consideration for it? We think there is no sensible answer to this question. The Restatement rejects the rule that insulates junior mortgagees from liability for their assumption agreements. See Restatement (Third) of Property (Mortgages) § 5.1(c) & cmt. f (1997).

Incidentally, can you construct an argument that Downs actually *did* give consideration for the doctors' assumption agreement? In fact, why would a junior mortgagee ever give an assumption agreement benefitting the senior lender, unless the senior were giving up something of value in return— typically forbearance in foreclosing even though the senior debt is in default?

2. *Burden of proof for grantees.* The *Downs* case is unusual in that the grantee is the party attempting to recharacterize the transaction as a mortgage. Should the burden of proof be the same for the grantee as for the grantor?

Additional reasons, beyond the rather odd one involved in *Downs*, may occasionally motivate a grantee to seek to characterize an absolute deed or conditional sale as a mortgage transaction. For example, suppose a third party is injured on the real estate and the grantee is sued on a negligence theory in his or her status as a "landowner." Because a mortgagee normally will not be liable to third parties for unsafe conditions on mortgaged real estate unless he or she exercises dominion and control over it, a grantee in such circumstances may understandably attempt to argue that the deed created only a mortgage. See, e.g., Smith v. Fried, 98 Ill.App.3d 467, 53 Ill.Dec. 845, 424 N.E.2d 636 (1981).

3. *Language disclaiming mortgage intent.* Note that the grantees in *Downs* included specific mortgage-negating language in the documents. Should such language have been dispositive? If courts treat such provisions as determinative, what would be the impact on the substantive rules considered in this section? Would it make more sense to treat such provisions as merely relevant to the issue of intent? See Fraser v. Fraser, 702 N.W.2d 283 (Minn.Ct.App.2005) (language in agreement that it "shall not be construed and interpreted as an 'equitable mortgage' as that term is defined by Minnesota law" not deemed conclusive as to the question of intent). Should it have made a difference in *Downs* that the grantees were attacking the provision that *they* probably insisted on including in the agreement? Cf. Restatement (Third) of Property (Mortgages) § 3.3, illus. 7 and cmt. d (1997) ("If the grantee was the party who insisted on insertion of the mortgage-negating language, the grantee probably should be estopped from attacking his or her own attempt to negate mortgage intent.").

B. THE INSTALLMENT LAND CONTRACT

The most commonly used substitute for the mortgage or deed of trust as a land financing device is the installment land contract. This device is also known variously as the "contract for deed" or the "long term land contract." The installment land contract carries out the same economic function as a purchase money mortgage—financing by the seller of the unpaid portion of the purchase price of the land. Under the installment land contract, the vendee normally goes into possession and agrees to make monthly installment payments of principal and interest until the principal balance is paid off. The contract may amortize the unpaid balance over a term as short as a few years or as long as 30 or 40 years. Even if the contract has a long amortization period, it may nevertheless require the vendee to pay off the balance by a "balloon payment" after only a few years. During the period of the contract, the vendee usually must pay the taxes, maintain casualty insurance and keep the premises in good repair—all customarily obligations of the "owner" of the land. Nevertheless, the vendor retains legal title until the vendee makes the final payment, at which time the vendor must execute and deliver a deed to the land.

The installment land contract should be distinguished from the ordinary executory or "earnest money" contract for the sale of land which was the primary focus of Chapter One. The earnest money contract establishes the rights and liabilities of the parties as seller and buyer during the time period between the date of the contract and the date of closing, at which time title passes (and security agreements, if any, are executed). By contrast, the installment land contract governs the parties throughout the life of the debt.

1. THE NATURE OF THE INSTALLMENT LAND CONTRACT AND REMEDIES FOR VENDEE DEFAULT

When a vendee under an installment land contract defaults, the vendor, under traditional remedies, may sue "(1) for the installments which are due with interest thereon; (2) for specific performance of the contract; (3) for damages for the breach; (4) to foreclose his vendee's rights; (5) to quiet title; or if he should desire, he may merely rescind the contract." See Comment, Installment Contracts for the Sale of Land in Missouri, 24 Mo.L.Rev. 240, 243 (1959). Most of these remedies, however, tend to be slow and expensive, and some of them depend on the vendee's being able to satisfy a money judgment. As a consequence vendors most frequently rely on the forfeiture clause contained in virtually every installment land contract. This clause typically will provide that "time is of the essence" and that upon vendee default, the vendor has the option to declare the contract terminated, to retake possession of the premises, and to retain all of vendee's prior payments under the contract as liquidated damages.

Moreover, this clause also purports to relieve the vendor from further obligations under the contract.

Historically, many buyers resorted to installment land contracts because they did not have enough money to make the down payment needed to obtain a conventional mortgage loan. See Frank R. Lacy, Land Sale Contracts in Bankruptcy, 21 U.C.L.A.Rev. 477 (1973). Indeed, as high loan-to-value-ratio (95% to 100%) loans from institutional lenders became more widely available, the use of installment land contracts declined. But they have not faded away, because vendors are often willing to supply credit to purchasers whose poor credit scores and relatively low incomes would disqualify them from getting institutional loans. Indeed, with the tightening of underwriting standards in the wake of the mortgage crisis post-2007, the use of installment land contracts has increased in some states.

Vendors view the installment land contract as a "pro-vendor" financing device. In considering the following material, you should focus on the remedies available to the installment contract vendor and on the rights of the vendee. These remedies and rights will vary greatly from jurisdiction to jurisdiction. Is the installment contract device, in fact, really as "pro-vendor" as the common perception of it? Or does it perhaps seriously disadvantage the vendee without giving the vendor the swift creditor remedy that he or she was counting on?

RUSSELL V. RICHARDS
Supreme Court of New Mexico, 1985
103 N.M. 48, 702 P.2d 993

WALTERS, JUSTICE. Mary V. Russell filed this action against John R. and Beth Richards for damages resulting from the default and forfeiture of her interest in a real estate contract and for loss of personal property. The trial court entered judgment for Russell and awarded damages in the amount of approximately $64,000. The Richardses filed this appeal. We affirm in part and reverse in part.

The Richardses present the following issues on appeal: (1) whether the trial court's refusal to enforce the forfeiture was an abuse of discretion; and (2) whether the trial court erred in awarding damages.

Russell was an assignee-purchaser under a standard form real estate contract with the Richardses, who were the original sellers of the real property. Russell paid $11,188 to the assignors and assumed $37,938 under the contract. At the time of her default, Russell had made 72 payments to the Richardses and had reduced the principal owed by $10,782, leaving a principal amount of $26,504. The real property, by that time, had increased in value from $48,989 at time of purchase to $82,735.

At trial, Russell presented evidence on the circumstances of her default, the valuation of the real property subject to the contract and the value of her personal property not recovered after default. She asserted that the forfeiture of her interest under the contract should shock the conscience of the trial court. Although the trial court found that Russell's interest under the contract was forfeited, it also found that the forfeiture shocked its conscience. The trial court entered judgment in favor of Russell, awarding damages of $56,724 for her equity in the real property and $7500 for the loss of her personal property.

The Richardses contend that the trial court's failure to enforce the forfeiture of Russell's interest under the contract was an abuse of discretion. We agree. The rule is well settled in New Mexico that the forfeiture provision in this type of real estate contract is enforceable, *Eiferle v. Toppino,* 90 N.M. 469, 565 P.2d 340 (1977), absent unfairness which shocks the conscience of the court. *Bishop v. Beecher,* 67 N.M. 339, 355 P.2d 277 (1960). To determine whether a forfeiture shocks the conscience of the court, this Court has applied the following equitable considerations: the amount of money already paid by the buyer to the seller; the period of possession of the real property by the buyer; the market value of the real property at the time of default compared to the original sales price; and the rental potential and value of the real property. *See Huckins v. Ritter,* 99 N.M. 560, 661 P.2d 52 (1983).

Russell's reliance on the equitable exception to enforcement of forfeiture is misplaced. Not every case of default and forfeiture presents circumstances which shock the conscience of a court. *Compare Huckins v. Ritter,* 99 N.M. 560, 661 P.2d 52 (1983) (forfeiture not enforced), with *Manzano Industries, Inc. v. Mathis,* 101 N.M. 104, 678 P.2d 1179 (1984) (forfeiture enforced). The parties to a real estate contract and their assignees agree to be bound by its terms and provisions, and to accept the burdens of the contract together with its benefits. A subpurchaser takes the land subject to the terms of the contract of which he has knowledge. *Campbell v. Kerr,* 95 N.M. 73, 618 P.2d 1237 (1980). The courts will enforce a real estate contract except where enforcement, under the equitable circumstances of the case, would result in an unconscionable forfeiture. *Huckins v. Ritter.* Such equitable circumstances as would avoid forfeiture are not present here.

In this case, Russell was in possession of the premises approximately 6 years and paid a total of $10,782 on the contract principal to the Richardses over that period; and the trial court properly considered that amount. The trial court's further consideration of Russell's down payment was not proper, however, because that amount was paid to Russell's assignors. The Richardses received no part of that payment. The trial court's inclusion of the down payment in the damage amount placed the financial responsibility on the Richardses to return money that was never paid to them.[1]

Similarly, the trial court's consideration of the increased market value of the real property was erroneous. The inclusion of any portion of the market value amount in the damage amount gave Russell the benefit of the enhancement in the value of the property, contrary to established law. This court has held that "during the life of the real estate contract any risk of loss or enhancement in value accrues to the purchaser." *MGIC Mortgage Corp. v. Bowen,* 91 N.M. 200, 202, 572 P.2d 547, 549 (1977). Upon default and forfeiture, the buyer's interest is terminated and there is no enhancement value to be recovered by the buyer. *Id.*

We note that Russell had received benefit and profit during her possession. She rented out three units of the property and, at the time of default, the entire property was leased for a monthly payment far in excess of the payment due under the contract. Russell had been in default several times before the forfeiture and each time she had cured the default. She knew the consequences of default.

We also agree with the Richardses that the trial court erred in awarding damages for Russell's loss of her interest under the contract. In order to recover damages there must be a right of action for a wrong inflicted on the party claiming damages; damage without wrong does not constitute a cause of action. *See Jomack Lumber Co. v. Grants State Bank,* 75 N.M. 787, 411 P.2d 759 (1966). Russell's loss of her interest under the contract did not result from a wrong committed by the Richardses, but from her default under the real estate contract for failure to make timely payment. The usual consequence of default, as clearly stated in the contract assumed by Russell, is forfeiture of all interest; only unusual equitable circumstances create an exception to that rule. . . .

[The court upheld the trial court's award of $7500 for Russell's loss of personal property, although one judge dissented from this conclusion, and the court remanded the case for modification of the judgment.]

WATKINS V. EADS
Court of Appeals of Kentucky, 2014
2014 WL 2154901

TAYLOR, JUDGE. On September 24, 1998, Joe (Jody) S. Watkins entered into an installment land sale contract with Elizabeth Stipp Eads for the purchase of residential property owned by Elizabeth located at 531 Main Street, Paris, Kentucky. Although not documented in the record, Elizabeth subsequently conveyed her interest in the property to Richard and Deanna

---

[1] Editors' Note: Do you agree with the court's analysis on this point? Did Russell's down payment inure to the benefit of the Richardses and, if so, how?

Eads. The contract stated a total purchase price of $125,000 with a down payment of $5,000 to be paid upon execution of the contract. The $120,000 balance was to accrue interest at the rate of 9.5 percent per annum, simple interest, and was to be paid in 180 equal monthly installments of $1,253.07. Watkins was also responsible for paying the *ad valorem* taxes on the property conveyed under the contract. The contract further provided that in the event of default, the Eads could declare the total balance due, and if such balance was not paid within ten days, the contract could be terminated. The contract also contained the following forfeiture clause which is the genesis of this appeal:

> [I]n the event that the amount then owing is not paid within ten (10) days payments made by Purchaser hereunder and the value of any repairs and/or improvements made by Purchaser may retained to the benefit of the Seller as fixed and liquidated damages for nonperformance by Purchaser of this agreement and as rent and compensation for use and occupancy of said property by Purchaser, as Purchaser specifically waives their right to foreclosure sale of the property.
>
> However, if the above remedy of Seller, upon default by Purchaser, is determined to be unenforceable by a court of competent jurisdiction, then in that event Seller may, at his option, declare all of the unpaid purchase money herein, the interest due thereon and all other amounts due hereunder to be immediately due and payable without further notice of demand to Purchaser, and Seller may thereupon institute proceedings to collect the same as if Seller had a purchase money lien on said property, pursuant to the holding and guidelines of *Sebastian v. Floyd,* Ky., 585 S.W.2d 381 (1979), and Purchaser agrees to pay all costs thereof, including reasonable attorney's fees.

It is undisputed that Watkins eventually defaulted under the terms of the contract. On June 4, 2010, the Eads sent Watkins a letter notifying him the contract would be terminated in ten days unless all arrearages (payments, taxes, and interest) were paid in full. There is a dispute between the parties as to the actual amount owed including interest. The arrearages were not paid; consequently, the Eads filed a complaint in Bourbon Circuit Court in June of 2011. Therein, the Eads alleged that Watkins was in default under the terms of the contract, and that per the contract's forfeiture clause, Watkins forfeited any right to a foreclosure sale or recoupment of payments made thereunder.

Watkins filed an answer and counterclaim, asserting that he had not forfeited the right to a foreclosure sale and was entitled to recoupment of payments made under the land contract. Specifically, Watkins argued that a foreclosure sale of the real property was legally mandated and that he was entitled to receive approximately $86,984.72 from the proceeds of the sale of the real property.

By opinion and order entered April 17, 2012, the circuit court granted summary judgment in favor of the Eads. The circuit court determined that Watkins was in default, had forfeited his right to a foreclosure sale per the contract, and waived any payments made under the land contract. . . . These appeals follow.

Watkins contends the circuit court erred by concluding that the forfeiture clause in the contract was enforceable and that he waived his right to a foreclosure sale of the real property. Watkins relies upon *Sebastian v. Floyd,* 585 S.W.2d 381 (Ky.1979), for the proposition that a forfeiture clause in an installment land contract is *per se* invalid. The Eads respond that Watkins voluntarily waived his right to a foreclosure sale of the real property under the contract and, therefore, *Sebastian,* 585 S.W.2d 318, is inapposite. . . .

Installment land sale contracts, also commonly referred to as contracts and bond for deed, are recognized as valid and enforceable contracts to finance the purchase of real property. *Sebastian,* 585 S.W.2d 381. These contracts are common in owner-financed transactions. Upon execution of an installment land sale contract, legal title to the real property remains with the seller, and equitable title to the real property passes to the purchaser. *Id.* However, Kentucky law is clear that upon default by the purchaser in an installment land contract, the purchaser does not "forfeit" his interest in the real property and, most importantly, a purported forfeiture clause stating otherwise is considered void and unenforceable. *Sebastian,* 585 S.W.2d 381.

This Court recently revisited *Sebastian* in *Slone v. Calhoun,* 386 S.W.3d 745 (Ky.App.2012). As noted in *Slone, Sebastian* remains the controlling precedent in Kentucky regarding installment land sale contracts. Under the *Sebastian* rule, a real estate purchaser, who defaults under an installment land sale contract, still retains an equitable interest in the real property and further possesses redemption rights therein pursuant to Kentucky Revised Statutes (KRS) 426.530. The Kentucky Supreme Court held in *Sebastian* that the forfeiture provision in an installment land sale contract that provided for the forfeiture of the buyers' payment upon the buyers' default was invalid and otherwise not enforceable in Kentucky. The Supreme Court noted that there was no practical distinction between a land sale contract and a purchase money mortgage. The Court made the following observation regarding this issue:

> There is no practical distinction between the land sale contract and a purchase money mortgage, in which the seller conveys legal title to the buyer but retains a lien on the property to secure payment. The significant feature of each device is the seller's

financing the buyer's purchase of the property, using the property as collateral for the loan.

Where the purchaser of property has given a mortgage and subsequently defaults on his payments, his entire interest in the property is not forfeited. The mortgagor has the right to redeem the property by paying the full debt plus interest and expenses incurred by the creditor due to default. In order to cut off the mortgagor's right to redeem, the mortgagee must request a court to sell the property at public auction. *See* Lewis, Reeves, How the Doctrine of Equitable Conversion Affects Land Sale Contract Forfeitures, 3 Real Estate Law Journal 249, 253 (1974). *See also* KRS 426.005, 426.525. From the proceeds of the sale, the mortgagee recovers the amount owed him on the mortgage, as well as the expenses of bringing suit; the mortgagor is entitled to the balance, if any. [*Sebastian,* 585 S.W.2d at 383.]

Effectively, grantors who finance the sale of real property are treated like banks or mortgage institutions that finance real estate transactions and retain mortgages against the property to secure the payment of the indebtedness owed. This public policy is consistent with the legislative mandate that "strict foreclosure" in Kentucky has been abolished, regardless of the method of financing. KRS 426.525. Prior to passage of this statute at common law, a lien holder could unilaterally take possession and control of mortgaged property, thereby eliminating any equity of the mortgagor or owner of the property, as well as extinguishing statutory redemption rights provided for in KRS 426.530. *Sebastian* extended the policy of strict foreclosure prohibition to installment land sale contracts.

The forfeiture clause at issue in this case clearly violates the holding in *Sebastian* and *Slone* and also contravenes KRS 426.525 and KRS 426.530. The forfeiture clause in Watkins' contract is void and of no effect. The circuit court erred as a matter of law in enforcing the same.

We would further note that the circuit court's conclusion that the contract states that "he [Watkins] is waiving his rights that were established by *Sebastian v. Floyd.* . . ." is also erroneous on its face for two reasons. First, the contract does not contain any language whatsoever regarding the waiver of "*Sebastian* rights." Second, had the contract expressly waived any "rights" from *Sebastian,* this waiver would also have been void on its face. We must emphasize that *Sebastian* did not create "rights" that are subject to waiver. Rather, *Sebastian* established and applied the long-standing law in Kentucky that strict foreclosure is prohibited in any real estate financing transaction, including owner-financed transactions that utilize installment land sale contracts. Until the Supreme Court directs otherwise, any attempt to waive the protections afforded by *Sebastian* are void as a matter of law and the only judicial remedy available to address the alleged breach of an installment land sale contract is a judicial sale of the property. *Sebastian,* 585 S.W.2d 381.

Under the authority of *Sebastian,* 585 S.W.2d 381, a forfeiture clause in an installment land contract is void and will not be given legal effect in this Commonwealth. *See also Slone,* 386 S.W.3d 745. . . .

Upon remand and entry of judgment, the circuit court shall direct that a judicial sale of the real property be conducted in accordance with applicable law, and from the proceeds, the Eads are entitled to recover the balance owed under the land contract as determined by the circuit court in accordance with this opinion. Any remaining balance will be paid to Watkins. . . .

NOTES

1.   *The strict enforcement approach.* The *Richards* decision reflects the traditional hostility many state courts demonstrated toward efforts by installment contract vendees to avoid forfeiture. See also Burgess v. Shiplet, 230 Mont. 387, 750 P.2d 460 (1988) ("When a purchaser enters into a contract for deed with a seller, he or she runs the risk of defaulting on the required payments and facing the consequences of losing the property along with forfeiting the amount already paid. If this produces a harsh or unwanted result, it is for the legislature to remedy and not the job of this court to change the plain meaning of the contract. . . . Buyers cannot look to mortgage law for alternative remedies but must accept the remedies set forth in their contract with sellers.").

2.   *The "installment land contract as a mortgage" approach.* By contrast, *Watkins* reflects the view that because the vendor is retaining title simply for the purpose of securing the vendee's payment of future installments, the installment contract is the functional equivalent of a purchase money mortgage and its enforcement should be governed by mortgage law. This approach is consistent with how the Uniform Commercial Code treats installment credit sales of personal property. See, e.g., U.C.C. § 1–201(b)(35) (2016) (" 'Security interest' means an interest in personal property or fixtures which secures payment or performance of an obligation. . . . The retention or reservation of title by a seller of goods notwithstanding shipment or delivery to the buyer . . . is limited in effect to a reservation of a 'security interest.' "). This is likewise the approach adopted by the Restatement. Restatement (Third) of Property (Mortgages) § 3.4(b) (1997) ("A contract for deed creates a mortgage."). As a result, in any jurisdiction adopting the Restatement, an installment land contract will be "governed procedurally and substantively by the law of mortgages." Id. at cmt. c. Under this approach, what should have happened in *Russell v. Richards*?

There is support in case law in several states for this view. Indiana generally treats the installment contract as a mortgage, Skendzel v. Marshall, 261 Ind. 226, 301 N.E.2d 641 (1973), but Indiana courts still permit forfeiture to occur where the vendee (1) has abandoned the premises or (2) has paid only a minimal amount toward the contract price and has jeopardized the vendor's security (e.g., commission of waste). What is the rationale for these exceptions? If an installment vendee that has leased the premises to a tenant defaults to the vendor, tells the vendor to "stick it up your ass" and directs the tenant to make future rent payments to the vendor, has the vendee abandoned the premises? See McLemore v. McLemore, 827 N.E.2d 1135 (Ind.Ct.App.2005). If the vendee has made payments for four years on a contract that requires thirty years of installments payments, has the vendee paid more than a "minimal amount"? See, e.g., *Skendzel* (vendee who paid 29% of principal made more than minimal payment); *McLemore* (18.2% of principal over three years of payments more than minimal); but see Huber v. Sering, 867 N.E.2d 698 (Ind.Ct.App.2007) (forfeiture affirmed where less than 20% of contract price had been paid and vendee had violated insurance and maintenance covenants). Would Indiana be better off if it treated all installment land contracts as mortgages irrespective of the amount paid on the contract or such issues as abandonment or security impairment?

The Florida Supreme Court has not yet held that a vendee has an absolute right to insist on foreclosure of an installment land contract, but numerous intermediate appellate decisions in Florida so hold. See, e.g., Kubany v. Woods, 622 So.2d 22 (Fla.Ct.App.1993) ("This agreement for deed is treated under Florida law as a mortgage and is subject to the same rules of foreclosure."); Luneke v. Becker, 621 So.2d 744 (Fla.Ct.App.1993); White v. Brousseau, 566 So.2d 832 (Fla.Ct.App.1990).

The New York Supreme Court, Appellate Division, in a 1983 case where vendees had paid almost half of the contract purchase price of a house, reversed a trial court forfeiture decree, stating that there was "no reason why these vendees should be treated any differently than the mortgagor at common law" and holding that "vendors may not summarily dispossess the vendees of their equitable ownership without first bringing an action to foreclose the vendees' equity of redemption." Bean v. Walker, 95 A.D.2d 70, 464 N.Y.S.2d 895 (1983). See also Call v. LaBrie, 116 A.D.2d 1034, 498 N.Y.S.2d 652 (1986) (payment by vendee of over 12% of the contract price deemed sufficient to convert contract for deed into an equitable mortgage).

Both Nebraska and Vermont follow the Restatement approach. See, e.g., Wintroub v. Nationstar Mortg. LLC, 303 Neb. 15, 927 N.W.2d 19 (2019) ("[B]ecause a seller in a land contract retains the title as security for the unpaid purchase money and has an equitable lien on the land to the extent of the debt, a seller has, for all intents and purposes, a purchase-money mortgage."); Prue v. Royer, 193 Vt. 267, 67 A.3d 895 (2013) (citing Restatement § 3.4(b) approvingly).

In Colorado, trial courts have the discretion to require that a contract for deed be foreclosed as a mortgage. See Grombone v. Krekel, 754 P.2d 777 (Colo.App.1988) ("The decision whether an installment land contract is to be treated as a mortgage is committed to the sound discretion of the trial court, based on facts presented. . . . The factors to be used by the trial court in determining whether to treat an installment land contract as a mortgage include the amount of the vendee's equity in the property, the length of the default period, the willfulness of the default, whether the vendee has made improvements, and whether the property has been adequately maintained.").

3. *Statutory reforms requiring foreclosure.* Several states have adopted legislation requiring the installment contract vendor to foreclose the vendee's interest after default. Oklahoma's statute requires this in all cases. See, e.g., Okla.Stat.Ann. tit. 16, § 11A (1998) ("All contracts for deed . . . shall be subject to the same rules of foreclosure and to the same regulations, restraints, and forms as are prescribed in relation to mortgages."). Others require foreclosure only for residential real property and/or only after the vendee has met certain payment thresholds. See, e.g., 735 Ill.Comp.Stat. §§ 5/15–1206, 5/9–102 (residential real estate where contract period exceeds five years and amount due is less than 80% of contract price); Md. Code Ann. Real Prop. § 10–105 (once vendee has paid 40% or more of cash price of residential property, vendee may demand deed provided vendee executes purchase money mortgage for the then-outstanding balance); Ohio Rev. Code Ann. § 5313.07 (judicial foreclosure required if installment contract for dwelling has been in effect for five years or more and vendee has paid more than 20% of price); Tex.Prop.Code Ann. § 5.066 (forfeiture not available to vendor, and nonjudicial foreclosure required, once installment vendee of residential property "has paid 40% or more of the amount due or the equivalent of 48 monthly payments" under contract).

4. *Statutes institutionalizing the forfeiture remedy.* By contrast, some state legislatures have elected to permit forfeiture after default in accordance with the terms of the contract, but only if the vendor complies with certain substantive and procedural requirements. Most of these statutes provide that notwithstanding the terms of the contract, the vendor cannot terminate the contract and enforce a forfeiture without first providing the defaulting vendee with notice of the vendor's intent to terminate the contract as well as a "cure period" during which the vendee can cure the default and reinstate the contract. In Minnesota, for example, the vendee cannot enforce a forfeiture against a defaulting vendor unless the vendee has provided a written notice of default and the default has remained uncured for 60 days after service of the notice. Minn.Stat.Ann. § 559.21, subd. 2a. To cure, the vendee must pay all of the missed installments, as well as 2% of the unpaid principal, costs of serving the notice, and attorney fees actually expended by the vendor (subject to caps that vary depending upon the amount in default). Id. The written notice must contain statutorily-mandated language conspicuously advising the vendee that if the vendee fails to cure, "YOUR CONTRACT WILL TERMINATE AT THE END OF THE PERIOD AND YOU WILL LOSE ALL THE MONEY YOU HAVE PAID ON THE CONTRACT; YOU WILL LOSE YOUR RIGHT TO POSSESSION OF THE PROPERTY; YOU MAY LOSE YOUR RIGHT TO ASSERT ANY CLAIMS OR DEFENSES THAT YOU MIGHT HAVE; AND YOU WILL BE EVICTED." Id. subd. 3. Is such a statute sufficient to protect a vendee's equitable interest in the property? Why or why not?

In the states that have codified the forfeiture remedy, there is a good deal of variation in the specifics. For example, Iowa's statute requires only a 30-day cure period, but does not require the vendee to pay the vendor's attorney fees to prevent forfeiture. Iowa Code Ann. §§ 656.1 to 656.9. Washington's statute requires a 90-day cure period unless the contract itself requires a longer period. Wash.Rev.Code § 61.30.070(1)(e). In some states, the grace period required for cure increases depending on the amount the vendee had paid prior to default. Ariz.Rev.Stat. § 33–742 (30 days if vendee had paid less than 20% of the price; 60 days if vendee paid 20 to 30%; 120 days if vendee paid 30–50%; 9 months if vendee paid more than 50%). See also N.D.Cent.Code §§ 32–18–01 to 32–18–06 (six months cure period, extended to one year if vendee has paid more than one-third of original indebtedness); Or.Rev.Stat.Ann. §§ 93.905 to 93.945 (60 days if unpaid balance exceeds 75% of price; 90 days if balance is between 50% and 75% of price; otherwise 120 days). In other states already discussed in note 3, the statutes codify the vendor's ability to obtain forfeiture where the vendee has not met the payment threshold necessary to trigger a foreclosure requirement. See, e.g., Ohio Rev.Code §§ 5313.01–5313.10; Tex.Prop. Code §§ 5.061–5.066.

Courts in these states sometime suggest that judicial relief from an "unconscionable forfeiture" may be available. See, e.g., Coddon v. Youngkrantz, 562 N.W.2d 39 (Minn.App.1997) (recognizing that equity may intervene where strict application of statutory cancellation would be "unjust"). Moreover, statutory forfeiture may sometimes be held inappropriate for certain relatively minor defaults. See, e.g., Lett v. Grummer, 300 N.W.2d 147 (Iowa 1981) (statutory forfeiture refused where failure to make minor repairs did not threaten security). Nevertheless, judicial intervention in statutory termination contexts tends more often to focus more on technical statutory compliance than on the inherent fairness of the forfeiture itself. See Nelson, Whitman, Burkhart & Freyermuth, Real Estate Finance Law § 3.28 (6th ed.2015). Indeed, Professor Durham's observations with respect to Ohio legislation may well have national relevance: "[u]nlike defaults on land contracts not covered by [Ohio Rev.Code §§ 5313.01–5313.10] where Ohio courts have clearly been inclined to give vendees equitable relief, the vendee subject to statutory forfeiture may find himself faced with a judge who either feels constrained by the statute from granting equitable relief or takes comfort in the simplicity of the statute and ignores the possibility of equitable action." James Geoffrey Durham, Forfeiture of Residential Land Contracts in Ohio: The Need for Further Reform of a Reform Statute, 16 Akron L.Rev. 397 (1983). See also Miller v. American Wonderlands, Inc., 275 N.W.2d 399 (Iowa 1979) (upholding forfeiture for $10.48 default on a $30,000 contract); ExtraOrdinary Learning and Educ. Complex/Minneapolis Communiversity, Inc. v. New Bethel Baptist Church, 430 N.W.2d 184 (Minn.Ct.App.1988) (forfeiture upheld where vendee was, at most, one day late).

5. *Waiver or estoppel as a defense against forfeiture.* An additional ameliorative judicial approach, conceptually less drastic than the foregoing theories, is the waiver concept:

> Frequently a vendor will accept one or several late payments from the vendee without taking action to declare a forfeiture. When the vendor finally runs out of patience and informs the vendee that forfeiture has occurred, the vendee may argue that the vendor's prior behavior constitutes a waiver of the time provisions of the contract and that the vendor is legally bound to accept the late payments. This dispute often surfaces in a vendee's suit or counterclaim for specific performance of the contract. The vendee may be willing to tender the entire purchase price, or he may insist upon an opportunity to make up his arrearages and resume the original payment schedule.

> Many courts have adopted the vendee's position in this situation. In effect, these courts hold that the vendor's waiver avoids the effect of the forfeiture clause and creates in the vendee a right analogous to an equity of redemption. According to this view, if the vendor had given the vendee clear notice that no further delinquencies would be tolerated, and if this notice had been given in adequate time to allow the vendee to get back on schedule, the vendor might thereby have preserved his right of forfeiture as to future installments. Since the vendor did not do so, the court itself will generally fix a reasonable time within which the vendee must cure the delinquencies.

Nelson & Whitman, Installment Land Contracts—The National Scene Revisited, 1985 B.Y.U. L. Rev. 1. See Turley v. Staley, 372 S.W.3d 821 (Ark.Ct.App.2009) (vendor waived the forfeiture remedy by accepting late payments over a ten year period).

Even where there is no prior pattern of forbearance, a vendor may occasionally be *estopped* to invoke forfeiture based on a single claimed default. In Danelson v. Robinson, 317 Mont. 462, 77 P.3d 1010 (2003), a defaulting vendee asserted that the vendor, in response to the vendee's offer to cure the contract by obtaining a loan from vendee's mother-in-law, assured vendee that "he was not worried about the payment and that taking out a loan from [vendee's] mother-in-law was not necessary." 77 P.3d at 1011. Two months later vendor initiated a forfeiture of the contract. Vendee then sought a judicial declaration that vendor was estopped to assert a forfeiture. The trial court rejected vendee's estoppel argument, but the Montana Supreme Court reversed, holding that the vendee should be permitted "to show that the [vendor] . . . waived [the right to forfeiture] for at least a period of time; that the [vendee] relied on this waiver; and that the [vendor] should be estopped thereby." Id. at 1013.

———————

Many states have not adopted the Restatement view that treats the installment contract as a mortgage. Further, many states do not have comprehensive legislation regulating the vendor's exercise of the forfeiture remedy. Nevertheless, courts in many of these states do acknowledge that the installment contract is a financing device, and have expressed concern that strict forfeiture (as reflected in *Richards v. Russell*) can be inequitable. As we have noted:

> [N]umerous state courts have in recent years refused to enforce against a defaulting vendee forfeiture clauses that the courts have deemed unreasonable or inequitable. These courts have employed several approaches to save the vendee from forfeiture. Some cases, for example, have in effect conferred on the vendee a mortgagor's equity of redemption, permitting him to tender the remainder of the purchase price (or even his arrearages) in a suit or counterclaim for specific performance of the contract. Where the vendee was unable or unwilling to redeem, courts have occasionally ordered the judicial foreclosure of the land contract. Finally, some courts, after determining that a particular forfeiture clause is unfair, have extended to the defaulting vendee the right to restitution—the right to recoup his payments to the extent that they exceed the vendor's damages caused by the vendee's default. Of course, many state courts have not considered the forfeiture clause in all of the remedial contexts described above, nor have they always been theoretically precise. Some courts have utilized contract principles to protect the defaulting vendee from an inequitable forfeiture provision. Other courts have gone a long way toward simply treating the installment land contract as a mortgage . . . . Still others have employed a confusing amalgam of mortgage and contract law.

Nelson, Whitman, Burkhart & Freyermuth, Real Estate Finance Law 76 (6th ed.2015).*

With this in mind, reconsider the facts of *Russell v. Richards*. If Russell could pay the entire outstanding balance of $26,504 (although not in the timely manner required by the contract), should the court have allowed her to do so? If she could not, should the court have required the Richardses to make restitution of all or any portion of Russell's prior payments? If so, how should the court calculate that amount? Keep these questions in mind in connection with the following material.

---

* Reprinted with permission of LEG, Inc. d/b/a West Academic.

PETERSEN V. HARTELL
Supreme Court of California, 1985
40 Cal.3d 102, 219 Cal.Rptr. 170, 707 P.2d 232

REYNOSO, JUSTICE. . . .

I

Defendant is administratrix of the estate of Juanita Gaspar who, upon the death of her first husband in 1946, succeeded to sole ownership of a 160-acre tract of unimproved land southeast of Fort Bragg in Mendocino County. In the late 1960's she entered into agreements with three of her grandchildren to sell small portions of the land at $1,500 per acre, with no down payment and monthly installments of $50 or less. The agreement now relied on by plaintiffs was embodied in a written contract, executed in November 1967, providing for the sale to granddaughter Kathy Petersen and her husband, Richard Petersen, of slightly more than six acres for a total purchase price of $9,162, payable at $50 per month. The buyers were given the right to pay the entire balance of the purchase price at any time. There was no provision making time of the essence or specifying remedies in the event of default.

Although the contract was drafted by Richard Petersen, who was then a recent law school graduate, the trial court found that no undue influence or overreaching was employed by either of the Petersens in the preparation or execution of the agreement. The price of $1,500 per acre was set by Mrs. Gaspar, who wished to give her grandchildren the opportunity to acquire small portions of her property. She was dependent, however, on income from the land contract payments, along with her social security benefits, to make ends meet.

The Petersens missed occasional payments in 1968, 1969, 1971, and 1972. Of the 65 payments due from November 1967 through March 1973, they made 58 payments totaling $2,900. In April 1973 the couple separated and their payments ceased. Kathy Petersen testified that about that time she spoke about the separation to her grandmother, who said it was important to take care of the children first and that she (the grandmother) would "get by."

In September 1975 Kathy Petersen sent Mrs. Gaspar a check for $250 as "back payments." Mrs. Gaspar's attorney then wrote the Petersens, stating that Mrs. Gaspar elected to terminate the contract. In February 1976 Mrs. Gaspar wrote to Kathy Petersen, returning the latter's check and explaining that she considered the contract broken. In September 1976 Richard Petersen wrote to the attorney requesting reinstatement of the contract and a statement of the amounts due, and enclosing a $250 money order, which the attorney promptly returned on instructions from Mrs. Gaspar.

In October 1976, Mrs. Gaspar died. Kathy Petersen then assigned all her interest under the contract to Carol Ranta as trustee for the two minor children of the Petersen marriage. Thus, the plaintiffs in the present action are Richard Petersen and the two children, who appear through Ranta as their guardian ad litem. By their amended complaint against Mrs. Gaspar's administratrix, plaintiffs seek specific performance, declaratory relief, damages, and the quieting of title to an easement of necessity to connect the property with a public road. They further tender the entire balance due under the contract on condition that defendant deliver a good and sufficient deed.

After a nonjury trial, the trial court denied plaintiffs' prayer for specific performance. It concluded that (1) plaintiffs' breach of the contract was grossly negligent and wilful, (2) plaintiffs failed to tender full performance until April 1, 1977, when the action was commenced, (3) defendant is entitled to restitution of the property, and (4) plaintiffs are entitled to restitution of $2,900 plus interest from April 1, 1977. Judgment was entered accordingly with costs to defendant.

II

In *MacFadden v. Walker,* 5 Cal.3d 809, 97 Cal.Rptr. 537, 488 P.2d 1353, this court affirmed a judgment for specific performance in favor of a vendee whose default in monthly payments we found wilful as a matter of law. The trial court had found the default to be neither wilful nor grossly negligent and so had granted relief under Civil Code section 3275, which provides that a party may be relieved from a forfeiture incurred for nonperformance of a contractual obligation "upon making full compensation to the other party, except in case of a grossly negligent, willful, or fraudulent breach of duty." That section was the basis for the prior holding in *Barkis v. Scott* (1949) 34 Cal.2d 116, 208 P.2d 367, that a vendee who had made substantial payments and improvements on the property and then as a result of simple negligence defaulted in two payments was entitled to have the contract reinstated. In *MacFadden,* however, this court concluded that relief under section 3275, as construed in *Barkis,* was not available because the trial court's finding that the vendee's default had been nonwilful was not supported by evidence. The issue on appeal, therefore, was "whether a vendee who would otherwise be entitled to specific performance of an installment land sale contract in which time is declared to be of the essence forfeits the right to that remedy because of her wilful failure to make installment payments when due after there has been substantial part performance of the contract." (5 Cal.3d at p. 811, 97 Cal.Rptr. 537, 488 P.2d 1353.)

To resolve that issue, *MacFadden* turned to *Freedman v. The Rector* (1951) 37 Cal.2d 16, 230 P.2d 629, explaining that there, "we held that section 3275 is not the exclusive source of the right to relief from forfeiture.

We concluded that the prohibition of punitive damages for breach of contract (Civ.Code, § 3294), the strict limitations on the right to provide for liquidated damages (Civ.Code, §§ 1670, 1671), and the provision that 'Neither specific nor preventive relief can be granted to enforce a penalty or forfeiture in any case . . .' (Civ.Code, § 3369) together established a policy that precludes any forfeiture having no reasonable relation to the damage caused by the vendee's breach even when that breach is wilful. (See also *Baffa v. Johnson* (1950) 35 Cal.2d 36, 37–39 [216 P.2d 13].) Since in the *Freedman* case, however, the vendor had sold the property to a third party in reliance on the vendee's repudiation of the contract, specific performance was not an available remedy, and relief from forfeiture was necessarily limited to awarding the defaulting vendee restitution in the amount of the excess of his part payment over the damages caused by his breach. We believe that the anti-forfeiture policy recognized in the *Freedman* case also justifies awarding even wilfully defaulting vendees specific performance in proper cases. . . .

Unlike the trial court in *MacFadden,* the trial court below denied plaintiff vendees specific performance. Since that remedy is discretionary (*Pasqualetti v. Galbraith* (1962) 200 Cal.App.2d 378, 382, 19 Cal.Rptr. 323; *Lind v. Baker* (1941) 48 Cal.App.2d 234, 245, 119 P.2d 806), we must consider whether the denial was an abuse of discretion and, if not, whether plaintiffs are entitled to relief on some other ground.

To be entitled to specific performance of a contract, a plaintiff must plead and prove that the contract is just and reasonable and the consideration adequate, as required by section 3391. Yet here, the trial court's findings of fact and conclusions of law fail to decide those issues even though they were properly raised in the complaint. There are indications in the findings and the trial court's memorandum of intended decision, however, that had the court reached those issues, it would have resolved them in plaintiffs' favor. . . . Accordingly, we infer that the trial court omitted any determination that the contract was just and reasonable and the consideration adequate not because of any lack of support for those conclusions in the record but because, in the court's view, those determinations would not have altered the court's ultimate conclusion that specific performance should be denied. . . .

The more likely connection between the [trial court's] findings of the Petersens' derelictions as to payments and the denial of specific performance is that the trial court weighed the seriousness of plaintiffs' defaults against them in a balancing of equities. That that was the court's theory seems likely from its citation of *Kosloff v. Castle* (1981) 115 Cal.App.3d 369, 171 Cal.Rptr. 308, where the Court of Appeal declared that whereas the wilfully defaulting vendee's right to restitution of installment payments made in excess of the seller's damages is unqualified, such vendee's right to specific performance is discretionary and dependent on a balancing of equities that include the seriousness of the vendee's defaults. (*Id.,* at p. 376, 171 Cal.Rptr. 308. Accord, *Bartley v. Karas* (1983) 150 Cal.App.3d 336, 344–345, 197 Cal.Rptr. 749.)

If that theory were correct, there would be ample basis in the evidence and findings to support the denial of specific performance. The Petersens' monthly payments were erratic and delinquent almost from the beginning even though the seller made clear her need of the payments for her support. By April 1973 the Petersens had made only 58 out of the 65 payments then due, and their first attempt to reinstate the contract was not until 29 months later, when they tendered only $250 out of the $1,800 that was by then overdue and unpaid.

The issue, therefore, is whether plaintiffs, despite their wilful defaults in payments, now have an absolute right to a conveyance of the property in exchange for payment of the entire balance of the purchase price (together with interest and any other damages) in light of their substantial part performance and the seller's notice of election to terminate the contract on account of such defaults.

III

Although we treated factors mitigating the seriousness of the vendee's default as relevant in upholding the judgment of specific performance in *MacFadden v. Walker,* supra, 5 Cal.3d 809, 813, 97 Cal.Rptr. 537, 488 P.2d 1353, we took care to explain that "[s]ince we have concluded . . . that Mrs. Walker [the vendee] is entitled to the remedy of specific performance, we need not decide whether she might also be entitled to some other remedy under the law governing security transactions" (*id.,* at p. 816, 97 Cal.Rptr. 537, 488 P.2d 1353). For at least a century in this state, a seller of land being sold under an installment contract who sues to quiet title because of the vendee's default in installment payments has been required to give the vendee a reasonable opportunity to complete performance. . . .

In those early cases, however, the vendee who failed to exercise the right to redeem by completing the payments forfeited payments already made, apparently without regard to whether the amounts paid exceeded the seller's damages. . . . Thereafter, this court decided that even a wilfully defaulting vendee may be entitled to restitution under section 3369, which provides that "[n]either specific nor preventive relief can be granted to enforce a penalty or forfeiture in any case." That section "precludes the court from quieting the vendor's title unless he refunds the excess of the part payments over the damage caused by the vendee's breach." (*Freedman v. The Rector* (1951) 37 Cal.2d 16, 22, 230 P.2d 629.) Such restitution is a matter of right for the wilfully defaulting vendee who proves that the payments made to the seller exceed the amount necessary to give the seller the benefit of his bargain. (*Honey v. Henry's Franchise Leasing Corp.,* supra, 64 Cal.2d 801, 805, 52 Cal.Rptr. 18, 415 P.2d 833; *Bartley v. Karas,* supra, 150 Cal.App.3d 336, 345, fn. 5, 197 Cal.Rptr. 749; *Kosloff v. Castle,* supra, 115 Cal.App.3d 369, 376, 171 Cal.Rptr. 308.)

While recognizing that the wilfully defaulting vendee's right to restitution is unqualified, some post-*Freedman* decisions have treated such vendee's right to a reasonable opportunity to redeem the property by paying the entire balance owed, plus damages, before title is quieted in the seller, as merely discretionary. Thus, in *Bartley v. Karas,* supra, 150 Cal.App.3d 336, 197 Cal.Rptr. 749, the court interpreted the *Keller* line of cases as allowing such relief "*where the circumstances indicated* that it would be 'in consonance with equity' " (*id.,* at p. 344, 197 Cal.Rptr. 749, emphasis added) and as holding that the relief "*may* . . . be proper where the seller's conduct contributed to the default and where there is some good faith, but imperfect excuse, for the buyer's conduct" (*id.,* at p. 345, 197 Cal.Rptr. 749, emphasis added). Other decisions similarly have weighed the seriousness of the vendee's defaults in determining the propriety of granting the relief. . . .

We think that as a matter both of stare decisis and of sound public policy, a vendee who has made substantial payments on a land installment sale contract or substantial improvements on the property, and whose defaults, albeit wilful, consist solely of failure to pay further amounts due, has an unconditional right to a reasonable opportunity to complete the purchase by paying the entire remaining balance plus damages before the seller is allowed to quiet title. We read *Keller* and its earlier progeny as so holding. As *Keller* itself observes, "the legal title is retained by the vendor as security for the balance of the purchase money, and if the vendor obtains his money and interest he gets all he expected when he entered the contract." (53 Cal. at p. 118.) To that statement we add that the seller may be entitled to damages in addition to interest.[4] Whatever the amounts due, their payment in full makes the seller whole regardless of the nature of the vendee's defaults in payments.

In the present case, of course, the seller did not sue to quiet title but instead gave the vendees written notice of election to terminate the contract because of their failure to make timely payments. When plaintiffs sued for specific performance, defendant merely answered, praying that plaintiffs take nothing. Thus, the right of redemption asserted by plaintiffs cannot be justified as a condition to the granting of relief sought in this action by the seller.

If Mrs. Gaspar had been entitled to foreclose the Petersens' interest in the land by a unilateral declaration of termination on account of wilful

---

[4] Compare Code of Civil Procedure section 726, subdivision (a), providing for application of the proceeds of a mortgage foreclosure sale to "the payment of the costs of court, the expenses of levy and sale, and the amount due plaintiff, including, where the mortgage provides for the payment of attorney's fees, such sum for attorney's fees as the court shall find reasonable, not exceeding the amount named in the mortgage."

default, leaving the Petersens with only a right to monetary restitution of payments in excess of seller's damages, there would appear no basis for allowing plaintiff vendees to enforce an absolute right of redemption in an action in which defendant sought no affirmative relief. Arguably supporting the trial court's apparent conclusion that the seller had such a right of nonjudicial foreclosure were (1) the absence of equities requisite to a vendee's right of specific performance under *MacFadden* and (2) facts that appear to have empowered the seller to convey to a bona fide purchaser: the contract was not recorded; the land was unoccupied; and the seller paid the property taxes.

Other circumstances, however, both factual and legal, lead us to conclude that Mrs. Gaspar had only a security interest (see Note, *Contracts: Forfeiture Clauses: Relief to Vendee in Default in California* (1952) 40 Calif.L.Rev. 593, 597), and that the vendees' right to purchase the property by completing payment of the purchase price and any other amounts due could be terminated only by a foreclosure sale or by strict foreclosure, i.e., a judicial proceeding quieting the seller's title against the vendees' right of redemption. Seller's counsel acknowledged at least the possibility that such foreclosure might be necessary by (1) accompanying the formal notices of termination with requests for a quitclaim deed and (2) including in the judgment prepared for, and signed by, the trial judge, a provision that "plaintiffs have no right, title, or interest in" the property.

Moreover, sections 2985 and 2985.1, enacted in 1961 and 1963, prohibit one who has contracted to sell land under a long-term installment contract from conveying title in complete disregard of the vendees' interest. Section 2985 defines a "real property sales contract" as "an agreement wherein one party agrees to convey title to real property to another party upon the satisfaction of specified conditions set forth in the contract and which does not require conveyance of title within one year from the date of formation of the contract." Section 2985.1 provides in pertinent part: "A real property sales contract may not be transferred by the fee owner of the real property unless accompanied by a transfer of the real property which is the subject of the contract, and real property may not be transferred by the fee owner thereof unless accompanied by an assignment of the contract." The seller is thus prohibited from making any transfer that would sever the direct contractual relationship between the vendee and the owner of the fee. The intended protection of the vendees' interest is best served by interpreting section 2985.1 to require continuation of that linkage between seller's title and vendee's contractual interest until the latter has been affirmatively terminated by conveyance of title to the vendee, by a foreclosure sale, or by strict foreclosure.

Finally, we think that to retain specific performance under *MacFadden v. Walker,* supra, 5 Cal.3d 809, 97 Cal.Rptr. 537, 488 P.2d 1353, as the utmost remedy available in a suit initiated by a wilfully defaulting vendee unduly burdens courts and litigants with time-consuming and expensive legal proceedings. The present case is illustrative. To settle a dispute over land sold for a total price of only $9,162 required two days of nonjury trial in which eight witnesses (only two of whom were parties) testified to circumstances bearing on whether the vendees' defaults were sufficiently egregious to bar them from specific performance under *MacFadden.* Yet, as already explained, if defendant seller had sued to quiet title, plaintiffs would have been entitled as a matter of right to a conveyance of title in exchange for payment of the balance of the purchase price with interest and damages. Such redemption by plaintiff would give defendant the entire benefit bargained for, free of any dependence on further performance by plaintiff vendees. The outcome will be no less fair to both parties if, as we hold, the vendees under a real property sales contract, as defined in section 2985, are entitled to judicial enforcement of the same absolute right of redemption in response to the seller's notice of election to terminate the contract for default in payments. The complaint initiating the vendee's action for that purpose, rather than being designated as one for specific performance, is more appropriately referred to as one to redeem the vendee's interest in real property.

Accordingly, we conclude that plaintiffs are entitled to a conveyance of title to the property in exchange for payment of the entire remaining balance due under the contract together with interest and any consequential damages as determined by the court. Should plaintiffs fail to make such payments within a reasonable time fixed by the court, the adjudication that plaintiffs have no further interest in the property should become effective only upon defendant's payment of the sums due to plaintiffs as restitution. Statements in *Bartley v. Karas,* supra, 150 Cal.App.3d 336, 197 Cal.Rptr. 749, and *Kosloff v. Castle,* supra, 115 Cal.App.3d 369, 171 Cal.Rptr. 308, inconsistent with this conclusion are disapproved.

The judgment is reversed.

BIRD, CHIEF JUSTICE, concurring and dissenting.

I agree with the majority that an unconditional right of redemption exists for most wilfully defaulting vendees under security device installment land sale contracts.

However, there is no reason to deny the right of redemption to vendees whose payments prior to default amount to less than "a substantial part of the purchase price." . . .

The majority also fail to discuss the cogent arguments raised by Professor Hetland, who appeared as amicus curiae for plaintiffs. Professor Hetland argues that the installment land sale contract, when employed as a security device, is the functional equivalent of a mortgage or deed of trust and should generally be subject to the same rules. This view has much to recommend it.

Treating the installment land sale contract as the equivalent of a mortgage under Civil Code section 2924[1] would bring the procedures for foreclosure of the vendee's equity of redemption into line with those permitted for foreclosure under a mortgage or deed of trust. (See Civ.Code, § 2924 [private foreclosure sale]; Code Civ.Proc., § 700.010 et seq. [judicial foreclosure sale].) Moreover, the vendee, like a mortgagor or trustor under a deed of trust, would not be restricted to an equity of *redemption*, i.e., the right to conveyance of title only upon payment of the *full* amount of the debt. The vendee would also be entitled to *reinstatement* of the contract upon payment of any *delinquent* amounts. (See Civ.Code, § 2924c.)

Providing installment contract vendees the same protections that are afforded to mortgagors would eliminate some abusive practices of vendors, who have exploited the lack of legal sophistication and limited capacity to litigate of their low-income clients. Most important, defaulting vendees would be able to avoid the loss of their homes by paying only the delinquent amounts. Under the majority's holding, a wilfully defaulting vendee may avoid this fate only by paying the outstanding balance in full. This is an unjustifiably harsh burden to place on the low-income and middle-income families and individuals who will be most affected.

[The dissenting opinion of Mosk, J. is omitted.]

NOTES

1.   *Judicial recognition of a right of redemption.* A substantial number of states, like California, afford the tardy vendee a final opportunity to tender the contract balance before losing the land. See Lewis v. Premium Inv. Corp., 341 S.C. 539, 535 S.E.2d 139 (2000); Lamberth v. McDaniel, 131 N.C.App. 319, 506 S.E.2d 295 (1998). This specific performance or "equity of redemption" right is sometimes viewed as unconditional, while other courts enforce it only if the vendee has paid a "substantial" amount of the contract price. See Nelson, Whitman, Burkhart & Freyermuth, Real Estate Finance Law § 3.29 (6th ed.2015). Moreover, many courts impose a "good faith" requirement on the vendee. According to the Hawaii Supreme Court, for example, specific performance should be available where "the vendee's breach has not been due to gross negligence, or to deliberate or bad-faith conduct on his part, and the vendor can reasonably and adequately be compensated for his injury." Jenkins v. Wise, 58 Hawaii 592, 574 P.2d 1337 (1978). For a clear-cut example of the denial of specific performance to a grossly negligent vendee, see Curry v. Tucker, 616 P.2d 8 (Alaska 1980) (affirming forfeiture decree where vendee

---

[1]   Section 2924 provides in part that "Every transfer of an interest in property, other than in trust, made only as a security for the performance of another act, is to be deemed a mortgage. . . ."

had retained possession "rent free" despite making no monthly payments for over seven years).

Going back to the facts of *Russell v. Richards*, if Russell could have paid off the entire $26,504 balance of the contract, a court following the *Petersen* approach would have awarded Russell specific performance and required the Richardses to tender a deed to the property. In that case, though, Russell could not merely have cured the prior defaults and reinstated the contract. As Chief Justice Bird's opinion recognizes, cure and reinstatement would have been available to a defaulting purchase money mortgagor. Having acknowledged the similarity between the installment contract and the purchase money mortgage, why do you think the majority was reluctant to take the final step and treat the contract as a mortgage for all purposes?

2.   *Restitution as an alternative form of relief for the vendee.* In some circumstances, the vendee will be unable to pay off the entire balance of the contract, and no applicable state statute provides the vendee with a right to cure the defaults and reinstate the contract. In this situation, forfeiture would occur, with the vendor not only keeping all of the vendee's prior payments, but also recovering possession of the land. Such a result may be particularly harsh for the vendee, especially in a case like *Russell v. Richards*, where the vendee had made substantial payments and the land had appreciated in value during the contract period. In such a case, the vendor's retention of prior payments would appear to enrich the vendor unjustly to the extent that those payments exceed any loss the vendor actually suffered due to the vendee's breach. In this situation, as *Petersen* implies, the vendee could obtain restitution:

> Increasingly [many courts] are holding that "forfeiture may not be 'free' and that the vendor must return the payments he has received insofar as they exceed his actual damages. Some courts . . . take this position only in cases in which they conclude that an outright forfeiture would be 'unconscionable' but this may simply mean that the purchaser would suffer a substantial net loss if no restitution were ordered.

Nelson, Whitman, Burkhart & Freyermuth, Real Estate Finance Law 84 (6th ed.2015). See, e.g., Moran v. Holman, 501 P.2d 769 (Alaska 1972); K.M. Young & Assocs., Inc. v. Cieslik, 4 Hawaii App. 657, 675 P.2d 793 (1983); Bellon v. Malnar, 808 P.2d 1089 (Utah 1991).

The restitutionary remedy described in *Petersen* sounds deceptively simple—calculate the vendor's damages due to the vendee's breach and, if the vendee's prior payments exceed that amount, the vendor must pay the difference to the vendee. But exactly how should one calculate the vendor's damages for this purpose? In Honey v. Henry's Franchise Leasing Corp., 64 Cal.2d 801, 52 Cal.Rptr. 18, 415 P.2d 833 (1966), the California Supreme Court held that the vendor of a defaulted installment contract had an option to rescind the contract and measure the vendor's damages by the "rental value" approach or to enforce the contract and measure the vendor's damages by the "difference value" approach. Under the rental value approach, the vendor would have to make restitution of the amount by which the vendee's prior payments exceeded the fair rental value of the property while the vendee was in possession. By contrast, under the difference value approach, the vendor would make restitution of the amount by which the vendee's prior payments exceeded the difference between the land's market value at the time of the breach and the original contract price. Which approach the vendor would take in any particular case would depend significantly on whether the land had appreciated or depreciated during the term of the contract. If the land had appreciated significantly in value prior to the vendee's breach, as in *Russell v. Richards*, the vendor would minimize its restitution liability by rescinding the contract and measuring its damages using the rental value approach. [Can you explain why this would minimize the vendor's restitution liability?] See, e.g., J. Hetland, Secured Real Estate Transactions 52 (1974) ("rarely ... has the value of property dropped so that the vendor prefers difference value to his alternative measure—rental value"). In this situation, why should the vendor have this choice—rescind or enforce—when the purchase money mortgagor would be limited to foreclosure?

      While restitution is available in theory, defaulting vendees rarely obtain it. First, courts in some states will require restitution only if the vendor's retention of "excess" payments through forfeiture would be "unconscionable" or a "penalty." See, e.g., Warner v. Rasmussen, 704 P.2d 559 (Utah 1985) (excess of prior payments forfeited over vendor's actual damages was only 6% of sales price, which did not rise to level of unconscionability), *abrogated on other grounds*, Commercial Real Estate Inv., L.C. v. Comcast of Utah II, Inc., 285 P.3d 1193 (Utah 2012). Second, courts often conclude that the vendor's actual damages exceed the defaulting vendee's prior payments. This commonly occurs where the value of the land has declined during the contract period (either by market value declines or by physical damage to the land or its improvements), and the decline exceeds the total of the vendee's prior payments. See, e.g., Park Valley Corp. v. Bagley, 635 P.2d 65 (Utah 1981) ($145,000 decline in land's value during contract period exceeded vendee's payments under contract; no restitution required). Even if the value of the land has not declined, or has increased, courts very frequently find that the vendor's damages exceed the vendee's prior payments. For an example, see Clampitt v. A.M.R. Corp., 109 Idaho 145, 706 P.2d 34 (1985). In that case, after forfeiting under a $2.3 million dollar installment contract for the purchase of a farm (which the vendor resold two years later for $3.8 million), the vendee sought restitution of over $750,000 expended in connection with the contract, including $510,000 in principal payments, $221,753 in interest payments, $13,783 in real estate taxes, and $7,338 for irrigation equipment installed by the vendee on the property. The court found that the vendor's damages included both the rental value of the vendee's possession (which the court valued at $447,000) and costs of repossession and resale, including attorney fees and the cost of a brokerage commission upon resale (which the court valued at approximately $300,000). When comparing these damages to the prior payments forfeited, the court concluded that "the application of the liquidated damage clause in this case appears fair and reasonable" and held that no restitution was required. 706 P.2d at 40.

Another (and perhaps more egregious) example is Long v. Smith, 776 S.W.2d 409 (Mo.Ct.App.1989). Smith purchased a home from Long for a price of $20,000 on a contract for deed. Under the contract, Smith was to pay the $17,000 contract balance (which bore a 10% interest rate) in monthly installments of $450; on this schedule, Smith would pay off the contract in six and one-half years. The contract also provided a forfeiture clause that stated

> it is further agreed that upon such default the buyer shall then become a tenant of the seller as tenant from month to month and agrees to pay *four hundred fifty* Dollars per month as rent for such premises, said rent becoming due and payable monthly in advance.

During the contract period, Smith's payments reduced the contract balance to $4,117. Following defaults by Smith, Long declared a forfeiture and filed an unlawful detainer action seeking possession. The court granted judgment for Long and rejected Smith's argument that the forfeiture exacted a penalty, noting that the rental value of the home was $450 per month and thus that "[t]he payment amounts forfeited by Smith were exactly proportionate to the rental value of the property." 776 S.W.2d at 415. [Query: If the rental value of the home was really $450/month, why would Long have agreed to sell the home in exchange for only six and one-half years of payments in that amount? Should the court have accepted the contract's stipulation of $450/month as the land's true rental value?]

If the vendor of an installment contract for a residence invokes a forfeiture and the defaulting vendee seeks restitution, is it appropriate to give the vendor credit for the rental value of the land for the duration of the vendee's possession? Does this effectively convert the installment contract into a "rent-to-own" contract? Keep in mind that under the typical installment contract, the vendor has no duty with respect to the condition of the premises (unless the vendor expressly agrees to such a duty); it is the vendee who would have the responsibility for the maintenance and repair of the premises. By contrast, under most residential leases, the landlord has an implied warranty of habitability that cannot be waived and imposes a duty to keep the premises in habitable condition. Do cases like *Long v. Smith* permit a vendor to have it both ways, i.e., to get the benefit of treating the defaulting vendee as a tenant without the corresponding burdens of being a landlord?

———————————

Even in states where the forfeiture remedy is available to the vendor, it is sometimes an undesirable option. This is especially true in cases where the land is worth less at the time of default than the balance of the contract price. If the vendor was a mortgagee, the vendor's remedies would be clear: the vendor could (1) foreclose and, if the sale yielded less than the balance due, obtain a deficiency judgment (except in states, like California, that would protect the vendee from liability for a deficiency), or (2) sue on the contract obligation, obtain a judgment for that amount, and collect the judgment out of the purchaser's nonexempt assets (including the land). Unfortunately, the vendor's options are less clear. As *Russell* and *Petersen* demonstrate, courts commonly apply either contract law or a confusing combination of contract and mortgage law principles. See Grant S. Nelson, The Contract for Deed as a Mortgage: The Case for the Restatement Approach, 1998 B.Y.U. L. Rev. 1111. The following materials address the vendor's remedial options other than forfeiture and some of the pitfalls associated with these remedies.

SUMMIT HOUSE CO. V. GERSHMAN

Court of Appeals of Minnesota, 1993
502 N.W.2d 422

ANDERSON, CHIEF JUDGE. . . . In 1986, respondents Bruce and Karen Gershman (Gershmans) entered into a contract for deed to sell their condominium to appellant Summit House Co., a Minnesota general partnership consisting of Melvin C. Gittleman and Donald W. Anderson (Summit). The contract required Summit to make a balloon payment on October 31, 1987. On September 10, 1987, with the market value of condominiums declining, Summit sued to terminate the contract. The Gershmans counterclaimed for specific performance of the contract and were awarded summary judgment in the amount of $107,605.25. The district court stated the Gershmans were to convey the property to Summit upon payment of the judgment.

Summit failed to pay the judgment. The Gershmans proceeded to levy execution on Summit's contract for deed vendee's interest in the condominium and purchased that interest for $73,130.18 at a sheriff's sale on February 22, 1991. Summit failed to bid at the sheriff's sale and failed to redeem the condominium within the one-year redemption period provided by Minn.Stat. § 550.25 (1990). On May 14, 1992, Summit moved for an order that the judgment had been satisfied by the sheriff's sale. The district court denied Summit's motion, concluding the execution sale had not canceled the contract.

The district court held the judgment against Summit for $107,605.25 was only partially satisfied by the sheriff's sale of the condominium for $73,130.18, and that Summit still owed the Gershmans $34,475.07, the balance of the judgment. The district court stated there is no reason why the Gershmans should be treated differently from any other creditor. It noted the sheriff's sale was an execution on a money judgment and that Summit had a full year to redeem its contract for deed vendee's interest, but failed to exercise that option. The district court held that Summit would be entitled to a satisfaction of the judgment under Minn.Stat. § 548.15 (1990) as soon as it satisfied the balance of the judgment. . . .

1.   Did the Gershmans' execution on Summit's contract for deed vendee's interest at a sheriff's sale, after having obtained a judgment for specific performance of the contract for deed, constitute a cancellation of the contract for deed that satisfied the judgment? . . .

A contract for deed vendor has a choice of remedies when the contract for deed vendee defaults on the contract. The vendor may either seek specific performance on the contract or may cancel the contract. The doctrine of election of remedies is designed to prevent double recovery for a single wrong, and therefore the vendor cannot seek both specific performance and contract cancellation. Covington v. Pritchett, 428 N.W.2d 121, 124 (Minn.App.1988). A contract can be canceled either by judicial termination or by statutory cancellation under Minn.Stat. § 559.21 (1990). Blythe v. Kujawa, 177 Minn. 79, 224 N.W. 464 (1929); Kosbau, 400 N.W.2d at 108.

The Gershmans chose the remedy of specific performance in response to Summit's attempt to rescind the contract. The district court entered a judgment in favor of the Gershmans' claim for specific performance. By pursuing specific performance to a determinative conclusion, the Gershmans chose not to cancel the contract, but to affirm it.

Summit claims the Gershmans, by executing on Summit's interest in the condominium at the sheriff's sale, obtained all that they were equitably entitled to under the contract for deed. It argues that, because the Gershmans have resold the property, they would be unable to convey title to Summit in the event that Summit satisfied the balance of the judgment. Summit further argues that paragraph 5 of the district court's order of November 30, 1988 requires the Gershmans to convey the condominium to Summit upon payment of the judgment in full. This argument fails because it ignores the sequence of events which led to the execution sale.

Had Summit satisfied the money judgment prior to the sheriff's sale, it would have retained the right to receive title to the condominium. Summit's failure to pay the judgment forced the Gershmans to seek satisfaction of the judgment at an execution sale which netted less than the amount of the judgment. Summit had the opportunity to bid for the condominium at the sheriff's sale and could have exercised its right to redeem the condominium within the statutory period of one year from the date of sale. It failed to pursue either option. Once the execution sale took place in an attempt to satisfy a money judgment and the condominium was not redeemed within the one-year redemption period, the action was taken out of the context of a contract for deed. It then became an action to enforce a money judgment.

Summit argues that because the Gershmans reacquired the property as a result of the sheriff's sale, the contract was canceled and the judgment has been satisfied. We disagree. Summit has provided no authority to support its contention that the sheriff's execution sale, which was to enforce a money judgment against a defaulting buyer on a contract for deed, cancels the contract which formed the basis of the money judgment. . . .

To hold that the Gershmans' judgment for specific performance was satisfied because they bought the condominium at an open sheriff's sale after Summit refused to satisfy the judgment would be an incongruous result. Such a result would in effect eliminate specific performance as a viable remedy for a contract for deed vendor and eviscerate the election of remedies doctrine. The choice of remedies would be effectively eliminated if the vendor knew that the vendee could simply refuse to pay a money judgment and force the seller to accept the return of the property as full satisfaction of the judgment. Summit asks us to hold, in effect, that cancellation of the contract and the return of the property is the vendor's only remedy against the defaulting vendee. We agree with the district court and refuse to follow that line of reasoning. . . .

Affirmed.

NOTES

1.   *Damages for breach of contract and the election of remedies doctrine.* In theory, an installment contract seller, like her earnest money contract counterpart, could sue the defaulting buyer for the seller's actual damages for breach of contract (to be measured by the difference between the contract balance and the fair market value of the property at the date of breach, along with any foreseeable consequential damages occasioned by the buyer's breach). If the installment seller's actual damages exceed the buyer's prior payments, could the installment seller seek a judgment for the excess? The election of remedies doctrine provides a significant barrier to such an action, in two key respects. First, if the contract's forfeiture provision articulates that the seller may retain the buyer's prior payments as "liquidated damages"—as most installment contracts do—a court may conclude (as discussed in Chapter One) that the seller has contractually elected retention of prior payments as its exclusive damages remedy. Further, if the buyer has not abandoned or relinquished possession of the land voluntarily, and the seller brings an action to recover possession (e.g., eviction or unlawful detainer), a court may likewise treat the filing of such an action as an election of remedies that would bar other relief, such as an judgment for the contract price. See, e.g., Rogers v. Triple S Ventures, Inc., 752 So.2d 1220 (Ala.Ct.App.1998); NC Properties, LLC v. Lind, 797 N.W.2d 214 (Minn.Ct.App.2011). Courts have even held that the election to enforce a forfeiture bars a subsequent attempt by seller to recover for physical damages for waste or for failure to pay real estate taxes as required by the contract. See, e.g., Rudnitski v. Seely, 452 N.W.2d 664 (Minn.1990); Hepperly v. Bosch, 172 Ill.App.3d 1017, 123 Ill.Dec. 70, 527 N.E.2d 533 (1988) (after vendors elected forfeiture remedy, they could not recover for damage to the premises for vendees' failure to "maintain, repair and renovate the

premises" as required by the contract); Michigan Nat'l Bank v. Cote, 451 Mich. 180, 546 N.W.2d 247 (1996).

Setting aside the legal problems posed by election of remedies doctrine, the installment seller seeking additional damages also faces a pragmatic problem:

> the factfinder (very often a jury) must be convinced that the property, as of the date of the breach, was worth less than the contract price. In other words, the vendor may be in the unenviable position of persuading the fact finder that he or she convinced the purchaser to enter into a "bad deal."

Grant S. Nelson, The Contract for Deed as a Mortgage: The Case for the Restatement Approach, 1998 B.Y.U. L. Rev. 1111, 1133.

Some courts alleviate the harshness of the election of remedies concept by means of their determination of when an election takes place. For example, the Michigan Supreme Court has held that "while the [vendor] may not accept or take possession and still seek money damages, he may, even after sending notice of forfeiture, refuse tender of possession and either commence an action for money damages or for foreclosure of the land contract." Gruskin v. Fisher, 405 Mich. 51, 273 N.W.2d 893 (1979). But see Mazur v. Young, 507 F.3d 1013 (6th Cir.2007) (guarantors' obligations to vendor did not survive forfeiture— applying Michigan law). For a full explanation of Michigan law, see Mayes v. Mathews, 2011 WL 5964615 (Mich.Ct.App. 2011).

Some state statutes ameliorate somewhat the vendor's election of remedies dilemma by authorizing, in certain limited circumstances, the award of damages to the vendor even though a contract termination election has already been made. See, e.g., Ohio Rev.Code § 5313.10 (even if judgment for cancellation of the contract has taken place, damage award may be entered against vendee who "has paid an amount less than the fair rental value plus deterioration or destruction of the property occasioned by the vendee's use"; James Geoffrey Durham, Forfeiture of Residential Land Contracts in Ohio: The Need for Further Reform of a Reform Statute, 16 Akron L.R. 397 (1983).

Finally, some courts reject the election rule entirely in the installment land contract context and have substituted for it an estoppel concept. Under this approach, "the proper inquiry should be whether the [vendee] has relied on [acts or statements by the vendor] and therefore would be unfairly prejudiced by assertion of a different inconsistent remedy. If so, the [vendor] should be bound to the remedy earlier chosen. . . . Absent estoppel, he should be free to choose a different remedy." Keesee v. Fetzek, 106 Idaho 507, 681 P.2d 600 (Ct.App.1984).

2.   *Specific performance for the purchase price.* The buyer in *Gershman* (who it appears had the money to satisfy the contract) made a decision that would appear to be perfectly rational—to relinquish the condo and stop "throwing good money after bad." This was unacceptable to the Gershmans, who did not want to take back the condo unit in a "down" market and also lose

the benefit of their bargain (the favorable sale price). By allowing the Gershmans to sue for specific performance of the price, the court allowed the Gershmans to maintain the economic benefit of their bargain while avoiding both the election of remedies problem [Query: can you explain why?] and the burden of proving actual damages.

The earnest money seller almost always receives specific performance when a buyer fails or refuses to perform under an earnest money contract. Likewise, most courts will grant specific performance to the installment contract seller, either as a matter of course or upon a showing that the seller's legal remedy is inadequate. See, e.g., McCollam v. Cahill, 766 N.W.2d 171 (S.D.2009); Steinhoff v. Fisch, 847 P.2d 191 (Colo.Ct.App.1992). But see Holman v. Hansen, 773 P.2d 1200 (Mont.1989) (specific performance denied where extrinsic evidence indicated installment seller had requested contract clause granting seller the right of specific performance, but buyer had refused to consent to such language in the contract).

Note that there can be conceptual roadblocks to specific performance that are more troublesome for the installment seller than for the earnest money contract seller. When a buyer under an earnest money contract defaults on the closing date, the contract can be treated as completely repudiated, and a specific performance decree for the full contract price follows. By contrast, when a contract for deed purchaser defaults, a suit for more than the past due installments can be problematic; many contracts for deed, unlike most mortgage documents, contain no acceleration clause permitting the seller to declare the entire contract balance due and payable upon buyer default. In this case, the seller may only be able to sue for the past due installments plus interest, unless the court allows the seller to apply the contract doctrine of anticipatory repudiation as a basis for acceleration. [This issue was irrelevant in *Gershman*; as the facts indicate, the full balance of the contract had already come due via a required "balloon" payment.]

3.   *Foreclosure of the buyer's rights.* In states that do not treat the installment contract as a mortgage, courts nevertheless sometimes give the vendor the option to foreclose the contract for deed by judicial sale. This approach seems conceptually problematic, because the vendor is seeking a mortgage remedy under a device that is ostensibly governed by contract law. In any event, where such a sale occurs, if the sale yields more than the contract balance, the defaulting buyer is entitled to the surplus. Where the sale brings less than the contract balance, the vendor normally will be entitled to a deficiency judgment.

Note that such a foreclosure is economically similar to the specific performance remedy. In each situation, the seller obtains a judgment for the full contract balance, which may be satisfied out of the contract real estate. In addition, the buyer in each setting bears the risk of postcontract decline in the value of the real estate. For further discussion of the judicial foreclosure remedy, see Nelson, Whitman, Burkhart & Freyermuth, Real Estate Finance § 3.32, at 97–98 (6th ed.2015).

4. *Premises liability of vendors.* To what extent should an installment contract vendor be liable to third parties for the condition of the premises or personal injuries that occur on them? See, e.g., Kreher v. Bertucci, 814 So.2d 614 (La.Ct.App.2002) (vendor not liable in tort to tenant of vendee who is injured on premises); Jackson v. Scheible, 902 N.E.2d 807 (Ohio 2009) (contract vendor not liable for injuries where bicyclist's view is blocked by failure to trim tree located on contract premises—vendor is not liable as owner under ordinance requiring tree trimming); Romel v. Reale, 155 A.D.2d 747, 547 N.Y.S.2d 691 (1989) (vendor has no liability for injury to guest of vendee who fell on contract premises after possession had been delivered to vendee). But see City of Webster Groves v. Erickson, 763 S.W.2d 278 (Mo.Ct.App.1988) (vendor liable as "owner" under public nuisance ordinance for failing to clear premises of debris even though vendee was in possession). Normally, a mortgagee is not be liable for unsafe conditions on mortgaged real estate unless she is in possession or otherwise exercises dominion and control over it. See, e.g., Smith v. Fried, 98 Ill.App.3d 467, 53 Ill.Dec. 845, 424 N.E.2d 636 (1981).

2. TITLE ISSUES AND THE RIGHTS OF CREDITORS

JOHN MIXON, INSTALLMENT LAND CONTRACTS: A STUDY OF LOW INCOME TRANSACTIONS WITH PROPOSALS FOR REFORM AND A NEW PROGRAM TO PROVIDE HOME OWNERSHIP IN THE INNER CITY
7 Houston L.Rev. 523, 545–548 (1970)*

When a buyer finances his purchase by a mortgage, one of the transactional costs covers title search or a title insurance policy guaranteeing that the buyer will get good title to the land. The system of land titles in this country is such that a purchaser cannot easily tell who owns or claims title to the land. Unless he is willing to take the seller's word that title is good, a purchaser must get expert assistance. Failure to do so can result in his paying the full purchase price for land and then losing it to a superior claimant.

Although individual middle income purchasers might be willing to take the title risk, or they might lack knowledge about the weakness of the system, their mortgagees are neither willing to take the risk nor do they lack knowledge. Hence, before a mortgagee will lend money for the purchase, the borrower will have to produce a policy of title insurance or other reliable assurance that title is good. The title policy brings title up to date at the time of the sale, and it offers considerable assurance to the buyer that he will be able to keep and enjoy the land which he buys. It also guarantees to the mortgagee that his lien has priority over any other claims.

---

* Reprinted with permission of Houston Law Review.

On the other hand, the low income installment land contract buyer does not know about the need for title insurance, and he would be unlikely to persuade his seller to pay for a policy or for a title search. Without title insurance or other protection, the installment purchaser runs the risk that the seller's title is no good. In the case of older housing which the vendor may have bought as a purely speculative venture, this risk can be very high. On the other hand, title to a large tract of land which the seller puts together as a new housing development is likely to be good into the seller, but it will probably have another defect, that of development cost financing.

When an installment land seller puts together a subdivision, he borrows money to finance both his purchase and construction of the houses he plans to sell. His mortgagee will probably require a title insurance policy or other means of title assurance be provided. Even without the mortgagee's insistence, the developer would be knowledgeable enough to get good title to the land. The contract vendee in a large scale development therefore probably need not worry too much about title into his vendor. Title out of the vendor, however, is another matter. The vendor will develop the subdivision, and build his houses with money borrowed from a mortgagee. He will plan to sell the houses on contracts and use the cash flow from contract receipts to pay off the purchase price and construction mortgages. If the payoff occurs as indicated, the vendee may indeed get good title because the vendor's debt will eventually be extinguished. However, if the subdivision does not succeed, all contract vendees may lose their entire investment. This will occur if the vendor does not get enough cash flow in receipts from his sales to make his payments, or if he pockets the cash and skips town. In either event, the mortgagee will foreclose. Because the mortgagee's rights are prior in time to the rights of the contract vendees, they will lose their rights or claims in the foreclosure, whether they are current on their payment or not.[2]

Another title problem which can plague an installment contract vendee is the operation of the real property recording act. When a buyer purchases under a mortgage-financed transaction, his deed is immediately recorded to show he has claim to the land. The public record protects the buyer from anyone who might later deal with the former owner. However, if the buyer's claim is not recorded, a later purchaser who takes a deed from the former owner may cut off the interest of the first (unrecorded) purchaser. Installment land contracts are virtually never recorded. Thus, the vendee's claim is vulnerable to a later purchaser from the vendor. Although in the study area, the vendee's possession would give him legal protection against a subsequent purchaser, the conflict presented by such a conveyance almost certainly would require a lawsuit to establish that the vendee had good title. The reason for lack of recordation of installment contracts is that the vendor anticipates the vendee probably will miss a

---

[2] Editors' Note: Does this depend on when the contracts were entered into?

payment, and the property will eventually be repossessed. In that situation the vendor will not want any indication on the record that there was once an installment contract to a prior claimant. If the record title is clear (that is, if the installment contract has not been recorded), the only concern a vendor has is evicting the defaulting vendee from the land. This he usually is able to do either by threats or by the tenant eviction procedure. The vendor then has clear record title which he can convey or contract to sell to some new buyer.

Even if an installment vendee were willing to spend the money to have a title search made, he could not protect himself from most of the potential title difficulties under an installment land contract. For example, the vendee would still run the risk that his seller might go bankrupt, suffer a tax lien, or make title questionable by conveying to a subsequent purchaser. The title search would, of course, turn up prior liens which the vendor had placed on the property, and it would show whether the base title into the seller was good.

NOTES

1. *When must the vendor perfect the title?* Suppose the vendor does not have marketable title at the time vendor enters the contract. Is the vendor in default if the title is defective? The usual view is that the vendor has no duty to perfect the title until the vendee makes the final payment. See Weeks v. Rowell, 289 Ga.App. 507, 657 S.E.2d 881 (2008); Luette v. Bank of Italy, 42 F.2d 9 (9th Cir.1930). But consider Marlowe Inv. Corp. v. Radmall, 26 Utah 2d 124, 485 P.2d 1402, 1403 (1971):

> It is true that ordinarily such a vendor does not necessarily have to have marketable title until the purchaser has made his payments. Nevertheless, if it plainly appears that he has so lost or encumbered his ownership or his title that he will not be able to fulfill his contract, he cannot insist that the purchaser continue to make payments when it is obvious that his own performance will not be forthcoming.

2. *Installment contract purchase of a parcel subject to a blanket mortgage.* Suppose you represent a potential contract for deed vendee who desires to purchase a subdivision lot from a developer. There is a blanket first mortgage on the subdivision, and the mortgagee will not agree to release the lot from that mortgage lien at the time the parties enter into the contract. What provisions would you insist on in the contract to protect the vendee if the vendor defaults and the mortgage is foreclosed?

3. *Clearing the vendor's title after a forfeiture.* Installment land contracts can also pose title problems for the vendor. Suppose that vendor and vendee are in a state that does not have a statutory non-judicial method for terminating the vendee's interest. Suppose further that the vendee has recorded the contract prior to default. Even if a forfeiture would be valid under the circumstances, as a practical matter the vendor will have to bring a judicial

proceeding to obtain a determination that forfeiture has occurred before the vendor will be able to sell the land to a new buyer. Most title examiners will not accept title for a subsequent purchaser on the mere affidavit from the vendor that the prior vendee has defaulted under the contract; instead, most would require a valid release by the vendee. This cloud on the vendor's title gives a vendee (even one with little or no equity) enough bargaining leverage to demand something of a *quid pro quo* from the vendor in exchange for a release. See Nelson, Whitman, Burkhart & Freyermuth, Real Estate Finance Law § 3.33 (6th ed.2015).

Vendors often seek to avoid this predicament by trying to ensure that the vendee cannot record the contract. Vendors do this by having the parties execute the contract without an acknowledgment (so that the contract would not be capable of recording). Some contracts will even state that recording of the contract invalidates it, though the legal effectiveness of such a provision is doubtful. Warren, California Installment Land Sales Contracts: A Time for Reform, 9 U.C.L.A.L.Rev. 609, 629 (1962). If the vendee cannot record the contract itself, the vendee may record an affidavit or other notice that incorporates the essential terms of the contract, including the legal description, parties, and the important terms. Such a document would only contain the vendee's signature and acknowledgment, but may put a practical cloud on the vendor's interest if the jurisdiction allows such a document to impart constructive notice to subsequent persons whose interests arise through the vendor. See Coggins v. Mimms, 373 So.2d 964 (Fla.Ct.App.1979) (recording of an affidavit by vendee did not provide constructive notice to subsequent purchasers due to absence of an acknowledgment by vendors).

Some states have enacted legislation requiring residential installment land contract vendors to record their contracts. See, e.g., Iowa Code Ann. § 558.46 (seller must record within 90 days; failure to record results in fine of up to $100/day and loss of right to forfeiture while contract remains unrecorded); Ohio Rev. Code Ann. § 5313.02(C) (vendor must record with within 20 days of signing). Is such a requirement a reasonable quid pro quo for the vendor's retention of a possible forfeiture remedy?

4.   *Use of deeds in escrow.* Suppose that simultaneously with the execution of the installment contract, the vendee executes a deed conveying all of vendee's right, title and interest in the land to the vendor. The deed is placed in escrow, to be recorded only in the event of a default by the vendee. From the vendor's perspective, this approach presumably terminates the vendee's contract rights and clears up any title problems occasioned by vendee's recording of the contract. Is this a sensible solution for vendors? To what extent is the "anti-clogging" doctrine we studied earlier in this chapter relevant to this problem? See Nelson, Whitman, Burkhart & Freyermuth, Real Estate Finance Law § 3.31 (6th ed.2015).

5.   *The vendee's possession as notice.* Suppose Vendee does not record the contract for deed but takes possession of the real estate. Vendor later borrows money from Bank and grants Bank a mortgage on the land, which Bank

records. To what extent is Vendee protected against subsequent liens arising through Vendor, like Bank's mortgage? As Professor Mixon suggests, possession by the vendee normally will prevent such a lien from attaching to the vendee's interest in the land. See, e.g., Hentges v. P.H. Feely & Son, Inc., 436 N.W.2d 488 (Minn.Ct.App.1989). However, in a few states, possession can only provide *actual* and not constructive notice, so that a mortgagee or judgment creditor of the vendor who acquires her interest without actual knowledge of the vendee's interest, may take free and clear of the vendee's interest. See, e.g., Drey v. Doyle, 99 Mo. 459, 12 S.W. 287 (1889); Note, 16 Mo.L.Rev. 142 (1951).

Mortgaging the vendee's interest. As the vendee pays off the installments under a contract for deed, the vendee's interest can become a significant economic asset, especially if the land increases in value. For example, suppose Vendee's original contract balance was $100,000, the current balance is $50,000, and the land has appreciated in value to $150,000. If Vendee needs a loan to pay medical or educational expenses, can Vendee use the $100,000 of "equity" in the contract as collateral for a loan? Virtually all cases hold that the vendee can mortgage her interest. See Nelson, Whitman, Burkhart & Freyermuth, Real Estate Finance Law § 3.35 (6th ed.2015). Note that functionally a mortgage on the vendee's interest is the economic equivalent of a second mortgage, because the vendor holds an interest analogous to a first purchase money mortgage on the land.

NOTES

1.   *Protecting the vendee's mortgagee from forfeiture or foreclosure by the vendor.* While a lender can take a mortgage on the vendee's interest, the lender's position is tenuous unless it has some way to protect itself against a declaration of forfeiture by the vendor. The cases provide some measure of protection for the lender; most courts hold that where a vendor has actual knowledge of a mortgage on the vendee's interest, the vendor cannot invoke forfeiture of the contract without giving the lender notice of the vendor's intention to forfeit and an opportunity to protect its position. See, e.g., In re Coffelt, 395 B.R. 133 (Bankr.D.Kan.2008); Fincher v. Miles Homes of Mo., Inc., 549 S.W.2d 848 (Mo.1977); Yu v. Paperchase Partn., 114 N.M. 635, 845 P.2d 158 (1992). Contra: In re Cox, 68 B.R. 788 (Bankr.D.Or.1987).

What if the vendee's mortgage has recorded the mortgage, but the vendor has no actual knowledge of it? The weight of authority is that the vendor would have no duty in such circumstances to notify the mortgagee of the vendor's intent to terminate the contract. See, e.g., Kendrick v. Davis, 75 Wash.2d 456, 452 P.2d 222 (1969); Dirks v. Cornwell, 754 P.2d 946 (Utah App.1988); Shindledecker v. Savage, 96 N.M. 42, 627 P.2d 1241 (1981). But see Stannard v. Marboe, 159 Minn. 119, 198 N.W. 127 (1924). Washington legislation has abrogated *Kendrick* and now requires the vendor to give notice to any claimant holding an interest of record at the time of the notice to forfeit. Wash.Rev. Code Ann. § 61.30.040(2)(a). Which approach is preferable? See Note, Mortgages— Mortgage of a Vendee's Interest in an Installment Land Contract— Mortgagee's Rights Upon Default, 43 Mo.L.Rev. 371, 374 (1978) ("The better policy would be to protect the mortgagee's interest if the mortgage has been recorded. . . . Adoption of the actual notice rule would reward ignorance. A vendor who did not search the public record would be in a better position than one who checked the record and discovered the mortgage.").

2.   *The rights of the vendee's mortgagee.* Suppose that vendor gives notice to the vendee's mortgagee of the vendee's default and the vendor's intent to declare a forfeiture. What rights does the vendee's mortgagee have to protect its interest? In theory, if the vendee's mortgage is the functional equivalent of a second mortgage, one might presume that the mortgagee should be able to conduct a foreclosure and sell the vendee's interest subject to the vendor's rights under the installment contract. Nevertheless, some courts have indicated that the mortgagee can acquire title to the land without a foreclosure sale, simply by paying the vendor the balance due under the installment land contract. See, e.g., First Mortg. Corp. of Stuart v. deGive, 177 So.2d 741 (Fla.Ct.App.1965); Shindledecker v. Savage, 96 N.M. 42, 627 P.2d 1241 (1981). Does this approach treat the mortgagee too favorably?

If the vendee's mortgage is entitled to notice of intent to forfeit but the vendor fails to provide it, the law is clear that the rights of the vendee's mortgagee are not affected (i.e., the mortgagee's rights are not forfeited). This is analogous to the treatment that the law provides to a junior mortgagee who is not joined as a party to a judicial foreclosure by a senior mortgagee. See Nelson, Whitman, Burkhart & Freyermuth, Real Estate Finance Law § 3.32 (6th ed.2015). We will return to this subject in greater detail in Chapter Six, Section C infra.

3.   *Documentation for mortgaging the vendee's interest.* Because lenders are often unclear about the nature of the vendee's interest and because the law governing installment land contracts varies so significantly from state to state, lenders employ a variety of problematic and nonstandard devices. Some use an "assignment of purchaser's interest for security purposes." Notwithstanding the use of the word "assignment," it is typically apparent from the face of the document that the intent is to create a mortgage lien on the vendee's interest. Some lenders, however, may attempt to disguise the true nature of the transaction by characterizing it as a sale of the vendee's interest. These lenders may take from the vendee both an assignment (containing no security language) and a quitclaim deed; they assume that on vendee default, they can record the quitclaim deed and thus obviate the need for foreclosure. As explained earlier in this chapter, both the "clogging" and "absolute deed as mortgage" doctrines should defeat such attempts to avoid mortgage law.

Prudent lenders instead will use standard financing forms such as a mortgage or a deed of trust to create a security interest in the vendee's interest.

Moreover, where local law permits, the lender should ensure the forms contain a power of sale to obviate the need for judicial foreclosure in the event of vendee default.

4.   *Prohibition on assignment by the vendee.* Suppose a contract for deed expressly denies the vendee the power to assign or mortgage its interest without the vendor's consent. Such a provision is conceptually similar to so-called "due-on-sale" or "due-on-encumbrance" clauses in mortgages, discussed in Chapter Five, Section B infra. The courts tend to construe such prohibitions on assignment very narrowly. See, e.g., Murray First Thrift & Loan Co. v. Stevenson, 534 P.2d 909 (Utah 1975) (prohibition on "assignment" did not disable the vendee from assigning, but merely gave rise to an action for damages; in any event, the prohibition did not apply to a collateral or security assignment, as distinct from an outright assignment). Such a prohibition may even be struck down as an unreasonable restraint on alienation. See, e.g., Terry v. Born, 24 Wash.App. 652, 604 P.2d 504 (1979) (where contract prohibited both assignment and prepayment, an unreasonable restraint on alienation existed).

———

Judgments against the vendor or the vendee. In nearly every state, a judgment creates a lien on all of the real property of the judgment debtor.[3] By contrast, a judgment does not automatically create a lien against the debtor's personal property; a judgment lien arises against personal property only by "attachment," which typically requires the sheriff to "levy" on particular items of personal property by seizing them and thus taking them out of the debtor's control. For further background, see Epstein, Bankruptcy and Related Law 387–397 (8th ed.2013). Consequently, when the judgment debtor is either a vendor or a vendee under a contract for deed, the characterization of the debtor's interest (as either real or personal property) can be crucial in determining the rights of the judgment creditor.

CASCADE SECURITY BANK V. BUTLER
Supreme Court of Washington, 1977
88 Wash.2d 777, 567 P.2d 631

BRACHTENBACH, ASSOCIATE JUSTICE. The issue here is whether the interest of a real estate contract purchaser constitutes "real estate" within the meaning of the judgment lien statutes, RCW 4.56.190 and 4.56.200. Those statutes provide:

———

[3]   The mechanics for how this lien arises varies by jurisdiction. In most states, the lien arises as soon as a judgment is docketed in a county and applies to all land in that county. In other states, the lien may not arise or be effective against other creditors of the debtor unless the evidence of the lien is recorded in the real property records.

RCW 4.56.190:

> The *real estate* of any judgment debtor, and such as he may acquire, not exempt by law, shall be held and bound to satisfy any judgment of the district court of the United States rendered in this state, any judgment of the supreme court, court of appeals, or superior court of this state, and any judgment of any justice of the peace rendered in this state . . . .

We hold, prospectively, that judgments are liens upon the interest of a real estate contract purchaser within the meaning of those statutes. This holding, at long last, constitutes the demise of Ashford v. Reese, 132 Wash. 649, 233 P. 29 (1925).

The facts are that in 1968 the judgment debtors (defendants) became contract vendees of real estate. In March of 1973 the plaintiff obtained a judgment against those vendees-defendants who were then in possession of the property with their contract in good standing. Ten days later, for good consideration, the vendees' interest was assigned to third parties who are not involved here. Some months later the then vendees-assignees assigned their interest to the respondent-intervenors, who are now the holders of the contract vendees' interest. Almost a year after the present contract vendees-respondent intervenors acquired all of the vendees' interest in the contract, the judgment creditor-plaintiff applied for a writ of execution on the judgment and against the vendees' interest. The sheriff executed and published notice of sale. The respondents intervened. The trial court granted their motion for summary judgment and enjoined the sale.

The trial court based its decision in favor of the contract vendees upon Ashford v. Reese, supra, wherein we said at page 650, 233 P. at page 29:

> [A]n executory contract of sale in this state conveys no title or interest, either legal or equitable, to the vendee . . . .

If the holding of Ashford v. Reese, supra, were still the law, the contract vendee did not hold a real estate interest within the scope of the judgment lien statute. It would follow that the judgment debtor's interest was not subjected to the automatic lien when the judgment was entered and, because the debtor's interest had been assigned to another before execution, that interest was free from the lien. We overrule Ashford v. Reese, supra, but only prospectively, and therefore affirm. . . .

We have identified the vendee's interest as "substantial rights", as a "valid and subsisting interest in property", as a "claim or lien" on the land and as rights "annexed to and . . . exercisable with reference to the land." Oliver v. McEachran, 149 Wash. 433, 438, 271 P. 93 (1928) . . . .

These characterizations are patently at odds with the *Ashford* language. Additionally, we have held the vendee to have certain rights totally inconsistent with the concept that a vendee has no title or interest, legal or equitable. For example, we have held that: a vendee may contest a suit to quiet title; under the traditional land sale contract, the vendee has the right to possession of the land, the right to control the land, and the right to grow and harvest crops thereon; a vendee has the right to sue for trespass; a vendee has the right to sue to enjoin construction of a fence; a vendee's interest constitutes a mortgageable interest; a vendee is a necessary and proper party for purposes of a condemnation proceeding; a vendor's interest for inheritance tax purposes is personal property; a vendor's interest for purposes of succession and administration is personal property; a vendee may claim a homestead in real property; a vendee is a real property owner for attachment purposes.

Specifically we here hold that a real estate contract vendee's interest is "real estate" within the meaning of the judgment lien statute. Other jurisdictions have so held, for example, Mutual Bldg. & Loan Ass'n v. Collins, 85 N.M. 706, 516 P.2d 677 (1973), and Fridley v. Munson, 46 S.D. 532, 194 N.W. 840 (1923).

We are urged to embrace the doctrine of equitable conversion as the proper characterization of the respective interests of the vendor and vendee. That is a theory by which the vendee's interest is at once converted into real property and the vendor's interest is strictly personal property. It is premised upon the maxim that equity regards that as done which ought to be done. 2 S. Spencer, Pomeroy's Equity Jurisprudence §§ 370–372, pages 31–33 (5th ed. 1941). To adopt that doctrine would merely substitute a new set of uncertainty for the confusion which has followed *Ashford*.

It is true that many jurisdictions have adopted it. It cuts a wide swath for it is deemed applicable to contracts, devolution, wills and trusts. It is the uncertainty of the doctrine which is of concern to us. Its application theoretically depends upon the intent of the parties. Parr-Richmond Indus. Corp. v. Boyd, 43 Cal.2d 157, 272 P.2d 16 (1954); Atkinson v. VanEchaute, 236 Ark. 423, 366 S.W.2d 273 (1963). Some states do not favor it. In re Shareff's Estate, 143 Pa.Super. 465, 17 A.2d 623 (1941). Its nebulous character is evidenced by those decisions which hold that it applies only when necessity and justice require it, or that it applies only to the extent necessary to accomplish equity. National Bank of Topeka v. Saia, 154 Kan. 740, 121 P.2d 251 (1942); Chicago v. Salinger, 384 Ill. 515, 52 N.E.2d 184 (1943). It has been held that the parties may contract away application of the doctrine. Eade v. Brownlee, 29 Ill.2d 214, 193 N.E.2d 786 (1963). . . .

To base our decision upon this fiction would embark us upon a case-by-case determination of the boundaries of the doctrine in this State. Rather we are content to limit ourselves to the pertinent issue at hand, which is to overrule Ashford v. Reese, supra, and declare that a vendee's interest is real estate within the meaning of the judgment lien statutes. It

is apparent from our many cases cited above that we have defined and
classified the interests of vendors and vendees for a variety of purposes.
That body of case law is based upon a realistic examination of the nature
of the interest in a particular context. We need not adopt a fiction to
buttress the rationale of those cases or the present one. . . .

NOTES

1.   *Is the vendee's interest real estate?* Consistent with *Butler*, most courts
hold that a vendee's interest is real estate for purposes of judgment lien
legislation and that a lien arises on that interest as soon as the judgment is
docketed or recorded. See Nelson, Whitman, Burkhart & Freyermuth, Real
Estate Finance Law § 3.36 (6th ed.2015). See also In re Griffin, 397 B.R. 356
(Bankr.W.D.Va.2008) (in Virginia, a judgment lien attaches to a vendee's
equitable interest regardless of whether he also possesses legal title). However,
there is some case law that holds that a judgment lien does not attach to
equitable interests in real estate and, accordingly, that a vendee's interest,
being equitable, is not subject to the lien. See In re Estate of Ventling, 771 P.2d
388 (Wyo.1989); FCX, Inc. v. Long Meadow Farms, Inc., 269 S.C. 202, 237
S.E.2d 50 (1977).

2.   *Judgment creditor of vendee vs. vendee's mortgagee.* Suppose that
Vendee has paid off $40,000 of the original installment contract price of
$100,000, and that the unencumbered fair market value of the land is also
$100,000. Creditor obtains and dockets a judgment against Vendee in the
amount of $30,000. Vendee later borrows $30,000 from Mortgagee, who records
a mortgage. Vendee then defaults to Mortgagee, which forecloses its mortgage
and conducts a sale at which Vendee's interest is sold to Buyer. In this
situation, Buyer would take Vendee's interest in the land subject to Creditor's
lien (which had temporal priority over the mortgage). In this scenario, then,
what should be the maximum price that Buyer would pay at the foreclosure
sale to acquire Vendee's interest?

3.   *The impact of a judgment against the vendee.* Suppose that Vendee
has paid off $40,000 of the original installment contract price of $100,000, and
that Creditor has obtained and docketed a $100,000 judgment against Vendee.
Suppose further that Vendee then assigns its interest in the land to Buyer,
who takes over making payments under the contract and who spends an
additional $150,000 building a new cabin on the land. After the cabin is
complete, Creditor seeks an execution sale of the land and the cabin. At that
sale, the land and the cabin sell for $190,000. Buyer asks the court to limit
Creditor's lien to the first $40,000 of the sale proceeds, arguing that this was
the amount of Vendee's equity in the land at the time of the assignment and
thus was the "limit" of Vendee's interest (and thus the limit of the Creditor's
lien). Is Buyer's argument sound? Consider the reasoning of the Court of
Appeals of New Mexico in Bank of Santa Fe v. Garcia, 102 N.M. 588, 698 P.2d
458 (1985), rejecting this argument:

Under [Buyer's] definition of a debtor's "interest," the trial court should have determined the amount of [Vendee's] equity and precluded their judgment lien creditors from reaching any of the proceeds in excess of that amount. . . . The case law regarding the relationship between judgment liens and real estate contracts, together with the plain statutory language, indicates that defendants' position is incorrect.

Under a real estate contract, the purchaser holds equitable title, while the seller retains legal title in trust until the contract is paid. A judgment lien against the purchaser attaches to the equitable interest under the contract.

The seller's interest is considered personalty. . . . During the life of a real estate contract any risk of loss or enhancement of value accrues to the purchaser. In short, when the vendor has not exercised his contractual rights to declare a forfeiture, our cases support recognizing that the debtor's estate in the property is an equitable fee simple, subject to the vendor's lien for the unpaid purchase price. Therefore, because a judgment lien is a lien on the real estate of the debtor from the date of filing of the transcript of judgment, and a purchaser under a real estate contract is treated as the owner of the property, the debtor's interest in the property to which the lien attaches, when he holds equitable title under a real estate contract, is the full value of his estate in the property, not just the amount of his payments and the value of improvements as defendants here contend.

. . . The rule is consistent with the strong public policy in favor of satisfaction of judgments. The language of *Cochran v. Cutler*, 39 Ill.App.3d 602, 350 N.E.2d 59 (1976), in an analogous situation, is applicable to [Buyer] here. "By failing to make arrangements for the satisfaction of the lien at the time of the conveyance, they took the risk that the property might increase in value and that such increase might be reached by the judgment creditors should they choose to enforce the lien." 39 Ill.App.3d at 609, 350 N.E.2d at 64. Knowing that risk, they contributed to the equity in the property at their peril. [Citations omitted]

Would the result have been any different if the Buyers had not had actual knowledge of the judgment lien?

4. *Judgments against the vendor.* There is a split of authority as to whether a judgment against the vendor creates a lien against the land subject to the contract. Some jurisdictions treat the vendor's interest as real estate for the purpose of judgment lien statutes. See First Sec. Bank of Idaho, N.A. v. Rogers, 91 Idaho 654, 429 P.2d 386 (1967) ("The majority rule is that a judgment lien against a vendor after the making of the contract of sale, but prior to making and delivery of the deed, extends to all of the vendor's interest remaining in the land and binds the land to the extent of the unpaid purchase

price."); see also Chain O'Mines v. Williamson, 101 Colo. 231, 72 P.2d 265 (1937); Bedortha v. Sunridge Land Co., Inc., 312 Or. 307, 822 P.2d 694 (1991). A growing number of jurisdictions treat the vendor's interest as personal property, either because the vendor's interest is considered personalty by virtue of the equitable conversion doctrine or because it is illogical to treat both the vendee and the vendor as having "real estate" for purposes of a judgment lien statute. See, e.g., Bank of Hawaii v. Horwoth, 71 Haw. 204, 787 P.2d 674 (1990); Marks v. City of Tucumcari, 93 N.M. 4, 595 P.2d 1199 (1979); Cannefax v. Clement, 818 P.2d 546 (Utah 1991).

The latter view is preferable as a conceptual matter. Under the Uniform Commercial Code, which governs secured transactions in personal property, the vendor's interest under an installment contract is an "account," meaning "a right to payment of a monetary obligation . . . for property that has been or is to be sold . . . ." U.C.C. § 9–102(a)(2) (2016). The vendor's right to payment under the contract is thus considered personal property, even if the vendee's obligation to make those payments is also secured by an interest in land. Thus, if a lender makes a loan to the vendor and uses the vendor's right to receive payments under the contract as collateral for repayment of the loan, Article 9 governs the loan transaction—even though real estate law, and not Article 9, governs the rights and obligations of the vendor and the vendee vis-a-vis each other. Conceptually, it seems more sensible to say that if the vendor's interest is personal property vis-a-vis voluntary secured creditors, it should likewise be treated as personal property vis-a-vis judgment creditors.

Suppose Vendee has recorded a contract for deed and has paid a significant amount on the contract but has several more years of payments remaining. Now suppose two different creditors (A and B) obtain judgments against Vendor. If Vendee is not aware of the judgments, and Vendee continues making payments to Vendor, these payments will be sufficient to discharge Vendee's liability on the contract to the extent of the payments. But now suppose that Creditor A demands that Vendee begin making installment payments to Creditor A; Creditor B makes a comparable demand. In this circumstance, with knowledge of the respective judgment liens, Vendee cannot continue to satisfy its liability by making payments to Vendor. Does Vendee risk forfeiture if Vendee does not figure out which Creditor is entitled to priority (and if Vendee pays the wrong one)? What would you suggest Vendee do in this situation? See Splittorff v. Fehn, 810 N.E.2d 385 (Ind.Ct.App.2004).

5. *Perfection of security interests in vendors' rights under installment contracts.* Suppose Bank makes a loan to Vendor, and takes as security the Vendor's interest under a contract for deed. The question arises as to how Bank should "perfect" this interest, i.e., how it should give notice of the interest to subsequent third parties dealing with Vendor. Perfection is important in two contexts for Bank. First, if Vendor makes another assignment to a different creditor, the Bank will prevail over the second only if Bank had first properly "perfected" its interest. Second, if Vendor later becomes bankrupt, the trustee in bankruptcy will have the rights of a lien creditor of Vendor, see 11 U.S.C.

§ 544(a), and will be able to invalidate Bank's security interest if it was not perfected.

Some courts have held that a vendor's interest is an interest in real property and thus the lender can perfect only by recording evidence of the security interest in the real property records in the county where the land is located. See, e.g., In re Hoeppner, 49 B.R. 124 (Bankr.E.D.Wis.1985); Reardon v. Alsup, 114 N.M. 95, 835 P.2d 811 (1992); In re Shuster, 784 F.2d 883 (8th Cir.1986). This view is egregiously wrong; it is plainly inconsistent with U.C.C. Article 9, which governs in all 50 states. Under Article 9, the vendor's interest is an "account," and a lender can perfect a security interest in an account by filing a financing statement in the state's central U.C.C. filing office in the state where the vendor is located. Furthermore, Article 9 makes clear that filing a financing statement covering the vendor's interest is sufficient to perfect the secured party's interest in both the right to collect the vendee's payments and the vendor's right to pursue its remedies against the land in the event of vendee's breach. U.C.C. § 9–308(e) ("perfection of a security interest in a right to payment or performance also perfects a security interest in a security interest, mortgage, or other lien on personal or real property securing the right, notwithstanding other law to the contrary").

One recent federal court of appeals decision nevertheless reveals that courts continue to struggle with the curious nature of the contract for deed. See In re Blanchard, 819 F.3d 981 (7th Cir. 2016). In *Blanchard*, Bank took a security interest in the vendor's rights under a contract for deed, documenting that security interest with a mortgage and recording that mortgage in the land records. Bank did not file a financing statement in the U.C.C. records. When the vendor went bankrupt, the bankruptcy trustee sued to invalidate the Bank's interest as unperfected. The Seventh Circuit rejected the trustee's argument:

> But we do not need to decide in this case whether, under Wisconsin law, UCC filing is now one effective way to perfect a mortgage on a land contract vendor's interest. What we must decide is only whether recording in the county land records remains one effective way to perfect a mortgage on a land contract vendor's interest. Our answer is yes. Revised Article 9 might make it unnecessary to record a mortgage on a land contract vendor's interest in the county land records, as it is possible that UCC filing would be sufficient. But that does not mean that recording in the county land records is not also effective. We see nothing in Revised Article 9 that restricts the scope of Wisconsin's land recording statute, which applies broadly to "every transaction by which any interest in land is created, aliened, mortgaged, assigned or may be otherwise affected in law or in equity." A vendor's interest includes the right to receive the land contract payments. The vendor also holds legal title to the land, and his interest therefore is "still an interest in . . . real estate." [819 F.3d at 988; citations omitted]

Does it make sense to say that the vendor's rights under an installment contract can be governed by both real and personal property security systems?

If Bank properly perfects its interest under Article 9, should it nevertheless also record an assignment of the vendor's contract interest in the real estate records? From the viewpoint of Article 9, such a recording is unnecessary and irrelevant. But for other practical reasons, recording is important and desirable. First, if the vendor defaults, the lender steps into the vendor's shoes, and the contract purchaser eventually pays off the contract, then the lender must deliver a deed to the land to the purchaser. But unless there is also a recorded assignment to the lender, the lender's deed to the purchaser will appear in the public records to be "wild"—i.e., not connected with the preexisting chain of title—and hence the purchaser's title may be unmarketable. Second, if the lender does not record an assignment from the vendor, the lender subjects itself to the risk that a dishonest vendor might later purport to convey title to the land to a good faith purchaser without notice of the lender's unrecorded interest. This could occur if the vendor (without informing or consulting the lender) declares a forfeiture of the land contract on account of the vendee's default. After the forfeiture, the vendor might purport to make a competing outright sale of the real estate by deed to some other purchaser. A court might well hold that, once the land contract has been forfeited, there is no longer an "account" in existence in U.C.C. terms, and hence Article 9 no longer applies at all. Thus, if the vendor didn't record its assignment in the real estate records, and the subsequent purchaser did record, the subsequent purchaser might prevail over the lender under the normal operation of the recording act. Alternatively, the dishonest vendor might collude with the vendee to issue a deed to the vendee and thus facilitate the vendee's transfer of the land to a bona fide purchaser. Obviously, such a deed is improper if the vendee has not fulfilled the contract and the lender has not consented to it. However, if the lender has not recorded evidence of its assignment, the deed will appear to be proper and a bona fide purchaser could later acquire the land without notice of the dishonest vendor's collusive behavior. The only way the lender can guard against this risk with certainty is to record the assignment. See Dale A. Whitman, Transfers by Vendors of Interests in Installment Land Contracts: The Impact of Revised Article 9 of the Uniform Commercial Code, 38 Real Prop., Prob. & Tr. J. 421, 443 (2003); Larry M. Wertheim, Revised Article 9 of the U.C.C. and Minnesota Contracts for Deed, 28 Wm. Mitchell L. Rev. 1483 (2002).

6. *Bankruptcy of a party to the contract.* When either vendor or vendee goes into bankruptcy prior to the conveyance of legal title to the vendee, it can have important consequences for the other party. Because they are better understood in the context of a more extensive consideration of the impact of the Bankruptcy Code on real estate security, such problems are explored in Chapter Six, Section J infra.

C. THE NEGATIVE COVENANT AS A MORTGAGE

DALE A. WHITMAN, MORTGAGE DRAFTING: LESSONS FROM THE RESTATEMENT OF MORTGAGES
33 Real Prop. Prob. & Tr. J. 415, 429–30 (1998)

Rather than obtaining a mortgage, creditors sometimes require the borrower to covenant not to convey or encumber certain real estate held by the borrower. A creditor may consider covenants not to convey or encumber real estate superior to a mortgage because they are not supposed to be subject to the jurisdiction's antideficiency, one-action, or other similar procedural limitations on recovery against defaulting borrowers.[41] If the creditor, at its option, may later characterize the negative pledge as a mortgage, then it seems to have an opportunity to have its cake and eat it too.[42]

However, under the Mortgages Restatement a negative covenant is not a mortgage.[43] The case law widely agrees.[44] Thus, the covenant cannot be foreclosed. Indeed, whether the creditor has any satisfactory remedy for breach of a negative covenant is unclear. Of course, the creditor may sue for damages if the borrower breached the covenant by conveying or encumbering the real estate. But if the original debt was recourse in nature, a suit for damages adds nothing significant to the creditor's action on the debt.[45] That a court would order specific performance of a negative covenant by literally preventing the borrower from transferring the land is

---

[41] *See* Nelson, Whitman, Burkhart & Freyermuth, Real Estate Finance Law, § 3.39 (6th ed.2015).

[42] *See* John R. Hetland, Secured Real Estate Transactions 73 (1974).

[43] According to the Restatement (Third) of Property (Mortgages) § 3.5 (1997), absent "other evidence of intent to create a mortgage, a promise by a debtor to a creditor not to encumber or transfer an interest in real estate does not create a mortgage, equitable lien, or other security interest in that real estate." Only if the promise "is accompanied by specific language of grant or conveyance or by words such as 'mortgage,' 'security,' 'security interest,' 'lien,' or language of similar import to refer to the lender's interest, will extrinsic evidence normally be admissible to establish that a mortgage in real estate was intended." Id., cmt. b.

[44] *See, e.g.,* Chase Manhattan Bank v. Gems-By-Gordon, Inc., 649 F.2d 710 (9th Cir. 1981); Sorran Bank v. United States (*In re* Aumiller), 168 B.R. 811 (Bankr. D.C. 1994); Crystal City State Bank v. Goldstein (*In re* Slover), 71 B.R. 9 (Bankr. E.D. Mo. 1986); *In re* Friese, 28 B.R. 953 (Bankr. D. Conn. 1983); Weaver v. Tri City Credit Bureau, 557 P.2d 1072 (Ariz. Ct. App. 1976); Tahoe Nat'l Bank v. Phillips, 480 P.2d 320 (Cal. 1971); Equitable Trust Co. v. Imbesi, 412 A.2d 96 (Md. 1980); Perpetual Fed. Sav. & Loan Ass'n v. Willingham, 370 S.E.2d 286 (S.C. Ct. App. 1988).

[45] Professor Gilmore stated it as follows:

    [t]he debtor's covenant not to encumber property . . . should be treated, as on the whole case law has done, as a covenant "merely personal"—good enough to give rights against the covenantor for breach, to bring an acceleration clause into play, to constitute an "event of default" under a loan agreement, but not good enough to give rights, whether they be called legal or equitable, in property.

Grant Gilmore, Security Interests in Personal Property 1017 (1965).

highly unlikely because doing so would require the court to impose a direct and egregious disabling restraint on alienation.[46]

In light of the limited and dubious nature of the remedies available to a lender on a negative pledge, the wisest course is simply not to use them. They are subject to the charge of being too cute. An ordinary mortgage or deed of trust is almost certainly a better choice, regardless of the procedural limitations imposed upon them by local law.

---

[46] The closest any court has come to granting specific performance of a negative covenant is the California Supreme Court's dictum in *Coast Bank v. Minderhout*, 392 P.2d 265, 268 (Cal. 1969), *overruled by Wellenkamp v. Bank of America*, 582 P.2d 970 (Cal. 1978):

> Whether the promise not to transfer or encumber the property would be directly [enforceable] by injunction, specific performance or an action for damages is another question. It is open to doubt whether such a promise would be a reasonable restraint when, as in this case, plaintiff had the additional protection of a security interest and the right to declare the entire debt due in the event of default. It is unnecessary, however, to decide this question now.

This is not a ringing endorsement of specific enforcement of the negative covenant.

CHAPTER FOUR

RIGHTS AND DUTIES OF THE PARTIES PRIOR TO FORECLOSURE: SOME PROBLEM AREAS

∎ ∎ ∎

A. FUNDAMENTALS OF THE MORTGAGE CONTRACT

At its heart, the mortgage is a contract that is structured much like a deed. Since the mortgage deals with the transfer of an interest in real property, the statute of frauds applies to these agreements. See Restatement (Third) of Property: Mortgages § 1.1 (1997); 72 Am. Jur. 2d Statute of Frauds § 77.

Historically, the minimum requirements of a mortgage contract consisted of: the names of the parties, a description of the mortgaged property, language evidencing an intent to grant a mortgage, the signature of at least the mortgagor (i.e., the party granting the mortgage), and delivery of the mortgage to the mortgagee. The contours of these individual items have varied from jurisdiction to jurisdiction. Indeed, for purposes of providing certainty, some states have adopted statutory forms that reduce the necessary information to the smallest amount possible. See, e.g., Iowa Code Ann. § 558.19; Minn. Stat. Ann. § 507.15; Tenn. Code Ann. § 66–5–103. Additionally, over time these common law requirements have been codified or expanded through special statutes to include other information, such as a description of the secured obligation. Sometimes the additional information is not required for the validity of the mortgage between the parties themselves, but rather it is a prerequisite for the mortgage to be recordable. See, e.g., La. Civ. Code Ann. art. 3352 (requiring, among other things, a mailing address, marital status of the parties, and the last four digits of the mortgagor's social security or taxpayer identification number).

One might be surprised to read that the precise requirements of a mortgage contract are not solidified—that, indeed, they vary from state to state and are even somewhat open-ended within a given jurisdiction. This is due to the fact that most of the time a financial institution is the mortgage lender. This means that in addition to basic information, the mortgage contracts contain a significant amount of other information on items such as foreclosure, rights of the parties, insurance, and property taxes.

The following case raises problems relative to the description of the secured obligation in mortgage contracts.

DEVLIN V. WIENER
Connecticut Supreme Court, 1995
232 Conn. 550, 656 A.2d 664

CALLAHAN, ASSOCIATE JUSTICE. This appeal requires us to determine whether a mortgage deed and the underlying obligation that the deed purports to secure are sufficiently definite to sustain the plaintiff's foreclosure action. The trial court concluded that a debt is owed the plaintiff and that the debt is secured by a valid mortgage. We agree.

The record reveals the following facts. The plaintiff, Gerald Devlin, owned a nine acre parcel of real estate in Branford, on which his residence was located. The defendants Pine Orchard Associates, Inc., and Pine Orchard Development Corporation (collectively, Pine Orchard), sought to acquire and then subdivide the plaintiff's land. On February 18, 1984, the plaintiff executed a written contract to sell the nine acre parcel and his residence to Pine Orchard. The agreement entered into by the parties, although convoluted, essentially provided that the plaintiff would convey his interest in his Branford real estate to Pine Orchard for a cash payment of $86,000 and a promise by Pine Orchard either (1) to convey to the plaintiff a finished three bedroom condominium, cooperative apartment unit or single-family residence in the planned subdivision, or (2) to transfer to the plaintiff a building lot in the planned subdivision together with sufficient building materials for the plaintiff to erect a three bedroom single-family residence on the lot, or (3) to return to the plaintiff his Branford residence together with one half of one acre of land. The agreement further provided that, as security for Pine Orchard's additional promise, Pine Orchard would mortgage the transferred property back to the plaintiff. Finally, the agreement provided that the mortgage would secure a debt of Pine Orchard to the plaintiff in the amount of $84,000.[3] The $86,000 was paid to the plaintiff at the time of the closing and, as required by the agreement, was used to extinguish an existing first mortgage held by the Branford Savings Bank. No other consideration has been paid to the plaintiff.

On February 29, 1984, the plaintiff conveyed his interest in the Branford real estate to Pine Orchard Development Corporation and, on the

---

[3] The document itself, which was fashioned by the parties without the aid of counsel, is several pages in length and contains various crossouts, insertions and initialed modifications. As aptly noted by the trial court, the agreement "graphically demonstrates the potential for disaster in documents prepared by laypersons without the assistance of lawyers."

same date, that defendant mortgaged the same real estate to the plaintiff in accordance with paragraph twenty-nine of the purchase and sale agreement. Daniel J. Wiener executed the mortgage instrument in his capacity as president of the corporation. The mortgage deed expressly stated that it was given to secure the obligation of Pine Orchard to "transfer certain properties" to the plaintiff pursuant to "a contract dated February 18, 1984." Although the deed itself was silent as to the amount of the secured debt, paragraph twenty-nine of the purchase and sale agreement specifically indicated that the mortgage was to secure an obligation of the corporation in the amount of $84,000.

On July 8, 1985, Pine Orchard Development Corporation conveyed all of its interest in the Branford property to Pine Orchard Development Associates, a partnership in which Daniel J. Wiener was a general partner. Thereafter, Pine Orchard Development Associates transferred the property to Daniel J. Wiener and Gloria Maddox Wiener, jointly as husband and wife with a right of survivorship. On April 13, 1990, Daniel J. Wiener transferred his interest in the Branford property, by quitclaim deed for no consideration, to his wife, the named defendant, Gloria Maddox Wiener.

On January 31, 1992, the plaintiff filed suit against Pine Orchard Associates, Inc., Pine Orchard Development Corporation and Gloria Maddox Wiener for foreclosure of his mortgage, claiming that the defendants' obligation to the plaintiff, as set forth in the February 18, 1984 purchase and sale agreement and as secured by the mortgage deed given by Pine Orchard Development Corporation to the plaintiff on February 29, 1984, was in default. The named defendant filed an answer and various special defenses, including the defense that the "Mortgage Deed does not refer to a 'Mortgage Note' and fails to define any other obligation or debt in sufficient detail," and therefore does not secure an enforceable obligation.

After a hearing, the trial court concluded that "[a]s between the parties . . . there is an indebtedness due to the plaintiff on the mortgage in the amount of $84,000. While the defendants have cited deficiencies in the document in question, the court notes that . . . the document is susceptible to 'a reasonable and precise interpretation.' . . . The court finds there is an underlying obligation due to the plaintiff in the amount of $84,000.00 and that this amount is secured by a valid mortgage." Thereafter, on motion by the plaintiff, the trial court ordered a foreclosure by sale and rendered judgment accordingly. The named defendant appealed from the judgment of the trial court to the Appellate Court, and we transferred the appeal to this court pursuant to Practice Book § 4023 and General Statutes § 51–199(c).

On appeal, the named defendant claims only that the trial court improperly concluded that the mortgage deed and the obligation purportedly secured by the mortgage deed were sufficiently definite to sustain the plaintiff's foreclosure action. At the outset, the named defendant challenges the trial court's finding that she was a party, or in privity with a party, to the mortgage transaction. She claims, therefore, that the trial court improperly applied the law governing the enforceability of mortgages between parties to the mortgage, instead of applying the law governing the enforceability of mortgages between mortgagees and nonparties. Moreover, the named defendant claims that the mortgage deed is invalid because it does not secure a note, but rather, the performance of affirmative acts by Pine Orchard under the February 18, 1984 purchase and sale agreement, and because the deed does not recite the specific amount of the debt allegedly owed. Finally, the named defendant contends that the obligation contained in paragraph twenty-eight of the purchase and sale agreement is insufficient because it is too indefinite as to time for performance, subject matter and method of performance. We conclude that the mortgage is sufficiently definite as to be enforceable against the named defendant even if she is properly viewed as a third party, and we therefore affirm the judgment of the trial court.

We begin by reviewing the well established common law governing the sufficiency of mortgage deeds as between a mortgagee and a nonparty to the mortgage. "In [*Dart & Bogue Co. v. Slosberg*, 202 Conn. 566, 578–79, 522 A.2d 763 (1987)], we stated that the dispositive question in examining the validity of a mortgage is whether it provides 'reasonable notice' to third parties of the obligation that is secured. . . . The purpose of such 'reasonable notice' is to prevent parties that are not privy to the transaction from being defrauded or misled. . . . A corollary of this proposition is that errors and omissions in the recorded mortgage that would not mislead a title searcher as to the true nature of the secured obligation do not affect the validity of the mortgage against third parties. . . . In other words, the recorded mortgage deed does not need to recite with particularity all of the details of the underlying transaction. . . ."

> "In *Dart & Bogue Co.* [*v. Slosberg, supra*, 202 Conn. at 579, 522 A.2d 763], we defined 'reasonable notice' as notice of the nature and amount of the encumbrance which the mortgagor intends to place upon the land. . . . The 'nature' of a secured debt includes such fundamental characteristics as whether the debt is absolute or contingent, liquidated or unliquidated, or whether it is given to secure an existing liability or future advances. . . . The 'amount' of the debt is the dollar value of the obligation secured, to the extent that it can be ascertained at the time the mortgage is executed. If the debt cannot be definitively ascertained at that time, such data must be set out with respect to that debt as will put anyone interested in the inquiry upon a track leading to discovery. . . . Significantly, in *Dart & Bogue Co.* [*v. Slosberg, supra*, at 580, 522 A.2d 763], we recognized that [t]he record is the starting point for

inquiry, not . . . the starting and ending point. . . . In sum, if a party is able by common prudence and by the exercise of ordinary diligence, [to] ascertain the extent of the encumbrance from information set out in the land records, then the mortgage is valid." (Citations omitted; internal quotation marks omitted.)

Connecticut National Bank v. Esposito, 210 Conn. 221, 227–28, 554 A.2d 735 (1989).

We initially note that we will not declare the mortgage deed invalid, as the named defendant urges us to do, simply because the deed itself lacks a statement of the specific amount of the debt secured. As in *Esposito*, the deed in the present case omits "documents that contain important details about the obligation but the existence of which documents [is] expressly referred to in the recorded mortgage deed. The mortgage deed does not affirmatively misidentify the characteristics of the obligation, thus leading a title searcher to believe that the obligation is something that it is not, nor does the omission of the documents leave a title searcher without any indication of the obligation's nature or without a reasonable direction to discover the terms of the mortgage." *Id.* at 230, 554 A.2d 735. In fact, the mortgage deed expressly states that the obligation secured is set forth in the February 18, 1984 purchase and sale agreement between the plaintiff and Pine Orchard Associates, Inc., and further states that the agreement is on file at the office of the attorney for Pine Orchard. Thus, because the mortgage deed sufficiently puts a title searcher on notice of the location of the underlying agreement that contains the substance of the secured debt, the efficacy of the mortgage deed may be determined by analyzing the sufficiency of the underlying agreement.

Moreover, the mortgage deed is not invalid simply because it purports to secure a "performance" instead of a stated monetary obligation. "The condition of a mortgage may be the payment of a debt, the indemnity of a surety, or the doing or not doing any other act. *Cook v. Bartholomew*, 60 Conn. 24, 25, 22 A. 444 (1891); see *State v. Hurlburt*, 82 Conn. 232, 236, 72 A. 1079 (1909); *Jarvis v. Woodruff*, 22 Conn. 548, 550–51 (1853); *Gagan v. Leary*, 14 Conn.Sup. 468, 470 (1946); see also 9 G. Thompson, Real Property (Grimes 1958) § 4659, p. 32." (Internal quotation marks omitted.) *Connecticut National Bank v. Esposito, supra*, 210 Conn. at 225–26, 554 A.2d 735. Thus, if we determine that the underlying agreement contains a sufficiently definite obligation, whether that obligation be for the payment of a specific dollar amount or for the performance of some act, we may also determine that the mortgage deed is adequate to sustain the plaintiff's foreclosure action.

We now turn to the parties' February 18, 1984 purchase and sale agreement. Although the named defendant contends that the agreement is insufficient to support the mortgage deed at issue because the obligation contained in paragraph twenty-eight is too indefinite as to time for performance, subject matter and method of performance, the trial court, after viewing all of the evidence, concluded otherwise. On appeal, we are limited to determining whether this legal conclusion finds support in the record and is "legally and logically correct." *Pandolphe's Auto Parts, Inc. v. Manchester*, 181 Conn. 217, 221–22, 435 A.2d 24 (1980); see also *RK Constructors, Inc. v. Fusco Corp.*, 231 Conn. 381, 384–85, 650 A.2d 153 (1994).

The trial court concluded that paragraph twenty-eight of the parties' purchase and sale agreement creates an obligation due the plaintiff in the amount of $84,000. Our review of the various subsections to paragraph twenty-eight of the original agreement, which was made a trial exhibit by the plaintiff, reveals that Pine Orchard agreed to compensate the plaintiff for the Branford property, in addition to the $86,000 payment made to extinguish the existing encumbrance, by one of three alternate methods. First, under paragraph twenty-eight (a) Pine Orchard could have chosen to return to the plaintiff his Branford residence together with one half of one acre of land. Second, under paragraph twenty-eight (a)(i), Pine Orchard could have chosen to transfer to the plaintiff a building lot together with sufficient building materials for the plaintiff to erect a three-bedroom single-family residence on the lot. Third, under paragraph twenty-eight (a)(ii), Pine Orchard could have chosen to convey to the plaintiff a finished three bedroom condominium, cooperative apartment unit or single-family residence in the subdivision that the defendants planned to construct on the Branford property. We further note that paragraph twenty-nine of the agreement provides that, as security for Pine Orchard's obligations to the plaintiff under paragraph twenty-eight, Pine Orchard granted the plaintiff a mortgage interest in the Branford property in the amount of $84,000.

Our review of the agreement between the plaintiff and Pine Orchard, which was part of the record before the trial court, persuades us to conclude that the trial court properly found that Pine Orchard Development Corporation had executed a mortgage securing a debt to the plaintiff in the amount of $84,000. Although the named defendant claims that the agreement is insufficient because it does not specify a time for performance, we note that both subsections (a) and (b) of paragraph twenty-eight of the agreement refer to a requirement that any conveyance to the plaintiff be made within two years from the date of closing. Likewise, although the named defendant contends that the method of performance and the subject matter constituting the substance of the agreement are not sufficiently specified, the parties specifically agreed that each of the three options that Pine Orchard could have chosen to satisfy its obligation to the plaintiff had a value of $84,000. Thus, we conclude that the trial court's determination that there is an underlying obligation owed the plaintiff in the amount of $84,000, and that this amount is secured by a valid mortgage, is supported by the record and is "legally and logically correct." *Pandolphe's Auto Parts, Inc. v. Manchester, supra,* 181 Conn. at 221–22, 435 A.2d 24.

The judgment of the trial court is affirmed and the case is remanded to that court to set new law days and to order appropriate notice.

In this opinion the other justices concurred.

NOTES

1. *Definiteness of obligation.* There are two distinct issues in the *Devlin* case, and it is useful to consider them separately. One issue is whether the obligation that a mortgage secures is described with sufficient clarity. The Connecticut court (wisely, we think) takes the view that the obligation must be definite, but that the definition does not necessarily have to appear in the mortgage itself, so long as the mortgage contains "data . . . with respect to that debt as will put anyone interested in the inquiry upon a track leading to discovery." The details may be in another agreement or set of agreements between the parties. Restatement (Third) of Property (Mortgages) § 1.5(a) (1997) is even more forgiving: "A mortgage need not describe the obligation whose performance it secures, provided the parties have otherwise reached agreement identifying that obligation." Obviously, describing the obligation, or at least identifying the documents that describe it, is a sound practice.

Not all courts are so accommodating as the Restatement and the Connecticut court. In Kalange v. Rencher, 136 Idaho 192, 30 P.3d 970 (2001), the parties entered into a note and a deed of trust, but also signed a separate "loan agreement," not mentioned in the deed of trust, which required the borrower to pay an additional $50,000 under certain circumstances. The court refused to recognize that the "loan agreement" was secured by the deed of trust, even though it was quite obvious that the parties understood it to be secured. See also, Wilson v. Ledger, 97 A.D. 1028, 949 N.Y.S.2d 515 (App.Div.2012) (the plans and specifications for the residence to be constructed, as well as the size and location of the lot upon which it would be built and conveyed to plaintiff, were essential terms of the note and mortgage inasmuch they represented the manner of repayment of the debt—the parties left these material terms for future negotiation and agreement and failed to set forth in the documents any objective method for supplying these missing terms, resulting in only an unenforceable agreement to agree); see also La. Civ. Code art. 3288 (requiring that the mortgage "state the amount of the obligation, or the maximum amount of the obligations that may be outstanding at any time and from time to time that the mortgage secures.").

2. *Non-monetary obligations.* The second issue in *Devlin* is whether the non-monetary obligation is capable of being reduced to a money equivalent. If it cannot, it cannot be secured by a mortgage. See Nelson, Whitman, Burkhart & Freyermuth, Real Estate Finance Law § 2.2 (6th ed.2015); Restatement (Third) of Property (Mortgages) § 1.4 (1997). For example, a variety of construction agreements have been held capable of being mortgaged and the

cost of completion of the contract has been deemed *prima facie* evidence of the mortgage debt. See Pawtucket Inst. for Sav. v. Gagnon, 475 A.2d 1028 (R.I.1984) (promise to build apartment house); Jeffrey Towers, Inc. v. Straus, 31 A.D.2d 319, 297 N.Y.S.2d 450 (1969) (promise to build driveway and sewer line). In *Devlin*, the parties made this issue relatively easy by stipulating to the $84,000 value for the obligation.

What is the reason for requiring that the obligation be reducible to a monetary equivalent? As the comment to Restatement § 1.4 observes,

> Mortgage enforcement would break down if mortgages were permitted to secure performance of obligations that could not be measured in terms of money. There would be no means of determining whether a foreclosure sale produced a surplus or a deficiency. If a junior lienholder desired to redeem, there would be no means of determining the amount necessary to accomplish a redemption.[*]

3. *Support mortgages.* Restatement (Third) of Property (Mortgages) § 1.4 (1997) Illustration 4 comments that when a mortgage is given both to secure a promise of financial support, and also a promise of "love, affection, and kindness," the mortgage is valid to secure the first obligation but not the second. The reason, of course, is that a promise of emotional support cannot be reduced to a monetary equivalent. Yet people fairly often enter into mortgages that purport to require such "emotional" obligations. See, e.g., Thompson v. Glidden, 445 A.2d 676 (Me.1982).

LEONARD A. JONES, A TREATISE ON THE LAW OF MORTGAGES OF REAL PROPERTY
Vol. I (8th ed. 1928)[1]

§ 77. Trust deeds. A deed of trust to secure a debt is in legal effect a mortgage. It is a convenience made to a person other than the creditor, conditioned to be void if the debt be paid at a certain time, but if not paid that the grantee may sell the land and apply the proceeds to the extinguishment of the debt, paying over the surplus to the grantor. It is in legal effect a mortgage with a power of sale, but the addition of the power of sale does not change the character of the instrument any more than it does when conditioned in a mortgage. Such a deed has all the essential elements of a mortgage; it is a conveyance of land as security for a debt. It passes the legal title just as a mortgage does, except in those states with a natural effect of a conveyance is controlled by statute; and in states where a mortgage is considered merely as a security, and not a conveyance, a deed of trust is apt to be regarded in this respect just like a mortgage . . . .

---

*   © 1997 by The American Law Institute. Reprinted with permission.

1   Editors' Note: Footnote citations omitted.

The only important difference between them is, that in the [mortgage] the conveyance is directly to the creditor, while in the [deed of trust] it is to a third person for his benefit. Another practical difference is that the deed of trust with power of sale may be foreclosed according to its terms by the trustee without authority of court, whereas a simple mortgage can be foreclosed only under decree of court. The instrument evidences a contract between the debtor and a creditor, and it is not binding upon anyone until accepted by the beneficiary.

NOTES

1. *Purpose of the deed of trust.* The primary reason for the birth and development of the deed of trust is to provide speed and financial efficiency to the foreclosure process. The judicial foreclosure of a regular mortgage can be both time consuming and expensive. Specifically, a residential mortgage lender will typically wait until it has been anywhere from three to six months since a borrower failed to make payment before initiating a judicial foreclosure proceeding. At that point, the length of time until the sale occurs and the process is complete ranges from state to state (both by law and by the court's docket). A 2020 study found that it took an average of 685 days from the first notice of the foreclosure to the completion of the process. See Midyear 2020 U.S. Foreclosure Market Report, ATTOM Data Solution/RealtyTrac (Aug. 2020). Also, judicial foreclosure sales rarely yield the fair market value of the property. See Debra Pogrund Stark, Facing the Facts: An Empirical Study of the Fairness and Efficiency of Foreclosures and A Proposal for Reform, 30 U. Mich. J.L. Reform 639, 663 (1997) ("Third parties successfully bid in only 11.2% of the 1993 judicial sales cases and only 9.6% of the 1994 judicial sales cases."). On the other hand, non-judicial foreclosures using a deed of trust can be accomplished "in as little as thirty to forty-five days." See R. Wilson Freyermuth, Foreclosure by Arbitration?, 37 Pepp. L. Rev. 459, 467 (2010).

2. *The three parties.* The deed of trust contract is between three parties: the borrower (the trustor), the lender (the beneficiary), and the trustee. The trustee is the extra person who is not present in the traditional mortgagor-mortgagee transaction. In a deed of trust transaction, the borrower executes a deed of trust in the name of the trustee. This deed purports to actually convey legal title to the trustee who holds it for the special purpose of serving as security for the debt. If the borrower defaults, then upon notice by the lender/beneficiary, the trustee will conduct a foreclosure sale of the property (rather than it being conducted by a sheriff or other public officer). Typically, state law will require publication of the upcoming sale in a local periodical followed by the public auction. The winning bidder at the auction (including the lender if applicable) will receive a trustee's deed conveying title.

3. *Trustee duties.* Importantly, the law provides that the trustee is obligated to act on behalf of both the borrower and the lender—in other words, to be a disinterested party. This means that the trustee must act with absolute impartiality. Only the trustee may cancel the deed of trust (which involves

recording an instrument of cancelation into the same county land records where the deed of trust is recorded) when the secured obligation has been paid in full or when the trustee otherwise receives direction to do so from the beneficiary. A trustee who impermissibly cancels a deed of trust is personally liable.

Although the trustee must technically be jointly appointed in most cases, practically the lender picks the trustee. Some states also impose restrictions on who can serve as trustee—for example, the trustee cannot be affiliated with either the borrower or the lender. In most cases, the trustee will be an attorney or some kind of real estate-related company, such as the title company that conducted the closing of the sale and the mortgage loan.

B. THEORIES OF TITLE: POSSESSION, RENTS, AND RELATED CONSIDERATIONS

RESTATEMENT (THIRD) OF PROPERTY (MORTGAGES)
§ 4.1, Comment a (1997)*

American courts have traditionally recognized one of three theories of mortgage law. Under the title theory, legal "title" to the mortgaged real estate remains in the mortgagee until the mortgage is satisfied or foreclosed; in lien theory jurisdictions, the mortgagee is regarded as owning a security interest only and both legal and equitable title remain in the mortgagor until foreclosure. Under the intermediate theory, legal and equitable title remain in the mortgagor until a default, at which time legal title passes to the mortgagee. * * *

(1) *The title theory.* English legal history is crucial to understanding the title theory. * * * [W]hen the mortgage transaction became the conveyance of a fee on condition subsequent, with defeasance based on performance by the mortgagor on law day, the mortgagee obtained legal title to the land, and, with it, acquired the right to possession and to collect rents and profits. Thus, actual possession became the norm. * * * [U]nder English law at this time, any collection of interest was deemed usurious. Consequently, possession and its access to rents and profits proved to be an economic substitute for interest. Indeed, until the middle of the 17th century the usual practice was for the mortgagee to take possession upon execution of the mortgage; only thereafter did it become common for the mortgagor to be left in possession.

In all probability, the development of mortgagor possession coincided with the creation by equity of the mortgagor's equity of redemption. * * * This was a logical development because, with the acceptance of the mortgagor as the equitable owner of the real estate, there was an implicit

---

*   © 1997 by The American Law Institute. Reprinted with permission.

recognition that, notwithstanding the mortgagee's legal title, its major interest in the real estate was that of security. With the acceptance of this view, the mortgagee who actually exercised the right to possession was held to strict standards of accountability. Consequently, the exercise of the possessory right became relatively infrequent. Nevertheless, while seldom used, the right to possession was, as it still is in a few states today, a fundamental element of the mortgagee's legal title. As a result, the mortgagee could maintain ejectment against the mortgagor until the mortgage was satisfied * * *.

The American states initially adopted the title theory in substantially the same form it had developed in England. Usually, however, there was an express agreement permitting the mortgagor to stay on the mortgaged real estate. * * * Even without such express agreements, courts often found from the other terms and conditions of the mortgage documents an implicit right in the mortgagor to remain in possession.

Today, however, title jurisdictions differ in only a few respects from their lien theory counterparts. Such states recognize that mortgagees hold title for security purposes only, and for both practical and theoretical purposes they usually view the mortgagor as the owner of the land. * * * In addition, two other developments have placed significant limitations on the title theory. First, statutes in some title states give the mortgagor the right to possession until default. Second, commonly used mortgage forms containing similar provisions achieve the same result.

This is not to say that the title theory is now irrelevant. As legal titleholder, in the absence of agreement to the contrary, the mortgagee has a right to immediate possession against the mortgagor. This right is occasionally asserted after the mortgagor has defaulted and incident to the commencement of foreclosure. Its assertion can be important where a lengthy foreclosure proceeding could mean a substantial period during which mortgagor could divert the rents and profits of the land to purposes other than service of the mortgage obligation. * * * However, these advantages for the title theory mortgagee are more apparent than real, since a lien theory mortgagee is often able to accomplish similar results through the appointment of a receiver or enforcement of an assignment of rents agreement. * * *

(2) *The lien theory.* The substantial majority of American jurisdictions follow the lien theory. Under this theory, the mortgagee acquires only a "lien" on the mortgaged real estate and the mortgagor retains both legal and equitable title and the right to possession until foreclosure or a deed in lieu of foreclosure. Given the early acceptance of the title theory by American courts, the adoption of the lien theory was largely the product of legislation. Some lien theory statutes provide that the mortgagee is not entitled to maintain a possessory action for the

mortgaged real estate; some also state that the "mortgagor shall be deemed to be the owner of the land." Others accomplish the same result by slightly different terminology. Several statutes state that a mortgage shall not be deemed a conveyance so as to allow the mortgagee to obtain possession other than by foreclosure. Identical results usually follow even if a deed of trust, rather than a mortgage, is employed, and likewise where an absolute deed or conditional sale is intended as a security device.

Lien theory jurisdictions have been far from uniform as to the effect of mortgage language that purports to give the mortgagee a right to possession of the mortgaged real estate before foreclosure. While some states enforce such agreements, others invalidate them on the theory that they contravene the public policy in favor of mortgagor possession underlying lien theory statutes. However, where such language is either absent or ineffective, the lien theory means that a mortgagor, prior to foreclosure, may prevail against the mortgagee for any interference with the mortgagor's possession of the mortgaged real estate to the same extent that any owner of land would prevail against a trespasser.

(3) *The intermediate theory.* A few states purport to follow a compromise position between the title and lien theories. Under this "intermediate" approach, the mortgagor is deemed to have legal title until default occurs; after default, legal title passes to the mortgagee. In other words, the mortgagee has the right to possession and to collect rents and profits after mortgagor default. This approach is grounded variously in statutes and case law. Since it is uncommon for title theory mortgagees to assert a right to possession prior to default, in practice the intermediate theory seems to differ, little, if at all, from its title theory counterpart.

NOTES

1. *Classification of states.* At least 32 states follow the lien theory, with the balance adhering either to the title or intermediate theory. The Restatement adopts the lien theory. See Restatement (Third) of Property (Mortgages) § 4.1(a) (1997) ("A mortgage creates only a security interest in real estate and confers no right to possession of that real estate on the mortgagee.").

2. *Mortgagee in possession in lien states.* Even in a lien theory jurisdiction, a mortgagee may sometimes acquire possession of the mortgaged property legally by means other than foreclosure. First, the mortgagee may acquire possession with the consent of the mortgagor. See, e.g., Kelley/Lehr & Assoc., Inc. v. O'Brien, 194 Ill.App.3d 380, 141 Ill.Dec. 426, 551 N.E.2d 419 (1990). Specifically, the standard residential mortgage contract, used by nearly all lenders in the United States, contains provisions that grant such a right. Section 9 of that document provides that "If [the] Borrower fails to perform the covenants and agreements" or if the "Borrower has abandoned the Property" then the mortgagee may "do and pay for whatever is reasonable or appropriate to protect [the mortgagee's] interest in the Property." Iowa, Single Family,

Fannie Mae/Freddie Mac Uniform Instrument: Mortgage § 9 (This includes, among other things, "entering the Property to make repairs, change locks, replace or board up doors and windows, drain water from pipes, eliminate building or other code violations or dangerous conditions," as well as having the "utilities turned on or off."). Id.

Second, a mortgagee who enters into peaceable possession in good faith after purchasing at an invalid foreclosure sale may remain in possession until a valid foreclosure takes place. In addition, where the mortgagor abandons the mortgaged real estate, the mortgagee's security interest alone (even absent contract language like that quoted above) has historically been deemed sufficient to permit the mortgagee to take and retain possession until foreclosure. This is due to the fact that courts have long held that to the extent "legal title vests in the mortgagee" that it is "for the protection of his interest." See Leonard A. Jones, A Treatise on the Law of Mortgages of Real Property § 10 (Vol. I, 5th edition, 1904) (quoting Glass v. Ellison 9 N.H. 69 (1837)). In this setting, public policy clearly supports possession by the mortgagee to protect the abandoned real estate against vandalism and deterioration. Moreover, society is benefited by its productive use. See generally Nelson, Whitman, Burkhart & Freyermuth, Real Estate Finance Law § 4.24 (6th ed.2015). The Restatement authorizes mortgagee possession in each of the foregoing situations. See Restatement (Third) of Property (Mortgages) § 4.1(c) (1997). Note, however, that the mortgagee's claim to possession must be on account of being a mortgagee—in other words, by virtue of the security interest. Thus, mortgagee in possession status does not arise where the mortgagee acquires possession as a tenant or agent of the mortgagor.

3. *Mortgagee taking possession without judicial process.* The improper taking of possession by a mortgagee can sometimes prove costly. This can of course arise in a situation where the mortgage contract's provisions on entry have not been properly triggered and where a given jurisdiction's law places more limits on the ability of a mortgagee to engage in possessory acts absent such an event. Moreover, some states will not even enforce mortgage contract provisions that allow for entry even when the necessary default or other event has occurred. Consider the case of Jordan v. Nationstar Mortg., LLC, 185 Wash. 2d 876, 879, 374 P.3d 1195, 1197 (2016):

After defaulting on her home mortgage payment, plaintiff Laura Jordan returned home from work one evening to discover she could not enter her own house: the locks had been changed without warning. A notice informed her that in order to gain access to her home, she must call defendant Nationstar Mortgage LLC to obtain the lockbox code and retrieve the new key inside . . . . Jordan's home loan was secured by a deed of trust, a commonly used security instrument that was created as an alternative to traditional mortgages to provide for a simpler method of foreclosure. The deed of trust contained provisions that allowed Nationstar to enter her home upon default without providing any notice to the homeowner.

... Jordan represents a certified class of 3,600 Washington homeowners who were locked out of their homes pursuant to similar provisions in their deeds of trust with Nationstar. This case presents an important issue for these homeowners and the thousands of others subject to similar provisions, as well as the many mortgage companies that have a concern with preserving and protecting the properties in which they have an interest . . . .

[The question before us is whether,] [u]nder Washington's lien theory of mortgages and RCW 7.28.230(1), can a borrower and lender enter into a contractual agreement prior to default that allows the lender to enter, maintain, and secure the encumbered property prior to foreclosure? . . . While we recognize an overarching freedom to contract, provisions are unenforceable where they are prohibited by statute. . . Our case law is clear that Washington law prohibits a lender from taking possession of property before foreclosure of the borrower's home. . . Under any definition, the conduct allowed under the [mortgage contract] entry provisions constitutes possession because Nationstar's actions satisfy the key element of possession: control. . . Changing the locks is akin to exercising control, which is the key element of possession. By changing the locks, Nationstar took possession of the property.

Because Washington law prohibits lenders from taking possession of the borrower's property before foreclosure, the provisions are in conflict with state law. Therefore, we must answer the first certified question in the negative and find that the entry provisions are unenforceable.

Is the foregoing decision correct? Is it too broad? In other words, should there be at least some circumstances in which a mortgagee can enter the property for purposes of preserving its value? Also, does the court perhaps implicitly recognize a "residential-nonresidential" distinction? For that matter, should there be a different rule or standard for when a mortgagee can take possession of residential property—someone's home—compared to when the property is commercial in nature, like an office building or retail center?

4.   *Liability of a mortgagee in possession.* Even where the mortgagee has the right to take possession, the decision whether to exercise that right must be influenced by a careful consideration of the rights and liabilities of a mortgagee in possession. For example, mortgagee-in-possession status makes the mortgagee liable in tort "for injuries resulting either through its actionable fault in utilizing the property or by reason of its failure to perform duties imposed by law upon the owner of land." Nelson, Whitman, Burkhart & Freyermuth, Real Estate Finance Law § 4.26, at 211 (6th ed.2015). One court held that "where a mortgagee lawfully takes possession . . ., he or she takes the rents received from the use of the premises in the quasi character of trustee or bailiff of the mortgagor." Mandel v. Strickland, 287 A.D.2d 695, 735 N.Y.S.2d 553 (2001). As a result, the mortgagee must operate the property "not only to

protect its own interest but also for the benefit of the mortgagor to pay off the debt." In addition, the mortgagee in possession bears a significant responsibility to the mortgagor for maintenance of the mortgaged premises. In this connection, consider the language of the court in New York & Suburban Fed. Sav. & Loan Ass'n v. Sanderman 392 A.2d 635 (Ch. Div. 1978). In that case, the first mortgagee sought reimbursement for various expenditures it had made in caring for the property while in possession.

[The mortgagee] urges that under the decisions in Zanzonico v. Zanzonico, 66 A.2d 530 (1949), cert. den. 338 U.S. 868 (1949); Newark v. Sue Corp., 124 N.J.Super. 5, 7–8 (App. Div. 1973), a mortgagee in possession has a duty to protect against vandalism or be held liable for loss or destruction of the property. It points to the following statement in *Zanzonico*:

> A mortgagee who goes into possession of the mortgaged lands assumes a grave responsibility for the management and preservation of the property. It is notorious that in Newark untenanted property is apt to be wrecked by vandals. When the tenants in the six-family house vacated the premises on the order of the public authorities [Tenement House Commission], complainant could have surrendered the house to [mortgagor's] devisee or he could have made the necessary repairs and alterations and charged the cost against future rents. But he did neither; he allowed the house to remain empty and took inadequate means to protect it. He is liable for the resulting damage. * * * [at 316, 66 A.2d at 533]

A mortgagee who goes into possession is under a duty to maintain and preserve the property. The standard by which the discharge of that duty should be judged is that of a provident owner. Essex Cleaning Contractors, Inc. v. Amato, 127 N.J.Super. 364, 366 (App. Div. 1974), certif. den. 65 N.J. 575 (1974); * * *. However, until the mortgagee has foreclosed he is not the owner and must act with due regard to the interests of the junior encumbrancers and the holder of the equity of redemption. Shaeffer v. Chambers, 6 N.J.Eq. 548 (Ch. 1847); cf. Taylor v. Morris, 1 N.J.Super. 410 (Ch. Div. 1948).

It is suggested in 4 American Law of Property, § 16.100 at 190, that there is a limit on the duty of the mortgagee in possession:

> He must, therefore, conserve its value by making repairs, and this duty is recognized on the one hand by charging him for any loss that flows from his failure to act and, on the other hand, by allowing him credit for expenditures in carrying it out. There are, however, limitations on this. One is that he is not bound to dig into his own pocket and so need not expend more than the rents and profits he receives. Another is that he does not have to make good or prevent the depreciation caused by ordinary wear and tear—"the silent effect of waste and decay from time."

Indeed, in casting upon him this duty of affirmative conduct the standard for its invocation is "willful default," "gross negligence," or "recklessness and improvidence," a rather low standard of responsibility whose [sic] mildness is explained by the fact that the mortgagor, the owner, also should look after the upkeep of his own property.

* * *

Judge Bigelow, who wrote the language quoted by the Supreme Court in *Zanzonico,* supra, in essence gave the mortgagee an option either to take possession, expending funds and collecting the expenditures from future rents, or not take possession but proceed quickly to foreclosure and sale of the real property. Under the first alternative the mortgagee, like a provident owner, would have to weigh the probability of collecting rents against the cost of repairs, taxes, insurance and the mortgagor redeeming the property. Under the second the mortgagee could proceed to foreclosure quickly and rely upon the right to collect any deficiency from the mortgagor. In no circumstance was the mortgagee to take possession and then allow the real property to be dissipated before foreclosure. In other words, the mortgagee was under a duty to evaluate what to do in the same manner as a provident owner would do.

5.   *Avoiding mortgagee in possession status.* Because of the foregoing responsibilities and liabilities associated with being a mortgagee in possession, mortgagees frequently use other mechanisms, such as receiverships, to gain access to the rents and profits and control over the mortgaged real estate pending foreclosure. We consider these matters in Section C of this chapter.

DOVER MOBILE ESTATES V. FIBER FORM PRODUCTS, INC.

California Court of Appeal, Sixth District 1990
220 Cal.App.3d 1494, 270 Cal.Rptr. 183

ELIA, ASSOCIATE JUSTICE.

* * *

In 1985, tenant Fiber Form entered into a five year lease with landlord Old Town Properties, Inc. The lease provided that it was subordinate to any deeds of trust or mortgages placed on the property unless the mortgagee or beneficiary elected to have the lease be superior.

Old Town subsequently encumbered the property with a second deed of trust to Saratoga Savings & Loan Association. Old Town defaulted. Saratoga Savings & Loan foreclosed and, at a December 3, 1986 trustee's sale, Income Property Investments, Inc. (hereafter Dover) purchased the property. Dover knew of Fiber Form's lease before it purchased the property. In fact, the lease was of "supreme importance to its decision to purchase." A trustee's deed was recorded on December 5, 1986.

On December 4, 1986, Dover notified Fiber Form that it had purchased the property. It told Fiber Form to direct future rent payments to Dover's management company. The parties did not enter into a new lease but Fiber Form continued to pay rent per the lease.

On March 9, 1987, Fiber Form and Dover discussed reducing the monthly rental. The discussion was prompted by a downturn in Fiber Form's business. Fiber Form allegedly advised Dover that the foreclosure extinguished the lease and contended that it was operating under a month to month lease. Dover denies that such notice occurred but alleges that Fiber Form requested a one-year delay in the rent increase scheduled to take effect, pursuant to the lease, on May 1, 1987. Dover offered to delay the increase if Fiber Form extended the lease an additional year. This proposal was never accepted.

On June 1, 1987, Fiber Form gave Dover 30 days written notice of its intent to vacate. Fiber Form subsequently vacated the premises and stopped paying rent.

Dover filed suit against Fiber Form for rent and conversion. The trial court determined that the trustee's sale terminated the lease and entered judgment for Fiber Form in the action to recover rent. Costs for attorney's fees in the amount of $7,255.95 were awarded to Fiber Form. This appeal ensued.

* * *

Fiber Form argues that it became a month to month tenant after the trustee's sale because the sale extinguished the lease. Dover, on the other hand, contends that the lease was not terminated but was ratified because Fiber Form continued to pay rent after the trustee's sale. For reasons we shall state, we conclude that the trustee's sale extinguished the lease so that Fiber Form became a month to month tenant, thereby allowing Fiber Form to terminate on 30 days notice.

Title conveyed by a trustee's deed relates back to the date when the deed of trust was executed. (*Bank of America v. Hirsch Merc. Co.* (1944) 64 Cal.App.2d 175, 184, 148 P.2d 110.) The trustee's deed therefore passes the title held by the trustor at the time of execution. (*Hohn v. Riverside County Flood Control etc. Dist.* (1964) 228 Cal.App.2d 605, 612, 39 Cal.Rptr. 647.) Liens which attach after execution of the foreclosed trust deed are extinguished. The purchaser at the trustee sale therefore takes title free of those junior or subordinate liens. * * *

A lease is generally deemed to be subordinate to a deed of trust if the lease was created after the deed of trust was recorded. (*Bank of America v. Hirsch Merc. Co., supra,* 64 Cal.App.2d at p. 184, 148 P.2d 110; Miller & Starr, Cal.Real Estate 2d; § 8:82, p. 422.) On the other hand, "when the lease was executed and recorded prior to the recordation of the deed of trust, or if the beneficiary of the deed of trust had notice of an unrecorded lease at the time the trust deed was recorded, the lien of the trust deed is junior to the estate of the lessee." * * *

A lease may also be deemed subordinate by virtue of a subordination agreement. * * * "Subordination agreements are often used to adjust the priorities between commercial tenants and the mortgagee of the real estate, * * * Absent such an adjustment, priorities will be governed by the recording acts and related common law principles." (Nelson & Whitman, Real Estate Finance Law (2d ed. [Lawyer's Ed.] 1985) § 15.11, p. 1114.)

A lease which is subordinate to the deed of trust is extinguished by the foreclosure sale. * * * A foreclosure proceeding destroys a lease junior to the deed of trust, as well as the lessee's rights and obligations under the lease. (Nelson & Whitman, Real Estate Finance Law (2d ed. [Lawyer's Ed.] 1985) § 15.11, p. 1114.) As stated in section 15.1 of the Restatement Second of Property, "[i]f the sale of the landlord's interest is forced by one having a paramount title to that of the tenant, such as a mortgagee whose interest existed at the time the lease was made, the tenant's interest will be defeated by the sale." (*Id.* at p. 90.)

In this case the lease itself provides that it is subordinate to the deed of trust. Section 21.1 provides, "[t]enant agrees that this Lease shall be subordinate to any mortgages or deeds of trust * * * that may hereafter be placed upon the premises, * * *" Although section 21.1 does give the mortgagee or beneficiary the option to elect "to have this Lease superior to its mortgage or deed of trust * * *," that option was never exercised. Accordingly, it is clear that the lease is subordinate to the deed of trust and was therefore extinguished by the trustee's sale.

* * *

We find no reason to question the continued validity of this rule. The fact that foreclosure terminates a subordinate lease comports with basic notions of priorities and notice. If the trust deed is recorded before the lease is created, then the tenant enters into the lease with notice that the lease will be subordinate. Alternatively, if the tenant and landlord expressly agree that the lease should be subordinate, as is the case here, then the tenant is aware of the possibility that its lease could be extinguished by foreclosure. Indeed, Fiber Form expressly agreed that the lease was subordinate to any trust deeds and therefore it risked having foreclosure terminate the lease. That Fiber Form, rather than Dover, ultimately desired that the lease be terminated upon foreclosure should be of no import.

Dover argues that foreclosure should not automatically terminate the lease but should give the purchaser the option of terminating it. However, if this were the rule, then the purchaser could evict the tenant if rent values increased or hold the tenant to the lease if rent values decreased. In other words, the purchaser could do whatever was most profitable. We decline to allow the purchaser this option. To the contrary, we think it more equitable to follow the rule that the trustee's sale automatically terminates the lease. Of course, even though the lease is extinguished, the tenant and purchaser are not precluded from entering into a new lease agreement.

Finally, we note that the tenant under a subordinate lease can obtain some protection by requiring the landlord to obtain from its lender a nondisturbance agreement in favor of the tenant. Such an agreement provides that the lender with a superior lien will not, "by foreclosure or otherwise, disturb the tenant's possession, as long as the tenant is not then in default under the lease." (Johnson & Moskovitz, Cal.Real Estate Law & Practice, § 153.50, p. 153–94.) In addition, the tenant could bargain with its landlord for the right to cure the landlord's default. (*Ibid.*)

We next consider what Fiber Form's status was once the lease was terminated. Did Fiber Form become a tenant under a new lease agreement? There was evidence that in March 1987 Fiber Form notified Dover that it had been advised by counsel that the foreclosure extinguished the lease and therefore it was operating under a month to month tenancy. In addition, there was evidence that Dover believed the prior lease continued in effect after the foreclosure sale and, as a consequence, Dover did not attempt to obtain a new lease. We conclude that the foregoing constitutes substantial evidence in support of the trial court's conclusion that the parties did not enter into a new lease.

Having determined that no new lease agreement was reached, we conclude that Fiber Form was a month to month tenant. The prior lease was extinguished and a new lease was not entered into. Fiber Form paid rent monthly, with Dover's consent, but there was no agreement reached regarding the term of the hiring. Accordingly, Fiber Form must be deemed a month to month tenant, thereby entitled to terminate upon 30 days notice. (Civ.Code, § 1944; Civ.Code, § 1946; *Linnard v. Sonnenschein* (1928) 94 Cal.App. 729; *Vavuris v. Pinelli* (1957) 147 Cal.App.2d 390, 394, 305 P.2d 149.) Fiber Form gave such notice, vacated the premises and therefore was not obligated to pay any further rental.

* * *

The judgment is affirmed.

NOTES

1.   *Senior vs. subordinate leases.* As the principal case indicates, whether a lease is senior or junior/subordinate to a foreclosing mortgage can have significant consequences for both the lessee and the foreclosure sale purchaser. Moreover, the interplay between lease-mortgage priority and the mortgage

theory followed by the jurisdiction can also sometimes be important outside the context of foreclosure. Consider, in this regard, the following analysis:

LEASES SENIOR TO THE MORTGAGE

A lease that antedates a mortgage, if duly recorded, is prior and superior to the mortgage. In most states this would also be the case even if the lease were not recorded, for normally the lessee is in possession and in most states possession gives all the world notice of the tenant's rights. With respect to these prior leases the following points should be kept in mind:

1.   Such a lease, since it is prior and superior to the mortgage, cannot be extinguished by foreclosure of the mortgage.

2.   If such a lease contains an option to purchase the property, the mortgagee will want the option to be subordinated to the mortgage. Otherwise there is danger that exercise of the option would extinguish the mortgage.

3.   Complete subordination of a prior lease to a subsequent mortgage is legally possible. A subordination agreement signed by the lessee makes his lease junior to the mortgage, subject to extinguishment by foreclosure of the mortgage, just as if the lease had been signed after the recording of the mortgage. Oddly enough subordination of the lease to the mortgage in some respects weakens the mortgagee's position, as is evident from the subsequent discussion.

4.   In title and intermediate states, on default in the mortgage payments, the mortgagee has the right to serve a demand on a senior lessee (one whose lease antedates the mortgage) and the lessee must thereafter pay rent to the mortgagee.[2] The lessee has no right to move out, as is true of junior lessees, as hereinafter explained. This rule stems from the notion in title and intermediate states that the mortgage is a transfer of some sort of title to the mortgagee, a notion previously referred to herein. Because of this mysterious transfer of title, there is created between the lessee and the subsequent mortgagee an equally mysterious link called "privity of estate." It is this privity of estate that makes the lessee liable to a subsequent mortgagee for rents. While it has its benefits, this rule also carries some burdens as we shall subsequently see. This rule, it is evident, has one unusual consequence, namely, it helps the mortgagee collect rent where his mortgage is junior to the lease. Naturally, the tenant has no obligation to pay rent to such mortgagee until the mortgagee serves a demand on the tenant to pay such rent.

---

[2]   Editors' Note: A mortgagee in a title state has a common law right to collect rents as soon as its mortgage becomes effective. The text accompanying this footnote assumes that the mortgagee's right has been modified as described in the Restatement excerpt at the beginning of this chapter.

In lien theory states, the mortgagee ordinarily is not entitled to make such a demand on the tenant. This follows from the fact that in these states a mortgage conveys no title; hence privity of estate is lacking.

LEASES JUNIOR TO THE MORTGAGE

With respect to leases that are junior to the mortgage (e.g., leases made by the mortgagor after the recording of the mortgage) the following rules are applicable:

1. Such a lease can be extinguished by foreclosure of the mortgage.

2. Occasionally a mortgagee will wish to foreclose his mortgage without extinguishing the lease. In some states this is possible and in others not. In states where it is legally impossible to preserve a junior lease when a mortgage is foreclosed, a mortgagee must be wary of placing reliance on such leases.

3. In title and intermediate states, the mortgagee has the right to evict junior leases as soon as default occurs in the mortgage payments.[3] This is also true in lien states where a clause is inserted in the mortgage giving the mortgagee the right to possession on default and the state is one that recognizes the validity of such a provision. Alternatively the mortgagee may serve a demand which gives the tenant a choice as between moving out or paying rent to the mortgagee. However, the mortgagee cannot compel the tenant to remain and pay rent to him. This is so because where the lease is subsequent to the mortgage, there is no privity of estate between the mortgagee and the lessee. For this reason, it is better for the mortgagee to proceed in such a situation under the assignment of rents, for then the tenant must stay and pay rent to the mortgagee.[4]

4. If the mortgagee enters under his mortgage, as stated in paragraph three, and the tenant chooses to remain and pay rent, in many states the result is to terminate the lease and create a month-to-month or year-to-year tenancy. Here again if the mortgagee wishes to preserve the leases it is best for him to proceed under his assignment of rents rather than under the mortgage.

---

[3] Editors' Note: This statement again assumes that the title state mortgagee's common law rights have been modified.

[4] Editors' Note: An assignment of rents is an agreement, separate from the mortgage, that grants a security interest in the rents from mortgaged real estate. "[I]ts most significant purpose is to provide a mortgage lender with the ability to collect rents that accrue from the mortgaged real property between the mortgagor's default and a completed foreclosure." See R. Wilson Freyermuth, Modernizing Security in Rents: The New Uniform Assignment of Rents Act, 71 Mo. L. Rev. 1, 5 (2006). A more complete discussion of this device is provided below under "Security Interests in Rents."

Robert Kratovil, *Mortgages—Problems in Possession, Rents and Mortgagee Liability*, 11 DePaul L. Rev. 1, 8–10 (1961).*

2. *Priority preferences.* As *Dover* illustrates, it is problematic to generalize about the priority preferences of the parties in commercial lease settings. Our first reaction is probably to assume that a tenant normally desires protection against a foreclosure wiping out its lease rights. After all, a tenant often makes a substantial investment in the leasehold and he or she would seem to have a strong interest in ensuring that the investment is fully realized over the complete term of the lease. On the other hand, as *Dover* illustrates, where the tenant's business is precarious or the rent or other lease terms prove to be unduly pro-landlord, the tenant may be only too willing to see the lease and its attendant liabilities destroyed by foreclosure.

The mortgagee's self-interest is also not always readily apparent. In many cases it may prefer senior status for its mortgage because if foreclosure occurs, the foreclosure purchaser often wants to have the option of compelling a renegotiation of leases that it desires to retain. On the other hand, if a prime tenant is bound by a long term lease that is very favorable to the landlord, the last thing the mortgagee desires is for foreclosure to take the tenant "off the hook."

3. *Varying priorities by agreement.* A variety of devices are used to readjust the rights and responsibilities of the mortgagee and lessee in the commercial lease context. Two of these, the *subordination agreement* and the *nondisturbance agreement,* are described in *Dover.*

Subordination is an act by which one having an interest in particular real estate consents to a reduction in priority as against another holding an interest in the same real estate. See Miscione v. Barton Dev. Co., 61 Cal. Rptr. 2d 280, 285 (1997). In the mortgage-lease setting described above, for example, the subordination agreement may provide that "the Lease, the leasehold estate created thereby, together with all rights and privileges of Tenant thereunder, are hereby unconditionally subjected, and made subordinate, to the lien or charge of the Mortgage." Note that usually such a subordination is contained in a separate document executed by the tenant and the mortgagee. However, as in *Dover*, sometimes boilerplate language in the lease accomplishes the same result.

In a *nondisturbance* agreement, a mortgagee holding a senior lien agrees that "in the event of foreclosure, the foreclosure purchaser will permit the lease to continue and allow the tenant to remain on the leased premises so long as the tenant continues to comply with the terms of the lease and is not in default."

The *attornment* is an agreement by which a tenant agrees with the mortgagee that "if the interest of the Landlord under the Lease shall be transferred by reason of foreclosure or deed in lieu thereof, Tenant shall be bound to the Purchaser under all of the terms, covenants and conditions of the

---

* Reprinted with permission of DePaul University and the author.

Lease for the balance of the term thereof with the same force and effect as if the Purchaser were the original landlord under the lease." It may further provide that "Tenant does hereby attorn to Purchaser, including Lender if it be Purchaser, as the landlord under the lease, said attornment to be effective and self-operative without the execution of any further instruments upon Purchaser's succeeding to the interest of the landlord under the Lease."

All three of these devices may be combined, and often are, in a Subordination, Nondisturbance, and Attornment Agreement. This agreement is normally executed by the lessee and mortgagee, but sometimes by the landlord-mortgagor as well. Note carefully the impact of this agreement. First, the lessee specifically subordinates the lease to the mortgage. Next, the mortgagee grants the lessee the protection of a nondisturbance clause so that any foreclosure purchaser agrees to recognize lessee's rights under the lease. Finally, the lessee, by attorning, agrees to be bound under the terms of the lease to any foreclosure purchaser even though, as junior party, a foreclosure would otherwise terminate his or her leasehold obligations.

4. *Junior residential leases and the Great Recession.* The overwhelming increase in foreclosures during the Great Recession caused legislatures to protect junior residential lessees whose leases would otherwise be destroyed by foreclosure of senior mortgages. Consider the following 2013 California statute:

(a) * * * [A] tenant or subtenant in possession of a rental housing unit under a month-to-month lease or periodic tenancy at the time the property is sold in foreclosure shall be given 90 days' written notice to quit pursuant to Section 1162 before the tenant or subtenant may be removed from the property as prescribed in this chapter.

(b) In addition to the rights set forth in subdivision (a), tenants or subtenants holding possession of a rental housing unit under a fixed-term residential lease entered into before transfer of title at the foreclosure sale shall have the right to possession until the end of the lease term, and all rights and obligations under the lease shall survive foreclosure, except that the tenancy may be terminated upon 90 days' written notice to quit pursuant to subdivision (a) if any of the following conditions apply:

(1) The purchaser or successor in interest will occupy the housing unit as a primary residence.

(2) The lessee is the mortgagor or the child, spouse, or parent of the mortgagor.

(3) The lease was not the result of an arms' length transaction.

(4) The lease requires the receipt of rent that is substantially less than fair market rent for the property, except when rent is reduced or subsidized due to a federal, state, or local subsidy or law.

(c)   The purchaser or successor in interest shall bear the burden of proof in establishing that a fixed-term residential lease is not entitled to protection under subdivision (b).

(d)   This section shall not apply if any party to the note remains in the property as a tenant, subtenant, or occupant.

(e)   Nothing in this section is intended to affect any local just cause eviction ordinance. This section does not, and shall not be construed to, affect the authority of a public entity that otherwise exists to regulate or monitor the basis for eviction.

West's Ann. Cal. C.C.P. § 1161b. Similarly, in May 2009 Congress enacted the Protecting Tenants at Foreclosure Act (PTFA) (Pub. L. 111–22, Div. A, Title VII, §§ 702–704, May 20, 2009, 123 Stat. 1660; amended by Pub. L. 111–203, Title XIV, § 1484, July 21, 2010, 124 Stat. 2204). The PTFA provides protections for bona fide tenants of residential real property at foreclosure following the date of its enactment, specifically by giving them the right to remain for the rest of the lease term or, if the foreclosure purchaser intends to occupy the property, then the right to 90-days notice prior to being evicted. (PTFA, §§ 702, 704.). These protections were made permanent in 2018. See Pub. L. 115–174, Title III, § 304, May 24, 2018, 132 Stat. 1339. Importantly, the PTFA sets a national floor for the eviction of tenants of foreclosed properties. To the extent state law conflicts with the PTFA's protections, they are preempted; however, it is permissible for state law to provide greater protections than under the PTFA. For a consideration of the California and Congressional enactments, see Nativi v. Deutsche Bank Nat'l Trust Co., 167 Cal. Rptr. 3d 173 (2014).

Security Interests in Rents

Mortgage lenders frequently view real property as providing two separate and distinct sources of security for the mortgage obligation. They rely not only on the real property itself, but also on the rents it produces. However, in lien theory states, it is important to realize that simply taking a garden-variety mortgage on the debtor's fee simple absolute will not adequately protect the lender with respect to rents and profits. As one federal judge aptly observed, "[i]n such instances, the logic is that the borrower has retained all the incidents of possession, including the right to rents, profits and crops, and these he may do with as he pleases. It is only when the lender takes possession, or does so constructively, as by having a receiver appointed, that he is entitled to the ordinary incidents of possession, like rents, profits and crops." First Fed. Sav. of Arkansas, F.A. v. City Nat'l Bank of Fort Smith, 87 B.R. 565, 566 (W.D.Ark. 1988).

Consequently, commercial mortgagees commonly require mortgage language or collateral agreements by which the mortgagor "assigns" or "mortgages" the rents as additional security for the mortgage loan. In relatively rare situations, such agreements give the mortgagee immediate access to the rents. In these situations, the mortgagee may, from the inception of the loan, actually collect the rents from mortgagor's tenants and apply them to the mortgage indebtedness. More commonly, however, the mortgagee's right of access to the rents is triggered by mortgagor default. See generally Keith D. Haroldson, Perfecting a Security Interest in Future Rents from Mortgaged Real Property, 40 Drake L. Rev. 287 (1991).

Today an assignment of rents agreement is enforceable in every jurisdiction, whether it follows the lien or title theory of mortgage law. This unanimity ends, however, as soon as courts confront the question of when such assignments become effective and at what point the mortgagee acquires the actual right to commence collection of the rents. As to these latter questions, mortgage law theory can sometimes play a significant role, as the following material illustrates. It is also unclear as to whether an assignment of rents agreement in the residential mortgage context would be enforced, considering some courts' rejection of mortgagee-in-possession clauses in residential mortgage contracts.

What recording or filing requirements must be followed with respect to an assignment of rents? Perhaps out of an excess of caution, mortgagees frequently not only record in the real estate records, but attempt to perfect a Uniform Commercial Code security interest in rents as well. This "belt and suspenders" approach stems from a concern that rents may be characterized as "personalty" and that recordation of an assignment in the real estate records will not provide the mortgagee with sufficient protection. In theory, this concern is misplaced. Under Article 9 of the U.C.C., the Code is inapplicable "to the creation or transfer of an interest in or lien on real property, including a lease or rents thereunder." U.C.C. § 9–109(d)(11). Thus, any attempted perfection under the U.C.C. seems both unnecessary and ineffective, although it probably does no harm so long as the assignment is also properly recorded in the real estate records.

IN RE MILLETTE

United States Court of Appeals, Fifth Circuit, 1999
186 F.3d 638

Before JONES and STEWART, CIRCUIT JUDGES, and DUPLANTIER, DISTRICT JUDGE.

EDITH H. JONES, CIRCUIT JUDGE:

* * *

BACKGROUND

Thomas Millette, Ted Millette, William Millette, and Charles Fridge own a commercial building in Pascagoula, Mississippi known as the

"Market Street Building." In August 1992, the owners executed a promissory note in favor of Eastover Bank in the principal amount of $445,198.71. As security for the note, the owners executed a deed of trust in favor of Eastover that contained the following assignment of rents clause:

> As additional security, Debtor hereby assigns to Secured Party all rents accruing on the Property. Debtor shall have the right to collect and retain the rents as long as Debtor is not in default as provided in Paragraph 9. In the event of default, Secured Party in person, by an agent or by a judicially appointed receiver shall be entitled to enter upon, take possession of and manage the Property and collect the rents. All rents so collected shall be applied first to the costs of managing the Property and collecting the rents, including fees for a receiver and an attorney, commissions to rental agents, repairs and other necessary related expenses and then to payment of the indebtedness.

The parties stipulated that the deed of trust securing the Market Street Building was properly recorded in the Jackson County property records. MTGLQ Investment, L.P. subsequently purchased the note and deed of trust from Eastover and retained Security National to service the loan.

In November 1993, O'Neal Steel obtained an Alabama judgment against Thomas, William, and Ted Millette in the amount of $164,335.89 plus interest. O'Neal enrolled the judgment in Jackson County, Mississippi on January 10, 1994. In May 1994, the Millettes, doing business as "Millette & Associates," entered into a commercial lease with Jackson County, which became the sole tenant in the Market Street Building. After discovering that the Millettes owned the building and were receiving rental income from it, O'Neal instituted a garnishment action in the Mississippi Circuit Court and served a writ of garnishment on Jackson County. As required by Mississippi law, the County answered the writ of garnishment, admitting it owed a debt to "Millette & Associates" under the lease. The County further stated that Security National claimed a prior interest in the rents pursuant to the recorded assignment of rents clause contained in the deed of trust.

When Security National learned of the garnishment action on January 4, 1995, it immediately served written notice and demand on Jackson County and ultimately intervened as a party in the garnishment action. Months later, Security National instituted foreclosure proceedings, but before it could complete the foreclosure, Thomas Millette filed for Chapter 7 bankruptcy, staying the foreclosure and all activity in the state court garnishment proceeding. The present adversary proceeding was commenced in bankruptcy court to determine the extent and priority of the competing liens on the rents.

O'Neal argues here * * * that it had a perfected interest in the Market Street Building's rents from the date it served its writ of garnishment on Jackson County. O'Neal contends that its lien has priority over Security National's lien because Security National failed to take the necessary steps to perfect its interest. According to O'Neal, under Mississippi law, a mortgagee must not only record its assignment of rents, but must also take "additional action," like appointing a receiver, to perfect its interest in rents. Therefore, because O'Neal served its writ of garnishment before Security National took the requisite additional action, O'Neal's interest in the rents should be superior.

The bankruptcy court disagreed with O'Neal's construction of Mississippi law and granted summary judgment in favor of Security National, holding that, based upon a then-recent Mississippi Supreme Court decision, Security National had a perfected interest in the rents when it recorded its deed of trust containing the assignment of rents clause. Although the district court disagreed with the bankruptcy court's legal analysis, it reached the same result. It held that an assignment of rents clause is not perfected upon recordation; instead, a mortgagee must take "additional steps" to perfect its interest. According to the district court, Security National's actions upon learning of the garnishment were sufficient to perfect its previously recorded assignment of rents. * * *

DISCUSSION

Whether a Mississippi mortgagee, which has obtained an assignment of rents, is perfected in the rents when the assignment is recorded, or whether it must take additional steps to perfect its interest in the rents, is an issue of first impression both in this court and the courts of Mississippi. This court must anticipate what the Mississippi Supreme Court would decide if the issue were before it. See *Free v. Abbott Labs.*, 176 F.3d 298, 299 (5th Cir.1999); *F.D.I.C. v. Abraham*, 137 F.3d 264, 268 (5th Cir.1998). * * *

O'Neal * * * advocates the older common law approach, which a minority of states continue to follow.[6] Under the older rule, an assignment of rents gives the mortgagee an inchoate lien which is perfected only when the mortgagee takes additional action to enforce it. In Texas, for instance, "an assignment of rentals does not become operative until the mortgagee obtains possession of the property, or impounds the rents, or secures the

---

[6] *See, e.g., Bevins v. Peoples Bank & Trust Co.*, 671 P.2d 875, 879 (Alaska 1983) ("The beneficiary must take some action to acquire possession of the property or the rents before the rent clause becomes operative."); *Martinez v. Continental Enter.*, 730 P.2d 308, 316 (Colo.1986) (en banc) ("[U]ntil the mortgagee takes some effectual step to subject the rents to the payment of the debt, . . . the mortgagee has but an inchoate right to the rents.").

appointment of a receiver, or takes some other similar action." *Taylor v. Brennan*, 621 S.W.2d 592, 594 (Tex.1981).

Several federal courts, while interpreting state law, have also followed the old rule. *See, e.g., In re Century Inv. Fund VIII L.P.*, 937 F.2d 371, 377 (7th Cir.1991) (Wisconsin law); *In re 1301 Conn. Ave. Assocs.*, 126 B.R. 1, 3 (D.D.C.1991) (District of Columbia law); *First Federal Savings and Loan Assoc. of Toledo v. Hunter (In re Sam A. Tisci, Inc.)*, 133 B.R. 857, 859 (N.D.Ohio 1991) (Ohio law); *Condor One, Inc. v. Turtle Creek, Ltd. (In re Turtle Creek, Ltd.)*, 194 B.R. 267, 278 (Bankr.N.D.Ala.1996) (Alabama law); *In re Mews Assocs., L.P.*, 144 B.R. 867, 868–69 (Bankr.W.D.Mo.1992) (Missouri law); *Drummond v. Farm Credit Bank of Spokane (In re Kurth Ranch)*, 110 B.R. 501, 506 (Bankr.D.Mont.1990) (Montana law); *Armstrong v. United States (In re Neideffer)*, 96 B.R. 241, 243 (Bankr.D.N.D.1988) (North Dakota law); *Ziegler v. First Nat'l Bank of Volga (In re Ziegler)*, 65 B.R. 285, 287 (Bankr.D.S.D.1986) (South Dakota law).

The majority of courts and legislatures have abandoned the "additional action" rule in favor of a rule analogous to those governing perfection of secured interest in personal property under the Uniform Commercial Code. Under the modern approach, the recording of a mortgage document containing an assignment of rents "gives the mortgagee rights superior to any subsequent third party who would seek to take a security interest in the leases and rentals pertaining thereto as a type of collateral." *O'Neil v. Carlson*, 135 N.H. 459, 608 A.2d 858, 861 (1992) (quoting *In re Rancourt*, 123 B.R. 143, 147 (Bankr.D.N.H.1991) (quotations omitted)). Several state legislatures have also rejected the old common law rule.[8] * * *

The recently published ALI *Restatement of Mortgages* has also adopted the position that a mortgage on rents is perfected when recorded. See Restatement (Second) of Property—Mortgages § 4.2(b) (1997). Under the Restatement, a mortgage on rents "is effective as against the mortgagor and, subject to the operation of the recording act, as against third parties, upon execution and delivery." *Id.* The Restatement's comments make it clear that, upon recordation, the mortgagee will be protected against competing claims by third parties and others claiming priority over the rents. *See id.* at § 4.2 cmt. b.

Public policy considerations weigh in favor of rejecting the old rule. The modern rule best protects diligent mortgagees from competing liens filed by subsequent creditors. Under the prior approach, a mortgagee with a lien on rents or an assignment of rents clause will nearly always lose a priority battle with a judgment creditor when the debtor has not defaulted

---

[8] *See, e.g.,* Cal. Civ.Code § 2938(a) (West 1993); Del.Code Ann. tit. 25, § 2121(a) (Supp.1998); Kan. Stat. Ann. § 58–2343(b) (1994); Md.Code Ann., Real Prop. § 3–204 (1996); Neb.Rev.Stat. § 52–1704 (1998); N.C. Gen.Stat. § 47–20(c) (Supp.1998); Tenn.Code Ann. § 66–26–116(a) (1993); Va.Code Ann. § 55–220.1 (Michie 1995); Wash. Rev.Code Ann. § 7.28.230(3) (West 1992).

on its payments under a mortgage. A judgment creditor can perfect its interest at any time by properly serving a writ of garnishment, while a mortgagee is prohibited from taking the requisite "additional action" to perfect until the debtor has defaulted. This leads to a bizarre result: A mortgagee, which has done all it could to secure its interest in the rents, loses priority to a judgment creditor who had constructive knowledge by the recordation of the mortgagee's assignment of rents. The case at hand illustrates this result.

Security National was unaware of O'Neal's judgment against the Millettes until after the writ of garnishment had already been served. Once Security National learned of the garnishment, it immediately served notice of its interest and intervened in the garnishment action. Before O'Neal served the writ of garnishment, the Millettes were not in default on the lease, and Security National had no justification for "further action" to perfect its assignment of rents. In spite of Security National's post-garnishment diligence, its interest would be subordinate to O'Neal's under the old common law rule.

Recognizing the inequity resulting from the application of the old rule, courts that continue to apply it have occasionally escaped its harsh result by liberally finding "additional action" of a mortgagee that sufficiently satisfied the rule. *See, e.g., In re Keller,* 150 B.R. 835, 839 (Bankr.N.D.Ga.1993) (holding that a mortgagee perfected its right to rents upon filing of a motion for relief from the automatic stay); *In re Mariner Enterprises of Panama City, Inc.,* 131 B.R. 190, 193 (Bankr.N.D.Fla.1989) (holding that a mortgagee's demand that the borrower turn over the rents is sufficient); *In re McCann,* 140 B.R. 926, 928–29 (Bankr.D.Mass.1992) (holding that filing a state foreclosure action is sufficient). The district court's opinion in this case typifies the approach. The court held that, although Security National was not perfected at the time O'Neal served its writ of garnishment, it soon became perfected by taking immediate steps to protect its interest in the rents.

Courts also avoid the old rule when it appears that, instead of receiving an inchoate lien on rents, the mortgagee received an "absolute assignment" of the rents. An absolute assignment passes title to the rents instead of granting a security interest and "operates to transfer the right to rentals automatically upon the happening of a specified condition, such as default." *Taylor,* 621 S.W.2d at 594. To be absolute, however, there must be "especially clear evidence that the parties intended to create such an assignment." *F.D.I.C. v. International Property Management, Inc.,* 929 F.2d 1033, 1036 (5th Cir.1991); *see also In re Century Investment Fund VIII L.P.,* 937 F.2d 371, 377 (7th Cir.1991) (Wisconsin law). Words such as "security" or "pledge" in the loan documents are insufficient to effect an absolute assignment. *FDIC,* 929 F.2d at 1036.

Because the perfection-upon-recordation rule for a mortgagee's security interests in rents is consistent with modern secured transaction law and unencumbered by the complexities, distinctions, and harsh results of the common law, we conclude that the Mississippi Supreme Court would reject the old rule and reward a diligent creditor, which records its assignment of rents and protects its lien by giving constructive notice to hypothetical third-parties. *See Mills v. Damson Oil Corp.*, 720 F.2d 874, 875 (5th Cir.1983) (recognizing that a recorded deed in Mississippi, even if defective, gives constructive notice of the deed's contents); *McMahon v. McMahon*, 247 Miss. 822, 157 So.2d 494, 500–01 (1963) (same).

* * *

CONCLUSION

Security National's interest in the rents was perfected when it recorded its deed of trust containing the assignment of rents clause. Accordingly, that interest primes the later garnishment lien asserted by O'Neal against the rents.

The judgments of the district and bankruptcy courts are, for the foregoing reasons, AFFIRMED.

NOTES

1. *State approaches to assignments.* As we noted earlier, every jurisdiction holds that rent assignments are valid and enforceable. However, this unanimity gives one cold comfort. The problem is that courts approach assignments in a variety of ways and are often hopelessly confused. To say that judicial and legislative treatment of assignments of rents lacks both uniformity and precision is a vast understatement. In trying to make sense of this bewildering situation, we need first to identify three crucial focal points in the creation and enforcement of a rents assignment. First, we need to ask ourselves when the assignment becomes *effective* between the mortgagor and mortgagee. In other words, when is a valid lien created as between those two parties? Second, we must determine when this lien becomes effective (*"perfected"*) against others who acquire interests in the real estate or its rents. This is the issue confronted by the *Millette* court. Third, we must identify when the mortgagee has the right to *collect* (to realize on or foreclose upon) the rents and profits. Unfortunately, while a growing number of courts and legislatures focus carefully on these three crucial issues, too many continue either to confuse or conflate them.

Some jurisdictions, as noted by *Millette*, claim to recognize the validity of so-called "absolute assignments" in situations where the language of the assignment is sufficiently sweeping. In such an assignment the mortgagee obtains a present title to the rents even though the assignment itself postpones the right to collect until mortgagor defaults. As one federal court stressed in interpreting New Jersey law:

An absolute assignment transfers title to the assignee upon its execution. * * * An assignment is absolute if its language demonstrates an intent to transfer immediately the assignor's right and title to the rents. * * * The instant assignment was quintessentially absolute, because it was a total assignment in *per verba de praesenti*: Jason Realty "hereby grants, transfers and assigns to the assignee the entire lessor's interest in and to those certain leases ... Together with all rents." * * * This exchange inescapably and unambiguously expressed an agreement to assign present title.

* * *

We are not moved by the fact that the assignment was part of a financing transaction and served as additional security for repayment of the note. An assignment clause within a mortgage may be independent of the mortgage security. * * * Moreover, we are impressed that the instant assignment was contained in an agreement separate from the mortgage.

In re Jason Realty, L.P., 59 F.3d 423, 427–28 (3d Cir. 1995). For similar reasoning, see, e.g., First Fed. Sav. of Arkansas, F.A. v. City Nat'l Bank of Fort Smith, 87 B.R. 565 (W.D. Ark. 1988); 801 Nolana, Inc. v. RTC Mortg. Trust 1994–S6, 944 S.W.2d 751 (Tex. App. 1997) ("An absolute assignment * * * operates to transfer the right to rents automatically upon the happening of a specified condition, such as default. It is a *pro tanto* payment of the obligation."). This approach supposedly requires no further affirmative action on the mortgagee's part either to perfect its interest or to commence collection.

A growing number of courts, however, have rejected the "absolute assignment" theory. Indeed, as one court aptly observed:

> To borrow a concept from tort law, but for the loan transaction, the Debtors would not have assigned rents to the Bank. No independent consideration was given for the assignments. The fact that the assignments are conditioned upon default and will terminate upon satisfaction of the debt indicates that they are merely additional security for the loan, and not an absolute transfer of the Debtor's interest in the rents to the Bank.

In re Lyons, 193 B.R. 637 (Bankr. D. Mass. 1996). Accord: In re S. Side House, LLC, 474 B.R. 391 (Bankr. E.D.N.Y. 2012) ("the majority of New York state cases are of the view that an absolute assignment is not permitted, regardless of the language in the agreement."); In re Cavros, 262 B.R. 206 (Bankr. D. Conn. 2001). In any event, many courts that purport to recognize "absolute assignments" start with a presumption an assignment of rents creates only a pledge of rents or a security interest in rents. See, e.g., In re 5877 Poplar, L.P., 268 B.R. 140 (Bankr. W.D. Tenn. 2001).

Opposite the states that allow absolute assignments are those (which are significant in number) that represent what is often referred to as the

"American common law" view, which was rejected by the *Millette* court. Under this view, according to one Colorado court:

> [A]ssignments of rents do not convey title to real property, but merely create liens against the property. Until a mortgagor defaults and a lender takes some "effectual step" subjecting the assigned rents toward the payment of the debt, for example, by gaining rightful possession of the property or by filing a foreclosure action, the lender has only an inchoate right to the rents. This is so even if the terms in a deed of trust grant the lender the right to receive rents in the event of default. * * *

Galleria Towers, Inc. v. Crump Warren & Sommer, Inc., 831 P.2d 908, 911 (Colo. App. 1991). Under the analysis of many of these "American common law" decisions, none of the three crucial steps we outlined in the first paragraph of this Note is regarded as satisfied until step three (the requisite "affirmative action") is accomplished by the mortgagee. For criticism of this approach, see In re Baltic Assocs., L.P., 170 B.R. 568 (E.D. Pa. 1994) (the foregoing view "confuses the issues of *perfection* of a security interest and *enforcement* of a security interest.").

Note also that the affirmative action required by this latter approach can sometimes be nominal. For example, some courts have held that a refused demand for possession or simply filing a request for a receivership (as opposed to obtaining its appointment) suffices. See Matter of Century Investment Fund VIII Ltd. Partn., 937 F.2d 371 (7th Cir. 1991); Long Island Bond & Mortg. Guarantee Co. v. Brown, 171 Misc. 15, 11 N.Y.S.2d 793 (1939); In re Flower City Nursing Home, Inc., 38 B.R. 642 (Bankr. W.D.N.Y. 1984). Sometimes it is enough that the mortgagee notify the mortgagor of default and demand payment of the rents. See, e.g., In re Fluge, 57 B.R. 451 (Bankr. D.N.D. 1985).

Between the foregoing extreme approaches, most states occupy a broad "middle ground" with respect to rent assignments. While there is great variety in this approach, most decisions and statutes focus on the three steps we outlined above. In general these jurisdictions hold that an assignment of rents is effective between the original parties upon execution and is perfected against third parties upon recording, but the right to commence collection (enforcement) requires subsequent affirmative action, albeit often relatively nominal, by the mortgagee. The Florida statute exemplifies this approach:

> (2) If such an assignment is made, the mortgagee shall hold a lien on the rents, and the lien created by the assignment shall be perfected and effective against third parties upon recordation of the [assignment].

> (3) Unless otherwise agreed to in writing by the mortgagee and mortgagor, the assignment of rents shall be enforceable upon the mortgagor's default and written demand for the rents made by the mortgagee to the mortgagor, whereupon the mortgagor shall turn

over all rents in the possession of the mortgagor at the time of the written demand or collected thereafter.

Fla.Stat. § 697.07(2),(3); Ginsberg v. Lennar Florida Holdings, Inc., 645 So.2d 490 (Fla. App. 1994) ("According to the statute an assignment of rents creates a lien on the rents in favor of the mortgagee, and the mortgagee will have the right to foreclose that lien and collect the rents without the necessity of foreclosing on the underlying mortgage."). See In re Bethesda Air Rights Ltd. Partn., 117 B.R. 202 (Bankr. D. Md. 1990); New York Life Ins. Co. v. Bremer Towers, 714 F.Supp. 414 (D. Minn. 1989) (in construing Minn. Stat. Ann. § 559.17); In re Fluge, 57 B.R. 451 (Bankr. N.D. 1985) ("Under applicable North Dakota case law, an assignment of rents clause may be enforced apart from the security in the property itself and in advance of foreclosure by affording either the lessee or mortgagor/lessor notification of an intention to invoke the assignment of rents clause."); In re McCutchen, 115 B.R. 126 (Bankr. W.D. Tenn. 1990) (foregoing statute "makes it clear that the perfected secured creditor is not entitled to the possession of the rents until a proper notice is received by the lessee, directing the lessee to pay the assignee.").

Note, however, that in some of these "middle ground" jurisdictions the affirmative action requirements that must be satisfied by the mortgagee to commence collection of the rents can be more substantial. See, e.g., 641 Avenue of the Americas Ltd. Partn. v. 641 Assocs., Ltd., 189 B.R. 583 (S.D.N.Y. 1995) ("a security interest in rents is perfected upon recordation;" however, "[it] becomes enforceable when the assignee takes affirmative steps to assert his rights, such as appointing a receiver to collect the rents, taking possession of the property, commencing foreclosure proceedings, or seeking an order for sequestration of the rents"); In re Park at Dash Point L.P., 121 B.R. 850 (Bankr. W.D. Wash. 1990) (In Washington, "assignments of rents are perfected by recording, and the mortgagee obtains the right to collect rents only after enforcing its security interest, which may be accomplished either by obtaining possession of the real property, or by the appointment of a receiver.").

2. *Restatement approach.* Now having a view of the variety and confusion in the case law on this matter, consider the Restatement approach to taking a security interest in rents:

§ 4.2   Mortgaging Rents

* * *

(b) A mortgage may be given on the rents of real property. Such a mortgage may be included in a mortgage on the real property or may be a separate instrument. The mortgage is effective as against the mortgagor and, subject to the operation of the recording act, as against third parties, upon execution and delivery.

(c) The mortgage may provide that the mortgagee may commence collection of the rents at any time or, in any event, upon mortgagor default. The mortgagee's right to actual possession of the rents arises upon:

(1)   satisfaction of any conditions in the mortgage; and

(2)   delivery of a demand for the rents to the mortgagor, the holder of the equity of redemption, and each person who holds a mortgage on the real property or on its rents of which the mortgagee has notice.

(d)   The delivery referred to in Subsection (c) is effective upon receipt and may be accomplished by personal service, the United States Mail, or any other means reasonably calculated to afford an addressee actual notice of the demand.

Restatement (Third) of Property (Mortgages) § 4.2 (1997).* Where does the Restatement fit with respect to the approaches to assignments outlined above? Is it significant that the Restatement uses the term "mortgages" rather than "assigns?" What type of "affirmative action" is required to commence collection of the rents?

COLEMAN V. HOFFMAN

Court of Appeals of Washington, 2003
115 Wash.App. 853, 64 P.3d 65

BRIDGEWATER, J.

* * *

In July 1997, Roberta Coleman lived with her six-month-old daughter, Makaliah Paige, at the Sound View II apartment complex in Pierce County. On July 4, as Coleman prepared food for the evening's celebration, an unrelated child named Paris, age 9 years, walked Makaliah in a stroller along the balcony. The offending balcony was located outside of Coleman's apartment and was thus part of a common area. As Paris pushed Makaliah, the stroller's wheel caught in a rotten portion of carpet, causing the stroller to lurch forward into the balcony's rotten railing. Makaliah fell through the broken railing and onto the ground one story below. She sustained a broken arm, fractured skull and other injuries.

OCI brokers secured real estate investments. In late 1996, OCI arranged a loan to David Brown and Steve Clem, who owned and were refinancing Sound View II. The loan was secured by a deed of trust, of which OCI was beneficiary, which carried a standard assignment of rents provision. Anderson Hunter, a law firm, funded the loan.

In early April, after Brown and Clem's default, Anderson Hunter commenced judicial foreclosure proceedings and directed that OCI begin collecting and forwarding rents (OCI remained as beneficiary under the deed of trust). To comply, OCI instructed Sound View II tenants to begin

---

*   © 1997 by The American Law Institute. Reprinted with permission.

making payments to OCI rather than Brown and Clem. And, to protect its investment, Anderson Hunter began paying utility and repair costs.

Sometime before Makaliah's injury, although disputed, Anderson Hunter hired Craig Hoffman to make repairs and manage the apartment complex. Hoffman previously tried to purchase the complex from Brown and Clem, but the transaction never closed. When Anderson Hunter hired Hoffman, which apparently occurred after the failed transaction, Hoffman expected to purchase the complex at the foreclosure sale.

On July 22, 1997, deciding against judicial foreclosure, Anderson Hunter sent a notice of default and of trustee's sale to Brown and Clem. The sale occurred on October 31, 1997. Hoffman was the purchaser.

Coleman, individually and as parent and guardian of Paige, sued Anderson Hunter, Hoffman, and OCI. She alleged several causes of action, including a common law premises liability claim. The trial court granted the defendants' summary judgment motions on all claims. * * *

Coleman appeals only the summary dismissal of her common law premises liability claim. Her theory is that the various respondents were mortgagees in possession and therefore can be held liable for the condition of the premises.

In an action for negligence, a plaintiff must prove four basic elements: (1) the existence of a duty, (2) breach of that duty, (3) resulting injury, and (4) proximate cause. Tincani v. Inland Empire Zoological Soc'y, 124 Wash.2d 121, 127–28, 875 P.2d 621 (1994). The threshold determination of whether a duty exists is a question of law. * * *

Although no Washington case is directly on point, other jurisdictions impose a duty of care on mortgagees in possession. See Mollino v. Ogden & Clarkson Corp., 243 N.Y. 450, 154 N.E. 307 (1926). Various treatises also support mortgagee liability:

"A mortgagee who properly acquires 'mortgagee in possession' status is held accountable for that possession . . . to third parties. In general, the mortgagee in possession is held to the standard of the provident owner to use reasonable diligence to keep the property . . . in a good state of repair." RESTATEMENT OF PROPERTY (THIRD), MORTGAGES, § 4.1, at 189 (1997).

In order for a mortgagee to be responsible for damages to third parties caused by unsafe conditions on the property, the mortgagee must exercise dominion and control over the property; a mortgagee out of possession of the mortgaged premises, with no management or control, is not liable for defects therein. Constructive possession is not sufficient to constitute control. 62 AM.JUR.2D Premises Liability, § 8, 356 (1990). * * *

"A possessor of land is (a) a person who is in occupation of the land with intent to control it or (b) a person who has been in occupation of land with intent to control it, if no other person has subsequently occupied it with intent to control it, or (c) a person who is entitled to immediate occupation of the land, if no other person is in possession under Clauses (a) and (b)." Ingersoll v. DeBartolo, Inc., 123 Wash.2d 649, 655, 869 P.2d 1014 (1994) (citing Restatement (Second) of Torts § 328E (1965)).

A.   Anderson Hunter

By its affidavits, Anderson Hunter established that it collected rents from the tenants after Brown and Clem's default. Clise v. Burns involved a trustee who, under a deed of trust, received rents, issues, and profits from mortgaged property. Clise v. Burns, 175 Wash. 133, 26 P.2d 627 (1933). The *Clise* court stated that the trustee's actions did not constitute possession and control for mortgagee in possession purposes. Clise, 175 Wash. at 136–37, 29 P.2d 1119.

However, Coleman produced two relevant letters and the deposition testimony of an Anderson Hunter attorney that, together, weigh heavily in our analysis. First, a May 24, 1999 letter prepared by Paul Carpenter, a member of the Anderson Hunter firm and Hoffman's attorney, states, "at the time of the alleged accident (7/4/97) we, together with [OCI], had, for all practical purposes taken over control of [the premises] in that we could not locate and/or communicate with [Brown and Clem]." (Emphasis added). * * * Although conclusory as to control, the letter is in the nature of an admission by Anderson Hunter and therefore factors into our analysis. Second, an October 1997 letter from OCI's senior vice-president to Carpenter states "that Craig Hoffman had been heading the 'facelift' since last April and Anderson Hunter pool was advancing funds to him for that purpose." * * * Finally, Carpenter indicated at his deposition that Anderson Hunter began paying utility bills on June 11 and paid repair costs to a plumbing company in May or June 1997.

B.   Hoffman

In his affidavit, Hoffman stated that he did not own the premises until November 1997, that he did not make any repairs or collect rents at the premises until August 1997, and that he did not fire the apartment manager until September 1997.

But Coleman produced several other documents that bear on our analysis of Hoffman's possession. First, the October 1997 letter stated that Hoffman had been making repairs since April 1997, which was before the accident. Second, in her declaration in opposition to summary judgment, Coleman states that, in May or June 1997, "Mr. Hoffman and Billy began tearing up the floorboard in front of my apartment. The work lasted for about two days. By the time they ended, the sinkhole was repaired[.]" * * * Third, in his deposition, Carpenter stated that "[m]y recollection is Craig

Hoffman terminated [the apartment manager's] service." * * * Although the record does not reflect the specific date of termination, the line of questioning at the deposition indicates that Hoffman fired the manager sometime in May, June, or July 1997.

C. OCI

OCI carried its burden of establishing the absence of an issue of material fact regarding its possession. In its summary judgment motion, OCI stated that it has never had an ownership interest in the premises; that it had no involvement in the repair, maintenance, control, or operation of the premises; and that, in servicing Anderson Hunter's loan to Brown and Clem, it activated the assignment of rents provision contained in the deed of trust and collected those rents during May, June, and July 1997. Coleman establishes no other issue of fact as to OCI's possession.

The mortgagee possession issue was addressed in two cases from other jurisdictions that involved facts similar to those presented here. Scott v. Hoboken Bank for Sav. in City of Hoboken, 126 N.J.L. 294, 19 A.2d 327 (1941), was a premises liability case where the plaintiff sued the mortgagee bank for injuries received in a fall on an ill-maintained stairway. The court stated that the bank "had in fact assumed complete control over the premises not alone as to the collection of rents and payment of bills but also as to the making of repairs . . . and . . . the owner, in the position of a rent paying tenant, had no control." 19 A.2d at 330.

Scott aligns perfectly with Pantano v. Erie County Sav. Bank of Buffalo, 257 A.D. 451, 13 N.Y.S.2d 932 (N.Y.App.Div.1939), which was also a personal injury suit against a mortgagee bank. In *Pantano*, the bank had "the exclusive right to lease the property, to bring, prosecute and settle summary proceedings for the removal of tenants, or actions at law for the recovery of rents or of any damage done [to the] premises or for the abatement of any nuisance thereon, [and] to make necessary repairs and alterations to the building." Pantano, 13 N.Y.S.2d at 934. The court allowed suit against the bank, holding that the bank possessed and controlled the premises. Pantano, 13 N.Y.S.2d at 934.

In an apartment building, factors indicating a mortgagee's possession include the indicia of control that landlords normally exhibit. *Scott* and *Pantano* demonstrate certain such factors: leasing, making repairs, and paying bills. Additional factors could include making management decisions and receiving and responding to tenant complaints.

Hoffman performed two acts that show possession and control: he made repairs and a managerial decision. Similarly, Anderson Hunter performed acts indicating possession and control: it paid utility bills and repair costs, collected rents, and hired Hoffman. But the facts show that OCI only collected rents; under *Clise*, this action alone does not establish possession and control. Thus, as to Hoffman and Anderson Hunter,

Coleman carried her burden in establishing genuine issues of fact regarding possession of the Sound View II. On her claim against OCI, Coleman has failed to establish an issue of fact. Therefore, the trial court erred in granting summary judgment in favor of Hoffman and Anderson Hunter, but it did not err in granting summary judgment to OCI.

* * *

The trial court's order of summary judgment on Coleman's common law premises liability claim is reversed as to Hoffman and Anderson Hunter but affirmed as to OCI.

We concur: HOUGHTON, P.J., and ARMSTRONG, J.

NOTES

1. *Does enforcing an assignment of rents create "mortgagee in possession" status?* Mortgagees are often concerned that they will become a "mortgagee in possession" simply because they enforce an assignment of rents provision. Under the Restatement, "the mere collection of rents pursuant to [an assignment of rents] does not constitute the mortgagee a 'mortgage in possession' with the duties and liabilities attendant to that status." Restatement (Third) of Property (Mortgages) § 4.2, comment c (1997). California takes the same position. See West's Ann. Cal. Civ. Code § 2938(e)(1). Accord: In re Olick, 221 B.R. 146 (Bankr. E.D. Pa.1998). But see United Nat'l Bank v. Parish, 750 A.2d 238 (1999) (assuming that mortgagee who collected rents pursuant to a rental assignment was a mortgagee in possession and therefore liable to pay real estate taxes during the period it collected rents). Consider the language of a recent Supreme Court of New Hampshire decision:

> Whether a mortgagee has exercised dominion and control over the property and, thus, possessed it, "is a factual issue." * * * For instance, collection of rent alone by a mortgagee may not render the mortgagee a mortgagee in possession; however, the collection of rent and active management of the real estate "will probably suffice." "In an apartment building, factors indicating a mortgagee's possession include the indicia of control that landlords normally exhibit," such as "leasing, making repairs, and paying bills." *Coleman v. Hoffman,* 115 Wash.App. 853, 64 P.3d 65, 69 (2003). "Additional factors could include making management decisions and receiving and responding to tenant complaints." *Id.;* see *Citizens' Savings & Trust Co. v. Rogers,* 162 Wis. 216, 155 N.W. 155, 159–60 (1915) (Mortgagee who "employed janitors, provided fuel and elevator service, and . . . collected rents from the tenants of the buildings" exercised "the dominion and control over the property that is usually . . . exercised by a landlord," and was mortgagee in possession.).

Case v. St. Mary's Bank, 63 A.3d 1209, 1215 (2013).

Coleman illustrates a major problem with enforcing an assignment of rents clause. If the mortgagee actually collects the rents, won't tenants invariably hold the mortgagee accountable for repairs and other management problems concerning the real estate? If the mortgagee responds to tenant concerns by making repairs or the like, then won't the mortgagee be treated as a mortgagee in possession? You should revisit these questions after we consider the receivership remedy in the next section.

2. *The Uniform Assignment of Rents Act.* There have been concentrated efforts to deal with the uncertainty around assignment of rents law. In 2005 the National Conference of Commissioners on Uniform State Laws promulgated the Uniform Assignment of Rents Act (UARA). Professor Freyermuth, its reporter, describes UARA as follows:

(UARA) * * * provides a comprehensive framework to govern the creation, perfection, and enforcement of security interests in rents arising from mortgaged real property. Without such a comprehensive statutory framework, courts (particularly bankruptcy courts) have struggled to establish clear and consistent rules governing security interests in rents—thereby encouraging needless and wasteful litigation over control of rents arising from mortgaged real property. Enactment of UARA in each state will provide much-needed clarity by establishing the following rules:

- In many states, statutes provide few (if any) standards to inform a court's exercise of discretion whether to appoint a receiver to collect rents from mortgaged real property. UARA establishes consistent standards to govern the appointment of a receiver for mortgaged real property. UARA § 7(a). In particular, UARA establishes the enforceability of a clause by which the assignor has agreed that the assignee can obtain the appointment of a receiver after the assignor's default. UARA § 7(a)(1)(A).

- Upon default by the assignor (or as otherwise agreed by the assignor), the assignee may collect all rents that have accrued but remain unpaid and all rents that accrue thereafter. UARA § 6(b). By its terms, UARA does not allow the assignee to require the assignor to turn over sums already collected from its tenants prior to enforcement by the assignee. * * *

- The assignee may enforce an assignment of rents by obtaining the appointment of a receiver, by notification to the assignor, by notification to the assignor's tenants, or by any other method permitted by other law. UARA provides specific rules governing the collection of rents by receivership, by notification to the assignor, and by notification to tenants. UARA also provides that an assignee could collect rents by any other method permitted by law (including by becoming a mortgagee-in-possession). UARA §§ 6(a), 7, 8, 9.

- The assignee's enforcement of its rights and remedies under UARA does not render the assignee as a "mortgagee in possession" or trigger other adverse statutory consequences. * * *

- An assignor that collects rents after it receives notification that the assignee has enforced its security interest in rents must turn over to the assignee the rents collected; if the assignor fails to do so, it is liable to the assignee for the amount not turned over. At common law, an assignor that refused to turn over rents to the assignee despite proper demand by the assignee could be held liable for "waste" (or conversion) of rents. The amount of such liability, however, varied depending upon whether the jurisdiction followed the lien theory of mortgages (damages recoverable only to the extent assignee was harmed) or the title theory of mortgages (damages measured by amount of rents collected and not turned over). * * *

- Most tenants that receive notification to make rent payments to the assignee cannot thereafter discharge their rental obligation by paying the assignor. Under the common law of contracts, the obligor can discharge its obligation by payment to the obligee until the obligor receives notification that the obligee has assigned the right to payment and the assignee directs the obligor to make payment to the assignee. UARA primarily tracks existing common law, providing that a tenant that receives notification to pay the assignee can only discharge its obligation by paying the assignee. UARA § 9(c)(1)–(2). UARA does provide an exception for a tenant that occupies the premises as its primary residence, permitting such a tenant to satisfy its rental obligation by payment to either the assignee or the assignor. UARA § 9(c)(2).

R. Wilson Freyermuth, Modernizing Security in Rents: The New Uniform Assignment of Rents Act, 71 Mo.L.Rev. 1, Appendix (2006).* To what extent is UARA similar to the Restatement? To date, five states, (Nevada, New Mexico, North Dakota, Texas and Utah) have adopted UARA.

3.   *Bankruptcy.* Assignment of rents issues become especially important when the mortgagor seeks the protection of the Bankruptcy Code. When this occurs, the rents mortgagee and the trustee (or the debtor-in-possession) will each claim priority as to rents collected during the bankruptcy proceeding. State law will often be determinative of that controversy. Thus, we will

---

*   Reprinted with permission of the Missouri Law Review.

consider rent assignments again in the bankruptcy context. See Chapter Six, Section J infra.

C. RECEIVERSHIPS

A mortgagee considering foreclosure may prefer an equitable receivership rather than attempting to obtain possession as mortgagee or direct collection of rents under an assignment of rents provision. While the scope of a receivership varies by state, it typically involves the court appointing a third party to take possession of the mortgaged property, to repair or preserve the property, and to collect rents.

As explained in the previous section, a mortgagee in a title theory state could obtain possession by an action at law for ejectment, but such an action is often drawn out and time-consuming. By comparison, a receiver may be appointed promptly incident to a foreclosure suit. Moreover, by using a receivership, a mortgagee avoids some of the strict accounting responsibilities associated with being a mortgagee in possession. Robert Kratovil, Mortgages—Problems in Possession, Rents, and Mortgagee Liability, 11 DePaul L.Rev. 1, 7 (1961). Also, "entry by a mortgagee may automatically terminate leases executed by the mortgagor [if they are subordinate to the mortgage], and if these leases are favorable to the landlord, such a course is to be avoided. Appointment of a receiver will ordinarily not have such a result." Id. Finally, the receivership generally will insulate a mortgagee from tort and related landowner-type liabilities normally imposed on mortgagees in possession. See Nelson, Whitman, Burkhart & Freyermuth, Real Estate Finance Law § 4.33 (6th ed.2015); Trustco Bank, N.A. v. Eakin, 256 A.D.2d 778, 681 N.Y.S.2d 410 (1998) (mortgagee not liable for damage to mortgaged property allegedly resulting from receiver's failure to secure premises due to lack of receivership funds). In lien theory states, the receivership may be an even more important remedy to the mortgagee because of the unavailability of ejectment to obtain possession for the mortgagee.

A receivership may also sometimes be preferable to reliance on enforcement of an assignment of rents provision. What if there are now no tenants paying rents? It may well be that such an assignment provision is of no practical remedy to the mortgagee. By contrast, a receiver can take possession and attempt to re-establish a cash flow from the mortgaged premises by entering into new tenant leases (with court approval). The following materials highlight some of the important issues involved in receiverships, beginning with the standards for appointment of a receiver (i.e., what evidentiary showing must the mortgagee make to obtain the appointment of a receiver?).

DART V. WESTERN SAVINGS & LOAN ASSOCIATION
Supreme Court of Arizona, 1968
103 Ariz. 170, 438 P.2d 407

STRUCKMEYER, JUSTICE. These two appeals, consolidated for this decision only, arise out of an action to foreclose a mortgage on a trailer park. Dart and his wife, together with Inland Western Mortgage Company, second mortgagee, were sued by Western Savings and Loan Association to foreclose a first mortgage. Western also sought the appointment of a receiver. Inland cross-claimed to foreclose its second mortgage and to foreclose a first mortgage on the Darts' home. It also sought a receiver.

William J. Dart, in answer to the complaint for foreclosure by Western, asserted that he was the beneficiary of a trust whose res was the subject matter of the foreclosure suit and he cross-claimed against Union Title Company, as trustee, alleging conversion of trust moneys (income from the trailer park deposited in escrow) so that the trust res was jeopardized. Union answered the cross-claim, admitting that it had converted trust moneys and stated there was an arrearage of $18,500 on the first mortgage. It further alleged that the Darts had, in March, 1964, unlawfully assumed the management and control of the trust estate. Union also urged the appointment of a receiver.

At the time of the hearing on the application by Western for a receiver, the property was of the estimated value between $500,000 and $800,000, and $244,478.69 was owed on the first mortgage and $55,000 on the second mortgage. A federal tax lien had been placed against the property in the approximate amount of $187,000. It is conceded, however, that this tax lien is junior to both mortgages. Real and personal property taxes are accruing against the trailer park at the rate of $1700 a year and interest on the first mortgage is accruing at the rate of $1600 a month.

William J. Dart, the residuary beneficiary of the trust, and his wife Dorothy entered into possession of the real property after it became known that Union had embezzled the trailer park income. Thereafter, they collected rentals at the rate of approximately $5,000 a month. Although some of the income was used by the Darts to improve the trailer court, none was applied to meet the payments due on either the first or second mortgages.

The Inland mortgage provides for an assignment of rents and profits as security for the mortgage. In addition, both mortgages provide that if an action to foreclose is brought, a receiver "shall be appointed" to take charge of the property and to receive and collect rents, issues and profits and apply them to the payment of the mortgages, taxes and other charges. The court, acting upon the above stated facts, did appoint receivers, first at the instigation of Western and later at the instigation of Inland. The appeals question the propriety of the trial court's actions in that respect.

It is clear that the appointments of the receivers were improvident.

A.R.S. § 33–703, subsec. A provides:

> "A mortgage is a lien upon everything that would pass by a grant of the property, but does not entitle the mortgagee to possession of the property unless authorized by the express terms of the mortgage. . . ."

Of this section, we have said:

> "The title to mortgaged property under our law remains in the mortgagor. The mortgagee's interest is that of a lienor." Mortgage Investment Co. of El Paso, Tex. v. Taylor, 49 Ariz. 558, 563, 68 P.2d 340, 342.

The principle applicable here has been discussed in 2 Glenn on Mortgages, § 173:

> "The mortgagee's equitable right to have a receiver, therefore, arises only when he shows something more than a default; . . . . Such, at least, is the prevailing rule with which we are now dealing; and so it remains to ask what is the 'something more' that is required.
>
> "The first point on which all are agreed, is that there should be no receivership if the security is adequate and no waste is threatened which is apt to impair the mortgagee's safety."

The reason for the rule that a mortgagee is not entitled to a receiver if the security is adequate and no waste is threatened is that, the mortgage being but a lien, the mortgagor is entitled to possession and to all the benefits, such as the income, which the possessor of property ordinarily enjoys. . . .

The evidence introduced at the hearing on the application by Western for a receiver makes it abundantly clear that the security is adequate. According to the uncontradicted statement of counsel for the Darts to the court at the hearing for the appointment of a receiver, the property is appraised at between $550,000 and $780,000. The attorney for Western made this statement to the court:

> "At this particular time it's obvious to Counsel here that the property at the present time, under the way in which it's being managed is probably not jeopardizing our particular loan in the amount of 250 some odd thousand dollars." . . .

It is, however, Western's position that because its mortgage provides a pledge of the rents and profits and an agreement for the appointment of a receiver that the court acted properly and within its discretion. Here again appellee's position runs counter to the weight of reason.

"We have seen that a receiver will not be appointed when the security is adequate and there is no danger of waste. The reason, of course, is that when the mortgagee does not stand in need of this interim measure an equity court will not deprive the mortgagor of the possession to which he is absolutely entitled under the lien theory; .... The question now is, whether the income and receivership clauses can overcome this rule. To say yes, would mean that although an equity court would properly refuse to thrust a mortgagee into possession when there is no necessity for it, yet the court should do that very thing if the mortgage so provides.

"The answer is that no such contract provision should force a court of equity to exercise its discretion in favor of a party who stands in no need of aid. ... If the security is plainly adequate, a receiver will not be appointed, despite the presence, in the mortgage, of a rent pledge or receivership clause, or both." 2 Glenn, Mortgages, § 175.1.

It is urged that the failure to pay taxes constitutes waste. But while it is true that taxes are accruing at the rate of $1700 a year, there is no evidence whatsoever that there has been a failure to pay taxes. And finally, Western suggests that the accrual of interest at the rate of $1600 a month is grounds for a receiver. We do not think so. Here again there is no showing that the security is insufficient to provide recoupment of interest.

The record is clear. The Union Title Company, as trustee, converted income from the property which if applied to the mortgages would have been sufficient to prevent them from being in default. Upon the failure of Union Title to make the mortgage payments, and it appearing that the property was being mismanaged by being permitted to fall into disrepair, appellant Dart, the residuary beneficiary of the trust, entered into possession. The testimony discloses, from Western's witness, Glenn Erickson, that when he first checked the property it was "badly run down. The recreation facilities were not operating. The pool was not operating, and it showed neglect throughout and they had quite a few vacancies out there." This was the condition of the property under the management of Union Title shortly before July 3, 1964. Thereafter, under the appellants' management and by September 3rd, the date of the receivership hearing, Erickson found "all the facilities operating nicely. The landscaping is well taken care of. It's neat and there seems—I talked to several people and there is lots of harmony out there now, and I would say it was running in first class condition right now" with "very few" vacancies.

We think it was within the prerogative of the residuary beneficiary to attempt to save the trust res and that he had sufficient equitable interest to enter upon the property for that purpose under the peculiar circumstances of this case. The operative facts which would empower the court below to appoint a receiver to take charge of the property were not present. It should have directed either that Union Title be immediately superseded as trustee and that the successor trustee take charge of the property, applying the income in accordance with the trust agreement; or, if it determined that appellant had been properly managing the property, it should have placed him in possession, under bond, to preserve the property with directions to distribute the income in accordance with the trust agreement. Irrespective, the lower court must direct that the net income of the trust property, both past and future, be distributed pursuant to the terms of the trust agreement.

The orders appointing the receivers are set aside and vacated and the cause is remanded for further proceedings consistent with this decision.

NOTES

1. *Standards for receivership.* One might suppose that a mortgagee might obtain a receivership more readily in a title theory state than in a lien theory state, because the title theory mortgagee has possessory rights not afforded its lien theory counterpart. Ironically, in some title jurisdictions this possessory right may have been an obstacle to obtaining a receivership, as some courts have required that the mortgagee establish that the legal remedy of ejectment is inadequate. See Nelson, Whitman, Burkhart & Freyermuth, Real Estate Finance Law § 4.34 (6th ed.2015).

However, today the articulated standard for the appointment of a receiver varies little among title, intermediate, and lien theory states. Under the most common statement of the rule, insolvency of the mortgagor and inadequacy of the security are not enough to justify the receivership. Rather, "there must be shown some additional, distinct equitable ground, such as danger of loss, waste, destruction, or serious impairment of the property, to warrant the appointment." Grether v. Nick, 193 Wis. 503, 508, 213 N.W. 304, 306 (1927). See Atco Constr. & Dev. Corp. v. Beneficial Sav. Bank, F.S.B., 523 So.2d 747 (Fla.App.1988) (appointment of receiver constitutes abuse of discretion in the absence of a showing of waste or serious risk of loss).

Under the Restatement, a mortgagee is entitled to the appointment of a receiver if "(1) the mortgagor is in default under the mortgage; (2) the value of the real estate is inadequate to satisfy the mortgage obligation; and (3) the mortgagor is committing waste." Restatement (Third) of Property (Mortgages) § 4.3(a) (1997). Note that while, in some jurisdictions, "waste" means affirmative physical destruction or at least failure to repair, in others the term has a much broader meaning. For example, under the Restatement approach, waste includes not only failing "to pay real estate taxes," but, in addition, "the failure to pay insurance premiums, if payment is required by the mortgage documents." Id., cmt. b. Finally, waste can even encompass "the improper taking by the mortgagor of rents which should be paid to the mortgagee" under an assignment of rents provision. Id.

In 2015, the Uniform Law Commission promulgated the Uniform Commercial Real Estate Receivership Act (UCRERA), enacted in 9 states as of 2021. Under UCRERA § 4(b)(1), appointment of a receiver in connection with mortgage enforcement is appropriate if "appointment is necessary to protect the property from waste, loss, transfer, dissipation, or impairment."

2. *Impact of receivership and rent assignment clauses.* Commercial mortgages often contain a clause in which the mortgagor consents to the appointment of a receiver after default, without regard to the mortgagor's solvency, the condition of the mortgaged property, or the adequacy of the security. As *Dart* illustrates, courts traditionally refused to enforce such a clause where the circumstances did not otherwise justify appointment in the absence of such a clause. These decisions reflect the view that the parties themselves may not contractually bind the discretion of the judge as to whether an equitable remedy is justified. See Nelson, Whitman, Burkhart & Freyermuth, Real Estate Finance Law 229 (6th ed.2015). By contrast, some courts have been more willing to enforce receivership clauses irrespective of whether a receivership would be justified in their absence. See, e.g., Dover Assocs. Joint Venture v. Ingram, 768 A.2d 971 (Del.Ch.2000); Fleet Bank of Maine v. Zimelman, 575 A.2d 731 (Me.1990); Metropolitan Life Ins. Co. v. Liberty Center Venture, 437 Pa.Super. 544, 650 A.2d 887 (1994); Federal Home Loan Mortg. Corp. v. Nazar, 100 B.R. 555 (D.Kan.1989). Other courts, while not willing to enforce receivership clauses automatically, do give such clauses some evidentiary weight. See, e.g., Barclays Bank of Cal. v. Superior Court, 69 Cal.App.3d 593, 137 Cal.Rptr. 743 (1977) ("although a trust deed's recital that upon default the beneficiary shall be entitled to the appointment of a receiver is not binding upon the courts, such a recital nevertheless has some evidentiary weight" and "presents a prima facie, but rebuttable, evidentiary showing of the beneficiary's entitlement to appointment of a receiver"); Wellman Sav. Bank v. Roth, 432 N.W.2d 697 (Iowa App.1988); Riverside Props. v. Teachers Ins. & Annuity Ass'n, 590 S.W.2d 736 (Tex.Civ.App.1979).

Courts also give receivership clauses in federally-insured mortgages substantial evidentiary weight. Some courts have indicated that such clauses alone may justify the appointment of a receiver in situations where the mortgagee cannot establish the traditional equitable conditions precedent for such an appointment. See, e.g., United States v. Berk & Berk, 767 F.Supp. 593 (D.N.J.1991); United States v. Mountain Village Co., 424 F.Supp. 822 (D.Mass.1976). It should be noted, however, that such cases are largely the product of the federal courts applying a "federal common law" instead of the substantive mortgage law of the forum state, a problem we will consider later in Chapter Eight.

Due to recent law reform efforts, many states now make such receivership clauses in nonresidential mortgages conclusively enforceable upon default. See, e.g., Ariz.Rev.Stat.Ann. § 33–702(B) (interpreted as superseding *Dart* in In re Scottsdale Medical Pavilion, 159 B.R. 295 (9th Cir. Bankr. 1993)); 735 Ill.Comp.Stat. 5/15–1702(a), 5/15–1704(a); West's Ann.Ind.Code § 32–30–5–1(4)(c); Minn.Stat.Ann. § 559.17(2); N.M.Stat.Ann. § 44–8–4(A); N.Y.Real

Prop.Law § 254(10). The Restatement, UARA, and UCRERA all provide support for this approach. See Restatement (Third) of Property (Mortgages) § 4.3(b) (1997) (mortgagee is entitled to appointment of a receiver if the mortgagor is in default "and the mortgage or other agreement contains either a mortgage on the rents or a provision authorizing appointment of a receiver to take possession and collect rents upon mortgagor default." UARA § 7(a)(1)(A); UCRERA § 6(b)(2). This trend reflects the reality that many nonresidential mortgage loans today are nonrecourse loans; every dollar of rent collected from the mortgaged property and not applied to payment of the debt is a dollar that the lender may not recover from the mortgagor. On such loans, conclusive enforcement of the receivership clause may be viewed as assuring specific performance of the assignment of rents.

3. *Ex parte receivership.* In some jurisdictions it is common for courts to appoint receivers by *ex parte* order. This entails the appointment of a receiver without providing either prior notice or a hearing for the mortgagor and other interested parties. Some jurisdictions reject this remedy unless the mortgage documents specifically authorize the appointment of a receiver without notice. See, e.g., GE Life & Annuity Assurance Co. v. Fort Collins Assemblage, Ltd., 53 P.3d 703 (Colo.App.2001). In any event, does such a practice violate the due process clause of the 14th Amendment? Under the significant weight of authority, the answer is no, at least as long as (a) the mortgagee's motion is supported by sworn evidence and (b) the mortgagor has a prompt opportunity for a hearing to challenge the propriety of the appointment. See, e.g., Friedman v. Gerax Realty Assocs., 100 Misc.2d 820, 420 N.Y.S.2d 247 (1979); Hartford Fed. Sav. & Loan Ass'n v. Tucker, 196 Conn. 172, 491 A.2d 1084 (1985); UCRERA § 3(b)(1). Cf. Manufacturers Life Ins. Co. v. Patterson, 51 Ohio App.3d 99, 554 N.E.2d 134 (1988) (mortgage provision authorizing the appointment of a receiver without notice constitutes waiver by mortgagor of due process objections). See generally Nelson, Whitman, Burkhart & Freyermuth, Real Estate Finance Law § 4.36 (6th ed.2015).

4. *Ability of receiver to terminate leases.* Suppose a receiver is appointed for rental property. To what extent should he or she be bound by rental prepayments or other collusive arrangements ("sweetheart" deals) between lessees and mortgagor? For an example of how New York, a lien jurisdiction, approaches this question, consider the following language from New York City Community Preservation Corp. v. Michelin Assocs., 115 A.D.2d 715, 496 N.Y.S.2d 530 (1985):

> As a general rule, a receiver of rents and profits in a mortgage foreclosure action is bound by the agreement between the tenant and the mortgagor landlord, and notwithstanding that the amount fixed as rent under the terms of the lease is less than the fair and reasonable rental value of the premises, the tenant may not be required to pay to the receiver a greater amount, even though the lease is subordinate to the lien of the mortgage. However, this rule presupposes the existence of a bona fide lease, and a court has "broad power" to prevent frustration of an order appointing a receiver of

rents "by a collusive or fraudulent lease for an inadequate rental or advance payment of rent in anticipation of a foreclosure action." [quoting Prudence Co. v. 160 West 73rd St. Corp., 260 N.Y. 205, 213, 183 N.E. 365 (1932)]

See generally Nelson, Whitman, Burkhart & Freyermuth, Real Estate Finance Law § 4.42 (6th ed.2015).

Under the Restatement, which adopts the lien theory of mortgages, a receiver generally has no authority to disaffirm pre-receivership leases. See Restatement (Third) of Property (Mortgages) § 4.4(a) (1997). Nevertheless, the receiver may "disaffirm any lease or related agreement between the mortgagor and a tenant that contravenes a provision of a prior recorded mortgage" or was "made while the mortgagor is in default under the mortgage that was not commercially reasonable when it was consummated." Id. § 4.4(b) & (c). A similar approach applies in states that have adopted UCRERA. UCRERA § 17(h).

Suppose that shortly before mortgagee obtained the appointment of a receiver, the mortgagor enters an agreement with tenant under which tenant agrees to and does extend tenant's lease in exchange for tenant's payment of the following year's rent in advance. Should the prepayment be binding on the receiver, or can the receiver properly demand that the tenant pay the agreed rent to the receiver notwithstanding the prepayment to mortgagor? Should it matter whether the mortgage and/or assignment of rents prohibited prepayment without the mortgagee's prior consent? See Dime Sav. Bank of New York, FSB v. Montague St. Realty Assocs., 229 A.D.2d 461, 645 N.Y.S.2d 533 (1996); Restatement (Third) of Property (Mortgages) § 4.4, cmt. c (1997).

5. *Competing receivers.* Suppose a junior mortgagee obtains the appointment of a receiver. Must rents collected by that receiver be used to reduce senior mortgage debt? Consider the language of the court in Vechiarelli v. Garsal Realty, Inc., 111 Misc.2d 157, 443 N.Y.S.2d 622 (1980):

> A receiver appointed at the instance of one mortgagee acts on behalf of that mortgagee and not generally on behalf of all lienholders. Therefore the senior mortgagee must either obtain the appointment of his own receiver or an extension of the junior receivership before rents may be collected for his benefit.

Similarly, the Restatement provides that "[w]hen a junior mortgagee obtains the appointment of a receiver, that receiver has the right, until a receiver is appointed under a senior mortgage, to collect rents from the mortgaged real estate and, after first using them to pay real estate taxes and other reasonable expenses associated with the maintenance and repair of the real estate, to apply the balance to the junior mortgage obligation." Restatement (Third) of Property (Mortgages) § 4.5(b) (1997). Is this sound policy? See id. cmt. b.

6. *Sale of mortgaged real estate by receiver.* Some commentators have advocated that receivership can be an effective way to dispose of real estate— and particularly, that it may in some cases provide a more effective way of

disposing of mortgaged real property than the foreclosure process. A receiver of mortgaged commercial real property could readily market that property to potential buyers in the context of operating the property during the receivership, permitting potential buyers to perform more meaningful due diligence. Further, a sale subject to judicial review and confirmation could produce greater finality regarding the title acquired by the buyer at the sale. Thus, there is some reason to expect that receiver sales of mortgaged real estate could produce higher sale prices than public foreclosure sales. In fact, a federal statute explicitly authorizes a receiver appointed by a federal court to sell mortgaged property in a private sale. 28 U.S.C. § 2001.

By contrast, under existing state laws, the authority for receiver sales has been much less clear. In many states, there is not a comprehensive statute governing real estate receiverships, or the applicable statutes do not explicitly address whether the receiver has a power of sale. In these states, there is some doubt as to whether or in what circumstances a state court receiver could conduct a sale of mortgaged property, and whether such a sale would be free and clear of liens and any applicable statutory redemption rights.

The litigation in *Shubh Hotels Boca, LLC v. Federal Deposit Insurance Corp* 46 So.3d 163 (Fla.Dist.Ct.App.2010), provides a good example. Shubh Hotels Boca, LLC (Shubh) owned a 180-room hotel in Boca Raton, subject to $28.8 million mortgage loan. In May 2009, the mortgagee instituted a judicial foreclosure proceeding following financial defaults by Shubh, and the lender obtained the appointment of a receiver to collect rents during the foreclosure proceeding. By January 2010, hotel operations were losing $28,000 each month and the receiver was unable to raise borrowed funds to continue operating the hotel. The mortgagee immediately moved to have the property sold as soon as a buyer could be identified. The trial court granted this motion, and the receiver identified a buyer willing to pay $9 million for the hotel, but Shubh objected to the proposed sale on the ground that the receiver had no legal authority to sell the hotel and could not convey title. The trial court rejected this objection and entered an order authorizing the sale, but the Florida District Court of Appeal reversed, noting that no Florida statute authorized a court-appointed receiver in a foreclosure case to sell the mortgaged property. The court also noted that the mortgage itself did not specifically authorize the receiver to sell the property, but only "to protect and preserve" the mortgaged property, to "operate [it] preceding foreclosure or sale," and to collect rents and apply them against the debt. More generally, the court noted that "the mere appointment of a receiver does not itself confer any of the owner's power or authority to sell such property," that "the role of a receiver in a foreclosure action is only to preserve the property's value," and that implying a power of sale would be inconsistent with that limited role. *Shubh*, 46 so.3d at 167. Finally, the court noted that under Florida law, every mortgagor has a statutory right of redemption until the issuance of a certificate of sale by the clerk of court, and held that "[r]ecognizing a general interim power of a receiver to sell mortgaged property in a foreclosure case would contravene" that redemption right. Id.

By contrast, courts in several other states have upheld receiver sales free and clear of liens and statutory redemption rights. See, e.g., CSB Bank v. Christy, No. 305869 (Mich.Ct.App. Oct. 18, 2012) (unpublished); Park Nat'l Bank v. Cattani, Inc., 187 Ohio App.3d 186, 931 N.E.2d 623 (2010); Huntington Nat'l Bank v. Motel 4 BAPS, Inc., 191 Ohio App.3d 90, 944 N.E.2d 1210 (2010); cf. Bogosian v. Foerderer Tract Committee, Inc., 264 Pa.Super. 84, 399 A.2d 408 (1979) (receiver may sell real estate free and clear of liens if there is "a reasonable prospect that a surplus will be left to be distributed among general creditors").

This uncertainty is a lamentable by-product of the outdated and inadequate state statutory provisions governing receiverships. In 2015, the Uniform Law Commission promulgated UCRERA, which clarifies this ambiguity by explicitly empowering the receiver, with court approval, to sell the mortgaged property with the same title-clearing effect as a foreclosure sale and without regard to statutory rights of redemption:

> With court approval, a receiver may transfer receivership property other than in the ordinary course of business by sale, lease, license, exchange or other disposition. Unless the agreement of sale provides otherwise, a sale under this section is free and clear of a lien of the person that obtained the appointment of the receiver, any subordinate lien, and any rights of redemption but is subject to a senior lien. [UCRERA § 16(c).]

As of May 2021, UCRERA has been enacted in 9 states (AZ, FL, MD, MI, NV, NC, OR, TN, UT). Nonuniform statutes in several other states explicitly recognize the receiver's power of sale. See, e.g., West's Ind.Code Ann. § 32–30–5–7; Wash.Rev. Code Ann. § 7.60.260. Minnesota's statute allows the receiver to sell the mortgaged property free and clear of liens in a general receivership, Minn.Stat.Ann. § 576.21(h), (k), but not in a custodial receivership, id. § 576.29(b), 576.46.

D. WASTE

PRUDENTIAL INSURANCE COMPANY OF AMERICA v. SPENCER'S KENOSHA BOWL, INC.
Court of Appeals of Wisconsin, 1987
137 Wis.2d 313, 404 N.W.2d 109

Before SCOTT, C.J., BROWN, P.J., and NETTESHEIM, J.

NETTESHEIM, JUDGE.

Spencer's Kenosha Bowl, Inc. (Spencer's) appeals from a judgment awarding $369,188.21 in damages to the Prudential Insurance Company of America (Prudential). The award is for waste committed by Spencer's upon real estate against which Prudential holds a mortgage.

* * *

The property involved in this litigation is a commercial building constructed in 1970 and situated on real estate located in the city of Kenosha. Spencer's purchased the property in 1975 from Delco Development Co. (Delco) which had previously mortgaged the property to Prudential. It is undisputed that Spencer's did not assume Delco's mortgage indebtedness when it purchased the property. Prudential subsequently foreclosed on the property after the mortgage note was in default.

In April, 1983, the Honorable Frederick Kessler, the judge then assigned to the case, granted Prudential's request for foreclosure of the property. The amount owed on the mortgage note at the time of the sheriff's sale was fixed at $994,497.80. The property sold for $635,000 in May, 1984. Following the sale, the Honorable Richard G. Harvey, Jr., the judge subsequently assigned to the case, held a hearing on Prudential's claim that Spencer's had committed waste upon the property. In his decision on the waste issue, Judge Harvey found that Spencer's had committed waste in the following amounts:

Property Taxes	$198,743.34
Roof	37,890.00
Ceiling Tile and Grid	103,064.52
Electric Facilities	14,647.16
Drywall-wood	36,251.85
Restroom	766.66
Exterior Canopy	13,090.83
Cleanup Costs	16,381.00
Floor Tile Damage	24,000.00
	$444,835.36

However, because the amount of the waste exceeded the amount of the debt less the foreclosure sale proceeds, Judge Harvey lowered Prudential's waste award so that it equaled the amount of the debt deficiency.

Spencer's initially argues that a grantee who does not assume the mortgage of a grantor-mortgagor cannot be held liable for any waste committed on the mortgaged property. Whether a mortgagee has a cause of action for waste is a question of law. *See Williams v. Security Savings & Loan Ass'n,* 120 Wis.2d 480, 482, 355 N.W.2d 370, 372 (Ct.App.1984). As a result, we review this question independently of any conclusions made by the trial court. *Id.*

Waste is a species of tort. *See Jaffe-Spindler Co. v. Genesco, Inc.,* 747 F.2d 253, 256 (4th Cir.1984). It is defined as "the unreasonable conduct by the owner of a possessory estate that results in physical damage to the real estate and substantial diminution in the value of the estates in which others have an interest." *Pleasure Time, Inc. v. Kuss,* 78 Wis.2d 373, 381, 254 N.W.2d 463, 467 (1977). Although a mortgagee only has a lien on the mortgaged property, *see* sec. 708.01, Stats.; *State v. Phillips,* 99 Wis.2d 46, 50, 298 N.W.2d 239, 241 (Ct.App.1980), he or she is entitled to maintain a legal action for waste against a mortgagor. *See Jones v. Costigan,* 12 Wis. 757 (677), 760–65 (1860).

We conclude that the waste doctrine permits a mortgagee to maintain an action for waste against a non-assuming grantee of a mortgagor. In *Scott v. Webster,* 50 Wis. 53, 6 N.W. 363 (1880), the supreme court held that senior mortgagees in possession of property were accountable to a junior mortgagee for waste committed on the property. *Id.* at 64, 6 N.W. at 365. There, the senior mortgagees removed a large amount of timber from the property which substantially diminished its value. *Id.* at 60–61, 6 N.W. at 363. Prior to the timber removal, the senior mortgagees purchased an equity of redemption which entitled them to possession of the property. *Id.* at 62, 6 N.W. at 364. Consequently, the senior mortgagees were both owners and mortgagees of the property. *Id.* at 63, 6 N.W. at 364–65. The court reasoned that with respect to the junior mortgagee, the senior mortgagees were mortgagees in possession and as such must be held liable for the waste they committed while in possession of the property. *Id.* at 63–64, 6 N.W. at 365.

Here, as in *Scott,* Spencer's legally had possession of the property and, under the trial court's findings, committed acts which resulted in a substantial diminution in the property's value. It is undisputed that Prudential, as a mortgagee, had an interest in the property. *See Phillips,* 99 Wis.2d at 50, 298 N.W.2d at 241. As a result, all of the essential ingredients for a waste cause of action as set out in *Pleasure Time* are met. *See Pleasure Time,* 78 Wis.2d at 381, 254 N.W.2d at 467. Moreover, we consider the court's reasoning in *Scott* as an indication of the liberality to be allowed a mortgagee when enforcing or protecting the lien interest. *See also Atkinson v. Hewett,* 63 Wis. 396, 23 N.W. 889 (1885) (mortgagee allowed to recover for wasteful conduct of trespasser). We do not deem the non-assuming grantee's status so unique that it warrants insulation from a waste action and prevents the mortgagee from preserving and protecting a security interest.

Our conclusion is also supported by the supreme court's language in *Edler v. Hasche,* 67 Wis. 653, 659–61, 31 N.W. 57, 59–61 (1887). There, Edler and Brandt were mortgagee and mortgagor, respectively. As in this case, Hasche purchased the mortgaged property from Brandt "subject to the mortgage." *Id.* at 659, 31 N.W. at 59. While the court left for a later proceeding the question of Hasche's liability for the mortgage debt and strongly suggested that the evidence might not support a finding that

Hasche had assumed the mortgage, the court nonetheless recognized that Hasche's removal of a building was waste for which he was liable to Edler. The court stated that "Hasche's liability for waste . . . upon every principle of justice is clear and must be affirmed." *Id.* at 661, 31 N.W. at 60–61.

The import of *Edler* on this case is clear. Regardless of successor liability on the mortgage debt, the court in *Edler* affirms the principle that a non-assuming grantee can be liable to a mortgagee for waste committed to the secured property. Consequently, Spencer's non-assuming grantee status does not affect its liability for waste.

As an extension of this issue, Spencer's attempts to draw a distinction between its liability for active and passive waste.[2] Passive or permissive waste results from negligence or omission to do that which would prevent injury. *See Finley v. Chain,* 176 Ind.App. 66, 374 N.E.2d 67, 79 (1978) (overruled on other grounds by *Morris v. Weigle,* 383 N.E.2d 341, 345 n. 3 (Ind.1978)). Active or voluntary waste requires an affirmative act which results in the destruction or alteration of property. *See Jowdy v. Guerin,* 10 Ariz.App. 205, 457 P.2d 745, 748 (1969). At common law, an individual could be held liable for waste only if the acts were tortious and intentional. *See* Leipziger, *The Mortgagee's Remedies for Waste,* 64 Calif.L.Rev. 1086, 1093–94 (1976). No waste cause of action lay for negligent waste. *Id.* at 1094, 1130–32.

Whether a particular act is waste depends upon the circumstances. *Pleasure Time,* 78 Wis.2d at 381, 254 N.W.2d at 467. Modern Wisconsin law does not distinguish between passive and active waste. However, early Wisconsin law recognized that waste could "be either voluntary or permissive." *Melms v. Pabst Brewing Co.,* 104 Wis. 7, 9, 79 N.W. 738, 739 (1899). Moreover, Wisconsin law has dealt with fact situations where the actions characterized as waste can be described as either active or passive. *See, e.g., Scott,* 50 Wis. at 53, 6 N.W. at 363 (waste resulting from removal of timber); *Jones,* 12 Wis. at 757 (removal of doors and windows from house); *Pleasure Time,* 78 Wis.2d at 381, 254 N.W.2d at 467–68 (waste alleged involved demolished and deteriorated buildings); *First Nat'l Bank v. Clark & Lund Boat Co.,* 68 Wis.2d 738, 741, 229 N.W.2d 221, 223 (1975) (failure to pay taxes).

We conclude that the modern waste definition is broad enough in Wisconsin to include both active and passive waste. The common law "limitations are not well rationalized in the cases and seem to have come about largely by accident." Leipziger, *supra,* at 1094. Conduct which results

---

[2] Spencer's bases its passive waste argument on *Camden Trust Co. v. Handle,* 132 N.J.Eq. 97, 26 A.2d 865 (1942), which recognized the common law rule that a non-assuming grantee cannot be liable for passive or permissive [waste]. We agree with the Indiana court that there is no logical or practical reason for support of this rule. *See Finley v. Chain,* 374 N.E.2d 67, 79 n. 7 (Ind.Ct.App.1978) (overruled on other grounds by *Morris v. Weigle,* 383 N.E.2d 341, 345 n. 3 (Ind.1978)).

either in active or passive waste "may injure or threaten property rendering the debt unsafe." *Finley,* 374 N.E.2d at 79. Consequently, the mortgagee's security may be impaired by either passive or active waste and the policy for allowing the mortgagee recovery is the same regardless of the type of waste involved.

Next, Spencer's argues that the entry of judgment was not warranted because the amount of the waste found to have been committed was less than the amount obtained from the sale of the property. Spencer's, however, cites no legal authority for this proposition and, as a result, we are not required to consider it. *See State v. Shaffer,* 96 Wis.2d 531, 545–46, 292 N.W.2d 370, 378 (Ct.App.1980). Moreover, Spencer's argument seems to be a distortion of the common law rule that, in lien jurisdictions, a mortgagee cannot recover until his security has been substantially impaired which occurs only when waste has reduced the value of the encumbered property to less than the unpaid balance of the debt. *See* Leipziger, *supra,* at 1097. It is undisputed in this case that the waste found by the trial court reduced the value of the encumbered property in the fashion required by this rule.

Spencer's also challenges the trial court's calculation of the damages based on the debt deficiency. Spencer's argues that this is in fact an award of a deficiency judgment on a mortgage which it never assumed. However, in lien jurisdictions, a trial court must determine the extent of reduction in the value of the security interest in the property, not just the amount of injury to the real estate. *See Finley,* 374 N.E.2d at 78. Where, as here, the amount of waste committed on the property is greater than the amount of the debt deficiency, the extent of reduction in the value of the mortgagee's security interest will always be equal to the debt deficiency. Consequently, we do not view the trial court's award as a deficiency judgment but, rather, as an independent award litigated within the context of a foreclosure proceeding.

* * *

Judgment affirmed.

NOTES

1.   *What constitutes waste?* As *Spencer's* suggests, waste was historically limited to cases of affirmative and intentional physical damage to the mortgaged real estate. Modern case law has expanded the concept markedly. The Restatement provides:

> Waste occurs when, without the mortgagee's consent, the mortgagor:
>
> (1) physically changes the real estate, whether negligently or intentionally, in a manner that reduces its value;

(2) fails to maintain and repair the real estate in a reasonable manner, except for repair of casualty damage or acts of third parties not the fault of the mortgagor;

(3) fails to pay before delinquency property taxes or governmental assessments secured by a lien having priority over the mortgage;

(4) materially fails to comply with covenants in the mortgage respecting the physical care, maintenance, construction, demolition, or insurance against casualty of the real estate or improvements on it; or

(5) retains possession of rents to which the mortgagee has the right of possession * * *.

See Restatement (Third) of Property (Mortgages) § 4.6(a) (1997).*

Spencer's clearly supports categories (1) and (2). How should damage from natural disasters, such as earthquakes and floods be treated? Is it really different from routine wear and tear caused by the elements? What about the mortgagor's failure to repair damage resulting from such disasters?

Spencer's also supports category (3), failure to pay real estate taxes. Other decisions also support liability for failure to pay property taxes, but there is not a great deal of authority. See Travelers Ins. Co. v. 633 Third Assocs., 14 F.3d 114 (2d Cir.1994) (New York law); North Am. Sec. Life Ins. Co. v. Harris Trust & Sav. Bank., 859 F.Supp. 1163 (N.D.Ill.1994) (Illinois law). Considerable contrary authority also exists. See Chetek State Bank v. Barberg, 170 Wis.2d 516, 489 N.W.2d 385 (App.1992); FGH Realty Credit Corp. v. Bonati, 226 A.D.2d 188, 641 N.Y.S.2d 12 (1996) (failure to pay taxes is waste only if "fraudulent"). If failing to pay prior property taxes is waste, why isn't failure to pay other prior liens, including prior mortgages, also waste? No substantial authority suggests that it is.

Is it different to hold a non-assuming grantee liable for demolishing a building on the mortgaged real estate than to hold the grantee liable for failing to pay real estate taxes? Does it help a mortgagee's case against a non-assuming grantee if the mortgage, as is almost always the case, contains a specific covenant to pay taxes? See generally Nelson, Whitman, Burkhart & Freyermuth, Real Estate Finance Law §§ 4.4, 4.5, 4.11 (6th ed.2015). What about other mortgage covenants that seem to expand the liability that would otherwise exist for waste? For example, suppose a mortgage covenant requires a particularly stringent type or level of maintenance of the property, failure of which would not be common-law waste. Is there a theory on which even a non-assuming grantee could be held liable for breach of such covenants? Couldn't they be said to "run with the land," so as to bind even non-assuming grantees? Almost no authority exists on this point, but a Maryland court has held that such covenants do run with the land. See Union Trust Co. v. Rosenburg, 171 Md. 409, 189 A. 421 (App.1937).

While damaging the property is waste, failing to take actions to maintain its value may not be. In Boucher Inv., L.P. v. Annapolis-West Ltd. Partn., 141 Md.App. 1, 784 A.2d 39 (2001), the mortgaged property was an office building. Its tenants had the use of an adjacent parking lot that was leased to the mortgagor. When the lease expired, the new owner of the office building made no attempt to renegotiate it. The mortgagee claimed waste because "the lack of parking resulted in a loss of tenants [and] . . . income to the property." The court characterized this argument as a "string of shaky inferences" and refused to find waste.

2.   *Waste liability of non-assuming grantees.* In most jurisdictions, when a foreclosure sale yields less than the mortgage debt, the mortgagee may obtain a deficiency judgment against anyone who is personally liable on the mortgage obligation. However, a grantee of mortgaged real estate is not personally liable if she took title "subject to" the existing mortgage but did not "assume" the debt. See Chapter Five, Section A infra. Thus, deficiency judgments are unavailable against non-assuming grantees. Does *Spencer's* suggest that a mortgagee can avoid this prohibition by successfully bringing an action for waste? If so, this can be an extremely important application of the concept of waste.

3.   *Waste liability when a mortgage clause or statute bars a deficiency judgment.* Can a mortgagee recover damages for waste if the mortgage note is "nonrecourse"—that is, the mortgagor has no personal liability on the debt? The answer may depend on the exact wording of the nonrecourse clause. See The Travelers Ins. Co. v. 633 Third Assocs., 973 F.2d 82 (2d Cir.1992), in which the court held that the particular nonrecourse clause was broad enough to bar an action for waste. Carefully drafted nonrecourse clauses often "carve out" liability for waste, making the mortgagor liable for waste though he is not liable for the mortgage debt. In Aozora Bank, Ltd. v. 1333 North California Blvd., 119 Cal.App.4th 1291, 15 Cal.Rptr.3d 340 (2004), the clause clearly made the mortgagor liable for waste, but it did not provide that the mortgagee could recover its attorneys' fees in the waste action, which was a rather glaring error by the mortgagee's counsel. The court refused to award the fees.

What about recovery of waste damages in a state with a statute barring deficiency judgments against mortgagors? In Cornelison v. Kornbluth, 15 Cal.3d 590, 125 Cal.Rptr. 557, 542 P.2d 981 (1975), the California court held that no damages for waste should be imposed unless the waste was committed "in bad faith," which the court defined as "reckless" or "malicious," rather than merely as a result of "economic pressures." The court reasoned that a mortgagor in financial distress often must choose between paying the mortgage debt service and keeping the property in repair. The policy of the California antideficiency statute clearly was to avoid personal liability if the mortgagor defaulted in mortgage payments. The court concluded that the mortgagor also should not be liable for failing to make repairs. While *Cornelison* represents a barrier to recovery for waste in California, it is not insuperable. See Nippon Credit Bank v. 1333 North Cal. Blvd., 86 Cal.App.4th 486, 103 Cal.Rptr.2d 421 (2001) (mortgagor's failure to pay property taxes though it had the money to do so was bad faith waste and justified award of punitive damages!).

4. *Waste committed by non-owners.* Suppose a third party that has no possessory interest in the mortgaged real estate, such as a trespasser, a licensee, or an easement holder, commits waste. If a person who has a present estate in the mortgaged real estate is liable for waste, shouldn't those who hold lesser interests also be liable? They normally are liable. See Turner v. Kerin & Assocs., 283 Mont. 117, 938 P.2d 1368 (1997) (mortgagee could recover in waste against contractor who installed water main line in noncompliance with code standards); McCorristin v. Salmon Signs, 244 N.J.Super. 503, 582 A.2d 1271 (1990) (mortgagee could recover for waste against a third party who caused damage while installing a billboard on the mortgaged premises).

However, suppose the third party is a demolition contractor that the owner hired to destroy a house or other improvements on the real estate. Obviously, the owner may be liable for waste, but what about the contractor? Restatement (Third) of Property (Mortgages) § 4.6(d) provides: "If the waste was committed with the mortgagor's consent, liability exists only if the person committing it had actual knowledge of the existence of the mortgage." In other words, the recorded mortgage does not give constructive notice, and demolition contractors do not have a duty to search the title of the real estate they work on. But should the contractor be liable if it *knows* that the land is mortgaged? Or can the contractor successfully argue that the owner's consent made the contractor's acts entirely legal and not actionable? See Stevensen v. Goodson, 924 P.2d 339 (Utah 1996) (adopting this argument).

5. *Limitations on recovery of damages for waste.* The mortgagee's recovery of waste damages may not exceed the least of:

(a) The actual harm caused by the waste, which normally is either the cost of repair or the diminution in the property's value;

(b) The mortgage debt amount or, if foreclosure has already occurred, the amount of any unpaid deficiency. The mortgagee must apply *all* waste damages it recovers against the mortgage debt. Also, if the mortgagee entered a "full credit bid" (a bid in the amount of the entire outstanding debt) and bought the property at the foreclosure sale, it cannot recover anything for waste, because its debt is considered to have been fully paid. See Cornelison v. Kornbluth, 15 Cal.3d 590, 125 Cal.Rptr. 557, 542 P.2d 981 (1975); or

(c) The amount by which the mortgagee's security has been impaired. This limitation is asserted mainly in lien theory states and is discussed in the next note.

6. *Measuring impairment of security.* Most mortgage loans are made for less than the full appraised value of the real estate. The ratio of the loan amount to the property's value is the "loan-to-value ratio" ("LTV ratio"). It is

an important indicator of the likelihood that the lender will suffer a loss on the loan. Lower ratios are safer. Thus, a loan with a 75% LTV ratio is much more secure than a loan with a 95% LTV ratio. A loan's LTV ratio generally improves (declines) gradually over time if the property's value is stable and the loan balance is gradually paid down by regular amortization payments.

This brings us to the problem of how to measure impairment of security resulting from waste. The courts have had considerable difficulty with this question and have used several approaches. The "hard-nosed" definition runs along these lines: "If the injury to the property does not reduce its value below the amount required to secure the debt, the mortgagee has suffered no injury." Frio Investments, Inc. v. 4M-IRC/Rohde, 705 S.W.2d 784 (Tex.App.1986). The difficulty with this definition is that it leaves no "cushion" or margin of security for the mortgagee. In effect, it makes the LTV ratio 100%, even though the original loan nearly always was made at a lower LTV ratio. Other courts, more sensitive to this issue, have said that the mortgagee is entitled to a "reasonable" margin of security or to the same LTV ratio that existed before the waste.

The Restatement's approach is novel. It provides that "an impairment of security exists if the ratio of the mortgage obligation to the real estate's value is above its scheduled level." Restatement (Third) of Property (Mortgages) § 4.6(c). In other words, the waste damage award should be sufficient, when applied to the mortgage balance, to maintain the LTV ratio as "scheduled"— that is, the ratio that would have existed if all payments had been made on schedule and if the property's value had remained stable over the life of the loan.

Apply the Restatement approach to compute the amount of damages the lender should recover on the following facts. Mortgagee ("ME") makes a mortgage loan of $80,000 to Mortgagor ("MR") that is secured by land worth $100,000. During the next five years, MR timely makes the scheduled amortization payments, which reduced the loan balance to $70,000. The land's value increased to $120,000. MR then committed waste, which reduced the land's value to $90,000.

Under the Restatement approach, the scheduled LTV ratio when the waste occurred was $70,000/$100,000 or 70%. After the waste is committed, the property's value is reduced to $90,000. Seventy percent of $90,000 is $63,000. The mortgagee is entitled to recover enough damages to reduce the loan balance from its present level ($70,000) to $63,000. Note that the $7,000 damage award is less than the total loan balance and also is less than the waste damage ($30,000). Thus, of the three limitations mentioned in Note 5, the impairment of security limitation is controlling.

An interesting feature of the Restatement approach is that the mortgagor who commits waste gets the benefit of increases in the property's value. As the value rises, more waste can be committed before damages begin to accrue. But the owner is disadvantaged if the property falls in value, because less waste can be committed before damages begin to accrue. If the lender has foreclosed before bringing the waste action, the "impairment of security" test and the scheduled LTV ratio are irrelevant, because the land is no longer security for the loan. Therefore, only the first two limitations mentioned in Note 5 are applicable.

Whether the courts will follow the Restatement approach to impairment of security is still unclear. In McNeese v. Hutchinson, 724 So.2d 451 (Miss.Ct.App.1998), the court called the Restatement analysis "helpful" but opted for the simpler approach of finding impairment if the waste diminished the property's value since the loan was made.

7.   *Other remedies*. The discussion above has focused on damages, but two other remedies are also generally available—an injunction and mortgage foreclosure. An injunction, which can prohibit further waste or order the mortgagor to correct the waste and thereby eliminate the impairment of security, may be thought of as a substitute for damages. But most mortgagees would probably rather have the money. Foreclosure is not permitted if a third party committed the waste without the mortgagor's consent.

8.   *Waste of rents*. The fifth type of waste mentioned in the Restatement, quoted in Note 1 above, might be termed "waste of rents." Of course, a mortgagor who retains the rents is committing waste only if the mortgagee has actuated its security interest in the rents (a so-called "assignment of rents"), as discussed in Sections A and B of this chapter. See, e.g., Ginsberg v. Lennar Florida Holdings, Inc., 645 So.2d 490 (Fla.App.1994) (rejecting a mortgage holder's claim of waste of rents because the mortgage holder had not demanded the rents, as required by the Florida statute, Fla.Stat.Ann. § 697.07).

Sometimes, unscrupulous persons buy real estate subject to an existing mortgage and then rent it, intending from the outset to retain all the rents and to pay nothing on the mortgage or for property maintenance. This practice, known as "rent skimming," can be particularly tempting in states that bar deficiency judgments. Rent skimming is a crime in California, Cal Civ. Code §§ 890–94, Colorado, Colo. Rev. Stat. § 18–5–802, Florida, Fla. Stat. Ann. § 697.08, Kansas, Kan. Stat. Ann. § 60–1011, and Washington, Wash. Rev. Code § 61.34.020–61.34.030. The California law applies to a person who acquires five or more parcels of residential real property in any two-year period. Section 890 defines "rent skimming" as "using revenue received from the rental of a parcel of residential real property at any time during the first year period after acquiring that property without first applying the revenue or an equivalent amount to the payments due on all mortgages and deeds of trust encumbering the property." This is a remarkable extension of the concept of "waste of rents". It makes the waste a *crime* and applies even if the mortgagee has not actuated an assignment of rents clause or even if an assignment of rents does not exist! In People v. Bell, 45 Cal.App.4th 1030, 53 Cal.Rptr.2d 156 (1996), the court upheld the law against a variety of constitutional challenges. It noted that "the rent skimming sections contain no language requiring the defined acts be done with any fraudulent or larcenous intent, nor do the sections require the defendant intend any additional act or future consequence.

The offense is thus one requiring general and not specific criminal intent." 53 Cal.Rptr.2d at 163.

E. MORTGAGEE LIABILITY FOR ENVIRONMENTAL PROBLEMS

Traditionally, a lender is not responsible to third parties, private or governmental, for the physical condition of the mortgaged real estate or injuries that occur on it. See, e.g., Solecki v. United States, 693 F.Supp. 770 (N.D.Iowa 1988) (mortgagee not liable for injury sustained by mortgagor's tenant in fall on mortgaged premises); Cantrell v. DuQuoin State Bank, 271 Ill.App.3d 291, 207 Ill.Dec. 621, 647 N.E.2d 1114 (1995) (mortgagee of building containing liquor establishment not liable under Dram Shop Act as "owner" where it exercises no dominion or control over the premises); Smith v. Fried, 98 Ill.App.3d 467, 53 Ill.Dec. 845, 424 N.E.2d 636 (1981) ("for a mortgagee to be responsible for damages to third parties caused by unsafe conditions on the property, the mortgagee must exercise dominion and control over the property"); Commonwealth v. Advantage Bank, 406 Mass. 885, 550 N.E.2d 1388 (1990) (mortgagee that was collecting rents pursuant to an assignment of rents clause not deemed an "owner" so as to be criminally liable under lead paint statute); Greenpoint Bank v. John, 256 A.D.2d 548, 682 N.Y.S.2d 438 (1998) (mortgagee who is not in possession is not liable to mortgagor's tenant for repairs under Multiple Dwelling Law); Edwards v. Van Skiver, 256 A.D.2d 957, 681 N.Y.S.2d 893 (1998) (installment land contract vendor not liable to tenant of vendee for injuries sustained on the contract premises); Hausman v. Dayton, 73 Ohio St.3d 671, 653 N.E.2d 1190 (1995) (even though mortgagee in an "intermediate" state acquires "title" after default, it is not liable for a nuisance on the premises unless it is in possession). Only by becoming a mortgagee in possession (as discussed earlier in this chapter) or by acquiring title and the right to possession through foreclosure or a deed in lieu of foreclosure does a mortgagee assume the normal responsibilities of an owner or possessor of real estate. See Kubczak v. Chemical Bank & Trust Co., 456 Mich. 653, 575 N.W.2d 745 (1998) (mortgagee foreclosure purchaser not liable for torts on mortgaged premises during statutory redemption period where mortgagor retained possession until the expiration of that period).

However, the federal Comprehensive Environmental Response, Compensation, and Liability Act ("CERCLA") and similar state legislation significantly increased the potential for mortgagee liability. See 42 U.S.C. §§ 9601–9675. The essence of this legislation has been summarized as follows:

> Congress enacted CERCLA to deal with hazardous waste dump sites that are polluting neighboring lands or water sources.

The Act and its related regulations authorize EPA either to order the responsible parties to contain the hazardous waste on the site or to clean the site and charge the responsible parties for EPA's response costs. The statutorily defined response costs include the cost of cleaning the site, any damages for injuries to natural resources, and the costs of any health assessment or health effects studies conducted pursuant to statutory authority. If EPA cleans the site, it may recover its response costs from any one or more of the persons enumerated in subsections 107(a)(1)–(4) of the Act, including: (1) the current "owner and operator" of the waste site, (2) any person who owned or operated the waste site when any hazardous dumping occurred; (3) the hazardous waste generators; and (4) the hazardous waste transporters. Liability for response costs is strict, joint, and several with limited exception.

Ann M. Burkhart, Lender/Owners and CERCLA: Title and Liability, 25 Harv.J.Legis. 317, 327 (1988).*

Why should a mortgagee be concerned about CERCLA? Mortgagees appear to be exempt from liability because CERCLA's definition of "owner and operator" excludes a "person, who, without participating in the management of a * * * facility, holds indicia of ownership primarily to protect his security interest in the * * * facility." 42 U.S.C. § 9601(20)(A).

Mortgagees were concerned for at least two reasons. The first is the preforeclosure period. Although the common law does not normally impose liability on the mortgagee for the mortgaged premise's physical condition, CERCLA could upset this normal assumption if the mortgagee's "participation in management" destroys its exemption from liability. To what extent does mortgagee oversight of the mortgagor's operations, which is common, represent impermissible "participation in management"?

The second potential liability problem for the mortgagee arises when it acquires ownership through foreclosure or by taking a deed in lieu of foreclosure. Clearly, the mortgagee is now the "owner" of the premises. At first blush, we would assume that the mortgagee takes on all liability that is inherent in being an owner in possession of real estate. However, the mortgagee may nevertheless be protected from liability if it can establish that even post-foreclosure ownership is held "primarily to protect his security interest in the * * * facility."

Avoiding CERCLA liability is critically important for mortgagees because the hazardous waste cleanup costs can far exceed the land's value even after it has been cleaned. Additionally, many insurance companies have refused to indemnify these costs. They argued that their comprehensive general liability policies did not insure against damages

---

caused by hazardous waste. The specter of such large liabilities caused many lenders to refuse to extend credit against any land that is or could be contaminated, including for cleanup costs. On the other hand, in determining whether mortgagees should be liable, the economic benefit that they enjoy from a cleanup is incontrovertible whether they own the land or hold only a mortgage.

Largely as a result of these competing considerations, the earliest judicial decisions concerning lender liability for hazardous waste cleanup costs varied greatly. With respect to a mortgagee's preforeclosure liability, courts have differed concerning the types of actions that constitute "participation in management." In one leading case, United States v. Mirabile, 15 Envtl. L. Rep. (Envtl. L. Inst.) 20992, 20995 (E.D.Pa. Sept. 6, 1985), the court said that a mortgagee was liable only if it participated in "operational, production, or waste disposal activities." In marked contrast, the Eleventh Circuit Court of Appeals stated that a mortgagee would be liable if it had the "capacity to influence the [borrower's] treatment of hazardous wastes" even if it did not "actually . . . involve itself in the day-to-day operations of the facility." United States v. Fleet Factors Corp., 901 F.2d 1550, 1557 (11th Cir.1990) (abrogated by 42 U.S.C. § 9601(20)(G)(i)(II); see also Monarch Tile, Inc. v. City of Florence, 212 F.3d 1219, 1222 n.2 (11th Cir. 2000).

The courts also markedly differed in considering the CERCLA liability of a mortgagee that has acquired the fee title to the mortgaged land. Some courts held that a mortgagee that acquired the land could have done so solely to protect its security interest. E.g., *Mirabile*. Other courts rejected that view. They held that, as a matter of straightforward statutory construction, a lender that acquires fee title is an "owner." These courts were also concerned with unjustly enriching the mortgagee. E.g., United States v. Maryland Bank & Trust Co., 632 F.Supp. 573 (D.Md.1986).

To provide clearer guidance on these issues, Congress enacted the Asset Conservation, Lender Liability, and Deposit Insurance Protection Act of 1996 ("1996 Statute"). As you review the following provisions from the 1996 Statute concerning mortgagee liability, consider which policies Congress considered to be most important and why. For example, what incentives was Congress attempting to create?

(F) Exclusion of lenders not participants in management

(i) Indicia of ownership to protect security

The term "owner or operator" does not include a person that is a lender that, without participating in the management of a * * * facility, holds indicia of ownership primarily to protect the security interest of the person in the * * * facility.

(ii) Foreclosure

The term "owner or operator" does not include a person that is a lender that did not participate in management of a * * * facility prior to foreclosure, notwithstanding that the person—

    (I)   forecloses on the * * * facility; and

    (II)   after foreclosure, sells, * * * or liquidates the * * * facility, maintains business activities, winds up operations, undertakes a response action * * * with respect to the * * * facility, or takes any other measure to preserve, protect, or prepare the * * * facility prior to sale or disposition,

if the person seeks to sell * * * or otherwise divest the person of the * * * facility at the earliest practicable, commercially reasonable time, on commercially reasonable terms, taking into account market conditions and legal and regulatory requirements. [The terms "foreclosure" and "foreclose" include acquiring title by a deed in lieu of foreclosure. § 9601(20)(H)(iii).]

(G) Participation in management

For purposes of subparagraph (F)—

    (i)   the term "participate in management"—

    (I) means actually participating in the management or operational affairs of a * * * facility; and

    (II) does not include merely having the capacity to influence, or the unexercised right to control, * * * facility operations;

    (ii) a person that is a lender and that holds indicia of ownership primarily to protect a security interest in a * * * facility shall be considered to participate in management only if, while the borrower is still in possession of the * * * facility encumbered by the security interest, the person—

    (I) exercises decisionmaking control over the environmental compliance related to the * * * facility, such that the person has undertaken responsibility for the hazardous substance handling or disposal practices related to the * * * facility; or

    (II) exercises control at a level comparable to that of a manager of the * * * facility, such that the person has assumed or manifested responsibility—

  (aa) for the overall management of the * * * facility encompassing day-to-day decisionmaking with respect to environmental compliance; or

  (bb) over all or substantially all of the operational functions (as distinguished from financial or administrative functions) of the * * * facility other than the function of environmental compliance;

(iii) the term "participate in management" does not include performing an act or failing to act prior to the time at which a security interest is created * * *; and

(iv) the term "participate in management" does not include—

  (I) holding a security interest or abandoning or releasing a security interest;

  (II) including in the terms of an extension of credit, or in a contract or security agreement relating to the extension, a covenant, warranty, or other term or condition that relates to environmental compliance;

  (III) monitoring or enforcing the terms and conditions of the extension of credit or security interest;

  (IV) monitoring or undertaking 1 or more inspections of the * * * facility;

  (V) requiring a response action or other lawful means of addressing the release or threatened release of a hazardous substance in connection with the * * * facility prior to, during, or on the expiration of the term of the extension of credit;

  (VI) providing financial or other advice or counseling in an effort to mitigate, prevent, or cure default or diminution in the value of the * * * facility;

  (VII) restructuring, renegotiating, or otherwise agreeing to alter the terms and conditions of the extension of credit or security interest, exercising forbearance;

  (VIII) exercising other remedies that may be available under applicable law for the breach of a term or condition of the extension of credit or security agreement; or

  (IX) conducting a response action * * *,

if the actions do not rise to the level of participating in
management (within the meaning of clauses (i) and (ii)).

42 U.S.C. § 9601(20)(F), (G). See Jeffrey B. Gracer & Jonathan Kalmuss-
Katz, Commercial Real Estate Loans: Minimizing the Environmental Risk
for Lenders under CERCLA, Practical Law Real Estate, Thomson Reuters
(2020), https://1.next.westlaw.com/Document/I5f59a00f1c8a11e38578f7ccc
38dcbee/View/FullText.html; Douglas A. Henderson, Andrea L. Rimer &
Andrew Perel, Environmental Liability in Commercial Real Estate and
Lending Transactions—Recent Litigation, New Statutory Defenses, 48
Real Est. L.J. 22 (2019); Bert Acken, Secured Creditors: Exempt from
Liability?, 46 Ariz. St. L.J. 489 (2014).

NOTES

1.   *Petroleum and underground storage tanks.* Note that petroleum
products and underground petroleum storage tanks are not covered by
CERCLA, but rather by the Resource Conservation and Recovery Act
("RCRA"). The 1996 Statute extended the protections afforded CERCLA
mortgagees to their RCRA counterparts. It amended RCRA to provide that the
terms "owner" and "operator" "do not include a person that, without
participating in the management of an underground storage tank and
otherwise not engaged in petroleum production, refining, or marketing, holds
indicia of ownership primarily to protect the person's security interest." 42
U.S.C. § 6991b(h)(9)(A). Moreover, the 1996 Statute makes it clear that the
specific CERCLA provisions that protect mortgagees against being
characterized as "participating in management" and that extend the
"protecting security interest" exemption to the post-foreclosure period also
apply to RCRA mortgagees. 42 U.S.C. § 6991b(h)(9)(B).

2.   *Does CERCLA overprotect the mortgagee-purchaser?* Suppose a
mortgagee forecloses a mortgage on a large apartment building and purchases
at the sale. A few weeks later, government authorities determine that the
building's electrical wiring system is defective and dangerous and must be
replaced. As the building owner, the mortgagee-purchaser would normally be
liable for the cost of replacement or repair. Similarly, if a person is injured on
real estate owned by a mortgagee-purchaser who is in the process of reselling
it, the mortgagee is liable. Travelers Property Casualty Co. of Am. v. Liberty
Mut. Ins. Co., 444 F.3d 217, 222 (4th Cir.2006) (mortgagee that purchased a
residential duplex at foreclosure sale and was in process of reselling it held
liable to injured third party for negligent failure to maintain stairway). Is there
a good reason why a mortgagee-purchaser should not also be liable for removal
of toxic substances? Does CERCLA afford too much protection for the
mortgagee-purchaser?

3.   *Advising the mortgagee.* Suppose you represent a mortgage lender.
What advice will you give with respect to future loans? Assuming that you are
satisfied that a proposed borrower's real estate is now free of environmental
contamination, how can the lender protect itself as to the future? What

provisions, if any, should be included in the mortgage documents to deal with potential environmental problems? See Fannie Mae/Freddie Mac Uniform Covenant No. 21 in Appendix, Form 3 infra. Is this language adequate?

Suppose, instead, that you represent a lender whose mortgage is already in default and you have a strong suspicion that the mortgaged real estate is contaminated. Assuming it is permitted in your jurisdiction, should the lender become a mortgagee in possession or should the mortgagee seek the appointment of a receiver? According to one commentator, the "benefit of having a receiver appointed is that the lender is arguably shielded by the fact that the receiver is the agent of the appointing court rather than the agent of the lender or property owner." Matthew L. Kimball, Environmental Strategies for the Real Estate Lender, 7 Real Est.Fin. 13, 22 (1991). Note also that a receiver is characterized under the 1996 Statute as a "fiduciary" and, as such, liability "for the release or threatened release of a hazardous substance at, from, or in connection with a * * * facility held in a fiduciary capacity shall not exceed the assets held in the fiduciary capacity." 42 U.S.C. § 9607(n)(1). James T. O'Reilly, Liability of Lending Institutions and Banks, 1 Superfund & Brownfields Cleanup § 8:24 (2019).

4. *CERCLA lien.* If the United States is not reimbursed for clean-up costs that it incurred, CERCLA gives it a lien on the real estate that was subject to the clean-up action if it belongs to a person who is liable for those costs. See 42 U.S.C. § 9607(*l*). Note that this lien is not given "superpriority" status vis á vis other security interests and liens on the real estate. Rather, it is "subject to the rights of any purchaser, holder of a security interest, or judgment lien creditor whose interest is perfected under applicable State law before notice of the lien has been filed in the appropriate office within the State (or county or other governmental subdivision)." 42 U.S.C. § 9607(*l*)(3). Thus, the CERCLA lien is a "standard lien"; its priority "is determined under traditionally applicable rules of lien priority. Thus, a CERCLA lien will be superior to liens held by unsecured creditors and those filed subsequently but will remain inferior to pre-existing liens." Jonathan Remy Nash, Environmental Superliens and the Problem of Mortgage-Backed Securitization, 59 Wash. & Lee L.Rev. 127, 146 (2002).

5. *State legislation.* More than forty states have enacted legislation similar to CERCLA. See, e.g., Mass.Gen.Laws Ann. c. 21C; Minn.Stat.Ann. § 115B.20; N.Y.—McKinney's State Finance Law § 97–b; Or.Rev.Stat. § 466.670. The statutes in a few of these states, unlike CERCLA, create "superliens" in favor of the state on real estate for which there are unreimbursed clean-up costs. These liens, like many real estate tax liens, are senior to pre-existing perfected mortgages on real estate. See, e.g., Mass.Gen.Laws Ann. c. 21E, § 13 (lien "shall have priority over any encumbrance theretofore recorded, registered or filed * * * other than on real property the greater part of which is devoted to single or multi-family housing."); N.J.Stat.Ann. 58:10–23.11f(f) (lien shall have priority "over all other claims or liens which are or have been filed against the property, except if the property comprises six dwelling units or less and is used for residential

purposes"). How should mortgage lenders react to the "superlien" approach? Should a state's superlien trump a pre-existing recorded purchase money mortgage? Consider Professor Nash's analysis:

> The underlying motive for these superlien statutes is manifest. Absent such a statute, the traditional rules of lien priority would allow a state to expend funds to clean up a contaminated property, with some or all of the benefit from those expenditures inuring to the senior secured lenders. These lenders would see the value of their security increase by virtue of the increase in property value resulting from the cleanup. If a state cannot recover its cleanup expenditures from the contaminating parties, it would be left to pursue any remaining equity in the property and other unencumbered assets of the property owner to recoup its expenses. Because environmental cleanup costs are generally quite large and the property owner is probably insolvent, the state, under these circumstances, will probably not recover much, if any, of the expenditures.

Jonathan Remy Nash, Environmental Superliens and the Problem of Mortgage-Backed Securitization, 59 Wash. & Lee L.Rev. 127, 148–49 (2002). Are there constitutional problems with superliens because they can trump previously recorded and perfected mortgages? See *id.* at 149–51.

How can mortgage lenders protect themselves against such liens? Can they require mortgagors to "escrow" for these liabilities as lenders normally do for real estate taxes? See Section E of this chapter. Can lenders predict potential environmental costs to the same extent that they can for real estate taxes?

6.   *State common law liability.* This section illustrates that lenders have generally succeeded in persuading Congress and many state legislatures to substantially exempt mortgagees from clean-up liability under CERCLA, RCRA, and similar state legislation. But the next case suggests that such mortgagees, as foreclosure purchasers, remain liable to adjoining landowners for environmental contamination on a variety of common law theories.

EDWARDS V. FIRST NATIONAL BANK OF NORTH EAST
Court of Special Appeals of Maryland, 1998
122 Md.App. 96, 712 A.2d 33

Argued before HARRELL, SALMON and BYRNES, JJ.

BYRNES, JUDGE.

* * *

Randy and Cynthia Edwards are the owners of residential real property in North East, Maryland known as 505 Mechanics Valley Road. Their property is adjacent to and downgrade from commercial property known as 513 Mechanics Valley Road. For approximately twenty years, the 513 Mechanics Valley Road site was used for a gasoline service station.

During part of that time, from 1981 until 1994, the property was owned by Jacqueline C. Yerkes. Mrs. Yerkes and her husband added a mini-market to the gasoline service station. The property came to be called the "T & C Mini Market."

First National Bank of North East ("the Bank") held a mortgage on the T & C Mini Market property. When Mrs. Yerkes defaulted on the mortgage, the Bank foreclosed on the property. Thereafter, on May 10, 1994, it purchased the property at the foreclosure sale and took possession of it. A few weeks later, the Bank conducted "tank tightness tests" on two 6,016 gallon underground storage tanks ("USTs") and one 3,000 gallon UST on the property. The tanks passed all of the tests and were judged to be tight.

The Bank then contracted with Edwards Service Station Equipment, Inc. ("ESSE") to remove the USTs. ESSE did so on October 24, 1994, under the watchful eyes of Maryland Department of the Environment ("MDE") employees. Removal of the USTs produced a strong smell of petroleum. Tests that were later performed on the property by MDE revealed the presence of petroleum byproducts in the soil at levels greater than permitted by law. MDE arranged for three testing wells to be installed on the T & C Mini Market property and ordered further testing to be undertaken. Those tests showed the continued presence of petroleum byproducts in the land.

In the meantime, on May 5, 1994, shortly before the Bank took possession of the T & C Mini Market property, Mr. and Mrs. Edwards installed a new deep well on their property. They did so in part because Mrs. Edwards was operating a day care center in their home and she needed to comply with certain local health regulations. The new well was approved by the Cecil County Health Department on September 9, 1994, after officials "completed multiple tests and personal inspections."

In late November, 1994, Mr. and Mrs. Edwards noticed the smell of gasoline in their house. When the smell intensified, they had their well-water tested. Tests performed on January 23, 1995 came up positive for PH-petroleum hydrocarbons. The MDE performed additional tests that confirmed the presence of petroleum byproducts in the Edwards's well.

On August 20, 1996, Mr. and Mrs. Edwards filed suit for damages against the Bank and against ESSE for injury to their real and personal property, in the Circuit Court for Cecil County. They pleaded causes of action against both defendants for * * * negligence, nuisance, trespass, and strict liability. On December 20, 1996, the Bank filed a motion to dismiss for failure to state a claim for which relief could be granted * * *. After hearing argument of counsel, the trial court granted the Bank's motion, from the bench. It subsequently issued a written order dismissing the Bank from the case and entering final judgment against Mr. and Mrs. Edwards in favor of the Bank * * *. Mr. and Mrs. Edwards then noted this appeal.

DISCUSSION

* * *

[Mr. and Mrs. Edwards] maintain * * * that the circuit court erred in ruling that the Water Pollution Control and Abatement Act in its entirety, and Env. § 4–401(i)(2)(i)(2) specifically, abrogated their common law causes of action for negligence, nuisance, trespass, and strict liability in tort.

Env. § 4–401 sets forth definitions for certain terms that are used in the Act. "Person responsible for the discharge," one such term, is defined at Env. § 4–401(i)(1) to include:

(i) The owner of the discharged oil[4];

(ii) The owner, operator, or person in charge of the oil storage facility, vessel, barge, or vehicle involved in the discharge at the time of or immediately before the discharge; and

(iii) Any other person who through act or omission causes the discharge.

The statutory language at issue in this case appears in Env. § 4–401(i)(2), which defines those who do *not* fall into the category of "Person responsible for the discharge:"

(i) A person who, without participating in the management of an underground oil storage tank, and who otherwise is not engaged in petroleum production, refining, or marketing, holds indicia of ownership in an underground oil storage tank primarily to protect its security interest in that underground oil storage tank if that person [. . .]

2. Abandoned that underground oil storage tank under regulations of the Department within 180 days of acquiring the tank through foreclosure or other means.[5]

---

[4] "Oil" is defined to include, inter alia, petroleum, petroleum by-products, and gasoline. Env. § 4–401(g).

[5] The February 27, 1997 amendment to Env. § 4–401(i)(2) added the following to those who are not included in the category of "Person not responsible for the discharge:"

(ii) A holder of a mortgage or deed of trust who acquires title to a property that is subject to a corrective action plan approved by the Department under this subtitle provided that the holder complies with the requirements, prohibitions, and conditions of the plan;

(iii) Subject to paragraph (3) of this subsection, a lender who extends credit for the performance of removal or remedial actions conducted in accordance with requirements imposed under this title who:

1. Has not caused or contributed to a discharge of oil; and

2. Previous to extending that credit, is not a person responsible for the discharge at the site; or

(iv) Subject to paragraph (3) of this subsection, a lender who takes action to protect or preserve a mortgage or deed of trust on a site or a security interest in property located on a site at which a discharge of oil has occurred, by stabilizing, containing, removing, or

The Bank contends that, on the facts alleged in the complaint and within the meaning of Env. § 4–401(i)(2)(i)(2), it "abandoned" the USTs at the T & C Mini Market site within 180 days of acquiring the property through foreclosure and thus it is not a "Person responsible for the discharge" under the Act. It argues further that because the legislative intent behind Env. § 4–401(i)(2)(i)(2) is, to use its words, "to protect a foreclosing lender from liability if the lender removes an underground storage tank within 180 days following foreclosure," the trial court properly ruled that the Act abrogated all common law causes of action against it arising out of contamination of adjacent property by oil kept in the USTs on the T & C Mini Market property. We disagree.

In determining the legislative intent of a statute, " '[t]he primary source . . . is, of course, the language of the statute itself.' " *State v. Pagano*, 341 Md. 129, 133, 669 A.2d 1339 (1996) * * *. "In some circumstances, [the courts] need not look beyond the statutory language to determine the legislative purpose. 'Sometimes the language in question will be so clearly consistent with apparent purpose (and not productive of any absurd result) that further research will be unnecessary.' " *Pagano*, 341 Md. at 133, 669 A.2d 1339 (quoting *Kaczorowski v. City of Baltimore*, 309 Md. 505, 515, 525 A.2d 628 (1987)).

The Bank urges us to construe Env. § 4–401(i)(2)(i)(2) broadly, as a general grant of immunity from suit in favor of commercial lenders. Yet, the statutory language states only that, under certain limited and defined circumstances, a lender is not a "Person responsible for the discharge." To the extent that a lender could face exposure to liability as a "Person responsible for the discharge," within the meaning of the Act, its exclusion from that category under Env. § 4–401(i)(2)(i)(2) would insulate it. To interpret Env. § 4–401(i)(2)(i)(2) to confer blanket immunity for lenders against common law liability for groundwater contamination, we would have to disregard the narrowly circumscribed language of the statute and illogically generalize its meaning. In interpreting the language of a statute, we must apply common sense and avoid unreasonable constructions. * * * We decline to find in the limited and specific exclusion spelled out in Env.

---

preventing the discharge of oil in a manner that does not cause or contribute to a discharge of oil if:

    1. The lender provides advance written notice of its actions to the Department or in the event of an emergency in which action is required within 2 hours, provides notice by telephone;

    2. The lender, previous to taking the action, is not a person responsible for the discharge at the site; and

    3. The action does not violate a provision of this article.

The amendment also added a new subsection, at Env. § 4–401(i)(3), which provides: "A lender taking action to protect or preserve a mortgage or deed of trust or security interest in property located on a site, who causes or contributes to a discharge of oil shall be liable solely for costs incurred in response to the discharge which the lender caused or to which the lender contributed unless the lender was a person responsible for the discharge before acquiring a mortgage, deed of trust, or security interest in the site or property located on the site."

§ 4–401(i)(2)(i)(2) the overarching and sweeping meaning that the Bank suggests.

In addition, Env. § 4–401(i)(2)(i)(2) must be read in conjunction with the remainder of the Act, * * * which includes a purpose clause expressly prohibiting any construction of the Act so as to abrogate or preempt common law remedies. Env. § 4–403, entitled "Construction and purpose of subtitle; remedies additional and cumulative," is explicit:

> ... It is the purpose of this subtitle to provide additional and cumulative remedies to prevent, abate, and control the pollution of the waters of the State. This subtitle may not be construed to abridge or alter rights of action or remedies in equity under existing common law, statutory law, criminal or civil, nor may any provision of this subtitle, or any act done pursuant to it, be construed as estopping any person, as riparian owner or otherwise, in the exercise of his rights in equity, under the common law, or statutory law to suppress nuisances or abate pollution.

The meaning of Env. § 4–403 is plainly apparent from its language. The words of the statute reflect the General Assembly's intention that the Act, which comprises subtitle 4 of the Environment Article, not be read to affect common law remedies. We need not search further for statutory meaning * * *. Moreover,

> Maryland courts adhere to the policy that statutes are not to be construed to alter the common-law by implication. The reason for this protection of common-law principles from statutory erosion is based on Article 5 of the Maryland Declaration of Rights, which guarantees to Maryland citizens the common-law of England. Thus, there is a presumption against statutory preemption of the common-law. The presumption is easily dissipated if the statute expressly overrides a common-law principle.

Hardy v. State, 301 Md. 124, 131–32, 482 A.2d 474 (1984) (citations omitted). * * * In this case, not only does the statute in question not expressly override the common law, it expressly states that it shall not be interpreted to override the common law.

Without making mention of Env. § 4–403 in its brief, the Bank argues that Env. § 4–401(i)(2)(i)(2) must be interpreted broadly so as to protect lenders against common law liability for two reasons: first, any other interpretation of the subsection would render it superfluous * * * and second, the legislative history surrounding the passage of the section evidences an intention on the part of the General Assembly to extend a broad grant of immunity to commercial lenders.

We agree that statutes should not be read so as to render their language superfluous. *See Bell Atlantic*, 346 Md. at 178, 695 A.2d 171; *City of Baltimore v. Hackley*, 300 Md. 277, 283, 477 A.2d 1174 (1984). * * * We disagree, however, that to give meaning to Env. § 4–401(i)(2)(i)(2), we must read it to abrogate common law causes of action against lenders, in direct contravention of the statutory purpose stated in Env. § 4–403. * * *

The legislative history that the Bank cites and the policy observations that it makes are not persuasive. To be sure, the 1992 enactment of what is now Env. § 4–401(i)(2)(i)(2) and the 1997 amendments to that section evidence legislative concern that commercial lenders not be disinclined to extend mortgages for fear of incurring legal responsibility and liability under the Act when they must take possession of mortgaged property to protect a security interest. Indeed, Env. § 4–401(i)(2)(i)(2) addresses those concerns by protecting lenders from remediation and clean up suits brought by the MDE when certain conditions are satisfied. The legislative history does not evidence an express or even an implied intention on the part of the General Assembly to abrogate, abolish, or preempt common law remedies against commercial lenders, however.

Finally, the Bank argues that we should affirm the circuit court's dismissal of the nuisance, trespass, negligence, and strict liability in tort claims against it because the facts alleged in the complaint do not support those causes of action. This argument was not raised in or decided by the circuit court. Accordingly, it is not properly before us for review. * * *

JUDGMENT REVERSED. CASE REMANDED TO CIRCUIT COURT * * * FOR FURTHER PROCEEDINGS CONSISTENT WITH THIS OPINION.

NOTE

Should mortgagees be exempt from common law liability? In the absence of such immunity, how should a mortgagee proceed as to a mortgage in default when it has reason to believe that the mortgaged premises are contaminated and potential owner liability exists to adjoining landowners or other third parties? To avoid becoming an owner of the contaminated premises and subject to the common law liabilities associated with ownership, should the mortgagee simply decline to foreclose? Should its decision be influenced by the amount of those potential liabilities? If the mortgagor or others who are personally liable for the mortgage debt have substantial other assets, should the mortgagee simply sue on the mortgage debt and avoid foreclosure entirely?

F. INSURANCE AND REAL ESTATE TAXES

Both the mortgagor and mortgagee have insurable interests for damage to the mortgaged property. The mortgagor's insurable interest is the value of the property; the mortgagee's insurable interest is the mortgage debt amount. See Nelson, Whitman, Burkhart & Freyermuth,

Real Estate Finance Law § 4.14 (6th ed.2015). Of course, a mortgagee cannot collect both the proceeds of its casualty insurance policy and the full debt as well, because it would result in a windfall and unjust enrichment. The mortgagee is limited to a single recovery of the debt amount. See Bank of Richmondville v. Terra Nova Ins. Co. Ltd., 263 A.D.2d 786, 694 N.Y.S.2d 206 (1999); Sotelo v. Washington Mut. Ins. Co., 734 A.2d 421 (Pa. Super. 1999); Benton Banking Co. v. Tennessee Farmers Mut. Ins. Co., 906 S.W.2d 436, 438 (Tenn. 1995).

In principle, both the mortgagor and mortgagee can purchase their own casualty insurance policies. However, the mortgagee normally requires the mortgagor to carry casualty insurance insuring the interests of both parties. An older type of policy, known as a "loss payable" policy or "open" policy, contained a clause providing simply that the loss would be payable to the mortgagor and the mortgagee "as their interests may appear." Today, the "standard mortgage" or "union mortgage" policy is used nearly universally. It contains language along the following lines:

> Loss or damage, if any, under this policy shall be payable to the mortgagee as his interest may appear, and this insurance, as to the mortgagee only therein, shall not be invalidated by any act or neglect of the mortgagor or owner of the within described property, nor by any change in the title or ownership of the property, nor by the occupation of the premises for purposes more hazardous than are permitted by this policy, provided, that in case the mortgagor or owner shall neglect to pay any premium under this policy, the mortgagee shall on demand pay the same.

You can see why lenders prefer this form of policy and have pressed for its widespread adoption. In essence, it ensures that the lender can recover on the policy no matter what the borrower has done. The lender is covered even if the borrower intentionally demolishes improvements on the land. Wells Fargo Bank, NA v. Null, 304 Mich.App. 508, 847 N.W.2d 657 (2014); Home Sav. of Am., F.S.B. v. Continental Ins. Co., 87 Cal.App.4th 835, 104 Cal.Rptr.2d 790 (2001). For an excellent review of the "standard mortgage" clause see Patrick A. Randolph, Jr., The Mortgagee's Interest in Casualty Loss Proceeds: Evolving Rules and Risks, 32 Real Prop., Prob. & Tr. J. 1 (1997).

Under the "standard mortgage" clause, it is entirely possible that the lender will recover on the insurance policy though the borrower has engaged in acts, such as arson or fraud, that bar the borrower from recovery. In this situation, if the insurer pays the mortgage debt in full, it is subrogated to the debt and the mortgage and can enforce them against the mortgagor. See, e.g., The Money Store/Massachusetts, Inc. v. Hingham Mut. Fire Ins. Co., 430 Mass. 298, 718 N.E.2d 840 (1999) (mortgagor blew up insured building; insurer paid off the mortgage and could enforce it against the mortgagor); 16 Couch, Insurance § 224:27 (Russ ed. 2002). The subrogation principle derives from general legal principles and is usually stated explicitly in the insurance policy as well. A typical clause, which applied in West Suburban Bank v. Badger Mut. Ins. Co., 947 F.Supp. 333 (N.D.Ill.1996), provides:

> We may pay the mortgagee the remaining principal and accrued interest in return for a full assignment of the mortgagee's interest and any instruments given as security for the mortgage debt.

An additional benefit of the standard mortgage clause is that, if the mortgagor fails to pay the premium, the insurer cannot cancel the policy against the mortgagee without first notifying the mortgagee of the default and making a demand that the mortgagee pay the delinquent premium. See, e.g., Farmers Home Mut. Fire Ins. Co. v. Bank of Pocahontas, 355 Ark. 19, 129 S.W.3d 832 (2003).

Does the existence of insurance coverage paid for by the mortgagor benefit the mortgagee? It will do so if either of two sets of facts is true: (1) the mortgage contains a covenant requiring the borrower to carry the insurance, or (2) in most courts, the mortgagee is named as an insured or loss payee in the insurance policy.

Here is a little more detail on those points. Courts universally hold that, "if the mortgagor promised the mortgagee, in the mortgage or otherwise, to purchase the insurance," the mortgagee has a right to the insurance proceeds to the extent the casualty has impaired the mortgagee's security. Restatement (Third) of Property (Mortgages) § 4.7(a)(1). This is true even if the mortgagee is not named as a "loss payee" in the policy. See Conrad Bros. v. John Deere Ins. Co., 640 N.W.2d 231 (Iowa 2001); Castle Ins. Co. v. Vanover, 993 S.W.2d 509 (Ky.App. 1999); General Star Indemnity Co. v. Pike County Nat'l Bank, 706 So.2d 227 (Miss. 1997). Courts often describe the mortgagee's right as an "equitable lien" on the insurance proceeds. The mortgagee's right also does not depend on the mortgagor being personally liable for the debt; the mortgagee is entitled to the benefits of the insurance policy even if the loan is "nonrecourse," see San Roman v. Atlantic Mut. Ins. Co., 250 A.D.2d 585, 672 N.Y.S.2d 396 (1998), and even if an antideficiency statute applies, see Redingler v. Imperial Sav. & Loan Ass'n, 47 Cal.App.3d 48, 120 Cal.Rptr. 575 (1975).

Nearly all mortgages contain clauses requiring the mortgagor to carry specified forms of insurance. However, the mortgagee may try to claim insurance proceeds for a loss not specified in the mortgage. For example, in Ziello v. Superior Court, 36 Cal.App.4th 321, 42 Cal.Rptr.2d 251 (1995), the mortgage stated that the mortgagor would carry a fire and "extended coverage" policy. In fact, the mortgagor also purchased earthquake coverage. The court held that, because the mortgage did not require that type of coverage, the mortgagee had no right to the insurance proceeds when the property was damaged by an earthquake.

If the mortgagee is named as an insured or loss payee in the policy, the mortgagee normally can benefit from the insurance proceeds to the extent necessary to pay the mortgage debt, even if neither the mortgage nor any other agreement required the borrower to carry the insurance. See, e.g., Singer v. American States Ins., 245 Mich.App. 370, 631 N.W.2d 34 (2001) (installment contract vendor was listed on declaration page of insurance policy as "contract vendor"; court held vendor could recover under the policy as a named insured). However, a California court has held that, unless the borrower promised to provide insurance for the mortgagee's benefit, the latter cannot claim the insurance proceeds even if it is a named insured in the policy. See Martin v. World Sav. & Loan Ass'n, 92 Cal.App.4th 803, 112 Cal.Rptr.2d 225 (2001).

The mortgagee's right to the insurance proceeds is only the beginning of the inquiry. Can the mortgagee elect to apply the proceeds toward a pay down of the mortgage debt, or must the mortgagee permit the mortgagor to use them to restore the damaged real estate, as most mortgagors doubtless expect? That is the issue in the following case.

STARKMAN V. SIGMOND
Superior Court of New Jersey, 1982
184 N.J.Super. 600, 446 A.2d 1249

DEIGHAN, J.S.C. The question to be resolved herein is whether plaintiff mortgagors are entitled to the proceeds of a fire insurance policy (which insures the interest of both the mortgagors and the mortgagees) to rebuild the residence or must the proceeds be applied in reduction of the mortgage where the value of the vacant land exceeds the balance due on the mortgage which has been kept current. Research has revealed no New Jersey case which addresses this problem of payment of the fire insurance proceeds where the security is not impaired and the mortgage is not in default. It is held that under the facts of this case the mortgagors are entitled to the proceeds to rebuild the residence.

Plaintiff mortgagors Tami Starkman and Dora Birnbaum executed a purchase money mortgage to defendant mortgagees Robert Sigmond and Barbara Sigmond, his wife, in the amount of $60,000. A fire loss occurred on the mortgaged premises; mortgagees demand that the insurance proceeds be applied to the outstanding mortgage balance. Plaintiff mortgagors seek the proceeds of the fire insurance to rebuild the residence. The essential facts are not in dispute and both parties move for summary judgment.

After the complaint was filed and before filing an answer, defendant mortgagees moved for summary judgment. At the time the motion was heard the insurance company, Prudential Property and Casualty Insurance (Prudential), was not a party to the action. The court determined it should have the benefit of Prudential's position on its obligation under the insurance policy, and on August 23, 1981 denied defendants' motion. Thereafter, plaintiffs filed an amended complaint against Prudential; defendants Sigmond filed an answer and crossclaim against Prudential. Prudential filed its answer, including a third-party complaint against plaintiffs' husbands, Morris Starkman and Simon Birnbaum, asserting they were the real parties in interest.

Subsequently, Prudential agreed to issue a $135,000 check in settlement of all claims made under the insurance policy. After application by plaintiffs, the court on December 21, 1981, by consent of the parties, ordered Prudential to issue the $135,000 in two drafts: one in the sum of $60,000 payable to both mortgagees and mortgagors and the other in the sum of $75,000 payable to plaintiff mortgagors only. Thereafter, plaintiffs, defendants Sigmond, and Prudential entered into a consent order to invest the $60,000 pending a determination by the court of the rights of the parties. Prudential required a release from the Sigmonds before it would issue the $60,000 check. On February 16, 1982 the court entered another consent order which provided that payment of the $60,000 would be in [the] nature of an interpleader. The Sigmonds were to execute the release and assert any claims against the fund which may have been asserted against Prudential.

On January 6, 1981 plaintiffs purchased a house and lot located at 112 South Sacramento Avenue, Ventnor, New Jersey from defendants for $150,000. Defendants took back a purchase money mortgage in the sum of $60,000 with interest at the rate of 10% payable in monthly amortization installments of $525. The mortgage is for a 30-year term but has a "balloon" at the end which requires full payment to be made on January 6, 1986, i.e., the entire mortgage is payable within five years. The mortgage also required the mortgagors to maintain hazard insurance on the premises for the benefit of the mortgagees. Prudential issued the insurance policy to plaintiffs as the "insureds"; defendants are listed as mortgagees on the face of the insurance policy. The loss payable clause to the mortgagee appears in the body of the policy and provides:

> Loss, if any, under this policy, shall be payable to the mortgagee * * *, named on the first page of this policy, as interest may appear * * *, and this insurance as to the interest of the mortgagee * * *, shall not be invalidated by any act or neglect of the mortgagor * * *.

This clause is known as a "union mortgage clause" because it insulates the mortgagee from policy defenses which may be available against the mortgagor. 5A Appleman, Insurance Law and Practice, § 3401 at 282

(1970). The union mortgage clause is to be distinguished from an "open loss payable clause." Under an open loss clause the policy merely identifies who is to collect the proceeds. Ibid. "In the open form, the indemnity of the mortgagee is subject to the risk of every act and neglect of the mortgagor which would avoid the original policy in the mortgagor's hands." 5A Appleman, op. cit., § 3401 at 293.[1]

On February 23, 1981 the house was substantially destroyed by fire. On November 17, 1981 plaintiffs received notification from the building inspector of Ventnor to demolish the dwelling because the fire damage amounted to total destruction creating a dangerous situation—the walls could collapse and youngsters were playing on the rotting floors. Plaintiffs submitted a certification from a real estate appraiser evaluating the vacant land at approximately $71,500, an amount which is at least $10,000 in excess of the outstanding balance on the mortgage. Plaintiffs have kept the monthly mortgage payments current.

Plaintiffs argue that since the mortgage is not in default and the security is not impaired, defendants cannot insist on applying the proceeds of the insurance to pay off the mortgage debt. Plaintiffs place primary reliance on the terms and conditions for acceleration in the mortgage and note. Plaintiffs observe that the provisions of the note and mortgage were negotiated[2] and these documents are silent as to acceleration in the event of fire. They contend that if defendants use the proceeds to satisfy the mortgage debt, they will be deprived of the loan from defendants and defendants are currently getting what they bargained for, i.e., continuous monthly payments over a period of time.

In contrast, defendants rely on the terms of the insurance policy. They argue that the policy is an independent agreement between the insurer and the mortgagees and that their rights cannot be affected by any acts of the mortgagors in rebuilding. Defendants claim their rights under the insurance policy became vested at the time of the fire and no subsequent act of the mortgagor can defeat their right to the proceeds. Defendants suggest that payment of the $60,000 to plaintiffs will result in a windfall to plaintiffs.[3] Defendants maintain that plaintiffs will have realized $56,000 profit within a few months. While defendants acknowledge that part of the proceeds of the insurance represent a loss of contents by

---

[1] For a short discussion of the two clauses, see 495 Corp. v. N.J. Ins. Underwriting Ass'n, 173 N.J.Super. 114, 117, n. 2, 413 A.2d 630 (App.Div.1980).

[2] Various provisions of the note were deleted pursuant to the negotiations.

[3]

$135,000	(insurance proceeds)
+71,500	(value of lot) =
206,500	
−150,000	(purchase price) =
$56,500	(profit)

plaintiffs, they suggest that the contents claim would not in any way approximate $56,000.

The standard mortgage clause creates an independent contract of insurance, for the separate benefit of the mortgagee, engrafted upon the main contract of insurance contained in the policy itself. 495 Corp. v. N.J. Ins. Underwriting Ass'n, supra, 173 N.J.Super. at 123, 413 A.2d 630, citing Reed v. Firemen's Ins. Co., 81 N.J.L. 523, 526, 80 A. 462 (E. & A.1910); 5A Appleman, op. cit., § 3401 at 292. An independent agreement exists between the mortgagee and the insurer. Employers' Fire Ins. Co. v. Ritter, 112 N.J.Eq. 418, 420, 164 A. 426 (Ch.1933). There are two beneficiaries of the insurance policy, the owner and the mortgagee, each with distinct and dissimilar rights. Id. at 421, 164 A. 426.

One line of cases and commentators state as a general rule that the mortgagee can recover the insurance proceeds regardless of the value of the remaining security once a fire loss occurs. E.g., Walter v. Marine Office of America, 537 F.2d 89, 97–99 (5 Cir.1976) (applying Louisiana law); Savarese v. Ohio Farmers' Ins. Co., 260 N.Y. 45, 53, 182 N.E. 665, 667 (Ct.App.1932); 5A Appleman, op. cit., § 3405 at 320; 29 N.J.Practice (Cunningham & Tischler, Law of Mortgages), § 164 at 756 (1975). The rationale of these cases results from a singular approach which focuses solely on the insurance policy. The policy is categorized as an independent contract[4] between the insurer and the mortgagee. Once a fire loss occurs, the mortgagee's right to the insurance proceeds vests. Any future act of the mortgagor which restores the property to its pre-fire condition is deemed irrelevant since the mortgagee is entitled to immediate payment after the fire.

Defendants Sigmond urge that the following section of the insurance policy requires direct payment to the mortgagee:

4. Mortgage Clause

Loss, if any, under this policy, shall be payable to the mortgagee (or trustee) named on the first page of this policy, as interest may appear, under all present or future mortgages upon the property herein described, in which the aforesaid may have an interest as mortgagee (or trustee), *in order of precedence of said mortgage* * * *. [Emphasis supplied]

---

4 See discussion of union mortgage clause, supra. One court has concluded that such a clause creates an *independent cause of action* by the mortgagee as a third-party beneficiary of the insurance policy, *not an independent contract*:

The fact that practically a limitless benefit is conferred by the standard clause [union clause] upon the mortgagee makes it none the less a benefit, and, however limitless a benefit may be, it can never reach the dignity of a contract. [Walker v. Queen Ins. Co., 136 S.C. 144, 160–163, 134 S.E. 263, 269 (1926), cited in 2 Williston, Contracts (3 ed. Jaeger 1959), § 401A at 1086, n. 6].

The foregoing clause does not establish that losses are to be paid to the mortgagees, but rather sets the order of priority for payment if there is more than one mortgagee. The clause negatives proportionate payment by the insurer as between the mortgagees in the event that the mortgage claims exceed the amount to be paid by the insurance company or in the event both mortgagees make a claim for the proceeds of insurance.

Other courts and commentators adopt the opposite rule of law and allow the mortgagor to recover the insurance proceeds in order to rebuild the damaged property. E.g., Schoolcraft v. Ross, 81 Cal.App.3d 75, 146 Cal.Rptr. 57 (D.Ct.App.1978); Fergus v. Wilmarth, 117 Ill. 542, 7 N.E. 508 (Sup.Ct.1886); Cottman Co. v. Continental Trust Co., 169 Md. 595, 182 A. 551 (Ct.App.1936); Osborne, Nelson & Whitman, Real Estate Finance Law (3d ed. 1979), § 4.15 at 150; 46 C.J.S., Insurance, § 1147 at 29 (under authority of a covenant to repair).

Various analytical approaches allow courts to reach this result. Some courts conclude that the purpose of the insurance is to maintain the security for the mortgage debt—if the property is restored, the security has not been impaired. Therefore, the purpose of the insurance has been fulfilled as to the mortgagee's interest and the mortgagor recovers the proceeds. Cottman v. Continental Trust Co., supra.

Osborne, Nelson and Whitman, in their treatise Real Estate Finance Law (3d ed. 1979), § 4.15 at 150, comment:

> At least in the absence of mortgage provisions to the contrary, it would seem that in the modern standard mortgage policy context where the mortgage is not in default, the mortgagor normally should be able, where rebuilding is practical, to insist upon the application of the insurance proceeds to rebuild the premises. To be sure, to permit the mortgagor to defeat the mortgagee's right to recovery by rebuilding may force the mortgagee to litigate the extent and sufficiency of repairs. On the other hand, it is almost always the mortgagor who is paying the premiums on the casualty insurance policy. Moreover, while permitting the mortgagee to utilize the insurance proceeds to pay the mortgage debt presumably benefits the mortgagor by rendering the property free from the mortgage lien to the extent of the loss, in many cases the mortgagor probably cannot afford to rebuild or is unable to obtain new mortgage financing for that purpose. Thus, on balance, it would seem more equitable in most cases to permit the mortgagor to rebuild and have the insurance applied to that purpose.

There is precedent for this view. One leading case is Cottman Co. v. Continental Trust Co., supra. There, plaintiff mortgaged its tugboats to secure a debenture with defendants as trustee (mortgagee). Pursuant to the requirements of the mortgage, insurance was taken out to protect the interest of the trustee (mortgagee). Thereafter, several of the tugs were damaged and repaired at plaintiff's expense. The insurer paid the claim of the trustee, who refused to reimburse plaintiff. Plaintiff sued the trustee for the proceeds of the insurance. In reversing a judgment for defendant trustee and holding that plaintiff mortgagor was entitled to the proceeds of the insurance, the Maryland Court of Appeals stated:

> Few cases, apparently, have reached appellate courts where the use of the insurance money for the repair and restoration of the security has been combatted by the recipient mortgagee. In such cases the argument is made that by virtue of the replacement or restoration, the creditor is left in the same position as he was before the loss, and therefore has no ground of complaint. It cannot be denied that if the restoration of the security, at the expense of the debtor, to the value it had before the loss or damage, leaves the parties in statu quo, then the retention of the insurance money by the creditor, mortgagee, or trustee, as additional security, would put the holder in a better position than he had originally bargained for. The theory of insurance, however, does not contemplate a resulting profit to the insured, or his mortgagee or other creditor. The interest of the mortgagee is to maintain the equilibrium of debt and security; and if, by the application of the insurance money to the upkeep of the security, that parity would be continued, it is not inequitable to require the payee of the fund to transfer the same to the debtor for that purpose, upon properly safeguarding its application to that end. [169 Md. at 601–02, 182 A. at 554]

In Schoolcraft v. Ross, supra, the deed of trust (mortgage) specifically gave the beneficiary (mortgagee) an option to use the insurance proceeds to rebuild or to apply in reduction of the mortgage debt. The mortgagee, relying on the option clause, elected to apply the proceeds to the debt despite the mortgagor's request to use the proceeds for rebuilding. The mortgagor could not afford to continue to pay the mortgage and also pay rent for an apartment, and thus defaulted in payment on the mortgage. In an action by the mortgagor for damages the California court held:

> [T]he right of a beneficiary (e.g., mortgagee) to apply insurance proceeds to the balance of a note secured by a deed of trust must be performed in good faith and with fair dealing and that to the extent the security was not impaired the beneficiary *must* permit those proceeds to be used for the cost of rebuilding. [81 Cal.App.3d at 77, 146 Cal.Rptr. at 58; emphasis supplied]

Since there was no evidence of the impairment of the security, the court held the mortgagee had no right to the funds. The court, even in face of the mortgagee's option, observed:

Forcing the buyer to pay off in advance would result in a buyer losing certain property rights contemplated by the parties, *among them the benefit of a long term loan which permits the buyer to spread the purchase price of the property over a long time.* [81 Cal.App.3d at 81, 146 Cal.Rptr. at 60; emphasis supplied]

The court found no evidence of impairment of the security and concluded "To the extent the security was not impaired, [mortgagee] had no right to the funds." Ibid.

Cottman and *Savarese*, both supra, demonstrate a general principle that hazard insurance is to protect the mortgagee's interest if the security for the debt is impaired. Absent an impairment, the mortgagee has no right to insist on payment from the insurer. The proceeds are to be paid to the insured mortgagor to effect the repair. New Jersey has recognized impairment of security as a rationale for recovery by mortgagees in other situations. "[T]he theory of recovery by a mortgagee is indemnity against an impairment of the mortgaged property * * *." 495 Corp. v. N.J. Ins. Underwriting Ass'n, supra, 173 N.J.Super. at 118, 413 A.2d 630 (foreclosure). A similar principle of impairment of security of mortgage has been applied to condemnation proceedings. In Transportation Comm'r v. Kastner, 179 N.J.Super. 613, 433 A.2d 448 (Law Div.1981), a part of the mortgaged property was taken by condemnation. The mortgage made no provision for payment of the condemnation award in the event of a partial taking. In holding that the mortgagees were not entitled to have the condemnation award paid the court stated:

[A] lienholder cannot enforce his lien against the condemnation award unless the remaining property is of insufficient value to satisfy his lien. [at 615, 433 A.2d 448]

If the proceeds are paid to the mortgagees in the present case, mortgagors will be damaged to the extent that they will lose the benefit of a long-term loan which was bargained for. The court takes judicial notice of the current prevailing high interest rates and the general scarcity of mortgage money, particularly for construction mortgages. If plaintiffs were forced to obtain a mortgage in the open market, it certainly would be greatly to their disadvantage and at a much higher interest rate than that to which plaintiffs and defendants Sigmond had bargained for. If construction mortgage financing were not available, plaintiffs could not even rebuild their home.

Moreover, there is evidence that the parties did not intend to accelerate the debt in case of fire. Under the insurance policy the insurer has the option to repair, rebuild or replace the property destroyed or damaged within a reasonable time and on giving notice of its intention to do so within 30 days after the receipt of the proof of loss. The dissent in Savarese v. Ohio Farmers' Ins. Co., supra, focused on the insurer's policy option to repair the property or to pay the loss as evidence of the purpose of the policy to maintain the security.

> [T]his clause [option to repair] in the agreement furnishes some indication that the purpose of the policy and the provision therein contained [to pay the mortgagee] *was to protect the mortgagee's interest in the property* only if such damage was not repaired. [260 N.Y. at 60, 182 N.E. at 670 (Lehman, J. dissenting); emphasis supplied]

If the insurer had elected to exercise that option, both mortgagees and mortgagors would be bound. See 5A Appleman, op. cit., § 3405 at 317. This provision, coupled with the covenant to repair in the mortgage, indicates that the purpose of the insurance was to protect the mortgagees' interest if the security was impaired. As a further indication of this intent the parties specifically deleted a provision in the note which would have permitted acceleration in the event of a breach of the covenant to repair. A similar provision in the mortgage was not deleted. Where acceleration provisions of a note and mortgage are in an irreconcilable conflict the note will prevail. See 55 Am.Jur.2d, Mortgages, § 176 at 304.

While a covenant to repair and a covenant to rebuild are not identical, the deletion of acceleration for breach of the covenant to repair in the note is indicative of the parties' intent. The mortgagees in the present case are attempting to accelerate the debt indirectly by demanding payment of the proceeds, a right which by negotiation they specifically gave up.

Lastly, defendant mortgagees are not prejudiced by permitting rebuilding of the residence and have sustained no damages. Property insurance is a contract of indemnity. 29 N.J.Practice, op. cit., § 164 at 737. The mortgagee collects the proceeds to compensate for its loss.

> It is an elementary principle of insurance law that fire insurance * * * is a contract of personal indemnity, not one from which a profit is to be realized * * * [T]he right to recover must be commensurate with the loss *actually* sustained. [Glens Falls Ins. Co. v. Sterling, 219 Md. 217, 222, 148 A.2d 453, 456 (Ct.App.1959); emphasis in original]

Since the vacant land remains as full security for the mortgage debt, it is difficult to identify any loss sustained by the mortgagee. This case differs from others in that, at the time the right to proceeds vested, unlike the *Savarese,* supra, rationale, the vacant land fully secured the debt. Cases which permit the mortgagee to recover refuse to take a hindsight view if the property has been restored by the trial date; the courts concentrate on the impairment of the security on the date of the fire. There has never been in this case impairment for purposes of the mortgagees interest.

The court looks to the substance of the whole transaction *rather
than to seek a metaphysical hypothesis upon which to justify a loss
that is no loss.* [Ramsdell v. Insurance Co. of N. Amer., 197 Wis.
136, 139, 221 N.W. 654, 655 (Sup.Ct.1928); emphasis supplied]

The court finds that mortgagees have suffered no damage as a result
of the fire, and until the building is commenced they have the security of
the $60,000 fund which is in escrow. They have no loss for which
indemnification is required nor have they been prejudiced. * * *

NOTES

1.   *The significance of mortgage language.* An extremely important
factual difference exists between the *Starkman* case and the *Schoolcraft* case,
which the court discussed in *Starkman.* In *Starkman,* the mortgage was silent
as to the disposition of the insurance proceeds between the mortgagor and
mortgagee. In *Schoolcraft,* on the other hand, an express mortgage clause
purported to give the mortgagee the right to capture the proceeds. Thus, the
New Jersey court merely had to reverse the traditional "default rule" to reach
its result, while the California court had to go farther and refuse to enforce the
mortgage language.

Even *Starkman* is a minority view, though the Restatement (Third) of
Property (Mortgages) § 4.6 adopts it. If the mortgagor promised the mortgagee
to insure the premises, courts in most cases give the mortgagee the option of
applying the insurance proceeds to the mortgage debt or to rebuilding the
mortgaged premises, if no mortgage language is to the contrary. The
mortgagee's right normally does not require a finding that rebuilding will
jeopardize the mortgage security. See Nelson, Whitman, Burkhart &
Freyermuth, Real Estate Finance Law § 4.15 (6th ed.2015).

The *Schoolcraft* approach, which endorses the use of insurance proceeds
to rebuild in the face of specific mortgage language giving the mortgagee the
option of compelling prepayment of the mortgage debt, is even more unusual;
indeed, it may be unique. Most courts seem to interpret even less precise
language in a more pro-mortgagee fashion. See, e.g., Giberson v. First Fed. Sav.
& Loan Ass'n of Waterloo, 329 N.W.2d 9 (Iowa 1983) (clause allowed proceeds
to be used for rebuilding "when authorized by the [mortgagee]"; court refused
to give summary judgment for mortgagors who sought the funds for rebuilding
without mortgagee's consent). Several courts have expressly rejected the
Schoolcraft approach. See, e.g., English v. Fischer, 660 S.W.2d 521 (Tex.1983)
(the "novel" doctrine of "good faith and fair dealing" is inapplicable when the
mortgage language affords the mortgagee the prepayment option); Loving v.
Ponderosa Systems, Inc., 479 N.E.2d 531 (Ind.1985).

On the other hand, California went even farther than *Schoolcraft.* In
Kreshek v. Sperling, 157 Cal.App.3d 279, 204 Cal.Rptr. 30 (1984), the court
required the lender to give the insurance proceeds to the borrower though the
borrower did not intend to rebuild! Because the mortgage debt was $320,000

and the property was worth more than $2 million despite the fire, the court concluded that the fire did not impair the lender's security. The California legislature subsequently overruled *Kreshek*, but it left *Schoolcraft* intact. See Cal. Civ. Code § 2924.7. Hence, if the borrower does not want to rebuild, the lender is entitled to the insurance proceeds, up to the amount of the debt. See California Fair Plan v. Boktor, 2003 WL 22883998 (Cal.Ct.App.2003, not reported in Cal.Rptr.).

2. *When should rebuilding be permitted with insurance proceeds?* As a practical matter, mortgagors and mortgagees probably routinely agree to use the insurance proceeds for rebuilding in most instances of casualty loss. The Fannie Mae/Freddie Mac Uniform Single-Family Mortgage form, reprinted as Form 3 in the Appendix, is very widely used for residential mortgage loans nationwide. Section 5 of that form provides: "Unless Lender and Borrower otherwise agree in writing, any insurance proceeds . . . shall be applied to restoration or repair of the Property, if the restoration or repair is economically feasible and Lender's security is not lessened."

In a similar vein, Restatement (Third) of Property (Mortgages) § 4.7(b) (1997)* provides that:

> Unless the mortgage effectively provides to the contrary, if restoration of the loss or damage . . . is reasonably feasible within the remaining term of the mortgage with the funds received by the mortgagee, together with any additional funds made available by the mortgagor, and if after restoration the real estate's value will equal or exceed its value at the time the mortgage was made, the mortgagee holds the funds received subject to a duty to apply them, at the mortgagor's request and upon reasonable conditions, toward restoration.

However, the view that restoration is a reasonable demand to which lenders should submit is not universal. In General G.M.C. Sales, Inc. v. Passarella, 195 N.J.Super. 614, 481 A.2d 307 (App.Div.1984), a sister court of the *Starkman* court rejected *Starkman's* reasoning:

> There may be cases in which the mortgagee will be adequately protected by a holding that allows the mortgagor to use the fire insurance proceeds to rebuild. But there will be times when the mortgagee will be placed at risk by having his mortgage on an existing building converted to a construction mortgage for a new building. The holding creates too much potential for dispute and litigation. . . . The parties could dispute the value of the security after a fire, especially if the property is not insured at full market value. Disagreement could also arise as to the value of the repairs or the replacement structure, the amount of progress payments, and other matters. For example, in the case at hand a question was raised as to the right to reconstruct a nonconforming building. The trial judge

---

* © 1997 by The American Law Institute. Reprinted with permission.

said that the mortgagee should not be forced into partnership with the mortgagor in rebuilding the structure, and the mortgage loan should not be converted into a construction loan. We agree with these observations.

The New Jersey Supreme Court affirmed the *Passarella* holding as it applies to commercial property but expressly reserved judgment on its applicability to residential property. 101 N.J. 12, 499 A.2d 1017 (1985). Are these objections to *Starkman* persuasive? Are the objections mitigated by the following, excerpt from § 4.7, comment d of the Restatement?*

> The mortgagee is entitled to impose reasonable conditions on the process of restoration of the real estate. For example, the mortgagee may reserve a power to review and approve the plans and specifications for the work to be done. Such a power is recognized if it is reasonably exercised. Likewise, the mortgagee may require reasonable provisions for the disbursal of the funds to ensure that they will in fact be used for restoration and not diverted to other purposes. If the mortgagee is experienced in construction lending, it may wish to administer the disbursal itself; alternatively, the mortgagee may require use of some external service, such as an escrow company, to disburse the funds and inspect the progress of the restoration. In either case, the reasonable administrative cost of these procedures may be charged against the funds.

Incidentally, the Restatement adopts *Starkman* but not necessarily *Schoolcraft*. The Restatement's provision for use of insurance proceeds for restoration is only a "default" rule, "unless the mortgage effectively provides the contrary." However, § 4.7 comment d observes that a mortgage clause allowing the mortgagee to capture the insurance proceeds when rebuilding is feasible may "be disregarded by the courts. For example, in jurisdictions following the Restatement, Second, Contracts the provision might be considered unenforceable on the ground that it is an unconscionable term of the contract (see Restatement, Second, Contracts § 208) or that enforcement would violate the mortgagee's duty of good faith and fair dealing (see Restatement, Second, Contracts § 205)."

3.   *How much of the insurance proceeds may the mortgagee capture?* Assume that rebuilding is not feasible, that the property is repaired without using the insurance proceeds, or that an effective mortgage clause provides that the lender need not allow rebuilding. Is the mortgagee entitled to *all* the insurance proceeds, up to the full amount of the mortgage debt? This is the majority view. See Grange Mut. Cas. Co. v. Central Trust Co., 774 S.W.2d 838 (Ky.App.1989). In many cases, this rule puts the mortgagee in a *more* secure position than it would have occupied without the casualty.

Restatement (Third) of Property (Mortgages) § 4.7(a) (1997) takes the view, supported by a substantial minority of cases, that the lender is entitled

---

*   © 1997 by The American Law Institute. Reprinted with permission.

to recover insurance proceeds only "to the extent that the mortgagee's security has been impaired by the loss or damage." This was the basis for the court's refusal to let the lender keep any of the insurance proceeds in Kreshek v. Sperling, note 1, *supra*. The Restatement measures impairment of security for this purpose in the same way as for waste—the mortgagee's recovery should be sufficient to restore the loan to its "scheduled" loan-to-value ratio. See the discussion in note 6 of Section C, Waste, in this chapter.

Here is an illustration of that principle on facts that parallel the illustration in note 6 of Section C. Mortgagee ("ME") makes a loan of $80,000 to Mortgagor ("MR"), secured by a mortgage on land with an appraised value of $100,000. MR purchases and maintains casualty insurance as required by the mortgage. During the next five years, MR makes all the scheduled payments, which reduces the mortgage debt balance to $70,000. At the same time, the land's value has increased to $120,000. A fire occurs, which reduces the land's value by $30,000 to $90,000. The insurer tenders $30,000. The scheduled loan-to-value ratio at the time of the fire was $70,000/$100,000 or 70 percent, so ME is entitled to a restoration of that loan-to-value ratio. Because the land is now worth $90,000, ME is entitled to a portion of the insurance proceeds necessary to reduce the debt balance to 70 percent of $90,000, which is $63,000. Therefore, ME can claim $70,000 minus $63,000, or $7,000 of the fire insurance proceeds.

4.   *Disposition of eminent domain awards.* When mortgaged property is taken in full by eminent domain, the mortgagee is entitled to the entire condemnation award, up to the debt balance, in the absence of a contrary agreement. See Nelson, Whitman, Burkhart & Freyermuth, Real Estate Finance Law § 4.12 (6th ed.2015). When only a partial taking occurs, the majority view is the same—the mortgagee may take the entire award, up to the debt balance. However, a growing and (we believe) well-reasoned trend suggests that the mortgagee should recover only enough to compensate for the impairment of its security. See People ex rel. Dept. of Transp. v. Redwood Baseline, Ltd., 84 Cal.App.3d 662, 149 Cal.Rptr. 11 (1978); State ex rel. Comm'r of Transp. v. Kastner, 179 N.J.Super. 613, 433 A.2d 448 (Law Div.1981); Restatement (Third) of Property (Mortgages) § 4.7(a) (1997). However, confusion exists concerning how impairment of security should be measured. See note 6 in Section C of this chapter. Additionally, courts that limit the mortgagee's recovery to the impairment of its security are divided on whether a mortgage clause that purports to give the mortgagee the full award can override this result. See, e.g., First Western Fin. Corp. v. Vegas Continental, 100 Nev. 710, 692 P.2d 1279 (1984) (it cannot). See generally David A. Leipziger, The Mortgagee's Remedies for Waste, 64 Cal.L.Rev. 1086, 1100 (1976); Harold Don Teague, Condemnation of Mortgaged Property, 44 Tex.L.Rev. 1535 (1966).

The Fannie Mae/Freddie Mac Uniform Single-Family Mortgage form that is reprinted as Form 3 in the Appendix, infra, takes quite a different approach to eminent domain awards than to casualty insurance proceeds. Section 11 of the form allows the mortgagee to capture the full award, up to the debt amount, when a total taking occurs. When a partial taking occurs, the form allows the mortgagee to recover "the amount of the proceeds multiplied by the following fraction: (a) the total amount of the sums secured immediately before the partial taking, divided by (b) the fair market value of the Property immediately before the partial taking."

If the mortgagee is entitled to the eminent domain award, must it allow the funds to be used for rebuilding by analogy to the *Starkman* decision? In many respects, eminent domain awards are similar to casualty insurance proceeds, but one obvious difference exists. In a total taking case, rebuilding is impossible because the real estate is gone! In a partial taking case, on the other hand, rebuilding may be feasible, though it is much less likely than with a casualty loss, because part of the real estate is unavailable. If rebuilding is feasible, the Restatement requires the lender to allow use of the eminent domain award for that purpose, in the absence of a contrary agreement. See Restatement (Third) of Property (Mortgages) § 4.7(b) (1997).

5. *Effect of a full credit bid on insurance recovery.* Assume that, after a casualty loss, a mortgagee purchases the mortgaged premises at a foreclosure sale by bidding the full debt amount. Can the mortgagee later recover the casualty insurance proceeds? See Arkansas Teacher Retirement System v. Coronado Props., Ltd., 33 Ark.App. 17, 801 S.W.2d 50 (1990) ("If the mortgagee has bid in the full amount of its secured debt at the sale, it thereby satisfies its lien and loses all entitlement to any insurance proceeds."); Helmer v. Texas Farmers Ins. Co., 632 S.W.2d 194, 196 (Tex.App.1982) ("The law in most jurisdictions seems to be that if the mortgage debt is satisfied by the proceeds of sale, as reflected in the mortgage or deed of trust in this case, the mortgagee is entitled to no further payment on account thereof."); Norwest Mortg., Inc. v. State Farm Fire & Cas. Co., 118 Cal.Rptr.2d 367 (App. 2002) (depublished); Fire Ins. Exchange v. Bowers, 994 S.W.2d 110 (Mo.App. 1999).

The court in Whitestone Sav. & Loan Ass'n v. Allstate Ins. Co., 28 N.Y.2d 332, 321 N.Y.S.2d 862, 270 N.E.2d 694 (1971) gave an alternative explanation for this result: "[T]he mortgagee has voluntarily converted the debt into the property and has done so by taking the property in satisfaction of the debt. It could have bid less, thus leaving a deficiency for which the mortgagor would be obligated and from which there would survive an insurable interest." Restatement (Third) of Property (Mortgages) § 4.8(a) (1997) agrees.

Does this rule seem too harsh? If the mortgagee knows that a fire or other casualty has reduced the property's value to less than the outstanding debt amount, a full credit bid would be unwise. Thus, the rule seems to penalize a mortgagee that is stupid or that carelessly failed to check the property's condition before the foreclosure sale. Consider the court's comment in Whitestone Sav. & Loan Ass'n v. Allstate Ins. Co.:

> The rule is not harsh and it is eminently practical. None disputes that the mortgagee is entitled to recover only his debt. Any surplus value belongs to others, namely, the mortgagor or subsequent lienors. Indeed, it is not conceivable that the mortgagee could recover a

deficiency judgment against the mortgagor if it had bid in the full amount of the debt at foreclosure sale. To allow the mortgagee, after effectively cutting off or discouraging lower bidders, to take the property—and then establish that it was worth less than the bid— encourages fraud, creates uncertainty as to the mortgagor's rights, and most unfairly deprives the sale of whatever leaven comes from other bidders.

Of course, the mortgagee also cannot claim insurance proceeds if it voluntarily accepted full payment of the mortgage debt. See Benton Banking Co. v. Tennessee Farmers Mut. Ins. Co., 906 S.W.2d 436 (Tenn.1995) (mortgagee had no right to fire insurance proceeds after it accepted promissory note from insured mortgagors' parent in satisfaction of debt). Similarly, if the mortgagee makes a successful partial credit bid, it can take only enough insurance proceeds to pay the deficiency, even if the bid exceeded the damaged property's value. See Rodriguez v. First Union Nat'l Bank, 61 Mass.App.Ct. 438, 810 N.E.2d 1282 (2004); Lenart v. Ocwen Fin. Corp., 869 So.2d 588 (Fla. Ct.App.2004).

If damage to the mortgaged building is not visible from its exterior, should a court refuse to award insurance proceeds to the mortgagee after a full credit bid even if the mortgagor refused to let the mortgagee inspect the interior before foreclosure? See Universal Mortg. Co. v. Prudential Ins. Co., 799 F.2d 458 (9th Cir.1986) (denying recovery to mortgagee on similar facts). How should a prudent mortgagee handle this situation? Virtually all well-drafted mortgages give the lender a right of reasonable inspection of the premises. See Patrick A. Randolph, Jr., The Mortgagee's Interest in Casualty Loss Proceeds: Evolving Rules and Risks, 32 Real Prop., Prob. & Tr. J. 1 (1997).

A few courts have been more sympathetic to mortgagees:

The "foreclosure after loss" rule requires an election of remedies. This Court has held that when making an election between remedies, a party must make the election with the full and clear understanding of the problem, facts and remedies essential to the exercise of an intelligent choice. . . . We conclude that implicit in the "foreclosure after loss" rule is the requirement that the mortgagee or purchaser at the foreclosure sale have knowledge of the loss before making an election. However, the mortgagee or purchaser must diligently seek facts that would enable it to make an informed election.

Ex parte Chrysler First Fin. Servs. Corp., 608 So.2d 734, 737 (Ala.1992). In that case, the house on the property had been destroyed five days before the foreclosure sale, but the court concluded that the lender was not "dilatory" or at fault for failing to discover the loss.

Incidentally, if the mortgagee's full credit bid prevents it from making a claim on the casualty insurance, who gets the benefit of the "unused" insurance coverage? In Lee v. Royal Indemnity Co., 108 F.3d 651 (6th Cir.1997), the mortgagee "erroneously" made a full credit bid at foreclosure. Under Tennessee law, it was therefore precluded from recovering anything from the insurance company. The court held that the homeowner/mortgagor could therefore collect the full face amount of the policy, though his home had been heavily encumbered by the mortgage when the loss occurred. The court stated that, "once a mortgagee's interest in the policy is extinguished through subsequent acts, any interest it had in the policy reverts back to the [mortgagor] policy holder." The insurer, of course, argued that this unjustly enriched the mortgagor, but the court commented that it was as if the mortgagor's "rich uncle" had paid off his mortgage loan. The court in Rodriguez v. First Union Nat'l Bank, 61 Mass.App.Ct. 438, 810 N.E.2d 1282 (2004), reached the same result.

6.   *Effect of full credit bid on other recovery by the mortgagee.* Full credit bids are dangerous for mortgagees in situations other than casualty loss. As we have already noted in Section C of this chapter concerning waste, a mortgagee that makes a full credit bid in foreclosure cannot recover anything for waste, even if it becomes apparent after the foreclosure that the property was not worth as much as the debt. See Evans v. California Trailer Court, Inc., 28 Cal.App.4th 540, 33 Cal.Rptr.2d 646 (1994) (disapproved of on other grounds by Black Sky Capital, LLC v. Cobb, 439 P.3d 1149 (Cal. 2019).

Mortgagees sometimes sue their former mortgagors after foreclosure on a variety of other grounds—fraud in the mortgage application process, conversion of rents received before foreclosure ("waste of rents"), and improper receipt of eminent domain proceeds, to mention a few. Should a full credit bid also bar the mortgagee's recovery on these grounds? We will confront this question later in Chapter Six, Section H infra.

7.   *Insurance recovery for losses occurring after foreclosure.* Who is entitled to the insurance proceeds when the casualty loss occurs after a foreclosure purchase by the mortgagee? The mortgagee, of course, regardless of the amount it bid at the sale, because the mortgagee now owns the real estate and is insured by the policy. The policy may say that the proceeds are payable to the mortgagor and mortgagee "as their interests may appear," but the mortgagee's interest is now the fee title. See, e.g., Liberty Mut. Fire Ins. Co. v. Alexander, 374 N.J.Super. 340, 864 A.2d 1127 (App.Div.2005); Disrud v. Arnold, 167 Wis.2d 177, 482 N.W.2d 114 (App.1992); J. Burke McCormick, Note, Fire Insurance Recovery Rights of the Foreclosing Mortgagee: Is His Lien Lost in the Ashes?, 8 Ford.Urb.L.Rev. 857 (1980); Nelson, Whitman, Burkhart & Freyermuth, Real Estate Finance Law § 4.16 (6th ed.2015).

8.   *Insurance purchased by the mortgagee.* Many mortgages provide that, if the mortgagor does not carry the required insurance, the mortgagee can purchase insurance to protect itself and charge the premiums to the mortgagor. This is often termed "force-placing" the insurance. See, e.g., Custer v. Homeside Lending, Inc., 858 So.2d 233 (Ala.2003), in which the court approved the lender's force-placing of flood insurance. However, the insurance obtained

by the lender may be far from ideal from the borrower's viewpoint. One lender sent the following disclaimer to its borrower:

> Please note this is not a homeowners policy. * * * No attempt was made to duplicate any insurance you may have had in the past. The insurance coverage we have obtained may be more expensive, may not be enough to cover your loss and provide less coverage than you could obtain from an agent or company of your choice.

Hickman v. SAFECO Ins. Co., 695 N.W.2d 365 (Minn.2005) (force-placed policy language evidenced intent to benefit borrower, as well as lender).

Force-placed insurance has generated a great deal of litigation against lenders, servicers, and insurance companies. Property owners have alleged that insurance companies pay kickbacks to lenders and servicers, which inflates the premiums. Even without a kickback, plaintiffs claim that excessive premiums are charged and that lenders and servicers buy excessive insurance. Plaintiffs have brought these actions on a number of grounds, including state common law, federal and state lending laws, and RICO. See, e.g., Montoya v. PNC Bank, N.A., 94 F. Supp. 3d 1293 (S.D. Fla. 2015); Hamilton v. Suntrust Mortg. Inc., 6 F. Supp. 3d 1300 (S.D. Fla. 2014); Cannon v. Wells Fargo Bank N.A., 917 F. Supp. 2d 1025 (N.D. Cal. 2013); Ellsworth v. U.S. Bank, N.A., 908 F. Supp. 2d 1063 (N.D. Cal. 2012).

Escrow Accounts for Taxes and Insurance

The preceding material suggests that mortgagees have a strong and legitimate concern that their mortgagors maintain and pay the premiums for casualty insurance on the mortgaged premises. Mortgagees are perhaps even more insistent that mortgagors promptly pay the real estate taxes and special assessments accruing against the property. The reason for this concern, as Professor Durfee once aptly pointed out, is that "in most tax systems * * * the burden of the ordinary tax on land and the burden of special assessments for local improvements rest on both mortgagor and mortgagee in the sense that unless these charges are satisfied by someone before the axe falls, the interests of both parties will be rubbed out. The state goes after the land and its claim overrides *all* prior interests whatever their character." Edgar N. Durfee, Cases on Security 136 (1951) (emphasis added). In other words, even a "first" mortgage on real estate will be wiped out by a sale under a subsequently arising real estate tax lien.

For this reason, most mortgages include clauses that require the mortgagor to pay taxes and insurance premiums and make the failure to do so grounds for acceleration of the mortgage debt. As additional protection, many mortgagees demand that mortgagors set up accounts with the mortgagee into which the mortgagor will pay 1/12 of the annual taxes and insurance premiums each month (along with the regular monthly payment of principal and interest) and out of which the mortgagee will make the tax and insurance payments as they fall due. You can see the typical residential loan provision in Section 3 of the Fannie Mae/Freddie Mac Uniform Mortgage Form, reproduced as Form 3 in the Appendix. Loans on commercial real estate often have similar requirements.

These accounts are usually called "escrow," "impound," or "reserve" accounts. The usual obligations paid from escrow accounts are ad valorem property taxes, special assessments, and casualty insurance premiums. Sometimes other items are included, such as condominium or PUD homeowner association assessments and ground rents if the security property is ground-leased land. Use of escrow accounts ensures that the mortgagor will have enough money to pay these expenses and provides the lender with an "early warning system"; as soon as the mortgagor misses even one monthly payment, the lender is immediately aware of the default and can take measures to protect itself.

Escrow accounts are also an important source of revenue for loan servicers. If the mortgagee is not required to pay interest on the account to the mortgagor, it can invest the funds and earn interest on them for its own benefit until they need to be paid out. For an average account balance of, say, $1,000, the annual earnings at a 4% return would be $40.

When a mortgagee sells a loan to a secondary market investor, such as Fannie Mae or Freddie Mac, the investor normally will employ the mortgagee to "service" the loan, which involves maintaining relations with the borrower, collecting and remitting the monthly payments to the investor, and administering the escrow account. Secondary market investors pay a fee to their servicers for these functions. A typical fee on a residential loan might be 25 to 50 "basis points." A "basis point" is one-hundredth of a percent. Twenty-five basis points would produce a servicing fee of $250 annually on a $100,000 loan. When this fee is combined with the "float" or investment income from the escrow account, an efficient servicer can earn a very attractive income from a portfolio of loans.

Mortgagee liability for interest on escrow accounts. Formerly, mortgagees often voluntarily paid interest on escrow accounts. Some lenders allowed their borrowers to set up interest-bearing savings accounts to receive the monthly escrow payments. Others credited the borrower's escrow payments to the mortgage loan balance and debited the loan balance when the lender paid the taxes and insurance premiums. This approach was very advantageous to borrowers, because it effectively allowed them to earn interest on their escrowed money at the mortgage debt rate.

However, these practices have largely faded away, and few lenders today pay or credit interest to their borrowers except when they are required by law to do so. As a result, attorneys for borrowers filed a spate of class action suits in an attempt to establish that lenders have a duty to pay interest on escrowed funds though the mortgage documents do not clearly require them to do so. These plaintiffs employed a variety of creative theories, such as express trust, constructive trust, pledge, "special deposit," unjust enrichment, and quasi-contract. At first it seemed that they might be successful, because a few significant cases allowed borrowers to recover interest. See Derenco, Inc. v. Benjamin Franklin Fed. Sav. & Loan Ass'n, 281 Or. 533, 577 P.2d 477 (1978); Buchanan v. Brentwood Fed. Sav. & Loan Ass'n, 457 Pa. 135, 320 A.2d 117 (1974); Madsen v. Prudential Fed. Sav. & Loan Ass'n, 558 P.2d 1337 (Utah 1977).

However, this trend was short-lived. Lenders quickly revised their mortgage clauses concerning escrow accounts to delete words like "pledge," "trust," and "deposit." Today, most state courts refuse to order lenders to pay interest to borrowers. See Kronisch v. Howard Sav. Institute, 161 N.J.Super. 592, 392 A.2d 178 (1978); Michael E. Kaemmerer, Comment, Tax and Insurance Escrow Accounts in Mortgages—The Attack Presses On, 41 Mo.L.Rev. 133 (1976); Nelson, Whitman, Burkhart & Freyermuth, Real Estate Finance Law §§ 4.17–4.18 (6th ed.2015).

To some extent, borrowers won in the legislatures what they lost in the courts. Several states enacted legislation regulating escrow accounts. The statutes are summarized in Nelson, Whitman, Burkhart & Freyermuth, Real Estate Finance Law § 4.19 (6th ed.2015). Little uniformity exists among them. They typically apply only to residential mortgages (one- to four-family dwellings). The required interest rate may be fixed by the statute or by a state regulatory agency, such as the Commissioner of Banking.

CHAPTER FIVE

TRANSFER AND DISCHARGE

■ ■ ■

A. TRANSFER OF THE MORTGAGOR'S INTEREST

Most buyers of real estate do not pay the entire purchase price in cash but, instead, obtain financing for a significant portion of the price. One way for a purchaser to do so is to obtain a new loan from a third-party lender, such as a bank or savings association. Another way, the subject of this section, is for the purchaser to "take over" an existing mortgage loan on the property. Here the title to the land is transferred to the purchaser, but the existing mortgage is not paid off or satisfied. The purchaser is ordinarily given credit toward the purchase price in an amount equal to the outstanding balance of the loan being taken over. She may pay the remainder of the price in cash or may finance part or all of it by other means, such as a second mortgage loan.

Why would a purchaser prefer to take over an existing mortgage loan, rather than obtain a new one? The most obvious reason is that, if interest rates have been rising, the rate on the old loan may be lower than on any comparable loan available in the current market. Of course, in that setting, lenders are loath to see their loans "taken over" at existing rates. They would prefer to adjust those rates upward or to have the loans paid off so the funds could be lent again at a higher rate. Whether lenders have the legal power to gain these advantages depends largely on the existence and enforceability of "due on sale" clauses, which are the subject of Section B of this chapter.

Even if the existing mortgage loan does not have a lower interest rate than currently-available financing or if the lender will increase the lower rate to the current market level, there may still be advantages to a real estate purchaser in taking over an existing mortgage loan. The purchaser can usually avoid paying a number of "closing costs" associated with obtaining a new loan, such as title insurance, an appraisal of the real estate, and perhaps some loan fees. The purchaser may also be able to take over the loan though he or she does not meet lenders' usual credit and income standards for new loans. However, this advantage, like the interest rate advantage mentioned in the previous paragraph, will likely not be realized if the mortgage contains a "due on sale" clause, as virtually all modern mortgages do. Even if the purchaser will not enjoy any of these benefits by taking over an existing loan, she may not have a choice if the loan prohibits prepayment.

When a purchaser takes over an existing mortgage loan, the sale can be handled in one of two ways. The purchaser can either take "subject to" the mortgage (which is, in a sense, an inevitable conclusion, because the mortgage continues to encumber the land's title) or the purchaser can "assume" it. While people sometimes refer to "assumption of the mortgage", the assumption is really an assumption of liability on the debt, as represented by the promissory note. To be perfectly accurate, we should say that a sale or other transfer is always "subject to" the mortgage and that sometimes there is also an assumption of the debt.

An assumption is the purchaser's promise to make the payments and perform the other covenants in the note and mortgage. It must be an express promise. In most states, an assumption is not implied merely from the facts that the property was encumbered by the mortgage and that the purchaser paid the difference between the agreed price and the mortgage balance in cash.[1] Even if the original mortgage contains a promise to pay and boilerplate language to the effect that it binds and benefits the "successors and assigns" of the property, the covenant to pay does not run with the land and does not bind a future owner in the absence of an assumption.

Any clear expression of the purchaser's agreement to become personally liable for the debt is sufficient. The purchaser need not expressly "assume" the debt so long as his intent to do so is clear. Compare Yager v. Rubymar Corp., 35 Misc. 2d 517, 230 N.Y.S.2d 609 (1962) (grantees "hereby covenant to pay" outstanding debt—assumption), with Hyde Wholesale Dry Goods Co. v. Edwards, 255 Ark. 211, 500 S.W.2d 85 (1973) (grantee "hope[s] to be able to make arrangements to take care of the mortgage holders"—no assumption).

The promise need not be written, although it is obviously a good practice to use a writing. One might suppose that an assumption agreement would fall within the section of the Statute of Frauds dealing with a promise "to answer for the debt, default, or misdoings of another." But the courts almost never so hold. They usually adopt the reasoning of the Virginia Supreme Court in Langman v. Alumni Assoc. of the University of Virginia, 247 Va. 491, 442 S.E.2d 669 (1994):

> A grantee who assumes an existing mortgage is not a surety. The
> grantee makes no promise to the mortgagee to pay the debt of

---

[1]   First Interstate Bank v. Nelco Enterprises, 822 P.2d 1260 (Wash.App. 1992). A few states, notably Pennsylvania and Oklahoma, differ, finding an "implied assumption" if the mortgage balance is deducted from the price. In those states, while a "subject to" conveyance creates no direct obligation to the mortgagee, the grantee is obligated by implication to indemnify the grantor if the latter is forced to pay the mortgage obligation. See Heaney v. Riddle, 23 A.2d 456 (Pa. 1942); Dick v. Vogt, 162 P.2d 325 (Ok. 1945).

another, but promises the grantor to pay the mortgagee the debt the grantee owes to the grantor. This is an original undertaking.

However, many courts require that "the obligation of the grantee to assume and pay the mortgage debt be established by evidence which is clear and convincing." Cassidy v. Bonitatibus, 5 Conn.App. 240, 497 A.2d 1018 (1985). An oral assumption could be highly problematic under this standard.

The promise may be in a separate document, or it may appear in the contract of sale or the deed. No separate consideration need be given for the assumption. It is simply part of the larger package of mutual promises, including the seller's promise to sell the real estate and the buyer's promise to pay the purchase price.

The following two decisions describe the legal consequences of taking title "subject to" a mortgage or of assuming the debt that it secures.

VINCENT V. GARLAND

District Court of Appeal, Fourth District, California, 1936
14 Cal.App.2d 725, 58 P.2d 1320

TURRENTINE, JUSTICE pro tem.

Defendants William J. Garland et ux. mortgaged certain real property to Grover T. Garland. Thereafter, mortgagors conveyed the property to plaintiff, Marcella A. Vincent, subject to the mortgage. The mortgage becoming due and unpaid, the mortgagee, Grover T. Garland, instituted an action to foreclose the mortgage and in the action Grover T. Garland was plaintiff and William J. Garland et ux., the mortgagors, and Marcella A. Vincent, the grantee of the mortgagors and plaintiff herein, were made defendants. After filing suit and duly serving the defendants, but before judgment, the mortgagor William J. Garland paid the sum due on said mortgage to Grover T. Garland whereon the action was dismissed as to William J. Garland et ux., and the action was continued in the name of Grover T. Garland pursuant to agreement between Grover T. Garland and William J. Garland. The foreclosure decree was entered October 3, 1931. November 2, 1931, the sheriff, pursuant to the decree of foreclosure, sold the property to Grover T. Garland. This was done on the promise of Grover T. Garland that he would purchase the property for William J. Garland. Plaintiff herein brought this action to quiet her title to the property covered by said mortgage against the defendants shortly prior to the expiration date of the equity of redemption. The lower court entered its decree that she take nothing by virtue of this action and that she has no right, title, interest, or estate in the property covered by said mortgage. From such judgment, plaintiff appeals.

* * *

Jones on Mortgages, § 768, lays down the following rule: "And so a mortgagor, who has sold subject to the mortgage debt, upon being compelled to pay it, is subrogated to the benefit of the security, without any formal assignment of it to him. He thereby becomes an equitable assignee of it, and may enforce it against the property." This rule is quoted with approval in Beach v. Waite, 21 Cal.App. 304, 131 P. 880. "If such vendee takes subject to the mortgage the land thereupon becomes, so far as the mortgagor is concerned, and as between him, the creditor, and the vendee, primarily liable for the payment of the debt. * * * When such conveyance is made, the relation of principal and surety springs up between the land and the mortgagor, he being the surety and the land the principal debtor. * * * He becomes at once entitled to all the protection which the law gives to sureties." Braun v. Crew, 183 Cal. 728, 192 P. 531, 533.

"The principal question in the case is whether the transfer of the note, and the assignment of the mortgage to the original mortgagor, after the premises had been sold subject to the mortgage, constituted in law a discharge of the mortgage, so that it could not be enforced against the property. We think it very clear that they did not. When the estate was sold subject to the mortgage, the mortgage was left as a primary charge upon the land, although the grantee did not make herself personally liable for it by assuming it. The grantor, who was the maker of the mortgage note, was entitled to have the mortgaged property applied in payment of it. To protect her own interests, she might take an assignment of the mortgage and the debt, and enforce the mortgage by a foreclosure, as effectually as if she was not the maker of the note." Pratt v. Buckley, 175 Mass. 115, 55 N.E. 889.

"The distinction between the rights and liabilities of a grantee assuming a mortgage and a grantee who merely takes subject to a mortgage without assuming the payment of the mortgage is quite plain. See Pomeroy, Equity Jurisprudence (4th Ed.) §§ 1205, 1206; 15 Harv.L.Rev., p. 398; Stearns on Suretyship (3d Ed.) § 90. When the grantee assumes the mortgage debt as between the grantee and the mortgagor, not only is the land a primary fund for the payment of the debt, but likewise the personal liability thus assumed by the grantee. On the other hand, when the grantee merely takes subject to the mortgage, while it is true that the grantee assumes no personal liability whatever, nevertheless the security in his hands is liable for the payment of the mortgage debt, which liability as between the grantee and the mortgagor is primary. Therefore, to the extent of the value of such security properly applicable to the mortgage debt, the original mortgagor and the grantee subject to the mortgage stand in a relation one to another, which, while not a true suretyship, is nevertheless equitably analogous thereto and subject to the operation of the same principles. The original mortgagor is entitled to pay the debt at any time and to be immediately subrogated to the right of the mortgagee to foreclose the mortgage, although he has no personal claim against the grantee, and the mortgagee has no personal claim against such grantee to which the mortgagor could be subrogated." Zastrow v. Knight, 56 S.D. 554, 229 N.W. 925, 930, 72 A.L.R. 379.

In our opinion the judgment entered in this action was correct. If the action could be maintained at all after payment by the original mortgagors as set forth in the statement of facts, it could be maintained in the name of the original party. "In case of * * * transfer of interest, the action or proceeding may be continued in the name of the original party." Code Civ.Proc. § 385.

Judgment affirmed.

NOTE

Liability of a "subject to" grantee. Neither the mortgagor nor the mortgagee can sue a "subject to" grantee personally, because she did not agree to become personally liable for the secured debt. However, as the *Vincent* opinion illustrates, a mortgagee can foreclose even after the mortgagor transfers the mortgaged property to a "subject to" grantee. Furthermore, if the mortgagee does not foreclose, the mortgagor can do so based on the doctrine of subrogation. Subrogation is an assignment, by operation of law, of the mortgagee's right to foreclose to the mortgagor. Its fundamental purpose is to make the ultimate responsibility for paying the debt fall where it should. When the mortgagor transfers "subject to" the mortgage, the land becomes the primary fund for payment of the debt, and the mortgagor is a surety to that extent.

The major disadvantage of subrogation is that it is available only if the mortgagor pays the outstanding debt in full. No subrogation right exists for a partial payment. Restatement (Third) of Suretyship and Guaranty §§ 27–31 (1996). The reason is that, if partial subrogation was available to a surety that paid only part of the debt, the real estate collateral would be divided between two parties—the mortgagee and the surety—who may have quite divergent interests and views about when and how to foreclose. The law simply will not impose on the mortgagee the burden of negotiating with the surety about when and how the remedies under the mortgage will be exercised. To do so would, in effect, force the Bank into a loan participation relationship without any participation agreement. See Sawyer v. Zacavich, 178 Cal. App. 2d 605, 611 (1960); Comment, Subrogation of Mortgages in California: A Comparison with the Restatement and Proposals for Change, 48 UCLA L. Rev. 1643 (2000).

McRAE V. POPE

Supreme Judicial Court of Massachusetts, 1942
311 Mass. 500, 42 N.E.2d 261

COX, JUSTICE.

When this bill in equity was filed on May 9, 1939, the plaintiffs, husband and wife, sought reformation of a deed that they had given the defendant Robert D. Pope, hereinafter referred to as Pope, that he be ordered to pay a mortgage that covered the premises described in the deed and other premises owned by the plaintiffs, and that the defendant Mabel D. Pope, the mother of said Pope, hereinafter referred to as Mrs. Pope, be enjoined from foreclosing that mortgage. The bill alleged that prior to July 17, 1935, the plaintiffs were the owners of certain real estate in this Commonwealth on which they had given a mortgage; that on that date they conveyed a portion of the premises to Pope, who assumed and agreed to pay the unpaid taxes and the amount of said mortgage, with interest, as a part of the consideration for his deed, but that, by error and mistake of the scrivener, the deed did not set out the true agreement, but, on the contrary, contained the provision merely that the premises conveyed were subject to unpaid taxes and the mortgage, with interest. Further allegations were that Mrs. Pope, on January 7, 1939, received an assignment of the mortgage; that on March 28, 1939, she demanded of the plaintiffs the amount due on the mortgage; that, although the plaintiffs offered to pay the amount, she refused to assign the mortgage to them; that on April 24, 1939, she gave her son a partial release of the mortgage, without consideration, and on April 28, 1939, commenced foreclosure proceedings.

The copy of the deed that is annexed to the bill, which Pope admits that he received, recites the conveyance 'for consideration paid,' and that the premises conveyed are subject to the unpaid taxes and also to the mortgage. The notice of foreclosure proceedings recites that the premises, excepting therefrom so much of them as had been released from the mortgage on April 24, 1939, will be sold on May 29, 1939. Mrs. Pope admitted in her answer, as did, in effect, her son, that foreclosure proceedings had been commenced by publication in accordance with a copy thereof annexed to the bill. Mrs. Pope was temporarily restrained from proceeding with the foreclosure, and the suit was referred to a master.

The master found that Pope did agree to assume and pay the mortgage and taxes; that the transaction between the plaintiffs and him was, in fact, an exchange of equities in properties, each of which was encumbered for $3,650; and that Mrs. Pope, as guardian of her son, who was at that time a minor, petitioned the Probate Court for license to sell his real estate which was the subject matter of the exchange. About two years after the exchange, Pope was requested to change the mortgage in question, so that the new mortgage would cover only the premises then owned by him, but he refused to do this. During the entire period from the date of the conveyance to him until January, 1939, he regularly paid the interest and amounts due on principal. In January, 1939, his mother paid the full amount of the mortgage and took an assignment of it, and, in the following April, she gave her son a partial release of the mortgage covering that portion of the premises that had been conveyed to him, as a 'part of a plan to foreclose the mortgage, after execution of the partial release and force the plaintiffs to pay the amount due on the mortgage or lose their property through foreclosure.' No consideration was paid for this partial release. On March 27, 1939, the mortgage being in default, Mrs. Pope demanded that the plaintiffs pay the amount due. On the question of mistake, the master found that the mistake or error was due to the failure of the plaintiff Arthur A. McRae, or the plaintiffs' agent, to properly inform the attorney who drew the deed of the full details of the transaction. This report was filed on June 30, 1939, and on July 7, 1939, by interlocutory decree, the 'temporary injunction' was dissolved.

On July 21, 1939, the plaintiffs moved to amend their bill by striking out the paragraph in which it was alleged that through mistake and error of the scrivener, the deed did not set forth the true agreement of Pope to assume and pay the taxes and mortgage, and by inserting allegations to the effect that the mistake was that of the plaintiff Arthur A. McRae or of the plaintiffs' agent. Further allegations by way of amendment were that the temporary restraining order had been dissolved, that the plaintiffs, in order to prevent the foreclosure, were compelled to pay Mrs. Pope the sum of $2,988.67 for a discharge of the mortgage, and that, when she gave the partial release, she knew that the mortgage covered not only the property owned by her son, but also that owned by the plaintiffs. Additional prayers were that Mrs. Pope be ordered to repay the plaintiffs the sum they had paid her with interest and costs, and that she account to them for all moneys received under the mortgage. On December 6, 1940, the motion to amend was allowed, and the suit was recommitted to the master to make further findings of fact with reference to the issues raised by the amendment to the bill.

Facts appearing in the master's report after recommittal are that Pope, as a part of the consideration of the deed to him, agreed to assume and pay the outstanding mortgage and unpaid taxes; that the plaintiffs, in order to prevent the foreclosure sale, paid Mrs. Pope the amount alleged for the discharge of the mortgage; that the value of the parcel owned by Pope on the date that he received the partial release was $5,600; that the value of the property not conveyed by the plaintiffs was $1,800; 'that the mortgage that the plaintiffs were compelled to pay covered in part the same premises partially released'; and that Mrs. Pope knew, when she executed the partial release to her son, that the mortgage covered not only the property owned by him, but also the property owned by the plaintiffs. Both reports were confirmed by interlocutory decree, and a final decree was entered adjudging that the defendants were jointly and severally indebted to the plaintiffs in the sum that the plaintiff had paid to prevent the foreclosure of the mortgage, together with interest, which sum and interest the defendants were ordered to pay with costs. The defendants appealed from the order for final decree (see Carilli v. Hersey, 303 Mass. 82, 87, 20 N.E.2d 492), and from the final decree.

* * *

It is the general rule that a grantor is not absolutely bound by the consideration or the acknowledgment of its payment expressed in his deed, and that the true consideration may be shown by parol or other evidence. Under the exception to the parol evidence rule that admits evidence to show the consideration for a deed, it has been generally held, in the absence of an assumption clause in the deed or a covenant affecting the result, that parol evidence is admissible, even as between immediate parties to the instrument, to prove an assumption by the grantee of a mortgage debt that is secured by the premises conveyed. Drury v. Tremont Improvement Co., 13 Allen 168, 171; Wigmore on Evidence, 3d Ed., § 2433; Williston on Contracts, Rev.Ed., § 115A; Am.Law Inst., Restatement: Contracts, §§ 82, 243, 244. The importance of the application of this rule in the case at bar is that in this Commonwealth, where land is conveyed subject to a mortgage, the grantee does not become bound by mere acceptance of the deed to pay the mortgage debt, but if the deed contains a stipulation that the land is subject to a mortgage which the grantee assumes and agrees to pay, a duty is imposed upon him by the acceptance of the deed, and the law implies a promise to perform his undertaking.

Upon the record in the case at bar, we are of opinion that the finding of the master that Pope assumed and agreed to pay the mortgage in question must stand. Furthermore, the subsequent conduct of Pope could be found to be consistent with this undertaking. For a period of about three and one half years he regularly paid the interest and amounts due on principal. Drury v. Tremont Improvement Co., 13 Allen, 168, 172.

The case therefore, in so far as Pope stands, is that he assumed and agreed to pay the mortgage, with the result that, as between him and the plaintiffs he became the principal debtor, and the plaintiffs became sureties. The plaintiffs were not only entitled to have the land freed from the lien of the mortgage, but they could also enforce Pope's promise to pay the mortgage note and discharge them from any liability upon that indebtedness. Lynn Five Cents Savings Bank v. Portnoy, 306 Mass. 436, 438, 28 N.E.2d 418, and cases cited. As between Pope and the plaintiffs the burden of the mortgage was thrown on the parcel conveyed to him to the exoneration of the land that was retained by the plaintiffs. The obligation assumed by Pope was to pay the note secured by the mortgage at its maturity It appears that there was a default, and, accordingly, a cause of action for the amount due thereon immediately accrued to the plaintiffs, although they had not then paid the note or sustained any loss by reason of non-payment. In the case at bar, the plaintiffs have already paid the mortgage debt, and here seek to recover the amount so paid. They are entitled to recover. The measure of damages is the amount of the mortgage debt that Pope should have paid. Furnas v. Durgin, 119 Mass. 500, 506, 507, 20 Am.Rep. 341.

* * *

As the case stands against Mrs. Pope, she was the assignee of a mortgage that covered not only the land owned by the plaintiffs, but also the parcel that had been conveyed by them to her son, as she well knew. As between the plaintiffs and her, the former were liable to her on the mortgage note, the security of which comprised both parcels of land. The burden of the mortgage rested upon all of the land, and Mrs. Pope attempted, by the partial release to her son, to cast the entire burden upon the plaintiffs, and, by so doing, to deprive them of the benefit of a portion of the security. This she cannot do in disregard of the equities of the case which require that she must abate such proportionate part of the mortgage debt as is necessary to protect the plaintiffs.

The master found that the value of the parcel owned by Pope on the date that his mother gave him the partial release of the mortgage was $5,600. Mrs. Pope received nothing from her son for this partial release. In the circumstances, she is equitably chargeable with the proper contributory share of the debt that she should have received from him. The plaintiffs paid $2,988.67 for the discharge of the mortgage that covered land found by the master to be worth $7,400. Mrs. Pope is equitably chargeable on account of the partial release to her son with 5600/7400 of this amount, together with interest from the date when the mortgage was paid, unless the payment of the mortgage debt was in such circumstances that the plaintiffs are not entitled to recover anything from Mrs. Pope, who contends that the payment was voluntarily made.

We are of opinion that the case at bar does not come within the established rule of law that money voluntarily paid under a claim of right, with full knowledge of the facts on the part of the one making the payment, cannot be recovered back. Mrs. Pope commenced foreclosure proceedings on April 28, 1939, and the premises were advertised to be sold in pursuance thereof on May 29, 1939. She was temporarily restrained from proceeding with the foreclosure, and this restraining order was continued in force on May 16, 1939. After the master made his first report, this restraining order was dissolved on July 7, 1939, and then the plaintiffs, as the master found, were compelled to pay the mortgage. Mrs. Pope had demanded of the plaintiffs the full amount due on the mortgage, and had refused to give the plaintiffs an assignment of it. She had already given her son a partial release of the mortgage, and she must be held to have known that, because of this partial release, she was not entitled to demand of the plaintiffs the full amount of the mortgage. The plaintiffs can hardly be said to have been remiss in their efforts to obtain relief, and it does not appear that they could have done very much to prevent the foreclosure after the injunction had been dissolved that restrained Mrs. Pope from proceeding with the foreclosure. The payment of the mortgage, in the circumstances, cannot be said to have been made voluntarily. Moreover, it could have been found that Mrs. Pope was acting in bad faith. She knew that her mortgage covered both parcels of land, and the partial release to her son, without consideration paid, was part of a plan to foreclose the mortgage and to force the plaintiffs to pay the amount due on the mortgage or lose their property through foreclosure. The commencement of foreclosure proceedings was something more than a mere threat. The proceedings were an actuality and designed to deprive the plaintiffs of substantial rights. General Laws (Ter.Ed.) c. 244, § 36, provides, among other things, that if a mortgagee, or a person claiming or holding under him, receives more than is due on the mortgage, the mortgagor entitled to such excess may recover it in an action of contract. In the case at bar, no question has been raised as to the adequacy of any remedy at law.

The final decree makes no distinction between the amount due from the defendants respectively. It adjudges that they are jointly, and severally indebted to the plaintiffs in the full amount of the mortgage, together with interest, and orders them to pay the plaintiffs that amount with costs. The liabilities of the defendants to the plaintiffs depend upon different rules of law. All necessary parties are before the court, and there is no difficulty in determining their respective rights and obligations, and no difficulty in enforcing them.

Both defendants are indebted to and should be ordered to pay the plaintiffs that proportionate part of the mortgage debt represented by the value of so much of the real estate as was released to the son, in accordance with what has already been said. Pope is further indebted to and should pay the plaintiffs in addition thereto the difference between this sum and the total amount of the mortgage, together with interest. It should be understood that the order requiring both defendants to pay the identical proportion of the mortgage debt does not amount to the imposition of a double liability, inasmuch as a payment by one would discharge the other.

The decree, as modified in accordance with this opinion, is affirmed with costs.

Ordered accordingly.

NOTES

1. *Mortgagor's recourse against an assuming grantee.* The principal-surety principle governs the relationship between the mortgagor and the grantee. If the grantee assumed, the mortgagor who pays the debt has three forms of recourse—reimbursement and exoneration, which are based on the assumption agreement, and subrogation.

Reimbursement. A mortgagor-surety that pays the mortgage obligation in whole or in part when it is due or delinquent is entitled to reimbursement (or "indemnity," as some cases put it) from the assuming grantee-principal. The mortgagor-surety is also entitled to reimbursement for any incidental costs of performance. Unlike subrogation, full payment of the debt is unnecessary to the mortgagor-surety's right of reimbursement. A partial payment is sufficient. However, reimbursement is an unsecured right. The mortgagor-surety can demand payment, but if the grantee-principal is insolvent or disappears, the real estate does not stand as collateral for the right of reimbursement. Restatement (Third) of Suretyship and Guaranty §§ 22–25 (1996).

Exoneration. If an assuming grantee does not pay the mortgage obligation when due, the mortgagor-surety can get a court order that compels the grantee to pay. One may think of this as specific performance of the assumption agreement. The mortgagor-surety need not pay in advance of getting such an order, because the assumption agreement shifted that burden to the grantee. Restatement (Third) of Suretyship and Guaranty § 21 (1996).

Subrogation. In addition to enforcing the assumption agreement, the mortgagor-surety can subrogate to the mortgagee's right to foreclose, if the mortgagee has not done so, and to enforce the assumption agreement, including for any deficiency that the mortgagee recovered from the mortgagor.

2. *Mortgagee's recourse against an assuming grantee.* The mortgagee can recover the entire debt from an assuming grantee or a deficiency after foreclosing the mortgage. If the mortgagee was a party to the assumption agreement, its recourse is based on privity of contract.

If the mortgagee was not a party, it can enforce the assumption based on one of two legal doctrines. The great majority of jurisdictions characterize the mortgagee as a third-party beneficiary of the assumption agreement, which enables the mortgagee to enforce it. Based on this doctrine, a technical difference exists between the lender suing the mortgagor, which is an action on the promissory note, and suing the grantee, which is an action on the assumption agreement. However, little practical difference exists between them.

In those jurisdictions that do not characterize the mortgagee as a third-party beneficiary, the mortgagee can enforce the assumption on a different basis—the equitable subrogation doctrine, which is also called the suretyship subrogation theory or the derivative rights theory. Unlike the third-party beneficiary doctrine, which vests the mortgagee with its own cause of action against an assuming grantee, the equitable subrogation doctrine allows the mortgagee to enforce the mortgagor-surety's rights against the grantee. The purpose is to avoid circuity of action, because a mortgagor that transfers the property to an assuming grantee becomes a mere surety for the debt. As such, a mortgagor that has to pay off the secured debt has a right of subrogation against the assuming grantee. However, for the mortgagor to have a right of subrogation against the grantee, the grantee must be personally liable to the mortgagee on the debt. As the California Supreme Court once explained:

> * * * [T]o avoid circuity of action, and to protect the mortgagor, as the intermediate party, from being compelled to pay the debt, and then to seek redress from his grantee who has assumed the mortgage debt, equity permits the mortgagee to bring all the parties who are liable for the debt, whether principally or ultimately, before the court, and have their rights adjusted in a single suit. In such an action the mortgagee represents the mortgagor for the purpose of enforcing this obligation of the purchaser to him, and his right to enforce this obligation has the same extent and is subject to the same limitations as would be that of the mortgagor in a separate action against his grantee.

Hopkins v. Warner, 109 Cal. 133, 41 P. 868, 869 (1895).

If this logic strikes you as being circular, we can only agree. Professor Corbin once called this theory "a cumbrous intellectual expedient for holding that a contract between two parties can create an enforceable right in a third." Arthur L. Corbin, Contracts for the Benefit of Third Persons, 27 Yale. L.J. 1008, 1015 (1918). Calling the mortgagee a third-party beneficiary seems a great deal more straightforward to us. The good news is that the mortgagee's right of recovery against the grantee is the same regardless of which theory the jurisdiction applies with two notable exceptions: (1) rescission of the assumption agreement, as described in note 3 and (2) a break in the chain of liability, as described in note 4.

3. *Rescission of the assumption agreement.* Suppose the mortgagor/ grantor gets an assumption agreement from the grantee but subsequently purports to rescind it, to waive the grantee's duties under it, or to release the grantee from it. Is the mortgagee bound by this action, so that it loses its claim against the grantee? It depends on whether the jurisdiction follows the third-party beneficiary doctrine or the equitable subrogation doctrine. If it follows the third-party beneficiary doctrine, the mortgagee may not.

> Assuming that [the mortgagee has a direct right of action against the grantee under a third-party beneficiary theory], it can well be argued that the mortgage holder receives an immediate vested right under the assumption agreement which cannot be defeated by the grantor's subsequent release of the grantee. While there is authority for this view in other jurisdictions, the weight of authority requires acceptance or adoption of the assumption agreement for the mortgage holder's right to vest. What constitutes acceptance or adoption remains unsettled. Some courts require the

mortgage holder to give notice of acceptance to the assuming grantee; others seem to require a material change of position making it inequitable to deprive the mortgage holder of his rights under the assumption agreement; still others presume acceptance, enabling the mortgage holder to acquire a vested right when the assumption occurs, subject, however, to a power of disaffirmance. But in no case would an attempted release be effective after the mortgage holder has begun an action on the assumption agreement.

See Roger A. Cunningham & Saul Tischler, Transfer of the Real Estate Mortgagor's Interest, 27 Rutgers L.Rev. 24, 46 (1973).* The Restatement (Third) of Property (Mortgages) § 5.1(c)(5) also adopts the "material change of position" approach to this question. As an example of such a change of position, see Federal Land Bank of Wichita v. Krug, 253 Kan. 307, 856 P.2d 111 (1993).

In contrast, if the jurisdiction follows the equitable subrogation doctrine, the mortgagee is bound by the mortgagor's release of rights unless the release constitutes a fraudulent conveyance or the mortgagee substantially changed its position in reliance on the assumption, such as by releasing the mortgagor from liability.

4. *A break in the chain.* What is the effect of a chain of assumptions? If A, the original mortgagor, sells to B, who assumes and later sells to C, who also assumes, all three parties are personally liable to the mortgagee. The mortgagee can bring an action on the debt or for a deficiency against any or all of them. See Swanson v. Krenik, 868 P.2d 297 (Alaska 1994). In addition, if A or B pays the mortgage, either of them has suretyship rights against the person to whom they sold the land. In the final analysis, if A and B assert this right, C will and should be left "holding the bag."

Matters get more complicated if there is a break in the chain of assumptions. Suppose we change the foregoing facts. A sells to B, who merely takes "subject to" and does not assume. B then sells to C, who gives B an assumption agreement. You may think this is irrational. If B has no personal liability on the debt, why would B bother to get C to assume such liability? But irrational or not, it sometimes happens.

The issue is subtle and may depend on precisely what C's assumption agreement says. For example, suppose C merely promises "to keep, observe, and perform all of the terms, conditions, and provisions of A's agreement with the mortgagee that are to be kept, observed, and performed by B." If B didn't assume, then the foregoing promise by C to assume B's duties is a promise to assume nothing at all! See Chambers v. Thomas, 123 Idaho 69, 844 P.2d 698 (1992), holding that C had no personal liability on these facts. Incidentally, much the same issue can arise when a grantee purports to assume a non-recourse mortgage debt. If the promise is to pay the note "according to the terms thereof" and if the note's terms exclude personal liability, the "assuming"

* Reprinted with permission of Rutgers University, The State University of New Jersey, West Publishing Co. and the authors.

party has assumed nothing. See Schultz v. Weaver, 780 S.W.2d 323 (Tex.App.1989).

However, suppose that the note provides for full personal recourse and that C's agreement is to pay the note itself, not merely B's nonexistent obligation. The courts have divided on the question of whether C is liable to the mortgagee, generally depending on whether the jurisdiction follows the third-party beneficiary doctrine or the equitable subrogation doctrine. Compare Somers v. Avant, 244 Ga. 460, 261 S.E. 2d 334 (1979) (assuming grantee following break in chain is liable on debt—third-party beneficiary doctrine) with Dail v. Campbell, 191 Cal.App.2d 416, 12 Cal.Rptr. 739 (1961) (assuming grantee, following break in chain of assumptions, has no personal liability—equitable subrogation doctrine). See generally Garrard Glenn, Mortgages § 271 (1943); Nelson, Whitman, Burkhart & Freyermuth, Real Estate Finance Law § 5.15 (6th ed.2015); Annot., 12 A.L.R. 1529 (1921). The Restatement (Third) of Property (Mortgages) § 5.1(c)(1) (1997) takes the view that the assuming grantee should be liable even if his or her predecessor was not.

The suretyship defenses. The law has traditionally been highly solicitous of sureties and has taken the view that the surety should not be liable for a different "deal" than he or she originally made, unless the surety consents to the change in the terms. Therefore, a surety is generally discharged from his or her duties in a variety of situations in which the mortgagee's actions change the terms in a way that impairs the surety's position.[2] Such changes can include:

- releasing the grantee from personal liability,
- releasing some or all of the real estate from the mortgage,
- impairing the mortgagee's right to realize on the security of the mortgage, such as by agreeing to forbear from taking action on a default,
- modifying the interest rate or terms of payment, or
- extending the time to maturity of the mortgage loan.

The mortgagor-surety is said to have a "suretyship defense" in such cases. The mortgagor-surety's discharge is granted on the grounds that the actions of the mortgagee (1) have made it less likely that the grantee or the land will satisfy the debt and (2) have made it more difficult for the mortgagor to assert recourse (subrogation, reimbursement, and

---

[2] Traditional suretyship doctrine even discharged uncompensated sureties, such as an uncompensated guarantor, when the modification was *beneficial* to the surety;. See Thomas-Sears v. Morris, 278 Ga.App. 152, 628 S.E.2d 241 (2006). This view has now lost much of its weight.

exoneration) against the grantee and the land if the mortgagor has to pay the debt.

To see why these acts by the mortgagee can impair the mortgagor's rights of recourse against the grantee, you must understand that such acts are *binding on the mortgagor in asserting recourse against the grantee* (unless the mortgagee has "preserved" the recourse of the mortgagor by an express agreement with the grantee, a technique that is probably seldom used). This conclusion may seem counterintuitive; why should the mortgagor be bound by an agreement or act to which she or he was not a party? But it is well established.

For example, if the mortgagee gives the grantee an additional year to pay the debt, the mortgagor may not assert recourse against the grantee until that extra year has elapsed. This may be extremely harmful to the mortgagor's position if, for example, the grantee becomes insolvent or the real estate declines in value during that year.

Similarly, if the mortgagee releases some of the real estate from the mortgage, the mortgagor may not assert recourse (by way of subrogation) against that part of the real estate. If the remaining real estate is not sufficient in value to fully cover the mortgage debt, the mortgagor is harmed, both because the risk of the grantee's defaulting is increased and because, if the mortgagor is required to pay the debt, the mortgagor's subrogation claim against the remaining real estate will be inadequate to reimburse the mortgagor's payment.

While there is consensus that acts of the mortgagee that impair the mortgagor-surety's position should result in a discharge of the mortgagor-surety, there is great disagreement as to the *amount* of the discharge. Traditional suretyship law nearly always gives a complete discharge, even if the impairment of the surety's position is minor. However, an increasingly widespread viewpoint holds that a discharge should be recognized only to the extent that the surety would suffer actual loss as a result of the impairment. The Restatement (Third) of Suretyship and Guaranty § 37, Introductory Note (1997) and ensuing sections take this view, as does Restatement (Third) of Property (Mortgages) § 5.3 (1997). Consider how the court handles it in the following case. Pay particular attention to the footnotes.

Of course, if a mortgagor consents to a change in the terms of the loan by the grantee and the mortgagee, he or she cannot complain about continuing to be held liable as a surety. The mortgagee argued that such consent existed in the following case.

FIRST FEDERAL SAVINGS AND LOAN
ASSOCIATION OF GARY v. ARENA
Court of Appeals of Indiana, Fourth District, 1980
406 N.E.2d 1279

CHIPMAN, JUDGE.

* * *

On May 26, 1965, the Arenas executed a note, mortgage, and supplemental agreement with First Federal. The note provided for a loan of $32,000 at an interest rate of 5¾%, and the mortgage securing this note provided for advances of up to $6,400. March 11, 1966, the Arenas were granted an advance of $5,100, and in consideration, they executed a modification and extension agreement which provided they would owe a new balance of $36,664.81, and the interest rate would be increased to 6%. A separate note, mortgage, and supplemental agreement were also executed by the Arenas in relation to this advance.

March 10, 1969, the Arenas conveyed the real estate which was the subject of both the May 26, 1965, and March 11, 1966, mortgages to Sanford G. Richardson by warranty deed subject to the two mortgages to First Federal.[1] The same day, without notice to or the consent of the Arenas, Mr. Richardson and First Federal entered into a modification and extension agreement, under the terms of which Richardson assumed both of the mortgages in question, and the time for payment was extended to twenty years; there was also a change in the interest rate from 6% to 7¼%. Thus, this agreement, signed only by Richardson and First Federal, was designed to be a modification of First Federal's earlier agreement with the Arenas by extending the time of payment and modifying the terms of payment to which the Arenas and First Federal had agreed.

After June 27, 1975, Richardson failed to make the payments due under the March 10, 1969, modification and extension agreement. As a result, a default on the mortgages and notes occurred and a suit in foreclosure was filed on behalf of First Federal against the Arenas, Richardson, and several lienholders.

* * *

---

[1] Although the grantee's preliminary offer to purchase provided Mr. Richardson would "assume" the existing mortgages on the property, the warranty deed evidencing the consummated contract recited the conveyance was "subject to" the Arenas' mortgages to First Federal. Based upon the general rule that any inconsistencies between the terms in the preliminary contract and the deed are to be settled by the deed alone, since all prior negotiations are considered merged in that instrument, *Wayne International Building & Loan Ass'n v. Beckner*, (1922) 191 Ind. 664, 134 N.E. 273; *Guckenberger v. Shank*, (1941) 110 Ind.App. 442, 37 N.E.2d 708, along with the fact none of the parties argued there was any mistake in drawing the deed or that they intended to make it read other than as in fact it was written, we have concluded, for purposes of this opinion, the conveyance was "subject to" the mortgage.

By reason of an expressed provision to that effect in the supplemental agreements between the Arenas and First Federal, the Arenas were not released from liability upon [the time] extension of the mortgage in the agreement between Mr. Richardson and First Federal; however, this agreement not only extended the time for payment, but it also modified the terms of payment by increasing the interest rate. It is our opinion the trial court properly found the Arenas had not consented to such a change in interest rates and, therefore, were released from liability.[3] Arenas' grantee and First Federal could not modify the original mortgagors' agreement without the mortgagors' consent.

The focal point in this controversy is the meaning to be accorded a reservation of rights clause which appeared in the supplemental agreement executed by the Arenas when they obtained the initial mortgage and later secured the advance. The agreement provided:

* * * THE MORTGAGOR COVENANTS: 6. That in the event the ownership of said property or any part thereof becomes vested in a person other than the Mortgagor, the Mortgagee may, without notice to the Mortgagor, deal with such successor or successors in interest with reference to this mortgage and the debt hereby secured in the same manner as with the Mortgagor, and may forbear to sue or may extend time for payment of the debt, secured hereby, without discharging or in any way affecting the liability of the Mortgagor hereunder or upon the debt hereby secured.

First Federal asserts the reservation of rights language set out above permitted it, in dealing with Richardson, to increase the interest rate and extend the time of payment without first obtaining the Arenas' consent while still retaining their liability. Appellant takes the position that the portion of paragraph six providing for no discharge modified forbearing to sue and extending time for payment as well as dealing in the same manner as with the mortgagor; therefore, since the interest rate was increased when the Arenas were given their additional advance, according to First Federal, raising the interest rate in its agreement with Richardson would

---

[3] If the full amount due on foreclosure did not exceed the value of the property at the time of the execution of the Modification and Extension Agreement, it was proper for the trial court to completely discharge the Arenas. *Mutual Ben. Life Ins. Co. v. Lindley*, (1932) 97 Ind.App. 575, 183 N.E. 127; Stevens, *Extension Agreements in the "Subject-To" Mortgage Situation*, 15 U.Cin.L.Rev. 58 (1941). As a corollary, if the value of the land at the time of this agreement was less than the amount of the mortgage on the property, the Arenas should have remained liable to the extent of this difference. Although it was improper for the trial court to hold there was a complete discharge without also holding the value of the land at the time of the March 10, 1969, agreement fully supported the mortgage loan, First Federal never raised any error regarding the extent to which the Arenas were discharged; consequently, we can only assume the amount due on foreclosure on March 10, 1969, would have been less than the value of the property at that time. We note, since Mr. Richardson offered to purchase the real estate in question for $37,000, and the aggregate balance remaining unpaid when Mr. Richardson and First Federal executed the Modification and Extension Agreement was $33,393.83, it appears the value of the land, in fact, did exceed the amount due, and thus, a complete discharge would have been proper.

merely be dealing with him in the same manner as it had dealt with the Arenas and, consequently, should not result in a discharge.

The Arenas, on the other hand, contend the reservation of rights clause in the Supplemental Agreement made no reference to the alteration or modification of the interest rate but rather, referred only to an extension of the time for payment or the decision to forbear to sue.

While it is true paragraph six indicates First Federal could deal with successors in interest to the mortgage in the same manner as with the mortgagor, we hold the resolution of whether this meant First Federal and the Arenas' grantee would be permitted to increase the interest rate without affecting the Arenas' liability was a question of law for the trial court since the rules applicable to construction of contracts generally apply to the construction of an agreement whereby a purchaser of mortgaged premises assumes the payment of the mortgage. 20 I.L.E. Mortgages § 193.

* * *

The essence of the appeal before us then is whether the trial court correctly concluded that as a matter of law, the scope of the reservation of rights clause found in paragraph six did not include altering or modifying the interest rate, and consequently, First Federal did not reserve the right to modify and increase the interest rate from 6% to 7¼% without the consent of the Arenas. We hold the trial court's entry of summary judgment in favor of Arenas was proper.

When the Arenas conveyed the real estate to Richardson subject to the existing mortgages to First Federal, the land became as to said parties, the primary source of funds for payment of the debt. *Mutual Ben. Life Ins. Co. v. Lindley*, (1932) 97 Ind.App. 575, 183 N.E. 127. No technical relation of principal and surety arose between the Arenas and their grantee from this conveyance, but an equity did arise which bears a close resemblance to the equitable rights of a surety. As a result, the Arenas assumed a position analogous to that of a surety, and the grantee became the principal debtor to the extent of the value of the land conveyed. *Mutual Ben. Life Ins. Co. v. Lindley, supra*; Warm, *Some Aspects of the Rights and Liabilities of Mortgagee, Mortgagor and Grantee*, 10 Temple L.Q. 116 (1936).

While a mortgagor in such a situation may consent in advance to future modifications or agree his liability will not be discharged by subsequent agreements between his grantee and the mortgagee, such clauses are to be strictly construed against the mortgagee, see Friedman, *Discharge of Personal Liability on Mortgage Debts in New York*, 52 Yale L.J. 771, 788 (1943), since it would be unjust to subject the mortgagor to a new risk or material change to which he has not consented. Consequently, a reservation of rights clause will not prevent a discharge of liability where the modification in question exceeds the scope of the consent in the clause.

This should come as no surprise since the mortgagor occupies the position of a surety, and the law of suretyship provides that a surety is entitled to stand on the strict letter of the contract upon which he is liable, and where he does not consent to a variation and a variation is made, it is fatal, see *American States Insurance Co. v. Floyd I. Staub, Inc.*, (1977) Ind.App., 370 N.E.2d 989; *White v. Household Finance Corp.*, (1973) 158 Ind.App. 394, 302 N.E.2d 828; therefore, an agreement between the principals for a higher interest than called for by the original contract will, if made without the surety's consent, release him from all liability. 74 Am.Jur.2d Suretyship § 47 (1974); see also 4 Am.Jur.2d Alteration of Instruments § 55 (1962).

The fact First Federal dealt with the grantee shows it knew of the Arenas' conveyance, and knowing of this conveyance, it was incumbent upon First Federal not to deal with the grantee in such a manner as would jeopardize or alter the surety-principal relationship. Warm, *Some Aspects of the Rights and Liabilities of Mortgagee, Mortgagor and Grantee*, 10 Temple L.Q. 116 (1936). The modification and extension agreement in question provided Mr. Richardson would personally assume the mortgage debt and thus, inured to the benefit of First Federal, but at the same time, the terms of the Arenas' earlier mortgage were changed to the detriment of the Arenas. If this increase in the interest rate was beyond the scope of the reservation of rights clause, the Arenas were thereby discharged, and the grantee became the sole debtor on the mortgages.

We hold the trial court properly rejected First Federal's argument that by increasing the interest rate it was merely dealing with Mr. Richardson in the same manner as it had dealt with the Arenas, and therefore, according to paragraph six, the Arenas should not have been discharged.

While it is true paragraph six indicated First Federal could deal with successors in interest to the mortgage in the same manner as with the mortgagor, this provision did not say First Federal could do so with impunity. We agree with the trial court that the portion of this paragraph providing for no discharge only modified forbearing to sue or extending the time for payment; consequently, the mortgagor would not be discharged from liability if the mortgagee simply extended the time for payment of the debt or opted not to bring suit, but these were the only situations where the mortgagee knew to a certainty his actions in dealing with the grantee would not discharge the mortgagor. The reservation of rights clause in paragraph six did not apply to activities which allegedly came within the ambit of dealing in the same manner as with the mortgagor. At the risk of being redundant, we again note, paragraph six stated in part: "6. (T)he Mortgagee may, without notice to the Mortgagor, deal with * * * successors in interest with reference to this mortgage and the debt hereby secured in the same manner as with the Mortgagor, and * * *." The punctuation used clearly sets this portion of paragraph six apart from the remainder of the paragraph which then goes on to provide the mortgagee "may forbear to sue or may extend time for payment of the debt, * * * without discharging or in any way affecting the liability of the Mortgagor hereunder or upon the debt hereby secured."

In order to give the reservation of rights clause the expanded application urged by First Federal so that it also applied to dealing in the same manner as with the mortgagor, it would be necessary to ignore the punctuation used and the maxim that such clauses should be strictly construed against the mortgagee. Further, such a construction would change the reservation of rights provision from applying in two definite situations to an open-ended invitation to argue there was no discharge because the mortgagee either could have or in fact had dealt with the mortgagor in the same manner; the possible activities which arguably could then come within this clause's application would be indefinite.

We hold the construction of the supplemental agreement between the Arenas and First Federal was a question of law for the trial court, which correctly held paragraph six did not authorize First Federal and the Arenas' grantee to alter the terms of payment on the mortgage debt by increasing the interest rate without affecting the Arenas' liability.

Judgment affirmed.

MILLER, P. J., and YOUNG, J., concur.

NOTES

1. *Scope of reservations of rights in the original mortgage.* It is perhaps amazing that a lender's lawyer, drafting a clause in a mortgage that reserves the mortgagee's rights against the mortgagor despite a modification entered into with a grantee, would fail to take into consideration *all* the possible modifications—the whole range listed in the introductory note just before the *Arena* case! For another example of such sloppy drafting (or thinking), see Moss v. McDonald, 772 P.2d 626 (Colo.App.1988) (because original note language consented to extensions of time granted *after* maturity of the note, it did not serve as a consent to an extension granted *prior* to maturity).

2. *Extent of the discharge.* The *Arena* case raises the fundamental question of the *extent* to which the grantor should be discharged when the mortgagee and grantee modify the obligation. The court holds that, after a "subject to" transfer, an increase in the interest rate without the grantor's consent discharges the grantor to the extent of the property's value. The discharge is only in the amount of the property's value because, in a "subject to" transfer, the Arenas would have had recourse only to the property. In contrast, if Richardson had assumed the mortgage debt, the Indiana court's view is that the Arenas would have been totally discharged, because they would have been sureties for the entire debt. This is the traditional approach.

But surely the Arenas would not have been harmed to this extent by the unconsented modification, which merely increased the interest rate from 6% to 7.25%. By the time of Richardson's default, about six years later, the mortgage balance was probably less than $3,000 higher because of the increased interest than it would have been at the old interest rate. Why isn't this the proper limit of the Arenas' discharge? The Restatement (Third) of Property (Mortgages) § 5.3 comment d and illustration 8, assert that it is.

To counter this argument, the Arenas could assert that the increased interest rate resulted in higher monthly payments for Richardson and that he would not (or, at least, might not) have defaulted if his payments had remained at their original level? Therefore, they should be completely discharged because they would (might?) never have had to pay the debt if the interest rate had not increased. Is this position too speculative to be worth adopting?

The Restatements, as mentioned above, grant a discharge to the mortgagor/surety only to the extent that the modification of the loan's terms would otherwise harm him or her. Here's an additional illustration. Assume Mortgagor ("MR") borrows $50,000 from Mortgagee ("ME") on a one-year note secured by a mortgage on MR's house. MR then sells the house to Grantee ("GE"), who does not assume the mortgage debt. GE then persuades ME to grant a time extension of one additional year to pay the loan. At the end of the second year, when the note falls due, GE does not repay the $50,000 loan and ME demands that MR pay the debt. The value of the house has fallen during the second year from $60,000 to $40,000. As a result of the time extension, the loan is now undersecured by $10,000, and MR's recourse is impaired by that amount. Therefore, under the Restatement view, MR is discharged in the amount of $10,000 and is liable to ME for only $40,000.

3.   *The effect of modifications and time extensions on the mortgagor.* If the mortgagor is not completely discharged, how do modifications of the loan's terms or maturity impact the mortgagor as against the mortgagee? The mortgagor is entitled to the benefit of any advantageous modifications but is not bound by any disadvantageous modifications (unless the mortgagor consented to them, of course). In effect, the mortgagor is entitled to perform either the original or the modified version of the obligation. For example, if the interest rate is increased, the mortgagor can still pay off the loan at the original rate. Restatement of Suretyship and Guaranty § 1(c). If the loan maturity is extended, the mortgagor has the choice of paying on the original or the modified schedule. Restatement of Suretyship and Guaranty § 40(c).

4.   *How can mortgagees avoid the suretyship defenses?* Mortgagees would naturally like to preserve their rights against original mortgagors when they elect to grant releases or modifications to grantees. Three fairly obvious methods will do so:

(a)   Include a clause in the mortgage that preserves the mortgagee's claim against the mortgagor. The drafter of the *Arena* mortgage tried to do that, but did not do it very well. No doubt exists that this sort of provision (sometimes termed a "survival" clause or a "waiver of defenses" clause) is effective, but the courts tend to construe such clauses narrowly, as *Arena* illustrates;

(b)   Get the mortgagor's consent to the modification after the mortgage is entered into, but before (or at the time that) the modification is made; or

(c)   Get the mortgagor's consent after the modification is made.

Think about choices (b) and (c). A common context is the situation in which the mortgagee, acting under authority of a due-on-sale clause, approved a grantee's assumption of a mortgage loan subject to the condition that the interest rate be increased by, say, 1.5%. A simple way to obtain the mortgagor's consent to the increase is simply to ask the mortgagor to join in executing the amendment to the promissory note that changes the rate. That implements choice (b) above. The mortgagor/seller may very well be happy to cooperate, because she wants to sell the real estate.

On the other hand, suppose the mortgagee does not get the mortgagor's consent at the time of the sale and modification. Instead, the mortgagee comes back to the mortgagor after the sale is completed and asks him to consent to the rate change. Do you think that the mortgagor will be cooperative now? At this point, the sale is a "done deal" and the mortgagor is perfectly satisfied with the status quo. The mortgagee no longer has any leverage to convince the mortgagor to sign a consent form.

B.   RESTRICTIONS ON TRANSFER BY THE MORTGAGOR

The Due-On Clauses—Introduction*

The law of real property usually develops in an evolutionary fashion. Change is often measured in terms of decades and centuries rather than in months and years. Yet economic turmoil can accelerate this process. Just as the Great Depression of the 1930s spurred the enactment of mortgage moratoria and antideficiency legislation, so too the inflationary economic climate of the 1970s and early 1980s and the Great Recession that began in 2008 produced new mortgage law.

A major focus during the 1970s to early 1980s was the due-on-sale clause, a mortgage provision that affords the mortgagee the right to accelerate the mortgage debt and to foreclose if the mortgaged real estate is transferred without the mortgagee's consent.[3] Such clauses have two distinct functions from a lender's viewpoint. First, they are used to protect mortgagees against transfers that endanger mortgage security or increase

*   This material is adapted from Nelson, Whitman, Burkhart & Freyermuth, Real Estate Finance Law §§ 5.21 & 5.22 (6th ed.2015), reprinted with permission of LEG, Inc. d/b/a West Academic.

3   A typical due-on-sale clause provides, in part: "If all or any part of the Property or an interest therein is sold or transferred by Borrower without Lender's prior written consent, * * * Lender may, at Lender's option, declare all the sums secured by this mortgage to be due and payable." Fannie Mae/Freddie Mac, Clause 18 (one-to-four family).

the risk of default, typically because the proposed transfer is to a person with a poor credit rating or inadequate income to make the loan payments. Second and more importantly, they enable mortgagees to recall lower-than-market interest rate loans during periods of rising interest rates. Use of the due-on-sale clause in this context pits lenders against borrowers and real estate buyers, who would like to be able to sell and purchase mortgaged real estate by assuming existing loans. During the 1970s and early 1980s, the due-on-sale clause became a major economic, political, and legal issue. It was confronted and evaluated by most state supreme courts, many legislatures, several federal regulatory agencies, the United States Supreme Court, and, ultimately, Congress. It was also the subject of a great deal of scholarly commentary.[4]

Given the prevailing economic conditions, this close scrutiny was hardly surprising. Due to exceptionally high interest rates and the limited availability of home financing, large numbers of potential home buyers were excluded from the housing market. For many purchasers, the assumption of an existing lower-than-market interest mortgage represented one of the few practical financing alternatives. The financial climate also made it much more difficult for owners to sell. Many sellers were forced either to reduce significantly the price of their properties to enable buyers to qualify for institutional high-interest financing or to suffer an effective price reduction by financing part of the purchase price themselves at lower-than-market interest rates. Thus, for those sellers with lower-than-market interest rate mortgages on their properties, assumability of the mortgage was a key to obtaining a higher price for the property.

On the other hand, the economic stake of institutional lenders in upholding due-on-sale clauses was also great. Institutional lenders, especially savings and loan associations, were experiencing severe economic difficulty. Because they held portfolios that included large numbers of fixed rate, lower-yielding mortgage loans, they were hard pressed to pay the higher short-term rates demanded by depositors. Many savings and loan associations and similar institutions failed, and others were left in precarious financial positions. Because the due-on-sale clause provided one means of eliminating lower-interest mortgage loans from institutional portfolios, and doing so without resort to expensive federal "bailout" or other subsidy schemes, federal regulators considered its enforceability critical to the economic health of the thrift industry.

---

[4] See, e.g., Gorinson & Manishin, Garn-St. Germain: A Harbinger of Change, 40 Wash. & Lee L. Rev. 1313 (1983); Nelson & Whitman, Congressional Preemption of Mortgage Due-on-Sale Law: An Analysis of the Garn-St. Germain Act, 35 Hast.L.J. 241 (1983); Volkmer, The Application of the Restraints on Alienation Doctrine to Real Property Security Interests, 58 Iowa L.Rev. 747 (1973).

Due-on-Encumbrance Restrictions

Mortgages may restrict mortgagor transfers by means other than a due-on-sale clause. For example, a mortgage may contain a clause authorizing the mortgagee to accelerate the debt if the mortgagor "further encumbers" the mortgaged real estate. Such language is usually referred to as a "due-on-encumbrance" provision. While due-on-encumbrance language is often included as part of a due-on-sale clause, it is not uncommon for a mortgage to contain a separate due-on-encumbrance clause. Unlike the due-on-sale situation, in which the mortgagee's desire to increase the interest rate predominates, due-on-encumbrance language is utilized mainly to protect against impairment of mortgage security by a debtor who incurs a junior mortgage debt and thus reduces his or her economic stake in the mortgaged real estate.

Increased-Interest-on-Transfer Clauses

Another provision closely related to the due-on-sale clause authorizes the mortgagee to increase or adjust the mortgage interest rate in the event of a transfer by the mortgagor (an "increased-interest-on-transfer" clause). This type of clause fulfills the same economic function as the due-on-sale clause because it enables the mortgagee to use a transfer by the mortgagor as the basis for increasing the interest yield on the mortgage. However, unlike a due-on-sale clause, it does not confer on the mortgagee an absolute right to accelerate the mortgage debt upon a transfer. Therefore, it gives no direct protection against transfer to an uncreditworthy buyer. Only if the transferee fails to pay the increased mortgage payments can the mortgagee declare a default and accelerate the debt.

Installment Land Contract Prohibitions on Transfer

Transfer restrictions may also appear in installment land contracts, which are probably the most commonly used mortgage substitute. Installment land contracts frequently include a provision that prohibits assignment by the vendee without the vendor's permission. Violation of the provision constitutes a default and might result in vendor termination of the contract and loss of the purchaser's equity. In this respect, the provision differs from a due-on-sale clause, under which an unapproved transfer will at most trigger an acceleration of the mortgage debt and, if the accelerated debt is unpaid, a foreclosure sale of the mortgaged real estate.

Events Triggering Acceleration

A common question is what kind of event triggers acceleration of a debt under a due-on-sale or other transfer restriction clause. While some early clauses used a "sale" alone as a triggering event, most recent forms employ broader language that is often modeled after the Fannie Mae/Freddie Mac mortgage form. That form permits the lender to accelerate "if all or any part of the Property or any interest in it is sold or transferred (or if a beneficial interest in Borrower is sold or transferred and Borrower is not a natural person)." Under this language, standing alone, even a short-term lease or a grant of an easement or other limited interest in the land would trigger the lender's right to accelerate.

Perhaps the most significant question is whether a sale by installment land contract permits acceleration. The answer depends on the exact wording of the clause in question, but under broad language like that of the Fannie Mae/Freddie Mac clause, the courts have nearly uniformly permitted acceleration.[5]

Due-On Clauses—Pre-Garn-St. Germain Act
State Judicial and Legislative Response

Due-on-Sale Clauses

Due-on-sale clauses came under judicial attack as unreasonable restraints on alienation in many jurisdictions. While the results of these cases are now primarily of historical interest because of the federal legislation to be discussed below, a brief review of them will be helpful to an understanding the present legal context.

No court held that a due-on-sale clause is *per se* unlawful as a restraint on alienation. Indeed, some courts suggested that it was not a restraint on alienation at all. While many courts probably viewed the clause as an indirect restraint on alienation, all courts recognized that there were circumstances in which enforcement of the clause was reasonable and thus permissible. Some courts, however, were more sympathetic to enforcement than others, and two broad judicial approaches to the clause emerged.

Under the predominant judicial approach, the clause was deemed *per se* reasonable unless the borrower could show that the lender had engaged in unconscionable conduct.[6] The courts employing this approach recognized the desirability of protecting the mortgagee from the vagaries of the interest rate market. The mortgagee was not required to establish that a proposed transfer would impair security. The validity of the due-on-sale clause was not normally judged by the facts of an individual case. Under one variant of this approach, such facts were relevant only to the extent that the mortgagor attempted to meet the burden of proving that

---

5 See Income Realty & Mortgage, Inc. v. Columbia Savings and Loan Association, 661 P.2d 257, 259–60 (Colo.1983); Century Savings Association v. C. Michael Franke & Co., 9 Kan.App.2d 776, 689 P.2d 915 (1984) (contract for deed transfer deemed "transfer of title" for due-on-sale purposes); Mutual Federal Savings & Loan Association v. Wisconsin Wire Works, 58 Wis.2d 99, 101, 110, 205 N.W.2d 762, 769 (1973), appeal after remand, 71 Wis.2d 531, 239 N.W.2d 20 (1976). But see Fidelity Federal Savings and Loan Association v. Grieme, 112 Ill.App.3d 1014, 1019, 68 Ill.Dec. 558, 561, 446 N.E.2d 292, 295 (1983) (entering into agreement for deed held insufficient to trigger clause allowing lender to accelerate upon "change of ownership"); Peoples Federal Savings and Loan Association of East Chicago, Indiana v. Willsey, 466 N.E.2d 470 (Ind.App.1984) (transfer by contract for deed not a sale or conveyance for purposes of due-on-sale clause).

6 See, e.g., Tierce v. APS Co., 382 So.2d 485, 487 (Ala.1979); Income Realty & Mortgage Inc. v. Columbia Savings & Loan Association, 661 P.2d 257, 265 (Colo.1983).

enforcement was unconscionable or inequitable in his or her case. An increase in the market interest rate was thought to be insufficient to meet this burden, and due-on-sale clauses in such jurisdictions were usually enforced.

Under the minority approach, followed by about a dozen jurisdictions, the courts held that enforcement of due-on-sale clauses must be reasonable in individual cases, necessitating a case-by-case determination.[7] Under this approach, the mortgagee's desire to increase interest rates was not considered a sufficient reason to justify enforcement of the clause. The mortgagee had the burden to establish reasonableness, which normally meant that the transfer would result in security impairment or an increased risk of default. Because this was usually hard to prove, lenders rarely sought due-on-sale enforcement in jurisdictions that followed this approach.

As noted above, majority or "automatic enforcement" jurisdictions often stated that due-on-sale clauses would be unenforceable if the mortgagor could establish that enforcement would be "unconscionable" or "inequitable." While it is difficult to articulate precisely when enforcement would be so categorized, most courts probably would have been unwilling to enforce the clauses in "non-substantive" or "non-sale" transfers. For example, one court indicated that enforcement should be denied in situations such as transfers to a spouse who becomes a co-owner, transfers to a spouse incidental to a marriage dissolution proceeding or settlement, and transfers to an inter vivos trust of which the mortgagor was a beneficiary.

No-Transfer Provisions in Installment Land Contracts

While there was some early support for enforcement of no-transfer provisions in installment land contracts, later decisions were much less sympathetic. This attitude was reflected in two ways. First, no-transfer clauses were often construed narrowly against the vendor. Second, in contrast to the majority approach to due-on-sale clause enforcement, courts often eschewed an "automatic enforcement" approach; the "no-transfer" language was enforced only when it was established that the transfer would impair the vendor's security. Moreover, even when a vendor demonstrated such an impairment, it was likely that a court would avoid forfeiture by permitting the transferee to pay off the contract balance or by ordering that the real estate be foreclosed by public sale.

---

7   See, e.g., Baltimore Life Insurance Co. v. Harn, 15 Ariz.App. 78, 81, 486 P.2d 190, 193 (1971); Wellenkamp v. Bank of America, 21 Cal.3d 943, 953, 148 Cal.Rptr. 379, 385–86, 582 P.2d 970, 976–77 (1978); Magney v. Lincoln Mutual Savings Bank, 34 Wn.App. 45, 659 P.2d 537, 541 (1983).

State Legislation

Several states imposed legislative limitations on due-on-sale clauses.[8] While the details of these statutes varied considerably, they commonly prohibited due-on-sale enforcement in residential mortgages unless the mortgagee could establish that a transfer would impair mortgage security. Most statutes permitted the mortgagee to condition transfer of the property on payment of a limited assumption fee or on an increase in the mortgage interest rate by a modest amount, usually no more than one percent. Some statutes imposed similar restrictions on increased-interest-on-transfer provisions.

Due-On Clauses—Pre-Garn-St.
Germain Act Federal Regulation

In 1976, the Federal Home Loan Bank Board (the Board), the federal agency that regulated federally-chartered and federally-insured savings and loan associations, became concerned about the increasing controversy over whether federally-chartered associations had the authority to enforce due-on-sale clauses. The Board issued a regulation effective July 31, 1976 (the 1976 Regulation) that provided that a federal association "continues to have the power to include * * * a provision in its loan instrument whereby the association may, at its option, declare immediately due and payable sums secured by the association's security instrument if all or any part of the real property securing the loan is sold or transferred by the borrower without the association's prior written consent."[9]

In this regulation, the Board authorized federal associations to exercise the due-on-sale option, except in the case of certain types of "minor" transfers, and provided that all rights and remedies of the association and borrower "shall be exclusively governed by the terms of the loan contract." In the preamble to the 1976 Regulation, the Board also expressed its intent that the due-on-sale practices of federal associations be governed exclusively by federal law and emphasized that federal associations "shall not be bound by or subject to any conflicting state law which imposes different * * * due-on-sale requirements."[10]

While lower federal courts concluded that the 1976 Board Regulation preempted the application of state due-on-sale law to federal associations, a few state courts reached contrary results. Ultimately, this conflict was resolved by the United States Supreme Court in Fidelity Federal Savings & Loan Association v. de la Cuesta,[11] a case that addressed the effect of the

---

[8]   See Ariz.Rev.Stat. § 33–1571; West's Colo.Rev.Stat.Ann. § 38–30–165; O.C.G.A. § 44–14–5; Iowa Code Ann. § 535.8; N.M.Stat.Ann.1981, §§ 48–7–15 to 48–7–20; Minn.Stat.Ann. § 47.20; Utah Code Ann.1981, §§ 57–15–1 to 57–15–10 (repealed).

[9]   12 C.F.R. § 545.8–3(f) (1983).

[10]   41 Fed.Reg. 18,286, 18,287.

[11]   458 U.S. 141, 102 S.Ct. 3014, 73 L.Ed.2d 664 (1982).

1976 Regulation on California law. California generally limited due-on-sale enforcement to situations in which impairment of mortgage security was established. In *de la Cuesta*, the Supreme Court held that: (1) The Board intended to preempt state law; (2) The 1976 Regulation conflicted with California law, though it merely authorized but did not require federal associations to use due-on-sale clauses; (3) The Board acted within its statutory authority under section 5(a) of the Home Owner's Loan Act, which authorized the Board to promulgate rules for the operation and regulation of federal associations; and (4) Though the 1976 Regulation's merits might be debatable, it was a reasonable and, therefore, a valid exercise of the Board's authority.

Though *de la Cuesta* confirmed the validity of the Board's response to the needs of federally-chartered savings associations with respect to due-on-sale clauses, it did nothing for other types of lenders. Hence, these lenders, particularly state-chartered savings and loan associations, sought a uniform national solution—congressional preemption of state laws restricting the enforcement of due-on-sale clauses. Their efforts culminated in the passage of the Garn-St. Germain Depository Institutions Act.

SECTION 341, GARN-ST. GERMAIN DEPOSITORY INSTITUTIONS ACT OF 1982

96 Stat. 1505, 12 U.S.C.A. § 1701j–3, as amended, November 30, 1983, 97 Stat. 1237

Sec. 1701j–3.   Preemption of due-on-sale prohibitions

(a) Definitions

For the purpose of this section—

(1) the term "due-on-sale clause" means a contract provision which authorizes a lender, at its option, to declare due and payable sums secured by the lender's security instrument if all or any part of the property, or an interest therein, securing the real property loan is sold or transferred without the lender's prior written consent;

(2) the term "lender" means a person or government agency making a real property loan or any assignee or transferee, in whole or in part, of such a person or agency;

(3) the term "real property loan" means a loan, mortgage, advance, or credit sale secured by a lien on real property, the stock allocated to a dwelling unit in a cooperative housing corporation, or a residential manufactured home, whether real or personal property; and

(4) the term "residential manufactured home" means a manufactured home as defined in section 5402(6) of Title 42 which is used as a residence; and

(5) the term "State" means any State of the United States, the District of Columbia, the Commonwealth of Puerto Rico, the Virgin Islands, Guam, the Northern Mariana Islands, American Samoa, and the Trust Territory of the Pacific Islands.

(b) Loan contract and terms governing execution or enforcement of due-on-sale options and rights and remedies of lenders and borrowers; assumptions of loan rates

(1) Notwithstanding any provision of the constitution or laws (including the judicial decisions) of any State to the contrary, a lender may, subject to subsection (c) of this section, enter into or enforce a contract containing a due-on-sale clause with respect to a real property loan.

(2) Except as otherwise provided in subsection (d) of this section, the exercise by the lender of its option pursuant to such a clause shall be exclusively governed by the terms of the loan contract, and all rights and remedies of the lender and the borrower shall be fixed and governed by the contract.

(3) In the exercise of its option under a due-on-sale clause, a lender is encouraged to permit an assumption of a real property loan at the existing contract rate or at a rate which is at or below the average between the contract and market rates, and nothing in this section shall be interpreted to prohibit any such assumption.

* * *

(d) Exemption of specified transfers or dispositions

With respect to a real property loan secured by a lien on residential real property containing less than five dwelling units, including a lien on the stock allocated to a dwelling unit in a cooperative housing corporation, or on a residential manufactured home, a lender may not exercise its option pursuant to a due-on-sale clause upon—

(1) the creation of a lien or other encumbrance subordinate to the lender's security instrument which does not relate to a transfer of rights of occupancy in the property;

(2) the creation of a purchase money security interest for household appliances;

(3) a transfer by devise, descent, or operation of law on the death of a joint tenant or tenant by the entirety;

(4) the granting of a leasehold interest of three years or less not containing an option to purchase;

(5) a transfer to a relative resulting from the death of a borrower;

(6) a transfer where the spouse or children of the borrower become an owner of the property;

(7) a transfer resulting from a decree of a dissolution of marriage, legal separation agreement, or from an incidental property settlement agreement, by which the spouse of the borrower becomes an owner of the property;

(8) a transfer into an inter vivos trust in which the borrower is and remains a beneficiary and which does not relate to a transfer of rights of occupancy in the property; or

(9) any other transfer or disposition described in regulations prescribed by the Federal Home Loan Bank Board.

(e) Rules, regulations, and interpretations; future income bearing loans subject to due-on-sale options

(1) The Federal Home Loan Bank Board, in consultation with the Comptroller of the Currency and the National Credit Union Administration Board, is authorized to issue rules and regulations and to publish interpretations governing the implementation of this section.

(2) Notwithstanding the provisions of subsection (d) of this section, the rules and regulations prescribed under this section may permit a lender to exercise its option pursuant to a due-on-sale clause with respect to a real property loan and any related agreement pursuant to which a borrower obtains the right to receive future income.

NOTES

1. *Non-sale transfers.* To what extent does the Garn Act permit a lender to enforce a due-on-sale clause in "non-sale" or "non-substantive" family transfers that do not involve 1-to-4 family residences? Consider the following examples; in each case, assume that the mortgage in question contains a due-on-sale clause identical to the one contained in the Fannie/Freddie Uniform Instrument.

(a) A husband and wife own a store building in joint tenancy which they operate as a grocery store. Wife dies and her husband becomes the sole owner. If the building is mortgaged, can the lender enforce the due-on clause?

(b) A mother dies, leaving a 20-unit apartment building to her daughter under her will. If the building is mortgaged, can the lender enforce the due-on clause? See In re Smith, 469 B.R. 198 (Bankr. S.D.N.Y. 2012) (refusing enforcement); In re Cady, 440 B.R. 16 (Bankr. N.D.N.Y. 2010) (same). Can these decisions be reconciled with the language of the Garn Act?

(c) Husband and Wife own a 640-acre farm parcel in joint tenancy, subject to a mortgage. Husband dies. Can the mortgagee accelerate the loan? Should it make a difference if the land contains a farmhouse in which Wife still lives? How might a lender have drafted the mortgage documents to address such a situation?

2.   *Transfers of stock or partnership interests.* Suppose that the majority of the shares of a closely-held corporate mortgagor are sold to a new owner. If the mortgage contains a due-on-transfer clause, is it enforceable in this setting even though the legal owner of the real estate is still the corporation? Because the clause is a restraint on alienation, a court might construe the clause against enforcement on the ground that no "transfer" had occurred. See, e.g., Fidelity Trust Co. v. BVD Assocs., 196 Conn. 270, 492 A.2d 180 (1985) (transfer of limited partnership interests in borrower not a violation). A similar question arises if the title to the real estate is held by a trustee, and there is a change in the identity of the trust beneficiary. As a practical matter, beneficial ownership has been transferred, but legal title remains unchanged. Does such a transfer trigger a due-on-sale clause? See Mercado v. Calumet Fed. Sav. & Loan Ass'n, 196 Ill.App.3d 483, 143 Ill.Dec. 370, 554 N.E.2d 305 (1990) (summarizing Illinois cases).

The due-on-sale provision in the uniform covenants of the Fannie Mae/Freddie Mac mortgage/deed of trust form (reproduced in the Appendix of this book) provides, in pertinent part: "If all or any part of the Property or any interest in it is sold or transferred (or if a beneficial interest in Borrower is sold or transferred and Borrower is not a natural person) without Lender's prior written consent, Lender may require immediate payment in full of all sums secured by this Security Instrument." Does the parenthetical language solve the problem? Is a clause permitting acceleration upon the sale of corporate stock or a partnership interest really a "due-on-sale" clause as the Garn Act defines the term? If so, why? If not, does federal pre-emption apply?

3.   *Coverage of successive transfers.* Does a due-on-sale clause run with the land? Suppose A borrows money from a bank and gives it a mortgage with a due-on-sale clause on A's house. Subsequently, A sells the house to B with the bank's consent. B later wants to sell the house to C. Is the bank's consent necessary, or did its previous consent relinquish its right to accelerate for the remainder of the loan's life? Would it matter whether (a) the mortgage contained a statement that it bound the successors and assigns of the original mortgagor, or (b) the mortgagee, in granting consent to the A-B sale, expressly reserved the right to approve all future transfers? See Esplendido Apts. v. Metropolitan Condo. Ass'n, 161 Ariz. 325, 778 P.2d 1221 (1989), in which the court relied on the "successors and assigns" clause in finding that B's transfer to C triggered the due-on-sale clause; Howell v. Murray Mortg. Co., 890 S.W.2d 78 (Tex.App.1994) (clause held binding on mortgagor's administrator). But see In re Ormond Beach Assocs. Ltd. Partn., 184 F.3d 143 (2d Cir. 1999).

4.   *Waivers by lenders.* Lenders can and frequently do waive their right to accelerate under due-on-sale clauses. Commonly, a lender waives its right in return for the payment of an assumption fee, an increased interest rate on the loan, or both. See Gruber v. Federal Nat'l Mortg. Ass'n, 2003 WL 1091046 (Cal.App.2003) (not reported in Cal.Rptr.2d), in which the court upheld

imposition of an assumption fee. Sometimes, the grantee will argue that a waiver or estoppel should be implied from the lender's action, inaction, or ambiguous words. See In re Ramos, 357 B.R. 669 (Bankr.S.D.Fla.2006) (lender waived debtor's transfer of the property by failing to raise it properly in Chapter 13 bankruptcy proceeding); In re Mini, 2009 WL 3756827 (Bankr. N.D.Cal.2009) (lender's prepetition conduct made enforcement of due-on-sale clause unfair and inequitable when it would trump the debtor's attempts to reorganize in bankruptcy). Do you think a waiver or estoppel should be found on the following facts?

(a)   A loan officer for the lender stated "there will be no problem" with a loan assumption if the purchaser's financial condition proves to be as represented to the lender. Compare Destin Sav. Bank v. Summerhouse of FWB, Inc., 579 So.2d 232 (Fla.App.1991) (no waiver found) with Great Northern Sav. Co. v. Ingarra, 66 Ohio St.2d 503, 423 N.E.2d 128 (1981), noted 11 Capital U.L.Rev. 380 (1981) (waiver found).

(b)   The parties do not notify the lender of the sale, but the lender receives a hazard insurance binder that shows that the real estate has a new owner. The lender takes no action to enforce the due-on-sale clause for many months afterwards. See Rakestraw v. Dozier Assocs., Inc., 285 S.C. 358, 329 S.E.2d 437 (1985) (17-month delay; waiver and estoppel found); Cooper v. Deseret Fed. Sav. & Loan Ass'n, 757 P.2d 483 (Utah App.1988) (28 month delay; estoppel found). In cases such as this, should a court require some evidence that the purchaser has been damaged or harmed by the lender's delay? Suppose that, immediately after learning of the transfer, the lender demands that the purchaser assume the loan, which the purchaser refuses to do, but then delays for 12 months before accelerating and commencing foreclosure. If this is a waiver, as a court has held it to be, see Rubin v. Los Angeles Fed. Sav. & Loan Ass'n, 159 Cal.App.3d 292, 205 Cal.Rptr. 455 (1984)), isn't the court penalizing the lender for being patient and attempting to work out the dispute?

(c)   Suppose the parties fail to notify the lender of the transfer, and the lender does not receive any document disclosing the ownership change. Should the lender be deemed to have constructive notice that a deed to the property has been recorded? See Stenger v. Great Southern Sav. & Loan Ass'n, 677 S.W.2d 376 (Mo.App.1984) (no notice imputed).

5.   *Concealment of transfers.* Most due-on-sale clauses do not include an express covenant that the borrower must disclose to the lender that a transfer is taking place, though this type of covenant certainly makes sense for the lender. No cases impose an implied duty to disclose. See Medovoi v. American Sav. & Loan Ass'n, 89 Cal.App.3d 244, 152 Cal.Rptr. 572 (1979) (depublished). When current interest rates are significantly higher than the rate on an

existing loan, borrowers are often tempted—and are sometimes advised by real estate brokers—to transfer without telling their lender. They may go to some lengths to conceal sales. For example, they may arrange for the grantee to make the monthly mortgage payments to the grantor and for the grantor to continue remitting them to the lender.

However, concealment is tricky, and a good chance exists that the lender will discover the transaction sooner or later. Some lenders have contracted with title companies to watch their properties and report any recorded transfers. A lender may also discover that a transfer has occurred because it receives a tax bill or homeowner's insurance binder that shows the name of a new owner. Lenders may even have properties visited to determine whether the original borrowers are still in residence.

A borrower may try to circumvent these means of detection. For example, the borrower may agree with the grantee that the deed will not be recorded, that the taxing authorities will not be notified of the sale, and that the hazard insurance will continue to be carried in the old owner's name. But these techniques are obviously risky and can give rise to serious problems.

If a lender discovers a concealed transfer, what are its remedies? Obviously, it can accelerate the loan if it acts within a reasonable time after discovery. The acceleration might be quite devastating, particularly if interest rates have risen substantially or if the present owner cannot qualify for new financing. Can the lender also successfully claim damages for its lost interest between the time of the transfer and the time of its discovery? Could a lender predicate a damages claim on some theory of breach of an implied covenant, such as the covenant of good faith and fair dealing? No reported case seems to have adopted these arguments, but a court conceivably could do so.

Suppose a lender discovers the concealed transfer and accelerates. The brunt of the lender's action falls on the grantee, of course. Could the grantee bring a successful action against the grantor, perhaps on the theory that the grantor had implicitly warranted that the financing taken over by the grantee would continue to be available for its full stated term? What if the grantee cannot qualify for new financing, and ends up losing the property in foreclosure? Again, no case law imposes liability on the grantor in these situations, but the argument is not a frivolous one.

On the whole, we think concealment is a bad strategy, full of risks for both parties. The wiser course is to discuss the proposed transaction with the lender and to make the best deal possible.

6. *Concealment by lawyers.* Should a lawyer be troubled by the ethical implications of counseling a client to conceal a transfer or of arranging the details of the transaction? Two issues exist: (1) Does a lawyer have an ethical obligation either to inform or not to inform the lender that a transfer has occurred? (2) Does a lawyer have an ethical obligation to refrain from advising or assisting in the concealed transfer? The comments below are based on the

Model Rules of Professional Conduct (1983) (MRPC) and the Restatement (Third) of the Law Governing Lawyers (2000) ("Restatement").

The lawyer's duty of disclosure or nondisclosure. A lawyer has a duty not knowingly to reveal a confidence of his or her client. See MRPC 1.6. Exceptions are made for disclosures necessary to prevent the client from committing a crime that would result in death or bodily harm, or that are based on "fraudulent" conduct by the client; see Restatement § 67(1). The relevant opinions consistently treat "fraudulent" as referring only to criminal conduct or something very close to it. Therefore, a lawyer probably has a duty not to disclose a real estate transfer to a mortgage lender against a client's wishes.

The lawyer's duty to avoid advising or assisting in the transfer. The concealment of a transfer is at most a breach of contract and perhaps not even that if the mortgage does not specifically require the borrower to report the transfer. The relevant rules require a lawyer to withdraw from representation only when the client's conduct is "illegal" or "fraudulent." MRPC 1.2(d); Restatement § 94(2). A lawyer is not prohibited from advising a client to breach a contract. Again, the term "fraudulent" is generally taken to include only criminal or quasi-criminal activity. This approach is adopted in the due-on-sale situation by Oregon Ethics Opinion 464, which exonerated a lawyer who assisted a client in a concealed real estate sale and commented that "the transaction, although legally precarious for both the buyer and seller, is not fraudulent or illegal." The "terminology" section of MRPC's Preamble provides:

> "Fraud" or "fraudulent" denotes conduct having a purpose to deceive and not merely negligent misrepresentation or failure to apprise another of relevant information.

It is difficult (though not impossible) to conceive of a court's finding nondisclosure of a real estate transfer to be fraudulent in this sense. State bar ethics opinions have generally agreed with Oregon. See Alaska Bar Ass'n Ethics Opinion #88–2; Illinois Bar Advisory Opinion No. 728; Virginia Bar Opinion 471 (1983).

A lawyer nevertheless may feel uncomfortable in assisting a client in a concealed transfer. If the client insists on proceeding contrary to the lawyer's advice, the lawyer is plainly entitled to withdraw from representation. See Restatement § 32(3)(f) (lawyer who considers client's action to be "repugnant or imprudent" may withdraw); Mark E. Roszkowski, Drafting Around Mortgage Due-on-Sale Clauses: The Dangers of Playing Hide-and-Seek, 21 Real Prop.Prob. and Tr. J. 23, 41–58 (1986).

C. TRANSFER OF THE MORTGAGEE'S INTEREST

In this section we discuss the legal aspects of transactions in which one lender (for example, the one who has "originated" or made a mortgage loan) sells or assigns the note and mortgage to another lender, typically termed an "investor." Such a transaction is known as a secondary sale, and the market in which transactions between lenders occur is called the secondary mortgage market. The economic aspects of the secondary market, and the involvement of government agencies in such transactions, are discussed in Chapter Eight. Secondary market transactions can take many forms, but they generally fall into four categories.

1. OUTRIGHT SALE TO AN INVESTOR WHO WILL HOLD THE MORTGAGE LOAN IN ITS PORTFOLIO

The transaction may involve a single (usually large) mortgage loan, or a pool of smaller (e.g., residential) mortgages loans. The investor is a company or institution with substantial funds to invest, such as a savings bank, a life insurance company, or a pension fund. In their earlier years as private entities, Fannie Mae and Freddie Mac acted as investors in this sort of transaction; they held in their portfolios a large share of the mortgage loans they purchased. The funds they used to make these purchases were raised largely by selling debentures in the capital markets. The debenture would come in the form of a certificate that would entitle the owner to certain payments of principal and interest for a term. Debenture, Black's Law Dictionary (11th ed. 2019). Payment, however, was guaranteed merely by the general solvency of Fannie and Freddie; it was not tied to the mortgage loans themselves, as would come later with the rise of securitization.

2. PARTIAL ASSIGNMENTS OF A MORTGAGE LOAN SOLD TO MULTIPLE INVESTORS

With a partial assignment (in other words, a partial sale), the investor who purchases the mortgage loan or loans typically only retains a portion of the ownership interest and sells partial interests (literally, tenancy in common interests) to other investors. For example, on a single large commercial loan, say $50 million, the investor might retain a 1/4 interest ($12.5 million) and sell the other three 1/4 ($12.5 million) shares to three other investors. In this way, credit and interest rate risk are spread around to others. Commercial banks and thrift banks often engage in this sort of transaction as a way of diversifying their portfolios and reducing risk. Sometimes the original mortgagee will itself act as the "lead" lender in the transaction, instead of selling the entire loan to a separate investor who would arrange the transaction as shown above. This should be distinguished, however, from the sale of so-called "loan participations." In a loan participation, ownership of the loan (or loans) remains with one individual, but the economic rights and liabilities related to that loan are partially transferred to others. Unlike in the partial assignment depicted above, a pure participation transaction does not create a relationship between the participants and the borrower-mortgagor. "The participant is not a lender to the borrower and has no contractual relationship with the borrower." See Natwest USA Credit Corp. v. Alco Standard Corp., 858 F. Supp. 401, 408 (S.D.N.Y. 1994). "The participant's only contractual relationship is with the lender; the participant has no ability to seek legal recourse against the borrower." See In re AutoStyle Plastics, Inc., 269 F.3d 726, 736 (6th Cir. 2001).

Note that in either form of the transaction just described, the partial interest investors will ordinarily receive pro-rata pass-through shares of the payments of principal and interest made by the mortgagor(s), less certain fees earned by the lead lender or entity that arranged the transaction. It is possible for the parties to agree that some interest holders will have a higher priority than others (or higher than the lead lender), and thus will have first right to the payments if a partial default by the mortgagor occurs. In addition, the lead lender may (or may not) guarantee receipt of the principal and interest payments to the participants.

3. SALE OF MORTGAGE-BACKED SECURITIES

The sale of mortgage-backed securities (MBS) is, in some ways, similar to the transaction above but involves the creation of a new asset separate from the mortgage loan itself. In this sort of transaction, the ultimate investors do not purchase fractional shares of ownership in the underlying mortgage loan or in a pool of mortgage loans. Instead, they purchase securities, issued by the secondary market investor, and those securities are *collateralized* (i.e., backed-up) by the mortgage loan or loans. The payments received by the securities investors are "pass-throughs," meaning that they correspond on a pro-rata basis to the payments made on the underlying mortgage loans. That means that each payment a securities investor receives will be partly interest and partly a return of the invested principal.

This type of transaction was popularized by the Government National Mortgage Association ("Ginnie Mae"), a government agency and a part of the Department of Housing and Urban Development (HUD). For pools of residential mortgage loans that are individually insured or guaranteed by the Federal Housing Authority (FHA), the Department of Veterans Affairs (VA), the Department of Agriculture's Rural Development Program (USDA), and the HUD's Office of Public and Indian Housing (PIH), Ginnie Mae does not issue the securities itself but instead issues guaranties to securities investors, assuring them that they will receive monthly payments corresponding to the payments due on the underlying mortgage loans even if some of the loans experience default. In essence, this places the full faith and credit of the United States behind the securities, making them highly liquid and salable at relatively low interest yields. In a securitization transaction, the loans are acquired by a sponsoring investor who then engages in a series of transfers that ultimately results in the mortgage loans being titled in the name of a corporate trustee. The trust then issues the pass-through securities (called mortgage-backed securities), which are then sold to investors in the capital markets. Here, the investors do not own the loans or even a fractional interest in them. Rather, the purchased securities are legally connected to the mortgage loans (which are titled in the name of the trustee) such that payments made on those loans flow through the trust to the investors. In the residential mortgage market, Fannie Mae and Freddie Mac are the two primary sponsors of mortgage securitizations. These government-controlled entities both purchase mortgage loans and arrange the securitization and issuance of the mortgage-backed securities. See Christopher K. Odinet, Foreclosed: Mortgage Servicing and the Hidden Architecture of Homeownership in America 25–31 (2019).

4. SALE OF MULTICLASS MORTGAGE-BACKED SECURITIES

When used with commercial mortgage loans, the mortgage securitization transaction involves large pools (commonly 100 loans or more) of large mortgage loans (commonly $20 million each or more.) The securities, which are widely sold and traded in the capital markets, are not "pass-throughs," but instead represent a variety of combinations of principal and interest payments which, in the aggregate, can be covered by payments made by the borrowers on the underlying loans. For example, some classes of securities may pay interest only; some classes may pay out early in the life of the underlying loans, and some later; some classes may have priority over others. The securities are called "Commercial Mortgage-Backed Securities" ("CMBS"), and the loans themselves are often called "conduit" loans. Each class of securities is called a "tranche," and a CMBS pool may give rise to as many as ten or twenty different tranches.

Issuers of these sorts of securities are often major Wall Street investment banks. The transactions are complex, and because the securities are "rated" prior to marketing, the details of the underlying mortgage transactions are largely governed by the requirements of the three Wall Street rating agencies (Moody's, Fitch's, and Standard and Poor). Substantial fees are captured by various parties, including the rating agencies and various trustees and loan servicers. (The diagram above is merely conceptual, and does not show all of these parties.)

Despite the cost of creation, complexity, and inflexibility of these loans, they are often sought by real estate entrepreneurs because they carry interest rates that are significantly lower than are usually available from other sources of funds, such as bank loans. This is possible because the carving of the securities into multiple "tranches" allows the creation of security classes that appeal to a wide variety of investors.

The growth of residential mortgage-backed securities. The securitization of commercial mortgages, which became common in the 1990s, proved to be an effective and successful vehicle for raising commercial mortgage funds. Securitization of residential loans had a slower start—the first securitization was sponsored by Ginnie Mae in February 1970; Fannie Mae and Freddie Mac followed over the next decade. However, growth happened over time. A relatively small proportion (a little over 10%) of residential mortgage debt had been held in securitized pools at the beginning of the 1980s. See Chicago Fed Letter, The Role of Securitization in Mortgage Lending (Nov. 2007). The decades that followed saw a significant rise in home mortgage securitizations. By the early 2000s, nearly 60% of home mortgages were held in securitized pools. The graph below shows the rise of mortgage-backed securities as a percentage of all mortgage debt outstanding between 1980 and 2006.

MBS share of total mortgage debt outstanding

Source: Inside Mortgage Finance Publications, Inc., 2007, *The 2007 Mortgage Market Statistical Annual*, 2 vols., Bethesda, MD.

Because there was such market demand for residential mortgage-backed securities, private Wall Street financial institutions began sponsoring their own securitizations, called "private-label" securitizations, with the first being sponsored by Bank of America in 1977. Brent J. Horton, In Defense of Private-Label Mortgage-Backed Securities, 61 Fla. L. Rev. 827, 875 (2009). These securitizations were strikingly different from the government-related ones discussed above. The mortgage loans in these new pools were nearly all conventional, meaning they were not FHA and VA-backed. The securities themselves were not guaranteed by the federal government, and they were multiclass (like the commercial mortgage-backed securities discussed above)—not pass-throughs. The Ginnie Mae, Freddie Mac, and Fannie Mae programs were carefully regulated and monitored by the federal government and had very few defaults. The new securitizations of the 2000s were quite the opposite.

In 2008 the residential mortgage market (and to a significant degree, the credit markets in general) collapsed, accompanied by drastically reduced liquidity, the de-privatization of Fannie Mae and Freddie Mac (which were placed in federal conservatorship), and the failure of a number of other large investment bankers and institutional lenders. The story of this collapse is complex, with many interlocking factors, some of which may yet only be dimly understood, but it revolves around the growth of private-label residential mortgage-backed securities.

Housing inflation and deflation. The problems arose because of the confluence of two factors. The first was a prolonged period of exceptionally low interest rates—rates that, beginning in 2001, were lower than at any time in the Twentieth Century. The low rates were a result of the exceptionally loose monetary policy pursued by the Federal Reserve Board. Because housing demand is highly influenced by (and negatively correlated to) interest rates, the result was a huge upswing in demand. This increase in demand drove housing prices into an extraordinary inflationary spiral, especially in the Sunbelt states (particularly California, Arizona, Nevada, and Florida). For example, the average annual home pricing jump in California was 6.1% between 1995 and 2000. From 2000 to 2003, the annual average increased to 13.6%. See Christopher K. Odinet, Foreclosed: Mortgage Servicing and the Hidden Architecture of Homeownership in America 16 (2019). Such inflation tends to feed on itself, as people conclude, "I *have* to buy a house (or upgrade to a larger house) now, before price inflation puts houses out of my reach."

This inflationary spiral would, without doubt, have reversed itself within a few years, leading to a corrective period of price stagnation or deflation. After all, most people can only afford so much housing, and when prices get out of reach, demand has to drop. But the "correction" proved much more severe than might have been expected because of another factor: a fundamental structural realignment in the mortgage lending industry.

Mortgage industry restructuring. Traditionally, mortgage loans were made by "portfolio lenders," mainly banks, insurance companies, and thrifts. All aspects of a loan were handled by the same—usually local—institution: the loan application, loan closing, collection of payments, and maintenance of escrow accounts for taxes and insurance. Starting in the 1930s with the creation of Fannie Mae and becoming more robust in the 1970s, this pattern began to change as more and more lenders began selling their loans on the secondary market. But these secondary market buyers, particularly Fannie Mae and Freddie Mac, generally maintained high quality standards, insisting that the loans they purchased be made only to borrowers who had a strong likelihood of making the payments.

This structure began to break down in two ways at the beginning of the Twenty-first Century. First, more and more loans were made by independent "mortgage brokers." These brokers would arrange to find and bring borrowers to "wholesale" lenders. The broker would take the applicant's loan application, "qualify" the borrower, and arrange for the loan closing. The broker received a commission, which was generated from the "yield spread premium"—in essence, the present value of the difference between the interest rate the borrower was paying and the (lower) interest yield demanded by the wholesale lender.

Commissions were fat during the early to mid-2000s. In high-cost areas like much of California, a broker might earn $20,000 or more on a single loan. And since the broker had no funds invested in the loan, many brokers simply did not care whether the borrower might later default or not; the emphasis was on making immediate commissions. The wholesale lenders and secondary market buyers had (and tried to exercise) little control over the actions of loan brokers, who were typically small, very numerous, and able to enter and leave the market readily.

Some brokers and lenders were tempted to encourage borrowers to give "creative" answers to questions on loan applications (i.e., to lie) to help falsify information about income and ability to repay, and even to engage in outright fraud. See, e.g., In re First All. Mortg. Co., 471 F.3d 977 (9th Cir. 2006), in which Lehman Brothers, Inc., which issued mortgage-backed securities collateralized by a pool of residential mortgages, was charged with liability for "aiding and abetting" the fraudulent practices of the mortgage originator. One former employee of the pre-2008 subprime mortgage lender Long Beach Mortgage reported that "higher-ups at the company would frequently offer gifts to the loan reviewers in exchange for looking the other way on questionable loan applications." See Christopher K. Odinet, Foreclosed: Mortgage Servicing and the Hidden Architecture of Homeownership in America 20 (2019).

The practice of making "Alt-A" loans (colloquially, "liar's loans") grew: loans which did not require the traditional forms of documentation of credit, employment and income for the borrower. And because interest rates and hence commissions were higher on "subprime" mortgages—those that did not require borrowers to meet traditional credit and income standards—brokers increasingly emphasized subprime lending, even pushing borrowers into subprime loans who could readily have qualified for prime loans. A Wall Street Journal investigation revealed that up to a little more than 50% of all subprime borrowers in 2005 actually had very healthy credit profiles and could ostensibly have qualified for more affordable loans. Rick Brooks & Ruth Simon, Subprime Debacle Traps Even Very Credit-Worthy, Wall St. J. (Dec. 3, 2007).

Notably, subprime lenders included not only nonbank finance companies such as New Century, Countrywide Financial, and Ameriquest, but mainstay banks like Citigroup, Merrill Lynch, and Morgan Stanley also got into the subprime game, usually by purchasing subprime lending companies to hold as subsidiaries. See Christopher K. Odinet, Foreclosed: Mortgage Servicing and the Hidden Architecture of Homeownership in America 21 (2019).

At the same time, things were changing at the other end of the mortgage process, the secondary market, with the advent of the private label residential mortgage securitizations noted above. Large numbers of pools of Alt-A and subprime mortgages were formed, in addition to pools of prime mortgages. Investors were dazzled by the high returns they could earn on these securities. In theory, they should have been concerned about the quality of the underlying mortgage loans, but it was impractical for them to investigate thousands of individual loans. As a fallback, the investors relied on the ratings given to the securities issues by the three New York rating agencies (Moody's, Standard and Poor, and Fitch's), but these agencies' methods of verifying loan quality were entirely inadequate. Moreover, they were busy earning fees for providing high ratings and realized that down-rating a particular security could cost them in lost business as the issuer "shopped" the rating with the other agencies.

Thus, a large share the residential mortgage industry had restructured itself into three components: mortgage brokers, subprime lenders/securities issuers, and mortgage-backed securities investors. Each of these components was making huge profits, but none of them cared much about mortgage loan quality; it was a far cry from the days when a single bank or savings association made the loan and took the loss if it went sour.

A perfect storm. This situation might have gone on for a very long time if housing prices had continued to rise, for rising prices can cover mortgage weaknesses very effectively, for several reasons. If prices rise, borrowers have increasing equity (i.e., the difference between how much the mortgage property is worth and the amount due on the mortgage loan), and hence have an incentive to try very hard to avoid foreclosure. If they cannot continue to make the loan payments, they can usually sell the property for enough to fully pay off the loan balance. And if lenders must foreclose in a rising market, they will usually recover enough in the foreclosure sale to pay the loan balance and perhaps even make a profit.

But when prices began to stagnate or fall in 2006 and 2007, borrowers who had difficulty making their payments could no longer sell their houses for enough to cover their indebtedness. It all started in October 2006 when a chief economist at the credit rating agency Moody's predicted that nearly one-half of the U.S. housing stock was set to experience a decline in value. See Mark Zandi, Celia Chen, & Brian Carey, Moody'sEconomy.com,

Housing at the Tipping Point 7 [Oct. 2006]. This proved to be all too true. By March 2008, about 11% of all homeowners owed more on their mortgage loans than what their homes were now worth. By September 2010, that amount rose to 23%. See Christopher K. Odinet, Foreclosed: Mortgage Servicing and the Hidden Architecture of Homeownership in America 32 (2019). Moreover, many borrowers had obtained adjustable rate mortgages that carried artificially low "teaser" rates for the first two or three years. When these loans began to reset to market rates, the resulting higher payments made default inevitable in many cases. For example, in one account of a borrower in Boston, the adjustable rate mortgage loan produced an initial monthly payment of $2,100. However, once the rate reset a few years into the loan term, the payment went up to $2,400, and then again later to more than $2,800. See Christopher K. Odinet, Foreclosed: Mortgage Servicing and the Hidden Architecture of Homeownership in America 19 (2019).

Thus, the large upswing in foreclosures was caused by a combination of housing price deflation and an industry characterized by a huge "moral hazard"—a structure in which no one had a sufficient stake in ensuring that the mortgage loans being originated could and would be paid back. Anyone reasonably familiar with the mortgage business would have predicted that many of the loans made during the 2002–2006 period were headed for almost certain default. And of course, houses that were foreclosed were dumped back on the market, further increasing supply and driving down prices. It was a "perfect storm"—a set of conditions that would inevitably lead to disaster.

In many cases, these loans might have been "saved" by restructuring their payments in "workout" agreements (i.e., by amending the terms of the loan to make the payments more affordable or by giving the borrower more time to pay). However, the loans were being serviced by companies hired by the trustees of the securitized mortgage pools. These companies, called mortgage servicers, had significant authority to enter into modifications or workouts but typically very limited guidance on whether to do so. Mortgage servicers also had financial incentives built into their servicing contracts that made foreclosure a more likely choice than a workout. See Christopher K. Odinet, Foreclosed: Mortgage Servicing and the Hidden Architecture of Homeownership in America 47–54 (2019) (chronicling loss mitigation gone wrong in connection with how servicers get paid). In the end, few loans were modified and saved from foreclosure.

The problems of loan default were not confined to the investors who purchased mortgage-backed securities. In many cases, institutional investors had attempted to hedge their default risk by entering into "credit default swap" agreements, mainly with commercial banks, insurance companies, and investment banks. One of the biggest companies in the business of selling these derivative contracts was the American Insurance

Group (AIG). A holder of mortgage-backed securities would enter into a swap contract and would pay a fee in exchange for a promise that, if a default occurred, the counterparty would cover the loss. These providers of "swaps" were, in essence, selling insurance against mortgage defaults to the securities holders. So long as housing prices were rising, defaults were low and selling such insurance was highly profitable. But when the housing market turned negative and defaults began to rise, the institutions that had sold the credit default swaps were forced to begin paying off in amounts far beyond their expectations and capacities. The issuance of these swaps was completely unregulated, either by the Securities and Exchange Commission or by state insurance commissioners. The issuers had provided no, or inadequate, reserves to cover the claims they received, and they simply lacked the funds to pay them.

The size of the "credit default swap" market was difficult to grasp. There are no firm data (since the market was unregulated), but it is estimated that there were credit default swap agreements of $45 to $60 trillion by mid-2007—more than twice the size of the U.S. stock market! Perhaps it is fair to say that the issuers of these swaps had little idea of how to price the risk that they had assumed—a risk that was far greater than they had anticipated. Moreover, the credit default swap agreements themselves were widely traded, often with little attention to whether the original issuer had the financial strength to cover its obligations.

The results of this debacle were felt heavily by a wide group of investors in the private-label mortgage-backed securities market, such as pension funds, commercial banks, insurance companies, and sovereign wealth funds throughout the world, not to mention individuals who had acquired mortgage-backed securities for their own investment accounts. Some insurance companies and banks received a double hit, both as investors in mortgages or mortgage-backed securities and as issuers of credit default swap agreements. Indeed, at the time, nearly every bank and financial institution in the United States had entered into swap agreements with AIG (and AIG simply couldn't pay). The devastation was widespread. As insurance companies weakened, concerns arose as to their ability to pay their obligations on other lines of insurance, such as municipal bond credit insurance.

The federal government's reaction to the mortgage crisis was complex, slow to develop, and initially inadequate. It is nicely summarized in U.S. Dep't of the Treasury, The Financial Crisis Five Years Later: Response, Reform, and Progress (Sept. 2013). In Chapter Eight of this book you will encounter many of the federal initiatives.

5. COLLATERAL OR SECURITY TRANSFER OF NOTES AND MORTGAGES

This type of transfer by the mortgagee, unlike all of the others described above, is not intended to be permanent. The mortgagee is seeking a loan from another lender, who demands collateral. The mortgagee pledges the note and mortgage as security for repayment of the new debt, documented by some form of loan and security agreement. The parties expect that, when the new debt is repaid, the security given by the mortgagee will be discharged and the note and mortgage returned to the mortgagee.

One of the most common users of this transaction is a mortgage banker who makes large numbers of residential loans, intending to sell them on the secondary market to Fannie Mae, Freddie Mac, or some other investor as described in examples 1 and 2 above, or to securitize them as described in examples 3 and 4. However, it may take the mortgage banker considerable time—several weeks or months, depending on its lending volume—to accumulate enough mortgages to form a pool of acceptable size. While the mortgage banker is accumulating a package of loans of sufficient size to sell, it may temporarily pledge the loans (i.e., the notes and mortgages) it has already originated to another lender, commonly a local commercial bank, as collateral for a line of credit. The funds drawn down on this line of credit will be used by the mortgage banker to continue making additional loans. This is sometimes termed a "warehouse" line of credit, since the mortgage loans are "parked" in the bank's "warehouse" for a few days or weeks until the mortgage company is ready to sell them to secondary market investors or securitize them. The practice is nicely explained in Rodgers v. Seattle-First Nat'l Bank, 40 Wash.App. 127, 697 P.2d 1009 (1985).

Legal Aspects of Mortgage Transfer

While mortgage loans have been sold in secondary market transactions for centuries, it is surprising how widely courts and lawyers have misunderstood or misconceived the process. Indeed, a benefit of the otherwise dismal mortgage crisis, and the litigation that it spawned, was to clarify the law of loan and related mortgage transfers. One of the most helpful documents in achieving this clarification was published by the Permanent Editorial Board of the Uniform Commercial Code in November, 2011, entitled "Application of the Uniform Commercial Code to Selected Issues Relating to Mortgage Notes," and referred to here simply as the "PEB Report." It's an excellent source for those who need a carefully-written, thoughtful explanation of many aspects of the process.

What rights does the secondary market purchaser of a mortgage loan want to obtain? Obviously, the purchaser wants rights to *both* the promissory note (which embodies the obligation to repay the loan) and the mortgage, since without the mortgage, the note would be unsecured (making its collection more difficult and doubtful), and without the note, the mortgage would be unforeclosable (since the holder of the mortgage could not experience a default on the secured obligation). More about this in a moment.

First, in today's market, a promissory note secured by a residential mortgage is generally said to meet the very special requirements under Article 3 of the Uniform Commercial Code such that the note is considered *negotiable*. U.C.C. 3–104. This is important for the remainder of our discussion because negotiable notes (as opposed to non-negotiable ones) are subject to very special rules that separate *ownership* of the note on the one hand from the ability to *enforce* the note on the other. Thus, there are two distinct set of rights that can be transferred in a single note: the *right to enforce*, and *ownership* (or "title") to the note. These two sets of rights are distinct from one another, and a great deal of confusion and nonsense has been created by muddling the two concepts. In other words, it is possible to have *ownership* of a note but not the power to *enforce* the note. Likewise, one can have the power to enforce a note but not be its owner.

Entitlement to enforce a note means that one can sue on it or (if applicable foreclosure requirements are met) foreclose the mortgage that secures it. The maker of the note (i.e., the mortgagor who first signs it) is the party most concerned with who is entitled to enforce the note. After all, as a borrower, one wants to know who the correct person is to pay. The concept of enforcement entitlement is designed to protect the maker against having to pay twice or defend against multiple claims to payment on the note. If the maker pays in full the person entitled to enforce the note, the debt is discharged and the mortgage that secures it is extinguished.

On the other hand, *ownership* of the note means that one is entitled to its economic value (i.e., the money). The owner of the note is the person who can claim the payments, including regular installment payments, a voluntary payoff, and the proceeds of a short sale or a foreclosure.

As the PEB Report (at p. 4, footnote 15) observes, "The concept of "person entitled to enforce" a note is not synonymous with "owner" of the note. * * * A person need not be the owner of a note to be the person entitled to enforce it, and not all owners will qualify as persons entitled to enforce." This is so because, as we will see, entitlement to enforce and ownership are governed by two separate legal regimes that establish different criteria. It is absolutely critical, when speaking or writing about note transfers, to make is clear whether one is referring to a transfer of ownership, a transfer of the right to enforce, or both. See Nationstar Mortg., L.L.C. v. West, 2014 WL 820008 (Ohio Ct. App. Feb. 28, 2014), in which the court did a nice job of explaining the distinction.

While people in casual conversation may talk generically about "transferring the note," doing so can easily lead to confusion, or even to nonsensical conclusions, if one does not specify whether ownership or the right of enforcement (or both) is to be transferred. For an excellent example, in which the legislature jumbled the two concepts but the court intelligently parsed them, see Trujillo v. Nw. Tr. Services, Inc., 183 Wash.2d 820 (2015).

As we have indicated above, a secondary market purchaser of a mortgage loan ordinarily not only wants both ownership of the *note* and the right to enforce it, but also want both ownership of the *mortgage* and the right to foreclose it. As it happens, transfers of the right to enforce have been controversial and the subject of a great deal of litigation in recent years, while transfers of ownership have been straightforward and rarely litigated. We will consider transfers of the right to enforce at length below. First, however, two brief notes appear below—one on how ownership is transferred, and one on MERS.

Transferring ownership. U.C.C. Article 9 governs transfers of ownership of promissory notes (including those secured by real estate mortgages). A note is an "instrument" in the lexicon of Article 9, and the definition is broad; under § 9–102(a)(47), an "instrument" is "a negotiable instrument or any other writing that evidences a right to the payment of a monetary obligation . . . and is of a type that in ordinary course of business is transferred by delivery with any necessary endorsement or assignment." Thus, both negotiable and nonnegotiable notes are covered.

Unfortunately for our purposes, Article 9 is written in the terminology of creating security interests in personal property. The Code then (rather obliquely) defines "security interest" to include transfers of ownership; under § 1–201(b)(35), "security interest" includes "an interest of a *buyer* of . . . a promissory note." This peculiarity makes Article 9's wording confusing and difficult to follow as applied to outright sales of notes. To avoid this problem, we have rewritten § 9–203(b), the section dealing with creation of security interests, as though it were solely about sales of notes. As so rewritten, 9–203(b) reads as follows:

> a [sale of an interest in a promissory note] is enforceable against the [seller] and third parties with respect to the [note] only if:
>
> (1) value has been given;
>
> (2) the [seller] has rights in the [note] or the power to transfer rights in the [note] to a [buyer]; and
>
> (3) one of the following conditions is met:
>
>> (A) the [seller] has authenticated a [sale] . . . agreement that provides a description of the [note] . . .; [or]
>>
>> (B) the [note] is in the possession of the [buyer] under Section 9–313 pursuant to the [seller's] agreement.

Thus, assuming the seller has rights in the note (or is an agent of someone who has such rights), and assuming the buyer gives value, ownership can be transferred in either of two ways: (A) by a signed, written agreement (or its electronic equivalent), such as a contract of sale or a written assignment, or (B) by delivering possession of the note to the buyer, provided that there is some agreement indicating that ownership is to be transferred.

But here we return to our main question: what happens to the *mortgage* when ownership of a note is sold? Under § 9–203(g) (also rewritten to focus on outright sales of notes) "The attachment of [ownership] in a right to payment or performance [i.e., a note] secured by a security interest or other lien on personal or real property is also attachment of [ownership] in the security interest, mortgage, or other lien." Thus, a sale of ownership rights in the note also *automatically* transfers the corresponding ownership rights in a real estate mortgage securing that note.

We haven't yet discussed transfers of the right of *enforcement* of notes; that comes next. But we can forecast a bit of that discussion by saying that, while a delivery of the original note will transfer *both* ownership and the right to enforce, the use of a separate document of assignment alone can be used to transfer ownership but will *not* transfer the right to enforce (at least if the note is negotiable).

MERS: A brief description. Because the next case deals with MERS (the Mortgage Electronic Registration System), we precede the case opinion with a bit of background on MERS. In the mid-1990s, the major players in the mortgage market (including Fannie Mae, Freddie Mac, the Mortgage Bankers Association, and several large banks) founded MERS to hold mortgages as a "nominee" for the note-holders (notably, the term "nominee" is not a legal one and has no meaning in American property law). Under the MERS system, each residential mortgage contract either names MERS as the original mortgagee, or the listed original mortgagee assigns the mortgage to MERS immediately after origination. When the loan is subsequently sold on the secondary market, MERS simply continues to be the holder of the mortgage, always serving as the nominee of the party who holds the note from time to time. MERS maintains a data base of note holders and servicers, and a borrower can query this data base to determine who holds and who services his or her mortgage loan.

The point of this system is to avoid the need for recording an assignment of the mortgage each time the loan is sold. This was an important objective, for recording assignments in the more than 3,600 local recording offices in the United States had become a major burden to secondary market investors. Under the MERS system, MERS is always the mortgage holder as shown in the local public records, and one needs to consult MERS's own records to determine who actually holds the loan. If a suit is filed that affects a MERS mortgage or the real estate it covers, MERS (as the mortgagee of record) is served with process, and it in turn notifies the actual holder of the note.

It is significant that MERS does not hold or take possession of the promissory notes (except in the case of electronic notes). Its responsibility is exclusively to hold the mortgages as nominee for the note holders. In most cases no further assignment of the mortgage is ever recorded by MERS, unless the note is transferred to a non-MERS member or an assignment is made to the mortgage servicer in preparation for a foreclosure.

MERS served its function relatively smoothly and efficiently until the mortgage market largely collapsed in 2007. In the ensuing years, foreclosure defense lawyers launched a tide of litigation attacking numerous aspects of MERS's operations, largely based on the amorphous nature of MERS, the true meaning of a nominee, and conflicting legal arguments made by MERS attorneys in court as to the company's status vis-à-vis mortgage loans. Among the issues they raised were the following:

- Is MERS a "real party in interest" or otherwise entitled to notice of suits or administrative actions that might affect the interests of mortgagees?

- As a "nominee" for the mortgage holder, does MERS have authority to execute assignments or (in states using deeds of trust) to appoint substitute trustees?

- Does MERS have standing to foreclose mortgages in its own name? (This practice was dropped in 2011, but was remarkably controversial while it lasted.)

- Is MERS wrongfully depriving local recorders of the revenue they would earn if mortgage assignments were still being recorded locally?

- Does the placement of a mortgage with MERS somehow improperly separate the note from the mortgage, thus making the mortgage unenforceable?

- Are assignments by MERS valid, given the fact that they are typically executed by employees of the secondary market participants, who serve as nominal (and unpaid) officers of MERS? (There were also many attacks on the technical aspects of these assignments, often alleging them to be "robo-signed.")

For an excellent discussion of the MERS litigation, see Christopher L. Peterson, Two Faces: Demystifying the Mortgage Electronic Registration System's Land Title Theory, 53 Wm. & Mary L. Rev. 111 (2011); see also Christopher L. Peterson, Foreclosure, Subprime Mortgage Lending, and the Mortgage Electronic Registration System, 78 U. Cin. L. Rev. 1359, 1371 (2010).

U.S. BANK, N.A. V. BURNS
Missouri Court of Appeals, 2013
406 S.W.3d 495

GARY M. GAERTNER, JR., JUDGE.

Introduction

Jeana Burns (Appellant) appeals the trial court's summary judgment in favor of U.S. Bank National Association (U.S. Bank), as Indenture Trustee for the Registered Holders of Aegis Asset Back Securities Trust 2005–2, Mortgage Backed Notes (Securities Trust). Appellant also appeals the trial court's judgment on the pleadings in favor of Trustees of Wildhorse (Subdivision). Appellant argues that there are disputed issues of material fact that precluded summary judgment, and that the judgment on the pleadings erroneously included an unrelated party. We affirm the summary judgment and modify the judgment on the pleadings under Rule 84.14.

Background

On August 24, 1999, Appellant obtained title through a Missouri Warranty Deed to property located at 1536 Honey Locust Court in Chesterfield, Missouri (Property). Appellant recorded the warranty deed in the St. Louis County Records. The deed contained the Property's address as well as a correct legal description of the Property. Title to the Property is solely in Appellant's name. Also on August 24, 1999, Daryl Burns executed an Assent to Execution of Deeds and Waiver of Marital Rights, waiving any right to the Property. This document was also recorded in the St. Louis County Records.

On April 1, 2005, Appellant executed a promissory note (Note) in favor of Aegis Funding Corporation (Aegis) in the amount of $496,300.00. Attached to the Note was a deed of trust (Deed of Trust) for the Property that Appellant executed in favor of Aegis, to secure repayment of the loan. The Deed of Trust listed Mortgage Electronic Registration Systems, Inc. (MERS) as the beneficiary, and it stated that MERS acted as a nominee for Aegis. The Deed of Trust listed the Property's correct address but contained an incorrect legal description of the Property. Again, Daryl Burns executed an Assent to Execution of Deeds and Waiver of Marital Rights (Second Waiver), which was recorded in the St. Louis County Records on April 8, 2005. This document contains the same incorrect legal description of the Property.

On January 31, 2008, MERS, as nominee for Aegis, executed an Assignment of Deed of Trust (Assignment) assigning all of its rights, title, and interest in the Deed of Trust "together with any and all notes and obligations therein described or referred to" to U.S. Bank, as Indenture Trustee for the Securities Trust. This Assignment was recorded in the St. Louis County Records, and it contained the same incorrect legal description of the Property.

On August 18, 2010, U.S. Bank filed suit against Appellant, Daryl Burns, and Subdivision, seeking in Counts I through III to reform the Deed of Trust, the Second Waiver, and the Assignment, respectively, to reflect the correct legal description of the Property. In Count IV, U.S. Bank requested that the trial court declare the Deed of Trust the first-priority lien against the Property and quiet title to the Property in Appellant's name, subject to the Deed of Trust.

In November 2011, Subdivision filed a cross-claim against Appellant and Daryl Burns requesting payment of outstanding subdivision assessments, late fees, and collection costs. Subdivision had previously recorded in the St. Louis County Records a lien against the Property for such fees, pursuant to Subdivision's policies applicable to the Property.

US Bank moved for summary judgment on all counts of its petition, and Subdivision moved for judgment on the pleadings regarding its cross-claim. The trial court granted both motions. In its summary judgment, the trial court ordered that the incorrect legal descriptions described above be reformed and declared the Deed of Trust a valid and enforceable lien against the Property. The trial court quieted title to the Property in the name of Appellant, subject to the Deed of Trust. In its judgment on the pleadings, the trial court ordered Appellant and Daryl Burns jointly and severally liable for subdivision fees and attorney's fees in the amount of $14,929.00. This appeal follows.

Discussion

Appellant raises two points on appeal. First, she argues that the trial court erred in granting summary judgment in favor of U.S. Bank, because a genuine dispute exists regarding a material fact, namely, whether U.S. Bank had an interest in the Property. In Point II, Appellant argues the trial court erred in granting Subdivision's motion for judgment on the pleadings against Daryl Burns, because he has no ownership interest in the Property. Subdivision agrees that Daryl Burns has no interest in the Property and should therefore have no liability for fees awarded by the trial court in its judgment on the cross-claim. Thus, Point II is granted. We consider Appellant's remaining point below.

Point I

Appellant argues the trial court erred in granting summary judgment because a genuine factual dispute exists regarding whether U.S. Bank was entitled to enforce the Deed of Trust. We disagree.

The trial court made the following finding:

> The Deed of Trust is held by [US Bank] and is a valid and enforceable lien against the Property and [US Bank] is entitled to enforce the provisions thereof.

Appellant's primary argument is that MERS' attempt in the Assignment to transfer the Deed of Trust together with the Note, when MERS was not a party to the Note, was ineffective. See *Bellistri v. Ocwen Loan Servicing, LLC*, 284 S.W.3d 619, 623 (Mo.App.E.D.2009) (invalidating attempted assignment of note with deed of trust where assignor was not party to note). However, given the circumstances here and applicable law, a different question requires threshold consideration.

In Missouri, "[a] deed of trust securing a negotiable note passes with it. . . ." *Goetz v. Selsor*, 628 S.W.2d 404, 405 (Mo.App.S.D.1982) (citing *Smith v. Holdoway Constr. Co.*, 129 S.W.2d 894, 899 (Mo.1939)). "[A] party entitled to enforce a note is also entitled to enforce the deed of trust securing that note. . . ." *In re Washington*, 468 B.R. 846, 853 (Bankr.W.D. Mo. 2011) (applying Missouri law). Thus, regardless of the Assignment, we first consider whether U.S. Bank is entitled to enforce the Note, and thereby the Deed of Trust with it.

Missouri has adopted the Uniform Commercial Code (UCC), which governs commercial transactions. Chapter 400, RSMo. (Supp.2012). Application of the UCC is straightforward regarding this question of who may enforce the Note. See *Washington*, 468 B.R. at 853. The holder of a negotiable instrument is entitled to enforce it. Section 400.3–301. A holder is one (1) who possesses the instrument, and (2) to whom the instrument is made payable. Section 400.1–201(20). Here, the Note was payable "to the order of Lender." "Lender," as defined by the Note, is Aegis. Aegis originally possessed the Note, and thus, Aegis was the original holder of the Note. Neither party disputes this fact.

US Bank contends it then became the holder of the Note by virtue of the endorsements on the Note made by Aegis. Endorsements made by the holder of a negotiable instrument are either "special" or "blank." Section 400.3–205. A special endorsement identifies a person to whom it makes the instrument payable. Section 400.3–205(a). Any endorsement by the holder that is not a special endorsement is a blank endorsement. Section 400.3–205(b). When an instrument is endorsed in blank, it becomes payable to its bearer and may be negotiated by transfer of possession alone until specially endorsed. Section 400.3–205(b); *Wohlschlaeger v. Dorsey*, 206 S.W.2d 677, 680 (Mo.App.1947).

US Bank attached a copy of the Note to its petition. U.S. Bank attached in its motion for summary judgment an affidavit by Nicole Melton, the Contract Management Coordinator of U.S. Bank's loan servicer, attesting that the copy of the Note attached to the petition was a "true and correct copy of the Note." That copy of the Note shows a special endorsement by Aegis, the original holder of the Note, to Aegis Mortgage Corporation. There is also a blank endorsement by Aegis Mortgage Corporation on the Note. U.S. Bank asserted in its reply memorandum in support of its motion for summary judgment that the Note was in its counsel's possession. U.S. Bank argues that the blank endorsement coupled with its possession of the Note makes U.S. Bank the holder of the Note. See Sections 400.3–205(b), 400.1–201(20).

Appellant disputes the validity of these endorsements. In her response to U.S. Bank's motion for summary judgment, Appellant offered a different copy of the Note. This copy did not contain any endorsements, and Appellant argues that a genuine factual dispute exists regarding whether the Note was endorsed to U.S. Bank. However, Appellant's copy of the Note had an attached allonge,[3] specially endorsing the Note to U.S. Bank, as Indenture Trustee of the Securities Trust.[4] Appellant also attached the affidavit of Johnna Miller, an authorized signer for Ocwen Loan Serving, LLC, the servicer for U.S. Bank. Ms. Miller attested that U.S. Bank was in

---

[3] An allonge is "[a] piece of paper annexed to a negotiable instrument or promissory note on which to write endorsements for which there is no room on the instrument itself." *Bremen Bank & Trust Co. of St. Louis v. Muskopf*, 817 S.W.2d 602, 607 (Mo.App.E.D.1991) (quoting Black's Law Dictionary 100 (4th ed.1968)). An allonge is considered part of the note, and an endorsement on an allonge is effective even if there is room on the note for an endorsement. Section 400.3–204(a), Comment 1.

[4] Appellant also argues that U.S. Bank did not prove it was the Indenture Trustee for the Securities Trust, and therefore, U.S. Bank has no standing to enforce the Deed of Trust. In each document in the record relevant to the issue on appeal, where U.S. Bank appears, it is listed as the Indenture Trustee for the Securities Trust. Regardless, Appellant has not demonstrated how that fact, even if U.S. Bank was not the Indenture Trustee, is material to the determination of whether U.S. Bank is the holder of the Note under the UCC.

physical possession of the Note and was the holder of the Note. Appellant does not dispute the validity of the allonge.[5]

Therefore, documents submitted by both parties in the record confirm U.S. Bank is in possession of the Note. Both copies of the Note contain endorsements: one specially to U.S. Bank on the attached allonge, and one in blank on the Note itself. Appellant has failed to establish the existence of a genuine factual dispute regarding either the endorsement of the Note to U.S. Bank or U.S. Bank's possession of the Note. These facts qualify U.S. Bank as the holder of the Note under U.C.C. Section 400.1–201(20). As such, U.S. Bank is also the holder of the Deed of Trust, and therefore entitled to enforce the Deed of Trust. See *Washington*, 468 B.R. at 853. Thus, whether the Assignment effectively transferred the Deed of Trust to U.S. Bank is irrelevant. Point denied.

Conclusion

We find no genuine issue of material fact and no error of law in the trial court's conclusion that U.S. Bank was entitled to summary judgment as a matter of law. We affirm the summary judgment.

Regarding the trial court's judgment on the pleadings in favor of Subdivision, as neither the facts nor this Court's legal conclusion are in dispute, we exercise our ability to enter the proper judgment under Rule 84.14. See *Mitalovich v. Toomey*, 206 S.W.3d 361, 365 (Mo.App.E.D.2006) (modification of judgment is especially appropriate where there are no disputed facts). Therefore, we modify the trial court's judgment on the pleadings to remove Daryl Burns, and we affirm the judgment as modified in favor of Subdivision and against Appellant.

ROBERT M. CLAYTON, III, C.J., MICHAEL K. MULLEN, S.J., concur.

NOTES

1.   *The mortgage "follows the note."* The borrower's principal argument in the *Burns* case was that since MERS was not a party to the note, it had no right to assign the deed of trust securing it. This argument was consistent with the same court's earlier decision in Bellistri v. Ocwen Loan Servicing, LLC, 284 S.W.3d 619, 623 (Mo. Ct. App. 2009). There the court had said:

> When the holder of the promissory note assigns or transfers the note, the deed of trust is also transferred. An assignment of the deed of trust separate from the note has no "force." Effectively, the note and the deed of trust are inseparable, and when the promissory note is

---

[5] In the summary judgment proceedings below, Appellant disputed the validity of the allonge based on its effective date in relation to a servicing agreement applicable to the Securities Trust. Appellant does not make this argument on appeal. Regardless, neither the date of any endorsement nor any provision of an outside servicing agreement is relevant to the determination under the UCC of whether U.S. Bank is the holder of the Note. See *Washington*, 468 B.R. at 852–53.

transferred, it vests in the transferee "all the interest, rights, powers and security conferred by the deed of trust upon the beneficiary therein and the payee in the notes." . . . MERS never held the promissory note, thus its assignment of the deed of trust to [the secondary market investor] separate from the note had no force.

But in the *Burns* case, the court's response to the borrower's argument that the assignment was ineffective was, "so what?" Since the note, which represents the debt, is the principal thing being sold, and since the mortgage is merely security for, or an accessory to, the note, any transfer of the right to enforce the note will *automatically* serve to transfer the right to enforce mortgage or deed of trust as well. No separate assignment of the mortgage or deed of trust is necessary in order to transfer the right to foreclose judicially (or in this case, nonjudicially). This is indeed the view of the vast majority of American courts. Dozens of cases could be cited; See, e.g., Deutsche Bank Nat'l Tr. Co. v. Matthews, 273 P.3d 43 (Okla. 2012); Restatement (Third) of Property (Mortgages) § 5.4(a) (1997). Sometimes courts explain this result by saying that a transfer of the right to enforce the note brings about an equitable assignment of the mortgage as well; see, e.g., Dow Fam., LLC v. PHH Mortg. Corp., 838 N.W.2d 119 (Wis. Ct. App. 2013). Likewise, if there is an assignment of the mortgage but the note (assuming it is negotiable) is not delivered, the right of enforcement will not pass to the assignee; see In re Am. Equity Corp. of Pinellas, 332 B.R. 645 (Bankr. M.D. Fla. 2005).

Indeed, it is well nigh impossible to separate the mortgage from the note, and it is not clear why anyone would want to do so. After all, the note without the mortgage would be far less secure than with it, while the mortgage without the note would be essentially worthless, since the person who held the mortgage could not experience a default, and hence could never foreclose. The doctrine that the mortgage follows the note fulfills the important objective of keeping the two together, which is what the parties to the transfer want and expect in virtually all cases. It also follows the theory, prevalent in the civil law system, that the mortgage is an accessory right attached to the principal obligation (the note). See European University Institute, Real Property Law and Procedure in the European Union 18 (2005). An accessory cannot exist without attachment to the principal.

Observe carefully that here we are talking about the right to *enforce*: under the common law principle discussed in *Burns*, whoever obtains the right to enforce the note will also be able to enforce—that is, foreclose—the mortgage. This is quite distinct from the principle of U.C.C. § 9–203(g), discussed prior to the *Burns* case, which says that ownership of the mortgage will follow ownership of the note. That principle deals with the economic benefits of the note and mortgage, not the right to enforce them. In effect, it says that whoever is entitled to the financial proceeds of a suit on the note is also entitled to the financial proceeds of a foreclosure of the mortgage. Thus, just as there are two distinct aspects of the note (ownership and the right of enforcement) that can be transferred, there are two distinct ways in which the mortgage can "follow the note" (realization of the proceeds of foreclosure, on the one hand, and the right of foreclosure on the other). The right to enforce the mortgage follows the right to enforce the note under the common law principle used by the court in the *Burns* case. The ownership of the mortgage follows ownership of the note under U.C.C. § 9–203(g). This distinction between the two different ways that "the mortgage follows the note" is a subtlety that is often lost on lawyers and judges.

This, of course, raises the question: why does one ever have to execute an assignment of a mortgage? As noted above, MERS was created to avoid the recordation of these documents. If the mortgage follows the note, what purpose does this additional document serve? Legally, it would seem it serves no purpose. Yet, to say that a written assignment of a mortgage is unessential to foreclosure is not to say that it is a bad idea. On the contrary, use of mortgage assignments is an excellent practice, primarily because of the operation of the recording acts. Only a written mortgage assignment can be recorded, and recording, for reasons we will examine later, is very desirable from the viewpoint of the assignee. But, as noted above, an assignment is unnecessary to confer the right to foreclose judicially. Maine seems to be an exception with respect to judicial foreclosure; see Deutsche Bank Nat'l Tr. Co. v. Wilk, 76 A.3d 363 (Me. 2013) and Wells Fargo Bank, NA v. deBree, 38 A.3d 1257 (Me. 2012), apparently requiring proof of each link in the chain of mortgage assignments as a prerequisite to foreclosure. New Jersey has taken the same position by court rule, N.J. Ct. R. 4–64–1(b)(1–13), although the legal basis for the rule is uncertain since the relevant statute, N.J. Stat. Ann. § 46:9–9, permits—but does not require—recording of assignments. But in nearly all other states, the note-holder can pursue judicial foreclosure without proof of an assignment of the mortgage. See, e.g., JP Morgan Chase Bank, N.A. v. Murray, 63 A.3d 1258 (Pa. Super. Ct. 2013) (holder of negotiable note can pursue foreclosure despite defects in chain of mortgage assignments).

Nonjudicial foreclosures are another matter. The Missouri court in *Burns* was quite willing to recognize the traditional rule that the right to foreclose the deed of trust follows the right to enforce the note, but at least a dozen nonjudicial foreclosure states have refused to do so, construing their statutes to require a chain of mortgage assignments as a prerequisite to foreclosure. We will return to this issue.

The other side of the coin, of course, is that one must have the right to enforce the note in order to foreclose the mortgage. See Kluge v. Fugazy, 536 N.Y.S.2d 92 (1988) (where mortgage was assigned but note was excluded from assignment, assignee of mortgage could not foreclose); Restatement (Third) of Property (Mortgages) § 5.4(c): "A mortgage may be enforced only by, or in behalf of, a person who is entitled to enforce the obligation the mortgage secures." As we will see below, however, this concept is not always followed in nonjudicial foreclosures.

2.   *Negotiability.* The *Burns* case seems to hold that the transfer of the right to enforce a note is governed by Article 3 of the Uniform Commercial Code. But this holding is correct only if, as described above, the note in question

is *negotiable*; Article 3 governs only negotiable notes, since it applies only to "instruments," and under U.C.C. § 3–104(b), " 'Instrument' means a negotiable instrument." Negotiability is a highly technical matter, and each note must be examined carefully to determine whether it is negotiable or not. It is disappointing, but not unusual, that the Missouri court simply assumed that the note in question was negotiable (it may not have been and thus ownership and enforcement would not be capable of separation). That is a sloppy practice, but courts often do it. See Dale A. Whitman, How Negotiability Has Fouled Up the Secondary Mortgage Market, and What To Do About it, 37 Pepp. L. Rev. 737 (2010).

We will examine the requirements for negotiability in a moment. But suppose a particular note does not satisfy them, and therefore is not governed by U.C.C. Article 3? In that case, a transfer of the right to enforce the note is presumably controlled by common law principles. There is, unfortunately, very little modern case law as to just what those principles are—a fact that may explain why courts so readily assume that notes are negotiable. Other examples of cases in which courts made that assumption without analysis include Provident Bank v. Cmty. Home Mortg. Corp., 498 F.Supp.2d 558 (E.D.N.Y. 2007) and In re Woodberry, 383 B.R. 373 (Bankr. D.S.C. 2008).

Now, back to Article 3. Under U.C.C. § 3–104(a), in order to be negotiable, the instrument must:

- contain an unconditional promise * * * to pay a fixed amount of money, with or without interest or other charges;

- be payable to bearer or to order;

- be payable on demand or at a definite time;

- not state any other undertaking or instruction * * * to do any act in addition to the payment of money.

- Notwithstanding the foregoing, under U.C.C. § 3–104(a)(3), a note can be negotiable even though it contains:

- an undertaking or power to give, maintain, or protect collateral;

- an authorization or power to the holder to confess judgment or realize on or dispose of collateral;

- a waiver of the benefit of any law intended for the advantage or protection of an obligor.

Finally, a note is considered conditional (hence, nonnegotiable) if it states an express condition, states that it is subject to or is governed by another writing, or states that rights or obligations with respect to its promise are stated in another writing. However, negotiability is not impaired by:

- a reference to another writing for a statement of rights with respect to collateral, prepayment, or acceleration;

- the fact that payment is limited to resort to a particular fund or source.

From these rules, one can see that, if negotiability is to be preserved, care must be taken in including references to mortgages in the notes they secure. A general statement that the note is secured by the mortgage is permissible, since it is merely a "statement of rights with respect to collateral." See Countrywide Home Loans, Inc. v. Randy St. Louis, 290 B.R. 1 (Bankr. E.D.N.Y. 2003); Swindler v. Swindler, 355 S.C. 245, 584 S.E.2d 438 (Ct. App. 2003). It is also acceptable to incorporate by reference in the note any specific terms of the mortgage that deal with "rights with respect to collateral, prepayment, or acceleration." See, e.g., In re Knigge, 479 B.R. 500 (8th Cir. 2012), finding that undertakings such as occupying the property, refraining from wasting or destroying the property, maintaining insurance on the property, and giving notice to lender of any losses related to the property were all within the Code's "give, maintain, or protect collateral" language and did not impair negotiability. But a general incorporation of the mortgage into the note will destroy negotiability, since Section 3–106 provides that the note is regarded conditional if "rights or obligations with respect to the promise or order are stated in another writing." See Resol. Tr. Corp. v. 1601 Partners, Ltd., 796 F.Supp. 238 (N.D. Tex. 1992). The same is true of incorporation of other sorts of documents.

Nonrecourse notes, which provide that the borrower has no personal liability and that the debt may be collected only from foreclosure on the real estate, were long held to be nonnegotiable on the ground that the promise to pay was not unconditional. However, the current version of Article 3, promulgated in 1990, reversed that rule, providing instead that a promise to pay is viewed as unconditional despite the fact that "payment is limited to resort to a particular fund or source." Likewise, under older versions of Article 3, adjustable rate notes were usually held nonnegotiable, but the current version of § 3–112(b) provides:

> Interest may be stated in an instrument as a fixed or variable amount of money or it may be expressed as a fixed or variable rate or rates. The amount or rate of interest may be stated or described in the instrument in any manner and may require reference to information not contained in the instrument.

3. *Is the standard residential note negotiable?* Virtually every residential mortgage loan made in the United States is written on the Fannie Mae/Freddie Mac Uniform Single Family Note. Hence, whether or not that particular note form is negotiable is a matter of crucial importance. In 1997 Professor Ronald Mann argued that the Fannie Mae/Freddie Mac Uniform Single-family Note form was nonnegotiable because Paragraph 4 of the note contains the statement, "When I make a prepayment, I will tell the Note Holder in writing that I am doing so." Mann observed,

> [T]hat provision appears to constitute an "undertaking . . . to do a[n] act in addition to the payment of money." For historical reasons codified in section 3–104(a)(3) of the UCC, a promissory note cannot be an instrument if it contains such an undertaking: the rules of

negotiability apply only to promises to pay money, not to other, nonmonetary undertakings. Sending a notice certainly is an act "in addition to the payment of money," and the note's language seems to constitute an "undertaking" to perform that act (albeit only on certain conditions).

Ronald J. Mann, Searching for Negotiability in Payment and Credit Systems, 44 UCLA L. Rev. 951 (1997).

This argument went undiscovered by lawyers and the courts until 2010, but it has now been considered by perhaps a dozen courts, beginning with HSBC Bank USA, Nat'l Ass'n v. Gouda, 2010 WL 5128666 (N.J. Super. Ct. App. Div. 2010) (not reported in A.3d). All of them have rejected Mann's position and found the uniform residential note to be negotiable. They typically adopt this view on the grounds that: (1) the borrower's decision to prepay principal is voluntary, not required; (2) the prepayment notification requirement imposes no additional financial liability on the borrower, and adds nothing to the promise to pay the debt; and (3) there is no penalty if the borrower fails to give the notification.

Whether this is correct in any ultimate sense is hard to say; none of the decisions come from the highest court of a state. The prepayment notice obligation in the Fannie Mae-Freddie Mac form is, by its nature, conditional; it applies only if the borrower elects to make a prepayment. As a matter of general principle, it is uncertain whether such an obligation falls under Section 3–104's proscription against "other undertakings" or not. But for the present, at least, it seems reasonable to assume that the standard residential note is negotiable (even if analytically questionable).

4. *Transferring the right to enforce a negotiable note*. Reading the *Burns* case, one would likely conclude that under Article 3 the proper way to transfer the right of enforcement of a negotiable note is to endorse it (either in blank, or specially to the transferee) and deliver it, giving the transferee possession. This will work, but it is not the only way. Article 3 provides three methods of transferring the right of enforcement:

(a) *Becoming a holder*. As *Burns* indicates, this will occur if the note has been delivered to and is in the possession of the person enforcing it, with an appropriate endorsement (either in blank—which makes the note a "bearer note," or specially—an endorsement that specifically identifies the person to whom the note is delivered). These actions will constitute the person who takes the note a "holder," entitling him or her to enforce the note. See, e.g., In re Walker, 466 B.R. 271, 280–81 (Bankr. E.D. Pa. 2012). No endorsement is necessary if the note was originally payable to "bearer;" see Bank of N.Y. v. Raftogianis, 10 A.3d 236, 240 (N.J. Super. Ct. Ch. Div. 2010). Original bearer notes are virtually never used in real estate financing, but a note that has been endorsed in blank becomes a bearer note, so that the right of enforcement can then be further transferred by delivery of possession without the need for any additional endorsements.

(b) *Becoming a nonholder who has the rights of a holder*. Under U.C.C. § 3–301(ii), this will occur if the note has been delivered to and is in the possession of the person enforcing it, but without an endorsement. In the absence of an endorsement, the person taking delivery cannot be a holder, but can still get the right of enforcement if the delivery was made for the purpose of transferring that right. The latter requirement may complicate enforcement or foreclosure, since the party in possession may be put to the burden of proving exactly how it acquired the note, and that the transfer to it was made for the purpose of giving the right of enforcement. See Leyva v. Nat'l Default Servicing Corp., 255 P.3d 1275, 1281 (Nev. 2011), requiring the servicer to provide specific, affirmative proof that the note was delivered to it for the purpose of transferring the right of enforcement. Avoiding this burden is the primary reason that endorsement of the note is wise and desirable. However, meeting the burden is usually possible; proof of the purpose of the delivery of the note might be provided through a mortgage assignment, a pooling and servicing agreement, or affidavits of the transferor's employees. See, e.g., Ulster Sav. Bank v. 28 Brynwood Lane, 41 A.3d 1077, 1085 (Conn. App. Ct. 2013).

(c) *Providing a "lost note affidavit."* Under U.C.C. § 3–309, a person who does not qualify to enforce the note under (a) or (b) above because of a lack of possession may still enforce it by providing a "lost note affidavit." See, e.g., Svrcek v. Rosenberg, 40 A.3d 494 (Md. Ct. Spec. App. 2012). However, the requirements for the affidavit are quite strict: (1) the note must have been destroyed, (2) its whereabouts not discoverable, or (3) it must be in the wrongful possession of an unknown person or one who cannot be served. Before accepting such an affidavit, a court might well demand evidence as to the efforts that have been made to locate the note. See Correa v. U.S. Bank Nat'l Ass'n, 118 So.3d 952 (Fla. Dist. Ct. App. 2013) (affidavit was insufficient, where foreclosing plaintiff did not prove the content of the note or the circumstances under which it was lost). In addition, the court can require the enforcing party to provide assurance (typically in the form of a bond or indemnity) against the possibility that the borrower will have to pay twice. See, e.g., First Constr. Co. v. Tri-S. Mortg. Investors, 308 N.W.2d 298, 299 (Minn. 1981), approving requirement of a bond.

Florida, uniquely, has a statutory definition of what will constitute adequate protection against the borrower's having to pay twice. The list includes:

(a) A written indemnification agreement by a person reasonably believed sufficiently solvent to honor such an obligation;

(b) A surety bond;

(c) A letter of credit issued by a financial institution;

(d) A deposit of cash collateral with the clerk of the court; or

(e) Such other security as the court may deem appropriate under the circumstances.

Any security given shall be on terms and in amounts set by the court, for a time period through the running of the statute of limitations for enforcement of the underlying note, and conditioned to indemnify and hold harmless the maker of the note against any loss or damage, including principal, interest, and attorney fees and costs, that might occur by reason of a claim by another person to enforce the note.

Fla. Stat. 702.11. See Delia v. GMAC Mortg. Corp., 161 So.3d 554 (Fla. Dist. Ct. App. 2014), refusing to grant foreclosure where the lender failed to produce proof that it had provided adequate protection.

5. *Endorsement is essential to becoming a holder.* If one wishes to be a holder of negotiable note (method (a) above), an endorsement of the note, either in blank or special, is essential. A separate written assignment of the note or the mortgage plainly does not qualify; see Bremen Bank & Tr. Co. of St. Louis v. Muskopf, 817 S.W.2d 602 (Mo. Ct. App. 1991); Bank of N.Y. Mellon v. Deane, 970 N.Y.S.2d 427 (Sup. Ct. 2013).

6. *Transferring the right of enforcement of nonnegotiable notes.* On the other hand, if the note is not negotiable, and hence Article 3 does not apply, the right to enforce it can be transferred by assignment; see Kent v. Kent, 44 P.2d 445 (Cal. Ct. App. 1935). The assignment may be carried out in any of several ways: by endorsement on the note by the original payee-mortgagee; by the use of a separate document which the payee-mortgagee executes, stating that rights under the note are transferred to the assignee; or even by an oral statement to the assignee that a transfer is being made, at least if accompanied by a delivery. See Hill v. Alexander, 41 P. 1066 (Kan. Ct. App. 1895). Thus, the methods of transferring nonnegotiable notes are extremely flexible. However, there is very little modern authority on the transfer of nonnegotiable notes.

7. *Defenses and claims.* A critical aspect of negotiability is how it relates to claims that can be made on the note and defenses that the borrower/maker can raise in relation to the note's enforcement. U.C.C. § 3–305, which points out that a holder in due course ("HIDC") is insulated from certain *defenses* that the maker of the instrument might raise. But a HIDC also takes free of *claims,* of which there are two different types. One is a "claim in recoupment," which is in essence an offset asserted by the maker of the note to an attempted enforcement. A claim in recoupment must arise from the transaction that gave rise to the instrument itself; see Hathorn v. Loftus, 726 A.2d 1278 (N.H. 1999). Under § 3–305(b), claims in recoupment are treated like personal defenses; hence, if a claim in recoupment is based on the conduct of someone other than the present holder, it can't be asserted against an HIDC.

The other type of claim against which a HIDC is protected (by U.C.C. § 3–306) is a claim *to the instrument.* By "claim," § 3–306 means "a claim of a property or possessory right in the instrument or its proceeds." Thus, HIDCs are protected with respect to their ownership. Non-HIDCs, on the other hand, take subject to preexisting claims; see In re Valentine, 146 B.R. 945 (Bankr. E.D. Va. 1991). Cases involving ownership claims against HIDCs are not as common as those involving defenses, but they do arise.

One fairly recent example is In re AppOnline.com, Inc., 321 B.R. 614 (E.D.N.Y. 2003). A mortgage company that was in serious financial straits sent a check to a title company to fund a loan the mortgage company was making, with the title company acting as the closing agent. The title company disbursed the funds, but the bank on which the check was drawn refused to pay it because the mortgage company had insufficient funds in its account. The title company sued, claiming that it was entitled to an equitable lien on the note and mortgage to help the title company reimburse itself for the loss that it had suffered as a result of the bad check. However, the mortgage company had transferred the note to an HIDC, and on the basis of U.C.C. § 3–306 the court held that that HIDC prevailed over the title company's claim.

Another example is Provident Bank v. Cmty. Home Mortg. Corp., 498 F.Supp.2d 558 (E.D.N.Y. 2007). Community was a mortgage banker that obtained a warehouse line of credit from Southwest Bank. Community adopted a practice of having its residential borrowers execute two original copies of each promissory note, a practice known as "double-booking" the loans. It then delivered one copy of each note to Southwest as collateral for the line of credit, and at about the same time sold the other copies on the secondary market to Netbank. The court resolved the conflict by noting that the notes received by Netbank had been endorsed by Community, while the notes delivered by Southwest had not. Hence, it found that Netbank was a holder in due course, Southwest was not, and Netbank prevailed. Oddly, the court never cited § 3–306, although it seems directly applicable and supports the court's conclusion.

Because ownership of a note is ordinarily the province of Article 9, but claims of ownership against a HIDC are governed by § 3–306, you might wonder whether these two provisions of the Uniform Commercial Code could lead to disparate or inconsistent results. For example, suppose the note had been delivered to a HIDC, but the original payee had also assigned its ownership to a different party by a written assignment (as Article 9 would permit). As it turns out, no inconsistency is possible, for § 9–331(a) provides "This article does not limit the rights of a holder in due course of a negotiable instrument, a holder to which a negotiable document of title has been duly negotiated, or a protected purchaser of a security." Thus, if a claim against a HIDC arises, § 3–306 will override Article 9.

8. *Non-holders in due course and patent equities.* Suppose a mortgage note is non-negotiable, or is negotiable but is transferred to one who does not qualify as a HIDC. Under these circumstances the freedom from the maker's personal defenses granted by the U.C.C. to HIDCs will not apply. If the note is negotiable but the holder is not a HIDC, U.C.C. § 3–305(a)(2) makes the assignee subject to any "defense of the obligor that would be available if the person entitled to enforce the instrument were enforcing a right to payment under a simple contract." If the note is non-negotiable, the common law reaches the same result. See Lapis Enterprises, Inc. v. Int'l Blimpie Corp., 84 A.D.2d 286, 445 N.Y.S.2d 574 (N.Y. App. Div. 1981) (fraud defense can be asserted against assignee in good faith of a nonnegotiable note); Nelson, Whitman, Burkhart & Freyermuth, Real Estate Finance Law § 5.32 (6th ed.2015).

The assignee of a note who believes that HIDC protection may be lacking often wisely demands that the maker provide an "estoppel certificate" at the time of the transfer, averring that the note is valid and not subject to defenses by the maker. These certificates are generally effective; see Soler v. Klimova, 774 N.Y.S.2d 126 (2004); Tinnes v. Immobilaire IV, Ltd., 2001 WL 122073 (Ohio Ct. App. Feb. 13, 2001) (not reported in N.E.2d) (person who relies on estoppel certificate may assert it whether or not identified in it). If they are broadly drafted, they can provide even better protection for the assignee than would the HIDC doctrine, since they can insulate the assignee from both real and personal defenses of the maker. The maker's defenses in this context are often termed "patent" defenses or "patent equities," since by demanding an estoppel certificate the assignee of the note can bring them to light. By contrast, a "latent" defense or equity is a claim to the instrument, or a claim that will defeat it, by someone other than the maker—so that an estoppel statement by the maker is of no value in ferreting it out.

However, even for patent equities, an estoppel certificate is not always a panacea. As the New York Court of Appeals pointed out in Hammelburger v. Foursome Inn Corp., 54 N.Y.2d 580, 446 N.Y.S.2d 917, 431 N.E.2d 278 (1981), the assignee must actually rely on the certificate, and must not know that the facts differ from the certificate's recitations. Moreover, if the certificate itself was obtained by fraud or duress, the mortgagor will not be estopped by it and can later contradict its statements.

9. *The "close-connectedness" doctrine.* Certain other judge-made limitations on the holder-in-due course doctrine may have implications for the assignment of real estate mortgage debt. One such doctrine is the "close connectedness" concept. Under this theory, holder-in-due-course status is lost if the purchaser of a negotiable note is too closely connected with the transferor; the purchaser is regarded as lacking "good faith." Professors White and Summers have delineated several factors that tend to point toward "close connectedness." (The term "lender" refers to the assignee of the note.)

(1) Drafting by the lender of forms for the seller.

(2) Approval or establishment or both of the seller's procedures by the lender (e.g., setting of the interest rate, approval of a referral sales plan).

(3) An independent check by the lender on the credit of the debtor or some other direct contact between the lender and the debtor.

(4) Heavy reliance by the seller upon the lender (e.g., transfer by seller of all or a substantial part of his paper to one lender).

(5) Common or connected ownership or management of seller and lender.

See James J. White & Robert S. Summers, Uniform Commercial Code § 14–6 (6th ed. 2010); The doctrine was developed in the context of consumer credit transactions, and the courts have been quite reluctant to apply it in commercial loans. See, e.g., Equico Lessors, Inc. v. Ramadan, 493 So.2d 516 (Fla. Dist. Ct. App. 1986) ("In a commercial setting, more than just a close connection must be shown before an assignee will be denied the status of a holder in due course."); A.I. Trade Fin., Inc. v. Altos Hornos de Vizcaya, S.A., 840 F.Supp. 271 (S.D.N.Y. 1993) (in a commercial loan, "although a close connection may facilitate the holder's actual discovery and notice of fraud, the close relationship alone cannot create an issue of the holder's notice.)"

On the other hand, close-connectedness is alive and well in consumer transactions. Indeed, if the connection is close enough, one might ask whether it might form a basis, not merely for allowing the mortgagor to resist the lender's foreclosure action or suit on the note, but for permitting the mortgagor an affirmative recovery against the lender. That is precisely what happened in Union Mortg. Co. v. Barlow, 595 So.2d 1335 (Ala. 1992). The mortgagor was defrauded by a home improvement contract who had very close and long-standing ties to the mortgage company that purchased its mortgage loans. The jury awarded her $6 million in punitive damages against the mortgage company!

10. *The decline of the HIDC doctrine.* During the past several decades, a number of states have reversed or modified the holder in due course doctrine in consumer transactions by individualized statutes. See, e.g., 9 Vt. Stat. Ann. § 2455 ("indebtedness of a consumer"); Wash. Rev. Code Ann. § 63.14.020 (retail installment contracts). In addition, the Uniform Consumer Credit Code (UCCC), drafted by the National Conference of Commissioners on Uniform State Laws, abolishes the HIDC doctrine in "consumer loan" and "consumer credit sale" transactions. The UCCC was originally promulgated in 1968. The UCCC (or something close to it) has been adopted by at least eleven states: Colorado, Idaho, Indiana, Iowa, Kansas, Maine, Oklahoma, South Carolina, Utah, Wisconsin, Wyoming.

The demise of the HIDC doctrine in consumer credit transactions was predicted to be cataclysmic, but in fact was absorbed by credit providers with scarcely a hiccup. See Ralph J. Rohner, Holder in Due Course in Consumer Transactions: Requiem, Revival, or Reformation? 60 Cornell L. Rev. 503 (1975); James J. White & Robert S. Summers, Uniform Commercial Code § 14–1 (4th ed. 1995).

The impact of the UCCC and the other state statutes mentioned above on mortgage transactions is rather marginal. Most mortgages are given to secure repayment of loans of money or payment for the real estate itself, rather than payment for goods or services; hence, they are not regarded as "consumer credit" transactions, and the statutes mentioned have no effect on them at all. Perhaps the UCCC's greatest mortgage law consequences arise when a consumer enters into a contract for home improvement services (e.g., the installation of aluminum siding), and gives a note secured by a mortgage in payment.

11. *The FTC rule.* The Federal Trade Commission virtually eliminated the HIDC doctrine in consumer credit transactions by a "trade regulation rule"

adopted in 1975 entitled "Preservation of Consumers' Claims and Defenses." Under this rule, it is an unfair trade practice under Section 5 of the Federal Trade Act for a seller of goods or services to finance a sale without including in the note or other evidence of debt ("consumer credit contract") language that makes the seller and any subsequent assignee subject to the consumer's claims and defenses. 16 C.F.R. § 433 1–2; 15 U.S.C. § 45. This language must be in at least ten point bold face type and reads as follows:

"NOTICE. ANY HOLDER OF THIS CONSUMER CREDIT CONTRACT IS SUBJECT TO ALL CLAIMS AND DEFENSES WHICH THE DEBTOR COULD ASSERT AGAINST THE SELLER OF GOODS OR SERVICES OBTAINED WITH THE PROCEEDS HEREOF. RECOVERY HEREUNDER BY THE DEBTOR SHALL NOT EXCEED AMOUNTS PAID BY THE DEBTOR HEREUNDER."

See Hempstead Bank v. Babcock, 115 Misc.2d 97, 453 N.Y.S.2d 557 (Sup. Ct. 1982). While the primary impact of the rule is on seller financing, third party purchase-money loans are also covered if a type of close-connectedness test is satisfied. Under this requirement, a third party lender comes within the rule if the seller of goods or services "refers consumers to the lender or is affiliated with the creditor by common control, contract, or business arrangement." 16 C.F.R. § 433.1(d).

To be sure, the FTC rule has significant limitations. It covers only natural persons purchasing goods or services for personal, family, or household use, and only purchases of $25,000 or less. 16 C.F.R. §§ 433.1(b), 433.1(d)(e). Real estate mortgages are affected only to the extent that they secure payment for such goods and services. 16 C.F.R. § 433.1(c); Associates Home Equity Services, Inc. v. Troup, 343 N.J.Super. 254, 778 A.2d 529 (N.J. Super. Ct. App. Div. 2001). Consequently, a mortgage loan used to buy a house, whether it has first or junior lien status, is untouched by the rule.

12. *The federal holder-in-due-course doctrine.* A bulk purchaser of a lender's inventory of loans cannot be a holder in due course; see U.C.C. § 3–302(c); Bankers Tr. (Del.) v. 236 Beltway Inv., 865 F.Supp. 1186 (E.D. Va. 1994). However, when a federally-insured financial institution becomes insolvent and its assets are transferred in bulk to the Federal Deposit Insurance Corp. (FDIC), a different rule obtains:

> The federal holder in due course doctrine bars makers of promissory notes from asserting personal defenses against the FDIC and its successors in connection with purchase and assumption transactions involving troubled financial institutions. * * * The FDIC enjoys this protection as a matter of federal common law so that it may achieve the congressional mandate of the "sound, effective, and uninterrupted operation of the [nation's] banking system with resulting safety and liquidity of bank deposits."

Sunbelt Sav., FSB, Dall., Tex. v. Montross, 923 F.2d 353 (5th Cir. 1991) (holding that *non*-negotiable notes are not protected by the federal HIDC doctrine). The HIDC doctrine protects the federal agencies both when they are acting as receivers for insolvent institutions and when, in their corporate capacities, they acquire ownership of an institution's assets. It has also been held to protect parties who acquire notes from the federal agencies; see Hudspeth v. Inv. Collection Services. Ltd. P'ship, 985 S.W.2d 477 (Tex. Ct. App. 1998).

13. *Predatory lending.* Both federal and state statutes that attempt to control or penalize predatory mortgage lenders may withdraw the protection of the holder in due course doctrine from secondary market purchasers of predatory loans. The federal statute, the Home Ownership and Equity Protection Act of 1994 ("HOEPA") provides that:

> Any person who purchases or is otherwise assigned a mortgage referred to in section 1602(aa) of this title shall be subject to all claims and defenses with respect to that mortgage that the consumer could assert against the creditor of the mortgage, unless the purchaser or assignee demonstrates, by a preponderance of the evidence, that a reasonable person exercising ordinary due diligence, could not determine, based on the documentation required by this subchapter, the itemization of the amount financed, and other disclosure of disbursements that the mortgage was a mortgage referred to in section 1602(aa) of this title.

15 U.S.C. § 1641(d)(1).

HOEPA's definition of covered loans was expanded by the 2010 Dodd-Frank Act and the ensuing regulations of the Consumer Financial Protection Bureau. Effective January 10, 2014, loans were covered if they met any of the following criteria (with the dollar figures adjusted annually for inflation):

- The transaction's annual percentage rate (APR) exceeds the applicable average prime offer rate by more than 6.5 percentage points for most first-lien mortgages, or by more than 8.5 percentage points for a first mortgage if the dwelling is personal property and the transaction is for less than $50,000;

- The transaction's APR exceeds the applicable average prime offer rate by more than 8.5 percentage points for subordinate or junior mortgages;

- The transaction's points and fees exceed 5 percent of the total transaction amount or, for loans below $20,000, the lesser of 8 percent of the total transaction amount or $1,000; or

- The credit transaction documents permit the creditor to charge or collect a prepayment penalty more than 36 months after transaction closing or permit such fees or penalties to exceed, in the aggregate, more than 2 percent of the amount prepaid.

More detail about HOEPA is found in Chapter Eight, Section E of this book.

14. *Possible changes.* The Holder in Due Course doctrine continues to be controversial. Consumer advocates generally oppose it, believe it should have been eliminated for mortgage loans by the FTC when it adopted its 1975 rule discussed above, and continue to press for its repeal or substantial weakening with respect to mortgage loans today. Secondary market investors, and especially the securitization industry, claim to view it as sacrosanct and predict dire consequences if it is weakened or eliminated. In 2014 the American Law Institute created an advisory group to consider possible significant changes in the HIDC doctrine in the context of home mortgage notes. At the same time, the drafting committee for the Uniform Home Foreclosure Procedures Act, a project of the Uniform Law Commission, was also considering making changes in HIDC. Where these efforts will lead, and whether they will come to fruition, is uncertain, but it seems likely that change is in the wind.

15. *Nonjudicial foreclosures.* About 30 states, by statute, provide a procedure for foreclosing mortgages without the necessity of a judicial action. In about half of these states, the security document is called a "deed of trust" instead of a mortgage, and the foreclosure is handled by the trustee (a private individual, often an attorney) named in the deed of trust. All of the U.S. states continue to allow traditional common-law judicial foreclosures as well, so the nonjudicial procedure is only an option. However, in most of the states permitting them, nonjudicial foreclosures are highly popular among lenders because they are regarded as cheaper and quicker than judicial proceedings. You'll learn a great deal more about nonjudicial foreclosures in Chapter Six of this book.

Under most nonjudicial foreclosure procedures, having standing to foreclose is established in exactly the same way as in a judicial foreclosure— by producing proof that the party seeking to foreclose has the right of enforcement of the promissory note. The proof is commonly by means of an affidavit or a statement or notice that the foreclosing party must record in the public records and serve on the borrower. For example, in the *Burns* case above, you'll recall the court pointing out that in Missouri "a party entitled to enforce a note is also entitled to enforce the deed of trust securing that note. . . ." Most states using nonjudicial foreclosure continue to follow this perfectly sensible approach.

Over the past few years, however, the courts of eight states have construed their nonjudicial foreclosure statutes as *not* requiring any proof, evidence, or even allegation that the foreclosing party has the right to enforce the promissory note. In those states, all of our discussion above concerning the methods of transferring the right of enforcement of a negotiable note under U.C.C. Article 3 are simply irrelevant in a nonjudicial foreclosure. The result is bizarre; it stems from inadequate drafting of the original statutes (whose drafters in most cases seem to have been unaware that secondary mortgage market existed), combined with an unwillingness on the part of the courts to recognize that the statutes should be read *in pari materia* with the Uniform Commercial Code.

The states reaching this result are Alabama, Arizona, California, Georgia, Idaho, Minnesota, Michigan, and Texas. The cases are discussed in Dale A. Whitman & Drew Milner, Foreclosing on Nothing: The Curious Problem of the Deed of Trust Foreclosure Without Entitlement to Enforce the Note, 66 Ark. L. Rev. 21 (2013). The conclusion these courts have reached is by no means inevitable; the Massachusetts Supreme Judicial Court, faced with the same issue, read its foreclosure statute as effectively incorporating U.C.C. Article 3's principles for transferring the right of enforcement of the note. See Eaton v. Fed. Nat'l Mortg. Ass'n, 969 N.E.2d 1118 (Mass. 2012).

If holding the note is not the relevant indicium of the right to foreclose, what is? Surely there is *some* form of evidence that must exist to confer the right to foreclose—even if there is no court in which to present it unless the borrower brings an action to enjoin the foreclosure. The recent decisions in the group of eight states identified above often do not make this question easy to answer. Depending on the jurisdiction, it may be a photocopy of the note, a chain of assignments (possibly recorded, possibly not), or perhaps either a chain of assignments or possession of the note. California is a particular mystery, since it appears that neither the right to enforce the note nor a recorded chain of assignments is necessary to give one authority to instruct the trustee of a deed of trust to foreclose. See Debrunner v. Deutsche Bank Nat'l Tr. Co., 138 Cal.Rptr.3d 830 (2012) (no proof of the right to enforce the note is required to foreclose nonjudicially); Haynes v. EMC Mortg. Corp., 140 Cal. Rptr. 3d 32 (2012) (recorded assignment of deed of trust unnecessary to foreclose nonjudicially); Johnson v. PNC Mortg., 2014 WL 6629585 (N.D. Cal. Nov. 21, 2014) (party may foreclose even if assignment of deed of trust is defective).

NOTE ON SECONDARY MARKET REPURCHASE OBLIGATIONS

Contracts between mortgage loan originators and secondary market purchasers almost invariably contain numerous representations and warranties by the originator/seller. Among the common ones are the following:

- The seller is a properly formed entity, licensed to do business in the state where the loans were made, with legal authority to originate and to sell the loans.

- The seller is solvent and the information concerning its financial condition that has been provided to the purchaser is true and correct.

- The sale of the loans will not violate any law or breach any contract or duty of the seller, or any court order.

- The sale of the loans is in the ordinary course of business and is not a "bulk transfer."

- The seller's originating and servicing practices are legally proper, and the escrow accounts for taxes and insurance have been properly set up and maintained. The seller is an approved seller/servicer by Fannie Mae and Freddie Mac (even though this may be a sale to a private entity).

- The seller has not made any materially inaccurate or misleading statements concerning the loans to the purchaser.

- The seller is a member in good standing of MERS, and has complied and will comply with all MERS rules and procedures.

- All mortgages being sold have the priority (first or second) that has been attributed to them.

- All payments due from the loan escrow accounts for taxes, insurance, etc. have been paid.

- None of the notes or mortgages has been modified, and no mortgagor has been released from liability.

- The notes and mortgages are not subject to any defense or setoff; none of the mortgagors was in bankruptcy when the loan was originated.

- All of the properties are insured in a manner complying with Fannie Mae and Freddie Mac guidelines.

- The loans are not in default, or subject to any event that would become a default with the passage of time.

- None of the loans are "high cost" loans under HOEPA, and none are subject to any state or local predatory lending law.

There may be many more "reps and warranties," but these give a flavor of what can be expected. If the loans being sold are "subprime," the last of the reps and warranties listed above may need to be modified.

The agreement will typically provide that if a breach of the reps and warranties is discovered by the purchaser, it will give the seller a limited time (e.g., 60 days) to correct the breach. If the breach is not corrected within that time, the purchaser can require the seller to repurchase the loan.

Repurchase by the seller may also be required if the loan goes into "early default." Definitions of "early default" vary; under one version, the seller must buy back the loan if any of the first three mortgage payments after the sale becomes more than 30 days delinquent, or if the mortgagor files bankruptcy within the first three months after the sale of the loan.

Fannie Mae and Freddie Mac follow similar procedures, but with some variations. For example, if Freddie Mac determines that a loan is deficient and requests the seller to repurchase it, the seller has 60 days to file an appeal. If the appeal is denied, the servicer must then repurchase or file a second appeal (if new material information becomes available since the original appeal) within 15 days. See Freddie Mac, Appealing a Repurchase Request or

Repurchase Alternative Issued due to Servicing Violations (Dec. 1, 2016), https://guide.freddiemac.com/app/guide/section/3602.9.

A large number of lawsuits were filed after the 2008 financial crisis by secondary market purchasers who alleged that mortgage originators had failed to repurchase mortgage loans as required by their contracts. In some cases, however, the originators had become insolvent, so that it was unlikely that recovery by the secondary market investors would come close to equaling their losses. The claims were based on both loans in default when the secondary market sale occurred, thus breaching the warranties and representations in the contract, and loans that defaulted soon after the sale, triggering an "early default" repurchase obligation. See, e.g., DLJ Mortg. Cap. Corp. v. Fairmont Funding, Ltd., 920 N.Y.S.2d 1 (N.Y. App. Div. 2011) (court refused to find that purchaser had waived or was estopped to assert repurchase provision); Bank of Am., Nat'l Ass'n. v. Wells Fargo Bank, N.A. by & through Midland Loan Services, 2014 WL 3639190 (N.D. Ill. July 23, 2014) (not reported in F.Supp.2d) (finding that the purchaser had a duty to mitigate its damages by proper servicing while it held the loan, and such duty could affect the amount it was entitled to recover in the repurchase transaction). This litigation serves as a cautionary tale as to the effectiveness of relying on representations and warranties in policing bad behavior in financial transactions. See generally Patricia A. McCoy & Susan M. Wachter, Evidence and Innovation in Housing Law and Policy (L. Fennell & B. Keys, eds., Cambridge University Press, 2017) (explaining how the existence of representations and warranties and the potential penalties associated with them did not deter lax mortgage loan underwriting).

NOTE ON TRANSFERS OF MORTGAGE SERVICING

As we have already noted, the process of collecting and accounting for mortgage loan payments, maintaining escrow or reserve accounts to pay property taxes and hazard insurance, and dealing with defaults and foreclosures is known loosely as "servicing" of a loan. When a portfolio lender makes a loan and retains it in portfolio, it is both the "investor" and the "servicer." But quite frequently the functions of investor and servicer are split from one another. For example, lender A may originate the loan, transfer ownership of it to B, and retain the servicing. Alternatively, lender A may originate the loan, transfer ownership to B, and sell the servicing rights to C.

The servicer is, of course, the agent of the owner or investor, and represents it in dealing with the borrower. Servicers earn fees for their work; a typical annual fee for a residential loan might be in the range of .0020 to .00375 (20 to 37½ "basis points") of the loan amount. Thus, a servicer might earn $200 to $375 per year for servicing a $100,000 loan. In addition to the servicing fee, the servicer earns interest on the balance in the tax and insurance escrow accounts it holds. This "float" can be quite significant, and is a material attraction to lenders who seek servicing contracts. For example, the mortgage servicer Ocwen Financial noted in public filings that in 2007 it held $677 million in escrow accounts on behalf of various borrowers. The servicer invested this money and the yield ended up accounting for 9% of its overall servicing income for that year. See Adam J. Levitin & Tara Twomey, Mortgage Servicing, 28 Yale J. on Reg. 1, 39 (2011). Servicers are also allowed to keep late fees, inspection fees, and some other miscellaneous fees.

There are obvious economies of scale in servicing. In an age of computer-based systems, it is more expensive to service a smaller number of performing loans than it is to service a much larger amount of performing loans. This is due to the fact that investing in servicing software and other resources requires significant upfront costs, while the fee for servicing an individual loan is relatively small. But, once the initial investment is made, there are little additional costs incurred for adding substantially more loans to the servicing program (thus earning significantly more in fees). Hence there are economic incentives for large servicers to become even larger, purchasing servicing rights from smaller entities. Servicing rights can be freely transferred, and a very active market in servicing rights exists in the United States.

But transfers of servicing can be confusing and frustrating to borrowers. They may find that they can no longer deal with the "friendly" local institution that originated their loans, but instead must contend with faceless bureaucrats in Detroit or Dallas, reachable only by toll-free numbers that seem always to be busy or that connect to endless voicemail chains. Payments may be miscredited or lost when servicing is transferred. Smooth, careful transfers seem the exception rather than the rule.

As a result of consumer complaints about servicing transfers, Congress, in the Cranston-Gonzalez Affordable Housing Act of 1990, added to the Real Estate Settlement Procedures Act (RESPA) a new Section 6 that deals with transfers of servicing. It requires that at the time of loan application, the borrower must be informed of the lender's practices in terms of servicing transfers—that is, how likely it is that the servicing of the loan will be transferred. See Rochester Home Equity, Inc. v. Upton, 1 Misc.3d 412, 767 N.Y.S.2d 201 (Sup. Ct. 2003). In addition, if an actual transfer of servicing occurs, the borrower must be given notice by the transferor 15 days before, and by the transferee 15 days after the transfer. Section 6 also contains a grievance procedure and a provision for civil damages and penalties against lenders who fail to comply with it.

In addition, Section 404(a) of the Helping Families Save Their Homes Act of 2009 requires an assignee of residential loan to notify the borrower of the transfer within 30 days after it occurs, even if there is no change of servicing. The borrower may recover actual or statutory damages for a breach of this duty. Note that this obligation to provide notice of loan transfers imposes a duty only on the transferee and not the transferor, and in this way differs from the 1990 statute discussed above requiring notification of changes in servicing, under which both parties must provide notice. Both statutes are analyzed carefully in Gale v. First Franklin Loan Services, 701 F.3d 1240 (9th Cir. 2012).

One important limitation relative to procedural violations under these consumer financial protection statutes deals with Article III standing. As noted above, failure to provide a specific notice can, by itself, result in the imposition of statutory damages under the plain language of the statute. However, the U.S. Supreme Court in Spokeo v. Robins held that the simple failure to provide a written notice or the mere commission of some "bare procedural violation" does not meet constitutional standing (regardless of what a statute provides). Spokeo, Inc. v. Robins, 136 S.Ct. 1540, 1550 (2016), as revised (May 24, 2016). This case, much criticized by consumer advocates, serves as a serious barrier to recovery for plaintiffs who can show that they were not furnished with the legally-required notices or were not given the stipulated process but who cannot show a "concrete and particularized" harm that is "actual or imminent." See Casillas v. Madison Ave. Associates, Inc., 926 F.3d 329, 333 (7th Cir. 2019) (citing Spokeo to reject the plaintiff's claim for damages on account of a debt collector's failure to provide notice under the Fair Debt Collection Practices Act).

NOTE ON THE PAYMENT PROBLEM

Suppose you borrow money from a bank and secure that loan with a mortgage. Subsequently, you desire to pay off the loan. You then send the bank a check or other form of payment for the total balance due, which the bank duly accepts. What you do not know is that the bank assigned your note and mortgage to another investor some months earlier. If the bank fails to remit your payment to the present holder of your note (i.e., the new owner), are you liable to the holder to pay it again? At first blush, the question seems absurd; how can you be held responsible for failing to pay the assignee when you had not been informed that any assignment had been made or that any assignee existed? Surely you cannot be forced to pay twice.

Amazingly, under traditional legal principles, this conclusion is wrong! Payment to the assignor is ineffective against the assignee, even though the payor had no idea that there *was* an assignee. Of course, the assignor is liable for failing to forward or refund the payment; see Hilgeman v. Am. Mortg. Sec., Inc., 994 P.2d 1030 (Ariz. Ct. App. 2000). But if the assignor is missing or insolvent, the payor is out of luck! The precise reason for this result depended on whether the promissory note was or was not negotiable.

Nonnegotiable notes. If the note was nonnegotiable, the common law of "symbolic writings" governed. Under this concept, the note was regarded as a physical reification of the debt itself. The Contracts Restatement put it this way:

> [A]n obligor who renders performance without requiring production of such a symbolic writing takes the risk that the person receiving performance does not have possession of the writing either because he has assigned it or because his right is defective. Non-production has the same effect as receipt of notification of assignment or reason to know of a defect in an assignee's right. In addition, the obligor who performs without surrender or cancellation of or appropriate notation

on the writing takes the risk of further obligation to an assignee who takes possession of the writing as a bona fide purchaser.

Restatement (Second) of Contracts § 338, cmt. h, at 80 (1981). In effect, this rule meant that the payor was expected to demand to see the note before making each payment, and demand its surrender before making a final payoff. However, the rule does admit three exceptions. A payor who pays without first requiring production of the note will nevertheless not have to pay again to the assignee if (i) the assignor may offer a plausible explanation for not producing the documents; (ii) the assignor may have been given authority to collect payments and thus be the agent of the assignee; or (iii) through the course of the parties' dealings, the assignee may be estopped from claiming payment from the payor or otherwise denying satisfaction of the mortgage. See Rodgers v. Seattle-First Nat. Bank, 40 Wash. App. 127, 133, 697 P.2d 1009, 1012 (1985).

Negotiable notes. If the note was negotiable, Article 3 governed, and produced the same result. U.C.C. § 3–602 (1990) provides that an instrument is paid, and the payor is discharged, "to the extent that payment is made . . . to a person entitled to enforce the instrument." Under § 3–301, the phrase "person entitled to enforce" includes a holder to whom the instrument has been negotiated. Significantly, it also includes any person to whom the instrument is delivered for the purpose of giving the right of enforcement, even if that person is not a holder; U.C.C. § 3–203(a), (b). Thus, a transfer by delivery of the instrument without an indorsement will not constitute the transferee a holder, but the transferee is still entitled to enforce the instrument. See Comment 1 of U.C.C. § 3–203.

Although the U.C.C. never explicitly stated that delivery of the instrument vests the power to discharge the obligation *exclusively* in the person "entitled to enforce" the instrument, but that was the widespread understanding. Consequently, if the original payee delivered possession of the instrument to someone else for the purpose of transferring the right of enforcement, a subsequent payment to the original payee would not discharge the obligation. This result followed whether the new possessor of the instrument was a holder or was "in due course" or not. In effect, the payment had simply been made to the wrong person—a person who no longer had the power to discharge the obligation. See Whitehead v. Am. Sec. & Tr. Co., 285 F.2d 282, 284 (D.C. Cir. 1960).

In theory, no lawyer, title company, or escrow company should ever conduct a closing in which a mortgage loan is being paid off without first demanding to see the existing note. But it is often very inconvenient for the lender to produce the note. Remember that the original note, and not merely a photocopy, must be examined. It may be held in a vault in the lender's (or, more accurately, the mortgage servicer's) home office in another city, for example, or (more commonly these days) in the vault of a custodian company in New York or Chicago. Producing it takes time and costs money. As a practical matter, closing agents usually don't bother; they trust the lender/servicer, and sometimes that trust is misplaced. And if the "payment" rule is impractical with regard to final payments, it is obviously even more out of touch with reality with respect to regular monthly payments. In Equity Bank v. Gonsalves, 44 Conn.Supp. 464, 691 A.2d 1143 (Super. Ct. 1996), the court described the standard doctrine discussed above, and then commented:

> The reason given [for the payment rule] is that the maker can protect himself by demanding production of the instrument and refusing to pay a party not in possession of it. * * * To this court that reason does not make sense as to a mortgage note payable monthly. A mortgagor cannot be expected every month he makes a payment to ask a mortgagee bank to prove [its] possession of the note. See Dale A. Whitman, Reforming the Law: The Payment Rule as a Paradigm, 1998 B.Y.U. L. Rev. 1169 (1998).

Changing the rule: nonnegotiable notes. For a long time there was widespread agreement among real estate lawyers (and some courts) that the "payment" rule described above was undesirable and introduced unnecessary risk and complexity in financing transactions. However, changing it proved to be a slow process. When Restatement (Third) of Property (Mortgages) was issued in 1997, § 5.5 rejected the "payment" rule, providing instead that "performance of the obligation to the transferor is effective against the transferee if rendered before the obligor receives notice of the transfer." This language, if followed by the courts, should eliminate the "payment" rule with respect to nonnegotiable notes. Of course, only time will tell whether courts will do so; there are as yet no cases under § 5.5. See EMC Mortg. Corp. v. Chaudhri, 946 A.2d 578 (N.J. Super. Ct. App. Div. 2008), purporting to reject the Restatement and finding that recording of the mortgage assignment gave constructive notice of the transfer. However, the case involves not payment to the transferor, but the right to foreclose of the transferee.

In addition, the Mortgages Restatement recognizes that the traditional rule continues to operate with respect to negotiable notes, since they are governed by U.C.C. Article 3, and Restatements can't repeal statutes. Only an amendment to Article 3 could accomplish that purpose.

Changing the rule: negotiable notes. In 2002, the Permanent Editorial Board of the U.C.C. adopted a change involving the first four subsections of U.C.C. § 3–602. The key change is in subsection (b).

> (a) Subject to subsection (e), an instrument is paid to the extent payment is made by or on behalf of a party obliged to pay the instrument, and to a person entitled to enforce the instrument.

> (b) Subject to subsection (e), a note is paid to the extent payment is made by or on behalf of a party obliged to pay the note to a person that formerly was entitled to enforce the note only if at the time of the payment the party obliged to pay has not received adequate notification that the note has been transferred and that payment is to be made to the transferee. A notification is adequate only if it is signed by the transferor or the transferee, reasonably identifies the

transferred note, and provides an address at which payments subsequently are to be made. Upon request, a transferee shall seasonably furnish reasonable proof that the note has been transferred. Unless the transferee complies with the request, a payment to the person that formerly was entitled to enforce the note is effective for purposes of subsection (c) even if the party obliged to pay the note has received a notification under this subsection.

(c) Subject to subsection (e), to the extent of a payment under subsections (a) and (b), the obligation of the party obliged to pay the instrument is discharged even if payment is made with knowledge of a claim to the instrument under Section 3–306 by another person.

(d) Subject to subsection (e), a transferee, or any party that has acquired rights in the instrument directly or indirectly from a transferee, including a party that has rights as a holder in due course, is deemed to have notice of any payment that is made under subsection (b) after the note is transferred to the transferee but before the party obliged to pay the note receives adequate notification of the transfer.

The need for subsection (d) might not be apparent in light of subsection (b), which seems to do the trick by itself. A new Official Comment to subsection (d) explains that its purpose is to prevent holders in due course from losing the other immunities from defenses that their status would otherwise give them.

Subsection (d) assures that the discharge provided by subsection (c) is effective against the transferee and those whose rights derive from the transferee. By deeming those persons to have notice of any payment made under subsection (b), subsection (d) gives those persons "notice of the discharge" within the meaning of Section 3–302(b). Accordingly, the discharge is effective against those persons, even if any of them has the rights of a holder in due course. * * * The deemed notice provided by subsection (d) does not, however, prevent a person from becoming, or acquiring the rights of, a holder in due course. * * * Thus, such a person does not become subject to other defenses described in Section 3–305(a)(2), claims in recoupment described in Section 3–305(a)(3), or claims to the instrument under Section 3–306.

Unfortunately, this amendment has been enacted in only twelve states at this writing (Kentucky, Washington DC, Mississippi, South Carolina, Michigan, Arkansas, Nevada, New Mexico, Oklahoma, Indiana, Texas, and Minnesota).

The effect of the "payment" rule. Although the "payment" rule may seem harsh, its practical effect is largely limited to transactions among natural persons rather than institutions. While the transfer of institutional mortgages on the secondary market is pervasively common, so also is the practice of designating the originating mortgagee or some other firm as the agent of the assignee for purposes of "servicing" the loan. As we have already seen, servicing entails, among other things, receiving the mortgage payments from the mortgagor. It is perfectly plain that the mortgagor will be protected in continuing to make payments to the servicer so long as an agency relationship exists. See Skott v. Bank of Am. Ill., 468 S.E.2d 359 (Ga. 1996).

NOTE ON RECORDATION OF MORTGAGE ASSIGNMENTS

Is it necessary or relevant to record an assignment of a mortgage? We have already seen that, as between the parties to a transfer of a note and mortgage, no assignment of the mortgage is necessary; a transfer of the note (usually by endorsement and delivery of it) will, under the laws of most states, automatically transfer the mortgage rights as well. Nonetheless, use of an separate assignment of the mortgage is customary. As we have suggested above, the document may be either in the form of an outright transfer or an assignment for security purposes, depending on the nature of the transaction.

The notes below discuss whether and when recording of an assignment is significant. More detail on each of these situations is found in Nelson, Whitman, Burkhart & Freyermuth, Real Estate Finance Law § 5.33 (6th ed.2015). The following notes draw on scenarios between a mortgagor, mortgagee, grantee, and assignee(s). The relationship of these parties may be diagramed as follows:

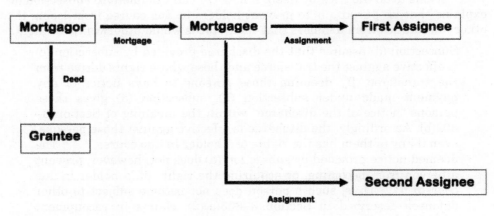

Bear in mind that not all of these parties are necessarily involved in each of the following situations. In fact, the second assignee and the grantee do not appear in most of them.

1. *Validity of the assignment as between the parties.* General principles of recording law make it clear that recordation is unnecessary to the validity of any instrument as between the parties to it. See Stoebuck & Whitman, Property § 11.9 (3d ed. 2000). Thus, the mortgagee and the assignee are bound by the assignment whether it is recorded or not. In any event, as we have already discussed, the assignment is not essential to the assignee's ability to foreclose the mortgage judicially; that ability follows from the assignee's ability to enforce the note.

Perhaps it goes without saying that recordation of a mortgage assignment is not necessary to preserve the priority of the mortgage as against other interests in the land. That priority is established by the original recording of the mortgage itself, and simply continues if the loan is sold or pledged on the secondary market; see In re Cook, 457 F.3d 561 (6th Cir. 2006); In re Patton, 314 B.R. 826 (Bankr. D. Kan. 2004).

2. *Failure to record as excusing the mortgagor's default.* Assume a mortgagor mortgages land to a mortgagee, and the mortgagee assigns the mortgage loan to an assignee. The assignment is not recorded. Then the mortgagor defaults, the assignee institutes foreclosure, and the mortgagor defends by pointing out the assignee's failure to record. This defense will fail, of course; the recording acts are intended to protect subsequent purchasers of either the land or (arguably) the mortgage, and the mortgagor is neither. As the court put it in Rowe v. Small Bus. Admin., 446 N.E.2d 991 (Ind. Ct. App. 1983), "We fail to see how the [mortgagors] needed notice from the record to be aware of their obligations."

3. *Recording as giving notice of the assignment to the mortgagor.* If a mortgagor mortgages land to a mortgagee and the mortgagee gives the recorded assignment to an assignee, does the recordation act as constructive notice of the assignment to the mortgagor? Why do we care about notice? If the note is negotiated to the assignee, we have already seen that, under the payment rule embodied in Article 3 (in states that have not adopted the 2003 amendments), the mortgagor is bound to discover the assignment by insisting on seeing the note before making each payment; recording the assignment can hardly add anything to this already burdensome duty.

But if the note is not negotiable or the traditional payment rule has been reversed by the 2002 amendments to Article 3, the question whether the mortgagor has notice of the assignment becomes more important, since it is easier to argue that payment to the mortgagee is good until the mortgagor has such notice. Does recording the assignment give notice? The answer surely should be no, since finding notice on these facts would mean that the mortgagor would be expected to examine the title before making each payment on the loan. As one court put it,

> To require any [person] to run a title search before making any disbursements to a payee named in a note held for collection and secured by a deed of trust, or to pay at its peril, would impose an impractical and crushing burden. * * *

Giorgi v. Pioneer Title Ins. Co., 454 P.2d 104 (Nev. 1969). A few statutes and cases disagree and impose this burden; see Rucker v. State Exch. Bank, 355 So.2d 171 (Fla. Dist. Ct. App. 1978); EMC Mortg. Corp. v. Chaudhri, 946 A.2d 578 (N.J. Super. Ct. App. Div. 2008) (dictum); see Nelson, Whitman, Burkhart & Freyermuth, Real Estate Finance Law § 5.33 (6th ed.2015). The far preferable and much more widely held view is represented by the following New York statute:

McKINNEY'S CONSOL. LAWS OF NEW YORK, Real Prop.Law, § 324 (1968): The recording of an assignment of a mortgage is not in itself a notice of such assignment to a mortgagor, his heirs or personal representatives, or to an owner of the mortgaged premises, where such assignment is recorded subsequent to the recording of the conveyances of such premises to such owner, so as to invalidate a payment made by either of them to the mortgagee or to a prior assignee of the mortgage.

4.   *Recording as notice to a grantee taking title from the mortgagor.* Now add to the foregoing facts a deed of the land from the mortgagor to the grantee, delivered *after* the assignment to the assignee. If the mortgage note is nonnegotiable, so that it is relevant to determine whether the grantee has notice of the assignment, should the recordation be held to give the grantee notice? Here there is no great burden in so holding, since the grantee is expected to examine the public records anyway as part of the normal process of purchasing the land. The grantee is precisely the sort of third party who is held to notice of a previously-recorded conveyance. If the assignment is unrecorded on these facts, it is well established that the grantee is entitled to assume that the mortgagee still holds the note and mortgage, and a payoff by the grantee to the mortgagee is binding against the assignee. See Sixty St. Francis St., Inc. v. Am. Sav. & Loan Ass'n of Brazoria Cnty., 554 So.2d 1003 (Ala. 1989) (unclear whether note was negotiable or not).

5.   *Failure to record as facilitating a wrongful release by the original mortgagee.* Read this note with extra care; it explains the most important reason that assignment of mortgages should record. Assume a mortgagor mortgages land to a mortgagee, who assigns the mortgage to an assignee. However, the assignee fails to record. Now the mortgagee connives with the mortgagor to execute and record a release of the mortgage. There is in fact no payoff of the loan, and the assignee is unaware of the scheme. The crooked mortgagor, having now appeared to clear the land's title of the mortgage, sells it to a bona fide purchaser (the grantee) and splits his unlawful gains with the mortgagee. Is the assignee bound by the release?

The answer is plainly that the assignee is bound. The reason is that, if the assignment is unrecorded, it is entirely impossible for the grantee to protect herself against this form of skullduggery. See Kalen v. Gelderman, 66 S.D. 53, 278 N.W. 165 (1938); Brenner v. Neu, 28 Ill.App.2d 219, 170 N.E.2d 897 (1960). This is perhaps the best and most obvious reason that the assignee should record an assignment.

A similar problem can arise if the mortgagor conveys title to the land to a mortgagee (i.e., as a deed in lieu of foreclosure) after the mortgagee has made an unrecorded assignment to the assignee. If the mortgagee now sells the land, the buyer who checks the records will find no assignment, and hence will naturally assume that the mortgage has merged with the title in the mortgagee's hands, and hence has been extinguished. This seems the proper result, but the cases are divided as to whether the buyer from the mortgagee will take free of or subject to the mortgage held by the assignee. See Curtis v.

Moore, 152 N.Y. 159, 46 N.E. 168 (1897), discussed in Nelson, Whitman, Burkhart & Freyermuth, Real Estate Finance Law § 5.33 (6th ed.2015).

6. *Wrongful release by the trustee under a deed of trust.* Suppose that, instead of a mortgage, the mortgagor gives a deed of trust to a trustee to secure a note to a mortgagee. The mortgagee then assigns the note and the beneficial interest in the deed of trust to the assignee. Subsequently, the trustee, who turns out to be a crook, improperly executes a reconveyance of the deed of trust to the mortgagor, even though the mortgagor has not paid the underlying debt. The mortgagor then sells the land to a grantee, a bona fide purchaser.

Here, perhaps surprisingly, the grantee will prevail whether the assignment is recorded or not. The reason lies in the role of the trustee, who is in many jurisdictions the only party who *can* reconvey the title to the mortgagor. In effect, the trustee represents (for the limited purposes of reconveyance and foreclosure) whomever may hold the beneficial interest in the note from time to time. See Marsh v. Stover, 363 Ill. 490, 2 N.E.2d 559 (1936), noted 31 Ill. L. Rev. 350 (1936).

Note that this rule applies only if it is the trustee who issues the reconveyance. In some jurisdictions in which deeds of trust are used, satisfactions are customarily given by the beneficiary directly, rather than by the trustee. There the rule for mortgages discussed in the previous notes will govern.

7. *Recording as ensuring notice to assignee of new litigation.* Suppose a secondary market investor buys a mortgage loan, but records no assignment. Then a suit is filed that could jeopardize the validity or priority of the mortgage. One obvious example is a foreclosure of a mortgage senior to the one in question, but there are many other possibilities: a quiet title action by someone claiming better title to the land, a building or housing code enforcement proceeding, or an action to force cleanup of hazardous waste on the land, for example. The plaintiff in that action may perform a title examination, discover the identity of the original mortgagee or previous holder of the mortgage, and make service of process on that party. But the actual (though unrecorded) holder of the mortgage will get no direct service (since there is no obvious way for the plaintiff to identify the holder), and hence the holder may not learn of the suit from the party who was actually served.

In Fifth Third Bank v. NCS Mortg. Lending Co., 860 N.E.2d 785 (Ohio Ct. App. 2006), a foreclosure action was filed by a prior mortgage holder. The court found the foreclosure judgment binding on the assignee of the junior mortgage, which had never learned of or entered an appearance in the litigation, despite its claim that it had instructed its predecessor to record an assignment of the mortgage—an act that was "inexplicably" never done. Because most secondary market investors use independent servicers to manage their mortgage portfolios, an investor may prefer to have a recorded assignment run to its servicer rather than itself. In this way, any notice issued will find its way directly to the entity that is responsible for management of the loan, rather than having to take the circuitous route of going first to the investor, who will then need to notify the servicer. But in *Fifth Third Bank*, no assignment at all was recorded, and hence no notice of the litigation was directed either to the investor or its servicer. The case illustrates that failing to record a mortgage assignment can have disastrous consequences. For a similar example, in which the prior lien being foreclosed was a mechanics lien, see R.I. Constr. Services, Inc. v. Harris Mill, LLC, 68 A.3d 450 (R.I. 2013).

As an alternative to recording an assignment to itself, the investor may prefer to have an assignment recorded to MERS, the Mortgage Electronic Registration Systems. MERS is merely a nominee for the investor, but it operates a "mail room" function, keeping a record of all investors and servicers, and redirecting to the relevant servicer any notice that it receives with respect to a particular mortgage. Unfortunately, this notion is not foolproof, for it depends on the courts taking the same view of MERS that MERS itself takes. In Landmark Nat'l Bank v. Kesler, 216 P.3d 158 (Kan. 2009), the original mortgagee named in the junior mortgage was MERS, as nominee for the actual lender. A senior mortgagee filed a foreclosure action, but never served either MERS or the junior lender, and a default judgment was entered against both of them, wiping out the second mortgage. The Kansas Supreme Court found no error in the trial judge's refusal to set aside the default judgment. The junior mortgagee was not entitled to notice because there was no assignment to it in the public records; the court found that MERS was not entitled to notice because it was merely a nominee, had advanced no funds under the mortgage loan, and was therefore not a real party in interest. This conclusion seems absurd, but Indiana and Arkansas courts have followed it.

8. *Effect of recording on successive conflicting assignments by the mortgagee.* Assume a mortgagor mortgages land to a mortgagee. The mortgagee now makes two conflicting assignments of the mortgage, the first to a first assignee and the second to a second assignee. Which of them is considered to hold the mortgage?

The first question is whether the mortgage note is negotiable. If this is so, we have already seen that under Article 3, the right of enforcement of both the note and the mortgage will normally follow possession of the note (provided the note is endorsed or the assignee can prove that possession was delivered for the purpose of transferring the right of enforcement). Obviously if the first assignee has obtained actual possession of the note, the second assignee cannot obtain it from the mortgagee; this should be enough to "tip off" the second assignee that the proposed assignment to them is of dubious validity, and the first assignee will prevail. All of this follows whether the first assignee records or not. The first assignee's position will be buttressed by the "claims" language of U.C.C. § 3–306 if the first assignee is a HIDC, but that factor doesn't seem necessary to their position.

In theory, the second assignee could argue that he or she is just the sort of "subsequent purchaser" who is protected by the recording acts against a prior unrecorded assignment, but the courts, faced with this apparent conflict between the U.C.C. and the recording acts, should and usually will opt to apply the U.C.C. and disregard the recording act, reasoning (as always) that the mortgage follows the note. See Am. Bank of the S. v. Rothenberg, 598 So.2d 289 (Fla. Dist. Ct. App. 1992); Jan Z. Krasnowiecki, J. Gregg Miller & Lloyd R. Ziff, The Kennedy Mortgage Co. Bankruptcy Case: New Light Shed on the Position of Mortgage Warehousing Banks, 56 Am. Bankr. L.J. 325, 333–39 (1982), arguing strenuously for the preeminence of the U.C.C. in this situation.

If the note is negotiable but the first assignee does not take possession of it (perhaps taking a mere written assignment rather than the endorsed note itself), and if the second assignee does take the note, then the second assignee will prevail. Again, this result should, and usually does, follow irrespective of whether the first assignment is recorded. In other words, a recordation by the first assignee will not be considered constructive notice to the second, so as to deprive the second assignee of title to the note and mortgage. See Foster v. Augustanna Coll. & Theological Seminary, of Rock Island, Ill., 92 Okl. 96, 218 P. 335, 37 A.L.R. 854 (1923); Nelson, Whitman, Burkhart & Freyermuth, Real Estate Finance Law § 5.34 (6th ed.2015). This conclusion is supported by U.C.C. § 3–302(b), which provides:

> Public filing or recording of a document does not of itself constitute notice of a defense, claim in recoupment, or claim to the instrument.

Incidentally, in this setting the first assignee, not getting possession of the note, obviously can't become a HIDC, thus ruling out the protection against adverse claims provided by § 3–306.

Things change drastically if the note is nonnegotiable. Now Article 3 does not apply, and the state's recording act is usually held to control. If the first assignee fails to record and the second assignee qualifies as a BFP under the recording acts (and in notice-race states, records first), then the second assignee will prevail. See Fannin Inv. & Dev. Co. v. Neuhaus, 427 S.W.2d 82 (Tex. Civ. App. 1968); Second Nat'l Bank of New Haven v. Dyer, 121 Conn. 263, 184 A. 386 (1936). Does this contravene the general notion that the note or indebtedness is the primary right of the mortgagee, and the mortgage is merely an adjunct which follows it? Should the second assignee prevail only if they get actual possession of the original note from the mortgagee? The *Dyer* case did not so require; see Nelson, Whitman, Burkhart & Freyermuth, Real Estate Finance Law § 5.33 (6th ed.2015).

9. *Recording as a prerequisite to foreclosure.* In about a dozen states, by statute, a party who claims to hold a mortgage by virtue of an assignment cannot foreclose unless the assignment has been recorded. Except for Maine, virtually all of these statutes apply only to nonjudicial foreclosures. See, e.g., Minn. Stat. Ann. § 580.02(3), requiring that any assignments be recorded as a prerequisite to a nonjudicial foreclosure. Maine does indeed construe its statute to require a chain of recorded assignments for a judicial foreclosure; see Deutsche Bank Nat'l Tr. Co. v. Wilk, 76 A.3d 363 (Me. 2013).

It's not at all obvious what policy these statutes serve, other than to give title insurance companies some "comfort" by providing a clear public chain of title to rely upon when they insure the title of a foreclosure purchaser. There is no strong reason to regard recording of assignments as essential, and a number of other nonjudicial foreclosure states do not require it, along with nearly all judicial foreclosure states. Moreover, the presence or absence of a recorded assignment proves nothing about who holds or has the right to enforce the promissory note, which (properly understood) is the critical issue in a mortgage foreclosure.

The statutes requiring recording of assignments as a precondition to foreclosure amount to little more than a formality. The recording can take place immediately prior to the foreclosure, which may be many months or years after the actual assignment. Hence, these statutes are essentially useless in informing borrowers about who holds their mortgages. See, e.g., WM Specialty Mortg., LLC v. Salomon, 874 So.2d 680 (Fla. Dist. Ct. App. 2004) (assignee may foreclose despite late-executed assignment). Moreover, courts tend to treat the recording requirement as irrelevant if no one is injured by the failure to record (as is usually the case); see Fed. Home Loan Mortg. Ass'n v. Kelley, 858 N.W.2d 69 (Mich. Ct. App. 2014); Dixon v. Windsor, 596 So.2d 898 (Ala. 1992).

NOTE ON THE CREATION OF A NATIONAL MORTGAGE REGISTRY

Thus far in this chapter, we have spent a good deal of effort to explain the existing system for transferring mortgages (and notes secured by mortgages). In this note, we step back to appraise the system, and ask whether something better might not be created.

In theory, the requirement of Article 3 for delivery of possession of negotiable notes, as the exclusive way to transfer the right of enforcement, serves two purposes. First, it ensures that two (or more) competing parties cannot assert the same right of enforcement against the borrower (since there can be only one party in possession of the original note), and thus protects the borrower against double enforcement. Second, it allows the borrower to determine, by demanding to see the original note, whether a party attempting to enforce the note actually has the right of enforcement.

The system works reasonably well to achieve the first objective, except in the eight states (discussed in note 9) that don't require proof of the right to enforce the note as a prerequisite to nonjudicial foreclosure. At the same time, the system imposes significant costs on secondary market participants to move original notes around the country (with the attendant risks of lost notes) and to store them in a network of custodians' vaults.

Unfortunately, the system is almost completely useless to achieve the second objective. In an era in which nearly all mortgages are sold on the secondary market, and in which loans are managed by servicers who are seldom located near the borrowers, any request by a borrower to see the original note is likely to be met with incredulous silence or a polite chuckle. The note is likely held by a custodian for the secondary market investor, and is located far away in a vault to which the servicer has no simple means of access. If the borrower were insistent, the servicer might be able to e-mail or fax a copy of the note to the borrower, but a copy, of course, would prove nothing. As a practical matter, there is simply no convenient mechanism by which a borrower can verify that the servicer who is demanding payment of the note actually holds it or represents the holder.

Substantial additional costs grow from the need to record mortgage assignments in the local real estate records (which, as we saw above, is obligatory in order to use nonjudicial foreclosure in about a dozen states, and is a wise precaution everywhere). The party making the assignment must discover which local recording jurisdiction is applicable (of the more than 3,600 in the United States) and determine what its document standards and fees are. It must then hand tailor the assignment (which must, of course, bear the names of the parties to the original mortgage, its recording data, a signature of the assignor, and a notarial acknowledgment) and transmit it to the correct recording office with the appropriate fee. None of this is impossible, but it is sufficiently burdensome that it's easy to see why many secondary market participants forego recording of assignments unless and until it becomes necessary in order to foreclose the mortgage.

Both the process of physically shipping notes around the country and the need to record assignments in one of thousands of local jurisdictions seem archaic, rooted in the technology of the eighteenth and nineteenth centuries. Indeed, the whole idea of having one system (delivery) for transferring notes and another (recording assignments or MERS) for transferring mortgages seems dull-witted, when everyone agrees that the right to enforce the note and the mortgage should remain together. Couldn't transfers of notes and mortgages be tracked together with a single system? Surely in an era of nationwide digital networks and electronic documents we can do better.

At this point, no successor system is at hand. MERS was created as an attempt to ameliorate the problems of recording mortgage assignments, but MERS does not address the issue of note delivery at all (except in the case of electronic notes, currently a small subset of all notes), and as we have seen, MERS has had many problems of its own.

But some progress is being made. There have been serious academic efforts to describe an integrated nationwide system of registration for notes and mortgages traded on the secondary market. See Dale A. Whitman, A Proposal for a National Mortgage Registry: MERS Done Right, 78 Mo. L. Rev. 1 (2013); Adam J. Levitin, The Paper Chase: Securitization, Foreclosure, and the Uncertainty of Mortgage Title, 63 Duke L.J. 637 (2013); Christopher K. Odinet, Foreclosed: Mortgage Servicing and the Hidden Architecture of Homeownership in America (2019); Alan M. White, Losing the Paper— Mortgage Assignments, Note Transfers and Consumer Protection, 24 Loy. Consumer L. Rev. 468 (2012). Some considerations that would go into creating such a registry include: whether the law should come from the federal government or from a uniform state law; what role existing law would play in the operation of the registry; who would be eligible to use the registry; how the registry would interact with the U.C.C. and state foreclosure law; and what kind of warranties a party who used the registry would automatically give to those who might come to rely on the registered information.

At the time of this writing, it is difficult to say when or whether a national registry system will become a reality. The barriers, both political and in terms of garnering industry support and consensus, are formidable. On the other hand, our experience with the existing system during the mortgage crisis that began in 2007 has demonstrated just how dysfunctional and inefficient it is. The need for change is strong.

NOTE ON COLLATERAL (SECURITY) ASSIGNMENTS OF MORTGAGE LOANS

Collateral assignments and the "payment" rule. There are two quite distinct types of assignments of notes and mortgages. The first is an "outright" assignment—a sale of the loan, usually for cash, to an investor who plans to hold it for the long term or securitize it. The second is a "collateral" assignment, in which the loan is pledged by the mortgagee as collateral for *another* loan, one made by the assignee to the mortgagee. As mentioned above, "servicing" contracts, in which some entity (sometimes the local lender who originated the loan) is appointed an agent to collect payments and remit them to the secondary market investor are very common with outright assignments. However, such formal contracts for servicing are much less common in collateral assignments; instead, the originating mortgagee simply continues to service the loans.

As we have already noted, nonbank mortgage lenders frequently obtain much of their operating capital by borrowing funds from commercial banks on lines of credit. They then use these funds to originate mortgage loans, which they ultimately package and sell on the secondary mortgage market or securitize. While a nonbank mortgage lender is accumulating a package of loans of sufficient size to sell, it may temporarily pledge the loans (i.e., the notes and mortgages) it has already originated to the commercial bank as collateral for the line of credit.[12]

Suppose the nonbank mortgage lenders receive a repayment on one of these loans while it is pledged or "warehoused" with the bank. If the nonbank has been designated as the bank's agent to receive such payments, all is well from the borrower's viewpoint. But if there is no formal agency agreement, and if the nonbank becomes insolvent and fails to pay off the bank's line of credit, the bank may claim that it is not bound by the payment made by the mortgagor, and that the note and mortgage are still in effect. In such cases,

---

[12] The warehouse line of credit is not the only way nonbank mortgage lenders obtain financing. Some, especially smaller, nonbank mortgage lenders act as "correspondents" for commercial banks or other larger lenders. The correspondent will originate residential loans meeting the larger institution's specifications, and will fund the loan at closing; the larger institution will then immediately reimburse the correspondent for the loan amount and will take ownership of the loan. This approach is sometimes called "table funding" because the larger institution's check is available virtually at the closing table.

courts are inclined to work hard to find or imply an agency relationship; see In re Royal W. Properties, Inc., 441 B.R. 158 (Bankr. S.D. Fla. 2010); Rodgers v. Seattle-First Nat'l Bank, 697 P.2d 1009 (Wash. Ct. App. 1985). As we saw in the previous section of this book, ultimately the combination of Restatement § 5.5 and the revisions to U.C.C. § 3–602 should eliminate this problem, whether the notes are negotiable or nonnegotiable.

How does the pledgee of a mortgage "foreclose?" Assume that a default occurs in payment on the debt for which a note and mortgage have been pledged as security. How should the pledgee "foreclose" or realize on the security? One approach is for the pledgee to put the underlying note and mortgage on the secondary mortgage market and sell them. This follows from U.C.C. § 9–610, which provides that:

(a) After default, a secured party may sell, lease, license, or otherwise dispose of any or all of the collateral * * *.

(b) Every aspect of a disposition of collateral, including the method, manner, time, place, and other terms, must be commercially reasonable. If commercially reasonable, a secured party may dispose of collateral by public or private proceedings, by one or more contracts, as a unit or in parcels, and at any time and place and on any terms.

Another option is found in U.C.C. § 9–607(a)(1), which provides:

If so agreed, and in any event upon default, a secured party may notify an account debtor or other person obligated on collateral to make payment or otherwise render performance to or for the benefit of the secured party.

Hence the pledgee of the note and mortgage may simply notify the mortgagor on the underlying debt to begin making payments on that debt directly to the pledgee. See Columbus Investments v. Lewis, 48 P.3d 1222 (Colo. 2002). Of course, if the mortgagor was unaware of the pledge or is unwilling to accept the pledgee's word that a default by the mortgagee has occurred, the pledgee may need to obtain a court order directing the mortgagor to make future payments to the pledgee.

Suppose the underlying mortgage debt is also in default. Can the pledgee foreclose the mortgage on the land, or must the pledgee first engage in some sort of "foreclosure" of the security interest *in* the note and mortgage? If the note is negotiable (and perhaps even if it is not), these questions should be answered by first inquiring who has possession of the note, the pledgor or the pledgee. This inquiry would fit with our earlier discussion of transfers of the right of enforcement of a negotiable note. If possession has been transferred to the pledgee, it's highly likely that a court would find the pledgee has the right to enforce the note and the mortgage. See Bank of Tokyo Tr. Co. v. Urb. Food Malls Ltd., 650 N.Y.S.2d 654 (1996), agreeing with this conclusion, but requiring the pledgee to join the pledgor in the foreclosure action if the balance on the debt secured by the pledge is less than the balance owing on the mortgage. See also Prairie Properties, L.L.C. v. McNeill, 996 S.W.2d 635 (Mo. Ct. App. 1999) (collateral assignee of mortgage who obtained possession of note had authority to release it).

Even if possession of the note has been transferred to the pledgee, the pledgor might still have the power to foreclose the mortgage under an agency or servicing agreement, express or implied, with the pledgee. See Poseidon Dev., Inc. v. Woodland Lane Estates, LLC, 62 Cal.Rptr.3d 59, 69 (2007) (holding that a lender who had made an assignment of the mortgage could no longer foreclose or enforce it). The assignor claimed the assignment was only as collateral, but on its face the assignment appeared absolute.

NOTE ON MORTGAGE PARTICIPATIONS

In a mortgage loan participation transaction, a "lead lender" originates a mortgage loan and then sells fractional interests in it to one or more other lenders. For example, the lead lender may loan $10 million to a shopping center developer, and may then sell four $2 million participations to four other lenders, keeping a $2 million investment for itself. Similar arrangements are often made for packages of much smaller loans on residential properties.

Why do lenders engage in participations? In some cases, each lender may be limited by governmental regulation in the amount of lending it can make to a particular borrower or secured by a particular type of property. Commercial banks are examples of institutions with these kinds of limitations. In the example above, the $2 million participation shares may be within this limit, while the entire $10 million loan, if made by a single lender, might exceed it. In addition, each lender, by diversifying its portfolio, spreads the risk of loan default; it is generally safer for a lender to invest $2 million in each of five different projects (especially if they are located in five different market areas) than to invest $10 million in a single project in a single market.

A participation is not, however, the only way for a group of lenders to pool their funds in making loans. Alternatively, they might form a partnership or a joint venture, or they might enter into a multi-lender agreement or "syndication," in which each lender has a direct relationship with the borrower, advancing part of the total loan funds and becoming a direct creditor of the borrower for repayment of these funds, with separate collateral. But in real estate lending, participations are much more commonly employed than these other approaches. See John C. Murray, Recharacterization Issues in Participating Loans, 19 Prob. & Prop. 36 (Sept./Oct. 2005).

How is a participation structured mechanically? In the past, a very common method involved one mortgage securing a series of notes or bonds, each one for a fractional part of the total debt. Some or all of these notes or bonds were then sold to third party assignees. The most common method in use today, however, involves the use of a single note and mortgage for each loan. The originating mortgagee or "lead lender" will generally retain the original note and mortgage and sell "participation certificates" to the other institutions. These certificates will detail the fractional interests sold and the specific mortgage loan involved. Thus, the participation is really a partial assignment of the note and mortgage (making the assignees tenants in common of the note and mortgage).

If the participation involves the sale of fractional interests in a large pool of smaller mortgage loans, the originating mortgagee will sell "participation certificates" delineating the fractional interest being sold and specifically identifying which mortgage loans are involved. In both of the above situations, the participation certificates will be governed more specifically by the terms of a detailed "participation agreement." The following material will highlight some of the legal issues that arise with participations and participation agreements.

Priority among the participants. Suppose the loan goes into default and foreclosure ensues. As among the participants, and as against the lead lender, who will have priority as to the foreclosure proceeds and any collectible deficiency judgment? Today, almost all courts grant a pro-rata priority among the participants in the absence of a contrary agreement. See generally Nelson, Whitman, Burkhart & Freyermuth, Real Estate Finance Law § 5.35 (6th ed.2015). Likewise, the participants have no special priority vis á vis the lead lender unless the agreement provides otherwise; see Domeyer v. O'Connell, 364 Ill. 467, 4 N.E.2d 830 (1936).

However, these common law priority rules are seldom significant today, because participation agreements almost always deal with these matters in detail. Clauses that establish priorities between the participants themselves, and between them and the lead lender, are very common—often called an intercreditor agreement. But disputes can still arise if the language of the agreement is not entirely clear; see, e.g., Bank of Chicago v. Park Nat'l Bank, 640 N.E.2d 1288 (Ill. App. Ct. 1994).

Managing the mortgage loan. In any participation, someone must be in charge. Decisions about management of the underlying loan or loans must be made. Who will have this authority? The following provision provides one possible answer:

> Seller [lead lender] shall give prompt notice to Purchaser as to any default under the terms of any mortgage in which the Purchaser has a participation interest. Seller may act upon any loan in default and the security property by any procedure which may be necessary in its sole discretion, including the acceptance of a deed in lieu of foreclosure or the purchase at a foreclosure sale or trustee's sale. Seller shall exercise the judgment of a prudent lender in Seller's lending area. Seller shall make an appraisal of the property within a reasonable time before taking any action affecting such loan in default. Seller may manage, maintain or dispose of property so acquired in any manner which it shall deem necessary, the parties hereto sharing ratably with Seller in the net proceeds of sale to the extent of Purchaser's share in the unpaid principal balance due on the loan. It is further understood that it shall be within the sole

discretion of Seller, after 10 days written notice to Purchaser, to determine whether foreclosure shall be pursuant to a power of sale, or through court action, and as to whether or not a deficiency judgment shall be obtained.

While this language gives the lead lender full decision-making authority, one can easily imagine cases in which such an arrangement is unacceptable to the participants—particularly if the lead lender retains only a small fraction of ownership of the underlying loan. The participants may insist that the lead lender at least consult with them before making critical decisions. They may even want one of their number to have authority instead of the lead lender, or may want to subject all important decisions to majority or supermajority vote.

Nevertheless, lenders sometimes enter into participation agreements that are vague or silent as to who will make managerial decisions concerning the loan. The question of whether to be lenient or tough, to forbear or foreclose, is often a close one on which the participants may have very different opinions. For examples of such disputes, see S. Pac. Thrift & Loan Ass'n v. Sav. Ass'n Mortg. Co., 70 Cal.App.4th 634, 82 Cal.Rptr.2d 874 (1999); Capitol Sav. & Loan Ass'n v. First Fin. Sav. & Loan Ass'n, 364 N.W.2d 267 (Iowa Ct. App. 1984). Even well-drafted agreements often end up in litigation. See, e.g., Mark Twain Bank v. Cont'l Bank, 817 F.Supp. 792 (E.D. Mo. 1993), in which the agreement required the participant's agreement before the lead bank could "extend the final maturity" of the underlying loan. The court held that a decision by the lead bank to defer certain payments by the borrower was outside the scope of this phrase, and was proper even if the participant did not agree.

One implication of the participation's structure is that the individual participants cannot pursue independent remedies against the borrower, but rather must count on the lead lender (or other servicer hired by the lead lender) to do so. See Beal Sav. Bank v. Sommer, 8 N.Y.3d 318 (2007).

Lead lender liability. When a participation goes sour, the participants often attempt to find some theory of liability that will allow them to shift their losses to the lead lender. Sometimes this is easy. For example, the lead lender in a participation ordinarily services the underlying mortgage loan or loans, collecting payments, escrowing taxes and insurance, maintaining accounts, and remitting to the participants their share of the payments received. Suppose the lead bank collects payments from the borrower(s) and simply refuses to forward to the participants a part of the share to which they are entitled under the agreement. Pretty obviously, this conduct will breach the lead lender's contractual duty. See Resol. Tr. Corp. v. Heights of Tex., FSB, 1991 WL 205040 (D. Kan. Sept. 17, 1991) (not reported in F.Supp.)

The participation agreement will sometimes state that the lead lender, in its capacity as servicer, will hold the funds collected from the borrower "in trust" for the participants. Again, it seems obvious that if the lead lender misappropriates these funds or deals with them negligently, liability for breach of fiduciary duty will result. However, the courts have been most reluctant to extrapolate from this limited "trust" language a general fiduciary duty that extends, for example, to the lead lender's management of relations with the borrower. See S. Pac. Thrift & Loan Ass'n v. Sav. Ass'n Mortg. Co., 70 Cal.App.4th 634, 82 Cal.Rptr.2d 874 (1999); First Citizens Fed. Sav. & Loan Ass'n v. Worthen Bank & Tr. Co., 919 F.2d 510 (9th Cir. 1990). Of course, a general fiduciary duty may be found if the language of the participation agreement is broad enough. See Guar. Sav. & Loan Ass'n v. Ultimate Sav. Bank, F.S.B., 737 F.Supp. 366 (W.D. Va. 1990), where the agreement stated, "Seller * * * is to act in all matters hereunder for the Buyer * * * as a trustee with fiduciary duties to administer the loans hereunder."

Participations as securities. Participants sometimes attempt to establish that their shares are "securities" under the federal securities acts, hoping that this characterization will make it easier for them to blame the lead lender for the failure of the underlying loan. However, virtually all of the cases refuse to treat a participation sold to a financial institution as a security. See, e.g., First Fin. Fed. Sav. & Loan Ass'n v. E.F. Hutton Mortg. Corp., 834 F.2d 685 (8th Cir. 1987); McVay v. W. Plains Serv. Corp., 823 F.2d 1395 (10th Cir. 1987). On the other hand, if the participation interest is sold to an unsophisticated private individual, it is relatively easy to convince a court that it is a security. See, e.g., Pollack v. Laidlaw Holdings, Inc., 27 F.3d 808 (2d Cir. 1994). The details of the analysis are not within the scope of our present treatment; see J. Thomas Cookson, Loan Participation Agreements as Securities: Judicial Interpretations of the Securities Act of 1933 and the Securities Exchange Act of 1934, 24 Wm. & Mary L. Rev. 295 (1983). The unsophisticated consumer who invests in participation interests is at a particular disadvantage, often finding himself or herself in a swimming pool operated by a shark.

Misrepresentation or concealment by the lead lender. Many of the conflicts that arise between the lead lender and the participants revolve around the fact that the characteristics of the underlying borrower and the real estate never matched the participants' beliefs or assumptions. For example, the borrower may have had weaker credit, less real estate management experience, lower net worth, or a poorer track record in repaying past loans than the participants understood. The real estate may have had a lower value, been in a more risky location, or been more difficult to develop than the participants realized. Ideally the parties would make it perfectly clear whether the participants were relying on the lead lender's representations about such matters, or whether they had made their own investigation of the facts. But the extent of such reliance is often left quite unclear and gives rise to litigation. See, e.g., Commonwealth Mortg. Corp. v. First Nationwide Bank, 873 F.2d 859 (5th Cir. 1989); First Fed. Sav. & Loan Ass'n v. Twin City Sav. Bank, FSB, 868 F.2d 725 (5th Cir. 1989).

Misdealing by the lead lender. As the foregoing material suggests, modern participation agreements are characterized by a high degree of flexibility and informality. The underlying loan documents, including notes and mortgages, are usually left in the hands of the lead lender. Normally neither the participation agreement nor the participation certificates are recorded in the real estate records, nor is a financing statement filed under Article 9 of the

U.C.C. Indeed, no filing seems necessary, since a participation interest is evidently a "payment intangible" under Article 9, and perfection of security interests in payment intangibles is automatic under § 9–309(3). Moreover, the participants are clearly not holders in due course of the mortgage note or notes. Most of the time this informality simplifies what otherwise could be an inherently complex transaction. It creates few problems where, as is usual, the lead lender is a solvent, reputable and reasonably competent lending institution.

On the other hand, what if the lead lender is incompetent or crooked? Suppose, for example, that a lead lender reassigns the note or notes or sells additional participation interests in them (a double-dealing problem)? Or suppose the loan documents are pledged as security for unrelated borrowing by the lead lender? Even assuming that such acts are not conscious misdealing, what if they occur by mistake? What if the lead lender becomes insolvent and goes into bankruptcy? In each of these cases, a potential conflict exists between the claims of the participants and those of third parties whose interests arise through the lead lender.

These problems have the potential to come about simply because the lead lender continues to hold the underlying mortgage note or notes. Hence, one obvious precaution the participants can take is to relieve the lead lender of possession of the notes. Of course, it is not easy for the parties to agree that one of several participants will be the "lucky" one who holds the notes. A more even-handed approach is to appoint a custodian (typically a commercial bank that has no other connection with the transaction) and transfer the notes to it with an accompanying agreement. This will prevent the lead lender from improperly releasing the underlying mortgages or "double-selling" or "double-pledging" the notes. An alternative, somewhat simpler but less neat, is to mark the notes with a legend stating that participation shares in them have been sold, to whom they were sold, and in what amounts. This approach is more practical if the participation is of a single large mortgage loan rather than a pool of small loans.

D. DISCHARGE OF THE DEBT AND MORTGAGE: BY PAYMENT OR OTHERWISE

When a borrower pays off a mortgage debt in full, the mortgage automatically is extinguished. The popular mythology of the borrower "burning the mortgage" reflects this basic concept. The concept is indeed correct, but it is a bit more complex and requires some further explanation.

To begin, a mortgage may be paid off by either of two classes of persons: those who are primarily responsible for payment and those who are not. Who is "primarily responsible" The concept does not depend on the existence of personal liability for the debt. Most obviously, mortgagors are primarily responsible if they still own the mortgaged real estate, whether the debt is recourse or not. Similarly, if the real estate is transferred, the grantees become "primarily responsible," whether they assumed personal liability on the debt or not. Even tenants in common, life tenants, or other holders of a limited interest in the real estate are primarily responsible, except to the extent that someone else has a duty to reimburse them for part of the payment they make.

If someone who is primarily responsible pays off a mortgage loan, the mortgage is indeed extinguished. Legally, it no longer exists. Because it still appears in the public records, the mortgagee has a duty to provide a suitable document in recordable form that shows that the mortgage has been released. The person making the payoff can then record it to clear the title. We can correctly refer to the payoff as a "redemption" of the land from the mortgage.

The great majority of states statutorily require mortgagees to provide a recordable document discharging the mortgage. The customary name for the document varies among the jurisdictions. It may be called a release, a satisfaction-piece, a discharge, or, particularly where deeds of trust are commonly used, a reconveyance. The name has little significance. These statutes often provide a fixed time period, such as 10 to 90 days, within which the lender must provide the discharge document. Many statutes impose financial penalties on mortgagees who fail to comply and allow the payor to recover any actual damages resulting from the mortgagee's failure to provide a discharge.

Most statutory penalties are imposed only after the borrower submits a specific request for the satisfaction. The penalties are generally modest, such as $100 to $1,000, but some are quite draconian. For example, the Missouri statute imposes a penalty of the lesser of $300 per day or ten percent of the loan balance. Mo. Ann. Stat. § 443.130. The Oklahoma penalty is the lesser of $100 or one percent of the loan balance, for each day after ten days. Okla. Stat. tit. 46, § 15; Tucker v. FSB Mortgage of Little Rock, 886 P.2d 498 (Okl.App.1994) (penalty of $16,400). In South Carolina, the trial court has discretion to impose a penalty of up to one-half of the loan balance. See Kinard v. Fleet Real Estate Funding Corp., 319 S.C. 408, 461 S.E.2d 833 (App.1995) (penalty of $72,500). The worst (or best) jurisdiction is Pennsylvania, which provides for the mortgagee to forfeit any amount up to the full mortgage debt, in the court's discretion. Pa. Stat. Ann. tit. 21, § 682. The Model Residential Mortgage Satisfaction Act, promulgated by the Uniform Law Commission, imposes a flat penalty of $500 if the mortgagee does not provide a satisfaction within 30 days after a written demand. However, the payor may not send the demand until 30 days after the payoff, which effectively gives the mortgagee at least 60 days before the penalty becomes effective. § 203. The Act has been adopted in Alabama, North Carolina, U.S. Virgin Islands, Virginia and Wisconsin.

Normally, only a complete payoff extinguishes a mortgage. However, the mortgagor and mortgagee may include e a "partial release" clause in the mortgage. This clause is commonly included in a blanket mortgage on a subdivision of lots. The mortgagee agrees to release the mortgage on individual lots as the mortgagor sells them and pays the mortgagee a specified amount for the release. A similar clause may be used when an apartment building is converted to condominiums.

What about payoffs by people who are not primarily responsible, such as a mortgagor who has transferred the land subject to or with an assumption of the mortgage, a junior mortgagee or other junior lienor, a tenant under a subordinate lease, and conceivably even people holding easements or covenant rights that are subordinate to the mortgage. If the mortgage is due, they have the right to pay it. Their payment is properly known as a redemption. However, redemption by such a person has a very different consequence than redemption by one who is "primarily responsible." Their redemption does not *extinguish* the mortgage but, rather, *assigns* both the obligation (the note or other evidence of debt) and the mortgage to the payor.

This assignment takes place by operation of law and is based on the principle of subrogation. Its purpose is to avoid unjust enrichment by helping the payor get reimbursed by the person who *should* have paid—the person who is primarily responsible for payment. Although the assignment takes place automatically, the mortgagee is obligated upon request to give the payor an actual paper document of assignment showing that the payor now has the rights the mortgagee had before.

Perhaps the most common illustration of this principle involves a second mortgagee that learns that the borrower has defaulted in payment on the first mortgage. The second mortgagee can pay off the first mortgage in full. By doing so, the second mortgagee acquires the first mortgage and the right to enforce the note that it secures, if it is a recourse obligation. Why would a second mortgagee exercise this right? The primary reason is to gain control of the timing and procedure of foreclosure of the first mortgage. The second mortgagee can now determine whether and when to foreclose and whether foreclosure will be judicial or by power of sale, if the jurisdiction permits the latter. If property values are presently low but the second mortgagee expects them to rise, gaining this control may mean the difference between the second mortgagee being wiped out by a foreclosure of the first and being able to recover, in the long run, at least part of its debt.

Tender. Suppose a person that is entitled to pay the debt offers to pay it in full, but the lender refuses to accept the money. If the offeror has the ability to pay, its offer to do so is a tender. For many purposes, a tender is as good as an actual payment. It immediately stops interest from accruing on the mortgage debt and entitles the payor to a release or an assignment of the mortgage.

The tender must be in cash or "good funds;" a tender of a new promissory note for the balance owing on the old note does not extinguish the mortgage. See FNMA v. McAuliffe, 226 A.D.2d 497, 641 N.Y.S.2d 115 (1996). Moreover, the tender must be "kept good" in the sense that the party who tenders must continue to be ready, willing, and able to pay. The tender must also be unconditional, except for the condition that the lender provide a document of release or assignment).

On all these matters involving discharge and tender, see Restatement (Third) of Property (Mortgages) § 6.4 (1997).

Mortgagees' disclosures. A person that is ready to pay off a mortgage debt needs to know the debt amount. Lenders often keep better records than borrowers, and, even if the prospective payor has calculated the payoff amount, it would like to be certain that the lender agrees. Therefore, lenders customarily provide "payoff letters" or statements upon request, usually for a fee.

In addition to the person who is paying off the loan, a number of other people may have a legitimate need to know the balance and status of the mortgage debt. For example, a buyer who intends to assume or take subject to an existing debt needs to know its amount. A bidder at the foreclosure sale of a junior mortgage also needs to know the amount of the senior mortgage debt, as does a junior lienor that intends to redeem a senior mortgage to protect against its foreclosure.

Perhaps 15 or so jurisdictions statutorily require lenders to provide payoff statements, but they are often poorly drafted. The Restatement (Third) of Property (Mortgages) § 1.6 (1997) takes the view that lenders have a common-law obligation to provide a statement of the amount owing, the current interest rate, the basis of adjustment if the rate is adjustable, any additional fees and charges the lender claims, and whether the loan is in default or has been accelerated. The lender must also disclose the balance in any escrow account to pay taxes and insurance, for example, and the identity of any person that the lender knows has acquired an interest in the mortgage or the debt.

A request for this information must be made for good cause by the mortgagor, another person whose performance is secured by the mortgage, the holder of any interest in the real estate, or a prospective bidder at a foreclosure sale. A mortgagee that fails to disclose within a reasonable time after such a request is liable for damages. In addition, an incorrect disclosure may estop the lender to deny its accuracy as against someone who has reasonably and detrimentally relied on it. Note that a mortgagor may have difficulty proving that it detrimentally relied on an incorrect statement, because the mortgagor knows or should know at least the approximate balance owing. See, e.g., In re Royal Meadows Stables, Inc., 187 B.R. 516 (Bankr.E.D.Va.1995) (borrower had at least "constructive knowledge" of the actual debt amount). Compare Freedom Fin. Thrift & Loan v. Golden Pacific Bank, 20 Cal.App.4th 1305, 25 Cal.Rptr.2d 235 (1993), in which a new lender paid off an existing loan on the basis of a payoff statement that the old lender later claimed was erroneously low. The court held the old lender was estopped against the new lender but could still recover the remaining amount of the debt from the borrower.

Section 201(d) of the Model Residential Mortgage Satisfaction Act contains language similar to that of the Restatement. It requires the payoff statement to include "(1) the date on which it was prepared and the payoff amount as of that date, including the amount by type of each fee, charge, or other sum included within the payoff amount; (2) the information reasonably necessary to calculate the payoff amount as of the requested payoff date, including the per diem interest amount; and (3) the payment cutoff time, if any, the address or place where payment must be made, and any limitation as to the authorized method of payment."

1. PREPAYMENT

Contrary to the pervasive popular belief, a mortgagee has a common law right to refuse an early tender or "prepayment" of principal or interest. This rule is derived from the classic case of Brown v. Cole, 14 L.J. (N.S.) Ch. 167, Chancery, 1845, in which the court stated that, if mortgagors "were allowed to pay off their mortgage money at any time after the execution of the mortgage, it might be attended with extreme inconvenience to mortgagees, who generally advance their money as an investment." For many mortgagees, prepayment creates more than a problem of reinvesting the prepaid funds. If the mortgage is held by a vendor who desires installment sale reporting of his gain on the sale under § 453 of the Internal Revenue Code, unanticipated prepayment can result in greatly increased tax liability.

In an attempt to buttress their common law rights, mortgagees sometimes include "lock-out" mortgage provisions that specifically prohibit prepayment for a fixed period of time or even for the entire life of the loan. See, e.g., Hartford Life Ins. Co. v. Randall, 283 Or. 297, 583 P.2d 1126 (1978) (mortgage note provision that prohibited any payoff for eleven years is not an unreasonable restraint on alienation); George v. Fowler, 96 Wash.App. 187, 978 P.2d 565 (1999) (upholding a lock-out for the entire life of the loan). Of course, even if the loan is "locked out" and gives the borrower no prepayment privilege, the lender may still accept a prepayment voluntarily if the borrower sweetens the deal by agreeing to pay a fee. See Tyler v. Equitable Life Assur. Socy., 512 So.2d 55 (Ala.1987). But under common law principles, a "lock-out" clause is unnecessary, because a lender has no duty to accept a prepayment, unless the mortgage or note expressly authorize prepayment.

The common law rule, called "perfect tender in time," has been widely criticized as contrary to most borrowers' expectations. The Restatement (Third) of Property (Mortgages) § 6.1 (1997) rejects it, providing instead that: "In the absence of an agreement restricting or prohibiting payment of the mortgage obligation prior to maturity, the mortgagor has a right to make such payment in whole or in part." It seems little enough to ask of mortgagees, who nearly always draft the loan documents, to expressly restrict prepayment if that do not want it. However, only two jurisdictions have agreed. See Mahoney v. Furches, 503 Pa. 60, 468 A.2d 458 (1983); Skyles v. Burge, 789 S.W.2d 116 (Mo.App.1990). The arguments are nicely set out in Metropolitan Life Ins. Co. v. Promenade Towers Mut. Housing Corp., 84 Md.App. 702, 581 A.2d 846 (1990), which follows "perfect tender in time." See also, Ex parte Brannon, 683 So.2d 994 (Ala.1996); Poommipanit v. Sloan, 1 Neb.App. 1132, 510 N.W.2d 542 (1993) (applying the common law rule to a real estate installment contract).[13]

As a matter of practice, many mortgagees permit prepayment and provide for it in their mortgage documents. However, they may exact a "prepayment penalty" or "yield maintenance fee" for the privilege of prepaying the loan. Much of the following material focuses on judicial and legislative attempts to deal with such fees. For comprehensive treatments of mortgage prepayment, see Megan W. Murray, Prepayment Premiums: Contracting for Future Financial Stability in the Commercial Lending Market, 96 Iowa L.Rev. 1037 (2011); Dale A. Whitman, Mortgage Prepayment Clauses: A Legal and Economic Analysis, 40 U.C.L.A. L.Rev. 851 (1993); Frank S. Alexander, Mortgage Prepayment: The Trial of Common Sense, 72 Cornell L.Rev. 288 (1987).

LOPRESTI V. WELLS FARGO BANK, N.A.

Superior Court of New Jersey, Appellate Division, 2014
435 N.J.Super. 311, 88 A.3d 944

The opinion of the court was delivered by PARRILLO, P.J.A.D.

* * * On March 1, 2002, Body Max executed and delivered a Promissory Note to defendant's predecessor, First Union, as evidence of a $550,000 loan. The terms of this note included an interest rate of 6.75% and required Body Max to make "consecutive monthly payments of principal and interest in the amount of $4,898.00 commencing on April 1, 2002 and continuing on the same day of each month thereafter until fully

---

[13] Courts rarely depart from the "perfect tender in time" rule, but it can occur. See Littlejohn v. Parrish, 163 Ohio App.3d 456, 839 N.E.2d 49 (2005), in which the court held that, if the borrower was willing to pay a fee that would fully compensate the lenders for their lost interest income, the lenders' refusal to accept prepayment breached the implied contractual duty of good faith and fair dealing.

paid." The total principal and interest accrued on the loan was "due and payable on March 1, 2007." In addition, this original note contained a prepayment provision setting a fee of 1% in the event Body Max paid the loan prior to the termination date:

> PREPAYMENT COMPENSATION. Principal may be prepaid in whole or in part at any time; *provided, however,* if principal is paid before it is due under this Note, whether voluntary, mandatory, upon acceleration or otherwise, such prepayment shall include a fee equal to 1% of the amount prepaid.

> Any prepayment in whole or in part shall include accrued interest and all other sums then due under any of the Loan Documents. No partial prepayment shall affect the obligation of Borrower to make any payment of principal or interest due under this Note on the due dates specified.

This note was executed by Salvatore Lopresti (Lopresti) in his capacity as President of Body Max.

In order to secure payment of its obligations under the original note, Body Max executed a Mortgage and Absolute Assignment of Leases dated March 1, 2002 to First Union. This mortgage covered Body Max's principal place of business, a gymnasium located on Delsea Drive in Washington Township. This document was also executed by Lopresti as President of Body Max.

Additionally, on March 1, 2002, Lopresti executed and delivered to First Union an Unconditional Guaranty to provide assurance that Body Max would fulfill its obligations under the original note. To secure payment and performance of the guaranty, plaintiffs executed and delivered a Mortgage and Absolute Assignment Agreement of Leases to First Union, covering the premises where their primary residence was located, also in Washington Township.

Pursuant to the loan transaction of March 1, 2002, First Union advanced the full $550,000 loan proceeds to Body Max. Body Max then transferred the funds to TD Bank in order to pay off a prior loan borrowed by Body Max. Plaintiffs did not personally receive any of the loan proceeds.

Thereafter, on December 20, 2005, Body Max modified the terms of its original note with Wachovia Bank, First Union's successor and Wells Fargo's immediate predecessor. Lopresti, as President of Body Max, executed and delivered the modified note of December 20, 2005 in the amount of $460,195.41. The modified note stated that it "renew[ed], extend[ed] and/or modifie[d] that [Original Note of March 1, 2002], evidencing an original principal amount of $550,000.00." The terms of the modified note included an interest rate of 7.25% and called for "consecutive monthly payments of principal and interest in the amount of $4,228.19

commencing on January 20, 2006, and continuing on the same day of each month thereafter until fully paid." All of the principal and interest on this modified note were "due and payable on December 20, 2020." Further, the modified note defined "loan documents" as "all documents executed in connection with or related to the loan evidenced by this Note and any prior notes which evidence all or any portion of the loan evidenced by this Note . . . guaranty agreements, . . . [and] mortgage instruments. . . ."

The December 20, 2005 modified note also contained a prepayment provision, structured to compensate Wachovia for an early payoff of the loan, in the event market interest rates had fallen. The provision states:

COMPENSATION UPON PREPAYMENT OR ACCELERATION.

In addition to principal, interest and any other amounts due under this Note, Borrower shall on demand pay to Bank any "Breakage Fee" due hereunder for any voluntary or mandatory prepayment or acceleration, in whole or in part, of principal of this Note occurring prior to the date such principal would, but for that prepayment or acceleration, have become due. For any date of prepayment or acceleration ("Break Date"), a Breakage Fee shall be due if the rate under "A" below exceeds the rate under "B" below and shall be determined as follows:

Breakage Fee = the sum of the products of $((A-B) \times C)$ for each installment of principal being prepaid, where:

A = A rate equal to the sum of (i) the bond equivalent yield (bid side) of the U.S. Treasury security with a maturity closest to the Maturity Date as reported by *The Wall Street Journal* (or other published source) on the funding date of this Note, plus (ii) 1/2%.

B = A rate equal to the bond equivalent yield (bid side) of the U.S. Treasury security with a maturity closest to the Maturity Date as reported by *The Wall Street Journal* (or other published source) on the Break Date.

C = The principal installment amount being prepaid times (the number of days remaining until the scheduled due date for such installment divided by 360).

"Maturity Date" is the date on which the final payment of principal of this Note would, but for any prepayment or acceleration, have become due.

Breakage Fees are payable as liquidated damages, are a reasonable pre-estimate of the losses, costs and expenses Bank would incur in the event of any prepayment or acceleration of this

Note, are not a penalty, will not require claim for, or proof of, actual damages, and Bank's determination thereof shall be conclusive and binding in the absence of manifest error.

Any prepayment in whole or in part shall include accrued interest and all other sums then due under any of the Loan Documents. No partial prepayment shall affect Borrower's obligation to make any payment of principal or interest due under this Note on the date specified in the Repayment Terms paragraph of this Note until this Note has been paid in full.

On May 19, 2010, Body Max attempted to refinance the original 2002 loan, as modified by the 2005 loan, in order to obtain a lower interest rate and to reduce the prepayment fees on the loan. However, about two months later, Wachovia declined Body Max's request due to the company's "negative equity positions and losses."

Subsequently, Body Max was able to obtain refinancing from TD Bank Commercial Lending (TD Bank) and requested a payoff amount from Wachovia for the balance of the loan. On July 21, 2010, Wachovia provided Body Max with a payoff of all amounts due on the loan. TD Bank then transferred the total payoff amount of $416,838.78 directly to Wells Fargo, which included $368,383.99 of principal, $148.38 of accrued interest and $48,306.41 in prepayment fees. A Settlement Statement was executed by TD Bank and Body Max evidencing the total amount of the loan owed to Wells Fargo, including the prepayment fee, that was advanced by TD Bank on behalf of Body Max.

According to Wells Fargo, plaintiffs did not issue any personal checks from any of their personal accounts to pay the principal loan or the $48,306.41 prepayment fee due to the Bank. Rather, as noted, the prepayment fees were paid by TD Bank directly to Wells Fargo out of the proceeds of its loan to Body Max.

As noted, plaintiffs filed a complaint alleging that defendant violated both the Prepayment Law and the New Jersey Consumer Fraud Act, *N.J.S.A.* 56:8–1 to –20, by assessing and collecting a prepayment charge as provided for in the promissory note executed in connection with the business loan to Body Max. In its summary judgment motion, defendant maintained that plaintiffs lacked standing because they did not have a sufficient stake in the matter inasmuch as Body Max paid the prepayment fee through its refinancing arrangement with TD Bank. Substantively, defendant argued that the protection of the Prepayment Law allowing for prepayment *without* penalty to any "mortgagor," other than a corporation, simply does not apply to commercial loans between sophisticated business parties, such as the transaction at issue here. Additionally, defendant contended that the formula used to calculate the prepayment fee was reasonable and designed to protect the Bank's interests in the event that interest rates had fallen prior to the maturity of the loan. Finally, defendant maintained that there was no evidence of unlawful conduct to support the consumer fraud count.

Plaintiffs countered that they have standing as personal guarantors of the bank loan; that the Prepayment Law applies to this transaction because the initial loan was secured by their personal residence and they were personally liable for the obligations under the loan; that the prepayment fee was unreasonable because the modification of more than 13% was greater than the initial bargained for prepayment fee of 1% and Wells Fargo failed to provide documentation evidencing how it reached the amount charged; and finally that the prepayment penalty amounted to a violation of the Consumer Fraud Act.

In granting summary judgment for defendant, dismissing plaintiffs' complaint in its entirety, the motion judge held that the Prepayment Law did not apply, reasoning:

> The corporation willingly negotiated the terms of [its] loan with the banks that were involved here. . . . There were sophisticated parties. Certainly the reason why a prepayment penalty cannot be imposed on the individual is to protect that individual, but it is not felt it was necessary when we have a corporation involved.

The court further explained "that there was a guaranty executed, which did involve the plaintiffs in this matter, but . . . the guaranty never came into play, the individuals never came into play in this matter, [because] there was no default."

The judge also found no Consumer Fraud Act violation:

> When we're dealing with the New Jersey Consumer Fraud Act, . . . a plaintiff must allege three elements under the Consumer Fraud Act. One, unlawful conduct by the defendant, and then we go on to an ascertainable loss and a causal relationship. . . .

> I find that the plaintiff in this matter is unable to provide the [c]ourt with any evidence whatsoever of unlawful conduct by the defendant in this matter and, therefore, that cause of action cannot be sustained either in this instance. They have failed on the first prong of the three-part test under the Act.

This appeal by plaintiffs followed. * * *

Pursuant to *N.J.S.A.* 46:10B–2, "[p]repayment of a mortgage loan may be made by or on behalf of a mortgagor at any time without penalty." Consequently, "[a]ny holder of a mortgage loan . . . who shall knowingly demand and receive prepayment fees . . . shall be liable to the mortgagor for the return of the whole amount of the prepayment fees so received, plus interest. . . ." *N.J.S.A.* 46:10B–5.

Thus, the Prepayment Law prohibits the charging of a prepayment fee on a "mortgage loan," which is defined as "a loan secured by an interest in real property consisting of land upon which is erected or to be erected, in whole or in part *with the proceeds of such loan,* a structure containing . . . dwelling units. . . ." *N.J.S.A.* 46:10B–1(a) (emphasis added). Moreover, a "mortgagor" is defined as "any person *other than a corporation* liable for the payment of a mortgage loan, and the owner of the real property which secures the payment of a mortgage loan[.]" *N.J.S.A.* 46:10B–1(b) (emphasis added).

The Prepayment Law applies to individual consumers, not commercial mortgagors, as the Legislature clearly "intended to protect individual mortgagors from being locked into long-term mortgages with excessive interest rates, but felt that more sophisticated commercial mortgagors needed no such protection." *Shinn v. Encore Mortg. Servs., Inc.,* 96 *F.Supp.*2d 419, 422 (D.N.J.2000). Indeed, we have upheld the use of prepayment fees negotiated on commercial loans between sophisticated parties. See, e.g., *Westmark Commercial Mortg. Fund IV v. Teenform Assocs., L.P.,* 362 *N.J.Super.* 336, 347–48, 827 *A.*2d 1154 (App.Div.2003) (holding that the prepayment premium on a commercial loan was permissible where the debtor freely entered into the contract, the terms of the contract were clear and unambiguous, and the parties were experienced and sophisticated); *Mony Life Ins. Co. v. Paramus Parkway Building, Ltd.,* 364 *N.J.Super.* 92, 105, 834 *A.*2d 475 (App.Div.2003) (holding that a clear and unambiguous prepayment premium clause was "valid and enforceable under New Jersey law[ ]").

In *Westmark, supra,* the debtor challenged the prepayment premiums that were charged after the creditor accelerated the payout under the loan contract. 362 *N.J.Super.* at 343, 827 *A.*2d 1154. We noted, at the outset, that "[a] borrower does not have the right, under New Jersey law, to prepay a commercial loan, unless the documents afford that right." *Id.* at 343–44, 827 *A.*2d 1154 (citing *Norwest Bank Minnesota v. Blair Road Assocs.,* 252 *F.Supp.*2d 86, 97 (D.N.J.2003)). Thus, " '[s]ince a lender has the right not to have the loan prepaid but rely on collecting the interest contracted for, the lender is entitled to charge a penalty to the borrower for the privilege of the prepayment.' " *Id.* at 344, 827 *A.*2d 1154 (quoting *Norwest, supra,* 252 *F.Supp.*2d at 97). Further, we determined that prepayment clauses were "designed to protect a lender against potential losses it may incur if a loan is paid earlier than contracted for." *Ibid.* (citing *United States v. Harris,* 246 *F.*3d 566, 573 (6th Cir.2001)).

In holding that the prepayment fee in *Westmark, supra,* was enforceable, we relied, in part, on the *Restatement (Third) of Property:*

Mortgages § 6.2 (1997). *Id.* at 347, 827 *A.*2d 1154. Specifically, the Restatement notes that "if the borrower fully understood and had the opportunity to bargain over the clause, either with the assistance of counsel or by virtue of the borrower's own experience and expertise, the clause will ordinarily be enforced." *Restatement (Third), supra,* § 6.2 comment c. In addition, we reasoned that "to deem the [prepayment] clause unenforceable[ ] . . . would be providing defendants with a better contract than they were able to negotiate for themselves. . . ." *Id.* at 347, 827 *A.*2d 1154; *see also Karl's Sales & Serv. v. Gimbel Bros., Inc.,* 249 *N.J.Super.* 487, 493, 592 *A.*2d 647 (App.Div.) (finding that courts may not "remake a better contract for the parties than they themselves have seen fit to enter into, or to alter it for the benefit of one party and to the detriment of the other [ ]"), *certif. denied,* 127 *N.J.* 548, 606 *A.*2d 362 (1991).

Here, it is undisputed that the subject matter of plaintiffs' complaint involves a commercial loan to a business, and the loan proceeds were used for business, and not personal, much less residential home, purposes. Plaintiffs offer no proof to the contrary.

Nevertheless, plaintiffs argue that they fall within the Prepayment Law's definition of "mortgagor" because they are "any person other than a corporation" and they were liable for payment of the loan in the event Body Max defaulted. Specifically, they point to the guaranty executed as part of the initial promissory note, which provided their residential property as collateral security in the event Body Max defaulted on the loan. Plaintiffs' statutory interpretation is simply wrong.

On March 1, 2002, Body Max executed and delivered a Promissory Note to First Union as evidence of a $550,000 loan. Significantly, the borrower under the promissory note was not plaintiffs but their business, Body Max. In fact, the 2002 and 2005 loan documents that contained the prepayment provisions explicitly designate Body Max as the borrower.

Just as significant, the full amount of the loan was advanced to Body Max under the original note. In other words, Wells Fargo transferred the loan proceeds directly to Body Max's corporate account, not to plaintiffs' personal accounts, and the proceeds were not used in connection with plaintiffs' real property. Also, to secure the amounts advanced under the original note, Body Max executed and delivered a mortgage on the commercial property where the corporation conducts business.

Even more fatal to plaintiffs' position, the mortgage referred to in their complaint, although it covers their residence, does not secure a personal loan, since, as noted, the loan proceeds were not used in connection with plaintiffs' real property. Rather, the mortgage secures plaintiffs' personal guarantee of the obligations of their business, Body Max, under the Wells Fargo commercial loan. As such, because the loan proceeds from the bank were not used in connection with plaintiffs' real property, their residential mortgage is not a "mortgage loan" within the definition of *N.J.S.A.* 46:10B–1(a), and therefore Wells Fargo is not the "holder of a mortgage loan" subject to the protections against prepayment fees in the Prepayment Law.

In fact, neither plaintiffs' guarantee nor the mortgage on their residence provide for a prepayment fee, and plaintiffs did not pay the prepayment fee in this matter. Rather, the prepayment fee is expressly provided for in the note executed by Body Max and naming Body Max as the borrower. Pursuant to that contractual provision, it was Body Max that was charged the prepayment fee, and Body Max that paid all accounts owed to Wells Fargo, including the prepayment fee, when Body Max refinanced the loan with TD Bank.

To reiterate then, Body Max was the actual borrower and "mortgagor" under the Wells Fargo loan. The 2002 initial loan and the 2005 loan modification were both executed by Body Max and required the corporation to fulfill the loan obligations, including the prepayment fee. And to that end, Body Max fulfilled its obligations to Wells Fargo, including payment of the contractual prepayment fee, through its refinanced loan with TD Bank. And because of Body Max's corporate status, Wells Fargo, as holder of the mortgage loan, was exempted from the Prepayment Law's proscription against charging such a fee. *N.J.S.A.* 46:10B–1(b). Thus, we concur with the motion judge's holding that the Prepayment Law is inapplicable to the instant transaction.

We are therefore left with plaintiffs' alternative contention that the prepayment fee in the 2005 modified loan was excessive. Specifically, plaintiffs argue that the modified prepayment provision, which increased the 1% fee to over 13%, was unreasonable, and that the $48,306.41 prepayment charge amounted to an unlawful penalty or stipulated damage clause.

Defendant maintains that the "breakage fee" formula used to calculate the prepayment charge was structured to do nothing more than compensate the Bank for the investment value lost in the event Body Max paid the loan off early at a time when interest rates had fallen. Specifically, Wells Fargo contends that if the interest rates at the time of refinancing were higher than the interest rates when Body Max received funding for the loan, there would have been no prepayment fee. Thus, Wells Fargo asserts that the formula was not an arbitrary penalty, but rather a mechanism to protect its investment. We agree.

In asserting that the prepayment charge was unreasonable, plaintiffs rely exclusively on *MetLife Capital Financial Corporation v. Washington Avenue Associates L.P.,* 159 *N.J.* 484, 495–501, 732 *A.*2d 493 (1998), which addressed the reasonableness of a 5% late fee on a commercial loan. At the outset, the Court determined that "liquidated damages provisions in a commercial contract between sophisticated parties are presumptively reasonable and the party challenging the clause bears the burden of proving its unreasonableness." *Id.* at 496, 732 A.2d 493. The Court found that the reasonableness of a stipulated damages provision requires a review of the totality of the circumstances. *Id.* at 495, 732 A.2d 493. After considering several factors regarding this late fee, including (1) the normal industry standard; (2) the use of the fee to compensate the lender for administrative costs; (3) the fact that the "loan involved an arms-length, fully negotiated transaction between two sophisticated commercial parties, each represented by counsel[,]"; and (4) the absence of fraud, duress or unconscionability on the part of the lender, the Court concluded that the borrower was unable to overcome the presumptive reasonableness of the fee. *Id.* at 500, 732 A.2d 493.

Here, too, plaintiffs have not overcome the presumptive reasonableness of the prepayment fee. As the trial court noted, the loan transaction involved sophisticated parties, who freely negotiated the terms of the loan, and the prepayment provision was "clearly spelled out" in the 2005 loan modification. In addition, as Wells Fargo asserts, the "breakage fee" was not an arbitrary penalty, but rather a carefully constructed formula used to protect the Bank's loan investment in the event interest rates dropped prior to the termination date. The formula sought to protect Wells Fargo's investment by accounting for the market interest rates at the time of prepayment in comparison to the interest rates at the time the loan was first advanced.[3] According to this formula, if the interest rates at the time Body Max prematurely paid the loan were higher than when it first received the loan, then there would have been no prepayment fee. Thus, the totality of the circumstances concerning the prepayment provision, including the sophistication of the parties involved, the use of the fee to compensate Wells Fargo, and considering that the formula used to calculate the breakage fee was "clearly spelled out," demonstrate that the charge was neither excessive nor unreasonable.

Finally, having found no violation by defendant of the Prepayment Law, and therefore no unlawful conduct or unconscionable commercial practice, plaintiffs simply have not established a viable, valid claim under the Consumer Fraud Act. Therefore, the dismissal of this count of plaintiffs' complaint was also proper.

Affirmed.

---

[3] For each monthly installment payment due on the loan, the breakage fee was calculated as the difference between the yield on Treasuries with the same maturity as the loan, as of the date the loan was originally funded, and the yield on Treasuries as of the date the loan was prepaid. The result is a measure of the difference in the investment value of funds on the date of the loan and the date of the prepayment. This figure was then multiplied by the amount of each principal installment being prepaid times the number of days remaining until the scheduled due date for such installment divided by 360.

NOTES

1. *Language permitting prepayment.* Even under the common law rule, lenders sometimes include language permitting prepayment without realizing that they have done so. If the promissory note provides for payments of X dollars per month "or more" or if it states that the entire balance must be paid by X date "if not sooner paid," the borrower can prepay the balance owing at any time. See Latimer v. Grundy County Nat'l Bank, 239 Ill.App.3d 1000, 180 Ill.Dec. 400, 607 N.E.2d 294 (1993); Acord v. Jones, 211 Ga.App. 682, 440 S.E.2d 679 (1994). The casual use of such boilerplate phrases can backfire against the lender.

2. *Types of prepayment clauses.* Many mortgages expressly permit prepayment, but only if the borrower pays an additional fee or "penalty." Such fees are relatively rare in home mortgage loans but are widely used in loans on commercial property. A variety of formulas may be used to calculate the fee, such as:

- Six months' interest on the amount by which prepayments in any 12 month period exceed 20% of the original principal amount.

- A fixed percentage, such as 2% of the amount being prepaid. The percentage may decline over time as the loan gets closer to maturity, such as, 2% during the loan's first five years and 1% thereafter.)

- The present value of difference between the interest the lender would have earned on the mortgage loan for the remaining term and the interest it would earn on the same sum if invested in some alternative investment, such as U.S. government securities of an equivalent term. This type of clause is sometimes referred to as a "yield maintenance" fee. The wording of such clauses tends to be complex and filled with mathematical jargon that is unintelligible to many readers. Here is an example of a relatively clear and simple version, with the definitions of the terms omitted:

> "Required Yield Maintenance" shall mean an amount equal to the positive excess of (i) the present value ("PV") of all future installments of principal and interest due under this Note, including the principal amount due at maturity (collectively, "All Future Payments"), discounted at an interest rate per annum equal to the Treasury Constant Maturity Yield Index published during the second full week preceding the date on which such premium is payable for instruments having a maturity coterminous with the remaining term of this Note, over (ii) the principal amount of this Note outstanding immediately before such

prepayment [(PV of All Future Payments) − (principal balance at time of prepayment) = prepayment fee].

This sort of clause is now widely used and enforced by the courts. See, e.g., Great Plains Real Estate Devel., L.L.C. v. Union Central Life Ins. Co., 536 F.3d 939 (8th Cir.2008); In re AE Hotel Venture, 321 B.R. 209 (Bankr. N.D.Ill.2005). The use of the yield on U.S. Treasury securities is obviously unrealistic. In all probability, the lender is going to invest the prepaid funds in another mortgage loan, not in Treasury bonds. Nonetheless, the courts applying state law have nearly always approved the use of a "Treasury Flat" reference rate in yield maintenance clauses. See, e.g., River East Plaza, L.L.C. v. Variable Annuity Life Ins. Co., 498 F.3d 718 (7th Cir.2007).

3. *Attacking prepayment fees.* Borrowers have been almost completely unsuccessful in attacking prepayment fees in state courts. This does not seem surprising. After all, if a clause "locking out" the loan and allowing no prepayment at all is enforceable, as it clearly is, then a clause allowing prepayment for a fee should be enforceable as well.

The usual statement is that a court will refuse to enforce a prepayment fee only if it "shocks the conscience," and fees that are shocking enough are so rare as to be virtually nonexistent. See, e.g., Shadoan v. World Sav. & Loan Ass'n, 219 Cal.App.3d 97, 268 Cal.Rptr. 207 (1990). Perhaps the most extreme case is Williams v. Fassler, 110 Cal.App.3d 7, 167 Cal.Rptr. 545 (1980), which involved a seller-financed mortgage that provided for a fee of 50% of the prepayment amount. The mortgagee-seller testified that he wanted to avoid the negative income tax consequences that could have resulted if more than 30% of the total purchase price had been paid during the year of sale and that his accountant advised him that the 50% fee would protect him. The court said: "We * * * hold that in a transaction between private parties, an agreement specifying a 50 percent prepayment penalty is valid if the penalty is reasonably related to the obligee's anticipated risk of incurring increased tax liability upon the occurrence of the prepayment."

Other grounds for attack have been asserted but without much success. Sometimes, borrowers argue that the fee is a form of liquidated damages, and, therefore, must be a reasonable advance estimate of the probable damages the lender will suffer from prepayment. We agree that a prepayment fee is liquidated damages. However, state courts have been quite unreceptive to the use of this liquidated damages/penalty analysis. See Lazzareschi Inv. Co. v. San Francisco Fed. Sav. & Loan Ass'n, 22 Cal.App.3d 303, 99 Cal.Rptr. 417 (1971). Even when they adopt the analysis, they nearly always find the fee to be a reasonable estimate and uphold it. See TMG Life Ins. Co. v. Ashner, 21 Kan.App.2d 234, 898 P.2d 1145 (1995).

Occasionally, a borrower tries to convince a court that a prepayment fee is a form of excessive interest and violates the state's usury statute. However, this argument nearly always fails, as it should. Interest is a charge for the *use* of money, while a prepayment fee is a charge for *giving back* the money, rather than using it. See C.C. Port, Ltd. v. Davis-Penn Mortg. Co., 891 F.Supp. 371 (S.D.Tex.1994).

In sum, attacks on prepayment fees in state courts seem doomed to failure. The Restatement (Third) of Property (Mortgages) § 6.2 agrees. It provides that, except for the application of the general contract law principles of good faith, fair dealing, and unconscionability, "an agreement that prohibits payment of the mortgage obligation prior to maturity is enforceable, and * * * an agreement requiring the mortgagor to pay a fee or charge as a condition of such payment is enforceable."

4. *Prepayment fees in bankruptcy.* A borrower who is in bankruptcy often tenders a prepayment, typically in a Chapter 11 reorganization. In this situation, the question is not so much whether the fee is enforceable under state law (though obviously it must be for the lender to collect it) as whether the fee is collectible as a *secured* claim in bankruptcy. If the fee is recognized as enforceable but unsecured, the lender will stand in line with the debtor's general creditors and may recover only a few cents on the dollar. But if the fee is regarded as a secured claim and if the real estate has enough value above the amount of the mortgage debt itself, the lender will recover the full fee.

Whether the fee can be treated as a secured claim is governed by Bankruptcy Code § 506(b), which simply requires that such fees be "reasonable." This standard is a far cry from the "shock the conscience" test usually employed under state law. The bankruptcy courts usually treat the fee as a species of liquidated damages, and they initially were quite aggressive in finding prepayment fees to be unreasonable. Indeed, yield maintenance clauses often came in for sharp criticism in the bankruptcy courts. For example, a rather crude and simplistic yield maintenance formula might set the fee as the amount prepaid, times the number of years remaining on the loan, times the difference between the contract interest rate and the interest rate on U.S. government securities of the same maturity as the remaining loan term. For example, assume a loan with a $1 million balance, an 6% interest rate, and a 10 year term is being prepaid. Further assume that the current interest yield on ten-year U.S. government bonds is 3%. Under the formula above, the prepayment fee would be $1 million × 10 years × 3%, or $300,000.

However, some features of this clause tend to exaggerate the lender's damages, including:

(a) The formula above does not take the time value of money into account. It imposes the fee immediately, while the lender's interest yield would have been earned only over the next ten years. It thus overcompensates the lender. The interest differential should be discounted to present value terms.

(b) In most cases, the mortgage loan calls for monthly payments that will fully or at least partially amortize it over its term. Thus, if $1 million is being prepaid, that $1 million would not have been outstanding for the next ten years even in the absence of prepayment. A yield maintenance formula that assumes the amount being prepaid would otherwise have been the loan's balance for its full remaining term is usually unrealistic and tends to overcompensate the lender.

Bankruptcy courts are highly unreceptive to formulas that to overcompensate lenders in these ways. As one court put it: "The damage formula is simple and well established. It is the difference in the interest yield between the contract rate and the market rate at the time of prepayment, projected over the term of the loan and then discounted to arrive at present value. * * * Any prepayment charge should be wholly or largely dependent upon such a calculation." In re A.J. Lane & Co., 113 B.R. 821 (Bankr.D.Mass.1990). Similar criticisms are found in In re Kroh Bros. Dev. Co., 88 B.R. 997 (Bankr.W.D.Mo.1988); In re Skyler Ridge, 80 B.R. 500 (Bankr.C.D.Cal.1987). Even when the bankruptcy courts treat the enforceability issue as entirely one of state law, they often take an aggressively pro-borrower view of state law. See In re Wiston XXIV Ltd. Partn., 170 B.R. 453 (D.Kan.1994), aff'd, 45 F.3d 441 (10th Cir.1994).

An additional objection to many yield maintenance clauses is that they use the current rate on U.S. Treasury obligations of the same maturity as the remaining loan term as a "reference" or discount rate in computing the present value of the fee. It is quite arguable that this is unreasonable, because the lender will very likely use the funds to make another real estate loan, rather than to purchase government bonds. The lender may have a shortfall in return for a brief period until another real estate lending opportunity arises. but, in the long run, the rate on similar mortgage loans, not the government bond rate, is the relevant rate.

However, more recently, yield maintenance provisions have been faring better in bankruptcy courts. Several more recent decisions accept the use of the U.S. obligation rate as a reference rate. See In re CP Holdings, Inc., 332 B.R. 380 (W.D.Mo.2005):

> The Court rejects CP Holdings' [borrower's] argument that the interest rate on commercial first-mortgage loans should be used when calculating the reinvestment yield, rather than the yield on a U.S. Treasury issue, for two reasons. First, this substitution would be offensive to the basic notion of freedom of contract as the parties agreed that the yield on a U.S. Treasury issue would be used to calculate the reinvestment yield CP Holdings and CALPERS [lender], two "sophisticated and experienced business parties," contracted to have the prepayment premium calculated using the yield on a U.S. Treasury issue. (Hr'g Tr. 132:20–143:2; 138:7–140:1). The Court, in deference to long-standing principles of contract law, declines CP Holdings' request to impermissibly rewrite the contract in contravention of the parties bargained-for agreement.
>
> Second, the testimony of both experts supports a finding that the use of the yield on a U.S. Treasury issue to calculate the reinvestment

yield is reasonable. Randolph, CALPERS expert, testified that the yield on a U.S. Treasury issue provides a stable and relatively secure interest rate. Pflaum, CP Holdings' expert, recognized that "only Treasury instruments are absolutely default free," can be "move[d] with the press of a button," "are held as reserve by central banks," and are used "to develop and structure financial derivatives." (Pflaum Test. 84:19–85:3). Accordingly, the parties made a reasonable attempt to forecast the damages anticipated by acceleration by using the yield on a U.S. Treasury in the prepayment premium formula because such an investment is safe, easy to obtain and provides a relatively stable and secure rate of return.

Do you think the borrower's expert witness did a good job in this case? The applicable U.S. Treasury yield was 3.8687%, while the current rate on new commercial mortgages was alleged to be 6.5%. The choice of rates had an enormous impact on the amount of the resulting fee.

Unfortunately, no standard index exists for commercial mortgage loan rates. Arguably, creating such an index is infeasible, because these loans vary so widely. By contrast, the market for U.S. Treasury obligations is extremely liquid, and their rates are widely reported. Other decisions that have upheld the use of a U.S. Treasury rate include In re Doctors Hospital of Hyde Park, 508 B.R. 697 (Bankr.N.D.Ill. 2014); In re Vanderveer Estates Holdings, Inc., 283 B.R. 122 (Bankr.E.D.N.Y.2002). For a state court case upholding the use of a U.S. Treasury rate, see Santa Rosa KM Associates, Ltd., P.C. v. Principal Life Ins. Co., 41 Kan.App.2d 840, 206 P.3d 40, 48–49 (2009).

Incidentally, what happens if the bankruptcy court disallows the fee as a secured claim under § 506(b) on the basis of its unreasonableness? Does the court then substitute a fee of a reasonable amount? No such luck! The lender does not have a secured claim for the prepayment fee and must take its chances with the other unsecured creditors. This outcome is a stiff penalty for a lender that was too greedy in negotiating the loan.

5. *Prepayment caused by the mortgagee's acceleration.* An extremely important problem arises when a prepayment occurs, not because the borrower wants to prepay, but because lender accelerates the debt. Under the typical mortgage, at least four causes for acceleration may exist: (1) borrower's default; (2) exercise of a due-on-sale clause when the borrower transfers the real estate without the lender's approval; (3) payment of insurance proceeds due to a casualty that damages the property; and (4) payment of an eminent domain award due to a government taking of the property.

In all these settings, borrowers have argued that the prepayment was involuntary and, therefore, not within the scope of the prepayment clause. Courts in several early cases agreed with this argument and denied the fee, but recent cases seem to reflect a judicial change in attitude.

(a) *Acceleration on default.* When the prepayment clause clearly applies to prepayments resulting from acceleration for default, the courts will enforce it. See Willow Grove, Ltd., v. Fed. Nat'l Mortgage Ass'n, 2013 WL 6865127 (D.Colo. 2013); Planned Pethood Plus, Inc., 228 P.3d 262 (Colo.App.2010); Feinstein v. Ashplant, 961 So.2d 1074 (Fla.App.2007); In re AE Hotel Venture, 321 B.R. 209 (Bankr. N.D.Ill.2005); Citicorp Mortg., Inc. v. Morrisville Hampton Village Realty Ltd. Partn., 443 Pa.Super. 595, 662 A.2d 1120 (1995); Biancalana v. Fleming, 45 Cal.App.4th 698, 53 Cal.Rptr.2d 47 (1996). If the clause is unclear, a court is unlikely to enforce it. See In re Denver Merch. Mart, Inc., 740 F.3d 1052 (5th Cir.2014); In re Tri-State Ethanol, LLC, 369 B.R. 481 (D.S.D.2007); Broadway Bank v. Star Hospitality, Inc., 695 N.W.2d 43 (Table) (Iowa Ct.App.2004); In re McClung, 2003 WL 23807834 (Bankr. D. Kan. 2003). This distinction is now so well understood that a lender's lawyer who fails to make the point clear in the documents would be suspected of having lived in a cave for the past twenty years!

Does imposing the fee upon default violate any important public policy? The fee's purpose is to shift to the borrower the risk of prepayment and injury to the lender. That is the very risk that occurs when the borrower defaults and the lender accelerates. One can hardly expect the lender to forbear accelerating indefinitely in the face of a default.

(b) *Acceleration upon payment of casualty insurance or eminent domain proceeds.* Mortgages usually provide that the lender, at its option, may require application of casualty insurance or eminent domain proceeds to the outstanding mortgage debt. Whether such clauses are enforceable is a matter of debate. See Chapter Four, Section E supra. If such payments are applied to the loan balance they are, in a sense, prepayments. Can the lender demand a prepayment fee?

Courts traditionally refused to enforce the fee in this situation. However, courts in several recent cases have enforced it when the prepayment clause clearly required payment. See, e.g., Melin v. TCF Fin. Corp., 1995 WL 265064 (Minn.Ct.App.1995) (not reported in N.W.2d).

The Restatement (Third) Property (Mortgages) § 6.3 (1997) agrees that the fee should be collectible if the mortgage so provides but with an important exception. Suppose the mortgagor requests that the insurance or eminent domain funds be used to restore the real estate, rather than applied to the debt. Further suppose that restoration is economically feasible with the proceeds and would restore the property to at least its original value, but the mortgagee refuses this request. On these facts, no prepayment fee should be collectible, because the lender does not need the proceeds to protect its loan or security. The lender's demand is probably being made because interest rates have risen and the money can be relent at a higher rate. For the lender to collect the prepayment fee at the same time would be an unwarranted windfall.

(c) *Acceleration under a due-on-sale clause.* If the loan is secured by a one- to four-family home that is occupied by the owner, a federal regulation prohibits imposition of a prepayment fee. 12 C.F.R. § 191.5(b)(2), (b)(3). A few state also disallow a prepayment fee when a lender exercises a due-on-sale clause. See, e.g., N.Y. Real Prop.L. § 254–a. Suppose, however, that the property is not a 1- to 4-family residence and that no state statute applies. Courts usually treat the prepayment as "involuntary and refuse to impose the fee. See, e.g., McCausland v. Bankers Life Ins. Co., 110 Wash.2d 716, 757 P.2d 941 (1988); Tan v. California Fed. Sav. & Loan Ass'n, 140 Cal.App.3d 800, 189 Cal.Rptr. 775 (1983). However, in most of these cases, the documents did not clearly impose the prepayment fee when the lender accelerated under the due-on-sale clause.

If the loan documents clearly provide for a prepayment fee in this situation, how should the courts respond? There seem to be no recent cases, but the correct analysis, by analogy to our discussion of insurance and condemnation proceeds, is to ask why the lender accelerated. If the lender has a legitimate objection to the proposed real estate buyer's creditworthiness, the lender should be entitled to the prepayment fee, because it isn't the lender's fault that the borrower decided to sell to an unqualified person. On the other hand:

> If a lender elects to accelerate the debt upon sale because interest rates have increased [and not because the proposed buyer is unqualified], the lender should not also be allowed to collect a prepayment fee. The function of the prepayment fee or prohibition is to protect lenders from borrower refinancing in times of falling interest rates and should not be used to penalize borrowers who refuse to accept lender's [sic] increased interest rates at resale in times of rising rates. It is only fair that the lender be prohibited from demanding prepayment fees upon acceleration of the debt since, in that instance, it is the lender who is insisting on prepayment.

Warrington 611 Assocs. v. Aetna Life Ins. Co., 705 F.Supp. 229 (D.N.J.1989).

6. *Statutory limitations on residential prepayment fees.* State legislation in this area is widespread but varies in content. One common element is that the legislation is usually limited to loans secured by residential real estate, which is variously defined by terminology such as "single family dwellings," "owner-occupied single family dwellings," "one to four family dwellings," or "an owner-occupied one to six family residence."

Beyond this common qualification, the legislation varies considerably. For example, at one extreme is the Pennsylvania statute, which prohibits all prepayment penalties in residential mortgage loans. 41 Pa.Stat. § 405. New Jersey has similar legislation. N.J.Stat.Ann. §§ 46:10B–1, 10B–3. See *Lopresti, supra.* Illinois achieves the same practical effect by prohibiting prepayment penalties in all residential mortgages with an interest rate in excess of 8%. 815 Ill. Comp. Ann. Stat. 205/4. See also Vernon's Ann.Mo.Stat. § 408.036 (prohibits prepayment penalties in residential real estate loans after five yearsfrom when the loan was made); Mich.Comp.Laws Ann. § 438.31c (no prepayment penalty after three years for single family dwellings and charges limited for first three years to 1% of the prepayment amount); N.Y.— McKinney's Banking Law § 393(2);. N.Y.—McKinney's Gen.Obl.Law § 5–501(3)(b); Miss.Code Ann. § 75–17–31; West's Ann.Cal.Civ. Code § 2954.9(b).

A federal savings association may "impose a fee for any prepayment of a loan." 12 C.F.R. § 160.34. This regulation's effect is to preempt any contrary state law. Similarly, the Comptroller of the Currency has preempted application of state law on prepayment fees to national banks that offer or purchase adjustable rate mortgages. See 12 C.F.R. § 34.23.

Two major quasi-federal entities purchase residential mortgage loans on the secondary market, Fannie Mae and Freddie Mac. They generally do not enforce prepayment clauses in mortgages they own, and their standard note and mortgage forms permit prepayment without a fee. Mortgagees using the standard form may attach a prepayment clause by rider, but the rider must state that it becomes void if Fannie or Freddie purchase the mortgage. Fannie's and Freddie's practices and rules tend to have a significant impact on mortgage lending practices because many mortgagees either sell mortgages to them or want the option to do so. Therefore, prepayment fees in prime home mortgage loans have become quite rare, although they are common in subprime loans.

Finally, prepayment fees in mortgage loans guaranteed by the Department of Veterans Affairs or insured by the Federal Housing Administration are prohibited, and the loans may be prepaid at any time. See 38 C.F.R. § 36.4311; 24 C.F.R. § 203.22(b).

2. LATE FEES AND DEFAULT INTEREST

Mortgage lenders often provide incentives for their borrowers to pay loan installments on time. Two commonly-used incentives are late fees and default interest.

WESTMARK COMMERCIAL MORTGAGE FUND IV v. TEENFORM ASSOCIATES, L.P.

Superior Court of New Jersey, Appellate Division, 2003
362 N.J.Super. 336, 827 A.2d 1154

The opinion of the court was delivered by WEFING, J.A.D.

This is a mortgage foreclosure action in which defendants appeal from certain aspects of a Final Judgment of Foreclosure entered on January 15, 2002. After reviewing the record in light of the contentions advanced on appeal, we affirm but remand for entry of a corrected judgment.

On July 28, 1999 defendants executed a promissory note to plaintiff for the sum of $3,145,000. The note carried an interest rate of eight percent and called for equal monthly payments of $23,076.90 for a period of five years, at which point the balance was due in full. To secure their obligation, defendants granted plaintiff mortgages on three parcels of commercial property, one in Carlstadt, in Bergen County, one in Brick, in Ocean County and one in Phillipsburg, in Warren County.

Less than a year later, defendants fell behind in their payments. Plaintiff filed a complaint in foreclosure in July 2000 and venued the matter with the Chancery Division in Bergen County. In November 2000, plaintiff was granted partial summary judgment and the matter was forwarded to the Office of Foreclosure, where plaintiff sought entry of final judgment. Defendants disputed the amounts due under the note and mortgages and the matter was returned to the Chancery Division for a hearing. Following that hearing, the Chancery Division concluded that the amounts sought, in excess of $200,000, were reasonable and were due and owing. A Final Judgment of Foreclosure was entered thereafter, from which defendants have appealed.

The matters in dispute fall into four categories: late fees, default interest, prepayment fees and attorney fees. The July 28 note provided for all four items. Defendants contend that the amounts allowed in each category are unreasonable and unwarranted. For the reasons stated in this opinion, we disagree.

I

Paragraph 5 of the July 28, 1999 note provides as follows:

> 5. If any installment under this Note shall not be received by Holder on the date due, Holder may at its option impose a late charge of six percent (6%) of the overdue amount. Considering all of the circumstances on the date of this Note, such late charge represents a fair and reasonable estimate of the costs that will be sustained by Holder due to the failure of Borrower to make a timely payment. The parties further agree that proof of actual damages would be costly or inconvenient. Such late charge shall be paid without prejudice to the right of Holder to collect any other amounts due or to declare a default under this Note or the other Loan Documents or to exercise any other rights and remedies of Holder. If the late charge provided for herein exceeds the maximum late charge provided by applicable law, such late charge shall be automatically reduced to the maximum late charge permitted by applicable law.

Defendants contend this paragraph is invalid, under the settled principle stated in *Westmount Country Club v. Kameny*, 82 N.J.Super. 200, 205, 197 A.2d 379 (App.Div.1964), that "[p]arties to a contract may not fix a penalty for its breach . . . . such a contract is unlawful."

Our analysis of the question presented must perforce begin with the Supreme Court's recent opinion in *MetLife v. Washington Avenue Associates, L.P.*, 159 N.J. 484, 732 A.2d 493 (1999). That also was a foreclosure action involving commercial property. The Note in question in that case called for the debtor to pay a late fee of five percent of any delinquent payments. The debtor challenged that as unreasonable. The Supreme Court, however, disagreed.

The Court noted that liquidated damages clauses in a commercial context between sophisticated parties are presumptively reasonable. *Id.* at 496, 732 A.2d 493. The Court held that the burden of establishing a particular clause as unreasonable rests upon the party challenging it as such. *Ibid.* No one factor is determinative whether a clause is reasonable; rather, a reviewing court must look at the totality of the circumstances. *Id.* at 495, 732 A.2d 493. In conducting its review, the Court deemed it appropriate to look to what is permitted by statute and what constitutes common practice within the industry. *Id.* at 497, 732 A.2d 493. After completing that survey, the Court concluded that late fees based upon a percentage of the delinquent installment are generally allowed and that five percent was not an unusually large or unreasonable fee in commercial transactions. The Court noted that defendants had presented no evidence to overcome the presumption of reasonableness or to suggest fraud, duress or unconscionability on the part of the lender. The Court thus concluded the five percent late charge was reasonable. *Id.* at 500, 732 A.2d 493.

Here, defendants argue that plaintiff did not present any evidence that the late fees charged were related to any actual or anticipated damages to plaintiff flowing from late payment. The argument misapprehends *MetLife*, however. The burden of proof rested squarely on defendants, who presented no evidence at all on the question of the reasonableness of the late fees. We recognize that the late fee in question here is six percent, as opposed to the five percent deemed reasonable in *MetLife*. In light of the defendants' total failure of proof, however, we have no basis to conclude that an increase of one percentage point is sufficient to overcome the presumption of reasonableness and, thus, affirm the decision of the Chancery Division judge that six percent was reasonable in the context of this case.

There is an additional aspect to defendants' challenge to the award of late fees. They cite *Crest Savings & Loan Ass'n v. Mason*, 243 N.J.Super. 646, 649, 581 A.2d 120 (Ch.Div.1990), for the proposition that a lender cannot collect late charges "for nonpayments of installments claimed to be due after the filing of the complaint." We have no quarrel with the principle, but it is inapplicable. This complaint was filed in July 2000 and we have no indication in this record of any late fees charged for any period after that date.

II

Paragraph 6 of the note provides as follows:

6.   If the unpaid balance hereof is not received by Holder on the Maturity Date, or on the Acceleration Date (defined below) such amount shall bear interest at the Note Rate plus two (2%) per annum (the "Default Rate") from such date until paid in full. Considering all of the circumstances on the date of this Note, such interest represents a fair and reasonable estimate of the costs and

> expenses that will result from the loss of use of the money due. The parties further agree that proof of actual damages would be costly or inconvenient. Interest at the Default Rate shall be paid without prejudice to the right of Holder to collect any other amounts due or to declare a default under this Note or the other Loan Documents or to exercise any other rights or remedies of Holder.

Defendants challenge this clause on default interest on the same basis that they challenged the clause on late fees. We apply the same analysis that we did to the question of the reasonableness of the late fees and reach the same conclusion.

The *MetLife* Court also considered the validity of a clause increasing the rate of interest upon default in payment. The Court found that default interest rates are a common tool utilized by lenders to offset a portion of the damages incurred as a result of delinquent loans. *Id.* at 501, 732 A.2d 493. The Court held that default interest rates should be measured for reasonableness and if found to be unreasonable, struck down as a penalty. *Ibid.* In *MetLife*, the default interest rate was 12.55%, three percentage points higher than the contract rate. The Court determined that the three percent increase in the interest rate was a reasonable estimate of the lender's potential costs of administering a defaulted loan, as well as the potential difference in interest rates between the defaulted loan and a replacement loan the lender may be able to place. *Ibid.*

Here, the note called for an increase of two percentage points in the interest rate upon default, raising it from eight percent to ten percent. Based upon the result reached in *MetLife* and defendants' total failure to present any proof to the contrary, the Chancery Division judge correctly determined the ten percent default interest rate to be reasonable.

[The court's discussion of the prepayment fee and attorney's fees is omitted.]

NOTES

1.   *Theories of attack.* As *Westmark* illustrates, both late fees and default interest are subject to attack on the ground that they are invalid liquidated damages clauses, because they violate the requirement that the clauses must represent a reasonable advance estimate of the lender's actual damages.

An additional challenge exists if the late fees and default interest make the loan usurious. Of course, not all states have usury statutes, and some states have statutes that do not apply to mortgage loans. Moreover, nearly all state usury ceilings on first lien loans secured by residential property are preempted by federal law. See 12 U.S.C. § 1735f–7. However, a few states have exercised the right to "un-preempt" their usury laws from this federal statute.

Clearly, if default interest causes a loan to violate a state usury law, the default interest is invalid. After all, default interest *is* interest, and interest is what usury statutes are all about. On the other hand, applying usury analysis to a late fee is more subtle. Late fees are not denominated as interest, and they usually do not accrue on the basis of the number of days, weeks, or months that a payment is late. Rather, the late fee is a fixed amount regardless of how late the payment is, typically after some brief grace period, such as 5 to 15 days. But see Smiley v. Citibank (South Dakota), N.A., 517 U.S. 735 (1996) (National Bank Act defines "interest" to include late fees, which can make interest rate usurious).

The Arkansas Supreme Court characterized a late fee as usurious interest in Bunn v. Weyerhaeuser Co., 268 Ark. 445, 598 S.W.2d 54 (1980). North Carolina agreed in Swindell v. FNMA, 330 N.C. 153, 409 S.E.2d 892 (1991) (5% late fee usurious). However, in Clermont v. Secured Inv. Corp., 25 Cal.App.3d 766, 102 Cal.Rptr. 340 (1972), the court concluded that "while the late charge here * * * must constitute either damages or interest, it may not * * * constitute both." Having determined that the clause was a liquidated damages provision, the court believed it was unnecessary to look at the usury allegation and remanded the case for a decision on the liquidated damages issue.

A usury attack on a late fee may be difficult to sustain for another reason. Usury statutes often impose harsh penalties on usurious transactions, such as total loss of interest or sometimes even loss of principal. Such severe consequences may make courts reluctant to take a broad view of the usury approach.

2. *Unconscionability as a standard.* The doctrine of unconscionability is an alternative approach to the liquidated damages "reasonableness" approach that the New Jersey court employed in *Westmark*, to analyze late fees and default interest. The unconscionability doctrine is typically extrapolated from the well-known statement of that doctrine in U.C.C. § 2–302. However, courts do not widely employ it

Unconscionability may be substantive, such as an extreme and oppressive term, procedural, such as unfair surprise because the borrower did not realize the nature of the term agreed to, or a combination of the two. Use of the unconscionability standard is advocated in Steven W. Bender & Michael T. Madison, The Enforceability of Default Interest in Real Estate Mortgages, 43 Real Prop. Prob. & Trust J. 199 (2008).

It is usually more difficult to get a court to intervene and refuse enforcement based on the unconscionability standard. See, e.g., Four J. Funding v. Land Pres., L.L.C., 2004 WL 3130562 (Conn.Super. 2004) (default interest at 24% was not unconscionable); Bekins Bar V Ranch v. Huth, 664 P.2d 455 (Utah 1983) (default interest at 36% and 58% was not unconscionable). Sometimes, a court fails to draw a clear distinction between the reasonableness and unconscionability standards. See, e.g., Cantamar, L.L.C. v. Champagne, 142 P.3d 140 (Utah App. 2006) (default interest clause would be an unreasonable liquidation of damages if it were unconscionable; 30% default rate was not unconscionable).

3. *Rationales for late fees and default interest.* Late fees are perhaps most naturally understood as compensating the lender for the past harm of the administrative expense and difficulty of dealing with the borrower's default. Default interest, on the other hand, may be regarded as compensating the lender for future harm resulting from the fact that a defaulted loan is riskier than had been anticipated. The lender may incur losses due to the necessity of placing reserves against the loan, the adverse impact on the lender's balance sheet, the potential for penalties from regulatory authorities, and the need to implement increased monitoring of the defaulted loan. See Bender & Madison, supra note 2, at 201–02. In addition, a loan that has defaulted may be regarded as "damaged goods," which makes it more difficult to sell on the secondary market, even if the default has been cured. See Harris Ominsky, Real Estate Lore: Modern Techniques and Everyday Tips for the Practitioner 68 (2006).

4. *What default interest rate is excessive?* A court is almost certain to uphold a default interest clause that increases the contract rate by three or four percent. See, e.g., Flojo Int'l, Inc. v. Lassleben, 4 Cal.App.4th 713, 6 Cal.Rptr.2d 99 (1992) (4% increase upheld); Norwest Bank Minnesota v. Blair Road Assocs., L.P., 252 F.Supp.2d 86 (D.N.J.2003) (prime rate plus 4% upheld). Courts usually strike down a default interest clause that involves much larger increases. See, e.g., Feller v. Architects Display Bldgs., Inc., 54 N.J.Super. 205, 148 A.2d 634 (App.Div.1959) (increase from 17% to 33% struck down); Stuchin v. Kasirer, 237 N.J.Super. 604, 568 A.2d 907 (App.Div.1990) (increase from 9% to 24% struck down). But the cases are hard to reconcile, and some courts have approved quite high rates. See, e.g., In re Dixon, 228 B.R. 166 (W.D.Va.,1998) (increase from 18% to 36% upheld); Casaccio v. Habel, 14 Ill.App.3d 822, 303 N.E.2d 548 (1973) (increase from 18% to 24% upheld).

5. *What amount of late charge is excessive?* The *Westmark* case is typical; courts routinely uphold late fees up to 5% or 6% of the missed installment. See McKeever v. Fiore, 78 Conn.App. 783, 829 A.2d 846 (2003) (5% fee upheld); Mattvidi Assocs. Ltd. Partn. v. NationsBank of Virginia, 100 Md.App. 71, 639 A.2d 228 (1994) (5% fee upheld, with a comprehensive listing of other decisions). Cases involving larger fees are rare.

However, suppose the fee is based not on the missed installment but on the *outstanding principal balance* of the loan! In that case, even a small percentage amount can produce a very large fee indeed. In Garrett v. Coast & Southern Fed. Sav. & Loan Ass'n, 9 Cal.3d 731, 108 Cal.Rptr. 845, 511 P.2d 1197 (1973), the court applied a liquidated damage/penalty analysis and concluded that the lender had "made no 'reasonable endeavor * * * to estimate a fair average compensation for any loss that might be sustained' by the delinquency in the payment of the installment." It struck down the fee.

Much the same result follows if the late fee is applied to a late "balloon" payment—that is, a payment of the full balance, as required by the loan documents. In 1300 Ave. P Realty Corp. v. Stratigakis, 186 Misc.2d 745, 720

N.Y.S.2d 725 (Sup.Ct.2000), a 4% fee clause was applied in such a setting, producing a fee of nearly $15,000, but the court enforced it. Contrast Art Country Squire, L.L.C. v. Inland Mortg. Corp., 745 N.E.2d 885 (Ind.Ct.App.2001), in which the court worked hard to construe the fee as applicable only to monthly payments and not to the balloon.

Sometimes, the lender's characterization of the fee may give the game away. In Hitz v. First Interstate Bank, 38 Cal.App.4th 274, 44 Cal.Rptr.2d 890 (1995), credit card customers attacked the issuing bank for charging both late fees and "overlimit" fees, that applied to borrowers whose account balances exceeded their credit limits. A bank executive had written a memo when the fees were introduced that projected "new revenue" of $250,000 annually from the fees without any mention of costs. The executive also testified that he considered the fees "a good source of revenue" and that he expected the bank to "make a profit" from the fees. That was enough to convince the court that the fees were not a "reasonable endeavor to estimate fair compensation for loss."

6. *The effect of acceleration on late fees.* Assume that a mortgagor defaults on monthly payments and that the mortgagee accelerates the loan. If the acceleration had not occurred, a number of additional monthly payments would have fallen due by the time the foreclosure is completed. Is the lender entitled to a late fee on these payments? Courts generally hold that no further fees are collectible after acceleration. As one court put it:

> Upon such acceleration, installment payments are no longer due, and [mortgagee] is entitled to the amount of the debt and interest provided for in the mortgage documents. There is then no basis for allowing [mortgagee] compensation for administrative expenses in connection with alleged late payments. [Mortgagee] is relegated to its rights in the foreclosure action.

Crest Sav. & Loan Ass'n v. Mason, 243 N.J.Super. 646, 581 A.2d 120 (1990). Accord Shadhali, Inc. v. Hintlian, 41 Conn.App. 225, 675 A.2d 3 (1996); Fowler v. First Fed. Sav. & Loan Ass'n, 643 So.2d 30 (Fla.App.1994); Green Point Sav. Bank v. Varana, 236 A.D.2d 443, 653 N.Y.S.2d 656 (1997); Security Mut. Life Ins. Co. v. Contemporary Real Estate Assocs., 979 F.2d 329 (3d Cir.1992) (Pennsylvania law). Some of these cases suggest that the court would reach a contrary result if the mortgage documents clearly provided for the continued accrual of late fees after acceleration. Can this be correct?

Courts that follow the reasoning outlined above sometimes assert that, if a late fee *were* applied to a balloon payment or an accelerated balance, it would produce an unconscionable penalty. See Poseidon Devel., Inc. v. Woodland Lane Estates, L.L.C., 152 Cal.App.4th 1106, 62 Cal.Rptr.3d 59 (2007); LaSalle Bank N.A. v. Shepherd Mall Partners, L.L.C., 140 P.3d 559 (Okl.Civ.App.2006).

7. *State statutory limitations on late fees.* A number of states statutorily regulate late payment charges. All require that the fee be calculated on the

amount of the late installment and not on the outstanding principal amount of the loan. For example, New York limits late payment penalties for mortgages on owner-occupied one- to six-family dwellings to a maximum of 2% of the past due installment and requires a fifteen day grace period after an installment due date before the penalty may be assessed. See N.Y.—McKinney's Real Prop.Law § 254–b. See also Mass.Gen.Laws Ann. c. 183, § 59 (fifteen day grace period and late penalties limited to 3% of the late installment for first mortgages on owner-occupied dwellings of four or less households or on a residential condominium unit); West's Cal.Civ.Code § 2954.4 (ten day grace period and maximum late charge for single family, owner-occupied dwellings limited to the greater of 6% of each delinquent installment or $5).

8.   *Federal regulatory limitations on late fees.* No limitation exists on the amount of late fees that a federal savings association can charge. See 12 C.F.R. § 160.33. Moreover, the no-limitation regulation preempts any conflicting state law, so that federal savings associations may be able to charge larger late fees than other lenders in the state. See Collins v. Union Fed. Sav. & Loan Ass'n, 99 Nev. 284, 662 P.2d 610 (1983).However, 12 C.F.R. § 160.33 imposes certain procedural and notice limitations:

> A Federal savings association may not impose a late charge more than one time for late payment of the same installment, and any installment payment made by the borrower shall be applied to the longest outstanding installment due. A Federal savings association shall not assess a late charge as to any payment received by it within fifteen days after the due date of such payment. No form of such late charge permitted by this paragraph shall be considered as interest to the Federal savings association and the Federal savings association shall not deduct late charges from the regular periodic installment payments on the loan, but must collect them as such from the borrower.

With respect to all loans made to consumers, lenders generally may not charge a late fee when the only delinquency is the borrower's failure to pay a previously-assessed late fee. See 16 C.F.R. § 444.4.

3.   DEEDS IN LIEU OF FORECLOSURE

When foreclosure is impending, the borrower may offer to deed the property to the lender, rather than go through a foreclosure sale. Deeds in lieu of foreclosure may seem attractive to both parties for several reasons. The mortgagee can avoid the delay and expense associated with foreclosure. This motivation is especially strong when a judicial proceeding is the only foreclosure method or when the state has a long post-foreclosure redemption period. Moreover, if the mortgagor is of dubious solvency, the mortgagee may be willing to forego seeking a deficiency judgment. In any event, legislation in some jurisdictions prohibits or severely restricts deficiency judgments.

The mortgagor may want to avoid the possibility of a personal judgment that, though currently uncollectible, can create future problems if his financial fortunes ultimately improve. Sometimes, the mortgagor can persuade the mortgagee who accepts a deed in lieu not to take action to impair the mortgagor's credit rating. In any event, a notation of a deed in lieu on a credit report can be less damaging than a foreclosure.

Due diligence. When a mortgagee is considering whether to accept a deed in lieu, it should take all the same precautions as any well-advised property purchaser. This is especially so in the case of income-producing rental real estate:

> The mortgagee's investigation should include an environmental audit to determine whether the property is or may be contaminated by hazardous waste; a determination whether the property complies with the Americans with Disabilities Act, is the subject of any existing lawsuits or tort claims, and complies with local zoning and other codes; a check for unpaid trade creditors and, if they exist, a determination whether the mortgagor or mortgagee will be responsible for paying them; and a review of the content and assignability of all vendor service contracts. The mortgagee also should identify any other liabilities or restrictions on the real estate.

Nelson, Whitman, Burkhart & Freyermuth, Real Estate Finance Law § 6.19 (6th ed.2015).

Deed in lieu not a clog. The deed in lieu does not normally constitute an invalid clog on the equity of redemption, because the prohibition against clogging applies only to agreements given when the lender makes the loan and not to transactions designed to wind up and terminate the mortgage relationship. See Panagouleas Interiors, Inc. v. Silent Partner Group, Inc., 2002 WL 441409 (Ohio Ct.App.2002) (not reported in N.E.2d); Levenson v. Feuer, 60 Mass.App.Ct. 428, 803 N.E.2d 341 (2004).

Nonetheless, a court can recharacterize a deed in lieu as an equitable mortgage ("additional security for the loan"), though the borrower did not give the deed at the same time as the mortgage. This result is particularly likely if the borrower gave the deed as part of a workout agreement, in which the lender gave the defaulting borrower additional time to perform on the loan, and if the borrower kept possession of the property. The key fact is that the borrower did not give the deed as an immediate and final conveyance of the property title.

The lender sometimes tries to improve the appearance of this transaction by putting the deed in lieu of foreclosure into escrow, with instructions that the escrow agent record and deliver it only if the borrower defaults again. This really does not improve matters. The borrower is still at risk of being persuaded by the mirage of hope to sign anything—

including the deed—to keep the loan alive a little longer, which is exactly what the clogging doctrine will not allow. Courts sometimes invalidate the deed or give it effect only as "additional security" and not as an actual transfer of title. See, e.g., Basile v. Erhal Holding Corp., 148 A.D.2d 484, 538 N.Y.S.2d 831 (1989); Panagouleas Interiors, Inc. v. Silent Partner Group, Inc., 2002 WL 441409 (Ohio App. 2002) (not reported in N.E.2d). Contra, see Ringling Joint Venture II v. Huntington Nat'l Bank, 595 So.2d 180 (Fla. Dist. Ct. App. 1992); Wensel v. Flatte, 27 Ark.App. 5, 764 S.W.2d 627 (1989).

In addition to the possibility that a court will recharacterize the deed in lieu as being an equitable mortgage, a lender that accepts such a deed faces two other potential challenges—the deed grantee's bankruptcy and unconscionability.

Bankruptcy. When a borrower is experiencing sufficient financial difficulties that it gives a deed in lieu, a significant chance exists that it subsequently will declare bankruptcy. Under some circumstances, a deed in lieu may be avoidable under the Bankruptcy Code. It is arguably a *preference* under § 547 if the mortgagor was insolvent when it delivered the deed and entered bankruptcy within 90 days of delivery and if the outstanding debt was less than the property's value. Alternatively, it may be a *fraudulent transfer* under § 548 of the Bankruptcy Code if the borrower went into bankruptcy within two years after the conveyance and did not receive "reasonably equivalent value" for it. See In re 1701 Commerce, LLC, 511 B.R. 812 (Bankr. N.D. Tex. 2014); Sensenich v. Molleur, 328 B.R. 675 (Bankr.D.Vt.2005) (treating a Vermont strict foreclosure like a deed in lieu for purposes of § 548); Ann M. Burkhart, Freeing Mortgages of Merger, 40 Vand.L.Rev. 283, 339–41 (1987).

Unconscionability. Even if a court does not find an equitable mortgage: "[T]here is an underlying idea that the mortgagor and mortgagee are not of equal bargaining strength. Therefore, it is entirely possible, especially if the consideration paid is disproportionately less than the value of the equity or if none is paid where the equity has value, that the whole transaction will be construed as unfair or unconscionable. The courts will either permit the mortgagor to redeem at this point or restore the original mortgagor-mortgagee relationship." Note, Mortgages—Improvements— Absolute Deed in Lieu of Foreclosure, 31 Mo.L.Rev. 312, 315 (1966); Francie Cohen Spahn, Deeds in Lieu of Foreclosure, 26 No. 4 Prac. Real Est. Law. 47 (2010). See, e.g., Robar v. Ellingson, 301 N.W.2d 653, 657–58 (N.D.1981).

To provide some protection against challenges to the deed in lieu based on the equitable mortgage doctrine, bankruptcy, and unconscionability, a mortgagee should accept a deed in lieu only if it also gets a property appraisal and the mortgagor's affidavit. What is the point of the appraisal? What should the affidavit say?

The mortgagee also must protect itself against the possibility that a court will recharacterize or invalidate the deed in lieu by preventing application of the doctrine of merger, because it would eliminate the original mortgage. Without the original mortgage, the mortgagee may find itself to be unsecured if a court invalidates the deed in lieu or in a junior lien position if a court treats it as an equitable mortgage. Ann M Burkhart, Freeing Mortgages of Merger, 40 Vand.L.Rev. 283 (1987). As described in the next excerpt, the mortgagee also must be concerned about the existence of junior liens. Fortunately, a successful challenge based on the merger doctrine generally can be prevented by the simple expedient of including a statement in the deed in lieu that the mortgagee does not intend the mortgage to merge into the fee title.

NELSON, WHITMAN, BURKHART & FREYERMUTH, REAL ESTATE FINANCE LAW
541–542 (6th ed.2015)*

Merger—General Considerations

The doctrine of merger is one of the most complex and confusing areas of the law of mortgages. The basic doctrine itself can be stated in a few sentences and is deceptively simple. When a mortgagee's interest and a fee title coincide and meet in the same person, the lesser estate, the mortgage, merges into the greater, the fee, and is extinguished. Courts state that "whether a merger has occurred depends on the intent of the parties, especially the one in whom the interests unite. If merger is against that party's best interest, it will not be deemed intended by the parties."

Once having stated the basic doctrine, the confusion begins. The confusion often arises because merger can be used either as a defense to the mortgage debt or as an argument that the mortgage no longer exists. For example, suppose that in lieu of a foreclosure action, a mortgagor agrees to convey the mortgaged property to the mortgagee. Does the merger of the two estates in the mortgagee extinguish the mortgage debt so that the mortgagee cannot pursue the mortgagor personally? On the other hand, the same facts may result in a merger problem with the focus on the *mortgage* and not on the debt. Suppose that our mortgagee was a first mortgagee and that, through inadvertence, took a deed in lieu of foreclosure without first checking to see if junior liens existed on the real estate. If a junior lienor did exist, is it now a senior lien because merger destroyed the former first mortgage or can the original first mortgagee foreclose it to eliminate the junior lien?

---

*   Reprinted with permission of LEG, Inc. d/b/a West Academic.

Merger of the Mortgage

Merger of the *mortgage* is an important issue, especially when junior liens exist. Unlike foreclosure, a deed in lieu of foreclosure does not eliminate those liens. Therefore, a mortgagee that is considering accepting a deed in lieu should have the title examined to determine whether junior interests exist. If they do, the lender normally should foreclose, rather than accept a deed in lieu.

If a senior mortgagee accepts a deed in lieu without having the title examined or if the title examiner misses a junior lien, the junior lienor may assert that the senior mortgage has merged into the fee title and that the junior lien now has first priority! This argument, while often made, seldom succeeds. Courts usually hold that the senior mortgage still exists and can be foreclosed to eliminate the subsequently-discovered junior lien. The Texas Supreme Court reached this conclusion in North Texas Bldg. & Loan Ass'n v. Overton, 126 Tex. 104, 86 S.W.2d 738 (1935):

> It is often true, as no doubt it was in the instant case, that it is decidedly to the advantage of the mortgagor and mortgagee to avoid the necessity of a foreclosure suit by a conveyance of the premises to the mortgagee. A rule penalizing them for so doing would be contrary to our policy that litigation is not to be encouraged. The junior lienholder suffers no injury thereby, but is in the same position as if there had been a foreclosure without his having been made a party. His equity of redemption is not affected, neither is his lien thereby elevated to a first lien.
>
>   * * *
>
> It is immaterial, as between the senior and junior lienholders, whether the mortgagee retains the note and mortgage in his possession or surrenders them to the mortgagor. It is likewise immaterial whether or not the deed of conveyance from the mortgagor to the mortgagee recites, as did the one in the instant case, that the cancellation of the note and mortgage was a part of the consideration for the conveyance.

Professor Durfee has described the theoretical justification for this result as follows: "[T]he classical approach to a case of this sort takes several steps. (1) At common law there is a merger of the mortgage in the equity of redemption. (2) Equity will prevent merger if the party in whom the interests unite is found to have intended to keep both interests on foot. (3) In the absence of evidence of a contrary intent, equity will presume the existence of that intent that is most beneficial to the party holding the two interests." Durfee, Cases on Security 396 (1951). These arguments are obviously sound, and courts widely accept them. Representative cases include Decon Group, Inc. v. Prudential Mortgage Capital Co., LLC, 174 Cal. Rptr. 3d 205 (Cal. Ct. App. 2014); Federal Land Bank v. Colorado Nat'l Bank, 786 P.2d 514 (Colo.App.1989); GBJ, Inc., II v. First Avenue Inv. Corp., 520 N.W.2d 508 (Minn.App.1994); London Bank & Trust Co. v. American Fidelity Bank & Trust Co., 697 S.W.2d 956 (Ky.App.1985); Altabet v. Monroe Methodist Church, 54 Wash.App. 695, 777 P.2d 544 (1989).

However, courts in deed in lieu cases hold that merger has extinguished the senior mortgage just often enough to entice some junior lienors to make that argument. See, e.g., Citizens State Bank of New Castle v. Countrywide Home Loans, Inc., 949 N.E.2d. 1195 (Ind. 2011); Janus Properties, Inc. v. First Florida Bank, N.A., 546 So.2d 785 (Fla.App.1989) (court found merger and elevated the junior mortgage to first priority). In *Janus*, the court placed some reliance on the fact that the first mortgagee, after accepting the deed in lieu, "solemnized its intent by executing and recording a satisfaction of mortgage." What should the mortgagee have done instead?

Eliminating the doctrine of merger. For an analysis of the merger doctrine's applicability to mortgages and arguments for its abolition, see Ann M. Burkhart, Freeing Mortgages of Merger, 40 Vand.L.Rev. 283 (1987). The Restatement also takes the position that the merger doctrine "does not apply to mortgages or affect the enforceability of a mortgage obligation." Restatement (Third) of Property (Mortgages) § 8.5 (1997). If a court adopts the Restatement approach and rejects the merger doctrine, will the intervening lien problem be obviated? "[A] conveyance of the equity of redemption by a mortgagor or subsequent grantee to a mortgagee will not, except in extremely rare circumstances, terminate the latter's mortgage as against liens or other interests that prior to the conveyance were junior to it." Restatement (Third) of Property (Mortgages) § 8.5 cmt. b (1997). Suppose the mortgagee who takes the deed in lieu assumes that an intervening lien exists or takes with actual knowledge of it. Should the mortgagee still be able to foreclose? See id.

Use of nominee. If a court is inclined to enforce the merger doctrine though a junior lien exists, can merger be avoided by having the deed in lieu run to a nominee of the mortgagee, such as its attorney or affiliated corporation, rather than to the mortgagee? See Alden Hotel Co. v. Kanin, 88 Misc.2d 546, 387 N.Y.S.2d 948 (1976).

Merger of the Debt

Merger (or, more properly, extinguishment) is more often a *debt* problem when the controversy is between the person who holds the debt, mortgage, and property title and the person who is liable for the debt. See Nelson, Whitman, Burkhart & Freyermuth, Real Estate Finance Law § 6.16 (6th ed.2015).

MID KANSAS FEDERAL SAVINGS AND LOAN ASSOCIATION V. DYNAMIC DEVELOPMENT CORPORATION

Supreme Court of Arizona, 1991
167 Ariz. 122, 804 P.2d 1310

FELDMAN, VICE CHIEF JUSTICE.

A construction lender held notes secured by first and second deeds of trust on a residential developer's property. The lender acquired title to the property at a trustee's sale on the second trust deed and thereafter brought an action against the developer for the balance due on the first notes. The court of appeals held that the lender was precluded from doing so under A.R.S. § 33–814(G) and the rationale of our decision in *Baker v. Gardner*, 160 Ariz. 98, 770 P.2d 766 (1988).

We must determine whether the anti-deficiency statutes apply to a residential developer and whether a lender may recover the balance owing on the first notes after it has acquired title to the property at the foreclosure sale of its second deed of trust.

* * *

[W]e hold that by its terms, the anti-deficiency statute does not apply to Dynamic in this case and A.R.S. § 33–814(G) does not preclude Mid Kansas from waiving its security and bringing a debt action on the notes.

C.   The Doctrine of Merger and Extinguishment

Because we hold that the anti-deficiency statute does not apply, we must reach the merger and extinguishment issue that is the basis of the concurring opinion in the court of appeals.* * *

Where the same mortgagee holds both a first and second mortgage on the mortgagor's land, and becomes the purchaser at the foreclosure sale of one of the mortgages, the question of merger of rights—often called extinguishment—arises. The merger of rights doctrine addresses the narrow question of whether the mortgagor's personal liability on the senior debt has been discharged. *Wright v. Anderson*, 62 S.D. 444, 253 N.W. 484, 487 (1934). The primary issue in the doctrine of merger of rights is whether the lender would be unjustly enriched if he were permitted to enforce the debt. See generally Burkhart, *Freeing Mortgages of Merger*, 40 Vand.L.Rev. 283, 382 (1987).

Although the mortgagee's purchase of the property at the foreclosure of the senior mortgage will not extinguish the debt secured by a junior mortgage, the reverse is true where the junior mortgage is foreclosed. If one holding both junior and senior mortgages forecloses the junior and purchases the property at the foreclosure sale, the long-standing rule is that, absent a contrary agreement, the mortgagor's personal liability for the debt secured by the first mortgage is extinguished. G. Nelson & D.

Whitman, Real Estate Finance Law § 6.16, at 467 (2d ed. 1985). The rule has been followed for generations. See *Board of Trustees of the Gen. Retirement Sys. v. Ren-Cen Indoor Tennis & Racquet Club*, 145 Mich.App. 318, 377 N.W.2d 432 (1985), appeal denied, 425 Mich. 875, 388 N.W.2d 680 (1986); [additional citations omitted].

The basis of the merger of rights doctrine is that the purchaser at a foreclosure sale of a junior lien takes subject to all senior liens. *Ren-Cen Club*, 377 N.W.2d at 434; *Wright*, 253 N.W. at 487; see also Burkhart, *supra*, 40 Vand.L.Rev. at 377. Although the purchaser does not become personally liable on the senior debt (as does an assuming grantee), the purchaser must pay it to avoid the risk of losing his newly acquired land to foreclosure by the senior lienholder. Therefore, the land becomes the primary fund for the senior debt, and the purchaser is presumed to have deducted the amount of the senior liens from the amount he bids for the land. *Tri-County Bank*, 449 N.W.2d at 541. As the court in *Wright* explained, when the same mortgagee holds both the junior and senior mortgages on the land and buys at the foreclosure sale of the junior mortgage:

> The mortgagor * * * has an equitable right to have the land pay the mortgage before his personal liability is called upon and the purchaser will not be permitted to retain the land * * * and enforce the same against the mortgagor personally.

253 N.W. at 487. Similarly, the court in *Ren-Cen Club* noted that

> [t]he indebtedness will be presumed to have been discharged so soon as the holder of it becomes invested with title to the land upon which it is charged, on the principle that a party may not sue himself at law or in equity. The purchaser is presumed to have bought the land at its value, less the amount of indebtedness secured thereon, and equity will not permit him to hold the land and still collect the debt from the mortgagor.

377 N.W.2d at 435 (quoting *Belleville Savings Bank v. Reis*, 136 Ill. 242, 26 N.E. 646, 647 (1891) (citations omitted)).

Thus, the merger of rights doctrine holds that the senior lien is merged into—or extinguished by—the title acquired by the lienholder when he acquires the mortgagor's equity of redemption under a sale on the junior lien. * * *

As we have previously noted, even where a merger would otherwise occur at law, an express agreement between the parties that no merger shall occur often precludes such a finding by the court. Nelson & Whitman, *supra*, § 6.16, at 467 (citing *Toston v. Utah Mortgage Loan Corp.*, 115 F.2d 560 (9th Cir. 1940); *Continental Title & Trust Co. v. Devlin*, 209 Pa. 380, 58 A. 843 (1904); *Van Woerden v. Union Improvement Co.*, 156 Wash. 555,

287 P. 870 (1930)). Of course, where the mortgagee acquires title to the property through an involuntary conveyance, such as foreclosure, the parties obviously will not have formed a mutual intent concerning the continued enforceability of the debt. Burkhart, *supra*, 40 Vand.L.Rev. at 377.

However, such an intent may be implied under circumstances that would make a finding of merger inequitable to the parties. The dissent in *Wright*, for instance, argued that where the mortgagee paid the full value of the property without deducting the amount of the prior lien, the rule of merger should not apply. 253 N.W. at 489 (Polley, J., dissenting). This argument was adopted by a recent decision that allowed a bank to retain its claim for the unsecured deficiency remaining on the first mortgage even though the bank purchased the property at the foreclosure sale on the second mortgage. *In re Richardson*, 48 B.R. 141 (Bkrtcy.E.D.Tenn. 1985). The court found that the bank had not tried to take unfair advantage of the debtor because its bid had reflected the value of the property and the bank had, in addition, credited the debtors with the amount beyond the bid it received on reselling the property. *Id.* at 142. A different result would obtain where the mortgagee is permitted to keep land that is worth as much as the two mortgage debts and also allowed to collect on the senior debt. In the latter situation, the mortgagee would be unjustly enriched, and the merger doctrine is appropriately applied to destroy the senior debt. Nelson & Whitman, *supra*, § 6.16, at 467–68.

The facts in this case clearly illustrate and require application of the doctrine of merger and extinguishment; they also demonstrate that no equitable exception is appropriate here. Mid Kansas held the four first deeds of trust and the second blanket deed of trust on the four lots. Mid Kansas purchased all four pieces of property with a credit bid of the amount due on the second lien, $101,986.67. Mid Kansas thus acquired free and clear title to improved property apparently worth between $555,750 and $608,000.[9] Even accepting the lower figure, it is apparent that the sum of the junior and senior liens ($527,236.67 exclusive of interest and costs) on the property at the relevant time—the date of the foreclosure sale—was probably less than the value of the property. Mid Kansas obviously tendered a credit bid that was discounted by the amount of the senior liens. Therefore, Mid Kansas would be unjustly enriched were we to allow it to acquire, for $100,000, property worth over $500,000 and also sue Dynamic for another $400,000 under the first notes. Mid Kansas does not contend

---

9   The value of the properties, as listed on the IRS Statements of Acquisition or Abandonment of Secured Property filed by Mid Kansas, totalled $555,750. Mid Kansas submitted appraisals to the trial court estimating the value of the lots, if completed in accordance with the plans and specifications, at $608,000. Ironically, the IRS statements filed by Mid Kansas stated that the "borrower was not personally liable for repayment of the debt," although Mid Kansas attributes this to "clerical error" and has since "corrected" the forms.

that the property it acquired was worth less than the total owed on the first and second liens.

On these facts, we hold that the doctrine of merger and extinguishment applies. See *Ren-Cen Club*, 377 N.W.2d at 436 (equity will not assist plaintiff in obtaining the price advantage of purchasing at a second mortgage sale without the disadvantage of having to satisfy the debt secured by the first mortgage). Because the holder of the senior lien acquired title, free from any equity of redemption, on the foreclosure of the junior lien, the doctrine of merger extinguishes the maker's liability on the senior notes.[10] This result is supported by other courts that have applied the doctrine of merger and extinguishment and held that the debt secured by the first mortgage is discharged when the senior mortgagee acquires the property at a sale on the second mortgage and the price at foreclosure sale is depressed to reflect the outstanding first mortgage. See, e.g., *Ren-Cen Club*, 377 N.W.2d 432; *Tri-County Bank*, 449 N.W.2d 537; see also authorities cited in Annot., supra, 95 A.L.R. at 104–105.

CONCLUSION

The anti-deficiency statute, A.R.S. § 33–814(G), does not apply to Dynamic in this case because the homes under construction were not utilized for single-family dwellings. We vacate the court of appeals' opinion and reverse the trial court's judgment. The case is remanded to the trial court for proceedings consistent with this opinion. On remand, the parties will have the opportunity to present evidence as to the value of the property at the time of the foreclosure sale. If the facts are as they appear on this record, equity will require no exception to the doctrine of merger and extinguishment. If Dynamic prevails, it will be eligible for its attorney's fees subject to Rule 21, Ariz.R.Civ.App.P., 17B A.R.S.

GORDON, C.J., and MOELLER and CORCORAN, JJ., concur.

CAMERON, JUSTICE, dissenting in part, concurring in part. [Justice Cameron's dissenting opinion, which is based on the view that the majority misconstrued the antideficiency statute, is omitted.]

NOTES

1. *What should the* Mid Kansas *mortgagee have done?* When a mortgagee holds two mortgages on the same property and both are in default, how should she proceed? Does the solution lie in foreclosing both mortgages judicially at the same time and seeking a single deficiency judgment against the mortgagor? Assuming that both mortgages are in default, should the mortgagee instead foreclose on the senior mortgage and purchase at that

---

[10] We note that our legislature has specifically curtailed a lender's ability to obtain a judgment against the debtor in excess of the fair value of the land in those cases where a deficiency judgment is permitted. See A.R.S. § 33–814(A). We find this legislative proscription against unjust enrichment persuasive in our present holding.

foreclosure sale? See Black Sky Capital, LLC v. Cobb, 246 Cal. Rptr. 3d 583, 439 P.3d 1149 (Cal. 2019); In re Trustee's Sale of Real Property of Ball, 319 P.3d 844 (Wash. Ct. App. 2014); Nelson, Whitman, Burkhart & Freyermuth, Real Estate Finance Law § 6.16 (6th ed.2015).

2. *Is merger needed to reach the* Mid Kansas *result?* If a court adopts the Restatement approach, what result would it reach in a case like *Mid Kansas*? What analysis would it use in reaching that result? See TD Bank, N.A. v. Dunbar Tower LLC, 976 N.Y.S. 2d 703 (N.Y. App. Div. 2013); Restatement (Third) of Property (Mortgages) § 8.5 cmt. c(2) (1997).

3. *Deed in lieu and merger of the debt.* Similarly, if the mortgagee in *Mid Kansas* had accepted a deed in lieu, rather than foreclosing, would merger of the debt be an issue? If, as is usual, the conveyance to the mortgagee is made and accepted as payment of the mortgage debt, no question of merger of the debt is either possible or necessary. The debt is certainly eliminated but not because of merger. It was discharged by payment or, more accurately, by substituted performance or accord and satisfaction. Nelson, Whitman, Burkhart & Freyermuth, Real Estate Finance Law § 6.16 (6th ed.2015).

4. *Is a deficiency judgment available?* When negotiating with the mortgagee to accept a deed in lieu, the mortgagor should attempt to obtain the mortgagee's covenant not to sue on the note. If the mortgagee does not give the covenant and subsequently concludes that the property's value is less than the debt balance, can the mortgagee sue for the deficiency? Or should merger of the debt always be inferred? See Nash Finch Co. v. Corey Dev., Ltd., 669 N.W.2d 546 (Iowa 2003); Prigal v. Kearn, 557 So.2d 647 (Fla.App.1990). The courts in both cases recognized that the deficiency liability continues to exist, unless the parties specifically agree to cancel it. In contrast, Illinois statutorily provides that acceptance of a deed in lieu eliminates personal liability for the debt unless the parties expressly agree otherwise. 735 Ill.Comp.Stat. 5/15–1401.

4 SHORT SALES

During difficult economic times, real estate values can decline substantially, as they did during the Great Recession. If a property becomes worth less than the owner owes on the mortgage, the owner may decide that continuing to make mortgage payments does not make economic sense. The owner also may be unable to continue making payments due to job loss, for example. Rather than stopping loan payments and waiting for foreclosure, the owner can try to sell the property. To do so, the owner has to convince the mortgagee and other lienors to release their liens in exchange for the sale proceeds, though the proceeds are insufficient to pay the secured debts in full. Because these "short sales" or "preforeclosure sales" can be advantageous for the lienors and for the landowner, they became as common as foreclosures during the most recent economic downturn, though the number of short sales has now declined as property values have increased. Brumfield, The "Short Cut" to the

Stabilization of the Underwater Housing Market: How the New FHFA Short Sale Guidelines Promote Economic Efficiency, 41 Real Est. L.J. 456 (2013); Real Estate Economy Watch, Short Sales Peak, Then Plummet, available at www.realestateeconomywatch.com/2013/09/short-sales-peak-then-plummet/.

The biggest advantage of a short sale is that the real estate usually sells for more than it would at a foreclosure sale. A short seller typically lists the property for sale with a real estate agent, who actively markets the property. In contrast, foreclosure sales normally involve very limited, if any, marketing. Additionally, a short sale is safer for the purchaser than a foreclosure sale. For example, short sale purchasers can physically inspect the property before agreeing to buy it and, after agreeing to buy, have time to arrange financing and a title examination. In contrast, a foreclosure purchaser normally cannot inspect the property before the sale and, in many states, must pay the purchase price immediately.

Another significant advantage of a short sale is that it often can occur much more quickly than a foreclosure sale. A lender can process a short sale request in 60–90 days after the seller has found a buyer. Dunaway, Babbitt, Gerth & McGrane, Law of Distressed Real Estate § 3B:8. In contrast, the average time for a foreclosure nationally can be over a year; in some states, it can be substantially longer. Notice, State-Level Guarantee Fee Pricing, Federal Housing Finance Agency (Sept. 25, 2012), 77 Fed. Reg. 58,991, 58,992. Even in states in which the speedier nonjudicial foreclosure is available, a statutory right of redemption may allow the borrower to retain possession of the property for months or years after the foreclosure. If the borrower cannot redeem during that time, he may stop maintaining the property and paying the taxes and insurance premiums.

Short sales are less expensive for lenders than foreclosure sales, especially in states that require judicial foreclosure. Because the foreclosing lender often purchases the property at the sale, the lender can incur not only the costs of foreclosure, but also of owning and selling the property.

Borrowers also can benefit from a short sale. They avoid the embarrassment and stigma of going through foreclosure. Additionally, some, though not all, commentators believe that a borrower's credit rating is not as adversely affected by a short sale as by a foreclosure sale. With a short sale, the borrower has actively attempted to sell the property and pay at least part of the debt, rather than putting the lender to the task of foreclosing. Dunaway, Babbitt, Gerth & McGrane, Law of Distressed Real Estate § 3B:8; Miller, Short Sales Overview with an Emphasis on Broker Issues, 26 No. 3 Prac. Real Est. Law. 9 (2010).

A common stumbling block to a short sale is getting every lienor to agree to release its lien. Particularly if a lienor won't receive any of the sale proceeds, it may be content to wait and see if the property's value increases in the future, rather than agreeing to a short sale now. Any private mortgage insurer also has to agree to the sale and also may prefer to wait for the property's value to increase. Moreover, the borrower has to get all these consents before the purchase agreement expires.

An additional concern for the borrower is whether it will be liable for a deficiency after the short sale. If so, the borrower may prefer foreclosure, so that it can keep possession of the property rent-free for a longer period of time. Courts are divided on whether a state's antideficiency statute protects a borrower after a short sale, as well as after a foreclosure.

COKER V. JPMORGAN CHASE BANK, N.A.
Supreme Court of California, 2016
62 Cal.4th 667, 364 P.3d 176

LIU, J.

Under Code of Civil Procedure section 580b, when an individual borrows money from a bank to buy a home and the bank forecloses on the home, the bank can collect proceeds from the foreclosure sale but nothing more. The bank may not obtain a deficiency judgment against the borrower if the sale proceeds are not enough to repay the loan. At issue here is whether the statute's antideficiency protection applies not only when a bank initiates a foreclosure sale, but also when a defaulting borrower arranges a short sale. In a short sale, the borrower sells the home to a third party for an amount that falls short of the outstanding loan balance; the lender agrees to release its lien on the property to facilitate the sale; and the borrower agrees to give all the proceeds to the lender. We hold, as the Court of Appeal did below, that the statute applies to short sales just as it does to foreclosure sales.

I.

The operative complaint here alleges that on May 20, 2004, Carol Coker purchased a condominium in San Diego County with the help of a $452,000 loan from Valley Vista Mortgage Corporation. The loan was secured by a deed of trust recorded against the condominium. A few years later, Coker fell behind on her payments. On March 10, 2010, she received a "notice of default and election to sell" from Chase Home Finance, LLC, or JPMorgan Chase Bank, N.A. (Chase), Valley Vista's successor in interest on the loan. As Chase began the foreclosure process, Coker asked Chase if it would release its security interest so that she could sell her property to a third party for $400,000.

In a June 21, 2010, letter to Coker, Chase provisionally approved the sale and agreed to release its security interest, subject to several conditions. First, "[t]he borrower (seller) must net zero [from the sale]. All proceeds are to be remitted to the lender. . . . *Neither the borrower nor any other party may receive any sales proceeds or any other funds as a result of this transaction.*" Second, the letter identified the "Total Proceeds to be received by Chase" as "$375,061.86" (the sale price minus closing costs) and said that "Chase shall not accept less than the stated net amount." Third, Chase reserved the right to rescind its approval of the sale "should any variances occur in the approved transaction," including any additional costs that reduce Chase's net proceeds, postponement of the closing, or untimely delivery of the final settlement statement to Chase. Fourth, the letter said: "The amount paid to Chase is for the release of Chase's security interest(s) only, and the Borrower is still responsible for all deficiency balances remaining on the Loan, per the terms of the original loan documents." Coker accepted Chase's terms and sold her condominium to a third party for $400,000 on July 22, 2010.

In January 2011, Coker received a collection letter from an authorized agent of Chase, demanding the $116,686.89 balance remaining on her loan. Coker brought this declaratory action, claiming (among other things) that Code of Civil Procedure section 580b prohibited Chase from collecting the deficiency. (All statutory references are to this code unless otherwise specified.) The trial court sustained Chase's demurrer without leave to amend. But the Court of Appeal reversed, holding that any effort by Chase to recover the deficiency would be barred by section 580b and that Coker's agreement to pay the deficiency balance was an unenforceable waiver of the statute's protections. In so holding, the court explained that section 580b's "protections apply after any sale, not just a foreclosure." The court also rejected Chase's contention that because Coker waived her rights under section 726, which requires a secured creditor to foreclose on a borrower's property before seeking a personal judgment, section 580b does not apply. We granted review.

II.

When a borrower defaults on a loan secured by real property, the lender can use one of three procedures to recover the debt. First, the lender can initiate a judicial foreclosure by filing a lawsuit. (§ 725a.) As the plaintiff in the suit, the lender must prove that "the subject loan is in default and the amount of default." (*Arabia v. BAC Home Loans Servicing, L.P.* (2012) 208 Cal.App.4th 462, 470, 145 Cal.Rptr.3d 678 (*Arabia*).) If the lender proves its case, the court can order the sale of the property to satisfy the borrower's debt. (§ 726.)

Second, the lender can initiate a nonjudicial foreclosure. (See *Alliance Mortgage Co. v. Rothwell* (1995) 10 Cal.4th 1226, 1236, 44 Cal.Rptr.2d 352,

900 P.2d 601.) The instrument that secures the loan (i.e., the deed of trust or mortgage) usually contains a power-of-sale clause, which gives the lender the right to sell the property without judicial supervision after the borrower defaults. (*Ibid.*) "Nonjudicial foreclosure is less expensive and more quickly concluded than judicial foreclosure, since there is no oversight by a court, '[n]either appraisal nor judicial determination of fair value is required,' and the debtor has no postsale right of redemption." (*Ibid.*) As a result, "nonjudicial foreclosure is 'overwhelmingly preferred by lenders' and is far more common than judicial foreclosure in California." (*Arabia, supra,* 208 Cal.App.4th at p. 471, 145 Cal.Rptr.3d 678; see *Mabry v. Superior Court* (2010) 185 Cal.App.4th 208, 221, fn. 5, 110 Cal.Rptr.3d 201.)

Third, the lender can recover money from the defaulting borrower by facilitating a short sale. In a short sale, the lender agrees to release its lien on the borrower's property so that the borrower can sell the property to a third party. In exchange, the borrower agrees to give the lender all of the proceeds from the sale. Both parties know that the sale proceeds will fall short of the total amount that the borrower owes. The Assembly Committee on Judiciary has observed that short sales "save banks millions in foreclosure costs" and can help homeowners "feel like they took responsibility for the obligation to pay [their creditors] back." (Assem. Com. on Judiciary, Analysis of Sen. Bill No. 931 (2009–2010 Reg. Sess.) p. 61.) Although there were virtually no short sales in California in 2007, the number grew to a few thousand in 2008, to 90,000 in 2009, and to approximately 110,000 in 2010. (See Sen. Com. on Banking & Financial Insts. Sen. Bill No. 412 (2011–2012 Reg. Sess.) as amended on Mar. 21, 2011, p. 2.)

Our Legislature has enacted a cluster of statutes to protect borrowers who default on a loan secured by real property. (See 4 Witkin, Summary of Cal. Law (10th ed. 2005) Security Transactions in Real Property, § 179, p. 983.) Section 580d prohibits the holder of a note secured by a deed of trust from obtaining any deficiency judgment after the holder has exercised the power of sale in the trust deed. Section 580a limits any deficiency judgment that a junior lienholder can obtain after a nonjudicial foreclosure sale to the difference between the fair market value of the property and the amount of the outstanding debt. (See *Walter E. Heller Western, Inc. v. Bloxham* (1985) 176 Cal.App.3d 266, 272, 221 Cal.Rptr. 425.) Section 726 imposes a similar fair market value limitation on any deficiency judgment after a judicial foreclosure sale. The case before us concerns another statute in this cluster, section 580b.

When an individual obtains a loan to purchase real property and uses the property as collateral, the transaction is called a purchase money loan. Section 580b addresses what happens when the proceeds from the sale of real property are not enough to satisfy the outstanding balance on a purchase money loan. In 2010, when Coker arranged the short sale of her condominium, section 580b read in relevant part: "No deficiency judgment shall lie in any event after a sale of real property or an estate for years therein for failure of the purchaser to complete his or her contract of sale, or under a deed of trust or mortgage given to the vendor to secure payment of the balance of the purchase price of that real property or estate for years therein, or under a deed of trust or mortgage on a dwelling for not more than four families given to a lender to secure repayment of a loan which was in fact used to pay all or part of the purchase price of that dwelling occupied, entirely or in part, by the purchaser." (As amended by Stats.1989, ch. 698, § 12, p. 2289; in this opinion, the term "section 580b" refers to this version of the statute.)

The statutory text indicates that when a homeowner defaults on a purchase money loan, section 580b prevents the lender from obtaining a deficiency judgment against the borrower. We have said this protection is "a stabilizing factor in land sales" for two reasons. (*Roseleaf Corp. v. Chierighino* (1963) 59 Cal.2d 35, 42, 27 Cal.Rptr. 873, 378 P.2d 97 (*Roseleaf*).) First, lenders are less likely to overvalue the homes they finance when they cannot hold homeowners personally liable for any deficiency. (*Ibid.*) Second, when an economic downturn causes widespread depression of property values, section 580b "prevents the aggravation of the downturn that would result if defaulting purchasers were burdened with large personal liability." (*Ibid.*)

It is well established that section 580b protects a purchase money borrower after a judicial or nonjudicial foreclosure sale. (See *Kurtz v. Calvo* (1999) 75 Cal.App.4th 191, 194, 89 Cal.Rptr.2d 99; *Birman v. Loeb* (1998) 64 Cal.App.4th 502, 506, 75 Cal.Rptr.2d 294.) The question here is whether the antideficiency protection of section 580b also applies after a short sale.

III.

* * *

Chase reads section 580b to govern three scenarios in which there has been a sale of real property: "No deficiency judgment shall lie in any event after a sale of real property or an estate for years therein [1] for failure of the purchaser to complete his or her contract of sale, or [2] under a deed of trust or mortgage given to the vendor to secure payment of the balance of the purchase price of that real property or estate for years therein, or [3] under a deed of trust or mortgage on a dwelling for not more than four families given to a lender to secure repayment of a loan which was in fact used to pay all or part of the purchase price of that dwelling occupied, entirely or in part, by the purchaser." (Bracketed numbers added.) On this reading, the term "under a deed of trust" in section 580b modifies the word "sale." Chase argues that "a sale . . . under a deed of trust" plainly means a foreclosure sale, where the lender sells the home after default without the borrower's consent; it does not mean a short sale, where the borrower voluntarily sells the home to a third party for less than the loan balance and the lender reconveys the deed of trust. According to Chase, "Section 580b does not apply to a short sale because such transactions are *not* involuntary sales conducted by a trustee or by the sheriff 'under a deed of trust.'"

In an amici curiae brief, Housing and Economic Rights Advocates and other groups contend that the text of section 580b may be parsed differently so that the term "under a deed of trust" does not modify the word "sale." They read the statute as follows: "No deficiency judgment shall lie in any event [1] after a sale of real property or an estate for years therein for failure of the purchaser to complete his or her contract of sale, or [2] under a deed of trust or mortgage given to the vendor to secure payment of the balance of the purchase price of that real property or estate for years therein, or [3] under a deed of trust or mortgage on a dwelling for not more than four families given to a lender to secure repayment of a loan which was in fact used to pay all or part of the purchase price of that dwelling occupied, entirely or in part, by the purchaser." (Bracketed numbers added.) On this reading, no sale is required to trigger section 580b's protection; the statute simply provides that "[n]o deficiency judgment shall lie in any event . . . under a deed of trust. . . ."

In 2012, the Legislature reformatted section 580b to expressly parse the text in the manner urged by amici curiae. (Stats.2012, ch. 64, § 1, subd. (a); see Stats.2014, ch. 71, § 18 [same parsing in current version of the statute].) Chase concedes that the statutory text, when parsed this way, does not limit antideficiency protection to foreclosure sales and bars a purchase money lender from obtaining a deficiency judgment against a defaulting homeowner after a short sale. But Chase argues that the Legislature's decision to reformat the statute in 2012 does not illuminate what section 580b meant at the time of Coker's short sale in 2010. Chase observes that section 580b, as originally enacted in 1933, unambiguously referred to "any sale under a deed of trust" (Stats.1933, ch. 642, § 5, p. 1673) and that there is no indication the Legislature intended to sever the semantic linkage between "sale" and "under a deed of trust" when it amended the statute in 1949 to apply to "any sale of real property for failure of the purchaser to complete his contract of sale, or under a deed of trust" (Stats.1949, ch. 1599, § 1, p. 2846). Chase's briefing also points out that "short sales were unknown when Section 580b was passed in 1933."

In considering these competing interpretations of the "sale" clause in section 580b, we do not write on a blank slate. For more than half a century, this court has understood the statute to limit a lender's recovery on a standard purchase money loan to the value of the security, no matter how the security has been exhausted—indeed, even if *no sale* has occurred under the deed of trust securing the unpaid loan. * * * [O]ur cases assigning to section 580b this broad construction have consistently looked to the purposes of the statute and to the substance rather than the form of loan transactions in deciding the statute's applicability. The Legislature has never repudiated our basic approach to interpreting section 580b despite ample opportunities to do so. (See *IBP, Inc. v. Alvarez* (2005) 546 U.S. 21, 32, 126 S.Ct. 514, 163 L.Ed.2d 288 ["Considerations of *stare decisis* are particularly forceful in the area of statutory construction, especially when a unanimous interpretation of a statute has been accepted as settled law for several decades."]; *Cel-Tech Communications, Inc. v. Los Angeles Cellular Telephone Co.* (1999) 20 Cal.4th 163, 178, 83 Cal.Rptr.2d 548, 973 P.2d 527 (*Cel-Tech*).).

* * *

1.

The loan at issue in this case was a standard purchase money mortgage. As amici curiae observe, Coker "did nothing more than buy a home to live in using purchase money financing. She did not buy the property as investment or commercial property, did not develop it, and did not refinance it or obtain construction financing to materially increase its value. There is nothing distinctive to remove her purchase money mortgage from the mass mainstream of home purchase transactions." The parties do not dispute that when Coker obtained the loan, "[t]he present security value of the property . . . [was] a reliable indicator of its actual fair market value," and Coker was in no better position than Chase to assess any future risk to the security's value resulting from an economic downturn. (*Spangler, supra,* 7 Cal.3d at p. 611, 102 Cal.Rptr. 807, 498 P.2d 1055.) Because this case involves a standard purchase money loan, section 580b "applies automatically" here. (*Ibid.*)

* * *

2.

Our analysis above reaffirms and applies the rule that section 580b "applies automatically" to a standard purchase money loan, thereby obviating the need to "determine whether it subserves the purposes of section 580b." (*Spangler,* 7 Cal.3d 603 at p. 611, 102 Cal.Rptr. 807, 498 P.2d 1055.) But Chase contends that we should not extend this established rule to short sales because it would not further section 580b's purpose of deterring overvaluation of property or its purpose of stabilizing the economy in times of distress. We disagree with Chase's policy arguments for exempting short sales from the analytical framework set forth in *Spangler.*

As to the first purpose, Chase argues that "[a] holding that Section 580b applies to short sales will have no effect on future loan decisions" because section 580e, enacted after Coker's short sale, prospectively bars lenders from recovering any deficiency on a purchase money home loan after a short sale. But whether or not our decision in this case will affect future loan decisions, the question before us is whether section 580b's applicability to short sales would have deterred overvaluation *before* section 580e came into existence, when Coker obtained her loan and bought her home. On this question, Chase argues that applying section 580b to short sales would have fueled borrower speculation and overvaluation, citing Justice Kennard's observation in *DeBerard* that "section 580b encourages buyers to offer more than the market value of the property because they know that in the case of default they will not be personally liable for any deficiency." (*DeBerard,* 20 Cal.4th 659 at p. 672, 85 Cal.Rptr.2d 292, 976 P.2d 843 (conc. opn. of Kennard, J.).) But this is a general argument against our settled understanding that section 580b serves to deter overvaluation; the same criticism applies to antideficiency protection after a foreclosure sale, and we have implicitly rejected it in our cases construing section 580b, including *DeBerard.* (See *DeBerard,* at p. 663, 85 Cal.Rptr.2d 292, 976 P.2d 843.) Further, Chase says section 580b's applicability to foreclosure sales "provides ample deterrence to overvaluation." But even if so, Chase's assertion that section 580b's applicability to short sales "would not provide *additional* deterrence to lender overvaluation of real property" does not follow.

As to the statute's further purpose of economic stabilization, Chase argues that a defaulting borrower who wants antideficiency protection always has the option to insist that the lender foreclose. But section 580b is not merely concerned with the welfare of individual borrowers. We have said it is "a macroeconomic stabilization measure" to ensure that "purchasers *as a class* are harmed less than they might otherwise be during a time of economic decline [so that] the economy benefits." (*DeBerard, supra,* 20 Cal.4th at p. 663, 85 Cal.Rptr.2d 292, 976 P.2d 843, italics added.) This purpose is equally served by applying section 580b whether defaulting borrowers have lost their homes by foreclosure or a short sale. Chase further contends that it is "highly debatable and far from certain" that applying section 580b to short sales would prevent aggravation of an economic downtown, citing studies claiming that "antideficiency laws incentivize borrowers otherwise capable of maintaining their debt payments to strategically default in numbers that saturate the market" and "create additional downward pressures on residential housing values." But again, this is a general argument against antideficiency laws that our cases have implicitly rejected; it is not an argument for why our settled understanding of section 580b's macroeconomic stabilization purpose should apply only to foreclosure sales and not short sales. Indeed, none of the studies cited by Chase even mentions short sales, much less distinguishes them from foreclosure sales.

Chase's overall argument with respect to statutory purpose is that "resolv[ing] the debate as to the wisdom of extending antideficiency protections to short sales" is "a legislative task." Although this is true, it remains our responsibility to decide whether section 580b, properly construed, had already resolved the debate at the time of Coker's sale. The rule then, as now, is that section 580b "applies automatically" to a standard purchase money loan * * *, and Chase has not convinced us that the rule should govern only foreclosure sales and not short sales. Because Coker's short sale did not change the standard purchase money character of her loan, section 580b applies automatically here.

3.

Having concluded that section 580b applies to Coker's short sale, we further hold that Coker could not validly waive section 580b's protection in exchange for Chase's approval of the short sale. "Any one may waive the advantage of a law intended solely for his benefit. But a law established for a public reason cannot be contravened by a private agreement." (Civ.Code § 3513.) "[A] key purpose of section 580b is to stabilize the state's economy, to the benefit of all. The public benefit section 580b provides is one of its primary purposes." (*DeBerard, supra,* 20 Cal.4th at p. 669, 85 Cal.Rptr.2d 292, 976 P.2d 843.)

* * *

D.

Chase makes two additional arguments based on legislative history and context: first, that the Legislature could not have intended section 580b to apply to short sales because short sales were unknown when section 580b was passed in 1933, and second, that the Legislature's recent enactment of section 580e casts doubt on section 580b's applicability to short sales. We address each in turn.

1.

Even if short sales were unknown in 1933 (or in 1989 when the Legislature enacted the version of section 580b that controls this case), that does not mean section 580b cannot apply to a lender whose secured interest is exhausted in a short sale. "Fidelity to legislative intent does not 'make it impossible to apply a legal text to [transactions] that did not exist when the text was created. . . . Drafters of every era know . . . that the rules they create will one day apply to all sorts of circumstances they could not possibly envision.' " (*Apple, supra,* 56 Cal.4th at p. 137, 151 Cal.Rptr.3d 841, 292 P.3d 883, quoting Scalia & Garner, Reading Law: The Interpretation of Legal Texts (2012) pp. 85–86.)

Our holding that section 580b applies when a lender's security is exhausted in a short sale follows from principles elaborated in our case law over several decades. The Legislature has never cast doubt on our repeated articulation of section 580b's purposes or our consistent approach of evaluating the statute's applicability in light of those purposes—even as the Legislature has amended section 580b twice between 1953, when we decided *Brown*, and 2010, when Coker sold her home.

* * *

2.

Chase further argues that when the Legislature finally decided to address short sales, it enacted section 580e in 2010 after Coker's sale and intended that provision to be the only source of antideficiency protection for borrowers who conduct a short sale. As originally enacted, section 580e said in relevant part: "No judgment shall be rendered for any deficiency under a note secured by a first deed of trust or first mortgage for a dwelling of not more than four units, in any case in which the trustor or mortgagor sells the dwelling for less than the remaining amount of the indebtedness due at the time of sale with the written consent of the holder of the first deed of trust or first mortgage. Written consent of the holder of the first deed of trust or first mortgage to that sale shall obligate that holder to accept the sale proceeds as full payment and to fully discharge the remaining amount of the indebtedness on the first deed of trust or first mortgage." (Stats.2010, ch. 701, § 1; the statute was later amended in ways not relevant here.)

According to Chase, section 580e does not apply retroactively to protect borrowers who, like Coker, arranged a short sale before the statute was enacted. In addition, section 580e does not extend antideficiency protection to corporations, limited liability companies, limited partnerships, or political subdivisions (§ 580e, subd. (d)(1)), nor does it protect borrowers who commit waste (§ 580e, subd. (c)). Chase argues that it would have made no sense for the Legislature to enact this nuanced, forward-looking statute "if the Legislature had believed that Section 580b already prohibited deficiency judgments after a short sale even if the borrower was a corporation, LLC or partnership."

But whatever the Legislature may have believed about section 580b's applicability to short sales when it enacted section 580e cannot dictate the proper construction of section 580b as it stood at the time of Coker's short sale. That is because the statute then in effect was enacted by the Legislature in 1989. (See *Bruesewitz v. Wyeth LLC* (2011) 562 U.S. 223, 242, 131 S.Ct. 1068, 179 L.Ed.2d 1 ["[p]ost-enactment legislative history (a contradiction in terms) is not a legitimate tool of statutory interpretation" because "by definition [it] 'could have had no effect on the [legislature's] vote' "].) Even assuming the Legislature intended section 580e to operate prospectively, the fact is that the Legislature did not limit or otherwise alter section 580b when it enacted section 580e. Although the Legislature may have believed that henceforth only section 580e and not section 580b would govern short sales, "a legislative declaration of an existing statute's meaning is neither binding nor conclusive in construing the statute. Ultimately, the interpretation of a statute is an exercise of the judicial power the Constitution assigns to the courts." (*Western Security Bank v. Superior Court* (1997) 15 Cal.4th 232, 244, 62 Cal.Rptr.2d 243, 933 P.2d 507.)

* * *

CONCLUSION

For the reasons above, we affirm the judgment of the Court of Appeal.

NOTES

1. *Lender's right to recover a deficiency after a short sale.* In marked contrast to the *Coker* decision, some courts strictly construe the language of antideficiency laws in determining whether a lender can recover a deficiency after a short sale. For example, the court in Espinoza v. Bank of America, N.A., 823 F. Supp. 2d 1053 (S.D. Cal. 2011), permitted recovery of a deficiency after a short sale because the relevant statute expressly prohibited a deficiency only after property was sold "under power of sale contained in the mortgage or deed of trust." Does it make sense to hold that a lender can recover a deficiency after agreeing to a short sale but cannot after foreclosing? This holding creates a strong incentive for borrowers to forego a short sale in favor of the slower and more expensive foreclosure process. Strict construction of antideficiency statutes also seems inappropriate because legislatures probably did not foresee the widespread use of short sales when they enacted the statutes.

For these reasons, other courts, like the court in *Coker*, have been more lenient in their interpretation of an antideficiency statute. For example, in Enloe v. Kelso, 217 Cal. App. 4th 877, 158 Cal. Rptr. 3d 881 (2d Dist. 2013), the court held that the short seller was protected by the antideficiency statute because it should be "liberally construed to effect its purpose" and should be applied based on the transaction's substance, rather than its form. In Tanque Verde Anesthesiologists L.T.D. Profit Sharing Plan v. Proffer Group, Inc., 172 Ariz. 311, 836 P.2d 1021 (Ct. App. Div. 2 1992), the court assumed that the antideficiency statute applied to a short seller, though the statute provided that it applied when land is "sold pursuant to the trustee's power of sale." See Nelson, Whitman, Burkhart & Freyermuth, Real Estate Finance Law § 6.20 (6th ed.2015).

2. *Short sale antideficiency statute.* As described in the opinion, California has enacted an antideficiency statute for short sales. Cal. Civ. Proc. Code § 580e. The statute also prohibits (1) lenders from requiring the borrower to pay any consideration, other than the sale proceeds, for the lender's consent to the short sale and (2) waiver of the borrower's protections under the statute. The stated statutory purposes are to limit the borrower's liability, to "mitigate the impact of the ongoing foreclosure crisis and to encourage the approval of short sales as an alternative to foreclosure." Some commentators have argued

that prohibiting a deficiency judgment and additional compensation from the borrower will prevent the third goal from being achieved. Bernhardt, Short Sales and Deficiency Liability: The Pointlessness of Purposes, Sept. 2013 Real Prop. L. Rep. 1 (2013); Ornstein & Maree, California Senate Bill 458, 65 Consumer Fin. L.Q. Rep. 291 (2011).

3. *Short sale process.* To encourage the use of short sales in lieu of foreclosure and to speed up the process, the Federal Housing Finance Agency and other government agencies involved in housing finance have promulgated standard forms and servicing guidelines for short sales. The guidelines address a variety of issues, including seller eligibility, methods for processing short sale applications, and permitted closing costs. HUD, the Department of the Treasury, Fannie Mae, and Freddie Mac also provide financial incentives for borrowers and junior lienors to encourage the use of short sales. See Nelson, Whitman, Burkhart & Freyermuth, Real Estate Finance Law § 6.21 (6th ed.2015). Additionally, some states now statutorily require lenders to respond in a timely manner to short sale requests. See, e.g., 735 Ill. Comp. Stat. 5/15–1401.1; Ind. Code §§ 24–4.4–2–201 & 24–9–3–6; Nev. Rev. Stat. § 668.051.

CHAPTER SIX

FORECLOSURE

• • •

A. ACCELERATION AND MARSHALING

1. ACCELERATION

GRAF V. HOPE BLDG. CORP.
Court of Appeals of New York, 1930
254 N.Y. 1, 171 N.E. 884

O'BRIEN, J. Plaintiffs, as executors of Joseph L. Graf, are the holders of two consolidated mortgages forming a single lien on real property the title to which is vested in defendant Hope Building Corporation. According to the terms of the agreement consolidating the mortgages, the principal sum is made payable January 1, 1935. Nevertheless, a clause provides that the whole shall become due after default for twenty days in the payment of any installment of interest. David Herstein is the controlling stockholder and also president and treasurer of defendant. He alone was authorized to sign checks in its behalf. Early in June, 1927, he went to Europe. Before his departure a clerical assistant who was also the nominal secretary of the corporation computed the interest due July 1, and through an error in arithmetic incorrectly calculated it. Mr. Herstein signed the check for the erroneous amount but before the date upon which the interest became due, the secretary discovered the error, notified the mortgagee of the shortage of $401.87, stated that on the president's return from Europe the balance would be paid and on June 30 forwarded to the mortgagee the check as drawn. It was deposited by the mortgagee and paid by defendant. On July 5 Mr. Herstein returned, but, through an omission in his office, he was not informed of the default in the payment of interest. At the expiration of twenty-one days this action of foreclosure was begun. Defendant made tender of the deficiency but the mortgagee, strictly insisting on his contract rights, refused the tender and elected to assert the power created by the acceleration clause in the consolidation agreement.

On the undisputed facts as found, we are unable to perceive any defense to the action and are, therefore, constrained to reverse the judgment dismissing the complaint. Plaintiffs may be ungenerous, but generosity is a voluntary attribute and can not be enforced even by a chancellor. Forbearance is a quality which under the circumstances of this case is likewise free from coercion. Here there is no penalty, no forfeiture (Ferris v. Ferris, 28 Barb. 29; Noyes v. Anderson, 124 N.Y. 175, 180), nothing except a covenant fair on its face to which both parties willingly consented. It is neither oppressive nor unconscionable. (Valentine v. Van Wagner, 37 Barb. 60.) In the absence of some act by the mortgagee which a court of equity would be justified in considering unconscionable, he is entitled to the benefit of the covenant. The contract is definite and no reason appears for its reformation by the courts. (Abrams v. Thompson, 251 N.Y. 79, 86.) We are not at liberty to revise while professing to construe. (Sun P. & P. Assn. v. Remington P. & P. Co., 235 N.Y. 338, 346.) Defendant's mishap, caused by a succession of its errors and negligent omissions, is not of the nature requiring relief from its default. Rejection of plaintiff's legal right could rest only on compassion for defendant's negligence. Such a tender emotion must be exerted, if at all, by the parties rather than by the court. Our guide must be the precedents prevailing since courts of equity were established in this State. Stability of contract obligations must not be undermined by judicial sympathy. To allow this judgment to stand would constitute an interference by this court between parties whose contract is clear. One has been unfortunately negligent but neither has committed a wrong. If defendant's president had left some person in charge with authority to deal with affairs as they might arise, the first error could have been immediately corrected and the second would not have occurred. Even after Mr. Herstein's return on July 5, two weeks remained before the expiration of the twenty days. The secretary's forgetfulness during this time is not sufficient excuse for a court of equity to refuse to lend its aid to the prosecution of an action based upon an incontestably plain agreement. Such a refusal would set at nought the rules announced and enforced for a century in such cases as Noyes v. Clark (7 Paige, 179); Hale v. Gouverneur (4 Edw.Ch. 207); Ferris v. Ferris (supra); Valentine v. Van Wagner (supra); Malcolm v. Allen (49 N.Y. 448); Bennett v. Stevenson (53 N.Y. 508); Hothorn v. Louis (52 App.Div. 218; affd., 170 N.Y. 576). The words of Chancellor Walworth in Noyes v. Clark (supra) express the rule which has since prevailed in respect to the rights of a mortgagee against a defaulting mortgagor under an acceleration clause: "The parties * * * had an unquestionable right to make the extension of credit dependent upon the punctual payment of the interest at the times fixed for that purpose. And if, from the mere negligence of the mortgagor in performing his contract, he suffers the whole debt to become due and payable, according to the terms of the mortgage, no court will interfere to relieve him from the payment thereof according to the conditions of his own agreement. (Steel v. Bradfield, 4 Taunt.Rep. 227; James v. Thomas, 5 Barn. & Adol. 40.)" Ferris v. Ferris (supra) illustrates the application of that rule when the court, holding that the acceleration clause works neither a forfeiture nor a penalty, rejected a defense founded upon the fact that the mortgagor was unacquainted with business and suffered the day of payment to arrive sooner in consequence of her own negligence than she would otherwise have done. This court has never departed from that rule. Cases can be found in other courts where the facts may be so distinguished as to take them out of the rule or where other theories have been applied in a way which fails to meet with our approval. We feel that the interests of certainty and security in real estate transactions forbid us, in the absence of fraud, bad faith or unconscionable conduct, to recede from the doctrine that is so deeply imbedded in equity.

Reliance is placed by respondent upon Noyes v. Anderson (supra), but we think that the reasoning in that case requires a reversal here. There the issue related to the effect upon a collateral agreement of a default in the payment of an assessment, and the court, giving full recognition to the principles of the cases above cited, decided that the breach of a condition subsequent in that agreement, unlike a default in the payment of interest on the principal of a mortgage debt, resulted in a forfeiture. * * *

The judgment of the Appellate Division and that of the Special Term should be reversed and judgment ordered in favor of plaintiff for the relief demanded in the complaint, with costs in all courts.

CARDOZO, CH. J. (dissenting).

The action is one for the foreclosure of a consolidated mortgage.

The principal of the mortgage is $335,000, payable in quarter-annual installments of $1,500, beginning April 1, 1925, and continuing until January 1, 1935, when there is to be payment of the residue ($276,500). Interest computed at the rate of 5¾ per cent per annum is payable quarter-annually, like the installments of the principal. At the option of the mortgagee the whole of the principal is to become due after default for twenty days in the payment of any installment of the interest.

On July 1, 1927, there became due the quarterly installment of principal ($1,500), and interest ($4,621.56), in all $6,121.56. The interest payments were not constant in amount, for the debt on which interest was to be computed varied each quarter with the reduction of the principal. At this time, the owner of the equity of redemption was the Hope Building Corporation, which was not a signer of the bond nor personally bound for the payment of the debt. The corporation was owned and controlled by its president, Mr. Herstein, who sailed for Europe June 2, 1927, on a hurried trip for business. Before leaving he requested his bookkeeper, who was nominally the secretary of the corporation, to make out the checks for the principal and interest payable in July. Through an error in arithmetic, she computed the interest as $4,219.69, which was $401.87 short of the correct amount. Mr. Herstein signed a check for the interest so computed and also one for $1,500, the installment of the principal. After he had gone, the bookkeeper recalculated the interest and discovered her mistake. There was no one authorized to sign checks when the president was away.

Accordingly on June 24 she mailed the two checks to the plaintiff mortgagee, stating that a mistake in arithmetic had been made, and that the president was expected to return about July 5, at which time a check for $401.87 would be promptly forwarded. The president of the corporation returned at the appointed time, but unfortunately the bookkeeper forgot about the error, and failed to bring it to his attention. The twenty-day period of grace expired July 21. On July 22, without warning or demand, the plaintiff began this action for the foreclosure of its mortgage, electing to declare the principal indebtedness to be due by reason of the default in the payment of the interest. Promptly the same day, the corporation, thus advised of its default, tendered the overdue installment. The tender, being rejected, was kept good by payment into court. These facts being proved, the trial judge held that there has been a mere mistake in computation, against which equity would relieve by refusing to cooperate with the plaintiff in the effort to collect the accelerated debt. The Appellate Division unanimously affirmed. Upon appeal by the plaintiff the case is now here by allowance of this court.

There is no undeviating principle that equity shall enforce the covenants of a mortgage, unmoved by an appeal *ad misericordiam*, however urgent or affecting. The development of the jurisdiction of the chancery is lined with historic monuments that point another course. * * *

To all this, acceleration clauses in mortgages do not constitute an exception. They are not a class by themselves, removed from interference by force of something peculiar in their internal constitution. In general, it is true, they will be enforced as they are written. In particular this has been held of a covenant in a mortgage accelerating the maturity of the principal in default of punctual payment of an installment of the interest. If the quality of a penalty inheres in such a covenant at all, it is not there to such a degree as to call, in ordinary circumstances, for mitigation or repression (Noyes v. Clark, 7 Paige, 179; Ferris v. Ferris, 28 Barb. 29; Malcolm v. Allen, 49 N.Y. 448; Bennett v. Stevenson, 53 N.Y. 508). Less favor has been shown to a provision for acceleration of a mortgage in default of punctual payment of taxes or assessments. We have held that such a provision, though not a penalty in a strict or proper sense, is yet so closely akin thereto in view of the forfeiture of credit that equity will relieve against it if default has been due to mere venial inattention and if relief can be granted without damage to the lender (Noyes v. Anderson, 124 N.Y. 175; followed in Ver Planck v. Godfrey, 42 App.Div. 16; Germania Life Ins. Co. v. Potter, 124 App.Div. 814, and of Trowbridge v. Malex Realty Corp., 198 App.Div. 656). In the one case as in the other, in foreclosure for default of taxes just as in foreclosure for default of interest, the privilege of acceleration is absolute in the event of a default, if the privilege is to be measured by the language of the covenant. The distinction lies in this only, that the punctual payment of interest has an importance to the lender as affecting his way of life, perhaps the very means for his support, whereas the importance of payment of the taxes is merely as an assurance of security. The difference is not one of kind, for the provision is enforcible even as to taxes if the default is continuous or willful; it is a difference merely of degree, the purpose of the payment being referred to as a test wherewith to gauge the measure of the hardship, the extent of the oppression.

There is neither purpose nor desire to impair the stability of the rule, which is still to be enforced as one of general application, that nonpayment of interest will accelerate the debt if the mortgage so provides. The rule is well understood, and is fair to borrower and lender in its normal operation. Especially is it fair if there is a period of grace (in this case twenty days) whereby a reasonable leeway is afforded to inadvertence and improvidence. In such circumstances, with one period of grace established by the covenant, only the most appealing equity will justify a court in transcending the allotted period and substituting another. There is a difference, however, between a denial of power, without heed to the hardship calling for its use, and a definition of hardship that will limit the occasions upon which power shall be exercised. In none of the cases cited as indicative of lack of power was there any need to determine the effect of accident or mistake apparent to a mortgagee who has preferred default to payment. * * *

When an advantage is unconscionable depends upon the circumstances. It is not unconscionable generally to insist that payment shall be made according to the letter of a contract. It may be unconscionable to insist upon adherence to the letter where the default is limited to a trifling balance, where the failure to pay the balance is the product of mistake, and where the mortgagee indicates by his conduct that he appreciates the mistake and has attempted by silence and inaction to turn it to his own advantage. The holder of this mortgage must have understood that he could have his money for the asking. His silence, followed, as it was, by immediate suit at the first available opportunity, brings conviction to the mind that he was avoiding any act that would spur the mortgagor to payment. What he did was almost as suggestive of that purpose as if he had kept out of the way in order to avoid a tender (Noyes v. Clark, supra). Demand was, indeed, unnecessary to bring the debt to maturity at law. There is not a technical estoppel (Thompson v. Simpson, 128 N.Y. 270, 291; Spencer Bower on Estoppel by Representation, pp. 61, 352, 358; cf. Williston, Contracts, vol. 3, §§ 1497, 1548, 1557). The consequence does not follow that, in conditions so peculiar, the omission to make demand is without significance in equity. Significant it may then be in helping the court to a determination whether the conduct of a suitor in taking advantage of a default, so easily averted and so plainly unintentional, is consistent with good conscience (cf. Retan v. Clark, 220 Mich. 493). True, indeed, it is that accident and mistake will often be inadequate to supply a basis for the granting or withholding of equitable remedies where the consequences to be corrected might have been avoided if the victim of the misfortune had ordered his affairs with reasonable diligence (United States v. Ames, 99 U.S. 35, 47; Grymes v. Sanders, 93 U.S. 55; Noyes v. Clark, supra). The restriction, however, is not obdurate, for always the gravity of the fault must be compared with the gravity of the hardship (Noyes v. Anderson, supra; Lawrence v. American Nat. Bank, 54 N.Y. 432; Ball v. Shepard, 202 N.Y. 247, 253). Let the hardship be strong enough, and equity will find a way, though many a formula of inaction may seem to bar the path. * * *

* * * The court will stand aside when by intervening it will make itself an instrument of injustice (Thomas v. Brownville, etc., R.R. Co., supra). There is no occasion to define the situations in which it will be ready to go farther and stay the remedy at law. Enough for present purposes that it may withhold a remedy in equity. If justice exacts an acceptance of a tender, the relief to be granted will be subject to that condition, and the decree will be limited to the overdue installments, with costs accruing to the date of tender and refusal. * * *

POUND, CRANE, and HUBBS, JJ., concur with O'BRIEN, J.

CARDOZO, C.J., dissents in opinion in which LEHMAN and KELLOGG, JJ., concur.

Many courts, like the *Graf* majority, hold that a mortgagor will not be relieved from enforcement of an acceleration clause if he defaulted as a result of his negligence or mistake or by accident, at least in the absence of fraud, bad faith, or other mortgagee conduct that renders use of the clause unconscionable. This judicial attitude is perhaps best exemplified by the following language from Verna v. O'Brien, 78 Misc.2d 288, 356 N.Y.S.2d 929 (1974), a post-*Graf* New York decision: "[M]ere improvidence or neglect or poverty or illness is not sufficient basis for relief in equity from foreclosure under a mortgage acceleration clause. A mortgagee may be ungenerous, perhaps even uncharitable, but generosity and charity are voluntary attributes and cannot be enforced by the court."

The Restatement takes a similar approach. It limits judicial discretion to defeat acceleration to situations in which "the mortgagee has waived its right to accelerate" or "has engaged in fraud, bad faith, or other conduct making acceleration unconscionable." Restatement (Third) of Property (Mortgages) § 8.1(d)(2), (3) (1997). Thus, "a mortgagee who is guilty of no misconduct is *ex ante* permitted to rely on its contract acceleration right without being subject to the vagaries of mortgagor's financial and personal situation, a matter over which mortgagee usually has little control." Id., cmt. e.

In contrast, other courts take the view that "equity has the power to relieve a mortgagor for an inadvertent default in the payment of principal or interest where acceleration would work extreme hardship upon him." Robert R. Rosenthal, The Role of Courts of Equity in Preventing Acceleration Predicated upon a Mortgagor's Inadvertent Default, 22 Syr.L.Rev. 897, 904 (1972). See also Steven W. Bender, Equity in Times of Mortgage Crisis, 48 Real Prop. Tr. & Est. L.J. 543, 550–51 (2014). Indeed, at least one court has specifically endorsed Justice Cardozo's characterization of the appropriate approach as a "balancing process;" when deciding whether equitable relief should be granted, "the gravity of the fault must be weighed against the gravity of the hardship." Redding v. Gibbs, 203 Neb. 727, 280 N.W.2d 53 (1979). Even New York courts can have difficulty with the *Graf* holding, as seen in the next opinion.

As you read *Mabry*, consider which approach to acceleration makes the most sense, including from a judicial economy perspective.

BNH CALEB 14 LLC v. MABRY

Supreme Court, Queens County, New York, 2015
49 Misc.3d 402, 11 N.Y.S.3d 844

MARTIN E. RITHOLTZ, J.

In a renowned song, popularized by singer Dinah Washington, the opening lyrics proclaim: "What a Difference a Day Makes, Twenty-four little hours." As demonstrated by the facts of this case, a wait of a few days in making a mortgage payment—that to some and to defendant mortgagor may have seemed minuscule—can potentially have devastating and catastrophic events. As a result of a late monthly payment of a mortgage by defendant mortgagor Karen C. Mabry ("Mabry"), plaintiff BNH Caleb 14 LLC ("BNH"), the assignee of a mortgage note from the mortgagee Greenpoint Mortgage Funding, Inc., seeks to foreclose on a mixed use property located at 113–33 Farmers Blvd., St. Albans, N.Y. 11412, located in Queens County.

Under the clear terms of the mortgage note, all payments had to be made on the first of each month. The check for the payment due on April 1, 2014, was not written until April 8, 2014, and was allegedly not received by plaintiff until April 14, 2014. The mortgage note allowed only a ten day grace period. Contrary to BNH's claims, the mortgage note, is not plainly clear on a "Grace Period." Nowhere is there a phrase, placed in boldface or otherwise, that defines a "Grace Period" as a 10-day period. Instead, the Note, dated August 22, 2005, states:

1.   In the event that any payment shall become overdue for a period of 10 days, a late charge of five percent (5%) of the total monthly payment of principal, interest and escrow so overdue may be charged by the Lender for the purpose of defraying the expense incident to handling such delinquent payment. (Emphasis in the original).

It would appear that paragraph 5 of the mortgage note assumes that a "Grace Period" had been clearly defined when it states that, in the event of a default, "including any grace period set forth therein," the payment of the "whole of the Principal Sum . . . shall, forthwith or thereafter, at the option of the lender, become due and payable."

Mabry's check, dated April 8, 2014, made to the order of plaintiff's counsel, Harry Zubli, Esq., was allegedly received on April 14, and endorsed by him to another entity on April 24, 2014, according to the back of the check. Mabry did not include a late fee of $118.15. For this failure by Mabry to include a monthly late fee of 5%—namely 5% of $2,363.42 or approximately $118.15—BNH seeks to accelerate the entire sum due and foreclose on the mortgage, notwithstanding the fact that Zubli did not reject the payment, but, instead, endorsed it to his client, and it was accepted and deposited.

The very next month, a late payment by the defendant mortgagor was rejected by the plaintiff mortgagee. The plaintiff, by its counsel, Harry Zubli, Esq., sent out a letter to defendant mortgagor, deeming her in default under the mortgage note and accelerating all other payments. Mr. Zubli, by letter dated May 13, 2014, rejected the May 2014 mortgage payment which was offered on a check written on May 10. Although not raised by either party, the Court notes that the check written by Mabry— from a different account and bank than the one sent out a month earlier— was improperly dated, reciting "May 10, 2013," instead of 2014. Having rejected the May check, not for the improper date, but for the alleged lateness coupled with the failure to include the $118.15 in the prior month's alleged lateness, BNH seeks to foreclose on the mortgage, thus moving for summary judgment in this foreclosure litigation.

The law of New York in this area, in short, is fact specific. The Appellate Division, Third Department, in New York Guardian Mortgagee Corp. v. Olexa, 176 A.D.2d 399, 574 N.Y.S.2d 107 (1991), in pertinent part, stated: "The law is clear that when a mortgagor defaults on loan payments, even if only for a day, a mortgagee may accelerate the loan, require that the balance be tendered or commence foreclosure proceedings, and equity will not intervene." Id. at 401, 574 N.Y.S.2d 107, quoted with approval in Home Sav. of Am. v. Isaacson, 240 A.D.2d 633, 633, 659 N.Y.S.2d 94 (2nd Dept.1997).

The Appellate Division, Second Department, in the last cited case, Home Sav. of Am. v. Isaacson, 240 A.D.2d 633, 633, 659 N.Y.S.2d 94 (1997), held that the appellant mortgagor did not tender the entire balance due within the relevant contractual time so as to stave off foreclosure.

Notwithstanding the aforementioned holdings, the Appellate Division, in several cases, has held that a summary judgment motion should be denied where the mortgagor asserts a valid defense, including tender of the entire amount then due, the mortgagee's opportunistic bad faith, or an unconscionable act. See, e.g., Grand Pacific Fin. Corp. v. 97–111 Hale, LLC, 123 A.D.3d 764, 1 N.Y.S.3d 115 (2nd Dept.2014) (fact issues existed as whether mortgagee acted in bad faith and engaged in oppressive and unconscionable conduct); New York Guardian Mortgagee Corp. v. Olexa, 176 A.D.2d at 402, 574 N.Y.S.2d 107, supra; European American Bank v. Harper, 163 A.D.2d 458, 461, 558 N.Y.S.2d 155 (2nd Dept.1990) (equitable remedy of foreclosure may be denied to prevent overreaching or other unconscionable conduct by mortgagee); DiMatteo v. North Tonawanda Auto Wash, Inc., 101 A.D.2d 692, 693, 476 N.Y.S.2d 40 (4th Dept.1984) ("Unconscionability on the part of the mortgagee, however, has long been recognized as a defense to enforcement of an acceleration provision."), appeal dismissed, 63 N.Y.2d 675 (1984).

In DiMatteo v. North Tonawanda Auto Wash, Inc., 101 A.D.2d 692, 476 N.Y.S.2d 40, supra, the Appellate Division found that an inadvertent default by the mortgagor raised factual questions that might prevent foreclosure. The monthly mortgage installments in DiMatteo were due on the first day of the month, with a seven-day grace period. A monthly mortgage payment was timely written, but later found to have been made on insufficient funds. The mortgagor claimed that had the check been deposited when issued, it would have cleared. The mortgagor also claimed, in that case, that the mortgagee gave no opportunity to cure the default.

The Supreme Court in DiMatteo granted the mortgagee's motion for summary judgment. In a substantial modification, basically amounting to a reversal, the Fourth Department ruled that summary judgment should not have been granted to either party, invoking the defense of unconscionability. The appellate court stated:

Defendant here has attempted to show that its default was the result of innocent and inadvertent mistake and, by implication at least, that it attempted to cure the default upon learning of it. Defendant claims that its default resulted from error in the balancing of its checking account, and that plaintiffs were but slightly inconvenienced with respect to only one installment payment. There has been no showing that the default prejudiced plaintiffs in any way. Defendant, therefore, has raised factual questions which, if resolved in its favor, could prevent foreclosure.

DiMatteo v. North Tonawanda Auto Wash, Inc., 101 A.D.2d at 693, 476 N.Y.S.2d 40. Just as in DiMatteo, there has been no showing in the case at bar that the mortgagee was prejudiced in any way by the late payment.

Plaintiff BNH, in the present case, has established its prima facie case for foreclosure on its motion for summary judgment, under the current facts. See, Grand Pacific Fin. Corp. v. 97–111 Hale, LLC, 123 A.D.3d at 766, 1 N.Y.S.3d 115, supra. In opposition to the movants' prima facie showing, defendant Mabry has demonstrated a lack of any prejudice by the plaintiff in the late mortgage payment or that the default prejudiced the plaintiff in any way. See, DiMatteo v. North Tonawanda Auto Wash, Inc., 101 A.D.2d at 693, 476 N.Y.S.2d 40, supra.

Concerning New York Court of Appeals decisions relating to the enforceability of acceleration clauses, compare 172 Van Duzer Realty Corp. v. Globe Alumni Student Assistance Ass'n, Inc., 24 N.Y.3d 528, 2 N.Y.S.3d 39, 25 N.E.3d 952 (2014) (tenant entitled to hearing on whether collection of undiscounted acceleration rent was an enforceable penalty) with Fifty States Mgt. Corp. v. Pioneer Auto Parks, 46 N.Y.2d 573, 415 N.Y.S.2d 800, 389 N.E.2d 113 (1979) (equity will not intervene in a provision in 20-year lease term between commercial parties providing for the acceleration of the rent due for the entire lease term upon the tenant's default in a monthly rent installment). See discussion in 172 Van Duzer Realty Corp. v. Globe Alumni Student Assistance Ass'n, Inc., 24 N.Y.3d at 534, 2 N.Y.S.3d 39, 25 N.E.3d 952 distinguishing Fifty States Mgt. Corp. v. Pioneer Auto Parks, 46 N.Y.2d at 575–578, 415 N.Y.S.2d 800, 389 N.E.2d 113.

In this Court's opinion, defendant Mabry has set forth a meritorious defense based upon the unconscionability of the plaintiff BNH, whose attorney, Mr. Zubli, accepted the April, 2014 check and caused it to be deposited. Instead of defaulting on a previous occasion, Mabry, in fact, had been lulled into a sense of belief that her tardy payment would be accepted, albeit with the imposition of additional late fees. See exhibit G to the moving affirmation of Mr. Zubli, of his letter to Mabry dated August 19, 2013. No warning had previously been given her that a future late payments would result in default.

This case shows, as alluded by the Court's opening paragraph, that in mortgage foreclosure cases, a day's passage may, indeed, make a very big difference. This Court, however, will not lend its imprimatur to a stratagem designed to accelerate an entire loan balance and deprive the mortgagor of her real property for the failure to include a late fee of $118.15. The branch of plaintiff BNH's motion seeking summary judgment is, therefore, denied.

* * *

NOTES

1. *Tender before or after acceleration.* When or if acceleration occurs can have crucial consequences for the parties. If the mortgagor tenders the arrearages (past-due installments) before acceleration, the mortgage is reinstated. See, e.g., Delandro v. America's Mortg. Servicing, Inc., 674 So.2d 184 (Fla.App.1996); Kent v. Pipia, 185 Mich.App. 599, 462 N.W.2d 800 (1990). After acceleration, only tender of the full accelerated mortgage debt will suffice, unless a statute provides to the contrary. See, e.g., United Companies Lending Corp. v. Hingos, 283 A.D.2d 764, 724 N.Y.S.2d 134 (2001); City Savings Bank of Bridgeport v. Dessoff, 3 Conn.App. 644, 491 A.2d 424 (1985); Dime Savings Bank of New York v. Glavey, 214 A.D.2d 419, 625 N.Y.S.2d 181 (1995). A mortgagee's post-acceleration acceptance of arrearages only reduces the mortgage obligation but does not defeat the acceleration. See Ryder v. Bank of Hickory Hills, 146 Ill.2d 98, 165 Ill.Dec. 650, 585 N.E.2d 46 (1991).

When does acceleration take place? Most acceleration clauses are "optional," as opposed to "automatic," in the sense that acceleration does not automatically occur when the mortgagor defaults. In some states, both notice of intent to accelerate and notice of acceleration itself are required unless the parties agree otherwise. See, e.g., Karam v. Brown, 407 S.W.3d 464 (Tex. Ct. App. 2013); Shumway v. Horizon Credit Corp., 801 S.W.2d 890 (Tex.1991); Ogden v. Gibraltar Sav. Ass'n, 640 S.W.2d 232 (Tex.1982). However, in most jurisdictions, notice is not mandatory. Rather, the mortgagee "must perform some affirmative, overt act evidencing his intention to take advantage of the accelerating provision. 650 Brooklyn LLC v. Hunte, 3 N.Y.S.3d 909 (N.Y. Sup. Ct. 2015). Such affirmative action must be taken before the debtor tenders what is actually due, or the creditor loses his right to treat the entire debt as due because of that particular default." Rajic v. Faust, 972 N.Y.S.2d 146 (N.Y. Sup. Ct. 2013) (unreported); Spires v. Lawless, 493 S.W.2d 65, 73 (Mo.App.1973). In some states, the affirmative action must be a notice to the mortgagor. See, e.g., Mass. Gen. Laws ch. 244, § 35A; 4518 S. 256th, LLC v. Karen L. Gibbon, P.S., 195 Wash. App. 423, 382 P.3d 1 (2016); Wells Fargo Bank, N.A. v. Girouard, 123 A.3d 216 (Me. 2015); In re Crystal Properties, Ltd., 268 F.3d 743 (9th Cir.2001) (California law).

Mortgagees often use notice to the mortgagor to establish the requisite affirmative action. In many states, commencement of a foreclosure proceeding is sufficient evidence of an election to accelerate. See Nelson, Whitman, Burkhart & Freyermuth, Real Estate Finance Law § 7.6 (6th ed.2015). Under the Restatement, acceleration is "effective on the date specified in a written notice delivered by mortgagee to mortgagor after the latter's default. The notice may provide that the acceleration is effective immediately or at some future specified date." Restatement (Third) of Property (Mortgages) § 8.1, cmt. b (1997).

2. *Waiver, abandonment, and estoppel.* Virtually all courts recognize that acceleration may sometimes be defeated by mortgagee *waiver.* For examples in which acceleration was precluded by the mortgagee's consistent

past pattern of accepting late payments, see Alderman v. Davidson, 326 Or. 508, 954 P.2d 779 (1998) (repeated acceptance of late installment payments constituted waiver of right to accelerate); Rosselot v. Heimbrock, 54 Ohio App.3d 103, 561 N.E.2d 555 (1988); McGowan v. Pasol, 605 S.W.2d 728 (Tex.Civ.App.1980). See generally, Nelson, Whitman, Burkhart & Freyermuth, Real Estate Finance Law § 7.7 (6th ed.2015).

Sometimes, mortgagors assert that the mortgagee has *abandoned* or *waived* an otherwise valid acceleration. As stated in Note 1, the mortgagee's post-acceleration acceptance of arrearages normally only reduces the mortgage debt and does not impair the validity of the acceleration and foreclosure. Of course, a mortgagor and mortgagee can agree to undo or "abandon" an earlier acceleration. To what extent, however, can the parties' post-acceleration actions cause abandonment? For example, suppose that, after acceleration, a mortgagee accepts arrearages and several monthly installment payments from the mortgagor but forecloses nonjudicially almost a year later for the then mortgage balance. In this situation, a court arguably could conclude that the parties' post-acceleration actions evidence an agreement to abandon the earlier acceleration and, therefore, that the foreclosure based on that acceleration is invalid. However, courts rarely find abandonment. See generally, Martin v. Federal National Mortgage Ass'n, 814 F.3d 315 (5th Cir. 2016); Holy Cross Church of God in Christ v. Wolf, 44 S.W.3d 562 (Tex.2001); Fitzgerald v. Harry, 2003 WL 22147557 (Tex.App.2003, not reported in S.W.2d) (post-acceleration letter from mortgagee to mortgagor stating "in the event you do not pay your note payments . . . your unpaid note balance will be accelerated" together with a "vague assertion" that the mortgagee accepted subsequent note payments were insufficient to constitute abandonment). But see Jatera Corp. v. U.S. Bank National Ass'n, 917 F.3d 831 (5th Cir. 2019); Bank of New York Mellon v. Peterson, 442 P.3d 1006 (Colo. Ct. App. 2019).

Is it good public policy to be generous in finding waiver or abandonment? Will forbearance by mortgagees be discouraged? Suppose the note or mortgage contains "anti-waiver" language. According to the Restatement, while "such a provision may, in close cases, tip the balance against a finding of waiver, it usually is not dispositive on the waiver issue." Restatement (Third) of Property (Mortgages) § 8.1 cmt. e (1997). But see Gaul v. Olympia Fitness Center, Inc., 88 Ohio App.3d 310, 623 N.E.2d 1281 (1993) ("a mortgagee's past acceptance of late loan payments does not constitute a waiver of mortgagee's right to accelerate * * * following a subsequent default where the relevant loan documents contain 'anti-waiver' provisions."). Consider the following language of the Connecticut Supreme Court:

[U]nder this court's interpretation of nonwaiver clauses * * * the plaintiff's conduct in affording the defendant eight additional days to stave off the consequences of acceleration and foreclosure by curing the default cannot be construed as a waiver of its option to accelerate the mortgage loan. Indeed, a conclusion by this court that a lender, by giving a borrower one more opportunity to cure a default, has not clearly and unequivocally exercised its right to accelerate the debt, ultimately would militate against persons in the defendant's position; such a conclusion surely would eviscerate any inclination or incentive that a lender might have to extend any kind of generosity or flexibility to borrowers in default, on the eve of commencing litigation. Moreover, the letter from the plaintiff's attorney was not contradictory, as the defendant claims, because beyond affording the defendant a few more days to cure her default, *it did not retract expressly the previous notice of acceleration.*

Webster Bank v. Oakley, 265 Conn. 539, 551, 830 A.2d 139, 147–48 (2003).

Even if no consistent prior pattern of forbearance exists, a mortgagee may sometimes be *estopped* to accelerate based on a single transaction. For example, a mortgagee may be estopped if it attempts to accelerate after orally assuring a mortgagor in default that acceleration and foreclosure will be postponed while the mortgagor attempts to sell the mortgaged property. Unless the mortgagee gives reasonable notice that it is withdrawing the extension, the mortgagor has a defense to acceleration if she detrimentally relied on the assurance. See Nelson, Whitman, Burkhart & Freyermuth, Real Estate Finance Law § 7.7 (6th ed.2015).

3. *Defaults other than failure to pay installments.* Depending on the language of the acceleration clause, acceleration may be triggered not only by failure to pay installments of principal or interest, but also by such derelictions as failure to insure or pay taxes. When a non-debt related default triggers acceleration, should reinstatement of insurance or payment of taxes before the foreclosure sale be sufficient to avoid acceleration, or must the mortgagor also pay the accelerated debt? Compare Jeffery v. Seven Seventeen Corp., 461 A.2d 1009 (Del.1983) and Parrott v. Wallace, 127 Idaho 306, 900 P.2d 214 (App.1995) with Balducci v. Eberly, 304 Md. 664, 500 A.2d 1042 (1985) and Eisen v. Kostakos, 116 N.J.Super. 358, 282 A.2d 421 (App.Div.1971).

Under the Restatement view, only tender of the accelerated debt will defeat acceleration in the non-debt related default context. See Restatement (Third) of Property (Mortgages) § 8.1(c) & cmt. c (1997). Interestingly, a few courts have held that impairment of security is needed to justify acceleration when the mortgagor fails to pay taxes or maintain casualty insurance on the mortgaged premises. See Mid-State Trust II v. Jackson, 42 Ark.App. 112, 854 S.W.2d 734 (1993) (insurance); Vonk v. Dunn, 161 Ariz. 24, 775 P.2d 1088 (1989) (taxes); Freeman v. Lind, 181 Cal.App.3d 791, 226 Cal.Rptr. 515 (1986) (insurance), *abrogated by* Cal. Civ. Code § 2924.7.

4. *Note and mortgage inconsistency.* Problems arise when the note and mortgage are inconsistent with respect to acceleration. Suppose the mortgage contains an acceleration clause, but the note does not. Most courts permit acceleration in the event of default and allow foreclosure for the full amount of the mortgage debt. This is the Restatement approach. See Restatement (Third) of Property (Mortgages) § 8.1(a) (1997). However, some courts do not permit a deficiency judgment under these circumstances. See Robert Kratovil, Modern Mortgage Law and Practice 84 (1988).

5. *Absence of acceleration clause.* Suppose that the note and mortgage do not include an acceleration clause or that the clause is unenforceable for some reason. If the mortgagor defaults on its payment obligation, courts occasionally permit acceleration based on the contract concept of anticipatory repudiation. See Barnett v. Oliver, 18 Kan.App.2d 672, 858 P.2d 1228 (1993) (trial court did not abuse its equitable discretion by accelerating balance in absence of acceleration clause). However, in the absence of an enforceable acceleration clause, the mortgagee normally can foreclose only for the installment in default. When this occurs, what does the foreclosure purchaser get? How much should he or she pay? What happens to the surplus, if any? See Nelson, Whitman, Burkhart & Freyermuth, Real Estate Finance Law § 7.8 (6th ed.2015). Some jurisdictions address these issues statutorily. See, e.g., Minn.Stat.Ann. § 580.09; West's Ann.Cal.Code Civ.Proc. § 728; Golden v. Ramapo Imp. Corp., 78 A.D.2d 648, 432 N.Y.S.2d 238 (1980) (interpreting New York statute).

6. *Arrearages legislation.* Many states have enacted "arrearages" legislation that permits the mortgagor to defeat acceleration by curing the default that existed before acceleration. See, e.g., Alaska Stat. § 34.20.070(b); West's Ann.Cal.Civ.Code § 2924c; Minn. Stat. Ann. § 580.30; Pa.Stat. tit. 41, § 404; Utah Code Ann. § 57–1–31. These statutes authorize the landowner to stop a foreclosure by paying the arrearages.

Can a junior lienor also exercise that right after the lender has accelerated the loan? The Alaska Supreme Court was confronted with this issue when interpreting Alaska Stat. § 34.20.070(b), which provides in pertinent part:

> At any time before the sale, if the default has arisen by failure to make payments required by the trust deed, the default may be cured by payment of the sum in default other than the principal that would not then be due if no default had occurred, plus attorney fees or court costs actually incurred by the trustee due to the default.

According to the court:

> [T]he language admits of two possible interpretations. The legislature may have omitted express mention of obligors because it assumed that the reference would apply only to obligors; alternatively, it may have omitted express mention because it wished to include other interested parties * * *. From the plain text either interpretation is plausible.

> Because the statute is written in the passive voice—it states that the "default may be cured"—its meaning is ambiguous. * * *

> Especially when statutory language and legislative history are ambiguous, we look to the common law as a useful tool to discern legislative intent and to interpret statutes. * * *

> The equity of redemption * * * is analogous to the right of cure granted [by § 34.20.070(b)]. If a lienholder is able to redeem the property, then that person should also be able to cure a default. * * *

We have characterized cure as a type of redemption: "If the party who executes the deed of trust defaults the obligation, the party nonetheless has a right of redemption. In other words, the party has the opportunity to cure the default at any time *before* a nonjudicial sale." Therefore just as the junior lienholder has the right to redeem a mortgage, we determine that the junior lienholder also possesses the right to cure default on a deed of trust before the foreclosure sale. Our conclusion is further buttressed by the twin principles that redemption statutes should be construed liberally and that equity abhors a forfeiture.

Young v. Embley, 143 P.3d 936, 944–46 (2006).

Under the Minnesota statute, the mortgagor can reinstate the mortgage by paying, before the foreclosure sale, "the amount actually due thereon and constituting the default actually existing in the conditions of the mortgage at the time of the commencement of the foreclosure proceedings * * *." Minn.Stat.Ann. § 580.30. Do the terms "amount actually due" and "default actually existing" mean the amount due and the default existing now that the mortgagee has accelerated? See Davis v. Davis, 293 Minn. 44, 196 N.W.2d 473 (1972).

Are arrearages statutes subject to abuse by mortgagors who may default repeatedly, knowing they can defeat acceleration by simply tendering the arrearages? Will the requirement that, in addition to arrearages, the mortgagor pay statutory attorney's fees and certain other costs deter potential abuse? Should the number of reinstatements be limited? See Pa.Stat.Ann. tit. 41, § 404 (mortgagor limited to three reinstatements per year). Will commercial mortgagors be willing repeatedly to accept the economic penalties of reinstatement, especially in the case of mortgages of substantial dollar amount? Should statutory reinstatement rights be accorded only to residential mortgagors? See the Pennsylvania statute, supra.

7. *Bankruptcy Code.* Suppose a mortgagee accelerates the debt and the mortgagor does not have a statutory or contractual right to defeat acceleration by a pre-foreclosure tender of arrearages. If the mortgagor files a Chapter 13 bankruptcy proceeding before foreclosure, the bankruptcy court has ample authority to permit the mortgagor to reinstate the mortgage by paying the arrearages. See Section J of this chapter, infra.

8. *Fannie Mae/Freddie Mac mortgage form language.* The Fannie Mae/Freddie Mac standard residential mortgage or deed of trust form contains important limitations on the acceleration process. It requires the mortgagee to give the mortgagor a detailed mailed notice and a thirty-day grace period before acceleration, and it permits the mortgagor to defeat acceleration until five days before foreclosure by paying the arrearages and the mortgagee's reasonable costs and attorney's fees. See Appendix, Form 3, ¶ 19 and Forms 4 and 6, ¶ 22. These provisions may be omitted from the Fannie Mae/Freddie Mac form only if state law is more protective of the mortgagor. Because most institutional lenders want the option of selling their home mortgages to these

two secondary market purchasers, the Fannie Mae/Freddie Mac form is very widely used. Therefore, even in states that do not statutorily regulate acceleration, vast numbers of mortgagors have substantial protection against abuse of the acceleration process.

2. MARSHALING

If a mortgage covers more than one parcel of land, should the mortgagee sell them together or separately at a foreclosure sale? If the mortgagee should sell them separately, which parcel should it sell first? These questions are particularly important if some parcels are encumbered by junior liens or other subordinate interests, while others are not. Naturally, the junior interest holders would like the mortgagee to foreclose first on the parcels without junior interests, because those foreclosures may generate enough money to satisfy the mortgagor's outstanding debt and thereby extinguish the mortgage on the other parcels.

Marshaling is an equitable doctrine that may dictate the order in which a mortgagee must foreclose. The first rule of marshaling, called the "two funds" rule, represents an attempt, when possible, to avoid the unnecessary elimination of junior interests. The term "two funds" is a bit misleading; it is more accurate to say that are two items of collateral. In the following case, the two items are (1) the surface estate in certain parcels of land and (2) the mineral estate in the same parcels.

MATTER OF ESTATE OF HANSEN
Supreme Court of North Dakota, 1990
458 N.W.2d 264

MESCHKE, JUSTICE.

* * *

In February 1975, Albert Hansen borrowed $53,000 from the Bank of North Dakota [BND] and, to secure the debt, mortgaged 1,040 acres of property in McKenzie County. The mortgage covered both the surface and minerals. In July 1981, Albert and Dianna Hansen gave the State Bank of Towner [SBT] a $200,000 promissory note in settlement of pending legal actions. See State Bank of Towner v. Hansen, 302 N.W.2d 760 (N.D.1981). To secure this debt, the Hansens gave SBT a second mortgage on the surface of the property earlier mortgaged to BND. The SBT mortgage expressly provided that the minerals "shall not be subject to this mortgage." The Hansens defaulted on the debt to SBT in November 1984. [Editors' Note: Subsequently, Hansen also defaulted to BND. Albert Hansen died, and Dianna Hansen appears here representing his estate.]

* * *

BND began foreclosure of its mortgage in August 1988 when Hansen was indebted to it for more than $70,000. The BND mortgage covered both the minerals and the surface of the Hansen property. In its answer to the BND complaint, SBT requested that BND marshal its security under NDCC 13–01–04 and 35–01–15 and sell the minerals first at the foreclosure sale because SBT's junior mortgage covered only the surface. Hansen answered and requested that the surface be sold first in seven separate parcels and that the minerals be sold second in the same sequence. BND objected and argued that the minerals could not be sold separately from the surface.

The trial court ruled that the minerals could be sold separately from the surface and ordered that the minerals be sold before the surface, but in separate parcels and in the sequence designated by Hansen. At the foreclosure sale on April 28, 1989, the minerals were sold to Williams, Walter F. Gehrts, Kenneth Henry, and Raymond Sharkey for a total of $74,680. Because that amount equaled the foreclosure judgment, BND was not aggrieved and did not appeal. Hansen appealed, however, urging that the trial court erred in ordering the minerals sold before the surface. * * *

[W]e conclude that the trial court properly marshaled the mortgaged property for the protection of SBT as a junior lienholder in this case.

The rules for marshaling mortgaged property to pay distinct debts are codified in this state. NDCC 13–01–04 sets forth the basic principle:

> Marshaling funds—Rights of creditors. When a creditor is entitled to resort to each of several funds for the satisfaction of his claim and another person has an interest in, or is entitled as a creditor to resort to, some but not all of them, the latter may require the former to seek satisfaction from those funds to which the latter has no such claim so far as it can be done without impairing the right of the former to complete satisfaction and without doing injustice to third persons.

The pertinent part of NDCC 35–01–15 is to the same effect:

> Order of resort for payment—Marshaling securities. When a person has a lien upon several things and other persons have subordinate liens upon or interests in some but not all of the same things, the person having the prior lien, if he can do so without the risk of loss to himself or of injustice to other persons, on the demand of any party interested, must resort to the property in the following order:
>
> 1. To the things upon which he has an exclusive lien.

These enactments codify the long-recognized equitable duty owed by a senior lienholder to a junior lienholder. See Aberle v. Merkel, 70 N.D. 89,

291 N.W. 913, 918 (1940); Union Nat'l Bank v. Milburn & Stoddard Co., 7 N.D. 201, 73 N.W. 527 Syllabus 4 (1897). The principle applies here.

Assuming that sale of the minerals separately from the surface was correct, these marshaling statutes entitled SBT to have the minerals, on which it had no lien, sold before the surface if it could be done without risk of loss to BND or injustice to Hansen. Hansen and SBT agreed that the surface and minerals should be sold separately and do not challenge this part of the decision on appeal.

The trial court partially granted Hansen's request as to the sequence of the sale of the parcels but, contrary to her request, ordered that the minerals be sold before the surface. Hansen asserts that this violated her right to designate the sequence of sale of the parcels authorized by 1987 N.D.Sess.Laws Ch. 194 and NDCC 28–23–07. Section 5 of 1987 N.D.Sess. Laws Ch. 194 said that "[a]t the foreclosure sale, or in writing at least ten days prior to sale, the debtor may direct the division of the property into known lots or parcels and may direct the order in which the lots or parcels and the remaining property, or other property may be sold, as provided by section 28–23–07." NDCC 28–23–07 says that the "debtor, if present at the sale, may direct the order in which property, real or personal, shall be sold, when such property consists of several known lots or parcels or of articles which can be sold to advantage separately, and the sheriff or other officer must follow such directions."

These two statutory rights of the debtor to designate the sequence of sale "of known lots or parcels" do not differ substantially. See Production Credit Ass'n v. Henderson, 429 N.W.2d 421, 425 (N.D.1988). The purpose of these laws is "to give the [debtor] an opportunity to redeem from any, or all parcels or lots, to sell only so much of the property as is necessary to pay the debt, and to get the highest possible price for the land sold." Figenskau v. Wiege, 56 N.D. 768, 219 N.W. 471, 472 (1928). They are also intended to assist a debtor in protecting homestead rights. See First Security Bank, Underwood, N.D. v. Enyart, 439 N.W.2d 801, 806–807 (N.D.1989). Absent any other rights, these provisions authorized Hansen to direct that the surface be sold before the minerals if it could be sold to advantage separately.

Neither Hansen nor SBT has cited any precedent assessing the interplay between a marshaling statute and a like manner-of-sale statute, and we have not discovered any. However, "when two statutes relating to the same subject matter appear to be in conflict, they should, whenever possible, be construed to give effect to both if such can be done without doing violence to either." O'Fallon v. Pollard, 427 N.W.2d 809, 811 (N.D.1988); NDCC 1–02–07. Inconsistent statutes should be construed, if possible, to give effect to both.

This court has indicated that the manner-of-sale statute is not paramount in all events. In Michael v. Grady, 52 N.D. 740, 204 N.W. 182, 184 (1925), the court said that not every sale where property consisting of several known lots or parcels is sold en masse is subject to attack, "particularly in those cases where the several parcels are first offered separately but no bids are received thereon." Likewise we do not believe the Legislature intended that the debtor's right to designate the sequence of sale of parcels invariably overrides and defeats a junior lienholder's right to invoke equitable principles of marshaling.

The marshaling statutes and the manner-of-sale statutes are both designed to achieve equitable results for their intended beneficiaries. Where there exists more than one lien on the property, the trial court should balance the competing equities of the junior lienholder and of the debtor in settling the sequence of sale of parcels. We believe this approach harmonizes these provisions.

The trial court in this case properly weighed the equities in directing that the minerals be sold before the surface, in separate parcels and in the sequence requested by Hansen. Hansen was not injured by sale of the minerals first to pay the debt inasmuch as both the surface and minerals secured the BND mortgage. Hansen's attempt to free the minerals from the BND mortgage and make the junior lienholder, SBT, entirely subordinate to the BND debt would have placed SBT in a position nearly comparable to an unsecured creditor.

We are aware of statements in Douglas County State Bank v. Steele, 54 N.D. 686, 210 N.W. 657, 659 (1926), to the effect that, under the marshaling statutes, a homestead claimant could require a senior lienholder "to resort first to the nonhomestead quarter, even though to have done so would have wholly defeated the rights of the junior lienholder upon that quarter." However, Hansen's assertion that her homestead rights were violated is unpersuasive. In this case, we agree with the trial court that Hansen's homestead rights were adequately protected. Because the sale of minerals satisfied the BND mortgage, the surface was not sold and no redemption from the BND foreclosure was required for the mortgagors to retain the surface of the homestead parcel. Having requested a separate sale of the minerals, Hansen cannot object to the separate sale of the homestead minerals. Hansen did not request that the homestead minerals and the homestead surface be the very last parcels sold to satisfy the debt. * * * We conclude that the trial court's directions for the sequence of sale fairly balanced SBT's right to require marshaling and Hansen's right to specify the sequence of sale.

We therefore affirm the trial court's orders directing the sequence of sale and confirming the sheriff's sale.

NOTE ON THE INVERSE ORDER OF ALIENATION RULE

The form of marshaling involved in *Hansen* is the "two funds" rule. See Nelson, Whitman, Burkhart & Freyermuth, Real Estate Finance Law § 10.9 (6th ed.2015). See also In re Bay Circle Properties, LLC, 577 B.R. 587 (Bankr. N.D. Ga. 2017); In re Schantz, 2017 WL 3972451 (Bankr. N.D. Iowa). Courts often apply another form of marshaling when an owner gives a mortgage on real estate and then sells a portion of that real estate. For example, suppose that mortgagor borrows money and gives a "blanket" mortgage on her land, which consists of three residential lots. She then sold parcel 1 to A. Later, she sold parcel 2 to B. She retained parcel 3. Neither A nor B assumed the mortgage. Based on the mortgagor's promise to make the full payment on the mortgage debt, A and B both paid the full fair market value for their parcels, with no credit to the price for any part of the mortgage debt.

Is this a wise transaction for A or B? They purchased land subject to a mortgage but had no direct control of the payments due under it. If the mortgagor defaults, they may not even learn about the default until the foreclosure process is set in motion. Moreover, if A and B wish to redeem, they must pay the entire outstanding debt if the mortgagee has accelerated, which could be a great hardship or impossible for them. Most observers would conclude that, unless the mortgagor is exceptionally creditworthy and reliable, A and B have entered into a very risky transaction. Nevertheless, people sometimes agree to this arrangement. Can you see a safer way to structure it, assuming that the mortgagee will cooperate?

If the mortgagor defaults on the mortgage debt, in what order should the mortgagee foreclose on the three parcels?

> The traditional rule or doctrine of inverse order of alienation provides that where a portion of lands subject to a lien has been alienated, the grantees may insist that the land retained by the grantor or original owner be sold first to satisfy the lien * * * and that where the original owner has alienated all of the land subject to the lien in separate parcels successively, the parcels alienated or encumbered be sold in the reverse order of alienation. * * *

> The reason for this rule is that if the last parcel had been retained by the grantor, it would have been liable first to satisfy the judgment lien. * * * The purchaser of the parcel last alienated, who had notice of the prior alienation of other parcels encumbered by the judgment liens, "sits in the seat" of the common grantor, and has precisely the same rights and incurs the same obligations as the common grantor. Therefore, that purchaser's property must be sold first in order to satisfy the judgment lien.

Commonwealth Land Title Co. v. Kornbluth, 175 Cal.App.3d 518, 220 Cal.Rptr. 774 (1985). Under this reasoning, which is widely, though not universally, followed, the mortgagee must foreclose first on parcel 3, because the mortgagor still owns it. If this foreclosure does not produce sufficient funds to pay the mortgage debt in full, the mortgagee must foreclose next on B's parcel. If the debt is still unsatisfied, the mortgagee can foreclose on A's parcel.

Why does the grantor have to suffer foreclosure first? And why, as between the two grantees, should B suffer before A? Is this latter result harder to rationalize than the notion that the mortgagee should first foreclose on the mortgagor's land? Finally, do you see why a court will not protect A from immediate foreclosure if A assumed the entire debt or received credit for it against the purchase price for parcel 1?

Should the mortgagee be legally required to foreclose on B before A only if B had knowledge of A's position before buying parcel 2? Courts uniformly agree that B's knowledge is a prerequisite to marshaling. But how will B learn about A's position? The mortgagor obviously does not want to tell B, because doing so may discourage B from buying the land. If A's deed is recorded, should B be held to have constructive notice? The court in Commonwealth Land Title Co. v. Kornbluth, supra, commented: "The notice required is actual notice or notice presumed from circumstances and not constructive notice arising from recordation." See also BancorpSouth Bank v. Brantley, 156 So.3d 822 (Miss. 2014).

Why should this be the rule? If B does an ordinary title examination, B will discover the mortgage. Additionally, it will be obvious to B's title examiner that the mortgage covers more land than B is buying. Is it too much to ask that the title examiner further check the records to determine whether the mortgagor has already transferred some of the mortgaged real estate to a person like A? Or does that assume that the title examiner will understand the doctrine of marshaling?

While we have described the "inverse order of alienation" rule with respect to deeds from the mortgagor to A and B, the same principle applies when the mortgagor executes a blanket first mortgage on parcels 1 and 2, then gives A a second mortgage on parcel 1, and then later gives B a second mortgage on parcel 2. In this situation, the "two funds" rule does not apply to A and B, because parcels 1 and 2 are both encumbered by the blanket first mortgage and by either A's or B's second mortgage. But the "inverse order" rule requires the first mortgagee to foreclose on parcel 2 before foreclosing on parcel 1. See In re Shull, 72 B.R. 193 (Bankr.D.S.C.1986).

The Restatement (Third) of Property (Mortgages) § 8.6 (1997) endorses both the "two funds" rule and the "inverse order of alienation" rule. The Restatement notes that a court should order marshaling only if it would benefit the holders of subordinate interests. For example, a court should not require marshaling when the total value of the parcels is less than the outstanding first mortgage debt. Because the first mortgagee will have to foreclose on all the parcels, the order of foreclosures makes little difference to the junior lienholders. See Restatement § 8.6 cmt. d.

Putting marshaling aside for a moment, consider the foreclosure of a single mortgage that covers two or more parcels. Who should decide whether the mortgagee can sell them together ("in bulk") or separately? If the mortgagee will sell them separately, who should decide the order of sale? We consider this issue in Section D of this chapter.

B. MISCELLANEOUS FORECLOSURE METHODS

As mentioned previously, the two major methods of mortgage foreclosure in the United States are *judicial foreclosure* and *nonjudicial foreclosure*. Judicial foreclosure is available in every state and, in many states, is the only type of permitted foreclosure. It is an equitable action with a judicially supervised sale of the mortgaged property. In about 35 states, the prevailing method is a nonjudicial foreclosure under a power of sale. Depending on the state, the "power of sale" in a mortgage is vested in the mortgagee or in a public official, such as the sheriff or the "public trustee" in Colorado. In a deed of trust, which is used in most power of sale states, the power of sale is in the trustee. These two predominant methods, judicial sale and power of sale, will receive considerable emphasis in this chapter.

A relatively minor foreclosure method is *strict foreclosure*. Under this method, foreclosure is in court, but no foreclosure sale is held. Instead, the court gives the defaulting mortgagor a period of time to pay the mortgage debt. If the mortgagor fails to do so, title to the mortgaged property vests in the mortgagee without a sale. If the property is worth more than the mortgage debt, the mortgagor has no right to the excess. On the other hand, if the mortgaged real estate is worth less than the mortgage debt, the mortgagor is liable for the deficiency. See, e.g., Eichman v. J & J Bldg. Co., Inc., 216 Conn. 443, 582 A.2d 182 (1990). This method is still used in Vermont and in Connecticut. See, e.g., Conn.Gen.Stat.Ann. § 49–15; Farmers & Mechanics Bank v. Arbucci, 24 Conn.App. 486, 589 A.2d 14 (1991); Pacific Mut. Life Ins. Co. v. Broad Assocs. Ltd. Partn., 24 Conn.App. 42, 585 A.2d 115 (1991); Vt. Stat. Ann. tit. 12, § 4941; Vt.R.Civ.P., Rule 80.1(a)–(*l*); Stowe Center, Inc. v. Burlington Sav. Bank, 141 Vt. 634, 451 A.2d 1114 (1982). On the other hand, if the mortgagor or a junior lienholder makes a strong showing that the mortgaged real estate is worth more than the mortgage debt, the court may require a foreclosure sale. See, e.g., Brann v. Savides, 48 Conn.App. 807, 712 A.2d 963 (1998) (foreclosure by sale should have been ordered because the real estate's fair market value exceeded the obligation by more than $200,000). Strict foreclosure, as we shall see, is also available in many other jurisdictions to deal with the rather limited problem of how to handle a junior lienor who has been omitted from a judicial foreclosure suit.

NOTES

1. *Entry Without Process and Actions at Law for a Writ of Entry.* Some New England states permit two related foreclosure methods—*Entry Without*

Process and *Actions at Law for a Writ of Entry.* Under the former method, a mortgagee may take possession of the premises without legal help after the mortgagor defaults. If the mortgagee maintains possession for a time period varying from one to three years, the mortgagor's equity of redemption terminates. The mortgagee's entry must be peaceable. Its possession can be constructive, so that the mortgagor essentially becomes the mortgagee's tenant.

In the Action at Law for a Writ of Entry, the mortgagee initiates a judicial action and alleges that the mortgage is in default. After an accounting for what is due and owing, the court enters a judgment for possession of the premises. If the mortgagee takes and maintains possession for one to three years, depending on the jurisdiction, the mortgagor's equity of redemption terminates. Both of these methods result in strict foreclosure, because they do not require a property sale. Moreover, the mortgagee can obtain a deficiency judgment if the property is worth less than the mortgage debt. See generally, Nelson, Whitman, Burkhart & Freyermuth, Real Estate Finance Law § 7.11 (6th ed 2015).

2.   *Scire facias.* Scire facias is a type of judicial foreclosure at law that is used, for the most part, only in Delaware. It is similar to the remedy at law available to the ordinary execution creditor. After a default, the mortgagee can obtain a judicial writ of scire facias, which is an order for the mortgagor to show cause why the land should not be taken in execution to satisfy the defaulted mortgage obligation. If the mortgagee prevails, the court issues a judgment for the amount owing and a writ of *levari facias,* which directs that the judgment be satisfied from the proceeds of a public execution sale. See Gelof v. First Nat'l Bank of Frankford, 373 A.2d 206 (Del.Super. 1977). See also Nelson, Whitman, Burkhart & Freyermuth, Real Estate Finance Law § 7.12 n.259 (6th ed.2015).

3.   *Constitutionality of strict foreclosure.* Does vesting title to the mortgaged property in the mortgagee without a sale create constitutional problems? Does strict foreclosure violate the Due Process and Equal Protection Clauses of the United States Constitution because the mortgagee can obtain a deficiency judgment against the mortgagor if the mortgaged property's value is less than the mortgage debt, but the mortgagor has no claim if the property's value is greater than the debt?

In Dieffenbach v. Attorney General of Vermont, 604 F.2d 187 (2d Cir.1979), the United States Court of Appeals for the Second Circuit rejected both constitutional challenges to Vermont's strict foreclosure. The court emphasized that strict foreclosure does not violate substantive due process because it is rationally related to a legitimate state interest. According to the court, "[o]ne possible purpose of strict foreclosure is to make it easier for banks or other creditors to lend by giving them a speculative interest in the property, for the bank realizes that it may retain the excess if the property's value happens to exceed the debt. Another purpose might be to compensate the bank for its expense * * * in a foreclosure suit and subsequent sale. A third possibility is that, in an implicit quid pro quo, the legislature has granted the banks this speculative interest in return for requiring the banks to lend money at lower interest rates, and to permit prepayment without penalty." Id. at 196.

The court also rejected the equal protection challenge that strict foreclosure impermissibly burdens only those mortgagors whose property is worth more than the mortgage debt. The court reasoned that the "legislature may reasonably have concluded that strict foreclosure laws equitably distribute the commercial costs of mortgages because every mortgagor * * * is equally subject to the risk that his property's value will exceed the portion of his debt that he is unable to pay. The state's failure to 'insure' against the unequal actual incidence of this risk by permitting banks to absorb the risk in their interest rates does not amount to a violation of equal protection." Id. at 197.

C. JUDICIAL FORECLOSURE

NELSON, WHITMAN, BURKHART & FREYERMUTH, REAL ESTATE FINANCE LAW
605–606 (6th ed.2015)*

Judicial foreclosure, which is an equitable action, is a major method of foreclosure in the United States. It is the exclusive or generally used foreclosure method in 30% of the states. Moreover, it is available in every state, either by express statutory enactment or as an incident to the inherent jurisdiction of courts of equity. Even in jurisdictions where power of sale foreclosure is dominant, judicial foreclosure is necessary in certain special situations, such as when the mortgage does not authorize a power of sale foreclosure. For example, if a court holds that a document in the form of a deed is actually an equitable mortgage, the deed will not contain a power of sale clause and, therefore, must be foreclosed judicially. A mortgagee also should judicially foreclose when lien priority is disputed. In that situation, a judicial determination of lien priority will enable potential foreclosure purchasers to know the state of the title they will be bidding on. On the other hand, if the mortgagee foreclosed by power of sale, uncertainty as to lien priority would discourage bidding and create title problems for the sale purchaser. In some jurisdictions, deficiency judgments are unavailable after a power of sale foreclosure. Consequently, if the mortgagee believes that the foreclosure sale will yield less than the debt and wishes to retain the option of obtaining a deficiency judgment, judicial foreclosure is mandatory.

---

*   Reprinted with permission of LEG, Inc. d/b/a West Academic.

NOTES

1. *The "necessary-proper party" distinction.* Judicial foreclosures are subject to the same rules of civil procedure as other cases, including the rules concerning "necessary" and "proper" parties. Unfortunately, no unanimity exists concerning their meaning. However, the terminology is useful in the context of the basic purposes of a foreclosure proceeding. Two purposes are often articulated. First, a successful foreclosure should terminate the rights of all holders of interests that are "subject to" the mortgage being foreclosed. However, to state this proposition begs the question "why"? The answer is found in the more fundamental and descriptive purpose of foreclosure, which is to give the foreclosure sale purchaser essentially the title to the land "as it stood at the time of the time of the execution of the mortgage." Scharaga v. Schwartzberg, 149 A.D.2d 578, 540 N.Y.S.2d 451 (1989). Or, as the Restatement puts it, the purpose of foreclosure is to put "the foreclosure purchaser into the shoes of the mortgagor at the time the mortgage being foreclosed was executed." Restatement (Third) of Property (Mortgages) § 7.1 cmt. a (1997). In this sense, a party is "necessary" if failing to join it will defeat this purposes.

If a junior interest holder is not joined, "that interest is neither terminated nor otherwise prejudiced by the foreclosure." Id. cmt. b. For example, if a first mortgagee judicially forecloses and does not join the second mortgagee, the latter's mortgage remains on the land. In that case, the sale purchaser's title to the land is fundamentally different than the mortgagor's title when he executed the first mortgage. Thus, as a general rule, "necessary parties" are all persons who hold an interest in the mortgaged real estate that is junior to the mortgage being foreclosed. For a catalogue of these persons, see Nelson, Whitman, Burkhart & Freyermuth, Real Estate Finance Law § 7.13 (6th ed.2015). We will consider a little later in this section the rights of an omitted "necessary" party.

The reason judicial foreclosure does not terminate unjoined junior interests is constitutional. Consider the language of the following Kansas decision, holding that an unjoined junior lease is not terminated by foreclosure:

> There is no logic and no order to a theory which binds a tenant and automatically terminates his or her interest in real estate by a court decision to which he or she was not a party. Indeed, our sense of due process is offended by a rule which forecloses an interest in real estate where the holder of that interest is not given an opportunity to be heard on the issue. The Kansas rule is designed to ensure that a tenant may not have his or her leasehold interest in property automatically forfeited without the due process right of a day in court. We reject the argument that expediency and the complexities of modern society require that we abandon our present process for one which would adjudicate the property interests of non-parties to an action and bind them without having an opportunity to present their claims in court.

Citizens Bank & Trust v. Brothers Const. & Mfg., Inc., 18 Kan.App.2d 704, 859 P.2d 394, 398 (1993). Accord Como, Inc. v. Carson Square, Inc., 648 N.E.2d 1247 (Ind.App.1995).

2. *Impact of foreclosure on senior interests.* What is the status of a *senior* lien or other *senior* interest when a junior lienor forecloses? A senior lienor is not a "necessary" party because it is not subject to or subordinate to the mortgage being foreclosed. The senior lienor's interest will not be terminated or otherwise prejudiced by the junior foreclosure. See, e.g., Ruby Valley National Bank v. Wells Fargo Delaware Trust. Co., N.A., 317 P.3d 174 (Mont. 2014). To omit the senior from a foreclosure suit by the junior lienor will not defeat the purposes of foreclosure, because the senior's lien existed when the mortgagor executed the mortgage being foreclosed. Indeed, it is often said that only junior interest holders can be made parties-defendant without their consent.

On the other hand, can a senior lienor be joined, against its will, as a "proper" party? If so, to what extent will it be bound by the proceeding? Clearly, the foreclosing mortgagee can join a senior lienor for certain limited purposes. For example, a foreclosing junior lienor can join a senior lienor to determine the amount and terms of the senior lien. Do you see why this would be important from the foreclosing junior lienor's perspective? The foreclosing lienor also can join a person who claims to hold a senior lien if the foreclosing lienor claims that its lien is senior. The foreclosure proceeding can be used to determine this priority dispute.

On the other hand, will a court ever force a senior lienor to be joined for the purpose of selling the property free and clear of its lien, with the sale proceeds distributed according to lien priority? Normally, the answer is no. Should the result be different if the senior lien is in default? Even in that situation, shouldn't the senior mortgagee be able to choose its own time for selling and not be forced to do so in a market that, in its judgment, is unfavorable? Only a few courts have upheld such "free and clear" foreclosures over the senior lienor's objection, even when the senior mortgage is in default. For a discussion of these problems, see Nelson, Whitman, Burkhart & Freyermuth, Real Estate Finance Law § 7.15 (6th ed.2015); Durfee, Cases on Security §§ 203–204 (1951). For a thoughtful argument that junior lienors should normally have the power to foreclose "free and clear" of senior liens, see David Gray Carlson, Simultaneous Attachment of Liens on After-Acquired Property, 6 Cardozo L.Rev. 505, 530–34 (1985).

3. *Junior lessee as a necessary party.* The presence of lessees in a foreclosure proceeding, judicial or otherwise, presents special problems. In this connection reconsider *Dover Mobile Estates v. Fiber Form Products, Inc.* supra Chapter Four, Section B. If a lease is senior to the mortgage, the lessee and lease are unaffected by foreclosure. The sale purchaser obtains the mortgagor's interest and becomes the lessee's landlord. See Annot., Effect of Foreclosure of Mortgage as Terminating Lease, 14 A.L.R. 664. Because the foreclosure does not affect the lease, the lessee is not a "necessary" party in a judicial foreclosure

proceeding. On the other hand, if the mortgage is senior to the lease, the general rule is that the foreclosure of the leased premises:

> nullifies and extinguishes the lease * * *. No contract of lease which the mortgagor may make with respect to the mortgaged premises either inures to the benefit of the mortgagee or is binding on him. There is no privity of either estate or contract between the mortgagee and the lessee of the mortgagor to bind either, and the foreclosure of the mortgage avoids the lease and releases the lessee from any obligation. The tenancy created by attornment between the mortgagor's lessee and the purchaser under the foreclosure is an entirely new tenancy, and not a continuation of the old tenancy with the substitution of a new landlord. Whenever the estate which the lessor had at the time of making the lease is defeated or determined, the lease is extinguished with it.

Roosevelt Hotel Corp. v. Williams, 227 Mo.App. 1063, 56 S.W.2d 801, 802 (1933). Accord Reilly v. Firestone Tire & Rubber Co., 764 F.2d 167 (3d Cir.1985).

If a foreclosing mortgagee does not join a junior lessee, one would assume that the lessee's interest would be unaffected by the foreclosure. Indeed, that is the majority and clearly correct rule. See, e.g., Como, Inc. v. Carson Square, Inc., 648 N.E.2d 1247 (Ind.App.1995); Citizens Bank & Trust v. Brothers Const. & Mfg., Inc., 18 Kan.App.2d 704, 859 P.2d 394 (1993); Nelson, Whitman, Burkhart & Freyermuth, Real Estate Finance Law § 7.13 (6th ed.2015). However, a few courts hold that, while most unjoined junior interests survive foreclosure, junior leases do not. One Ohio court described the rationale for this holding:

> Where interests are of a type properly determinable in foreclosure proceedings, they survive the foreclosure if not joined. Among that type are title, liens, or similar interests. Where interests are not of that type, among which are to be found the personal rights of possession and quiet enjoyment conveyed by lessor to lessee, joinder is not necessary and they are foreclosed absolutely. * * *

> We agree with the analysis * * * that the rights of possession and quiet enjoyment through the lease are personal rights; their existence derives from the lessor's title, and they are extinguished upon the foreclosure of that title and the interests incident to it.

Hembree v. Mid-America Federal Sav. & Loan Ass'n, 64 Ohio App.3d 144, 154–55, 580 N.E.2d 1103, 1109–10 (1989). See Menard, Inc. v. 1945 Cornell, LLC, 991 N.E.2d 360 (App. Ct. 2013); New York Life Ins. Co. v. Simplex Products Corp., 135 Ohio St. 501, 21 N.E.2d 585 (1939). Does this reasoning satisfy you? Don't all junior interests "derive from" the mortgagor's title?

If, as most courts hold, an omitted junior lessee's interest is unaffected by a foreclosure sale, can the foreclosing mortgagee choose whether to sell the property subject to the lease or free and clear of it? Does this rule encourage mortgagees intentionally to omit a junior lessee whose lease is substantially more pro-landlord than would be possible if negotiated under current market conditions?

The cases are divided about equally on whether the mortgagee may "pick and choose" which leases "live" or "die." See Nelson, Whitman, Burkhart & Freyermuth, Real Estate Finance Law § 7.13 (6th ed.2015). In states that don't allow the mortgagee to pick and choose, the courts permit an unjoined tenant to intervene in the foreclosure proceeding to get its (presumably undesirable from the tenant's viewpoint) lease wiped out.

Do the pick-and-choose states confer "a bonus on a mortgagee that violates the normal foreclosure maxim encouraging joinder of all junior interest holders"? Nelson, Whitman, Burkhart & Freyermuth, Real Estate Finance Law 612 (6th ed.2015). On the other hand, when a junior lessee enters into a lease for a fixed term, why should the fortuity of a default in the landlord's mortgage allow him or her to escape the lease obligation? If the mortgagor-landlord had voluntarily sold the reversion, the tenant would not be relieved of most lease obligations. Why should the result be different if the mortgagor-landlord's interest is transferred through the foreclosure process?

As *Dover Mobile Estates* and its note also illustrate, mortgagor-landlords, lessees, and mortgagees commonly adjust their relationships vis á vis each other through devices such as subordination, non-disturbance, and attornment agreements. Are these devices ultimately the better approach for dealing with the pick-and-choose issue?

In response to the massive number of foreclosures that occurred during the Great Recession that began in 2008, the federal government and several state and local governments enacted laws to help protect junior tenants after a senior lien has been foreclosed. See, e.g., Protecting Tenants at Foreclosure Act, 12 U.S.C. § 5220; Office of the Comptroller of the Currency, Bulletin 2020–9 (March 2, 2020); D.C. Code § 42–3505.01; Mass. Gen. Laws Ann. ch. 186A, § 2; N.H. Rev. Stat. Ann. § 540:2.

As stated in the preceding notes, if a junior interest holder is not joined in a judicial foreclosure on a senior lien, the junior interest is unaffected. What rights does the junior interest holder have? What rights does the purchaser at the senior foreclosure sale have?

ABDONEY V. YORK

District Court of Appeal of Florida, Second District, 2005
903 So.2d 981

STRINGER, JUDGE.

Emmett Abdoney seeks review of (1) the final summary judgment in favor of Janetta York in Abdoney's mortgage foreclosure action and (2) the final order that awarded York attorney's fees and costs. Because the trial court erred in determining that Abdoney's junior lien was extinguished by the filing of a certificate of sale in a prior foreclosure action concerning the same property, we reverse. In accordance with this ruling, we reverse the award of prevailing party attorney's fees and costs to York.

Emmett Abdoney, a practicing attorney, was given a second mortgage by Jason and Betty Peterson for $12,000 in attorney's fees and costs that they owed Abdoney. For personal reasons, Abdoney promised the Petersons that he would not foreclose the second mortgage. The Petersons failed to make payments on their first mortgage with Amerivest Corporation, and Amerivest instituted a foreclosure action against the Petersons and three junior lienors, one of which was Abdoney.

Abdoney entered into an agreement with Amerivest to buy out the first mortgage. Amerivest voluntarily dismissed Abdoney from the foreclosure suit, and the parties filed a joint stipulation for substitution of plaintiff. The court ordered the substitution, and Abdoney amended the foreclosure complaint but did not include himself in his capacity as a junior lienor.

The trial court entered a final judgment of foreclosure awarding Abdoney $11,269.27, and ordered a judicial sale. The final judgment did not specify a deadline for redemption. York was the successful bidder with a bid of $15,100, and the clerk filed a certificate of sale.

Shortly thereafter, Abdoney sent York a letter demanding satisfaction of his junior lien. In response, York filed a motion to declare junior lienor with notice barred in Abdoney's foreclosure action, which the court denied as premature. Abdoney subsequently made an offer and tendered a payment to York to either buy York out for her interest in the property or for her to buy Abdoney out. Additionally, Abdoney tendered payment as an offer of settlement in an attempt to preclude York from instituting foreclosure proceedings. York did not respond to Abdoney's offers.

Abdoney then filed a foreclosure action under a new case number. Abdoney's complaint sought (1) foreclosure against the Petersons, (2) foreclosure against York, (3) redemption, and (4) lien foreclosure. York filed an answer and counterclaim for (1) declaratory judgment, (2) quiet title, and (3) slander of title.

York subsequently filed a renewed motion to declare junior lienor with notice barred in the first foreclosure action. Abdoney moved to strike the motion to declare junior lienor barred for lack of standing, but the court denied the motion. The two cases were consolidated.

After a hearing, the court entered an order granting York's motion to declare junior lien barred. The court determined that Abdoney's junior lien was extinguished by the filing of the certificate of sale in the first foreclosure action. Both parties thereafter filed motions for summary judgment, and Abdoney filed a motion for rehearing of the court's order granting York's motion to declare junior lienor barred. York voluntarily dismissed her slander counterclaim. The court granted York's motion for final summary judgment and denied Abdoney's. The court also awarded York attorney's fees and costs pursuant to sections 57.041 and 57.105(1), Florida Statutes (2003), and an attorney's fee provision in the foreclosed mortgage.

On appeal, Abdoney argues that the trial court erred in granting York's motion for summary judgment and denying his motion for summary judgment because his junior lien was unaffected by the foreclosure sale. We agree and reverse and remand for further proceedings in Abdoney's foreclosure action.

Under the common law, the foreclosure of a senior mortgage extinguishes the liens of any junior mortgagees listed in the final judgment. Pinellas County v. Clearwater Fed. Sav. & Loan Ass'n, 214 So.2d 525, 527 (Fla. 2d DCA 1968). Thus, a junior mortgagee's right of redemption ceased at the entry of the final judgment of foreclosure if the junior mortgagee was made a party to the foreclosure of a senior mortgage. Shipp Corp., Inc. v. Charpilloz, 414 So.2d 1122, 1123 (Fla. 2d DCA 1982); Credithrift, Inc. v. Knowles, 556 So.2d 775, 777 (Fla. 1st DCA 1990); Islamorada Bank v. Rodriguez, 452 So.2d 61, 63 (Fla. 3d DCA 1984); Glendale Fed. Sav. & Loan Ass'n v. Guadagnino, 434 So.2d 54, 54 (Fla. 4th DCA 1983). In 1993, the legislature enacted section 45.0315, Florida Statutes, which lengthened the time for redemption by a junior mortgagee to "any time before the later of the filing of a certificate of sale by the clerk of the court or the time specified in the judgment, order, or decree." This statute abrogated the common law on the issue of the availability of redemption. Emanuel v. Bankers Trust Co., 655 So.2d 247, 249 (Fla. 3d DCA 1995).

When a junior mortgagee is omitted as a party to the foreclosure of a senior mortgage, the lien of the junior mortgagee is unaffected by the judgment. Quinn Plumbing Co. v. New Miami Shores Corp., 100 Fla. 413, 129 So. 690, 692 (1930); Hollingsworth v. Arcadia Citrus Growers Ass'n, 154 Fla. 399, 18 So.2d 159, 162 (1944); T-R Indian River Orange Co. v. Keene, 124 Fla. 343, 168 So. 408, 409 (1936). This is so because "while a sale has been held, it is not a sale in which the junior was a participant. He had no opportunity to bid for the property himself, nor to attempt to stir up other bidders in order to maximize the price paid for the property." Grant S. Nelson, Real Estate Finance Law, § 7.15, at 573 (4th ed. 2001). The lien of the senior mortgagee is likewise not extinguished by the irregular foreclosure action; instead, the purchaser at the foreclosure sale "becomes virtually an equitable assignee of the mortgage and of the debt it secured." Quinn Plumbing, 129 So. at 692. The purchaser "occupies the same position as the first mortgagee, . . . which may be enforced by such purchaser against the junior mortgagee to the same extent as they could have been enforced in the original foreclosure, had the junior mortgagee been made a party thereto." Id.

The only remedies of the purchaser against the omitted junior mortgagee are moving to compel redemption or re-foreclosure in a suit de novo. See Kurz v. Pappas, 116 Fla. 324, 156 So. 737, 741 (1934); Quinn, 129 So. at 692. The omitted junior mortgagee may defend in the same manner as if the foreclosure had not happened.[1] Quinn, 129 So. at 692.

The remedies of the omitted junior mortgagee against the purchaser are redemption and foreclosure. Nelson, supra, § 7.15, at 573–74. Foreclosure by the junior mortgagee with a resulting sale is subject to the first mortgage, which is revived. The purchaser will take the property subject to the first mortgage. Id. at 574. Pursuant to section 45.0315, the omitted junior mortgagee cannot independently exercise the right to redeem in the original foreclosure action after the certificate of sale has been filed. Burns v. Bankamerica Nat'l Trust Co., 719 So.2d 999, 1001 (Fla. 5th DCA 1998). If redemption is accomplished, the junior mortgagee holds both a senior and junior mortgage on the property, and he may foreclose either or both of them. Nelson, supra, § 7.15, at 575.

This case presents an unusual set of facts in that Abdoney, in his capacity as the senior mortgagee, omitted himself as a junior mortgagee from the original foreclosure action. Abdoney has admitted that this omission was intentional, but we cannot find any authority that would justify departing from the general rule that the lien of a junior mortgagee is not affected by a judgment of foreclosure to which he was not a party. Although Abdoney had notice of, and participated in, the judicial sale, he did so in his capacity as senior mortgagee and not as a junior mortgagee. Moreover, the evidence is undisputed that York was aware that Abdoney's junior mortgage was not listed in the final judgment of foreclosure.

As the purchaser of the property at the foreclosure sale, York is now equitably subrogated to the rights of the senior mortgagee, and Abdoney has retained his position as a junior mortgagee. Thus, the trial court erred in denying Abdoney's motion for summary judgment and granting York's motion for summary judgment based on its determination that Abdoney's junior lien was extinguished with the filing of the certificate of sale. Accordingly, we reverse and remand the final summary judgment for

---

[1] However, if the senior mortgagee omitted the junior mortgagee as a result of fraud or mala fides "so as to deprive [the junior mortgagee] of the opportunity (not the absolute right) of bidding the property up to an amount sufficient to cover its second mortgage, or to deprive it of the opportunity to contest the amounts devoted to 'costs and expenses' in order to conserve proceeds available to pay off the second mortgage," equity could support some other remedy. Quinn Plumbing Co. v. New Miami Shores Corp., 100 Fla. 413, 129 So. 690, 692–93 (1930). While the trial court found that Abdoney fraudulently omitted himself as a junior lienor, there is no evidence to support this finding. Abdoney's junior lien was recorded, and the record reflects that York had personal knowledge of the existence of Abdoney's junior lien.

further proceedings in Abdoney's foreclosure action. We also reverse the final order that awarded York attorney's fees and costs.

Reversed and remanded.

NELSON, WHITMAN, BURKHART & FREYERMUTH, REAL ESTATE FINANCE LAW
612–615 (6th ed.2015)*

The general rule is that lack of knowledge or notice of a subordinate interest in the mortgaged land does not excuse a foreclosing mortgagee from joining the holder of that interest to the suit. If the mortgagee does not join the subordinate interest holder, its interest, whether it is legal or equitable and whether it is an ownership interest or a lien, is not subject to the foreclosure decree. However, some exceptions exist. A foreclosure sale purchaser who pays value for the legal title without notice of the unjoined interest qualifies as a bona fide purchaser and takes free of that interest if it is only an equitable interest. Similarly, under a typical recording statute, a foreclosure sale purchaser who buys without knowledge or notice of an outstanding but unrecorded interest may take free and clear of it just as effectively as if its holder had been joined in the foreclosure action. Some courts have held that even the foreclosing mortgagee can qualify as a bona fide purchaser, though contrary authority exists. Some statutes, either explicitly or as interpreted, go further and terminate the unrecorded interest of an unjoined party as effectively as if he had been joined. Under the most extreme of these statutes, the foreclosure terminates the unrecorded interest though the mortgagee had actual knowledge of it when he began the foreclosure action. Protecting the foreclosing mortgagee and the foreclosure purchaser against unrecorded interests is very appropriate when they had no actual notice of the interest before suit or actual knowledge during the pendency of the litigation.

While the bona fide purchaser rule and the recording statutes aid the foreclosing mortgagee, the lis pendens doctrine also substantially serves his interests. That doctrine applies when a grantee acquires an interest in real estate that is the subject of a judicial action, such as a judicial foreclosure. If the property is within the court's jurisdiction and is specifically described, any grantee takes subject to the outcome of the judicial action, though she is not a party to it and had no actual knowledge of either the suit or the claim under litigation. Courts in some cases have erroneously failed to differentiate the lis pendens doctrine from situations in which the grantee had actual notice of the plaintiff's rights. Actual notice binds a grantee whether or not litigation is pending. Lis pendens also is different than the principle of privity of title, which applies to grantees after a judgment against a grantor, and the rule that property in judicial

---

*   Reprinted with permission of LEG, Inc. d/b/a West Academic.

custody cannot be transferred in derogation of the court's later order. Courts frequently describe the doctrine as resting on constructive notice, but its true basis is public policy. Lis pendens protects the court's jurisdiction. In the absence of lis pendens, a property owner could defeat the court's jurisdiction by transferring the property to a third party, which would force the plaintiff to commence a new action against the transferee.

However, the lis pendens doctrine can impose a hardship on innocent property purchasers who, as a practical matter, cannot discover the pending litigation concerning the property. Therefore, many states have enacted statutes that apply the lis pendens doctrine against third parties only if the plaintiff has filed a notice of the pendency of its suit ("lis pendens notice"). Nevertheless, even in those states, the doctrine can still create a trap for unwary purchasers who rely solely on a search for a lis pendens notice. Few of the statutes preempt the entire common law doctrine. As a result, it can still apply in many situations.

Even when the statute applies, the scope of its coverage can be problematic. The recorded lis pendens notice clearly binds subsequent mortgagees and grantees of the property, but what is its effect on prior unrecorded mortgages and other conveyances? If a foreclosing mortgagee has actual knowledge of an unrecorded mortgage when filing the lis pendens notice, the holder of the unrecorded mortgage will not be bound by the foreclosure proceeding unless joined to it. If the foreclosing mortgagee learns of the unrecorded mortgage after recording the notice but before judgment, at least one court has held that he must join the holder of the unrecorded mortgage. However, several other courts have held that the latter merely has a right to intervene and will be bound by the judgment if she fails to do so.

NOTE ON OMITTED PARTY PROBLEM

As the *Abdoney* describes, when a party that has the right to redeem is omitted from a foreclosure action, its interest is not terminated by that action. So far as the omitted party is concerned, the foreclosure is void and its right of redemption is the same as before the foreclosure. The foreclosure sale purchaser acquires the foreclosing mortgagee's rights and the rights of all junior interest holders who were joined in the foreclosure.

Rights of an omitted owner. If the omitted party is the property owner, she retains her title, but the foreclosure purchaser now owns the mortgage and may re-foreclose it against the omitted owner. See English v. Bankers Trust Co. of Cal., N.A., 895 So.2d 1120 (Fla.App.2005). The omitted owner may avoid foreclosure by exercising the equity of redemption and paying the mortgage debt to the foreclosure sale purchaser. See Pinto v. EMC Mortg. Corp., 700 So.2d 91 (Fla.App.1997). When the omitted owner redeems, she redeems the title to the land and, in doing so, cuts off the foreclosure sale purchaser's interest in the land. The foreclosure sale purchaser has no further right to redeem from or pay off the owner-mortgagor.

Rights of an omitted lienor. If the omitted party is a junior lienor, the situation becomes more complicated. Like the owner, the junior lienor has an equitable right to redeem. When he is omitted from the foreclosure, his lien and his equity of redemption are unaffected.

Why would it be unfair to terminate the junior lien when the lienor was not joined to the foreclosure action? After all, a judicially supervised sale has occurred, and, in the great majority of cases, the high bid does not exceed the amount of the foreclosed mortgage. If the high bid was no more than the amount of the foreclosed lien, is the bid amount adequate proof that the property's value was insufficient to cover the amount owing to the junior and that the junior must and should go away empty-handed?

No. Although a sale occurred, the junior was not a participant. The junior did not have an opportunity to bid for the property or to try to find other bidders to maximize the sale price. It is well known that, in most foreclosure sales, the bidding is scarcely spirited. The foreclosing senior lienor often is the only bidder. Of course, it is possible that even if the junior had been a party and present at the sale, no amount of effort on his part would have generated a higher bid. But this fact cannot be established by speculation. Instead, the junior lienor is entitled to a process that will duplicate, as much as possible, his right to have the value of the property tested at a sale *in which he is a participant.*

How can this result be achieved? Courts have granted two principal remedies to omitted junior lienors—foreclosure and redemption. E.g., *Abdoney.* The first remedy is the junior foreclosing his lien, subject to the first mortgage, which is revived for this purpose. Courts sometimes say that, with respect to the junior lienor, the original foreclosure sale never occurred. At the senior foreclosure sale, the buyer acquired both the mortgagor's and senior mortgagee's rights. If the junior subsequently forecloses his lien, the sale will convey the original mortgagor's interest to the buyer at the second sale, but the buyer at the original sale retains the original mortgagee's interest, which is revived for this purpose. For an excellent example of an omitted junior's foreclosure, see Pease Co. v. Huntington Nat'l Bank, 24 Ohio App.3d 227, 495 N.E.2d 45 (1985).

It is entirely possible that no one will bid for the property under these conditions. If the property's value is less than the senior lien amount, this should always be true. But even if no one bids, the junior lienor has had an opportunity to prove whether the property is worth more than the senior lien amount.

The amount of the revived first lien is the balance that was owed before the first foreclosure sale, which may be more or less than the foreclosure purchaser paid. If it is more, the purchaser at the first foreclosure sale gets a windfall when the debt secured by the first mortgage is paid. This is not improper, because the sale purchaser would have gotten the same windfall if she had been allowed to keep the property and sell it. On the other hand, if the purchaser paid more than the senior lien amount, the second foreclosure sale will deprive her of title to the property and replace it with a lien for a smaller amount. This could be a serious detriment to the original purchaser and may discourage foreclosure sale bidders from bidding more than the amount of the lien being foreclosed. Arguably, this detriment is a reasonable penalty to impose on the purchaser for failing to discover the junior lienor's omission before bidding at the first foreclosure sale. However, this argument is premised on the incorrect assumption that a careful search of the public records will always reveal the junior lien. For example, the junior lien may be a mechanic's lien that was unrecorded at the time of the senior foreclosure sale but that subsequently was recorded and related back to a time before the sale.

The omitted junior lienor's other principal remedy is redemption. See, e.g., United States Dept. of Hous. & Urban Dev. v. Union Mortg. Co., Inc., 661 A.2d 163 (Me.1995); Diamond Benefits Life Ins. Co. v. Troll, 66 Cal.App.4th 1, 77 Cal.Rptr.2d 581 (1998); Kuehl v. Eckhart, 608 N.W.2d 475 (Iowa 2000); Western Bank, Santa Fe v. Fluid Assets Dev. Corp., 111 N.M. 458, 806 P.2d 1048 (1991). Davis v. Cole, 193 Misc.2d 380, 747 N.Y.S.2d 722 (Sup.2002). The junior lienor may tender to the buyer at the senior foreclosure sale—in her capacity as the holder of the revived senior lien—the balance that was owed on the senior lien at the time of foreclosure. If the junior exercises this equity of redemption, he acquires the revived senior lien. As the holder of the senior and junior liens, he may foreclose either or both of them. Unlike the case in which an omitted *owner* redeems, the term "redemption" here does not refer to the vesting of the property title in the junior, but merely to the junior's power to acquire the senior lien. Sometimes it is said that, by tendering payment of the balance owing on the senior lien, the junior becomes subrogated to the senior mortgagee's rights—rights which have now, by the first sale, been vested in the sale purchaser.

Exercising the equity of redemption requires the omitted junior to come up with a substantial amount of money, and he cannot use the property itself as security to borrow the money. For this reason, omitted junior lienors do not commonly exercise the equity of redemption, and it certainly imposes a burden on a junior lienor that would not have existed if he had been named as a party to the original foreclosure action.

A third remedy is available to the omitted junior lienor, though it is seldom usable in practice. In some jurisdictions, if the foreclosure sale of the senior lien produced a surplus and if that surplus is still identifiable in the hands of the original mortgagor or of a lienor who is subordinate to the omitted junior, the junior can assert a lien on the surplus funds. Obviously, cases in which these circumstances exist are very rare indeed.

Rights of the foreclosure purchaser. Let us now turn to the methods that are available to the purchaser at the senior sale to protect her interests if an omitted junior lienor forecloses or exercises the equity of redemption, as

123

described above. The purchaser may have three options—the equity of redemption, re-foreclosure, and, in some states, strict foreclosure. Let us look first at redemption. If the omitted junior has not taken any action, the senior sale purchaser may pay off the junior lien and thereby clear the property title. As we noted earlier, the senior foreclosure purchaser succeeds not only to the rights of the senior mortgagee, but also to the rights of the foreclosed mortgagor. Because the mortgagor had the right to pay off the junior lien, the senior foreclosure purchaser has the same right, until the junior lienor forecloses his lien. Whether this is an attractive alternative to the senior purchaser obviously depends on how large the junior lien is. If the senior purchaser doubts that the property is worth the additional investment, she may be well-advised to allow the junior to foreclose, because she will still have a first mortgage on the property in the amount of the original senior lien.

Even if the junior lienor redeems the senior debt from the original sale purchaser, the parties' position is not significantly changed. The senior purchaser can simply pay off the senior lien in the junior's hands, using the very dollars that the junior paid the purchaser when the junior redeemed. The senior foreclosure purchaser's redemption has priority because the purchaser stands in the shoes of the foreclosed mortgagor. When an owner exercises her equity of redemption, the lienor's debt has been paid off, and he no longer has an interest in the land. His only right is to be paid. Thus, the transaction is a wash. If the senior purchaser is willing to pay enough money out of her own pocket, she can also pay off the junior lien. Therefore, the senior sale purchaser can easily nullify an omitted junior lienor's redemption. If the senior purchaser does not wish to take the next step and pay off the junior lien as well, the omitted junior lienor still has the power to compel a test of the property's value in his own foreclosure sale.

An alternative route that the senior sale purchaser may take is to re-foreclose the first mortgage. See, e.g., Ordones v. American Interstate Ins. Co., 950 So.2d 427 (Fla.App.2006); United States Dept. of Hous. & Urban Dev. v. Union Mortg. Co., Inc., 661 A.2d 163 (Me.1995); Western Bank, Santa Fe v. Fluid Assets Dev. Corp., 111 N.M. 458, 806 P.2d 1048 (1991); Ahern v. Pierce, 236 A.D.2d 343, 653 N.Y.S.2d 620 (1997); First Fed. Sav. & Loan Ass'n v. Nath, 839 P.2d 1336 (Okla.1992); U.S. Bank of Washington v. Hursey, 116 Wash.2d 522, 806 P.2d 245 (1991). This time, we may be sure that the senior sale purchaser will not omit the junior lienor. The purchaser takes this action in her capacity as the senior mortgagee. The junior can participate in the sale and thus has the right that he was denied when the senior mortgagee originally foreclosed. The proceeds of the sale will be used to pay off both liens in the order of their priority, with any additional surplus going to the re-foreclosing party in her capacity as the property owner.

However, if the original sale purchaser re-forecloses the first mortgage and if the successful bid at the second sale does not produce a surplus above the total of both liens, the original sale purchaser stands to lose any amount she bid at the first sale in excess of the balance owing on the senior lien. She should have the right to sue the original mortgagor for the loss, but such a right is not well-established. In any event, we may well imagine that it is not worth much as a practical matter in most cases.

The third method that may be available to the senior sale purchaser to deal with an omitted junior lienor is usually termed "strict foreclosure." In substance, it is a judicial decree that the junior lien will be canceled unless the junior pays off the senior debt within a court-specified time period.

In jurisdictions where strict foreclosure is allowed, courts take a variety of approaches to the use of strict foreclosure against an omitted lienor. Courts in some cases suggest that the remedy is automatically available, unless the senior mortgagee intentionally omitted the junior lienor. See Tejedo v. Secretary of Veterans Affairs, 673 So.2d 959 (Fla.App.1996). Other courts have held that strict foreclosure is unavailable to deal with an omitted junior lienor. See United States Dept. of Hous. & Urban Dev. v. Union Mortg. Co., Inc., 661 A.2d 163 (Me.1995) ("We conclude that any attempt to subsequently foreclose against the junior mortgagee must preserve the junior mortgagee's right to redeem from the senior mortgage and the right to participate in a second public sale.").

However, courts in most jurisdictions do not follow either extreme approach. In many jurisdictions, to have strict foreclosure against an omitted junior lienor, the original foreclosure purchaser must establish that (1) she bought in good faith without knowledge of the outstanding interest and (2) the junior lienor knew of the sale and permitted the purchaser to buy without disclosing the junior lien.

Courts in other decisions follow a flexible rule that requires equitable grounds for relief. These courts generally require that the foreclosing senior mortgagee omitted the junior through inadvertence or mistake untinged with bad faith. Moreover, some courts look at the property's value or the sale price at the prior foreclosure sale. If the premises are worth no more than the senior encumbrances, a court should allow strict foreclosure of the junior lien. See, e.g., Mesiavech v. Newman, 120 N.J.Eq. 192, 184 A. 538 (Ch.1936). According to the Restatement:

> Because strict foreclosure deprives the omitted junior of the right to participate in a public foreclosure sale and to receive any potential surplus from it, there is a presumption against this remedy. Thus, strict foreclosure should be available only where the senior purchaser can establish that the omission was the result of inadvertence or mistake and that the fair market value of the mortgaged real estate does not exceed the amount of encumbrances senior to the junior lien.

Restatement (Third) of Property (Mortgages) § 7.1 cmt. b (1997).* Some states statutorily provide for strict foreclosure. See, e.g., 735 Ill. Comp. Stat. 5/15–1603.5; 2035 Realty Co. v. Howard Fuel Corp., 77 A.D.2d 870, 431 N.Y.S.2d 57 (1980). For an excellent and extensive analysis of the omitted junior lienor problem and the rights and remedies of the parties, see George M. Platt, The

---

Dracula Mortgage: Creature of the Omitted Lienholder, 67 Ore.L.Rev. 287 (1988).

D. POWER OF SALE FORECLOSURE

1. SOME GENERAL CONSIDERATIONS

NELSON, WHITMAN, BURKHART & FREYERMUTH, REAL ESTATE FINANCE LAW
634–638 (6th ed.2015)*

The other main foreclosure method—power of sale foreclosure—is available in thirty-five jurisdictions. After varying types and degrees of notice, the property is sold at a public sale, either by a public official, such as a sheriff, by some other third party, or by the mortgagee. Almost no power of sale foreclosure statutes provide an opportunity for a hearing before the foreclosure sale. Power of sale foreclosure is also called nonjudicial foreclosure or foreclosure by advertisement.

In some states that authorize power of sale foreclosures, the deed of trust is the most commonly used mortgage instrument. The mortgagor-trustor conveys the real estate to a trustee who holds it in trust for the mortgagee-beneficiary until the mortgage debt is paid in full. In the event of foreclosure, the trustee exercises the power of sale by a public sale of the mortgaged property. The sale usually is not judicially supervised.

The notice requirements for a power of sale foreclosure vary but are usually less rigorous than for a judicial foreclosure. The required notice may simply be notice of foreclosure or notice of default or both. While some states require the foreclosing mortgagee to give notice by mail or personal service to every person that has a junior record interest in the real estate, many do not. A few states require only notice by publication. Some of these states require a newspaper advertisement, but others require only public posting. Other states require published notice and notice by mail or personal service to the mortgagor and to the owner of the mortgaged real estate, but not to junior lienors and others holding an interest subordinate to the mortgage being foreclosed. A few states attempt to protect those interested parties who are neither mortgagors nor owners by requiring the foreclosing mortgagee to mail notice of foreclosure to any person who has previously recorded a request for such notice. In addition to the state notice requirements, federal legislation makes a power of sale foreclosure ineffective against a junior federal tax lien unless the foreclosing mortgagee gives the United States written notice at least 25 days before the sale by registered or certified mail or by personal service. . . .

---

*   Reprinted with permission of LEG, Inc. d/b/a West Academic.

Two federal statutes authorize power of sale foreclosure of all residential mortgages held by the Department of Housing and Urban Development ("HUD"). The Multifamily Mortgage Foreclosure Act (the "Multifamily Act") authorizes power of sale foreclosure for federally-insured and certain other mortgages on property, other than one-to-four family dwellings. 12 U.S.C. §§ 3701–3717. The Single Family Mortgage Foreclosure Act (the "Single Family Act") does the same for HUD-held mortgages on one-to-four family dwellings. 12 U.S.C. §§ 3751–3758. The Acts' provisions are similar. Regulations implementing both Acts were streamlined and consolidated in one regulation in 1996. 24 C.F.R. §§ 27.1–27.123, 61 Fed.Reg. 48546 (1996). . . .

The underlying theory of power of sale foreclosure is simple. By complying with the statutory requirements, the mortgagee can achieve the same results as judicial foreclosure without the substantial additional burdens that judicial foreclosure entails. Like judicial foreclosure, power of sale foreclosure terminates all interests junior to the mortgage being foreclosed and gives the sale purchaser the same title that the mortgagor had when she gave the mortgage. Moreover, where it is commonly employed, power of sale foreclosure has provided an effective foreclosure remedy that usually is substantially faster and cheaper than judicial foreclosure.

Although power of sale foreclosure generally works and is more efficient and less costly than judicial foreclosure, the titles it produces have been less stable than those resulting from judicial foreclosure for at least three reasons. First, court supervision in judicial foreclosure prevents many defects. Second, the defendants in a judicial foreclosure will bring possible defects to the court's attention, which provides additional protection. Finally, the concept of judicial finality insulates even technically defective judicial foreclosure proceedings against subsequent collateral attack. None of these protections are inherent in power of sale foreclosure. Moreover, as we will examine in detail later in this chapter, power of sale foreclosure has been subject to constitutional challenge because of its alleged notice and hearing deficiencies. . . .

Another troubling distinction between judicial and power of sale foreclosures has been frequently litigated during the past several years. To have standing to foreclose a mortgage judicially, the plaintiff has to prove that it has the right to enforce the debt. However, courts in several states have held that the same standing requirement does not exist for power of sale foreclosures, as well illustrated by the decision in You v. JP Morgan Chase Bank, 293 Ga. 67, 743 S.E.2d 428 (2013). In that case, the borrowers borrowed money to buy a home and signed a note and deed to secure debt. The lender transferred the note to "an unidentified entity" and then assigned the security deed to JP Morgan Chase's predecessor. When the borrowers defaulted, Chase foreclosed nonjudicially and was the highest bidder. The borrowers then sued Chase for wrongful foreclosure.

In their suit, the borrowers argued that Chase could not foreclose because it did not own the note. The Georgia Supreme Court stated that the plaintiffs' argument would have been correct if Chase had foreclosed judicially, because Chase would have had to prove that it had the right to enforce the note. However, the court held that the same rule does not apply to a power of sale foreclosure because the Georgia power of sale statutes do not expressly include that requirement. The court stated that the owner of a security deed can foreclose by power of sale even if it does not hold the note *or have any beneficial interest in the debt.*

2. DEFECTS IN EXERCISE OF POWER OF SALE

BASKURT V. BEAL

Supreme Court of Alaska, 2004
101 P.3d 1041

Before: BRYNER, CHIEF JUSTICE, MATTHEWS, EASTAUGH, and FABE, JUSTICES.

OPINION

MATTHEWS, JUSTICE.

* * *

FACTS

This case involves two parcels of land originally owned by Marion and Mortimer Moore. * * * In 1991 Mortimer and Marion simultaneously sold their respective parcels to Charles McAlpine. The following day, McAlpine conveyed the parcels to Annette Beal by quitclaim deed. These transactions were financed by two separate promissory notes signed by McAlpine: Note A for $95,000 payable to Mortimer; and Note B for $135,000 payable to Marion. Each note was to be paid to the respective seller through its own separate escrow account.

The two promissory notes were secured by a single deed of trust covering both parcels * * *. In 1994 Annette paid off the $95,000 owed on Note A for Parcel 1 to Mortimer. At that time, there was some discussion regarding paying off Note B, but Marion preferred to continue to receive monthly payments rather than being paid off in a single lump sum. Marion did agree to a reduction of the interest rate on Note B. The 1991 deed of trust was modified to reflect the payoff of the note to Mortimer and the change in interest rate on Marion's note.

In the fall of 1999, after an erratic payment history, Annette fell behind in her payments. Sarah Baskurt the Moores' daughter, took steps to commence foreclosure, including contacting attorney Jim Christie to conduct the foreclosure. Christie and Land Title Company of Alaska, Inc., made the arrangements for the foreclosure. At that time, Annette owed $26,780.81 on Parcel 2, having paid approximately eighty percent of the original $135,000 purchase price.

The foreclosure sale was held on April 26, 2000, inside the main entrance of the Nesbett Memorial Courthouse in Anchorage. Prior to arriving at the sale, Baskurt, who wanted to bid on the property but believed she lacked the financial strength and knowledge of property development to do so on her own, contacted friends to see if they would be interested in bidding on the property as her partner. Robert and Joyce Wainscott agreed and Baskurt and Joyce Wainscott formed a partnership for the purpose of acquiring and developing or reselling the property. Baskurt, who believed the property was worth at least $250,000, brought a check for $151,000 to the sale. The Wainscotts brought a check for $100,000 to the sale. The trio had at least $251,000 available to put toward the purchase price of the property.

At the sale Baskurt recognized her neighbor, Allen Rosenthal, whom Baskurt knew to have considerable experience in home construction. Rosenthal had learned of the foreclosure sale about a week earlier and had contacted Land Title, who referred him to Christie. Christie provided Rosenthal with general information about the property and the foreclosure. Rosenthal, who believed the property could be subdivided for family residences or condominiums, thought that if he could purchase the land for under $160,000 he would have gotten a "good deal." He had with him cashier's checks for $60,000 and $100,000.

Baskurt approached Rosenthal and asked why he was at the sale. Rosenthal testified that he told Baskurt he was interested in bidding on the property but denies that he told Baskurt how much he was willing to bid. Baskurt claims Rosenthal told her he would be willing to bid up to $95,000 on the property. Baskurt asked Rosenthal to join her partnership with Joyce, and Rosenthal tentatively agreed. Baskurt spoke with Joyce, and the three cemented their partnership. There was little discussion regarding bidding strategy or tactics, and the three assumed that each would be a one-third partner, contributing an equal portion to the sale price. Immediately following the expansion of the partnership, Leslie Plikat, Land Title's agent, inspected Baskurt's and Rosenthal's cashiers checks. Plikat registered two bidders, Baskurt and Rosenthal.

The foreclosure sale, conducted by Christie, was by public outcry. Baskurt made the opening and only bid for $26,781.81, a dollar over the remaining debt owed on the property, on behalf of the partnership. There were no other bids, and the property was sold to Baskurt, Joyce, and Rosenthal via a trustee's deed.

PROCEEDINGS

On May 17, 2000, Annette filed a complaint against Baskurt, Wainscott, Rosenthal, McAlpine, and Land Title seeking to have the foreclosure sale set aside. * * * After a three-day bench trial, the superior court set aside the foreclosure sale as both void and voidable. Final judgment setting aside the foreclosure sale and awarding attorney's fees and costs to Annette was entered on February 28, 2003. Purchasers appeal. * * *

The Foreclosure Sale Was Voidable

Pursuant to AS 34.20.070 a trustee under a deed of trust executed as security for the payment of an indebtedness may, in the case of default or noncompliance with the terms of the deed, foreclose and sell the property according to the terms provided in the deed. However, defects in the mechanics of the trustee's exercise of the power to foreclose may render the foreclosure sale voidable.[7] Generally, mere inadequacy of price is not sufficient by itself to require setting aside a foreclosure sale.[8] However, if the inadequacy of the sale price is (1) "so gross as to shock the conscience and raise a presumption of fraud or unfairness," or (2) is coupled with other irregularities in the sale procedures, then invalidation of the sale may be justified.[9]

Gross inadequacy is measured by reference to the fair market value of the property at the time of the sale.[10] Fair market value for these purposes has been defined as

> not the fair "forced sale" value of the real estate, but the price which would result from negotiation and mutual agreement, after ample time to find a purchaser, between a vendor who is willing, but not compelled to sell, and a purchaser who is willing to buy, but not compelled to take a particular piece of real estate.[11]

---

[7] *See Rosenberg v. Smidt*, 727 P.2d 778, 784 (Alaska 1986) (distinguishing void and voidable sales; in case of latter, alleged defect goes "not to the trustee's right to proceed with the foreclosure but only to the mechanics of exercising that power") (internal citations omitted).

[8] *See McHugh v. Church*, 583 P.2d 210, 213 (Alaska 1978) (holding mere inadequacy of price insufficient to set aside foreclosure sale in context of judicial sale); *see also* GRANT S. NELSON & DALE A. WHITMAN, REAL ESTATE FINANCE LAW § 7.21, at 672 (4th ed. 2002) ("All jurisdictions adhere to the recognized rule that mere inadequacy of the foreclosure sale price will not invalidate a sale, absent fraud, unfairness or other irregularity.").

[9] *McHugh*, 583 P.2d at 213–14.

[10] RESTATEMENT 3D OF PROPERTY (MORTGAGES) § 8.3 cmt. b, at 584, 593 (1997).

[11] *Id.* at 584; *see also BFP v. Resolution Trust Corp.*, 511 U.S. 531, 537–38, 114 S.Ct. 1757, 128 L.Ed.2d 556 (1994) ("The market value of . . . a piece of property is the price which it might be expected to bring if offered for sale in a fair market; not the price which might be obtained on a sale at public auction or a sale forced by the necessities of the owner, but such a price as would be fixed by negotiation and mutual agreement, after ample time to find a purchaser, as between a vendor who is willing (but not compelled) to sell and a purchaser who desires to buy but is not compelled to take the particular . . . piece of property.") (citing BLACK'S LAW DICTIONARY 971 (6th ed.1990)).

Courts determine adequacy of price by comparing the fair market value to the purchase price of the property at the foreclosure sale. Jurisdictions vary on what percentage of fair market value renders the purchase price grossly inadequate. Foreclosure sale prices of fifty percent or more of fair market value are routinely upheld.[12] Even prices garnering less than fifty percent of fair market value are often upheld.[13] However, several courts have upheld the invalidation of a foreclosure sale that produced a price of twenty percent of fair market value or less.[14] The New Mexico Supreme Court has enunciated the standard that when the price falls into the ten to forty percent range, it should not be confirmed "absent good reasons why it should be."[15]

The Restatement adopts the position that although " 'gross inadequacy' cannot be defined in terms of a specific percentage of fair market value," generally, "a court is warranted in invalidating a sale where the price is less than twenty percent of fair market value and, absent other foreclosure defects, is usually not warranted in invalidating a sale that yields in excess of that amount."[16]

Even where the foreclosure sale price is not grossly inadequate, a low price coupled with some other irregularity in the foreclosure proceeding can be sufficient to render the sale voidable. As explained by the United States Supreme Court in *Schroeder v. Young*[17] and noted by this court in *McHugh:*

> While mere inadequacy of price has rarely been held sufficient in itself to justify setting aside a judicial sale of property, courts are not slow to seize upon other circumstances impeaching the fairness of the transaction, as a cause for vacating it, especially if the inadequacy be so gross as to shock the conscience. If the sale

---

[12] *See, e.g., Fed. Deposit Ins. Corp. v. Villemaire*, 849 F.Supp. 116 (D.Mass.1994); *Kurtz v. Ripley County State Bank*, 785 F.Supp. 116 (E.D.Mo.1992); *Danbury Savings & Loan Ass'n v. Hovi*, 20 Conn.App. 638, 569 A.2d 1143 (1990); *Moody v. Glendale Fed. Bank*, 643 So.2d 1149 (Fla.3d DCA 1994); *Guerra v. Mutual Federal Savings & Loan Ass'n*, 194 So.2d 15 (Fla. 1st DCA 1967); *Long Island Sav. Bank v. Valiquette*, 183 A.D.2d 877, 584 N.Y.S.2d 127 (N.Y.App.Div.1992); *Glenville & 110 Corp. v. Tortora*, 137 A.D.2d 654, 524 N.Y.S.2d 747 (N.Y.App.Div.1988); *Zisser v. Noah Indus. Marine & Ship Repair, Inc.*, 129 A.D.2d 795, 514 N.Y.S.2d 786 (N.Y.App.Div.1987); *S & T Bank v. Dalessio*, 429 Pa.Super. 282, 632 A.2d 566 (1993); *Cedrone v. Warwick Fed. Sav. & Loan Ass'n*, 459 A.2d 944 (R.I.1983).

[13] *See, e.g., Moeller v. Lien*, 25 Cal.App.4th 822, 30 Cal.Rptr.2d 777 (1994) (25% of fair market value); *Shipp Corp., Inc. v. Charpilloz*, 414 So.2d 1122 (Fla. 2d DCA 1982) (33% of fair market value); *Hurlock Food Processors Inv. Assocs. v. Mercantile-Safe Deposit & Trust Co.*, 98 Md.App. 314, 633 A.2d 438 (Md.1993) (35% of fair market value); *Frank Buttermark Plumbing & Heating Corp. v. Sagarese*, 119 A.D.2d 540, 500 N.Y.S.2d 551 (N.Y.App.Div.1986) (30% of fair market value).

[14] *See, e.g., Ballentyne v. Smith*, 205 U.S. 285, 27 S.Ct. 527, 51 L.Ed. 803 (1907) (14% of fair market value); *Crown Life Ins. Co. v. Candlewood, Ltd.*, 112 N.M. 633, 818 P.2d 411 (1991) (15% of fair market value); *United Oklahoma Bank v. Moss*, 793 P.2d 1359 (Okla.1990) (approximately 20% of fair market value); *Rife v. Woolfolk*, 169 W.Va. 660, 289 S.E.2d 220 (1982) (14% of fair market value).

[15] *Armstrong v. Csurilla*, 112 N.M. 579, 817 P.2d 1221, 1234–35 (1991).

[16] RESTATEMENT § 8.3 cmt. b, at 584.

[17] 161 U.S. 334, 337–38, 16 S.Ct. 512, 40 L.Ed. 721 (1896).

has been attended by any irregularity, as if several lots have been sold in bulk where they should have been sold separately, or sold in such manner that their full value could not be realized; if bidders have been kept away; if any undue advantage has been taken to the prejudice of the owner of the property, or he has been lulled into a false security; or, if the sale had been collusively, or in any other manner, conducted for the benefit of the purchaser, and the property has been sold at a greatly inadequate price, the sale may be set aside, and the owner may be permitted to redeem.[18]

Other commentators agree. Professors [Nelson and Whitman] explain that problems connected with foreclosure sales, including

problems associated with the notice of the sale, sale by parcel or in bulk, and adequacy of the foreclosure price ... have their greatest impact in a cumulative sense. While one of these problems may not always be sufficient to set aside a sale, the more of them that are present in one fact situation, the greater the likelihood that a new sale will be ordered.[19]

The Restatement adopts a sliding-scale approach to the cumulative effect that price and irregular procedures have on the fairness of the sale:

Even where the foreclosure price for less than fair market value cannot be characterized as "grossly inadequate," if the foreclosure proceeding is defective under local law in some other respect, a court is warranted in invalidating the sale and may even be required to do so. Such defects may include, for example, ... selling too much or too little of the mortgaged real estate. For example, even a slight irregularity in the foreclosure process coupled with a sale price that is substantially below fair market value may justify or even compel the invalidation of the sale.... On the other hand, even a sale for slightly below fair market value may be enough to require invalidation of the sale where there is a major defect in the foreclosure process.[20]

In *McHugh,* we considered the effect of selling property in bulk as opposed to by parcel.[21] Though we declined to adopt "a flat rule requiring the trustee to sell real property in separate lots or parcels, rather than as a whole unit,"[22] we recognized that a trustee under a deed of trust is a dual

---

[18] *McHugh v. Church,* 583 P.2d 210, 213 (Alaska 1978) (quoting *Schroeder,* 161 U.S. at 337–38, 16 S.Ct. 512).

[19] GRANT S. NELSON & DALE A. WHITMAN, REAL ESTATE FINANCE LAW § 7.16, at 657 (4th ed.2002).

[20] RESTATEMENT 3D OF PROPERTY (MORTGAGES) § 8.3, at 587.

[21] *See McHugh,* 583 P.2d at 213–18.

[22] *Id.* at 218.

fiduciary owing duties to both the trustor and the beneficiary.[23] Among the duties owed by the trustee is the duty to take reasonable and appropriate steps to avoid sacrifice of the debtor's property and interest.[24]

Bearing these principles in mind, we turn to the facts of this case. Purchasers contend that there was no basis to set the foreclosure sale aside as voidable. They argue, among other things, that the sale should not have been set aside on the basis of an inadequate price since under *McHugh*, an inadequate price is an insufficient basis for setting aside a foreclosure sale. Further, they contend that the sale should not have been set aside on the ground that the parcels were sold together because under *McHugh*, the trustee was under no duty to sell the parcels separately.

We are not convinced by Purchasers' argument. The test for whether a sale is voidable based on price inadequacy is whether the price paid was *grossly* inadequate when compared to the fair market value of the property on the date of the foreclosure sale. The trial court found that the 1991 sales price of $225,000 was the best indicator of fair market value. The fact that the foreclosure purchase price of $26,781.10 was less than fifteen percent of the sale price indicates that the gross inadequacy standard was met. The trial court so found, and Purchasers identify no circumstances indicating that this finding is erroneous.

The superior court also found that the sale of either parcel alone would likely have generated sufficient proceeds to satisfy the amount due. By conducting the sale in bulk rather than selling only one parcel, the court found that the trustee failed in its duty to act reasonably to protect Beal's interests. This finding is supported by the evidence and is in accordance with our observation in *McHugh* that a trustee has a duty to take reasonable steps to act impartially and in such a way as "not to sacrifice the debtor's property."[26] When coupled with the inadequacy of the price, the trustee's unreasonable failure to sell only one parcel initially justifies invalidating the sale.[27]

We conclude that the superior court properly set aside the sale based on the grossly inadequate sale price and the trustee's failure to sell only one parcel in breach of its duty to act reasonably to protect Beal's interests.

For the above reasons we conclude that the sale was voidable and AFFIRM the decision of the superior court.

CARPENETI, JUSTICE, not participating.

---

[23] *Id.* at 214.

[24] *Id.* at 218.

[26] *McHugh*, 583 P.2d at 218.

[27] *Id.* Our conclusion should not be read as implying that the gross inadequacy of the sale price alone would not be a sufficient ground to set aside the sale. It is not necessary to reach that question in this case because of the additional flaw in the sale process.

NOTES

1.   *The "void"-"voidable"-"inconsequential" distinction.* Defects in a power of sale foreclosure can be categorized in at least three ways. Some defects are so substantial that they render the sale *void.* In this situation, the sale transfers no title to the sale purchaser or subsequent grantees, except perhaps by adverse possession. A forged mortgage, for example, is in this category. Similarly, a foreclosure is void if the lender did not validly accelerate the debt or if the debt was otherwise not yet due.

Most defects render the foreclosure *voidable,* rather than void. See, e.g., Rosenberg v. Smidt, 727 P.2d 778 (Alaska 1986). In a voidable sale, bare legal title passes to the sale purchaser, subject to the redemption rights of those who were injured by the sale defect. For example, a sale is voidable in some jurisdictions if the mortgagee purchases at its own power of sale foreclosure. However, if the defect only makes the sale voidable, the redemption rights can be eliminated if a bona fide purchaser acquires the land for value. In that situation, an action for damages against the foreclosing mortgagee or trustee may be the only remedy.

Finally, some defects are so *inconsequential* that the sale is neither void nor voidable. Such defects include minor typographical or similar errors that do not prejudice any of the affected parties. As such, they do not affect the validity of the sale. For a thorough consideration and classification of defects in the exercise of a power of sale, see Nelson, Whitman, Burkhart & Freyermuth, Real Estate Finance Law § 7.21 (6th ed.2015).

2.   *Common foreclosure defects.* A variety of defects are used with varying degrees of success to challenge power of sale foreclosures. Sometimes, the challenge is to the *mortgagee's right to foreclose.* For example, a mortgagor may assert that no default exists in the mortgage obligation or that the mortgagee did not have the right to accelerate. On the other hand, many challenges are to the *foreclosure process,* rather than to the mortgagee's substantive right to foreclose. Procedural challenges may be based on defects such as intentional and negligent chilled bidding, improper time or place of sale, defective notice of sale, and selling either too much or too little of the mortgaged land. For further consideration of these grounds, see Nelson, Whitman, Burkhart & Freyermuth, Real Estate Finance Law § 7.22 (6th ed.2015).

3.   *Inadequate foreclosure price.* Perhaps the most commonly asserted, but least successful, challenge to power of sale foreclosure is inadequacy of the sale price. Nationally, "it is well-settled that in the absence of irregularity in the conduct of the foreclosure sale, mere inadequacy of price will not operate to set the sale aside, unless the consideration is so grossly inadequate as to shock the conscience of the court." Lake Hillsdale Estates, Inc. v. Galloway, 473 So.2d 461 (Miss.1985). As one commentator has noted with respect to his jurisdiction, "sales have been upheld where the price paid for the property was only one-half, one-third, one-fourth, one-fifth, or even one-twentieth of its reasonable value." Larry D. Dingus, Mortgages—Redemption After

Foreclosure Sale in Missouri, 25 Mo.L.Rev. 261, 263–64 (1960). Indeed, one court, convinced that the "conscience shocking test" was "impractical and should be abandoned," held that "[i]f a foreclosure sale is legally held, conducted and consummated, there must be some evidence of irregularity, misconduct, fraud, or unfairness on the part of the trustee or the mortgagee that caused or contributed to an inadequate price, for a court of equity to set aside the sale." Holt v. Citizens Central Bank, 688 S.W.2d 414 (Tenn.1984). Finally, the Single Family Mortgage Foreclosure Act of 1994, which applies to one- to four-family mortgages held by HUD, provides that the foreclosure "sale price shall be conclusively presumed to be reasonable and equal to the fair market value of the property." 12 U.S.C. § 3760(e).

The *Beal* court adopted the Restatement's "grossly inadequate" standard. Under that standard, a court is "warranted in invalidating a sale where the price is less than 20 percent of fair market value and * * * is usually not warranted in invalidating a sale that yields in excess of that amount." Restatement (Third) of Property (Mortgages) § 8.3, cmt. b (1997). The Arizona Supreme Court has agreed. See Krohn v. Sweetheart Properties, Ltd., 203 Ariz. 205, 52 P.3d 774 (2002).

The "grossly inadequate" standard applies only if no other defects existed in the foreclosure process: "[E]ven where the foreclosure price * * * cannot be characterized as 'grossly inadequate,' if the foreclosure proceeding is defective under local law in some other respect, a court is warranted in invalidating the sale and may even be required to do so." Id. § 8.3 cmt. b (1997). See Pizza v. Walter, 345 Md. 664, 694 A.2d 93 (1997) (sale yielding slightly more than 50% of fair market value set aside when coupled with inadequate advertising).

Finally, "adequacy of the sale price looms larger on its own when the mortgagee is seeking to validate it for purposes of seeking a deficiency judgment. Courts scrutinize the sale price much more closely if the mortgagee wants a deficiency judgment in addition to the land." Nelson, Whitman, Burkhart & Freyermuth, Real Estate Finance Law 647 (6th ed.2015).

4. *Chilled bidding.* Irregular conduct by a mortgagee or trustee that suppresses bidding is often characterized as "chilled bidding" and is the basis for setting aside a sale. Chilled bidding can be categorized in two ways:

> The first occurs when the mortgagee or trustee and potential purchasers collude or engage in other intentional conduct to suppress the bidding. The second type encompasses inadvertent and unintentional acts by the trustee or mortgagee that suppress bidding.

> The first type of chilled bidding occurs in a myriad of fact situations and arguably voids the sale, rather than merely rendering it voidable. For example, a mortgagee or trustee can attempt to guarantee that it will be the successful sale bidder by paying off potential third party bidders or by agreeing to share the resale profits with them. Alternatively, the mortgagee or trustee can discourage bidding by

intentionally misrepresenting the state of the title or the property's physical condition.

Nelson, Whitman, Burkhart & Freyermuth, Real Estate Finance Law 652–53 (6th ed.2015). Even though the *Beal* opinion does not mention chilled bidding, would the "partnership" among Baskurt (the mortgagees' daughter), Joyce, and Rosenthal have provided an independent basis for setting aside the sale?

Chilled bidding issues can also arise in the context of inadvertent or "innocent" erroneous statements by the mortgagee or trustee at the foreclosure sale or in the foreclosure notice. See id. at 649–50.

5. *State court remedies to attack power of sale foreclosure.* Three remedies normally are available to challenge the validity of a power of sale foreclosure: (1) an injunction suit against a pending foreclosure, (2) a suit in equity to set aside the sale, and (3) an action for damages against the foreclosing mortgagee or trustee. See Nelson, Whitman, Burkhart & Freyermuth, Real Estate Finance Law § 7.23 (6th ed.2015). Not only the mortgagor, but also the holders of interests that were junior to the foreclosed mortgage, can seek these remedies. A particular remedy's availability depends on several factors, including "whether the defect is discovered before or after the sale, the nature of the defect, and importantly, if the sale has already been completed, whether the sale purchaser or any subsequent grantee is a bona fide purchaser." Id.

6. *Damages for wrongful foreclosure.* Suppose a defect renders a power of sale foreclosure voidable, but the foreclosure purchaser is a bona fide purchaser. The owner cannot recover the land and only has an action for damages against the foreclosing mortgagee. In these circumstances, what is the appropriate measure of damages? Many courts hold that the measure of damages is the difference between the property's fair market value and the aggregate amount of liens thereon as of the date of the sale. See Munger v. Moore, 11 Cal.App.3d 1, 89 Cal.Rptr. 323 (1970); Adkison v. Hannah, 475 S.W.2d 39, 43 (Mo.1972). Other courts describe the measure of damages as the value of the mortgagor's equity in the property at the time of the foreclosure sale. See, e.g., Guay v. Brotherhood Bldg. Ass'n, 87 N.H. 216, 177 A. 409 (1935). See generally, Annot., 97 A.L.R. 1059. Should the appropriate measure of damages instead simply be the property's fair market value at time of sale, less the value of any senior liens and the foreclosure sale price? Cf. Murphy v. Financial Dev. Corp., 126 N.H. 536, 495 A.2d 1245 (1985). Or should it be the fair market value, less any senior lien and the mortgage that was wrongfully foreclosed? See Nelson, Whitman, Burkhart & Freyermuth, Real Estate Finance Law 669–70 (6th ed.2015). Which measure of damages will make the mortgagor whole for her loss of the land?

Let's apply the foregoing variations to the following hypothetical. Suppose that a second mortgage foreclosure is voidable but that a bona fide purchaser now owns the land. Immediately before the sale, the title was encumbered by a first mortgage of $10,000, a second mortgage of $5,000, and a third mortgage of $3,000. Suppose the second mortgagee purchased at the foreclosure sale for

$4,000. The land's fair market value was $20,000. How much should the mortgagor recover from the second mortgagee?

Suppose the land's value has increased since the defective foreclosure sale. In calculating damages, should the mortgagor be able to use the property's fair market value at the time of the damage action? Who should have the benefit of any appreciation in land value between the sale date and the damages action? See Nelson, Whitman, Burkhart & Freyermuth, Real Estate Finance Law § 7.23 (6th ed.2015).

Suppose a junior lienor brings the damages action. What is the proper measure of damages? What should the *maximum* recovery be? See id. at 667.

Should a plaintiff who succeeds in setting aside a foreclosure sale also be permitted to recover damages? Should she be able to recover permanent damages? See Calhoun First Nat'l Bank v. Dickens, 264 Ga. 285, 443 S.E.2d 837 (1994) (mortgagor may not recover both the property and the value of her equity). If not, what damages, if any, should be recoverable? Consider the following language from Clark v. West, 196 Ga.App. 456, 395 S.E.2d 884 (1990):

> The gist of appellees' argument is that an injured party must elect between an equitable action for cancellation of the foreclosure sale and a suit for damages, and pursuit of one to satisfaction results in the exclusion of the other. We agree that this principle applies if the injured party is seeking to redress only the loss of the value of the property. That is, the injured party may not *both* set aside or cancel the foreclosure *and also* recover damages for the value of the property. However, this court has approved actions in which both cancellation and damages were sought. See *Andrews v. Holloway,* 140 Ga.App. 622, 231 S.E.2d 548 (1976); *Gilbert v. Cherry,* 136 Ga.App. 417, 221 S.E.2d 472 (1975). In those cases, cancellation was sought to recover the property, and *in addition,* damages were sought for other breaches of duty and other losses. The latter procedure applies in the case at bar, because appellant sought both cancellation of the foreclosure sale to recover the property and also damages for her mental anguish, which resulted from the intentional nature of defendant's acts, alleging that appellees clearly knew the note was not in default and they had no right to foreclose. It strains credulity to insist that the recovery of appellant's wrongfully foreclosed residence has made her whole, and we find no bar in law or in logic to a recovery of damages for her humiliation and emotional distress should evidence at trial establish the truth of the allegation in her pleadings that the foreclosure was instituted intentionally and without basis. Accordingly, we do not agree that because the foreclosure sale had been canceled, appellant could not pursue her separate claim for damages.

7.   *Action for damages vs. suit to set aside.* If a bona fide purchaser has not acquired the foreclosed property, should a mortgagor nevertheless have the

option of a suit to set aside the sale or an action for damages? In Rogers v. Barnes, 169 Mass. 179, 47 N.E. 602, 604 (1897), the court stated the predominant view:

> On principle, we think it must be considered that in this commonwealth a mortgagee, when there has been no default or breach of the conditions of the mortgage, cannot sell the land mortgaged under the usual power of sale contained in a mortgage, so as to pass a good title even to a bona fide purchaser for value, or to any subsequent purchaser from him. * * * A majority of the court, however, do not think that the decision of this case necessarily depends upon the question whether Rice [a bona fide purchaser] took a good, absolute title or not. The case of the plaintiff, taken most favorably for the defendant, somewhat resembles that of a conversion of personal property, where the owner can sue the wrongdoer, and recover the full value of the property converted, even though the title to the property did not pass by the conversion, or can recover the property; or that of a misappropriation or unauthorized investment or sale of trust property, where the cestui que trust can compel the trustee to account for the full value of the property, even although the property, or some of it, can be recovered. In neither of these cases can the plaintiff recover both the property and full damages for the conversion or misappropriation of it, but if he recover judgment for full damages, and they are paid, the title to the property passes to the wrongdoer and his grantees. A mortgagee, in executing the power of sale contained in a mortgage, is, in a sense, trustee for the mortgagor. So, in the present case, a majority of the court think that the plaintiff, if he so elect, can recover full damages of the defendant, whether he can or cannot redeem the premises from Rice. If the damages recovered are paid, the effect is to make Rice's title good as against the plaintiff's. The defendant, for the purpose of mitigating damages, cannot be heard to say that he has not done what he intended to do, and what, on the face of the transaction, he appears to have done, when what he has done will become valid and effectual if he pays the damages.

For a contrary view, see Bowen v. Bankers' Life Co., 185 Minn. 35, 239 N.W. 774, 776 (1931) ("to recover damages at law it is necessary to show that the land went to an innocent holder so that plaintiff's interest in it was lost"). Which position is preferable from a public policy perspective? For a general consideration of the cases, see Annot., 97 A.L.R. 1059.

8. *The tender requirement.* When a mortgagor seeks injunctive relief or to set aside a sale, some courts require him to tender into the court the outstanding mortgage debt. See, e.g., Ginther-Davis Center, Ltd. v. Houston Nat'l Bank, 600 S.W.2d 856 (Tex.Civ.App.1980); Smith v. Citizens & Southern Fin. Corp., 245 Ga. 850, 268 S.E.2d 157 (1980). When the amount is in dispute, these courts require the mortgagor to tender at least the amount he concedes is due. The tender requirement is premised on the maxim that one who seeks

equity must do equity. Whatever the underlying equitable basis for the tender requirement, does it make sense when applied in this situation? Is it not implicit in the mortgagor's equity of redemption and in the prohibition against clogging it, that a mortgagor's interest can only be terminated by a foreclosure? See Nelson, Whitman, Burkhart & Freyermuth, Real Estate Finance Law § 3.1 (6th ed.2015). Is it not also implicit in the concept of foreclosure that a mortgagor, whatever his economic condition, is entitled to an orderly liquidation of the mortgage security? If so, shouldn't the mortgagor have the right to one valid foreclosure sale? See id. §§ 7.22–7.23.

A few courts apparently also require tender of the mortgage debt by junior lienors seeking equitable relief against a power of sale foreclosure. See Arnolds Mgmt. Corp. v. Eischen, 158 Cal.App.3d 575, 205 Cal.Rptr. 15 (1984) (full tender required). Does a junior lienor have a stronger argument against tender than a mortgagor? Should it make a difference that the mortgagor normally is personally liable on the mortgage debt but the junior lienor is not?

The deed of trust is the most commonly used land security instrument in most power of sale jurisdictions. Why use a deed of trust, which requires a trustee to foreclose, rather than a mortgage with a power of sale in the mortgagee? The reason is that courts in many of these states have held that, if a mortgagee exercises a power of sale and purchases the property at that sale, the sale is voidable. See Nelson, Whitman, Burkhart & Freyermuth, Real Estate Finance Law § 7.22 (6th ed.2015).

Foreclosure of a deed of trust raises issues that are not present in a mortgage foreclosure, as described in the following case and notes.

MONTEREY S.P. PARTNERSHIP V. W.L. BANGHAM, INC.
Supreme Court of California, 1989
49 Cal.3d 454, 777 P.2d 623, 261 Cal.Rptr. 587

LUCAS, C.J.

We consider whether the interest of the beneficiaries under a deed of trust is affected by a default judgment in a mechanic's lien foreclosure suit in which the trustee under the deed of trust was served with the summons and complaint, but the beneficiaries were not served. We conclude that the beneficiaries' interest was not affected by the default judgment, and that the successor to the beneficiaries' interest under the deed of trust therefore owns the property in question free and clear of the mechanic's lien and default judgment.

I.   *Facts*

By a deed of trust recorded in February 1981, Oak Knoll Partnership (Oak Knoll) encumbered property it owned in South Pasadena, California (the property) as security for repayment of a $2 million promissory note.

The deed of trust named Oak Knoll as trustor, Hallmark Reconveyance Corporation as trustee, and Hallmark Acceptance Corporation as beneficiary. Hallmark Acceptance Corporation assigned its beneficial interest in the deed of trust to 252 beneficiaries (the beneficiaries) by an assignment recorded in early March 1981. By recorded substitutions, the beneficiaries substituted Western Mutual Corporation (Western) as trustee in place of Hallmark Reconveyance Corporation.

When Oak Knoll missed payments on the promissory note, the beneficiaries recorded a series of notices of default. On May 4, 1984, after Oak Knoll failed to cure its default, Western conducted a trustee's sale under the deed of trust. The beneficiaries purchased the property at the sale for $650,000. Following two intermediate conveyances, plaintiff Monterey S.P. Partnership (Monterey) obtained title to the property by a quitclaim deed recorded in early August 1985.

Meanwhile, in June 1982, defendant W. L. Bangham, Inc. (Bangham) had recorded a mechanic's lien claim of $44,310.83 against the property. That claim was based on engineering design, drafting, field survey work, and construction layout that Bangham performed, commencing in 1979, at the direction of Oak Knoll and prior owners of the property. In September 1982, Bangham filed an action for a money judgment and to foreclose its mechanic's lien. Bangham recorded a lis pendens in January 1984. On May 3, 1984, the day before Western conducted the trustee's sale to the beneficiaries, Bangham served Western with a summons and complaint as "Doe 1" in its mechanic's lien foreclosure action. Although the beneficiaries were named as defendants in the complaint, they were not served. That October, Bangham amended its complaint to substitute Western in the place of the fictitious "Doe 1," and concurrently filed a request to enter default against Western. The following April, Bangham recovered judgment by default against Western.

In early November 1985, pursuant to the default judgment, the sheriff conducted a public sale of the property. Bangham, the highest bidder, acquired the property for $56,254.23, and received a sheriff's deed. Monterey then sued Bangham for a judgment (1) quieting title to the property; (2) declaring that the sheriff's deed to Bangham was of no force and effect against Monterey's interest in the property; and (3) allowing Monterey to redeem the property from the sheriff's sale. The superior court granted Monterey's motion for summary judgment on the first two counts of its complaint (quiet title and declaratory relief).

Bangham appealed and the Court of Appeal reversed, holding that former section 369 of the Code of Civil Procedure (hereafter former section 369) entitled Bangham to prosecute a binding mechanic's lien foreclosure against Western, as trustee under the deed of trust, without joining the beneficiaries. That section provided: "An executor or administrator, or trustee of an express trust, or a person expressly authorized by statute, may sue without joining with him the persons for whose benefit the action is prosecuted. *A person with whom, or in whose name, a contract is made for the benefit of another, is a trustee of an express trust,* within the meaning of this section." (Italics added.) The Court of Appeal held that Western, as trustee under the deed of trust, was a "trustee of an express trust" as defined in former section 369, and that former section 369, by implication, authorized a trustee to defend an action against the trust without joining with him the beneficiaries of the trust.

II. *Discussion*

Monterey asserts that Bangham's default judgment and the subsequent sheriff's sale could affect only the interests of the parties named in the complaint *and* served with summons. Monterey therefore concludes that, because the beneficiaries under the deed of trust from which Monterey claims title were not served with summons, it now owns the property free and clear of the mechanic's lien and default judgment in favor of Bangham. We agree.

It has long been established in this state that all persons with an interest in the subject real property at the time suit is brought to enforce a mechanic's lien on that property must be made parties to the suit. If they are not made parties, "they are, in no respect, bound by the decree or proceedings thereunder." (*Whitney v. Higgins* (1858) 10 Cal. 547, 551.) As the Court of Appeal recognized, that principle endures to this day. (See, e.g., *Frank Pisano & Associates v. Taggart* (1972) 29 Cal.App.3d 1, 22–230).

Although *Whitney, supra,* 10 Cal. 547, involved the effect of a mechanic's lien foreclosure on the rights of a mortgagee, the holding applies equally to a beneficiary under a deed of trust. As we explained in describing "the anomalous nature of deeds of trust in this state" (*Bank of Italy etc. Assn. v. Bentley* (1933) 217 Cal. 644, 657 [20 P.2d 940]), "deeds of trust, except for the passage of title for the purpose of the trust, are practically and substantially only mortgages with a power of sale . . . ." (*Ibid.*) In practical effect, if not in legal parlance, a deed of trust is a lien on the property.

It would be inconsistent with *Bank of Italy, supra,* 217 Cal. 644, to deny the beneficiaries the rights of mortgagees recognized in *Whitney, supra,* 10 Cal. 547, merely because the beneficiaries' security interest took the form of a deed of trust, which conveys "title" to a trustee. The deed of trust conveys "title" to the trustee "only so far as may be necessary to the execution of the trust." (*Lupertino v. Carbahal* (1973) 35 Cal.App.3d 742, 748 [111 Cal.Rptr. 112].) Thus, as trustee, Western had only two duties with respect to the property. Had the trustor, Oak Knoll, satisfied the debt secured by the deed of trust, Western would have been obligated to reconvey its interest in the property to Oak Knoll. (Civ. Code, § 2941, subd.

(b).) In practical effect, that reconveyance is nothing more than the release of the lien of the deed of trust. When, as actually occurred, Oak Knoll defaulted on its obligation, Western was required on proper request from the beneficiaries to exercise the power of sale contained in the deed of trust. That power is carefully circumscribed by statute. (See *id.*, §§ 2924–2924h.)

The limited nature of Western's function as trustee is perhaps best illustrated by the fact that the beneficiaries, by employing statutory procedures for judicial foreclosure in response to the trustor's default, could have foreclosed without any involvement whatever of Western and its power of sale. (See Code Civ. Proc., § 725a [beneficiary or trustee under a deed of trust may bring suit to foreclose]; *Field* v. *Acres* (1937) 9 Cal.2d 110, 113 [69 P.2d 422] [trustee "has no right to complain if the beneficiary takes advantage of a statute allowing a judicial foreclosure of the deed of trust"].)

Nor does the Subdivision Map Act (Gov. Code, § 66430) indicate that a trustee under a deed of trust is the sole real party in interest for our purposes here. Section 66430 provides: "No final map or parcel map required by this chapter or local ordinance which creates a subdivision shall be filed with the local agency without the written consent of all parties having any record title interest in the real property proposed to be subdivided, except as otherwise provided in this division." As stated in an Attorney General's opinion (59 Ops.Cal.Atty.Gen. 386, 389 (1976)), "[a] trustee under a deed of trust encumbering property to be subdivided is a party who has a record title interest in property for purposes of the Subdivision Map Act."

In no way, however, does the trustee's record title interest—or its role under the Subdivision Map Act generally—divest the beneficiary of its security interest in the property, nor does it suggest that the beneficiary need not be named and served in an action in order for the security of the deed of trust to be affected. Because a deed of trust typically secures a debt owed the beneficiary, it is the beneficiary, not the trustee, whose economic interests are threatened when the existence or priority of the deed of trust is challenged. Even before we declared a deed of trust to be equivalent to a mortgage with a power of sale in *Bank of Italy, supra,* 217 Cal. 644, we held that when the beneficiary of the deed of trust, but not the trustee, was a party, "[t]he real party in interest was before the court." (*Anderson v. Alexander* (1920) 184 Cal. 265, 266 [193 P. 241].)

Thus, mortgagees and trust deed beneficiaries alike hold security interests in property encumbered by mortgages and deeds of trust, and those interests are not affected by a mechanic's lien foreclosure action filed after the recordation of those encumbrances unless the mortgagees or beneficiaries are themselves named and served in that action. Merely serving the trustee is insufficient because a trustee's interest in the property is not the same as a beneficiary's.

In this case, the beneficiaries under the deed of trust were named as defendants in Bangham's suit to foreclose its mechanic's lien, but they were never brought within the court's jurisdiction by service with summons and complaint. In holding that the beneficiaries nonetheless were bound by the judgment in Bangham's lien foreclosure action, the Court of Appeal relied on former section 369. We disagree that former section 369 created an exception to the general rule that beneficiaries are necessary parties to an action affecting the security of a deed of trust.

Although former section 369 did not expressly authorize a trustee to *defend* a suit on behalf of the beneficiaries, the Court of Appeal held that, "by implication," former section 369 authorized such a defense. (See *Straube v. Security First Nat. Bank* (1962) 205 Cal.App.2d 352, 360 [23 Cal.Rptr. 213] [dictum].) We have not previously addressed this issue, and we need not reach it here. * * *

[W]e conclude that Western, as trustee under the deed of trust, was not a "trustee of an express trust" within the meaning of former section 369. The similarities between a trustee of an express trust and a trustee under a deed of trust end with the name. "Just as a panda is not a true bear, a trustee of a deed of trust is not a true trustee." (*Stephens, Partain & Cunningham v. Hollis* (1987) 196 Cal.App.3d 948, 955 [242 Cal.Rptr. 251].) Thus, the trustee of an express trust must consent to serve as trustee (see Prob. Code, § 15600); must not "use or deal with trust property for the trustee's own profit or for any other purpose unconnected with the trust ..." (*id.*, § 16004, subd. (a) [former Civ. Code, § 2229]); and must not knowingly obtain interests adverse to the trust (Prob. Code, § 16005 [former Civ. Code, § 2232]). In addition, and significantly, the trustee of an express trust has broad powers over trust property. The trustee is statutorily empowered to acquire or dispose of trust property (Prob. Code, § 16226 [former Civ. Code, § 2261, subd. (a)(1); former Prob. Code, § 1120.2, subd. (5)]) and to "manage, control, divide, develop, improve, exchange, partition, change the character of, or abandon trust property or any interest therein" (Prob. Code, § 16227 [former Prob. Code, § 1120.2, subds. (1), (5)]). Perhaps most important to the case at hand, the trustee of an express trust *must* "take reasonable steps to defend actions that may result in a loss to the trust." (Prob. Code, § 16011; see also *Estate of Duffill* (1922) 188 Cal. 536, 554–555 [206 P. 42]; Rest.2d Trusts (1957) § 178.)

A trustee under a deed of trust, by contrast, can be appointed as trustee without its consent. (*Burns v. Peters* (1936) 5 Cal.2d 619, 623 [55 P.2d 1182].) As discussed above, the trustee under a deed of trust does not have a true trustee's interest in, and control over, the trust property. Nor is it bound by the fiduciary duties that characterize a true trustee. For example, "a trustee under a deed of trust is not absolutely prohibited from purchasing the trust property at the trustee's own sale." (*Stephens, Partain & Cunningham, supra*, 196 Cal.App.3d at p. 955.)

In light of these distinctions between the rights and obligations of a trustee of an express trust and Western's rights and obligations as trustee under the deed of trust, it would be unreasonable to deem Western "a trustee of an express trust" within the meaning of former section 369. Indeed, the Court of Appeal's interpretation of former section 369 would blur the consistent statutory distinction between deeds of trust and strict or voluntary trusts. (See 3 Witkin, Summary of Cal. Law (9th ed. 1987) Security Transactions in Real Property, § 73 Witkin, Summary of Cal. Law (9th ed. 1987) Security Transactions in Real Property, § 7, pp. 520–521.)

* * *

Regrettably, it appears to be too late in the development of our vocabulary to rename deeds of trust and the "trustees" who act under those instruments. We can only emphasize that those terms are ill-suited under modern practice to describe the true nature of trust deeds and the limited role of trustees such as Western.

The decision of the Court of Appeal is reversed.

NOTES

1. *Trustee as a fiduciary.* As in *Beal,* courts often stress that a trustee under a deed of trust is a fiduciary for both the mortgagor and mortgagee and must act impartially between them. See, e.g., Meyers Way Dev. Ltd. Partn. v. University Sav. Bank, 80 Wash.App. 655, 910 P.2d 1308 (1996); Nelson, Whitman, Burkhart & Freyermuth, Real Estate Finance Law § 7.22 (6th ed.2015). Yet the trustee clearly represents two parties whose interests are often antithetical. Consequently, he is not a traditional trustee, and some courts, such as the court in *Monterey,* do not accept the traditional fiduciary label. Another California court characterized "the role of such trustee" as "more nearly that of a common agent of the parties to the instrument." Lancaster Sec. Inv. Corp. v. Kessler, 159 Cal.App.2d 649, 324 P.2d 634 (1958). Consider these different characterizations of a trustee as you think about the following notes.

2. *Trustee obligation to verify default.* Before foreclosing, does a trustee have a duty to investigate whether the debt is in default? In Spires v. Edgar, 513 S.W.2d 372 (Mo.1974), the Missouri Supreme Court held that "in the absence of unusual circumstances known to the trustee, he may, upon receiving a request for foreclosure from the creditor, proceed upon that advice without making any affirmative investigation and without giving any special notice to the debtor."

3. *Trustee as foreclosure purchaser.* It is a widely accepted rule that a trustee may not purchase the premises at a sale she conducts, at least without the mortgagor-trustor's express consent. See, e.g., Smith v. Credico Indus. Loan Co., 234 Va. 514, 362 S.E.2d 735 (1987) ("a co-trustee under a deed of trust cannot purchase property on behalf of herself or another at the foreclosure sale, even where that sale is conducted by another trustee, and

even where the trustee who makes the purchase was not an active participant in conducting the sale"); Nelson, Whitman, Burkhart & Freyermuth, Real Estate Finance Law § 7.22 (6th ed.2015). But see Stephens, Partain & Cunningham v. Hollis, 196 Cal.App.3d 948, 242 Cal.Rptr. 251 (1987) ("It has long been recognized that a trustee under a deed of trust is not absolutely prohibited from purchasing the trust property at the trustee's own sale.").

4. *Trustee closely related to mortgagee-purchaser.* The trustee sometimes is an officer or employee of the beneficiary or the beneficiary's attorney or the holder of an equity interest in it. In many jurisdictions, this close connection may cause closer judicial scrutiny of the sale, but it usually will not invalidate it. See, e.g., Perry v. Virginia Mortg. & Inv. Co., Inc., 412 A.2d 1194 (D.C.App.1980); Boatmen's Bank of Pulaski County v. Wilson, 833 S.W.2d 879 (Mo.App.1992) (sale upheld though trustee was officer of bank-mortgagee).

However, other courts will set aside the sale in these situations. These courts analyze the situation in at least two ways. Some courts take the position that, when a substantial connection exists between the trustee and beneficiary, the beneficiary's purchase in reality is an indirect purchase by the trustee that is voidable. See, e.g., Whitlow v. Mountain Trust Bank, 215 Va. 149, 207 S.E.2d 837 (1974). Alternatively, some courts hold that an "instrument—in form a deed of trust—executed to the chief executive officer of a corporation is, in effect, a mortgage, and the law relating to foreclosure of mortgage deeds rather than the law relating to trust deeds is applicable." Mills v. Mutual Bldg. & Loan Ass'n, 216 N.C. 664, 6 S.E.2d 549 (1940). The sale is voidable because the beneficiary is treated as if he had purchased from himself at his own foreclosure sale.

Other states have attempted to deal with the foregoing problem by statute. For example, a Utah statute authorizes a bank or savings and loan association to be both a trustee and beneficiary under the same deed of trust. Utah Code Ann. § 57–1–21. Another Utah statute states that "[a]ny person, including the beneficiary or trustee, may bid at the sale." Utah Code Ann. § 57–1–27. See also Va.Code Ann. § 64.2–1423.

5. *Trustee or mortgagee liability to foreclosure purchaser.* To what extent is the trustee or mortgagee responsible to the foreclosure sale purchaser for title defects in the mortgaged real estate? Consider the language of Stuart v. American Sec. Bank, 494 A.2d 1333 (D.C.App.1985):

> The general rule is that a foreclosure purchaser takes a property subject to prior liens and interests accruing prior to consummation of the sale. *See Patron v. American National Bank of Jacksonville*, 382 So.2d 156, 158 (Fla.App.1980); 55 Am.Jur.2d *Mortgages* § 780 (1971); 3A R. Powell, The Law of Real Property, ¶ 466 at 696.64(4) (1984) (deed given without warranty). The recording of the assessments operates as constructive notice to all purchasers. *Ivrey v. Karr*, 182 Md. 463, 473, 34 A.2d 847, 852 (1943). Moreover, a trustee generally has no obligation to disclose liens or interests which the purchaser

could have discovered by his own investigation. *Id.* at 852 (quoting *Wicks v. Westcott,* 59 Md. 270, 277 (1883)). Prior liens are not affected by a foreclosure sale and are normally not payable out of the proceeds of such sale. *Gunton v. Zantzinger,* 3 MacArthur (10 D.C.) 262, 264–65 (1879); *Baltimore Federal Savings & Loan Association v. Eareckson,* 221 Md. 527, 528–31, 158 A.2d 121, 123–24 (1960) (prior first mortgage). In other words, the doctrine of *caveat emptor* applies to foreclosure sales because a trustee makes no warranty of title and is generally subject to no duty to investigate or describe outstanding liens or encumbrances. *See Ivrey v. Karr, supra,* 182 Md. at 473, 34 A.2d at 852; *Feldman v. Rucker,* 201 Va. 11, 19–21, 109 S.E.2d 379, 385–86 (1959); G. Bogert & G. Bogert, The Law of Trust & Trustees, § 745 at 487 (rev. 2d ed. 1982). The purchaser must therefore make his own investigation and determine what liens or encumbrances may exist against the property prior to turning over his deposit. *Cf. Garland v. Hill,* 28 Md.App. 622, 624, 346 A.2d 711, 713 (1975) (notice for purpose of allowing further investigation by interested person), *aff'd,* 277 Md. 710, 357 A.2d 374 (1976).

Should it make a difference if the trustee has actual knowledge of a title defect? According to McPherson v. Purdue, 21 Wash.App. 450, 585 P.2d 830 (1978):

> In this state, the rule of caveat emptor is no longer rigidly applied to the complete exclusion of any moral and legal obligation to disclose material facts not readily observable upon reasonable inspection by the purchaser. Hughes v. Stusser, 68 Wash.2d 707, 415 P.2d 89 (1966). The material fact here was the absence of any title to an easement which the deed of trust purported to convey. Examination of the chain of title would have revealed this defect. [The purchaser] could have readily discovered this material fact by an inspection of the chain of title in the object case, and he was not entitled to rely on the trustee's silence in this matter.

Courts have also applied this analysis to the failure to disclose physical defects in the mortgaged real estate. See Karoutas v. HomeFed Bank, 232 Cal.App.3d 767, 283 Cal.Rptr. 809 (1991) (mortgagee with actual knowledge of defective soil conditions liable for damages and rescission for failing to disclose conditions to a foreclosure purchaser who could not reasonably be expected to discover them).

GLIDDEN v. MUNICIPAL AUTHORITY OF TACOMA
Supreme Court of Washington, en banc., 1988
111 Wash.2d 341, 758 P.2d 487

DURHAM, JUSTICE.

In October 1986, Patricia Rourke, as trustee under a deed of trust, conducted a nonjudicial foreclosure sale of property in Pierce County. Appellant Municipal Authority of the City of Tacoma (Municipal Authority) was the successful bidder at the sale and received from Rourke a trustee's deed containing recitals that notice of the sale had been sent "to all persons entitled thereto", and that the sale complied in all respects to the notice requirements of Washington's deeds of trust act, RCW 61.24.

The issue presented for decision is what protection these recitals, and the "conclusive evidence" standard of RCW 61.24.040(7), afford Municipal Authority against a claim to the property asserted by respondent Old Stone Bank (OSB), a junior lienor who was not notified of the sale in the manner required by the deeds of trust act. Municipal Authority asserts that because it is a bona fide purchaser for value (BFP), RCW 61.24.040(7) vests it with clear title. OSB contends that because Municipal Authority is itself a junior lienor, the "conclusive evidence" rule of RCW 61.24.040(7) does not protect it from challenges based on flawed foreclosure procedures. OSB also asserts that Municipal Authority does not qualify as a BFP.

* * *

I

The property in dispute, by means of separate deeds of trust, secured debts owed by the Mount Bay Corporation to plaintiff Marian Glidden ($37,640.16), respondent OSB ($88,500), and appellant Municipal Authority ($38,605). Glidden is the senior lienholder, with OSB and Municipal Authority, respectively, occupying the second-and third-order lienholder positions. There are at least two other junior lienors.

When Mount Bay defaulted on its debt to Glidden in 1986, Rourke, as trustee, initiated foreclosure proceedings pursuant to the power of sale provision in the Glidden deed of trust. In May 1986, Rourke notified Mount Bay that it was in default. On June 5, Rourke served on Mount Bay notice that the trust property would be sold at public auction on October 17, 1986, if Mount Bay's default was not cured before October 7. Rourke recorded this notice with the county auditor and posted it on the property but did not notify any of the junior lienholders about the impending foreclosure sale as required by RCW 61.24.040(1)(b).

Municipal Authority learned of the sale from the posted notice, and called Rourke on June 16 to request copies of the notice and of her foreclosure report. Between June 16 and October 17, the scheduled date of Rourke's sale, Municipal Authority and Rourke communicated on several occasions. On at least two of these occasions, Bryan Chushcoff, an attorney for Municipal Authority, asked Rourke if she had given notice of the planned foreclosure sale to junior encumbrancers. Rourke responded each time by saying: "Of course, Bryan, I always do." On the day of the sale, another Municipal Authority official asked Rourke if she had notified junior lienholders. Again she said that she had.

While Rourke's foreclosure plans were going forward, OSB set in motion its own foreclosure of the property. OSB initiated foreclosure proceedings in June and scheduled a sale for December. Rourke first learned of OSB's sale on June 20 in a phone conversation with OSB's attorney and received further notice of it in September, when an updated title report disclosed the recording of a notice of trustee's sale under OSB's deed of trust. Municipal Authority in September of OSB's plans to foreclose when it received a copy of this notice of trustee's sale.

Municipal Authority and Glidden were the only bidders at Rourke's sale. Glidden bid $37,640.19, the amount of Mount Bay's indebtedness to her. Municipal Authority bid $37,845. Rourke accepted Municipal Authority's bid.

Immediately after the sale, Chushcoff appeared at Rourke's law office to tender the purchase price. He received a receipt for the payment, and returned later in the day to pick up the trustee's deed. During this second visit, Chushcoff and Rourke speculated as to why OSB had not entered a bid. Terry McCarthy, a partner in Rourke's firm, happened into the conversation and asked Rourke if she had served OSB with notice. Rourke asserted that she had and told McCarthy and Chushcoff that OSB representatives had indicated to her that they knew about the sale.

The trustee's deed Municipal Authority received contained the following recitals:

7.   The Trustee * * * in accordance with law, caused copies of the statutory "Notice of Trustee's Sale" to be transmitted by mail to all persons entitled thereto and either posted or served prior to ninety days before the sale * * *

* * *

9.   All legal requirements and all provisions of said Deed of Trust have been complied with, as to acts to be performed and notices to be given, as provided in Chapter 61.24 RCW.

On October 29, Rourke learned from OSB's title company that OSB had not received notice of the sale and after checking her records realized that other junior lienholders also had not received proper notice. Rourke immediately called Municipal Authority and asked that the sale be undone. After some weeks of discussions, Rourke tendered to Municipal Authority its purchase price and a quitclaim deed. Municipal Authority refused the tender.

Glidden and Rourke commenced this action in December 1986, seeking a judgment declaring void the October 17 sale and the trustee's deed Rourke issued to Municipal Authority following the sale on the basis that Rourke had failed to serve proper notice on the junior lienholders. In its answer, Municipal Authority asserted that as a BFP it acquired clear title to the sale property pursuant to RCW 61.24.040(7). Municipal Authority asked that title be quieted in its favor, or in the alternative that Rourke and her law firm be held liable for damages in the amount of the fair market value of the property, at a minimum of $146,000.

OSB, impleaded by Municipal Authority as a third party defendant, answered Municipal Authority's claims by contending that as a junior lienor it was entitled to, but did not receive, statutory notice of the foreclosure sale, and that Rourke's failure to comply with statutory notice requirements renders the sale void as to OSB's interests in the property. Had it known of the sale, OSB asserted, it would have cured Mount Bay's default and thus preserved its interests. OSB also refuted Municipal Authority's claim to being a BFP and requested a ruling that Rourke's sale is void and that OSB's interests in the property remain valid.

On OSB's motion for summary judgment, the trial court ruled OSB's second priority lien to be "a valid, existing, enforceable lien" notwithstanding Municipal Authority's purchase because OSB "was an omitted junior lienor in that it was not notified of the sale[.]" Thus, the court held, OSB "may proceed to foreclose its Deed of Trust or exercise any rights under the Old Stone Deed of Trust and promissory note secured thereby." The trial court made no finding on Municipal Authority's status as a BFP. We granted Municipal Authority's petition for direct review.

II

Washington's deeds of trust act, RCW 61.24, authorizes nonjudicial foreclosures of deeds of trust as a time-efficient alternative to judicial mortgage foreclosure proceedings. *See* Gose, *The Trust Deed Act in Washington,* 41 Wash.L.Rev. 94 (1966). We have previously identified three principal goals of the deed of trust private sale program:

> First, the nonjudicial foreclosure process should remain efficient and inexpensive. Second, the process should provide an adequate opportunity for interested parties to prevent wrongful foreclosure. Third, the process should promote the stability of land titles.

(Citation omitted.) *Cox v. Helenius,* 103 Wash.2d 383, 387, 693 P.2d 683 (1985).

As this case well illustrates, these goals "are often difficult to reconcile." Comment, *Court Actions Contesting the Nonjudicial Foreclosure of Deeds of Trust in Washington,* 59 Wash.L.Rev. 323, 330 (1984). Permitting "omitted junior lienors" such as OSB to retain collateral interests in land that has been sold at auction, while advancing the second objective, would undermine the third. Conversely, preventing such omitted parties from challenging nonjudicial foreclosures in order to protect the title obtained by a sale purchaser such as Municipal Authority would favor the third objective over the second.

We would find the proper balance of objectives difficult to achieve in this case if it were not for RCW 61.24.040(7). That provision requires the foreclosing trustee to issue to the foreclosure sale purchaser a deed which:

> shall recite the facts showing that the sale was conducted in compliance with all of the requirements of this chapter and of the deed of trust, which recital shall be prima facie evidence of such compliance and conclusive evidence thereof in favor of bona fide purchasers and encumbrancers for value[.]

The deed Rourke issued to Municipal Authority contains recitals that notice was properly served "to all persons entitled thereto", "as provided in Chapter 61.24 RCW." Thus, if Municipal Authority is a BFP, RCW 61.24.040(7) renders these recitals conclusive as to the correctness of the foreclosure sale procedures and Municipal Authority would be entitled to clear title. If Municipal Authority is not a BFP, however, the deed recitals would be only prima facie evidence that the sale was conducted properly, subject to rebuttal by omitted junior lienholders seeking preservation of their interests.[3] *See Steward v. Good*, 51 Wash.App. 509, 512, 754 P.2d 150 (1988); Comment, 59 Wash.L.Rev. at 339; Comment, *In Deed An Alternative Security Device: The Nebraska's Trust Deeds Act*, 64 Neb.L.Rev. 92, 127–28 (1985).

In the posture in which this case comes to us, therefore, the issue we must decide is this: Viewed in a light most favorable to the nonmoving party (Municipal Authority), does the evidence on which the trial court based its ruling establish that Municipal Authority is not a BFP as a matter of law?

III

Before considering how the evidence bears out OSB's claim that Municipal Authority is not a BFP, we address two legal arguments advanced by OSB, which, if correct, would make resolution of the BFP issue unnecessary. First, OSB contends that, as an "omitted junior lienor", it is entitled to preservation of its interest regardless of whether Municipal Authority is a BFP. The trial court apparently accepted this argument, concluding, without addressing the BFP question:

1. That at the Trustee's sale, Old Stone Bank was an omitted junior lienor in that it was not notified of the sale;

2. As an omitted junior lienor, Old Stone Bank's lien was not affected by the Trustee's sale[.]

---

[3] Ordinarily, a nonjudicial foreclosure sale would extinguish all junior liens. *See* RCW 61.24.050. As the trial court correctly observed, however, the "omitted junior lienor" rule of mortgage law may operate in the nonjudicial foreclosure context to preserve the interest of a junior lienor who has not had an opportunity to contest foreclosure or participate at the foreclosure sale. *See* RCW 61.24.020 (deeds of trust are "subject to all laws relating to mortgages on real property", except when the act provides otherwise).

We cannot agree that OSB's interest may be sustained without consideration of Municipal Authority's status as a BFP. While lack of notice undeniably prejudices omitted junior lienors whose interests are extinguished by foreclosure, *see* RCW 61.24.050, the Legislature has determined that on balance the rights of the bona fide purchaser are paramount. See earlier discussion of RCW 61.24.040(7). Post-sale challenges are thus improper; the omitted lienors must seek other remedies. *See* Comment, 59 Wash.L.Rev. at 337–40; Comment, 64 Neb.L.Rev. at 122.

OSB argues also that RCW 61.24.040(7) cannot protect Municipal Authority even if Municipal Authority is a BFP because the provision does not apply to "lienholder insiders". In support of this argument, OSB notes that "conclusive recitals" provisions such as that contained in RCW 61.24.040(7) have been interpreted as affording no protection to trust beneficiaries who purchase the trust property at a procedurally flawed nonjudicial foreclosure sale. *See Johnson v. Johnson*, 25 Wash.2d 797, 172 P.2d 243 (1946) (applying California law to "conclusive recitals" clause contained in deed of trust). Such recitals should also afford no protection to other junior lienholders, OSB asserts.

We find this argument to be without merit. The reason a trust beneficiary might be denied the benefits of "conclusive recitals" clauses is that the beneficiary is in a position to conduct the sale in a manner calculated to serve his own interests. *See Johnson*, at 840, 172 P.2d 243 ("conclusive recitals" clause should not protect "the beneficiary of the trust who purchased at the sale brought about by it"); Comment, 64 Neb.L.Rev. at 128 n. 150. But nothing inherent to the relationship between a junior lienholder and the foreclosing party, and certainly nothing that has been established about Municipal Authority's relationship to Glidden or Rourke here, enables the junior lienholder to rig a sale to its benefit. Thus, there is no cause to deny lienholders, as a class, the protection the "conclusive evidence" standard of RCW 61.24.040(7) affords.

We are persuaded against OSB's proposed "lienholder insider" exception to the recitals provision in RCW 61.24.040(7) also because such an exception is unnecessary to the proper operation of the statute. Textually, RCW 61.24.040(7) does not distinguish lienholders from other purchasers. The only distinction that is drawn is that between purchasers who are BFPs and those who are not, and this we find sufficient to protect third parties from prejudice caused by procedural flaws in foreclosures. A lienholder/purchaser who acts in reliance on flawed sale procedures would not be a BFP, and thus would not be insulated by the "conclusive evidence" rule.[4]

---

[4] Significantly, scholarly discussions of conclusive recitals provisions make no mention of the need for a "lienholder insiders" exception. *See* G. Nelson & D. Whitman, *Real Estate Finance Law* § 7.20, at 537–39 (2d ed. 1985); Comment, *Court Actions Contesting the Nonjudicial*

A broad brush exclusion of "lienholder insiders" is not only unjustified, it appears to be unwise. By limiting the availability of post-sale challenges to foreclosure, the "conclusive evidence" rule of RCW 61.24.040(7) plays a critical role in removing the disincentives to investment that had existed under prior mortgage foreclosure laws. *See* Gose, 41 Wash.L.Rev. at 95–96. The promise of clear title helps attract purchasers to land sale auctions, and the swiftness and certainty of the nonjudicial foreclosure process encourages land-backed financing by assuring lenders a reliable method for realizing on their security interests. We would do almost certain damage to an essential aspect of the deed of trust program, therefore, if we were to deny post-sale protections to what is likely the broadest class of sale participants—the junior lienholders. *See Rosenberg v. Smidt,* 727 P.2d 778, 787 (Alaska 1986) (Moore, J., dissenting in part).

IV

We turn now to the bona fide purchaser question. A BFP is one who purchases property without knowledge, actual or constructive, of competing interests. *Miebach v. Colasurdo,* 102 Wash.2d 170, 175–76, 685 P.2d 1074 (1984). At issue here is Municipal Authority's knowledge that OSB had not received notice of Rourke's sale. OSB does not contend that Municipal Authority had actual knowledge of Rourke's failure to notify OSB, but argues that Municipal Authority should be charged with constructive knowledge of Rourke's error.

Two questions of fact must be answered to respond to OSB's contention. First, did the events surrounding Rourke's sale create in Municipal Authority a duty to inquire into possible flaws in the foreclosure process? Second, if Municipal Authority did have such a duty, did it satisfy that duty? *See generally Miebach,* at 175–77, 685 P.2d 1074 (discussing "inquiry notice"). Only the second of these questions is at issue here, since Municipal Authority concedes that "the circumstances surrounding the Glidden sale were such as to require it to make inquiry."

The question of whether Municipal Authority satisfied its duty of inquiry cannot properly be answered on summary judgment, however, because on this question, "the evidence is such that different inferences might reasonably be drawn therefrom". *Hudesman v. Foley,* 73 Wash.2d 880, 889, 441 P.2d 532 (1968) (quoting 92 C.J.S. *Vendor & Purchaser* § 374 (1955)); *see Fleming v. Stoddard Wendle Motor Co.,* 70 Wash.2d 465, 423 P.2d 926 (1967). That Municipal Authority had not received proper notice of Rourke's sale; that it knew about OSB's planned December sale; that junior lienholders did not attend the sale—these facts might suggest that Municipal Authority could not reasonably rely on Rourke's claim that she "always" notifies junior lienholders. On the other hand, knowing as much as Municipal Authority, Rourke persistently stood by her claims that she had notified OSB.

More also needs to be known about the communications between Municipal Authority and Rourke before it can be said with certainty that Municipal Authority acted unreasonably in relying on her. For example, did Rourke have a reputation for carelessness in performing her duties as trustee? Was she known to respond hastily and incorrectly to inquiries put to her? What more can be determined about the timing and substance of Rourke's assurances that would reflect on the reasonableness of Municipal Authority's reliance? From a fuller appreciation of the circumstances of Rourke's interactions with Municipal Authority, the trial court will better be able to determine the reasonableness of Municipal Authority's reliance.

Urging us not to worry about this unresolved factual question, OSB offers the following principle of law: "Reasonable inquiry means inquiry of the party possessing the potential claim against the property." While obviously of value to OSB here, hard and fast rules of this sort are not generally recommended for questions of reasonableness. *Cf.* W. Keeton, D. Dobbs, R. Keeton, & D. Owen, *Prosser and Keeton on Torts* § 35 (5th ed. 1984) (disapproving rigid rules of conduct in tort law where reasonableness is in issue). What Municipal Authority reasonably should have done, and what a future foreclosure sale purchaser reasonably should do to prevent challenges to its title, can be determined only from the particular circumstances that obtain in each case.

We cannot accept OSB's proffered rule in any event because we find it to be unsupportable as a matter of law. The only case OSB cites for the rule is *Enterprise Timber, Inc. v. Washington Title Ins. Co.,* 76 Wash.2d 479, 457 P.2d 600 (1969), in which a mortgagee was charged with constructive knowledge of a fraud perpetrated by the mortgagor in acquiring the mortgaged property. The basis for the imputation of constructive knowledge was the mortgagee's actual knowledge of the mortgagor's bad reputation and prior illegal conduct in similar transactions.

> This knowledge apparently prompted [the mortgagee] to take unusual precautions to protect itself, and should have prompted a reasonable investigation of [the mortgagor's] purchase of the property. A simple inquiry of [the previous owner] would have revealed the fraud in procuring the conveyance. The record amply supports the [trial] court's finding that plaintiff unreasonably failed to make this investigation and was thus charged with constructive notice of the fraud . . .

Enterprise Timber, at 483, 457 P.2d 600.

OSB would read this language to mean that inquiry concerning other interests in property *must* be made of the interested parties themselves. We do not believe the holding of *Enterprise Timber* is that broad. The

Enterprise Timber opinion merely observes that such inquiry would have disclosed a fraud in the transaction there at issue; at most, it suggests that inquiry of the previous owner was necessary under the circumstances that obtained in that case because whatever assurances the mortgagor might have made concerning the validity of his title were patently unreliable. Because there is no evidence that Rourke had a reputation for failing to give notice or being untruthful, this case is distinguishable.

The order on summary judgment is reversed and the case remanded for further proceedings.

PEARSON, C.J., and ANDERSEN, UTTER, BRACHTENBACH, CALLOW, GOODLOE, DOLLIVER and DORE, JJ., concur.

NOTES

1. *Presumption statutes.* Like Washington, several states have presumption statutes that are designed to enhance the finality of power of sale foreclosures and the marketability of titles that they produce. See, e.g., Ala. Code §§ 35–10–5, 12–21–99; West's Ann.Cal.Civ.Code § 2924; Mo. Ann. Stat. § 443.380; Nev.Rev.Stat.Ann. § 107.030(8); S.D. Codified Laws § 21–48–23; Utah Code Ann. § 57–1–28. Consider the following analysis of these statutes:

> Though these statutes vary significantly, they nevertheless seem to fall into three general categories. The first type, which we characterize as *"rebuttable presumption"* legislation, is exemplified by the Missouri statute: "[T]he recitals in the trustee or mortgagee's deed concerning the default, advertisement, sale or receipt of the purchase money, and all other facts pertinent thereto, shall be received as prima facie evidence in all courts of the truth thereof." [Mo.Rev.Stat. § 443.380] This type of statute, which is found, with minor variations, in over a dozen states, contains neither "conclusive presumption" language nor any specific protection for bona fide purchasers. Indeed, a few of these statutes claim to deal only with the *notice* requirements of the foreclosure and not with other aspects that might be carried out improperly. At most, the recitals create a rebuttable presumption that there was a valid basis for foreclosure and that the necessary procedural requirements have been satisfied. These statutes seem to do little more than restate the common law notion that the party attacking the validity of a foreclosure sale has the burden of proof. Presumably the rights of a bona fide purchaser under this type of statute would be no greater than those afforded under the common law "void-voidable" classification of power of sale foreclosure defects considered above. Such statutes contribute only slightly to the stability of power of sale titles.

> In the second category of statutes, the inclusion of appropriate recitals creates a conclusive presumption in favor of bona fide purchasers, but this presumption extends only to notice requirements

of the sale. We label this type of statute *"conclusive presumption for bona fide purchasers—notice only."* The California statute is typical; it states:

> [A] recital in the deed executed pursuant to the power of sale of compliance with all requirements of law regarding the mailing of copies of notices or the publication of a copy of the notice of default or the personal delivery of the copy of the notice of default or the posting of copies of the notice of sale or the publication of a copy thereof shall constitute prima facie evidence of compliance with these requirements and conclusive evidence thereof in favor of bona fide purchasers and encumbrancers for value and without notice.

[Cal.Civ.Code § 2924]. * * * [I]n the absence of such a statute, the failure to mail a statutorily required notice to a mortgagor renders the foreclosure sale void. That the property is sold to a bona fide purchaser is irrelevant. No title, legal or equitable, passes at the sale. The statute, however, reduces the impact of the notice defect. In effect, the notice defect is deemed to render the sale only *voidable*. Consequently, a foreclosure sale purchaser or subsequent grantee who qualifies as a bona fide purchaser will hold an indefeasible title despite the failure to give proper notice.

On the other hand, it is unclear whether the [foregoing] statute will benefit a bona fide purchaser when the defect in the sale process is *procedural* but does not deal with the statutory notice requirements. For example, suppose the person who conducts a foreclosure sale under a deed of trust was improperly replaced as trustee by another person a few days before the sale. Under the traditional analysis, the sale is void regardless of the sale purchaser's being a bona fide purchaser. The California statute does not appear to aid the purchaser in that context because a sale by an unqualified trustee does not constitute the type of notice defect that is within the literal purview of the statute. * * *

The third category, which we characterize as *"conclusive presumption for bona fide purchasers—all aspects of foreclosure"* affords the greatest protection for bona fide purchasers. At least fourteen states have this type of legislation. Washington's statute typifies this category. It requires the foreclosing trustee to issue the foreclosure purchaser a deed that

> shall recite the facts showing the sale was conducted in compliance with all of the requirements of this chapter and of the deed of trust, which recital shall be prima facie evidence of such compliance and conclusive evidence thereof in favor of bona fide purchasers and encumbrancers for value.

[Wash.Rev.Code Ann. § 61.24.040]. * * *

The literal language of this type of statute is breathtakingly broad in its impact on bona fide purchasers. Not only does it purport to protect a bona fide purchaser from notice and other procedural defects in the foreclosure process, it is arguably applicable even when the mortgagee had no substantive right to foreclose. * * * Suppose, for example, that a mortgage is foreclosed even though the obligation that it secures is not in default, or that the mortgage was forged. Under traditional state, the foreclosure would be void in either instance, and would be set aside even against a sale purchaser who was a bona fide purchaser. The literal language of ["category three"] statutes suggest a different result. * * *Limiting the conclusive impact of [such statutes] to procedural defects in the foreclosure process clearly makes sense. To allow a bona fide purchaser to prevail over a mortgagor who was not in default or a person who never executed a mortgage to begin with would be fundamentally unfair, a normative result that legislatures adopting "category three" statutes probably did not intend.

Grant S. Nelson & Dale A. Whitman, *Reforming Foreclosure: The Uniform Nonjudicial Foreclosure Act*, 53 Duke L.J. 1399, 1503–07 (2004).

2.   *Washington statute amended.* Shortly after *Glidden* was decided, the Washington legislature amended West's Rev.Code Wash.Ann. § 61.24.040(7) to provide that "these recitals shall not affect the lien or interest of any person entitled to notice under RCW § 61.24.040(1), if the trustee fails to give the required notice to such person. In such case, the lien or interest of such omitted person shall not be affected by the sale and such omitted person shall be treated as if such person was the holder of the same lien or interest and was omitted as a party defendant in a judicial foreclosure proceeding." Why do you think the response to *Glidden* was so swift?

3.   *Intentional omission of junior parties in a power of sale foreclosure.* Earlier in our consideration of judicial foreclosure, we observed that, in some jurisdictions, a foreclosing mortgagee can keep a pro-landlord junior lease alive by intentionally not joining the lessee. Should this be possible in the power of sale context? Suppose, for example, a state power of sale statute requires a foreclosing mortgagee to mail notice to each person holding a junior interest in mortgaged land. Suppose further that the foreclosing mortgagee mails notice to everyone entitled to it except junior lessees that the mortgagee wants to keep. Should the foreclosure be effective against everyone but the "un-notified lessees"? Or should the foreclosure be invalid as to everyone? Does the amendment to the Washington statute discussed in Note 2 permit a foreclosing mortgagee to keep favorable junior leases alive after the power of sale foreclosure by intentionally failing to give them the required statutory notice?

3. CONSTITUTIONAL PROBLEMS WITH POWER OF SALE

As we noted earlier, power of sale foreclosure statutes vary considerably in the degree and nature of notice that the foreclosing mortgagee must give the mortgagor and other interested parties. Moreover, power of sale legislation almost never provides for a hearing, judicial or otherwise, before foreclosure. To what extent do these attributes of power of sale foreclosures create constitutional problems under the due process clauses of the Fifth and Fourteenth Amendments to the federal Constitution? The following materials examine these issues. It is important to remember that the Fourteenth Amendment's due process clause applies only when "state action" exists ("significant state involvement") and that the due process clause of the Fifth Amendment applies only when sufficient "federal action" exists.

GARCIA V. FEDERAL NATIONAL MORTGAGE ASSOCIATION

United States Court of Appeals, Sixth Circuit, 2015
782 F.3d 736

MERRITT, CIRCUIT JUDGE.

This case presents another appeal from a home foreclosure in Michigan. Plaintiffs raise one issue on appeal: Whether the district court erred in dismissing plaintiffs' due process claim because it found that the Federal National Mortgage Association,[1] commonly referred to as Fannie Mae, was not a state actor for constitutional purposes when it foreclosed upon their home? We affirm the district court's judgment dismissing the due process claim as without merit, but on the ground that the Michigan foreclosure procedure does not violate due process.

I.

Plaintiffs Angel and Estela Garcia obtained a home loan in 2003 from First Guaranty Mortgage Corporation and granted a mortgage to Mortgage Electronic Registration Systems, Inc., sometimes referred to as "MERS,"[2] as mortgagee and nominee for lender First Guaranty and its successors and assigns. The mortgage was duly recorded with the Leelanau Register

---

[1] Fannie Mae, and its twin brother Freddie Mac, are government-sponsored private enterprises that purchase and securitize residential mortgages. Specifically, Fannie Mae is a federally chartered corporation that operates in the secondary mortgage market, purchasing and securitizing residential mortgages to provide mortgage lenders with capital to use to fund additional mortgages.

[2] MERS is a system for electronically tracking interests in mortgages that are traded on the secondary market. MERS members (approximately 6,000) agree that MERS serves as mortgagee or beneficiary, and when loan ownership or servicing rights are sold from one MERS member to another, MERS remains the titleholder to the security instrument as nominee on behalf of whoever owns the loan. The language on a standard mortgage or deed of trust reads: "MERS is the mortgagee [or beneficiary] of this security instrument. MERS is a separate corporation that acts solely as nominee on behalf of the lender and its successors and assigns."

of Deeds. In January 2011, Mortgage Electronic Registration Systems assigned the mortgage to BAC Home Loans Servicing, LP, and the assignment was recorded. BAC Home Loans merged into Bank of America on July 1, 2011, and Bank of America became the mortgage holder. As successor by merger, Bank of America was not required to record the assignment.

Plaintiffs do not dispute that in 2007 they fell behind on their mortgage payments and defaulted on the loan. In January 2011, plaintiffs received a letter regarding the default and containing information explaining their rights, including the right to seek a loan modification. Plaintiffs sought foreclosure-related assistance from the Northern Michigan Community Action Agency, and Mr. Garcia and his son attended a workshop offered by the agency on how to prevent foreclosure. Plaintiffs also attended a meeting with Bank of America's legal counsel in April 2011, providing counsel with financial information and forms prepared with help from the Northern Michigan Community Action Agency.

Plaintiffs were offered a loan modification by Bank of America allowing for reduced payments for a three-month trial period. The letter offering the loan modification directed plaintiffs to make the lowered payments on time for three months and stated that if all the trial period payments were timely made, the loan would be permanently modified. Plaintiffs allege that they made the three payments in accordance with the letter, but that they did not receive any further information regarding a new payment amount after the three modified payments were made. They also allege that Bank of America returned two payments they attempted to make in March 2012. Despite the returned payments, Bank of America offered plaintiffs a permanent loan modification in May 2012 and instructed them to execute and return the loan modification agreement sent to them. Plaintiffs do not allege that they ever executed or returned the loan modification agreement to Bank of America, and Bank of America confirms that it never received any of the required loan modification documents.

In August 2012, Bank of America's legal counsel sent plaintiffs a letter informing them that because they were in default and had not accepted the loan modification agreement, a non-judicial foreclosure would proceed. Notice of the foreclosure was published in accordance with Michigan law and the property was sold at a sheriff's sale on October 12, 2012. Bank of America was the high bidder and purchased the property. It then executed a quitclaim deed to Fannie Mae that was recorded on November 29, 2012. The six-month statutory redemption period under Michigan law expired on April 12, 2013. In June 2013, Fannie Mae filed a possession action in the local court. On October 15, 2013, more than six months after the statutory redemption period had expired, plaintiffs filed this action in Michigan state court against defendants Fannie Mae, Mortgage Electronic Registration

Systems, BAC Home Loans Servicing, LP, and Bank of America, N.A. Defendants removed the case to federal court pursuant to both diversity and federal-question jurisdiction. The Federal Housing Finance Agency, the federal "conservator" for winding up the affairs of Fannie Mae, was permitted to intervene.

Plaintiffs brought four claims in their complaint: (1) Quiet Title pursuant to Mich. Comp. Laws § 600.2932; (2) violations of Fifth and Fourteenth Amendment Due Process Rights; (3) illegal/improper foreclosure and sheriff's sale pursuant to Mich. Comp. Laws § 600.3204; and (4) violation of Mich. Comp. Laws § 600.3205 *et seq.* Defendants Fannie Mae, Mortgage Electronic Registration Systems, BAC Home Loans Servicing and Bank of America filed a motion to dismiss, as did the intervenor, Federal Housing Finance Agency. The district court granted the motions to dismiss on all claims. Plaintiffs appeal only the dismissal of Count II, which claims violation of their Fifth and Fourteenth Amendment Due Process Rights.

* * *

III.

The Fifth and Fourteenth Amendments prohibit the deprivation of property by a state actor without due process of law. Our previous decisions concerning the Due Process Clause as it relates to foreclosures by Freddie Mac and Fannie Mae have focused on whether Freddie Mac and Fannie Mae have been transformed into state actors in light of the conservatorship of the Federal Housing Finance Agency. We have not addressed the questions of whether the Federal Housing Finance Agency is a state actor and what restrictions the Due Process Clause may impose on the Agency in its direction of Fannie Mae. We find it unnecessary to wade into that discussion in this case. Even if the Due Process Clause constrains the Federal Housing Finance Agency in its direction of Fannie Mae, its compliance with Michigan's foreclosure-by-advertisement procedures satisfied the requirements of the Due Process Clause.

We begin with a brief look at the historical development of foreclosure and redemption at common law. At early common law, the mortgagee had the right to confiscate the mortgaged property at the time of the first missed payment. If the mortgagor had made a number of payments, the mortgagee received a windfall because it kept all payments made up to the time of default and then also received full title to the property as well. Accordingly, the Court of Chancery in the sixteenth century sought to mitigate this harsh result by granting the mortgagor an equitable period of time to redeem the property by coming current with the payments. The mortgagor's equity of redemption demonstrates the equity courts' reluctance to permit unfair or inequitable loss of a person's property. However, the ambiguity surrounding the equitable redemption process, particularly the uncertainty of the amount of time to redeem the property, prompted states to regularize the process with statutory redemption periods starting in the early 1800s. *See* Theodore F.T. Plucknett, *A Concise History of the Common Law* 603–08 (1956); Thomas W. Bigley, Comment, *Property Law—The Equity of Redemption: Who Decides When It Ends?*, 21 Wm. Mitchell L.Rev. 315, 319–22 (1995); Grant Nelson & Dale Whitman, *Real Estate Finance Law* §§ 7:1–7:5 (3d ed.1994).

As a result, two types, or phases, of the right to redemption now generally exist in the United States. The first is an "equitable" redemption period that occurs before the foreclosure and sale of the property. It allows the mortgagor to pay the outstanding debt and have his rights to the property restored. This opportunity may not be waived by contract and is a creation of the Court of Chancery four centuries ago. The right to redeem *after* the foreclosure and sale is a "statutory right of redemption." Statutory redemption provides that even after the equitable right of redemption has been foreclosed, the borrower has one more opportunity to regain the property by paying the purchaser at the foreclosure sale the price paid at the sale. The statutory redemption period is in fact an *additional* period granted to the property owner after the equitable redemption period ends at the time of sale.

The requirement for "due process of law" functions somewhat like equity to require procedural fairness and to prohibit the state from conducting unfair or arbitrary proceedings. "Procedural due process" at its core requires notice and an opportunity to be heard "at a meaningful time and in a meaningful manner." *Armstrong v. Manzo*, 380 U.S. 545, 552, 85 S.Ct. 1187, 14 L.Ed.2d 62 (1965); *see also Mathews v. Eldridge*, 424 U.S. 319, 333, 96 S.Ct. 893, 47 L.Ed.2d 18 (1976). Accordingly, the Due Process Clause is flexible and calls for such procedural protections as the particular situation demands. Due process is required to prevent, to the extent possible, an *erroneous* deprivation of property. *See Gilbert v. Homar*, 520 U.S. 924, 930–32, 117 S.Ct. 1807, 138 L.Ed.2d 120 (1997) (due process calls for such procedural protections as the situation demands). The extent to which procedural due process must be afforded the plaintiff is influenced by the extent to which he may suffer loss and depends upon whether his interest in avoiding that loss outweighs the governmental interest in summary adjudication. *Cafeteria & Rest. Workers Union v. McElroy*, 367 U.S. 886, 81 S.Ct. 1743, 6 L.Ed.2d 1230 (1961), tells us that "consideration of what procedures due process may require under any given set of circumstances must begin with a determination of the precise nature of the government function involved as well as of the private interest that has been affected by governmental action." *Id.* at 895, 81 S.Ct. 1743.

Although we find no Supreme Court opinion ruling on what procedures satisfy due process in this foreclosure context, lower courts, scholars, Congress, and agencies have taken varied approaches to the question of whether, and how, federally related entities, including the Department of Veterans Affairs, and its predecessor the Veterans Administration, the Farmers Home Administration, and the Department of Housing and Urban Development are subject to due process constraints when they foreclose mortgages. These agencies, which sometimes are direct lenders and other times only insure loans to borrowers, may utilize nonjudicial foreclosures that provide specified notice requirements but no hearing before the property is sold. *See* Florence Wagman Roisman, *Protecting Homeowners from Non-Judicial Foreclosure of Mortgages Held by Fannie Mae and Freddie Mac,* 43 Real Estate L.J. 125 (2014).

A. *Notice*

The traditional assumption in the United States has been that the required notice for a foreclosure is a contractual or statutory matter and not a constitutional problem. *See Scott v. Paisley,* 271 U.S. 632, 635, 46 S.Ct. 591, 70 L.Ed. 1123 (1926) (notice to a mortgagor is sufficient if a sale of mortgaged property is conducted in accordance with the terms of a contract). More recent Supreme Court decisions have required that to satisfy the Due Process Clause, the notice must be "reasonably calculated . . . to apprise interested parties. . . ." *Mullane v. Cent. Hanover Bank & Trust Co.,* 339 U.S. 306, 314, 70 S.Ct. 652, 94 L.Ed. 865 (1950); *see also Mennonite Bd. of Missions v. Adams,* 462 U.S. 791, 798, 103 S.Ct. 2706, 77 L.Ed.2d 180 (1983) ("When the mortgagee is identified in a mortgage that is publicly recorded, constructive notice by publication must be supplemented by notice mailed to the mortgagee's last known available address, or by personal service.").

The Michigan foreclosure-by-advertisement statute's notice requirements are not at odds with notions of due process under both common law and Supreme Court precedent. The statute requires notice and opportunities to cure the default or redeem the property at several points before the borrower's rights are fully extinguished. The process begins with written notice to the borrower by the foreclosing party, by first-class mail and certified mail, return receipt requested, both sent to the borrower's last-known address. The notice must set forth the reasons that the mortgage is in default and state the amount that is due and owing, and inform the borrower that he has 30 days to request a meeting to attempt to work out a loan modification. If the borrower requests such a meeting within 30 days of receiving notice of the default, foreclosure proceedings will not commence until at least 90 days after the notice is mailed to the borrower. The default notice must also inform the borrower of the number of days in the redemption period that will be available to the borrower if the property is eventually sold at a foreclosure sale. Mich. Comp. Laws §§ 600.3205a-.3205e, 600.3212 (2012).

The foreclosing party must then give notice to the borrower of the date of foreclosure and sheriff's sale by publishing a notice for four successive weeks, at least once in each week, in a newspaper published in the county where the premises are located. A copy of the notice must also be posted in a conspicuous place upon the premises described in the notice. *Id.* § 600.3208. The notice must also include a statement that if the property is sold at a foreclosure sale, the borrower may bid on the property at the sheriff's sale. *Id.* § 600.3228.

Following the date of the sheriff's sale, the borrower has a six-month, post-foreclosure statutory redemption period in which he may redeem the property pursuant to the procedures set forth in the Michigan law. Mich. Comp. Laws § 600.3240. As noted above, the borrower must be given notice of this six-month statutory period for residential properties in the notice of default. Mich. Comp. Laws § 600.3205a(j).

During the six-month post-foreclosure redemption period, if the borrower believes there has been "fraud or irregularity" in the foreclosure process that has prejudiced his right to retain or redeem his property, he may bring an action in a court of law requesting that the foreclosure be stayed and that the sale be set aside. *Kim v. JPMorgan Chase Bank, N.A.,* 493 Mich. 98, 825 N.W.2d 329, 337 (2012). The borrower also has the full complement of Michigan common law remedies regarding fraud, misrepresentation or other unfair practices or dealings, within their applicable statutes of limitation, under which to bring legal action against appropriate parties if the facts so warrant.

Plaintiffs do not dispute that they received the required statutory notice of the foreclosure and subsequent sheriff's sale by both notice posted on the property and notice in the local newspaper. Thus, the Michigan statute provides notice to the homeowner of the default, foreclosure, and sale, as well as notice regarding how to cure the default, notice of an opportunity to seek a loan modification, and notice of how to redeem the property. The plaintiffs do not plead any erroneous deprivation of property through lack of notice that the Due Process Clause seeks to avoid.

B.   *Right to a Hearing*

Plaintiffs' main argument is that—despite actual notice of default and a six-month redemption period before foreclosure—due process entitles them to a judicial hearing before foreclosure. Where only property rights are involved, however, the postponement of a structured judicial hearing is not a denial of due process if there is adequate opportunity after the foreclosure for such a hearing. *Phillips v. Comm'r,* 283 U.S. 589, 596–97, 51 S.Ct. 608, 75 L.Ed. 1289 (1931) ("Where only property rights are involved, mere postponement of the judicial enquiry is not a denial of due process, if the opportunity given for ultimate judicial determination of liability is adequate."); *see also Mitchell v. W.T. Grant Co.,* 416 U.S. 600,

611, 94 S.Ct. 1895, 40 L.Ed.2d 406 (1974) (upholding Louisiana statute for seizure of personal property as satisfying due process because the state has a legitimate interest in enabling the creditor to enforce his security interest in the debtor's property); *see also Parratt v. Taylor,* 451 U.S. 527, 539, 101 S.Ct. 1908, 68 L.Ed.2d 420 (1981) (state prison inmate unsuccessfully sued prison officials alleging that the officials' negligent loss of his mail deprived him of his property without due process of law). Although no Supreme Court case we have found addresses the right to a hearing in the foreclosure context, at least two circuit courts have held that where a borrower defaults on a mortgage where the security interest is held by the government, a hearing is not required. *Vail v. Brown,* 39 F.3d 208, 209 (8th Cir.1994) (Department of Veterans Affairs was not obligated, as matter of due process, to hold a pre-deprivation hearing if it provides notice that is "sufficient to permit the [borrower] to participate in the foreclosure sale and to exercise his or her preforeclosure options."); *McCachren v. U.S. Dep't of Agric., Farmers Home Admin.,* 599 F.2d 655, 657 (5th Cir.1979) (landowners entitled to a hearing only if the matter of default is in question).

In the foreclosure context, these principles do not require a preforeclosure judicial hearing because the mortgagor is given timely and adequate notice of the reasons for the default in advance of the foreclosure and an opportunity to cure any default, followed by a six-month period to redeem the property, as well as an opportunity to stop the foreclosure and set aside any resulting sale for "fraud or irregularity" in the process. The Michigan statute provides adequate process in both the period following notice of the default but prior to any sale of the property, and then further opportunity by giving the homeowner another six months to set aside the sale if there has been "fraud or irregularity" in the process. *Kim,* 825 N.W.2d at 337; Mich. Comp. Laws § 600.3240 (2012). This ability to bring an action before expiration of the statutory redemption period satisfies the requirement that there be a hearing "at a meaningful time and in a meaningful manner" before permanent deprivation of property that the homeowner does not yet own free and clear of debt due to the existence of a mortgage on the property.

Plaintiffs here simply have not alleged facts that would demonstrate that they were erroneously deprived of their property years after they first defaulted on the mortgage. Plaintiffs signed a mortgage and a note that allowed for the use of summary foreclosure proceedings in the event of default. Plaintiffs do not contest that they had actual notice of the default and subsequent foreclosure. They contacted the lender several times about loan modification after the foreclosure process was initiated. They met with Bank of America's counsel and were offered a permanent loan modification, which they did not accept. What plaintiffs here would be able to demonstrate if given a pre-foreclosure hearing is left unstated. They acknowledge defaulting on the loan. They do not dispute that they did not accept the offered loan modification. They did not redeem the property during the six-month statutory redemption period. Nor have they alleged any facts demonstrating fraud or irregularity in the process they received that prevented them from taking any of these many opportunities to keep their home. Thus, on the merits of the case, plaintiffs have not stated a Fifth or Fourteenth Amendment due process claim.

For the foregoing reasons, we affirm the judgment of the district court.

NOTES

1. *The notice requirement.* In Mennonite Bd. of Missions v. Adams, 462 U.S. 791, 103 S.Ct. 2706, 77 L.Ed.2d 180 (1983), a county sold land for nonpayment of taxes. It did not send notice of the sale to a mortgagee that held a junior lien. The United States Supreme Court relied on *Mullane* to hold that the mortgagee's due process rights were violated because notice that the mortgaged property was being sold for nonpayment of taxes was only published and posted in the county courthouse. The Court emphasized that "when the mortgagee is identified in a mortgage that is publicly recorded, constructive notice by publication must be supplemented by notice mailed to the mortgagee's last known available address, or by personal service. But unless the mortgagee is not reasonably identifiable, constructive notice alone does not satisfy the mandate of *Mullane*." Id. Does the *Garcia* decision satisfy this standard?

Other courts also have held that, when state or federal action is present, such as in a tax sale, the government has to send a notice to a person that will lose its property interest. E.g., Davis Oil Co. v. Mills, 873 F.2d 774, 782–84 (5th Cir. 1989); Turner v. Blackburn, 389 F. Supp. 1250 (W.D.N.C. 1975) (Power of sale legislation required only notice by newspaper publication and posting. The court invalidated the legislation: "To propose to a homeowner that he trek to the courthouse or spend 20 cents to examine fine-print legal notices, *daily* for the duration of a twenty-year mortgage, as his sole protection against summary eviction, seems to us to offer him nothing of value."). Contra Federal Deposit Ins. Corp. v. Morrison, 747 F.2d 610, 615 (11th Cir. 1984).

For the view that the Eleventh Circuit's opinion in *Morrison* reflects "an understanding of the practical problems faced by foreclosing mortgagees, practicalities not taken into account in * * * *Mennonite* or the district court in *Morrison,* and that it reflects 'a clarity of insight into the complexities of Alabama mortgage law rarely accorded the depth of analysis that body of law deserves,' " see Romaine S. Scott, *Mennonite*: What Does It Mean to Alabama Mortgagees After *Federal Deposit Insurance Corp. v. Morrison*, 36 Alabama L.Rev. 969, 998 (1985). On the other hand, the Fifth Circuit sharply criticized the Eleventh Circuit's approach in *Morrison*.

Are junior lienors constitutionally entitled to more than notice by publication? The junior lienor often has a greater financial stake in the mortgaged real estate than the mortgagor. If notice by publication or posting is insufficient when a tax lien sale will terminate a junior lien, shouldn't it also be insufficient when a senior mortgage foreclosure will do the same? Can commercial junior lienors keep themselves informed concerning the status of senior liens? What about noncommercial junior lienors? See generally, Nelson, Whitman, Burkhart & Freyermuth, Real Estate Finance Law § 7.25 (6th ed.2015). Consider the language of a Maryland decision in which the court held that *Mennonite* requires junior lienors to get at least mailed notice of a power of sale foreclosure:

> A simple title scan from the time the property was acquired by the current owner to the initiation of the foreclosure proceedings would have provided notice of [the junior mortgagee's] interest in the property. Also, [the junior mortgagee's] name and address appear on the top page of the deed of trust which is recorded in the land records * * *. Certainly, this process is not oppressive to the foreclosing party in terms of the amount of time, money or effort expended.

Island Fin., Inc. v. Ballman, 92 Md.App. 125, 607 A.2d 76 (1992). Accord, USX Corp. v. H.H. Champlin, 992 F.2d 1380 (5th Cir.1993); Teschke v. Keller, 38 Mass.App.Ct. 627, 650 N.E.2d 1279 (1995).

2. *"Request for notice" statutes.* Some power of sale statutes require mailed notice not only to the mortgagor and the real estate owner, but also to any person who has recorded a request to receive it. See, e.g., Vernon's Ann.Mo.Stat. § 443.325. Does this type of statute obviate the constitutional notice problem with respect to junior lienors? Consider a typical judicial response to this question:

> The [request for notice] statute is designed to go hand in hand with [the] constitutional protection so that no property interest will be unfairly extinguished. In this instance [the junior lienor] did not receive notice solely for the reason that it had not filed a request for notice of sale. It is clear, however, that with little effort or diligence, [mortgagee] could have obtained [the junior lienor's] address and mailed notice to [it]. After taking into consideration the holdings of *Mennonite* and its progeny, we believe that [a request for notice statute] protects the due process rights of those parties whose interests and addresses are not "reasonably ascertainable," by providing a mechanism through which such parties can be assured that they will receive notice. If an interest of a party is reasonably ascertainable, however, the minimum requirements of due process dictate that actual notice be given without a formal request for notice being filed.

Island Fin., Inc. v. Ballman, 92 Md.App. 125, 607 A.2d 76 (1992). Accord Bank of America, N.A. v. Arlington West Twilight Homeowners Ass'n, 920 F.3d 620, 623–24 (9th Cir. 2019); Davis Oil Co. v. Mills, 873 F.2d 774 (5th Cir.1989); USX Corp. v. H.H. Champlin, 992 F.2d 1380 (5th Cir.1993). Contra Tagaban v. City of Pelican, 358 P.3d 571, 577–78 (Alaska 2015); M & M Investment Group, LLC v. Ahlemeyer Farms, Inc., 994 N.E.2d 1108 (Ind. 2013).

3. *Supplemental notice by foreclosing mortgagee.* To what extent can a foreclosing mortgagee obviate the notice argument by providing more extensive notice than the statute requires? Some courts and commentators have maintained that "the fact that mortgagees alert mortgagors to their rights will not satisfy the requirements of due process or cure a constitutionally infirm statute." Kathleen Barry, Comment, The Constitutionality of Maine's Real Estate Mortgage Foreclosure Statutes, 32 Maine L.Rev. 147, 171 (1980). See also Wuchter v. Pizzutti, 276 U.S. 13, 48 S.Ct. 259, 72 L.Ed. 446 (1928) (nonresident motorist service of process statute that required only service on the secretary of state violated the Fourteenth Amendment due process clause though the secretary of state actually mailed notice to the nonresident motorist). On the other hand, if notice is actually provided to all interested parties, does anyone have the requisite injury required by Article III of the Constitution to confer standing to litigate the statute's constitutional infirmity? See Nelson, Whitman, Burkhart & Freyermuth, Real Estate Finance Law § 7.26 (6th ed.2015).

4. *The hearing requirement.* Several courts that have reached the hearing issue directly have cited *Fuentes v. Shevin,* 407 U.S. 67 (1972)to invalidate power of sale statutes. See, e.g., Turner v. Blackburn, 389 F.Supp. 1250 (W.D.N.C.1975); Garner v. Tri-State Dev. Co., 382 F.Supp. 377 (E.D.Mich.1974); Northrip v. Federal Nat'l Mortg. Ass'n, 372 F.Supp. 594 (E.D.Mich.1974), *rev'd on other grounds,* 572 F.2d 23 (6th Cir. 1975); Valley Dev. at Vail, Inc. v. Warder, 192 Colo. 316, 557 P.2d 1180 (1976). However, in Guidarelli v. Lazaretti, 305 Minn. 551, 233 N.W.2d 890 (1975), the Minnesota Supreme Court upheld that state's power of sale statute against a *Fuentes* hearing argument. The court stated:

> Unlike the due process problems raised by [*Sniadach v. Family Finance Corp. of Bay View,* 395 U.S. 337 (1969) and *Fuentes*] the statutory scheme for mortgage foreclosure by advertisement, Minn.St. c. 580, provides for 4 weeks' prior notice before sale, it permits the mortgagor to redeem his property within either 6 months or 1 year, and most importantly, he is not deprived of the use and possession of the property prior to the public foreclosure sale.

Do you agree? Which is more burdensome to a debtor, being deprived of temporary possession of a refrigerator or automobile until a final hearing on the merits or being deprived of title to real estate with no statutory requirement of a hearing at all?

In many jurisdictions, a mortgagor or junior lienor often challenges a pending power of sale foreclosure by bringing a suit to enjoin it. The basis for the injunction suit is found either in the common law or in a general statutory authorization that is not part of the power of sale legislation. A few power of sale statutes specifically authorize an injunction suit by the mortgagor. See Wash. Rev.Code § 61.24.130. Does the ability to bring a suit satisfy the constitutional hearing requirement? Or do the power of sale statutes have to provide an opportunity for a hearing? See Nelson, Whitman, Burkhart & Freyermuth, Real Estate Finance Law § 7.26 (6th ed.2015).

A state constitution may provide greater hearing rights than the federal constitution. In Anderson v. Alaska Housing Finance Corp., 462 P.3d 19 (Alaska 2020), the Alaska Supreme Court held that the Alaska Constitution requires a foreclosing state agency to provide a pre-deprivation hearing. It also held that the property owner's ability to bring an independent lawsuit or counterclaim in a subsequent eviction proceeding does not satisfy the due process hearing requirement.

The hearing probably does not have to be judicial. As the *Turner* court indicated, a hearing before a "clerk or a similar neutral official" is sufficient. Turner v. Blackburn, 389 F.Supp. 1250 (W.D.N.C.1975). Moreover, in United States v. Ford, 551 F.Supp. 1101 (N.D.Miss.1982), a federal district court held that a federal agency's administrative hearing procedure can supplement state power of sale legislation that fails to satisfy due process hearing requirements. The neutrality of the administrative official conducting the hearing is an important issue. Indeed, in reversing a trial court's refusal to issue preliminary injunctive relief against an FmHA power of sale foreclosure, the Eleventh Circuit said:

> A fair hearing requires an impartial arbiter. We have serious reservations about the neutrality of the hearing officers. The regulations establish that the hearing officer is a nearby district director. On its face, the regulation appears less than neutral. The nearby director will be evaluating a decision to foreclose made by a peer and already approved by his boss, the state director. * * * On the surface, the [mortgagors] have shown a substantial likelihood that a conflict may exist that impinges the hearing officer's impartiality.

Johnson v. U.S. Dept. of Agric., 734 F.2d 774 (11th Cir.1984).

5.   *Waiver of due process rights.* Assuming that many power of sale statutes violate procedural due process requirements, is waiver a possible solution? In Anderson v. Alaska Housing Finance Corporation, 462 P.3d 19, 28–29 (Alaska 2020), the Alaska Supreme Court held that a mortgagor had not waived his right to a hearing because (1) his waiver was not knowing and voluntary, (2) the waiver language in the loan documents was not clear and was not the subject of negotiation, and (3) the loan documents were adhesion contracts. Accord Fuentes v. Shevin, 407 U.S. 67 (1972); Ricker v. United States, 417 F. Supp. 133 (Me. 1976). For further consideration of waiver in power of sale foreclosures, see Johnson v. U.S. Dept. of Agric., 734 F.2d 774 (11th Cir.1984); Rau v. Cavenaugh, 500 F.Supp. 204 (D.S.D.1980).

If a valid waiver depends only on making the waiving party aware of what rights he is waiving, it could be argued that carefully drafted language in a mortgage or deed of trust can constitute a waiver of procedural due process rights. On the other hand, if a valid waiver depends on factors such as equality of bargaining power, doesn't a subsequent title examiner have an impossible burden? If bargaining inequality invalidates the power of sale clause in a particular mortgage, can this claim be used against any purchaser or only against the foreclosing lender if it buys at the sale? One commentator has pointed out:

> If as the *Fuentes* and *Overmyer* cases suggest, not all waivers will be effective, then the power of sale foreclosure may be rendered of doubtful utility because of the problems of establishing marketable title. Defects of the type described above will not appear of record. How will a title examiner be able to distinguish a valid exercise of a power for sale from an ineffective one? Would such a defect render a sale void or merely voidable? If the sale is rendered void, then no title passes in law or equity. Thus, the purchaser at the sale, whether the noteholder or a third party, cannot get title of any kind and *a fortiori* no title would pass to subsequent purchasers. If, however, the defect renders the sale only voidable the mortgagor or grantor's right to challenge is cut off as against any purchaser for value without notice. Thus the grantor or mortgagor will be able to set aside the sale as against the noteholder as purchaser, but not as against a sale purchaser or subsequent grantee who would otherwise qualify as a purchaser for value without notice.

Grant S. Nelson, Deed of Trust Foreclosure Under Power of Sale— Constitutional Problems—Legislative Alternative, 28 Mo.Bar J. 428, 434 (1972).

How could an effective waiver by subsequent junior mortgagees or judgment creditors be established? Is the mortgagor's waiver in recorded documents sufficient to bind junior interest holders? Can constitutional rights be waived in such an indirect fashion? See Nelson, Whitman, Burkhart & Freyermuth, Real Estate Finance Law § 7.27 (6th ed.2015).

6. *Federal power of sale legislation.* As mentioned earlier, the federal Multifamily Mortgage Foreclosure Act ("Multifamily Act") and the Single Family Mortgage Foreclosure Act ("Single Family Act") authorize power of sale foreclosure of all residential mortgages held by the Department of Housing and Urban Development ("HUD"). Under the Acts, the Notice of Default and Foreclosure must be sent by certified mail, return receipt requested, at least twenty-one days before the foreclosure sale, to the original mortgagor, any other person liable for the mortgage debt, the property "owner," and, at least ten days before the sale, all lienors. 12 U.S.C. §§ 3708(1) & 3758(2). Unless one takes a broad view of who is an "owner," neither the Acts nor the related regulations require mailed notice to holders of leases, easements, and similar junior interests. Is this a constitutional defect? As we noted earlier, a junior interest holder who is not joined to judicial foreclosure is not bound by the proceedings, because of due process principles. Should we apply similar reasoning to power of sale foreclosures?

The Acts do not provide for a hearing. However, the regulations for the Multifamily Act require HUD to "provide to the mortgagor [and current owner] an opportunity informally to present reasons why the mortgage should not be foreclosed. Such opportunity may be provided before or after the designation of a foreclosure commissioner but before service of the notice of default and foreclosure." 24 C.F.R. § 27.5. The regulations for the Single Family Act do not include a similar requirement. Does even the Multifamily Act requirement satisfy due process? At least one court has held that is does with respect to mortgagors. See Lisbon Square v. United States, 856 F.Supp. 482 (E.D.Wis.1994) ("By offering a mortgagor a chance to explain the failure to make mortgage payments, HUD provides all the due process required by the Fifth Amendment. * * * A mortgagor who fails to respond to notices of delinquency waives the right to be heard.") Are you convinced? In any event, are the Acts constitutionally defective because other junior interest holders are not afforded a right to a hearing?

For an analysis of the Acts and of Congress' attempts to expand their coverage to other federally-held mortgages, see Patrick A. Randolph, The New Federal Foreclosure Laws, 49 Okla.L.Rev. 123 (1996).

As stated at the beginning of this section, due process applies only to "state action" and "federal action." One of the most significant issues with respect to federal action is whether Fannie Mae and Freddie Mac are federal agencies because they are now in federal conservatorship. The answer to this question has very important consequences, because Fannie Mae and Freddie Mac own the majority of residential mortgages in this country.

FEDERAL HOME LOAN MORTGAGE ASSOCIATION V. KELLEY
Court of Appeals of Michigan, 2014
306 Mich. App. 487, 858 N.W.2d 69

PER CURIAM.

In this foreclosure-related litigation, plaintiff, Federal Home Loan Mortgage Association (Freddie Mac), appeals by leave granted an Ingham Circuit Court opinion and order reversing the 55th District Court's July 31, 2012 order terminating the possession by defendants Michael R. and Kathryn M. Kelley of residential property located in East Lansing. For the reasons set forth in this opinion, we reverse and remand for reinstatement of the district court's order.

I. BACKGROUND

A. UNDERLYING MORTGAGE TRANSACTION

This dispute involves real property located at 2458 Barnsbury Road, in East Lansing, Michigan. On March 21, 2003, First National Bank of

America loaned defendants $240,000 for the purchase of the property. Defendants executed a mortgage encumbering the property to First National. The mortgage was recorded on April 24, 2003. On March 26, 2003, First National assigned the mortgage to ABN-AMRO Mortgage Group, Inc. The assignment was recorded on November 25, 2003. On September 1, 2007, CitiMortgage, Inc. and ABN-AMRO merged and maintained the name CitiMortgage (hereinafter CMI).

B. FREDDIE MAC AND THE FEDERAL HOUSING FINANCE AGENCY CONSERVATORSHIP

Freddie Mac is a federally chartered corporation that was created as part of the Emergency Home Finance Act of 1970. See 12 U.S.C. § 1451 *et seq.; American Bankers Mtg. Corp. v. Fed. Home Loan Mtg. Corp.*, 75 F.3d 1401, 1404 (C.A.9, 1996). Freddie Mac operates in the secondary mortgage market, purchasing and securitizing residential mortgages. *Sonoma Co. v. Fed. Housing Fin. Agency*, 710 F.3d 987, 989 (C.A.9, 2013). Freddie Mac is governed by the Federal Housing Enterprises Financial Safety and Soundness Act, 12 U.S.C. § 4501 *et seq. Sonoma Co.*, 710 F.3d at 989.

In 2008, Congress amended the Financial Safety and Soundness Act by enacting the Housing and Economic Recovery Act (HERA), 12 U.S.C. § 4511 *et seq.* "HERA established the Federal Housing Finance Agency [FHFA], an independent agency charged with supervising [Fannie Mae and Freddie Mac] and the Federal Home Loan Banks." *Sonoma Co.*, 710 F.3d at 989. HERA empowered the FHFA to act, under certain circumstances, as a conservator or receiver of Freddie Mac or the Federal National Mortgage Association (Fannie Mae) for purposes of "reorganizing, rehabilitating, or winding up the affairs" of either entity. 12 U.S.C. § 4617(a)(2). It is undisputed that the FHFA placed Freddie Mac into conservatorship in September 2008.

C. FORECLOSURE OF THE PROPERTY

In June 2011, defendants defaulted on the mortgage and CMI foreclosed on the property under Michigan's foreclosure by advertisement statute, MCL 600.3201 *et seq.* Freddie Mac purchased the property at an October 20, 2011 sheriff's sale. Defendants failed to redeem the property within the six-month statutory redemption period, and the property vested in Freddie Mac on April 20, 2012. See MCL 600.3236.

On May 1, 2012, after expiration of the statutory redemption period, Freddie Mac initiated eviction proceedings in district court pursuant to MCL 600.5704. Defendants challenged the foreclosure, arguing in part that the foreclosure violated their Fifth Amendment due process rights. Defendants maintained that Freddie Mac was a federal actor by virtue of FHFA's conservatorship and was subject to the due process requirements of the Fifth Amendment, and therefore could not foreclose by advertisement.[5] * * *

The district court granted Freddie Mac's motion for summary disposition under MCR 2.116(C)(9) (failure to state valid defense) and MCR 2.116(C)(10) (no genuine issue of material fact). The district court held in relevant part that Freddie Mac was not a governmental actor subject to Fifth Amendment * * *.

Defendants appealed, and the circuit court reversed. The circuit court held that Freddie Mac was a governmental entity subject to the Fifth Amendment's notice and hearing requirements. The circuit court reasoned that Freddie Mac filed tax exemptions as the United States under MCL 207.526(h)(*i*) and 505(h)(*i*) and that the federal government retained permanent control over all aspects of Freddie Mac. Noting that "FHFA controls every aspect of [Freddie Mac's] business and its Board of Directors is appointed by and answers to the Director of the FHFA," the court concluded that "the procedures and provisions in place in this case make the conservatorship, in all practicality, permanent." * * *

The circuit court reversed the district court's order awarding possession to Freddie Mac and dismissed the complaint. Freddie Mac applied for leave to appeal and the FHFA moved to intervene. This Court granted both applications. On appeal, Freddie Mac argues that the circuit court erred by holding that it was a governmental entity for constitutional purposes * * *.

III. ANALYSIS

A. DUE PROCESS

The Fifth Amendment "appl[ies] to and restrict[s] only the Federal Government and not private persons." *Pub. Utilities Comm. of D.C. v. Pollak,* 343 U.S. 451, 461, 72 S.Ct. 813, 96 L.Ed. 1068 (1952). Therefore, the threshold question in this case is whether Freddie Mac is a governmental entity subject to a Fifth Amendment claim.

The circuit court concluded that Freddie Mac is a governmental entity subject to Fifth Amendment claims for two reasons: (1) Freddie Mac "filed tax exemptions as the United States under MCL 207.526(h)(*i*) and 505(h)(*i*)"; and (2) Freddie Mac is a governmental entity under *Lebron v. Nat'l. R. Passenger Corp.,* 513 U.S. 374, 377, 115 S.Ct. 961, 130 L.Ed.2d 902 (1995). Both of these conclusions are erroneous.

With respect to Freddie Mac's tax status, while MCL 207.505(h)(*i*) and MCL 207.526(h)(*i*) provide tax exemptions for certain instruments and transactions involving the United States, Freddie Mac is specifically

---

[5] Defendants' brief on appeal explains that at the time of the foreclosure, Freddie Mac was the investor of defendants' mortgage, and CMI was selected by Freddie Mac to service the mortgage.

authorized by federal statute to be exempt from "all taxation now or hereafter imposed by any . . . State," except for real property taxes. 12 U.S.C. § 1452(e). Thus, Freddie Mac would have been exempt regardless of whether it sought an exemption "as the United States." Moreover, the circuit court did not cite, and defendants do not provide, any authority supporting the position that seeking a tax exemption "as the United States" subjects federally created corporations to constitutional claims under the Fifth Amendment. As the United States Court of Appeals for the Ninth Circuit stated in *Hall v. American Nat'l. Red Cross,* 86 F.3d 919, 922 (C.A.9, 1996), "Government-created corporations are often held to be tax-immune government instrumentalities, but courts have also frequently found them not to be subject to constitutional treatment as government actors." Thus, the mere fact that Freddie Mac filed for tax exemptions as "the United States" was not dispositive of whether Freddie Mac is a governmental entity for constitutional purposes. Instead, *Lebron,* 513 U.S. 374, 115 S.Ct. 961, is controlling on this issue, and under the *Lebron* framework, we conclude that Freddie Mac is not a governmental entity.

In *Lebron,* the United States Supreme Court addressed whether the National Railroad Passenger Corporation (commonly known as Amtrak) was a governmental entity for constitutional purposes. In that case, Amtrak refused to display the plaintiff's political advertisement on a large billboard at Penn Station commonly known as "the Spectacular." The plaintiff sued, alleging violations of his First and Fifth Amendment rights. *Id.* at 377–378, 115 S.Ct. 961. At issue was whether Amtrak was a governmental entity subject to the plaintiff's constitutional claims. *Id.* at 378–379, 115 S.Ct. 961.

In resolving this issue, the Supreme Court held that, "where . . . the Government creates a corporation by special law, for the furtherance of governmental objectives, and retains for itself permanent authority to appoint a majority of the directors of that corporation, the corporation is part of the Government" for constitutional purposes. *Id.* at 400, 115 S.Ct. 961. Although Amtrak's authorizing statute expressly stated that Amtrak was not a federal entity, the *Lebron* Court concluded otherwise. The Court reasoned that Amtrak was created by special statute explicitly for the furtherance of a governmental goal—specifically, the preservation of passenger trains in the United States. *Id.* at 383, 397–398, 115 S.Ct. 961. Furthermore, six of the eight Amtrak board members were directly appointed by the President of the United States. *Id.* at 397, 115 S.Ct. 961. Moreover, the Court reasoned, the government's control of Amtrak was permanent in nature, explaining:

> Amtrak is not merely in the temporary control of the Government (as a private corporation whose stock comes into federal ownership might be); it is established and organized under federal law for the very purpose of pursuing federal governmental

objectives, under the direction and control of federal governmental appointees. It is in that respect no different from the so-called independent regulatory agencies such as the Federal Communications Commission or the Securities Exchange Commission, which are run by Presidential appointees with fixed terms. [*Id.*]

In concluding that Amtrak was a federal entity, the *Lebron* Court distinguished *Regional Rail Reorganization Act Cases,* 419 U.S. 102, 95 S.Ct. 335, 42 L.Ed.2d 320 (1974), wherein the Supreme Court held that Conrail was not a federal instrumentality "despite the President's power to appoint . . . 8 of [Conrail's] 15 directors." *Lebron,* 513 U.S. at 399, 115 S.Ct. 961. The *Lebron* Court noted that, in *Regional Rail,* the federal appointees were appointed to the Conrail board to protect federally backed debt obligations. *Id.* Furthermore, the appointees were required to operate Conrail "at a profit for the benefit of its shareholders," and full control of the board would shift back to the shareholders once federally backed debt obligations fell below 50 percent of total indebtedness. *Id.* (quotation marks and citations omitted). In contrast, "[t]he Government exerts its control [over Amtrak] not as a creditor but as a policymaker, and no provision exists that will automatically terminate control upon termination of a temporary financial interest." *Id.*

In this case, there is no dispute that the government created Freddie Mac by special statute for the purpose of furthering governmental objectives.[8] Defendants do not argue, nor can they prove that, preconservatorship, Freddie Mac was a governmental entity. See *American Bankers Mtg. Corp. v. Fed. Home Loan Mtg. Corp.,* 75 F.3d 1401, 1406–1409 (C.A.9, 1996) (holding that preconservatorship Freddie Mac lacked sufficient government control under *Lebron* because 13 of its 18 directors were elected annually by common shareholders and its 60 million shares of common stock were publicly traded on the New York Stock Exchange).

Instead, defendants argue that the FHFA's 2008 conservatorship served to transform Freddie Mac into a governmental entity. This argument is not novel and has been repeatedly rejected by federal courts including the United States Court of Appeals for the Sixth Circuit, which recently held that "[u]nder the *Lebron* framework, Freddie Mac is not a government actor who can be held liable for violations of the Fifth Amendment's Due Process Clause." *Mik v. Fed. Home Loan Mtg. Corp.,* 743 F.3d 149, 168 (C.A.6, 2014). This holding aligned with numerous decisions by federal courts across the country, which have soundly rejected the same argument. For the following reasons, we now similarly hold that Freddie

---

[8]   See, e.g., 12 U.S.C. § 4501; *American Bankers Mtg. Corp. v. Fed. Home Loan Mtg. Corp.,* 75 F.3d 1401, 1406–1407 (C.A.9, 1996) ("The congressional purposes for Freddie Mac are clearly designed to serve the public interest by increasing the availability of mortgages on housing for low- and moderate-income families and by promoting nationwide access to mortgages.").

Mac, under the conservatorship of the FHFA, is not a governmental entity for constitutional purposes.

As conservator, the FHFA succeeded to "all" of Freddie Mac's "rights, titles, powers, and privileges," with authority to operate all of its business "with all the powers of the shareholders, the directors, and the officers. . . ." 12 U.S.C. § 4617(b)(2)(A), (B)(i). Although these powers are sweeping, importantly, Congress did not appoint FHFA as *permanent* conservator over Freddie Mac. Instead, the purpose of the conservatorship is to reorganize, rehabilitate, or wind up Freddie Mac's affairs. 12 U.S.C. § 4617(a)(2). These terms connote a temporary period of control, and defendants identify no statutory language showing that the government intended to effectuate a permanent takeover of Freddie Mac.

The circuit court concluded that although "conservatorship is described as a temporary status of a company, the procedures in place in this case make the conservatorship, in all practicality, permanent," noting that "there is no determined end date in which [Freddie Mac] will become a private entity, nor is there an automatic provision that will revert [Freddie Mac] to a private entity." Similarly, defendants point out that in *Regional Rail,* 419 U.S. at 102, 95 S.Ct. 335, the Court held that Conrail was not a federal instrumentality in part because the government's full voting control would *automatically* shift back to Conrail's shareholders once the corporation's federal debt obligations fell below 50 percent of its indebtedness. *Lebron,* 513 U.S. at 399, 115 S.Ct. 961, citing *Regional Rail,* 419 U.S. at 152, 95 S.Ct. 335. Defendants argue that, unlike Conrail, in this case there is no triggering mechanism that terminates the conservatorship. These arguments are unpersuasive.

The *Lebron* Court noted that with respect to Conrail the government was merely acting as its creditor and exerted control over Conrail for the purpose of ensuring a profit for Conrail's shareholders. *Lebron,* 513 U.S. at 399, 115 S.Ct. 961. Notably, the *Lebron* Court did not state that government control would be deemed permanent unless the government's involvement was scheduled to terminate on a specified date or upon the satisfaction of a specified condition. To the contrary, the *Lebron* Court recognized that the indefinite government control over Conrail, pending the satisfaction of certain conditions, did not equate to permanent government control. *Id.* With respect to permanence, the conservatorship of Freddie Mac is analogous to the government's control of Conrail, as it is similarly of indefinite duration pending the satisfaction of certain conditions. See 12 U.S.C. § 4617(a)(2). Thus, Congress's failure to specify a termination date does not render the FHFA's control permanent under the *Lebron* framework. This is especially true considering that the government's control of Freddie Mac was imposed for the inherently temporary purpose of "reorganizing, rehabilitating, or winding up" its affairs. 12 U.S.C. § 4617(a)(2).

In sum, Freddie Mac was created by special law for governmental purposes; however, although the federal government, through the FHFA, exercises control over Freddie Mac, that control is not permanent in nature. Accordingly, under the *Lebron* framework, Freddie Mac is not a federal entity for constitutional purposes, and defendants' due process claim fails as a matter of law. See *Nat'l. Airport Corp. v. Wayne Bank,* 73 Mich.App. 572, 574, 252 N.W.2d 519 (1977) ("It is unquestioned that state action is required in order to assert a denial of due process under both the Michigan and United States Constitutions.").

* * *

IV. CONCLUSION

In summary, we conclude that Freddie Mac is not a governmental entity for constitutional purposes and defendants' due process claim therefore failed as a matter of law. * * * Therefore, defendants were not entitled to any relief, and the district court properly entered an order terminating defendants' possession of the property. Accordingly, we reverse the circuit court's order and remand for reinstatement of the district court's order terminating defendants' possession of the property.

Reversed and remanded for proceedings consistent with this opinion. No costs are awarded in this matter. MCR 7.219(A). We do not retain jurisdiction.

SISTI V. FEDERAL HOUSING FINANCE AGENCY

United States District Court, D. Rhode Island, 2018
324 F. Supp. 3d 273

JOHN J. MCCONNELL, JR., UNITED STATES DISTRICT JUDGE.

The Plaintiffs in these cases seek a ruling that Defendants Federal Housing Finance Agency ("FHFA"), Federal National Mortgage Association ("Fannie Mae"), and Federal Home Loan Mortgage Corporation ("Freddie Mac") are government actors, and thus, violated the Plaintiffs' Fifth Amendment due process rights when they conducted non-judicial foreclosures on the Plaintiffs' homes. The Defendants have moved for judgment on the pleadings. For the following reasons, their motions are DENIED.

I. BACKGROUND

A. Fannie Mae, Freddie Mac, and FHFA

* * *

While acting as conservator, FHFA controls all of the rights, titles, powers, and privileges of the shareholders and boards of directors of the GSEs. FHFA elects the entirety of both boards of directors; the shareholders do not. FHFA also determines the boards' size and scope of authority.

FHFA controls the business activities of the GSEs, and manages them to serve public ends. It does not manage the GSEs to maximize profitability or shareholder returns. FHFA prohibits the GSEs from paying any dividends to their common shareholders.

There is no date certain for when the conservatorship will end, nor will it end upon the completion or attainment of predetermined criteria. Instead, FHFA's director has total authority and discretion over whether its control of the GSEs will end.[1]

Presently, the United States government owns all of the senior preferred stock of the GSEs; this stock is senior in right for both dividends and liquidation to all other preferred or common stock. The government also has warrants to purchase 79.9% of the GSEs' common stock. The GSEs cannot issue new shares, declare dividends, or dispose of assets without approval of the U.S. Treasury. In exchange, Fannie Mae has received some $116 billion from the Treasury to maintain liquidity; Freddie Mac has received some $71 billion.

Both GSEs have paid more dividends into the Treasury than they received in the bailout: Fannie Mae has paid approximately $151 billion and Freddie Mac has paid approximately $98 billion. However, under the senior preferred stock purchase agreement, these dividend payments do not reduce the government's ownership interest in the GSEs, The Congressional Budget Office considers payments from the GSEs into the Treasury to be "intragovernmental payments."

The GSEs cannot redeem the senior preferred stock prior to the termination of the government's funding commitment; that will not occur until all of the GSEs' liabilities have been satisfied.

After appointing itself conservator of the GSEs, FHFA created the Servicer Alignment Initiative ("SAI"), which directs actions taken by the GSEs' mortgage servicers when servicing a delinquent mortgage. The SAI requires servicers of GSE-owned mortgages to follow specific timelines for processing foreclosures. The SAI directed the GSEs' servicers to use non-judicial foreclosure procedures when foreclosing in Rhode Island.

* * *

III. DISCUSSION

The Court begins by briefly addressing the relevant case law. The Court next examines the claims as to Fannie Mae and Freddie Mac.

---

[1] The director of FHFA can either issue an order terminating the conservatorship, or can appoint FHFA receiver of the GSEs. If the latter action is taken, the conservatorship ends, but FHFA would maintain control as receiver.

Finally, the Court turns its analysis to FHFA as the conservator of the GSEs.

A. The relevant case law

The Court holds that the Plaintiffs can prove that the GSEs and FHFA-as-conservator are government actors, and thus, can prove that the Defendants denied Plaintiffs due process by conducting non-judicial foreclosures. This Court is aware that this holding is contrary to every other court to reach the issue. Numerous district courts, as well as the Sixth and D.C. Circuits, have concluded that the Defendants are not government actors for purposes of constitutional claims—a fact the Defendants emphasized throughout their briefing and at oral argument (as well they should have). *See, e.g.,* Defs.' Reply at 29–33 (listing decisions of other courts).

Nevertheless, none of those cases is binding on this Court; they are only available to the Court for any persuasive value they may have. This Court, however, is duty-bound to conduct an independent inquiry of the matter before it, bound by the law that controls it. *See D'Arezzo v. Providence Ctr., Inc.,* 142 F.Supp.3d 224, 228–29 (D.R.I. 2015). In so doing, the Court is not persuaded by the reasoning of prior cases—discussed more below—and instead concludes that the Defendants can be found to be government actors.

B. The Plaintiffs can prove that Fannie Mae and Freddie Mac are government actors for purposes of constitutional claims.

The starting point for the Court's analysis is *Lebron v. National Railroad Passenger Corp.,* 513 U.S. 374, 115 S.Ct. 961, 130 L.Ed.2d 902 (1995). In *Lebron,* the United States Supreme Court announced that, where "the Government [1] creates a corporation by special law, [2] for the furtherance of governmental objectives, and [3] retains for itself permanent authority to appoint a majority of the directors of that corporation," then the corporation is "part of the Government" for constitutional claims. *Id.* at 400, 115 S.Ct. 961.

* * *

Both Plaintiffs and Defendants agree that *Lebron*'s three-part test controls whether Fannie Mae and Freddie Mac are government entities. The parties do not dispute that the first two prongs are satisfied, and the Court accepts at this stage of the litigation the Plaintiffs' factual allegation that FHFA currently has authority to appoint a majority of the Fannie Mae and Freddie Mac boards. The only disputed issue is whether the government has retained "permanent authority" to make these appointments. *Lebron,* 513 U.S. at 400, 115 S.Ct. 961.

* * *

Plaintiffs argue that HERA gave FHFA complete and total control over Fannie Mae and Freddie Mac, and that this authority will continue uninterrupted until the government decides to end conservatorship (if, indeed, it ever does), rendering government control effectively permanent. The Defendants, however, argue that HERA gives FHFA *indefinite*, but not *permanent*, control over the GSEs, and that *Lebron* implies that any form of government control short of a statutory grant of power is merely temporary.

* * *

The practical reality here is that the government effectively controls Fannie Mae and Freddie Mac permanently. The government appoints all of the members of the GSEs' boards of directors and controls every operational aspect of the entities. It owns all of the GSEs' senior preferred stock and owns warrants to purchase 79.9% of their common stock. The government does not allow the GSEs to pay dividends to shareholders; rather, they must be paid directly into the U.S. Treasury. Indeed, to date the GSEs have paid more into the Treasury than they received in the 2008 bailout.

But perhaps most important is the unchecked control the government has over the duration of its total takeover of the GSEs. Absent an act of Congress, the conservatorship will only *end* in one of two ways: the director of FHFA can decide to end the conservatorship, or it can appoint FHFA receiver, whereupon FHFA will retain control of the GSEs as receiver. Either way, the decision to end the conservatorship is left entirely to the discretion of the government. This is "worlds apart" from other scenarios in which the Supreme Court has found or suggested government control is only temporary. *See Reg'l Rail*, 419 U.S. at 152, 95 S.Ct. 335 (provision automatically terminating government control); *Lebron*, 513 U.S. at 398, 115 S.Ct. 961 (government ownership of private corporation's stock where corporation not organized under federal law for public purpose). The practical reality, then, is that the government can control Fannie Mae.

IV. CONCLUSION

For the foregoing reasons, the Court DENIES the Defendants' motions for judgment on the pleadings.

IT IS SO ORDERED.

NOTE

Which decision—*Kelley* or *Sisti*—do you find more persuasive in terms of whether Fannie and Freddie should be viewed as "state actors"? What if the foreclosing mortgagee is a corporation wholly-owned by the federal government, such as Ginnie Mae? See, e.g., Warren v. Government Nat'l Mortg. Ass'n, 611 F.2d 1229 (8th Cir. 1980) (holding that foreclosure by GNMA was not the exercise of "powers of a governmental nature" and was thus not state action despite GNMA being wholly-owned by federal government); Daniel E. Blegen, The Constitutionality of Power of Sale Foreclosures by Federal Government Entities, 62 Mo.L.Rev. 425 (1997) (criticizing *Warren* and concluding that after Lebron, GNMA is a state actor); Nelson, Whitman, Burkhart & Freyermuth, Real Estate Finance Law § 7.29 (6th ed.2015). Putting aside the constitutional question, is it good policy to make foreclosure more difficult for federal entities than it is for their private counterparts? Blegen, supra, at 446–47.

E. DISBURSEMENT OF FORECLOSURE SALE PROCEEDS

BANK OF AMERICA, N.A. v. BA MORTGAGE, LLC

Court of Appeals of New Mexico, 2005
137 N.M. 368, 111 P.3d 226

VIGIL, JUDGE.

A fund was created when BA Mortgage, LLC foreclosed on its mortgage and the subsequent sale of the property resulted in a surplus of $28,467.43. This appeal requires us to determine whether a junior mortgagee or the debtor's assignee of her rights of redemption and surplus is entitled to the surplus. The district court ruled that the debtor's assignee was entitled to the surplus. * * *

Entitlement to the Surplus

G. Nelson and D. Whitman, *Real Estate Finance Law* § 7.31, at 588 (2d ed. 1985), states the rule regarding the right to surplus after foreclosure:

> The major underlying principle is that the surplus represents the remnant of the equity of redemption and security wiped out by the foreclosure. Consequently, the surplus stands in the place of the foreclosed real estate and the liens and interests that previously attached to that real estate now attach to the surplus. They are entitled to be paid out of the surplus in the order of priority they enjoyed prior to foreclosure. The claim of the foreclosed mortgagor or the owner of the equity of redemption normally is junior to those of all valid liens wiped out by the foreclosure. (footnotes omitted).

Restatement (Third) of Property: Mortgages § 7.4 (1997), states the same rule, providing that "the surplus is applied to liens and other interests terminated by the foreclosure in order of their priority and the remaining balance, if any, is distributed to the holder of the equity of redemption." Therefore, "the claim of the holder of the foreclosed equity of redemption to the surplus is subordinate to the claims of all other holders of liens and interests terminated by the foreclosure." *Id.* cmt. b.

It is undisputed that Junior Mortgagee recorded its lien before Assignee obtained its assignment of right of redemption and made a claim to the right to any surplus. Applying the foregoing rule, Junior Mortgagee has a higher priority claim to the surplus than Assignee. *See Pacific Loan Mgmt. Corp. v. Superior Court,* 196 Cal.App.3d 1485, 242 Cal.Rptr. 547, 551–52 (1987) (stating that a junior lienor had the right to have its secured debt paid from surplus); *W.A.H. Church, Inc. v. Holmes,* 46 F.2d 608, 611 (D.C.1931) (stating that surplus arising from foreclosure must be used to satisfy subordinate mortgages, liens, and judgments before any surplus can be turned over to the mortgagor); *Builders Supply Co. v. Pine Belt Sav. & Loan Ass'n,* 369 So.2d 743, 745 (Miss.1979) (stating that "the surplus arising from a sale under a senior lien should be applied on a junior lien"); *Morsemere Fed. Sav. & Loan Ass'n v. Nicolaou,* 206 N.J.Super. 637, 503 A.2d 392, 394 (Ct.App.Div.1986) (stating that "surplus funds take on the character of the land, at least with respect to junior encumbrancers whose liens existed at the time of the foreclosure").

Assignee persuaded the district court, and makes the argument on appeal, that Junior Mortgagee's failure to obtain a judgment on its lien means that Junior Mortgagee lost any right it had to the surplus. The court's view was that the junior lien was wiped out in the foreclosure, and because there was no judgment on the junior lien, the lien did not survive the foreclosure.

We disagree. Under the general rule, the surplus stands in the place of the foreclosed real estate and the liens and interests that previously attached to the real estate now attach to the surplus. Nelson & Whitman, *supra,* § 7.31, at 589; Restatement of Prop. § 7.4. Junior Mortgagee was timely and proactive in asserting its right to any surplus. It filed a cross-claim in the foreclosure action, appeared, and argued its position. When questioned by the court, it explained that it had not yet obtained a judgment because there was no reason to do so until after the foreclosure and after it became clear there was a surplus. It explained that to maintain its status as a lienor, it only needed to have a valid lien, not a judgment. We agree with this proposition. *See* Nelson & Whitman, *supra,* § 7.31, at 589 (stating, "[i]n order to qualify for lienor status, it must be established that the claim was reduced to a lien prior to the foreclosure sale." (footnote omitted)). Moreover, in addition to its express reservation of jurisdiction, the court's order granting foreclosure recognized that there still might be additional matters to resolve, including the parties' rights to any surplus that might result from the sale. This would include the distribution of any possible surplus that might result from the sale. Junior Mortgagee's decision to make its claim and lien known, but to wait and see how things developed, was reasonable. We therefore also reject Assignee's additional argument that Junior Mortgagee did not exercise the diligence required because it never served its cross-claim on the mortgagor.

Foreclosure is an equitable action, and the distribution of foreclosure proceeds should be governed by equitable considerations. *See Las Campanas Limited Partnership v. Pribble,* 1997–NMCA–055, ¶ 9, 123 N.M. 520, 943 P.2d 554; *see also Kankakee Federal Savings & Loan Association v. Mueller,* 134 Ill.App.3d 943, 89 Ill.Dec. 781, 481 N.E.2d 332, 334 (1985) (noting that the distribution of proceeds from foreclosure is equitable). Junior Mortgagee timely appeared and made its claim and lien known well before the sale, and continued to press its point before the surplus was distributed. We conclude that the steps taken by Junior Mortgagee, including filing its motion for judgment for foreclosure and priority claim to surplus money proceeds, were sufficient to preserve its claim to the surplus. *See id.* 89 Ill.Dec. 781, 481 N.E.2d at 333–34 (holding that junior mortgagee was entitled to its share of the surplus from foreclosure even though it initially defaulted in the senior's foreclosure action and did not appear until it filed a motion, after the foreclosure, where the junior mortgage had been set forth in the senior mortgagee's petition, the junior mortgage was admitted in the answer, and the court had preserved its right to control the future distribution of the surplus); *Morsemere,* 503 A.2d at 394–95 (allowing a junior claimant to share in the surplus even though it did not move to intervene in the senior mortgagee's foreclosure action until after the sale); *Cowan v. Stoker,* 100 Utah 377, 115 P.2d 153, 155 (1941) (holding that a motion made before the proceeds of the foreclosure sale have been distributed "and served on all parties to the suit who are thereafter given an opportunity to plead and be heard, is a proper means for opening up the judgment for the purpose of allowing a junior mortgagee to make claim to surplus funds" because the "law is interested not so much in form as in substance").

We conclude that Junior Mortgagee is entitled to the surplus because it has a higher priority claim to the surplus than Assignee unless, on remand, it is determined that its lien is invalid. For these reasons, we reverse and remand for further proceedings.

IT IS SO ORDERED.

We concur: JAMES J. WECHSLER and JONATHAN B. SUTIN, JUDGES.

NOTES

1. *Statutory modifications.* Statutes often regulate the distribution of surplus, especially in the power of sale setting. Some statutes codify the principles described in the preceding case.[1] Other statutes, by their express

---

[1] See, e.g., Ariz.Rev.Stat. § 33–727(B): "If there are other liens on the property sold, or other payments secured by the same mortgage, they shall be paid in their order * * *"; Cal. Civ. Code § 2924j(e) (after payment of expenses, the lien being foreclosed, any excess goes to "satisfy the

terms, give the surplus to the mortgagor and do not refer to the junior lienors' rights.[2] However, courts generally interpret this type of statute as giving junior lienors rights in the surplus that are superior to the property owner's rights.[3] A few statutes do not mention priorities but simply authorize the mortgagee or trustee to pay the surplus "to the person or persons legally entitled to the proceeds."[4] Nelson, Whitman, Burkhart & Freyermuth, Real Estate Finance Law 700 (6th ed.2015).

2.   *Procedural requirements for junior lienor to preserve claim to surplus in judicial foreclosure.* Most foreclosures do not yield a surplus. Therefore, does it make sense to require a junior lienor to appear and plead in every senior foreclosure simply to preserve a possible claim to surplus? Do any policy reasons justify this expenditure of legal fees and other costs? Is this burden especially problematic for vendor purchase money junior lienors? Why not allow the foreclosed junior to assert its claim for the first time after the foreclosure sale, like in power of sale foreclosures?

3.   *Senior lien claim on junior surplus.* An important corollary of the above rules governing surplus is that only those whose interests were cut off by the foreclosure have a valid claim on surplus. Is that rule fair to senior lienors? Should a senior lienor be able to use the surplus produced by a junior lien foreclosure sale to pay the senior debt? Should it make a difference if the foreclosed mortgagor is insolvent? See Armand's Engr., Inc. v. Town & Country Club, Inc., 113 R.I. 515, 324 A.2d 334 (1974). See generally, Bohra v. Montgomery, 31 Ark.App. 253, 792 S.W.2d 360 (1990) ("upon a sale of a junior mortgage, the surplus belongs to the mortgagor, and is not applied to the satisfaction of the prior mortgage"); Davis v. Huntsville Prod. Credit Ass'n, 481 So.2d 1103 (Ala.1985) ("a first mortgagee has no right to any surplus upon foreclosure of the second mortgage, particularly in the absence of default of the first mortgage"); Members Equity Credit Union v. Duefel, 295 Ill.App.3d 336, 229 Ill.Dec. 876, 692 N.E.2d 865 (1998); Restatement (Third) of Property (Mortgages) § 7.4 cmt. c (1997) ("Senior lienors have no claim to a surplus produced by the foreclosure of junior mortgage.").

4.   *Payment of surplus to holders of nonpossessory junior interests.* If a foreclosure terminates an easement, the easement holder has a valid claim to any foreclosure surplus. See Anderman v. 1395 E. 52nd Street Realty Corp.,

---

outstanding balance of obligations secured by any junior liens or encumbrances in order of their priority").

    [2] See, e.g., Minn. Stat. Ann. § 580.10; Ind. Code Ann. § 32–30–10–14; Wash. Rev. Code Ann. § 61.12.150.

    [3] See, e.g., White v. Shirk, 20 Ind. App. 589, 51 N.E. 126 (1898); United Bank v. Mani, 81 Mass. App. Ct. 75, 959 N.E.2d 452, 455 n.8 (2011) (mortgagee is mortgagor's success or assign); Brown v. Crookston Agr. Ass'n, 34 Minn. 545, 26 N.W. 907 (1886); Fuller v. Langum, 37 Minn. 74, 33 N.W. 122 (1887).

    [4] See Utah Code Ann. § 57–1–29. Courts typically interpret this language to incorporate the common law of surplus. See Timm v. Dewsnup, 2003 UT 47, 86 P.3d 699 (Utah 2003) ("[A]lthough [the statute] does not specifically mention junior trust deeds or lienholders, the surplus from the sale stands in the place of the foreclosed real estate and is subject to the same liens and interests that were attached to it. . . . In other words, any excess left over from the nonjudicial foreclosure sale on the trust deed property belongs not to [mortgagor], but to other valid lienholders.").

60 Misc.2d 437, 303 N.Y.S.2d 474 (1969). Should the mortgagor or the easement holder have priority in the surplus? Should the surplus be allocated between them on some type of pro rata basis? Consider the same questions when the mortgagor and a lessee claim the surplus. According to the Restatement: "[S]uch persons are entitled to receive, in order of their pre-foreclosure priority, the fair market value of their interests as of the date of foreclosure. Fair market value for the foregoing purpose is determined in the same manner as in eminent domain proceedings." Restatement (Third) of Property (Mortgages) § 7.4 cmt. b.

5. *Acceptance of surplus as ratifying foreclosure.* Suppose that a power of sale foreclosure yields a surplus but that the mortgagor believes grounds exist for having the sale set aside. Would you advise the mortgagor to accept the surplus? Consider the consequences for one mortgagor who did so:

> It has been held that acceptance of a surplus derived from a foreclosure sale waives the right of the mortgagor to attack the foreclosure. Flake v. High Point Perpetual Building and Loan Association, 204 N.C. 650, 169 S.E. 223 (1933); 55 Am.Jur.2d Mortgages § 665 (1971). By endorsing the check and reaping the benefits of the surplus toward the satisfaction of other debts, plaintiffs elected to ratify the sale. They may not now treat the sale as a nullity and have it set aside, or sue the trustee for wrongfully conducting the sale. *Flake,* supra.

Leonard v. Pell, 56 N.C.App. 405, 289 S.E.2d 140, 142 (1982).

6. *Effect of other security on competing surplus claims.* Suppose that a first mortgage foreclosure sale produces a surplus but that it is insufficient to satisfy the second and third mortgagees' claims. If the third mortgagee can prove that the second mortgage debt is more than adequately secured by other property, should the third mortgagee have a superior claim to the surplus if its debt is not otherwise secured? See United States v. Century Fed. Sav. and Loan Ass'n, 418 So.2d 1195 (Fla.App.1982). This argument is a variation on the marshaling principle discussed in Section A of this chapter. Good authority exists for marshaling foreclosure surplus. See, e.g., Pongetti v. Bankers Trust Sav. & Loan Ass'n, 368 So.2d 819 (Miss.1979).

F. REACQUISITION OF TITLE BY MORTGAGOR AND RELATED ISSUES

OLD REPUBLIC INSURANCE CO. v. CURRIE

Superior Court of New Jersey, 1995
284 N.J.Super. 571, 665 A.2d 1153

BOYLE, P.J.CH.

Allen and Ruthie Currie were the owners of property at #16 West End Avenue, Plainfield, New Jersey. On or about July 16, 1974, the Curries executed a home repair contract and mortgage of even date which was subsequently assigned to plaintiff, Old Republic Insurance Company ("Old Republic"). The Curries thereafter filed a petition in bankruptcy. On December 4, 1978, the U.S. Bankruptcy Court entered an order declaring the lien of plaintiff to the Plainfield property fixed in the amount of $6,476.

After the bankruptcy, Allen and Ruthie Currie lost the Plainfield property through a foreclosure. However, on January 19, 1981, defendant, Allen Currie, reacquired the property. Ruthie Currie was not named on this later deed. No payments have been made toward the satisfaction of this debt since the date of the bankruptcy order.

Sometime during the month of April 1984, plaintiff ran a search of the property which disclosed that the Secretary of the Department of Housing and Urban Development conveyed the property to an Allen Currie. Plaintiff claims that it was unable to ascertain whether this Allen Currie was the same Allen Currie who had been indebted to Old Republic because this time Ruth Currie was not on the deed. Plaintiff responded to this information by rerecording its mortgage. However, plaintiff made no further attempt to verify the identity of the new owner until May, 1993. At some point thereafter, plaintiff confirmed that Allen Currie had reacquired the property and commenced this action on August 10, 1994.

Plaintiff argues that, by operation of law, its mortgage is revived, and that it is entitled to simple interest on the $6,476, plus simple interest at the contract rate of 12.5% to the date of judgment, together with counsel fees and costs as allowed by the court rules.

Defendant's sole defense to this action is that the above bankruptcy proceeding extinguished defendant's indebtedness to plaintiff. However, there is no authority to support this proposition. Plaintiff asserts that defendant's answer has failed to interpose a validly recognized defense and therefore brings this motion to strike defendant's answer. * * *

* * *

Generally, the purchaser at a foreclosure sale acquires the entire interest of the mortgagor and mortgagee unaffected by the rights of junior mortgagees or encumbrancers who are parties to the foreclosure. Atlantic City National Bank v. Wilson, 108 N.J.Eq. 213, 154 A. 537 (E. & A.1931). However, if the mortgagor is the purchaser or subsequently reacquires the property, there is authority that the junior mortgages revive as liens on the property. For example, it is clear that if the mortgagor and the first mortgagee contrive to extinguish the second mortgage, the court will restore the second mortgage. Stiger v. Mahone, 24 N.J.Eq. 426 (Ch. 1874). But even in the absence of fraud, the reacquisition is held to revive the second mortgage on three distinct theories.

First, under the payment theory, when the mortgagor purchases the property at the sale, the mortgagor is in effect paying the first mortgage and the second mortgage moves into first position. This is what would have occurred if the mortgagor had paid the first mortgage when it became due. If payment after foreclosure were to alter this result, the mortgagor would be profiting by its own wrong in failing to pay when due. Elkind v. Pinkerton, 294 Mass. 502, 2 N.E. 2d 456 (1936).

Second, is the covenant to defend title theory. Under this approach, the second mortgage that is revived usually contains a warranty that the mortgagor agrees that he will defend the title against all lawful claims. Permitting the foreclosure of the first mortgage is a breach of the warranty to defend the title. Even if the second mortgagee takes subject to the first mortgage, it has been held that the warranty to defend is not affected by the reference to the first mortgage. Merchants' National Bank v. Miller, 229 N.W. 357 (N.D.1930); cf. Dorff v. Bornstein, 277 N.Y. 236, 14 N.E. 2d 51 (1938).

Third, the warranty of title theory is based upon the warranty of title contained in the second mortgage. The mortgagor has warranted that the mortgaged premises shall be security for the debt and that the mortgagor will produce the property if the debt is not paid. If, for some reason (such as the foreclosure of the first mortgage with the title vesting in a third party), the mortgagor is prevented from producing the security, the obligation remains and is merely postponed until the mortgagor can fulfill it. When the mortgagor reacquires the property, it then must provide the property as security for the debt. This after-acquired title doctrine is an ancient equitable remedy designed to effectuate the intention of the parties. It has long been settled that an after-acquired title inures to the benefit of the mortgagee. Decker v. Caskey, 3 N.J.Eq. 446 (Ch. 1836); Tully v. Taylor, 84 N.J.Eq. 459, 94 A. 572 (E. & A. 1915). It is also treated as an obligation founded on the warranty. Robinson-Shore Development Co. v. Gallagher, 26 N.J. 59, 138 A. 2d 726 (1958). Even if the mortgagor's personal liability for the debt which is secured by the mortgage has been extinguished by bankruptcy, the warranty obligation is not nullified and he must produce the property. Baird v. Chamberlain, 60 N.D. 784, 236 N.W. 724 (1931).

Based upon the foregoing, this court is satisfied that (1) plaintiff is entitled to have its mortgage revived and (2) that defendant's answer does not contest the validity or priority of plaintiff's mortgage. Accordingly, this court will grant plaintiff's motion to strike defendant's answer.

This court, on its own motion, has decided to address the issue as to the proper amount to which plaintiff is entitled. While plaintiff contends that it is entitled to simple interest at the contract rate of 12.5% to the date of judgment, this court cannot agree. Plaintiff was on notice in April, 1984 that Allen Currie had reacquired the subject property. At that point, plaintiff should have asserted its rights. Had plaintiff done so, defendant would have had the opportunity to satisfy his debt without paying an additional eleven years of accrued interest, totaling $8,904.50. Therefore, plaintiff's inaction prejudiced defendant by $8,904.50, as plaintiff concededly did not notify defendant that it had rerecorded its mortgage. There is no evidence to suggest that defendant had occasion to become aware of the lien. In light of the above, this court holds that it would be unconscionable to permit plaintiff to benefit from its own dereliction to the tune of 12.5% interest over a period of eleven years. Consequently, plaintiff's claim is barred in part by laches. Laches is a "delay for a length of time, which, unexplained and unexcused, is unreasonable under the circumstances and has been prejudicial to the other party." West Jersey Title and Guaranty Co. v. Industrial Trust Co., 27 N.J. 144, 153, 141 A. 2d 782 (1958) (citing Hinners v. Banville, 114 N.J.Eq. 348, 168 A. 618 (E. & A.1933)).

Plaintiff's entire claim is not barred by laches. Instead, its claim is barred to the extent defendant has been prejudiced. Defendant was prejudiced in this matter to the extent that plaintiff did not assiduously pursue its rights after the April 1984 title search. Accordingly, this court awards plaintiff interest on its claim from the date of the bankruptcy judgment (December 4, 1978), to January 1, 1985, which this court deems to be a reasonable time within which plaintiff could have asserted its right. Therefore, plaintiff's judgment is in the reduced amount of $11,395, plus attorney's fees and costs as provided in the Rules.

NOTES

1. *Moral issues.* The principal case, more than most, raises basic questions of fairness and morality. Although a senior lien foreclosure normally eliminates junior liens and other junior interests, should the rule apply when the mortgagor purchases at the senior sale? The principal case articulates three traditional reasons why it should not apply. However, this case boils down to an intuitive notion of fairness—a person should not profit by defaulting. The relief afforded the redeemed junior lienor is also constrained by an intuitive notion of fairness. Because the junior lienor unreasonable delayed in asserting its claim, the court substantially reduced the accrued interest on the revived mortgage. This is a classic application of the equitable principle of laches. For further exploration of the "fairness-morality" issue, see Grant S. Nelson, The Foreclosure Purchase by the Equity of Redemption Holder or Other Junior Interests: When Should Principles of Fairness and Morality Trump Normal Priority Rules?, 72 Mo.L.Rev. 1259 (2007).

For a subsequent New Jersey decision rejecting the reasoning of *Old Republic*, see Mooney v. Provident Sav. Bank, 308 N.J.Super. 195, 705 A.2d 816 (1997).

2. *Reacquisition by nonrecourse mortgagor or subsequent grantee.* If the mortgagor who reacquires title was not personally liable on the mortgage obligation, should the junior liens be revived? The usual answer is "yes." "Even where the mortgage obligation is completely" nonrecourse, "the mortgagor agrees to the satisfaction of that obligation out of the mortgaged real estate. Thus, actions by the mortgagor that undermine the ability of the mortgagee to realize on the benefits of that agreement should be discouraged." Restatement (Third) of Property (Mortgages) § 4.9 cmt. b (1997).

Should the answer be the same when the person who reacquired the title was a subsequent grantee? The answer clearly is "yes" in the case of an assuming grantee, but what about a "subject to" grantee? According to the Restatement:

> Strong policy considerations also compel the application of the same rule to transferees of the mortgagor who take subject to the mortgage, but who do not assume liability on existing liens. In this type of transaction, the purchase price paid by the transferee is almost always reduced by the value of any liens that the transferee agrees are to remain on the real estate. To permit the transferee under such circumstances to acquire title through a senior lien foreclosure and, in so doing, to destroy junior liens, would enable the transferee to acquire the real estate for less than originally contemplated. Such unjust enrichment of the transferee should be discouraged.

Id.*

3. *Mortgagor reacquisition from bona fide purchaser.* The easiest cases for revival are when the mortgagor purchases at the foreclosure sale or when the purchaser acts on the mortgagor's behalf. On the other hand, if the sale purchaser is a bona fide purchaser who does not know the mortgagor or her plan to terminate junior interests and later sells the property to the mortgagor, should the junior interests revive? "[T]here are good reasons to allow the [mortgagor] to reacquire title from a bona fide purchaser free and clear of previously foreclosed interests." Restatement (Third) of Property (Mortgages) § 4.9 cmt. b (1997) What are they? See id; 1 Nelson, Whitman, Burkhart & Freyermuth, Real Estate Finance Law § 4.44 (6th ed. Practitioner Series 2014).

In the principal case, Curry, the mortgagor, did not reacquire title by purchasing at the foreclosure sale, but rather from the Secretary of HUD who apparently was the foreclosure purchaser and the original senior mortgagee. Usually, a mortgagee-purchaser does not qualify as a bona fide purchaser. See Nelson, Whitman, Burkhart & Freyermuth, id. Therefore, Curry probably could not qualify as a transferee from a bona fide purchaser.

4. *Junior interest holders acquire title.* Generally, when a junior interest holder purchases at a senior foreclosure sale, the other junior interests do not revive. Under the Restatement, "a purchase by a junior lienor or other junior interest at a validly conducted foreclosure of a senior lien cuts off the rights of

---

* © 1997 by The American Law Institute. Reprinted with permission.

both the holder of the equity of redemption and other junior interests as well." Restatement (Third) of Property (Mortgages) § 4.9(b) cmt. c (1997).

Greater controversy exists when the senior foreclosure is of a real estate tax lien. While the Restatement applies the foregoing rule in the tax foreclosure context, substantial case law disagrees. See id. comment c and the reporters' note. If a mortgagee purchases at a senior tax sale, shouldn't the sale terminate the mortgagor's and the juniors' interests?

G. STATUTORY REDEMPTION

When a valid foreclosure has taken place, the equitable right of redemption ends. However, about thirty three states have provided for a statutory right of redemption that provides an additional time period for mortgagors, their successors in interest, and, in some instances, junior lienors, to pay a certain sum of money to redeem the title to the property. To some extent we have already considered the impact of such statutes in the omitted lienor situation. Under statutory redemption, the redemption amount is normally tied to the foreclosure sale price, rather than to the mortgage debt, as is the case with respect to equitable redemption.

During the period of statutory redemption the mortgagor usually will have the right to possession. A few states, however, require the mortgagor to post bond as a condition precedent to acquiring the right to redeem and the right to possession. See, e.g., Vernon's Ann.Mo.Stat. § 443.410. The statutes vary greatly from state to state both as to time period and as to whether parties other than mortgagors and their successors have redemption rights. Moreover, in some states statutory redemption is available only after a power of sale foreclosure (see, e.g., Vernon's Ann.Mo.Stat. § 443.410), whereas in others it is available only after judicial foreclosure (see, e.g., Utah Code Ann.1953, § 78B–6–906; West's Rev.Code Wash.Ann. § 61.24.050). In the majority of states, however, it is available in both types of foreclosure. See, e.g., Minn.Stat.Ann. §§ 580.23, 580.24 and 581.10.

While there is great variation in these statutes, most fall into two broad categories—the "strict priority" or "ordered redemption" approach and the "scramble method." The Minnesota statute, reprinted below, follows the "strict priority" approach.

MINN. STAT. ANN. §§ 580.23, .24

580.23. Redemption by mortgagor * * *

Subdivision 1. Six-month redemption period. (a) When lands have been sold in conformity with the preceding sections of this chapter, the mortgagor, the mortgagor's personal representatives or assigns, within six months after such sale, except as otherwise provided in subdivision 2 or section 582.032 or 582.32, may redeem such lands, as hereinafter provided, by paying the sum of money for which the same were sold, with interest from the time of sale at the rate provided to be paid on the mortgage debt as stated in the certificate of sale and, if no rate be provided in the certificate of sale, at the rate of six percent per annum, together with any further sums which may be payable as provided in sections 582.03 and 582.031.

(b) Delivery of funds and documents for redemption must be made at the normal place of business of the recipient, on days other than Sunday, Saturday, and legal holidays, between the hours of 9:00 a.m. and 4:00 p.m.

* * *

Subd. 2. 12—month redemption period. Notwithstanding the provisions of subdivision 1 hereof, when lands have been sold in conformity with the preceding sections of this chapter, the mortgagor, the mortgagor's personal representatives or assigns, within 12 months after such sale, may redeem such lands in accordance with the provisions of payment of subdivision 1 thereof, if:

(1) the mortgage was executed prior to July 1, 1967;

(2) the amount claimed to be due and owing as of the date of the notice of foreclosure sale is less than 66–2/3 percent of the original principal amount secured by the mortgage;

(3) the mortgage was executed prior to July 1, 1987, and the mortgaged premises, as of the date of the execution of the mortgage, exceeded ten acres in size;

(4) the mortgage was executed prior to August 1, 1994, and the mortgaged premises, as of the date of the execution of the mortgage, exceeded ten acres but did not exceed 40 acres in size and was in agricultural use as defined in section 40A.02, subdivision 3;

(5) the mortgaged premises, as of the date of the execution of the mortgage, exceeded 40 acres in size; or

(6) the mortgage was executed on or after August 1, 1994, and the mortgaged premises, as of the date of the execution of the mortgage, exceeded ten acres but did not exceed 40 acres in size and was in agricultural use. * * *

* * *

Subd. 4. Waiver; 12-month redemption for ag use. A mortgagor, before or at the time of granting a mortgage executed on or after August 1, 1994, may waive in writing the mortgagor's right under subdivision 2, clause (6), to have a 12-month redemption period based upon the premises being in agricultural use as of the date of execution of the mortgage. The written waiver must be either a document separate from the mortgage or a separately executed and acknowledged addendum to the mortgage on a separate page. * * * Where there is a waiver of the rights under subdivision 2, clause (6), the redemption period in subdivision 1 applies.

580.24. Redemption by creditor

(a) If no redemption is made by the mortgagor, the mortgagor's personal representatives or assigns, the most senior creditor having a legal or equitable lien upon the mortgaged premises, or some part of it, subsequent to the foreclosed mortgage, may redeem within seven days after the expiration of the redemption period determined under section 580.23 or 582.032, whichever is applicable; and each subsequent creditor having a lien may redeem, in the order of priority of their respective liens, within seven days after the time allowed the prior lienholder by paying the amount required under this section. However, no creditor is entitled to redeem unless, one week or more prior to the expiration of the period allowed for redemption by the mortgagor, the creditor:

(1) records with each county recorder and registrar of titles where the foreclosed mortgage is recorded a notice of the creditor's intention to redeem;

(2) records with each county recorder and registrar of titles where the notice of the creditor's intention to redeem is recorded all documents necessary to create the lien on the mortgaged premises and to evidence the creditor's ownership of the lien, including a copy of any money judgment necessary to create the lien; and

(3) after complying with clauses (1) and (2), delivers to the sheriff who conducted the foreclosure sale or the sheriff's successor in office a copy of each of the documents required to be recorded under clauses (1) and (2), with the office, date and time of filing for record stated on the first page of each document.

* * *

(b) Saturdays, Sundays, legal holidays, and the first day following the expiration of the prior redemption period must be included in computing the seven-day redemption period. When the last day of the period falls on Saturday, Sunday, or a legal holiday, that day must be omitted from the computation. The order of redemption by judgment creditors subsequent to the foreclosed mortgage shall be determined by the order in which their judgments were entered as memorials on the certificate of title for the foreclosed premises or docketed in the office of the district court administrator if the property is not registered under chapter 508 or 508A, regardless of the homestead status of the property. All mechanic's lienholders who have coordinate liens shall have one combined seven-day period to redeem.

(c) The amount required to redeem from the holder of the sheriff's certificate of sale is the amount required under section 580.23. The amount required to redeem from a person holding a certificate of redemption is:

(1) the amount paid to redeem as shown on the certificate of redemption; plus

(2) interest on that amount to the date of redemption; plus

(3) the amount claimed due on the person's lien, as shown on the affidavit under section 580.25, clause (3).

The amount required to redeem may be paid to the holder of the sheriff's certificate of sale or the certificate of redemption, as the case may be, or to the sheriff for the holder.

For an excellent description of how the Colorado "ordered redemption" system operates, see Wyse Fin. Servs., Inc. v. National Real Estate Inv., LLC., 92 P.3d 918 (Colo.2004), *superseded by statute as stated in* Oakwood Holdings v. Mortgage Investments Enterprises, 410 P.3d 1249, 1254 (Colo. 2018) (noting that subsequent versions of the statute had removed references to the owner's right of redemption after foreclosure).

The second approach, the "scramble method," has been described as follows:

Here again, once the mortgagor redeems, all others are preempted from exercising their right. The difference is that there is no priority order in which redemptions may be made from the purchaser. If a junior lienor redeems first, then the next redeeming party, whether it is the mortgagor or another junior lienor, must pay the previously redeeming lienor the foreclosure sale price and sometimes the amount of the lien of that junior lienor (depending on whether the prior redemptioner had preforeclosure priority over the second redemptioner). Once the previously redeeming junior lienor has been fully paid so that his lien is satisfied, he has no further redemption rights. If, however, the originally redeeming junior lienor had preforeclosure priority that was subordinate to the next redeeming junior lienor, then he may take another opportunity to redeem if his lien is still unsatisfied.

3 Richard R. Powell & Patrick A. Rohan, Powell on Real Property § 470 (1997). For a thorough examination of this redemption method, represented by the Iowa model, see Patrick B. Bauer, Statutory Redemption Reconsidered: The Operation of Iowa's Redemption Statute In

Two Counties Between 1881 and 1980, 70 Iowa L.Rev. 343 (1985); Lee B. Blum, Iowa Statutory Redemption After Mortgage Foreclosure, 35 Iowa L.Rev. 72 (1949); Iowa Code Ann. Ch. 628.

UNITED STATES v. STADIUM APARTMENTS, INC.

United States Court of Appeals, Ninth Circuit, 1970
425 F.2d 358, cert. denied, 400 U.S. 926, 91 S.Ct. 187, 27 L.Ed.2d 185 (1970)

[FHA had insured the mortgage given by the developer of an apartment project to Prudential Insurance Co. When the developer defaulted, Prudential assigned the mortgage to FHA, as it was legally entitled to do under 12 U.S.C. § 1743, and FHA paid Prudential the balance owing on the mortgage. FHA then obtained a default judgment in federal district court foreclosing the mortgage. The district judge framed the foreclosure decree to allow a one-year period of redemption as provided by Idaho statute. FHA appealed this aspect of the decree, arguing that under principles of federal pre-emption and supremacy, it was not subject to the Idaho statutory redemption provisions. Although the developer did not participate in the appeal, the Ninth Circuit invited the attorneys general of the states within the circuit to submit amicus curiae briefs, and several did so. The court held that federal law should apply, and that no redemptive period should be permitted following foreclosure. The discussion of federalism is deleted from the portion of the opinion reproduced below, but the concepts are treated in Chapter Eight, Section G infra.]

* * *

Reasons of policy dictate the same result. In the first place, only 26 [now 33] of the states provide for post-foreclosure redemption. The periods of redemption vary widely. So do other conditions to redemption and the rules governing right to possession, right to rents, making repairs, and other matters arising during the redemption period.

* * *

There is a split of authority as to whether the right of redemption can be waived. Similarly, there is a split of authority as to the right of the mortgagee to recover the value of improvements made during the redemption period. It would be contrary to the teaching of every case that we have cited to hold that there is a different federal policy in each state, thus making FHA "subject to the vagaries of the laws of the several states." Clearfield Trust Co. v. United States, 1943, 318 U.S. 363, 367, 63 S.Ct. 573, 575, 87 L.Ed. 838. Which policy is to be the federal policy, that of the states which do not provide for a period of redemption, or that of those which do? And if the policy is to be the latter, is it to embrace, in each state, all of the special rules applicable in that state alone? Is it to be expanded to establish a federal right of redemption in each state where none exists under local law?

In response to our request, the government has informed us of the views of federal agencies involved in the lending or insuring of funds for private housing purposes. These include, in addition to the Federal Housing Administration, the Farmers Home Administration of the Department of Agriculture, acting under 42 U.S.C. § 1471 ff., and the Veterans Administration, acting under 38 U.S.C. § 1800 ff. We quote the government's response:

> "The Farmers Home Administration, the Federal Housing Administration, and the Veterans Administration have informed us that their experience has indicated that the imposition of post-foreclosure-sale redemption periods makes the foreclosure remedy more costly and administratively time-consuming in those states whose local law so provides. Generally, the reasons given in support of this conclusion are * * * that existence of a post-sale period for redemption chills bidding at the foreclosure sale, forcing the United States to buy the property at the sale and to hold it (paying meanwhile the costs of maintenance) until the expiration of the period, when it finally can give good title to a purchaser."

Additional reasons stated by the government are quoted in the margin.[7] We do not find the policy arguments presented by California convincing.

---

[7] "The Farmers Home Administration has stated that where post-sale redemption periods have been imposed, the mortgaged property may, after sale and before expiration of the redemption period, 'stand unoccupied and unattended for considerable periods of time and consequently [may] deteriorate substantially in value, to the detriment of the financial interest of the United States and without concomitant benefit to any other party.' Similarly, the Veterans Administration reported to us that where a post-sale redemption period is imposed unless the former owner redeems timely, the mortgagee or his assignee are obligated to pay holding costs during the redemption period, i.e., taxes, public improvements, if any, the cost of repairs to preserve the security, and the cost of hazard insurance premium when necessary. There is also for consideration the interest normally accruing on the outstanding investment. Moreover, many of these properties have been abandoned and must remain vacant during redemption periods. In many instances they are subject to extreme vandalism during these periods which is, of course, costly to the holder."

"Most pertinent to the present case, of course, were the comments of the Federal Housing Administration concerning foreclosures on multi-family projects like that involved here. The Federal Housing Administration reported to us:

'It is perhaps the normal situation to find any project in foreclosure to be in need of substantial repair. Many mortgagors, during a period of diminishing income, utilize the net income to keep the mortgage current as long as possible, keeping maintenance expenses to a bare minimum. When the evil day arrives that the income will no longer cover the mortgage payments, he falls into default, and the subject of the foreclosure action is a property which requires substantial expenditures to place it in properly habitable condition, and to make it attractive to the rental market. With the notable exception of Alabama, redemption statutes permit a foreclosure purchaser to receive from a redemptioner little more than the price bid at the foreclosure sale, so that a purchaser is well advised to keep rehabilitation expenses to an absolute minimum until the redemption period expires. As a practical matter, this delays the day when FHA, as such purchaser can safely embark on a program involving capital expenditures, thereby delaying the day when the property may be placed in condition for its best use and for

First, it is argued that the purpose of the redemption statutes is to force the mortgagee and others to bid the full market price at the sale. We assume that this is the purpose; we are not convinced that the statutes accomplish it. What third party would bid and pay the full market value, knowing that he cannot have the property to do with as he wishes until a set period has gone by, and that at the end of the period he may not get it, but instead may be forced to accept a payment which may or may not fully reimburse him for his outlays? In some states he cannot get possession. E.g., California Code Civ.Proc. § 703, Mau, Sadler & Co. v. Kearney, 143 Cal. 506, 77 P. 411; Haynes v. Treadway, 133 Cal. 400, 65 P. 892. In some states if he does get possession and collects rents, they will be deducted from his reimbursement, e.g., Idaho, Clark Investment Co. v. United States, supra. In some states, if he makes repairs, he will not be repaid for his outlays. These are precisely the problems which the federal government should not have to face. It is not in the real estate business. It should not have to hold and manage properties for any period longer than is absolutely necessary for it to get back its money. It should not be subjected to the risk that the property will deteriorate, and it should not be left with no means to protect itself against such losses.

Our doubts as to whether the statutes accomplish the purpose is reinforced by the fact that in many states, partly because of those statutes, real estate financing is almost exclusively secured by trust deeds with power of sale. This is certainly true in California, and the statutory right of redemption does not apply to such sales. Py v. Pleitner, 1945, 70 Cal.App.2d 576, 161 P.2d 393; Roberts v. True, 1908, 7 Cal.App. 379, 94 P. 392. See also, as to Idaho, n. 5, supra. One is tempted to inquire why, if public policy so strongly favors a post-sale period of redemption, the legislature has not applied it to sales under trust deeds? Perhaps it is because the redemption statute has, in some states, made the use of mortgages almost a dead letter.

Moreover, the policy of FHA is to bid the fair market value at the foreclosure sale. For this purpose, it has the property carefully appraised before bidding. See Book 2, Volume VII, Sec. 72926 of the FHA Manual. It is authorized by 12 U.S.C. § 1713(k) to "bid any sum up to but not in excess of the total unpaid indebtedness secured by the mortgage, plus taxes, insurance, foreclosure costs, fees, and other expenses * * *." It bids fair market value for its own protection as well as that of the mortgagor and other lienors. It is limited to the amount specified because the objective is to recover its loss on the mortgage insurance, not to put the government in the business of buying and speculating in real property. Presumably, if the property is worth more, others will increase the bid, the government will

---

advantageous sale which will reimburse the insurance fund for a portion of the loss incurred as a result of the mortgagor's default.' "

be paid in full, and the excess will go to junior lien holders and, if there be sufficient funds, to the mortgagor.

It is also suggested that a purpose of the redemption statutes is to protect junior lienors. Perhaps. But if the objective of the statutes is to obtain bids equal to market value, and if as is argued, the bidding would be lower in the absence of the statutes, then junior lienors could more easily protect themselves in the latter situation. They could buy the property at the sale for less. It is always open to the junior lienors to protect themselves by bidding. They take with notice of the senior lien. Here, the government's judgment was for $93,804.97; its bid was $55,100. The court found the value of the property to be $58,000. The deficiency judgment is for $37,728.88. This is a singularly inappropriate case in which to be concerned about junior lien holders. They simply have no equity in the property. * * *

Nor is it accurate to say that the application of state redemption rights does not tie up government funds; as this case illustrates, it does do so. Under 12 U.S.C. § 1743(c) the mortgagee has the option of assigning the mortgage to the Secretary and being paid the full amount of the guarantee, instead of itself foreclosing. As might be expected, that is what Prudential did in this case. Why would any mortgagee do otherwise, when by so assigning it can receive the full benefit of the insurance without having to incur the expense and risk attendant upon foreclosure? Under the statute, Prudential received the full benefit of the insurance—government obligations equal to the then total value of the mortgage, in this case more than $90,000. If the redemption period applies, the government must wait a year to get its money back—and it may not then get it all, or even as much as it bid.

We conclude that the Idaho statute providing for right of redemption is not here applicable.

* * *

ELY, CIRCUIT JUDGE (dissenting).

The statutes can best be understood through a brief review of their historical development. * * *

The harshness of strict foreclosure led to the concept of foreclosure by sale. Theoretically, the property was to be sold to the highest bidder with the mortgagee having first claim to the proceeds and the mortgagor obtaining his equity in the form of whatever surplus remained. This approach was expected to yield more even results by allowing the competitive market to set the value of the land instead of the "value" being set at the amount of the unpaid debt as was the fact under strict foreclosure. Unfortunately, this expectation was frustrated by reason of the immense advantages favoring the mortgagee at the sale. First, it was unnecessary for the mortgagee to raise and expend any cash up to the amount of the unpaid debt. Secondly, there would not often be an interested outside buyer, or junior lienholder with cash, at the precise time of the sale. Thus, the senior mortgagee was assured of being almost always the only bidder at the sale. The junior lienors, in particular, suffered under this method since their interests were cut off by the judicial sale. Since they had no weapons with which to force the sale price above the amount of the senior's claim, they often realized nothing on their claims.

The response of many jurisdictions to the unsatisfactory results of the foreclosure-by-sale procedure was the adoption of a statutory redemption period. The basic design of statutory redemption consists of giving the mortgagor and those claiming under him (including junior lienors) the right to redeem the property from the purchaser at the sale within a specified period by paying, *not* the balance of the debt secured, but the price paid at the sale. The objective of the redemption right is that the mortgagee or other bidders, if any, shall bid not less than the fair market value of the land, since otherwise the purchaser risks being divested of the land by redemption at less than its market value.

The key to understanding the statutory redemption right lies in the proposition that the statute's operation is in the nature of a threat. When redemption is exercised, it is thereby evidenced that the mortgagee has not bid adequately at the sale and the statute has not had its intended effect. On the other hand, if the threat functions successfully and the mortgagee does bid adequately, then the mortgagor and junior lienors, if any, will have been satisfied to the full value of the property and there will be no reason for exercising the redemption right. If he bids the full market value of the property, then the mortgagee may rest secure in the knowledge that it will not be redeemed. See generally Durfee & Doddridge, Redemption From Foreclosure Sale, 23 Mich.L.Rev. 825, 827–834 (1925); Note, Redemption From Judicial Sales, 5 U.Chi.L.Rev. 625, 626 (1938).

* * *

The Government, and also the majority, make several arguments designed to show that redemption statutes are neither important nor necessary. The first is that the statutes do not work because no third party will bid at the sale, knowing that he will be subject to redemption. The statutes, as I have tried to explain, are not the least bit concerned with the actions of third parties since they were necessitated by the observation that third parties do not ordinarily bid at foreclosure sales in any event. Instead of trying to stimulate bidding at the sale, they set up the more realistic possibility that the property will be redeemed if the mortgagee's bid is inadequate.

NOTES

1. *No statutory redemption under federal foreclosure acts.* As the foregoing indicates, the federal government views statutory redemption as contrary to its interest as a mortgagee. See generally 12 U.S.C. § 1710. ("notwithstanding any state law to the contrary, there shall be no right of redemption * * * in the mortgagor or any other person subsequent to the foreclosure sale in connection with a Secretary-held single family mortgage"). Specifically, the Single Family Mortgage Foreclosure Act, which authorizes power of sale foreclosure of federally-insured mortgages on one- to four-family dwellings held by the Secretary of Housing and Urban Development, provides that, as to any foreclosure under it, "there shall be no [post-sale] right of redemption, or right of possession based upon a right of redemption in the mortgagor or others." 12 U.S.C. § 3763(e). Also, The Multifamily Mortgage Foreclosure Act, which authorizes power of sale foreclosure for HUD-held mortgages on property other than one- to four- family dwellings, has an identical prohibition on statutory redemption. 12 U.S.C. § 3713(d).

2. *Federal government as junior lienor.* When the federal government finds itself in the role of a junior lienor, it finds the statutory redemption concept much more to its liking. By federal statute, the United States, as a foreclosed junior lienor, is generally afforded by statute "one year from the date of sale within which to redeem." 28 U.S.C. § 2410. As to federal tax liens, the redemption period is the longer of 120 days or the state redemption period, if any. 26 U.S.C. § 7425; 28 U.S.C. § 2410(c). To the extent that state legislation is less protective of the interests of junior lienors, it is preempted by the federal statutes. See United States v. John Hancock Mut. Life Ins. Co., 364 U.S. 301, 81 S.Ct. 1, 5 L.Ed.2d 1 (1960). Consider the following description of the aim of this federal redemption scheme:

> The statutory purpose is to encourage the lienholder to bid at least a fair price on the property being foreclosed by allowing the government to redeem the property at the same price that the lienholder pays for it (plus interest); if the superior lienholder pays the debtor at least a fair price, this somewhat inures to the benefit of the government as a creditor by reducing the debtor's obligations; the government is not obliged to redeem; if the lienholder pays less than a fair price, the government in redeeming the property is able to capture any differential between the price paid and the property's fair market value.

Delta Sav. & Loan Ass'n, Inc. v. IRS, 847 F.2d 248, 251 (5th Cir.1988). In view of the federal government's arguments in *Stadium Apartments,* do you see some irony in the foregoing language?

3. *Improvements by purchaser during the redemption period.* In a few states, the foreclosure sale purchaser has the right to possession during the redemption period. If you were a purchaser in possession should you make repairs or improvements to the real estate? If the foreclosed mortgagor redeems will you be reimbursed for such expenditures? Ultimately, this issue

must be resolved by the language of redemption statute. Consider how the New Mexico Supreme Court approached this problem:

> There is no mention of improvements or betterments in the statute. Thus the only funds that a purchaser may recover under the redemption statute are those funds that the purchaser paid to acquire the property. Those funds include the amount the purchaser paid for the property, with interest [10% per annum], plus any taxes and penalties. Section 39–5–18(A)(1) * * * Those funds also include any amount paid by the purchaser to satisfy outstanding liens or mortgages on the property, with interest, plus taxes and penalties. Section 39–5–18(A)(1). The statute does not allow the purchaser to recover for any funds paid for improvements.
>
> We also agree * * * that requiring the redeemer to pay for such improvements would contravene the public policy embodied in the redemption statute. One of the purposes of the redemption statute is to give the property owner * * * a reasonable opportunity to redeem the property. * * * This purpose would be defeated if redeemers were required to pay purchasers for improvements, in addition to those costs provided for in the redemption statute. Purchasers could make it more burdensome for redeemers to redeem their property by investing significant amounts of money into improvements, almost ensuring that the redeemer would be unable to redeem their

Chase Manhattan Bank v. Candelaria, 135 N.M. 527, 90 P.3d 985 (2004). On the other hand, a few state statutes appear to require the redeeming mortgagor to pay for improvements made by a sale purchaser while in possession. See, e.g., Ala. Code § 6–5–252. Suppose the property is rental residential real estate and repairs are necessary during the redemption period. Is it good public policy to deny reimbursement for such repairs?

FARMERS PRODUCTION CREDIT ASSOCIATION v. McFARLAND

Supreme Court of Iowa, 1985
374 N.W.2d 654

Considered en banc.

SCHULTZ, JUSTICE.

In this appeal a mortgagors' assignee and a junior mortgage lienholder compete for final redemption rights in a senior mortgagee's foreclosure action. Daniel and Linda McFarland (mortgagors) owned real estate that was subject to two mortgages. On June 9, 1983, the junior mortgage-holder, Production Credit Association (PCA), filed an action to foreclose its mortgage. Shortly thereafter, the senior mortgage-holder, American Federal Savings & Loan Association (AFS), filed a separate foreclosure action against the McFarlands naming PCA as a junior lienholder and party defendant. On November 11, 1983, a decree of foreclosure was entered in the latter action in favor of AFS and it stated PCA had a valid second lien. The property was sold to AFS at a January 10, 1984, sheriff's sale and the mortgagors were granted a six-month period of redemption. *See* Iowa Code § 628.26. On April 6, 1984, the mortgagors conveyed their redemption rights to Daniel's mother, Dorothy McFarland. On that date Dorothy (assignee) tendered a check for redemption of the property. The junior mortgage holder, PCA, on May 3, 1984, tendered its own check in an attempt to redeem the property. No issue is advanced concerning the validity of either tender; however, the assignee claims her redemption precluded further redemptions.

In its June 9, 1983, petition for foreclosure PCA alleged Daniel and Linda McFarland had entered into a collateral agreement and mortgage in the amount of $40,000 to secure other notes contracted between the parties. PCA prayed for judgment in rem against the mortgaged premises in the amount of $40,000 plus interest and other costs and requested the mortgage be foreclosed. In their answer the mortgagors requested the court to determine the amount they owed PCA. Following PCA's attempt to redeem the property foreclosed in the AFS action, Dorothy McFarland intervened in PCA's foreclosure action and claimed her redemption in the AFS foreclosure had extinguished PCA's lien. At the same time, the mortgagors amended their answer and requested the court to enter a decree denying PCA's petition for foreclosure or, in the alternative, hold their mortgage obligation was limited to $40,000 if foreclosure was ordered.

* * *

On October 1, 1984, the trial court entered a three-pronged ruling: (1) PCA was entitled to recover the principal and interest on its note; (2) PCA could redeem the property from the mortgagors' assignee; and (3) PCA was entitled to a sheriff's deed to the property.

On appeal the mortgagors and assignee maintain the trial court erred in ruling PCA was entitled to redeem. They claim a junior lienholder cannot redeem after an assignee of the mortgagor has redeemed because a redeeming assignee takes the property unencumbered by liens on the property. Although we hold the junior lienholder cannot redeem in this case, the reason for our decision is different from that asserted by the mortgagors and assignee. Since the assignee redeemed within the exclusive statutory period granted a debtor, we hold the junior lienholder has no right to redeem. However, we further hold that a redemption by the debtor or assignee during the exclusive period does not allow either party to take the property free and clear of liens on the property.

Several sections of Iowa Code chapter 628 are relevant. Under section 628.3 the debtor's right to redeem is for a period of one year from the date of a sale "and for the first six months thereafter such right of redemption is exclusive." Section 628.5 provides for redemption by creditors: "If no redemption is made by the debtor as above provided, thereafter, and at any time within nine months from the day of sale, said redemption may be made by a mortgagee * * *" The "as above provided" is an obvious reference to the debtor's exclusive right to redeem pursuant to section 628.3. Section 628.26 permits an agreement to reduce the period of redemption, as in this case, so that the mortgagor's period of redemption set forth in section 628.3 is reduced from twelve to six months, the exclusive right to redeem is the first three months, and the creditors' period of redemption is after three months and within four months from the date of sale.

The plain language of section 628.3 gives the debtor the exclusive right to redeem during the appropriate six or three month period. "An exclusive right is one which only the grantee thereof can exercise, and from which all others are prohibited or shut out." *Black's Law Dictionary* 507 (rev. 5th ed. 1979). We interpret the use of the term "exclusive" to vest the right of redemption in the debtor only and to shut out all creditors. In the instant case the mortgagors have assigned their redemption rights to Dorothy McFarland. Such assignments are permitted under section 628.25 which provides "[t]he rights of a debtor in relation to redemption are transferable, and the assignee has the like power to redeem." "Like" is defined as "[e]qual in quantity, quality, or degree or exactly corresponding." *Black's Law Dictionary* at 834. The plain words of the statute give the assignee the same quantity and quality of rights as the debtor, which would include the "exclusive" right to redeem within three months of the sheriff's sale.

* * *

Although redemption by the mortgagor or assignee during the exclusive period prevents redemption by a junior lienholder, it does not provide the redeemer complete relief from junior liens. We do not agree with the claim of the mortgagors and assignee that the assignee is the owner of the property free and clear of liens. The trial court did not address this issue because it ruled PCA's redemption was valid. In equity our review is de novo and our responsibility is to decide as the trial court should have. *Farmers Savings Bank, Joice, Iowa v. Gerhart*, 372 N.W.2d 238, 242 (Iowa 1985). Consequently, we determine the respective rights of a mortgagor's assignee and junior lienholders in a foreclosure action.

Before addressing this issue, however, we find it necessary to review the rights of a junior lienholder. After the debtor's exclusive period of redemption has expired, any creditor can redeem the property as long as its claim against the debtor has matured into a lien before the creditor's period of redemption has ceased. Iowa Code § 628.5. A creditor's period of redemption is either after six months and within nine months from the date of sale pursuant to section 628.5 or after three and within four months from the sale under section 628.26. Creditors can even redeem from each other. Iowa Code § 628.8.

A judgment creditor who fails to redeem within the statutory period of time loses his lien on the property. *Paulsen v. Jensen,* 209 Iowa 453, 458, 228 N.W. 357, 359 (1929). Additionally, a junior mortgagee who is a party to the foreclosure action and fails to redeem has his lien on the property extinguished. *Anderson v. Renshaw,* 229 Iowa 93, 98–99, 294 N.W. 274, 277–78 (1940). A judgment lien, lost by the failure to redeem by the junior judgment lienholder, will attach again to the property when the debtor redeems the property, but the junior mortgage lien is not re-established. *Id.* at 99, 294 N.W. at 278. This is because a judgment lien automatically attaches to after acquired real estate of the debtor. *Id.; see* Iowa Code § 624.23(1). The extinguishment of the junior mortgage lien, however, does not destroy the debt itself and the mortgagee can later obtain a judgment against the debtor. *Anderson,* 229 Iowa at 99, 294 N.W. at 278.

There is no question that our decisions have distinguished between redemption by a mortgagor and that by an assignee with respect to the rights of junior lienholders that have failed to redeem within the statutory period. Under those circumstances we have indicated that while a judgment creditor's lien is re-established when the mortgagor redeems, neither the judgment creditor nor junior mortgagee's rights attach to property redeemed by the assignee. *Cadd v. Snell,* 219 Iowa 728, 733–35, 259 N.W. 590, 592–93 (1935); *Paulsen,* 209 Iowa at 458, 228 N.W. at 359 (1929); *Cooper v. Maurer,* 122 Iowa 321, 326–27, 98 N.W. 124, 125–26 (1904); *Moody v. Funk,* 82 Iowa 1, 4, 47 N.W. 1008, 1009 (1891). In *Cooper* we gave the reason for the distinction when we stated:

> If, when the process of redemption is complete, the property is again vested in the debtor either by his having been the last to redeem or by conveyance from the holder of a sheriff's deed, then the unsatisfied creditor may reach it, for the simple reason that all the debtor's property is liable for the payment of his debts unless specifically exempted by statute. If, however, when the last redemption has been made, the property is in a third person, it cannot be so subjected for the equally simple reason that the property of one man cannot be subjected to the payment of the debts of another.

122 Iowa at 327, 98 N.W. at 126.

These cases, however, do not benefit the assignee in this action. All those cases addressed the issue of whether liens that have been extinguished become re-established when the assignee redeems. Under the facts in the present action, the mortgagors had subjected their property to the PCA lien, which was in force at the time of the assignment. By redeeming within three months of the sheriff's sale the assignee prevented any redemption by the mortgagor's creditors. Therefore, PCA's lien was not extinguished because no creditor redemption period existed. PCA's lien remained viable and the assignee's right to the property is subject to the PCA lien. The titleholders could not divest PCA's lien on the property merely by assigning their redemption rights to Daniel's mother.

The mortgagors and assignee assert our language in *Tirrill* [v. Miller, 206 Iowa 426, 218 N.W. 303 (1928)] indicates that when a mortgagor's assignee redeems, the assignee takes the property free from liens and debts of the mortgagor and the property is subjected only to the debts of the assignee. 206 Iowa at 429, 218 N.W. at 304. Although the assignee's redemption in that case was within the exclusive period, we note again that the issue of the exclusive right to redeem was neither raised nor discussed in *Tirrill*. Additionally, under the facts in that case the court acknowledged the creditor had a right to redeem. *Id.* Therefore, statements made in the *Tirrill* decision were under circumstances in which the court recognized the lienholders could have protected themselves by redeeming. In the present case PCA attempted to redeem, but we determined PCA had no right of redemption. Despite language in *Tirrill* to the contrary, we hold the liens of a junior lienholder or creditor are not extinguished when a mortgagor or assignee redeems during the exclusive statutory period.

It could be argued that junior creditors' liens are extinguished either by the entry of the foreclosure decree or the completion of the sheriff's sale. Under such an argument the creditors then possess only a statutory right of redemption which is cut off when the debtor or the debtor's assignee redeems during the exclusive period. Although this cut-off theory was not advanced by either party at trial or on appeal, we deem it necessary to address it. We conclude, however, that such a theory is not in line with our statutory scheme and is contrary to our case law.

Our statutes indicate that junior creditors' liens are still in effect after the entry of a foreclosure decree and the sheriff's sale. Chapter 654 of the Code outlines procedures for the foreclosure of real estate mortgages and makes reference to "liens upon the property" at a time subsequent to the foreclosure decree and sale. *See* Iowa Code § 654.7 (disposal of over-plus "if there is no other lien upon the property"); § 654.8 (providing "a person having a lien on the property which is junior to the mortgage" can be assigned the interest of the holder of the mortgage); § 654.9 (provision for the payment of "any other liens on the property sold"). Likewise, the chapter on executions, chapter 626, recognizes liens on the property after the foreclosure and sale. *See* Iowa Code § 626.82 (overplus paid to the debtor "unless there are liens upon the property").

Our case law also supports the proposition that junior creditors' liens continue after the foreclosure decree and sheriff's sale. We have determined that the purchaser at a foreclosure sale acquires only an equitable lien for the amount of the purchase money, and legal title remains in the mortgagor and is not divested until the expiration of the statutory periods of redemption. *In re Jensen's Estate,* 225 Iowa 1249, 1252–53, 282 N.W. 712, 714 (1938); *Wissmath Packing Co. v. Mississippi River Power Co.,* 179 Iowa 1309, 1324, 162 N.W. 846, 851 (1917); *Greenlee v. North British & Mercantile Insurance Co.,* 102 Iowa 427, 429, 71 N.W. 534, 535 (1897). Language in our cases indicates that the junior lienholders' rights are extinguished with the expiration of their period of redemption. *See Anderson,* 229 Iowa at 99, 294 N.W. at 278 ("the lien of appellee's mortgage upon the foreclosed property was lost at the expiration of nine months"); *Paulsen,* 209 Iowa at 458, 228 N.W. at 359 ("[w]hen the junior creditor fails to redeem before the expiration of nine months, he loses his lien upon that property").

In light of our statutory scheme and case law addressed to mortgage foreclosures, we conclude that junior creditors' liens continue after the foreclosure decree and sheriff's sale. Junior lienholders can protect their claims either by bidding at the foreclosure sale or redeeming in a deliberate manner. *See* Iowa Code chs. 626 and 628; * * *

In summary, the trial court erred in allowing PCA to redeem the property from Dorothy McFarland, and PCA is not entitled to a sheriff's deed from the foreclosure sale in the AFS action. Although Dorothy McFarland has a right to title under the assignment, her title is subject to the rights of PCA against the property in this action. The district court should amend its order to allow foreclosure in rem on the PCA lien.

AFFIRMED IN PART, REVERSED IN PART AND REMANDED.

All Justices concur except UHLENHOPP, CARTER and WOLLE, JJ., who concur in part and dissent in part.

UHLENHOPP, JUSTICE, concurring in part, dissenting in part.

I concur in the holding of the majority that the junior mortgagee cannot redeem from the assignee, but dissent from the holding that the junior mortgagee can foreclose against the property. I join in Justice Carter's dissent, but add the following.

* * *

When the sheriff's sale was held under the senior mortgage foreclosure judgment, the junior mortgagee could have protected itself by bidding on the property if it believed the property had value in excess of the senior mortgage. It did not do so, and the senior mortgagee bid in the property. If the *mortgagor* had thereafter redeemed at any time during the six-month redemption period and if the junior mortgagee had meantime obtained judgment against the mortgagor on the mortgagor's note, the junior mortgagee would have had a lien on the property *under its judgment*

*against the mortgagor by virtue of the statute which makes a judgment a
lien against the debtor's real property.* Iowa Code § 624.23.

The *assignee,* however, redeemed. A judgment in favor of the junior
mortgagee against the mortgagor would not be against the assignee, and
would not be a lien on the assignee's real property. The junior mortgagee
therefore would have no judgment lien to enforce against the property in
the assignee's hands.

I would affirm the district court's judgment that the junior mortgagee
is entitled to judgment on the mortgagor's note, but would otherwise
reverse the judgment.

CARTER and WOLLE, JJ., join this concurrence in part and dissent in
part.

CARTER, JUSTICE, dissenting.

I dissent.

The majority opinion unnecessarily and without articulating a single
policy ground supporting its result significantly retracts the protection
previously afforded mortgagors under our redemption laws. It is
particularly unfortunate that this occurs at a time when, because of
prevailing economic conditions, mortgagors are particularly in need of such
protection.

* * *

Within the context of our established system of foreclosure by judicial
sale, our decisions have followed a consistent course in declaring that
junior liens are extinguished at the conclusion of the statutory redemption
process. *E.g., Anderson v. Renshaw,* 229 Iowa 93, 98–99, 294 N.W. 274,
277–78 (1940); *Cadd v. Snell,* 219 Iowa 728, 733–35, 259 N.W. 590, 592–93
(1935); *Paulsen v. Jensen,* 209 Iowa 453, 458, 228 N.W. 357, 359 (1929);
Cooper v. Maurer, 122 Iowa 321, 326–27, 98 N.W. 124, 125–26 (1904). In
the present case, the statutory redemption process terminated upon
redemption from sale by the mortgagor's assignee.

The majority seeks to escape from the inevitable consequence of the
cited cases by completely ignoring the mechanics of foreclosure by judicial
sale. It is axiomatic in a system of foreclosure by sale that any interest of
the mortgagors in the real estate is extinguished by the sale in order that
the purchaser at the sale may obtain a clear title. All that remained in the
mortgagor or junior lienholders following the sale was a mere incorporeal
hereditament derived from the statutes governing redemption from sale.
The majority opinion misinterprets the language in some of our decisions
as establishing the time for extinguishment of junior liens as the expiration
of the redemption period for creditors. One need only recognize foreclosure
by sale for what it is in order to realize that such reliance is misplaced. The

extinguishment of all liens at the time of sale is essential to the successful operation of that system. 5 G. Thompson, *Real Property* § 4838 (1924); Comment, 27 Iowa L.Rev. 482, 485 (1942). Moreover, in reviewing the policy reasons underlying extinguishment of liens of junior lienholders upon foreclosure, there is absolutely no reason to turn the issue on the timing of the redemption made by the mortgagor or the mortgagor's assignee.

It is significant that, to the extent some courts have sought to establish the liens of junior creditors against property held by redeeming mortgagors, such cases do not suggest that the liens were not extinguished upon sale. The protection of liens in these cases has developed under theories in which the junior liens may be "revived." *See* Durfee & Doddridge, *Redemption from Foreclosure Sale—The Uniform Mortgage Act,* 23 Mich.L.Rev. 825, 850 (1925) (hereinafter cited as *Durfee & Doddridge*). There is no authority in our cases for holding as the majority does that, if a mortgagor or a mortgagor's assignee redeems during the exclusive period, they take the property subject to the junior liens. Indeed, as the majority concedes, *Tirrill v. Miller,* 206 Iowa 426, 429, 218 N.W. 303, 304 (1928) holds otherwise.

If the law really is as the majority suggests, this is a matter of critical importance in the functioning of mortgage foreclosure litigation. Vital property interests turn on the timing of the mortgagor's redemption. Given this circumstance, it is strange that in more than 100 years of litigation this court has never before suggested that the timing of the mortgagor's redemption is of any significance in determining the status of junior liens. Moreover, at least four critical examinations of our redemption system by legal commentators have been undertaken not one of which has suggested that the timing of the mortgagor's redemption makes any difference in determining the status of junior liens. *See* Bauer, *Statutory Redemption Reconsidered: The Operation of Iowa's Redemption Statute in Two Counties Between 1881 and 1980,* 70 Iowa L.Rev. 343, 379–84 (1985) (hereinafter cited as *Bauer*); *Osborne[, Mortgages,]* § 309, at 642–44; Blum, *Iowa Statutory Redemption After Mortgage Foreclosure,* 35 Iowa L.Rev. 72, 73 (1949); *Durfee & Doddridge* at 857.

Indeed, *Osborne* and *Durfee & Doddridge* suggest the contrary. The former states:

> The [preferred] scheme is designed to put pressure on the foreclosing mortgagee at the time of the sale to bid what he thinks the property is worth, up to the amount of his debt; and it puts pressure on a junior lienor during the period of his right to redeem to bid more than the price paid by the senior mortgagee. Iowa at the present time comes closest to this suggested solution. Under

its statute the mortgagor's assignee on redemption clearly takes free of all liens against the mortgagor.

Osborne at 642 (footnotes omitted). Similarly, *Durfee & Doddridge* have suggested that under the Iowa decisions the redemptioner simply succeeds to the rights of the purchaser. *Durfee & Doddridge* at 857. They see this as a desirable result and suggest that junior lienors like senior lienors should be forced to bid at the sale at their peril in order to preserve their security interest. * * *

It is difficult to suggest any reason for the provisions of section 628.3 which give the mortgagor an exclusive right of redemption for the first six months, except as a vehicle for exerting pressure on junior lienors to bid at the sale. Under the majority's approach, the mortgagee's exclusive right now becomes meaningless in any case where there are junior liens. In addition, the presence of such an illusory right in our statutes creates a trap for the unwary debtor who will often be acting without advice of counsel.

A major flaw in the majority's approach is the resulting overbreadth of the category of creditors who will be afforded protection. The majority concedes that junior lienors who have been afforded an opportunity to redeem and have not done so should lose their liens, but holds that it is otherwise when the mortgagor's redemption during the exclusive period precludes redemption by creditors. This distinction is impossible to justify based on the realities of junior lien status. A recent study indicates that more than ninety percent of all junior lienholders fail to make redemption. *See Bauer,* 70 Iowa L.Rev. at 370, 377. Under the majority's holding in the present case, there is no method for distinguishing legitimate redemption rights from purely illusory redemption rights. The result will be to give a windfall to those junior lienors whose security interests are worthless based upon the value of the property and who would not have redeemed from the sale even if they had enjoyed an opportunity to do so.

If it were the intent of chapter 628 to protect junior lienholders in the manner that the majority proposes, they and not the mortgagor would logically have been given the exclusive right of redemption at the outset of the redemption process thereby permitting them to establish their position if the value of the property warranted such action but extinguishing their liens in those cases where it did not. The fact that our legislature has granted to the mortgagor an exclusive right to go forward in the redemption tug-of-war and has denied to junior lienors the right to redeem from a previously redeeming mortgagor leads to the inescapable conclusion that it had no intent to protect junior lienors in the situation presented in the present case.

UHLENHOPP and WOLLE, JJ., join this dissent.

NOTES

1. *Lien revival after statutory redemption.* Courts take a variety of approaches to lien revival when the mortgagor or her successor redeems. Many, for example, endorse revival of all junior liens that existed before the sale. See, e.g., Franklin v. Spencer, 309 Or. 476, 789 P.2d 643 (1990) ("redemption by the mortgagor * * * 'reinstates' the lien of any unsatisfied docketed judgment the instant that the mortgagor * * * redeems"); Newman v. American Nat'l Bank, 780 P.2d 336 (Wyo.1989) ("Public policy requires [the] revival of junior mortgages. The potential for a mortgagor to eliminate junior mortgagees by allowing a foreclosure by the senior mortgagee and then [redeeming] is a solid basis for such public policy."). Indeed, in some states, even the lien of the foreclosed mortgage is revived to the extent of any unpaid deficiency. See Nelson, Whitman, Burkhart & Freyermuth, Real Estate Law § 8.6 (6th ed.2015).

At the opposite extreme are states like California, where its statute provides: "Liens extinguished by the sale * * * do not reattach to the property after redemption and the property that was subject to the extinguished lien may not be applied to the satisfaction of the claim or judgment under which the lien was created." West's Ann.Cal.Code Civ.Proc. § 729.080(e). According to its legislative history, the foregoing statute "changes the prior rule that liens subordinate to that under which the sale was held reattach upon redemption by the judgment debtor or a successor in interest. The prior rule that upon redemption by the judgment debtor the judgment lien under which the property was sold reattaches for the amount of the deficiency is also not continued. * * * This encourages the judgment creditor and subordinate lienholders to protect their interests by looking to the property sold. * * * [This legislation] makes it clear that once a lien is extinguished a lien may not be created on the same property to enforce the same claim or judgment. Hence, for example, a judgment creditor whose judgment lien is extinguished may not again record the judgment to create a lien on the same property, nor may the judgment creditor obtain an execution lien by levy of a writ of execution on the property." Cal. Legislative Committee Comment, § 729.080(e) (1982). See Cal.L.Rev.Comm. Reports 2001.

A few pages back, we learned that, when the mortgagor or other holder of the equity of redemption purchases the property at the foreclosure sale, junior liens and other interests are not terminated. See Section F of this chapter supra. Is this policy subverted by California's approach to lien revival in the statutory redemption context?

2. *Assignee of mortgagor as redeeming party.* In most jurisdictions, the mortgagor's statutory redemption right is assignable. See, e.g., Chess v. Burt, 87 So.3d 1201 (Ala.App. 2011); Western Bank of Las Cruces v. Malooly, 119 N.M. 743, 895 P.2d 265 (App.1995); 4 Richard R. Powell & Patrick A. Rohan, Powell on Real Property § 470 (1997). However, courts differ on the effect of a redemption by the assignee. In some, previously existing junior liens against the mortgagor revive against the redeeming assignee. See, e.g., Donovan v.

Farmers Home Admin., 19 F.3d 1267 (8th Cir.1994) (applying South Dakota law). In others, the redeeming assignee takes free of such liens even though they revive where the mortgagor is the redeeming party. See, e.g., Turner v. Les File Drywall, Inc., 117 N.M. 7, 868 P.2d 652 (1994). Why should the mortgagor be able to transfer to her assignee a better title than she possessed? Is this good policy? See Nelson, Whitman, Burkhart & Freyermuth, Real Estate Finance Law § 8.6 (6th ed.2015).

Is the majority in *McFarland* influenced by *who* the mortgagor's assignee is? Would it have reached the same result had the assignee been unrelated to the mortgagor?

3. *Redemption by junior lienor.* Suppose a junior lienor redeems under an applicable statutory redemption system. Do other junior liens revive? Under most statutes, redemption by a junior lienor gives it the same title the foreclosure sale purchaser would have obtained had there been no redemption. See Nelson, Whitman, Burkhart & Freyermuth, Real Estate Finance Law § 8.7 (6th ed.2015). In other words, junior liens do not revive. Is this good policy?

PORTLAND MORTGAGE CO. V. CREDITORS PROTECTIVE ASS'N

Supreme Court of Oregon, 1953
199 Or. 432, 262 P.2d 918

BRAND, JUSTICE.

This is an appeal by the Creditors Protective Association from an order denying a motion made by it for an order requiring the sheriff of Multnomah County to accept an offer of redemption made by it for the real property described in these proceedings.

The Portland Mortgage Company, a corporation, held a first mortgage upon the real property involved in this case. Katherine M. and Byron L. Randol were the mortgagors. The appellant Creditors Protective Association, a corporation, obtained a judgment against the Randols, which became a lien against said property, subsequent in time and inferior to the lien of the plaintiff's mortgage. The judgment was entered on 21 March 1950. On 24 March 1950 the plaintiff brought suit to foreclose its mortgage, but did not join the judgment lienholder as a party. The mortgage was foreclosed by decree on 25 May 1950 and the plaintiff purchased the property at the foreclosure sale for $6,214.72, being the amount of the mortgage plus costs. On 3 July 1950 the sheriff executed and delivered to the plaintiff a certificate of sale to the property. The sale was confirmed on 20 July 1950. On 17 August 1950 the plaintiff filed a suit in equity against the defendant Creditors Protective Association, the judgment lienholder. The complaint alleged that the judgment lien of the defendant, which had not been foreclosed in the original suit, constituted a cloud upon the plaintiff's title, and that it was subsequent in time and inferior to the interest of the plaintiff as purchaser at the mortgage foreclosure sale, except for the statutory right of redemption possessed by the defendant as a judgment lien creditor. The complaint prayed for the entry of an interlocutory judgment and decree requiring that the defendant redeem from the sheriff's sale to the plaintiff "within such time as the court shall deem reasonable in the manner and mode provided by statute for the redemption by a lien creditor from a sale of real property on execution, and in the event of the failure of the defendants so to redeem said property, that a final judgment and decree be entered herein forever barring * * *" the claim of the defendant in or to the real property.

On 16 July 1951, more than a year after the sale of the mortgaged property to the plaintiff, and pursuant to the foreclosure decree, the sheriff executed and delivered to the plaintiff a deed conveying the premises. On 20 August 1951 the circuit court entered an interlocutory decree reciting the entry of a default against the defendant and providing that said defendant should have a period of 60 days from the date of the decree within which to redeem the property "in the manner and mode provided by the statutes of the State of Oregon for redemption by a lien creditor from an execution sale of real property from the Sheriff's sale to plaintiff", and providing further that in the event of failure of the defendant to redeem within the time allowed, a final judgment would be entered, barring and foreclosing the right of the defendant in the property. On 20 September 1951 the defendant judgment lienholder filed with the sheriff of Multnomah County a notice addressed to the plaintiff, its attorneys, the contract purchasers from the plaintiff and the sheriff, by the terms of which the parties mentioned, were notified that the defendant claimed a judgment lien against the property, which was due and unpaid. The notice further provided:

> "* * * that pursuant to Chapter 6–1605, O.C.L.A. 1940, you are hereby requested to account on or before the expiration of ten days of the receipt of this notice for all rents, issues and profits from the following described property * * * [describing it] and you are further notified of redemption of said property, and that on the 9th day of October, 1951, at 10:00 o'clock A.M., Creditors Protective Association, an Oregon corporation, will apply to the Sheriff of Multnomah County to redeem the above described real property pursuant to Chapter 6–1607, O.C.L.A. 1940."

* * *

On 9 October 1951 at the hour of 9:30 a.m., being one-half hour before the time specified by the defendant as the time at which it would "apply to the sheriff of Multnomah County to redeem * * *" the property, the plaintiff paid to the clerk of Multnomah County the sum of $321.50 which was sufficient to constitute full satisfaction of the judgment of the defendant, and thereupon the clerk satisfied said judgment on the margin of the record. It is stipulated that said funds are still being held by the county clerk. At the hour of 10 o'clock a.m., being the time set in the so-called notice of redemption, the defendant applied to the sheriff to redeem the real property and tendered to the sheriff the sum of $7,037.88, being the amount set out in the accounting as the amount necessary to redeem the property. The plaintiff, through its attorney, then exhibited the receipt of the county clerk for the sum of $321.50, received as satisfaction of the defendant's judgment. The defendant, by its attorney, refused said sum of $321.50. The sheriff denied the application of the defendant to redeem, for the reason that the judgment records showed that the judgment held by the defendant had been satisfied in full prior to the tender of the redemption money by the defendant, basing his decision upon the provisions of O.C.L.A. §§ 6–1602, subsection (2), 6–1607, subsections (1)(b) and (1)(c). * * *

On 22 October 1951 the defendant filed a motion for an order requiring the sheriff to accept the offer of redemption made by it. That motion was made and filed in the case which the plaintiff had instituted on 17 August 1950 for the purpose of foreclosing the interest of the defendant judgment lienholder, and in which case the defendant had defaulted. The offer was accompanied by an affidavit reciting the facts and stating that the payment of $321.50 to the clerk by the plaintiff was made without the knowledge or consent of defendant. On 12 December 1951 the court denied the motion of the defendant, from which order the defendant appeals. * * *

Only one assignment of error is presented by the defendant for consideration here, namely, that the court erred in denying the motion of the defendant for an order directing the sheriff of Multnomah County to accept the tender of defendant and to allow it to redeem the subject real property. The defendant maintains that the right of a lien creditor to redeem is a valuable and absolute right granted by statute which cannot be abridged or defeated by the purchaser at a mortgage foreclosure sale without the consent of the lien creditor. He relies upon the provisions of O.C.L.A. §§ 6–1602 to 6–1607 inclusive as the basis of the asserted right.

* * *

The defendant intimates that a lien creditor is a necessary party to a mortgage foreclosure. This is true only in a limited sense. The statute provides that any person having a lien subsequent to the plaintiff upon the same property shall be made a defendant in a suit to foreclose a mortgage. O.C.L.A. §§ 9–501, 9–502. But it is established that although junior lien claimants are necessary parties if the decree is to affect them, nevertheless the decree of foreclosure is valid as to all parties who are properly joined even though other lienors are not joined. The omitted junior lienholder is in the same position as if no foreclosure had ever taken place, and he has the same rights, no more and no less, which he had before the foreclosure suit was commenced. * * * One of the rights available to the junior lienholder is to redeem the mortgage and thus become subrogated to the position of the senior mortgagee. Brown v. Crawford, D.C., 252 F. 248; Coughanour v. Hutchinson, 41 Or. 419, 69 P. 68. This right was therefore available to the defendant unless it was cut off by the act of the plaintiff in paying into court the amount of the judgment which was a lien on the mortgaged property. * * *

Just as the omitted junior lienholder retains the rights he had in the property subject to the lien, so the senior mortgagee retains rights with respect to the junior lienholder which are the equivalent of those held by him before the foreclosure of his mortgage. The purchaser at the foreclosure sale, whether he be the mortgagee or a third party, is vested with the rights of the mortgagee as against any omitted parties in the foreclosure suit, and may proceed to cut off the junior lien by suit for strict foreclosure. By the decree the junior lienor will be required to redeem or be barred of any rights in the property. This is the procedure sanctioned by the courts of this state. * * *

The defendant claims that his right to redeem in this case is granted by statute and relies on O.C.L.A. § 6–1602(2), which provides that a creditor having a lien by judgment may redeem property sold subject to redemption. It is evident from defendant's argument and brief that it has confused the equitable right of redemption or equity of redemption with the statutory right of redemption. A clear distinction must be made between these two concepts.

The difference between the equity of redemption and statutory redemption has been made clear by the decisions of this court. Higgs v. McDuffie, 81 Or. 256, 157 P. 794, 158 P. 953; and Sellwood v. Gray, supra. The classic statement is that of Mr. Justice Lord in Sellwood v. Gray [11 Or. 534, 5 P. 196]. We quote:

"* * * His equity of redemption is the right to redeem from the mortgage—to pay off the mortgage debt—until this right is barred by a decree of foreclosure; but until this right is barred, his estate, in law or in equity, is just the same after as it was before default. It is a right, though, of which the law takes no cognizance, and is enforceable only in equity, and has nothing to do with our statute of redemptions. [Citing cases.] This is a valuable right, and exists not only in the mortgagor himself, but in every other person who has an interest in, or legal or equitable lien upon, the mortgaged premises, and includes judgment creditors, all of whom may insist upon a redemption of the mortgage. [Citing authorities.] Nor can one against his consent be deprived of this right without due process of law. To bar his right of redemption he must be made a party to the foreclosure, or the proceeding as to him will be a nullity. * * *"

The exercise of the equitable right of redemption has the effect of discharging the lien if the redemption is by the mortgagor or his successor in interest, but if a junior lien claimant redeems, the effect is to substitute the junior for the senior lienholder. In the latter case, the aggregate of the liens will be unchanged, but the persons holding the liens will be different. A junior lien, and the right of redemption which is an incident thereof, will remain in existence unless and until the same is foreclosed by a senior lienholder. When the junior lien is foreclosed, then the statutory right of redemption as to junior lien creditors given by O.C.L.A. § 6–1602(2) comes into existence. If there has never been a foreclosure of the junior lien, then there is no statutory right of redemption, only the equitable right of redemption. Concerning the rights of an omitted junior lienholder, a learned author states:

> "* * * This man's rights remain as they were, because the foreclosure does not bind him; and so, as a participant in the equity of redemption which, as to him, was never foreclosed, he can redeem in equity. That, indeed, is not only his proper course, but it is the only procedure that should be open to him. He cannot resort to statutory redemption, because he is not within the terms of the statute. The latter comes into effect at and with foreclosure, as we have seen, but the statute envisages those only whom the foreclosure has barred. It follows that one who has never been foreclosed cannot resort to statutory redemption. His remedy remains where it always was, regardless of whether the particular State had provided for statutory redemption. The remedy is redemption in equity after the ancient mode." 2 Glenn on Mortgages, § 238.

It is apparent, therefore, that the defendant cannot rely on the statutory provisions as a basis for his claim of an absolute right to redeem. The obvious purpose of the statutory right of redemption is to give an additional opportunity to the mortgagor to recover his land and to the subsequent lien creditors to protect their interests. But, as has been indicated, the defendant herein can protect his interests without resort to the statutory right of redemption, and we therefore hold that the defendant does not come within the provisions of O.C.L.A. § 6–1602(2). The provisions of O.C.L.A. § 6–1603 limiting the right of a lien creditor to redeem to the period of 60 days from date of sale clearly indicates that the statutory right of redemption does not apply in cases such as the one at bar. It was provided in the interlocutory decree that the defendant "shall have a period of sixty days from the date of this decree within which to redeem in the manner and mode provided by the statutes of the State of Oregon for redemption by a lien creditor from an execution sale of real property * * *."

The quoted provision did not constitute a holding that the defendant had a statutory right of redemption. The decree only adopted the procedure of statutory redemption as that which should be followed by the defendant if it should choose to redeem.

The junior lienor, who was omitted in the foreclosure of the senior mortgage, still has the valuable right of redemption available to him, but, when such a right is exercised, the authorities are clear that the redeeming junior lienholder is not entitled to a conveyance of the property, but rather to an assignment of the security interest of the senior mortgage. Renard v. Brown, 7 Neb. 449; Smith v. Shay, 62 Iowa 119, 17 N.W. 444; O'Brien v. Perkins, Tex.Civ.App., 276 S.W. 308; Shelton v. O'Brien, Tex.Com.App., 285 S.W. 260. This rule is stated in 2 Jones, Mortgages, 8th ed, § 1376, as follows:

> "A junior incumbrancer who, not having been made a party to a foreclosure of a prior mortgage, afterward redeems, redeems not the premises, strictly speaking, but the prior incumbrance; and he is entitled, not to a conveyance of the premises, but to an assignment of the security. Therefore if the prior mortgagee in such case has become the purchaser at the foreclosure sale, and has thus acquired the equity of redemption of the mortgaged premises, the junior mortgagee upon redeeming is not entitled to a conveyance of the estate, but to an assignment of the prior mortgage; whereupon the prior mortgagee, as owner of the equity of redemption, may, if he choose, pay the amount due upon the junior mortgage, redeeming that. * * *"

When a junior lienholder has redeemed the senior incumbrance and steps into the shoes of the prior mortgagee, he must foreclose his lien and have the property sold, in order to realize on his security, unless the purchaser at the prior foreclosure, who has acquired the mortgagor's equity of redemption, chooses to redeem from him. The equity of redemption acquired by the purchaser at the foreclosure sale, when perfected by delivery of a sheriff's deed, constitutes the basis of his right to re-redeem from a junior lienholder who by redemption from the purchaser has acquired the rights of the senior mortgagee but has not acquired the property. We quote:

> "Redemption by a junior lienor, however, means a correlative privilege on the part of the senior whose mortgage has gone through foreclosure. The junior lien, in the beginning, was subject to redemption on the part of the mortgagor. The latter, of course, lost all his rights and interest when the decree of foreclosure was entered against him. But let us remember that the junior's security consisted only of the equity of redemption, or a share in it. Hence if he redeems after a foreclosure from which he has been

omitted, he is not redeeming the premises as the mortgagor would have done, but is merely acquiring the senior mortgage for the protection of his own interest. It follows that he can be met at the gate by the purchaser at the sale, whether he be the senior mortgagee or a third party, with a tender of money in payment of his debt with interest. In other words, the purchaser at the sale can dispose of the junior mortgagee by redeeming the land from his lien." 1 Glenn, Mortgages, § 86.5.

* * *

The authorities cited control the decision in the pending case. Since the sheriff's deed to the plaintiff conveyed all the interests in the property except the judgment lien held by the defendant, the plaintiff acquired an owner's interest in the property entitling it to pay off the judgment of defendant and free the land of the lien. O.C.L.A. § 6–1001. No question is raised in this court as to the right of the clerk of the court to enter the satisfaction of judgment as permitted by O.C.L.A. § 6–1001. Since the purchaser, having a sheriff's deed, could redeem from the junior lienholder if the latter had redeemed from the senior mortgage, and could thereby acquire unencumbered and unclouded title, we can see no reason why such junior lienholder cannot be paid off prior to any redemption. In the view we take of this case, it therefore makes no difference whether the notice of redemption by the junior lienholder was given prior to the time plaintiff paid the judgment, or how far such proceedings had been carried.

* * *

We hold that the payment by the plaintiff to the county clerk pursuant to the provisions of O.C.L.A. § 6–1001 and the entry of satisfaction on the margin of the record discharged defendant's judgment and that thereupon the defendant ceased to be a lienholder. Having been fully paid he had no right to redeem.

The order of the trial court denying defendant's motion to require the sheriff to accept defendant's offer of redemption is affirmed.

NOTE

Equitable redemption vs. statutory redemption. As the court in Portland Mortgage Co. held, when a senior lienor judicially forecloses its lien and fails to join a junior lienor, the junior lien is not eliminated and the junior lienor retains the same rights as before the foreclosure. The junior lienor still has its equitable right of redemption, rather than a statutory right of redemption. The choice can make a difference for several reasons. For example, a junior lienor who redeems under a statutory right of redemption normally gets fee title to the property, rather than just the revived first lien. Moreover, to exercise statutory redemption, the junior must usually pay the price paid at the original foreclosure sale, rather than the balance that was owed on the first lien. Unlike equitable redemption, the mortgagor in many states has the first right to statutorily redeem, and the junior lienors can redeem only if the mortgagor does not. Additionally, statutory redemption has a fixed time period, while equitable redemption is cut off only by the doctrine of laches or a foreclosure in which the person seeking to redeem is a party. Some commentators have argued that the omitted junior should have a choice of proceeding under either form of redemption.

H.　LIMITATIONS ON DEFICIENCY JUDGMENTS

Under the traditional approach followed in many jurisdictions, once the mortgage goes into default and the obligation is accelerated, the mortgagee has two options. The mortgagee may either (1) obtain a judgment on the personal obligation and enforce it by levying upon any of the mortgagor's property and, if a deficiency remains, foreclose on the mortgaged real estate for the balance or (2) foreclose on the real estate first and if the proceeds are insufficient to satisfy the mortgage obligation, obtain a deficiency judgment thereafter. Some jurisdictions following the above approach require the mortgagee to elect one of the two options. The Restatement agrees; see Restatement (Third) of Property (Mortgages) § 8.2 (1997). Other states, however, reject this "election of remedies" requirement; the mortgagee is permitted to follow both options simultaneously with the only limitation being that the mortgage obligation may only be satisfied once.

Under the traditional approach, a deficiency judgment is calculated by subtracting the foreclosure sale price from the mortgage obligation. If the foreclosure is judicial, the deficiency judgment is obtained in the same proceeding after the foreclosure sale. Where the foreclosure is by power of sale, the mortgagee obtains a deficiency judgment by filing a separate judicial action against the mortgagor.

As we have seen earlier in this chapter, a forced sale, even under stable economic conditions, normally will not bring a price that will reflect the reasonable market value of the property if it were marketed outside the foreclosure context. Moreover, in times of severe economic downturn, mortgaged property often sells for substantially depressed prices. To make matters worse, mortgagees occasionally purchase at the foreclosure sale for a deflated price, obtain a deficiency judgment, and resell the real estate at a profit.

The great depression of the 1930s, as might be expected, produced a substantial amount of varied state legislation to provide relief for mortgagors, as did the recession in the early 1980s and the Great Recession that began in 2008. Perhaps best-known were the various moratoria statutes. Such legislation differed from state to state. Some statutes gave courts authority to grant foreclosure postponements on petition of mortgagors in individual cases. Other statutes extended the period of statutory redemption beyond the usual period or stretched out the periods of time in a foreclosure action. See generally George E. Osborne, Handbook on the Law of Mortgages § 331 (1970). Most of this legislation was upheld against federal and state constitutional attack. Constitutional law students are familiar with Home Building & Loan Ass'n v. Blaisdell, 290 U.S. 398, 54 S.Ct. 231, 78 L.Ed. 413 (1934), which upheld the Minnesota legislation, finding it not to be an unconstitutional impairment of the obligation of contracts.

However, as the economy recovered, most of the moratoria legislation either lapsed, was repealed, or became moribund. The more lasting legacy of the 1930s depression, as well as prior and subsequent economic downturns, is the wide variety of procedural and substantive limitations on deficiency judgments imposed by legislatures and, less frequently, by the courts. The following material is intended to provide you with a general overview of these limitations.

GRANT S. NELSON, DEFICIENCY JUDGMENTS AFTER REAL ESTATE FORECLOSURES IN MISSOURI: SOME MODEST PROPOSALS
47 Mo.L.Rev. 151, 152–54 (1982)*

The majority of states limits the mortgagee's right to a deficiency judgment. Some limitations are procedural. For example, many states impose strict notice requirements[5] and time limits[6] on the mortgagee. Failure by the mortgagee to comply with these limitations can destroy the right to obtain a deficiency judgment.[7]

Likewise, failure to comply with "one action" rules also can destroy the mortgagee's right to a deficiency judgment. Under such rules, the mortgagee's only remedy on default is foreclosure, and he must obtain any deficiency judgment incident to the foreclosure proceeding.[8] Two justifications are often cited for this rule:

---

* Reprinted with permission of The Missouri Law Review.

[5] See, e.g., Me.Rev.Stat.Ann. tit. 14, § 6203–E (1980).

[6] See, e.g., Nev.Rev.Stat. § 40.455 (1979) (three months after sale); N.J.Stat.Ann. § 2A:50–2 (West Cum.Supp.1981–1982) (three months after sale or confirmation); N.D.Cent.Code § 32–19–06 (1976) (ninety days after sale). Some states limit the time for completing execution on a deficiency judgment. See, e.g., id. (three years).

[7] See N.Y.Real Prop.Acts.Law § 1371(3) (McKinney 1979); Okla.Stat.Ann. tit. 12, § 686 (West 1960).

[8] Cal.Civ.Proc.Code § 726 (West 1980) provides:

There can be but one form of action for the recovery of any debt, or the enforcement of any right secured by mortgage upon real property, which action must be in accordance

One is to protect the mortgagor against multiplicity of actions when the separate actions, though theoretically distinct, are so closely connected that normally they can and should be decided in one suit. The other is to compel a creditor who has taken a mortgage on land to exhaust his security before attempting to reach any unmortgaged property to satisfy his claim.[9]

Similar restrictions sometimes apply to power of sale foreclosures.[10] In such situations, the exercise of the power of sale is a condition precedent to a subsequent action at law for a deficiency. Some commentators refer to this restriction as the "security first" principle.[11]

There also are important substantive limitations on deficiency judgments. As a result of the depression of the 1930s, many states enacted "fair value" legislation, and most of this legislation is still in force. Fair value statutes usually define the deficiency as the difference between the mortgage debt and the fair value of the foreclosed land, rather than as the difference between the mortgage debt and the foreclosure sale price of the land.[12] Depending on the statute, a court[13] or a jury[14] may determine the fair value. Most of these statutes were designed to deal with depression conditions, when foreclosure sales typically yielded nominal amounts. This legislation, however, also assumes that even in a stable economic climate, a forced sale of real estate will yield a price significantly lower than otherwise would be obtained by private sale.

Closely related to the fair value approach are the appraisal statutes used in a few states.[15] This legislation requires the court or the person conducting the foreclosure sale to appoint an appraiser, who determines the value of the property. For example, in South Carolina, a statute reduces

---

with the provisions of this chapter. In such action the court may, by its judgment, direct the sale of the encumbered property * * *.

Four other states—Idaho, Montana, Nevada, and Utah—have one action statutes copied from California. *See* Idaho Code § 6–101 (1979); Mont.Code Ann. § 71–1–222 (1981); Nev.Rev.Stat. § 40.430 (1979); Utah Code Ann. § 78–37–1 (1977).

[9] G. Osborne, G. Nelson & D. Whitman, Real Estate Finance Law § 8.2, at 526.

[10] *See, e.g.,* Walker v. Community Bank, 10 Cal.3d 729, 733–34, 518 P.2d 329, 331–32, 111 Cal.Rptr. 897, 899–900 (1974); Nevada Land & Mortgage Co. v. Hidden Wells Ranch, Inc., 83 Nev. 501, 504, 435 P.2d 198, 200 (1967).

[11] G. Osborne, G. Nelson & D. Whitman, *supra* note 9, § 8.2, at 527. Many states also have "election of remedies" statutes under which the mortgagee can foreclose and seek a deficiency judgment or sue on the note and then foreclose, but cannot bring both actions simultaneously. *See, e.g.,* N.Y.Real Prop.Acts.Law §§ 1301, 1401 (McKinney 1979). For a complete compilation of the 15 states with such statutes, see Washburn, *The Judicial and Legislative Response to Price Inadequacy in Mortgage Foreclosure Sales,* 53 S.Cal.L.Rev. 843, 928 n. 467 (1980).

[12] *See, e.g.,* Cal.Civ.Proc.Code § 726 (West 1980); N.Y.Real Prop.Acts.Law § 1371 (McKinney 1979); Utah Code Ann. § 57–1–32 (1974).

[13] *See, e.g.,* N.Y.Real Prop.Acts.Law § 1371 (McKinney 1979).

[14] *See, e.g.,* N.D.Cent.Code §§ 32–9–04,–06,–07 (1979). For an analysis of this statute, see First State Bank v. Ihringer, 217 N.W.2d 857, 859–63 (N.D.1974).

[15] *See, e.g.,* Ark.Stat.Ann. § 51–1112 (1971); La.Code Civ.Proc.Ann. art. 2336–2337 (West 1961); S.C.Code § 29–3–660 to –760 (1976).

the deficiency by the difference between the foreclosure sale price and the appraisal amount.[16] Other state appraisal statutes establish two-thirds of the appraisal value as an upset price and prohibit deficiency judgments if the upset price satisfies the mortgage debt and costs.[17]

Numerous other types of antideficiency legislation are common. For example, some states prohibit deficiency judgments after a power of sale[18] or a purchase money mortgage[19] foreclosure. Some of these latter statutes limit the definition of a purchase money mortgage to those held by the vendor as the mortgagee,[20] while others also include purchase money mortgages held by a variety of third party lenders.[21] Many such statutes also apply only to purchases of residential property.[22]

––––––––––

For a more detailed and comprehensive consideration of the antideficiency concepts treated in this subsection, see Kristen Barnes, "Pennies on the Dollar": Reallocating Risk and Deficiency Judgment Liability, 66 S.C. L. Rev. 243 (2014); Marianne M. Jennings, From the Courts: Foreclosure, Anti-Deficiency Statutes, and Confusion, 42 Real Est. L.J. 493 (2014); Robert M. Washburn, Judicial and Legislative Response to Price Inadequacy in Mortgage Foreclosure Sales, 53 So.Cal.L.Rev. 843 (1980). For an insightful economic analysis of antideficiency legislation, see Michael H. Schill, An Economic Analysis of Mortgagor Protection Laws, 77 Va.L.Rev. 489 (1991). For a strong brief for barring deficiency judgments in the home foreclosure setting, see John Mixon, Deficiency Judgments Following Home Mortgage Foreclosure: An Anachronism That Increases Personal Tragedy, Impedes Regional, Economic Recovery and Means Little to Lenders, 22 Tex.Tech.L.Rev. 1 (1991).

The California antideficiency regulatory scheme is probably more complex and pervasive than that of any other jurisdiction. Consequently, you should study carefully the description of this regulatory framework contained in Cornelison v. Kornbluth, 15 Cal.3d 590, 125 Cal.Rptr. 557, 542 P.2d 981 (1975):

> Prior to 1933, a mortgagee of real property was required to exhaust his security before enforcing the debt or otherwise to waive all right to his security (§ 726; see Walker v. Community

––––––––––

[16] S.C.Code § 29–3–740 (1976).

[17] *See, e.g.,* Ohio Rev.Code Ann. § 2329.19 (Page 1981); Wyo.Stat. § 1–17–316 (1977).

[18] *See, e.g.,* Cal.Civ.Proc.Code § 580d (West 1976); Wash.Rev.Code Ann. § 61.24.100 (Cum.Supp.1981). For a discussion of the Washington statute, see Helbling Bros. v. Turner, 14 Wash.App. 494, 496–98, 542 P.2d 1257, 1258–59 (1975).

[19] *See, e.g.,* N.C.Gen.Stat. § 45–21.38 (1976); S.D.Comp.Laws Ann. §§ 44–8–20 to –24 (1967).

[20] *See, e.g.,* N.C.Gen.Stat. § 45–21.38 (1976).

[21] *See, e.g.,* Ariz.Rev.Stat.Ann. § 33–729(A) (1974).

[22] *See, e.g., id.* §§ 33–729,–814; Or.Rev.Stat. §§ 88.070–.075 (1979).

Bank (1974) 10 Cal.3d 729, 733–734, 111 Cal.Rptr. 897, 518 P.2d 329). However, having resorted to the security, whether by judicial sale or private nonjudicial sale, the mortgagee could obtain a deficiency judgment against the mortgagor for the difference between the amount of the indebtedness and the amount realized from the sale. As a consequence during the great depression with its dearth of money and declining property values, a mortgagee was able to purchase the subject real property at the foreclosure sale at a depressed price far below its normal fair market value and thereafter to obtain a double recovery by holding the debtor for a large deficiency. (Roseleaf Corp. v. Chierighino (1963) 59 Cal.2d 35, 40, 27 Cal.Rptr. 873, 378 P.2d 97; see Glenn, Mortgages (1943) § 156, pp. 857–861.) In order to counteract this situation, California in 1933 enacted fair market value limitations applicable to both judicial foreclosure sales (§ 726) and private foreclosure sales (§ 580a) which limited the mortgagee's deficiency judgment after exhaustion of the security to the difference between the fair value of the property at the time of the sale (irrespective of the amount actually realized at the sale) and the outstanding debt for which the property was security. Therefore, if, due to the depressed economic conditions, the property serving as security was sold for less than the fair value as determined under section 726 or section 580a, the mortgagee could not recover the amount of that difference in his action for a deficiency judgment. (See Hetland, Secured Real Estate Transactions (Cont.Ed.Bar 1974) § 9.3, pp. 183–184.)

In certain situations, however, the Legislature deemed even this partial deficiency too oppressive. Accordingly, in 1933 it enacted section 580b which barred deficiency judgments altogether on purchase money mortgages. "Section 580b places the risk of inadequate security on the purchase money mortgagee. A vendor is thus discouraged from overvaluing the security. Precarious land promotion schemes are discouraged, for the security value of the land gives purchasers a clue as to its true market value. [Citation.] If inadequacy of security results, not from overvaluing, but from a decline in property values during a general or local depression, section 580b prevents the aggravation of the downturn that would result if defaulting purchasers were burdened with large personal liability. Section 580b thus serves as a stabilizing factor in land sales." (Roseleaf Corp. v. Chierighino, supra, 59 Cal.2d 35, 42, 27 Cal.Rptr. 873, 877, 378 P.2d 97, 101; see also Spangler v. Memel (1972) 7 Cal.3d 603, 612, 102 Cal.Rptr. 807, 498 P.2d 1055; Bargioni v. Hill (1963) 59 Cal.2d 121, 123, 28 Cal.Rptr. 321, 378 P.2d 593.)

Although both judicial foreclosure sales and private nonjudicial foreclosure sales provided for identical deficiency judgments in nonpurchase money situations subsequent to the 1933 enactment of the fair value limitations, one significant difference remained, namely property sold through judicial foreclosure was subject to the statutory right of redemption (§ 725a), while property sold by private foreclosure sale was not redeemable. By virtue of sections 725a and 701, the judgment debtor, his successor in interest or a junior lienor could redeem the property at any time during one year after the sale, frequently by tendering the sale price. The effect of this right of redemption was to remove any incentive on the part of the mortgagee to enter a low bid at the sale (since the property could be redeemed for that amount) and to encourage the making of a bid approximating the fair market value of the security. However, since real property purchased at a private foreclosure sale was not subject to redemption, the mortgagee by electing this remedy, could gain irredeemable title to the property by a bid substantially below the fair value and still collect a deficiency judgment for the difference between the fair value of the security and the outstanding indebtedness.

In 1940 the Legislature placed the two remedies, judicial foreclosure sale and private nonjudicial foreclosure sale on a parity by enacting section 580d. Section 580d bars "any deficiency judgment" following a private foreclosure sale. "It seems clear that section 580d was enacted to put judicial enforcement on a parity with private enforcement. This result could be accomplished by giving the debtor a right to redeem after a sale under the power. The right to redeem, like proscription of a deficiency judgment, has the effect of making the security satisfy a realistic share of the debt. [Citation.] By choosing instead to bar a deficiency judgment after private sale, the Legislature achieved its purpose without denying the creditor his election of remedies. If the creditor wishes a deficiency judgment, his sale is subject to statutory redemption rights. If he wishes a sale resulting in nonredeemable title, he must forego the right to a deficiency judgment. In either case the debtor is protected." (Roseleaf v. Chierighino, supra, 59 Cal.2d 35, 43–44, 27 Cal.Rptr. 873, 878, 378 P.2d 97, 102.)

Now consider carefully a specific application of West's Ann.Cal.Code Civ.Proc. § 580b:

DeBERARD PROPERTIES, LTD. V. LIM

Supreme Court of California, 1999
20 Cal.4th 659, 85 Cal.Rptr.2d 292, 976 P.2d 843

MOSK, J.

We must decide whether, notwithstanding the protection against deficiency judgments conferred by Code of Civil Procedure section 580b (hereafter section 580b), a purchaser may waive, by contract term, that protection in exchange for new consideration following the original purchase money sale. * * *

In 1990, Myo Za Theresa Lim and Bun Raymond Lim agreed to buy a shopping center from DeBerard Properties, Ltd., for $3.2 million. The Lims tendered a $1,120,000 down payment, assumed a first trust deed securing an obligation of $1,913,266.92 held by a bank, and signed a promissory note for $170,000 secured by a second trust deed in favor of DeBerard.

By September 1993 the Lims could no longer make payments on the obligations secured by the first and second trust deeds. The Lims hired an accountant to renegotiate their obligations to the holders of the trust deeds. The accountant renegotiated both obligations. As a result, the parties to this case executed a forbearance agreement.

The agreement halved the monthly payments from $1,416.67 to $708.33 and the interest rate from 10 to 5 percent. Also, DeBerard agreed not to foreclose, and it agreed to subordinate its trust deed to any modification of the bank loan, in order to facilitate the Lims' renegotiations with the bank. In turn, the Lims waived the protection provided by section 580b.

Despite these changes, the Lims soon defaulted on their obligations to the bank and DeBerard. The bank foreclosed and extinguished DeBerard's junior security interest. DeBerard then filed this suit on the promissory note.

In a bench trial, the court concluded that section 580b may be waived as a matter of law and found that the Lims had voluntarily, knowingly, and intelligently waived it. The court awarded DeBerard $241,075.81 plus costs.

The Court of Appeal reversed. It concluded that section 580b's language precluded its protection from being waived.

We begin with section 580b's text. As relevant here, the statute provides: "No deficiency judgment shall lie in any event after a sale of real property . . . for failure of the purchaser to complete his or her contract of sale, or under a deed of trust or mortgage given to the vendor to secure payment of the balance of the purchase price of that real property . . . ."

The language of section 580b is plain. A vendor is barred from obtaining a deficiency judgment against a purchaser in a purchase money secured land transaction. "[I]n the case of a seller-financed loan for real property, i.e., a purchase money obligation, a deficiency judgment is prohibited." (*Ghirardo v. Antonioli* (1996) 14 Cal.4th 39, 49, 57 Cal.Rptr.2d 687, 924 P.2d 996.) "The explicit language of section 580b brooks no interpretation other than that deficiency judgments are prohibited by the purchase money mortgagee so long as a purchase money mortgage or deed of trust is in effect on the original property. To allow a purchase money creditor to circumvent the absolute rule by enforcing a . . . waiver of section 580b in exchange for other concessions would [flout] the very purpose of the rule. If the purchase money creditor retains an interest in the original property, the debtor cannot be held for a deficiency. If the purchase money creditor does not wish to accept the risk that the property will be lost through foreclosure by another secured creditor, the remedy is to either foreclose himself or destroy the purchase money nature of the transaction. . ." (*Palm v. Schilling,* 199 Cal.App.3d at p. 76, 244 Cal.Rptr. 600 * * *).

Historically we have discerned two reasons for the Legislature's decision to protect purchasers in purchase money secured land transactions. First, section 580b is a transaction-specific stabilization measure: it stabilizes purchase money secured land sales by keeping the vendor from overvaluing the property and by suggesting to the purchaser its true value. Second, it is a macroeconomic stabilization measure: if property values drop and the land is foreclosed upon, the purchaser's loss is limited to the land that he or she used as security in the transaction, purchasers as a class are harmed less than they might otherwise be during a time of economic decline, and the economy benefits. * * *

DeBerard correctly observes that in *Spangler v. Memel* (1972) 7 Cal.3d 603, 102 Cal.Rptr. 807, 498 P.2d 1055 (*Spangler*), we held that section 580b did not apply to the facts at issue, notwithstanding the statute's absolute bar to deficiency judgments in purchase money secured land sales. It contends that we should hold the statute may be waived in cases such as this.

Spangler, however, creates only a narrow exception to the scope of section 580b, and we decline to create another one here.

In *Spangler*, the vendor conveyed a single-family residence on Sunset Boulevard in Los Angeles to the purchaser for $90,000, consisting of $26,100 in cash and a $63,900 note secured by a purchase money deed of trust, which the vendor agreed to subordinate to future construction loans of as much as $2 million so that the residence could be replaced by an office building. The purchasers in turn agreed to waive the antideficiency judgment protection of section 580b, so that the vendor would have recourse against them should the lender of the construction loans foreclose on an anticipated higher priority encumbrance. The purchasers found a lender that, as expected, extended a $408,000 loan on condition that its deed of trust have priority over the vendor's.

Once built, the office building proved to be a commercial failure, and the lender foreclosed on its deed of trust, extinguishing the value of the vendor's subordinated security. The vendor sued the purchasers to recoup the deficiency, and we held that she could recover it.

We explained that section 580b's protection "applies automatically only to the standard purchase money situation. We are of the view that if the transaction in question is a variation on the standard purchase money mortgage or deed of trust transaction, it should be examined so as to determine whether it subserves the purposes of section 580b ..." (*Spangler, supra*, 7 Cal.3d at p. 611, 102 Cal.Rptr. 807, 498 P.2d 1055.) Thus, *Spangler* created a two-part inquiry: does the sale vary from a standard purchase money transaction, and if so, does applying section 580b's antideficiency protection comport with the Legislature's intent? Section 580b applies unless the answer to the first question is yes and the answer to the second question is no.

In *Spangler*, we held that "a sale of real property for commercial development in which the vendor agrees to subordinate his senior lien under the purchase money deed of trust to the liens of lenders of the construction money for the commercial development is a variation on the standard purchase money mortgage transaction." (*Spangler, supra*, 7 Cal.3d at p. 611, 102 Cal.Rptr. 807, 498 P.2d 1055.) And we held that applying section 580b would not comport with the Legislature's intent. "[T]he success of the commercial development depends upon the competence, diligence and good faith of the developing purchaser. It would seem proper, therefore, that the purchaser[—]not the vendor[—]bear the risk of failure, particularly since in the event of default, the junior lienor vendor will lose both the land and the purchase price." (7 Cal.3d at p. 613, 102 Cal.Rptr. 807, 498 P.2d 1055.)

Moreover, "[i]n the subordination clause context, the amount of the construction loan is usually extremely large. This is illustrated by the case at bench[,] where the subordination clause provided that the vendor would agree to subordinate for construction loans up to $2 million, and a loan of $408,000 was actually obtained. It is clear that the typical vendor in this context cannot possibly raise the astronomical sums needed to buy in at the senior sale and thereby protect his junior security interest. The only possible protection available to the vendor[,] other than careful and sometimes fortuitous choice of purchasers, is to allow a deficiency judgment against the commercial developer." (*Spangler, supra*, 7 Cal.3d at p. 614, 102 Cal.Rptr. 807, 498 P.2d 1055.)

The Court of Appeal has, in various decisions, properly recognized that *Spangler's* application is limited. "*Spangler* does not make the mere presence of a subordination agreement a push button that defeats the rule of automatic application of section 580b. It is only when a subordination agreement signals a pronounced change in the use to which the property is devoted—thus making it a variation on the standard purchase money security transaction—that the transaction is removed from the reach of the rule." (*Thompson v. Allert* (1991) 233 Cal.App.3d 1462, 1466, 285 Cal.Rptr. 367.) * * *

In sum, *Spangler's* rule is limited to those situations in which a pronounced intensification of the property's anticipated post-sale use both requires and eventually results in construction financing that dwarfs the property's value at the time of sale. Furthermore, the purchaser must be in a much better position than the vendor to assess the property's possible value and to understand the risks involved in capitalizing on the property's potential. Finally, under all the circumstances of the sale, including the property's development and the financing for that development, conferring section 580b's protection must unfairly thrust "the risk of the failure of the commercial development . . . upon the vendor" (*Spangler, supra,* 7 Cal.3d at p. 613, 102 Cal.Rptr. 807, 498 P.2d 1055), imposing on it a commercially unreasonable burden because "the success of the commercial development depends upon the competence, diligence and good faith of the developing purchaser" (*ibid.*). In a situation in which all three factors are found, stability in secured land transactions is deemed to be better maintained by creating an exception to section 580b's safe harbor.[3] * * *

This case, however, is unlike *Spangler*. DeBerard sold the Lims a shopping center. The Lims continued to operate a shopping center—they did not obtain a construction loan that dwarfed the property's value at the time of sale and then proceed to build a more intensive use. Merely renegotiating the sale's terms in an effort to salvage the transaction did not take it outside the scope the Legislature intended section 580b to have.

With commendable candor, DeBerard acknowledges that this case is different from *Spangler* in some respects, but nonetheless it advances

---

[3]   Significant risks attach to vendors' interests that are subordinated to construction loans. In *Budget Realty Inc. v. Hunter,* supra, 157 Cal.App.3d 511, 204 Cal.Rptr. 48, the court noted: "The subordination of a seller's purchase money lien to construction financing exposes the seller to unique risks. Construction financing is extremely short-term financing. Further, the amount financed for construction of improvements generally dwarfs the value of the land. Thus, for a seller to salvage his position from the foreclosing construction lender, the seller must pay a 'balloon payment' typically exceeding the entire value of the land he sold. Permanent or interim 'take out' financing is not accessible until the project is substantially completed. Further, the costs of the improvements are reflected only fractionally in the project's value until the improvements are substantially completed. A half-completed office building generally does not have one-half the market value of a completed office building. Subordination to construction financing substantially aggravates the jeopardy to the seller's security." (*Id.* at p. 516, 204 Cal.Rptr. 48.) * * *

several reasons in favor of its view that we should permit the Lims to waive section 580b.

First, DeBerard discerns that the Lims' agreement to waive section 580b's protection enabled the "dramatic" change in the terms of their obligation to DeBerard. "The workout agreement, and the renegotiation of the senior and junior loans, reallocated the risks and dramatically changed the financial nature of the commercial development. The success or failure of the workout agreement was in the hands of the borrowers and the senior lender."

As stated, however, we cannot justify permitting a waiver in disregard of the language of section 580b just because DeBerard eased the terms of the Lims' obligation to it. The fact is that the same property secured its note. * * * And there was no large construction loan in furtherance of an intensified use. Nor do we agree that there was a dramatic change in the financial arrangements that might conceivably bring this case within *Spangler*'s ambit. DeBerard began with a relatively risky subordinated security interest, and ended in the same position. * * *

Next, DeBerard contends that we should take into account that the Lims were sophisticated purchasers and borrowers. The record supports its factual contention. Nevertheless, section 580b does not distinguish between sophisticated and unsophisticated purchasers, just as the relevant portion does not distinguish between residential and commercial sales. * * *

Next, DeBerard invokes policy. Enforcing "post-default waivers of [section] 580b would encourage vendors holding junior purchase money trust deeds to execute subordination agreements in favor of the senior lender, thus enabling the senior lender to modify the senior debt. Without such a subordination, the senior lender is forced to choose between a unilateral modification . . . or foreclosure." In sum, DeBerard argues that allowing waivers of section 580b's protection will encourage flexibility in negotiating modifications of purchase money secured land sales.

In our view, DeBerard's policy argument must be addressed to the Legislature, which can consider in detail the benefit, if any, of permitting a purchaser to waive section 580b's protection in exchange for easing the terms of its obligation to its secured creditor or creditors. * * *

Finally, DeBerard notes that *Russell v. Roberts*, 39 Cal.App.3d 390, 114 Cal.Rptr. 305, is authority for its view. We recognize that a few Court of Appeal decisions have declared that a purchaser's post-sale waiver of section 580b's protection in exchange for consideration is generally valid— i.e., even when, unlike the facts of *Spangler*, the property is not distinctly improved by means of a construction loan to which the vendor's interest is subordinated. * * *

The only decision to discuss the point is *Russell*. That court stated that section 580b may be waived "after the sale and deed of trust transaction are completed." (*Russell v. Roberts, supra,* 39 Cal.App.3d at p. 395, 114 Cal.Rptr. 305.) *Russell* drew an analogy to *Salter v. Ulrich* (1943) 22 Cal.2d 263, 138 P.2d 7, which stated: "Since necessity often drives debtors to make ruinous concessions when a loan is needed, [Code of Civil Procedure] section 726 should be applied to protect them and to prevent a waiver in advance. This reasoning, however, does not apply after the loan is made, when all rights have been established and there remains only the enforcement of those rights." (*Id.* at p. 267, 138 P.2d 7.)

Russell also found a policy reason to support its conclusion. "We note also . . . *Spangler v. Memel,* 7 Cal.3d 603, 610 [102 Cal.Rptr. 807, 498 P.2d 1055], which expresses the conclusion, 'that section 580b automatically applied only to the standard purchase money transaction and that with respect to variants from this standard purchase money transaction, section 580b would apply only if the factual circumstances came within the purposes of the section . . .' It seems clearly not 'within the purposes of the section' to deny a vendee whose rights have long been established, and who is no longer subject to the coercion of the lender, the privilege of waiving for a new consideration one of those earlier attained rights." (*Russell v. Roberts, supra,* 39 Cal.App.3d at p. 395, 114 Cal.Rptr. 305.) * * *

With regard to the policy reasoning of *Russell v. Roberts, supra,* 39 Cal.App.3d 390, 114 Cal.Rptr. 305, we agree with *Palm* that " '[r]uinous concessions' are, if anything, easier to obtain when the debtor is in default. Then, the temptation to 'press the bet' is likely to be stronger than the poor decision to purchase the property in the first instance." (*Palm v. Schilling, supra,* 199 Cal.App.3d at p. 73, 244 Cal.Rptr. 600.) * * *

We therefore disapprove the discussion in *Russell v. Roberts, supra,* 39 Cal.App.3d at pages 394–395, 114 Cal.Rptr. 305, and the dicta in [prior Court of Appeal decisions].

We affirm the Court of Appeal's judgment.

GEORGE, C.J., and BAXTER, J., WERDEGAR, J., CHIN, J., and BROWN, J., concur.

Concurring Opinion by KENNARD, J.

I concur in the majority opinion. I write separately to comment further on the purposes of Code of Civil Procedure section 580b. As the majority notes, * * * this court [has] articulated two purposes for section 580b: preventing sellers from overvaluing real property and moderating the economic dislocation caused by downturns in property values.

As to the first purpose, commentators and the Court of Appeal have noted the lack of economic logic to the argument that Code of Civil Procedure section 580b reduces overvaluation of properties. (See *Budget*

Realty, Inc. v. Hunter (1984) 157 Cal.App.3d 511, 515–516, 204 Cal.Rptr. 48; Harris, *California Code of Civil Procedure Section 580b Revisited: Freedom of Contract in Real Estate Purchase Agreements* (1993) 30 San Diego L.Rev. 509, 516–517; Bernhardt, Cal. Mortgage and Deed of Trust Practice (Cont. Ed. Bar 2d ed.1990) One-Action and Antideficiency Rules, § 4.27, pp. 207–208; Hetland, Cal. Real Estate Secured Transactions (Cont. Ed. Bar 1970) p. 270.) Assume the fair market value of the property is X. If the seller finds a buyer willing to pay 2X or 3X for the property, the seller is no worse off selling for that price (and often will be better off) than selling for X. In either case, if default occurs, the price the seller will be able to resell the property for is the same regardless of the initial selling price (assuming a stable property market, that price will be X). The seller gains nothing by refusing to sell its property for the higher price, and loses nothing by selling the property for more than its value as security. Although overvaluing may increase the risk of default in property bought for commercial purposes (by increasing the income stream the property must generate in order to pay for itself), the increased selling price may well compensate the seller for the increased risk. Moreover, section 580b encourages buyers to offer more than the market value of the property because they know that in the case of default they will not be personally liable for any deficiency. In my view, the criticisms of the overvaluation rationale * * * described above are well founded.

NOTES

1.　*Waivers of 580b. DeBerard* tells us that virtually all post-default waivers of section 580b are unenforceable. Thus, vendors may rely only on the *Spangler* construction lending exception and perhaps unique settings involving a "special relationship between the parties."

Nickerman v. Ryan, 93 Cal.App.3d 564, 155 Cal.Rptr. 830 (1979), represents a "special relationship" case. In that case the court limited the impact of section 580b on a mortgage transaction that was incident to a post-dissolution agreement adjusting the interests of an ex-wife and ex-husband in property held as tenants in common. The agreement provided for the conveyance of the ex-wife's interest in a motel and certain other real estate to the ex-husband. In return, ex-husband delivered to her a promissory note for $25,000 secured by a deed of trust on the motel and conveyed to her his interest in the former family home and certain other property. Later, foreclosure of a senior lien on the motel wiped out her junior deed of trust lien. She then sued him for a deficiency judgment on the note. The ex-husband asserted that section 580b barred such a judgment because the deed of trust was given to secure the "purchase" by him of her interest in the motel and other real estate.

The trial court found that the "note and deed of trust were not given to [ex-wife] to secure payment of the balance of the purchase price of the [motel], but rather to equalize a division of community property after a decree of divorce." In affirming this trial court finding, the Court of Appeal also determined that "the transaction * * * is such a variation on the standard purchase money mortgage or deed of trust transaction that it would not subserve the purposes of section 580b * * * to deny a deficiency judgment in this case." According to the court, "it would be ironic to hold that the [ex-wife] who entered into the transaction to be free of the vicissitudes of the commercial enterprises, and so surrendered her joint right of control, should find that her fair share of the joint property was lost because of the sole management of the [ex-husband] who assumed the risks of the motel and apartment business. She is deserving of the same consideration given the vendor in Spangler v. Memel."

2. *Refinancing purchase money home mortgages.* Perhaps more important to California homeowners is the fact that § 580b not only bars deficiency judgments in favor of vendor-mortgagees, but also "(3) *under a deed of trust, or mortgage, on a dwelling for not more than four families given to a lender to secure repayment of a loan which was in fact used to pay all or a part of the purchase price of that dwelling occupied, entirely or in part, by the purchaser.*" (emphasis supplied). As a result, virtually all California homeowners are protected against deficiency judgments on institutional purchase-money mortgages. In effect, such loans are "nonrecourse;" mortgagors are not personally liable on them.

However, homeowners may have unwittingly lost this 580b protection when, due to falling interest rates, they refinanced their existing purchase money loans. Millions of California homeowners did so during the unusually low interest period during the past decade. Was the new loan "in fact used to pay all or a part of the purchase price"? Should the new loan be treated as a continuation of its predecessor for this purpose? While the California Supreme Court has not addressed these questions, one California Court of Appeals has determined that refinanced mortgages are not "purchase money" and represent a variation on the standard purchase money transaction to which 580b is inapplicable. See Union Bank v. Wendland, 54 Cal.App.3d 393, 126 Cal.Rptr. 549 (1976). For a comprehensive consideration of this potentially important problem, see Carol Burns, Comment, Will Refinancing Your Home Mortgage Risk Your Life Savings?: Refinancing and California Code of Civil Procedure Section 580b, 43 UCLA L.Rev. 2077 (1996).

The California legislation resolved the foregoing issue in favor of the refinancing mortgagor:

> No deficiency judgment shall lie in any event on any loan, refinance, or other credit transaction (collectively a "credit transaction") which is used to refinance a purchase money loan, or subsequent refinances of a purchase money loan, except to the extent that in a credit transaction, the lender or creditor advances new principal (hereafter "new advance") which is not applied to any obligation owed or to be owed under the purchase money loan, or to fees, cost, or related expenses of the credit transaction. Any new credit transaction shall be deemed to be a purchase money loan except as to the principal amount of any new advance.

As a result, a refinancing of a purchase money mortgagor or deed of trust receives protection under section 580(b) except to the extent it is a "cash out" transaction. The foregoing language was effective January 1, 2013. It is partially retroactive because it applies to refinancing of a purchase money loans that existed prior to the effective date. Nevertheless it does not apply to any refinancing that was consummated prior to the January 1, 2013 effective date.

3. *The short-sale and deficiency judgment issues.* During the Great Recession that began in 2008 the short-sale has been a common foreclosure alternative. This practice is considered in detail elsewhere in this casebook. See Chapter Five, Section D4 supra. Instead of conveying the real estate to the mortgagee in lieu of foreclosure, as is the practice in a deed in lieu transaction, the mortgagor, with lender's consent, sells the property to a third person for less than the mortgage balance. The mortgagee then releases its lien from the real estate. The lender finds this type of transaction advantageous because it avoids the expense and delay of foreclosure as well as the possessory obligations (repair and maintenance costs) associated with a deed in lieu of foreclosure. In most states, the mortgagee will have the ability to recover from the mortgagor the difference between the short sale amount and the mortgage obligation. Consequently, prudent mortgagors will negotiate a release of this deficiency.

The California legislature has now protected such mortgagors by enacting section 580(e) of the Code of Civil Procedure which bars deficiencies incident to short sales on all loans (whether purchase money or otherwise) on dwellings containing not more than four dwelling units "in any case in which the trustor or mortgagor sells the dwelling for a sale price less than the remaining amount of the indebtedness outstanding at the time of sale in accordance with the written consent of the holder of the deed of trust or mortgage."

4. *Guarantors and section 580b.* As the foregoing illustrates, most California purchase money mortgagors are protected against personal liability on their mortgage obligations. But suppose a mortgagee insists that the purchase money mortgage obligation be guaranteed by a third party. To what extent are guarantors of such mortgages similarly shielded? The next principal case deals with this issue. We will also consider this issue in the national context later in this section.

TALBOTT V. HUSTWIT

California Court of Appeal, Fourth District, Division 3, 2008
164 Cal.App.4th 148, 78 Cal.Rptr.3d 703

ARONSON, J.

* * *

The Hustwits are guarantors of a loan plaintiff Cynthia D. Talbott, trustee of the Cynthia D. Talbott Separate Property Trust (Talbott), made to Pacific West Investment Trust (Trust). A trust deed against certain

Newport Beach real property secured the Trust's loan obligations. The Trust defaulted and Talbott instituted a nonjudicial foreclosure under the power of sale provision in the trust deed. A trustee sale was held in March 2005. Talbott purchased the property with a $900,000 credit bid, subject to a senior loan. Talbott then sued the Hustwits under their guaranty agreements for the difference between the $900,000 credit bid and the unpaid balance of the loan, $1,288,042.36, plus interest. After a bench trial on stipulated facts, the court issued a written statement of decision awarding Talbott $432,628.40, plus interest. The Hustwits now appeal.

A. *Section 580a Does Not Apply to Guarantors*

California's antideficiency statutes (§§ 580a, 580b, 580d, 726), enacted during the depression, limit or prohibit lenders from obtaining personal judgments against borrowers where the lender's sale of real property security produces proceeds insufficient to cover the amount of the debt. (*See Cornelison v. Kornbluth* (1975) 15 Cal.3d 590, 600–602, 125 Cal.Rptr. 557, 542 P.2d 981.) Section 580a provides in relevant part:

> Whenever a money judgment is sought for the balance due upon an obligation for the payment of which a deed of trust or mortgage with power of sale upon real property or any interest therein was given as security, following the exercise of the power of sale in such deed of trust or mortgage, the plaintiff shall set forth in his or her complaint the entire amount of the indebtedness which was secured by the deed of trust or mortgage at the time of sale, the amount for which the real property or interest therein was sold and the fair market value thereof at the date of sale and the date of that sale. . . .

> Before rendering any judgment the court shall find the fair market value of the real property, or interest therein sold, at the time of the sale. The court may render judgment for not more than the amount by which the entire amount of the indebtedness due at the time of sale exceeded the fair market value of the real property or interest therein sold at the time of sale with interest thereon from the date of the sale. . . .

The Hustwits contend section 580a applied to them, and the trial court erred in failing to consider evidence that the property's fair market value exceeded the total amount owed Talbott. We disagree.

The Hustwits were held liable as guarantors of the Trust's loan obligation to Talbott. A guarantor is one who promises to answer for the debt or perform the obligation of another when the person ultimately liable fails to pay or perform. (Civ.Code, § 2787.) "A contract of guaranty gives rise to a separate and independent obligation from that which binds the principal debtor." (*Security-First Nat. Bank v. Chapman* (1940) 41 Cal.App.2d 219, 221, 106 P.2d 431.) "Since section 580a has to do solely with actions for recovery of deficiency judgments on the principal obligation [it] has no application to an action against a guarantor [citations]. . . ." (*Mariners Sav. & Loan Assn. v. Neil* (1971) 22 Cal.App.3d 232, 234, 99 Cal.Rptr. 238 (*Mariners*); *Bank of America etc. Assn. v. Hunter* (1937) 8 Cal.2d 592, 67 P.2d 99; *Loeb v. Christie* (1936) 6 Cal.2d 416, 57 P.2d 1303; see also *Dreyfuss v. Union Bank of California* (2000) 24 Cal.4th 400, 407, 101 Cal.Rptr.2d 29, 11 P.3d 383 ["a creditor's resort to any and all security on a debt does not implicate the antideficiency provisions"].)

The Hustwits do not address the case law holding that guarantors cannot claim the protection of section 580a, and concede they were unable to discover any case law to the contrary. Instead, they cite two cases which recognize a general state policy to prevent secured creditors from obtaining excess recoveries. (See *Bank of Hemet v. United States* (9th Cir.1981) 643 F.2d 661; *Walter E. Heller Western, Inc. v. Bloxham* (1985) 176 Cal.App.3d 266, 221 Cal.Rptr. 425.) Neither of these cases concern guarantors, and the general policy statements contained in them does not persuade us to abandon Supreme Court precedent.[2] Accordingly, we conclude section 580a has no application to guarantors.

B. The Hustwits Are True Guarantors

Although case law is uniform in holding section 580a does not apply to guarantors, the question remains whether the Hustwits were true guarantors. Courts have recognized a distinction between true, independent contracts of guaranty and guaranties executed by the primary obligor. (*Mariners, supra*, 22 Cal.App.3d at p. 234, 99 Cal.Rptr. 238.) "It is well established that where a principal obligor purports to take on additional liability as a guarantor, nothing is added to the primary obligation. [Citations omitted.] The correct inquiry set out by the authority is whether the purported debtor is anything other than an instrumentality used by the individuals who guaranteed the debtor's obligation, and whether such instrumentality actually removed the individuals from their status and obligations as debtors." (*Torrey Pines Bank v. Hoffman* (1991) 231 Cal.App.3d 308, 319–320, 282 Cal.Rptr. 354 (*Torrey Pines*); *Cadle Co. II v. Harvey* (2000) 83 Cal.App.4th 927, 933, 100 Cal.Rptr.2d 150.)

In *Torrey Pines*, a bank sued a husband and wife on personal guaranties signed in connection with a construction loan the bank made to a revocable living trust in which the defendants were the trustors, trustees, and primary beneficiaries. The court determined the structure of the trust

---

[2] As the concurrence recognizes, the case law supporting liability here has remained unchanged for over 60 years. We can thus safely assume virtually all of the loan guaranties now in existence were made in reliance upon the current state of the law. Although we share our concurring colleague's observations and concerns, we believe any change in the law affecting liability of guarantors for deficiency judgments should originate with the Legislature, which is better able to measure the impact of altering commercial arrangements by into account the views of experts and affected parties.

made any distinction between the guarantors and the debtor insignificant, thus barring the bank from recovering on the guaranties. Specifically, the court noted that under the trust law at the time, trustees were personally liable on contracts entered into on behalf of their trusts. Accordingly, the trust was deemed a " 'mere instrumentality.' " (*Torrey Pines, supra*, 231 Cal.App.3d at p. 321, 282 Cal.Rptr. 354.) The court, however, did not enunciate a blanket rule applying to all living trusts, clarifying: "We emphasize that our holding is necessarily limited to these facts. While it would be possible in a living trust to create a greater degree of separation of interest between settlor, trustee, and beneficiary (e.g., by the use of a separate trustee), this particular trust device did not accomplish enough division between these interests to enable us to say that the purpose of the antideficiency law would be served by enforcing these personal guaranties as 'true' guaranties, as opposed to 'purported' guaranties." (*Id.* at p. 323, 282 Cal.Rptr. 354.)

Similarly, *Riddle v. Lushing* (1962) 203 Cal.App.2d 831, 836, 21 Cal.Rptr. 902, involved a situation in which partners had individually guaranteed a partnership note. Because the partners were already jointly and severally liable on the note as general partners, the court held the guaranty did not change the partners' status as principal obligors. (*Ibid.*)

In contrast, *Mariners, supra*, 22 Cal.App.3d 232, 99 Cal.Rptr. 238, involved a situation where the wife took out a loan secured by her separately-owned real property, and the husband signed a personal guaranty. The court recognized that in many ways a husband and wife are partners, but nonetheless held the husband became a true guarantor because he would not have been personally liable for the loan made to the wife absent the guaranty. (*Id.* at p. 235, 99 Cal.Rptr. 238.)

Here, the trust arrangement provided the Hustwits a significantly greater degree of separation than that in *Torrey Pines*. Although the Hustwits are the settlors of the Trust, they are secondary, not primary, beneficiaries. More importantly, the Hustwits are not trustees of the Trust; instead, the Hustwits used a limited liability company as trustee, thus limiting their personal liability for the Trust's obligations. The Hustwits became true guarantors because the Hustwits' trust arrangement "actually removed the[m] from their status and obligations as debtors." (*Torrey Pines, supra*, 231 Cal.App.3d at p. 320, 282 Cal.Rptr. 354.) Accordingly, we conclude the trial court did not err in holding the protections of section 580a inapplicable in the present case.

The judgment is affirmed. * * *

SILLS, P.J., Concurring.

I agree with the reasoning and result of the majority opinion, because both are compelled by Supreme Court authority. However, I write separately to voice concerns about the potential danger for the easy circumvention of the protections offered consumers under California's statutory antideficiency legislation by the use of loan guarantees. (See Code Civ., Proc., §§ 580a, 580b, 580d & 726.)[1] The current "subprime mortgage crisis" at a time of generally declining real estate prices illustrates the public importance of the issue.[2]

* * *

As the majority opinion correctly decides—well, correctly under the current state of the case law—the Hustwits simply outwitted themselves. They have to take the rough with the smooth, and, more specifically, cannot avail themselves of the protections of limited liability corporations and at the same time claim an obligation is really theirs at the same time. Sometimes piercing the veil can actually help you.

* * *

Given [the contemporary sharp decline in real estate values] there is a real danger that, under the effect of current case law, lenders will seize the non-coverage of guarantors as a loophole to circumvent antideficiency protections otherwise afforded homeowners: Just get the parents or other relatives to guarantee the loan. Since the guarantee obligation has been held "independent" of the loan, the lender can obtain a deficiency judgment under deflationary conditions.

The Legislature, of course, can readily cure this danger (as it can cure any non-Constitutionally created anomaly in the law with the right drafting). * * *

NOTES

1. *Jurisdictional split.* A great deal of case law exists concerning the applicability of antideficiency legislation to guarantors. The outcomes of these cases are often very different and tend to depend on the exact language of the statute or the court's determination of the legislative intent. However, courts in the majority of cases deny antideficiency protection to guarantors. See, e.g., Horizon Bank, N.A. v. Marshalls Point Retreat LLC, 908 N.W.2d 797 (Wis.

---

[1] As explained by the California Supreme Court in *Cornelison v. Kornbluth* (1975) 15 Cal.3d 590, 600, 125 Cal.Rptr. 557, 542 P.2d 981, antideficiency was a Depression-era response to the potential for "double recovery" by lenders. At a time of declining property prices, lenders would be able to purchase the real property securing the debt at a price below normal market value, and then hold the debtor liable "for a large deficiency." Later, the incentive on the part of the lender to bid too low was removed by creating a right of redemption (bid too low and the debtor could get the property back for that amount!) and the right of redemption was extended to both private and judicial foreclosures. The point being: If a lender wanted a deficiency judgment, the lender would be subject to statutory redemption rights. (*Id.* at pp. 601–602, 125 Cal.Rptr. 557, 542 P.2d 981.)

[2] See Posting of Gary Becker to The Becker-Posner Blog, http://www.becker-posner-blog.com/archives/2007/12 (Dec. 23, 2007) ["The vast majority of economists, including me, were surprised by the extent of the subprime mortgage crisis. This needs to be recognized when evaluating the numerous proposals about how to prevent the next housing crisis, and also about how to help those who are in danger of having their homes foreclosed."] (as of June 9, 2008).

2018); LSREF2 Clover Property 4, LLC v. Festival Retail Fund 1, LP, 3 Cal. App. 5th 1067 (2016); Inland Mortgage Capital Corporation v. Chivas Retail Partners, LLC, 740 F.3d 1146 (7th Cir. 2014); JP Morgan Chase Bank, N.A. v. Winthrop Properties, LLC, 94 A.3d 622 (Conn. 2014). Courts that hold against guarantors frequently reason that the guarantor is not liable on the note and mortgage but on the separate guaranty contract.

However, other courts hold that a guarantor is protected by the antideficiency statute for the same reason that the borrower is protected—to eliminate the incentive for a foreclosing lender to bid a low price at the foreclosure and then sue for a deficiency. Courts are especially likely to protect the guarantor if it is in essence the borrower, such as a partner in a partnership that borrows money. See, e.g., High Point Bank and Trust Co. v. Highmark Properties, LLC, 776 S.E.2d 838 (N.C. 2015); First-Citizens Bank & Trust Co. v. Cornerstone Homes & Development, LLC, 314 P.3d 420 (Wash. Ct. App. 2013).

2. *Actions for fraud or waste and antideficiency legislation.* To what extent, if any, should antideficiency legislation bar mortgagee actions against mortgagors based on fraudulently induced loan transactions? Suppose, for example, that in an application to a Bank for financing to acquire a $600,000 single family house, the borrower falsely represented that he or she owned over $300,000 in stocks and bonds. Indeed, the borrower submitted falsified statements from a brokerage house. The Bank then made $450,000 loan and took back a deed of trust on the house. Two years later, after a steep decline in real estate values, the loan went into default, the Bank foreclosed, and the property sold at the foreclosure sale for $375,000. Suppose now the Bank files an action for fraud against the borrower to recover $75,000 on the theory that, but for the fraudulent misrepresentation as to his or her net worth, Bank would not have made the loan and would not have suffered the foreclosure deficiency.

Most courts have been reluctant to allow antideficiency statutes to shield a borrower from a recovery based on fraud and have reasoned that "a suit for fraud is a completely separate remedy from a suit on a promissory note secured by a deed of trust. This [fraud] action is not a suit on a note. * * * It would be wrong to apply a bar of recovery against plaintiff based on a transaction that was fraudulently induced. To do so would be to condone the fraud." Manson v. Reed, 186 Cal.App.3d 1493, 231 Cal.Rptr. 446 (1986). On the other hand, at least one decision cast doubt on the viability of such fraud actions. See First Fed. Sav. & Loan Ass'n of Phoenix v. Lehman, 159 Cal.App.3d 537, 205 Cal.Rptr. 600 (1984) (fraud action barred by antideficiency statutes because there was no causal relationship between the alleged fraud and the damages sustained).

In response to the foregoing apparent uncertainty, California enacted legislation specifying that, notwithstanding antideficiency statutes, a lender "may bring an action for the recovery of damages, including exemplary damages not to exceed 50 percent of actual damages, against a borrower" based on fraud when the latter's conduct induced the making of the loan. West's Ann.Cal.Fin.Code §§ 1301, 7459, 7460, 15102. The legislation exempts single-family residential real property "when the property is actually occupied by the borrower as represented to the lender in order to obtain the loan and the loan is for $150,000 or less * * *." Id. The legislature later added language to section 726 of the Code of Civil Procedure that not only restates this legislation, but also makes it clear that it covers "any person authorized by this state to make or arrange loans or any successor in interest thereto, that originates, acquires, or purchases * * * any loan secured * * * by a mortgage or deed of trust on real property." West's Ann.Cal.Code Civ.Pro. §§ 726(f), (g). To what extent does this legislation clarify the problem?

Courts employ similar reasoning when a borrower commits bad faith waste on the property, which "requires evidence of the reckless, intentional or malicious destruction, misuse, alteration or neglect of real property." Bowen v. Yniguez, 2005 WL 1324773 (Cal. Ct. App.) (not officially published). The court distinguished bad faith waste from waste resulting from an owner's financial inability to maintain the property: "[A] purchaser caught in such circumstances may be compelled in the normal course of events to forego the general maintenance and repair of the property in order to keep up his payments on the mortgage debt. If he eventually defaults and loses the property, to hold him subject to additional liability for waste would seem to run counter to the purpose of [the anti-deficiency statute] and to permit the purchase money lender to obtain what is in effect a deficiency judgment."

Is this distinction between bad faith waste and waste due to financial straits legally valid? Does it matter to the lender why the property is in a deteriorated physical condition? Perhaps the facts of Bowen will cast some light on this issue. The borrower bought an inn that he used as a "party house." "[S]ignicant parts of the establishment had been removed and put in the yard", the back yard looked like "a disaster had hit," and the kitchen floor had a "gaping hole." That's just the beginning of the list of damages.

3. *Antideficiency statutes and the "full credit bid" problem.* As the previous note describes, antideficiency legislation does not bar most actions against the mortgagor for fraud or bad faith waste. See Dale A. Whitman, The Risks of a Full Credit Bid, 2 ACREL News 14 (2017); Gary L. Barr, Wasteland: The Antideficiency Rule in Foreclosures Does Not Apply in Cases of Bad Faith Waste, 30 L.A. Law 20 (2008). But this is not the end of the story. A mortgagee may be barred from recovery if it purchases the mortgaged real estate at the foreclosure sale by making a "full credit bid"—one that is an amount equals or exceeds the mortgage obligation. The theory is that, when the mortgagee purchases in such a fashion, the mortgage obligation is satisfied and no further claim against the mortgagor is justified.

But should this be an iron-clad rule? Consider the language of a California Supreme Court opinion in which a mortgagee that purchased at the foreclosure sale by a full credit bid later sued not the mortgagor, but a real estate broker, an appraiser, and a title insurance company on the theory that they had conspired to defraud the lender by submitting inflated appraisals and other false information about the properties and borrowers when the mortgagee made the loan::

As with any purchaser at a foreclosure sale, by making a successful full credit bid or bid in any amount, the lender is making a generally irrevocable offer to purchase the property for that amount. The lender, perhaps more than a third party purchaser with fewer resources with which to gain insight into the property's value, generally bears the burden and risk of making an informed bid.

It does not follow, however, that being intentionally and materially misled by its own fiduciaries or agents as to the value of the property prior to even making the loan is within the realm of that risk. * * * Most lenders, such as [plaintiff] in this case, are corporate entities, and rely on their agents to provide them material information. Here, [plaintiff] did obtain appraisals, and attempted to make informed loan decisions. It alleges, however, that its appraiser, Rothwell, in conspiracy with defendants, fraudulently misrepresented the nature of the properties and the existence and qualifications of the buyers, and that it did not discover the fraud until after it acquired title to the properties. The full credit bid rule was not intended to immunize wrongdoers from the consequences of their fraudulent acts.

We conclude therefore that in order to establish reliance, [plaintiff] need only demonstrate that its full credit bids were a proximate result of defendants' fraud, and that in the absence of such fraud it would not, in all reasonable probability, have made the bids. * * * As for the question of whether this reliance was justifiable, a generally fact-based inquiry, we reiterate that "Negligence on the part of the plaintiff in failing to discover the falsity of a statement is no defense when the misrepresentation was intentional rather than negligent." * * * "Nor is a plaintiff held to the standard of precaution or of minimum knowledge of a hypothetical, reasonable man." * * * "If the conduct of the plaintiff in the light of his own intelligence and information was manifestly unreasonable, however, he will be denied a recovery." * * *

Thus, to the extent [plaintiff's] full credit bids were proximately caused by defendants' fraudulent misrepresentations, and this reliance without independent or additional inquiry was either appropriate given the context of the relationship or was not otherwise manifestly unreasonable, Alliance's bids cannot be deemed an admission of the properties' value. * * * Hence, the full credit bid rule would not apply.

In the alternative, to the extent [plaintiff's] full credit bids were not proximately caused by defendants' fraudulent misrepresentations, or its reliance without independent or additional inquiry was either inappropriate given the context of the relationship or was otherwise manifestly unreasonable, the full credit bid rule applies, and [plaintiff's] bid would then constitute an irrevocable offer to purchase the property for that amount. * * * Hence, under these circumstances, [plaintiff] would not be entitled to recover the difference between its bid, which by definition is "an amount equal to the unpaid principal and interest of the mortgage debt, together with the costs, fees and other expenses of the foreclosure," and the actual value of the property. (Cornelison, supra, 15 Cal.3d at p. 606, fn. 10, 125 Cal.Rptr. 557, 542 P.2d 981.) It would, however, still be able to recover any other damages flowing from the defendants' fraud.

Alliance Mortg. Co. v. Rothwell, 10 Cal.4th 1226, 44 Cal.Rptr.2d 352, 359–65, 900 P.2d 601, 608–14 (1995). What would those other damages be? See also Bank of America, NA v. First American Title Ins. Co., 878 N.W.2d 816 (Mich. 2016) (mortgagee could recover from title company and closing agents for fraud though mortgagee made full credit bid at its foreclosure sale). For a case where a mortgagee making a full credit bid was held to be unjustified in relying on allegedly fraudulent appraisal issued before the consummation of the loan, see Michelson v. Camp, 72 Cal.App.4th 955, 85 Cal.Rptr.2d 539 (1999).

However, the result may be different if the fraud occurred at the time of the foreclosure bid, rather than at the time of the loan. In Fed. Deposit Ins. Corp. v. Chicago Title Ins. Co., 2015 WL 5276346 (N.D. Ill.), a federal district court upheld the traditional rule that a full credit bid represents conclusive proof of the property's value. The court stated:

> [A]pplying the credit bid rule to limit recovery against third parties makes sound policy sense: absent proof of fraud or negligence that caused the lender to submit a credit bid that was too high, "[t]o allow the [lender], after effectively cutting off or discouraging lower bidders, to take the property—and then establish that it was worth less than the bid—encourages fraud, creates uncertainty as to the [borrower]'s rights, and most unfairly deprives the sale of whatever leaven comes from other bidders.

One-Action Rule

Like the antideficiency laws, the one-action rule is designed to offer some relief to mortgagors and other owners of mortgaged land. One-action rules and antideficiency laws often operate together, as you will see in *Mid Kansas*, infra.

NELSON, WHITMAN, BURKHART & FREYERMUTH, REAL ESTATE FINANCE LAW
710–711, 722–724 (6th ed.2015)*

This rule means, in general, that in the event of a default, the mortgagee's sole remedy is a foreclosure action and that any deficiency claim must be sought in that proceeding. The purpose of this rule is two-fold. One is to protect the mortgagor against a multiplicity of actions when the separate actions, though theoretically distinct, are so closely connected that normally they can and should be decided in one suit. The other is to compel a creditor who has taken a mortgage on land to exhaust the security before attempting to reach any unmortgaged property to satisfy the claim. The mortgagee * * * cannot disregard the security even if it wishes to do so, and sue upon the note or debt. Nor may the requirement of the statute be waived by the mortgagor through a provision in the mortgage. * * *

Procedurally, a mortgagor may use the rule both defensively and as a sanction. If the mortgagor successfully raises the rule as an affirmative defence, the mortgagee will be required to exhaust the security before obtaining a deficiency judgment. On the other hand, suppose the mortgagor does not raise the rule in the personal action. As the California Supreme Court has stated, the mortgagor "may still invoke it as a sanction against the mortgagee on the basis that the latter by not foreclosing on the security in the action brought to enforce the debt, has made an election of remedies and waived the security."

* * *

One of the most (in)famous cases involving a one-action rule is Security Pacific National Bank v. Wozab, 51 Cal.3d 991, 275 Cal.Rptr. 201, 800 P.2d 557 (1990). The California one-action rules provides that "[t]here can be but one form of action for the recovery of any debt . . . ." Cal. Civ. Proc. Code § 726(a). The Wozabs owed the mortgagee over $1,000,000. The debt was secured by the Wozabs' home. When the mortgagee became concerned that the Wozabs were about to file for bankruptcy, it took approximately $2,800 as a setoff from a deposit account that the Wozabs had with the mortgagee.

Based on the one-action rule, the Wozabs then contended that the setoff caused the mortgagee to lose its security interest in their residence. After considering this claim, the mortgagee reconveyed the deed of trust to the Wozabs but sought to recover the unpaid debt of approximately $976,000 from them. The Wozabs then asserted that the setoff not only resulted in a waiver of the security, but also in a destruction of the underlying debt as well.

---

*   Reprinted with permission of LEG, Inc. d/b/a West Academic.

The Supreme Court disagreed, holding that the appropriate sanction was loss of the security only. In reaching this result, the court stressed that § 726(a) not only embodies a one-action rule, but a "security first" principle as well. The former rule was not violated in *Wozab* because a setoff was not deemed an "action," the latter being defined by the Civil Procedure Code as "an ordinary proceeding in a court of justice by which one party prosecutes another for the declaration, enforcement, or protection of a right, the redress or prevention of a wrong, or the punishment of a public offense." Presumably, had the setoff represented an "action," destruction of the underlying debt would have been an appropriate sanction. Rather, the court opted to find a violation of the security first concept. In so doing, it did not completely rule out loss of the underlying debt for a "security first" violation, but clearly was inclined to view such a sanction as acceptable only in extreme cases. According to the court:

> Allowing the bank to sue on the debt does not violate the two fundamental purposes of section 726: (1) preventing a multiplicity of lawsuits against the debtor, and (2) requiring exhaustion of the security before a resort to the debtor's unencumbered assets. The present action is the only lawsuit against the Wozabs, and they freely chose not to have the bank foreclose the security interest.

> Finally, the result advocated by the Wozabs—allowing them to evade their debt almost in its entirety—would be a gross injustice to the bank and a corresponding windfall to the Wozabs. * * *

> The result we reach is also fair and workable in future cases. Because a debtor can object to an improper setoff and require the bank to return it and proceed first against the security interest, a bank cannot *unilaterally* waive its security interest by taking an improper setoff and then proceeding directly on the underlying debt. The debtor retains the right to require the bank to return the improper setoff and proceed against the security interest before bank attempts to recover on the underlying debt. Of course, if the bank refused the debtor's demand and retained the setoff funds, the security-first rule * * * would preclude the bank from foreclosing the security interest or proceeding on the underlying debt. Conversely, if the bank complied with the debtor's demand to return the funds and to proceed first against the security, the debtor could not thereafter assert the bank had waived its security interest. [Id. at 51 Cal.3d 991, 1005, 275 Cal.Rptr. 201, 210, 800 P.2d 557, 566.]

You should note, however, what a potential trap the one-action rule is for lenders. The trial court and intermediate appellate court both held for the Wozabs! The supreme court split 4–3. The lesson here is to be extremely careful!

NOTES

1.   *Letters of credit and section 726(a).* "Standby letters of credit" are increasingly used to partially secure obligations where the prime security is a mortgage or deed of trust on real estate. Professors White and Summers describe this device as follows:

> A standby letter of credit * * * acts as a "backup" against [debtor] defaults on obligations of all kinds. For example, it might be issued to a bank that financed a real estate transaction of the [debtor]. It might provide for payment of certain amounts on presentation of a document which stated that the [debtor] had defaulted and that a specific amount was owing to the beneficiary.

James J. White and Robert S. Summers, Uniform Commercial Code 703 (4th ed.1995). Such letters of credit are commonly issued by banks in favor of a mortgagee. The premium for its issuance is paid by the mortgagor-debtor. Thus, for example, suppose mortgagee lends $10,000,000 to mortgagor, the obligation being secured by a deed of trust on mortgagor's office building. As additional security mortgagee demands a $2,000,000 letter of credit from a bank acceptable to mortgagee. Thus, the mortgagee can look to the letter of credit as well as the real estate as security for the obligation. Note that the letter of credit is governed by something called the "independence principle." This means that the obligation of the issuer of the letter of credit to the mortgagee is independent of the mortgagee's performance under its agreement with mortgagor. In other words, the issuer normally must pay upon mortgagee presenting the appropriate written demand even though mortgagor may be justified in not performing its obligation to mortgagee. Id.

Note further how the obligation of the issuer of the letter of credit differs from that of a guarantor. "In the typical secondary guarantee, the guarantor can defend against a claim by the beneficiary [Lender] by showing that its customer [Debtor] had a justifiable basis for failing to perform." Id. at 704. Thus, a typical mortgagee would generally prefer to have their mortgagor's obligation backed up by a standby letter of credit than a guarantee.

To what extent does the presence of a letter of credit together with a deed of trust on real estate as security for an obligation raise section 726(a) problems? In 1994 California enacted legislation which provides that when an obligation is secured by both a deed of trust and a letter of credit, a draw against the letter of credit does not violate the one action rule. See West's Ann.Cal.Civ.Code § 580.5. See also 1111 Prospect Partners, L.P. v. Superior Court, 45 Cal.Rptr.2d 338 (App.1995) (a draw against a letter of credit followed by a nonjudicial foreclosure of the deed of trust is not a violation of section 726(a); thus pre-1994 law was held to be consistent with section 580.5).

2. *CERCLA.* As we already know, some one-action rules give the mortgagor the right to force foreclosure of the mortgaged real estate as a condition precedent to seeking a deficiency judgment. However, until recently, foreclosure and purchase by a mortgagee of contaminated real estate created the concern that it would become liable for massive cleanup costs under CERCLA. This concern was allayed in California by the enactment of an amendment to section 726 that permits the mortgagee, subject to certain limitations, to waive its security interest in "environmentally impaired" real estate and to proceed against the mortgagor as an unsecured creditor. This election is available to the mortgagee if (1) the costs of cleanup exceed 25% of the fair market value of the real estate (ignoring the impact of the contamination on that value) and (2) the mortgagor had actual knowledge of the contamination when the obligation was created or (3) the mortgagor caused, contributed to, or permitted it to occur. See West's Ann.Cal.Code Civ.Proc. § 726.5. Consequently, a mortgagee can often obtain a judgment on the underlying debt while avoiding any potential CERCLA liability that could accrue from taking possession of contaminated real estate incident to foreclosure.

3. *The Nevada approach to the one-action rule.* As the foregoing notes illustrate, both California courts and its legislature have taken an ad hoc approach to defining what is not an "action" for purposes of § 726(a). Nevada represents an interesting contrast. While the core of Nevada's one-action rule has its origin in California's § 726(a), the Nevada legislature has taken a more global approach in specifically identifying sixteen acts that do not constitute an action:

As used in this section, an "action" does not include any act or proceeding:

(a) To appoint a receiver for, or obtain possession of, any real or personal collateral for the debt or as provided in NRS 32.015.

(b) To enforce a security interest in, or the assignment of, any rents, issues, profits or other income of any real or personal property.

(c) To enforce a mortgage or other lien upon any real or personal collateral located outside of the State which does not, except as required under the laws of that jurisdiction, result in a personal judgment against the debtor.

(d) For the recovery of damages arising from the commission of a tort, including a recovery under NRS 40.750, or the recovery of any declaratory or equitable relief.

(e) For the exercise of a power of sale pursuant to NRS 107.080.

(f) For the exercise of any right or remedy authorized by chapter 104 of NRS or by the Uniform Commercial Code as enacted in any other state.

(g) For the exercise of any right to set off, or to enforce a pledge in, a deposit account pursuant to a written agreement or pledge.

(h) To draw under a letter of credit.

(i) To enforce an agreement with a surety or guarantor if enforcement of the mortgage or other lien has been automatically stayed pursuant to 11 U.S.C. § 362 or pursuant to an order of a federal bankruptcy court under any other provision of the United States Bankruptcy Code for not less than 120 days following the mailing of notice to the surety or guarantor pursuant to subsection 1 of NRS 107.095.

(j) To collect any debt, or enforce any right, secured by a mortgage or other lien on real property if the property has been sold to a person other than the creditor to satisfy, in whole or in part, a debt or other right secured by a senior mortgage or other senior lien on the property.

(k) Relating to any proceeding in bankruptcy, including the filing of a proof of claim, seeking relief from an automatic stay and any other action to determine the amount or validity of a debt.

(*l*) For filing a claim pursuant to chapter 147 of NRS or to enforce such a claim which has been disallowed.

(m) Which does not include the collection of the debt or realization of the collateral securing the debt.

(n) Pursuant to NRS 40.507 or 40.508.

(*o*) Pursuant to an agreement entered into pursuant to NRS 361.7311 between an owner of the property and the assignee of a tax lien against the property, or an action which is authorized by NRS 361.733.

(p) Which is exempted from the provisions of this section by specific statute.

(q) To recover costs of suit, costs and expenses of sale, attorneys' fees and other incidental relief in connection with any action authorized by this subsection.

Nev.Rev.Stat. § 40.430(6). The fact that Nevada's legislature found it necessary to create the foregoing "laundry list" of exceptions raises the question whether lawyers, rather than mortgagors, are the primary beneficiaries of the one-action rule. For an example of Nevada courts applying the rule in its traditional setting, see Bonicamp v. Vazquez, 120 Nev. 377, 91 P.3d 584 (2004) (when a debt incurred in Colorado was secured by a deed of trust on Nevada real estate, the mortgagee was barred from foreclosing on the deed of trust after it had previously obtained a default judgment on the debt against the debtor in Colorado).

The following case illustrates the interaction of antideficiency statutes with an election of remedies statute.

MID KANSAS FEDERAL SAVINGS AND LOAN ASSOCIATION V. DYNAMIC DEVELOPMENT CORPORATION

Supreme Court of Arizona, 1991
167 Ariz. 122, 804 P.2d 1310

FELDMAN, VICE CHIEF JUSTICE.

A construction lender held notes secured by first and second deeds of trust on a residential developer's property. The lender acquired title to the property at a trustee's sale on the second trust deed and thereafter brought an action against the developer for the balance due on the first notes. The court of appeals held that the lender was precluded from doing so under A.R.S. § 33–814(G) and the rationale of our decision in *Baker v. Gardner*, 160 Ariz. 98, 770 P.2d 766 (1988).

We must determine whether the anti-deficiency statutes apply to a residential developer and whether a lender may recover the balance owing on the first notes after it has acquired title to the property at the foreclosure sale of its second deed of trust. Rule 23, Ariz.R.Civ.App.P., 17B A.R.S. We have jurisdiction under Ariz. Const. art. 6, § 5(3) and A.R.S. § 12–120.24.

FACTS AND PROCEDURAL HISTORY

A. *Factual Background*

Dynamic Development Corporation (Dynamic) is a developer that builds and sells residential and commercial property. In May 1985, Dynamic secured financing from Mid Kansas Federal Savings and Loan Association (Mid Kansas) for the construction of ten "spec" homes on lots Dynamic owned in a Prescott subdivision. The total loan, amounting to $803,250, was disbursed in the form of ten separate loans, each evidenced by a separate note and secured by a separate deed of trust on a single unimproved lot. Unable to complete construction with the amounts financed under the first notes, Dynamic obtained an additional $150,000 loan from Mid Kansas in January of 1986. This loan was evidenced by a single promissory note and a blanket deed of trust on the seven lots remaining unsold.

The first and second notes came due in the summer of 1986. Two more lots were sold and released from the liens. In the fall of 1986, Mid Kansas notified Dynamic that the five remaining properties would be sold at a trustee's sale if the total debt on the first and second notes was not paid. Dynamic was unable to pay the total balance due, but did sell one more lot prior to the trustee's sale and applied the proceeds to the second note.

Mid Kansas noticed a trustee's sale on the four remaining properties, each of which was by then improved by a substantially finished residence. At the time of the trustee's sale, Dynamic owed Mid Kansas approximately $102,000 on the second note and $425,000 on the four first notes. Originally, the sales on the first deeds were scheduled for the day after the sale on the second deed. On January 20, 1987, the second-position blanket deed of trust was foreclosed by the sale of the four parcels. Mid Kansas purchased the property with a credit bid of the balance owed on the second note. The four first-position sales were postponed and ultimately never held. Having thus acquired title to the property, Mid Kansas now seeks to waive the security of the first liens and sue for the balance due on the first notes.

B. Procedural Background

Mid Kansas's amended complaint stated causes of action for recovery of the balance due under each of the four promissory notes. Mid Kansas moved for partial summary judgment on the four debt claims. The trial court granted the motion and entered judgment for Mid Kansas pursuant to Rule 54(b), Ariz.R.Civ.P., 16 A.R.S.

The court found that Dynamic was in default on the four construction notes in the principal amount of $425,250 plus interest at thirteen percent. The court rejected Dynamic's claim that Mid Kansas had "artificially created a deficiency and now seeks a deficiency judgment against the maker of the notes." The court determined that

> under the holding of *Southwest Savings and Loan v. Ludi*, 122 Ariz. 226 [594 P.2d 92 (1979)], Plaintiff can maintain an action on these notes notwithstanding there was a Trustee's Sale instituted by Plaintiff on a separate deed of trust involving the [same] subject properties.

On appeal, Dynamic argued that Mid Kansas was prohibited from recovering on the promissory notes by the Arizona anti-deficiency statute, A.R.S. § 33–814(G). After the release of our opinion in *Baker*, Dynamic filed a supplemental brief asserting that *Ludi* could no longer be read to permit a residential mortgage holder to waive its security and sue on the note. *See Southwest Sav. & Loan Ass'n v. Ludi*, 122 Ariz. 226, 594 P.2d 92 (1979). Dynamic argued that *Baker* prohibited any attempt to waive the security and sue on the note as a disguised action for deficiency. Therefore, Mid Kansas could not both foreclose the second deed by power of sale and elect to sue Dynamic on the first notes covering the same property.

The court of appeals reversed and remanded the case for entry of judgment for Dynamic. *Mid Kansas Fed. Sav. & Loan Ass'n v. Dynamic Dev. Corp.*, 163 Ariz. 233, 787 P.2d 132 (Ct.App.1989). The court held that under *Baker*, Mid Kansas's attempt to waive the security and sue on the debt was an action for a deficiency, barred after a trustee's sale under § 33–814(G).

* * *

Mid Kansas petitioned for review in this court, presenting the following issues for our consideration:

1.   Whether commercial developers of residential property who borrow for business purposes are entitled to the benefit of Arizona's consumer anti-deficiency statutes, A.R.S. §§ 33–729(A) and 33–814(G).

2.   Whether Arizona's anti-deficiency statutes apply when the encumbered properties are not actually used as residences.

3.   Whether a lender's election to waive its security and sue upon a construction loan note secured by a deed of trust constitutes an action for a deficiency prohibited by Arizona's anti-deficiency statutes, A.R.S. §§ 33–729(A) and 33–814(G).

DISCUSSION

A.   The Applicability of the Anti-deficiency Statutes

Arizona has two anti-deficiency statutes. A.R.S. § 33–729(A) applies to purchase money mortgages and purchase money deeds of trust foreclosed judicially pursuant to the authority of A.R.S. § 33–807(A). A.R.S. § 33–814(G) applies to deeds of trust that are foreclosed by trustee's sale, regardless of whether they represent purchase money obligations. Both sections prohibit a deficiency judgment after sale of a parcel of "property of two and one-half acres or less which is limited to and utilized for either a single one-family or single two-family dwelling." A.R.S. §§ 33–729(A), 33–814(G).

Arizona also has an election of remedies statute within the general law applicable to mortgages. Under A.R.S. § 33–722, a mortgagee can foreclose and seek a deficiency judgment or can sue on the note and then execute on the resultant judgment but cannot bring both actions simultaneously. *See* Washburn, *The Judicial and Legislative Response to Price Inadequacy in Mortgage Foreclosure Sales,* 53 S.Cal.L.Rev. 843, 928 (1980). The election statute is intended to protect the debtor from multiple suits and at the same time grant the creditor the benefit of the security.

The election statute alters the traditional common law rule that a holder of a note secured by a mortgage has the right to sue on the note alone, to foreclose on the property, or to pursue both remedies at once (although there may be only one recovery on the debt). *See Paramount Ins., Inc. v. Rayson & Smitley,* 86 Nev. 644, 472 P.2d 530, 533 (1970).[2] However, the reach of the statute, as applied to most mortgages, is quite limited. In *Smith v. Mangels,* 73 Ariz. 203, 207, 240 P.2d 168, 170 (1952), this court

---

[2]   Under the statutory scheme, the provisions within the law of mortgages (chapter 6 of A.R.S. Title 33) are not applicable to deeds of trust unless the deed of trust is judicially foreclosed as a mortgage pursuant to A.R.S. § 33–807(A). *See* A.R.S. § 33–805. The election statute is within chapter 6. Therefore, the election statute is not applicable to deeds of trust foreclosed by trustee's sale, and there is no analogous statute within the law applicable to deeds of trust. Dynamic does not contend that the lender lost its common law right to elect among its remedies. *See generally Universal Inv. Co. v. Sahara Motor Inn, Inc.,* 127 Ariz. 213, 215, 619 P.2d 485, 487 (Ct.App.1980) (deed of trust statute does not mandate foreclosure by trustee's sale, but allows option to foreclose as mortgage or bring action on debt).

held the election statute does not preclude a subsequent foreclosure action after judgment on the debt, as is the case in some other states. *See, e.g.,* Neb.Rev.Stat. §§ 25–2140 and 25–2143 (1989); N.Y. Real Prop.Acts.Law § 1301 (McKinney 1979); S.D. Codified Laws Ann. §§ 21–47–5 and 21–47– 6 (1987).

In *Baker,* we held the election statute was limited by the subsequently enacted purchase money mortgage anti-deficiency statute, A.R.S. § 33– 729(A), which barred the lender from waiving the security and suing on the debt. 160 Ariz. at 104, 770 P.2d at 772. In so holding, we joined the courts of California and North Carolina in finding that such an election is inconsistent with the anti-deficiency statutes, which limit the lender to recovery from the land itself. *Id.*

Baker held that the lender should not be allowed to circumvent the anti-deficiency statute by electing to sue the debtor on the note, thereby realizing any difference between the value of the real property and the amount owed on the debt. As our supplemental opinion pointed out, *Baker's* holding applies whenever the anti-deficiency statutes apply and therefore is not always limited to the purchase money situation. 160 Ariz. at 106–07, 770 P.2d at 774–75. Assuming that the deed of trust falls within one of the anti-deficiency statutes, an action for a deficiency is prohibited after a trustee's sale on any deed of trust and after judicial foreclosure on purchase money deeds of trust. *See* A.R.S. §§ 33–814(G) and 33–729(A). If a lender holds a non-purchase money deed of trust, he *may* recover a deficiency *if* he does so through an action for judicial foreclosure because A.R.S. § 33– 729(A) applies only to purchase money liens. In this latter case, of course, the debtor receives the protections of judicial foreclosure, including a statutory redemption right.

Read together, therefore, the statutes enact the following scheme: when the holder of a non-purchase money deed of trust of the type described in A.R.S. § 33–814(G) forecloses by non-judicial sale, the statute protects the borrower from a deficiency judgment. The lender therefore may not waive the security and sue on the note. *Baker,* 160 Ariz. at 106, 770 P.2d at 774. The holder may, however, seek to foreclose the deed of trust as if it were a mortgage, as allowed by § 33–814(E); if he does so, the debtor is allowed redemption rights under §§ 33–726 and 12–1281 through 12–1289 and is thus protected from low credit bids, but the holder may recover a deficiency judgment—the difference between the balance of the debt and the sale price—unless the note is a purchase money obligation. In the latter case, the borrower is protected by the mortgage anti-deficiency statute, A.R.S. § 33–729(A), which applies only to purchase money obligations. *Baker,* 160 Ariz. at 106, 770 P.2d at 774.

Thus, if under *Baker* and the facts of this case Dynamic is protected by an anti-deficiency statute, Mid Kansas could not elect to waive its security and sue on the first notes after having already chosen to proceed by trustee's sale under the second deed of trust.

B. Persons and Properties Included Within the Statutory Definitions

Mid Kansas argues that neither Dynamic, as a developer, nor the property under construction is protected by an anti-deficiency statute. Neither of the statutes is limited to individual homeowners rather than residential developers. Rather, the statutes apparently protect any mortgagor, provided the subject property is a single one-or two-family residential dwelling on two and one-half acres or less.[5]

As we noted in *Baker,* both anti-deficiency statutes were enacted in 1971, along with several other laws designed to protect consumers. 160 Ariz. at 101, 770 P.2d at 769. As with virtually all anti-deficiency statutes, the Arizona provisions were designed to temper the effects of economic recession on mortgagors by precluding "artificial deficiencies resulting from forced sales." *Id.* (quoting Boyd and Balentine, *Arizona's Consumer Legislation: Winning the Battle But * * *,* 14 Ariz.L.Rev. 627, 654 (1972)). Anti-deficiency statutes put the burden on the lender or seller to fairly value the property when extending the loan, recognizing that consumers often are not equipped to make such estimations. *See generally Spangler v. Memel,* 7 Cal.3d 603, 102 Cal.Rptr. 807, 812–13, 498 P.2d 1055, 1060–61 (1972); Leipziger, *Deficiency Judgments in California: The Supreme Court Tries Again,* 22 U.C.L.A. L.REV. 753, 759–61 (1975). Indeed, the articulated purpose behind A.R.S. § 33–729(A) (and presumably behind its deed of trust counterpart, as we held in *Baker*) was to protect "homeowners" from deficiency judgments. *See Baker,* 160 Ariz. at 101, 770 P.2d at 769.

However, absent express limiting language in the statute or explicit evidence of legislative intent, we cannot hold that the statute excludes residential developers. Where the language of a statute is plain and unambiguous, courts must generally follow the text as written. *Mid Kansas,* 163 Ariz. at 238, 787 P.2d at 137 (citing *State Farm Mut. Ins. Co. v. Agency Rent-A-Car, Inc.,* 139 Ariz. 201, 203, 677 P.2d 1309, 1311

---

[5] The statutes read as follows (relevant portions emphasized):
A.R.S. § 33–729(A):

> [I]f a mortgage is given to secure the payment of the balance of the purchase price, or to secure a loan to pay all or part of the purchase price, of *a parcel of real property of two and one-half acres or less which is limited to and utilized for either a single one-family or single two-family dwelling* . . . [there shall be no deficiency judgment] . . .

A.R.S. § 33–814(G):

> If *trust property of two and one-half acres or less which is limited to and utilized for either a single one-family or single two-family dwelling* is sold pursuant to the trustee's power of sale, no action may be maintained to recover any difference between the amount obtained by sale and the amount of the indebtedness and any interest, costs and expenses.

(Ct.App.1983); *cf. Ritchie v. Grand Canyon Scenic Rides,* 165 Ariz. 460, 799 P.2d 801 (1990) (rule inapplicable where it would produce absurd result)). While we can infer that the legislature's primary intent was to protect individual homeowners rather than commercial developers, neither the statutory text nor legislative history evinces an intent to *exclude* any other type of mortgagor. Indeed, the North Carolina Supreme Court decided to apply a similar anti-deficiency statute to a commercial borrower, finding that the statute expressed no intent to exclude commercial transactions and therefore that the court could not read in such an intent. *Barnaby v. Boardman,* 313 N.C. 565, 330 S.E.2d 600, 603 (1985). Therefore, we hold that so long as the subject properties fit within the statutory definition, the identity of the mortgagor as either a homeowner or developer is irrelevant.

In contrast to the lack of legislative limitation as to the type of mortgagor protected, there is specific textual expression as to the type of property protected. Both statutes require that the property be (1) two and one-half acres or less, (2) limited to and utilized for a dwelling that is (3) single one-family or single two-family in nature. In applying a statute, we have long held that its words are to be given their ordinary meaning, unless the legislature has offered its own definition of the words or it appears from the context that a special meaning was intended. *State Tax Comm'n v. Peck,* 106 Ariz. 394, 395, 476 P.2d 849, 850 (1970).

A.R.S. § 33–814(g) calls for the property to be "limited to" a single one- or two-family dwelling. The word "dwelling" is susceptible to several interpretations, depending on the context of its use. *See* 28 C.J.S. *Dwelling* (1941 and 1990 Supp.). However, the principal element in all such definitions is the "purpose or use of a building for human abode," meaning that the structure is wholly or partially occupied by persons lodging therein at night or intended for such use. *Id.* * * *

The anti-deficiency statutes require not only that the property be limited to dwelling purposes, but also that it be "utilized for" such purposes. In *Northern Arizona Properties v. Pinetop Properties Group,* the court of appeals held that an investment condominium, which was occasionally occupied by the owners and occasionally rented out to third persons, fell within the statutory definition. 151 Ariz. 9, 725 P.2d 501 (Ct.App.1986). In deciding that the statute applied to a dwelling used for investment purposes and not as the mortgagor's principal residence, the court employed the definition of "dwelling" in Webster's Ninth New Collegiate Dictionary and in several housing codes as "a shelter * * * in which people live." Hence, although the condominium was held as an investment, it was also used (utilized) as a dwelling. *Id.* at 12, 725 P.2d at 504.

In contrast to the *Northern Arizona Properties* case, the property in question here had never been used as a dwelling, and was in fact not yet susceptible of being used as a dwelling. There is a difference between property intended for eventual use as a dwelling and property utilized as a dwelling. We hold that commercial residential properties held by the mortgagor for construction and eventual *resale* as dwellings are not within the definition of properties "limited to" and "*utilized* for" single-family dwellings. The property is not utilized as a dwelling when it is unfinished, has never been lived in, and is being held for sale to its first occupant by an owner who has no intent to ever occupy the property. *Cf. Northern Arizona Properties* (mortgagors intended to occupy property occasionally and rent it out).

Therefore, we hold that by its terms, the anti-deficiency statute does not apply to Dynamic in this case and A.R.S. § 33–814(G) does not preclude Mid Kansas from waiving its security and bringing a debt action on the notes.

[The court then held that Mid Kansas nevertheless was probably barred from recovering against Dynamic because of the merger doctrine.]

GORDON, C.J., and MOELLER and CORCORAN, JJ., concur.

CAMERON, JUSTICE, dissenting in part, concurring in part.

I concur in the result the majority ultimately reaches. However, because of my dissent in *Baker v. Gardner,* 160 Ariz. 98, 770 P.2d 766 (1988), I write separately. * * * It was my belief then, and now, that *any* creditor has the right under § 33–722 to elect either to foreclose on the mortgage *or* to sue on the note. *Id.* at 105, 770 P.2d at 774. Once the creditor chooses to foreclose, the anti-deficiency statutes apply, and he cannot seek a deficiency judgment. *Id.*

The majority reiterates the rationale of *Baker,* noting that if the anti-deficiency statutes include Dynamic, Mid Kansas would be precluded from waiving its security and could not sue on the first note after having foreclosed on the second note. Next, the majority determines whether Dynamic, as a commercial developer, is protected by the anti-deficiency statutes. Noting the statutes' purpose was to protect "homeowners" from deficiency judgments and to protect consumers who were not sophisticated enough to value property when seeking a loan, the majority includes commercial developers as mortgagors within statutory protection. Commercial developers, however, are business people who are capable of valuing their business enterprises when seeking commercial or construction loans. They are neither unsophisticated consumers nor "homeowners."

After determining that Dynamic falls within the class of persons protected by the statutes, the majority then notes that the property in question does not fit the statutory language. The majority stated that "commercial residential properties held by the mortgagor for construction and eventual *resale* as dwellings are not within the definition of properties 'limited to' and '*utilized* for' * * * dwellings." At 129, 804 P.2d at 1317. Commercial developers are generously included as mortgagors covered under the statutes, but excluded due to the type of property they hold. Again, I believe this is wrong. The majority's interpretation of "dwelling" and "utilized for" means that a commercial developer's property will never meet the statutory language. By applying the reasoning of my dissent in *Baker*, we could have more easily and clearly reached the majority's result, without having to extend empty statutory protection. I believe that the anti-deficiency statutes were not intended to cover commercial developers and, therefore, Mid Kansas has the right to elect to foreclose or to sue on the first note.

NOTES

1. *Absence of one-action rule.* In *Baker*, the supreme court held that Arizona's purchase money antideficiency legislation barred a mortgagee election to waive the security and sue on the note. Should the absence of a "one-action" rule in Arizona have made its decision in *Baker* more difficult?

2. *Florida approach.* Consider the following description of Florida's unique and confusing deficiency legislation:

> Florida deficiency legislation is both unique and ambiguous.[49] Under its language, where a deficiency judgment is sought, "the amount bid at the sale may be considered by the court as one of the factors in determining a deficiency under the usual equitable principles."[50] This language[51] has created substantial difficulty for Florida appellate courts. While one court has taken the position that "if the value of the foreclosed property exceeds the debt, the chancellor is authorized in denying a deficiency,"[52] other decisions emphasize that the granting of a deficiency judgment based on the foreclosure sale price "is the rule rather than the exception" unless

---

[49] See West's Fla.Stat.Ann. § 45.031(7).

[50] Id.

[51] The statutory language was in response to R.K. Cooper Construction Co. v. Fulton, 216 So.2d 11 (Fla.1968), a Florida Supreme Court decision which held:

"The value of the property as established by the sale is conclusive insofar as consideration to support title to the property in the purchaser, but the statutory automatic approval cannot bind the trial court when a suit at law is filed to enforce collection of the remaining amount due on the note. A shockingly inadequate sale price in the foreclosure proceeding can be asserted as an equitable defense and the trial judge has the discretion and duty to inquire into the reasonable and fair market value of the property sold, the adequacy of the sale price, and the relationship, if any, between the foreclosing mortgagee and the purchaser at the sale, before entering a judgment on the note." Id. at 13.

[52] Hamilton Investment Trust v. Escambia Developers, Inc., 352 So.2d 883, 884 (Fla.App.1977). See Trustees of Central States Southeast and Southwest Areas, Pension Fund v. Indico Corp., 401 So.2d 904 (Fla.App.1981). Cf. Withers v. Flagship Peoples Bank, 473 So.2d 789 (Fla.App.1985); Fara Manufacturing Co., Inc. v. First Federal Savings and Loan Association of Miami, 366 So.2d 164 (Fla.App.1979).

fraud or other inequitable conduct infects the sale process.[53] Even these latter cases suggest that a deficiency judgment may be denied or reduced where the foreclosure sale price is "shockingly inadequate" or "unconscionable."[54] Moreover, there is some evidence that Florida trial courts allow mortgagors to introduce evidence of the fair market value of foreclosed real estate and that those courts use their determination of value, rather than the foreclosure sale price, to calculate the amount of the deficiency judgment.[55] Consequently, while it would be inaccurate to assert that Florida is a "fair value" jurisdiction, it would also be misleading to suggest that Florida trial courts have no flexibility in determining whether to use the foreclosure sale price or the market value of the foreclosed real estate as the crucial factor in deficiency judgment proceedings.

Nelson, Whitman, Burkhart & Freyermuth, Real Estate Finance Law 715–16 (6th ed.2015).*

3. *Antideficiency statutes and installment land contracts.* To what extent will statutory prohibitions against purchase money mortgage deficiency judgments apply to installment land contracts? Suppose, for example, that a contract vendor, instead of invoking forfeiture, elects to seek specific performance in the form of a money decree for the contract price. For the view that such statutes do not prohibit "awarding specific performance by granting a money decree and further providing that in the event the decree is not paid the property shall be sold and the proceeds applied in satisfaction of the money decree", see Glacier Campground v. Wild Rivers, Inc., 182 Mont. 389, 597 P.2d 689 (1978); Renard v. Allen, 237 Or. 406, 391 P.2d 777 (1964).

Compare Venable v. Harmon, 233 Cal.App.2d 297, 43 Cal.Rptr. 490 (1965), in which the vendor repossessed the land after the purchaser's default, and then sued for damages. "[T]o allow the vendor to recover this judgment places him in a better position than under a trust deed or mortgage. It would allow him to recover a personal judgment and retain title to the land. This would accomplish the exact result which * * * the statute was designed to prevent." See also Ferguson v. Swanstrom, 2012 WL 3539123 (Cal.App. 2012) (unpublished).

4. *Restatement approach.* Under the Restatement, the mortgagee, after acceleration, may either (1) obtain a judgment on the personal obligation and enforce it by levying upon any of the mortgagor's assets and, if a deficiency remains, foreclose on the mortgaged real estate or (2) foreclose first on the

---

[53] Federal Deposit Insurance Corp. v. Circle Bar Ranch, Inc., 450 So.2d 921 (Fla.App.1984); Lloyd v. Cannon, 399 So.2d 1095, 1096 (Fla.App.1981), review denied, 408 So.2d 1092 (Fla.1981); Flagship State Bank of Jacksonville v. Drew Equipment Co., 392 So.2d 609, 613 (Fla.App.1981); S/D Enterprises, Inc. v. Chase Manhattan Bank, 374 So.2d 1121 (Fla.App.1979).

[54] Id. See Wilson v. Adams & Fusselle, Inc., 467 So.2d 345 (Fla.App.1985).

[55] See, e.g., Peoples Federal Savings & Loan Association of Tarentum, Pennsylvania v. Shoreline Garden Townhomes, II, Ltd., 538 So.2d 864 (Fla.App.1988); Coppola v. Housing Investment Corp. of Florida, 400 So.2d 112 (Fla.App.1981).

* Reprinted with permission of LEG, Inc. d/b/a West Academic.

mortgaged real estate and, if necessary, seek a deficiency judgment. Restatement (Third) of Property (Mortgages) § 8.2 (1997). The Restatement rejects the "one-action" rule. On the other hand, the mortgagor is substantially protected against a multiplicity of actions because mortgagee may not proceed under the above options concurrently or consecutively. "Once the mortgagee opts to proceed under one of the two [options], it is prohibited from utilizing the other." Id. cmt. b.

The Restatement permits deficiency judgments even though the mortgage is "purchase-money" or is being foreclosed by power of sale. On the other hand, it rejects the traditional common law view that the foreclosure sale price should automatically be used in measuring the deficiency. Instead, it adopts the "fair value" approach by giving the mortgagor "the right to insist that the greater of the fair market value of the real estate or the foreclose sale price be used in calculating the deficiency." Restatement (Third) of Property (Mortgages) § 8.4 cmt. a (1997).

> This approach enables the mortgagee to be made whole where the mortgaged real estate is insufficient to satisfy the mortgage obligation, but at the same time protects against the mortgagee purchasing the property at a deflated price, obtaining a deficiency judgment and, by reselling the real estate at a profit, achieving a recovery that exceeds the obligation. Thus, it is aimed primarily at preventing the unjust enrichment of the mortgagee. [It] also protects the mortgagor from the harsh consequences of suffering both the loss of the real estate and the burden of a deficiency judgment that does not fairly recognize the value of that real estate.

Id.*

5. *Should state antideficiency legislation be preempted by federal action?* Consider the following commentary:

> Strategic default—the practice of opting to default on an underwater home mortgage when the mortgagor has the ability to pay—has been a significant exacerbating factor in the mortgage crisis and its accompanying economic upheaval. The practice is aided and abetted by states such as California that limit or prohibit personal recourse on mortgage obligations. As a result, strategic default is a more pervasive problem in these states than in their recourse brethren. In effect, such states grant home mortgagors an option with respect to the mortgaged real estate. If market forces cause the property to increase in value, that increase inures to the benefit of the mortgagor. On the other hand, if the property value decreases and the mortgage is underwater, a mortgagor is able to avoid any personal liability through a deficiency judgment.

> Where state law permits such strategic behavior, we find it difficult to conclude that a mortgagor is acting immorally. On the

---

*   © 1997 by The American Law Institute. Reprinted with permission.

other hand, we believe that such activity should be made illegal. Thus, we conclude that Congress should preempt state non-recourse law by enacting legislation based on Section 8.4 of the Restatement (Third) of Property: Mortgages. Should Congress choose to take this course of action, it would pose no greater threat to federalism principles than when it opted in 1982, through the Garn Act, to invalidate state judicial decisions and statutes that enabled home purchasers to take over a seller's existing low interest rate mortgage without obtaining the mortgagee's consent. Indeed, the Garn Act was applicable to virtually all mortgages in the United States.

Should Congress find such preemption politically unappealing, we advocate that federal agencies such as FHFA accomplish the same result through the regulatory process.

Grant S. Nelson & Gabriel D. Serbulea, Strategic Defaulters Versus the Federal Taxpayer: A Brief for the Preemption of State Anti-Deficiency Law for Residential Mortgages, 66 Ark.L.Rev. 65, 108–109 (2013).

I. THE SERVICEMEMBERS CIVIL RELIEF ACT

From our country's early days, state and federal legislators have appreciated the need to relieve from or modify certain legal responsibilities of those who answer the call to serve in the military. The justification for this approach has been to allow these persons to perform their military duties without being hindered unnecessarily by pressing legal concerns at home. For example, during the War of 1812, Louisiana suspended all civil legal actions against soldiers for four months as the British marched on New Orleans. See H.R. Rep. 108–81. 108th Cong. 1st Sess. (2003). Later, during the Civil War, "Congress recognized the need to protect service members from civil obligations while on military duty away from home, * * * [and] [f]or the duration of the war * * * passed a total moratorium on civil actions brought against Union soldiers and sailors." Terry M. Jarrett, The Servicemembers Civil Relief Act: Important New Protections for Those in Uniform, 60 J.Mo.B. 174, 174 (2004).

When the United States entered World War I, Congress again felt the need to protect members of the armed forces and thus enacted the Soldiers' and Sailors' Civil Relief Act of 1918. See Soldiers and Sailors Civil Relief Act of 1918, ch. 20, 40 Stat. 440. While the World War I legislation was not as sweeping as its Civil War counterpart, it provided substantial protection to servicemembers on active duty against property seizure, foreclosure, bankruptcy, or similar actions. As World War II loomed on the immediate horizon, Congress enacted the Soldiers' and Sailors' Civil Relief Act of 1940 (the "SSCRA"). This statute largely renewed the 1918 bill which had expired shortly after the end of World War I. However, the SSCRA did not contain an expiration date and thus it survived for 63 years having been amended at least 13 times. Most recently, the SSCRA was amended in 1991 and 2002 in response to massive activations of military reserve forces in connection with Operation Desert Storm (the first Iraq War) and Operation Enduring Freedom (the Afghanistan operation in response to the 9–11 attack). See Jarrett, *supra*, at 175.

In 2003, in response to the Iraq War, Congress renovated and modified the SSCRA by enacting the Servicemembers Civil Relief Act ("SCRA" or the "Act") "[t]o restate, clarify, and revise the Soldiers' and Sailors' Civil Relief Act of 1940." While the SCRA deals with a wide variety of commercial transactions entered into by servicemembers, it does not make significant changes in its predecessor's treatment of real estate mortgage transactions. We briefly describe SCRA's impact in several important areas of interest to real estate lawyers and mortgagees.

Statutes of Limitation

Section 3936 automatically tolls all statutes of limitation during the period of service that would otherwise run against a servicemember. See 50 U.S.C. App. § 3936. It contains no language requiring that the servicemember be prejudiced by his or her military service. This section tolls not only properly denominated statutes of limitation, but also such periods relating to "the redemption of real property sold or forfeited to enforce an obligation, tax, or assessment." Id. Thus, section 3936 has been held to extend the time for redemption under state statutory redemption by a period equal to the mortgagor's period of service. See 1 Nelson, Whitman, Burkhart & Freyermuth, Real Estate Finance Law § 8.9 (6th ed. Practitioner Series 2014). Moreover, it also applies to redemption periods after real estate tax sales. See Hedrick v. Bigby, 228 Ark. 40, 305 S.W.2d 674 (1957). Equally important, the United States Supreme Court has unanimously rejected the contention that section 3936 requires "career" servicemembers to establish that their military service prejudiced their ability to redeem—rather, the Court concluded that "Congress included a prejudice requirement whenever it considered it appropriate to do so, and * * * its omission of any such requirement in [§ 3936] was deliberate." Conroy v. Aniskoff, 507 U.S. 511, 113 S.Ct. 1562, 123 L.Ed.2d 229 (1993).

Maximum Rate of Interest

Section 3937 limits interest to six percent during military service on obligations incurred before entering service, even though a higher rate was originally agreed upon. 50 U.S.C. § 3937. The interest rate is automatically reduced to the six percent maximum unless the mortgagee proves that military service has no material effect on the ability of the servicemember to pay a higher rate. For example, suppose a mortgagor executes a 8% mortgage note and is then called into active duty in the military. The burden then falls on the mortgagee to justify a rate higher than six percent. Anecdotal evidence suggests that during both the 1991–92 Persian Gulf War and the later Iraq and Afghanistan hostilities, institutional mortgage lenders frequently voluntarily agreed to collect six percent during the period of involuntary duty.

Installment Land Contracts (Contracts for Deed)

When a servicemember defaults on an installment land contract entered into before military service, the vendor may not terminate or rescind the contract or repossess the land except by judicial action. 50 U.S.C. § 3952. Forfeiture through nonjudicial means is a criminal act. Id. If the vendor files such a judicial action, the court may condition its order on repayment of all or part of the deposit and prior installments. If military service materially affected the servicemember's ability to comply with the terms of payment, the court may order an absolute stay or one conditioned on partial payment. The court also has the option to order the judicial sale of the real estate and an appropriate division of the proceeds.

Mortgages and Deeds of Trust

Section 3953 treats obligations secured by mortgages and deeds of trust in much the same fashion as its Section 3952 counterpart deals with installment land contracts. After a default in payment or other breach in a mortgage or deed of trust obligation that was consummated before service, the mortgagee may not sell, foreclose, or seize the mortgaged real estate during the term of service or for one year thereafter, except pursuant to a judicial order. Sibert v. Wells Fargo Bank, N.A., 863 F.3d 331 (4th Cir. 2017) (nonjudicial foreclosure valid because servicemember borrowed and gave mortgage during his service). The practical effect is that, in states where power of sale foreclosure is the predominant foreclosure method, mortgagees must, as a practical matter, foreclose judicially.

Waiver by Servicemember

A servicemember may waive the protections of the Act if the waiver is "made pursuant to a written agreement of the parties that is executed during or after the servicemember's period of military service. The written agreement shall specify the legal instrument to which the waiver applies * * *." 50 U.S.C. § 3918(a). This waiver may cover the rights conferred by the Act on both borrowers under mortgages and deeds of trust and vendees under installment land contracts. 50 U.S.C. § 3918(b)(1)(B). Note, however, that such a waiver is effective only if it is "executed *during or after* the servicemember's period of military service." 50 U.S.C. § 3918(a) (emphasis added). Consequently, pre-service waivers are ineffective. Thus, for example, if a servicemember purchases a home, executes a specific waiver of section 3953 rights, and is later called to active duty, the waiver is unenforceable. On the other hand, if the same purchase transaction is entered into while the servicemember is on active duty, the waiver is effective.

J. BANKRUPTCY

1. INTRODUCTORY CONCEPTS

When a mortgagor files for bankruptcy, the mortgagee's ability to enforce its lien becomes subject to the substantive and procedural limitations imposed by federal bankruptcy law. A variety of objectives motivate the bankruptcy system. The first is to provide an honest but unfortunate debtor with a "fresh start." See Jackson, The Fresh Start Policy in Bankruptcy Law, 98 Harv. L. Rev. 1393 (1985). For a consumer debtor, this usually means a discharge from otherwise unmanageable pre-bankruptcy debts; for some business debtors, this means the ability to restructure pre-bankruptcy debts and continue in business. A second objective is to provide a collective remedy for creditors of an insolvent debtor. Outside of bankruptcy, a debtor's financial distress can trigger a "race to the courthouse" in which creditors compete for the debtor's limited assets in judicial or nonjudicial collection processes. This race is potentially counterproductive in several respects. The distraction of responding to creditor collection activity may compromise the debtor's ability to carry out its business operations. Further, as noted earlier in this chapter, foreclosure sales often bring sale prices lower than the debtor might have obtained in an arms-length sale. By forcing creditors into a collective proceeding, bankruptcy seeks to protect the value of the debtor's assets for the benefit of the debtor (if reorganization is possible) or all creditors (if reorganization is impossible). In this way, bankruptcy law seeks to mitigate the adverse consequences of the "race to the courthouse" in a way that provides consistent treatment to similarly situated creditors. See generally Charles Tabb, The Law of Bankruptcy (2d ed. 2009); Elizabeth Warren, Bankruptcy Policy, 54 U. Chi. L Rev. 775 (1987); Thomas Jackson, The Logic and Limits of Bankruptcy Law (1986).

The Bankruptcy Code divides bankruptcy law into separate "Chapters." Three of these Chapters (1, 3, and 5) contain general provisions that apply in all types of bankruptcy cases. The remaining Chapters govern the specific types of bankruptcy cases. The most common is Chapter 7, which involves the liquidation of the debtor's non-exempt assets to satisfy creditors according to the priority and amount of their claims, typically in exchange for a discharge of most of the debtor's pre-bankruptcy debts. Chapter 11 provides for the reorganization of an individual or business debtor through the negotiation and confirmation of a "plan" that typically restructures the rights of both secured and unsecured creditors. Chapter 13 provides a reorganization process that permits individual wage earners to restructure or reduce unsecured claims and certain secured claims by committing all of their net disposable income for a period of three to five years toward the payment of such claims. Chapter 12, enacted in 1986, provides a similar reorganization procedure for family farmers. In this

Section, we focus on those aspects of bankruptcy law that have the most significant consequences for the mortgagor-mortgagee relationship.

The bankruptcy estate. The filing of a bankruptcy petition creates a bankruptcy estate. Subject to limited statutory exceptions, all of the debtor's interests in property (whether legal or equitable) at the moment of the bankruptcy petition become part of the bankruptcy estate. 11 U.S.C. § 541(a)(1). If, at that time, the mortgagee has started but not yet completed a foreclosure, the debtor's rights in the property have not yet been extinguished, and thus the mortgaged premises become property of the bankruptcy estate. See, e.g., In re Webb, 472 B.R. 665 (6th Cir. B.A.P. 2012). By contrast, if the foreclosure sale became final before the petition, the premises are not property of the bankruptcy estate. See, e.g., In re Ulrey, 511 B.R. 401 (Bankr. W.D. Va. 2014).[6]

The bankruptcy trustee/debtor-in-possession. The central figure in Chapter 7 cases is the trustee, who is the official representative of the bankruptcy estate. The Chapter 7 trustee collects and manages the property in the bankruptcy estate, investigates the bankrupt's financial affairs, invalidates any improper pre-bankruptcy transfers by the debtor, liquidates the property of the estate, and distributes the proceeds to creditors entitled to payment under the Code's distributive scheme. 11 U.S.C. § 704. By contrast, in reorganization cases under Chapters 11, 12, and 13, property of the estate remains in the hands of the debtor—who is called the "debtor-in-possession" or "DIP"—and the debtor may use that property while formulating a plan to pay the claims of creditors using the debtor's post-bankruptcy earnings. 11 U.S.C. §§ 1107(a), 1203(a), 1303. In Chapter 12 and 13 cases, a trustee is appointed, but the trustee's role is primarily administrative, i.e., the trustee collects the debtor's disposable post-bankruptcy income and uses it to make the payments due to creditors under the debtor's reorganization plan. 11 U.S.C. § 1202(b), 1302(b). In Chapter 11 cases, the court does not appoint a trustee at all, unless the debtor is engaging in fraudulent conduct or the court concludes that a trustee is needed to protect the bankruptcy estate and the interests of persons holding claims against the estate. 11 U.S.C. § 1104(a).

Contrasting secured and unsecured claims. Before making distributions to creditors, bankruptcy must identify those creditors holding valid claims against the debtor. Bankruptcy law respects most pre-

---

[6] If the mortgaged land is located in a state that allows for statutory redemption (see Section G supra), the trustee/debtor in possession has the power to exercise the mortgagor's redemption right for the time period remaining under the applicable state statute or for 60 days after the bankruptcy petition, whichever is longer. See 11 U.S.C. § 108(b); In re Thom, Inc., 95 B.R. 261 (Bankr.D.Me.1989). The bankruptcy petition, however, does not toll the running of the state statutory redemption period. See, e.g., In re Whispering Bay Campground, Inc., 850 F.2d 443 (8th Cir. 1988); Nelson, Whitman, Burkhart & Freyermuth, Real Estate Finance Law § 8.12, at 768 n.338 (6th ed.2015). Under what circumstances would a trustee choose to exercise the right of statutory redemption? Where would the money come from?

bankruptcy claims,[7] but disallows claims that are not enforceable under nonbankruptcy law (e.g., a claim evidenced by a forged promissory note or barred by the statute of limitations). 11 U.S.C. § 502(a), (b). Bankruptcy law also generally disallows claims for unmatured interest. 11 U.S.C. § 502(b)(2). Thus, if Debtor owed Bank $20,000 on an unsecured note bearing a 10% annual interest rate, the Bank's claim in bankruptcy would no longer accrue interest after the petition date.[8]

The Code separates claims into two primary categories—*secured* and *unsecured*. Generally, bankruptcy law takes secured creditors as it finds them on the petition date—a security interest that is valid under nonbankruptcy law is generally respected in bankruptcy. Thus, a creditor with a valid and recorded mortgage lien on the debtor's land is treated as the holder of a *secured claim*, and retains both its lien on the land and its pre-bankruptcy priority for any distribution from the proceeds of that land.[9] 11 U.S.C. § 506(a)(1). By contrast, the holders of *unsecured claims*— general creditors without any pre-bankruptcy lien against specific assets of the debtor—receive payment on their claims on a pro rata basis to the extent that assets remain after payment of secured claims and the expenses of bankruptcy administration. 11 U.S.C. §§ 507(b), 726(a).

In some cases, a mortgagee may hold an *undersecured claim*—i.e., one secured by a lien on land that is worth less than the total balance owed to the mortgagee. For example, suppose Bank holds a valid mortgage lien on Chapter 7 Debtor's land (worth $40,000) to secure a debt of $100,000. Outside of bankruptcy, the creditor would hold one legal claim against the debtor in the amount of $100,000. Section 506(a)(1) of the Bankruptcy Code, however, "bifurcates" Bank's claim, treating it as if it were two separate claims—a secured claim equal to the value of the collateral, and an unsecured claim to the extent of the deficiency balance of Bank's claim. In this example, Bank would thus have a secured claim of $40,000 and an unsecured claim of $60,000.

---

[7]   Claims are deemed valid or "allowed" unless the trustee, the debtor, or some other party in interest raises a valid objection. 11 U.S.C. § 502(a); In re Hemingway Transport, Inc., 993 F.2d 915 (1st Cir. 1993). Once a proper objection is raised, the court must conduct a hearing and determine the allowed amount of the creditor's claim.

[8]   The denial of claims for unmatured interest is based on administrative convenience. Usually, insolvent debtors cannot pay 100% of unsecured claims—much less interest on those claims. Disallowance of claims for unmatured interest permits the trustee/debtor-in-possession to avoid the accrual of interest (and the need to have to recompute claim amounts) as the bankruptcy case proceeds. Vanston Bondholders' Protective Comm. v. Green, 329 U.S. 156 (1946); In re Brooks, 323 F.3d 675 (8th Cir. 2003). Notwithstanding section 502(b)(2), however, creditors holding oversecured claims (claims secured by property with a value that exceeds the balance of the debt) are entitled to collect post-petition interest as part of their allowed claim, up to but not exceeding the value of the collateral. 11 U.S.C. § 506(a)(1), (b).

[9]   This principle is subject to two caveats, as discussed later in this section. First, even if the lien is valid, the bankruptcy petition prevents or "stays" the creditor from exercising its nonbankruptcy remedies during the bankruptcy. 11 U.S.C. § 362(a). Second, the Code gives the trustee/debtor-in-possession the power to avoid certain liens, including liens that the creditor failed to perfect prior to bankruptcy. 11 U.S.C. § 544(a).

2. THE AUTOMATIC STAY

The most immediate impact of a mortgagor's bankruptcy is the automatic stay. Under 11 U.S.C. § 362(a), the filing of a petition stays any effort by a mortgagee to foreclose a mortgage against property of the estate, whether judicially or nonjudicially. 11 U.S.C. § 362(a)(4); In re Kline, 472 B.R. 98 (10th Cir. B.A.P. 2012). The stay also prevents the mortgagee from taking any other collection efforts, such as suing for a personal judgment on the mortgage debt, seeking to execute on a judgment obtained prior to bankruptcy, seeking the appointment of a receiver for the mortgaged premises, or even sending a demand letter to the debtor. 11 U.S.C. § 362(a)(1), (2), (3), (6). The stay even prevents a mortgagee from recording a mortgage that debtor had granted (but that had not been recorded) prior to bankruptcy. 11 U.S.C. § 362(a)(4). The stay essentially forces the mortgagee and other creditors to resolve claims against the debtor through the collective bankruptcy process.

If the mortgagee violates the automatic stay, the mortgagor's rights in the property are unaffected; creditor actions in violation of the stay are void,[10] even if the creditor in question lacked knowledge or notice of the bankruptcy filing. See, e.g., In re Cueva, 371 F.3d 232 (5th Cir. 2004). Further, a creditor that knowingly violates the stay (i.e., that commits a "willful" violation) is liable for actual damages, including costs and attorney fees, and potentially punitive damages if the conduct is egregious or outrageous. 11 U.S.C. § 362(k)(1); Jones v. Wells Fargo Home Mortg., Inc., 489 B.R. 645 (E.D. La. 2013) (upholding $3.17 million punitive damage award for lender's willful violation of stay). Unless the court grants a creditor relief from the automatic stay, the stay remains in effect until the bankruptcy case is closed or dismissed or until the debtor receives a discharge, whichever occurs first. 11 U.S.C. § 362(c)(2).

Relief from the automatic stay. The Code provides a mechanism to allow the court, at the request of an affected creditor, to grant relief from the stay to permit that creditor to take action that would otherwise violate section 362(a). Section 362(d) sets forth four standards for relief from the stay that are relevant to mortgagees; each is discussed in turn below.

---

[10] Most federal circuits have held that actions taken in violation of the stay are void *ab initio.* See, e.g., In re Smith Corset Shops, Inc., 696 F.2d 971 (1st Cir.1982); Rexnord Holdings v. Bidermann, 21 F.3d 522 (2d Cir.1994); In re Graves, 33 F.3d 242 (3d Cir.1994); Matthews v. Rosene, 739 F.2d 249 (7th Cir.1984); By contrast, courts in the Fifth, Sixth, and Federal Circuits have held that actions taken in violation of the automatic stay are voidable, based on the power of the bankruptcy court to retroactively annul the automatic stay. Picco v. Global Marine Drilling Co., 900 F.2d 846 (5th Cir.1989); Easley v. Pettibone Michigan Corp., 990 F.2d 905 (6th Cir.1993); Bronson v. United States, 46 F.3d 1573 (Fed.Cir.1995). The distinction could matter if the mortgagee took action to begin a foreclosure (e.g., filing a complaint for judicial foreclosure) after the petition. If the complaint was void (the majority approach), the mortgagee would have to refile the complaint; by contrast, if the complaint was merely voidable, the court's grant of relief from stay could validate the initial complaint (in which case Mortgagee would not have to refile).

Relief from stay: lack of equity and capacity for reorganization. Under section 362(d)(2), a mortgagee can obtain relief from stay if "the debtor does not have an equity" in the collateral and the collateral "is not necessary to an effective reorganization." If these grounds are present, relief from stay is appropriate; neither the debtor nor general creditors would benefit if the mortgaged premises remained property of the estate. [Can you see why?]

In a Chapter 7 case, there is by definition no possibility of effective reorganization; thus, if a Chapter 7 debtor lacks equity in the mortgaged premises, the mortgagee is entitled to relief under section 362(d)(2). See, e.g., In re McFadden, 471 B.R. 136 (Bankr. D. S.C. 2012). We will give further consideration to section 362(d)(2) in Chapter 11 cases later, when discussing the requirements for confirming a Chapter 11 plan of reorganization.

Relief from stay: relief for "cause" and lack of "adequate protection." Section 362(d)(1) provides that the court shall grant relief from the stay if a creditor demonstrates "cause, including the lack of adequate protection of an interest in property" held by that creditor. Outside of bankruptcy, a mortgagee could foreclose after default, sell the mortgaged premises, and apply the proceeds to the debt. By preventing such a foreclosure and allowing the trustee or debtor-in-possession to retain and use the collateral during the bankruptcy,[11] the stay imposes on the mortgagee the risk that its collateral may depreciate during that period. This depreciation could result from market fluctuations in the value of the premises, use of the premises that reduces or exhausts its economic value, or from damage to the premises by an uninsured casualty. Such depreciation could ultimately result in a reduced recovery for the mortgagee.

Section 362(d)(1) allows the mortgagee to obtain "adequate protection" against this depreciation risk. The mortgagee can file a motion requesting that the court terminate the stay and permit the mortgagee to foreclose its lien immediately, or condition the continuation of the stay on the mortgagee receiving "adequate protection" of its lien. Once the mortgagee makes this request, the trustee/debtor-in-possession must either provide the mortgagee with adequate protection of its lien or surrender the premises to the mortgagee; if neither occurs, the bankruptcy court must lift the stay and permit the mortgagee to foreclose.[12] The trustee/debtor-in-possession can provide adequate protection by any action that eliminates

---

[11] The trustee generally may use property of the estate in the ordinary course of business, without the need for prior court approval. 11 U.S.C. § 363(c). The debtor-in-possession in a Chapter 11 case, or the debtor in a Chapter 12 or 13 case, also has a comparable power of use. 11 U.S.C. §§ 1107(a), 1203, 1303.

[12] The mortgagee must file a motion for relief from stay and/or adequate protection to trigger its right to adequate protection. See, e.g., In re Alliance Well Service, LLC, 551 B.R. 903 (Bankr. D. N.M. 2016) (creditor's right to adequate protection begins to accrue on date of motion, rather than petition date or date of default). As one bankruptcy court has noted, "if you don't ask for it, you won't get it." In re Vista Marketing Group, Ltd., 548 B.R. 502 (Bankr. N.D. Ill. 2016).

the risk that the stay will impose a depreciation loss upon the mortgagee. Thus, for example, if the risk arises from the mortgagor's failure to maintain casualty insurance on the premises, the court should lift the stay unless the trustee or debtor-in-possession puts adequate casualty insurance coverage in place. See, e.g., In re Spencer, 531 B.R. 208 (Bankr. W.D. Wis. 2015).

Section 361 provides an illustrative list of ways that the trustee/ debtor-in-possession can provide adequate protection. These could include periodic cash payments during the bankruptcy in an amount sufficient to offset expected depreciation in the collateral's value,[13] a "replacement lien" on other property,[14] or anything else that would provide the secured party with the "indubitable equivalent" of its interest in the collateral. The term "indubitable equivalent" includes the existence of an "equity cushion," meaning any surplus value (or "equity") in the collateral above the balance of the debt. Thus, suppose that Bank holds a mortgage on Debtor's land to secure an unpaid debt of $200,000, and that during Debtor's bankruptcy, the value of the land is expected to depreciate by as much as 20% due to local market conditions. If the value of the mortgaged land is $400,000, even a 20% depreciation of the collateral (e.g., a reduction in value to $320,000) would leave Bank more than fully secured. Under these circumstances, the Bank's "equity cushion" would provide adequate protection for the continuation of the automatic stay, and the trustee/ debtor-in-possession would not need to make cash payments or provide a replacement lien on other property.

Should the requirement for "adequate protection" encompass the mortgagee's lost opportunity cost? When a mortgagor files for bankruptcy, it often ceases making payments on its mortgage debt (if it had not already done so prior to bankruptcy). This means that during the bankruptcy case, the mortgagee is not collecting the interest that would otherwise have accrued on the mortgage debt. Outside of bankruptcy, the mortgagee could foreclose, sell the premises, and reinvest the sale proceeds in an alternative investment (e.g., a loan to a solvent borrower capable of paying interest). By delaying the mortgagee in pursuing this remedy, the stay imposes a lost opportunity cost on the mortgagee, and bankruptcy law generally compounds this burden by disallowing claims for unmatured interest. 11 U.S.C. § 502(b)(2).

For some mortgagees, bankruptcy mitigates this burden. Section 506(b) provides that an oversecured creditor (one with an equity cushion)

---

[13] 11 U.S.C. § 361(1). Cash payments to the mortgagee would reduce the amount of the mortgagee's claim, thus maintaining the value of the depreciated collateral relative to the unpaid balance of the mortgage debt.

[14] 11 U.S.C. § 361(2). For the replacement lien to provide adequate protection, the property subject to the replacement lien must be either unencumbered or the estate must have equity in the property that exceeds the expected depreciation loss in the original collateral.

may collect interest on its secured claim, up to (but not beyond) the total value of the collateral. But what about undersecured mortgagees?

UNITED SAVINGS ASSOCIATION OF TEXAS V. TIMBERS OF INWOOD FOREST ASSOCIATES, LTD.

Supreme Court of the United States, 1988
484 U.S. 365, 108 S.Ct. 626, 98 L.Ed.2d 740

JUSTICE SCALIA delivered the opinion of the Court. . . .

I

On June 29, 1982, respondent Timbers of Inwood Forest Associates, Ltd., executed a note in the principal amount of $4,100,000. Petitioner is the holder of the note as well as of a security interest created the same day in an apartment project owned by respondent in Houston, Texas. The security interest included an assignment of rents from the project. On March 4, 1985, respondent filed a voluntary petition under Chapter 11. . . .

On March 18, 1985, petitioner moved for relief from the automatic stay of enforcement of liens triggered by the petition, see 11 U.S.C. § 362(a), on the ground that there was lack of "adequate protection" of its interest within the meaning of 11 U.S.C. § 362(d)(1). At a hearing before the Bankruptcy Court, it was established that respondent owed petitioner $4,366,388.77, and evidence was presented that the value of the collateral was somewhere between $2,650,000 and $4,250,000. The collateral was appreciating in value, but only very slightly. It was therefore undisputed that petitioner was an undersecured creditor. Respondent had agreed to pay petitioner the postpetition rents from the apartment project (covered by the after-acquired property clause in the security agreement), minus operating expenses. Petitioner contended, however, that it was entitled to additional compensation. The Bankruptcy Court agreed and on April 19, 1985, it conditioned continuance of the stay on monthly payments by respondent, at the market rate of 12% per annum, on the estimated amount realizable on foreclosure, $4,250,000—commencing six months after the filing of the bankruptcy petition, to reflect the normal foreclosure delays. The court held that the postpetition rents could be applied to these payments. Respondent appealed to the District Court and petitioner cross-appealed on the amount of the adequate protection payments. The District Court affirmed but the Fifth Circuit en banc reversed.

We granted certiorari to determine whether undersecured creditors are entitled to compensation under 11 U.S.C. § 362(d)(1) for the delay caused by the automatic stay in foreclosing on their collateral.

II

When a bankruptcy petition is filed, § 362(a) of the Bankruptcy Code provides an automatic stay of, among other things, actions taken to realize the value of collateral given by the debtor. The provision of the Code central to the decision of this case is § 362(d), which reads as follows:

> On request of a party in interest and after notice and a hearing, the court shall grant relief from the stay provided under subsection (a) of this section, such as by terminating, annulling, modifying, or conditioning such stay—
>
> (1) for cause, including the lack of adequate protection of an interest in property of such party in interest; or
>
> (2) with respect to a stay of an act against property under subsection (a) of this section, if—
>
> (A) the debtor does not have an equity in such property; and
>
> (B) such property is not necessary to an effective reorganization.

The phrase "adequate protection" in paragraph (1) of the foregoing provision is given further content by § 361 of the Code, which reads in relevant part as follows:

> When adequate protection is required under section 362 . . . of this title of an interest of an entity in property, such adequate protection may be provided by—
>
> (1) requiring the trustee to make a cash payment or periodic cash payments to such entity, to the extent that the stay under section 362 of this title . . . results in a decrease in the value of such entity's interest in such property;
>
> (2) providing to such entity an additional or replacement lien to the extent that such stay . . . results in a decrease in the value of such entity's interest in such property; or
>
> (3) granting such other relief . . . as will result in the realization by such entity of the indubitable equivalent of such entity's interest in such property.

It is common ground that the "interest in property" referred to by § 362(d)(1) includes the right of a secured creditor to have the security applied in payment of the debt upon completion of the reorganization; and that that interest is not adequately protected if the security is depreciating during the term of the stay. Thus, it is agreed that if the apartment project in this case had been declining in value petitioner would have been entitled, under § 362(d)(1), to cash payments or additional security in the amount of the decline, as § 361 describes. The crux of the present dispute is that petitioner asserts, and respondent denies, that the phrase "interest in property" also includes the secured party's right (suspended by the stay) to take immediate possession of the defaulted security, and apply it in payment of the debt. If that right is embraced by the term, it is obviously not adequately protected unless the secured party is reimbursed for the use of the proceeds he is deprived of during the term of the stay.

The term "interest in property" certainly summons up such concepts as "fee ownership," "life estate," "co-ownership," and "security interest" more readily than it does the notion of "right to immediate foreclosure." Nonetheless, viewed in the isolated context of § 362(d)(1), the phrase could reasonably be given the meaning petitioner asserts. Statutory construction, however, is a holistic endeavor. A provision that may seem ambiguous in isolation is often clarified by the remainder of the statutory scheme—because the same terminology is used elsewhere in a context that makes its meaning clear, or because only one of the permissible meanings produces a substantive effect that is compatible with the rest of the law. That is the case here. Section 362(d)(1) is only one of a series of provisions in the Bankruptcy Code dealing with the rights of secured creditors. The language in those other provisions, and the substantive dispositions that they effect, persuade us that the "interest in property" protected by § 362(d)(1) does not include a secured party's right to immediate foreclosure.

Section 506 of the Code defines the amount of the secured creditor's allowed secured claim and the conditions of his receiving postpetition interest. In relevant part it reads as follows:

> (a) An allowed claim of a creditor secured by a lien on property in which the estate has an interest . . . is a secured claim to the extent of the value of such creditor's interest in the estate's interest in such property, . . . and is an unsecured claim to the extent that the value of such creditor's interest . . . is less than the amount of such allowed claim. . . .

> (b) To the extent that an allowed secured claim is secured by property the value of which . . . is greater than the amount of such claim, there shall be allowed to the holder of such claim, interest on such claim, and any reasonable fees, costs, or charges provided for under the agreement under which such claim arose.

In subsection (a) of this provision the creditor's "interest in property" obviously means his security interest without taking account of his right to immediate possession of the collateral on default. If the latter were included, the "value of such creditor's interest" would increase, and the proportions of the claim that are secured and unsecured would alter, as the stay continues—since the value of the entitlement to use the collateral from the date of bankruptcy would rise with the passage of time. No one suggests this was intended. The phrase "value of such creditor's interest" in § 506(a) means "the value of the collateral." H.R.Rep. No. 95–595, pp. 181, 356 (1977); see also S.Rep. No. 95–989, p. 68 (1978), U.S. Code Cong. & Admin.

News 1978, pp. 5787, 5854, 6141, 6312. We think the phrase "value of such entity's interest" in § 361(1) and (2), when applied to secured creditors, means the same.

Even more important for our purposes than § 506's use of terminology is its substantive effect of denying undersecured creditors postpetition interest on their claims—just as it denies *over* secured creditors postpetition interest to the extent that such interest, when added to the principal amount of the claim, will exceed the value of the collateral. Section 506(b) provides that "*[t]o the extent that* an allowed secured claim is secured by property the value of which . . . is greater than the amount of such claim, there shall be allowed to the holder of such claim, interest on such claim." (Emphasis added.) Since this provision permits postpetition interest to be paid only out of the "security cushion," the undersecured creditor, who has no such cushion, falls within the general rule disallowing postpetition interest. See 11 U.S.C. § 502(b)(2). If the Code had meant to give the undersecured creditor, who is thus denied interest on his *claim,* interest on the value of his *collateral,* surely this is where that disposition would have been set forth, and not obscured within the "adequate protection" provision of § 362(d)(1). Instead of the intricate phraseology set forth above, § 506(b) would simply have said that the secured creditor is entitled to interest "on his allowed claim, or on the value of the property securing his allowed claim, whichever is lesser." Petitioner's interpretation of § 362(d)(1) must be regarded as contradicting the carefully drawn disposition of § 506(b).

Petitioner seeks to avoid this conclusion by characterizing § 506(b) as merely an alternative method for compensating oversecured creditors, which does not imply that no compensation is available to undersecured creditors. This theory of duplicate protection for oversecured creditors is implausible even in the abstract, but even more so in light of the historical principles of bankruptcy law. Section 506(b)'s denial of postpetition interest to undersecured creditors merely codified pre-Code bankruptcy law, in which that denial was part of the conscious allocation of reorganization benefits and losses between undersecured and unsecured creditors. "To allow a secured creditor interest where his security was worth less than the value of his debt was thought to be inequitable to unsecured creditors." *Vanston Bondholders Protective Committee v. Green,* 329 U.S. 156, 164, 67 S.Ct. 237, 240, 91 L.Ed. 162 (1946). It was considered unfair to allow an undersecured creditor to recover interest from the estate's unencumbered assets before unsecured creditors had recovered any principal. See *id.,* at 164, 166, 67 S.Ct. at 240, 241; *Ticonic Nat. Bank v. Sprague,* 303 U.S. 406, 412, 58 S.Ct. 612, 615, 82 L.Ed. 926 (1938). We think it unlikely that § 506(b) codified the pre-Code rule with the intent, not of achieving the principal purpose and function of that rule, but of providing over-secured creditors an alternative method of compensation. Moreover, it is incomprehensible why Congress would want to favor undersecured creditors with interest if they move for it under § 362(d)(1) at the inception of the reorganization process—thereby probably pushing the estate into liquidation—but not if they forbear and seek it only at the completion of the reorganization.

Second, petitioner's interpretation of § 362(d)(1) is structurally inconsistent with 11 U.S.C. § 552. Section 552(a) states the general rule that a prepetition security interest does not reach property acquired by the estate or debtor postpetition. Section 552(b) sets forth an exception, allowing postpetition "proceeds, product, offspring, rents, or profits" of the collateral to be covered only if the security agreement expressly provides for an interest in such property, and the interest has been perfected under "applicable nonbankruptcy law." *See, e.g., In re Casbeer,* 793 F.2d 1436, 1442–1444 (CA5 1986); *In re Johnson,* 62 B.R. 24, 28–30 (CA9 Bkrtcy.App. Panel 1986); cf. *Butner v. United States,* 440 U.S. 48, 54–56, 99 S.Ct. 914, 917–18, 59 L.Ed.2d 136 (1979) (same rule under former Bankruptcy Act). Section 552(b) therefore makes possession of a perfected security interest in postpetition rents or profits from collateral a condition of having them applied to satisfying the claim of the secured creditor ahead of the claims of unsecured creditors. Under petitioner's interpretation, however, the undersecured creditor who lacks such a perfected security interest in effect achieves the same result by demanding the "use value" of his collateral under § 362. It is true that § 506(b) gives the *over* secured creditor, despite lack of compliance with the conditions of § 552, a similar priority over unsecured creditors; but that does not compromise the principle of § 552, since the interest payments come only out of the "cushion" in which the oversecured creditor *does have* a perfected security interest.

Third, petitioner's interpretation of § 362(d)(1) makes nonsense of § 362(d)(2). On petitioner's theory, the undersecured creditor's inability to take immediate possession of his collateral is always "cause" for conditioning the stay (upon the payment of market rate interest) under § 362(d)(1), since there is, within the meaning of that paragraph, "lack of adequate protection of an interest in property." But § 362(d)(2) expressly provides a different standard for relief from a stay "of an act against property," which of course includes taking possession of collateral. It provides that the court shall grant relief "if . . . (A) the debtor does not have an equity in such property [*i.e.,* the creditor is undersecured]; *and* (B) such property is not necessary to an effective reorganization." (Emphasis added.) By applying the "adequate protection of an interest in property" provision of § 362(d)(1) to the alleged "interest" in the earning power of collateral, petitioner creates the strange consequence that § 362 entitles the secured creditor to relief from the stay (1) if he is undersecured (and thus not eligible for interest under § 506(b)), *or* (2) if he is undersecured *and* his collateral "is not necessary to an effective reorganization." This renders

§ 362(d)(2) a practical nullity and a theoretical absurdity. If § 362(d)(1) is interpreted in this fashion, an undersecured creditor would seek relief under § 362(d)(2) only if his collateral was not depreciating (or he was being compensated for depreciation) and it was receiving market rate interest on his collateral, but nonetheless wanted to foreclose. Petitioner offers no reason why Congress would want to provide relief for such an obstreperous and thoroughly unharmed creditor.

Section 362(d)(2) also belies petitioner's contention that undersecured creditors will face inordinate and extortionate delay if they are denied compensation for interest lost during the stay as part of "adequate protection" under § 362(d)(1). Once the movant under § 362(d)(2) establishes that he is an undersecured creditor, it is the burden of the *debtor* to establish that the collateral at issue is "necessary to an effective reorganization." See § 362(g). What this requires is not merely a showing that if there is conceivably to be an effective reorganization, this property will be needed for it; but that the property is essential for an effective reorganization *that is in prospect.* This means, as many lower courts, including the en banc court in this case, have properly said, that there must be "a reasonable possibility of a successful reorganization within a reasonable time." 808 F.2d, at 370–371, and nn. 12–13, and cases cited therein. The cases are numerous in which § 362(d)(2) relief has been provided within less than a year from the filing of the bankruptcy petition. And while the bankruptcy courts demand less detailed showings during the four months in which the debtor is given the exclusive right to put together a plan, see 11 U.S.C. §§ 1121(b), (c)(2), even within that period lack of any realistic prospect of effective reorganization will require § 362(d)(2) relief.

III

A

Petitioner contends that denying it compensation under § 362(d)(1) is inconsistent with sections of the Code other than those just discussed. Petitioner principally relies on the phrase "indubitable equivalent" in § 361(3), which also appears in 11 U.S.C. § 1129(b)(2)(A)(iii). Petitioner contends that in the latter context, which sets forth the standards for confirming a reorganization plan, the phrase has developed a well-settled meaning connoting the right of a secured creditor to receive present value of his security—thus requiring interest if the claim is to be paid over time. It is true that under § 1129(b) a secured claimant has a right to receive under a plan the present value of his collateral. This entitlement arises, however, not from the phrase "indubitable equivalent" in § 1129(b)(2)(A)(iii), but from the provision of § 1129(b)(2)(A)(i)(II) that guarantees the secured creditor "deferred cash payments . . . of a value, *as of the effective date of the plan,* of at least the value of such [secured claimant's] interest in the estate's interest in such property." (Emphasis added.) Under this formulation, even though the undersecured creditor's "interest" is regarded (properly) as solely the value of the collateral, he must be rendered payments that assure him that value *as of the effective date of the plan.* In § 361(3), by contrast, the relief pending the stay need only be such *"as will result in the realization* . . . of the indubitable equivalent" of the collateral. (Emphasis added.) It is obvious (since §§ 361 and 362(d)(1) do not entitle the secured creditor to immediate payment of the principal of his collateral) that this "realization" is to "result" not at once, but only upon completion of the reorganization. It is *then* that he must be assured "realization . . . of the indubitable equivalent" of his collateral. To put the point differently: similarity of outcome between § 361(3) and § 1129 would be demanded only if the former read "such other relief . . . as will give such entity, *as of the date of the relief,* the indubitable equivalent of such entity's interest in such property." . . .

Petitioner also contends that the Code embodies a principle that secured creditors do not bear the costs of reorganization. It derives this from the rule that general administrative expenses do not have priority over secured claims. See §§ 506(c), 507(a). But the general principle does not follow from the particular rule. That secured creditors do not bear one kind of reorganization cost hardly means that they bear none of them. The Code rule on administrative expenses merely continues pre-Code law. But it was also pre-Code law that undersecured creditors were not entitled to postpetition interest as compensation for the delay of reorganization. Congress could hardly have understood that the readoption of the rule on administrative expenses would work a change in the rule on postpetition interest, which it also readopted.

Finally, petitioner contends that failure to interpret § 362(d)(1) to require compensation of undersecured creditors for delay will create an inconsistency in the Code in the (admittedly rare) case when the debtor proves solvent. When that occurs, 11 U.S.C. § 726(a)(5) provides that postpetition interest is allowed on unsecured claims. Petitioner contends it would be absurd to allow postpetition interest on unsecured claims but not on the secured portion of undersecured creditors' claims. It would be disingenuous to deny that this is an apparent anomaly, but it will occur so rarely that it is more likely the product of inadvertence than are the blatant inconsistencies petitioner's interpretation would produce. Its inequitable effects, moreover, are entirely avoidable, since an undersecured creditor is entitled to "surrender or waive his security and prove his entire claim as an unsecured one." *United States Nat. Bank v. Chase Nat. Bank,* 331 U.S. 28, 34, 67 S.Ct. 1041, 1044, 91 L.Ed. 1320 (1947). Section 726(a)(5) therefore requires no more than that undersecured creditors receive postpetition interest from a solvent debtor on equal terms with unsecured creditors rather than ahead of them—which, where the debtor is solvent, involves no hardship.

B

Petitioner contends that its interpretation is supported by the legislative history of §§ 361 and 362(d)(1), relying almost entirely on statements that "[s]ecured creditors should not be deprived of the benefit of their bargain." H.R.Rep. No. 95–595, at 339; S.Rep. No. 95–989, at 53, U.S. Code Cong. & Admin. News 1978, pp. 5839, 6295. Such generalizations are inadequate to overcome the plain textual indication in §§ 506 and 362(d)(2) of the Code that Congress did not wish the undersecured creditor to receive interest on his collateral during the term of the stay. If it is at all relevant, the legislative history tends to subvert rather than support petitioner's thesis, since it contains not a hint that § 362(d)(1) entitles the undersecured creditor to postpetition interest. Such a major change in the existing rules would not likely have been made without specific provision in the text of the statute, cf. *Kelly v. Robinson,* 479 U.S. 36, 47, 107 S.Ct. 353, 359–360, 93 L.Ed.2d 216 (1986); it is most improbable that it would have been made without even any mention in the legislative history. . . .

The Fifth Circuit correctly held that the undersecured petitioner is not entitled to interest on its collateral during the stay to assure adequate protection under 11 U.S.C. § 362(d)(1). Petitioner has never sought relief from the stay under § 362(d)(2) or on any ground other than lack of adequate protection. Accordingly, the judgment of the Fifth Circuit is

Affirmed.

NOTES

1. *Understanding the context of* Timbers. In a Chapter 11 case, there is typically an extended period of time between the petition date and the date that the debtor proposes and confirms a reorganization plan. As discussed later in this chapter, once the debtor begins to perform its confirmed plan of reorganization, the Code requires the debtor to repay any secured claim with interest. 11 U.S.C. § 1129(b)(2)(A)(i). Thus, *Timbers* focuses only whether an undersecured creditor is entitled to interest on the secured portion of its claim during the "pendency of bankruptcy," i.e., the period between the petition date and the effective date of the debtor's confirmed plan.

2. *The economic premises of* Timbers. Section 506(a) provides that a mortgagee's claim is secured "to the extent of the value of such creditor's interest in the estate's interest in the property." In interpreting this language, the Court defines the phrase "value of such creditor's interest" to mean "the value of the collateral." In other words, if the value of the mortgaged premises is $4 million, then the value of the mortgagee's interest is also $4 million. In light of the stay, is this correct as a matter of economics?

While commentators have criticized the *Timbers* decision both for its economic premises and its method of statutory interpretation, see, e.g.,

Douglas G. Baird, The Elements of Bankruptcy 204 (rev. ed. 1993); David Gray Carlson, Adequate Protection Payments and the Surrender of Cash Collateral in Chapter 11 Reorganizations, 15 Cardozo L. Rev. 1357 (1994), the Court's subsequent bankruptcy decisions have never questioned *Timbers*.

    3.   *Nonpayment of taxes as "cause" for relief from stay.* Suppose Bank holds a mortgage on the land of Mortgagor, who has filed a bankruptcy petition. On the petition date, Mortgagor owes Bank $1 million, and the mortgaged land has a value of $800,000. The land is not depreciating in value, but Mortgagor has not paid real estate taxes for the most recent year (totalling $20,000). Can Bank obtain relief from stay based on Mortgagor's nonpayment of taxes? Why or why not? See, e.g., In re Biltwood Props., LLC, 473 B.R. 70 (Bankr. M.D. Pa. 2012).

————————

Relief from stay under 11 U.S.C. § 362(d)(3). Frequently, developers structure commercial real estate projects as "single-asset" projects, i.e., the mortgagor is a business entity that owns no other assets and engages in no other business. Many have questioned whether bankruptcy law should provide *any* protection for such owners. The critique asserts that bankruptcy should facilitate the reorganization of active business concerns—ones that could not realistically negotiate a collective restructuring with hundreds or thousands of individual creditors without judicial intervention. By contrast, the "single asset" real estate project typically involves one debtor (the mortgagor) and few if any creditors other than the mortgagee—calling into question whether reorganization requires an intrusive (and expensive) federal judicial process. The Code did not exclude owners of "single asset" properties from seeking bankruptcy protection, however, and the owners of single-asset projects frequently sought bankruptcy protection during the real estate downturn of the late 1980s and early 1990s.

    This seriously frustrated mortgage lenders, particularly after *Timbers* confirmed that an undersecured mortgagee could not collect interest during the pendency of the bankruptcy. With no obligation to pay such interest, single-asset mortgagors would frequently "drag their feet" in proposing a plan of reorganization, hoping that market conditions would improve in the interim. Mortgagees complained bitterly about this pattern, arguing that the owner of a "single-asset" project should have a limited amount of time to "fish or cut bait."

    In 1994, Congress responded by adding § 362(d)(3), which applies only to single asset real estate.[15] If the mortgagee of single asset real estate

———

[15] The term "single asset real estate" means "real property constituting a single property or project, other than residential real property with fewer than 4 residential units, which generates substantially all of the gross income of a debtor who is not a family farmer and on which no substantial business is being conducted by a debtor other than the business of operating the real property and activities incidental thereto." 11 U.S.C. § 101(51B).

moves for relief from stay under § 362(d)(3), the debtor must either (1) propose a feasible reorganization plan within 90 days or (2) begin making monthly payments of interest on the secured portion of the mortgagee's claim (calculated using the nondefault interest rate specified in the mortgage note). If the debtor does neither, the court must grant relief from the stay and permit the mortgagee to foreclose. See, e.g., In re RYYZ, LLC, 490 B.R. 29 (Bankr. E.D.N.Y. 2013); In re RIM Dev., LLC, 448 B.R. 280 (Bankr. D. Kan. 2010). Query: Should Congress have required pendency interest payments at the default contract rate (or at the prevailing market rate) if that rate would be higher? Why or why not?

Relief from stay: bankruptcy abuse. During the 1980s and early 1990s, mortgagees often complained that mortgagors abused the bankruptcy process by filing "serial" bankruptcies—i.e., filing to prevent a foreclosure, confirming a reorganization plan, seeking bankruptcy protection again when the plan failed, and so on repeatedly. In 1994, Congress addressed this concern (whether real or perceived) by enacting section 362(d)(4), which now provides that the court shall grant a motion by a mortgagee for relief from stay:

> if the court finds that the filing of the petition was part of a scheme to delay, hinder, or defraud creditors that involved either (A) transfer of all or part ownership of, or other interest in, such real property without the consent of the [mortgagee] or court approval; or (B) multiple bankruptcy filings affecting such real property.

Further, if the court grants a mortgagee relief under section 362(d)(4), the mortgagee may record the order granting relief in the local real property records, and that recorded order will provide *in rem* relief from stay in any other bankruptcy filed in the ensuing two years.

NOTES

1.   *Other serial filings.* Many creditors complained that section 362(d)(4) did not sufficiently address the "serial filing" problem. Thus, in 2005, Congress also limited the protection of the automatic stay for some "repeat" filers. The Code now limits the stay for individual debtors in Chapters 7, 11, or 13 who, on the petition date, had been the debtor in another bankruptcy case that had been dismissed within the previous year. In such cases, the stay terminates with respect to the debtor 30 days after the filing of the later case, unless the court continues the stay upon motion of the debtor and the debtor establishes that the new filing was in "good faith as to the creditors to be stayed." 11 U.S.C. § 362(c)(3)(B). For cases in which the debtor failed to establish the requisite "good faith," see, e.g., In re Cannon, 375 B.R. 908 (Bankr. E.D. Mo. 2007); In re Kurtzahn, 337 B.R. 356 (Bankr. D. Minn. 2006); In re Collins, 335 B.R. 646 (Bankr. S.D. Tex. 2005).

2.   *Relief from stay—procedural considerations.* If a secured creditor files a motion seeking relief from the stay, the court must act on the motion within

thirty days; if not, the moving party automatically receives the requested relief. 11 U.S.C. § 362(e)(1). During this thirty-day period, the court conducts a preliminary hearing, after which it either (a) enters an order granting or denying the requested relief, or (b) continues the stay temporarily pending a later final hearing and determination. If the court continues the stay pending a final hearing, the court must conclude that final hearing within thirty days of the preliminary hearing, unless the court extends that thirty-day period with the consent of the parties or based upon "compelling circumstances." *Id.*

The moving party (usually the secured creditor) bears the burden of proof on the issue of the debtor's equity in the collateral (and thus on the value of the collateral). 11 U.S.C. § 362(g)(1). The party opposing relief (typically the trustee/debtor-in-possession) bears the burden of proof on all other issues. 11 U.S.C. § 362(g)(2). In exceptional circumstances, the court can order relief from the stay without notice, if the party seeking relief would suffer "irreparable damage" by the delay occasioned by notice and a hearing. 11 U.S.C. § 362(f).

In 2005, Congress amended section 362 to place an additional constraint upon an individual debtor's ability to delay a final determination of a secured party's motion for relief from stay. In the Chapter 7, 11, or 13 case of an individual debtor, the stay terminates sixty days after the secured party's motion, unless the court renders a final determination of the motion within that sixty-day period or the sixty-day period is extended by the secured party's consent or by the court—but the court may only extend this sixty-day period "for such *specific* time as the court finds is required for good cause," and the court must make specific factual findings justifying the extension. 11 U.S.C. § 362(e)(2) (emphasis added).

3. THE TRUSTEE'S AVOIDING POWERS

Because the trustee represents the interests of unsecured creditors, the trustee's primary goal is to maximize the size of the estate available to satisfy those claims. The trustee will thus investigate the debtor's financial affairs to identify any legal basis to challenge the validity of a creditor's claim or the validity of liens against property of the estate. The Code provides the trustee with an impressive arsenal of weapons in this effort. The most basic is 11 U.S.C. § 558, which gives the trustee "the benefit of any defense available to the debtor" against a creditor. Thus, to the extent that a debtor could have invalidated a mortgage based on fraud, usury, lack of capacity, or other grounds, so too can the trustee.

The Code also endows the trustee with a series of *avoiding powers*— causes of action that allow the bankruptcy trustee (or the debtor-in-possession in Chapter 11 or 12 cases)[16] to invalidate (or "avoid") certain

---

[16] In Chapter 11 and Chapter 12 cases, the debtor in possession receives the powers of a trustee, including the avoiding powers. 11 U.S.C. §§ 1107(a), 1203. The Code does not expressly delegate the avoiding powers to a Chapter 13 debtor, 11 U.S.C. § 1303. Because the legislative history indicates that section 1303 "does not imply that the debtor does not also possess other powers concurrently with the trustee," 124 Cong. Rec. 32,409 (floor statement of Rep. Edwards),

dispositions of property by the debtor or obligations incurred by the debtor during some period of time prior to bankruptcy or during bankruptcy. This section discusses the avoiding powers of greatest potential consequence to mortgagees.

The "strong-arm" power. Section 544(a) provides that the trustee has the status, as of the petition date, of a judgment lien creditor as to the debtor's personal property and a bona fide purchaser as to the debtor's land (other than fixtures). 11 U.S.C. § 544(a)(1) (personalty), § 544(a)(3) (land other than fixtures). Outside of bankruptcy, a bona fide purchaser of land would take that land free of an unrecorded mortgage. Section 544(a)(3) thus permits the trustee to invalidate (or "avoid") any mortgage against property of the estate if, on the petition date, that mortgage was not recorded under applicable state law. Thus, courts have permitted the trustee/debtor in possession to avoid a mortgage in cases where the mortgagee:

- failed to record until after the bankruptcy petition. See, e.g., In re Garrido Jimenez, 370 B.R. 878 (1st Cir. B.A.P. 2007). [Note that the mortgagee's action of recording the mortgage after the petition date would also constitute a violation of the automatic stay. 11 U.S.C. § 362(a)(4).]

- failed to record altogether. See, e.g., In re Sullivan, 387 B.R. 353 (1st Cir. B.A.P. 2008).

- tried to record the mortgage, but did not properly do so within the chain of title. See, e.g., In re Ramos, 493 B.R. 355 (Bankr. D. P.R. 2013); In re Thulis, 474 B.R. 668 (Bankr. W.D. Wis. 2012).

- filed the mortgage for recording in the wrong county. See, e.g., In re Simmons, 560 B.R. 308 (Bankr. S.D. Ohio 2016); In re Morgan, 449 B.R. 821 (Bankr. N.D. Ga. 2010).

- erroneously recorded a release of the mortgage prior to bankruptcy. See, e.g., In re Mammola, 474 B.R. 23 (Bankr. D. Mass. 2012).

Under § 544(a)(3), the trustee's knowledge is irrelevant; the strong-arm power bestows on the trustee the status of a bona fide purchaser *even if* the trustee has actual knowledge of the unrecorded mortgage.

---

numerous courts have concluded that a Chapter 13 debtor can exercise the avoiding powers. See, e.g., In re Dickson, 427 B.R. 399 (Bankr.6th Cir.2010); In re Fitzgerald, 237 B.R. 252 (Bankr.D.Conn.1999); In re Hernandez, 150 B.R. 29 (Bankr.S.D.Tex.1993). The trend in recent decisions, however, suggests a growing doubt that a Chapter 13 debtor can exercise the avoiding powers. See, e.g., In re Stangel, 219 F.3d 498 (5th Cir. 2000); In re Barbee, 461 B.R. 711 (6th Cir. B.A.P. 2011); In re Hansen, 332 B.R. 8 (10th Cir. B.A.P. 2005); In re Merrifield, 214 B.R. 362 (8th Cir. B.A.P. 1997); In re Scott, 572 B.R. 492 (Bankr. S.D.N.Y. 2017); In re Cole, 563 B.R. 526 (Bankr. W.D.N.C. 2017).

Avoidance of the mortgage typically allows the trustee to liquidate the mortgaged property and use the proceeds to pay administrative expenses and unsecured creditors. While the debtor's underlying obligation to the mortgagee remains valid, the mortgagee's claim is treated as unsecured, which will significantly reduce the mortgagee's recovery.

NOTES

1. *Defects in the execution or acknowledgment of mortgages.* The trustee/debtor-in-possession often invokes the strong-arm power in cases involving some defect in the execution of a mortgage. In these cases, the result turns on whether the defect defeats the ability of the mortgage to provide constructive notice to subsequent purchasers under applicable state law. Thus, similar defects can produce different results in different states. Compare In re Arnette, 584 B.R. 304 (Bankr. W.D. Wis. 2018) (under Wisconsin law, mortgage was sufficient to provide constructive notice even though it described the property using only a street address rather than a legal description) and In re Savage, 504 B.R. 921 (Bankr. W.D. Ark. 2014) (same result under Arkansas law) with In re Benton, 563 B.R. 113 (Bankr. D. Mass. 2017) (contrary result under Massachusetts law) and In re Dolven, 549 B.R. 386 (Bankr. D. Idaho 2016) (contrary result under Idaho law).

During the post-2008 real estate crisis, trustees frequently attempted to use the strong-arm power to avoid mortgages that were improperly acknowledged. Again, whether the trustee may avoid such a mortgage depends on whether state law treats it as sufficient to provide constructive notice to subsequent purchasers. If not, the trustee may use the strong-arm power to invalidate the mortgage. See, e.g., In re Kelley, 498 B.R. 342 (1st Cir. B.A.P. 2013); In re Kebe, 469 B.R. 778 (Bankr. S.D. Ohio 2012). Does it make sense to allow the trustee/debtor-in-possession to avoid such a mortgage? A defective acknowledgment does not defeat the validity of the mortgage between the mortgagor and the mortgagee; does it affect the ability of searchers to locate the mortgage in the land records?

2. *Preservation of an avoided mortgage lien for the benefit of the estate.* Suppose that First Bank takes a mortgage on Debtor's land but fails to record it. Debtor later grants a mortgage to Second Bank, which properly records. Debtor subsequently files a Chapter 7 case; on the petition date, Debtor owes each bank $100,000 but the mortgaged land is worth only $150,000. In this circumstance, Second Bank might try to argue that First Bank's failure to record the mortgage should result in Second Bank being promoted to first priority.

Under 11 U.S.C. § 551, however, the avoided transfer—i.e., the lien created by the unrecorded First Bank mortgage—is "preserved for the benefit of the estate." Section 551 thus allows the trustee to assert the lien of First Bank *as if that lien still had priority over Second Bank.* The trustee could thus take the first $100,000 of sale proceeds from the land—and could devote that sum to payment of administrative expenses and unsecured claims—before distributing the remaining proceeds to Second Bank on account of its junior lien. See, e.g., In re Guido, 344 B.R. 193 (Bankr. D. Mass. 2006).

The power to avoid fraudulent transfers. Sometimes, debtors deliberately frustrate the collection efforts of creditors by giving property (or transferring it at bargain prices) to friends, relatives, or third parties. The common law has always allowed an injured creditor to invalidate an intentionally fraudulent transfer, and the Uniform Voidable Transactions Act (UVTA) permits creditors to avoid transfers made by a debtor with the intent to hinder, delay, or defraud creditors. UVTA § 4(a)(1). Because such transfers also disadvantage an insolvent debtor's unsecured creditors, the Code permits the trustee to avoid intentionally fraudulent transfers made by the debtor within the two-year period prior to bankruptcy. 11 U.S.C. § 548(a)(1)(A).

More commonly, debtors make transfers by gift or for insufficient consideration without a specific intent to hinder, delay, or defraud one or more specific creditors. Because these transfers nevertheless have the same impact on creditors as intentionally fraudulent transfers, the common law has long deemed such transfers by *insolvent* debtors to be *constructively* fraudulent. The UVTA allows creditors to avoid constructively fraudulent transfers. UVTA § 4(a)(2), The Bankruptcy Code provides a similar rule in section 548(a)(1)(B), which permits the trustee to avoid any transfer of the debtor's property if the transfer was made within two years prior to the debtor's bankruptcy, the debtor received less than a "reasonably equivalent value" in exchange, and the debtor was insolvent at the time the transfer was made or was rendered insolvent as a result. 11 U.S.C. § 548(a)(1)(B)(i), (ii)(I). The trustee can recover the property from the transferee, even if the transferee acted in good faith and without knowledge that the transfer was fraudulent.[17]

For the most part, this avoiding power does not present a substantial threat to the typical mortgagee. The trustee cannot avoid pre-petition mortgage payments by the mortgagor as constructively fraudulent transfers, even if the debtor was insolvent, because the debtor received equivalent value for those payments in the form of *pro tanto* satisfaction of the debt. Likewise, because section 548 defines "value" to include "securing . . . [an] antecedent debt," 11 U.S.C. § 548(d)(2)(A), the trustee cannot use

[handwritten margin note: CL: transfers from insolvent debtors constructively fraudulent]

---

[17] 11 U.S.C. §§ 548(a)(1), 550(a)(1). Because this result may be harsh to the transferee, the Code provides some protection; if the transferee purchased the property in good faith, it receives a lien on the property to the extent of the amount paid to the debtor. 11 U.S.C. § 548(c). In addition, if the initial transferee has already conveyed the property to a third party, the trustee cannot recover the property from a third party who took the property for value, in good faith, and without knowledge of the fact that the initial transfer from the debtor was fraudulent. 11 U.S.C. § 550(b).

section 548 to avoid a mortgage simply because the debtor granted it to secure what previously had been an unsecured debt.[18]

The primary context in which section 548 has affected mortgagees involves attempts by trustees/debtors-in-possession to invalidate pre-bankruptcy foreclosure sales. For example, suppose that Bank foreclosed on its mortgage against Mortgagor's land and conducted a public sale at which Bank purchased the land for a full credit bid of $100,000. Three months later, Bank contracted to sell the land to a third person for $180,000, but before that sale can close, Mortgagor files a bankruptcy petition. One might argue that this foreclosure sale should be viewed as constructively fraudulent, at least if the $180,000 resale price accurately reflected the land's fair market value at the time of the foreclosure sale (in which case Mortgagor received $80,000 less than equivalent value for its interest in the land at foreclosure). In this instance, the foreclosure sale would have diminished Mortgagor's bankruptcy estate to the detriment of other creditors.

For many years, the weight of authority held that the trustee/debtor-in-possession could invalidate a pre-bankruptcy foreclosure sale as constructively fraudulent if the foreclosure sale price was less than 70% of the property's fair market value. The leading case for this view was *Durrett v. Washington Nat'l Ins. Co.*, 621 F.2d 201 (5th Cir. 1980). While *Durrett* was widely followed, reaction from the real estate community was hostile. Opponents argued that because *Durrett* created a long period of uncertainty about the validity of title purchased at a foreclosure sale, it "naturally inhibit[ed] a purchaser other than the mortgagee from purchasing at foreclosure," *Abramson v. Lakewood Bank & Trust Co.*, 647 F.2d 547, 549 (5th Cir. 1981) (Clark, J., dissenting), and in turn resulted in reduced sale prices and increased the likelihood of deficiency judgments.

In 1994, the United States Supreme Court rejected *Durrett* and its progeny in *BFP v. Resolution Trust Corp.*, 511 U.S. 531, 114 S.Ct. 1757, 128 L.Ed.2d 554 (1994). In a 5–4 decision, the Court held that "a fair and proper price, or a 'reasonably equivalent value,' for foreclosed property, is the price in fact received at the foreclosure sale, so long as all the requirements of the State's foreclosure law have been complied with." *BFP*, 511 U.S. at 544. As a result, § 548 no longer provides a basis to invalidate

---

[18] If a debtor granted a mortgage to secure the debt of an unrelated borrower, however, the debtor would not have received "value," and thus the trustee could avoid the mortgage as a fraudulent transfer if the debtor was insolvent or was rendered insolvent by granting the mortgage. See, e.g., In re Scheffler, 471 B.R. 464 (Bankr. E.D. Pa. 2012).

In determining whether a debtor is insolvent, the court must take into account both the debtor's fixed and contingent liabilities. In valuing the debtor's contingent liabilities, the court must consider the probability that the contingency will occur. See Covey v. Commercial Nat'l Bank of Peoria, 960 F.2d 657 (7th Cir.1992). Thus, if the debtor grants a mortgage to secure the obligation of a third party, valuation of this contingent liability requires the court to consider the likelihood of default by the third party.

a non-collusive foreclosure sale based on inadequacy of the price, so long as all other requirements of state foreclosure law have been satisfied.

NOTES

1. *The impact of* BFP *on installment land contract forfeitures.* Suppose Vendee defaults under an installment land contract on which Vendee owes a balance of $50,000, and Vendee's interest is forfeited. At the time, the land in question is worth $100,000. Six months later, Vendee files a Chapter 7 petition. Can the trustee set aside the contract termination as constructively fraudulent to Vendee's creditors? Some courts have held that *BFP* does not preclude the trustee from avoiding an installment contract forfeiture. See, e.g., In re Houston, 385 B.R. 268 (Bankr. N.D. Iowa 2008). Other courts have held that *BFP* prevents the trustee from setting aside contract forfeitures, however, concluding that "absent a debt so small as to shock the conscience, the cancellation of the remaining debt ... through a forfeiture proceeding regularly conducted pursuant to state law is 'reasonably equivalent value' for the debtor's interest in the property." See, e.g., In re Vermillion, 176 B.R. 563 (Bankr. D. Or. 1994); In re Butler, 552 N.W.2d 226 (Minn. 1996). Note that *BFP* involved a public auction foreclosure sale (which ostensibly serves as an opportunity for public valuation of the land). Should *BFP* apply to an installment contract forfeiture, where no such sale takes place?

2. *The impact of* BFP *on strict foreclosure.* One bankruptcy court in Connecticut held that "the value received by the debtors for their transfer of their interest in the property [pursuant to strict foreclosure] ... is the 'reasonably equivalent value' of the interest transferred." In re Talbot, 254 B.R. 63, 71 (Bankr. D. Conn. 2000). The court noted that "Connecticut strict foreclosure law provides a debtor with sufficient procedural safeguards to render it analogous to the foreclosure sale context of *BFP*." *Talbot*, 254 B.R. at 70. By contrast, another Connecticut bankruptcy court concluded that the mortgagee's compliance with strict foreclosure procedures did not conclusively establish that the mortgagor received "reasonably equivalent value." In re Fitzgerald, 255 B.R. 807 (Bankr. D. Conn. 2000). Which approach is more sensible? What sort of "procedural safeguards" are needed to make the context sufficiently analogous to *BFP*?

3. *The impact of* BFP *on deeds in lieu of foreclosure.* Suppose that Mortgagor executes and delivers to Bank a deed in lieu of foreclosure following default. Six months later, Mortgagor files a Chapter 7 case. Does BFP preclude the trustee from setting aside the deed in lieu of foreclosure as constructively fraudulent? See, e.g., In re 4100 West Grand LLC, 481 B.R. 444 (Bankr. N.D. Ill. 2012). Why or why not?

4. *Avoidance of fraudulent transfers under section 544(b).* The Code allows the trustee to set aside any transfer of the debtor's property that an actual unsecured creditor could have avoided under state law. 11 U.S.C. § 544(b)(1). As discussed earlier, state fraudulent transfer laws (e.g., the UVTA) permit a creditor harmed by an intentionally or constructively

fraudulent transfer to invalidate that transfer. Thus, if the trustee can identify an actual unsecured creditor of the debtor that is capable of asserting a state law fraudulent transfer claim, the trustee can use section 544(b) to assert that claim on behalf of the bankruptcy estate.

After *BFP*, the applicable standards for a fraudulent transfer are essentially the same under both section 548(a) and most applicable state fraudulent transfer laws. Thus, the trustee will use section 544(b) to attack a fraudulent transfer only if it occurred more than two years prior to bankruptcy (and thus outside section 548's two-year reach-back period). State law may provide a longer reach-back period for fraudulent transfers. For example, the UVTA generally allows creditors a period of four years in which to avoid a fraudulent transfer. UVTA § 9(a), (b).

The power to avoid preferential transfers. Suppose Debtor has only $1,000 in assets but has two unsecured creditors, X and Y, to whom Debtor owes $1,000 each. X reduces its claim to judgment and levies upon the $1,000 in assets shortly before Debtor files for bankruptcy. In this situation, X receives payment in full, and Y gets nothing; X has received a "preferential" payment relative to Y. Outside of bankruptcy, commercial law does not invalidate preferential transfers, but leaves creditors to their own collection efforts—"the race goes to the swiftest." Bankruptcy law cares about such transfers, however, because it seeks to discourage creditors from engaging in "eve-of-bankruptcy" collection activities and thus triggering the "race to the courthouse" that bankruptcy seeks to avoid or mitigate. Thus, section 547 allows the trustee or debtor-in-possession to avoid any voluntary or involuntary transfer of an interest in the debtor's property if the transfer:

- was made to a creditor or benefitted a creditor, 11 U.S.C. § 547(b)(1);

- was made on account of an antecedent debt, 11 U.S.C. § 547(b)(2);

- took place while the debtor was insolvent, 11 U.S.C. § 547(b)(3);[19]

- took place during the ninety-day period prior to bankruptcy (or within one year prior to bankruptcy if the benefitted creditor was an "insider"), 11 U.S.C. § 547(b)(4); and

- made the creditor better off than it would have been if the transfer had not occurred and the creditor had instead

---

[19] 11 U.S.C. § 547(b)(3). The Code applies a "balance sheet" test—the debtor is insolvent if the sum of its debts exceed the value of its assets. 11 U.S.C. § 101(32). Section 547(f) provides that in any preference action, the debtor is presumed to have been insolvent during the ninety days prior to bankruptcy. 11 U.S.C. § 547(f).

received payment on the debt only through a Chapter 7 liquidation of the debtor's assets, 11 U.S.C. § 547(b)(5).

For mortgagees, section 547 presents a risk in four discrete contexts: (1) payments by the mortgagor on the debt during the preference period; (2) mortgages taken during the preference period to secure previously unsecured debt; (3) delayed recording of the mortgage during the preference period; and (4) foreclosure sales during the preference period.

Preferences—payments on the mortgage debt. Suppose that on June 1, Debtor repays Bank the full $50,000 balance of an outstanding mortgage loan covering Blackacre. On July 1, Debtor files for bankruptcy. If Blackacre has a fair market value of $50,000 or more, Debtor's repayment to Bank was not a preference, because it did not improve Bank's position vis-à-vis other creditors. If the Debtor had not made the payment and had instead filed a Chapter 7 case, Bank (as a fully secured creditor) would have received full payment anyway. See, e.g., In re EDC, Inc. 930 F.2d 1275 (7th Cir. 1991); Braniff Airways, Inc. v. Exxon Co., U.S.A., 814 F.2d 1030 (5th Cir. 1987). By contrast, if Blackacre has a fair market value of only $30,000, then the trustee can avoid the $50,000 payment to Bank as a preference. In a Chapter 7 liquidation, Bank would have received less than $50,000; its $50,000 claim would have been bifurcated into a $30,000 secured claim (which would have been paid in full) and a $20,000 unsecured claim (on which Bank would have received only a pro rata dividend). The trustee could thus recover the entire $50,000 payment from Bank.

What about the more typical situation in which the debtor makes regular monthly payments of principal and interest? If the payments were in the scheduled amount and were made in a timely fashion, the trustee cannot avoid the payments. The Code provides an exception from the preference rule for payments made by the debtor if the debt was "incurred by the debtor in the ordinary course of business or financial affairs of the debtor and the transferee" and the payments were made "in the ordinary course of business or financial affairs of the debtor and the transferee" or "according to ordinary business terms." 11 U.S.C. § 547(c)(2).

Preferences—mortgage to secure previously unsecured debt. Section 547 permits the trustee to avoid a mortgage granted by the mortgagor within the preference period if the mortgage secures a pre-existing and previously unsecured debt. For example, suppose Debtor is in default in repayment of a $50,000 unsecured debt owed to Bank. Rather than seeking a judgment against Debtor, Bank agrees to forbear when Debtor executes a mortgage covering Blackacre (which is unencumbered and has a value exceeding $50,000). Two weeks later, Debtor files a bankruptcy petition. In this example, the mortgage (which is a transfer of an interest in Debtor's property) improved Bank's position vis-à-vis other creditors by securing an otherwise unsecured claim on which Bank would have received only a pro rata dividend in a Chapter 7 liquidation. Thus, the trustee can avoid Bank's mortgage lien as a preference, leaving Bank with an entirely unsecured claim.

Preferences—the late-recorded mortgage. There is usually a delay between the execution of a mortgage and its recording. In ideal circumstances, this delay is a matter of mere minutes or hours; however, due to inadvertence or neglect, the delay could extend for a greater period. During this delay, the mortgagee has a "secret" lien and third parties are at risk of transacting with the mortgagor in ignorance of the as-yet unrecorded mortgage. Bankruptcy policy discourages such secret liens, and this policy is reflected in the "timing" rule by which § 547 establishes when a transfer is deemed to occur for purposes of the preference rule:

> (A) at the time such transfer takes effect between the transferor and the transferee, if such transfer is perfected at, or within 30 days after, such time . . .;

> (B) at the time such transfer is perfected, if such transfer is perfected after such 30 days; or

> (C) immediately before the date of the filing of the petition, if such transfer is not perfected at the later of—

>> (i) the commencement of the case; or

>> (ii) 30 days after such transfer takes effect between the transferor and the transferee.

A transfer of real property is "perfected" when "a bona fide purchaser of such property from the debtor against whom applicable law permits the transfer to be perfected cannot acquire an interest that is superior to the interest of the transferee." 11 U.S.C. § 547(e)(1)(A). Thus, under any type of state recording act, a mortgage is "perfected" at the moment it is recorded.

This timing rule places a premium on timely recording of a mortgage. For example, suppose that on July 1, Debtor borrows $100,000 from Bank and grants Bank a mortgage on Blackacre. On September 1, Debtor files a bankruptcy petition. If Bank recorded its mortgage on or before July 31 (within thirty days after its execution), the mortgage is deemed to have been granted on July 1. 11 U.S.C. § 547(e)(2)(A). Thus, Debtor will not have granted the mortgage on account of an antecedent debt and the trustee cannot set aside the mortgage as a preference. By contrast, if the Bank did not record its mortgage until August 10, § 547(e)(2)(B) will deem the mortgage to have been granted on August 10 (even though the mortgage debt was actually incurred on July 1). As a result, Debtor will be deemed to have granted the mortgage on account of an antecedent debt and the trustee could avoid the mortgage as a preference (assuming it satisfies all of the other requirements of section 547(b)). See, e.g., In re Lee, 530 F.3d 458 (6th Cir. 2008) (72 day delay in recording); In re Flannery, 513 B.R. 1 (Bankr. D. Mass. 2014) (88-day delay); USAA Fed. Sav. Bank v. Hope, 589 B.R. 914 (M.D. Ga. 2018) (52-day delay). As a matter of policy, why allow the trustee to set aside a late-recorded mortgage as a preference? See, e.g., Nelson, Whitman, Burkhart & Freyermuth, Real Estate Finance Law § 8.16 (6th ed.2015).

Preferences—pre-bankruptcy foreclosure sales. As discussed earlier, *BFP* diminished the trustee's ability to avoid a pre-bankruptcy foreclosure sale as constructively fraudulent based on an inadequate sale price. After *BFP*, however, a number of courts have allowed the trustee to set aside pre-bankruptcy foreclosure sales at inadequate prices as preferences, at least where the mortgagee is the foreclosure sale purchaser. To appreciate the problem, consider the facts in In re Villareal, 413 B.R. 633 (Bankr. S.D. Tex. 2009). The mortgagee foreclosed following the debtor's default and purchased the premises for a credit bid of $70,000, even though the mortgagee's own appraiser had valued the premises at *$4.02 million*! Less than two months later, the debtor filed a Chapter 13 petition and sought to set aside the foreclosure sale as a preference. The debtor argued that by virtue of the foreclosure sale, the mortgagee received a transfer of the debtor's property than enabled the mortgagee to receive land worth $4.02 million—more than it would have received in a Chapter 7 liquidation, in which it would have received (at most) only the amount of the unpaid debt. The foreclosure sale in *Villareal* technically meets each element of section 547(b); should the trustee be able to use section 547 to set aside the sale when *BFP* would not have allowed the trustee to set aside the same sale under section 548?

In the case of In re Ehring, 900 F.2d 184 (9th Cir. 1990), the U.S. Court of Appeals for the Ninth Circuit held that the answer was no:

> If the petition had been filed before the foreclosure sale was complete, the automatic stay (11 U.S.C. § 362) would have prevented the sale. The creditor might have been able to lift the stay or might have had to wait for the trustee to liquidate the collateral. To the extent that the creditor is secured, it would receive 100% of its claim in dollar value—$199,746.41. The property appears to be worth $390,000 because the creditor sold it at that price a short time later, and it is well recognized that for various reasons foreclosure sales (and liquidation sales) do not bring the same value as a non-distress (fair market) sale. Because the creditor appears to have received value greater than the debt that was secured, it could be argued that the creditor has received "more" from the foreclosure than it would have under Chapter 7 liquidation.

This analysis, however, fails to consider the reality of the transaction. If the creditor received "more" it is only because the creditor elected to purchase the property at the foreclosure sale rather than simply accepting the receipts of a sale to a third party. Had the third party outbid the creditor, there could be no preference because the price paid would not have been transferred for an antecedent debt. Since section 547 does not reach a third-party purchaser, it is difficult to see why the existence of a preference should turn on the status of the purchaser as a creditor. If the sale was defective or the purchaser otherwise took unfair advantage of the debtor, the transfer may be voided under section 548, regardless of whether the purchaser was the creditor or a third party. We see no reason to construe section 547 to permit avoidance of an otherwise properly conducted sale based solely on the creditor being the highest bidder.

Furthermore, a close analysis of a foreclosure proceeding supports treating the creditor the same as the third-party buyer. Foreclosure is not a unitary event, but in fact two separate legal events. First, the creditor must exert its power or right to foreclose—to force the sale of the property. The creditor has no obligation to buy, let alone, bid at the sale. Moreover, the creditor in purchasing the property at the foreclosure sale assumes the risk of not being able to dispose of it for the amount of the debt. The sale is a separate, second transaction, the receipts of which will be used to satisfy the creditor.

A preference exists only when the creditor has received more under the foreclosure than it would have under Chapter 7 liquidation. There is nothing in the statute that prohibits the creditor from purchasing the property in a liquidation sale—just as at foreclosure. In fact, section 547(b)(5) likely presumes a liquidation sale similar to the foreclosure sale forced by the mortgagee. See 2 J. White & R. Summers, Uniform Commercial Code § 25–7, at 450. We conclude therefore that a creditor who purchases at a regularly conducted foreclosure sale has not received more than it would have under a Chapter 7 liquidation sale. . . .

A number of decisions have concurred with *Ehring.* See, e.g., In re Veltre, 562 B.R. 890 (Bankr. W.D. Pa. 2017); In re Cottrell, 213 B.R. 378 (Bankr. M.D. Ala. 1996). By contrast, a significant number of decisions have rejected *Ehring* and hold that the trustee can avoid a pre-bankruptcy foreclosure sale under section 547(b). See, e.g., In re Whittle Development, Inc., 463 B.R. 796 (Bankr. N.D. Tex. 2011); In re Villareal, 413 B.R. 633 (Bankr. S.D. Tex. 2009); In re Andrews, 262 B.R. 299 (Bankr. M.D. Pa.

2001); In re Park North Partners, Ltd., 80 B.R. 551 (N.D. Ga. 1987), on remand, 85 B.R. 916 (Bankr. N.D. Ga. 1988).

Some courts have argued that *BFP*'s policy of promoting finality also justifies prohibiting the trustee/DIP from using section 547(b) to set aside a pre-bankruptcy foreclosure sale. See, e.g., In re Pulcini, 261 B.R. 836, 844 (Bankr. W.D. Pa. 2001) (decision to set aside sheriff's sale as a preference would "profoundly affect Pennsylvania's interest in making title to real property stable and secure" because "title to real property purchased at a foreclosure sale 'would be under a federally created cloud' "). Is this concern legitimate? Would section 547(b) have the same potential chilling effect on foreclosure sale bidding as section 548? Why or why not? See generally Kenneth M. Misken & Juliana Bell, Preference Actions Arising Out of Foreclosure Sales, 31 Am.Bankr.Inst.J. 24 (April 2012); Averch & Berryman, Mortgage Foreclosure as a Preference: Does *BFP* Protect the Lender?, 7 J.Bankr.L. & Prac. 281 (1988).

Some commentators have argued that the *Ehring* approach is correct because preference law should address only those situations where a creditor gets paid up to the full amount of the debt, but not where the creditor receives a transfer in excess of full payment. Under this reasoning, the excess is not a preference but a fraudulent transfer—and thus avoidable only as a fraudulent transfer. In other words, if a creditor who is owed $1,000 would have received $300 in a Chapter 7 liquidation, but is paid $1,200 by the insolvent debtor within 90 days of bankruptcy, $1,000 of the transfer is preferential while the $200 excess can only be a fraudulent transfer. See, e.g., Kennedy, Involuntary Fraudulent Transfers, 9 Cardozo L.Rev. 531, 563–564 (1987); Zinman, Houle & Weiss, Fraudulent Transfers According to Alden, Gross & Borowitz: A Tale of Two Circuits, 39 Bus.Law. 977, 985 (1984). Is this argument persuasive? Is it consistent with the statutory language of the Bankruptcy Code? Can you make a persuasive argument for why bankruptcy policy justifies treating the entire $1,200 payment as a preference? See, e.g., Nelson, Whitman, Burkhart & Freyermuth, Real Estate Finance Law § 8.16 (6th ed.2015).

4. THE MORTGAGEE IN A CHAPTER 7 CASE

Chapter 7 is "liquidation" bankruptcy. A Chapter 7 debtor must turn over its nonexempt property[20] to the trustee in exchange for a discharge of

---

[20] Under the laws of each state, debtors are permitted to keep some amount of property free of the claims of general (unsecured) creditors seeking execution of a judgment. Each state's exemption law varies (and some are more generous than others), but the exemption permits the debtor to retain a certain amount of equity in a home, a car, clothing and household goods, personal effects such as jewelry, "tools of the trade," and some rights to payment (such as for child support or social security benefits). Thus, for example, if the applicable exemption allowed the debtor an exemption not to exceed $20,000 in its residence, and the debtor's residence was a manufactured home valued at $15,000, then the debtor could exempt the residence from the bankruptcy estate. 11 U.S.C. § 522(b). This means that the trustee could not take possession of the home, sell it, and

most of its pre-bankruptcy debts. The trustee gathers the debtor's nonexempt property, except for items that are valueless or burdensome to the estate, which the trustee will abandon under 11 U.S.C. § 554(a).[21] The trustee then liquidates the property of the estate and distributes the proceeds in accordance with the Code's distribution scheme. 11 U.S.C. §§ 725, 726.

One can best understand how Chapter 7 affects the rights of a mortgagee by considering a series of hypotheticals. Suppose Mortgagor owns a home subject to a recorded mortgage held by Bank. After being laid off from work, Mortgagor cannot make mortgage payments for several months and ultimately files a Chapter 7 petition. On the petition date, Mortgagor owes Bank $150,000, but the home is worth only $100,000. In this situation, the outcome is straightforward. The trustee will abandon the home, as there is no equity in it that could benefit the estate. Because Mortgagor is in default, Bank can move for relief from stay under § 362(d)(2) and will receive that relief because the debtor has no equity in the home.[22] Upon receiving relief from stay, Bank can foreclose its lien under applicable state law.

Suppose instead that on the petition date, the home is worth $300,000 and is located in a state in which Mortgagor may claim a $30,000 exemption in a residence. In this situation, the trustee will not abandon the home, because there is substantial equity in the home that could benefit the estate. Instead, using the power granted by 11 U.S.C. § 363(f),[23] the trustee will sell the home free and clear of liens, with Bank's mortgage lien being transferred to the proceeds of the sale. Thus, if the trustee sells the home for $300,000, Bank will receive the first $150,000 of proceeds to satisfy its secured claim; Mortgagor will receive the next $30,000 in

---

apply the proceeds to expenses of bankruptcy administration and payment of unsecured creditor clams.

[21] When the trustee abandons property of the estate, title to that property vests in the debtor. If the abandoned property is subject to a security interest, the creditor holding that security interest can enforce that security interest, but only after obtaining relief from stay as described earlier in Section J2.

[22] As explained in Section J2, section 362(d)(2)'s second prong—that the property not be "necessary to an effective reorganization" of the debtor—is irrelevant in Chapter 7 cases, in which the debtor is liquidating and not reorganizing. See, e.g., In re J & M Salupo Dev. Co., Inc., 388 B.R. 809 (Bankr. N.D. Ohio 2008).

[23] Section 363(f) provides:

The trustee may sell property . . . free and clear of any interest in such property of an entity other than the estate, only if—

(1) applicable nonbankruptcy law permits sale of such property free and clear of such interest;

(2) such entity consents;

(3) such interest is a lien and the price at which such property is to be sold is greater than the aggregate value of all liens on such property;

(4) such interest is in bona fide dispute; or

(5) such entity could be compelled, in a legal or equitable proceeding, to accept a money satisfaction of such interest.

proceeds on account of its exemption, and Trustee will apply the remaining $120,000 in proceeds to expenses of sale and then toward administrative expenses and the claims of unsecured creditors.[24]

Can the Chapter 7 mortgagor keep her home? In some cases, a mortgagor may file a Chapter 7 petition even if she is current on her mortgage, can afford to keep paying it, and wants to keep the home. This may occur, for example, if she is employed and can pay her ordinary expenses as they come due, but has become insolvent due to a catastrophic medical expense or a large tort judgment. The mortgagor's ability to retain her home in this situation will depend on its value relative to the balance of the mortgage debt and any exemption. For example, suppose Mortgagor's home is worth $300,000 but the remaining balance of the mortgage debt owed to Bank is only $150,000. In this situation, Mortgagor cannot retain its ownership of the home; the trustee will use its power under § 363(f) to sell the home (to capture Mortgagor's equity and apply it to payment of unsecured claims), and Mortgagor will be left with only the cash value of her residence exemption.

By contrast, suppose the home is worth $120,000 but Mortgagor owes Bank $150,000 on the mortgage debt. In this situation, the trustee will abandon the home. Yet under state law, Bank cannot foreclose if Mortgagor is not in default under the mortgage.[25] Further, Bank may prefer for Mortgagor to keep making her payments, as foreclosure now would result in a deficiency (for which Mortgagor's liability will be discharged in Chapter 7). Thus, in this situation, if Mortgagor keeps making her regular monthly payments in a timely fashion, she can keep her home. [Of course, if Mortgagor is "underwater" on the mortgage, she might rationally choose to default, let Bank foreclose on the mortgage, and take her Chapter 7 discharge of any personal liability to Bank. Given that, why might Mortgagor keep the home and continue making monthly payments?]

Ideally, Mortgagor would like to stay in her home and reduce the principal amount of her mortgage to $120,000 (probably reducing the

---

[24] What if the home was worth only $200,000 on the petition date? In this situation, the trustee's decision may depend upon how quickly (and at what price and cost) the trustee believes it can sell the home. If the trustee can sell the home immediately for $200,000 at a cost of only $10,000, the sale could net $10,000 for the benefit of unsecured creditors. But what if the trustee expects it to take six months to sell the home due to market conditions? In this situation, the trustee must recall that Bank, as an oversecured creditor, is entitled to post-petition pendency interest as part of its secured claim under § 506(b). Thus, the longer it takes trustee to sell the home, the higher Bank's claim will grow as that interest accrues! Thus, if the trustee is not confident in its ability to sell the home quickly and for an amount sufficient to generate a surplus for the estate, the trustee may instead abandon the home and allow Bank to foreclose (after Bank obtains relief from the automatic stay).

[25] You might ask: "Doesn't a mortgage typically provide that the mortgagor's bankruptcy would be an event of default?" Indeed, mortgages and other contracts typically provide that bankruptcy is an event of default, but the Bankruptcy Code does not permit enforcement of such clauses (known as "ipso facto" clauses). See, e.g., In re Pak, 252 B.R. 215 (Bankr. M.D. Fla. 2000) (mortgage clause treating bankruptcy filing as default unenforceable "ipso facto" clause).

corresponding amount of her monthly mortgage payments). Outside of bankruptcy, Mortgagor cannot restructure the mortgage in this way without Bank's consent. Can Mortgagor use the bankruptcy process to accomplish this result? At first blush, the Code seems to provide plausible authority in 11 U.S.C. § 506(d), which provides in pertinent part that "[t]o the extent that a lien secures a claim against the debtor that is not an allowed secured claim, such lien is void. . . ." Recall that § 506(a) would "bifurcate" Bank's claim into a secured claim for $120,000 and an unsecured claim for $30,000. Mortgagor thus might argue that Bank's lien is valid to the extent it secures the repayment of $120,000, but invalid to the extent that it would secure the $30,000 unsecured claim. If Mortgagor was correct, Mortgagor could thus "strip down" Bank's lien—meaning that once Mortgagor had repaid $120,000 to Bank, Bank's mortgage would be extinguished! Unfortunately for Mortgagor, the Supreme Court has rejected this argument.

DEWSNUP V. TIMM

Supreme Court of the United States, 1992
502 U.S. 410, 112 S.Ct. 773, 116 L.Ed.2d 903

JUSTICE BLACKMUN delivered the opinion of the Court. We are confronted in this case with an issue concerning § 506(d) of the Bankruptcy Code, 11 U.S.C. § 506(d). May a debtor "strip down" a creditor's lien on real property to the value of the collateral, as judicially determined, when that value is less than the amount of the claim secured by the lien?

I

On June 1, 1978, respondents loaned $119,000 to petitioner Aletha Dewsnup and her husband, T. LaMar Dewsnup, since deceased. The loan was accompanied by a Deed of Trust granting a lien on two parcels of Utah farmland owned by the Dewsnups.

Petitioner defaulted the following year. Under the terms of the Deed of Trust, respondents at that point could have proceeded against the real property collateral by accelerating the maturity of the loan, issuing a notice of default, and selling the land at a public foreclosure sale to satisfy the debt. See also Utah Code Ann. §§ 57–1–20 to 57–1–37 (1990 and Supp.1991).

Respondents did issue a notice of default in 1981. Before the foreclosure sale took place, however, petitioner sought reorganization under Chapter 11 of the Bankruptcy Code, 11 U.S.C. § 1101 *et seq.* That bankruptcy petition was dismissed, as was a subsequent Chapter 11 petition. In June 1984, petitioner filed a petition seeking liquidation under Chapter 7 of the Code, 11 U.S.C. § 701 *et seq.* Because of the pendency of these bankruptcy proceedings, respondents were not able to proceed to the foreclosure sale.

In 1987, petitioner filed the present adversary proceeding in the Bankruptcy Court for the District of Utah seeking, pursuant to § 506, to "avoid" a portion of respondents' lien. Petitioner represented that the debt of approximately $120,000 then owed to respondents exceeded the fair market value of the land and that, therefore, the Bankruptcy Court should reduce the lien to that value. According to petitioner, this was compelled by the interrelationship of the security-reducing provision of § 506(a) and the lien-voiding provision of § 506(d). Under § 506(a) ("An allowed claim of a creditor secured by a lien on property in which the estate has an interest . . . is a secured claim to the extent of the value of such creditor's interest in the estate's interest in such property"), respondents would have an "allowed secured claim" only to the extent of the judicially determined value of their collateral. And under § 506(d) ("To the extent that a lien secures a claim against the debtor that is not an allowed secured claim, such lien is void"), the court would be required to void the lien as to the remaining portion of respondents' claim, because the remaining portion was not an "allowed secured claim" within the meaning of § 506(a).

The Bankruptcy Court refused to grant this relief. *In re Dewsnup,* 87 B.R. 676 (1988). After a trial, it determined that the then value of the land subject to the Deed of Trust was $39,000. It indulged in the assumption that the property had been abandoned by the trustee pursuant to § 554, and reasoned that once property was abandoned it no longer fell within the reach of § 506(a), which applies only to "property in which the estate has an interest," and therefore was not covered by § 506(d).

The United States District Court, without a supporting opinion, summarily affirmed the Bankruptcy Court's judgment of dismissal with prejudice.

The Court of Appeals for the Tenth Circuit, in its turn, also affirmed. *In re Dewsnup,* 908 F.2d 588 (1990). Starting from the "fundamental premise" of § 506(a) that a claim is subject to reduction in security only when the estate has an interest in the property, the court reasoned that because the estate had no interest in abandoned property, § 506(a) did not apply (nor, by implication, did § 506(d)). *Id.,* at 590–591. The court then noted that a contrary result would be inconsistent with § 722 under which a debtor has a limited right to redeem certain personal property. *Id.,* at 592. . . .

II

[T]he parties and their *amici* are not in agreement in their respective approaches to the problem of statutory interpretation that confronts us. Petitioner-debtor takes the position that §§ 506(a) and 506(d) are complementary and to be read together. Because, under § 506(a), a claim is secured only to the extent of the judicially determined value of the real property on which the lien is fixed, a debtor can void a lien on the property pursuant to § 506(d) to the extent the claim is no longer secured and thus is not "an allowed secured claim." In other words, § 506(a) bifurcates classes of claims allowed under § 502 into secured claims and unsecured claims; any portion of an allowed claim deemed to be unsecured under § 506(a) is not an "allowed secured claim" within the lien-voiding scope of § 506(d). Petitioner argues that there is no exception for unsecured property abandoned by the trustee.

Petitioner's *amicus* argues that the plain language of § 506(d) dictates that the proper portion of an undersecured lien on property in a Chapter 7 case is void whether or not the property is abandoned by the trustee. It further argues that the rationale of the Court of Appeals would lead to evisceration of the debtor's right of redemption and the elimination of an undersecured creditor's ability to participate in the distribution of the estate's assets.

Respondents primarily assert that § 506(d) is not, as petitioner would have it, "rigidly tied" to § 506(a). They argue that § 506(a) performs the function of classifying claims by true secured status at the time of distribution of the estate to ensure fairness to unsecured claimants. In contrast, the lien-voiding § 506(d) is directed to the time at which foreclosure is to take place, and, where the trustee has abandoned the property, no bankruptcy distributional purpose is served by voiding the lien.

In the alternative, respondents, joined by the United States as *amicus curiae,* argue more broadly that the words "allowed secured claim" in § 506(d) need not be read as an indivisible term of art defined by reference to § 506(a), which by its terms is not a definitional provision. Rather, the words should be read term-by-term to refer to any claim that is, first, allowed, and, second, secured. Because there is no question that the claim at issue here has been "allowed" pursuant to § 502 of the Code and is secured by a lien with recourse to the underlying collateral, it does not come within the scope of § 506(d), which voids only liens corresponding to claims that have *not* been allowed and secured. This reading of § 506(d), according to respondents and the United States, gives the provision the simple and sensible function of voiding a lien whenever a claim secured by the lien itself has not been allowed. It ensures that the Code's determination not to allow the underlying claim against the debtor personally is given full effect by preventing its assertion against the debtor's property.

Respondents point out that pre-Code bankruptcy law preserved liens like respondents' and that there is nothing in the Code's legislative history that reflects any intent to alter that law. Moreover, according to respondents, the "fresh start" policy cannot justify an impairment of respondents' property rights, for the fresh start does not extend to an *in rem* claim against property but is limited to a discharge of personal liability.

III

The foregoing recital of the contrasting positions of the respective parties and their *amici* demonstrates that § 506 of the Bankruptcy Code and its relationship to other provisions of that Code do embrace some ambiguities. Hypothetical applications that come to mind and those advanced at oral argument illustrate the difficulty of interpreting the statute in a single opinion that would apply to all possible fact situations. We therefore focus upon the case before us and allow other facts to await their legal resolution on another day.

We conclude that respondents' alternative position, espoused also by the United States, although not without its difficulty, generally is the better of the several approaches. Therefore, we hold that § 506(d) does not allow petitioner to "strip down" respondents' lien, because respondents' claim is secured by a lien and has been fully allowed pursuant to § 502. Were we writing on a clean slate, we might be inclined to agree with petitioner that the words "allowed secured claim" must take the same meaning in § 506(d) as in § 506(a). But, given the ambiguity in the text, we are not convinced that Congress intended to depart from the pre-Code rule that liens pass through bankruptcy unaffected.

1. The practical effect of petitioner's argument is to freeze the creditor's secured interest at the judicially determined valuation. By this approach, the creditor would lose the benefit of any increase in the value of the property by the time of the foreclosure sale. The increase would accrue to the benefit of the debtor, a result some of the parties describe as a "windfall."

We think, however, that the creditor's lien stays with the real property until the foreclosure. That is what was bargained for by the mortgagor and the mortgagee. The voidness language sensibly applies only to the security aspect of the lien and then only to the real deficiency in the security. Any increase over the judicially determined valuation during bankruptcy rightly accrues to the benefit of the creditor, not to the benefit of the debtor and not to the benefit of other unsecured creditors whose claims have been allowed and who had nothing to do with the mortgagor-mortgagee bargain. . . .

2. This result appears to have been clearly established before the passage of the 1978 Act. Under the Bankruptcy Act of 1898, a lien on real property passed through bankruptcy unaffected. This Court recently acknowledged that this was so. See *Farrey v. Sanderfoot,* 500 U.S. 291, 297, 111 S.Ct. 1825, 1829, 114 L.Ed.2d 337 (1991) ("Ordinarily, liens and other secured interests survive bankruptcy"); *Johnson v. Home State Bank,* 501 U.S. 78, 84, 111 S.Ct. 2150, 2154, 115 L.Ed.2d 66 (1991) ("Rather, a

bankruptcy discharge extinguishes only one mode of enforcing a claim—
namely, an action against the debtor *in personam*—while leaving intact
another—namely, an action against the debtor *in rem*").

3.   Apart from reorganization proceedings, see 11 U.S.C. §§ 616(1)
and (10) (1976 ed.), no provision of the pre-Code statute permitted
involuntary reduction of the amount of a creditor's lien for any reason other
than payment on the debt. . . .

Congress must have enacted the Code with a full understanding of this
practice. See H.R.Rep. No. 95–595, p. 357 (1977), U.S. Code Cong. &
Admin. News 1978, pp. 5787, 6313 ("Subsection (d) permits liens to pass
through the bankruptcy case unaffected").

4.   When Congress amends the bankruptcy laws, it does not write "on
a clean slate." See *Emil v. Hanley,* 318 U.S. 515, 521, 63 S.Ct. 687, 690–
691, 87 L.Ed. 954 (1943). Furthermore, this Court has been reluctant to
accept arguments that would interpret the Code, however vague the
particular language under consideration might be, to effect a major change
in pre-Code practice that is not the subject of at least some discussion in
the legislative history. See *United Savings Assn. of Texas v. Timbers of
Inwood Forest Associates, Ltd.,* 484 U.S. 365, 380, 108 S.Ct. 626, 634, 98
L.Ed.2d 740 (1988). See also *Pennsylvania Dept. of Public Welfare v.
Davenport,* 495 U.S. 552, 563, 110 S.Ct. 2126, 2133, 109 L.Ed.2d 588 (1990);
United States v. Ron Pair Enterprises, Inc., 489 U.S. 235, 244–245, 109
S.Ct. 1026, 1032–1033, 103 L.Ed.2d 290 (1989). Of course, where the
language is unambiguous, silence in the legislative history cannot be
controlling. But, given the ambiguity here, to attribute to Congress the
intention to grant a debtor the broad new remedy against allowed claims
to the extent that they become "unsecured" for purposes of § 506(a) without
the new remedy's being mentioned somewhere in the Code itself or in the
annals of Congress is not plausible, in our view, and is contrary to basic
bankruptcy principles.

The judgment of the Court of Appeals is affirmed.

JUSTICE SCALIA, with whom JUSTICE SOUTER joins, dissenting.

With exceptions not pertinent here, § 506(d) of the Bankruptcy Code
provides: "To the extent that a lien secures a claim against the debtor that
is not an allowed secured claim, such lien is void. . . ." Read naturally and
in accordance with other provisions of the statute, this automatically voids
a lien to the extent the claim it secures is not both an "allowed claim" and
a "secured claim" under the Code. In holding otherwise, the Court replaces
what Congress said with what it thinks Congress ought to have said—and
in the process disregards, and hence impairs for future use, well-
established principles of statutory construction. I respectfully dissent. . . .

This case turns solely on the meaning of a single phrase found throughout the Bankruptcy Code: "allowed secured claim." Section 506(d) unambiguously provides that to the extent a lien does not secure such a claim it is (with certain exceptions) rendered void. See 11 U.S.C. § 506(d). Congress did not leave the meaning of "allowed secured claim" to speculation. Section 506(a) says that an "allowed claim" (the meaning of which is obvious) is also a "secured claim" "to the extent of *the value of [the] creditor's interest in the estate's interest in [the securing] property.*" (Emphasis added.) (This means, generally speaking, that an allowed claim "is secured only to the extent of the value of the property on which the lien is fixed; the remainder of that claim is considered unsecured." *United States v. Ron Pair Enterprises, Inc.,* 489 U.S. 235, 239, 109 S.Ct. 1026, 1029, 103 L.Ed.2d 290 (1989).) When § 506(d) refers to an "allowed secured claim," it can only be referring to that allowed "secured claim" so carefully described two brief subsections earlier.

The phrase obviously bears the meaning set forth in § 506(a) when it is used in the subsections of § 506 other than § 506(d)—for example, in § 506(b), which addresses "allowed secured claim[s]" that are oversecured. Indeed, as respondents apparently concede, even when the phrase appears outside of § 506, it invariably means what § 506(a) describes: the portion of a creditor's allowed claim that is secured after the calculations required by that provision have been performed. *See, e.g.,* 11 U.S.C. § 722 (permitting a Chapter 7 debtor to redeem certain tangible personal property from certain liens "by paying the holder of such lien the amount of the *allowed secured claim* of such holder that is secured by such lien"); § 1225(a)(5) (prescribing treatment of *"allowed secured claim[s]"* in family farmer's reorganization plan); § 1325(a)(5) (same with respect to *"allowed secured claim[s]"* in individual reorganizations). (Emphases added.) The statute is similarly consistent in its use of the companion phrase *"allowed unsecured claim"* to describe (with respect to a claim supported by a lien) that portion of the claim that is treated as "unsecured" under § 506(a). *See, e.g.,* 11 U.S.C. § 507(a)(7) (fixing priority of *"allowed unsecured claims* of governmental units"); § 726(a)(2) (providing for payment of *"allowed unsecured claim[s]"* in Chapter 7 liquidation); § 1225(a)(4) (setting standard for treatment of *"allowed unsecured claim[s]"* in Chapter 12 plan); § 1325(a)(4) (setting standard for treatment of *"allowed unsecured claim[s]"* in Chapter 13 plan). (Emphases added.) When, on the other hand, the Bankruptcy Code means to refer to a secured party's entire allowed claim, *i.e.,* to both the "secured" and "unsecured" portions under § 506(a), it uses the term *"allowed claim"*—as in 11 U.S.C. § 363(k), which refers to "a lien that secures an allowed claim." Given this clear and unmistakable pattern of usage, it seems to me impossible to hold, as the Court does, that "the words 'allowed secured claim' in § 506(d) need not be read as an indivisible term of art defined by reference to § 506(a)." We have often invoked the normal rule of statutory construction that identical words used in different parts of the same act are intended to have the same meaning. That rule must surely apply, *a fortiori,* to use of identical words *in the same section of the same enactment.*

The Court makes no attempt to establish a textual or structural basis for overriding the plain meaning of § 506(d), but rests its decision upon policy intuitions of a legislative character, and upon the principle that a text which is "ambiguous" (a status apparently achieved by being the subject of disagreement between self-interested litigants) cannot change pre-Code law without the *imprimatur* of "legislative history." Thus abandoning the normal and sensible principle that a term (and especially an artfully defined term such as "allowed secured claim") bears the same meaning throughout the statute, the Court adopts instead what might be called the one-subsection-at-a-time approach to statutory exegesis. . . .

The principal harm caused by today's decision is not the misinterpretation of § 506(d) of the Bankruptcy Code. The disposition that misinterpretation produces brings the Code closer to prior practice and is, as the Court irrelevantly observes, probably fairer from the standpoint of natural justice. (I say irrelevantly, because a bankruptcy law has little to do with natural justice.) The greater and more enduring damage of today's opinion consists in its destruction of predictability, in the Bankruptcy Code and elsewhere. By disregarding well-established and oft-repeated principles of statutory construction, it renders those principles less secure and the certainty they are designed to achieve less attainable. When a seemingly clear provision can be pronounced "ambiguous" *sans* textual and structural analysis, and when the assumption of uniform meaning is replaced by "one-subsection-at-a-time" interpretation, innumerable statutory texts become worth litigating. In the bankruptcy field alone, for example, unfortunate future litigants will have to pay the price for our expressed neutrality "as to whether the words 'allowed secured claim' have different meaning in other provisions of the Bankruptcy Code." Having taken this case to resolve uncertainty regarding one provision, we end by spawning confusion regarding scores of others. I respectfully dissent.

NOTES

1. Dewsnup *and the undersecured mortgagee.* Thanks to *Dewsnup,* an undersecured mortgagee in Chapter 7 still possesses the right to collect the full amount of the debt from the mortgaged property itself, even though the mortgagor's personal liability on the debt is discharged. Thus, the mortgagee will retain its lien on the mortgaged property until the mortgage is foreclosed or the mortgagor repays the mortgage debt in full. Full payment presumably would occur only if the mortgagor continues making all regularly scheduled installments, or if the mortgagor makes a full prepayment (as would occur if the mortgagor refinanced the mortgage, which could happen if the property

subsequently appreciated in value to the point that the loan was no longer "underwater").

As the facts in *Dewsnup* make clear, this principle applies not only if the mortgagor is not in default at the time of the bankruptcy petition, but also when the mortgagor is in default. In this regard, does *Dewsnup* help mortgagors by giving the mortgagee an incentive to delay foreclosure (hoping for a possible post-bankruptcy increase in the value of the land)?

2. *Dewsnup and "wholly underwater" junior liens.* Suppose that Mortgagor files a Chapter 7 petition. Mortgagor owns a home subject to two mortgages: a senior mortgage held by Bank1 (securing an unpaid balance of $200,000) and a junior mortgage held by Bank2 (securing an unpaid balance of $50,000). On the petition date, the home is worth only $150,000. Bank1's undersecured mortgage lien passes through the Chapter 7 case unaffected under *Dewsnup*. But what about Bank2's mortgage, which is entirely underwater on the petition date? Does *Dewsnup* also prohibit a Chapter 7 debtor from using section 506(d) to invalidate (or "strip-off") that lien?

Prior to *Dewsnup*, the Eleventh Circuit had ruled that section 506(d) permitted a Chapter 7 debtor to invalidate an entirely underwater junior lien. *Folendore v. United States Small Bus. Admin.*, 862 F.2d 1537 (11th Cir. 1989). After *Dewsnup*, however, the overwhelming weight of judicial authority held that section 506(d) does not permit "strip-off." See, e.g., *In re Talbert*, 344 F.3d 555, 560 (6th Cir. 2003); *Palomar v. First Am. Bank*, 722 F.3d 992 (7th Cir. 2013); *Ryan v. Homecomings Fin. Network*, 253 F.3d 778 (4th Cir. 2001); *In re Concannon*, 338 B.R. 90 (9th Cir. B.A.P. 2006); *In re Richins*, 469 B.R. 375 (Bankr. D. Utah 2012).

The Supreme Court finally resolved this split of authority in Bank of America, N.A. v. Caulkett, 575 U.S. 790 (2015), which held that § 506(d) did not permit a Chapter 7 debtor to avoid a junior mortgage lien that was wholly underwater. The Court refused to limit *Dewsnup* to undersecured liens, reasoning that "[u]nder the debtors' approach, if a court valued the collateral at one dollar more than the amount of a senior lien, the debtor could not strip down a junior lien under *Dewsnup*, but if it valued the property at one dollar less, the debtor could strip off the entire lien," and characterizing this as "arbitrary." Id. at 2001. Curiously, Justice Thomas (who dissented in *Dewsnup*) wrote the opinion in *Caulkett*, and he included a bizarre footnote acknowledging the long-standing criticism of *Dewsnup* but noting that the debtors "are not asking us to overrule *Dewsnup*."

5. THE MORTGAGEE IN A CHAPTER 13 CASE

Chapter 13 is to certain salaried or wage-earning individuals[26] what Chapter 11 is to the corporation or other business entity. A Chapter 13

---

[26] A Chapter 13 debtor cannot have secured debts exceeding $1,257,850 or unsecured debt exceeding $419,275. 11 U.S.C. § 109(e). These amounts are effective as of April 1, 2019, and they are automatically adjusted at three-year intervals based on the Consumer Price Index. 11 U.S.C. § 104(b). Individuals with debts exceeding these limits must seek reorganization in Chapter 11.

debtor can retain her pre-bankruptcy property and repay her creditors through a reorganization plan confirmed by the court and funded by her post-bankruptcy income. The debtor pays this income to a Chapter 13 trustee, who in turn makes payments to creditors in accordance with the confirmed plan. When the debtor completes performance of the plan, the debtor receives a discharge of her debts (even if creditors did not receive payment of their claims in full).[27] The following section addresses the impact of Chapter 13 on mortgagees.

The automatic stay and relief from stay in Chapter 13. In Chapter 13 cases, mortgagees are subject to the automatic stay. Chapter 13 also provides a special stay protecting third parties who have guaranteed a debtor's consumer debt[28] or put up collateral to secure such a debt. 11 U.S.C. § 1301(a)(1) ("a creditor may not act, or commence or continue any civil action, to collect all or any part of a consumer debt of the debtor from any individual that is liable on such debt with the debtor, or that secured such debt unless such individual became liable on or secured such debt in the ordinary course of such individual's business"). Thus, suppose Bank holds a purchase money mortgage on Mortgagor's home, and Mortgagor's father both guaranteed Mortgagor's repayment of the debt and executed a mortgage on his own home to secure that guaranty. The general automatic stay prevents Bank from foreclosing against Mortgagor's home, and section 1301 prevents Bank from suing Mortgagor's father on the guaranty or foreclosing on the father's home.

As explained earlier, section 362(d)(1) authorizes relief from the stay "for cause, including the lack of adequate protection of an interest in property of [the mortgagor]," and section 362(d)(2) authorizes relief if "(A) the [mortgagor] does not have an equity in such property; and (B) such property is not necessary to an effective reorganization." Courts have disagreed about whether both subsections apply in Chapter 13 cases. While a few courts have held that a mortgagee may seek relief in Chapter 13 only under section 362(d)(1), see, e.g., In re Fischer, 136 B.R. 819 (D. Alaska 1992),[29] the substantial weight of authority holds that a mortgagee can also seek relief under section 362(d)(2). See, e.g., In re McNeely, 366 B.R. 542 (Bankr. N.D. W.Va. 2007); In re Mellino, 333 B.R. 578 (Bankr. D. Mass.

---

[27] 11 U.S.C. § 1328(a). Section 1328(a) excludes certain debts from discharge, including domestic support obligations, student loan indebtedness, and installment debts where the final contract payment extends beyond the expiration of the plan (such as a mortgage debt where the remaining mortgage term exceeds the plan period). See 8 Collier on Bankruptcy ¶ 1328.02[3], at 1328–11 to 1328–24 (16th ed.).

[28] In this context, "consumer debt" means a debt incurred primarily for personal, family, or household purposes. 11 U.S.C. § 101(7).

[29] One commentator has argued that because section 362(d)(2) refers to a "reorganization," it should apply only to Chapter 11 (which is entitled "Reorganization") and not to Chapter 13 (which is entitled "Adjustment of Debts of an Individual with Regular Income"). Comment, Home Foreclosures Under Chapter 13 of the Bankruptcy Reform Act, 30 UCLA L.Rev. 637, 648 (1983). Can you explain why this argument is unpersuasive?

2005); In re Herrin, 325 B.R. 774 (Bankr. N.D. Ind. 2005). Where the mortgage covers the debtor's home, relief from stay under section 362(d)(2) is unlikely; courts will treat the debtor's home as being "necessary" to the debtor's ability to rehabilitate in Chapter 13. See, e.g., 3 Collier on Bankruptcy ¶ 362.07[4][b], at 362–121 (16th ed.).

Repayment under a Chapter 13 plan. Chapter 13 requires the debtor to propose a plan to repay creditor claims over a period of five years (reduced to three if the debtor's income is below the state's median income for households of similar size). 11 U.S.C. § 1325(b)(4)(A). Chapter 13 does not specify how much of her post-bankruptcy income the debtor must pay to the trustee; it merely requires that the debtor pay "such portion of future earnings or other future income . . . as is necessary for the execution of the plan." 11 U.S.C. § 1322(a)(1). This means that the debtor's contribution depends upon the plan's repayment terms, which must satisfy the confirmation requirements set forth in § 1325.

The debtor does not have to pay unsecured claims in full; however, the court may not confirm a Chapter 13 plan unless unsecured creditors will receive as much or more than they would have received in a Chapter 7 liquidation. 11 U.S.C. § 1325(a)(4). In addition, if the debtor does not pay unsecured claims in full, the court cannot confirm the plan over the objection of an unsecured creditor unless the debtor contributes *all* of her "disposable income" to fund the plan. 11 U.S.C. § 1325(b)(1). The court also may not confirm the plan unless it concludes that the debtor filed her petition and proposed her plan in good faith, 11 U.S.C. § 1325(a)(3), (7), and the plan is feasible, i.e., "the debtor will be able to make all payments under the plan and to comply with the plan." 11 U.S.C. § 1325(a)(6).

Modification of secured claims, cure of prepetition defaults and "de-acceleration." Sections 1322 and 1325 address how a Chapter 13 plan may treat secured claims. In particular, section 1322(b) provides that a Chapter 13 plan may:

> (2) modify the rights of holders of secured claims, other than a claim secured only by a security interest in real property that is the debtor's principal residence, or of holders of unsecured claims, or leave unaffected the rights of holders of any class of claims;

> (3) provide for the curing or waiving of any default; . . .

> (5) notwithstanding paragraph (2) of this subsection, provide for the curing of any default within a reasonable time and maintenance of payments while the case is pending on any unsecured claim or secured claim on which the last payment is due after the date on which the final payment under the plan is due. . . .

To understand the impact of these sections, consider this common example. Suppose Smith obtained a 30-year mortgage on a vacation home, at 8% annual interest. Five years into the mortgage, Smith lost his job and stopped making his $1,000 monthly mortgage payments. Bank (which holds the mortgage on the home) accelerated the mortgage and started a foreclosure proceeding. When Smith found a new job with an income sufficient to allow him to resume making mortgage payments, he filed a Chapter 13 petition to stop Bank's foreclosure. On the petition date, Smith had not paid his mortgage payment in six months (an arrearage of $6,000). Outside of bankruptcy, Smith could not keep the home and avoid foreclosure without either (1) paying off the accelerated balance of the debt in full or (2) paying the $6,000 arrearage to reinstate the mortgage, if applicable state law or the mortgage permitted reinstatement. Section 1322(b), however, permits Smith to "de-accelerate" the loan, resume making his $1,000 monthly installment payment, and cure the $6,000 arrearage by making an additional monthly installment payment under the Chapter 13 plan (e.g., by paying Bank an additional $100 each month for the 60 months of the plan).

"Cramdown." As noted above, section 1322(b)(2) also permits a plan to modify the rights of creditors holding secured claims (other than a claim secured only by real property that is the debtor's principal residence). In the previous example, this means that if prevailing interest rates are now 4%, Smith's plan might propose to modify the terms of Bank's mortgage to reduce the interest rate from 8% (the original contract rate) down to 5%— which would lower Smith's monthly payment amount.

If the plan proposes to modify a secured claim, the court can confirm the plan only if it satisfies one of the following requirements:

- the mortgagee accepts the plan, 11 U.S.C. § 1325(a)(5)(A);

- the plan proposes to surrender the property to the mortgagee, 11 U.S.C. § 1325(a)(5)(C); or

- the mortgagee will retain its lien on the collateral and the debtor will make future payments that have a present value that equals or exceeds the amount of the mortgagee's secured claim. 11 U.S.C. § 1325(a)(5)(B).

This third approach is known as "cramdown," i.e., the debtor crams its repayment plan down the throat of the unconsenting mortgagee.

The impact of the cramdown requirement is best understood through an another example. Assume that Smith owns a vacation condo subject to a mortgage loan held by Bank. The loan bears an 8% annual interest rate, is repayable in equal monthly installments of $1,400, has 20 years remaining to maturity, and an unpaid balance of $200,000. On the date Smith files a Chapter 13 petition, he is current on the mortgage, but due to market conditions, the vacation home has a value of only $120,000. As discussed earlier, section 506(a) bifurcates Bank's claim into a secured claim of $120,000 and an unsecured claim of $80,000. Bank will be paid on account of its unsecured claim to the same extent as other unsecured creditors. As for the Bank's secured claim, sections 1322(b)(2) and 1325 effectively permit Smith to "strip-down" that claim to the home's $120,000 current value. If Smith wants to strip-down the Bank's claim and retain the vacation home, Smith has two alternatives:

- Smith can make a lump-sum payment of $120,000 to Bank in full satisfaction of Bank's secured claim, thereby extinguishing Bank's lien.

- Smith can amortize the $120,000 secured claim through installment payments over five years under his plan. These payments must be in "equal monthly amounts," 11 U.S.C. § 1325(a)(5)(B)(iii)(I),[30] and must have a present value of $120,000 or more. Once Smith makes all installment payments under the plan in a timely fashion, Bank's mortgage lien will be extinguished—and if the condo should appreciate in value in the future, all of that appreciation will inure to the benefit of Smith.

Of course, Smith may be unable to accomplish either alternative. Smith may lack the ability to make a lump-sum payment of $120,000, or the post-bankruptcy income to make the installment payments necessary to amortize the full $120,000 balance in only five years. [At an 8% interest rate, the plan would require monthly installments of $2,433.] If so, Smith will be unable to modify or "strip-down" Bank's secured claim—at least over Bank's objection. In that case, to keep the house, Smith will have to continue to make all of the payments required under the original amortization schedule, unless he can convince the Bank to agree to modify the loan terms voluntarily. [This is often referred to as providing for payment of the mortgage "outside the plan."]

NOTES

1. *Determining the cram-down rate.* Because cram-down requires the court to calculate the present value of the debtor's plan payments, the court must determine what interest rate to use in making that calculation. The Code provides no explicit guidance, and courts have struggled to identify the appropriate rate. Because cram-down effectively forces the mortgagee to extend credit to a bankrupt debtor, mortgagees would prefer a "market" or "coerced loan" approach that would approximate the rate that a comparable

---

[30] Congress added this requirement in 2005, which prevents a Chapter 13 debtor from proposing to pay a secured creditor (over its objection) interest-only payments during the plan with a balloon payment of the entire secured claim in the plan's final month. See, e.g., In re Hamilton, 401 B.R. 539 (1st Cir. B.A.P. 2009). Why prohibit Debtor from proposing such a "balloon" plan?

debtor would have to pay to borrow an amount equal to the secured claim. By contrast, debtors have argued for a "cost of funds" rule that would set the cram-down rate based on the interest rate the creditor would have to pay to borrow a comparable amount. One might also take the view that the court should presumptively use the pre-bankruptcy contract rate as the cram-down rate, but allow either the debtor or the mortgagee to present evidence that might justify an upward or downward adjustment based upon the circumstances.

The Supreme Court attempted to resolve the confusion in Till v. SCS Credit Corp., 541 U.S. 465, 124 S.Ct. 1951 (2004). That case involved an attempt by a Chapter 13 debtor to modify a secured car loan from the pre-bankruptcy contract interest rate of 21% to a cram-down rate of 9.5%. The debtor proposed this as an appropriate cram-down rate because the existing "prime" rate was 8%, and an additional 1.5% adjustment was appropriate to account for the risk of the debtor's default. The Court's plurality decision ultimately upheld the bankruptcy court's confirmation of the plan, but it added little clarity. Four justices (Justices Stevens, Souter, Ginsburg, and Breyer) concurred with the bankruptcy court's "prime plus" formula approach, while the four dissenting judges (Justices Scalia, Kennedy, O'Connor and Rehnquist) would have adopted the presumptive contract rate approach. Justice Thomas did not agree with either approach, but concurred in the result (the 9.5% rate) because he believed that the Code did not require any adjustment for risk and thus that the secured creditor had no grounds to complain if the plan proposed any rate above the prime rate.

Commentators have roundly criticized _Till_, and justifiably so. The Court's opinions discuss the "prime" rate as if it were a "risk-free" rate (on top of which the court should then add an appropriate adjustment to account for the debtor's risk), but the prime rate is not a "risk-free" rate. The plurality opinion also provided no meaningful guidance as to how to calculate an appropriate risk premium, noting merely that courts have generally approved adjustments of 1% to 3%, and stating:

> Together with the cramdown provision, [the feasibility] requirement obligates the court to select a rate high enough to compensate the creditor for its risk but not so high as to doom the plan. If the court determines that the likelihood of default is so high as to necessitate an "eye-popping" interest rate, the plan probably should not be confirmed. [_Till_, 541 U.S. at 480–481.]

2.   _Cure and interest on arrearages._ Returning to the example on page 778, section 1322(b)(5) would permit Smith to cure the unpaid arrearage of $6,000 by paying it off in monthly installments under the plan. Prior to 1993, most courts held that the Chapter 13 debtor did not have to pay interest on the arrearage being cured. See, e.g., Landmark Fin. Servs. v. Hall, 918 F.2d 1150 (4th Cir. 1990). In 1993, the Supreme Court held in Rake v. Wade, 508 U.S. 464 (1993), that an oversecured creditor was entitled to post-petition interest on arrearages as a matter of right under section 506(b) (regardless of whether the creditor's contract provided for interest). In 1994, Congress added section

1322(e), which superseded *Rake* and provides that notwithstanding section 506(b), a creditor may collect interest on the arrearage being cured "in accordance with the underlying agreement and applicable nonbankruptcy law." Thus, because the loan in the example provided for 8% annual interest, Smith's cure of the $6,000 arrearage would require monthly installments under the plan of $121.66.

Some mortgage notes may provide both a pre-default (or "contract") interest rate and a higher post-default (or "default" rate). Under the weight of recent authority, if a Chapter 13 debtor proposes to cure a pre-petition arrearage in installments, the debtor must pay interest on the arrearage at the default rate (assuming that rate is valid under applicable law). See, e.g., Anderson v. Hancock, 820 F.3d 670 (4th Cir. 2016); In re Campbell, 513 B.R. 846 (Bankr. S.D.N.Y. 2014).

———————

Mortgages on primary residences and the "anti-modification rule." While section 1322(b)(2) generally allows a Chapter 13 plan to modify secured claims, the plan cannot modify a claim that is "secured only by a security interest in real property that is the debtor's principal residence." Without the mortgagee's consent, a Chapter 13 debtor cannot reduce the principal amount of the mortgage on its primary residence, regardless of its value. Likewise, the debtor can neither reduce the interest rate (even if market rates have declined) nor extend the loan term so as to reduce the monthly payment amount. Further, under the weight of authority, a junior mortgage enjoys the same protection against modification, as long as there is some equity in the home above the amount of the senior obligations. Congress adopted this rule "in response to perceptions, or to suggestions advanced in the legislative hearings . . . that home-mortgagor lenders, performing a valuable social service through their loans, needed special protection against modification." Grubbs v. Houston First Am. Sav. Ass'n, 730 F.2d 236, 246 (5th Cir. 1984).

Suppose Debtor owes $200,000 to Bank, secured by a mortgage on its primary home (worth only $150,000). Can Debtor modify the $50,000 unsecured portion of Bank's claim, or does section 1322(b)(2) protect the *entire claim* against modification? Relying upon section 506(d)—which invalidates a lien to the extent it "secures a claim against the debtor other than an allowed secured claim"—Debtor might propose to continue making the same monthly payment as before, but with that payment being applied toward a secured claim with a stripped-down balance of $150,000. If the Code permitted this approach, Debtor could get a release of the mortgage lien once Debtor had amortized the $150,000 balance of the secured claim.

Initially, the majority of courts upheld the ability of the debtor to bifurcate undersecured home mortgage claims and modify the unsecured portion of those claims. See, e.g., Bellamy v. Federal Home Loan Mortg.,

962 F.2d 176 (2d Cir. 1992); In re Hart, 923 F.2d 1410 (10th Cir. 1991); Wilson v. Commonwealth Mortg. Corp., 895 F.2d 123 (3d Cir. 1990); Lomas Mortgage USA v. Wiese, 980 F.2d 1279 (9th Cir. 1992). The leading case for the minority view was In re Nobleman, 968 F.2d 483 (5th Cir. 1992), which held that section 1322(b)(2) authorized modification of the "rights of holders of secured claims" rather than modification of secured claims themselves, and thus reasoned that the anti-modification rule prevented the debtor from modifying any of the rights of the mortgagee even if its claim was undersecured.

The Supreme Court unanimously resolved the split of authority by affirming the Fifth Circuit's reasoning and result. Nobleman v. American Savings Bank, 508 U.S. 324, 113 S.Ct. 2106 (1993). The *Nobleman* approach certainly treats the undersecured mortgagee more favorably than it would be treated under state law outside of bankruptcy. [Can you explain why?] Nevertheless, given the fragile state of lending institutions in the early 1990s and real estate values during that period, *Nobleman* may have represented a small judicial contribution to the solvency of the mortgage lending industry. See generally Scarberry & Reddie, Home Mortgage Stripdown in Chapter 13 Bankruptcy: A Contextual Approach to Sections 1322(b)(2) and (b)(5), 20 Pepperdine L.Rev. 425 (1993); Nassen, Bankruptcy Code § 1322(b)(2)'s No-Modification Clause: Who Does It Protect?, 33 Ariz.L.Rev. 979 (1991).

In 1994, Congress added section 1322(c)(2), which did not modify *Nobelman* but did affect its application in certain Chapter 13 cases. Section 1322(c)(2) permits the debtor to modify a secured claim despite the anti-modification rule if "the last payment on the original payment schedule . . . is due before the final payment under the plan is due. . . ." Most courts and commentators take the view that section 1322(c)(2) permits a debtor to bifurcate an undersecured home mortgage in this situation and cram-down the unsecured component of the claim. See, e.g., Hurlburt v. Black, 925 F.3d 154 (4th Cir. 2019); In re Paschen, 296 F.3d 1203 (11th Cir.), cert. denied, 537 U.S. 1097, 123 S.Ct. 696 (2002); 8 Collier on Bankruptcy ¶ 1322.17 (16th ed.). But section 1322(c)(2)'s practical effect is limited. In the typical Chapter 13 case, the debtor will have more than five years remaining on its mortgage term, and section 1322(c)(2) will not displace the anti-modification rule. As a result, section 1322(c)(2) will permit modification only for short-term mortgages, mortgages that are nearly paid off, and mortgages with impending balloon payments. Why might Congress have thought it appropriate to permit the debtor to modify the mortgage in these contexts, but not on the facts of *Nobleman*? See 8 Collier on Bankruptcy ¶ 1322.17; Nelson, Whitman, Burkhart & Freyermuth, Real Estate Finance Law § 8.18 (6th ed.2015).

NOTES

1. *Is de-acceleration and cure an impermissible "modification"?* Frequently, by the time a Chapter 13 filing occurs, the debtor has already defaulted on her home mortgage and the mortgagee has already accelerated the maturity of the debt. As noted previously, section 1322(b)(5) permits cure of a prepetition arrearage on a "secured claim on which the last payment is due after the date on which the final payment is due under the plan." If the mortgagee has already accelerated the debt pre-petition, however, the mortgagee might argue that the "last payment" is now due immediately, not at the originally scheduled maturity date, such that an attempted cure of the arrearage would be an impermissible modification! Nevertheless, the universal weight of authority holds that a Chapter 13 plan can defeat a pre-petition mortgage acceleration by cure and reinstatement. See, e.g., In re Taddeo, 685 F.2d 24 (2d Cir. 1982). This is entirely sensible; a contrary result would "encourage premature bankruptcy petitions rather than debtor attempts to resolve their financial problems by negotiation, mediation, or other extrajudicial means" and "encourage mortgagees to declare defaults and accelerate earlier to avoid the necessity of dealing with a Chapter 13 debtor." Nelson, Whitman, Burkhart & Freyermuth, Real Estate Finance Law § 8.18, at 826 (6th ed.2015) (quoting Zaretsky, Some Limits on Mortgagees' Rights in Chapter 13, 50 Brooklyn L. Rev. 433, 443 (1984)).

Suppose that at the time Mortgagor files a Chapter 13 petition, Mortgagor has missed the last six months of installment mortgage payments on his primary residence. Suppose further that the mortgage note provides that after default, the mortgage debt will accrue interest at the rate of 16% (rather than the pre-default contract rate of 8%). Can Mortgagor propose and confirm a plan that would cure the arrearage in installments over the life of the plan and have Mortgagor make ongoing monthly installment payments based on the pre-default contract rate of 8%. The Fourth Circuit has ruled "no," holding that this would violate the antimodification rule. Anderson v. Hancock, 820 F.3d 670 (4th Cir. 2016). What if the Mortgagor proposed to cure the arrearage in a lump sum? Would this entitle the Mortgagor to resume making payments at the pre-default contract rate? Why or why not?

2. *Balloon payments.* Suppose that at the time Smith files a Chapter 13 petition, the entire $100,000 balance of the mortgage on his primary home is due—not by virtue of acceleration, but because Smith's note provided for a "balloon payment" that is now due. Can Smith use *Taddeo* to "deflate" the balloon and pay it off in installments under the plan? That would appear to be a "modification," and for this reason, the weight of authority prior to 1994 held that the answer was no. See, e.g., In re Seidel, 752 F.2d 1382 (9th Cir. 1985). But in 1994, Congress added section 1322(c)(2), which (as noted in the text) would explicitly allow Smith to take the $100,000 balloon debt and pay it off in installments during the Chapter 13 plan. See, e.g., In re Paschen, 296 F.3d 1203 (11th Cir. 2002); In re Kelly, 283 B.R. 808 (Bankr. M.D. Fla. 2002).

But suppose Smith's home is worth only $75,000. Does section 1322(c)(2) only permit Smith to modify the *repayment period* for paying the entire balloon, or does it also allow Smith to modify the *entire claim* through cram-down under section 1325(a)(5)? On this question, the weight of authority and scholarly commentary permits modification of the entire claim. See, e.g., Hurlbut v. Black, 925 F.3d 154 (4th Cir. 2019); In re Paschen, 296 F.2d 1203 (11th Cir. 2002); 8 Collier on Bankruptcy ¶ 1322.17, at 1322–57 (16th ed.). Is that sensible?

3. *When is the debtor's cure right extinguished?* Section 1322(c)(1) provides that "a default with respect to . . . a lien on the debtor's principal residence may be cured . . . until such residence is sold at a foreclosure sale that is conducted in accordance with applicable nonbankruptcy law." Clearly, if a sale has divested the mortgagor of all interest in the property, cure is unavailable. But when is the residence "sold"? When the auctioneer's hammer falls? When the court enters an order confirming the sale? When a deed is delivered to the purchaser? What if the state allows statutory post-sale redemption?

The language of section 1322(c)(1) could have addressed these questions more explicitly. The most literal reading appears to prevent cure after a foreclosure sale has occurred—even if state law provides a post-sale redemption right—and the weight of judicial authority so holds. See, e.g., In re Cain, 423 F.3d 617 (6th Cir. 2005); In re McKinney, 344 B.R. 1 (Bankr. D. Me. 2006). Can you explain why cure during the statutory redemption period would be inappropriate? See Nelson, Whitman, Burkhart & Freyermuth, Real Estate Finance Law § 8.18 (6th ed.2015).

There remains judicial disagreement, however, regarding when the sale is final within the meaning of § 1322(c)(1). Some courts hold that the section established a federal "gavel" rule under which the cure right terminates when the hammer falls at the sale auction, as long as the sale complied with state law. See, e.g., In re Connors, 497 F.3d 314 (3d Cir. 2007); In re Cain, 423 F.3d 617 (6th Cir. 2005); In re Hubbard, 569 B.R. 188 (Bankr. M.D. Ala. 2017); In re Parker, 563 B.R. 650 (Bankr. E.D. Ky. 2017). The weight of authority requires that the court look to state law to determine whether any "post-gavel" actions—such as execution and delivery of a deed, or judicial confirmation of the sale—were required for the property to have been "sold." See, e.g., In re Vertullo, 593 B.R. 92 (Bankr. D. N.H. 2018) (execution and recording of deed); In re Ausburn, 524 B.R. 816 (Bankr. E.D. Ark. 2015) (confirmation of foreclosure sale); In re Howard, 351 B.R. 251 (Bankr. M.D. Ga. 2006) (delivery of deed); In re Wescott, 309 B.R. 308 (Bankr. E.D. Wis. 2004) (judicial confirmation of foreclosure sale).

4. *The limits of the anti-modification rule.* Section 1322(b)(2) prohibits modification of a claim that is secured "*only* by a security interest in real property that is the debtor's principal residence." This means that if a mortgage loan on the debtor's principal residence is also secured by other real estate or personal property, modification is permitted! See, e.g., In re Potts,

421 B.R. 518 (8th Cir. B.A.P. 2010) (modification permitted where mortgage covered both home and separate parcel used for grazing and growing crops). Under the weight of authority, modification is also permitted where the mortgage covers not only the debtor's principal residence but other rental property as well (i.e., a duplex in which the debtor lives in one unit but rents out the other). See, e.g., In re Scarborough, 461 F.3d 406 (3d Cir. 2006); Lomas Mortg. v. Louis, 82 F.3d 1 (1st Cir.1996); In re Picchi, 448 B.R. 870 (1st Cir. B.A.P. 2011); In re Berkland, 582 B.R. 571 (Bankr. D. Mass. 2018); In re Lopez, 511 B.R. 517 (Bankr. N.D. Ill. 2014). Can you identify a discernible rationale for this limitation?

Section 1322(b)(2)'s "only" qualification has proven to be a trap for many home mortgagees. The inclination of secured lenders is to take as much security as possible; indeed, it is normally considered prudent to do so. A mortgagee that succumbs to this temptation and takes an additional mortgage on other real estate or a security interest in the debtor's bank accounts, automobiles, boats or other chattels loses its protection against mortgage modification.

Prior to 2005, lenders often unwittingly threatened their anti-modification protection by including in the mortgage boilerplate language that extended the lender's security to include items reasonably related to the real estate, such as appliances, machinery, furniture, equipment, and fixtures installed on the mortgaged premises; rents, issues and profits of the mortgaged premises; and tax and insurance escrow funds held by the mortgagee. In 2005, Congress redefined "debtor's principal residence" to include "incidental property," which includes as "(A) property commonly conveyed with a principal residence in the area where the real property is located; (B) all easements, rights, appurtenances, fixtures, rents, royalties, mineral rights, oil or gas rights or profits, water rights, escrow funds, or insurance proceeds; and (C) all replacements or additions." 11 U.S.C. §§ 101(13A)(A) ("debtor's principal residence"); 101(27B) ("incidental property"). Thus, while additional security such as a mortgage on another tract of real estate or a security interest in the debtor's car will continue to destroy the mortgagee's protection against modification, the normal boilerplate provisions found in most residential mortgage forms should not have this effect. In re Birmingham, 846 F.3d 88 (4th Cir. 2017) (escrow funds and insurance proceeds constituted "incidental property"); In re Abdosh, 513 B.R. 882 (Bankr. D. Md. 2014) (same). How about a mortgage that also covers appliances such as a refrigerator? Could the mortgagee avoid the potential consequences of the "only" limitation by releasing the additional security before the debtor's Chapter 13 petition? See, e.g., In re Baker, 398 B.R. 198 (Bankr. N.D. Ohio 2008). What if the release comes after the petition? See, e.g., Wilson v. Commonwealth Mortg. Corp., 895 F.2d 123, 129 (3d Cir.1990). What if the lender initially took additional security but later foreclosed on or lost the additional security? See, e.g., In re Hueramo, 564 B.R. 604 (Bankr. N.D. Ill. 2017); In re Coyle, 559 B.R. 25 (Bankr. D. Conn. 2016).

5. *The timing of the "principal residence" determination.* Suppose that on the petition date, Debtor is renting the mortgaged premises to a third party, but moves into the premises as his primary home after the petition date. Does the anti-modification rule apply? Courts have not reached consensus. Some courts have ruled that the debtor's use on the loan date governs this question. See, e.g., In re Scarborough, 461 F.3d 406 (3d Cir. 2006); In re Proctor, 494 B.R. 833 (Bankr.E.D.N.C.2013). Others have held that the debtor's use on the petition date controls this determination, and this view reflects the weight of recent authority. See, e.g., In re Wong, 598 B.R. 827 (Bankr. D. Md. 2019); In re Berkland, 582 B.R. 571 (Bankr. D. Mass. 2018); In re Hueramo, 564 B.R. 604 (Bankr. N.D. Ill. 2017); see also In re Abdelgadir, 455 B.R. 896 (9th Cir. B.A.P. 2011) (using petition date in interpreting Chapter 11's analogous anti-modification rule). In 2010, Congress amended the definition of "debtor's principal residence" to read "if used as the principal residence by the debtor." 11 U.S.C. § 101(13A). Does this language provide a clear answer to the question? Why or why not?

6. *Does the anti-modification rule reflect sound policy?* In the wake of the economic crisis that began in 2007, home values in many markets plummeted, leaving many homeowners "underwater" (owing more than their homes were worth). The anti-modification rule effectively meant that homeowners could not use Chapter 13 to modify their mortgage loans and remain in their homes. The resulting crisis prompted significant responses by both states (foreclosure reform and the implementation of mediation programs designed to encourage loan modifications) and the federal government (including the HAMP and HARP programs designed to facilitate modification of home mortgage loans). Would these objectives be better facilitated by doing away with the anti-modification rule? Why or why not?

7. *Junior liens and "strip-off" of wholly unsecured junior liens.* Under the weight of authority, a junior mortgage on the debtor's primary residence enjoys the same protection against modification, as long as there is some equity in the home above the amount of the senior obligations. See, e.g., In re Brenneke, 441 B.R. 625 (Bankr. E.D. Mo. 2010); In re Rubottom, 134 B.R. 641 (9th Cir. B.A.P. 1991).[31] But what about the creditor holding a wholly "underwater" junior mortgage on the primary residence? Can the Chapter 13 debtor modify the mortgagee's claim, or does the anti-modification rule prohibit that result?

Following *Nobleman*, a few courts ruled that section 1322(b)(2) prohibited modification in this context. See, e.g., In re Hughes, 402 B.R. 325 (Bankr. D. Minn. 2009). However, the near-unanimous weight of authority permits the

---

[31] Courts have disagreed as to the appropriate valuation date for determining whether there is equity in the home over the balance of the senior debt. Most courts value the home for this purpose as of the petition date. See, e.g., In re DiMauro, 548 B.R. 685 (Bankr. D. Del. 2016); In re Hegeduis, 525 B.R. 74 (Bankr. N.D. Ind. 2015); In re Putman, 519 B.R. 491 (Bankr. N.D. Miss. 2016). Others have valued the home nearer to the time of the confirmation of the debtor's plan (which might benefit the junior lienholder if market values have increased since the petition date). See, e.g., In re Williams, 480 B.R. 813 (Bankr. E.D. Tenn. 2012). Which approach is more sensible as a matter of policy? Of fairness?

Chapter 13 debtor to use section 1322(b)(2) to strip-off a wholly underwater lien. *See, e.g.,* In re Zimmer, 313 F.3d 1220 (9th Cir. 2002); In re Lane, 280 F.3d 663 (6th Cir. 2002); In re Pond, 252 F.3d 122 (2d Cir. 2001); In re Tanner, 217 F.3d 1357 (11th Cir. 2000); In re Bartee, 212 F.3d 277 (5th Cir. 2000); TD Bank, N.A. v. Landry, 479 B.R. 1 (D.Mass.2012); In re Hall, 495 B.R. 393 (Bankr.N.D.Ill.2013). These decisions have reasoned that under *Nobelman,* the anti-modification rule cannot apply unless the mortgagee has a secured claim, and the wholly underwater junior lienor has no secured claim at all by virtue of section 506(a).[32]

8. *Manufactured homes.* Section 1322(b)(2) makes clear that the mortgagee must have a "security interest in *real property* that is the debtor's principal residence" to qualify for the protection of the anti-modification rule. A new mobile or manufactured home begins its life as personal property; in most states, upon the sale of a new manufactured home, the state issues a certificate of title for the home (as if the home were a vehicle). The home does not become "real property" under state law unless it has become a fixture or the owner complies with the state's "conversion" statute (which involves the surrender of the certificate of title and the permanent or quasi-permanent attachment of the home to a parcel of land). Thus, a lender or seller that provides purchase money financing for the purchase of a manufactured home takes (at least initially) a security interest in personal property and would not qualify for the protection of the antimodification rule unless and until the home becomes "real property." Compare In re Williamson, 400 B.R. 917 (Bankr. M.D. Ga. 2009) (mobile home deemed realty; lender's interest not modifiable) with In re Ennis, 558 F.3d 343 (4th Cir. 2009) (mobile home deemed personalty under Virginia law; lender's interest subject to modification).

In 2005, Congress amended the definition of "debtor's principal residence" to include a "mobile or manufactured home" used as the principal residence by the debtor, "without regard to whether it is attached to real property." 11 U.S.C. § 101(13A). At first blush, this might appear to give manufactured home lenders the benefit of the anti-modification rule, but Congress did not modify the language of § 1322(b)(2), which requires the lender to have a security interest in "*real property* that is the debtor's principal residence" to qualify for the anti-modification rule. As a result, most courts have held that unless the manufactured home has become a fixture or the lender has complied with the state's conversion statute (if any), a Chapter 13 debtor can modify the claim of a lender with a security interest in the home. *See, e.g.,* In re Coleman, 392 B.R.

---

[32] Courts have disagreed as to whether the authority for this strip-off lies within § 506(d) or § 1322(b)(2)'s anti-modification rule. As discussed earlier, the Supreme Court in *Dewsnup* concluded that a Chapter 7 debtor may not use § 506(d) to strip-down an undersecured lien. Some courts have concluded that *Dewsnup* does not apply in Chapter 13, and that a Chapter 13 debtor can use § 506(d) to strip-off an underwater junior lien. *See, e.g.,* Carroll v. Key Bank, 2011 WL 6338912 (D.Utah 2011); Hart v. San Diego Credit Union, 449 B.R. 783 (S.D.Cal.2010). The Tenth Circuit, however, has ruled that section 1322(b)(2) provides the exclusive authority for lien stripping in Chapter 13. In re Woolsey, 696 F.3d 1266 (10th Cir. 2012). See also In re Hernandez Diaz, 544 B.R. 471 (Bankr. D. P.R. 2016).

767 (8th Cir. B.A.P. 2008); In re Atchison, 557 B.R. 818 (Bankr. M.D. Ala. 2016).

What are the policy implications of this result? On the one hand, unlike normal single family real estate, many manufactured homes tend to depreciate over time regardless of market conditions. Thus, the reasoning of *Coleman* subjects manufactured home lenders to a significant risk of strip-down if the borrower files a Chapter 13. On the other hand, after such a strip-down, it may be less likely that the home will appreciate in value in the future, and therefore it will be less likely that the debtor could reap an "undeserved" windfall. In the wake of the recent real estate crisis, given the demand and need for affordable housing alternatives, should manufactured home lenders receive the same protection from modification as lenders holding liens on traditional "stick-built" homes? See Ann M. Burkhart, Bringing Manufactured Housing into the Real Estate Finance System, 37 Pepperdine L. Rev. 427 (2010).

9.   *"Chapter 20" cases: strip-off of a wholly unsecured junior lien by a Chapter 13 debtor after obtaining a discharge in a prior Chapter 7 case.* Some debtors are not eligible for Chapter 13 relief because their debts exceed the statutory debt limits for Chapter 13 relief. For example, suppose Smith owns a principal residence subject to an $800,000 first mortgage and a $200,000 second mortgage. Because of a severe drop in real estate values, the home is now valued at only $700,000. Because Smith also has $1 million in unsecured debt due to catastrophic medical expenses, he is not eligible for Chapter 13 relief. Smith would like to discharge the medical debt and retain the home while "stripping-off" the underwater second mortgage lien. A Chapter 7 filing would permit Smith to discharge the medical debt, but *Dewsnup* prevents a debtor from stripping-off a wholly underwater junior lien in Chapter 7. Smith may thus act strategically by attempting two successive bankruptcy filings. First, Smith might file a Chapter 7 petition to discharge the unsecured medical debt (and thereby bring himself within the permissible Chapter 13 debt limits). Then, after getting a Chapter 7 discharge, Smith might file a Chapter 13 petition and try to use section 1322(b)(2) to strip-off the underwater second mortgage lien (even though that relief was not available in his prior Chapter 7). In the bankruptcy vernacular, Smith's conduct is called "Chapter 20" bankruptcy.

In 2005, Congress amended the Code by adding 11 U.S.C. § 1328(f), which prohibits a Chapter 13 debtor from obtaining a discharge of debt in Chapter 13 if the debtor has obtained a Chapter 7 discharge during the preceding four years. But the Code does not prohibit a debtor from filing a Chapter 13 in this situation—it only prohibits the debtor from obtaining a Chapter 13 discharge. So can Smith use "Chapter 20" to strip-off the underwater junior lien?

IN RE CAIN

United States Bankruptcy Appellate Panel, Sixth Circuit, 2014
513 B.R. 316

MARIAN F. HARRISON, Bankruptcy Appellate Panel Judge. Debtor Andrea M. Cain (the "Debtor") appeals the August 9, 2013 order of the United States Bankruptcy Court for the Northern District of Ohio (the "Bankruptcy Court") denying the Debtor's unopposed Motion to Avoid the Mortgage Lien of Amerifirst Home Improvement Financial Company ("Amerifirst"). For the reasons that follow, the Panel REVERSES the Bankruptcy Court's denial of the Debtor's Motion to Avoid the Mortgage Lien of Amerifirst. . . .

The Debtor first filed a Chapter 7 petition and received a discharge on February 1, 2008. On July 3, 2008, the Debtor filed the present Chapter 13 case to pay an outstanding auto loan and tax obligations, to cure the default on her first mortgage, and to avoid a wholly unsecured second mortgage on her residence. The Debtor's Amended Chapter 13 Plan, dated August 21, 2008, was confirmed on September 18, 2008. The confirmed Chapter 13 plan included the following provision:

> Debtors will avoid the mortgage and/or judgment liens of Amerifirst Home Improvement Finance, Squires Construction Company, & Ohio Department of Taxation, which [are] wholly unsecured pursuant to 11 U.S.C. §§ 506(a), 1322(b)(2) & 1325(a)(5)(B), and which wholly impairs Debtors' exemption in their residence home pursuant to 11 U.S.C. § 522(f). Any unsecured claim filed by said creditor(s) shall be disallowed as discharged in Debtors' Chapter 7 Bankruptcy Case No. 08–10687 filed February 1, 2008 unless otherwise allowed by a separate order of the Court.

Because the Debtor had received a Chapter 7 discharge within the preceding four years, the Debtor was not eligible for a discharge in her Chapter 13 case. See 11 U.S.C. § 1328(f)(1). Accordingly, upon completion of the Debtor's payments under the plan, the Chapter 13 Trustee filed his Motion for Order Releasing Wages and Closing Case Without a Discharge. The Chapter 13 Trustee's motion was granted on May 6, 2013. On May 17, 2013, the Debtor filed a Motion to Avoid Mortgage Lien on Real Estate against Amerifirst in order to effectuate the provisions of her confirmed Chapter 13 Plan and to avoid Amerifirst's second mortgage lien on her residence. At the time of the Chapter 13 filing, the Debtor's residence was valued at not more than $100,800. The residence was encumbered by Everhome Mortgage Company's first mortgage in the amount of $106,306.38 and by Amerifirst's second mortgage in the amount of $9,415.28.

No party-in-interest objected to the Debtor's Motion to Avoid Mortgage Lien on Real Estate, however, the Bankruptcy Court denied the motion by order, dated August 9, 2013. The Bankruptcy Court held:

> The lien stripping power of 11 U.S.C. § 506 is unavailable to Debtor. She received a Chapter 7 discharge within four years of filing this case and is therefore ineligible for a Chapter 13 discharge. 11 U.S.C. § 1328(f)(1). Pursuant to § 1325(a)(5), the lien stays in place until discharge or payment of the underlying debt. Because the Debtor is ineligible for a discharge, the mortgage lien will stay in place until payment of the underlying debt.

The determinative issue in this appeal concerns the interplay between various provisions of the Bankruptcy Code affecting "Chapter 20" debtors. Specifically, the issue is whether a debtor may strip off a wholly unsecured, inferior mortgage lien on the debtor's primary residence in a Chapter 13 case filed less than four years after having received a Chapter 7 discharge.

This question has not been addressed by the Sixth Circuit. Two Circuit Courts and one Bankruptcy Appellate Panel have considered it, finding that a valueless lien can be stripped, regardless of discharge eligibility. *Wells Fargo Bank, N.A. v. Scantling (In re Scantling)*, [754] F.3d [1323], 2014 WL 2750349, at *5 (11th Cir. June 18, 2014); *Branigan v. Davis (In re Davis)*, 716 F.3d 331 (4th Cir.2013); *Fisette v. Keller (In re Fisette)*, 455 B.R. 177, 185 (B.A.P. 8th Cir.2011). Bankruptcy courts, however, are split on the question and on their approach. . . .

Courts utilizing the first approach refuse to allow stripping off wholly unsecured liens in Chapter 20 cases because doing so would amount to a "de facto discharge." *Lindskog v. M & I Bank*, 480 B.R. 916, 919 (E.D.Wis.2012). These courts rely on an interpretation of *Dewsnup v. Timm*, 502 U.S. 410, 417, 112 S.Ct. 773, 778, 116 L.Ed.2d 903 (1992) (holding that Section 506(d) does not allow a party to "strip down" a partially secured lien), and on Congress' inclusion of a discharge requirement in 11 U.S.C. § 1325(a)(5)(B)(i)(II). *See, e.g., In re Gerardin*, 447 B.R. 342, 352 (Bankr.S.D.Fla.2011) ("[D]ebtor who is ineligible for a chapter 13 discharge may not strip down or strip off a lien."), *abrogated by In re Scantling*, 2014 WL 2750349; *In re Fenn*, 428 B.R. 494, 500 (Bankr.N.D.Ill.2010) (allowing permanent strip off of junior mortgage lien after Chapter 20 debtor completes plan "results in a de facto discharge") (citation omitted); *Orkwis v. MERS (In re Orkwis)*, 457 B.R. 243, 252 (Bankr.E.D.N.Y.2011) (holding that junior lien is not removed until entry of discharge); *In re Winitzky*, No. 1:08–bk–19337–MT, 2009 WL 9139891, at *5 (Bankr.C.D.Cal. May 7, 2009) (holding that Code does not allow court to strip lien where debtor cannot receive a discharge).

Those courts adopting the second approach allow Chapter 20 lien stripping but hold that the parties' pre-bankruptcy rights are reinstated by operation of law after the plan has been consummated. *See, e.g., Victorio v. Billingslea,* 470 B.R. 545, 556 (S.D.Cal.2012) (finding that a Chapter 20 debtor must pay debt in full during course of Chapter 13 plan to permanently avoid liability on wholly unsecured lien); *In re Jarvis,* 390 B.R. 600, 605–06 (Bankr.C.D.Ill.2008) (holding that discharge is a necessary prerequisite to permanency of lien avoidance); *In re Lilly,* 378 B.R. 232, 236 (Bankr.C.D.Ill.2007) (citation omitted) ("Where a debtor does not receive a discharge . . . any modifications to a creditor's rights imposed in the plan are not permanent and have no binding effect once the term of the plan ends."); *In re Trujillo,* No. 6: 10–bk–02615–ABB, 2010 WL 4669095, at *2 (Bankr.M.D.Fla. Nov.10, 2010) (same), *aff'd sub nom. Trujillo v. BAC Home Loan Servicing, L.P. (In re Trujillo),* 2012 WL 8883694 (M.D.Fla. Aug.10, 2012), *abrogated by In re Scantling,* 2014 WL 2750349.

Courts applying the third approach "allow chapter 20 lien stripping because nothing in the Bankruptcy Code prevents it." *In re Jennings,* 454 B.R. at 257 (citations omitted). These courts contend that the mechanism that voids the lien is plan completion, and that Chapter 20 cases end in administrative closing rather than dismissal. *See, e.g., In re Scantling,* 2014 WL 2750349, at *5 (strip off of unsecured mortgage on debtor's principal residence "is accomplished through the § 506(a) valuation procedure that determines that the creditor does not hold a secured claim"); *In re Davis,* 716 F.3d at 338 (holding that Chapter 20 debtor can strip a worthless lien permanently upon completion of plan); *Zeman v. Waterman (In re Waterman),* 469 B.R. 334, 339 (D.Colo.2012) ("Chapter 20 debtor may strip off a wholly unsecured lien from his principal residence, despite being ineligible for a discharge."); *In re Fair,* 450 B.R. 853, 858 (E.D.Wis.2011) (citations omitted) ("[T]here is nothing in the bankruptcy code which ties the modification of an unsecured lien to obtaining a discharge under chapter 13."); *In re Fisette,* 455 B.R. at 185 (citations omitted) ("[N]othing in the Bankruptcy Code conditions a Chapter 13 debtor's ability to modify a wholly unsecured creditor's lien under § 1322(b) on his eligibility for a discharge."); *In re Wapshare,* 492 B.R. 211, 217–18 (Bankr.S.D.N.Y.2013) (citations omitted) ("[U]nsecured junior mortgage lien is permanently avoided in chapter 20 cases once a chapter 13 plan is confirmed and all plan payments have been made."); *Wong v. Green Tree Serv., LLC (In re Wong),* 488 B.R. 537, 551 (Bankr.E.D.N.Y.2013) (holding that where claim is unsecured under § 506(a), then claim is unsecured with respect to § 1322(b)(2) and § 1325(a)(5)); *In re Dolinak,* 497 B.R. 15, 22–23 (Bankr.D.N.H.2013) (citation omitted) ("Section 1328(f)(1) only prevents a chapter 20 debtor from receiving a discharge; it does not limit a chapter 20 debtor's rights under § 1322(b)."); *In re Gloster,* 459 B.R. 200, 205 (Bankr.D.N.J.2011) (holding that lien stripping allowed in "Chapter 20 setting so long as a subsequent Chapter 13 is filed in good faith and a plan is successfully completed.").

A growing consensus of courts have followed the third approach, holding that nothing in the Code prevents a Chapter 20 debtor from stripping a wholly unsecured junior lien on the debtor's principal residence. This approach is most consistent with the Sixth Circuit's decision in *In re Lane*, 280 F.3d 663, 669, because it starts by determining the status of the claim under 11 U.S.C. § 506(a).

In the present case, the Bankruptcy Court based its holding on 11 U.S.C. § 1325(a)(5)(B), which requires that the holder of a secured claim retain the lien securing the claim until the mortgage is satisfied or the debtor receives a discharge, whichever comes first. Thus, the Bankruptcy Court determined that because of the Debtor's ineligibility for a discharge, she must satisfy Amerifirst's lien in full. By failing to first determine the proper classification of Amerifirst's claim, the Bankruptcy Court's decision disregarded the road map set forth in *Nobelman* and *Lane*.

It is undisputed that under 11 U.S.C. § 506 Amerifirst's lien has no value because the amount owed under the first mortgage exceeds the value of the property. Consequently, pursuant to the holding in *Lane*, Amerifirst's claim is "unsecured" under 11 U.S.C. § 506(a). *Id.* at 669. Thus, Amerifirst's lien cannot be treated as a secured claim under 11 U.S.C. § 1322(b)(2) (protecting holders of "secured claims" secured only by a security interest in a debtor's principal residence). *In re Wong*, 488 B.R. at 551. Nor do the requirements of 11 U.S.C. § 1325(a)(5) (protecting the holder of a secured claim until the debt is paid or the debtor is discharged) apply. *Id.*

Applying the reasoning set forth in *Lane* to the facts of this case, the wholly unsecured status of Amerifirst's claim, rather than the Debtor's eligibility for a discharge, is determinative. *See In re Scantling*, 2014 WL 2750349, at *5 ("[S]trip off is accomplished through the § 506(a) valuation procedure that determines that the creditor does not hold a secured claim."). Nothing in 11 U.S.C. § 1328(f)(1) prohibits a Chapter 20 debtor from taking advantage of the protections and benefits (other than discharge) of Chapter 13. *Frazier v. Real Time Resolutions, Inc. (In re Frazier)*, 469 B.R. 889, 899 (E.D.Cal.2012) (citation omitted). Lien-stripping is an important tool in the Chapter 13 toolbox, and it is not conditioned on being eligible for a discharge. *In re Jennings*, 454 B.R. at 258 (citations omitted). *See also In re Frazier*, 469 B.R. at 895–96 ("[W]holly unsecured junior lien on the debtor's principal residence may be removed in Chapter 20 action despite the operation of § 1328(f)(1)."). Accordingly, a Chapter 20 debtor may avoid a wholly unsecured lien on the debtor's principal residence. . . .

NOTE

Which approach is preferable? At first blush, the *Cain* approach appears to sanction an end run around *Dewsnup*'s prohibition on lien-stripping. As one bankruptcy court noted, "allowing a debtor to file chapter 7, discharge all dischargeable debts and then immediately file chapter 13 to strip off a second mortgage lien would not be much different than simply avoiding the mortgage lien in the chapter 7 itself." In re Blosser, 2009 WL 1064455 (Bankr. E.D. Wis. 2009). Nevertheless, there are legitimate reasons why a "Chapter 20" debtor might want to use the restructuring tools of Chapter 13 even if she is not eligible for a discharge. Further, the Supreme Court has explicitly recognized that "Congress did not intend to categorically foreclose the benefit of Chapter 13 lien reorganization to a debtor who previously filed for Chapter 7 relief." Johnson v. Home State Bank, 501 U.S. 78, 87 (1991). As a result, courts should be properly reluctant to presume Congress intended for section 1328(f) to limit the availability of Chapter 13's other lien restructuring tools. See, e.g., In re Boukatch, 533 B.R. 292 (9th Cir. B.A.P. 2015) (allowing Chapter 20 strip-off notwithstanding debtor's ineligibility for Chapter 13 discharge); In re Rosa, 521 B.R. 337 (Bankr. N.D. Cal. 2014) (allowing Chapter 20 strip-off and holding that underwater junior held no unsecured claim in debtor's Chapter 13 case).

Still, note that 11 U.S.C. § 1325(a)(3) requires that a court may not confirm a Chapter 13 plan unless "the plan has been proposed in good faith and not by any means forbidden by law." If the debtor has no good reason for using "Chapter 20" other than stripping-off an underwater junior lien that could not have been avoided in Chapter 7, can the court properly conclude that the debtor's Chapter 13 plan lacks good faith and thus cannot be confirmed? See, e.g., In re Okosisi, 451 B.R. 90 (Bankr. D. Nev. 2011); In re Tran, 431 B.R. 230 (Bankr. N.D. Cal. 2010).

6. THE MORTGAGEE IN A CHAPTER 11 CASE

Chapter 11 establishes the process for reorganization of business debtors and individual debtors with debts that exceed the permissible limits for Chapter 13. As in Chapter 13, the Chapter 11 debtor-in-possession must propose a plan that explains how and to what extent it will pay its creditors on account of their claims. In Chapter 13 cases, all plans are either 3 or 5 years, and it is typical for the debtor to submit a plan at the same time he or she files the bankruptcy petition. By contrast, in Chapter 11, there is no fixed plan period, and there can be a significant delay between the petition date and the date that debtor proposes and seeks confirmation of a plan. The debtor has the exclusive right to submit a plan for the first 120 days of a Chapter 11 case, 11 U.S.C. § 1121(b), and for longer if the court extends this exclusivity period for "cause." 11 U.S.C.

§ 1121(d).[33] The need for this period derives from several factors. First, the financial affairs of Chapter 11 debtors are often more complex (and thus potentially more difficult to restructure) than those of individual debtors in Chapter 13. For this reason, Chapter 11 debtors often need time to adjust their operations to respond to the circumstances that resulted in the bankruptcy filing. Second, unlike in Chapter 13—where approval of the plan rests solely with the bankruptcy court—Chapter 11's provisions require that creditors vote on the plan, and judicial confirmation requires that the plan meet certain creditor approval thresholds. Thus, while the debtor negotiates with its creditors, a significant amount of time may pass between the petition date and the date on which the debtor begins repaying creditors under the terms of a confirmed plan.

Chapter 11, classification of mortgage claims, and nonrecourse mortgages. If the unpaid balance of the mortgage debt exceeds the value of the mortgaged property, § 506(a) "bifurcates" the mortgagee's claim into two claims—a secured claim equal to the value of the mortgaged property, and an unsecured claim for the difference between the value of the mortgaged property and the unpaid balance of the debt. Initially, one might assume that a commercial mortgagee might have no unsecured claim at all if the mortgage loan was "nonrecourse" (meaning that the mortgagor and mortgagee agreed in the loan documents that the mortgagor would have no personal liability on the debt). For distribution purposes in Chapter 11, however, nonrecourse mortgages are treated as if the mortgagee had recourse against the debtor. 11 U.S.C. § 1111(b)(1)(A) ("A claim secured by a lien on property of the estate shall be allowed or disallowed . . . the same as if the holder of such claim had recourse against the debtor on account of such claim, whether or not such holder has such recourse. . . .").

Thus, suppose Debtor owns an office building that is subject to a nonrecourse mortgage held by First Life Insurance Co. (First Life) that secures an unpaid balance of $20 million. On the Chapter 11 petition date, the office building is worth $15 million. Even though First Life could not have obtained a deficiency judgment against Debtor outside of bankruptcy, First Life still has an allowed unsecured claim of $5 million, and is entitled to receive a distribution in bankruptcy on account of that claim, along with other unsecured creditors. Can you explain why bankruptcy gives the nonrecourse mortgagee the right to assert an unsecured claim?

There are only two situations in which an undersecured nonrecourse mortgagee cannot assert an unsecured claim in Chapter 11. The first arises when the debtor proposes to sell the mortgaged property rather than to retain ownership of it. 11 U.S.C. § 1111(b)(1)(A)(ii). This exception makes sense, because in that case the mortgagee receives exactly what it bargained for in making a nonrecourse loan. The second arises when the

---

[33] If the debtor fails to file a plan, any other party (including a creditor) can file a plan after the exclusive period has expired.

undersecured mortgagee makes a "§ 1111(b) election" and chooses to waive its unsecured claim and have its entire claim treated as fully secured. 11 U.S.C. §§ 1111(b)(1)(A)(i), 1111(b)(2). In the above example, if First Life makes this election, First Life is deemed to have a secured claim of $20 million. It will retain its lien on the office building to secure the repayment of that entire amount, but it must forgo any right to share in any distribution made to unsecured creditors. The 1111(b) election thus allows an undersecured mortgagee like First Bank to avoid having its lien "stripped-down" in Chapter 11.[34]

The Chapter 11 plan. Section 1123 of the Code specifies in elaborate detail the contents of the plan, but two elements merit primary attention here. First, the plan must sort creditor claims into "classes"; second, the plan must describe in detail how it will treat each class of creditors (i.e., how it proposes to repay claims within that class). The debtor can place a claim into a particular class only if it is "substantially similar" to other claims in the same class. 11 U.S.C. § 1122(a). Thus, a Chapter 11 plan must classify secured and unsecured claims separately, and cannot place a senior mortgage claim and a junior mortgage claim on the same property in the same class. [This typically means that each secured claim must be placed in its own separate class.]

As in Chapter 13, a Chapter 11 plan may propose to repay unsecured creditors less than the full amount of their claims, and may modify a secured claim (unless the debtor is an individual debtor and the claim is secured only by the debtor's primary residence). 11 U.S.C. § 1123(b)(1), (5). In Chapter 11 vernacular, a claim that is modified by the debtor's plan is said to be "impaired." 11 U.S.C. § 1124 (a class is not "impaired" if the plan "leaves unaltered the legal, equitable or contractual rights" of all claims in the class). Importantly, a plan's mere cure of a pre-bankruptcy default and de-acceleration of a pre-bankruptcy acceleration is not impairment. 11 U.S.C. § 1124(2).[35] Thus, as in Chapter 13, the Chapter 11 debtor may cure the default by paying any arrearages in installments under its plan. However, if the plan proposes to modify the interest rate, extend the repayment term, or "strip-down" the principal balance to the current value of the collateral, such a modification impairs the mortgagee's secured claim.

---

[34] A mortgagee cannot make an 1111(b) election if the creditor's interest is of "inconsequential value." 11 U.S.C. § 1111(b)(1)(B)(i). Thus, if a junior mortgagee's debt is entirely "underwater" (i.e., the collateral's value is lower than the balance owed to the senior mortgagee), the junior cannot make an 1111(b) election. As a result, as in Chapter 13, the Chapter 11 debtor can "strip-off" the lien of an entirely underwater junior mortgagee. In re Heritage Highgate, Inc., 679 F.3d 132 (3d Cir. 2012); In re Johnson, 386 B.R. 171 (Bankr. W.D. Pa. 2008).

[35] If the plan proposes to pay the arrearage in installments, the debtor must pay interest on the arrearage "in accordance with the underlying agreement and applicable nonbankruptcy law." 11 U.S.C. § 1123(d).

Once the debtor files its proposed plan, the debtor must solicit the requisite creditor acceptance needed for court approval (or "confirmation") of the plan. Each creditor must receive a copy of the plan (or a plan summary) and a judicially-approved disclosure statement, and then each creditor votes whether to accept the plan. In general (and subject to the possibility of approval by "cram-down" as discussed later in this section), for the debtor to confirm its plan, each class of creditors must either (1) accept the plan or (2) not be impaired by it. 11 U.S.C. § 1129(a)(8). If a class is unimpaired, it is deemed to have accepted the plan. 11 U.S.C. § 1126(f). If the plan impairs a class of claims, the class is deemed to accept the plan if a majority in number and two-thirds in total amount of the claims in the class vote to approve the plan. 11 U.S.C. § 1126(c).

The confirmation requirements. Section 1129 establishes the requirements for the court to confirm a plan. As explained above, each class must accept the plan or must not be impaired. In addition, if even one creditor in an impaired class votes not to accept the plan, then the court may not confirm the plan unless it pays each creditor in that class an amount not less than the creditor would have received in a Chapter 7 liquidation. 11 U.S.C. § 1129(a)(7). Moreover, *at least one class* of impaired claims must accept the plan. 11 U.S.C. § 1129(a)(10). Finally, the court cannot confirm the plan unless it concludes that the plan was proposed in good faith, 11 U.S.C. § 1129(a)(3), and is "feasible," i.e., that confirmation "is not likely to be followed by the liquidation, or the need for further financial reorganization, of the debtor ... unless such liquidation or reorganization is proposed in the plan." 11 U.S.C. § 1129(a)(11). Under this standard, the court must examine the adequacy of the debtor's capital structure, its earning power, economic conditions, the ability of debtor's management and the probability of its continuation, and any other factors related to the debtor's ability to perform its plan successfully. See, e.g., In re Waterford Hotel, Inc., 497 B.R. 255 (Bankr. E.D. Mich. 2013).

Cram-down. If a plan satisfies all of the other requirements of § 1129, but an impaired class still fails to approve it, the court may nevertheless confirm or "cram-down" the plan over the objection of that class, as long as the plan "does not discriminate unfairly, and is fair and equitable" to that class. 11 U.S.C. § 1129(b)(1). To understand the implications of cram-down for the mortgagee, suppose Debtor owns a shopping center subject to a mortgage held by First Life Insurance Company (First Life) that secures an outstanding balance of $12 million. After losing several major tenants, Debtor files a Chapter 11 petition. The shopping center's current value is $10 million. First Life does not make an 1111(b) election, so it has a secured claim of $10 million and an unsecured claim of $2 million. As a result, First Life will have two votes on the plan: one as the only claimant in the class that contains its secured claim, and another as a member of a class of unsecured creditors. If First Life votes to reject the plan, then the class containing its secured claim will reject the plan; further, because of the size of its unsecured claim, its rejection may preclude Debtor from obtaining the necessary approval (two-thirds in amount) needed from the class of unsecured creditors. Thus, if First Life votes to reject the plan, Debtor cannot confirm it unless it satisfies the cram-down standards. The "fair and equitable" cram-down standard, however, applies differently to secured and unsecured claims.

Cram-down: the "fair and equitable" standard and secured claims. Section 1129(b)(2)(A) provides three standards under which a cram-down plan is considered "fair and equitable" in its treatment of an objecting mortgagee's secured claim, depending on how the plan proposes to treat the mortgagee. The first standard applies if the debtor plans to retain the mortgaged property; if so, the mortgagee must retain its lien and must receive present or deferred cash payments under the plan that (1) are at least equal to the amount of the total unpaid mortgage debt and (2) have a present value that is not less than the value of the mortgaged real estate. 11 U.S.C. § 1129(b)(2)(A)(i). Thus, in the above example, if Debtor wants to retain the shopping center over First Life's objection, First Life must retain its lien on the shopping center to secure the $10 million secured claim, the plan must make payments to First Life over the life of the plan that total at least $12 million, and these payments must have a present value of at least $10 million.

The second standard applies if the debtor's plan proposes to sell the real estate free and clear of the mortgage. In that case, the plan is considered "fair and equitable" as long as the mortgagee's lien is transferred to the sale proceeds, 11 U.S.C. § 1129(b)(2)(A)(ii), and the mortgagee has the opportunity (unless the court orders otherwise for cause) to "credit bid" at the sale—i.e., to bid by offsetting its successful bid against the unpaid balance of the debt. 11 U.S.C. § 363(k). The mortgagee's ability to credit-bid protects the mortgagee against the risk that the collateral is sold at a price below what the mortgagee considers to be the collateral's fair market value.

The third standard focuses on whether the debtor's cram-down plan provides for the mortgagee to realize the "indubitable equivalent" of its claim. 11 U.S.C. § 1129(b)(2)(A)(iii). The Code does not define "indubitable equivalence," but the Code's legislative history indicates that this term was intended to "give[ ] the parties and the courts flexibility by allowing such other relief as will result in the realization by the protected entity of the value of its interest in the property involved." H.R. Rep. No. 95–595, at 340 (1977), reprinted in 1978 U.S. Code Cong. & Admin. News 5962, 6296. The debtor will rely on this standard only when it cannot satisfy one of the other two standards. For example, in In re River East Plaza, LLC, 669 F.3d 826 (7th Cir. 2012), the debtor owned mortgaged real estate worth only $13.5 million in a case in which the mortgagee (which was owed $38.3 million) made an 1111(b) election. The debtor's plan proposed to "substitute" collateral, such that the debtor would keep the real estate free of the mortgagee's lien, while instead giving the mortgagee a first lien on $13.5 million in 30-year Treasury bonds. The court held that the bonds were not the "indubitable equivalent" of the mortgaged land (can you explain why not?) and that the plan's treatment of the mortgagee's secured claim was not fair and equitable.[36]

Section 1129(b) provides that the "fair and equitable" standard "includes" the three standards discussed above. The nonexclusive nature of the word "including" suggests that a court might conclude that a plan technically satisfies one of these standards and yet is still not "fair and equitable." See In re D & F Constr., Inc., 865 F.2d 673 (5th Cir. 1989) ("technical compliance with all the requirements in § 1129(b)(2) does not assure that the plan is 'fair and equitable.' . . . A court must consider the entire plan in the context of the rights of creditors under state law and the particular facts and circumstances in determining whether a plan is 'fair and equitable.' "). Thus, suppose that in the prior example, Debtor's plan proposes to pay First Life interest-only payments on its $10 million secured claim for 20 years, and then to pay the entire principal balance in a balloon payment after 20 years. The shopping center will need substantial refurbishment within the next 20 years, but the plan does not address how Debtor will accumulate the necessary reserves or obtain financing for such refurbishment. In such a case, a court will likely conclude that the plan is not fair and equitable because it defers repayment for too long a period and subjects the mortgagee to an unjustified risk of nonpayment. See, e.g., In re VIP Motor Lodge, 133 B.R. 41 (Bankr. D. Del. 1991).

Cram-down: the "fair and equitable" standard, unsecured claims, and the "absolute priority rule." If a class of unsecured creditors rejects a plan, the plan cannot satisfy the "fair and equitable" standard unless it also satisfies the "absolute priority rule." This rule—which is the product of early pre-Code case law and is now codified in section 1129(b)(2)(B)—requires that the claims of a class of unsecured creditors must be paid *in full* before any junior class of creditors or interest holders (including those holding ownership interests in the debtor) receives any property on account of those junior interests. Thus, in our prior example, suppose Debtor's plan proposes to retain full ownership of the shopping center without making

[36] Sometimes, debtors have proposed to sell mortgaged property free and clear of the mortgagee's lien, but via sales in which the mortgagee would not be allowed to credit bid. A few federal courts of appeal ruled that such sales offered the mortgagee the "indubitable equivalent" of its secured claim, as long as the asset was for a price at or above the judicially-determined value or in an arms-length public auction sale. See, e.g., In re Philadelphia Newspapers, 599 F.3d 298 (3d Cir. 2010); In re Pacific Lumber Co., 584 F.3d 229 (5th Cir. 2009). In 2012, however, the Supreme Court rejected these cases, holding that a plan that proposes to sell the collateral free and clear of the mortgagee's lien, but does not give the mortgagee the right to credit bid at that sale, cannot satisfy the indubitable equivalent standard. See, e.g., RadLAX Gateway Hotel, LLC v. Amalgamated Bank, 566 U.S. 639 (2012).

any additional equity investment, but to pay only 50% of First Life's $2 million unsecured claim. The plan would violate the absolute priority rule and could not be crammed-down over First Life's objection, even if every other class had voted to accept the plan.

As a result, a debtor normally cannot retain ownership of property of the estate solely on account of its pre-bankruptcy ownership interest unless unsecured creditors consent or receive full payment of their claims. Pre-Code case law, however, permitted deviation from the absolute priority rule if the holder of the junior interest injected new capital, in the form of money or money's worth, that was a reasonable equivalent of the ownership interest being received by the reorganized debtor. The Bankruptcy Code codified the absolute priority rule but did not explicitly codify the pre-Code "new value" exception. The Seventh and Ninth Circuits have ruled that a "new value" exception exists, see, e.g., In re 203 N. LaSalle St. Partn., 126 F.3d 955 (7th Cir. 1998); In re Bonner Mall Partn., 2 F.3d 899 (9th Cir. 1993), while the Second and Fourth Circuits have expressed doubt (but without definitively stating that it does not exist). See, e.g., In re Coltex Loop Central Three Partners, L.P., 138 F.3d 39 (2d Cir. 1998); In re Bryson Props., XVIII, 961 F.2d 496 (4th Cir. 1992). The remaining circuits have not ruled definitively, and the district and bankruptcy courts are divided. 7 Collier on Bankruptcy ¶ 1129.03[4][c], at 1129–94 n.166 (16th ed.) (collecting cases).

The Supreme Court has yet to rule directly on the question. Its most recent consideration of the "new value" exception came in Bank of America Nat'l Trust & Sav. Ass'n v. 203 North LaSalle St. Partnership, 526 U.S. 434 (1999). In that case, an undersecured mortgagee held a $38.5 million unsecured deficiency claim for which the plan proposed to pay only a 16% dividend. Under the debtor's plan, certain pre-bankruptcy partners of the debtor were to contribute $6.125 million in new capital in exchange for the full ownership interest in the reorganized debtor. Further, the plan was subject to the condition that the debtor's partners had the exclusive right to contribute the new capital. The mortgagee argued that the plan was not fair and equitable, because it proposed to vest ownership of the property in the reorganized debtor and its partners without giving anyone else (including the mortgagee) the opportunity to propose a larger investment or a competing reorganization plan. Without definitively addressing whether the Code contained a "new value" exception, the Court agreed that the plan could not be confirmed:

> If the price to be paid for the equity interest is the best obtainable, old equity does not need the protection of exclusiveness (unless to trump an equal offer from someone else); if it is not the best, there is no apparent reason for giving old equity a bargain. There is no reason, that is, unless the very purpose of the whole transaction is, at least in part, to do old equity a favor. And that, of course, is

to say that old equity would obtain its opportunity, and the resulting benefit, because of old equity's prior interest within the meaning of subsection [1129](b)(2)(B)(ii).

203 N. LaSalle St., 526 U.S. at 456. See also In re Castleton Plaza, LP, 707 F.3d 821 (7th Cir. 2013) ("Competition is essential whenever a plan of reorganization leaves an objecting creditor unpaid yet distributes an equity interest to an insider."). For further discussion of the "new value" exception, see Hoang, The New Value Exception to the Absolute Priority Rule After *In re 203 N. Lasalle Street Partnership*: What Should Bankruptcy Courts Do, and How Can Congress Help?, 149 U. Pa. L. Rev. 581, 612 (2000); Carlson & Williams, The Truth About the New Value Exception to Bankruptcy's Absolute Priority Rule, 21 Cardozo L. Rev. 1303 (2001); Watson, Left for Dead?: The Supreme Court's Treatment of the New Value Exception, 78 N.C. L. Rev. 1190 (2000); Markell, Owners, Auctions, and Absolute Priority in Bankruptcy Reorganizations, 44 Stan. L. Rev. 69 (1991).

Cram-down: "unfair discrimination." As noted earlier, the cram-down standard also requires that the plan must not "discriminate unfairly" with respect to the claims of an objecting impaired class. 11 U.S.C. § 1129(b)(1). The prohibition against unfair discrimination prevents the debtor from treating similar classes of claims differently, at least without appropriate justification for doing so. See, e.g., Markell, A New Perspective on Unfair Discrimination in Chapter 11, 72 Am. Bankr. L.J. 227 (1998); Polivy, Unfair Discrimination in Chapter 11: Comprehensive Compilation of Current Case Law, 72 Am. Bankr. L.J. 191 (1998).

The starting point for Chapter 11 claim classification is § 1122(a), which provides that "a plan may place a claim or interest in a particular class only if such claim or interest is substantially similar to the other claims or interests of such class." Thus, the debtor could typically classify unsecured claims in the same class, "whether [arising from] trade, tort, publicly held debt or a *deficiency of a secured creditor.*" In re Pine Lake Village Apt. Co., 19 B.R. 819, 830 (Bankr. S.D.N.Y. 1982). Nevertheless, the Code allows the debtor to create a separate class for unsecured claims that are "less than or reduced to an amount that the court approves as reasonable and necessary for administrative convenience." 11 U.S.C. § 1122(b). Thus, for example, Debtor's plan could have one class of unsecured creditors with claims over $500 (which it would pay in quarterly installments over a ten-year period) and another class for unsecured creditors with claims under $500 (which it would pay in full in a lump sum immediately after confirmation). The Code permits this treatment—even though it discriminates between smaller unsecured claims and larger ones—as a matter of convenience, permitting the debtor to avoid the administrative costs of paying small claims in small installments over a long period. See, e.g., 7 Collier on Bankruptcy ¶ 1122.03[4] (16th ed.).

Implicitly, the "unfair" discrimination standard suggests that a debtor can separately classify certain unsecured claims if the debtor can offer a sufficient justification for doing so. What justification would be sufficient? In considering this question, it is important to keep in mind that the cram-down standard requires that *at least one* impaired class must vote to confirm the plan. Thus, returning to our continuing example, suppose that Debtor's unsecured creditors include First Bank (which holds a $2 million unsecured deficiency claim) and twelve employees and trade creditors (which hold claims totalling $200,000 and ranging from $5,000 to $25,000). If Debtor classifies all of the unsecured creditors together in the same class, the two-thirds-in-amount requirement means that a "no" vote by First Bank will cause the class to reject the plan. If there is no other impaired class that approves the plan, Debtor cannot cram-down the plan over First Bank's objection, even if a court would conclude that it was "fair and equitable." For this reason, Debtor may attempt to classify First Bank's deficiency claim in one class and the employees and trade creditors in a different class, hoping that the employees and trade creditors will approve the plan and thus facilitate Debtor's cram-down.[37]

This type of classification is sometimes pejoratively called "artificial classification" or "gerrymandering." Some courts have traditionally demonstrated substantial hostility towards gerrymandering, most notably the Fifth Circuit in In re Greystone III Joint Venture, 995 F.2d 1274 (5th Cir. 1991). In *Greystone*, the debtor owed the mortgagee approximately $9,325,000 and trade creditors approximately $145,000. The bankruptcy court valued the mortgaged real estate at $5,825,000, leaving the mortgagee with an unsecured claim of $3,500,000. The debtor's plan classified the mortgagee's unsecured deficiency claim separately from the claims of trade creditors; the debtor would pay each class approximately 4% of their claims, but the plan also provided that the debtor's general partner would pay the balance of the trade creditors' claims in full. The mortgagee rejected the plan, but the trade creditor class voted to accept it, and the bankruptcy and district courts approved the plan (even though the mortgagee had proposed to fund a competing plan that would have paid all unsecured creditors in full). The Fifth Circuit reversed, holding that the debtor had classified the claims separately only to gerrymander an affirmative vote for plan and not for independent substantive reasons, pithily stating "thou shalt not classify similar claims differently in order to gerrymander an affirmative vote on a reorganization plan." *Greystone*, 995

---

[37] As discussed previously, an undersecured mortgagee may elect under § 1111(b) to waive its unsecured claim and have its claim treated as fully secured notwithstanding the current value of the collateral. Thus, the decision of an undersecured mortgagee like First Life whether to make a § 1111(b) election is not a simple one. If First Life makes the election, it must forgo any distribution on account of unsecured claims, but its lien will remain effective against the land until the entire $12 million unpaid debt is satisfied. However, because the election would leave First Life with no unsecured claim, First Bank will be unable to vote as an unsecured creditor, meaning it would have less leverage to prevent the cram-down of a plan to which it objects.

F.2d at 1279. The court noted that the record did not demonstrate the debtor's inability to obtain services if trade creditors did not receive preferential treatment, and thus concluded that the bankruptcy court was clearly erroneous to have found a good business reason for the separate classification. *Greystone*, 995 F.2d at 1281.

Consistent with *Greystone*, a number of courts have concluded that the debtor may not classify the unsecured deficiency claim of a mortgagee separately from the claims of other unsecured creditors (other than administrative convenience creditors). See, e.g., In re Bryson Props., XVIII, 961 F.2d 496 (4th Cir. 1992); In re Lumber Exchange Bldg. Partn., 968 F.2d 647 (8th Cir. 1992); In re Hanish, LLC, 570 B.R. 4 (Bankr. D. N.H. 2017). See also In re Village Green I, GP, 811 F.3d 816 (6th Cir. 2016) (artificial impairment of small class of unsecured claims was contrived solely to manufacture impaired accepting class and thus prevented a finding that the plan was proposed in good faith). Nevertheless, a few courts have reached the opposite result and have *required* the debtor to separately classify unsecured claims that would have been nonrecourse claims outside of bankruptcy, reasoning that these are significantly different from the claims of other unsecured creditors and thus cannot be classified together under § 1122. See, e.g., In re Woodbrook Assocs., 19 F.3d 314 (7th Cir.1994); Beal Bank SSB v. Waters Edge Ltd. Partn., 248 B.R. 668 (D. Mass.2000). See also In re Loop 76, LLC, 465 B.R. 525 (9th Cir. B.A.P. 2012) (claim guaranteed by a third party was not "substantially similar" to other claims that were not guaranteed; thus, not only could the claims be separately classified, they had to be separately classified). As a policy matter, which approach seems more sensible to you?

NOTES

1. *The cram-down interest rate.* To calculate the present value of the debtor's periodic plan payments, the court must determine what interest rate to use in making that calculation. As discussed earlier in this section, in Till v. SCS Credit Corp., 541 U.S. 465, 124 S.Ct. 1951, 158 L.Ed.2d 787 (2004), a plurality of the Supreme Court held that the Chapter 13 cram-down standard required the use of a "formula approach" that starts with the prime rate and adjusts that rate upwards to account for the debtor's risk of nonpayment. While *Till* was a Chapter 13 case, the plurality's opinion viewed the formula approach as applicable in the Chapter 11 cram-down context as well, and the weight of subsequent authority has used the *Till* formula approach in Chapter 11 cram-downs. See, e.g., In re Texas Grand Prairie Hotel Realty, L.L.C., 710 F.3d 324 (5th Cir. 2013); In re Charles Street A.M.E. Church of Boston, 578 B.R. 56 (Bankr. D. Mass. 2017); In re J.C. Householder Land Trust #1, 501 B.R. 441 (Bankr. M.D. Fla. 2013); In re LMR, LLC, 496 B.R. 410 (Bankr. W.D.Tex. 2013).

2. *Curing pre-bankruptcy arrearages—does interest accrue at the pre-default contract rate or the default rate?* If the plan proposes to cure a pre-bankruptcy arrearage through installment payments, § 1123(d) requires that the debtor must pay interest "in accordance with the underlying agreement and applicable nonbankruptcy law." The weight of authority holds that cure would require repayment of the arrearage at the applicable post-default rate. See, e.g., In re New Investments, Inc., 840 F.3d 1137 (9th Cir. 2016); In re Sagamore Partners, Ltd., 620 Fed. Appx. 864 (11th Cir. 2015); In re Moshe, 567 B.R. 438 (Bankr. E.D.N.Y. 2017); In re Moody Nat'l SHS Houston H, LLC, 426 B.R. 667 (Bankr. S.D. Tex. 2010). Does the Code's language adequately resolve the question?

3. *Cram-down—some examples.* Consider the following examples of proposed plans. In which, if any, should a court be willing to cram-down the plan over the objection of the mortgagee?

(a) Debtor owns an office building subject to a mortgage held by First Life Insurance Co. (First Life) that secures an unpaid balance of $20 million. On the date Debtor files its Chapter 11 petition, the office building is more than half vacant and is worth only $10 million. Debtor's plan proposes to make interest only payments on First Life's secured claim at 10% interest for fifteen years (assume the prevailing market interest rate is 8%), with a balloon payment of all outstanding principal at the end of fifteen years. However, due to current vacancy levels, net operating rentals are not sufficient to permit Debtor to pay the full amount of interest that will accrue on First Life's secured claim. Thus, Debtor's plan proposes to capitalize the unpaid portion of the interest, which will cause the total principal balance to increase each month until the property produces net rents sufficient to pay full debt service. [For reasons that should be clear, this is referred to as a "negative amortization" plan.] Can the court cram-down this plan over First Life's objection? Why or why not? What additional information, if any, would you want to ascertain in making this judgment? See, e.g., Great Western Bank v. Sierra Woods Group, 953 F.2d 1174, 1177–78 (9th Cir. 1992); In re D & F Constr. Inc., 865 F.2d 673, 675–76 (5th Cir. 1989); In re Spanish Lake Assocs., 92 B.R. 875 (Bankr. E.D. Mo. 1988); In re Edgewater Motel, Inc., 85 B.R. 989 (Bankr. E.D. Tenn. 1988); Schermer & Bartz, Negative Amortization and Plan Confirmation: Is It Fair and Equitable Under Section 1129(b) of the Bankruptcy Code?, 8 Bankr. Dev. J. 1 (1991).

(b) Debtor owns a 16-acre parcel of undeveloped land that is subject to a mortgage held by Bank that secures an unpaid balance of $1.4 million. Debtor's Chapter 11 plan proposes to transfer 5.6 acres of the land to Bank in full satisfaction of the debt. [This is referred to as a "dirt-for-debt" plan or an "eat dirt" plan.] Debtor offers an appraisal indicating that the 5.6 acre parcel is worth $1.6 million. Can the court cram-down this plan over Bank's objection? Why or why not? What additional information, if any, would you want to ascertain in making this judgment? See, e.g., In re Arnold & Baker Farms, 85 F.3d 1415 (9th Cir. 1996); In re National Truck Funding LLC, 588 B.R. 175 (Bankr. S.D. Miss. 2018); In re Richfield 81 Partners II, LLC, 447 B.R. 653

(Bankr. N.D. Ga. 2011); In re Riddle, 444 B.R. 681 (Bankr. N.D. Ga. 2011); Lurey & Berlin, When Can Less Than All of a Creditor's Collateral Serve as the Indubitable Equivalent of the Creditor's Secured Claim?, 28 Cumb. L. Rev. 333 (1998). Cf. In re Sagendorph, 562 B.R. 545 (D. Mass. 2017) (refusing to confirm Chapter 13 debtor's plan to force vesting of collateral in creditor in satisfaction of its claim).

(c)   Debtor owns a shopping center that is subject to a mortgage held by First Life that secures an unpaid balance of $12 million. On the date Debtor files its Chapter 11 petition, the center is worth only $10 million; First Life does not make an 1111(b) election. In its plan, Debtor separates its unsecured creditors into two classes—a "convenience" class of unsecured creditors holding claims under $1,500, and a "general" unsecured class (which is dominated by First Life's $2 million unsecured deficiency claim). Debtor has cash available to pay the convenience class creditors in cash in full on the effective date of its proposed plan, but if it does that, those creditors will not be impaired (and thus cannot vote on the plan). To obtain the approval of the convenience class (and thus obtain the approval of one class as required for cram-down), Debtor proposes to pay the convenience class creditors in full, but to delay that payment for 90 days after the plan's effective date. The convenience class is the only class of creditors that votes to approve the plan. First Life argues that the creditors in the convenience class were not truly "impaired" and thus were not entitled to vote, such that the court should hold Debtor ineligible to cram-down the plan. Should the court permit the Debtor's "artificial impairment" of the convenience class so as to allow cram-down? Compare In re Windsor on the River Assocs., Ltd., 7 F.3d 127, 132 (8th Cir. 1993) (no) with In re Village at Camp Bowie I, L.P. 710 F.3d 239 (5th Cir. 2013) and In re L&J Anaheim Assocs., 995 F.2d 940 (9th Cir. 1993) (yes). See also Brubaker, Artificial Impairment and the Single-Asset Real Estate Debtor, 33 Bankruptcy Law Letter 1 (No. 4, April 2013); Markell, Clueless on Classification: Toward Removing Artificial Limits on Chapter 11 Claim Classification, 11 Emory Bankr. Dev. J. 1 (1995); Carlson, Artificial Impairment and the Single Asset Chapter 11 Case, 23 Cap. U. L. Rev. 339 (1994).

4.   *The absolute priority rule and individual debtors.* Traditionally, the absolute priority rule applied in Chapter 11 cases involving individual debtors as well as those involving business entities. In 2005, Congress amended the cramdown standard for unsecured claims to state:

> the holder of any claim or interest that is junior to the claims of such class [of unsecured claims] will not receive or retain under the plan on account of such junior claim or interest any property, *except that in a case in which the debtor is an individual, the debtor may retain property included in the estate under section 1115* . . . .[38]

11 U.S.C. § 1129(b)(2)(B)(ii) (amendment language in italics). Section 1115 provides that in addition to property included within the estate under section

---

[38]   11 U.S.C. § 1129(b)(2)(B)(ii) (amendment language in italics).

541, in individual Chapter 11 cases property of the estate also includes property and earnings received by the debtor post-petition.

This amendment produced an interpretive quandary: Did Congress intend that an individual Chapter 11 debtor that did not pay unsecured creditors in full could keep only its post-petition property and earnings (not its pre-bankruptcy property)? Or did Congress instead mean that the individual Chapter 11 debtor could keep any property of the estate—including pre-bankruptcy property—even if it did not pay unsecured creditors in full? Under the former interpretation, the absolute priority rule would still apply to prevent the individual Chapter 11 debtor from retaining pre-bankruptcy property unless it paid unsecured creditors in full; under the latter interpretation, the absolute priority rule would no longer apply in individual Chapter 11 cases.

A few courts have concluded that the amendment abolished the absolute priority rule in individual Chapter 11 cases. See, e.g., In re O'Neal, 490 B.R. 837 (Bankr. W.D. Ark. 2013). The growing weight of authority, however, has concluded that the absolute priority rule still applies to an individual Chapter 11 debtor proposing to retain pre-bankruptcy property. See, e.g., Zachary v. California Bank & Trust, 811 F.3d 1191 (9th Cir. 2016); Ice House America, LLC v. Cardin, 751 F.3d 734 (6th Cir. 2014); In re Lively, 717 F.3d 406 (5th Cir. 2013); In re Stephens, 704 F.3d 1279 (10th Cir. 2013); In re Maharaj, 681 F.3d 558 (4th Cir. 2012); In re Summers, 594 B.R. 707 (Bankr. D. Colo. 2018).

5.   *Relief from stay in Chapter 11.* From the moment of the petition, the stay prohibits the mortgagee from foreclosing or otherwise seeking to enforce the mortgage debt unless the court grants relief from stay based on one of the grounds discussed earlier in Section J2. Mortgagees frequently file a motion for relief from the stay as quickly as possible after the petition is filed. The mortgagee may have a number of objectives in seeking relief. The mortgagee may want to proceed with foreclosure immediately, or may simply want to force the debtor to pay interest on the mortgagee's secured claim during bankruptcy. Alternatively, the mortgagee may file the motion to obtain leverage against the debtor in negotiations over the terms of the debtor's plan.

It is rare for a mortgagee to obtain relief from stay under section 362(d)(1)'s "cause, including lack of adequate protection" standard. As discussed earlier, this standard protects the mortgagee against the risk of depreciation in the value of the collateral during bankruptcy. Unless the mortgagee can demonstrate that the debtor's use of the real estate poses this risk, relief under section 362(d)(1) will not be forthcoming. Instead, a real estate mortgagee is more likely to seek relief under either section 362(d)(2) or 362(d)(3).

If the mortgaged property is single-asset real estate, the mortgagee will certainly seek relief under section 362(d)(3). As explained earlier, the debtor of single-asset real estate must either (1) propose a feasible reorganization plan within 90 days or (2) begin making monthly payments of interest on the secured portion of the mortgagee's claim. If the debtor does neither, the court must grant relief from the stay and permit the mortgagee to foreclose. Section 362(d)(3) thus forces the single-asset real estate debtor to propose its plan quickly, or to at least pay interest to the secured party to the extent that the debtor takes longer than 90 days to propose its plan.

Most frequently, the mortgagee will seek relief under section 362(d)(2), which entitles the mortgagee to relief if the debtor does not have an equity in the mortgaged property (i.e., the property is worth less than the outstanding balance of all encumbrances on the property) and the property is "not necessary to an effective reorganization." In this situation, the court should lift the stay and allow the mortgagee to foreclose, as continuing the stay would serve no purpose for either the secured creditor or unsecured creditors.

When a mortgagee seeks relief under section 362(d)(2), the burden is on the debtor to demonstrate that the collateral is "necessary to an effective reorganization." 11 U.S.C. § 362(g)(2). To meet this burden, the debtor need not actually have a finalized reorganization plan, but still must show that there exists "a reasonable likelihood of a successful reorganization within a reasonable time." United Savings Ass'n v. Timbers of Inwood Forest Assocs., Ltd., 484 U.S. 365, 375, 108 S.Ct. 626, 632, 98 L.Ed.2d 740 (1988). If the debtor has only been in Chapter 11 for a month, however, and is still negotiating its plan with creditors, how does the court make this determination? *Timbers* made clear that the court could and should grant relief from stay—even early in the case, during the debtor's "exclusivity" period—if the debtor has no equity and cannot demonstrate any realistic prospect of reorganization. But in the early stages of a Chapter 11 case, bankruptcy courts tend to give the debtor the "benefit of the doubt" and are reluctant to conclude that a successful reorganization is unlikely. By contrast, if the debtor has been in Chapter 11 for longer than the exclusivity period and has not yet managed to negotiate a feasible plan with creditors, relief under section 362(d)(2) becomes more likely. See, e.g., In re Ashgrove Apts. of DeKalb Cty., Ltd., 121 B.R. 752, 756 (Bankr.S.D.Ohio 1990) ("[A]s the case progresses, so too does the debtor's burden of proving that successful reorganization may be reasonably expected. . . . [T]he test should be viewed as a continuum with the scales tipping in favor of the debtor in the early stages and the burden of proof becoming greater in the later stages."). See also In re Gunnison Center Apts., L.P., 320 B.R. 391 (Bankr. D. Colo. 2005); In re Holly's, Inc., 140 B.R. 643 (Bankr.W.D.Mich.1992).

6.   *Valuation of mortgaged property in Chapter 11.* The value of mortgaged property is relevant in Chapter 11 for several reasons. In the context of a motion for relief from stay, it may be relevant in determining whether the mortgagee is oversecured or the debtor has equity in the collateral. In the context of plan confirmation, it may be relevant in terms of whether the debtor's plan meets the cram-down standard.

Unfortunately, the Code is not explicit as to the timing of such valuation. A few courts applied a "single valuation" approach that valued the collateral for all purposes as of the petition date. See, e.g., In re Torcise, 187 B.R. 18 (S.D.

Fla. 1995); In re Hulen Park Place Ltd., 130 B.R. 39 (N.D. Tex. 1991). Others used a "dual valuation approach" that valued the collateral at the petition date relief from stay purposes and again at plan confirmation for evaluating the debtor's plan. See, e.g., In re Addison Props. Ltd. Partn., 185 B.R. 766 (Bankr. N.D. Ill. 1995); In re Kennedy, 177 B.R. 967 (Bankr. S.D. Ala. 1995). The weight of recent authority adopts a flexible approach under which "valuation of the collateral and the creditor's claim should be flexible and not limited to a single point in time, such as the petition date or confirmation date." In re T-H New Orleans Ltd. Partn., 116 F.3d 790 (5th Cir. 1997) (claim that was initially undersecured on petition date held to become oversecured by virtue of post-bankruptcy appreciation in land value; mortgagee became entitled to post-petition interest only at the point the mortgagee became oversecured); In re SW Boston Hotel Venture, LLC, 479 B.R. 210 (1st Cir. B.A.P. 2012). This approach seems most consistent with section 506(a)(1), which states that the value of a creditor's collateral "shall be determined in light of the purpose of the valuation and of the proposed disposition or use of such property, and in conjunction with any hearing on such disposition or use or on a plan affecting such creditor's interest."

7. THE MORTGAGEE IN A CHAPTER 12 CASE

NELSON, WHITMAN, BURKHART & FREYERMUTH, REAL ESTATE FINANCE LAW
861–867 (6th ed.2015)*

For farmers unable to cope with the economic hardship of the severe agricultural recession of the 1980s, Chapters 11 and 13 provided little meaningful relief. Pursuing Chapter 11 reorganization involves substantial administrative expense, and the substantial creditor influence over the content of the reorganization plan made it extremely difficult for a family farmer to obtain approval of a plan that offered any significant chance of a successful rehabilitation. Further, while Chapter 13 could have provided an advantageous reorganization vehicle for family farmers, most were ineligible for Chapter 13 relief because they had secured and/or unsecured debts that far exceeded the eligibility limits.

In 1986, Congress responded by enacting a new Chapter 12 of the Bankruptcy Code entitled "Adjustment of Debts of a Family Farmer with Regular Annual Income" (hereinafter "Chapter 12").[860] In large measure,

---

*   Reprinted with permission of LEG, Inc. d/b/a West Academic.

[860] 11 U.S.C. §§ 1201 to 1231. Chapter 12 was set to expire in 1993, but was temporarily extended several times. In 2005, despite the relative rarity of Chapter 12 cases, Congress made Chapter 12 permanent and extended its provisions to cover family fishermen, incorporating aquaculture operations and effectively reversing prior decisions, such as In re Watford, 898 F.2d 1525 (11th Cir.1990), in which courts held that fishing operations were not "farming operations" within the meaning of Chapter 12. This section of the text will focus only upon family farmers.

For further discussion of Chapter 12, see Porter, Phantom Farmers: Chapter 12 of the Bankruptcy Code, 79 Am.Bankr.L.J. 729 (2005); Van Patten, Chapter 12 in the Courts, 38

Chapter 12 extends Chapter 13-like protections to family farmers, and thus the substance and structure of the two chapters are very similar. In general, Chapter 12 affords important powers to the debtor, including the ability to reduce secured indebtedness to the *current* value of the underlying security, to repay the reduced amount of those secured claims over an extended period of time, and to satisfy unsecured claims—including those that became unsecured by the foregoing "write down" of the security—by paying to the plan only his "disposable income" (income which is not reasonably necessary for family support and business operations). Further, the Chapter 12 debtor need not satisfy the absolute priority rule that would be applicable in Chapter 11, permitting the debtor to retain a family farm even without full repayment to objecting unsecured creditors.[861] Upon successful completion of the plan, the debtor is discharged of his or her unsecured indebtedness.[862]

Who qualifies for Chapter 12 relief?

Debtors are eligible to seek relief under Chapter 12 only if they are "a family farmer . . . with regular annual income."[863] The term "family farmer" can include an individual (or married couple), as well as a corporation or partnership in which more than 50% of the stock or equity is held by family members (including relatives) who conduct farming operations.[864] For individuals to be eligible, at least 50% of their debts must have arisen out of their farming operations;[865] for a corporation or

S.Dak.L.Rev. 52 (1993); Flaccus, A Comparison of Farm Bankruptcies in Chapter 11 and the New Chapter 12, 11 Ark.L.R.L.Rev. 49 (1989); Armstrong, The Family Farmer Bankruptcy Act of 1986: An Analysis for Farm Lenders, 104 Banking L.J. 189 (1987); King, Chapter 12: Adjustment of Debts of a Family Farmer with Regular Income, 29 So.Tex.L.Rev. 615 (1988); Matson, Understanding the New Family Farmer Bankruptcy Act, 21 U.Rich.L.Rev. 521 (1987); Norton, the New Family Farmer Bankruptcy Act, 3 Prac.Real Est.Law. 37 (1987); Wilson, Chapter 12: Family Farm Reorganization, 8 J.Agric.Tax. & L. 299 (1987); Comment, Protecting America's Farmers Under State Mediation Laws and Chapter 12: Who's Being Protected?, 72 Marq.L.Rev. 466 (1989); Comment, Bankruptcy Chapter 12: How Many Family Farms Can It Salvage?, 55 U.M.K.C.L.Rev. 639 (1987); Note, An Analysis of the Family Farmer Bankruptcy Act of 1986, 15 Hofstra L.Rev. 353 (1987). Comment, 57 Miss.L.J. 185 (1988), Note, 27 Washburn L.J. 495 (1988).

[861] 8 Collier on Bankruptcy ¶ 1200.01[4], at 1200–8 (16th ed.). Courts have even confirmed plans in which all disposable income was allocated to payment of secured claims, with no payment at all on unsecured claims. See In re Kjerulf, 82 B.R. 123 (Bankr.D.Or.1987).

[862] 11 U.S.C.A. § 1228(a).

[863] 11 U.S.C.A. § 109(f).

[864] 11 U.S.C.A. § 101(18). If the debtor is a corporation, its stock cannot be publicly traded. 11 U.S.C.A. § 101(18)(B)(iii). The term "farming operation" includes, inter alia, "farming, tillage of the soil, dairy farming, ranching, production or raising of crops, poultry, or livestock, and production of poultry or livestock products in an unmanufactured state." 11 U.S.C.A. § 101(21).

[865] 11 U.S.C.A. § 101(18)(A). In determining whether the debtor satisfies this threshold, a debt for the debtor's principal residence is excluded unless that debt arises out a farming operation. Courts have concluded that a mortgage debt on the debtor's principal residence arises out of a farming operation if the purpose of the debt has some connection to the debtor's farming activity. See, e.g., In re Woods, 465 B.R. 196 (Bankr.10th Cir.2012) (debtor's farmhouse was an integral part of farm operation when farm's books and records were maintained in there, and its proximity to the farming operation allowed debtor to take care of their livestock and irrigation system); In re Marlatt, 116 B.R. 703 (Bankr.D.Neb.1990) (mortgage on debtor's farmhouse arose out of farming operation where mortgage loan enabled debtor to retain farm in divorce settlement).

partnership, the eligibility threshold is 80%.[866] In any event, the debtor's aggregate debts cannot exceed $4,031,575;[867] a debtor exceeding the debt limitations must seek reorganization, if at all, in Chapter 11. These eligibility requirements reflect Congress's intent to exclude "large" farming operations, whether or not family-owned.

The debtor, the Chapter 12 trustee, and control of the farming operation

While a trustee is appointed in all Chapter 12 cases,[868] the farmer remains in possession of property of the bankruptcy estate (including any mortgaged real estate) and continues to operate the farm as a debtor-in-possession.[869] The debtor-in-possession has the rights, powers and duties of a Chapter 11 trustee, including the ability to assert any of the avoiding powers.[870] The Chapter 12 trustee has limited duties[871] unless the debtor-in-possession is removed from control of the farming operation and replaced by the Chapter 12 trustee, which can occur only for cause, including "fraud, dishonesty, incompetence, or gross mismanagement."[872] As in the Chapter 11 context, it is extremely rare for the debtor-in-possession to be removed.[873]

The automatic stay, relief from stay, and "adequate protection" in Chapter 12

As in other Chapters, section 362(a)'s automatic stay against enforcement of creditor claims applies in Chapter 12 cases,[874] thus precluding (for example) a mortgagee from foreclosing a mortgage on the debtor's farmland without first obtaining relief from stay. In addition, as in Chapter 13, Chapter 12 also extends the automatic stay to cover actions to collect consumer debts from co-debtors,[875] thus protecting the debtor from the risk of pressure from family members or friends who may have

---

[866] 11 U.S.C.A. § 101(18)(B)(i). A debt for a dwelling owned by the debtor and used as a principal residence by a shareholder/partner is excluded unless the debt arises out of a farming operation.

[867] 11 U.S.C.A. § 101(18)(A). This amount is effective as of April 1, 2013, and is automatically adjusted at three-year intervals based on the Consumer Price Index. 11 U.S.C.A. § 104(b).

[868] 11 U.S.C.A. § 1202(a).

[869] 11 U.S.C.A. § 1203.

[870] 11 U.S.C.A. § 1203. See, e.g., In re McClintock, 75 B.R. 612 (Bankr.W.D.Mo.1987) (Chapter 12 debtor-in-possession entitled to avoid fraudulent transfer under section 548); In re Jardine, 120 B.R. 559 (Bankr.D.Id.1990) (Chapter 12 debtor-in-possession entitled to avoid preferential transfer under section 547). For further discussion of the avoiding powers, see §§ 8.13 to 8.16 supra.

[871] See generally 8 Collier on Bankruptcy ¶ 1202.03 (16th ed.). Where the debtor in possession remains in control of farming operations, courts have held that the Chapter 12 trustee lacks standing to exercise the avoiding powers. See, e.g., In re Colvin, 2012 WL 1865562 (Bankr.W.D. Tex.2012); In re Tiegen, 123 B.R. 887 (Bankr.D.Mont.1991).

[872] 11 U.S.C.A. § 1204(a). By contrast, the Chapter 13 trustee may not displace the debtor from possession.

[873] See In re Jessen, 82 B.R. 490 (Bankr.S.D.Iowa 1988); 8 Collier on Bankruptcy ¶ 1204.01 (16th ed.).

[874] 11 U.S.C.A. § 362(a).

[875] 11 U.S.C.A. § 1201(a).

agreed to guarantee the debtor's obligations. The co-debtor stay applies only to individual family farmers, and does not cover debts arising from the debtor's farming operations.[876]

As explained previously, section 362(d)(2) requires the bankruptcy court to grant a secured creditor relief from stay if the debtor has no equity in the collateral and the collateral is not "necessary to an effective reorganization" of the debtor. Because the family farmer's reorganization will require its possession of the farmland and other farm-related collateral, a secured creditor can obtain relief from stay under section 362(d)(2) only if the court concludes that the debtor has no prospect for successful reorganization. As in the Chapter 11 context, courts are extremely reluctant to reach such a conclusion, particularly early in a case before the debtor has an opportunity to formulate a plan.

As also explained previously, section 362(d)(1) requires the bankruptcy court to grant a secured creditor relief from stay "for cause, including the lack of adequate protection" of the creditor's interest in the collateral. This permits a secured party to protect itself against the risk that the debtor's possession and use of the collateral during the pendency of the stay results in depreciation of the collateral to the creditor's detriment. In section 1205, however, Congress provided standards for providing adequate protection, applicable only in Chapter 12,[880] that could make it easier than in Chapter 11 for the debtor-mortgagor to keep the stay in effect. Like section 361, section 1205(b) permits the Chapter 12 debtor to provide adequate protection against depreciation of the collateral through cash payments, a replacement lien on other property, or other action deemed sufficient to provide adequate protection. However, section 1205(b) also permits the debtor to provide adequate protection to a mortgagee by paying the mortgagee the use value of the farmland, measured by "the reasonable rent customary in the community where the property is located, based upon the rental value, net income, and earning capacity or the property,"[881] even if that amount would not fully account for all anticipated depreciation in the farmland's value.[882] Thus, to keep

---

[876] 11 U.S.C.A. § 1201(a)(1). Relief from the Chapter 12 co-debtor stay is governed by 11 U.S.C.A. § 1201(c).

[880] 11 U.S.C.A. § 1205(a) ("Section 361 does not apply in a case under this chapter.").

[881] 11 U.S.C.A. § 1205(b)(3).

[882] At first blush, it is curious that section 1205(b)(3) should treat "use value" in the form of reasonable rental value as a measure of adequate protection—especially given the Supreme Court's *Timbers* decision . . . which held that "adequate protection" within the meaning of section 361 protects the creditor against depreciation of the collateral and does not require the debtor to pay an undersecured creditor interest on the secured portion of its claim. The explanation is that Congress added Chapter 12 in 1986—two years prior to *Timbers*—and at that time, there was substantial judicial authority that adequate protection of an undersecured claim *did* require payment of interest during the pendency of the stay, even if the collateral was not depreciating in value. See, e.g., In re American Mariner Indus., Inc., 734 F.2d 426 (9th Cir.1984). In that context of uncertainty, Congress might have viewed a "reasonable rental value" standard for adequate protection as more "pro-farmer" than a standard based upon prevailing interest rates—particularly at a time when mortgage interest rates were relatively high and farm rental values

the stay in place, the Chapter 12 debtor will need to provide the mortgagee with *no more* than the fair rental value of the land.[883] As the legislative history notes, "[i]f the lender cannot resell the property [after foreclosure], it typically will rent the property at a market rate. If the debtor pays market rent while he reorganizes, the lender will be getting only what it would realistically get as a result of a foreclosure."[884]

The Chapter 12 plan and treatment of creditor claims

The requirements for a Chapter 12 plan are largely similar to those for a Chapter 13 reorganization. The plan's term is typically three years, but can be extended to five years if the court approves with cause.[885] During the plan period, unless the plan will pay unsecured creditors in full, the court may not confirm the plan over the objection of an unsecured creditor unless the debtor pays to the trustee all of its "projected disposable income" to fund the plan.[886]

A Chapter 12 plan may modify the claim of an unsecured creditor, who need not be paid in full as long as the creditor receives no less under the plan that the creditor would have received in a Chapter 7 liquidation of the debtor.[887] Likewise, a Chapter 12 plan may modify secured claims (including claims secured only by the debtor's principal residence),[888] such as by extension of the maturity of the loan term, reduction of principal,[889] or a reduction of the interest rate.[890] The court cannot confirm the plan,

---

were relatively low. After *Timbers*, there is general agreement that the Chapter 12 debtor would need to pay rent as adequate protection only as necessary to protect the mortgagee against depreciation in the value of the mortgaged premises. Zink v. Vanmiddlesworth, 300 B.R. 394 (N.D.N.Y.2003); Van Patten, Chapter 12 in the Courts, 38 S.Dak.L.Rev. 52 (1993).

[883] In re Kocher, 78 B.R. 844, 850 (Bankr.S.D.Ohio 1987).

[884] 132 Cong.Rec. S3529 (daily ed. March 26, 1986) (statement of Sen. Grassley).

[885] 11 U.S.C.A. § 1222(c).

[886] 11 U.S.C.A. § 1225(b). A plan under which the debtor contributes all of its net disposable income satisfies this standard even if the debtor projects that it will have no net disposable income. See In re Rowley, 143 B.R. 547 (Bankr.D.S.D.1992); see also Gribbins v. Farm Credit Servs. of Mid-America, ACA, 43 Fed.Appx. 861 (6th Cir.2002) (where Chapter 12 debtor failed to comply with plan by making disposable income available to unsecured creditors, bankruptcy court was justified in dismissing the case).

[887] 11 U.S.C.A. §§ 1222(b)(2), 1225(a)(4). See also In re Borg, 88 B.R. 288 (Bankr.D.Mont. 1988). The court must make this determination based upon the value of the collateral as of the effective date of the plan, not the petition date. See, e.g., In re Novak, 252 B.R. 487 (Bankr.D.N.D. 2000); In re Hopwood, 124 B.R. 82 (E.D.Mo.1991).

[888] Unlike home mortgagees in Chapter 13, mortgagees of Chapter 12 debtors do not have the benefit of an anti-modification rule.

[889] In other words, a Chapter 12 debtor may "strip-down" an undersecured mortgage, reduce its principal balance to the then-current value of the land, and (after completing its plan and receiving a discharge) avoid the creditor's lien to the extent of the unpaid portion of the mortgagee's unsecured claim. See, e.g., In re Stidham, 292 B.R. 204 (Bankr.W.D.Okla.2003).

[890] 11 U.S.C.A. § 1222(b)(2). See, e.g., In re Citrowske, 72 B.R. 613 (Bankr.D.Minn.1987). Courts have even confirmed "negative amortization" plans of the type sometimes proposed in Chapter 11 . . . See In re Nauman, 213 B.R. 355 (Bankr.9th Cir.1997).

however, unless the plan is feasible.[891] Furthermore, if the plan modifies a secured claim, the court cannot confirm the plan unless the secured creditor accepts it, the debtor surrenders the collateral, or the plan allows the creditor to retain its lien and makes payments to the creditor the present value of which equal or exceed the amount of the creditor's secured claim.[892]

The foregoing is more readily understood in the context of the facts of Travelers Insurance Company v. Bullington.[893] In that case, the farmers owed the mortgagee approximately $645,000, secured by land worth only $475,000 on the petition date. The indebtedness was due in a balloon payment after five years and carried an interest rate that was fixed for the first year at 12.5% and thereafter floated at one point above an index of AAA-rated corporate bonds. The farmers' Chapter 12 plan bifurcated the mortgagee's claim into a secured claim of $475,000 and an unsecured claim for $170,000. The plan converted the pre-existing five-year obligation into a thirty-year fixed rate mortgage of $475,000 carrying a fixed interest rate of 10.75%. The $170,000 unsecured claim was to be discharged at the end of the four-year plan period after having any disposable income applied proportionately to its payment along with the farmers' other unsecured debts. The bankruptcy court approved the plan (and the Eleventh Circuit affirmed) notwithstanding the mortgagee's objections to the extension of the secured claim to thirty years and the mandated fixed interest rate.[894] The court held that the section 1222(b)(9) authorized the extension of the mortgage.[895] Moreover, it concluded:

---

[891] 11 U.S.C.A. § 1225(a)(6) (debtor must "be able to make all payments under the plan and comply with the plan"). For cases interpreting this requirement, see, e.g., In re Chambers, 2008 WL 5649690 (Bankr.E.D.Tenn.2008) (plan not feasible where debtor's projected income unreasonably exceeded historical income); In re Tofsrud, 230 B.R. 862 (Bankr.D.N.D.1999) (plan not feasible where debtor proposed to grow crop with which debtor had no experience); In re Sauer, 223 B.R. 715 (Bankr.D.N.D.1998) (plan not feasible where debtor's projected expenses were unreasonably low).

[892] 11 U.S.C.A. § 1225(a)(5). As in Chapters 11 or 13, this is referred to as the "cramdown" standard. See, e.g., In re Chickosky, 2013 WL 5434131 (Bankr.D.Conn.2013) (Chapter 12 plan could not eliminate cross-collateralization rights of lender that funded debtor's farming operations); In re Heath, 483 B.R. 708 (Bankr.E.D.Ark.2012) (same).

[893] 878 F.2d 354 (11th Cir.1989).

[894] This example is not meant to suggest that a Chapter 12 debtor could necessarily impose a thirty-year amortization schedule on the objecting mortgagee. As one commentator has noted, "[t]he court should not approve a thirty-year amortization if the debtor is capable of paying the claim over a 20-year period. A long-term payment should be permitted only to the extent that it is necessary to preserve the debtor's farming operation." 8 Collier on Bankruptcy ¶ 1225.03[4][b], at 1225–17 (16th ed.). As a result, Chapter 12 plans commonly may provide for long-term amortization but require the debtor to make a balloon payment at the end of a specified period. See, e.g., In re Schreiner, 2009 WL 924418 (Bankr.D.Neb.2009) (plan payments based on 20-year amortization but with 5-year balloon payment); In re Torelli, 338 B.R. 390 (Bankr.E.D.Ark.2006) (plan payments based on 10-year amortization but with 5-year balloon payment).

[895] 11 U.S.C.A. § 1222(b)(9) (plan may "provide for payment of allowed secured claims . . . over a period exceeding [the duration of the plan]").

> [S]imply because a creditor subjectively would not extend a mortgage on the same terms does not mean that objectively the mortgage does not have a given value. Given that [mortgagee] has pointed to no record evidence to show that the 10.75% interest rate does not give the mortgage a present value of $475,000, while [mortgagors'] chart does tend to support the interest rate, the bankruptcy court's finding ... is supported by sufficient evidence.[896]

There is substantial authority that the bifurcation and strip-down of undersecured claims reflected by *Bullington* does not operate as an unconstitutional taking of the mortgagee's property.[897]

A Chapter 12 plan may "provide for the curing or waiving of any default."[898] Thus, as in Chapters 11 and 13, pre-foreclosure mortgage accelerations may be de-accelerated and the original payment schedule reinstated.[899] Moreover, the "absolute priority" rule applicable in Chapter 11—which requires that a plan pay unsecured creditors in full before the debtor can retain property of the estate on account of the debtor's interest— does not apply in Chapter 12. A farmer-debtor in Chapter 11 could not keep its land after completion of its plan unless the plan paid unsecured creditors in full or the unsecured creditors agreed to accept the plan; thus, an undersecured mortgagee could use the threat of withholding its consent to obtain higher plan payments on the unsecured portion of its claim. Farmer-debtors in Chapter 12 are not subject to such mortgagee bargaining leverage.

Under Chapter 11, a mortgagee has the option to give up the unsecured part of his claim and instead have the mortgage treated as if it were fully secured. If the real estate goes up in value during the Chapter 11 case, the mortgagee who takes this election gets the benefit of that appreciation.[901] Under Chapter 12, the mortgagee loses this option. An appraisal at the time of plan confirmation will establish the amount of the

---

[896] Travelers Ins. Co. v. Bullington, 878 F.2d 354, 359 (11th Cir.1989). As in Chapters 11 and 13, calculating the present value of plan payments to a secured creditor requires selecting an appropriate interest rate. Because the Chapter 12 and 13 cramdown standards are comparable, it seems appropriate to conclude that the Supreme Court's analysis in *Till* will govern determination of the appropriate rate. The limited case authority so far has concluded that *Till's* formula approach applies in Chapter 12. See, e.g., In re Woods, 465 B.R. 196 (Bankr.10th Cir.2012).

[897] See, e.g., Travelers Ins. Co. v. Bullington, 878 F.2d 354 (11th Cir.1989); Dahlke v. Doering, 94 B.R. 569 (D.Minn.1989); In re Kerwin-White, 129 B.R. 375 (Bankr.D.Vt.1991), aff'd, 996 F.2d 552 (2d Cir.1993).

[898] 11 U.S.C.A. § 1222(b)(3).

[899] If the foreclosure sale has already occurred prior to the petition, de-acceleration is more problematic. While there is authority under Chapter 13 that de-acceleration is permissible, at least in statutory redemption states, at least one decision has held that such relief is unavailable in Chapter 12. See Justice v. Valley Nat'l Bank, 849 F.2d 1078 (8th Cir.1988). See also In re McKinney, 84 B.R. 748 (Bankr.D.Kan.1987) (de-acceleration not permitted after entry of foreclosure judgment).

[901] 11 U.S.C.A. § 1111(b).

secured claim. If the land goes up in value, the farmer-debtor will get the benefit of that appreciation at the completion of the plan.

NOTE

Write-downs of debt in the Farm Credit System. In addition to Chapter 12, many farm mortgagors can take advantage of the Agricultural Credit Act of 1987 (the "Act"). See 7 U.S.C. § 2001 et seq.; 12 U.S.C. § 2202 et seq. The Act affords delinquent borrowers from the Farmers Home Administration ("FmHA") significant substantive rights to have their mortgage loans "restructured," which generally entails the "write-down" of principal and interest. To be eligible for this assistance,

> (1) the delinquency must be due to circumstances beyond the control of the borrower . . .;

> (2) the borrower must have acted in good faith with the Secretary . . .;

> (3) the borrower must present a preliminary plan . . . that contains reasonable assumptions [with respect to the borrower's ability to meet living, farming and debt servicing expenses]; and

> (4) the loan, if restructured, must result in a net recovery to the Federal Government, during the term of the loan as restructured, that would be more than or equal to the net recovery to the Federal Government from an involuntary liquidation or foreclosure on the property securing the loan.

7 U.S.C. § 2001. If the borrower meets the foregoing requirements, the Secretary must "offer to restructure the loan obligations of the borrower . . . through primary loan service programs that would enable the borrower to meet the obligations (as modified) under the loan and to continue the farming operations of the borrower." *Id.* The Act confers similar rights on Farm Credit System borrowers, a large group of agricultural debtors who obtain land operational financing from Federal Land Bank Associations and Production Credit Associations. 12 U.S.C. § 2202a.

To the extent that the foregoing legislation mandates write-downs of delinquent farm mortgages, does it represent a form of "non-bankruptcy" bankruptcy? To what extent will eligible farm borrowers be able to achieve a bankruptcy result without having to suffer the possible stigma attached to a public filing of a Chapter 12 petition?

8.   RENTS IN BANKRUPTCY

As we noted in Chapter Four of this book, mortgagees frequently rely not only on the real estate itself as security, but also on the rents, issues and profits it produces. Thus, mortgagees frequently rely on assignments (or more accurately, "mortgages") of "rents, issues and profits" to create that desired additional security. Once a mortgagor files a bankruptcy petition, a dispute may arise between the mortgagee and the bankruptcy trustee (or the debtor in possession in a Chapter 11 proceeding) as to who has a prior claim to rents collected during the bankruptcy proceeding.

State law has traditionally governed the enforceability in bankruptcy of security interests in rents. Butner v. United States, 440 U.S. 48, 99 S.Ct. 914, 59 L.Ed.2d 136 (1979) (state law governs in determining whether mortgagee had valid security interest in rents collected during bankruptcy). Although *Butner* was decided under an earlier bankruptcy statute, courts have uniformly followed it in applying the current Code. See, e.g., Matter of Village Properties, Ltd., 723 F.2d 441 (5th Cir.1984); In re Rancourt, 123 B.R. 143 (Bankr.D.N.H.1991); In re Mid-City Hotel Assocs., 114 B.R. 634 (Bankr.D.Minn.1990). Consequently, at this point, you should now go back to Chapter Four, Section B and review carefully state law on rental assignments. Especially, refresh your understanding concerning the difference between "perfection" and "enforcement" concepts. The rest of this section addresses the specific impact of bankruptcy on the mortgagee's interest in rents.

The applicable provisions governing the security in rents in bankruptcy are found in Sections 363 and 552 of the Code:

§ 363.   Use, sale, or lease of property

(a) In this section, "cash collateral" means cash . . . or other cash equivalents whenever acquired in which the estate and an entity other than the estate have an interest and includes the proceeds, products, offspring, rents, or profits of property and the fees, charges, accounts or other payments for the use or occupancy of rooms and other public facilities in hotels, motels, or other lodging properties subject to a security interest as provided in section 552(b) of this title, whether existing before or after the commencement of a case under this title. . . .

(c) (1) . . . [U]nless the court orders otherwise, the trustee . . . may use property of the estate in the ordinary course of business without notice or a hearing.

(2) The trustee may not use, sell, or lease cash collateral under paragraph (1) of this subsection unless—

(A) each entity that has an interest in such cash collateral consents; or

(B) the court, after notice and a hearing, authorizes such use, sale, or lease in accordance with the provisions of this section. . . .

(4) Except as provided in paragraph (2) of this subsection, the trustee shall segregate and account for any cash collateral in the trustee's possession, custody, or control. . . .

(e) Notwithstanding any other provision of this section, at any time, on request of an entity that has an interest in property used, sold, or leased, or proposed to be used, sold, or leased, by the trustee, the court, with or without a hearing, shall prohibit or condition such use, sale, or lease as is necessary to provide adequate protection of such interest. . . .

§ 552. Postpetition effect of security interest

(a) Except as provided in subsection (b) of this section, property acquired by the estate or by the debtor after the commencement of the case is not subject to any lien resulting from any security agreement entered into by the debtor before the commencement of the case.

(b) (1) Except as provided in sections 363, 506(c), 522, 544, 545, 547, and 548 of this title, if the debtor and an entity entered into a security agreement before the commencement of the case and if the security interest created by such security agreement extends to property of the debtor acquired before the commencement of the case and to proceeds, products, offspring, or profits of such property, then such security interest extends to such proceeds, products, offspring, or profits acquired by the estate after commencement of the case to the extent provided by such security agreement and applicable nonbankruptcy law, except to any extent that the court, after notice and a hearing and based on the equities of the case, orders otherwise.

(2) Except as provided in sections 363, 506(c), 522, 544, 545, 547, and 548 of this title, and notwithstanding section 546(b) of this title, if the debtor and an entity entered into a security agreement before the commencement of the case and if the security interest created by such security agreement extends to property of the debtor acquired before the commencement of the case and to amounts paid as rents of such property or the fees, charges, accounts, or other payments for the use or occupancy of rooms and other public facilities in hotels, motels, or other lodging properties, then such security interest extends to such rents and such fees, charges, accounts, or other payments acquired by the estate after the commencement of the case to the extent provided in such security agreement, except to any extent that the court, after notice and a hearing and based on the equities of the case, orders otherwise.

Post-petition rents: mortgagee vs. trustee or debtor-in-possession. When a mortgagor files a Chapter 11 petition, the mortgagor hopes to control post-petition rents and use them to help fund its efforts to reorganize (e.g., by using them to pay operating expenses, marketing expenses needed to secure new tenants, and the attorney fees needed to secure experienced bankruptcy counsel). By contrast, the mortgagee views the post-petition rents as its cash collateral and wants to prevent their use, preserving them for application to the unpaid balance of the debt—particularly where the mortgagee is undersecured and accumulated post-petition rents can reduce the mortgagee's deficiency claim.

Mortgagees and trustee or debtors-in-possession have acted vigorously to protect their respective interests in post-petition rents, and these efforts have produced an enormous volume of litigation regarding the parties' respective rights to post-petition rents. The cases tend to fall into one of three basic scenarios, each discussed below.

Scenario 1. The mortgagee takes an assignment of rents, but fails to record it prior to the mortgagor's bankruptcy. In this relatively rare instance, the avoiding powers will permit the trustee or debtor in possession to invalidate the assignment and control post-petition rents. Under Bankruptcy Code § 544(a)(3), the trustee or debtor in possession has the status of a hypothetical bona fide purchaser of land. Under state law in all states, a bona fide purchaser of an interest in land takes that interest free of the unrecorded interest of third parties, such as the lien created by an unrecorded mortgage or assignment of rents. As a result, the mortgagee in this scenario will not have a security interest in the post-petition rents under § 552(b), and they will not constitute "cash collateral" under § 363(a). The trustee or debtor in possession can thus use them in its reorganization as it sees fit, without regard to the mortgagee's objection.

Scenario 2. The mortgagee takes and properly records an assignment of rents. After default, and before the mortgagor files a bankruptcy petition, the mortgagee takes the steps required under state law to enforce the assignment and begins collecting rents. In Scenario 2, courts have taken one of two basic approaches. Under the majority (and correct) approach, the post-petition rents constitute the mortgagee's cash collateral under §§ 552(b)(2) and 363(a); thus, the trustee or debtor-in-possession cannot control or use the post-petition rents without the mortgagee's consent or court approval, and the court cannot approve that use over the mortgagee's objection unless the mortgagee receives adequate protection of its interest in the cash collateral or unless the court determines that the "equities of the case" justify that use under § 552(b)(2). Under the minority (and incorrect) view, the post-petition rents do not constitute property of the estate, but instead belong to the mortgagee (who may apply them in reduction of the unpaid debt).

Courts adhering to the minority approach have concluded that "[w]hen a mortgagee completes all steps necessary to enforce its rights under an assignment of rent clause pre-petition, all interests of the [mortgagor] in the rents are extinguished and the rents do not become property of the estate or cash collateral." Sovereign Bank v. Schwab, 414 F.3d 450 (3d Cir. 2005); see also, e.g., In re Town Center Flats, LLC, 855 F.3d 721 (6th Cir. 2017); In re Cordova, 500 B.R. 701 (D. N.J. 2013); In re Soho 25 Retail, LLC, 2011 WL 1333084 (Bankr. S.D.N.Y. 2011); In re Robin Assocs., 275 B.R. 218 (Bankr. W.D. Pa. 2001). Many of the decisions adhering to this view involve assignments that the court characterized as "absolute" assignments rather than assignments intended for security. See, e.g., In re Jason Realty, L.P., 59 F.3d 423 (3d Cir. 1995); In re Village Props, Ltd., 723 F.2d 441 (5th Cir. 1984); 460 Tennessee Street, LLC v. Telesis Community Credit Union, 437 B.R. 306 (W.D. Tenn. 2010). Practically, a court following this approach must automatically deny the debtor in possession access to post-petition rents, regardless of the equities or whether the mortgagee's interest is or could be adequately protected.

The minority approach is both counter-intuitive and analytically unsound. Suppose the mortgagee had obtained the appointment of a receiver prior to bankruptcy (an action sufficient to enforce the assignment of rents in every state). This does not turn the receiver or the mortgagee into the beneficial owner of the rents. The receiver is accountable to the mortgagor for its management, and the net rents (after necessary expenses of the receivership) must be applied to the debt. Because the mortgagor retains a beneficial interest in the rents accruing during the receivership, even if it lacks control over them, the mortgagee's right is still appropriately characterized as a security interest. As a result, it is inappropriate to conclude that the mortgagor in Scenario 2 retains no interest in the rents that constitutes property of the estate. Under the correct view, the post-petition rents in Scenario 2 constitute property of the estate, but they also constitute the mortgagee's cash collateral (for which the mortgagee is entitled to adequate protection). See, e.g., In re Millette, 186 F.3d 638 (5th Cir. 1999); In re Buttermilk Towne Center, LLC, 442 B.R. 558 (6th Cir. B.A.P. 2010); In re Builders Group & Dev. Corp., 502 B.R. 95 (Bankr. D. P.R. 2013); In re MRI Beltline Industrial, L.P., 476 B.R. 917 (Bankr. N.D. Tex. 2012); In re South Side House, LLC, 474 B.R. 391 (Bankr. E.D.N.Y. 2012); In re Senior Housing Alternatives, Inc., 444 B.R. 386 (Bankr. E.D. Tenn. 2011); In re Village Green I, GP, 435 B.R. 525 (Bankr. W.D. Tenn. 2010).

Scenario 3. The mortgagee takes and properly records an assignment of rents. After the mortgagor's default, but before the mortgagee has taken steps sufficient to enforce its assignment, the mortgagor files a bankruptcy petition. In Scenario 3, the relative rights of the mortgagee and the trustee or debtor in possession depend upon whether state law on assignment of rents governs the mortgagee's rights and, if so, whether the mortgagee's lien on rents is considered "perfected" (by virtue of the recorded assignment) or "unperfected" (because the mortgagee has not yet taken steps to enforce the assignment).

The traditional "common law" approach in Scenario 3. If state law governs the mortgagee's rights, and the applicable state law follows the traditional "common law" view that an assignment of rents is not perfected—and is thus inchoate and ineffective—until the assignee has taken steps to activate that interest after default, then the trustee or debtor-in-possession in Scenario 3 may invalidate the mortgagee's unperfected interest under the strong-arm clause. Under this view, the post-petition rents would not constitute the mortgagee's cash collateral, and the trustee or debtor-in-possession could control and use the post-petition rents despite mortgagee's objection. As discussed in Chapter Four, during the 1980s and 1990s, a substantial number of federal courts reached this conclusion. See, e.g., In re Century Inv. Fund VIII L.P., 937 F.2d 371 (7th Cir. 1991) (applying Wisconsin law); In re Sam A. Tisci, Inc., 133 B.R. 857 (N.D. Ohio 1991); In re Turtle Creek, Ltd., 194 B.R. 267 (Bankr. N.D.Ala. 1996); In re Mews Assocs., L.P., 144 B.R. 867 (Bankr. W.D.Mo. 1992); In re Kurth Ranch, 110 B.R. 501 (Bankr. D. Mont. 1990); In re Neideffer, 96 B.R. 241 (Bankr. D. N.D. 1988); In re Ziegler, 65 B.R. 285 (Bankr. D. S.D. 1986).

Some court decisions in cases comparable to Scenario 3 followed the traditional common law rule, but nevertheless allowed the mortgagee to enforce its assignment of rents *after the bankruptcy petition* pursuant to section 546(b). Section 546(b)(1) provides that

> The [trustee's avoiding powers] are subject to any generally applicable law that (A) permits perfection of an interest in property to be effective against an entity that acquires rights in such property before the date of perfection. . . .

Section 546(b)(2) further provides that if that generally applicable law "requires seizure of such property or commencement of an action to accomplish such perfection . . . [and] such property has not been seized or such action has not been commenced before the date of the filing of the petition . . . [then] such interest in such property shall be perfected . . . by giving notice within the time fixed by such law for such seizure or such commencement." If section 546(b) applies, then the automatic stay does not prevent a mortgagee from perfecting its security interest after the petition date. 11 U.S.C. § 362(b)(3).

Mortgagees facing Scenario 3 have often asserted that section 546(b)(2) permitted them to perfect post-petition by seeking possession or a receivership in bankruptcy court or by giving notice of their intention to enforce the assignment of rents. By doing so, they argued, they thus perfected their interest in rents, making the post-petition rents "cash collateral." A substantial number of courts have accepted this argument.

See, e.g., Virginia Beach Fed. Sav. & Loan Ass'n v. Wood, 901 F.2d 849 (10th Cir. 1990); Saline State Bank v. Mahloch, 834 F.2d 690 (8th Cir. 1987); In re Casbeer, 793 F.2d 1436 (5th Cir. 1986). The argument is incorrect, however, and a substantial number of decisions have properly rejected it. See, e.g., In re Kurth Ranch, 110 B.R. 501 (Bankr. D. Mont. 1990); In re Wynnewood House Assocs., 121 B.R. 716 (Bankr. E.D. Pa. 1990); In re Multi-Group III Ltd. Partn., 99 B.R. 5 (Bankr. D. Ariz. 1989). By its terms, section 546(b)(1) permits post-petition perfection only when the relevant state perfection law allows the perfection to "relate back" so as to prevail over the interests of intervening third parties. Because state laws governing rent assignments do not provide this relation-back attribute, section 546(b) does not authorize a mortgagee to perfect its interest in rents after the petition date.

The modern majority approach in Scenario 3. Under the majority (and correct) view, as explained earlier, the recorded assignment is sufficient under state law to "perfect" the mortgagee's security interest in rents, see, e.g., In re Millette, 186 F.3d 638 (5th Cir. 1999), and thus the trustee or debtor-in-possession may not invalidate that security interest altogether using the strong-arm power. As a result, the post-petition rents constitute the mortgagee's cash collateral even if the mortgagee had not taken steps to begin collecting rents prior to bankruptcy. While this appears to permit post-petition enforcement of the mortgagee's interest in rents, the language of the Bankruptcy Code contemplates this result. As one court has observed:

> Section 363(c)(2) provides, in effect, for the automatic sequestration of rents that are subject to a perfected security interest. Under § 361(3), the bankruptcy court may provide adequate protection by "granting such other relief . . . as will result in the realization by such entity of the indubitable equivalent of such entity's interest," while § 105(a) grants the bankruptcy court the power to "issue any order . . . necessary or appropriate to carry out the provisions of [the Code]." We hold that under these authorities, the bankruptcy court's powers are sufficiently broad to allow it to enforce a mortgagee's security interest in rents when and to the extent a state court would do so.

In re Park at Dash Point L.P., 121 B.R. 850, 859 (Bankr. W.D. Wash. 1990).

Use of post-petition rents that constitute cash collateral. If the mortgagee's perfected security interest extends to post-petition rents under section 552(b)(2), those rents constitute "cash collateral" under section 363(a). Under section 363(c), the trustee or debtor in possession cannot use rents that are cash collateral without the consent of the mortgagee or court approval following notice and a hearing. If the mortgagee requests adequate protection of its cash collateral, the court must prohibit or condition use of the cash collateral "as is necessary to provide adequate protection of such interest." 11 U.S.C. § 363(e).

This does not mean that the mortgagee is automatically entitled to prevent the trustee or debtor from using the rents. If, for example, the mortgagee is oversecured and has a sizable equity cushion, the court will permit the debtor to use the post-petition rents so long as the equity cushion provides adequate protection of the mortgage debt. More commonly, however, the mortgagee finds itself undersecured. In that scenario, the Code permits the trustee or debtor-in-possession to use the post-petition rents only if either (a) the trustee or debtor in possession can provide adequate protection of the mortgagee's interest in the cash collateral or (b) the court concludes that the "equities of the case" justify the mortgagee's use.

As a result, the debtor's ability to use the post-petition rents may depend upon the debtor's intended use for them. If the debtor proposes to use a portion of the rents to pay the reasonable expenses of operating the property (i.e., paying the utilities, providing common area maintenance services), the court may well conclude that payment of these expenses is "necessary to protect the value of the creditor's interest in future rents and the real property, and therefore is not inconsistent with providing the creditor adequate protection, even if the creditor is undersecured." In re Park at Dash Point L.P., 121 B.R. 850, 859 (Bankr. W.D. Wash. 1990). See also In re Murray, 2011 WL 5902623 (Bankr. E.D.N.C. 2011); In re Cavros, 262 B.R. 206 (Bankr. D. Conn. 2001). Alternatively, the court might conclude that the "equities of the case" justify allowing the debtor to use the post-petition rents to pay for reasonable expenses of operating the property because the mortgagee would have to incur those expenses if it took over the property and became a mortgagee in possession. By contrast, if the debtor is proposing to use the post-petition rents to pay its Chapter 11 attorneys or other reorganization expenses unrelated to maintenance of the mortgaged premises, the court is unlikely to permit that use unless the debtor can provide adequate protection (such as some form of substitute collateral). See, e.g., Wolf v. FirstMerit Bank, N.A., 535 B.R. 772 (N.D. Ill. 2015).

Debtors have sometimes argued that they should be allowed to use the current month's rent, even if it constitutes cash collateral, as long as the mortgagee retains its lien on future rents. Most recent decisions, however, reject the view that future rents from the same property are an appropriate form of substitute collateral. As one court has noted:

> Where . . . there is a specific assignment of rents given as security, a diversion of any portion of the rents to a party other [than] the secured party is clearly a diminution of the secured party's interests in the assignment of rents portion of the

security. . . . The secured party has a security interest in the full amount of the future rents. Therefore, this court cannot accept that the use of future rents to replace the expenditure of the prior months rents somehow provides adequate protection for the secured party.

In re River Oaks Ltd. Partn., 166 B.R. 94, 99 (E.D. Mich. 1994). See also Putnal v. SunTrust Bank, 489 B.R. 285 (M.D. Ga. 2013); In re MRI Beltline Indus., L.P., 476 B.R. 917 (Bankr. N.D. Tex. 2012).

9. INSTALLMENT LAND CONTRACTS IN BANKRUPTCY

Suppose the party filing a bankruptcy petition is a vendor or vendee under an installment land contract rather than a mortgagee or mortgagor under a traditional mortgage or deed of trust. Here our starting point is 11 U.S.C. § 365(a). This section permits the trustee or debtor-in-possession to "assume" or "reject" any "executory contract" of the debtor.

Vendor bankruptcy. Assume that a vendor and vendee executed an installment land contract 7 years ago that provided for a purchase price of $100,000, payable in equal annual installments over 20 years. The vendee took possession immediately and has paid seven of the installments. Now the vendor experiences financial distress and files a bankruptcy petition. If the trustee or debtor-in-possession "rejects" the contract under § 365, what are the vendee's options?

If the vendee is in possession, as is typical, the right to reject the contract is trumped by the vendee's right to complete the payments over the term of the contract and to obtain legal title. See 11 U.S.C. § 365(i). If the vendee is not in possession, rejection means that the vendee cannot complete the contract and obtain title to the land; rather, the vendee will be left as an unsecured creditor with a claim for damages against the bankruptcy estate.

Vendee bankruptcy. In the more common scenario, it is the installment contract vendee that seeks bankruptcy protection. In this setting, the crucial question is whether the contract is an "executory contract" for purposes of § 365(a) or rather as a "mortgage" or "security device" not governed by § 365.

In determining whether a contract is "executory" for purposes of § 365, courts have traditionally applied the so-called "Countryman" test, under which a contract is executory if "the obligations of both parties are so far unperformed that the failure of either party to complete performance would constitute a material breach and thus excuse performance of the other." Countryman, Executory Contracts in Bankruptcy: Part 1, 57 Minn. L. Rev. 439 (1973). Taken literally, any installment land contract would satisfy this definition if the vendee has not completed all installment payments, as the vendor's failure to satisfy its obligation to tender title upon full performance by the vendee would constitute a material breach. See, e.g., In re Speck, 798 F.2d 279 (8th Cir. 1986) (installment land contract is executory); In re Terrell, 892 F.2d 469 (6th Cir. 1989); In re Ravenswood Apts., Ltd., 338 B.R. 307 (6th Cir. B.A.P. 2006). Because an installment land contract is in many respects functionally indistinguishable from a purchase money mortgage, however, other courts have held that it is a mortgage not governed by § 365, especially where the vendor has no contractual duty other than conveying legal title upon the vendee's full performance. See, e.g., In re Streets & Beard Farm Partn., 882 F.2d 233 (7th Cir. 1989); Heartline Farms, Inc. v. Daly, 934 F.2d 985 (8th Cir. 1991); In re Heward Bros., 210 B.R. 475 (Bankr. D. Idaho 1997). If the installment land contract is characterized as a mortgage, the vendor may not invoke section 365 and will be treated as a mortgagee in the vendee's bankruptcy. See, e.g., In re Booth, 19 B.R. 53 (Bankr. D. Utah 1982). If the land is worth more than the unpaid balance, the trustee will sell the land; the vendor will receive the unpaid balance and the surplus will be available for distribution to the vendee's unsecured creditors. By contrast, if the installment contract is considered executory, then 11 U.S.C. § 365(b) provides that if the debtor has defaulted, the trustee or debtor-in-possession can assume the contract, but must first cure the default, compensate the other party for any loss resulting from the default, and provide adequate assurance of future performance of the contract. If the trustee or DIP cannot do so, the contract is rejected and the vendee will lose the land; if the land is worth more than the contract balance, the vendor will gain that benefit. See, e.g., Nelson, Whitman, Burkhart & Freyermuth, Real Estate Finance Law 882–883 (6th ed.2015) ("[W]here the contract real estate is the debtor's sole or major asset, treatment of the contract as "executory" may well mean the failure of the reorganization and the inevitability of liquidation.").

Should the "executory contract or mortgage" issue be determined by state law (i.e., should an installment land contract be characterized as a mortgage or security device only to the extent that state law treats it as such in other contexts)? If so, a bankruptcy court in Indiana, Kentucky, or Oklahoma (where installment land contracts are essentially deemed mortgages) would reach a different result than in New Mexico (where state courts continue to resist such a characterization). See, e.g., In re Speck, 798 F.2d 279 (8th Cir. 1986) (state law controls). On the one hand, if bankruptcy courts uniformly took the position that installment land contracts are security or devices or mortgages as a matter of federal law, it may hasten the day when such contracts are uniformly treated as mortgages for all purposes (a result which we would generally applaud). See Grant S. Nelson & Dale A. Whitman, Installment Land Contracts— The National Scene Revisited, 1985 B.Y.U.L.Rev. 1, 63. On the other hand, does it unduly upset the expectations of the parties for a bankruptcy court to treat an installment land contract as a mortgage when local law clearly does not?

Should mortgage lenders in jurisdictions that treat installment land contracts as "executory" consider recasting their mortgage loan transactions so that they become installment land contract vendors rather than mortgagees? What would you advise?

CHAPTER SEVEN

SOME PRIORITY PROBLEMS

■ ■ ■

As noted in earlier in this book, real property law generally resolves priority between conflicting liens by reference to the doctrine of first-in-time, subject to the potential application of the recording act. The first lien to arise generally has priority over a subsequent lien, unless the holder of the subsequent lien qualifies for the protection of the recording act. There are exceptions to this basic priority rule, however. As we noted in Chapter Four, for example, a municipality's lien on a parcel for unpaid real estate taxes due on that parcel takes priority over an already existing and recorded mortgage on that parcel. Chapter Seven addresses a variety of priority disputes in which the law modifies the general first-in-time priority rule, either in whole or in part.

A. PURCHASE MONEY MORTGAGES

A purchase money mortgage is a mortgage that the mortgagor grants to enable the mortgagor to acquire ownership of the mortgaged land. A *vendor purchase money mortgage* arises when the seller of land agrees to extend credit to the buyer for some portion of the land's purchase price, and the buyer grants a mortgage on the land to secure its obligation to pay the rest of the price. A *third party purchase money mortgage* arises when the buyer of land obtains a loan from a third party (typically a bank, savings and loan, or other institutional lender), uses the loan proceeds to pay the purchase price of the land, and grants the third party a mortgage to secure the buyer's repayment of the loan.

Suppose that Jones purchases Blackacre from Seller using the proceeds of a loan obtained from First Bank and grants First Bank a purchase money mortgage. Shortly thereafter, First Bank discovers that Cathy Creditor asserts a judgment lien against Blackacre based on an unpaid judgment she obtained against Jones two years earlier. How should the law resolve a priority contest between First Bank and Cathy Creditor? Should it matter whether and/or when First Bank recorded its mortgage? Should it matter whether First Bank knew or should have known about the claims of Cathy Creditor?

KENTUCKY LEGAL SYSTEMS CORP. V. DUNN
Court of Appeals of Kentucky, 2006
205 S.W.3d 235

TACKETT, J. Kentucky Legal Systems Corporation (KLS) appeals from the judgment of the Fayette Circuit Court finding that its judgment lien against all property owned by N.E. Dunn and George E. "Ged" Dunn was inferior to the mortgage held by Community Trust Bank, where the mortgage enabled the purchase of the subject real property. KLS argues that Kentucky law requires that its first-recorded judgment lien have priority over the Community Trust mortgage. We disagree and affirm.

The property in question was purchased in October 2000, by Dunn, and the loan enabling the purchase was given by Community Trust Bank in exchange for a mortgage on the property. The judgment held by KLS was entered in 1992, and the judgment lien filed and properly recorded in 1998 against all real property owned by Dunn. KLS argues that the bank was on constructive notice of its judgment lien and that it failed to exercise due care before giving Dunn a loan. Dunn later defaulted on the mortgage and the bank sought foreclosure and a declaration that its mortgage held priority over the judgment lien. The circuit court agreed that the mortgage should be considered a purchase money mortgage in accord with the Restatement (Third) of Property, *Mortgages* § 7.2 (1997), quoting the following section:

> Under this section the vendor's purchase money mortgage is senior to any previous judgment liens that arise against the purchaser-mortgagor. This is true even though a judgment attaches as a lien to the judgment debtor's after-acquired real estate and the vendor takes the mortgage with actual knowledge of the judgment. . . .

> Because this long-established rule makes it unnecessary for a purchase money lender to examine for preexisting judgments and other liens against the purchaser-mortgagor, it reduces title risk in connection with such transactions and thus encourages purchase money financing by vendors. Moreover, the rule is justified on grounds of fundamental fairness. The vendor-mortgagee should prevail because the lien creditor has not extended credit or perfected the lien in reliance on the right to be repaid out of any specific property, much less out of the real estate previously owned by the vendor. This is obvious, since the judgment was obtained before the debtor acquired the real estate to which the judgment lien attached. . . .

> This section extends the same priority preference to third party purchase money lenders. . . . While it is true that such lenders, unlike vendors, do not give up ownership of specific real estate,

they nevertheless part with money with the expectation that they will have security in that real estate. Without this advance of money, the purchaser-mortgagor would never have received the property and the other claimants would never have had the opportunity to satisfy their claims from such a convenient source. As in the vendor purchase money context, this section seeks to avoid conferring a windfall on those claimants. [Restatement (Third) of Property (Mortgages) § 7.2 cmt. b.]

The circuit court adopted the Restatement's reasoning and held the bank's mortgage was superior to KLS's judgment lien. This appeal followed.

KLS's argument for its priority rests entirely on two statutes, KRS 382.270 which requires recording of all instruments affecting real property, and KRS 382.280, which provides that deeds and mortgages take effect in the order in which they are legally acknowledged and recorded. Coupled with the dearth of Kentucky cases on the subject, KLS argues that in the absence of a statutory mandate to do so, the courts should look only at the recording dates of instruments for guidance as to priority. Community Trust, citing the Restatement (Third) and other treatises, argues that the judgment was correct because without its grant of a loan with a mortgage reserved, the debtor would have no interest in the property at all to which KLS's judgment lien could attach, and cites many cases in other jurisdictions which follow this rule. KLS responds by saying that Kentucky only recognizes a limited exception to the ordinary rules on priority for purchase money mortgages, narrowly defining such an interest as a 'vendor's lien" where the grantor himself retains the mortgage.

KLS cites only two Kentucky cases, *Purdom v. Broach*, 210 Ky. 161, 275 S.W. 365 (1925) and *Minix v. Maggard*, 652 S.W.2d 93 (Ky.App.1983), in support of the above proposition. On closer examination, neither case is particularly useful to this determination. *Purdom* mentions vendor's liens only by saying 'no distinction can be made between a vendor's lien and a mortgage, as the former is simply a purchase-money mortgage, and therefore equivalent in legal effect." *Purdom* at 366. *Minix*, meanwhile, deals with an extraordinary set of facts involving an unrecorded purchase money mortgage from the grantor, but of which all of the relevant parties had actual notice, and a federal tax lien, and this Court held that due to the actual notice the purchase money mortgage had priority even though it was unrecorded. Neither case specifically defines a purchase money mortgage in the narrow way suggested by KLS, in that they do not involve a third-party lender at all.

Nor do the two statutes foreclose the possibility of an exception for purchase money mortgages to the ordinary rules of priority. The statutes are quite general and do not address the specific situation at all. In fact, the statutes only specifically mention mortgages and deeds, and not other interests created by liens such as the one held by KLS. We hold in the absence of definite guidance from case law or statute, the circuit court properly decided the question of priority based on guidance from the Restatement, which serves as a guiding star for courts and scholars alike on the state of the law. Considering also the many states which have adopted the Restatement (Third)'s view on this question,[1] either specifically by reference to the Restatement or by holding in accord with the reasoning behind the section, we hold that Kentucky should adopt this logical rule that third parties who lend money used to purchase real estate in exchange for a mortgage hold special priority over all other recorded liens and judgments except where agreed otherwise by the parties or specified by statute.

With respect to KLS's argument that Community Trust did not exercise due care in failing to discover its judgment lien, for the reasons stated in the Restatement (Third) we hold that Community Trust, as a purchase money lender, did not need to search for judgment liens, as they should be given first priority over a judgment lien regardless of whether they had notice of any kind of the interest. Even had Community Trust discovered the lien by exercise of due diligence, it should be granted priority over the judgment creditor's lien due to its status as a purchase money lender. . . .

NOTES

1.   *The general priority for purchase money mortgages.* Real estate law has traditionally accorded the purchase money mortgagee with a special priority over all other recorded liens and judgments. As noted in Fleet Mtge. Corp. v. Stevenson, 241 N.J.Super. 408, 575 A.2d 63 (1990):

> [P]riority of purchase money mortgages has been a fixture of N.J. law since 1820. . . . [T]heir special priority can be asserted against: (1) claims of dower [or] curtesy by the purchaser's spouse, (2) the lien of judgments, (3) mechanics liens, (4) mortgages executed before the purchase of the land, and (5) federal tax liens filed against the purchaser before he acquired title. The rationale behind such an historic and thoroughgoing priority is found essentially in the equity which results from providing the wherewithal to purchase the property. . . . [575 A.2d at 65]

Dunn is consistent with the Restatement and the overwhelming weight of American judicial authority. Ironically, it is no longer good law in Kentucky. See Hays v. Nationstar Mortg. LLC, 510 S.W.3d 327 (Ky.Ct.App. 2017). *Hays* involved a case essentially identical to *Dunn*, but the court wrongly reasoned

---

[1]   *See, Guffey v. Creutzinger*, 984 S.W.2d 219 (Tenn.Ct.App.1998); *see also, Belland v. O.K. Lumber Co., Inc.*, 797 P.2d 638 (Alaska 1990); *Garrett Tire Center, Inc. v. Herbaugh*, 294 Ark. 21, 740 S.W.2d 612 (1987); *Citibank Mortgage Corp. v. Carteret Savings Bank, F.A.*, 612 So.2d 599 (Fla.Dist.Ct.App.1992); *Aetna Cas. & Sur. Co. v. Valdosta Federal Savings & Loan Ass'n*, 175 Ga.App. 614, 333 S.E.2d 849 (1985).

that the Kentucky Supreme Court's decision in Mortgage Elec. Regis. Systems, Inc. v. Roberts, 366 S.W.3d 405 (Ky.2012)—a case which did not even involve purchase money priority—had impliedly overruled *Dunn* as being inconsistent with Kentucky's race-notice statute. Properly understood, the purchase money priority rule is a long-recognized, well-established exception to the recording statute.

2. *Construction loan as a purchase money mortgage.* Suppose Jones obtains a $300,000 loan from Bank, uses $50,000 of that loan to purchase Blackacre (an undeveloped lot), grants Bank a mortgage on Blackacre, and then uses the other $250,000 of loan proceeds to build a home on Blackacre. The part of the loan Buyer used to acquire title to Blackacre qualifies for purchase money mortgage treatment; thus, if Creditor had a pre-existing judgment against Jones, Bank's mortgage would have priority over Creditor's judgment lien, at least to the extent of the $50,000 used to purchase Blackacre.

But what about the $250,000 used for construction? The Restatement treats the entire amount of the loan as "purchase money," Restatement (Third) of Property (Mortgages) § 7.2 cmt. c (1997), but court decisions are not uniform. Compare Resolution Trust Corp. v. Bopp, 18 Kan.App.2d 271, 850 P.2d 939 (1993) ("[T]o split the mortgage would deny the lender its expected security interest and would, under modern lending practices, have a chilling effect on this type of building activity.") with Westinghouse Elec. Co. v. Vann Realty Co., 568 S.W.2d 777 (Mo.1978) (where part of the loan proceeds were used to acquire land and the rest to build apartment buildings on the land, the part that was used to acquire title was purchase money, but the rest was not). In a state like Missouri that does not provide the construction lender with purchase money priority for those funds directed to improvements, how should the lender structure the transaction to obtain the desired priority for the entire loan amount?

Now suppose Jones purchases Blackacre with previously saved cash, and then obtains a $300,000 construction mortgage loan which she uses to build a home on Blackacre. Should any of the loan proceeds be treated as "purchase money"? According to the Restatement, "[e]ven where the proceeds of the loan are used exclusively for improving the mortgaged real estate, the mortgage will receive purchase money treatment so long as it is given as part of the same transaction in which title to the real estate is acquired." Id. cmt. c. Is this a sensible position? Why or why not? What if Jones had purchased Blackacre six months before obtaining the construction loan? Id. (construction mortgage is part of the acquisition transaction only if the mortgagor commences "negotiations with the construction lender prior to mortgagor's acquisition of title, and the actual loan [is] 'made incident to the mortgagor's acquisition of title or within a reasonable time thereafter' ").

3. *Judgment searches against prospective mortgagors.* Purchase money lenders commonly conduct a search for judgments against prospective borrowers prior to making a loan. Given the purchase money priority rule, why bother? Would it be malpractice for a lawyer who represents such a lender to

fail to make a search? See Belland v. O.K. Lumber Co., Inc., 797 P.2d 638 (Alaska 1990).

The impact of recording acts and priority among competing purchase money mortgages. Remarkably, a purchase money mortgage need *not* be recorded to protect the mortgagee against judgment liens or other claims attaching to the real estate that arose against the purchaser-mortgagor before it acquired title. Restatement (Third) of Property (Mortgages) § 7.2 cmt. c (1997). However, *subsequent* interests that arise through the purchaser-mortgagor are another matter. Here the recording acts can be crucial. Under some circumstances, if a purchase money mortgagee is not careful, its lien could be superior to a prior judgment lien against the mortgagor, but inferior to a subsequent mortgage.

For example, suppose J has an outstanding judgment lien against P. L lends money to P to purchase Blackacre from S. S conveys Blackacre to P, who promptly records the deed. At the same time, P gives a mortgage for the purchase money to L, but L fails to record the mortgage. A few days later X lends money to P and X takes and records a mortgage on Blackacre, without actual knowledge of L's prior mortgage. In all probability, L's purchase-money mortgage will be prior to J's lien, but junior to X's subsequent mortgage. See Thorpe v. Helmer, 275 Ill. 86, 113 N.E. 954 (1916) (intervening judgment lien); Trigg v. Vermillion, 113 Mo. 230, 20 S.W. 1047 (1892) (intervening mortgage). See Restatement (Third) of Property (Mortgages) § 7.2 cmt. b & illus. 8 (1997). For a thoughtful analysis, albeit in a slightly different context, of how such a lien circularity problem could be resolved, see Santa Cruz Lumber Co. v. Bank of America, 160 Cal.App.3d 858, 207 Cal.Rptr. 28 (1984).

In some circumstances, a buyer of land may grant more than one purchase money mortgage. For example, suppose P buys Blackacre from S for a total price of $200,000. P pays $180,000 of the price in cash and executes to S both an installment note for the $20,000 balance and a mortgage to secure repayment of the note. But suppose P also obtained the $180,000 in cash by virtue of a mortgage loan from Bank. Here, both S and Bank have purchase money mortgages: which has priority? The Restatement, which reflects the substantial weight of authority, takes the view that a vendor purchase money mortgage has priority over its third party counterpart, unless the parties themselves have demonstrated a contrary intent (such as by a subordination agreement) or the state's recording act provides otherwise. Restatement (Third) of Property (Mortgages) § 7.2(c) (1997); ALH Holding Co. v. Bank of Telluride, 18 P.3d 742 (Colo.2000); Rothermich v. Weber's St. Charles Lanes, Inc., 957 S.W.2d 509 (Mo.App.1997).

By contrast, as demonstrated by the following case, courts in a few states accord no special priority to the vendor mortgagee and instead resolve priority based on the first-in-time principle and the state's recording act. As you read *Insight LLC v. Gunter,* which rejects the Restatement (wrongly, we believe), consider whether the court's approach is coherent and workable.

INSIGHT LLC V. GUNTER

Supreme Court of Idaho, 2013
154 Idaho 779, 302 P.3d 1052

[Editors' Note: We have included this opinion, although we believe Part C is wrongly decided, because one can learn valuable lessons from making mistakes or seeing others make them. As you read Part C, consider how the court's rule would encourage vendor and third-party purchase money mortgagees to behave in documenting similar transactions, particularly by comparison to the Restatement approach.]

W. JONES, JUSTICE. . . . This is an appeal from a district court trial regarding a dispute over two liens on real property: a deed of trust and a mortgage. Appellants ("Insight") are assignees of a mortgage secured by 160 acres of real property owned by Summitt, Inc. ("Summitt"), which includes an 18-acre parcel of land that Summitt purchased from the Respondents ("the Gunters"). The Gunters hold a deed of trust on the Gunter property. . . .

Summitt owned a 142-acre parcel of land that it intended to develop into a residential subdivision. Respondents, Pat and Monica Gunter owned an 18-acre plot of land that adjoined Summitt's 142 acres ("the Gunter property"). Not wanting to live next to a residential development, the Gunters solicited Summitt's president, Ron Hazel, to purchase the Gunter property; the parties agreed to a price of $799,000. On April 21, 2006, the Gunters and Summitt, through its president, Hazel, entered into a purchase and sale agreement for the Gunter property. The agreement, prepared by Summitt, identified EasyWay Escrow ("EasyWay") as the closing agent for the transaction. The agreement provided $1,000 earnest money and the balance of the purchase price was to be paid in "cash at closing." Possession of the land was to be delivered at closing on June 19, 2006.

After executing the purchase and sale agreement, Hazel contacted Independent Mortgage Ltd. Co. ("IM"), seeking a loan of $799,000. IM agreed to loan Summitt $616,000 so long as Summitt's principals executed personal guarantees and secured the mortgage with 160 acres of land including *both* the 142 acres already owned by Summitt and the 18 acres comprising the Gunter property.

Shortly after the execution of the agreement, Hazel contacted Monica Gunter and revealed that Summitt was unable to come up with the full amount of the purchase price. Hazel informed her Summitt could pay $599,000 and asked the Gunters to finance the remaining $200,000 of the purchase price, which the Gunters agreed to do. This conversation was documented by notes taken by Monica Gunter and delivered to EasyWay. These notes do not mention any other loan or financing contemplated by Summitt for the purchase of the Gunter property.

Sandpoint Title was responsible for recording and providing title insurance for both the IM mortgage and the Gunters' deed of trust. Stephanie Brown prepared the documents related to the IM/Summitt mortgage. Carol Sommerfeld, owner of EasyWay Escrow, prepared the documents related to the Gunter/Summitt deed of trust. The district court found that Sommerfeld was not aware of the mortgage executed between IM and Summitt. The district court also found that the Gunters lacked knowledge of the IM/Summitt mortgage at the time of the closing, because they were never informed of any financing by Summitt other than their own deed of trust. Also, there was no reference to the IM mortgage in any part of the closing file. As to the dispute of whether Hazel informed the Gunters or Sommerfeld of the IM/Summitt mortgage, the district court found credible Sommerfeld's and Monica Gunter's testimony that they were not informed of the IM/Summitt mortgage. It also found that IM knew of the Gunters' deed of trust because IM considered seeking a subordination agreement from the Gunters.

Hazel signed the IM/Summitt mortgage on June 19, 2006, at IM's offices in Sandpoint, Idaho. Later that same day Summitt executed a deed of trust in favor of the Gunters at EasyWay's office. All of the documents were delivered to Sandpoint Title by IM and EasyWay for recordation. IM instructed Sandpoint that the IM/Summitt mortgage was to be recorded first. The deed from the Gunters to Summitt was recorded on June 20, 2006, at 4:16 p.m. The IM/Summitt mortgage was recorded that same day at 4:17 p.m., and the Gunter/Summitt deed of trust was recorded at 4:18 p.m.

In 2007, Summitt defaulted on its obligations to both IM and the Gunters. Insight[1] filed a Complaint on August 27, 2008, naming Summitt, Summitt's principals, and the Gunters as defendants. On November 26, 2008, the Gunters answered and denied that their deed of trust was junior to the IM/Summitt mortgage. On February 17, 2009, Insight filed a motion for summary judgment. The district court denied the motion because there was an issue as to who was the initial encumbrancer. Insight filed a motion for reconsideration, which the district court denied. . . .

---

[1]   The IM/Summitt mortgage was assigned to Insight.

After trial, the district court found that the closing of the Gunter/Summitt deed of trust was a separate and independent transaction from the IM/Summitt mortgage. The court found that the separate closings were not part of "one continuous transaction." The district court further found that the Gunters' deed of trust effectively encumbered the Gunter property at the time the transaction between Summitt and the Gunters closed. However, it found the IM mortgage on the combined 160-acre parcel of land did not create an encumbrance on the Gunter property until after the Gunter/Summitt transaction closed. The rationale was that the mortgage could not encumber property that is not owned by the mortgagor. As a result, the Gunters' deed of trust was determined to be the "first encumbrance" on the Gunter property. The court also found that IM was not a good faith purchaser—even though it recorded first—because it was aware of the financing agreement between Summitt and the Gunters.

On appeal, Insight argues that the IM mortgage has priority as a matter of law because it was a purchase money mortgage that was first recorded thus rendering its "good faith" irrelevant. Insight also contends that the Gunters were not good faith purchasers and had imputed knowledge of IM's mortgage through the escrow agent, EasyWay. Respondents counter that the Gunters' deed of trust was the first encumbrance on the Gunter property; the IM mortgage was not a purchase money mortgage; and even if it was a purchase money mortgage, the Gunters' deed of trust effectively encumbered the land first and therefore had priority. . . .

A. The district court's finding that IM had notice of the Gunters' Deed of Trust is Clearly Erroneous. The district court found that IM had actual notice of the Gunters' deed of trust, because IM considered a subordination agreement and instructed Sandpoint Title to record the IM mortgage first. This finding is clearly erroneous.

The district court found that Summit executed the IM mortgage on June 19, 2006. The district court further found that Summit executed the Gunters' deed of trust also on June 19, 2006, but later in the day. It is not technically possible for IM to have notice of an encumbrance on property before that encumbrance actually comes into existence. Though IM knew that Summit was intending to execute a deed of trust, that was notice of an intent to subsequently encumber property, not notice of an actual encumbrance on property. Therefore, the district court's finding that IM had notice of the Gunters' deed of trust is clearly erroneous.

B. The IM/Summitt Mortgage Was a Purchase Money Mortgage. . . . Idaho Code § 45–112 requires that a purchase money mortgage be given "at the time of [the land's] conveyance." This statutory language reflects the commonly recognized requirement that a purchase money mortgage be granted as a part of "one continuous transaction involving the purchase" of land. The execution of the mortgage and the transfer of the deed need not be strictly contemporaneous. When a deed and mortgage are executed as part of the same transaction, the mortgage is not granted to the mortgagee after the mortgagor has obtained title; rather, the mortgagor takes title already encumbered by the mortgage.

Insight argues that the IM mortgage was part of one continuous transaction because security instruments were signed on the same day within hours of each other, the mortgage funds were sent to EasyWay, and all the documents were recorded together by Sandpoint Title. In other words, the mortgage was merely one step of several necessary to accomplish a single transaction. Respondents, however rely on the district court's finding that the IM mortgage closed separately from the Gunters' deed of trust, because the "IM mortgage could not encumber property before it is owned by the buyer." Thus, they argue the Gunter/Summitt deed of trust must have occurred before the IM mortgage.

The district court concluded that the IM mortgage was not a purchase money mortgage because it was not part of one continuous transaction. The district court reasoned that the mortgage and deed of trust closed at different times and at different locations. The district court noted that Carol Sommerfeld closed the Gunter/Summitt transaction at the office of EasyWay, while Stephanie Brown prepared all the documents related to the IM/Summitt transaction at the IM offices. This evidence, to the district court, did "not reflect coordination of a single closing effort" on the part of the parties. The district court noted that the Gunters did not have knowledge of the IM mortgage and were not informed of the mortgage. This conclusion was clearly erroneous.

The primary inquiry is whether the mortgage was intended as part of a single transaction. [*Estate of Skvorak v. Security Union Title Ins. Co.*, 89 P.3d 856 (Idaho 20014)] demonstrates that mortgages need not be executed in unison to be part of the same transaction. In *Skvorak*, the two mortgages were executed at different times on the same day and were not executed in the presence of all of the parties. In the current matter, Hazel executed the IM/Summitt mortgage on June 19 and the Gunter/Summitt deed of trust later that day. Also, the mere fact that the IM mortgage was signed at IM's offices and not in the presence of the Gunters is not fatal to the purchase money mortgage status of the IM mortgage, because in *Skvorak*, both parties had purchase money mortgages even though one of them was not signed in the presence of both the parties. Likewise, the present case involves one transaction with two mortgages enabling Summitt to purchase the Gunter property. A land-sale transaction concludes upon the delivery of the deed. Here, before the deed was delivered to Summitt, the proceeds and documents were delivered in escrow to the title company. Therefore, there was only one transaction.

The district court also found that the IM mortgage was not a purchase money mortgage because it was only able to encumber the Gunter property at the time Summitt gained an ownership interest in the Gunter property. But the district court's reasoning neglects the very nature of a purchase money mortgage, and presupposes that the mortgage was not a purchase money mortgage in order to find that IM did not encumber the property when executed. Under this standard, no purchase money mortgage could effectively encumber property before title passes to the mortgagor, because the purchase money *enables* the mortgagor to acquire title to the property. Insight rightly notes that applying the district court's reasoning—that "[the IM] mortgage could not encumber the Gunter property, because Summitt did not own the Gunter property when the mortgage was signed,"—would preclude any purchase money mortgage from being a purchase money mortgage. In a purchase money mortgage, title does *not* first pass to the mortgagor, which is then encumbered; rather, title passes to the mortgagor *already* encumbered. Nothing in Idaho's jurisprudence precludes more than one purchase money mortgage from being executed on land. Therefore, since the IM mortgage provided the funds necessary to enable Summitt to purchase the Gunter property, and since the money was not paid directly to Summitt but to EasyWay, the Gunter property passed to Summitt already encumbered by the Gunters' deed of trust *and* the IM mortgage.

In sum, the district court's finding that the IM mortgage and Gunters' deed of trust were not part of one continuous transaction is clearly erroneous. The mortgage granted by IM was a purchase money mortgage because it was executed to enable Summitt to purchase the property in question, in the same transaction as the acquisition of title. The question next becomes whether the taking of additional security by IM on the mortgage destroyed the purchase money status of the IM mortgage. . . .

Whether the taking of additional security on a mortgage, beyond the land being purchased, destroys the purchase money status of a mortgage, is a question of first impression. As early as the 1800s, courts have recognized purchase money mortgages, even though additional security was taken on a note. This additional security was often in the form of an assignment or a deed of trust. *See, e.g., Farmers' & Mech. Sav. Co. v. McCabe,* 73 Mo.App. 551, 553 (1898); *Bliss v. Crosier,* 159 Mass. 498, 34 N.E. 1075 (1893). One particular New York case from 1912 involved land given as additional security. *See Hubbard v. Lydecker,* 78 Misc. 80, 137 N.Y.S. 714, 716 (N.Y.S.1912). In *Hubbard,* a purchase money mortgage was given to purchase a lot on Prospect Street. The purchase money mortgage also included a lien on a lot on Greenridge Avenue as additional security. The court held that the mortgage was primarily a lien on the Prospect Street lot and that the Greenridge Avenue lot merely stood in the position of a guarantor.

The loan given by IM was given with the intent to enable Summitt to purchase the Gunter property. But after examining the property, Insight wanted additional security. Insight agreed to take a second mortgage on the adjoining 142 acres of Summitt property to guarantee the loan. The IM mortgage was primarily a purchase money mortgage designed to enable Summitt to purchase the property.

In sum, the IM mortgage was a purchase money mortgage that was not destroyed by the taking of additional security by IM.

C. The District Court Erred in Concluding the Gunter Deed of Trust Took Priority. Since both the IM/Summitt mortgage and the Gunter/Summitt deed of trust are purchase money mortgages, the next issue is which security interest has priority.

Insight argues that the IM mortgage has priority as a matter of law. Insight reads *Skvorak* as holding that as between two purchase money mortgages, the first to record has priority. Insight contends that the first party to record is the initial encumbrancer, and that the initial encumbrancer's knowledge is irrelevant. Second, Insight argues that the Gunters, even if they lacked actual knowledge, had constructive notice of IM's mortgage because it was recorded first, and constructive notice under I.C. § 55–811 is imparted at the time it is deposited with the recorder. Also, Insight contends that the Gunters had imputed inquiry notice of the IM mortgage, because EasyWay should have known from its past transactions with Summitt that Summitt was securing the purchase money with a mortgage from IM.

The Gunters contend that even if the IM mortgage is a purchase money mortgage, *Skvorak* does not support Insight's argument. The Gunters read *Skvorak* as only applicable when both mortgages were part of one continuous transaction, and where both parties knew of the other's mortgage. The Gunters contend they are the initial encumbrancer based on the district court's finding that the IM mortgage and the Gunters' deed of trust were not part of one continuous transaction. In the alternative, the Gunters urge this Court to reconsider its earlier rejection of § 7.2 of the Restatement.

The parties dispute who is the initial encumbrancer under *Skvorak*. Insight contends IM was the initial encumbrancer on the Gunter property, because the IM mortgage and the Gunters' deed of trust were not separate transactions, but one continuous transaction. IM was, therefore, the initial encumbrancer because it was the first to record. The Gunters argue the first encumbrancer is the first lien to be executed in one continuous transaction. Therefore, they argue IM was not the first encumbrancer, because it had knowledge of the Gunters' deed of trust, and its mortgage was a separate transaction. The district court concluded that because the IM mortgage was a separate transaction, it was not valid upon its execution but only after the Gunters' deed of trust closed and transferred title of the Gunter property. Consequently, the district court held that the Gunters' deed of trust was necessarily the first to encumber the property, and since IM had knowledge of the Gunters' deed of trust, its mortgage was subsequent to the Gunters' deed of trust.

In *Skvorak*, "initial encumbrancer" is merely the characterization of the party against whom subsequent purchasers are tested under the recording statutes. The court noted that the good faith of the initial encumbrancer is irrelevant. It should be clarified that the good faith of the initial encumbrancer is irrelevant as to subsequent encumbrancers, because the initial encumbrancer cannot technically have notice of an encumbrance before it comes into existence. But the issue presented in *Skvorak* was "the priority between a vendor purchase money mortgage and a third party purchase money mortgage, where the vendor has notice of the third party's mortgage and it was recorded first." 140 Idaho at 22, 89 P.3d at 862 (emphasis added). In *Skvorak*, "each party knew or had constructive notice of the other party's mortgage." Id. at 21, 89 P.3d at 861. Quite simply, in a dispute involving priority between two mortgages in a single transaction, where both parties are good faith encumbrancers of property for value, the first to record has priority against all other subsequent mortgages. *Id.* at 23, 89 P.3d at 863.

A purchase money mortgage is given priority against other liens subject to the recording laws. I.C. § 45–112. Idaho's race-notice statute provides that "[e]very conveyance of real property is . . . void as against any subsequent purchaser or mortgagee of the same property, or any part thereof, in good faith and for a valuable consideration, whose conveyance is first duly recorded." I.C. § 55–812. Our race-notice statute only voids a prior conveyance if (1) the subsequent conveyance was made in good faith and for valuable consideration; and (2) the subsequent conveyance is the first duly recorded. Idaho law defines "conveyance" as "the instrument in writing by which any estate or interest in real property is created, alienated, mortgaged or encumbered." I.C. § 55–813. A conveyance does not depend upon when it is recorded.

Here, the Summitt/IM mortgage was executed on June 19, 2006, before the Summitt/Gunter deed of trust was executed. Therefore, the IM mortgage was the prior conveyance and the Gunters' deed of trust was the subsequent conveyance. Since the Gunters' deed of trust was the subsequent encumbrance, the only way it could take priority over the IM mortgage as the first encumbrance—where IM by default is a good faith encumbrancer against subsequent encumbrancers—is if the Gunters were the first to record. The Gunters were not the first to record. Therefore, their deed of trust is junior to the IM mortgage. . . .

NOTES

1. *The rationale for vendor purchase money priority.* In providing priority for the vendor purchase money mortgagee over the third party purchase money mortgagee, the Restatement is consistent with Uniform Commercial Code Article 9, which provides comparable priority for a vendor purchase money secured party. See U.C.C. § 9–324(g)(1). As the Restatement explains:

> The preference for vendor purchase money mortgagees is arguably counterintuitive, at least from an economic perspective. After all, both the third party lender and the vendor make the sale transaction possible, and both rely upon the security of the same specific property for payment. Moreover, third party purchase money mortgagees, especially in residential transactions, often invest a substantially greater economic stake in the mortgaged property than that retained by the vendor.

> Nevertheless, the equities favor the vendor. Not only does the vendor part with specific real estate rather than money, but the vendor would never relinquish it at all except on the understanding that the vendor will be able to use it to satisfy the obligation to pay the price. This is the case even though the vendor may know that the mortgagor is going to finance the transaction in part by borrowing from a third party and giving a mortgage to secure that obligation. In the final analysis, the law is more sympathetic to the vendor's hazard of losing real estate previously owned than to the third party lender's risk of being unable to collect from an interest in real estate that never previously belonged to it.

Restatement (Third) of Property (Mortgages) § 7.2, cmt. d (1997).

2. *Rethinking* Gunter. The court in *Gunter* does not adopt Restatement § 7.2, but instead concludes that the priority of competing mortgages is governed by the state recording act. Under this approach, the court must decide which mortgagee was "first in time," and that mortgagee has temporal priority unless the recording statute protects the latter-in-time mortgagee. The *Gunter* court concluded that because the third-party IM mortgage was executed first, it was entitled to priority unless the Gunters' vendor mortgage qualified for the protection of the recording statute—which it did not, because the IM mortgage was recorded first.

In the context of this transaction, does it make sense to ascribe significance to which mortgage was executed first? See Restatement (Third) of Property (Mortgages) § 7.2 cmt. d (1997) (answering "no," where both mortgages arise in the context of the same transaction). Is the court's opinion internally consistent in this regard? How would you expect the result in *Gunter* to influence how third-party lenders like IM behave in similar transactions?

3. *Understanding the appropriate impact of notice and the recording acts on vendor vs. third party priority.* Suppose that both the vendor and the

third party lender are aware of each other. This is often the case, especially when the earnest money contract (which a third party lender routinely examines in reviewing the purchaser's loan application) mentions that the vendor is to finance a portion of the price. In this situation, the vendor's mortgage should be senior; the third party cannot gain priority simply by recording first. This is because in most states the recording acts confer priority only on a subsequent purchaser *without notice* and, in our situation, each party has notice of the other. Likewise, if *neither* party has notice of the other's mortgage, again vendor should prevail. The state's recording act should not change this result because it grants priority only to a *subsequent* purchaser without notice, and as discussed above, it makes little sense to treat the third-party lender as holding a subsequent mortgage if both mortgages arise in the same transaction. Restatement (Third) of Property (Mortgages) § 7.2 cmt. d (1997).

But suppose that only one of the parties has notice of the other. In this situation, even the Restatement agrees that the recording act should govern, and the party lacking notice should prevail. "Even though delivery of the mortgages is essentially simultaneous, the party lacking notice must in fairness be treated as the subsequent taker and thus eligible for the protection of the recording acts. Thus, in a jurisdiction having a notice type recording act, the lender who takes its mortgage without notice of the other's mortgage prevails. . . . In a race-notice type jurisdiction, the lender who takes without notice must also record first in order to prevail." Id.

Many institutional third party lenders are either required by law or the dictates of prudence to hold first mortgages. How can they obtain certain priority over the vendor?

The normal method is to have the vendor subordinate his lien to that of the third party lender. Ideally, this is usually done by including language in the vendor's mortgage specifically referring to the third party lender's mortgage and declaring its subordination to it. Normally, a vendor will agree to this for at least two reasons. First, he wants the third party mortgage transaction to be approved so that he can sell his property. Second, a vendor who takes a mortgage under such circumstances probably assumes, at the time of the initial transaction at least, that his will be a second mortgage.

Nelson, Whitman, Burkhart & Freyermuth, Real Estate Finance Law § 9.2, at 895 (6th ed.2015). A third party lender may also prevail if a court finds that the vendor's oral statements and conduct indicate an intent to subordinate the vendor's lien to the third party mortgage. See Pulse v. North Am. Land Title Co., 218 Mont. 275, 707 P.2d 1105 (1985). Suppose that there is no express subordination agreement, but the vendor has notice of the third party's mortgage and the third party mortgage is recorded before the vendor's mortgage. In this situation, should a court hold that the vendor has impliedly subordinated to the third party lender? See Restatement (Third) of Property (Mortgages) § 7.2 cmt. d (1997).

4. *Competing third party purchase money mortgages.* Sometimes the purchase money for a residential transaction is supplied by two third party lenders, one institutional (e.g., a bank) and one noninstitutional (e.g., a parent or employer). Suppose that the buyer, for example, is able to supply 5% of the purchase price. Then buyer arranges for a mortgage loan from a savings and loan association for 75% of the purchase price and a mortgage loan for the remaining 20% from his father. Should there be any underlying assumptions as to the priority of institutional lenders against private lenders? Should both mortgages share equal priority? While Article 9's "pure race" filing system gives priority to the first of the third party purchase money secured parties to file or perfect its security interest, U.C.C. § 9–324(g)(2), the case law provides little in the way of a common law answer in the mortgage law context. How do you assume this problem is handled in practice? Will recording first necessarily create priority? Should the savings and loan association require the father to take an explicit second mortgage or otherwise to subordinate? What happens if the savings and loan association is led to believe that the full 25% of the purchase price is to be supplied from purchaser's personal resources when in fact purchaser covertly gives a mortgage to his father for part of the 25%? See Nelson, Whitman, Burkhart & Freyermuth, Real Estate Finance Law § 9.2 (6th ed.2015).

B. THE AFTER-ACQUIRED PROPERTY CLAUSE

Article 9 of the Uniform Commercial Code, with limited exceptions, authorizes a debtor to grant a security interest in both present and after-acquired personal property. U.C.C. § 9–204(a). This provides significant transactional efficiencies for many business debtors. The classic example would be a retail seller of inventory such as a furniture store. Such a seller would typically finance its inventory of furniture either using a loan from a local bank or credit extended by furniture manufacturers. A creditor financing the seller's inventory may wish to take a security interest in the seller's furniture inventory to secure repayment of this credit.

In this situation, the *nemo dat* principle—which establishes that A cannot grant B any rights in an object of property that A does not have in the first place—presents a potential problem. Obviously, the seller will be selling items from its furniture inventory to customers, and then acquiring new items of furniture to replenish its inventory. The creditor may wish to take a security interest in this new inventory; however, at the time of the original loan, the seller doesn't own that new inventory yet. Without an "after-acquired property clause," the seller and the creditor would have to enter into a new security agreement each time the seller obtained a new shipment of inventory. U.C.C. § 9–204(a) instead permits the seller and the creditor to enter into one security agreement that is sufficient to cover both the seller's existing on-hand inventory and all inventory subsequently acquired by the seller. By virtue of the after-acquired property clause, the creditor's security interest will attach to each new item of inventory as the seller acquires it in the future.

Perhaps not surprisingly, it is less common for a real estate mortgage to contain an after-acquired property clause. Nevertheless, suppose that Jones borrows $250,000 from First Bank and grants First Bank a mortgage that covers not only Blackacre but "all other real property that Jones shall acquire in the future, until the mortgage debt is repaid." Three years later, while the mortgage remains unpaid, Jones acquires Whiteacre. Under the weight of judicial authority, First Bank's mortgage also creates a mortgage lien on Whiteacre as soon as Jones acquires Whiteacre. See, e.g., Hickson Lumber Co. v. Gay Lumber Co., 150 N.C. 282, 63 S.E. 1045 (1909). The Restatement likewise adopts this approach. Restatement (Third) of Property (Mortgages) § 7.5(b) (1997) ("An after-acquired property provision is effective between mortgagor and mortgagee."). The provision is effective between the parties even if the later-acquired parcels are in a different county or state than the land originally mortgaged. The rationale for enforcement is grounded in a specific performance theory; the provision is viewed as a promise by the mortgagor to mortgage after-acquired parcels, which promise is specifically enforced as soon the mortgagor acquires title to them. Id. cmt b.

NOTES

1. *Is an after-acquired property provision in a mortgage effective to cover after-acquired personal property?* Traditionally, some mortgages have included not only a description of the specific real estate being mortgaged, but also a clause purporting to cover all after-acquired realty and personalty of the mortgagor. Summarizing existing case law in 1963, Roger Cunningham and Saul Tischler noted:

> [In some states], the after-acquired property clause is effective to create an equitable lien upon both real and personal property subsequently acquired by the mortgagor regardless of the character of the business in which the mortgagor is engaged, provided the new property bears a functional relation to the property originally mortgaged. In other states, the after-acquired property clause is effective to create an equitable lien upon both realty and personalty if the mortgagor is a railroad company or other public utility company, but is effective only with respect to realty if not within that class.

Roger Cunningham & Saul Tischler, Equitable Real Estate Mortgages, 17 Rutgers L. Rev. 679, 718 (1963). Today, because U.C.C. Article 9 applies in all 50 states and validates after-acquired property clauses in personal property security agreements, a mortgagee that wants an enforceable lien upon after-acquired personal property can simply have the mortgagor sign a personal property security agreement containing a suitable after-acquired property clause. While a real estate mortgage could constitute an effective Article 9 security agreement if it met the necessary standards of Article 9 (i.e., if it sufficiently indicated the intent of the debtor to create a security interest in personal property and sufficiently identified that personal property), most prudent lenders would have the borrower execute both a real estate mortgage covering the land and an Article 9 security agreement covering the personal property.

2. *Relationship to accession and the law of fixtures.* Suppose X grants a mortgage on Blackacre, which is undeveloped land. X then builds a home on the land. Does the mortgage cover the home if the mortgage does not contain an after-acquired property clause? Yes; because of the doctrine of accession or the law of fixtures, an after-acquired property clause is normally not necessary for a mortgage on Blackacre to attach to subsequent improvements made on Blackacre. Hoyle v. Plattsburgh & M.R.R., 54 N.Y. 314 (1873); 3 Glenn, Mortgages, 1450 (1943).

A caveat: to state the foregoing principles does not resolve numerous substantial and complex priority questions. For example, to say that X's home becomes covered by the mortgage does not resolve the problem of what happens if X's building contractor is not paid. The question then becomes one of priority between the mortgage and a possible mechanic's lien. Or suppose that X installs a furnace in the home. The furnace is likely a fixture covered by the real estate mortgage, but this alone does not resolve priority as between the real estate mortgagee and the holder of a purchase-money security interest in the furnace. We will consider these problems later in this chapter.

3. *Recording act and "chain of title" problems.* Even if an after-acquired property provision is effective between the mortgagor and the mortgagee, is it effective against third parties who subsequently acquire an interest in the after-acquired parcel? Should such third parties have constructive notice of the after-acquired property provision? To frame the problem, suppose that R grants a mortgage (containing an after-acquired property clause) on Blackacre to X. R then acquires Whiteacre with his own money. Two months later, R borrows additional money from Z, who takes and records a mortgage on Whiteacre. X certainly has a valid mortgage on Whiteacre, but is it senior or junior to Z's mortgage?

It is tempting to say that if X's mortgage on Blackacre is recorded, then Z would have constructive notice of the after-acquired provision and thus X's lien would have priority. But this conclusion is not justified, despite the occasional judicial statement that recording is "effectual notice as against the world." Certainly, if Whiteacre and Blackacre are located in different counties or states, the land records in each county relate only to land within that county, so the recording of the mortgage on Blackacre in one county cannot provide constructive notice to Z when Z is searching title to Whiteacre in a different county. Even if Blackacre and Whiteacre *are* in the same county, the implication that X's mortgage should be senior to Z's mortgage is potentially problematic. Would a reasonable person in the position of Z (who is searching title to Whiteacre) be expected to find X's mortgage against Blackacre and realize that it contains an after-acquired property clause that might also cover Whiteacre? On the one hand, both recorded mortgages would appear in the grantor index under the name 'R'; thus, one might argue that Z should review any mortgage granted by R—including the mortgage on Blackacre—because any such mortgage could also cover Whiteacre (or any other parcel), either directly or by virtue of an after-acquired property clause. On the other hand, one might also argue that it would be unreasonable to expect Z (who, again, is searching title to Whiteacre) to search the records any further back in time than the date on which R acquired Whiteacre. If Z begins his search on the date R acquired Whiteacre and searches forward, Z will not discover the mortgage against Blackacre—which was recorded at an earlier date—and thus likely will not discover the after-acquired property clause. Cf. Glen Ellyn Sav. & Loan Ass'n v. State Bank of Geneva, 65 Ill.App.3d 916, 22 Ill.Dec. 569, 382 N.E.2d 1267, 1273 (1978) ("to constitute constructive notice to third persons an instrument must be in the chain of title to the property and will not be considered to be notice of record simply because it has been recorded at some time prior to acquisition of title [by such third parties].").

The Restatement resolves this question by treating a recorded mortgage containing an after-acquired property provision as being unrecorded as against those who later purchase interests in the after-acquired real estate. Restatement (Third) of Property (Mortgages) § 7.5 cmt. d (1997). Under this approach, if a state has either a "notice" or "race-notice" recording act, and Z takes its mortgage on Whiteacre without *actual* knowledge of X's mortgage, Z's mortgage will have priority. By contrast, if Z has actual knowledge of X's mortgage on Blackacre, X's lien on Whiteacre by virtue of the after-acquired provision will take priority over Z's lien on Whiteacre.

4.   *After-acquired property provision vs. purchase money mortgage.* Now suppose that in the problem in Note 3, the money supplied by Z was used by R to acquire Whiteacre, so that Z's mortgage on Whiteacre is a third party purchase money mortgage. Suppose further that when Z took his mortgage, he had *actual* knowledge of X's mortgage before advancing the funds to R. In this situation, Z's mortgage should be senior to X's mortgage by virtue of the purchase money mortgage rule which, in this setting, displaces the recording act. See Restatement (Third) of Property (Mortgages) § 7.5(b) cmt. e (1997). Is this good policy?

C. MECHANIC'S LIENS

Often, another creditor may obtain a lien against mortgaged property by virtue of a specific statute. In some cases, the statute may even give the statutory lien creditor priority over a conflicting mortgage that otherwise would have priority under first-in-time. We have encountered several such examples in earlier chapters, including a municipality's lien for unpaid real estate taxes (which always has priority over a conflicting mortgage) or a governmental agency's lien for environmental cleanup costs (which may or may not have priority over a conflicting mortgage lien, depending on the statute under which the cleanup lien arises).

The most common statutory lien involving real estate, however, is the mechanic's lien. If a contractor or subcontractor provides labor with regard to an improvement to land, or a supplier provides materials that become part of an improvement to land, the contractor, subcontractor or materials supplier can obtain a lien against the land if they are not paid for the work or supplies. Each state has its own statute that describes the process by which the creditor can assert and enforce a mechanic's lien, and which establishes the priority of that lien vis-a-vis a conflicting mortgage. Generalization is dangerous, because there is wide variation among each state's laws, but the following materials provide an overview of the principal statutory approaches and the general common features of these statutes.

NELSON, WHITMAN, BURKHART & FREYERMUTH, REAL ESTATE FINANCE LAW
§ 12.4 (6th ed.2015)*

The basic idea of a mechanic's lien is that a person whose work or materials improve real estate[167] and who has not been paid should be permitted to recover from that real estate.[168] Beginning with the original

---

* Reprinted with permission of LEG, Inc. d/b/a West Academic.

[167] Work done off-site may be lienable if it directly benefits the property. See In re Trilogy Development Co., 468 B.R. 854 (Bankr. W.D. Mo. 2011); John Wagner Associates v. Hercules, Inc., 797 P.2d 1123 (Utah Ct. App. 1990) (modular buildings, although removable, are part of real estate and provide basis for mechanic's lien); Alaska Cascade Financial Services, Inc. v. Doors Northwest, Inc., 52 Wash. App. 588, 762 P.2d 362 (Div. 2 1988) (modular buildings lienable, though constructed off-site); Vulcraft, a Div. of Nucor Corp. v. Midtown Business Park, Ltd., 1990–NMSC–095, 110 N.M. 761, 800 P.2d 195 (1990) (steel fabrication performed off-site); Northlake Concrete Products, Inc. v. Wylie, 34 Wash. App. 810, 663 P.2d 1380 (Div. 1 1983) (sewer line).

Mere maintenance or repair work is usually non-lienable. In re Payless Cashways, Inc., 230 B.R. 120 (B.A.P. 8th Cir. 1999), aff'd, 203 F.3d 1081, 35 Bankr. Ct. Dec. (CRR) 191 (8th Cir. 2000). See also Negvesky v. United Interior Resources, Inc., 32 A.D.3d 530, 821 N.Y.S.2d 107 (2d Dep't 2006) (installation of modular work stations not lienable); TPST Soil Recyclers of Washington, Inc. v. W.F. Anderson Const., Inc., 91 Wash. App. 297, 957 P.2d 265 (Div. 2 1998), opinion amended on reconsideration, 967 P.2d 1266 (Wash. Ct. App. Div. 2 1998) (Utah law) (cleanup of contaminated soil not lienable). . . .

In most jurisdictions, the lien is on the entire parcel of real estate, including land and improvements. However, in a few states, the improvement is legally separate from the land, and the lien attaches only to the improvement. See Provident Bank v. Tri-County Southside Asphalt, Inc., 804 N.E.2d 161 (Ind. Ct. App. 2004), on reh'g in part, 806 N.E.2d 802 (Ind. Ct. App. 2004). . . .

[168] If the work was done improperly, the lien may be for less or even zero. See Cashway Concrete & Materials v. Sanner Contracting Co., 158 Ariz. 81, 761 P.2d 155 (Ct. App. Div. 2 1988) (lien is for reasonable value of materials furnished; contract price is evidence of reasonable value). . . .

The lien is not the contractor's sole remedy. The contractor may get a personal judgment for the amount due or recover in quantum meruit or for unjust enrichment, though she failed to properly perfect a lien. See Pro Tech Air, Inc. v. NBGI Homes, LLC, 2010 WL 4227606 (Cal. App. 2d Dist. 2010), unpublished/noncitable; Brown Sprinkler Corp. v. Somerset-Pulaski County Development Foundation, Inc., 335 S.W.3d 455, 458 (Ky. Ct. App. 2010); Craft v. Stevenson Lumber Yard, Inc., 179 N.J. 56, 843 A.2d 1076 (2004). . . . The contractor may not recover both on

Maryland statute, "[t]hese laws grew, and their validity became established, as the courts held that the building business did not have the protection inherent in the widespread distribution of credit risk common to other businesses, and therefore needed this broader and special protection. Contractors, subcontractors, materialmen, and other building groups were frequently obliged to extend credit in larger amounts, and for longer time, than other businesses. Such parties might have their entire capital, or a substantial part of it, tied up in one or two, or ten or twenty, projects under construction."[169]

Originally, the mechanic's lien laws protected only general contractors or master-builders. But today "practically every segment composing the construction industry—including contractors, subcontractors, material dealers, laborers, artisans, architects, landscape architects, engineers, surveyors—is granted liens of varying extent under varying conditions for the labor, services, or materials furnished or contracted to be furnished for the particular improvement."[171] Because mechanic's lien statutes are in derogation of the common law, courts often state that they should be strictly construed. However, courts also often state that, because mechanic's lien statutes are remedial, they should be liberally construed to protect workers and materials suppliers. The court in *Ferguson Enterprises, Inc. v. Keybuild Solutions, Inc.*, 275 P.3d 741, 745 (Colo. App 2011), articulated the correct approach: "The mechanics' lien statute should be strictly construed with respect to those acts necessary to perfect the lien and should be construed liberally as to the provisions of the statute that are remedial in nature."

If the mechanic's lien was available only to those with whom the owner dealt directly, little question would exist as to the amount of the lien—it would be for the unpaid contract amount. When the acts extended their coverage to persons that had no direct dealings with the owner, they divided into two main types. One type, generally designated the "Pennsylvania" type,[175] gives the subcontractor a direct right for the value

---

the lien and in quantum meruit. See KC Excavating and Grading, Inc. v. Crane Const. Co., 141 S.W.3d 401 (Mo. Ct. App. W.D. 2004). . . .

[169] Stalling, Mechanics' Lien Laws as They Exist Today, 4 F.H.L.B. Rev. 232 (1938); see Cook v. Carlson, 364 F. Supp. 24 (D.S.D. 1973).

[171] Stalling, Mechanics' Lien Laws as They Exist Today, 4 F.H.L.B. Rev. 232 (1938); Smith, Note, Mechanic's Lien Priority Rights for Design Professionals, 46 Wash. & Lee L. Rev. 1035 (1989); Survey of Illinois Law for the Years 1951–1952: Property, 31 Chi.-Kent L. Rev. 61, 71 (1952). See In re Premier Hotel Development Group, 271 B.R. 813 (Bankr. E.D. Tenn. 2002) (engineers and architects are entitled to lien, but liens have priority over mortgage only if lien claimant gave notice of work to mortgagee, either directly or by recording notice, before mortgage recorded); Mark Twain Kansas City Bank v. Kroh Bros. Development Co., 14 Kan. App. 2d 714, 798 P.2d 511 (1990) (architect may have lien only if building is constructed); Mutual Savings Ass'n v. Res/Com Properties, L.L.C., 32 Kan. App. 2d 48, 79 P.3d 184 (2003) (engineering company entitled to lien for preliminary surveying and staking). . . .

[175] See Pa. Stat. Ann. tit. 49, § 1301. Approximately thirty states follow the Pennsylvania approach. See Comment: Mechanics' Liens and Surety Bonds in the Building Trades, 68 Yale L.J.

of its contributions. Some statutes in this group provide that the claims cannot exceed the contract price, less payments properly made to the contractor, or provide a method for the owner to limit them to that amount. However, other states permit the subcontractors' claims to exceed the contract price and to be payable though the owner has paid the general contractor in full. Courts have upheld their constitutionality. The other type of act, usually called the "New York" system, gives the subcontractor a derivative lien based on the contractor's rights. Because the lien rights are based on the contract between the owner and general contractor, the liability of the owner's property is limited to the contract price, less payments properly made to the contractor.[180]

The procedure that a lien claimant must follow varies widely among the states but typically requires filing a claim notice within a specified period of time, typically 60 to 180 days, after work completion.[181] The notice usually must be recorded, served personally on the owner, published in a newspaper, or some combination of these methods. If the claim is not paid within an additional specified period, typically six months to one year, the claimant usually must bring a judicial action to foreclose the lien in a manner similar to a mortgage foreclosure.

When the claimant perfects the lien by giving or recording the required notice, the lien's priority usually relates back to an earlier time. This relation-back feature is frequently litigated between construction mortgagees and mechanic's lienors that are attempting to prove senior priority status. Nearly half the states provide that mechanic's liens take priority from the date the building project began. In theory, this rule seems unobjectionable, because a property inspection will presumably disclose whether construction has begun. As a practical matter, however, commencement is often an ambiguous event. Courts disagree whether it has occurred when lumber is piled on the property, trees and brush have been cleared or grading has begun, or an electrical service pole and box are erected. In an attempt to ensure their priority over mechanic's liens that might be filed later, well-advised construction lenders photograph the

---

138, 144 n.30 (1958); Maurice T. Brunner, Annotation, Release or waiver of mechanic's lien by general contractor as affecting rights of subcontractor or materialman, 75 A.L.R.3d 505.

[180] See N.Y. Lien Law § 4; Fla. Stat. Ann. § 713.06(1); Ga. Code Ann. § 44–14–361(b). . . .

[181] . . . The date of completion is not always easy to determine. Suppose the owner calls the mechanic back to correct defective work that she discovered after nominal completion? See In re Trilogy Development Co., 468 B.R. 854 (Bankr. W.D. Mo. 2011); In re Jennerwein, 309 B.R. 385 (Bankr. M.D. Fla. 2004) (contractor's return to site to inspect fence and make list of unfinished items extended time to file); Creme de la Creme (Kansas), Inc. v. R & R Intern., Inc., 32 Kan. App. 2d 490, 85 P.3d 205 (2004) ("call-back" work was performed as a courtesy and did not extend contractor's time to file); Interstate Electrical Services Corp. v. Cummings Properties, LLC, 63 Mass. App. Ct. 295, 825 N.E.2d 1059 (2005) (call-back work was part of original contract and extended time to file); Stock Bldg. Supply, L.L.C. v. Parsley Homes of Mazuchet Harbor, L.L.C., 291 Mich. App. 403, 804 N.W.2d 898 (2011) (repair work does not confer any additional value and does not extend time to file); Rossi v. Pawiroredjo, 2004 MT 39, 320 Mont. 63, 85 P.3d 776 (2004) (contractor's return to site to remove floor stain extended time to file).

property on the day they record their mortgage to establish that construction has not begun.

The second most popular priority date is the day the particular lienor began furnishing labor or materials. The difficulties of determining the beginning of service or materials deliveries are considerably greater than those of determining when the whole building operation started. Additionally, an intervening mortgage can divide the lien claimants into prior and subsequent groups, which creates a problem when the mechanic's lien statute provides that all lien claimants have the same priority.

The third most common priority date, which exists in about six jurisdictions, is the day the claimant files the lien. In a few other states, the liens attach as of the date of the general contract or of the lienor's contract or when a notice of the contract is recorded. In some states, the liens attach at different times depending on various factors. In Missouri, the relative priorities of the construction mortgage and the mechanic's liens can differ for the land and for the improvements for which the lienors supplied labor or materials. Mechanic's liens on the land take priority from the date that work began, but the mechanic's liens on the improvement have first priority, regardless of when the construction mortgage is recorded. In some states, the mortgage is senior to the mechanic's liens if the loan proceeds were used to pay for the construction.

The statutes usually provide that property is lienable only if the improvements were constructed with the owner's consent. "Owner" is defined in a variety of ways. A tenant or life tenant often does not have the requisite power to consent. The owner "consents" if she signs a construction contract. Courts in some jurisdictions have held that a formal contract is not required and that the owner's acquiescence or even mere knowledge of the construction is sufficient. A number of these jurisdictions provide a procedure by which an owner who has not contracted for the improvement can record or post on the property a notice or disclaimer of responsibility within some fixed time after construction began. Depending on the statute, the notice can shift the burden of proving actual consent to the lienor or can entirely bar the filing of liens on the owner's property interest.[200]

NOTES

1. *Additional reading.* For further discussion of mechanic's liens from a national perspective, *see* Ethan Glass, Old Statutes Never Die . . . Nor Do They Fade Away: A Proposal for Modernizing Mechanics' Lien Law by Federal Action, 27 Ohio N.U.L.Rev. 67 (2000); Michael G. Walsh, A Mechanics' Lien Primer for the General Practitioner, 37 Prac.Law. 77 (July 1991); Nelson,

---

[200] Some statutes permit the lienor to remove the improvement notwithstanding the owner's notice of nonresponsibility, which may compel the owner to pay for the improvement to keep it. See, e.g., American Transit Mix Co. v. Weber, 106 Cal. App. 2d 74, 234 P.2d 732 (3d Dist. 1951).

Whitman, Burkhart & Freyermuth, Real Estate Finance Law § 12.4 (6th ed.2015).

2. *Risks for purchasers.* Although the above material focuses on the plight of the landowner, consider the position of a *purchaser*. For a brand new building, the possibility of a mechanic's lien is obvious. Even if the building is not new, sellers often have work done to a building to get it ready to sell; if such work has been done, potential mechanic's lien claims may exist. If the claimant need not file a lien notice until some months after the last work is done, how can a purchaser avoid taking title subject to a latent mechanic's lien? Obviously, a record title search is insufficient. The owner may try to obtain lien waivers from all the workers and materials suppliers, but how can the purchaser be certain that the owner knows the identity and location of all of them? And title insurance companies sometimes exclude mechanic's liens from the coverage of their policies, because an insurer's title search cannot disclose a lien of which there is as yet no evidence on the public records.

In some states, unrecorded mechanic's liens are binding on bona fide purchasers only if the contractor has filed a notice of the construction contract with the register of deeds or if the improvements are "visually evident." But the "visually evident" requirement is no panacea for buyers because it may provide little guidance. For example, if the seller has recently hired a heating contractor to replace the furnace, is that improvement "visually evident" to the buyer?

The courts' interpretation of the standard also can be difficult to predict. For example, in Carlson-Grefe Const., Inc. v. Rosemount Condo. Group Partn., 474 N.W.2d 405 (Minn.Ct.App.1991), the court found that neither the presence of a construction trailer containing plumbing supplies on the site nor a ceremonial groundbreaking was a sufficiently visible activity to establish the priority of a mechanic's lien. Many other cases deal with activities such as architectural, engineering, surveying, and legal work on the project. See also Himmighoefer v. Medallion Indus., Inc., 302 Md. 270, 487 A.2d 282 (1985), in which the court discusses the Maryland mechanic's lien statute amendments that protect bona fide purchasers who enter into contracts before the mechanic's lien is reduced to judgment.

The problem of unrecorded mechanic's liens affects not only purchasers, but also anyone acquiring an interest in the land. For example, a lender that takes a mortgage may find that it is subject to a mechanic's lien that was unrecorded and thus undiscoverable when the mortgage was given.

3. *Lien waivers.* Can mechanic's liens be waived and, if so, how? One must consider the question in two contexts. The first is whether a waiver can arise by virtue of a "no lien" clause in the construction agreement between the owner and the contractor. In most states, little doubt exists that this agreement binds the general contractor, but does it also bind subcontractors and suppliers? The jurisdictions are divided. In some states, the general contractor's agreement binds them if the provision meets the requirements provided by the statute; in some states, this may include a requirement that

the agreement be recorded. See, e.g., Feitler v. Springfield Enters., Inc., 978 N.E.2d 1160 (Ind.Ct.App.2012); 49 Pa.Stat. § 1402 (waiver in construction contract binds subcontractors and suppliers if they had notice of it). In other states, the rights of subcontractors and suppliers are independent of the general contractor's and cannot be waived without their consent. E.g., Cal. Civ. Code § 8122 (waiver in construction contract binds workers and suppliers only if they give written waiver and release); Lehrer McGovern Bovis, Inc. v. Bullock Insulation, Inc., 197 P.3d 1032 (Nev. 2008) (lien waiver in construction agreement does not bind subcontractor). Similarly, several states invalidate a lien waiver if the worker or supplier has not been paid. E.g., Nev.Rev.Stat. § 108.2457; Wis. Stat. § 779.135(1).

The second is whether a subcontractor or supplier can waive its right to assert a lien either during the course of construction or after the construction is completed. Courts in virtually all jurisdictions sustain these waivers, which is fortunate because they are extremely useful. For example, if you are buying a newly-constructed house or one on which work has recently been done, you would be very wise to get a list of the people that had worked on the project or had supplied materials and to insist that they provide you with lien waivers. Of course, a court might refuse to enforce a waiver if it was obtained by fraudulent representations or by bad faith conduct. See, e.g., Stringert & Bowers, Inc. v. On-Line Systems, Inc., 236 Pa.Super. 196, 345 A.2d 194 (1975). Likewise, a subcontractor or supplier might well refuse to provide a waiver if the subcontractor or supplier had not actually been paid for its work. Some jurisdictions prohibit the waiver of a lien arising from an *executory* contract. See National Glass, Inc. v. J.C. Penney Props., Inc., 336 Md. 606, 650 A.2d 246 (1994) (discussing Maryland statute). New York, Pennsylvania, and Florida have similar statutes. In effect, this means that a worker or materials supplier can waive a lien for work already performed or materials already delivered, but not for work or materials to be provided in the future. In these states, a buyer or lender must obtain waivers at the conclusion of the construction process to be certain that no lien claims will be filed.

A variation on this theme is the so-called "pay-if-paid" provision, which a general contractor may include in its agreements with subcontractors and suppliers. Under this provision, the worker or supplier is entitled to payment only if the owner pays the contractor. Some states invalidate this type of provision as contrary to the public policy underlying mechanic's lien statutes. E.g., 770 Ill.Comp.Stat. 60/21(e); Nev.Rev.Stat. §§ 624.624, 624.626; N.C.Gen.Stat. § 22C–2; Wis.Stat. § 779.135(3); West-Fair Elec. Contractors v. Aetna Cas. & Sur. Co., 87 N.Y.2d 148, 638 N.Y.S.2d 394, 661 N.E.2d 967 (1995). Other states enforce them. E.g., MidAmerica Constr. Mgmt., Inc. v. MasTec N. America, Inc., 436 F.3d 1257 (10th Cir. 2006) (pay-if-paid provisions enforceable under New Mexico and Texas law).

4. *Priority: mechanic's lienor vs. purchase money mortgagee.* Suppose that Buyer is in the process of acquiring Blackacre. On June 2, Buyer enters an agreement with Contractor to remodel the building on Blackacre. On June 4, Buyer acquires title to Blackacre, using the proceeds of a mortgage loan from

First Bank. On June 6, Contractor begins working on the remodeling. On July 1, Subcontractor begins work on some electrical work in conjunction with the remodeling. All of the work is done in September, but Buyer failed to pay Contractor for the work, and in turn Contractor did not pay Subcontractor. On November 18, Contractor filed a timely mechanic's lien claim; on November 20, Subcontractor likewise filed a timely mechanic's lien claim. Suppose that the jurisdiction follows the first priority rule described above, under which the mechanic's lien relates back to the day work began on the site (commonly known as the "first spade" rule). What is the relative priority of First Bank's mortgage and the two mechanic's liens, if:

    (a)   First Bank recorded its mortgage on June 4?

    (b)   First Bank recorded its mortgage on June 8?

    (c)   First Bank recorded its mortgage on November 19?

See Bob DeGeorge Assocs., Inc. v. Hawthorn Bank, 377 S.W.3d 592 (Mo.2012). How would your answers change if the jurisdiction followed the other two priority approaches described above?

D. DRAGNET CLAUSES AND FUTURE ADVANCES PROVISIONS

A mortgagor typically grants a mortgage to secure the repayment of a specific obligation to repay a fixed sum of money, as evidenced in a promissory note. In the typical home purchase, for example, the mortgagor borrows a fixed sum of money which she expects to repay in installments (such that the principal amount of the loan will decrease over time). But a mortgage can also provide that the mortgage lien will secure not only the repayment of one specific obligation, but also other debts that the borrower may owe to the lender, either arising out of past transactions or future transactions.

In some circumstances, the parties to a loan transaction will explicitly contemplate the strong likelihood or even certainty of additional future borrowings or "future advances." For example, a borrower may obtain a loan to finance the construction of improvements. In this situation, the borrower does not want to receive all of the loan proceeds immediately— and begin incurring interest charges on the entire amount—but instead to receive the loan in periodic "draws" as construction proceeds (so that the borrower incurs the debt only as it is needed to pay construction expenses). Likewise, a borrower may choose to obtain a "home equity line of credit," where the borrower may not need to draw on the line of credit (and begin incurring interest costs) immediately, but wishes to be able to draw on the credit line in the future as needed to pay certain expenses (such as future home repairs or a child's tuition expenses). In these situations, the mortgage loan documents typically contain an explicit "future advances" clause, which states that the mortgage will secure the repayment of advances made at the time the mortgage is granted and advances made in the future.

In other loan transactions—such as a thirty-year mortgage loan for an already-constructed home—the parties may not have specific expectations at the time of the loan that the borrower will obtain future loans as described above. Nevertheless, the mortgage may still include a provision that the mortgage will secure not only the obligation incurred by the mortgagor at the time the mortgage is granted, but also any other obligation that the mortgagor owes to the mortgagee. This kind of clause is often referred to as a "dragnet clause," and might read as follows: "The mortgage shall secure the mortgagor's obligations to pay the mortgage note of even date herewith and all other liabilities of mortgagor to mortgagee, now existing or hereafter incurred."

These kinds of provisions have generated two basic types of disputes. The first type (reflected by the *Shiew* case that follows) does not involve lien priority per se, but instead whether a dragnet clause is legally sufficient to secure an obligation that is of a different type or character than the one explicitly secured by the mortgage. The second type (to which we return after *Shiew*) is the lien priority dispute that arises when another creditor obtains an "intervening lien," e.g., when another creditor obtains a lien after the mortgage arises, but before the mortgagee makes a future advance to the mortgagor.

FIRST SEC. BANK OF UTAH v. SHIEW
Supreme Court of Utah, 1980
609 P.2d 952

MAUGHAN, JUSTICE. . . . In 1972, Bill and Linda Shiew purchased a home in Monticello, Utah. Plaintiff's branch in Monticello, Utah, loaned $6,342.48 to the Shiews; this loan was secured by a mortgage on the home. A standard printed provision in the mortgage recited it was "to secure the payment of any and all claims or demands now due or to become due now or hereafter contracted or incurred which the said mortgagee or the holder hereof, from time to time, may have or hold against the mortgagors or either of them, whether as maker, surety, guarantor, partner or otherwise, and whether contracted directly with or purchased by the holder hereof: . . ."

In 1974, in connection with a cattle-raising venture, the Shiews obtained a loan of $8,900.00 from plaintiff's branch in Price, Utah. The parties entered into a security agreement (Farm Products Chattel Mortgage) to secure this loan. The recited security was certain specified cattle and feed as well as all after acquired cattle and feed. The security agreement made no reference to the mortgage on the debtor's home as additional security. In fact, the security agreement recited: "This agreement constitutes the entire agreement between the parties."

In 1975, the Shiews were divorced, and Linda Shiew was awarded the home in Monticello. In April 1976, plaintiff filed an action against the Shiews in connection with the cattle business transaction. Plaintiff alleged that the security for payment of the note had *all* been disposed of in accordance with the terms of the security agreement, and the collateral was totally exhausted. Plaintiff claimed a deficiency of $4,369.25 and demanded judgment for that amount, plus interest and attorneys fees. It is significant that at the time of filing this action plaintiff did not claim the loan was further secured by a mortgage on the home in Monticello. Further, if the cattle loan were secured by the real estate mortgage as later claimed by plaintiff, under Section 78–37–1 (the single action rule), plaintiff would have been compelled to foreclose the real estate mortgage and exhaust that security rather than attempting to recover the debt directly by a money judgment.

Linda Shiew answered the complaint, but a judgment by default was entered against Bill Shiew on September 1, 1976. This judgment recited the facts concerning the loan transaction in 1974 in Price, Utah, and reiterated that the collateral securing the loan had been exhausted and a deficiency of $4,369.25 remained, and judgment against Bill Shiew was awarded in this amount to plaintiff.

Subsequently, on October 14, 1976, plaintiff filed a motion for leave to file an amended complaint and for an order making Utah Farm Bureau Insurance Company a defendant. This motion was granted.

The home in Monticello had been destroyed by fire in 1976. Plaintiff was a loss payee under the insurance policy. The insurance company issued a check payable to Linda Shiew and plaintiff in the sum of $10,000. The plaintiff requested Mrs. Shiew's endorsement so that it could satisfy the outstanding balance due on both the Price and Monticello loans. Mrs. Shiew refused to pay off the Price loan out of the fire insurance proceeds. Plaintiff notified the insurance company of this dispute.

On May 11, 1976, the insurance company issued two separate checks. One was payable to plaintiff in the amount of $2,843.80, the unpaid balance on the loan on the home in Monticello. The other check, payable to Linda Shiew, was in the amount of $7,156.20.

On November 10, 1976, plaintiff filed an amended complaint. In the first cause of action, plaintiff alleged the same facts and pleaded for a judgment against the Shiews, jointly and severally for the deficiency. In the second cause of action, plaintiff for the first time asserted that the dragnet provision in the mortgage on the home in Monticello made the mortgage security for any other indebtedness of Shiews. Plaintiff alleged that the insurance policy issued on the home contained a mortgage clause, and the house and its contents were destroyed by fire. Plaintiff alleged that the insurance company wrongfully paid the proceeds of the insurance to Linda Shiew, while Shiews were indebted to plaintiff in the sum of $4,369.25, together with interest and costs; plaintiff demanded judgment against the insurance company.

Upon trial before the court, plaintiff was awarded judgment against the insurance company and Linda Shiew. The insurance company alone appeals therefrom.

The primary issue submitted by defendant to the trial court and then to this Court concerns the proper interpretation of a dragnet clause in a mortgage. Defendant vigorously urged the dragnet clause should be interpreted according to the Kansas[1]-Hawaiian[2] rule, which provides:

> [I]n the absence of clear, supportive evidence of a contrary intention a mortgage containing a dragnet type clause will not be extended to cover future advances unless the advances are of the same kind and quality or relate to the same transaction or series of transactions as the principal obligation secured or unless the document evidencing the subsequent advance refers to the mortgage as providing security therefor.[3]

This Court has not previously undertaken a definitive interpretation of dragnet clauses in mortgages.

In Osborne, Nelson, Whitman, Real Estate Finance Law (1979), Section 12.8, p. 772, a dragnet clause is described as a mortgage provision which purports to make the real estate security for other, usually unspecified debts which the mortgagor may already owe or may owe in the future to the mortgagee. The lender usually has no particular future advances in mind and merely includes the clause for its potential future utility. Frequently, as in this case, the clause is included in the printed language of mortgages drafted by the mortgagee. These clauses are seldom the subject of negotiation and may go entirely unnoticed by the mortgagor until the mortgagee asserts them.

Osborne explains:

> . . . Dragnet clauses are generally upheld, but because their apparent coverage is so broad, and because the mortgagor is often unaware of their presence or implications, the courts tend to construe them narrowly against the mortgagee. Generalizations are difficult, since the language of the particular clause may be a decisive factor. However, the following illustrations show numerous ways in which the courts have narrowed the application

---

[1]   *Emporia State Bank and Trust Company v. Mounkes*, 214 Kan. 178, 519 P.2d 618 (1974).

[2]   *Akamine & Sons, Ltd. v. American Security Bank*, 50 Hawaii 304, 440 P.2d 262 (1968).

[3]   Note 1 *supra*, at p. 623 of 519 P.2d.

of dragnet clauses. Sometimes such holdings are said to be based on the intention of the parties, but in reality they usually represent the court's conceptions of fairness and equity. These illustrations are not intended to represent any majority rule, as there are many conflicting or contrary cases. They merely show the sort of judicial treatment dragnet clauses often receive.

1. The mortgage will only secure advances made or debts incurred in the future. If the mortgagor already owes debts to the mortgagee at the time the mortgage is executed, it would supposedly be easy to identify those existing debts specifically; if they are not so identified, it is assumed that the parties did not intend to secure them.

2. Only debts of the same type or character as the original debt are secured by the mortgage. For example, if the original loan is for home repairs, a future loan or advance for more repairs would be secured by the mortgage but a loan for an automobile purchase would not. It is easy to imagine grey areas in such a test. For example, what if the second loan were for adding a room to the house? The resolution of the matter is made easier if the documents on the second loan state that it is to be secured under the dragnet clause of the existing mortgage.

3. As an extension of the foregoing concept, it is sometimes held that the dragnet clause will cover future debts only if the documents evidencing those debts specifically refer back to the clause.

4. If the future debt is separately secured, whether by another mortgage or by a personal property security agreement, it may be assumed that the parties did not intend that it also be secured by the dragnet mortgage.

5. The clause is inapplicable to debts which were originally owed by the mortgagor to third parties, and which were assigned to or purchased by the mortgagee.

6. If there are several joint mortgagors, only future debts on which all of the mortgagors are obligated (or at least of which all were aware) will be covered by the dragnet clause.

7. Once the original debt has been fully discharged, the mortgage is extinguished and cannot secure future loans.

8. If the real estate is transferred by the mortgagor to a third party, any debts which the original mortgagor incurs thereafter are not secured by the mortgage. . . .

Osborne further admonishes:

> While the dragnet clause is usually regarded as advantageous to mortgagees, that is not necessarily the case. One reason is that the types of judicial limitations on the clause discussed above are very much open to debate and further development in most states; in this sense, the clause is an invitation to litigation. . . .

The foregoing illustrations indicate the diverse and numerous consequences which may flow from a dragnet clause. Although a clear majority rule has not evolved concerning the interpretation of these clauses, there is a consensus that dragnet clauses are not favored in equity and that they should be carefully scrutinized and strictly construed. As the court observed in the *Akamine* case: "Completely unrestricted enforcement of such mortgages would tend to reduce the borrower to the status of economic serf. . . ."

In the *Akamine* case the court ruled that unless the prior or subsequent advance related to the same transaction or series of transactions, the mortgage must specifically refer to it for the advance to be secured. The court explained it would not assist a lending institution in an attempt to captivate a borrower by inclusion in a mortgage of a broad all inclusive dragnet clause. The court observed contracts requiring one party to deal exclusively with one supplier have been viewed with great suspicion under the antitrust laws. The court stated: ". . . to attempt to foreclose, for example, on the mortgagor's home for debts incurred in operating a business and which debts are not specifically covered by the mortgage would be unconscionable and contrary to public policy." . . .

In the instant case the dragnet clause was a standard boiler plate provision inserted by the mortgagee in the mortgage on the Shiews' home in Monticello, Utah. There was no evidence this clause was a subject of negotiation between the parties, or that the attention of the mortgagors was directed to this provision. The mortgage was to secure a loan for the purchase of their home, and this transaction was with plaintiff's branch in Monticello, Utah, in 1972. In 1974, the Shiews entered into an entirely different type of transaction, a security agreement to finance a business venture, cattle raising. This transaction was conducted with a branch of plaintiff's bank in Price, Utah. The cattle and feed were recited as the security for this subsequent loan. Furthermore, the security agreement failed to mention the obligation was also secured by the real estate mortgage, and, in fact, refuted such a consequence by an integration clause which recited it constituted the entire agreement between the parties. The legal effect of this integration clause was the preclusion of any claim by the bank that it had accepted the mortgagors' continuing offer to secure future advances with the real estate mortgage on their home.

There is not a scintilla of evidence to support the inference the parties intended the second loan to be under the security of the first loan. The second loan was of an entirely different nature and type of transaction. The self-serving statements of the bank officer that he relied on the defendants' financial statement which specified their home as an asset is of no evidentiary value, for he did not claim he communicated an acceptance of the mortgagors' offer of the home as security, and, in fact, the integration clause of the security agreement would negate such an agreement.

In the instant case, when the dragnet clause is strictly construed against the mortgagee, who drafted it, and interpreted in accordance with afore-cited authority, there is an insufficient evidentiary basis to sustain the determination of the trial court that the mortgage on the Shiews' home constituted security for the subsequent security agreement concerning the financing of their cattle venture. . . .

HALL, JUSTICE (dissenting). . . . In adopting the holdings of certain other jurisdictions, the majority opinion fails to recognize that we have previously given a rather expansive meaning to open-end mortgage provisions for future advances. In Bank of Ephraim v. Davis, 559 P.2d 539 (1977), this Court unanimously held that advances made pursuant to such a provision take priority over all subsequent lien holders. The mortgage is to be interpreted as any other contract and if the future advance provision is sufficiently certain, it will be upheld.

The language of the clause held to secure future advances in Bank of Ephraim read as follows:

> To secure payment of any and all extensions or renewals, and successive extensions or renewals, of the note above described, or of the indebtedness represented by the same, and of any other indebtedness represented by the same, and of any other indebtedness at any time arising from the mortgagor to the mortgagee, whether represented by notes, drafts, open accounts or otherwise, ...

In the instant case, the clause reads as follows:

> . . . [T]his mortgage shall extend to and be security for . . . the payment of any and all claims or demands now due or to become due, now or hereafter contracted or incurred, which the said mortgagee . . . may have or hold against the mortgagors or either of them.

It is my opinion that the latter clause articulates with even greater clarity the meaning of the mortgage; hence it should be enforced according to its own terms. A party's subjective intent cannot alter the clear terms of a written contract and the 1972 loan clearly provides that the mortgage was to be security for future advances.

The majority opinion suggests that the fact that the 1974 loan made no reference to the 1972 loan, in some way weakens the effect of the open-end, future advance clause. The question is not whether the 1974 livestock loan refers to the future advance clause, but rather whether the 1972 mortgage loan refers to the advance made in 1974. The trial court concluded that the future advance clause of the open-end mortgage loan clearly covered the 1974 livestock loan. The court's decision was based, at least in part, on the fact that the mortgaged property was listed as an asset by the Shiews during the negotiations for the Price loan. The manager of the Price branch of First Security testified as follows:

Q. Now, prior to the making of that loan, did you well, you obtained from Bill Shiew, it's been admitted, a statement of his and Linda Shiew's assets, other than the cattle, is that right?

A. I did. He declared an $8,000 home in Monticello.

Q. What is the position of the bank with respect to the loan application that she took at the time?

MR. MORGAN: Objection, that calls for speculation and a legal argument as to what the position of the bank is.

THE COURT: He may answer that.

THE WITNESS: Because of the cattle situation, I had to look for other collateral, and I was aware of the open-end mortgage down in Monticello. And that's probably why it did not appear on the application, or the security document. It's very commonly used at First Security Bank, and we've used it many times. I'm very much familiar with it.

Q. When you negotiated the loan, Mr. Brown, with the Shiews, with respect to the cattle, and you took a financial statement from Mr. Shiew did you not?

A. Yes, I did.

Q. Was the granting of the loan influenced by the financial statement that you got?

A. It was.

Q. To what extent?

A. Well, the cattle market, as we've stated before, had weakened, and the Shiews had 50 ton of hay that wouldn't have taken these cattle through the winter, and it was real close. We checked for that as additional collateral, and it stated there that the home was $8,000 worth in Monticello, and we had less than half of that, and that was very much an influence because they wanted to take it through the winter. I wanted to sell it then, but they thought 50 ton of hay, and they wanted to go through the winter hoping that the cattle price would strengthen. They didn't do that.

The majority also holds that the future advance provision should not apply to unrelated future indebtedness which was not anticipated at the time the mortgage was signed. I believe the court's reasoning in First National Bank in Dallas v. Rozelle, 493 F.2d 1196 (10th Cir. 1974), was sound wherein it was held that an agreement to secure future advances must necessarily intend to secure sums that are indefinite and uncertain at the time the mortgage was executed. Furthermore, based on the uncontroverted testimony quoted supra, the trial judge specifically found that the two loans were related in the instant case when he ruled as follows:

> [T]he mortgaged property in San Juan County was set up by Bill Shiew as an asset when he applied for the livestock loan, and that said asset was relied upon by the plaintiff, and inducement to the plaintiff, in making the livestock loan. . .

In my opinion, the future advance of 1974 was therefore secured by the 1972 agreement. Furthermore, I believe Utah Farm should be held liable for First Security's loss, given the actual notice it had of the claim. The fire insurance policy, issued contemporaneously with the 1972 mortgage loan, named Bill Shiew as the insured and First Security as an additional insured, in its capacity as the mortgagee. The policy also contained the following provision:

> Loss (if any) under this policy, on buildings only, shall be payable to the mortgagee(s) . . . under any present or future mortgage upon the property described in and covered by this policy, as interest may appear, and in order of precedence of said mortgages. . . .

Rather than performing its contractual obligation of paying the insurance proceeds to the insured (designated by the policy to be Bill Shiew and First Security), Utah Farm unilaterally decided to adjudicate the rights of the parties and issued two separate checks. Given its knowledge of the conflicting claims it should have been more circumspect. Having wrongfully paid insurance proceeds to Linda Shiew, Utah Farm was found to be jointly liable with the Shiews for the balance of the 1974 loan. Such a decision is legally sound and is supported by the evidence.

I would affirm the trial court's ruling and judgment.

CROCKETT, C. J., concurs in the dissent of HALL, J.

NOTES

1. *To what extent is a dragnet clause enforceable, and why?* Traditionally, courts have held that dragnet clauses are enforceable in theory.

Nevertheless, courts have often found a reason to construe a dragnet clause narrowly—as in *Shiew*, where the majority applied the so-called "same class" rule and held that a dragnet clause in a home mortgage did not cover later business loans. Like many courts, the *Shiew* majority justified its decision as carrying out the intention of the parties; note that the court concludes that there is "not a scintilla of evidence" that the parties intended for the cattle loans to be secured by the mortgage. Given the language of the dragnet clause, and the testimony quoted by the dissent, is such a conclusion appropriate?

One can defend the traditional judicial hostility to dragnet clauses more plausibly on policy grounds. Expansive enforcement of a dragnet clause could hamper the mortgagor's ability to use its equity in the mortgaged property to obtain future credit. Consider the situation in *Shiew*, and imagine that when the Shiews needed credit for their cattle operations, First Security Bank refused to make the loan. If the Shiews then went to Bank of America to get a loan, Bank of America would be unlikely to make the loan if it learned of the dragnet clause—for fear that in the future, First Security Bank might agree to loan more money to the Shiews and that the additional borrowing would "soak up" the equity in the Shiews' land because of the dragnet clause. As an expansive reading of a dragnet clause might give a lender like First Security Bank a virtual monopoly on the borrower's access to future credit, courts used narrow construction rules like the "same class" rule to protect a mortgagor's access to future credit.

Reflecting this concern, the Restatement provides that for future loans to be secured under a dragnet clause, "[t]he advances must be made in a transaction similar in character to the mortgage transaction, unless (1) the mortgage describes with reasonable specificity the additional type or types of transactions in which advances will be secured; or (2) the parties specifically agree, at the time of the making of the advances, that the mortgage will secure them." Restatement (Third) of Property (Mortgages) § 2.4(b) (1997). A large body of case law agrees. See, e.g., In re Wollin, 249 B.R. 555 (Bankr. D. Or. 2000) (motor vehicle loan agreement did not secure credit card debt); In re Ballarino, 180 B.R. 343 (D.Mass.1995) (home mortgage containing dragnet clause did not secure later business loan); Nelson, Whitman, Burkhart & Freyermuth, Real Estate Finance Law § 12.8, at 1111 & n.404 (6th ed.2015) (collecting cases).

Should it be possible for the mortgagor to waive these limitations in the clause itself? Suppose the clause provides that future loans shall be secured by the mortgage "regardless of whether or not this instrument is specifically referred to in the evidence of indebtedness executed by Mortgagors with regard to such future advances, and further regardless of whether or not such future advances may be for purposes related or unrelated to the purpose for which the original indebtedness secured hereby is loaned." In Union Nat'l Bank of Little Rock v. First State Bank & Trust Co., 16 Ark.App. 116, 697 S.W.2d 940 (1985), this language was found to be an effective waiver of the same-class rule. The court observed: "[n]or do we find merit in the argument that the second quoted provision was in 'fine print.' The print was no different from any of the other printed portion of the mortgage in issue."

A final caveat is in order. Personal property secured lenders have long used dragnet clauses in their security agreements, and the Uniform Commercial Code contemplates that courts should enforce such clauses in accordance with their terms. U.C.C. § 9–204(c) ("A security agreement may provide that collateral secures . . . future advances or other value, whether or not the advances or value are given pursuant to commitment."). Historically, many courts addressing personal property security disputes also manifested substantial disfavor for dragnet clauses, often applying the "same-class" rule. See, e.g., In re Blair, 26 B.R. 228 (Bankr. W.D. Tenn. 1982). In 1999, however, during comprehensive revision of Article 9, the drafters inserted the following language in the Official Comments to Section 9–204 in an attempt to moderate this hostility to dragnet clauses:

> Determining the obligations secured by collateral is solely a matter of construing the parties' agreement under applicable law. This Article rejects the holdings of cases decided under former Article 9 that applied other tests, such as whether a future advance or other subsequently incurred obligation was of the same or a similar type or class as earlier advances and obligations secured by the same collateral. [U.C.C. § 9–204, cmt. 5]

As time passes, it seems plausible that this Comment will influence courts to give broader interpretation to dragnet clauses in mortgages. See, e.g., In re Alaska Fur Gallery, Inc., 457 B.R. 764 (Bankr.D. Alaska 2011) (applying Comment to give broad construction to dragnet clause in commercial mortgage, but acknowledging that narrow construction might be warranted in consumer context); In re Becker, 415 B.R. 360 (E.D.Wis.2009) (noting Comment in holding that dragnet clause in home mortgage secured three subsequent business loans). See also In re Willie, 157 B.R. 623 (Bankr.M.D.Tenn.1993) (under Tennessee law, dragnet clause in mortgage for personal purposes caused it to secure later loan for business purposes); First Commonwealth Bank v. West, 55 S.W.3d 829 (Ky.Ct.App.2000) (dragnet clause in mortgage on home and business real estate secured later debt to purchase tractor-trailer). See generally Ryan A. Hackney, Ripping Holes in the Dragnet: The Failings of U.C.C. § 9–204(c) as Applied to Consumer Transactions, 87 Tex. L.Rev. 1249 (2009).

2. *Other court-made limitations on dragnet clauses.* The extended Osborne quote in the *Shiew* case points out a number of limitations courts frequently impose on enforcement of dragnet clauses. Here is one more. Suppose land is subject to a mortgage containing a dragnet clause. The original mortgagor sells the property to a grantee who assumes the mortgage. The grantee then incurs an unrelated debt to the mortgagee. Is that debt secured by the mortgage? See In re Barnard, 1 B.R. 640 (Bankr.M.D.Fla.1979) (no), *overruled by* Uransky v. First Fed. Sav. & Loan Ass'n of Fort Myers, 684 F.2d 750 (11th Cir.1982) (yes). The Restatement would not recognize this advance

as being secured; it provides: "If mortgaged real property is transferred, the mortgage will secure only advances made prior to the mortgagee's gaining actual knowledge of the transfer." Restatement (Third) of Property (Mortgages) § 2.4(c) (1997). Note that Section 2.4(c) also eliminates coverage of advances made to the original mortgagor after the lender learns that mortgagor has transferred the real estate to a grantee.

3. *Estoppel by payoff statement.* Suppose a lender whose mortgage contains a dragnet clause issues a payoff statement. The statement gives only the balance owing on the direct mortgage debt, and fails to mention the additional non-mortgage debt that is swept under the mortgage by its dragnet clause. One court held the lender estopped by such a statement; in effect, it had eliminated the effectiveness of its own dragnet clause! See Regions Bank v. Wachovia Bank, 248 B.R. 201 (Bankr.S.D.Ga.2000). Do you agree?

4. *Statutory limitations on dragnet clause coverage.* Many states have statutes governing mortgages for future advances. A table describing them is found in Restatement (Third) of Property (Mortgages) § 2.1 (1997). The statutes typically require that a maximum amount be stated in the mortgage, and deny priority for any advances over that amount. Under such a statute, the "other" indebtedness secured under a dragnet clause could not, when added to the outstanding balance still due under the mortgage note itself, exceed the stated maximum amount. See, e.g., Mark Twain Kansas City Bank v. Cates, 248 Kan. 700, 810 P.2d 1154 (1991).

About a dozen statutes contain a "cutoff notice" provision, under which the debtor may record and/or serve on the lender a notice to the effect that he or she no longer wishes the future advances clause to be effective. See, e.g., Mo.Ann.Stat. § 443.055; Fla.Stat.Ann. § 697.04; Nev.Rev.Stat. §§ 106.300 to 106.400. Advances or loans made previously will still continue to be secured by the mortgage, but advances made after the cutoff notice are not secured. This allows the mortgagor to "escape" from the dragnet clause whenever desired— thus responding to the policy concern highlighted in note 1. However, a mortgagor who is initially unaware of the dragnet clause's existence or meaning is unlikely to assert this right until it is "too late"—i.e., until after incurring a large amount of other debt which is swept under the mortgage by the dragnet clause.

The second type of dispute involves priority contests between a mortgagee whose mortgage contains a future advances or dragnet clause and an "intervening lienor." Consider the following example: In 2015, Mortgagor obtains a $100,000 loan from First Bank, granting First Bank a mortgage on Blackacre; the mortgage includes a future advances clause. In 2017, Mortgagor goes to Second Bank, obtains a $50,000 loan to pay her child's school tuition, and grants Second Bank a mortgage on Blackacre (which has a value of $200,000). In 2019, Mortgagor borrows an additional $150,000 from First Bank. In 2020, Mortgagor defaults to First Bank, which starts a judicial foreclosure at which Blackacre sells for $200,000. At the time of the sale, Mortgagor owed a total of $250,000 to First Bank and $50,000 to Second Bank. How should the court distribute the sale proceeds? [For purposes of this example, let's assume that both mortgages were timely recorded and the costs of the foreclosure sale were zero.]

First Bank will argue that it should receive all $200,000 of the sale proceeds, because it should have the same priority for the 2019 advance as it had for the original 2015 loan (i.e., its priority for the future advance should "relate back" to the original mortgage date). It will argue that the mortgage had a future advances clause in it, and Second Bank had constructive notice of this—so Second Bank should have known that the principal amount secured by the 2015 mortgage could increase due to later advances (and thus made the loan at its own risk). By contrast, Second Bank will argue that First Bank's priority should be limited to the amount owed to First Bank in 2017 when Second Bank made the second mortgage loan. It will argue that when First Bank made its future advance in 2019, it knew or should have known of Second Bank's intervening lien. On this theory, the priority stack would look something like an Oreo®, with Second Bank as the "cream" between First Bank's two "cookies"—i.e., First Bank would receive the first $100,000 in proceeds (assuming this was the amount owed to First Bank in 2017), Second Bank would receive the next $50,000, and First Bank would receive the final $50,000.

As the following materials demonstrate, states have taken very different approaches to this problem, so the correct answer varies with the state in which the land is located.

ROSENTHAL & ROSENTHAL, INC. V. BENUN
Supreme Court of New Jersey, 2016
226 N.J. 41, 140 A.3d 547

JUDGE CUFF (temporarily assigned) delivered the opinion of the Court. This appeal addresses the priority of mortgages given [by Vanessa Benun] to secure financing for a group of related commercial entities [the Jazz Entities]. A factor [Rosenthal & Rosenthal, Inc. (Rosenthal)] purchased accounts receivable, advanced funds to the commercial entities, and agreed to make optional future advances. The financing was secured by personal guaranties and mortgages on the home of a guarantor [Benun]. Each mortgage was capped at $1 million.

Before the factor made additional advances to the commercial entities, it received actual notice that a law firm [Riker, Danzig, Scherer, Hyland & Perretti, L.L.P. (Riker)] representing the principal of the commercial entities had obtained a mortgage on the home of [Benun] to secure payment of current and future legal fees.[2] Notwithstanding actual notice of the intervening mortgage, the factor advanced additional funds. Eventually, the commercial entities defaulted and filed a bankruptcy petition. [Benun] also defaulted. At that time, the amount of indebtedness to the factor and to the law firm far exceeded the value of the security.

The factor commenced an action to foreclose on the mortgages it held. Although [Benun] did not appear in the foreclosure action, the law firm appeared to contest the priority of the liens on the secured property. The law firm contended that the factor's prior liens securing any funds advanced by the factor after receipt of actual notice of the law firm's intervening lien were subordinated to the law firm's mortgage.

The law governing mortgages securing optional, sometimes referred to as discretionary, future advances in this State is well-settled. When a lender holds a mortgage that secures optional future advances, the prior lien loses priority for advances made after actual notice of an intervening mortgage. Although the common law rule and the mortgage-priority statutory scheme adopted by the Legislature have been criticized by commentators and differ from the law in other states, any fundamental alteration of the law governing the priority of mortgages is best addressed by the Legislature.

Here, it is undisputed that the factor had advance notice of the law firm's intervening lien but nonetheless proceeded to make optional advances to the commercial entities. Having done so, its mortgages securing those optional future advances were subordinated to the law firm's intervening lien. Accordingly, we affirm the judgment of the Appellate Division, holding that the law firm's intervening lien takes priority over optional advances made by the factor after it received actual notice of the intervening lien.

I.

. . . [After default,] Rosenthal filed a foreclosure complaint against Benun, her husband, and Riker. Benun and her husband did not respond, and Rosenthal requested that a default judgment be entered against them. Riker answered, disputing the priority of Rosenthal's mortgages. Later, both Rosenthal and Riker filed cross-motions for summary judgment regarding the priority of their respective mortgages.

The trial court granted Rosenthal's motion for summary judgment. The trial court determined that the dragnet clauses in the Rosenthal mortgages were fully enforceable. Turning to the priority issue, the trial court held that Riker's argument that its mortgage displaced the two

---

[2] Editors' Note: Benun executed the mortgage to Riker to secure the repayment of unpaid legal fees for services provided by Riker to the Jazz Entities in the amount of $1,679,701.33 in unpaid legal fees. Riker continued to provide services thereafter, and its unpaid legal bills increased to over $3 million.

Rosenthal mortgages was legally flawed because the firm accepted a mortgage on the property with knowledge of two prior mortgages, each securing an obligation of up to $1 million, and with knowledge of the anti-subordination clauses. The court concluded that there was no convincing justification for rewarding Riker—a subsequent mortgagee—a superior priority.

Riker appealed, and the Appellate Division reversed in a published opinion. *See Rosenthal & Rosenthal, Inc. v. Benun,* 441 N.J.Super. 184, 117 A.3d 191 (App.Div.2015). The Appellate Division concluded that the common law rules of priority placed Riker ahead of Rosenthal. The panel relied on the long-standing New Jersey rule governing future advance mortgages: when the future advance is optional, actual notice of an intervening lien will subordinate advances made after such notice is received. *Id.* at 190, 117 A.3d 191 (citing *Ward v. Cooke,* 17 N.J. Eq. 93, 99 (Ch.1864)).

This Court granted Rosenthal's petition for certification. We also permitted the New Jersey Bankers Association (NJBA) and the New Jersey Land Title Association (NJLTA) to appear as amici curiae.

II.

. . . NJBA highlights the important role that future advances play in the financial industry. It asserts that the Appellate Division's opinion will defeat the primary purpose behind the use of future advances in the banking industry—allowing "lenders to lend money at the pace often required in commercial transactions, *i.e.,* at the point of economic necessity."

NJBA contends that the Appellate Division's focus on Rosenthal's actual notice of Riker's mortgage overlooks that Riker had actual notice of the Rosenthal mortgage. NJBA argues that Riker should have expected its lien to be subordinate to Rosenthal's two earlier-recorded liens.

NJBA expresses concern about three possible outcomes that could follow from the Appellate Division's decision: (1) lenders may avoid future advance transactions because of the risk that intervening liens will destroy their bargained-for security; (2) lenders will avoid checking title before future advances because, if they do, they risk losing priority; and (3) lenders may be unable to meet the rapidly fluctuating capital needs of borrowers in commercial transactions because of the time it takes to negotiate subordination agreements with intervening lenders. In all those situations, NJBA says that the burden is improperly placed on the first lender, rather than on the intervening lender, who is a newcomer to an existing contractual relationship.

In sum, NJBA argues for a rigid first-in-time, first-in-right rule. According to that rule, a lender that has a recorded mortgage securing future advances up to a specified amount should be treated the same as a lender who advanced the entire loan amount at one time.

NJLTA takes no position on the arguments advanced by either Rosenthal or Riker, but urges the Court to look closely at this case to protect the integrity of the recording system. It maintains that the recording system is "best supported and maintained by a determination that one may rely on the record in determining the priority of advances made under a recorded mortgage."

III. . . .

The term "future advance" is interpreted broadly. It covers "all situations in which a mortgagor's obligation . . . is enlarged after the mortgage becomes effective." *Restatement (Third) of Property: Mortgages* § 2.1 cmt. a (1997). Although that occurs most often when a mortgage secures a future advance loan, "an obligation secured by a mortgage may accrue by virtue of circumstances other than a monetary advance." *Ibid.* A personal guaranty falls under that definition.

In the typical future advance mortgage, "the borrower gives the lender a note and mortgage for the entire loan amount, though the lender will not advance all the funds to the borrower until a future date." 2 Grant S. Nelson et al., Real Estate Finance Law § 12.7 at 263 (6th ed.2014). The mortgaged property "stands as security not only for the funds advanced at the time the mortgage is executed and delivered, but also for any obligations incurred after the initial advance." James B. Hughes, Jr., *Future Advance Mortgages: Preserving the Benefits and Burdens of the Bargain*, 29 Wake Forest L.Rev. 1101, 1102 (1994).

Future advance mortgages are widespread in the construction-loan context, where the property, and in turn the lender's security interest in it, becomes more valuable as the work moves forward, lessening the risk of disbursing additional funds. 2 Nelson, *supra*, § 12.7 at 263. Moreover, as in this appeal, such financing vehicles can be used to secure commercial financing devices, such as letters of credit, factoring agreements, or lines of credit with an institutional lender. *See id.* at 263–64. Whatever their use and whatever their form, future advance mortgages have "substantial" advantages for both the borrower and the lender. *Id.* at 264. The borrower carries interest only on the funds that are presently needed, avoiding the need to reinvest received yet presently unneeded capital, and "[b]oth parties avoid the expense and paperwork involved in refinancing the initial loan or executing a series of junior mortgages." *Ibid.* The lender, moreover, can ensure that the initial advances are being put to a proper use before providing more cash to a borrower. A construction lender, for instance, can verify that the work is progressing, that contractors are being paid, and that the project is on budget.

The critical issue posed by future advance mortgages, and the one highlighted in this appeal, is the priority of a subsequent mortgage on the property obtained by intervening parties after the first mortgagee's initial advance but before future advances. That issue is of heightened importance when the value of the mortgaged property is insufficient to cover the outstanding principal of both mortgage loans. There are, broadly speaking, two considerations that bear on the priority issue: (1) whether the first mortgagee's subsequent advances were optional or obligatory; and (2) whether the first mortgagee had notice, either actual or constructive, of the intervening mortgage. *See* Hughes, *supra*, 29 Wake Forest L.Rev. at 1103. Under the traditional common law rule, if the advances are obligatory, the first mortgagee retains priority for all advances over all subsequent mortgagees, regardless of whether the first mortgagee had notice of an intervening lien. *Id.* at 1115–16. But if the advances are optional, then the first mortgagee retains priority only for advances made before the mortgagee had notice—usually actual notice—of the second, intervening mortgage. *Ibid.; see also* Grant S. Nelson & Dale A. Whitman, *Rethinking Future Advance Mortgages: A Brief for the Restatement Approach*, 44 Duke L.J. 657, 668–69 (1995).

The policy guiding that rule is straightforward—to protect the borrower "so that she can borrow from other lenders and can sell the property." 2 Nelson, *supra*, § 12.7 at 270. If optional advances were to retain priority over subsequent mortgages, the borrower would be doubly mistreated. The borrower "could not demand the contemplated additional loan funds[,]" because, again, they are made at the lender's discretion. Nor could she "obtain financing from another lender, because no one will lend on security that will be reduced or eliminated if the first mortgagee decides to make subsequent advances." Vesting the first mortgagee with priority, even over optional advances, thus creates the risk that the borrower will have substantial, but unavailable, equity.

The calculus changes, so the reasoning goes, when the advances are obligatory. Then the borrower "has a legal right" to the lender's performance, lessening the risk of stagnant equity. *Ibid.* Even if the lender fails to perform because the borrower has become too great a credit risk, "obtaining financing elsewhere normally will be unlikely." *Ibid.*

That explanation for the optional/obligatory and notice/no-notice distinctions undergirds much of the law governing future advance mortgages. The traditional common law rule "protects the mortgagor from being placed in the awkward and unfair position of being unable to use the real estate as security for additional financing, though it has value well in excess of the existing mortgage debt." *Ibid.* A number of states follow that approach through judicially crafted common law. *See, e.g., Idaho First Nat'l Bank v. Wells*, 100 Idaho 256, 596 P.2d 429, 433 (1979) (stating that Idaho follows "general rule in the United States" that if future advance "is optional, and if the mortgagee has notice when the advance is made that a subsequent creditor has acquired an interest in the land, then the advance loses its priority to that creditor" (citation omitted)); *Bank of Ephraim v. Davis,* 559 P.2d 538, 540–41 (Utah 1977) ("[A]n advance made pursuant to a mortgage to secure future advances which the mortgagee was not obligated to make . . . is subordinate in lien to an encumbrance intervening between the giving of the mortgage and the making of the advance, if the advance was made with actual notice or knowledge of the intervening encumbrance."); *Daniels v. Elks Club of Hartford,* 192 Vt. 114, 58 A.3d 925, 934 (2012) (noting that judicial decisions have long recognized optional/obligatory advance distinction). Other states have recognized the rule by statute. *See, e.g.,* 735 Ill. Comp. Stat. 5/15–1302 (stating that, with some exceptions, optional future advances "advanced or applied more than 18 months after a mortgage is recorded . . . shall be a lien as to subsequent purchasers and judgment creditors only from the time such monies are advanced or applied"); Me. Stat. tit. 9–B, § 436(1)(B) ("The priority of . . . future advances shall not include any future optional advances secured by such mortgage made by such institution after any such person, in addition to acquiring such subsequent right or lien, sends to the institution . . . express written notice[.]"); Neb.Rev.Stat. § 76–238.01(3)(b)(ii) ("If any optional future advance is made . . . after receiving written notice of the filing for record of any trust deed, mortgage, lien, or claim against such mortgaged real property, then the amount of such optional future advance shall be junior to such trust deed, mortgage, lien, or claim."); Vt. Stat. Ann. tit. 27, § 410(b)(3)(B) (stating that optional future advances take priority "to the extent of future advances that are outstanding before the mortgagee receives written notice of the intervening interest").

For the most part, New Jersey law tracks those common law distinctions, focusing on whether the subsequent advances were optional or obligatory and whether the first mortgagee had notice of the intervening mortgage. In *Ward, supra,* 17 N.J. Eq. at 99, the court held that a future advance mortgage "is entitled to priority over subsequent encumbrances, for all advances made prior to notice of the subsequent encumbrance." Only actual notice, not record or constructive notice, would suffice. . . .

In *Lincoln Federal Savings & Loan Ass'n v. Platt Homes, Inc.,* 185 N.J.Super. 457, 466–67, 449 A.2d 553 (Ch.Div.1982), the trial court permitted subordination of optional future advances secured by a prior mortgage to an intervening mortgage based on constructive rather than actual notice of the intervening lien, but limited the rule to construction loans. The bank advanced a portion of the funds committed for the project, retaining the right to make optional future advances. Before the bank advanced the second installment of construction financing, a third party loaned money to the builder and obtained a mortgage on the real property. The bank and the third party promptly recorded their respective mortgages contemporaneously with the advance of funds. The builder defaulted on both loans.

Although the bank lacked actual notice of the third party's mortgage, the trial court declined to follow the common law rule, holding that "constructive notice of intervening liens is sufficient to defeat the priority position of a construction mortgagee as to optional future advances." *Id.* at 463–67, 449 A.2d 553. The court reasoned that the bank should be charged with constructive notice of the intervening mortgage because it had been recorded before the bank made its second advance and that notice defeated the priority of the bank as to optional future advances. The court justified the departure from the prevailing common law rule because the construction lender can protect its interest by conducting a search prior to each advance and declining to make additional advances if it discovered intervening liens.

The trial court, however, limited the scope of its holding to the construction-loan context, explaining that it "cannot apply in general commercial loan situations, where commitments to make future advances may be secured by rapidly fluctuating collateral, such as inventory, accounts receivables or the like, with a mortgage on real property taken as side collateral only." *Id.* at 467 n. 5, 449 A.2d 553. In those cases, the future advance lender's priority in the other collateral, the collateral that is not real property, is protected by the Uniform Commercial Code. *Ibid.* (citing N.J.S.A. 12A:9–312(5) and (7)). That lender can therefore "make subsequent advances without each time having, as a condition of protection, to check for filings later than his." *Ibid.* (quoting Comment 5 to N.J.S.A. 12A:9–312(5) and (7)). . . .

IV.

The starting point for our resolution of the priority contest between Rosenthal and Riker is the common law rule. The general rule that a mortgage given to secure future advances retains its priority over a subsequent encumbrance only if the future advance is mandatory or if the prior mortgagee did not have actual notice of the intervening lien was established in *Ward*. That rule remains in effect except as altered by *Lincoln Federal* for construction loans.

Rosenthal's reliance on this exception in *Lincoln Federal* is misplaced because the trial court observed that its holding—that constructive notice of intervening liens was sufficient to defeat priority—could not apply to more fluid financing schemes, such as Rosenthal's factoring agreement. In fact, *Lincoln Federal* acknowledged that an optional advance made in the non-construction lending context following constructive notice only would retain the priority of the earlier mortgage. Here, however, Rosenthal had actual notice and made subsequent advances notwithstanding that notice.

We also reject Rosenthal's argument that the law of future advance mortgages does not apply to this case because the two mortgages obtained from Benun secured her personal guaranty rather than a direct loan to one of the Jazz Entities. The term future advance is defined broadly, covering "all situations in which a mortgagor's obligation . . . is enlarged after the mortgage became effective." *Restatement, supra,* § 2.1 cmt. a. Guaranty agreements fall under the umbrella of that definition, especially guaranty agreements that secure a future advance loan. Because the personal guaranty that secured the mortgages could, and did, expand after the mortgage became effective, the law that governs future advance mortgages controls. . . .

The common law rule governing future advance mortgages remains in force in this State. To be sure, there are policy reasons identified by Rosenthal and amici that question the continuing value of the common law rule and advocate for a rule that eliminates any ambiguity and fosters uniformity of interpretation and application, such as the *Restatement.* The common law rule also has been the subject of scholarly criticism. *See, e.g.,* Hughes, *supra,* 29 Wake Forest L.Rev. at 1125 ("[T]here should be a strictly defined rule to govern priority in future advance situations, but the present rule which relies upon the optional/obligatory distinction is simply not justified."); Robert Kratovil & Raymond J. Werner, *Mortgages for Construction and the Lien Priorities Problem—The "Unobligatory" Advance,* 41 Tenn.L.Rev. 311 (1974) (arguing that traditional optional/ obligatory test, as applied to construction context, impedes development); Matthew Lilly, Comment, *Subrogation of Mortgages in California: A Comparison with the Restatement and Proposals for Change,* 48 UCLA L.Rev. 1633, 1652 (2001) ("While encouraging future loans is sound public policy, making a distinction between optional and obligatory advances creates a cure that is often more onerous than the disease."); Nelson & Whitman, *supra,* 44 Duke L.J. at 659–60 (arguing that common law approach to priority of mortgages to secure future advances "has proved inadequate and should be discarded").

A number of states have modified or discarded the common law rule. Some states have statutorily redefined "notice" to include only written notice. *See, e.g.,* Me. Stat. tit. 9–B, § 436(1)(B) ("The priority of . . . future advances shall not include any future optional advances secured by such mortgage made by such institution after any such person, in addition to acquiring such subsequent right or lien, sends to the institution . . . express written notice[.]"); Neb.Rev.Stat. § 76–238.01(3)(b)(ii) ("If any optional future advance is made . . . after receiving written notice of the filing for record of any trust deed, mortgage, lien, or claim against such mortgaged real property, then the amount of such optional future advance shall be junior to such trust deed, mortgage, lien, or claim."); Vt. Stat. Ann. tit. 27, § 410(b)(3)(B) (stating that optional future advances take priority "to the extent of future advances that are outstanding before the mortgagee receives written notice of the intervening interest"). Some states have adopted a cutoff notice scheme. *See, e.g.,* Mo.Rev.Stat. § 443.055(6) (stating that mortgagor may give written notice that he "elects to terminate the operation of the instrument as security for future advances"); Nev.Rev.Stat. § 106.380(1) ("A borrower may at any time [give] written notice to the lender stating that the borrower elects to terminate the operation of an instrument as security for future advances[.]"). And some states have abolished the optional/obligatory distinction. *See, e.g.,* N.M. Stat. Ann. § 48–7–9 ("Every mortgage . . . may secure future advances and the lien of such mortgage shall . . . have priority from the time of recording as to all advances, whether obligatory or discretionary, made thereunder[.]"); Or.Rev.Stat. § 86.155(2) (stating that as to "principal advances made any time pursuant to the credit agreement," lien "shall have priority, regardless of the knowledge of the lienholder of any intervening lien, as of its date of recording . . . whether the advances are optional or obligatory advances").

Amici have also advanced persuasive reasons for departing from the common law rule. Where, however, the common law rule governing priority of optional future advances has been codified by statute, any plea to fundamentally alter the rule is best addressed to the Legislature.

V.

In sum, the law permits an intervening lender to insert itself into an existing contractual relationship and achieve priority over an earlier lender who retained the option to advance further funds. The rule grew out of a concern that a prior lender could preclude a borrower from obtaining capital to meet the needs of its business. The circumstances attendant to the execution of the mortgage in favor of Riker are akin to the need for financing to continue business operations under more favorable terms. Here, without some security to cover mounting legal fees, the Jazz Entities may not have been able to obtain legal representation to further their business operations.

Applying the well-settled law concerning the priority of a mortgage securing optional future advances against an intervening lienholder to the facts of this appeal is straightforward. Rosenthal does not dispute that its advances under the factoring agreements were optional. Nor does it dispute that it had actual notice of Riker's mortgage on the Benun property. Once Rosenthal had actual notice of Riker's intervening mortgage and continued to make advances to the Jazz Entities, it subjected itself to the common law priority rules. The amount that Rosenthal now claims has priority over the Riker mortgage was not only advanced at Rosenthal's discretion but also advanced after actual notice of Riker's mortgage. Those sums are therefore subordinated to the Riker mortgage. . . .

The judgment of the Appellate Division is affirmed.

NOTES

1. *Three approaches to the future advances priority problem.* The *Rosenthal* case reflects the traditional common law approach, often referred to as the "optional/obligatory" rule. If the mortgagee is obligated to make a future advance, the advance shares the mortgage's original priority (i.e., the advance is treated for priority purposes as if it had been made at the time of the mortgage), and will thus take priority over an intervening lien creditor. By contrast, if the advance was optional and the mortgagee knew that the intervening lien had arisen before making the advance, as in *Rosenthal*, the optional advance has priority only as of the date it is made. The common law rule continues to apply in approximately one-third of jurisdictions. Despite its ostensible justification (protecting a mortgagor's access to credit):

> [T]he common law rule has proved to be spectacularly confusing in practice. Its application is fraught with problems. There has been seemingly endless litigation about applying the distinction between optional and obligatory advances, particularly in the context of construction lending. More litigation has arisen over the sort of knowledge or notice on the part of the senior lender that is sufficient to cause a loss of priority for the advance. Is actual knowledge required or is constructive notice from the public records enough? If the intervening lien was a mechanic's lien, what sort of knowledge about the lien would result in loss of priority? Indeed, since the purpose of the doctrine is to facilitate junior mortgage borrowing, should it even apply to mechanics liens? In sum, there is sufficient uncertainty about how and when the common law rule is to be applied that only the rare junior lender would be willing to rely upon it. [R. Wilson Freyermuth & Dale A. Whitman, Residential Mortgage Default and the Constraints of Junior Liens, 57 U. Louisville L. Rev. 207, 216–17 (2019)]

The second approach is reflected in the Restatement, which rejects the common law rule and provides that if the mortgage explicitly secures future advances, then "all advances have the priority of the original mortgage"— without regard to whether those advances were optional or obligatory. Restatement (Third) of Property (Mortgages) § 2.3(a) (1997). No state courts have adopted the Restatement approach as a matter of the state's common law, but roughly fifteen states have enacted this approach by statute. See, e.g., Mo.Rev.Stat. § 443.055(5) ("As to any third party who may acquire or claim any rights in or a lien upon the encumbered real property, the priority of the lien of a security instrument securing future advances or future obligations shall date from the time the security instrument is recorded, whether or not any third party has actual notice of any such advances or obligations and whether or not such advances or obligations are optional or obligatory with the lender."). To protect the mortgagor's ability to obtain financing, these statutes allow the mortgagor to give a "cutoff notice" to the mortgagee. If the mortgagee makes a future advance to the mortgagor after receiving a cutoff notice, the mortgagee's priority for that advance will not relate back to the date of the mortgage, but will be determined by the date of the advance. See id. § 443.055(8). These statutes also typically require that a mortgage covering future advances must state explicitly the maximum principal balance that the mortgage can secure; advances that extended the principal balance beyond that stated cap would not receive relation-back priority. See id. § 443.055(2). Can you explain why this approach provides greater predictability for a junior mortgage lender?

A third approach is to give all future advances (whether optional or obligatory) the priority of the original mortgage, but without providing a "cutoff notice" procedure. Roughly one-third of the states have adopted this approach by statute, although many of these statutes apply only to construction loans and/or to "open-end" mortgages (like home equity lines of credit). See, e.g., Conn.Gen.Stat.Ann. § 49–3 (construction loans only); Mich.Comp. Laws Ann. § 565.902 (applicable to all types of mortgages containing future advances clause); N.Y. Real Prop. Law § 281 (credit line mortgages only). This approach provides the greatest predictability for the future advances lender, but does not address the problem of the mortgagor who has equity in the land but no way to borrow against it if the future advances lender refuses to make advances. Is this problem significant enough to worry about? See James B. Hughes, Jr., Future Advance Mortgages: Preserving the Benefits and Burdens of the Bargain, 29 Wake Forest L.Rev. 1101 (1994).

Ironically, the Restatement and several of the statutes after which it was patterned probably will not allow the mortgagor to issue a cutoff notice for a construction loan. As the Restatement provides, the mortgagor cannot issue a cutoff notice if "a termination or subordination of advances would unreasonably jeopardize the mortgagee's security for advances already made." The idea here is that a half-finished building is not worth one-half of the value of a finished building. Thus, a borrower who completes part of the work and issues a cutoff notice might never find the funds to complete the project, leaving the original construction lender seriously undersecured. Of course, a court might recognize the validity of a cutoff notice on a construction loan if the borrower provided satisfactory assurances to the lender that the project would be completed with funds from other sources. [Note also that even if the cutoff notice is effective, the borrower's refusal to borrow the remaining funds may breach the borrower's loan commitment or loan agreement, giving rise to potential damages liability.]

Does the Restatement approach expect too much lawmaking of the courts? Is recognition of a cutoff notice procedure in a state that does not statutorily provide for it beyond the appropriate authority of the judge? The common law optional/obligatory rule was developed by courts; may they not just as well invent or adopt a better approach? See Grant S. Nelson & Dale A. Whitman, Rethinking Future Advance Mortgages: A Brief for the Restatement Approach, 44 Duke L.J. 657 (1995).

2. *Advances to protect security.* Suppose that a mortgagee whose mortgage covers future advances spends $50,000 to pay real estate taxes and insurance premiums on the mortgaged property after the mortgagor failed to pay them in a timely fashion. The mortgagee is not obligated to make such advances, so it may be tempting to characterize these as "optional" advances. Nevertheless, even in states following the common law rule, advances such as these—which protect the mortgagee's security—have the same priority as the original mortgage loan. See Southern Trust Mortg. Co. v. K & B Door Co., 104 Nev. 564, 763 P.2d 353 (1988); Gerald L. Blackburn, Mortgages to Secure Future Advances, 21 Mo.L.Rev. 209 (1956); Restatement (Third) of Property (Mortgages) § 2.2(b) (1997).

3. *The optional/obligatory distinction and the mortgagee's failure to use loan agreement protections.* In many future advance mortgages, the loan documents will contain preconditions that the borrower must satisfy to obtain a future advance. In a construction loan, these preconditions are often extensive, and may include (for example) requirements that the mortgagor provide documentation evidencing that contractors and subcontractors have been paid for completed work. Such preconditions provide important protection against the risk of a construction lender having to make an advance on a project when progress does not justify that advance. The mere existence of such preconditions does not make future advances optional, as long as the mortgagee is obligated to make advances if the mortgagor satisfies the preconditions. See, e.g., Dempsey v. McGowan, 722 S.W.2d 848 (Ark.1987); Irwin Concrete, Inc. v. Sun Coast Props., Inc., 33 Wash.App. 190, 653 P.2d 1331 (1982). By contrast, if the lender retains the discretion whether to make an advance despite satisfaction of the preconditions, the advance is optional. See, e.g., National Bank of Washington v. Equity Investors, 81 Wash.2d 886, 506 P.2d 20 (1973).

Suppose that First Bank holds a mortgage given by Mortgagor to finance construction of a building on Blackacre. The construction mortgage requires Mortgagor to provide paid receipts for all completed work, but First Bank makes an advance without actually demanding to see paid receipts for work completed during the prior two months. In a state following the common law rule, would First Bank have priority for that advance over an intervening lienholder? Compare J. I. Kislak Mortg. Corp. v. William Matthews Builder, Inc., 287 A.2d 686 (Del.Super.Ct.1972), aff'd, 303 A.2d 648 (Del.1973) (where lender made advances without obtaining documentation required by construction loan agreement, advances were optional and lost priority) with Home Lumber Co. v. Kopfman Homes, Inc., 535 N.W.2d 302 (Minn.1995) (waiver of conditions by construction lender did not make advances optional). Should it matter in this situation whether the mortgagor could have satisfied the requirements if the construction lender had insisted? Why or why not?

4. *What constitutes notice?* As noted above, a further problem with the common law rule is determining when the future advances lender has "notice" that another lien has "attached" to the land. Whether "notice" exists can present different problems depending on the nature of the intervening lien. For

example, if the intervening lien is a mechanics' lien, when does the lender have "notice"? (a) When it knows the work has been done or materials have been supplied? (b) When it knows payment to the potential lienor has not been made? (c) When it knows that the mortgagor is in default to the potential lienor? (d) When it knows that the potential lienor is claiming a lien or has filed a lien notice? (e) When it has constructive notice from the filing of a lien notice in the appropriate records? The cases are divided. The majority view appears to be that the lender must have actual knowledge that the lien exists. *See, e.g.*, In re Johnson, 124 B.R. 648 (Bankr.E.D.Pa.1991); National Bank of Waterloo v. Moeller, 434 N.W.2d 887 (Iowa 1989); Drilling Serv. Co. v. Baebler, 484 S.W.2d 1 (Mo.1972); Grider v. Mutual Fed. Sav. & Loan Ass'n, 565 S.W.2d 647 (Ky.Ct.App.1978). Other courts treat constructive notice as sufficient. *See, e.g.*, Lincoln Fed. Sav. & Loan Ass'n v. Platt Homes, Inc.,185 N.J.Super. 457, 449 A.2d 553 (1982); J.I. Kislak Mortg. Corp., *supra* note 3. Some statutes require that the mechanics' lien claimant give written notice to the lender. Ohio Rev. Code § 5301.232.

If the competing junior lien is another mortgage, should the recording of the junior mortgage provide constructive notice to the senior? Should a future advance lender that has not received actual notice of an intervening lien have a duty to search the records prior to making a future advance? Why or why not? See, e.g., Bank of Ephraim v. Davis, 559 P.2d 538 (Utah 1977); Aaron E. Michel, Note, *Capital Mortgage Service Co. v. Southard*: A Change in Policy Concerning the Priority of Advances Over Intervening Liens in Protecting Mortgages, 9 Cap.U.L.Rev. 383 (1979).

5.   *Priority of future advances under home equity loans.* If the lender under a home equity line of credit is obligated to permit the borrower to draw on the line of credit at any time, the priority of the lender for those future advances is probably beyond question. But if the lender has too much discretion to cease making advances, future advances might be deemed optional and potentially subordinate to intervening liens. Several states have adopted statutes to protect lenders against this possibility. See, e.g., Mont.Code Ann. § 71–1–206; N.Y. Real Prop. Law § 281. While these statutes were enacted primarily with homeowner-mortgagors in mind, they may also apply to commercial lines of credit secured by real property as well.

6.   *Priority: mechanic's lien vs. construction mortgage.* If a construction lender uses sufficient care to record its construction mortgage before any work commences on the mortgaged land, it can usually preserve the priority of its mortgage against mechanic's liens in most jurisdictions. *See, e.g.*, GHB Constr. & Dev. Co., Inc. v. West Alabama Bank & Trust, 290 So.3d 793 (Ala.2019). This situation is highly unsatisfactory to mechanic's lien claimants because foreclosure of the construction mortgage will eliminate their liens, and leave them with only the tenuous hope that the foreclosure sale will generate some surplus proceeds to which their liens can attach. This hope is particularly tenuous because the construction lender is often the only bidder at the sale, and it rarely will bid more than it is owed.

Recognizing this dilemma, several states have provided the "stop notice" as an alternative means of recovery for mechanic's lienors. Under stop notice statutes, a mechanic's lienor (usually excepting the general contractor) may make a claim on any undisbursed construction funds in the hands of the lender and, under some statutes, of the borrower. This remedy is perhaps most fully developed in California, Cal.Civ.Code §§ 8500–60, but is also available in Alabama, Indiana, Mississippi, North Carolina, Rhode Island, Texas, and Washington.

In Missouri, courts have held that where a construction mortgagee can be said to have induced contractors or subcontractors to have furnished work or materials (such as by earmarking loan proceeds for the purpose of paying construction draws), the construction lender waives its priority as to mechanic's liens arising out of the development even if that work had not commenced at the time the construction mortgage was recorded. See, e.g., H.B. Deal Constr. Co. v. Labor Discount Center, Inc., 418 S.W.2d 940 (Mo.1967); Dave Kolb Grading, Inc. v. Lieberman Corp., 837 S.W.2d 924 (Mo.Ct.App.1992). For further discussion, see Chapter Nine, Section C2.

E. REPLACEMENT, MODIFICATION, AND REFINANCING OF SENIOR MORTGAGES: IMPACT ON JUNIOR LIENORS

Suppose that First Bank holds a recorded mortgage that covers both Blackacre and Whiteacre, while Second Bank holds a later-recorded mortgage that covers Blackacre. Now suppose that Mortgagor sells Whiteacre, and First Bank agrees to release its lien on Whiteacre in exchange for a partial prepayment of the loan. In that transaction, Mortgagor executes and First Bank records a new mortgage covering only Blackacre. After the transaction, someone reviewing the land records might be tempted to conclude that Second Bank's mortgage now has temporal priority over First Bank's new mortgage. As the following materials explain, such a conclusion would be premature and likely incorrect.

SOVEREIGN BANK V. GILLIS

Superior Court of New Jersey, Appellate Division, 2013
432 N.J.Super. 36, 74 A.3d 1

SABATINO, J.A.D. This appeal concerns whether a refinancing lender that discharges its own previous mortgage and issues another mortgage loan for a higher amount, and which simultaneously pays off the balance owed on a junior lienor's line of credit without having it closed, can rely upon equitable principles to maintain its priority over that junior lienor. This question of priority arises here in a context in which the borrowers, after obtaining the refinancing, drew additional funds on the line of credit and then defaulted on both the refinanced mortgage loan and the line of credit.

Applying principles of replacement and modification recognized in the Restatement (Third) of Property—Mortgages (1997) ("the Third Restatement"), we reverse the trial court's decision allowing the junior lienor that extended the line of credit to vault over the priority of the refinancing mortgage lender. We consequently direct the trial court, on remand, to determine the proper extent of the refinancing lender's priority, in an amount that avoids material prejudice to the junior lienor. . . .

The essential facts are substantially undisputed. On May 28, 1998, defendants Joseph and Eulalia Gillis ("the Gillises") borrowed $650,000 from Washington Mutual Bank, FA ("WaMu") to finance the purchase of a residential property in Warren Township. The mortgage loan had a thirty-year term through June 2028, with an adjustable interest rate initially set at 6.625%. WaMu secured the May 1998 loan with a purchase-money mortgage, which was recorded in the first position of priority.

Subsequently, in December 1998, the Gillises obtained a home-equity line of credit from Broad National Bank, secured by a mortgage recorded in the second position. In October 2001, the Gillises obtained additional funding from Crown Bank, NA ("Crown"), secured by a mortgage recorded in the third position.

On March 18, 2003, the Gillises obtained yet another home-equity line of credit, this time from Independence Community Bank ("Independence"), for the sum of $500,000, also secured by a mortgage. As a condition of closing, Independence required that the proceeds from the funds borrowed on the line of credit be used to discharge the two preexisting debts that the Gillises held with Broad and Crown. The amount remaining after the discharge (i.e., $58,252.58) was applied to pay down a portion of the outstanding purchase-money mortgage with WaMu, which at the time had a principal balance of about $534,000. Both the Broad and Crown mortgages were discharged shortly thereafter the payoff. Consequently, the March 18, 2003 line of credit with Independence stood in a second lien position behind the May 1998 WaMu purchase-money mortgage.

In January 2005, the Gillises sought to refinance their existing mortgage loans. To that end, they borrowed $1.19 million from WaMu, secured by another mortgage on their property ("the WaMu refinanced mortgage") dated January 13, 2005. The WaMu refinanced mortgage loan had a thirty-year term through February 2035, with an adjustable interest rate initially set at 4.027%. The WaMu refinanced mortgage was recorded on January 31, 2005. The principal amount from this refinancing was used to pay off the Gillises' remaining debt of $482,023.67 that the original May 1998 WaMu purchase-money mortgage secured, as well as the remaining debt of $499,921.93 that the Independence line of credit mortgage secured. . . .

For reasons that are not clear from the appellate record, WaMu failed to obtain written authorization from the Gillises to close out the Independence line of credit. Consequently, the mortgage on that line of credit was not discharged of record, despite an alleged intent to do so. The WaMu refinanced mortgage was instead recorded behind the Independence line of credit mortgage, which remained a lien of record even though the balance on that loan existing at the time of the January 2005 refinancing had been paid off by WaMu in full.

Thereafter, the Gillises continued to borrow funds under the Independence line of credit, starting on February 14, 2005 and continuing at least until August 15, 2006. Ultimately, however, the Gillises defaulted on both the WaMu refinanced mortgage loan and the Independence line of credit.

Pursuant to a January 2010 assignment, appellant Deutsche Bank National Trust Company ("Deutsche Bank") began holding the WaMu refinanced mortgage as the Trustee for WaMu Mortgage Pass Through Certificates, WAMU 2005–AR9. In addition, the mortgage on the Independence line of credit was assigned to respondent Sovereign Bank ("Sovereign").

In January 2010, Deutsche filed a foreclosure action in the Chancery Division against the Gillises on the defaulted WaMu refinanced mortgage. Sovereign likewise filed a foreclosure action in the Chancery Division in October 2010 on the defaulted line of credit. The trial court jointly managed the two foreclosure actions, but did not consolidate them. Consequently, the parties litigated their dispute under the caption of Sovereign Bank's foreclosure action.

Deutsche moved for summary judgment against Sovereign, arguing that, based upon equitable principles, the WaMu refinanced mortgage loan had priority over the Independence line of credit. Deutsche argued that the WaMu refinanced mortgage should be granted priority over the Independence line of credit mortgage under the doctrine of equitable subrogation because the debt on the line of credit existing at the time of the refinancing had been paid in full and was, in any case, intended to be discharged.

Sovereign cross-moved for summary judgment against Deutsche, conversely maintaining that the Independence line of credit, which had been recorded first, had priority over the WaMu refinanced mortgage loan. Among other things, Sovereign argued that the doctrine of equitable subrogation cannot be invoked to give the WaMu refinanced mortgage priority over the Independence line of credit because WaMu had actual knowledge of that pre-existing and recorded line of credit when the refinancing occurred. Sovereign further argued that because the line of credit had not been properly closed and that because the Gillises had subsequently withdrawn additional funds on it, the Independence mortgage should instead maintain priority over the WaMu refinanced mortgage.

Upon considering the lenders' competing arguments, the trial court granted summary judgment to Sovereign and held that the Independence line of credit has priority over the WaMu refinanced mortgage. In its written decision, the court applied case law instructing that a new mortgagee is not entitled to equitable subrogation if it "possesses actual knowledge of the prior encumbrance." First Union Nat'l Bank v. Nelkin, 354 N.J.Super. 557, 565–66, 808 A.2d 856 (App.Div.2002). Because WaMu obviously had such actual knowledge of the Independence line of credit when it paid off the balance on that loan in January 2005 as part of the refinancing, the court concluded that WaMu could not equitably maintain any priority over the Independence loan.

On appeal, Deutsche urges that we reverse the trial court and grant it an equitable remedy of priority, despite WaMu's admitted awareness of the Independence loan at the time of the refinancing. Deutsche contends that the "actual knowledge" exception recognized in *Nelkin* and other case law, at least as applied in these circumstances, unfairly bestows a windfall upon the original junior lienor, Independence, and its assignee, Sovereign. Deutsche argues that the actual knowledge principle wrongfully penalizes a refinancing lender such as WaMu that knowingly pays down a junior debt in full.

As part of its arguments, Deutsche relies upon principles of equity set forth in the Third Restatement, including comment (e) to Section 7.6, which states that "where a mortgage loan is refinanced by the same lender, a mortgage securing the new loan may be given the priority of the original mortgage under the principles of replacement and modification of mortgages." Because we endorse that approach, we reverse the trial court's decision and remand for further proceedings to determine the appropriate extent of appellant's priority. . . .

[Editors' Note: The court's discussion of whether a refinancing lender with actual knowledge of an intervening lien should be equitably subrogated to the priority of the refinanced mortgage is omitted. We focus on this issue in the context of third-party financing beginning on page 883.]

. . . [T]here is an alternative method for analyzing and resolving the priority question before us. Specifically, because the refinanced mortgage loan in 2005 was provided by the same lender—WaMu—as the original 1998 senior mortgage loan, the priority analysis can be guided by principles of "replacement" and "modification." . . .

In this present distinct context of modification and replacement, we conclude that the critical question of priority must revolve around whether the junior lienor, here Sovereign, has been materially prejudiced. As Section 7.3 of the Third Restatement provides as to replacement:

(a) If a senior mortgage is released of record and, as part of the same transaction, is *replaced* with a new mortgage, the latter mortgage *retains the same priority* as its predecessor, except

(1) to the extent that any change in the terms of the mortgage or the obligation it secures is *materially prejudicial* to the holder of a junior interest in the real estate, or

(2) to the extent that one who is protected by the recording act acquires an interest in the real estate at a time that the senior mortgage is not of record. [Emphasis added.]

Similar principles apply if the refinancing causes a modification of the original loan, as set forth in Section 7.3(b) and (c):

(b) If a senior mortgage or the obligation it secures is *modified* by the parties, the mortgage as modified *retains priority* as against junior interests in the real estate, except to the extent that the modification is *materially prejudicial* to the holders of such interests and is not within the scope of a reservation of right to modify as provided in Subsection (c).

(c) If the mortgagor and mortgagee reserve the right in a mortgage to modify the mortgage or the obligation it secures, the mortgage as modified retains priority even if the modification is *materially prejudicial* to the holders of junior interests in the real estate, except as provided in Subsection (d). [Emphasis added.]

We regard this as a sound approach. A proper judicial analysis of material prejudice will examine such aspects as the respective loan amounts involved, the interest rates, and, potentially the loan terms.[13] Actual or constructive knowledge by the refinancing lender, if it is the same original lender or its corporate successor, should be irrelevant. Consequently, summary judgment entered here in favor of Sovereign, which was predicated on a finding of WaMu's actual knowledge, must be reversed as a matter of law. To do otherwise would allow Sovereign to reap an undeserved windfall, particularly since WaMu paid off not only its original mortgage but also paid down in full the balance on the Independence line of credit.

That said, the priority of Deutsche, as WaMu's assignee, must be equitably calibrated to take into account the fact that the $1.19 million in

---

[13] Without resolving the issue conclusively, we tend to agree with the Third Restatement that an extension of the loan term in the refinanced loan is not likely to cause material prejudice to a junior lienor because the refinancing usually is staving off foreclosure on the senior loan.

refinancing provided by WaMu in 2005 exceeded the balance then due on WaMu's original $650,000 loan from 1998. A pro tanto "cap" on the new loan's priority appears to be appropriate in this respect, though we do not decide in the abstract on this record whether the cap should be (1) the original $650,000 loan amount, (2) the $534,000 balance at the time of the Independence loan in 2003, or (3) the roughly $482,000 balance when the refinancing occurred in 2005. Although the refinanced loan was extended at a lower interest rate than the 1998 loan, an analysis of the comparative adjustable rates also may have equitable implications.

We defer these equitable considerations to the trial court on remand, directing that the court evaluate these (and any other identified) matters of potential "material prejudice" to Sovereign, and then to ascertain an appropriate priority amount for Deutsche's lien that comports with these principles. . . .

NOTES

1. *Replacement of senior mortgages: impact on junior interests.* Replacement mortgages can arise in different contexts, but perhaps arise most frequently in construction lending. Often the construction lender for a project also becomes the permanent lender. Upon completion of construction, the construction lender will release the construction mortgage of record and either immediately or shortly thereafter record a permanent or "long term" mortgage. This will occur even though the original construction mortgage obligation remained unsatisfied. Once the construction mortgage is released of record, the intervening lienholders (e.g., holders of judgment liens, mechanic's liens or mortgage liens) may assert opportunistically that after the replacement transaction, they have been promoted in priority and are now senior to the permanent mortgage based on order of recording.

Normally, this assertion by the junior interests will be fruitless. The *Gillis* court articulates the pervasive rule that a senior mortgagee who discharges its mortgage of record and takes and records a replacement mortgage nevertheless retains the priority of the original mortgage, except to the extent that any change in the terms of the mortgage or the obligation it secures is materially prejudicial to the holder of the junior interest. What type of "material prejudice" must exist to trigger a loss of priority? There is one obvious situation where priority should be lost. Suppose that First Bank releases its construction mortgage *before* recording its permanent mortgage, and during the interim the borrower grants another mortgage to Second Bank, which does not know that First Bank has not been fully repaid. Here Second Bank's mortgage will enjoy priority over the replacement mortgage because of the operation of the recording acts. Restatement (Third) of Property (Mortgages) § 7.3(a)(2) (1997).

Putting aside this rather easy example, in what other situations will there be a loss of priority?

(a) *Extension of time for payment of the senior debt.* Generally, where the replacement mortgage extends the due date for repayment of the indebtedness, the extension is not deemed to create "material prejudice" and therefore no loss of priority occurs. Comment b to Restatement § 7.3 explains:

> There is a strong presumption under this section that a time extension on a senior mortgage or obligation, standing alone, is not materially prejudicial to intervening interests. A finding of material prejudice is justified only in the rare situation where the time extension can fairly be said to place the junior interest in substantially weaker position. The typical junior lienholder is normally grateful to have a time extension forestall the destruction of its lien by a senior foreclosure.

Can you articulate circumstances under which a time extension would "place the junior interest in a substantially weaker position"? Might a three-year time extension for repayment of a senior mortgage debt, granted in 2008, have materially prejudiced a junior mortgagee? If so, how?

(b) *Increase of principal balance of the senior debt.* Where the replacement mortgage secures an increased principal amount, there may be a loss of priority vis-a-vis junior interests. See, e.g., Skaneateles Savings Bank v. Herold, 50 A.D.2d 85, 376 N.Y.S.2d 286 (1975). If the original mortgage did not secure future advances, and the replacement mortgage secures an increased principal amount, the intervening lienholder is prejudiced to the extent of the increase in the principal balance. Can you explain why? By contrast, if the original mortgage secured future advances, under what circumstances (if any) would the intervening lienholder suffer prejudice as a result of the replacement transaction?

(c) *Increase in interest rate.* Where the replacement transaction results in an increase in the interest rate, an intervening lienholder can be materially prejudiced. Can you explain why? If the replacement transaction increases the interest rate by 2%, in what precise ways can this prejudice the intervening lienholder?

Can the mortgagee attempt to avoid the risk of potential subordination by including language in the replacement document that it represents a continuation and not a payment and discharge of the original debt and mortgage, and that no subordination to junior interests is intended? See Nelson, Whitman, Burkhart & Freyermuth, Real Estate Finance Law § 9.4 (6th ed.2015).

2. *Modification of senior mortgages: impact on junior interests.* It is common for a mortgagee and the mortgagor to agree to a variety of modifications in the terms of the mortgage or its obligation. Note that here, there is no "new" replacement mortgage. The original mortgage remains of record and the modifications are reflected in an amendment agreement (usually recorded). Often a modification arises because the mortgagor is in financial distress and the modification agreement is part of a "workout." In

other cases, the mortgagor will be financially healthy and the modifications may simply reflect business needs or changes in market conditions. Whatever the cause of such modifications, the priority questions they create are largely the same as in the replacement mortgage context, and the overwhelming weight of case authority applies comparable analysis. The senior mortgagee will be entitled to the same priority for the modified mortgage as for the original mortgage, except to the extent that the modification is materially prejudicial to the holder of an intervening junior interest. See, e.g., Shultis v. Woodstock Land Dev. Assocs., 188 A.D.2d 234, 594 N.Y.S.2d 890, 892 (1993); Burney v. McLaughlin, 63 S.W.3d 223 (Mo.Ct.App.2001); Shane v. Winter Hill Fed. Sav. & Loan Ass'n, 397 Mass. 479, 492 N.E.2d 92, 95 (1986). If the senior mortgagee fails to obtain the consent of the intervening lienholder to a prejudicial modification, the senior risks having its lien subordinated to the extent of the material prejudice. Shultis, 594 N.Y.S.2d at 892.

Consistent with this view, Restatement § 7.3(b) provides that "[i]f a senior mortgage or the obligation it secures is modified by the parties, the mortgage as modified retains priority as against junior interests in the real estate, except to the extent that the modification is materially prejudicial to the holders of such interests. . . ." A determination of when material prejudice occurs is a fact-specific inquiry. As discussed in the preceding note, a court would be unlikely to find material prejudice where the modification of the senior mortgage was merely an extension of time for payment. Restatement (Third) of Property (Mortgages) § 7.3 cmt. b (1997); Lennar Northeast Partners v. Buice, 49 Cal.App.4th 1576, 57 Cal.Rptr.2d 435 (1996).

By contrast, where the modification involves an increased interest rate and/or an increase in the principal amount of the indebtedness, a court is more likely to find material prejudice to the junior lienholder and grant the junior lienholder priority over the earlier mortgage to the extent of the modification. Restatement (Third) of Property (Mortgages) § 7.3 cmt. c (1997); Shultis, supra. Can you explain why? Suppose that the senior mortgage is a 30-year amortizing mortgage with an original principal balance of $120,000 and an original interest rate of 10%. Now suppose that the mortgagor defaults when the outstanding balance of the senior mortgage debt has been reduced to $100,000. After six months of negotiations, the mortgagor and senior mortgagee agree to modify the senior mortgage debt, restating the principal balance at $105,000 (i.e., to "capitalize" the $5,000 in unpaid interest that accrued during their negotiations) and increasing the interest rate to 12%. If this modification occurred without the consent of the junior lienholder, is the junior lienholder materially prejudiced by the modification? If so, how would you calculate the extent to which the junior lienholder was materially prejudiced? What additional information, if any, would you need to obtain to make this calculation? See R. Wilson Freyermuth & Dale A. Whitman, Residential Mortgage Default and the Constraints of Junior Liens, 57 U. Louisville L.Rev. 207, 226–233 (2019).

Courts sometimes suggest that a modification of a senior mortgage can be so substantial that complete loss of priority will result. See, e.g., Lennar

Northeast Partners and *Shultis, supra.* Suppose, for example, the modification of the senior mortgage obligation is so substantial that there is no value left in the real estate to secure the junior lien. Can you think of other similar situations?

3. *Senior mortgage language reserving the right to modify.* Can the mortgagee avoid these priority risks by thoughtful drafting techniques? Suppose the original mortgage contains the following language: "All those claiming by, through or under the mortgagor consent to any extensions, amendments, modifications, or alterations of the mortgage obligation agreed to by the mortgagor and mortgagee and their successors, including those that increase the principal amount or interest rate." Under the Restatement, this language is effective against junior interests. See Restatement (Third) of Property (Mortgages) § 7.3(c) (1997). Is this good policy? For the view that such a provision should be unenforceable, see Robert Kratovil & Raymond J. Werner, Mortgage Extensions and Modifications, 8 Creighton L.Rev. 595, 610 (1975). See generally Robert P. Giesen, "Routine" Mortgage Modifications: Lenders Beware, 17 Real Estate L.J. 221 (1989).

One concern expressed by Kratovil and Werner is that the enforcement of such mortgage language may prevent a mortgagor from obtaining junior mortgage financing (because of the potential for later modification of the senior mortgage). The Restatement addresses this concern in the same way it does the similar concern presented by future advances mortgages; it permits the mortgagor to issue a "cut-off notice" to the mortgagee that terminates the right to modify conferred by such a provision in the senior mortgage. Restatement (Third) of Property (Mortgages) § 7.3(d). Once the mortgagor provided the cut-off notice, any future modifications are governed by the "material prejudice" standard. Id. cmt. e.

Refinancing of senior mortgage by new lender. Suppose Jones owns Blackacre subject to a recorded first mortgage in favor of First National Bank and a recorded second mortgage in favor of State Savings Bank. Jones decides to refinance her first mortgage with a new lender, Regional Mortgage, to get the benefit of a favorable interest rate. In the process of the refinancing, Jones uses the loan proceeds obtained from Regional Mortgage to pay off the balance owed to First National Bank. Jones executes a new mortgage on Blackacre to Regional Mortgage, which records it promptly. First National Bank's mortgage is released of record.

Several months later, Jones loses her job and soon thereafter defaults to both Regional Mortgage and State Savings Bank. Both lenders institute foreclosure proceedings. Having paid off First National Bank's mortgage (which unquestionably had priority over the State Savings Bank mortgage) through the refinancing, Regional Mortgage argues that it should be subrogated to the priority First National Bank would have enjoyed prior to the refinancing (i.e., that it should "step into the shoes" of First National

Bank for priority purposes). By contrast, State Savings Bank argues that it now has priority under the recording acts, because it now holds the first-recorded mortgage of record. So which lender is entitled to priority? Should it matter whether Regional Mortgage knew or should have known of the existence of the State Savings Bank mortgage? Should the intent of Regional Mortgage at the time of the refinancing be relevant?

HOUSTON V. BANK OF AMERICA FEDERAL SAVINGS BANK

Supreme Court of Nevada, 2003
119 Nev. 485, 78 P.3d 71

PER CURIAM. . . . . Appellants, Edward R. Houston and Regina Houston, paid David Boone $740,000 for investment services. Boone converted the $740,000 to his own use. Shortly thereafter, on May 13, 1998, Boone and his wife Donna divorced. Pursuant to their property settlement agreement, Boone quitclaimed to Donna the real property located at 2100 Marina Bay Court, Las Vegas, Nevada (the property). At the time of the divorce, Norwest Mortgage, Bank of America's predecessor, held a deed of trust on the property for approximately $342,000.

On May 14, 1998, the Houstons filed a complaint against Boone to recover their $740,000. On June 1, 1998, the Houstons filed a notice of lis pendens on the property in the Clark County Recorder's Office. The Houstons also filed an ex parte motion for an order directing the issuance of a prejudgment writ of attachment, which the district court granted. Early on June 26, 1998, the writ of attachment was filed in the Clark County Recorder's Office. Ultimately, the Houstons obtained a judgment against Boone for $740,000. Boone filed for bankruptcy, but eventually stipulated that the money he owed the Houstons was a nondischargeable debt. The district court granted the Houstons a writ of execution on the property and scheduled a sale of the property. Bank of America intervened and the sale was enjoined.

Bank of America had refinanced the property for Donna on June 26, 1998, after the Houstons' writ of attachment was recorded. Bank of America had hired Nevada Title Company to perform a title search of the property, which was conducted on May 29, 1998, over a month before the refinancing.

After the district court enjoined the sale, both Bank of America and the Houstons filed motions for summary judgment. Bank of America argued that it held the priority lien on the property because it succeeded to the rights of Norwest. The Houstons contended, among other things, that Bank of America was negligent in failing to discover their interest in the property and that they would suffer an injury if the district court allowed Bank of America to succeed to Norwest's priority position. However, the Houstons did not provide the district court with the terms of the former deed of trust or any other evidence of prejudice. The district court granted summary judgment in favor of Bank of America and denied the Houstons' motion for summary judgment. The Houstons appeal. . . .

Equitable subrogation permits "a person who pays off an encumbrance to assume the same priority position as the holder of the previous encumbrance."[4] We have previously applied the doctrine of equitable subrogation, but not in the context presented by this case.[5] Other jurisdictions have adopted three different approaches[6] in determining whether to apply equitable subrogation under circumstances in which a third party held a lien on the property at the time the second lender paid off the former encumbrance.

The first approach, which a majority of states follow, is that actual knowledge of an existing lien precludes the application of equitable subrogation, but constructive knowledge does not.[8] The reasoning underlying this approach is that if a mortgagee did not possess actual notice of a junior lien holder, the mortgagee expected to step into the shoes of the previous creditor it had paid off.[9] In our view, however, this rule promotes willful ignorance; it encourages prospective mortgagees to avoid conducting title searches. Under this approach, if a prospective mortgagee performs a title search and discovers a junior lien holder, it will be barred from being subrogated. However, if a prospective mortgagee forgoes conducting a search, which would have uncovered a junior lien holder, and puts on blinders, it nevertheless will be subrogated. Thus, we decline to adopt this approach.

The second approach bars the application of equitable subrogation when a lien holder possesses either actual or constructive notice of an existing lien.[10] However, precluding equitable subrogation when a

---

[4]   *Mort v. U.S.*, 86 F.3d 890, 893 (9th Cir.1996).

[5]   *See, e.g., Laffranchini v. Clark*, 39 Nev. 48, 55–56, 153 P. 250, 251–52 (1915) (concluding that the holder of an invalid mortgage was not a volunteer, and thus, entitled to be equitably subrogated to the priority position of the lender whose loan it had paid).

[6]   Although there are generally three approaches the courts have adopted, some courts refuse to adopt a bright-line rule and simply consider constructive or actual knowledge as a factor in weighing the equities. *See, e.g., East Boston Sav. Bank v. Ogan*, 428 Mass. 327, 701 N.E.2d 331, 335 (1998) (refusing to adopt a bright-line rule regarding subrogee knowledge).

[8]   *Osterman v. Baber*, 714 N.E.2d 735, 739 (Ind.Ct.App.1999) (recognizing that the majority of jurisdictions hold that actual knowledge bars equitable subrogation, but constructive notice does not, but declining to adopt the majority view); *Rusher v. Bunker*, 99 Or.App. 303, 782 P.2d 170, 172 (1989) (acknowledging that the weight of authority is that constructive knowledge alone does not preclude equitable subrogation); *Restatement (Third) of Property: Mortgages* § 7.6 cmt. e (1997); *see, e.g., U.S. v. Baran*, 996 F.2d 25, 29 (2d Cir.1993) (applying New York law); *Dietrich Industries, Inc. v. U.S.*, 988 F.2d 568, 572 (5th Cir.1993) (applying Texas law); *Brooks v. Resolution Trust Corp.*, 599 So.2d 1163, 1165 (Ala.1992); *Smith v. State S & L Ass'n*, 175 Cal.App.3d 1092, 223 Cal.Rptr. 298, 301 (1985); *United Carolina Bank v. Beesley*, 663 A.2d 574, 576 (Me.1995); *Enterprise Bank v. Federal Land Bank*, 139 S.C. 397, 138 S.E. 146, 148–50 (1927).

[9]   George E. Osborne, *Mortgages* § 282, at 573 (2d ed.1970).

[10]   *See Harms v. Burt*, 30 Kan.App.2d 263, 40 P.3d 329, 332 (2002); *see also Independence One Mortg. v. Katsaros*, 43 Conn.App. 71, 681 A.2d 1005, 1007–08 (1996). Additionally, some courts

mortgagee discovered or could have discovered a junior lien holder runs contrary to the purposes underlying the doctrine. Equitable subrogation is an equitable remedy to avoid a person's receiving an unearned windfall at the expense of another. If there were no subrogation, a junior lien holder would be promoted in priority, giving that creditor/lien holder an unwarranted and unjust windfall. Neither negligence nor constructive notice of an existing lien is relevant as to whether the junior lien holder will be unjustly enriched or prejudiced. The "basis for subrogation in [the mortgage] context is the lender's justified expectation of receiving [a] security" interest in the property.[13] Even a lender with knowledge of an existing lien on the property ordinarily expects to step into the shoes of the creditor it paid off. Therefore, we also decline to adopt this approach.

The third approach, the view adopted by section 7.6 of the Restatement (Third) of Property: Mortgages, disregards actual or constructive notice if the junior lien holder is not prejudiced.[15] Under the Restatement, a mortgagee will be subrogated when it pays the entire loan of another as long as the mortgagee "was promised repayment and reasonably expected to receive a security interest in the real estate with the priority of the mortgage being discharged, and if subrogation will not materially prejudice the holders of intervening interests in the real estate."[16] Because the Restatement approach is the most persuasive, we adopt the view expressed by it.

Under the Restatement, notice of an intervening lien is not necessarily pertinent to whether a party should be subrogated, and a party can be subrogated even if the party possessed actual knowledge of the other lien

---

hold a sophisticated party to a higher standard in determining whether to apply equitable subrogation. *See, e.g., Universal Title Ins. Co. v. U.S.*, 942 F.2d 1311, 1317 (8th Cir.1991) (noting that "Minnesota courts impose stricter standards on professionals than lay persons in assessing whether mistakes are 'excusable' for purposes of the doctrine of legal subrogation"). Also, other courts hold that negligence in discovering an existing encumbrance bars equitable subrogation or at least consider a party's negligence in determining whether to apply equitable subrogation. *See Bankers Trust Co. v. U.S.*, 29 Kan.App.2d 215, 25 P.3d 877, 882 (2001); *Landmark Bank v. Ciaravino*, 752 S.W.2d 923, 929 (Mo.Ct.App.1988); *USLife Title Ins. Co. of Dallas v. Romero*, 98 N.M. 699, 652 P.2d 249, 252 (N.M.Ct.App.1982); *Kim v. Lee*, 145 Wash.2d 79, 31 P.3d 665, 671–72, as corrected, 43 P.3d 1222 (Wash.2001). However, in a number of these cases negligence merely appears to be another rationale for holding that constructive notice bars equitable subrogation. *See, e.g., Kim*, 31 P.3d at 671–72.

[13] 2 Grant S. Nelson & Dale A. Whitman, *Real Estate Finance Law* § 10.6, at 15–16 (4th ed. 2002).

[15] *See Suntrust Bank v. Riverside Nat. Bank*, 792 So.2d 1222, 1227 n. 3 (Fla.Dist.Ct.App.2001) (citing section 7.6 of the Restatement to support its decision that negligence in failing to discover an existing lien does not preclude the application of equitable subrogation as long as the existing interest does not suffer prejudice); *see also Trus Joist Corp. v. Nat'l Union Fire Ins. Co.*, 190 N.J.Super. 168, 462 A.2d 603, 609 (1983) (subrogating mortgagee notwithstanding its possessing actual knowledge of an existing intervening interest), *overruled on other grounds by Trus Joist Corp. v. Treetop Associates, Inc.*, 97 N.J. 22, 477 A.2d 817 (1984); *Klotz v. Klotz*, 440 N.W.2d 406, 407–10 (Iowa Ct.App.1989) (subrogating party to senior lien position despite party's having actual knowledge of junior lien holder). These latter two cases do not adopt the Restatement, but their holdings are similar to the Restatement view.

[16] *Restatement (Third) of Property: Mortgages* § 7.6(a)(4).

holder.[17] Pursuant to the Restatement, "[t]he question in such cases is whether the payor reasonably expected to get security with a priority equal to the mortgage being paid."[18] Further, "[a] refinancing mortgagee should be found to lack such an expectation only where there is affirmative proof that the mortgagee intended to subordinate its mortgage to the intervening interest."[19]

The Restatement reasons that an intervening lien holder will not be materially prejudiced by the application of equitable subrogation because the intervening lien holder will remain in the same position. The Restatement notes that "[t]he holders of intervening interests can hardly complain about this result, for they are no worse off than before the senior obligation was discharged."[21] Subrogation will not be granted if it would result in injustice or prejudice to an intervening lienor.

In this case, Bank of America fully paid off the former deed of trust on the property held by Norwest. In the district court's order granting Bank of America's motion for a preliminary injunction, it found that Bank of America paid off the entire former mortgage "with the intention and belief that it would acquire Norwest Mortgage's first-position deed of trust lien on the Property." Further, the record does not contain any evidence that Bank of America intended to subordinate its mortgage to the Houstons.[23]

The Houstons argue that there are issues of fact as to whether they will be prejudiced by the equitable subrogation of Bank of America to the priority lien position. Yet the Houstons did not produce any evidence that they would be prejudiced by equitably subrogating Bank of America, nor did they request time to produce such evidence. Both parties agree that Bank of America's loan is $5,000 more than the Norwest deed of trust, and therefore Bank of America is not entitled to equitable subrogation with regard to the $5,000 increase in its loan.

The mortgagor changed from Boone and Donna, to Donna alone, but the Houstons did not offer any evidence that this change prejudiced them. The Houstons did not show that Donna has a poor credit rating, makes so little money, or has so few assets that Bank of America will likely have to foreclose on the property, resulting in the Houstons' loss of their interest in the property. The Houstons did not provide the district court with the previous loan's terms to compare with the new loan's terms to determine if

---

[17]   *Id.* § 7.6 cmt. e.

[18]   *Id.*

[19]   *Id.*

[21]   *Id.* § 7.6 cmt. a.

[23]   The Houstons maintain that Bank of America should not be equitably subrogated to the priority position because it negligently failed to discover the lis pendens and writ of attachment the Houstons filed. Alternatively, they contend that there are issues of fact as to whether Bank of America was reasonable in relying on a twenty-seven day old title report. However, since we adopt the Restatement view, Bank of America's negligence in discovering the lis pendens and writ of attachment or its knowledge thereof is irrelevant.

there were modifications that materially prejudice the Houstons. Because there is no evidence in the record that the Houstons will be in a worse position than if Bank of America did not pay off the Norwest deed of trust, the district court did not err by granting Bank of America's motion for summary judgment and denying the Houstons' motion.

We affirm the judgment of the district court.

NOTES

1. *Should constructive notice of an intervening lien prevent subrogation?* As noted above, a few states have held that equitable subrogation is not available to a refinancing lender with constructive notice of an intervening lien. Consider the reasoning of the Wyoming Supreme Court in accepting this view:

> Having considered our statute and the cases from other states in which courts have applied equitable subrogation in the context of mortgage re-financing, we decline to adopt the Restatement. Unlike the trend in other courts, we are not persuaded any manifest injustice results from applying the express language of § 34–1–121 and adhering to the clear legislative intent that lien priority in Wyoming is to be determined by the date of recording. Here, the AWB mortgage was recorded in 1997, the First National Bank mortgage was recorded in 2002 and Countrywide's mortgage was recorded in 2003. Countrywide knew of the existence of First National Bank's lien before it extended the loan to the Ketchams. Thus, Countrywide knew First National Bank had a prior recorded lien on the property when it executed the 2003 mortgage. Countrywide was charged with knowing Wyoming is a "first in time" jurisdiction. We are charged with the duty of giving effect to the statutes our legislature has enacted. Where the language of a statute is plain and unambiguous and conveys a clear and definite meaning, the court has no right to look for and impose another meaning, but has the duty to give full force and effect to the legislative product. Contrary to Countrywide's assertion, it had no reason to expect under Wyoming law that its 2003 mortgage would be given priority over First National Bank's 2002 mortgage. Although Countrywide makes the policy argument that equitable subrogation will make refinancing more readily available to the public and thereby, serves the public interest, those arguments are properly directed to the legislature. In addition, the primary purpose of our recording statute is to secure certainty of title. *Condos v. Trapp*, 717 P.2d 827, 832 (Wyo.1986). This countervailing public policy interest in clarity and certainty in matters of land title arguably outweighs the interests of private lending institutions which can be protected by simple due diligence.

> As this Court stated in *Wyoming Bldg. & Loan Ass'n*, 269 P. at 48, equitable subrogation is "a creation of the court of equity, and is

given when otherwise there would be a manifest failure of justice." "It is a mode which equity adopts to compel the ultimate payment of a debt by one who in justice, equity and good conscience ought to pay it, though it is not exercised in favor of a mere intermeddler." *Id*. These factors, which may compel application of the doctrine of equitable subrogation in other contexts, simply are not present in the case of a mortgagee who agrees to refinance a prior mortgage. In this context, the mortgagee does not pay the debt (or extend the loan) because "in justice, equity and good conscience he ought to pay it." Nor in the context of mortgage re-financing does the mortgagee pay the debt because, as in *Gaub*, he must do so in order to protect his own interest. To the contrary, the mortgagee who refinances a prior mortgage more closely resembles a volunteer or intermeddler in whose favor courts have not been inclined to apply equitable subrogation. In our view equitable subrogation simply has no application where a financial institution extends a loan for the purpose of enabling a mortgagor to pay off an existing mortgage, knowing that a subordinate lien exists on the real estate. Other mechanisms are available for a re-financing lender to obtain first priority without invoking equity to achieve that result.

Countrywide Home Loans, Inc. v. First Nat'l Bank of Steamboat Springs, 144 P.3d 1224 (Wyo.2006). Does rejecting the Restatement approach *really* promote the integrity of the state's recording act? On what basis could First National Bank (the intervening lienholder) have reasonably expected to have priority, given that it knew or should have known it was in a subordinate lien position at the time it took its mortgage?

Note that Countrywide (the refinancing lender) could have avoided this priority problem through careful planning. It could have conditioned its willingness to make a refinancing loan on First National Bank's execution and delivery of a subordination agreement (i.e., an agreement acknowledging First National Bank's lien would be subordinate to the Countrywide refinancing lien). Alternatively, Countrywide could have taken an express assignment of the AWL note and mortgage, rather than having the AWL mortgage released of record. If Countrywide could have avoided the problem so easily, should the court be sympathetic to Countrywide's subrogation argument?

From a transaction cost perspective, perhaps so. When a mortgage is refinanced, it is customary for the refinancing lender, as a condition of making the loan, to obtain a new mortgagee's title insurance policy, the cost of which is borne by the borrower. The average cost of this title insurance to the refinancing homeowner on a $130,000 new mortgage is currently approximately $400. The cumulative cost nationally to homeowners runs in the billions of dollars annually, particularly during periods when large numbers of owners refinance because of falling interest rates. One of the major reasons a refinancing mortgagee requires title insurance is to be protected against the risk that intervening liens or other interests in real estate that may have been created since the original mortgage was recorded will have priority over the new refinancing mortgage. We have argued that the pervasive adoption of the Restatement approach has the potential to reduce or eliminate the title insurance company's risk in this situation. Would title insurers be forced by market pressures to pass the benefit of this reduced risk to homeowners in the form of substantially lowered title insurance premiums? See Grant S. Nelson & Dale A. Whitman, Adopting Restatement Mortgage Subrogation Principles: Saving Billions of Dollars for Refinancing Homeowners, 2006 B.Y.U. L.Rev. 305.

2. *Material prejudice to the intervening lienholder.* Even under the Restatement approach, the refinancing lender's priority would typically be limited to the balance of the original mortgage being refinanced. If the refinancing is a "cash-out" refinancing, where the lender is advancing additional funds to the borrower beyond the sum needed to pay off the original mortgage, the refinancing lender's lien would be subordinate to the extent of the additional amount. The "material prejudice" analysis in this context is comparable to the analysis in the replacement and modification context.

3. *Expanding subrogation to new purchasers.* Suppose a home or other real estate is sold and the proceeds of a loan from the purchaser's lender are used to pay off the seller's prior senior mortgage. As part of this transaction, the prior senior mortgage is released and the purchaser's lender records a new mortgage. Suppose the new lender or its title insurer fails to discover a pre-existing lien. Should that lien be promoted in priority? Or should subrogation protect the new mortgagee? Generally subrogation has not been available because it is assumed to apply only to debts incurred by the original debtor. However, the Massachusetts Supreme Court has adopted a broad, "no-fault" Restatement view of subrogation:

> Because we find that the equities are substantially similar in refinancing and sales transactions, and that application of equitable subrogation to a sale is consistent with our precedent, we hold that equitable subrogation applies in this case. . . . [T]he distinction between a sale and a refinancing exists, but subrogation arising out of either context yields the same result.

East Boston Sav. Bank v. Ogan, 428 Mass. 327, 701 N.E.2d 331, 335–36 (1998). As in the refinancing context, lenders to new home purchasers always require a separate title insurance policy insuring the priority and validity of its mortgage. The premium for this policy is usually paid for by the new home purchaser. Would pervasive adoption of the Restatement subrogation approach substantially reduce this cost to purchasers?

Suppose that the new purchaser does not obtain institutional financing but instead pays the purchase price in cash, part of which is used to pay off the seller's mortgage. If the purchaser later discovers the intervening lien, can the purchaser be equitably subrogated to the lien of the paid-off mortgage and thus claim priority over the intervening lien creditor? See, e.g., Sourcecorp, Inc. v. Norcutt, 229 Ariz. 270, 274 P.3d 1204 (2012).

F. FIXTURES

This section deals with the difficult problems of priorities that arise when otherwise moveable chattels (e.g., furnaces, machinery, central air conditioning, silos or grain bins) are annexed to real estate so as to become "fixtures." Although the problems are complex and varied, one of the most common fact situations involves a conflict between the seller or third party lender who takes a purchase money security interest in the chattel and a mortgagee who holds a mortgage on the real estate. Until the adoption of the Uniform Commercial Code, such problems were handled in a dozen or so states by section 7 of the Uniform Conditional Sales Act and elsewhere by the common law or by other specific state statutes. See Nelson, Whitman, Burkhart & Freyermuth, Real Estate Finance Law § 9.6 (6th ed.2015).

Today, all 50 states have enacted Article 9 of the Uniform Commercial Code, which addresses fixture priority questions in section 9–334. The following excerpts provide an overview of the rules by which Article 9 resolves priority disputes between a real estate mortgagee and a person holding an Article 9 security interest in an item that has become a fixture.

NELSON, WHITMAN, BURKHART & FREYERMUTH, REAL ESTATE FINANCE LAW
§ 9.7, at 910–913 (6th ed.2015)*

. . . [C]onflicts may arise between a creditor holding a claim against a fixture under personal property law (e.g., Article 9) and a creditor holding a claim against fixtures under real property law. The purpose of the UCC fixture provisions is to specify the order of priority in these disputes, based on state law definitions of what is a fixture.[154] In theory, there was no intent to promulgate a uniform definition of fixtures which would encroach upon local realty laws. Thus, much of the pre-UCC case law regarding whether a good has become a fixture remains relevant.[156] Two reasons were asserted for perpetuating this local law: (1) the generalized nature of a uniform law was inadequate to meet the needs of diverse local

---

*   Reprinted with permission of LEG, Inc. d/b/a West Academic.

[154] See, e.g., White and Summers, Uniform Commercial Code § 25.5 (6th ed.); In re Shelton, 35 B.R. 505, 508–509 (Bankr. E.D. Va. 1983).

[156] See, e.g., Alamosa Nat. Bank v. San Luis Valley Grain Growers, Inc., 756 P.2d 1022, 7 U.C.C. Rep. Serv. 2d 285 (Colo. App. 1988); Sears, Roebuck & Co. v. Bay Bank & Trust Co., 537 So. 2d 1041 (Fla. 1st DCA 1989); Community Bank of Homestead v. Barnett Bank of the Keys, 518 So. 2d 928, 5 U.C.C. Rep. Serv. 2d 239 (Fla. 3d DCA 1987); C.I.T. Financial Services v. Premier Corp., 1987 OK 101, 747 P.2d 934 (Okla. 1987); Courtright Cattle Co. v. Dolsen Co., 94 Wash. 2d 645, 619 P.2d 344 (1980); Wyoming State Farm Loan Bd. v. Farm Credit System Capital Corp., 759 P.2d 1230, 7 U.C.C. Rep. Serv. 2d 243 (Wyo. 1988); In re Black, 95 B.R. 223 (Bankr. N.D. Ala. 1988); Matter of Farrier, 61 B.R. 950, 1 U.C.C. Rep. Serv. 2d 1379 (Bankr. W.D. Pa. 1986); In re Shelton, 35 B.R. 505 (Bankr. E.D. Va. 1983); In re Boden Mining Corp., 11 B.R. 562, 33 U.C.C. Rep. Serv. 1550 (Bankr. S.D. W.Va. 1981); In re Avery, 7 B.R. 28 (Bankr. D. S.C. 1980); White and Summers, supra note 1 at 1055.

circumstances; and (2) laws pertaining to traditionally unique real property were deeply entrenched; a wholesale attempt at displacement would simply have caused omission of the fixture provisions from states' enactments of the UCC.

To maximize understanding of the ensuing topics, the fixture provisions of the Revised Article 9 are set out below.[158]

---

[158] The full text of the fixtures provision of Revised Article 9 is as follows:

§ 9–334. Priority of Security Interests in Fixtures * * *

(a)   **[Security interest in fixtures under this article.]** A security interest under this article may be created in goods that are fixtures or may continue in goods that become fixtures. A security interest does not exist under this article in ordinary building materials incorporated into an improvement on land.

(b)   **[Security interest in fixtures under real-property law.]** This article does not prevent creation of an encumbrance upon fixtures under real property law.

(c)   **[General rule: subordination of security interest in fixtures.]** In cases not governed by subsections (d) through (h), a security interest in fixtures is subordinate to a conflicting interest of an encumbrancer or owner of the related real property other than the debtor.

(d)   **[Fixtures purchase-money priority.]** Except as otherwise provided in subsection (h), a perfected security interest in fixtures has priority over a conflicting interest of an encumbrancer or owner of the real property if the debtor has an interest of record in or is in possession of the real property and: (1) the security interest is a purchase-money security interest; (2) the interest of the encumbrancer or owner arises before the goods become fixtures; and (3) the security interest is perfected by a fixture filing before the goods become fixtures or within 20 days thereafter.

(e)   **[Priority of security interest in fixtures over interests in real property.]** A perfected security interest in fixtures has priority over a conflicting interest of an encumbrancer or owner of the real property if: (1) the debtor has an interest of record in the real property or is in possession of the real property and the security interest: (A) is perfected by a fixture filing before the interest of the encumbrancer or owner is of record; and (B) has priority over any conflicting interest of a predecessor in title of the encumbrancer or owner; (2) before the goods become fixtures, the security interest is perfected by any method permitted by this article and the fixtures are readily removable: (A) factory or office machines; (B) equipment that is not primarily used or leased for use in the operation of the real property; or (C) replacements of domestic appliances that are consumer goods; (3) the conflicting interest is a lien on the real property obtained by legal or equitable proceedings after the security interest was perfected by any method permitted by this article; or (4) the security interest is: (A) created in a manufactured home in a manufactured-home transaction; and (B) perfected pursuant to a statute described in Section 9–311(a)(2).

(f)   **[Priority based on consent, disclaimer, or right to remove.]** A security interest in fixtures, whether or not perfected, has priority over a conflicting interest of an encumbrancer or owner of the real property if: (1) the encumbrancer or owner has, in an authenticated record, consented to the security interest or disclaimed an interest in the goods as fixtures; or (2) the debtor has a right to remove the goods as against the encumbrancer or owner.

(g)   **[Continuation of paragraph (f)(2) priority.]** The priority of the security interest under paragraph (f)(2) continues for a reasonable time if the debtor's right to remove the goods as against the encumbrancer or owner terminates.

(h)   **[Priority of construction mortgage.]** A mortgage is a construction mortgage to the extent that it secures an obligation incurred for the construction of an improvement on land, including the acquisition cost of the land, if a recorded record of the mortgage so indicates. Except as otherwise provided in subsections (e) and (f), a security interest in fixtures is subordinate to a construction mortgage if a record of the mortgage is recorded before the goods become fixtures and the goods become fixtures before the completion of the construction. A mortgage has this priority to the same extent as a construction mortgage to the extent that it is given to refinance a construction mortgage.

Although local law defining fixtures is still applicable, the UCC has to some extent influenced these local fixture concepts by its apparent recognition of three classes of goods. Authorities uniformly accept this so-called "tri-partite" concept, which consists of the three following classes situated on a continuum: (1) incorporated building materials; (2) fixtures; and (3) purely personal property.[159]

Under the UCC, no security interest exists in "ordinary building materials incorporated into an improvement on land" irrespective of whether local law classifies such materials as fixtures.[160] This prohibition does not affect rights of enforcement against the debtor personally as opposed to against the actual materials.[161] This provision derives from the [old] Uniform Conditional Sales Act and the policy underlying it is to prevent waste by prohibiting the dismantling of a completed structure.[162]

At the opposite extreme of the continuum is purely personal property. Upon first reading the UCC fixture scheme, one may form a common misconception that realty claimants can somehow prevail as to such property. Goods that are purely personal property do not become part of a real estate mortgage, even though a chattel security interest is never perfected, merely because the goods are located on the mortgaged property. For example, personalty such as stereo components or household furniture

---

§ 9–102(a)   Definitions

(40) "Fixture filing" means the filing of a financing statement covering goods that are or are to become fixtures and satisfying Section 9–502(a) and (b). The term includes the filing of a financing statement covering goods of a transmitting utility which are or are to become fixtures.

(41) "Fixtures" means goods that have become so related to particular real property that an interest in them arises under real property law.

(53) "Manufactured home" means a structure, transportable in one or more sections, which, in the traveling mode, is eight body feet or more in width or 40 body feet or more in length, or, when erected on site, is 320 or more square feet, and which is built on a permanent chassis and designed to be used as a dwelling with or without a permanent foundation when connected to the required utilities, and includes the plumbing, heating, air-conditioning, and electrical systems contained therein. * * *

(54) "Manufactured-home transaction" means a secured transaction: (A) that creates a purchase-money security interest in a manufactured home, other than a manufactured home held as inventory; or (B) in which a manufactured home, other than a manufactured home held as inventory, is the primary collateral.

[159] U.C.C. § 9–334, Comment 3; Adams, Security Interests in Fixtures Under Mississippi's Uniform Commercial Code, 47 Miss.L.J. 831, 836 (1976).

[160] U.C.C. § 9–334(a). The concept of "ordinary building materials" should be understood to cover lumber, wires, paint, nails, and other types of materials that would effectively lose their identity during the building process. Cf. In re Ryan, 360 B.R. 50, 62 U.C.C. Rep. Serv. 2d 58 (Bankr. W.D. N.Y. 2007) (specialty bathtub did not qualify as ordinary building material; security interest of seller continued in bathtub even after it became a fixture in debtor's home); In re Troutt, 62 Collier Bankr. Cas. 2d (MB) 1413, Bankr. L. Rep. (CCH) ¶ 81632, 70 U.C.C. Rep. Serv. 2d 424 (Bankr. S.D. Ill. 2009) (segments of insulation stapled into debtor's attic was a fixture).

[161] U.C.C. § 9–334(a).

[162] Henning, The Impact of Revised Article 9 on Missouri's Fixture Financing Scheme, 48 Mo.L.Rev. 63, 69–71 (1983).

would not be subject to a real estate mortgage simply because they were situated inside a mortgaged home.[163]

For the intermediate class of fixtures, Article 9 defers to state real estate law the question of when a good becomes a fixture,[164] and instead adopts in U.C.C. § 9–334 a set of rules to resolve priority conflicts between real estate mortgagees and parties holding conflicting interests arising under Article 9. . . .

NOTE

State law of fixtures. The traditional hornbook definition of a fixture is "a former chattel which, while retaining its separate physical identity, is so connected with the realty that a disinterested observer would consider it a part thereof." 5 Am. Law of Prop. § 19.1 at 3–4 (1952). Professor Steve Knippenberg has offered a more informal and intuitive (if somewhat impractical) definition: "You take the world, you shake it, and everything that doesn't fall off is [a fixture]." Lopucki, Warren & Lawless, Secured Credit: A Systems Approach 342 (9th ed. 2020). But the precise point at which a chattel becomes a fixture is left to the law of each state, and state court decisions have proven somewhat unpredictable. To the extent generalization is possible:

> Courts use a facts-and-circumstances test to determine whether a particular asset qualifies as a fixture, typically focusing upon three elements: (1) the intent of the annexor, (2) the degree of physical affixation to the realty, and (3) the degree of adaptation of the asset to the particular characteristics of the real estate. The first factor— the intent of the annexor—is important in disputes between a secured party and the party that owned the land at the time of affixation, but courts largely ignore this factor in disputes between a secured party and a subsequent purchaser of the land. In deciding whether to buy or lend, a purchaser typically will have relied upon the appearance that the fixture was part of the land, and the reasonable expectations of the purchaser outweigh the hidden intentions of the annexor. Accordingly, in most disputes involving whether goods constitute a fixture, the issue turns on the degree of affixation and adaptation. Goods that are plugged into the wall are "affixed" to the land, but a court is not likely to characterize the goods as a fixture. If a couple of screws connect goods to the land to keep the goods from vibrating, the goods may or may not be a fixture. If the goods are so extensively attached to or embedded in the land that the goods cannot be removed without intensive labor, the goods are almost certainly a fixture. Adaptation comes into play if the physical connection between the goods and the land is slight, but the goods have been specially

---

[163] The mortgagee could obtain a security interest in these items if the mortgage contained language sufficient to create a security interest in them under U.C.C. § 9–203(b).

[164] U.C.C. § 9–102(a)(41) (" 'Fixtures' means goods that have become so related to particular real property that an interest in them arises under real property law.").

designed to fit into a particular area. For example, drapes that are loosely attached but are specifically designed for a particular room may qualify as fixtures.

Lawrence, Henning & Freyermuth, Understanding Secured Transactions 304 (5th ed. 2012).

NELSON, WHITMAN, BURKHART & FREYERMUTH, REAL ESTATE FINANCE LAW
§ 9.7, at 913–917 (6th ed.2015)*

Subsequent real estate mortgages

[T]he default rule in U.C.C. § 9–334 is that an Article 9 security interest in fixtures is subordinate to the conflicting interest of a real estate mortgagee,[168] but the drafters provided a number of exceptions under which the Article 9 fixture secured party can establish first priority. The first such exception governs disputes between an Article 9 fixture security interest and the claim of a mortgagee whose lien arises after the goods become a fixture. In this situation, a "first to file" rule applies: as between a subsequent mortgagee and a prior Article 9 security interest in fixtures, the first party to make a fixture filing or record his real estate mortgage attains priority.[169] As a result, a subsequent realty mortgagee cannot obtain priority over an Article 9 security interest in fixtures so long as the Article 9 secured party has properly perfected its interest by a fixture filing. The fixture filing, as it appears in the land records, alerts subsequent purchasers and mortgagees. . . .

Prior real estate mortgages

Even if a real estate mortgage precedes the creation of an Article 9 security interest in a good that is later affixed to the real estate, Article 9 nevertheless awards priority to the Article 9 fixture security interest if (1) it is a purchase money security interest, and (2) a fixture filing is made before or within 20 days after the goods become fixtures.[170] Thus, suppose that Bank holds a recorded mortgage on P's home. On March 1, P purchases

---

*   Reprinted with permission of LEG, Inc. d/b/a West Academic.

[168] U.C.C. § 9–334(c).

[169] U.C.C. § 9–334(e)(1); Corning Bank v. Bank of Rector, 265 Ark. 68, 576 S.W.2d 949, 26 U.C.C. Rep. Serv. 1367 (1979); C.I.T. Financial Services v. Premier Corp., 1987 OK 101, 747 P.2d 934 (Okla. 1987); Matter of Farrier, 61 B.R. 950, 1 U.C.C. Rep. Serv. 2d 1379 (Bankr. W.D. Pa. 1986).

[170] U.C.C. § 9–334(d) and Comment 7; Yeadon Fabric Domes, Inc. v. Maine Sports Complex, LLC, 2006 ME 85, 901 A.2d 200, 60 U.C.C. Rep. Serv. 2d 367 (Me. 2006); WSFS v. Chillibilly's, Inc., 57 U.C.C. Rep. Serv. 2d 692 (Del. Super. Ct. 2005); M & M Development, Inc. v. LS Monticello JV Inc., 190 A.D.2d 392, 599 N.Y.S.2d 137, 21 U.C.C. Rep. Serv. 2d 1195 (3d Dep't1993); Parsons v. Lender Service, Inc., 1990 OK CIV APP 72, 801 P.2d 739, 13 U.C.C. Rep. Serv. 2d 1332 (Ct. App. Div. 3 1990); First Wisconsin Nat. Bank of Milwaukee v. Federal Land Bank of St. Paul, 849 F.2d 284, 6 U.C.C. Rep. Serv. 2d 975 (7th Cir. 1988); Schroeder, Security Interests in Fixtures, 1975 Ariz.St.L.J. 319, 320–329.

a furnace from X and grants S a security interest in the furnace to secure the unpaid balance of the purchase price. On March 2, P installs the furnace in his home, and the furnace becomes a fixture under applicable state law. On March 3, S makes a fixture filing in the appropriate real estate records. In this situation, S's purchase money security interest in the furnace takes priority over Bank's interest in the furnace as a mortgagee.

The historical preference for purchase money financing explains this "purchase-money" exception. In the above hypothetical, because the furnace was not part of the home at the time Bank took its mortgage, Bank did not rely upon the furnace as part of its security in the mortgage agreement. Further, the furnace likely enhances the value of the home and thus benefits the Bank by increasing the value of its security. To award Bank priority over S as to the furnace would arguably give Bank an undeserved, unbargained-for windfall.[171] . . .

In rare circumstances, an Article 9 security interest is created in a good after it has already become a fixture. For example, suppose that Bank holds a recorded mortgage on P's home. P purchases a furnace (paying in cash) and installs the furnace in his home, such that the furnace becomes a fixture under applicable state law. Later, P borrows money from X and grants X a security interest in the furnace. Even if X makes a timely fixture filing, Bank's mortgage takes priority, because X does not have a purchase money security interest and thus does not qualify for protection under U.C.C. § 9–334(d).[172] This result makes sense, because P is not buying and affixing new goods to improve the freehold, but is borrowing against existing property on which a lender could have relied in taking a real estate mortgage.[173]

Construction mortgages

Construction mortgagees, for a variety of reasons, pay out the proceeds of their loans on an installment basis as the construction of the building progresses. In an attempt to ensure that these subsequent advances relate back to the original date of the mortgage for priority purposes, construction mortgagees include "future advances" clauses in construction mortgages. In the typical construction loan, the borrower and construction lender expect that the borrower will use some of the construction funds advanced to acquire goods that will become fixtures upon installation. Naturally,

---

[171] Lawrence, Henning & Freyermuth, Understanding Secured Transactions 308 (5th ed. 2012).

[172] Schroeder, supra note 170, at 320–321. See McIlroy Bank & Trust Fayetteville v. Federal Land Bank of St. Louis, 266 Ark. 481, 585 S.W.2d 947 (1979). However, real estate mortgagees sometimes lose because of an inability to establish that the goods became fixtures. See, e.g., In re Avery, 7 B.R. 28 (Bankr. D. S.C. 1980).

[173] Schroeder, supra note 170, at 321. See McIlroy Bank & Trust Fayetteville v. Federal Land Bank of St. Louis, 266 Ark. 481, 585 S.W.2d 947 (1979).

therefore, the construction mortgagee wants to claim such fixtures as part of its security.

The "purchase money" priority rule discussed above, however, would create a potential trap for the construction mortgagee. For example, suppose that Bank holds a construction loan mortgage on an office building being constructed by P. During construction, P purchases $20,000 worth of cabinetry on credit from S, who takes a purchase money security interest to secure the purchase price. P then installs the cabinets into the building, and the cabinets become a fixture under applicable state law. On the same day, S makes an appropriate fixture filing covering the cabinets. In this situation, U.C.C. § 9–334(d) would give S priority over Bank as to the cabinets. Such a result may be inappropriate, however, because Bank may well have expected to finance all of the building's fixtures; granting priority to S would effectively allow P to "double-finance" the cabinets.

Article 9 addresses this dilemma by providing a special rule that provides the expected priority to the construction mortgagee so long as the mortgage is recorded before the goods are affixed.[175] As one commentator has noted, "as to any goods that become fixtures during the course of construction, the construction mortgagee enjoys priority to the extent of all advances made under the mortgage to finance the construction, including the cost of acquiring the land."[176] The construction mortgagee has priority for such advances even as against a purchase money security interest in fixtures;[177] moreover, it makes no difference whether the advances are "optional" or "obligatory."[178] The benefit of this priority is available to both assignees of the construction mortgage and to refinancing mortgagees.[179]

Other exceptions favoring fixture financers

A real estate mortgagee with priority may consent to subordinate his claim to the security interest of the fixture financier.[180] The mortgagee might agree to give such consent where the mortgagee has reasons to maintain the good will of the mortgagor, or where the mortgagee reasonably did not expect to have priority as to a particular fixture. For example, suppose that Bank holds a recorded construction mortgage on P's office building. P now wants to install certain fixtures during construction that were not part of the original construction budget and for which the Bank will not be advancing funds under its construction loan agreement. In such a case, the Bank might decide to consent to subordinate its priority

---

[175] U.C.C. § 9–334(g).

[176] Adams, supra note 159, at 908. To qualify as a construction mortgage, a mortgage must secure "an obligation incurred for the construction of an improvement on land." U.C.C. § 9–334(h).

[177] U.C.C. § 9–334(h); Funk, The Proposed Revision of Article 9 of the Uniform Commercial Code, 26 Bus.Law. 1465, 1472 (1972).

[178] U.C.C. § 9–334, Comment 11.

[179] U.C.C. § 9–334(h); Schroeder, supra note 170, at 332.

[180] U.C.C. § 9–334(f)(1).

to another secured party willing to provide financing for those particular fixtures.

In certain limited situations, U.C.C. § 9–334(e) enables an Article 9 fixture secured party to obtain priority over certain conflicting real estate interests by perfecting under Article 9's regular perfection rules rather than by making a fixture filing. For example, a security interest in fixtures has priority over a real estate mortgagee with respect to "readily moveable factory or office machines," "equipment that is not primarily used or leased for use in the operation of the real property," or "replacements of domestic appliances that are consumer goods" as long as that security interest is perfected "by any method permitted" in the UCC.[181] The drafters included this provision to alleviate the confusion in various jurisdictions as to whether these types of items are fixtures or pure personalty. In the drafters' judgment, commercial actors view office machines, stoves, refrigerators, and similar domestic appliances as being in the nature of chattels, even if a jurisdiction's real estate laws might characterize them as fixtures. The exception thus protects the expectations of an Article 9 secured party "who, perhaps in the mistaken belief that the readily removable goods will not become fixtures, makes a UCC filing ... rather than a fixture filing."[182] Note, however, that the priority guarantee for Article 9 secured parties as to domestic appliances extends only to replacement appliances, not original installations.[183] This limitation protects a construction lender that may have relied upon having a lien on the original appliances when it financed the home's construction.[184]

Likewise, the fixture secured party need not make a fixture filing to attain priority *vis-a-vis* lien creditors, including a trustee in bankruptcy.[185] Because such creditors typically do not rely on the real estate records, a fixture filing is not necessary and perfection by any other method is effective against them.[186] If the Article 9 secured party incorrectly assumes that goods will not become fixtures, she will be protected against nonreliance creditors as long as she takes the normal steps to perfect her interest under Article 9, even though she will be subordinated to recorded real estate mortgages because of her failure to make a fixture filing.

---

[181] U.C.C. § 9–334(e) and Comment 8. Perfection would ordinarily occur under Article 9 by the filing of a financing statement covering the goods in the appropriate filing office. U.C.C. § 9–310(a). However, if the security interest in question is a purchase-money security interest in consumer goods, that security interest is automatically perfected without the filing of a financing statement. U.C.C. § 9–309(1).

[182] U.C.C. § 9–334, Comment 8.

[183] U.C.C. § 9–334, Comment 8.

[184] Lawrence, Henning & Freyermuth, supra note 171, at 312.

[185] U.C.C. § 9–334(e)(3) and Comment 9. The term "lien creditor" is defined in U.C.C. § 9–102(a)(52) and includes creditors who acquire a lien on property "by attachment, levy, or the like." U.C.C. § 9–102(a)(52)(A).

[186] U.C.C. § 9–334(e)(3).

Finally, if fixtures are installed by a mortgagor's tenant, the UCC gives priority to the holder of an Article 9 security interest in those fixtures over conflicting interests in the realty if the tenant has the right as against the mortgagor to remove the fixtures from the mortgaged property.[187] This priority continues for a reasonable time even after the tenant/debtor's right of removal terminates.[188]

NOTES

1. *Some priority problems.* How would U.C.C. § 9–334 resolve the following priority problems?

(a) Bank holds a recorded mortgage on Butcher's land and building. On February 1, Manufacturer sells Butcher a walk-in refrigerator on credit, taking a purchase-money security interest in the refrigerator. On February 3, Butcher installs the refrigerator in its building, thereby rendering it a fixture. On February 9, Manufacturer makes a proper fixture filing covering the refrigerator. Who has priority in the refrigerator: Bank or Manufacturer?

(b) Same as problem (a), but now assume that Manufacturer simply files a regular Article 9 financing statement rather than making a fixture filing. Who has priority in the refrigerator: Bank or Manufacturer?

(c) On February 1, Manufacturer sells Butcher a walk-in refrigerator on credit, taking a purchase-money security interest in the refrigerator. On February 3, Butcher installs the refrigerator in its building, thereby rendering it a fixture. On February 5, Butcher borrows $500,000 from Bank and grants Bank a mortgage on its building, which Bank records that same day. On February 8, Manufacturer makes a proper fixture filing covering the refrigerator. Who has priority in the refrigerator: Bank or Manufacturer?

(d) On July 1, Manufacturer sells Butcher a walk-in refrigerator on credit, taking a purchase-money security interest in the refrigerator. On July 3, Butcher installs the refrigerator in its building, rendering it a fixture. Manufacturer does not make a fixture filing, but does file an Article 9 financing statement covering the refrigerator. On September 1, Customer obtains a judgment against Butcher arising out of a food-poisoning incident, and the judgment

---

[187] U.C.C. § 9–334(f)(2). This provision is consistent with the so-called "trade fixtures" doctrine, under which goods affixed to leased premises are treated as personal property as between the lessor and the lessee. Lawrence, Henning & Freyermuth, supra note 171, at 315; see also FL Receivables Trust 2002–A v. Arizona Mills, L.L.C., 210 Ariz. 388, 111 P.3d 430, 57 U.C.C. Rep. Serv. 2d 625 (Ct. App. Div. 1 2005), review denied and ordered depublished, 212 Ariz. 43, 127 P.3d 59 (2006).

[188] U.C.C. § 9–334(g). Although it could not remove the fixture, the Article 9 fixture secured party could still reduce its claim against the debtor to judgment and enforce that claim against the debtor's other assets (assuming that the debtor has personal liability on the debt).

constitutes a lien against Butcher's building. Who has priority in the refrigerator: Manufacturer or Customer?

(e) ABC Corp. (ABC) is building an office building financed by a construction loan from Bank, which holds a recorded mortgage. On November 1, Carpenter sells ABC 100 sets of cabinets for installation in the building; Carpenter takes a purchase-money security interest to secure ABC's obligation to pay the purchase price of the cabinets. On November 20, the cabinets are installed in the building and become fixtures. On November 22, Carpenter files a fixture filing covering the cabinets. Who has priority as to the cabinets: Carpenter or Bank?

(f) Same as problem (e), but assume that ABC had completed construction of the building on October 15. Would this change your answer? Why or why not?

2. *The fixture secured party's right to remove fixtures.* The priority recognized by U.C.C. § 9–334 becomes critical in the event of default—either a default on the mortgage obligation or the obligation owed to the fixture secured party (or both). Suppose that Manufacturer has a security interest in Butcher's walk-in refrigerator (which is a fixture under state law) and Bank holds a recorded mortgage on the building in which the refrigerator is installed. If Butcher defaults, Manufacturer wants to be able to remove the refrigerator (i.e., to "unaffix" it, thereby restoring its character as personalty) and conduct a foreclosure sale governed by Article 9. Manufacturer's ability to do so is governed by section 9–604, which provides:

(a) **[Enforcement: personal and real property.]** If a security agreement covers both personal and real property, a secured party may proceed: (1) under this part as to the personal property without prejudicing any rights with respect to the real property; or (2) as to both the personal property and the real property in accordance with the rights with respect to the real property, in which case the other provisions of this part do not apply.

(b) **[Enforcement: fixtures.]** Subject to subsection (c), if a security agreement covers goods that are or become fixtures, a secured party may proceed: (1) under this part; or (2) in accordance with the rights with respect to real property, in which case the other provisions of this part do not apply.

(c) **[Removal of fixtures.]** Subject to the other provisions of this part, if a secured party holding a security interest in fixtures has priority over all owners and encumbrancers of the real property, the secured party, after default, may remove the collateral from the real property.

(d) **[Injury caused by removal.]** A secured party that removes collateral shall promptly reimburse any encumbrancer or owner of the real property, other than the debtor, for the cost of repair of any physical injury caused by the removal. The secured party need not reimburse the encumbrancer or owner for any diminution in value of the real property caused by the absence of the goods removed or by any necessity of replacing them. A person entitled to reimbursement may refuse permission to remove until the secured party gives adequate assurance for the performance of the obligation to reimburse.

Thus (as should be intuitive), Manufacturer cannot remove the refrigerator if it lacks priority over Bank's mortgage. In other words, if Manufacturer is not first in line, its security interest in the refrigerator is of little value. Instead, Manufacturer could only (a) wait to enforce its lien until after Bank's senior mortgage lien is satisfied, (b) assert its lien against any surplus proceeds if Bank subsequently forecloses its senior mortgage, or (c) assert any rights it may be able to claim against the land under the jurisdiction's laws governing mechanics' liens.

By contrast, if Manufacturer has priority, it may remove the fixture and proceed to sell it in a foreclosure sale governed by Article 9, even over the objection of Bank. Bank could not complain that the removal of the refrigerator would lower the value of the land because of the absence of the refrigerator. If, however, removal of the refrigerator would do other physical damage to the building (e.g., if removal of the refrigerator would require removing and then replacing a wall at a cost of $1,500), Manufacturer would have to reimburse Bank for the cost to repair that damage.

3.   *The fixture secured party's rights in a real estate foreclosure sale.* Suppose that in the example in note 2, Butcher defaults to both Manufacturer and Bank, and Bank schedules a foreclosure sale of the building. Suppose further that Manufacturer has first priority in the walk-in refrigerator. Manufacturer could remove the refrigerator, but does not want to do that because it fears the refrigerator would bring a low price if removed and sold as used equipment. Instead, Manufacturer wants to leave the refrigerator in the building, allow the building to be sold at foreclosure, and then claim first priority against the foreclosure sale proceeds. Can Manufacturer do this?

Prior to the revision of Article 9 in 2000, the answer was no, at least according to the leading case, Maplewood Bank & Trust v. Sears, Roebuck & Co., 265 N.J.Super. 25, 625 A.2d 537 (App.Div. 1993). In *Maplewood*, the court held that a secured party's right to priority in a fixture was limited to its removal and that a secured party had no claim against the land itself—and thus no claim to the proceeds of the foreclosure sale. Instead, the court held, the secured party continued to have its priority in the fixture and could enforce its security interest by removing the fixture (even after the foreclosure sale).

This decision was understandably criticized, because in some cases certain fixtures (especially ones that are particularly adapted to a building) may be worth substantially more "in place" than they would be if removed. Thus, in the 2000 Article 9 revisions, the drafters overruled *Maplewood* by enacting section 9–604(b) (quoted in note 2 above). Section 9–604(b) allows a fixture secured party to choose to enforce its interest either under Article 9's enforcement provisions or under applicable state real estate law. If the secured party enforces its interest under real estate law, none of Article 9's enforcement provisions apply. Thus, if the state's real estate laws permitted Manufacturer to join in Bank's foreclosure action and enforce its interest in that proceeding, Manufacturer could claim first priority against the foreclosure-sale proceeds. By contrast, if the state's real estate law does not permit Manufacturer to join in the Bank's foreclosure, then the buyer at Bank's foreclosure sale would take title to the land subject to Manufacturer's security interest in the fixture, which Manufacturer could enforce pursuant to Article 9.

G. RIGHTS IN CROPS AND OTHER PRODUCTS OF LAND

FLETCHER V. STILLMAN

Missouri Court of Appeals, Southern District, 1996
934 S.W.2d 597

SHRUM, JUDGE. . . . On September 28, 1992, Plaintiffs bought a New Madrid County farm at a foreclosure sale. Located on the farm at the time of the foreclosure sale was a matured but unharvested soybean crop that had been planted by a renter. When the renter harvested the soybeans after September 28, 1992, the landlord's one-third share of the crop sale proceeds was placed in a joint account pending resolution of the dispute. Plaintiffs then filed this suit in which they claimed entitlement to the crop proceeds on the theory that any crops not yet harvested passed with the land. Contrarily, Defendant claims that she is entitled to the crop proceeds because the crops had matured before the foreclosure sale, i.e., they were ready for harvest even though they had not yet been severed. The trial court concluded that it was bound by the case of *Holdsworth v. Key*, 520 S.W.2d 637 (Mo.App.1975), and found for Plaintiffs.

Holdsworth contains this language:

"In Missouri, it is a settled legal principle of longstanding that unless otherwise provided in the deed of trust, unsevered crops standing on mortgaged land at the time of a foreclosure sale are subject to the lien of the deed of trust and pass to the purchaser of the land at the foreclosure sale. *Hayden v. Burkemper*, 101 Mo. 644, 14 S.W. 767 (1890); *Farmers' Bank of Hickory v. Bradley*, 315 Mo. 811, 288 S.W. 774 (banc 1926). The only way a growing crop can be relieved of the lien of a deed of trust is by an actual severance of the crop from the ground prior to the foreclosure sale."

Id. at 639[1–2].

Nevertheless, Defendant insists that the trial court erred in granting judgment for Plaintiffs because *Holdsworth* and other Missouri cases analyzed in her brief dealt with crops that were still growing at the time of sale and did not involve a matured crop as existed here. Defendant asserts that crop maturity distinguishes this case from any heretofore decided in Missouri, thus this is a case of first impression. With that as her premise, Defendant urges this court to adopt "the more equitable and fair rule, applied by numerous jurisdictions, [which] is that if the crop is mature and no longer drawing any nutrients or sustenance from the real estate, it is personalty, and does not pass with the land." Jurisdictions that adhere to this rule do so on the theory that once a crop matures and is no longer being supported by the soil, a constructive severance occurs so that the crop thereafter bears the same relation to the land on which it stood as it would if stored in a warehouse or barn. *See, e.g. Wood v. Wood*, 116 Colo. 593, 183 P.2d 889 (1947); *First National Bank v. Beegle*, 52 Kan. 709, 35 P. 814 (1894); *Hecht v. Dittman*, 56 Iowa 679, 7 N.W. 495 (1880). . . .

In response, Plaintiffs contend that this is not a case of first impression and that indeed the concept of constructive severance as contended for by Defendant is a doctrine that has been rejected by Missouri courts. In support of their argument, Plaintiffs cite *Farmers' Bank of Hickory v. Bradley*, 315 Mo. 811, 288 S.W. 774 (banc 1926); *Starkey v. Powell*, 315 Mo. 846, 288 S.W. 776 (banc 1926); and *Vogt [v. Cunningham]*, 50 Mo.App. 136 [(1892)]. We find that the three cases Plaintiffs rely on, when read together, settle the issue contrary to Defendant's contentions. . . .

In *Farmers' Bank of Hickory v. Bradley*, landowners gave a deed of trust on their farm to secure a note. After defaulting on the real estate note, they gave a chattel mortgage to [Bank] for "75 acres of corn located on the farm. . . ." After the chattel mortgage was given and while the corn was still standing and unharvested, the farm was sold to Bradley at foreclosure. Bradley took possession of the farm and its crops, which prompted [Bank] to file an action in replevin against Bradley to recover the corn. In effect, the trial court instructed the jury to return a verdict for [Bank]. When Bradley appealed, the Kansas City Court of Appeals reversed, holding that the deed of trust lien was superior to that of the chattel mortgage lien since the "growing corn crop" had not actually been severed from the ground at the time of the foreclosure sale. . . . Once *Bradley* was transferred [to the Supreme Court], the Supreme Court . . . sustained the decision of the Kansas City Court of Appeals and disapproved the contrary doctrine of constructive severance . . . . *Bradley*, 288 S.W. at 776. In so doing, the *Bradley* court said: "We have uniformly held that neither the owner of the land nor his grantee could free the growing crop of the lien of the deed of trust, except by an actual severance from the soil before possession taken or foreclosure had under the deed of trust." *Id.* at 775[2].

Starkey v. Powell was a case handed down on the same day as *Bradley*. In *Starkey*, a landowner gave a deed of trust on his farm in 1922. Later, in September 1923, while the farm was still subject to the lien of the deed of trust, the landowner sold a corn crop that was on the farm to Starkey at a public sale. On October 22, 1923, the holder of the deed of trust caused a foreclosure sale to be held and Powell bought the farm. When Powell bought the farm, a part of the corn crop purchased earlier by Starkey remained unsevered in the field. Within "a few days after November 1, 1923," Powell gathered and removed the corn, prompting Starkey to sue him for trespass and conversion. The trial court gave the jury a peremptory instruction to find for Starkey. Powell appealed, charging that the trial court "erred in holding that there was a constructive severance of the crop." *Id.* at 777. The Kansas City Court of Appeals agreed and reversed . . . . On transfer the Supreme Court held that the case was controlled by *Bradley*, thus clearly rejecting the doctrine of constructive severance of crops.

. . . *Bradley* and *Starkey* require that we reject Defendant's urging that she was entitled to the crop proceeds because the soybeans had matured prior to the foreclosure sale, an argument which is grounded upon the doctrine of constructive severance, a theory clearly rejected in *Bradley* and *Starkey*. Although Defendant claims her case is distinguishable from *Bradley* and *Starkey* because the crops in those cases were not matured at the time of the foreclosure sale, it is a distinction without a difference. *Bradley* and *Starkey* did not turn on the narrow question of crop maturity, but rather were decided on the broader basis that Missouri would not recognize the doctrine of constructive severance of crops and that a crop can only be freed from the lien of a deed of trust by actual severance. *Bradley*, 288 S.W. at 775[2]; *Starkey*, 288 S.W. at 777. The judgment is affirmed.

NOTES

1. *Foreclosure purchaser vs. mortgagor. Fletcher* represents the normal view that in a dispute about growing crops between a foreclosure sale purchaser and a mortgagor, the former usually prevails "on the theory that the mortgagor has pledged the crops, as well as the land itself, as security for the loan." 9 Richard R. Powell & Patrick J. Rohan, Powell on Real Property § 58.03(2) (1997). Some courts, as *Fletcher* also points out, temper the foregoing by applying "constructive severance" after the crop has matured.

2. *Foreclosure purchaser vs. mortgagor's lessee.* Suppose in *Fletcher* that the foreclosure purchasers had claimed the *tenant's* share of the soybean crop. Should the foreclosure purchasers prevail in that context? Here a somewhat different analysis is often applied. If the lease was senior to the foreclosed mortgage, the tenant is entitled to the crops because his or her lease rights were unaffected by the foreclosure. Where, however, a subordinate lease is destroyed by foreclosure, the results are less predictable. On the one hand,

some courts reject the lessee's post-foreclosure claim to the crop by using the severance analysis reflected in *Fletcher* and other foreclosure purchaser vs. mortgagor cases. On the other hand, many courts use the "emblements" concept to defeat the foreclosure purchaser. Under this approach, unsevered annual crops "produced primarily through the labor and industry of the land's possessor" are treated for this purpose as "personalty." 9 Richard R. Powell & Patrick J. Rohan, Powell on Real Property § 58.03 (1997). The latter concept is relied on because of the "uncertainty in the duration of the possessory right injected by the foreclosure of the mortgage." Id. at § 58.03(2).

3.   *Foreclosure purchaser vs. holder of Article 9 security interest in crops.* The crop entitlement question becomes more complex when a claim of a holder of an Article 9 security interest in crops is asserted against a real estate foreclosure purchaser. Note that the *Bradley* case, discussed in *Fletcher*, followed a traditional common law approach that the deed of trust lien trumped the chattel mortgage lien of the crop financer because "the 'growing corn crop' had not actually been severed from the ground at the time of the foreclosure sale." Under this approach, the creation of the chattel security interest in the crops did not represent a "constructive severance."

This analysis, however, pre-dated the adoption in every state of Article 9 of the Uniform Commercial Code. Article 9 governs security interests in "goods," and the drafters of Article 9 defined "goods" to include crops. Thus, Article 9 clearly contemplated that a lender could take and enforce a security interest in a farmer's crops under Article 9. This left open the question, however, of whether a lien could still arise against growing crops under real estate law—and, if so, the respective priority of a real estate mortgagee and a person holding an Article 9 security interest in crops.

Some courts and commentators took the view that by defining "goods" to include crops, the drafters of Article 9 intended for Article 9 to be the exclusive means of creating and enforcing a security interest in crops. See, e.g., Barkley Clark, The Law of Secured Transactions Under the Uniform Commercial Code ¶ 8.05[1] (1993) ("Article 9 is the exclusive statutory scheme to cover security interests in growing crops, and the mortgagee should not be able to claim a security interest under real estate law."); 4 White & Summers, Uniform Commercial Code § 30–7, at 44–45 (4th ed. 1995) ("Under a proper interpretation of Article 9, a real estate mortgagee cannot subject crops to his mortgage merely by complying with real estate mortgage law."). Certainly, it makes sense to conclude that by defining "goods" to include crops, the drafters of Article 9 intended for any priority conflicts as to crops to be governed by Article 9. Otherwise, farmers might have difficulty obtaining crop financing, because suppliers and farm lenders "would be forced to gamble upon the timing of foreclosure proceedings and even the weather in a race to sever crops" before a foreclosure sale of the land became final. Moritz Implement Co. v. Matthews, 265 Kan. 179, 959 P.2d 886 (1998). However, the statements of Clark and White and Summers may be overbroad to the extent they suggest that a real estate mortgagee could never claim an interest in crops under a mortgage. If a foreclosure sale occurs, there is a crop growing on the land at the time of the sale, and there is no conflicting Article 9 security interest in that crop, there is no good reason why ownership of the crop should not pass to the foreclosure sale purchaser under the general principle articulated in *Fletcher v. Stillman*.

To a significant extent, any lingering confusion has now been resolved by the 2000 amendments to Article 9, which provide clearly that a perfected security interest in crops has priority over the conflicting interest of the holder of a mortgage on the real property on which the crops are growing. U.C.C. § 9–334(i). Comment 12 to section 9–334 acknowledges that "[i]n some jurisdictions, a mortgage of real property may cover crops" under real estate law, but the mortgagee's interest is subordinate to a perfected Article 9 security interest in the crop. Given this clear statutory directive, a creditor "would be foolish indeed to rely on uncertain remnants of real estate law for creating consensual crop encumbrances." Eldon H. Reiley, Security Interests in Personal Property § 25:14 (3d ed. 2003).

4. *Timber*. Like crops, standing timber also creates a potential priority dilemma. Article 9 permits the creation of an Article 9 security interest in "standing timber that is to be cut and removed under a conveyance or contract for sale." U.C.C. § 9–102(a)(44) (such timber is "goods"). To perfect such a security interest under Article 9's rules, however, the secured party must file a "real-property related financing statement" in the real property records. Id. §§ 9–501(a)(1)(A), 9–502(b). Article 9's determination to include some standing timber as "goods," and ambiguities in its definitional scheme, have produced some uncertainty regarding the precise relationship of real estate law and Article 9.

Consider the facts of Feliciana Bank & Trust v. Manuel & Sessions, L.L.C., 943 So.2d 736 (Miss.2006). Bank held recorded mortgages on a parcel to secure two loans; later, Mortgagor entered into a timber contract with Buyer, who cut some of the timber. Bank sued the Buyer claiming it had a security interest in the timber; Buyer claimed that it had taken the timber free of any claim by Bank because Bank had not filed the necessary financing statement as required by Article 9. The court held that because the Bank had recorded its mortgage before Mortgagor and Buyer entered the timber contract, Bank's mortgage covered the timber and established Bank's priority vs. Buyer. This is plainly the correct result; can you explain why?

The *Feliciana* court then offered the following dicta: "if a typical deed of trust is executed after a contract for the cutting of the timber has been executed but before the actual harvesting of the trees, the deed of trust will either not apply to the timber at all because the timber is now personalty, or else the deed of trust will be subordinate to a prior UCC filing." Which is it? Should the execution of a timber contract effect a constructive severance of the timber so as to bring the timber exclusively within the Article 9 realm?

If the nature of the land in question is that it is used for growing timber to be cut as it matures, should the timber be considered "crops"? What if the timber is comprised of Christmas trees? See, e.g., Rainier Nat'l Bank v. Security State Bank, 796 P.2d 443, 445 (Wash.1990); In re Grogan, 2013 WL

5630627 (9th Cir. B.A.P. 2013). If you were making a loan to a Christmas tree farm, how would you go about documenting the loan?

H. FEDERAL TAX LIENS

NELSON, WHITMAN, BURKHART & FREYERMUTH, REAL ESTATE FINANCE LAW
§ 9.9, at 930–934 (6th ed.2015)*

The Federal Tax Lien Act (FTLA) grants to the United States a lien on all property belonging to a taxpayer who fails to pay federal taxes following proper demand.[242] This lien relates back to the date on which the taxes became due,[243] and attaches to all existing and after-acquired real and personal property in which the taxpayer has an interest.[244] Because the lien arises by operation of law, it is a "secret lien" of which third parties dealing with the taxpayer may be unaware. Thus, the FTLA requires the IRS to file a public notice of the lien to make it effective against the rights of subsequent purchasers, judgment creditors, mechanics' lienholders, and holders of consensual security interests.[245]

The first-in-time, first-in-right principle provides the baseline for establishing the priority of conflicting property interests, including federal tax liens. Nevertheless, there are several situations in which a federal tax lien may take priority over a prior-in-time lien. One situation involves an unperfected security interest. A security interest arising under state law is deemed to exist for FTLA purposes only if the collateral is "in existence" and the interest "has become protected under local law as against a subsequent judgment lien arising out of an unsecured obligation."[246] Thus, for example, the holder of an unperfected Article 9 security interest—whose claim is subordinate to a judgment lien creditor[247]—would have no "security interest" within the meaning of the FTLA, and thus would be subordinate to a later-filed federal tax lien.

By contrast, the priority of an unrecorded real estate mortgage vis-a-vis a federal tax lien depends upon the state's recording act. If the state's law requires recording to make a mortgage effective as against later judgment creditors, then the holder of an unrecorded mortgage would have no "security interest" within the meaning of the FTLA and would be

---

*   Reprinted with permission of LEG, Inc. d/b/a West Academic.

[242] 26 U.S.C.A. § 6321.

[243] 26 U.S.C.A. § 6322.

[244] 26 U.S.C.A. § 6321; Treas. Reg. § 301.6321–1.

[245] 26 U.S.C.A. § 6323(a).

[246] 26 U.S.C.A. § 6323(h)(1)(A).

[247] U.C.C. § 9–317(a)(2)(A).

subordinate to a later-filed federal tax lien.[248] In many states, however, even an unrecorded mortgage is effective against later judgment creditors, either because the judgment creditor is not considered to have paid value as a "purchaser" under the recording act or because the judgment lien statute imposes a lien only on the judgment debtor's actual real property, not his ostensible property as disclosed by a title examination.[249] In those states, an unrecorded mortgage would still have priority against a later-filed federal tax lien.

The "choateness" doctrine and construction financing

Another circumstance in which a federal tax lien may obtain priority over a prior-in-time lien involves lending secured by future advances. An understanding of this potential concern requires an explanation of the "choateness" doctrine under federal tax law. Even if a secured party has a perfected security interest before the government files notice of its tax lien, the secured party will not have priority over the tax lien unless its security interest is "choate." As explained in United States v. McDermott,[250] a security interest is choate if the identity of the secured party, the property to which the interest attaches, and the amount of the debt are all "established." In a typical residential mortgage transaction involving a single mortgage loan and a security interest in the borrower's home, the choateness doctrine poses no problem. For example, suppose Bank holds a recorded mortgage on Taxpayer's home securing repayment of the mortgage loan Taxpayer used to acquire the home. When Taxpayer fails to pay federal income taxes, the IRS files a tax lien notice. In this situation, the secured party (Bank), the collateral (the home), and the outstanding balance of the mortgage debt are all known.[251] Thus, Bank's mortgage unquestionably has priority over the federal tax lien.

The choateness doctrine presents a conceptual challenge, however, when a secured party attempts to enforce a lien against property securing future advances. For example, suppose that Bank holds a perfected security interest in all of the assets of ABC Company (ABC), securing a $2 million line of credit. At the time ABC fails to pay its payroll taxes and the IRS files a tax lien notice, the outstanding balance on the line of credit is $1.1 million. Over the next week, before Bank learns of the tax lien filing, ABC borrows another $200,000 under its line of credit, increasing the balance to $1.3 million. In this situation, the advances to ABC after the tax lien filing would not satisfy the choateness doctrine, as the debt had not

---

[248] See, e.g., Citizens State Bank v. United States, 932 F.2d 490 (6th Cir.1991) (applying Kentucky law).

[249] Stoebuck & Whitman, Property § 11.10 nn.13–16 (3d ed.2000).

[250] 507 U.S. 447 (1993).

[251] The fact that the balance of the debt might increase in the future with the accrual of interest is irrelevant to the choateness analysis. If the Bank has priority over the federal tax lien as to the principal amount of the debt, the Bank will likewise have priority as to interest accruing on that debt. 26 U.S.C.A. § 6323(e)(1).

been "established" at $1.3 million prior to the tax lien filing. As a result, under the FTLA, Bank would not have a "security interest" in the collateral to the extent of the $200,000 in future advances[252] on the date of the tax lien notice. Thus, without some exception to the choateness doctrine, while Bank would have priority in the collateral to the extent of the $1.1 million balance on the date of the tax lien filing, Bank's interest would be subordinate to the IRS to the extent of the additional advances.

The choateness doctrine thus creates a substantial practical problem for a construction mortgagee. As discussed in greater detail elsewhere,[253] a construction mortgagee typically advances the loan proceeds in stages (or "draws") as construction actually proceeds. Because the typical construction mortgage provides that the mortgage secures future advances, the construction mortgagee expects that it will have the same priority for each and every draw under the construction loan agreement. But the choateness doctrine creates the potential that the filing of a tax lien notice could "freeze" the mortgagee's priority as of the date of the tax lien notice and subordinate the mortgagee's lien with respect to later advances. This might seem particularly unwelcome to the mortgagee to the extent that the mortgagee made advances after the tax lien notice was filed but without actual knowledge of that filing.

To ameliorate the effect of the choateness doctrine and protect the reasonable expectations of the construction lender, the FTLA provides that a federal tax lien will not have priority over a conflicting security interest to the extent that it (a) secures certain post-tax-lien-notice advances under a "real property construction or improvement financing agreement" and (b) "is protected under local law against a judgment lien arising, as of the time of tax lien filing, out of an unsecured obligation."[254] Thus, suppose that O enters into a construction loan agreement with Bank to finance the construction of O's home on Blackacre, and grants Bank a construction mortgage on Blackacre. The mortgage, recorded on February 1, provides that Bank will make advances to O as construction proceeds. On March 1, the IRS files a tax lien notice against O based upon O's nonpayment of federal taxes. Construction continues, with Bank making advances on June 1, September 1, and upon completion on December 1. If under applicable state law, Bank would have had priority for these three advances over a

---

[252] Under 26 U.S.C.A. § 6323(h)(1), a security interest exists only to the extent that "[its] holder has parted with money or money's worth."

[253] See infra § 12.1.

[254] 26 U.S.C.A. § 6323(c)(1). The term "real property construction or improvement financing agreement" includes "an agreement to make cash disbursements to finance (i) the construction of improvement of real property, [or] (ii) a contract to construct or improve real property . . . ." 26 U.S.C.A. § 6323(c)(3)(A).

hypothetical judgment creditor who had acquired her lien as of March 1, then Bank's security interest will have priority over the federal tax lien.[255]

Non-construction-related future advances

In some cases, a mortgage may cover future advances even though such advances are unrelated to the construction of improvements on land. For example, suppose that Owner grants Bank a second mortgage on her home on February 1 to secure the repayment of a home equity line of credit that Owner intends to use to pay her child's college tuition expenses. Then, on March 1, the IRS files a tax lien notice against Owner. In this situation, the FTLA's exception for a "real property construction or improvement financing agreement" would not apply to protect any advances made by Bank after March 1 to pay the child's tuition expenses. Nevertheless, the choateness doctrine would present the same essential risks to Bank in this situation; Bank might expect its priority to date from February 1, but the March 1 tax lien filing could potentially "freeze" the Bank's priority as of that date and subordinate the Bank's lien with respect to advances made thereafter. Again, this would be unwelcome news to the Bank, particularly if the Bank made future advances without actual knowledge of the March 1 tax lien filing.

The FTLA also ameliorates the impact of the choateness doctrine in this situation, but only as to certain future advances. The FTLA provides that a federal tax lien does not have priority over

> a security interest which came into existence after tax lien filing by reason of disbursements made before the 46th day after the date of tax lien filing, or (if earlier) before the person making such disbursements had actual notice or knowledge of tax lien filing, but only if such security interest (1) is in property . . . covered by the terms of a written agreement entered into before tax lien filing, and (2) is protected under local law against a judgment lien arising, as of the time of tax lien filing, out of an unsecured obligation.[256]

This provision establishes a maximum 45-day window period in which a lender can obtain protection for future advances, subject to being shortened by actual knowledge of the tax lien filing. For example, suppose that when IRS files its tax lien notice against Owner on March 1, there is a zero balance on Owner's home equity line of credit. On April 1, Bank (which does not have knowledge of the tax lien) allows Owner to draw $5,000 on the line of credit to pay her child's tuition bill. On May 1, Bank (again without knowledge of the tax lien) allows Owner to draw an additional $5,000 on the line of credit to pay other college-related expenses. Further,

---

[255] See Treas. Reg. § 301.6323(c)–2(d), Example 1. For a detailed discussion of the state law rules governing future advances priority vis à vis intervening lien creditors, see § 12.7 infra.

[256] 26 U.S.C.A. § 6323(d).

assume that under state law, Bank would have priority over a judgment lien creditor as of March 1 with respect to both advances.[257] Under 26 U.S.C. § 6323(d), Bank will have priority over the IRS to the extent of the $5,000 advance of April 1, but not with respect to the $5,000 advance of May 1, which fell outside the 45-day window period. By contrast, suppose instead that on March 15, Bank had received a letter from the IRS advising Bank of its tax lien and providing a copy of its tax lien filing. In this situation, the Bank's knowledge of the tax lien terminates the window period for future advance priority, and thus Bank's mortgage would be subordinate to the federal tax lien with respect to both the April 1 and May 1 advances.

How can a mortgagee protect itself against this risk? Obviously, the lender can simply refuse to make advances to the borrower once the lender has knowledge of the federal tax lien. But because the window period never exceeds 45 days, the lender's mere lack of knowledge is not sufficient beyond that period. The lender thus cannot be certain of priority for a future advance unless it has checked the appropriate filing office within the preceding 45 days and did not find a tax lien notice on file against the borrower.[258]

NOTE

The choateness doctrine and rents. Suppose that Developer owns a building subject to a recorded deed of trust and assignment of rents in favor of Bank. The building is partially occupied by Tenant A, who is paying rent to Developer under a long-term lease entered into several years ago. Now suppose that the IRS files a notice of tax lien against Developer in the appropriate filing office, only days before Developer enters into a new lease for the remaining space in the building with Tenant B. As between Bank and the IRS, which has priority as to rents collected from Tenant A? From Tenant B?

As explained above, the FTLA recognizes a security interest only if the collateral is "in existence" and the interest "has become protected under local law as against a subsequent judgment lien arising out of an unsecured obligation." Developer's right to collect the rents accruing under Tenant A's lease arose upon the signing of the lease, prior to the tax lien. Because Bank holds a prior recorded assignment of rents, Bank has priority over the IRS as to those rents. But what about the rents accruing under Tenant B's lease? That lease did not come into existence until after the IRS filed its tax lien notice. In this situation, the IRS may argue that the choateness doctrine was not

---

[257] For a detailed discussion of the state law rules governing future advances priority vis à vis intervening lien creditors, see § 12.7 infra.

[258] In the case of real property, the IRS must file a tax lien notice in the office designated by the law of the state in which the property is situated. 26 U.S.C.A. § 6323(f)(1)(A)(i). Under the Uniform Federal Lien Registration Act (UFLRA), enacted in 39 states, the IRS must file a tax lien notice with respect to real estate in the real property recording office for the municipality where the land is located. UFLRA § 2(b).

satisfied and that the IRS thus had priority over Bank as to the rents arising under Tenant B's lease.

In making this argument, the IRS analogizes a lender's interest in post-tax-lien rents to a lender's interest in after-acquired accounts receivable. If the taxpayer sells goods or provides services on credit (and thus becomes entitled to be paid) after the IRS files a tax lien, the right to payment did not exist at the time of the tax lien notice. Thus, even if a lender had a prior perfected security interest in all of the taxpayer's present and after-acquired accounts receivable, the lender's lien would be "inchoate" as to the accounts that arose after the IRS tax lien filing. As a result, the lender's prior-perfected security interest in those particular accounts would not take priority over the tax lien, except to the limited extent provided in FTLA § 6323(c).

Technically, the right to collect rents under a lease of land does fit within the definition of "account" under U.C.C. Article 9. U.C.C. § 9–102(a)(2)(i) ("account" includes "a right to payment of a monetary obligation . . . for property that has been or is to be sold, leased, licensed, assigned, or otherwise disposed of . . ."). Does this mean that rents arising under the lease with Tenant B were like after-acquired accounts and thus inchoate so as to give the IRS priority as to those rents? Or should Bank's prior recorded assignment of rents give it priority over the IRS as to the rents arising under Tenant B's lease?

In Bloomfield State Bank v. United States, 644 F.3d 521 (7th Cir.2011), Judge Richard Posner provided the first and only reported appellate opinion addressing the issue, concluding that the prior recorded assignee of rents would have priority over the federal tax lien. Judge Posner rejected the argument that the rents were akin to after-acquired accounts receivable, instead treating the rents as "proceeds" of the land without regard to the timing of the lease:

> The real estate that generated the rental income at issue in this case existed when the mortgage was issued and thus before the tax lien attached; the rental income was proceeds of that property, which preexisted the tax lien. . . .
>
> . . . [B]ecause the bank had a lien on the real estate, the rentals were proceeds. By virtue of the rental-income provision in the mortgage [*i.e.*, the assignment of rents], the bank had a separate lien on the rents, but that is not the lien on which it is relying to trump the tax lien. The lien on which it is relying is the lien on the real estate. If an asset that secures a loan is sold and a receivable generated, the receivable becomes the security, substituting for the original asset. The sort of receivable to which the statute denies priority over a federal tax lien is one that does not match an existing asset; a month's rent is a receivable that matches the value of the real property for that month. [644 F.3d at 525–526.]

Do you agree with Posner's analysis? Why might it be appropriate to equate "rents" and "proceeds"? See R. Wilson Freyermuth, Of Hotel Revenues, Rents, and Formalism in the Bankruptcy Courts: Implications for Reforming Commercial Real Estate Finance, 40 UCLA L. Rev. 1461, 1533 (1993).

CHAPTER EIGHT

GOVERNMENT INTERVENTION AND PRIVATE RISK-SPREADING IN THE MORTGAGE MARKET

■ ■ ■

The preceding chapters of this casebook have developed the doctrines of real estate conveyancing and security law. The remaining chapters will describe how these doctrines are employed in the financing and development of land. In this chapter, we will discuss the real estate finance market and its regulation and support by government. The following chapters will address various types of real estate development.

A. MORTGAGE LENDING IN AMERICA: AN OVERVIEW

Mortgage debt in the United States exceeded $13.3 trillion dollars in mid-2014; this was nearly half of all outstanding debt. Clearly, mortgage finance is critically important for the economy and for effectuating certain policy goals, such as fostering homeownership. Unsurprisingly, the government is actively involved in regulating and facilitating the mortgage market in a number of ways. However, developing and implementing an optimal set of regulations and interventions has proven difficult, and failures in the government's regulatory system substantially contributed to the credit and real estate market crises that occurred in 2007 and succeeding years. Hence, a consideration of the government's role is an essential part of evaluating the real estate finance system.

This chapter begins with an overview of mortgage lending. This section of the book describes the various types of mortgage lenders, the government-sponsored mortgage market support institutions, and their regulators, with particular focus on the changes that occurred in response to the 2007 market failures. The next section examines governmental efforts to prevent lending abuses, such as class-based lending discrimination and predatory lending. The following section deals with government and private programs to spread mortgage risk by means of mortgage insurance and guarantees. Finally, this chapter considers the balance of regulatory power between the federal and state governments as it is adjusted through federal preemption of state law.

As we begin to look at the structure of the mortgage market, we must keep certain distinctions in mind. One is the difference between the *origination* and *holding* of mortgages. By origination, we mean the acts necessary to put the loan "on the books." Somewhat simplified, they include receiving the prospective borrower's loan application, making the necessary appraisal, credit, and employment checks, seeing that the documents (such as the note, mortgage, and Truth-in-Lending and RESPA disclosures) are prepared and executed, providing for title (and perhaps mortgage) insurance, recording of documents, and disbursing the loan funds to the borrower or, in the case of a purchase-money mortgage, to the seller. We often colloquially refer to these steps all together as "the loan closing" or simply "the closing."

When these steps have been completed, the mortgage loan has been "originated." What will the originating institution do with this new investment? It may continue to hold the note and the mortgage that secures it in its own portfolio, collect the monthly payments, and use them for its other business activities. In the early days of mortgage lending in the U.S., this was the most common business practice among mortgage lenders. See Christopher K. Odinet, The Unfinished Business of Dodd-Frank: Reforming the Mortgage Contract, 69 SMU L. Rev. 653, 694 n.58 (2016). Obviously, this is feasible only if the institution has a source of investment funds, such as savings account deposits, life insurance premium receipts, or pension fund contributions, that it can devote to investment in mortgages. For example, savings associations (a type of depositary institution) traditionally held most of the loans they originated in their own portfolios. *Id.*

As a second alternative, the originator may sell the note and mortgage (i.e., "sell the loan") to another institution. Indeed, a whole class of businesses (called mortgage banks or, more accurately, nonbank mortgage lenders) exists for the purpose of originating loans with the expectation of selling all of them to other investors. Depository institutions, such as commercial banks and savings associations, also sell loans, particularly when their deposit inflows are slow and demand for new loans is high in their market areas.

The business arrangements under which originators obtain the funds they need, and by which they transfer the loans they create to secondary market investors, can take several different forms, as the following excerpt illustrates.

CONSUMER FINANCIAL PROTECTION BUREAU
EXAMINATION PROCEDURES: MORTGAGE ORIGINATION
(2012)

Mortgage lending generally occurs through retail, wholesale, or correspondent lending channels. Sometimes there are no clear lines of demarcation among the channels, as a participant may operate in more than one of them. Each channel is described in more detail below.

1.   Retail Channel

In the retail channel, the lender conducts the origination process directly with the consumer, either in person or through an online application. An employee of the lender, generally called a loan officer, solicits the loan, takes the application, and tracks the application through to the closing process.

2.   Wholesale Channel—Mortgage Brokers

In the wholesale channel, a mortgage broker solicits the loan and takes the application from the consumer. Mortgage brokers are independent contractors and are not employees of the lender. The broker establishes relationships with multiple mortgage lenders and offers different mortgage loan products from these lenders. Mortgage brokers generally do not make underwriting decisions and do not actually fund the loans. In this channel, it is the mortgage lender that makes the underwriting decision, based on information provided by the broker. These mortgage lenders, called wholesale lenders, often are divisions of larger depository institutions. Generally, a wholesale lender requires a broker to enter into a wholesale lending agreement before the broker may originate loans on the lender's behalf.

In a variant of standard wholesale mortgage originations, some brokers "table fund" loans. In a table-funded transaction, the mortgage broker closes the loan as the lender of record and then assigns the loan to a purchaser at or immediately after the closing. The loan purchaser provides the funding for the loan, but the documents name the mortgage broker as the creditor.

3.   Correspondent Channel—Small Mortgage Lenders

Correspondent lending, a hybrid of retail channel and wholesale channel lending, often features smaller institutions, acting as correspondent lenders. Correspondent lenders are the primary interface with consumers, conducting all steps in the mortgage origination process and funding their own loans. They generally originate and deliver loans pursuant to underwriting standards set by other lenders or investors, usually larger depository lenders, upon advance commitment on price. In addition to soliciting consumers directly, correspondent lenders may receive applications and mortgage documents from mortgage brokers and subsequently speak directly with the consumer. Generally, a wholesale lender requires a correspondent to enter into a written correspondent lending agreement before the correspondent may originate loans for sale to the wholesale lender.

———————————

The graphic below shows residential mortgage debt in 2017 by type of originator. Over the past several years, credit unions have lost significant market share, and the share of mortgage originations by banking institutions has also fallen. Today, nonbank mortgage companies like QuickenLoans (the largest in 2019) and United Shore Financial have a majority of the market. Of the top 25 mortgage lenders in 2019 by total loan volume (which account for 37.2% of total loan originations that year), 17 were nonbanks. The top bank lenders in 2019 were Wells Fargo and Chase.

Residential Mortgage Debt by Originator Type (2017)

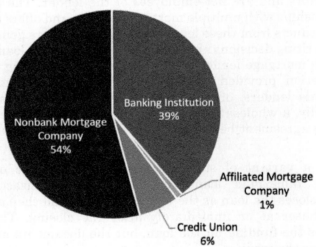

What sorts of institutions buy loans from originators? Three government sponsored enterprises (GSEs) have been active buyers in the so-called secondary mortgage market: Fannie Mae (formerly known as the Federal National Mortgage Association), Freddie Mac (formerly known as the Federal Home Loan Mortgage Corporation), and the Government National Mortgage Association ("GNMA" or "Ginnie Mae"). We will examine the activities of these entities in more depth later. Life insurance companies and pension funds have seen mortgage loans, especially on large income-producing projects, as attractive investments. Because they usually do not have local personnel outside the home office trained in loan origination, a symbiotic relationship often exists between a mortgage banker and the life insurance companies, pension funds, or other investors that buy its commercial loans. Depository institutions, especially those in capital-rich areas such as New England, also have been important mortgage loan purchasers.

A third alternative for the mortgage loan originator (or an investor to whom the originator sells the loan) is to place the loan in a pool with others having similar characteristics and to "securitize" them. This can be done in one of several ways. One method is to sell "participation certificates" to investors. Each of these certificates transfers a fractional share of ownership in the pool of loans, much like stock certificates in a corporation. The lender issuing the certificates may guarantee payment of them to the investors. A second method is for the investor to segregate a pool of mortgage loans into a separate entity altogether (usually a trust) and to then have the trust issue securities to be sold in the capital markets and that are backed by the mortgage loans themselves. This sort of security is known as a mortgage-backed security ("MBS"). Many different types of MBS exist. You will learn more about them in Section C of this chapter.

Two other distinctions must be kept in mind as we study the mortgage market. One is the difference between construction loans and long-term (sometimes called "permanent" or "take-out") loans. A construction loan is normally a short-term or demand loan made to a developer of real estate, who may or may not be the long-term owner of the building or subdivision being built. When the construction is completed, the permanent lender disburses the permanent loan funds, and the builder uses these funds to pay off (or "take out") the construction loan. The "permanent" loan is not literally permanent; it is a long-term loan (typically 8- to 20-year maturity for commercial property) made to the long-term owner of the property. Although permanent loans often are sold on the secondary market or are securitized, construction loans rarely are.

The other important distinction to consider is that between home loans (traditionally defined as loans on one-to-four family residential property) and loans on other types of real estate, such as apartment buildings, office buildings, shopping centers, industrial parks, farms, or undeveloped land (i.e., commercial loans). When we examine statistics about the mortgage market, we must be clear about the kind of property securing a particular loan. The following table, taken from data provided by the Federal Reserve Board, shows mortgage debt outstanding in the United States as of the end of the third quarter of 2019 by property type.

	Amount of Debt (Billions)	Percentage of Total Debt
Total Mortgage Debt, All Properties:	$15,841	
Farm Properties	254	1.6%
Nonfarm Properties by Type of Property:		
1-to-4 Family Houses	11,075	69.9%
Multifamily Housing	1,565	9.9%
Commercial Property	2,947	18.6%
Total Nonfarm Property	15,587	98.4%

These data show that approximately three-fourths of all mortgage debt is represented by what is undoubtedly the most familiar category to most Americans—the one-to-four family home mortgage loan. Mortgage loans on commercial properties are next largest in importance, while both farm mortgages and mortgages on apartment projects are far less significant in the overall picture.

The following chart, drawn from Federal Reserve System data, shows the types of mortgage debt holders and the percentage of overall mortgage debt that each type holds as of the third quarter of 2019.

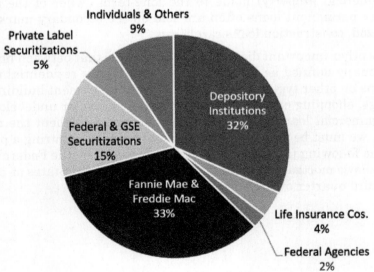

Holders of U.S. Mortgage Debt (Q3 2019)

- Individuals & Others 9%
- Private Label Securitizations 5%
- Federal & GSE Securitizations 15%
- Fannie Mae & Freddie Mac 33%
- Depository Institutions 32%
- Life Insurance Cos. 4%
- Federal Agencies 2%

It is interesting to see how overall mortgage debt has grown in the United States since the Great Depression. The following chart, which is derived from Federal Reserve Board data, shows total outstanding mortgage debt at five-year intervals.

Outstanding Mortgage Debt
(1940-2018)

Mortgage debt increased massively after the Second World War, especially during the 2000–2007 period, until the virtual collapse of the market in 2007. Growth since then started slowly but has since sped up. The rapid increase before 2007 was a result of many factors, including inflating land prices and construction costs, added real values as more real estate was developed, and a completely breakdown in loan underwriting.

B. MORTGAGE ORIGINATORS
AND THEIR REGULATORS

MARK JICKLIN & EDWARD V. MURPHY, WHO REGULATES WHOM? AN OVERVIEW OF U.S. FINANCIAL SUPERVISION

Congressional Research Service Report to Congress
December 8, 2010

Banking Regulators. Banking regulation in United States has evolved over time into a system of multiple regulators with overlapping jurisdictions. There is a dual banking system, in which each depository institution is subject to regulation by its chartering authority: state or federal. In addition, because virtually all depository institutions are federally insured, they are subject to at least one federal primary regulator (i.e., the federal authority responsible for examining the institution for safety and soundness and for ensuring its compliance with federal banking laws). The primary federal regulator of national banks is their chartering authority, the OCC [Office of the Comptroller of the Currency, within the U.S. Department of the Treasury]. The primary federal regulator of state-chartered banks that are members of the Federal Reserve System is the Board of Governors of the Federal Reserve System. State-chartered banks that are not members of the Federal Reserve System have the FDIC as their primary federal regulator. Thrifts (both state and federally chartered) had the Office of Thrift Supervision as their primary federal regulator, until the Dodd-Frank Act abolished the OTS and distributed its responsibilities among the OCC, the FDIC, and the Fed. All of these institutions, because their deposits are covered by FDIC deposit insurance, are also subject to the FDIC's regulatory authority. Credit unions—federally chartered or federally insured—are regulated by the National Credit Union Administration, which administers a deposit insurance fund separate from the FDIC's.

In general, lenders are expected to be prudent when extending loans. Each loan creates risk for the lender. The overall portfolio of loans extended or held by a lender, in relation to other assets and liabilities, affects that institution's stability. The relationship of lenders to each other, and to wider financial markets, affects the financial system's stability. The nature of these risks can vary between industry sectors, including commercial loans, farm loans, and consumer loans. Safety and soundness regulation encompasses the characteristics of (1) each loan, (2) the balance sheet of each institution, and (3) the risks in the system as a whole. Each loan has a variety of risk characteristics of concern to lenders and their regulators. Some of these risk characteristics can be estimated at the time the loan is issued. Credit risk, for example, is the risk that the borrower will fail to repay the principal of the loan as promised. Rising interest rates create another risk because the shorter-term interest rates that the lender often pays for its funds rise (e.g., deposit or CD rates) while the longer-term interest rates that the lender will receive from fixed-rate borrowers remain unchanged. Falling interest rates are not riskless either: fixed-rate borrowers may choose to repay loans early, reducing the lender's expected future cash flow. Federal financial regulators take into account expected default rates, prepayment rates, interest-rate exposure, and other risks when examining the loans issued by covered lenders.

Each lender's balance sheet can reduce or enhance the risks of the individual loans that make it up. A lender with many loans exposed to prepayment risk when interest rates fall, for example, could compensate by acquiring some assets that rise in value when interest rates fall. One example of a compensating asset would be an interest-rate derivative contract. Lenders are required to keep capital in reserve against the possibility of a drop in value of loan portfolios or other risky assets. Federal financial regulators take into account compensating assets, risk-based capital requirements, and other prudential standards when examining the balance sheets of covered lenders.

When regulators determine that a bank is taking excessive risks, or engaging in unsafe and unsound practices, they have a number of powerful tools at their disposal to reduce risk to the institution (and ultimately to the federal deposit insurance fund). They can require banks to reduce specified lending or financing practices, dispose of certain assets, and order banks to take steps to restore sound balance sheets. Banks have no alternative but to comply, since regulators have "life-or-death" options, such as withdrawing deposit insurance or seizing the bank outright.

NOTE ON NONBANK MORTGAGE LENDERS

Life insurance companies. The general insurance function of life insurance companies creates a steady and sizeable inflow of funds with a steady but relatively small and predictable outflow, which leaves large sums continually available for long-range investment. The investment pattern for these funds is based primarily upon the available return. As a result, mortgage loans must compete with other financial assets for life insurance companies' funds.

Until the 1950s, life insurance companies were significant lenders on single-family owner-occupied housing, but since then they have gradually withdrawn from this market and are now almost totally absent from it. However, life insurance companies remain a significant source of funding for commercial and multifamily apartment lending, accounting for 15.3% of all such mortgage loans held at the end of 2019. See Mortgage Bankers Association, Commercial/Multifamily Quarterly Databook 44 (Q4 2019).

Mortgage banking companies. Mortgage banking companies (which are really nonbanks but are colloquially referred to as "mortgage banks") originate loans in order to sell them to other investors or to securitize them. Hence, they hold loans only for the short term. While nonbank mortgage lenders make both residential and commercial loans, many specialize in single-family residential lending. The bulk of their business traditionally involved the origination of FHA-insured and VA-guaranteed mortgage loans. However, with the growth of private mortgage insurance companies, mortgage bankers increasingly expanded their activities into the field of conventional mortgages.

The growth and importance of these nonbank companies can hardly be understated. According to Home Mortgage Disclosure Act (HMDA) data from 2017, nonbank mortgage lenders originated 80% of all FHA loans, 70% of all VA loans, 64% of all USDA rural housing service loans, and nearly half of all conventional loans. These firms are quickly outpacing banks in the mortgage origination business, as well as in mortgage servicing. Importantly, 2017 HMDA data show that nonbank mortgage lenders originate 59% of all mortgage loans that go to low- and moderate-income households and over 64% of all mortgage loans that go to minority homebuyers.

Because mortgage bankers are not depository institutions, they cannot fund loans from customer deposits as can banks and savings associations. Instead, nonbank mortgage lenders fund loans with corporate capital and, more importantly, from warehouse loans, which are short-term lines of credit, usually from commercial banks. Some nonbank mortgage lenders have been started by or become affiliated with large financial institutions, such as bank holding companies.

Nonbank mortgage lenders sell their loans by soliciting commitments from large institutions to purchase substantial blocks of single-family loans and multifamily loans, and by selling mortgage-backed securities. Both Fannie Mae and Freddie Mac purchase large numbers of loans from mortgage bankers, and Ginnie Mae has had a great influence over nonbank mortgage lenders' operations through their use of the Ginnie Mae mortgage-backed security program. The nonbank's income is earned from borrower fees, servicing fees, profits from loan sales, and indirectly from large tax and insurance escrow deposits, which are often used as compensating balances for bank lines of credit. A nonbank also may earn income from sidelines, such as land development and construction loans and standby commitments.

Nonbank mortgage companies are typically corporations and, as such, are subject to state corporate laws and regulations. Historically, federal and state supervision of nonbank mortgage companies was minimal. However, many states have now adopted licensing laws for these firms, and they have become subject to heavier regulation (although nothing that nears the regulation of banks).

Mortgage brokers. During the past thirty years, the United States has witnessed huge growth in the use of mortgage brokers to originate residential loans. A mortgage broker, unlike the nonbank mortgage lender described above, does not actually fund the loan. Rather, the broker acts as an intermediary that finds a lender for the borrower. This has become an increasingly valuable service as the array of mortgages has become more varied. The broker takes the borrower's loan application, performs a preliminary financial and credit evaluation based on the lender's underwriting standards, produces the necessary documents, and supervises the loan closing. The lender may be a bank, nonbank lender, or a thrift institution. The loan is closed in the lender's name, and the lender underwrites, funds, and sometimes services the loan. The mortgage broker charges a fee that is paid by the borrower or the lender, usually in the form of a percentage of the loan amount. The way in which brokers were paid was once a very controversial matter because before the Dodd-Frank Act of 2010, brokers would disguise their fees in the form of an increased interest rate—typically in a way that was difficult for borrowers to understand. Today, all fees must be disclosed upfront and must be itemized, and they cannot be tied to the interest rate. Dodd-Frank § 1403(c)(4)(A), (2); see also 12 C.F.R. Part 1026. See also Nicole Olvera, Why the CFPB Should Reconsider Dodd-Frank's Prohibition on Yield Spread Premiums, 16 N.C. Banking Inst. 323 (2012).

C. GOVERNMENT-SPONSORED MORTGAGE MARKET SUPPORT INSTITUTIONS

HOUSING AMERICA'S FUTURE: NEW DIRECTIONS FOR NATIONAL POLICY

Housing Commission, Bipartisan Policy Center
February 2013, pages 40–46

Historical Context: The Path to Today's Housing Finance System. The Great Depression was a watershed period in the history of housing in the United States. Up until the mid-1930s, residential mortgages generally had short terms (usually three to ten years), variable interest rates, and featured "bullet" payments of principal at term. Borrowers would normally refinance these loans when they became due or pay off the outstanding loan balance. At the time, large down payments were common, and mortgages typically had very low loan-to-value (LTV) ratios of 60 percent or less. The homeownership rate, however, was significantly lower than it is today—around 45 percent, compared with 64.6 percent—as fewer families had the financial wherewithal to enter into mortgages with these more stringent terms. Homeownership was generally reserved for the wealthy or, in rural areas, for those who lived on and farmed their land.

As the Great Depression swept the nation, housing values declined by as much as 50 percent. Banks that held the mortgages on these homes refused to or were unable to refinance when the loans came due. Thousands of borrowers then defaulted, having neither the cash nor the home equity available to repay the loans. The consequence was a wave of about 250,000 foreclosures annually between 1931 and 1935.

In response to these events, the federal government established the Federal Home Loan Bank system in 1932 to increase the supply of mortgage funds available to local financial institutions and to serve as a credit reserve. Two years later, in 1934, the government created the FHA to help stabilize the mortgage market through its insurance programs. By insuring only mortgages that met certain limits on the maximum principal obligation, interest rate, LTV ratio, and loan duration, the FHA helped set the foundation for the modern standardized single-family mortgage. In 1944, the government established the VA loan guarantee program, similar in approach to the FHA loan-level insurance programs but targeted to helping military veterans and their families secure homeownership. In the years following World War II, the homeownership rate rose steadily, from 43.6 percent in 1940 to 55 percent in 1950 and to 66.2 percent in 2000, as measured by the Decennial Census.

In addition to ownership housing, the FHA also provides credit support for multifamily rental housing through a separate reserve fund first established by the National Housing Act of 1938. The FHA's authority to support multifamily housing was not widely exercised until the 1960s when several programs were created to encourage the construction and preservation of rental housing for moderate-income households.

In 1934, the government also authorized the FHA to create national mortgage associations to provide a secondary market to help mortgage lenders gain access to capital for FHA-insured loans. Only one such association was established, when the FHA chartered the Federal National Mortgage Association in 1937. In 1968, the Federal National Mortgage Association was partitioned into two separate entities—the Government National Mortgage Association, or Ginnie Mae, which remained in the government, and Fannie Mae, which became a privately owned company charged with the public mission of supporting the mortgage market by purchasing conventional (i.e., non-government-insured) mortgages. Until the 1980s, Fannie Mae carried out its mission by issuing debt—first as a government agency and after 1968 as a government-sponsored enterprise (GSE)—and using it to buy mortgages from their originators. In 1970, the secondary market grew with the creation of Freddie Mac, which was initially owned by the Federal Home Loan Banks and, with passage of the Financial Institutions Reform, Recovery and Enforcement Act (FIRREA) in 1989, reorganized as a private, for-profit corporation with a charter similar to that of Fannie Mae.

Over the years, Fannie Mae, Freddie Mac, and Ginnie Mae helped bring greater transparency and standardization to both the single-family and multifamily housing finance system, which has lowered mortgage costs. By setting clear benchmarks for loans eligible for securitization, the three institutions also helped improve the overall credit quality of the system. Moreover, by linking local financial institutions with global investors in the secondary market, they helped expand access to mortgage credit.

However, the companies' role was a sore point for the lending industry almost from the start. Acting as a giant thrift, Fannie Mae profited from the spread it earned between its cost of funds, which was lower than other private companies because of its government ties, and the interest rates on mortgages. The creation of the first MBS by Ginnie Mae in the 1970s led Fannie Mae and Freddie Mac, and then private Wall Street firms, to engage in securitization. Depositories viewed Fannie Mae as a competitor for balance-sheet lending, and, after MBS became the prevalent funding source, private-sector competitors likewise saw the GSEs as unfairly competing with them in the securities markets. Both institutions did enjoy a number of benefits because of their unique charters, including a line of credit with the U.S. Treasury, exemptions from certain state and local taxes, which provided favorable treatment for their portfolio business, and most importantly, an implied government guarantee of their securities as well as their own corporate debt. In return, the charters restricted Fannie

Mae and Freddie Mac only to residential mortgage finance in the United States, and the companies were expected to support mortgage markets throughout all market cycles, an obligation that did not apply to other fully private investors or guarantors.

In the wake of the Savings and Loan crisis in 1989, Congress imposed new capital requirements and strengthened the GSEs' mission requirements. But the pressure to deliver returns to shareholders, along with the mistaken view shared by actors throughout the mortgage market that housing prices would continue to rise without interruption, encouraged Fannie Mae and Freddie Mac to leverage their businesses to unsustainable levels. With insufficient capital buffers, both institutions suffered catastrophic losses when the housing market collapsed and the credit markets froze, leading to their conservatorship by the government in 2008. Notably, during the housing crisis, the multifamily businesses of Fannie Mae and Freddie Mac continued to generate a profit for both institutions, as the default rates on their multifamily loans were substantially lower than the loans in their single-family portfolios. It is also worth noting that the 12 Federal Home Loan Bank cooperatives, which were designed to provide countercyclical liquidity for U.S. mortgage and housing market participants, remained a reliable source of liquidity for their more than 7,700 member institutions during the crisis. The Home Loan Banks provide a reliable flow of funds and liquidity to local lenders for housing and community development through advances funded by debt the banks issue and collateralized by mortgages or mortgage bonds exchanged by members in return for the advances. In late 2008, while other sources of credit froze, Federal Home Loan Bank advances increased by $400 billion (reaching $1 trillion) as the Home Loan Banks continued to support their members' participation in the housing market.

Despite our current difficulties, households in the United States have enjoyed a wider range of mortgage financing options than those in most other nations of the world. For instance, the most common mortgage product in the United States—the long-term, fixed-rate mortgage—is relatively rare in other countries where shorter-term and variable-rate mortgages are the norm. The long-term, fixed-rate mortgage has been a tremendous boon to consumers who are provided with cost certainty and protection from the risks associated with fluctuating interest rates. The process of securitization has played an instrumental role in setting the standards for these mortgages and making them widely available on affordable terms for millions of American families. By taking individual mortgages—inherently illiquid and difficult-to-price assets—and combining them with millions of other loans in stable securities based on cash flows from a broadly diversified portfolio of assets, securitization has opened the residential finance market to investors who otherwise could not participate in this market. The flow of cash has helped fuel one of the most stable, transparent, and efficient capital markets in the world and assured American consumers of a steady and reliable source of mortgage credit.

Single-Family Housing Finance Trends. In the wake of the collapse of privately funded and nongovernment-insured mortgages, the federal government has emerged as a dominant presence in the housing finance market, a role it has played before when private capital has fled the mortgage market. The federal government currently insures and guarantees the largest share of mortgage-backed securities and assumes the major portion of credit risk in the U.S. mortgage market.

In 2011, securities backed by Fannie Mae, Freddie Mac, and Ginnie Mae (with credit insurance from the FHA and the VA) constituted 97 percent of all MBS, with non-agency funds less than 3 percent. By comparison, Fannie Mae, Freddie Mac, and Ginnie Mae accounted for 78 percent of the MBS market in 2000, with non-agency funds at 22 percent. Government and GSE shares of MBS remained relatively steady through the 1990s, a period of strong economic growth and stable interest rates.

The same general situation is true for all mortgage originations (whether originated to be held in portfolio or sold into the MBS market). In 2010, private-sector-related originations including jumbo loans, loans originated for private-label securities, and adjustable-rate mortgages (ARMs) to be held in portfolio constituted only 12 percent of originations (compared with 53 percent in 2000 and 44 percent in 1990), while FHA/VA loans and Fannie Mae and Freddie Mac conforming loans constituted 88 percent of originations (versus 47 percent in 2000 and 56 percent in 1990).

While there are nascent signs that we have turned a corner, the U.S. system of single-family housing finance continues to face serious challenges as significant problems related to the Great Recession persist. Sustained high unemployment, an unprecedented collapse in house prices—especially in certain highly affected states and metropolitan areas—the large volume of foreclosures, and a prolonged foreclosure process in some states continue to stand in the way of a full market recovery. Further, while in most of the country the cost of buying a home has never been more affordable, stringent underwriting requirements prevent many would-be borrowers from taking advantage of these conditions. Borrowers' credit scores at origination have increased by 40 to 50 points since 2001.

D. LENDING DISCRIMINATION

Class-based discrimination by mortgage lenders has been an ongoing problem in the United States. Some lenders have refused to make loans or have offered loans on less favorable terms to certain classes or races of loan applicants, or for homes in areas where the residents are predominantly members of racial minorities. Because of the perceived fundamental importance of housing and the usual need for financing to purchase it, a number of federal, state, and local laws prohibit lenders from engaging in these practices.

At the federal level, four principal statutes prohibit various types of discrimination in residential mortgage lending:

1.   *The Fair Housing Act*, 42 U.S.C. § 3605, which is part of the Civil Rights Act of 1968, provides:

(a) It shall be unlawful for any person or other entity whose business includes engaging in residential real estate-related transactions to discriminate against any person in making available such a transaction, or in the terms or conditions of such a transaction, because of race, color, religion, sex, handicap, familial status, or national origin.

(b) As used in this section, the term "residential real estate-related transaction" means any of the following:

(1) The making or purchasing of loans or providing other financial assistance—

(a) for purchasing, constructing, improving, repairing, or maintaining a dwelling; or

(b) secured by residential real estate.

2.   *The Fair Housing Act.* The Fair Housing Act's prohibition on sex discrimination was added by the Housing and Community Development Act of 1974, which also contains the following provision, 12 U.S.C. § 1735f–5:

No federally related mortgage loan, or Federal insurance, guaranty, or other assistance in connection therewith (under this chapter or any other Act), shall be denied to any person on account of sex; and every person engaged in making mortgage loans secured by residential real property shall consider without prejudice the combined income of both husband and wife for the purpose of extending mortgage credit in the form of a federally related mortgage loan to a married couple or either member thereof.

A "federally related mortgage loan" is defined as including loans on one-to-four family residences in which any federal, federally-chartered, or federally-insured financial institution or any federal mortgage insurance or guaranty is involved or that is eligible for purchase by a government-sponsored enterprise, such as Fannie Mae. This definition includes virtually all home mortgage loans. Enforcement of and rulemaking authority over the Fair Housing Act rests with the U.S. Department of Housing and Urban Development and private individuals. The U.S.

Department of Justice may enforce the Fair Housing Act if there is a pattern of violations. See 42 U.S.C. §§ 3610, 3612–14.

3.   *The Civil Rights Act of 1866*, 42 U.S.C. §§ 1981–82, provides in substance that all citizens have the same right to buy, sell, and own property and to make and to enforce contracts as white citizens. For a century, this language was interpreted to prohibit only governmental action, which significantly limited the law's effectiveness. Private lenders, landlords, and realtors, for example, were all outside the Act's purview. But, in Jones v. Alfred H. Mayer Co., 392 U.S. 409, 88 S.Ct. 2186, 20 L.Ed.2d 1189 (1968), the Supreme Court construed it to apply to private individuals as well—in that case, a real estate developer's refusal to sell houses to black citizens.

4.   *The Equal Credit Opportunity Act*, 15 U.S.C. § 1691 ("ECOA"), which was adopted in 1974, provides:

> It shall be unlawful for any creditor to discriminate against any applicant, with respect to any aspect of a credit transaction—
>
> (1) on the basis of race, color, religion, national origin, sex or marital status, or age (provided the applicant has the capacity to contract);
>
> (2) because all or part of the applicant's income derives from any public assistance program; or
>
> (3) because the applicant has in good faith exercised any right under this chapter.

The Consumer Financial Protection Bureau (CFPB), which was created by the Dodd-Frank Act of 2010 in the wake of the 2008 financial crisis, has the authority to issue regulations under ECOA. The CFPB also has the power to enforce ECOA, and federal law also empowers state attorneys general and state financial/banking commissioners to do the same. 12 U.S.C. §§ 5481(12)(D) and (14); 5564(a) (all dealing with enforcement); 5512(a) (dealing with rulemaking).

Two other federal statutes address the problem of lending discrimination, though they do not substantively prohibit it:

5.   *The Home Mortgage Disclosure Act of 1975*, 12 U.S.C. §§ 2801–2810 ("HMDA"), which has been described elsewhere in this chapter, requires both depository financial institutions and certain nonbank mortgage lenders (those with at least $10 million in assets and an office in a metropolitan statistical area) to maintain and to publish records showing, by census tract, loan amount, type of loan, borrower demographics and income level, and the locations of the properties that secure their mortgage loans. These requirements enable community organizations to determine whether mortgage lenders are (as has frequently been charged) taking

deposits out of central-city minority areas and relending them in "safe" all-white suburbs. The information is also useful to the examiners from the various federal and state banking agencies that audit financial institutions' overall performance.

6. *The Community Reinvestment Act of 1977*, 12 U.S.C. §§ 2901–2908 ("CRA"), requires each federally-related financial institution to adopt a delineation of the community that it serves and a statement of policy indicating how it will serve that community, with particular reference to meeting mortgage lending needs. The federal agencies that supervise financial institutions are instructed to take this information and the institution's performance under its statement into account in making decisions relevant to the institution's future plans, such as establishing new branch offices, M&A activity, and closing offices. See generally Craig E. Marcus, Note, Beyond the Boundaries of the Community Reinvestment Act and the Fair Lending Laws: Developing a Market-Based Framework for Generating Low- and Moderate-Income Lending, 96 Colum. L. Rev. 710 (1996). Federal financial regulatory agencies publicly release their ratings and evaluation reports of the lenders' performance under CRA. Lenders are rated on the basis of their awareness of community credit needs, marketing of credit availability, actual extension of credit to serve the needs, and community development activities. See Daniel Immergluck, Credit to the Community: Community Reinvestment and Fair Lending Policy in the United States (2004).

A final legal element bearing on discrimination in mortgage lending is the "disparate impact" concept. The Supreme Court first applied this concept in Griggs v. Duke Power Co., 401 U.S. 424, 91 S.Ct. 849, 28 L.Ed.2d 158 (1971). The case involved a company's employment and promotion practices under Title VII of the Civil Rights Act of 1964, which prohibits racial discrimination in employment. The company used intelligence and aptitude tests to determine which employees would be promoted. Black employees were less likely than whites to be promoted under this system, though no direct evidence existed that the employer intended to discriminate against blacks. The Court held that, if the plaintiffs could show that the company's tests and procedures had the *effect* of screening out disproportionate numbers of minorities, the burden would then shift to the employer to show that its practices were required by "business necessity" or by "genuine business need." Subsequent case development has indicated that the employer's burden is to show that it could not use other tests or criteria with a less discriminatory impact to accomplish the same business goal.

After much speculation, in 2015 the U.S. Supreme Court upheld the application of the disparate impact theory in Fair Housing Act cases. See Tex. Dep't of Hous. & Cmty. Affs. v. Inclusive Cmtys. Project, Inc., 576 U.S. 519 (2015). The disparate impact theory is significant because it does not require the plaintiff to prove that the defendant intended to discriminate (which is known as disparate treatment). With disparate impact, the defendant's intent does not matter—rather, the question is whether the defendant's policy or practice has, over time, had a discriminatory effect on a protected class. Indeed, many commonly-used mortgage lending criteria, such as length of time in present employment, length of residence in the community, and previous homeownership, probably have the effect of screening out more minorities than whites. The same may be true of traditional property appraisal standards, because members of racial minorities tend to have lower incomes and, hence, to seek housing in older and less costly neighborhoods. If it can be shown that these criteria have no or only slight power to predict mortgage loan default, does their use violate the Fair Housing Act? See David E. Teitelbaum & Clarke D. Camper, Developments in Fair Lending, 51 Bus. Law. 843 (1996) (suggesting that the statistical relevance of some factors used in credit scoring are questionable).

TEXAS DEPARTMENT OF HOUSING AND COMMUNITY AFFAIRS V. INCLUSIVE COMMUNITIES PROJECT, INC.

U.S. Supreme Court, 2015
576 U.S. 519, 135 S.Ct. 2507, 192 L.Ed.2d 514

KENNEDY, J.

The underlying dispute in this case concerns where housing for low-income persons should be constructed in Dallas, Texas—that is, whether the housing should be built in the inner city or in the suburbs. [Plaintiff nonprofit housing corporation alleged that the Texas Department of Housing and Community Affairs' had allocated too many housing tax credits for construction of low-income housing to predominantly black inner-city areas and not enough to predominantly white suburban neighborhoods with the result of continuing segregated housing patterns and discouraging housing for low-income blacks in the suburbs.] This dispute comes to the Court on a disparate-impact theory of liability. In contrast to a disparate-treatment case, where a "plaintiff must establish that the defendant had a discriminatory intent or motive," a plaintiff bringing a disparate-impact claim challenges practices that have a "disproportionately adverse effect on minorities" and are otherwise unjustified by a legitimate rationale. Ricci v. DeStefano, 557 U.S. 557, 577 (2009). The question presented for the Court's determination is whether disparate-impact claims are cognizable under the Fair Housing Act (or FHA), 82 Stat. 81, as amended, 42 U.S.C. § 3601 et seq. * * *

II.

The issue here is whether, under a proper interpretation of the FHA, housing decisions with a disparate impact are prohibited. * * *

Recognition of disparate-impact claims is consistent with the FHA's central purpose. The FHA...was enacted to eradicate discriminatory practices within a sector of our Nation's economy. See 42 U.S.C. § 3601 ("It is the policy of the United States to provide, within constitutional limitations, for fair housing throughout the United States"); H. R. Rep., at 15 (explaining the FHA "provides a clear national policy against discrimination in housing").

These unlawful practices include zoning laws and other housing restrictions that function unfairly to exclude minorities from certain neighborhoods without any sufficient justification. Suits targeting such practices reside at the heartland of disparate-impact liability. See, e.g., Huntington, 488 U.S., at 16–18 (invalidating zoning law preventing construction of multifamily rental units); Black Jack, 508 F. 2d, at 1182–1188 (invalidating ordinance prohibiting construction of new multifamily dwellings); Greater New Orleans Fair Housing Action Center v. St. Bernard Parish, 641 F. Supp. 2d 563, 569, 577–578 (ED La. 2009) (invalidating post-Hurricane Katrina ordinance restricting the rental of housing units to only " 'blood relative[s]' " in an area of the city that was 88.3% white and 7.6% black). The availability of disparate-impact liability, furthermore, has allowed private developers to vindicate the FHA's objectives and to protect their property rights by stopping municipalities from enforcing arbitrary and, in practice, discriminatory ordinances barring the construction of certain types of housing units. Recognition of disparate-impact liability under the FHA also plays a role in uncovering discriminatory intent: It permits plaintiffs to counteract unconscious prejudices and disguised animus that escape easy classification as disparate treatment. In this way disparate-impact liability may prevent segregated housing patterns that might otherwise result from covert and illicit stereotyping.

But disparate-impact liability has always been properly limited in key respects that avoid the serious constitutional questions that might arise under the FHA, for instance, if such liability were imposed based solely on a showing of a statistical disparity. Disparate-impact liability mandates the "removal of artificial, arbitrary, and unnecessary barriers," not the displacement of valid governmental policies. Griggs, supra, at 431. The FHA is not an instrument to force housing authorities to reorder their priorities. Rather, the FHA aims to ensure that those priorities can be achieved without arbitrarily creating discriminatory effects or perpetuating segregation.

* * *

It would be paradoxical to construe the FHA to impose onerous costs on actors who encourage revitalizing dilapidated housing in our Nation's cities merely because some other priority might seem preferable.

Entrepreneurs must be given latitude to consider market factors. Zoning officials, moreover, must often make decisions based on a mix of factors, both objective (such as cost and traffic patterns) and, at least to some extent, subjective (such as preserving historic architecture). These factors contribute to a community's quality of life and are legitimate concerns for housing authorities. The FHA does not decree a particular vision of urban development; and it does not put housing authorities and private developers in a double bind of liability, subject to suit whether they choose to rejuvenate a city core or to promote new low-income housing in suburban communities. As HUD itself recognized in its recent rulemaking, disparate-impact liability "does not mandate that affordable housing be located in neighborhoods with any particular characteristic." 78 Fed. Reg. 11476.

In a similar vein, a disparate-impact claim that relies on a statistical disparity must fail if the plaintiff cannot point to a defendant's policy or policies causing that disparity. A robust causality requirement ensures that "[r]acial imbalance . . . does not, without more, establish a prima facie case of disparate impact" and thus protects defendants from being held liable for racial disparities they did not create. Wards Cove Packing Co. v. Atonio, 490 U.S. 642, 653 (1989), superseded by statute on other grounds, 42 U.S.C. § 2000e–2(k). Without adequate safeguards at the prima facie stage, disparate-impact liability might cause race to be used and considered in a pervasive way and "would almost inexorably lead" governmental or private entities to use "numerical quotas," and serious constitutional questions then could arise. 490 U.S., at 653.

The litigation at issue here provides an example. From the standpoint of determining advantage or disadvantage to racial minorities, it seems difficult to say as a general matter that a decision to build low-income housing in a blighted inner-city neighborhood instead of a suburb is discriminatory, or vice versa. If those sorts of judgments are subject to challenge without adequate safeguards, then there is a danger that potential defendants may adopt racial quotas—a circumstance that itself raises serious constitutional concerns.

Courts must therefore examine with care whether a plaintiff has made out a prima facie case of disparate impact and prompt resolution of these cases is important. A plaintiff who fails to allege facts at the pleading stage or produce statistical evidence demonstrating a causal connection cannot make out a prima facie case of disparate impact. For instance, a plaintiff challenging the decision of a private developer to construct a new building in one location rather than another will not easily be able to show this is a policy causing a disparate impact because such a one-time decision may not be a policy at all. It may also be difficult to establish causation because of the multiple factors that go into investment decisions about where to construct or renovate housing units. And as Judge Jones observed below, if the ICP cannot show a causal connection between the Department's

policy and a disparate impact—for instance, because federal law
substantially limits the Department's discretion—that should result in
dismissal of this case. 747 F. 3d, at 283–284 (specially concurring opinion).

The FHA imposes a command with respect to disparate-impact
liability. Here, that command goes to a state entity. In other cases, the
command will go to a private person or entity. Governmental or private
policies are not contrary to the disparate-impact requirement unless they
are "artificial, arbitrary, and unnecessary barriers." Griggs, 401 U.S., at
431. Difficult questions might arise if disparate-impact liability under the
FHA caused race to be used and considered in a pervasive and explicit
manner to justify governmental or private actions that, in fact, tend to
perpetuate race-based considerations rather than move beyond them.
Courts should avoid interpreting disparate-impact liability to be so
expansive as to inject racial considerations into every housing decision.

The limitations on disparate-impact liability discussed here are also
necessary to protect potential defendants against abusive disparate-impact
claims. If the specter of disparate-impact litigation causes private
developers to no longer construct or renovate housing units for low-income
individuals, then the FHA would have undermined its own purpose as well
as the free-market system. And as to governmental entities, they must not
be prevented from achieving legitimate objectives, such as ensuring
compliance with health and safety codes. . . .

Were standards for proceeding with disparate-impact suits not to
incorporate at least the safeguards discussed here, then disparate-impact
liability might displace valid governmental and private priorities, rather
than solely "remov[ing] . . . artificial, arbitrary, and unnecessary barriers."
Griggs, 401 U.S., at 431. And that, in turn, would set our Nation back in
its quest to reduce the salience of race in our social and economic system.

It must be noted further that, even when courts do find liability under
a disparate-impact theory, their remedial orders must be consistent with
the Constitution. Remedial orders in disparate-impact cases should
concentrate on the elimination of the offending practice that "arbitrar[ily]
. . . operate[s] invidiously to discriminate on the basis of rac[e]." Ibid. If
additional measures are adopted, courts should strive to design them to
eliminate racial disparities through race-neutral means. See Richmond v.
J. A. Croson Co., 488 U.S. 469, 510 (1989) (plurality opinion) ("[T]he city
has at its disposal a whole array of race-neutral devices to increase the
accessibility of city contracting opportunities to small entrepreneurs of all
races"). Remedial orders that impose racial targets or quotas might raise
more difficult constitutional questions.

While the automatic or pervasive injection of race into public and
private transactions covered by the FHA has special dangers, it is also true
that race may be considered in certain circumstances and in a proper

fashion. Cf. Parents Involved in Community Schools v. Seattle School Dist. No. 1, 551 U.S. 701, 789 (2007) (Kennedy, J., concurring in part and concurring in judgment) ("School boards may pursue the goal of bringing together students of diverse backgrounds and races through other means, including strategic site selection of new schools; [and] drawing attendance zones with general recognition of the demographics of neighborhoods"). Just as this Court has not "question[ed] an employer's affirmative efforts to ensure that all groups have a fair opportunity to apply for promotions and to participate in the [promotion] process," Ricci, 557 U.S., at 585, it likewise does not impugn housing authorities' race-neutral efforts to encourage revitalization of communities that have long suffered the harsh consequences of segregated housing patterns. When setting their larger goals, local housing authorities may choose to foster diversity and combat racial isolation with race-neutral tools, and mere awareness of race in attempting to solve the problems facing inner cities does not doom that endeavor at the outset.

The Court holds that disparate-impact claims are cognizable under the Fair Housing Act * * *

[Chief Justice Roberts and Justices Alito, Scalia, and Thomas dissented in this opinion.]

MORTGAGE FINANCING: ACTIONS NEEDED TO HELP FHA MANAGE RISKS FROM NEW MORTGAGE LOAN PRODUCTS
U.S. Government Accountability Office
Report GAO–05–194, Feb. 2005, at 23–26

The mortgage industry is increasingly using mortgage scoring and automated underwriting. During the 1990s, private mortgage insurers, the GSEs, and larger financial institutions developed automated underwriting systems. Mortgage scoring is a technology-based tool that relies on the statistical analysis of millions of previously originated mortgage loans to determine how key attributes such as the borrower's credit history, the property characteristics, and the terms of the mortgage note affect future loan performance. Automated underwriting refers to the process of collecting and processing the data used in the underwriting process. FHA has developed and recently implemented a mortgage scoring tool, called the FHA TOTAL Scorecard, to be used in conjunction with existing automated underwriting systems. * * * The mortgage industry also uses credit scoring models for estimating the credit risk of individuals—these methodologies are based on information such as payment patterns.

Statistical analyses identifying the characteristics of borrowers who were most likely to make loan payments have been used to create a weight or score associated with each of the characteristics. According to Fair, Isaac and Company sources, credit scores are often called "FICO scores" because most credit scores are produced from software developed by Fair, Isaac and Company. FICO scores generally range from 300 to 850 with higher scores indicating better credit history. The lower the credit score, the more compensating factors lenders might require to approve a loan. These factors can include a higher down payment and greater borrower reserves.

The characteristics and standards for low and no down payment mortgage products vary among mortgage institutions. Standards to determine a borrower's eligibility differ from lender to lender. For example, one mortgage institution might have a limit on household income where another might not. Each of these mortgage products requires some form of borrower investment. Most mortgage institutions use automated systems to underwrite loans but differ on how they consider factors such as the borrower's credit score and credit history. Finally, mortgage institutions also try to mitigate the increased risk associated with these products by employing tools like prepurchase counseling and greater insurance coverage.

Economic research we reviewed indicated that LTV ratios and credit scores are among the most important factors when estimating the risk level associated with individual mortgages. We identified and reviewed 45 papers that examined factors that could be informative. Of these, 37 examined if the LTV ratio was important and almost all of these papers (35) found the LTV ratio of a mortgage important and useful. Nineteen research papers evaluated how effective a borrower's credit score was in predicting loan performance, and all but one reported that the credit score was important and useful. In addition, a number of the papers reported that other factors were useful when estimating the risk level. For example, characteristics of the borrower—such as qualifying ratios—were cited in several of the papers we reviewed. Finally, other research evaluated additional factors; however, we identified very few papers that investigated the same variables or corroborated these findings. Collectively, the research we reviewed appeared to concur that considering multiple factors was important and useful in estimating the risk level of individual mortgages. For example, some of the papers (7) reported that considering LTV ratio and credit score concurrently was important and useful when estimating the risk level of individual mortgages.

Many studies found that a mortgage's LTV ratio was an important factor when estimating the risk level associated with individual mortgages. In theory, LTV ratios are important because of the direct relationship that exists between the amount of equity borrowers have in their homes and the likelihood of risk of default. The higher the LTV ratio, the less cash borrowers will have invested in their homes and the more likely it is that they may default on mortgage obligations, especially during times of economic hardship (e.g., unemployment, divorce, home price depreciation). And, according to one study, "most models of mortgage loan performance emphasize the role of the borrower's equity in the home in the decision to default." We identified 45 papers that examined the relationship between default and one or more predictive variables; of these, 37 examined if LTV ratio was important and useful. Almost all of these papers (35) determined that LTV ratio was effective in predicting loan performance—specifically, when predicting delinquency, default, and foreclosure. Several papers reported that there was a strong positive relationship between LTV ratio and default. Specifically, one paper reported that the default rates for mortgages with an LTV ratio above 95 percent were three to four times higher than default rates for mortgages with an LTV ratio between 90 to 95 percent. Another paper found that, at the end of 5 years, the cumulative probability of default risks for mortgages with an LTV ratio less than 95 percent was 2.48 percent; however, the cumulative probability of default for mortgages with an LTV ratio greater than or equal to 95 percent was 3.53 percent.

While the majority of the empirical research found that LTV ratio mattered, four of the research efforts did not find that LTV ratio is important when estimating the risk level associated with individual mortgages. For example, one paper found that, for subprime loans, delinquency rates were relatively unaffected by the LTV ratio. Generally, subprime loans are loans made to borrowers with past credit problems at a higher cost than conventional mortgage loans. Additionally, some (7) research efforts examined the relationship between the LTV ratio and severity (losses), and all found that there was a positive relationship between the LTV ratio and severity. * * *

Despite the relatively recent use of credit score information in the mortgage industry, several studies found that credit score was an important and useful factor when estimating the risk level associated with individual mortgages. In general, credit scores represent a borrower's credit history.[33]

Credit histories consist of many items, including the number and age of credit accounts of different types, the incidence and severity of payment problems, and the length of time since any payment problems occurred. The credit score reflects a borrower's historic performance and is an indication of the borrower's ability and willingness to manage debt payments. Of the 45 papers we reviewed, 19 evaluated how effective a borrower's credit score was in predicting loan performance. Eighteen research efforts evaluated how effective a borrower's credit score was in predicting delinquency, default, and foreclosure; all of these efforts found that a borrower's credit score was important. Generally, the papers reported that higher credit scores were associated with lower levels of

[33] Generally, the mortgage industry began widely using credit score information in the late 1990s; therefore, considering credit score in empirical loan performance analysis is very recent. Further, there was a particularly strong housing market during this period.

defaults. Specifically, one study found that a mortgage with a credit score of 728 (indicating an applicant with excellent credit) had a default probability of 1.26 percent, while a mortgage with a credit score of 642 had a default probability of 3.41 percent—or more than two times higher.

Additionally, four research efforts examined the relationship between credit score and severity (losses), and three reported that there was a negative relationship between credit score and severity. For example, one study found that credit scores were also helpful in predicting the amount of losses resulting from foreclosed mortgages. In particular, the paper reported the loss rate for defaulted mortgages with high credit scores was lower than foreclosed mortgages with low credit scores.

NOTES

1.   *Intentional racial discrimination.* When race is a motivating factor in denial of mortgage financing for a home, the Fair Housing Act clearly has been violated. For example, in Green v. Rancho Santa Margarita Mortg. Co., 28 Cal.App.4th 686, 33 Cal.Rptr.2d 706 (1994), a mortgage broker failed to place a loan for a black couple though many lenders would have considered the couple to be qualified and though the broker had placed loans for less-qualified white couples in the same development. The court concluded that the broker's half-hearted efforts could be explained only by racial bias. See also Barber v. Rancho Mortg. & Inv. Corp., 26 Cal.App.4th 1819, 32 Cal.Rptr.2d 906 (1994).

However, such bias normally is difficult to prove. In Simms v. First Gibraltar Bank, 83 F.3d 1546 (5th Cir.1996), an apartment project owner, Simms, attempted to convince a lender to finance the conversion of the project into a cooperative that probably would be predominantly minority-owned. The bank refused, and the owner sued, claiming that the decision was racially motivated. The court was unconvinced:

> The fundamental flaw in this evidence is that Simms * * * presented absolutely no evidence that other, "non-protected" applicants or applications were treated any differently around the time of Simms' rejection. * * * Simms also did not present any evidence from which it might be inferred that First Gibraltar had a poor record of lending in minority areas or to minorities; furthermore, there was not the slightest evidence of racial bias presented on the part of any of First Gibraltar's personnel. Although Simms' expert, Smith, testified that it was industry custom to provide written notification of a rejection, and the district court ruled that First Gibraltar was required to give written notification of the rejection under Regulation B of the Equal Credit Opportunity Act, failure to provide written notification to Simms is insufficient to infer a racial motive on the part of First Gibraltar without some showing that other, "non-protected" applications were treated differently. In other words, failing to follow industry custom or federal regulations is not evidence from which a jury could infer racial animus unless Simms showed that First

Gibraltar normally conformed with industry custom or complied with federal regulations in handling similar, "non-protected" applications. [83 F.3d at 1558.]

The difficulty of proving that the defendant's actions are motivated by racial bias often leads plaintiffs to attempt to prove their case on the basis of disparate racial impact instead.

2. *Disparate impact*. There is no doubt that many lenders and mortgage loan servicers intensely dislike the disparate impact test. It can easily have the effect of delegitimizing credit standards and servicing practices that they have used for decades and that they consider essential to good lending practice. If they are attacked by a regulatory agency or the Department of Justice, they are faced with an unattractive choice—to spend the necessary time and resources to defend against the claim, perhaps unsuccessfully, or to settle, often for a substantial sum. Settlement is often the more attractive option.

3. *AI underwriting and alternative data*. A significant contemporary issue relative to the disparate impact theory and lending deals with the growing use of alternative data and machine learning in credit scoring. Alternative data refers to borrower information that does not appear on a traditional credit report, which typically consists of history with past credit services and products, foreclosures, bankruptcies, and evictions. See Josh Lauer, Creditworthy: A History of Consumer Surveillance and Financial Identity in America (2017), Non-traditional data includes things like a borrower's social media activity, digital footprint, purchasing habits, and personal preferences. A growing number of both banks and nonbanks are using these techniques to either enhance or replace their use of existing credit scoring methods. See Christopher K. Odinet, Securitizing Digital Debts, 52 Ariz. St. L.J. 477, 490–94 (2020) In these contexts, the correlations being drawn by these algorithms between seemingly irrelevant information about a borrower and a statistically significant propensity to repay a loan may be too remote or counterintuitive for human cognition. See Christopher K. Odinet, The New Data of Student Debt, 92 S. Cal. L. Rev. 1617, 1645–49 (2019). What sorts of unique lending discrimination issues does this raise and how does the disparate impact theory's burden shifting analysis work in these situations? See Mikella Hurley & Julius Adebayo, Credit Scoring in the Era of Big Data, 18 Yale J.L. & Tech. 148, 164–65 (2016); Andrew D. Selbst & Solon Barocas, The Intuitive Appeal of Explainable Machines, 87 Fordham L. Rev. 1085, 1131 (2018); Anya E.R. Prince & Daniel Schwarcz, Proxy Discrimination in the Age of Artificial Intelligence and Big Data, 105 Iowa L. Rev. 1257 (2020). Only time will tell as to whether the current disparate impact theory is sufficient to accommodate these new forms of artificial intelligence underwriting or if new theories (or laws) will be necessary.

4. *The "Qualified Mortgage" regulations*. The introduction of the Qualified Mortgage (QM) concept by the 2010 Dodd-Frank Act added a further layer of complexity to the equation. The applicable regulation was issued by CFPB on January 10, 2013; see 12 CFR Part 1026.

Adopted to implement Dodd-Frank's "ability to repay" concept, the initial definition of a QM, as formulated by the CFPB, included a provision that the ratio of the borrower's total installment debt to income cannot exceed 43 percent. While this percentage is relatively liberal and is equivalent to the current Federal Housing Administration requirement, there is little doubt that, because minority borrowers tend to have lower incomes and carry heavier debt service burdens that whites, the use of a 43% ratio will have the effect of rationing out more minority than white households. Home mortgage lenders are not required to confine their lending to QMs, but the definition represents a safe harbor in the sense that QM loans are automatically deemed to satisfy the "ability to repay" requirement. Moreover, the CFPB has issued a regulation that gives QM status to loans that exceed the 43% ratio if they are eligible for purchase by Fannie Mae or Freddie Mac (this regulation is called the "GSE patch"). This rule is important since so much of the mortgage market is dominated by Fannie and Freddie.

Under late 2020 rulemaking, however, the 43% ratio is being replaced with a price-based limit. In other words, rather than focusing on a ratio, the APR on the loan cannot exceed the average prime offer rate[1] for a comparable transaction within certain loan limits. For example, if the mortgage loan amount is $110,260 or more, then the APR cannot exceed the average prime offer rate by 2.25 or more percentage points.[2] However, this change is not without controversy, as some believe it will lead to weaker underwriting. See Patricia A. McCoy & Susan M. Wachter, The Macroprudential Implications of the Qualified Mortgage Debate, 83 L. & Contemp. Probs. 21 (2020).

On a related note, lenders who expected to limit their lending to loans complying with the QM standards worried that they might be open to a charge of illegal discrimination under a disparate impact analysis. The CFBP and the federal financial regulators attempted to quell these fears, issuing a joint statement that they did "not anticipate that a creditor's decision to offer only Qualified Mortgages would, absent other factors, elevate a supervised institution's fair lending risk." Joint Release: Federal Regulators Provide Guidance on Qualified Mortgage Fair Lending Risks (Oct. 2013). Many lenders were less than fully satisfied; HUD and the Department of Justice did not join in the statement, and in any event, a policy adopted by the federal agencies would not preclude a private action under ECOA or the Fair Housing Act.

E. PREDATORY LENDING

In recent decades concern has grown about the practice of "predatory" mortgage lending. Predatory loans may have terms that are highly

---

[1] The "average prime offer rate" means an annual percentage rate that is derived from average interest rates, points, and other loan pricing terms currently that are offered to consumers by a representative sample of creditors for mortgage transactions that have low-risk pricing characteristics. In other words, it's the APR on a mortgage loan offered to highly credit-worthy borrowers. See 12 C.F.R. § 1026.35(a)(2).

[2] CFPB, Executive Summary of the December 2020 Amendments to the ATR/QM Rule 3 (Dec. 2020).

disadvantageous—high interest rates, high front-end "points," excessive fees for front-end services, high prepayment penalties, and sometimes a "balloon" obligation after only a small portion of the original loan balance has been amortized. Some predatory loans are made to borrowers who could not qualify for more "normal" mortgage financing, but this is not always the case; sometimes the borrowers have had good credit and adequate income and would have been able to obtain a loan from other sources on much better terms. But, like a large number of borrowers, rich and poor, they did not shop the market to try to find better terms.

Should such loans be illegal, regardless of whether they have a discriminatory effect on racial minorities? In recent years, an increasing number of states and cities have adopted legislation making "predatory" loans illegal. But the meaning of the term "predatory" is not self-evident, and a wide variety of definitions have been adopted.

There is only one federal statute addressing predatory lending: The Home Ownership and Equity Protection Act, or HOEPA. The statute was substantially modified by the Dodd-Frank financial reform legislation of 2010. Its application is governed by rules promulgated by the CFPB. HOEPA loans consist of certain high-cost residential mortgage loans. A mortgage loan is deemed "high-cost" and thus subject to HOEPA when it is made above certain interest rate or fee thresholds. A HOEPA loan provides borrowers with special protections.

The new HOEPA rules are, to put it mildly, complex, and they illustrate the difficulties of formulating rules to curb abusive lending practices. Lenders who make HOEPA loans (and those who wish to avoid making such loans) will incur substantial training and supervision expenses to ensure compliance with the law, and those costs will be passed onto all borrowers in the form of higher loan costs. Lenders particularly complained about the provisions for including originator compensation (including salaries) as a loan fee; they argued that compensation was often formula-driven and that it was not easy to allocate it to individual loans.

The market impact of HOEPA. There is little doubt that most institutional lenders are not eager to make HOEPA loans, and that the expanded definitions of the CFBP's new rule will reduce the availability of low-balance mortgage loans. Lenders generally decried this result; see, e.g., Joseph A. Woodruff & Chris Driskill, Say Goodbye to Small Loans: The CFPB's Amendments to HOEPA Are Likely to Put A Chill on Lower-Balance Mortgage Lending, Mortgage Banking (July 2013). But is that a good thing or a bad thing? The question is not easy to answer. By definition, HOEPA loans have onerous terms, but if they are not available, where will consumers go for comparable credit? Perhaps to small loan companies or "payday" lenders? Will the terms of the alternative forms of credit be better or worse than HOEPA loans? These are questions to which we have seen no systematic or conclusive answers.

HOEPA was designed to curtail abusive and unfair practices by lenders in making new mortgage loans. There are, however, numerous other schemes for cheating homeowners, as the following excerpt indicates.

SOUTH BROOKLYN LEGAL SERVICES, PREDATORY LENDING INVESTIGATION CHECKLIST

Practicing Law Institute Real Estate Law and Practice Course Handbook Series
(May 13, 2008)*

First-Time Home-Buyer Scams/Property Flipping

Property flipping scams are a common abusive lending practice, often targeted at first-time and minority home-buyers. Property flipping occurs when a real estate speculator purchases a property cheaply, and then quickly "flips" or resells the property to an unsuspecting home-buyer at a price that exceeds the market value. Typically, the real estate speculator steers the home buyer to a group of real estate professionals (attorneys, lenders, etc.), all of whom are working in concert to deceive the home buyer (often known as a "one-stop shop"). In this way, the real estate speculator ensures that the home-buyer does not receive any independent advice regarding the terms of the purchase, the condition of the property, or the nature of the mortgage. In some cases, real estate speculators are selling houses for the fair market value to home buyers who will not be able to sustain the mortgage debt.

Loan Flipping

Many unsuspecting homeowners, predominantly minority and/or seniors, are victims of loan flipping. Loan flipping is equity stripping through refinances that have no tangible benefit to the homeowner.

In most loan flipping cases, homeowners are led to believe that they will get a reduction in their mortgage payment from the previous loan, a lower rate, debt consolidation, and cash-out. However, most homeowners end up in a higher-cost mortgage without the promised benefit; they lose significant home equity through exorbitant costs and fees; their previously unsecured debt is refinanced into a secured mortgage; and they are placed at increased risk of foreclosure.

Refinance/Home Improvement Scams

Like unscrupulous mortgage brokers, contractors also aggressively solicit homeowners by mail, phone calls and door-to-door solicitations. Unscrupulous contractors are known to provide financing through dishonest lenders, and typically get paid out of the loan closing before doing

---

* Reprinted with permission of the author.

any work. In some cases, the contractor begins work on the home before financing is made available, a tactic known as spiking, in order to pressure the homeowner to secure financing. It is not unusual for contractors to stop doing work or never begin any work after they receive payment.

Deed Theft/Foreclosure Rescue Scams

Foreclosure is public record information. Foreclosure rescue companies (which often operate out of real estate agencies) obtain these records and bombard homeowners with solicitations that promise foreclosure prevention assistance. Homeowners in foreclosure are often desperate and confused about the foreclosure process, and are therefore more susceptible to foreclosure rescue scams. Foreclosure rescue companies typically target low income and minority neighborhoods. Foreclosure rescue scams work in a few ways. Some homeowners are told that they can save their home from foreclosure with an affordable refinance mortgage, when in fact, the rescue entity tricks the homeowners into signing over the deed to their house to a straw-buyer who takes out a loan for significantly more than what the homeowner owed. Indeed, the new mortgage is frequently 100% of the property value. The unsuspecting homeowners no longer own the home, receive little or no money from the deed transfer, are forced to pay a much higher mortgage every month, and are eventually threatened with eviction.

The other type of rescue scam is when homeowners are instructed by a foreclosure rescue entity to sign the house over to a straw-buyer for a certain period of time, usually a year. The homeowners are then told that after that time expires, title will be transferred back into their name and their credit will be fixed. Instead, the foreclosure rescue entity takes out a mortgage for the full value of the home in the name of a straw-buyer, stealing all the equity and making it impossible for the homeowners to repurchase their home. Thus, the homeowners lose title to their home, receive little to no money from the transaction, and are placed at risk of eviction.

NOTES

1. *Licensing loan originators.* To help combat predatory lending, Congress enacted the Secure and Fair Enforcement for Mortgage Licensing Act ("S.A.F.E. Act") as part of the Housing and Economic Recovery Act of 2008, Pub. L. No. 110–289. The S.A.F.E. Act requires all residential mortgage originators, including mortgage brokers, to be licensed. To obtain a license, the originator must provide fingerprints, a personal history, including work experience, and permission for a background check. A license will be granted only if the applicant has not previously had a loan originator license revoked or been convicted of a felony and has demonstrated financial responsibility and good character. An applicant also must satisfy educational and testing requirements. The Act requires the creation of a mandatory nationwide

registration system for mortgage originators that will provide publicly-accessible information concerning the status of every originator's license. This system is called the Nationwide Multistate Licensing System & Registry (NMLS) and can be freely accessed online and searched by the public. However, the licensing requirements imposed by the S.A.F.E. Act do not impose the same kinds of safety and soundness requirements that are demanded of state- and federally-chartered banks

2. *State anti-predatory lending laws.* The great majority of states have anti-predatory lending laws. The laws vary widely with respect to the types of loans they cover and the types of practices they prohibit. Several state statutes prohibit or regulate prepayment penalties, balloon payments, mandatory arbitration clauses, and mortgage broker fees. The most common type of state law is a "mini-HOEPA" law. Some of these laws include the same or similar terms as the federal HOEPA, but others apply to a wider range of loans.

The state laws also differ on the available remedies. Some allow private actions, but others allow only government enforcement. Some allow damage multipliers, and loan assignees are liable for violations under some state laws but not others.

Commentators have disagreed on the efficacy and desirability of state anti-predatory lending laws. Opponents argue that these laws are counterproductive, because they restrict access to credit and increase loan costs. However, a number of studies indicate that the laws are effective. In one national study, the researchers found that, although weak state laws do not significantly affect lenders' behaviors, more restrictive state laws reduce subprime originations and increase the likelihood that a lender will reject a subprime loan application. Raphael W. Bostic, Kathleen C. Engel, Patricia A. McCoy, Anthony Pennington-Cross & Susan M. Wachter, State and Local Anti-Predatory Lending Laws: The Effect of Legal Enforcement Mechanisms (Aug. 7, 2007), *available at* http://ssrn.com/abstract=1005423.

F. SPREADING MORTGAGE RISK—
INSURERS AND GUARANTORS

MORTGAGE FINANCING: ACTIONS NEEDED TO HELP FHA MANAGE RISKS FROM NEW MORTGAGE LOAN PRODUCTS
U.S. Government Accountability Office
Report GAO–05–194, Feb. 2005, at 7–13, 23–26*

Mortgage insurance, a commonly used credit enhancement, protects lenders against losses in the event of default. Lenders usually require mortgage insurance when a homebuyer has a down payment of less than 20 percent of the value of the home. FHA, VA, the USDA's Rural Housing Service (RHS), and private mortgage insurers provide this insurance. * * *

---

*   Most footnotes, graphs, and charts have been omitted.

Private mortgage insurers generally offer first loss coverage—that is, they will pay all the losses from a foreclosure up to a stated percentage of the claim amount. Generally, these insurers limit the coverage that they offer to between 25 percent and 35 percent of the claim amount.

The insurance offered by the government varies in the amount of lender incurred losses it will cover. For example, VA guarantees losses up to 25 percent to 50 percent of the loan, while FHA's principal single-family insurance program insures almost 100 percent. FHA plays a particularly large role in certain market segments, including low-income and first-time homebuyers. * * * To cover lenders' losses, FHA collects insurance premiums from borrowers. These premiums, along with proceeds from the sale of foreclosed properties, pay for claims that FHA pays lenders as a result of foreclosures. * * *

Each mortgage institution we studied limits in some way the mortgages or the borrowers that may be eligible for their low and no down payment products, but the specific limits and criteria differ among institutions. Fannie Mae and Freddie Mac are constrained in the size of the mortgages they may purchase. Specifically, the Housing and Community Development Act of 1980 requires a limit (conforming loan limit) on the size of mortgages that can be purchased by either Fannie Mae or Freddie Mac. In [2021], the single unit dwelling conforming mortgage limit for Fannie Mae and Freddie Mac is [$548,250] for most of the nation.

FHA is also limited in the size of mortgages it may insure. The FHA loan limit varies by location and property type, depending on the cost of homes in an area and the number of units in a property. * * * [For a single-family home in 2021, the high-cost loan limit is $822,375 for a one unit dwelling.] FHA also has higher limits in Alaska, Hawaii, Guam, and the U.S. Virgin Islands because these are considered to be high cost areas.

[For VA-guaranteed loans, the loan amount depends on whether the eligible veteran, service member, or survivor has "full entitlement." If an individual has full entitlement, then there is no limit on loans over $144,000. The VA has a set of parameters to determine whether someone has a full entitlement. If an individual does not have a full entitlement, then the loan limit is based on one's county. In 2021, for the vast majority of counties the single unit dwelling loan limit was $548,250.]

NOTE ON MORTGAGE INSURANCE PREMIUMS

FHA mortgage insurance premiums. In recent years, FHA has taken several steps to restore its insurance fund's capital ratio to better than the statutory minimum. It tightened its underwriting standards, and it increased the minimum down payment for large loans—those above $625,000 (available only in high-cost areas)—from 3.5% to 5%. In 2013, it also imposed significant increases in its mortgage insurance premiums (MIPs). FHA charges both an up-front MIP, paid at closing of the loan (although it may be financed as part of the mortgage debt), and an annual MIP, paid in twelve monthly installments along with principal and interest. The increased up-front MIP is 1.75% of the base loan amount. (It was formerly 1.0%.) The annual MIP, computed as a percentage of the base loan amount, depends on the loan-to-value ratio and the loan's term, as indicated in the following table. (MIPs are higher for loans exceeding $625,000.)

Individuals who borrow loans insured by the FHA are considered to be at a higher risk of default, largely because they have lower credit scores and make lower down payments when they purchase a home. To account for this risk, FHA-loans are insured against loss. Borrowers, however, pay the premium for this insurance. The premium is paid once when the loan is made and then paid annually. Both are calculated as a percentage of the loan amount, with Congress setting the ceiling and HUD having the authority to lower it. For reference, in 2021 the upfront premium was 1.75% of the loan amount and the annual premium for a typical 30-year loan is as follows:

Base Loan Amount	Loan to Value Ratio	Annual Premium
≤ $625,500	≤ 95%	0.80%
≤ $625,500	> 95%	0.85%
> $625,500	≤ 95%	1%
> $625,500	> 95%	1.05%

Not all FHA borrowers must pay the annual premium for the entire term of the loan. For the average 30-year mortgage loan, if the loan's starting balance was 90% or less of the appraised value of the home, annual mortgage insurance premiums must only be paid for the first 11 years. However, if the starting balance was more than 90% of the appraised value, then the premiums must be paid annually for the entire term of the loan.

VA funding fee. VA charges a "funding fee" for its guaranty. The fee is used by the VA to cover losses on the loans that its guarantees. In 2020, the fee could be as high as 3.6% or as low as 1.4% of the amount borrowed, and is based on a variety of factors, including the type of military service in which the borrower was engaged, the loan-to-value ratio, and whether the loan is new or a refinance. For example, for a regular military veteran obtaining a first-time loan with no down payment, the 2020 fee was 2.3% of the loan amount.

PMI loan limits and mortgage insurance premiums. For those borrowers that obtain conventional loans (i.e., not FHA- or VA-backed), sometimes they, too, must pay a premium as part of their mortgage loan payments. This is called private mortgage insurance (PMI). PMI is usually required when a conventional loan borrower makes a down payment of less than 20% of the home's purchase price (i.e., the loan to value ratio is more than 80%).

Premiums are usually paid along with the principal and interest payment as a monthly fee. For a 30-year fixed-rate mortgage loan up to 85% of value, the premium might be 0.32% per year, divided into 12 monthly installments; on a $100,000 loan, this would amount to $29.17 per month. For a loan exceeding 95% of value, a typical premium would be 0.90% per year, or $75 per month on a $100,000 loan. Higher premiums are usually charged for graduated-payment and adjustable-rate loans, since they are believed to carry greater risk of default and loss. Rates may also vary on the basis of the borrower's credit score and the percentage of the original loan amount that the insurance contract covers. Some insurers offer single-premium upfront rates as an alternative to monthly payments.

G. FEDERAL PREEMPTION OF STATE MORTGAGE LAW

Although the vast preponderance of mortgage law is state law, we have seen in this chapter that the federal government is heavily involved in the mortgage market in a variety of ways: chartering and insuring mortgage lenders, purchasing mortgages on the secondary market, guaranteeing payment of securities backed by mortgages, and insuring or guaranteeing the repayment of individual mortgage loans. To what extent do federal contacts such as these permit the federal government or the courts to substitute federal law for state law when a mortgage is made, foreclosed, or otherwise the subject of legal action? If federal law is to be applied, what is its source? What is the effect on state law of the regulations of federal agencies that supervise financial institutions? These are the questions to be answered in this section.

Preemption of state mortgage law occurs in three distinct contexts: (1) when a federal agency is a market participant as the holder and enforcer of a note and mortgage; (2) when Congress adopts a statute that expressly preempts state law or creates an irreconcilable conflict with it; and (3) when a federal financial agency, acting under the authority given it by Congress, adopts a regulation that preempts state law or conflicts with it to such an extent that the state law must be deemed preempted.

1. FEDERAL AGENCIES AS MARKET PARTICIPANTS

No serious question exists that, when the federal government or its agencies foreclose a federally-held mortgage loan, federal law governs essentially all controversial aspects of the foreclosure, including confirmation of the sale, deficiency judgment liability, redemption rights, and rent assignments. The key question is not whether federal law applies, but rather what *is* the federal law? Should the court adopt the existing state rule as the federal rule, fashion a federal court-made rule, or derive a rule from the agency's regulations or documents? See *generally* Nelson,

Whitman, Burkhart & Freyermuth, Real Estate Finance Law § 11.6 (6th ed.2015).

The Supreme Court's controlling decision involving the federal government's preemptive rights as the holder of a debt or mortgage is United States v. Kimbell Foods, Inc., 440 U.S. 715, 99 S.Ct. 1448, 59 L.Ed.2d 711 (1979). The Court stated that, in deciding whether to adopt state law as the federal rule of decision when the government is enforcing an obligation, a court must determine:

1. Whether the federal program is one that, by its nature, requires nationwide uniformity;

2. Whether adopting the state law would frustrate the federal program's specific objectives; and

3. Whether applying a uniform federal rule would disrupt existing commercial relations predicated on state law.

See In re Bubert, 61 B.R. 362 (W.D. Tex. 1986). *Kimbell Foods* has often been viewed as embodying a strong preference for adopting state law as the federal rule. See, e.g., United States v. Stump Home Specialties Mfg., Inc., 905 F.2d 1117, 1119 (7th Cir. 1990). Much the same attitude is expressed in Frank S. Alexander, Federal Intervention in Real Estate Finance: Preemption and Federal Common Law, 71 N.C. L. Rev. 293 (1993):

When the federal government is acting simply as a market participant in real estate finance, and Congress has not expressly declared otherwise, state law should apply to the transaction. The federal interest in protecting the security and recovering the indebtedness is federal only because it identifies the holder of the interest; it is not federal because of any attribute of sovereignty. There is no inherent or obvious reason to displace state law and create judicially a federal rule which prefers the position of the government as creditor. To the contrary, when acting in the same capacity as a private creditor, the federal government "should fare no better, and no worse, than a private lender."

Nonetheless, the outcomes of the cases since *Kimbell Foods* have been varied, unpredictable, and chaotic. Typical points of controversy that arise when a federal agency forecloses a mortgage include:

1. Does the agency have to observe the same formalities for establishing lien priority as other lenders under state law?

2. Can the agency collect a deficiency judgment from a debtor under conditions in which state law would ordinarily bar deficiencies?

3. Does the agency have to recognize a post-foreclosure statutory right of redemption provided by state law?

4. Can the agency require a borrower to waive rights that are ordinarily nonwaivable under state law?

5. Does the agency have to provide all notices required by state law, such as a notice of default to borrowers?

Similar questions may arise after the FHA or VA pays a claim to a private lender. For example, if the VA pays a claim on a guaranteed loan, can it obtain reimbursement from the defaulting borrower despite a state antideficiency statute? Courts have been inconsistent in answering these types of questions, and we do not take the space here to summarize the case law. A good starting point is Professor Alexander's excellent article, cited above.

The notion that there should be general federal mortgage foreclosure statute has floated about the federal housing and financial regulatory agencies for many years. The idea is attractive to the agencies because they often find themselves taking losses on foreclosures as a consequence of slow and, in their view, outmoded state procedures. But despite this benefit, Congress has not enacted a comprehensive federal foreclosure statute.

However, Congress enacted a narrower bill, the Multifamily Mortgage Foreclosure Act, 12 U.S.C. §§ 3701–3717, in 1981. The Act created a nonjudicial foreclosure process for mortgages held by HUD on multifamily housing projects. It expressly preempts any state law granting post-foreclosure redemption rights. In 1994, Congress enacted a parallel act, the Single Family Mortgage Foreclosure Act, 12 U.S.C. §§ 3751–3768, which applies to HUD-held single-family home mortgages. For HUD's regulations under both acts, see 24 C.F.R. pt. 27, which was promulgated in 61 Fed.Reg. 48,546 (1996). See *generally* Patrick A. Randolph, Jr., The New Federal Foreclosure Laws, 49 Okla. L. Rev. 123 (1996); Nelson, Whitman, Burkhart & Freyermuth, Real Estate Finance Law § 11.4 (6th ed.2015).

2. EXPRESS CONGRESSIONAL PREEMPTION

Congress clearly has the power to preempt state law by direct statutory enactment if the subject matter is within the federal government's constitutional power. The Commerce Clause is the usual basis asserted for such action. During the 1980s, Congress preempted several aspects of state mortgage law:

1. Section 501 of the Depository Institutions Deregulation and Monetary Control Act of 1980, 12 U.S.C. § 1735f–7, preempts all state usury laws for "federally-related" loans secured by first liens on residential real estate. Grunbeck v. Dime Sav. Bank, 848 F.Supp. 294 (D.N.H. 1994) (§ 501 preempts New Hampshire statute requiring that interest on residential mortgage loans be computed on simple interest basis as a state law limiting rate or amount of interest).

2. Section 341 of the Garn-St. Germain Depository Institutions Act of 1982, 12 U.S.C. § 1701j–3, preempts state law restrictions on the enforceability of due-on-sale clauses in mortgages. The OCC regulations implementing the Act are in 12 C.F.R. pt. 591. See Chapter Five, Section B supra, for a complete discussion of the preemption.

3. The Alternative Mortgage Transactions Parity Act of 1982, 12 U.S.C. §§ 3801–3806 (the "AMTPA"), preempts state law restrictions on the structure of "alternative" mortgage instruments. The Act authorizes state-chartered financial institutions to make mortgage loans of types that the federal financial regulators have approved, even if state law does not allow them. See the following section of this chapter for a more thorough discussion of such mortgage loan formats.

In these statutes preempting state law, Congress permitted state legislatures, within some limited time period after enactment of the federal statute, to regain control of the field by "opting out" of the federal preemption. In each of the cases above, a few states did so. See, e.g., Doyle v. Southern Guaranty Corp., 795 F.2d 907 (11th Cir. 1986) (discussing Georgia's override of the 1980 federal usury preemption).

3. CONFLICT PREEMPTION

NELSON, WHITMAN, BURKHART & FREYERMUTH, REAL ESTATE FINANCE LAW
§ 11.6 (6th ed.2015)*

The term "conflict preemption" refers to cases in which a federal statute or program's purposes cannot be achieved if state law is also followed. The conflict may be purely statutory, as in cases in which federal law specifically approves conduct that state law prohibits. However, most of the litigation has dealt with the question whether a federal banking regulator may issue regulations that preempt state law and thereby may immunize conduct that state law would prohibit or punish. Historically there was a sharp difference between the treatment of national banks under the Office of the Comptroller of the Currency (OCC) and savings associations under the Office of Thrift Supervision (OTS). Savings associations were governed by the 1933 Home Owners Loan Act,[332] which permitted the OTS to grant them a remarkably comprehensive form of preemption, governing every aspect of their operations "from the cradle to the grave,"[333] and fully occupying the field. This "field preemption,"

---

* Reprinted with permission of LEG, Inc. d/b/a West Academic.

[332] 12 U.S.C. §§ 1461–1468.

[333] A good illustration is Fidelity Fed. Sav. & Loan Ass'n v. De la Cuesta, 458 U.S. 141 (1982), upholding, under the authority of the Home Owners Loan Act, the regulation of the Federal Home Loan Bank Board preempting state law with respect to due-on-sale clauses. See Meyers v. Beverly Hills Fed. Sav. & Loan Ass'n, 499 F.2d 1145 (9th Cir. 1974). When state courts "deal with the

however, did not apply to national banks. The 1864 National Bank Act[334] under which they operated contained no specific preemption language, and the courts were forced to develop principles to guide the OCC in its preemptive efforts.

The standard statement governing the OCC's preemptive authority is found in the Supreme Court's opinion in Barnett Bank of Marion County v. Nelson.[335] The Court held that a Florida statute prohibiting banks from selling insurance in certain towns was preempted by a 1916 federal law which authorized such actions because the state insurance law stood as an "obstacle to the accomplishment and execution of the full purposes and objectives of Congress." This is a classic example of "conflict preemption." As applied to OCC, it would mean that agency had authority to preempt state law that "prevents or significantly interferes" with a national bank's exercise of its powers.

In practice, the OTS (and its predecessor, the Federal Home Loan Bank Board) pressed its preemptive authority over savings associations very broadly. As early as 1994, its implementing regulation[336] listed a large number of examples of preempted features of loan transactions and lender operations, and the courts upheld its authority in each instance. For example, regulations concerning prepayment penalties,[337] interest on tax escrow accounts[338] on home loans, and many other mortgage law topics[339]

internal affairs of federal savings and loan associations * * * they are nonetheless applying federal law." Murphy v. Colonial Federal Savings and Loan Association, 388 F.2d 609, 612 (2d Cir. 1967). See Community Title Co. v. Roosevelt Federal Savings & Loan Association, 670 S.W.2d 895, 903 (Mo.App. 1984). On control by OTS' predecessor, the FHLBB, of S & L mergers, see Federal Home Loan Bank Board: Preemptive Rights or Unbridled Powers?, 12 Cap.U.L.Rev. 529 (1983).

[334] 12 U.S.C. §§ 85–86.

[335] 517 U.S. 25, 116 S.Ct. 1103 (1996). See also Association of Banks in Ins., Inc. v. Duryee, 270 F.3d 397 (6th Cir. 2001) (federal statute preempted state insurance regulation as applied to national banks).

[336] 12 CFR § 560.2(a).

[337] Toolan v. Trevose Federal Savings & Loan Association, 462 A.2d 224 (Pa. 1983); Meyers v. Beverly Hills Federal Savings and Loan Association, 499 F.2d 1145 (9th Cir. 1974); see generally § 6.4, supra.

[338] First Federal Savings & Loan Association v. Greenwald, 591 F.2d 417 (1st Cir. 1979); Wisconsin League of Financial Institutions, Ltd. v. Galecki, 707 F.Supp. 401 (W.D.Wis. 1989); Olsen v. Financial Federal Savings & Loan Association, 434 N.E.2d 406 (Ill.App. 1982). See generally § 4.19 supra.

[339] The following cases found the indicated state laws preempted by 12 CFR § 560.2, the OTS preemption regulation, or its predecessors: Flagg v. Yonkers Sav. and Loan Ass'n, 396 F.3d 178 (2d Cir. 2005) (state law requiring payment of interest on escrow account balances); State Farm Bank v. Burke, 445 F.Supp.2d 207 (D.Conn. 2006) (state law regulating use of agents by lender to perform marketing, solicitation, and customer service activities); Silvas v. E*Trade Mortg. Corp., 421 F.Supp.2d 1315 (S.D.Cal. 2006) (false advertising in violation of California unfair competition law); Stoneking v. Bank of America, 43 P.3d 1089 (N.M.App. 2002) (state law restricting collection of prepayment fees); Washington Mutual Bank v. Superior Court, 115 Cal.Rptr.2d 765 (Cal.App. 2002) (state law restrictions on the charging of pre-closing interest); Bright v. Washington Mut. Bank, 2002 WL 453725 (Cal.App. 2002) (not published in Cal.Rptr.) (state law restricting hazard insurance requirements); Chaires v. Chevy Chase Bank, F.S.B., 748 A.2d 34 (Md.App. 2000) (state law limitations on front-end loan fee charges); Turner v. First Union Nat. Bank, 740 A.2d 1081

were held to prevail over contrary state law. Consumer advocates complained of these rules, for the federal regulations often granted savings associations latitude and power that would have been denied them under state law.

The OCC was determined not be left behind in the preemption race. In 2004 it followed the lead of OTS, adopting its own broad preemption of state law for national banks.[340] The list of preempted areas of the law was nearly identical to that of the OTS discussed above,[341] and it was far from nuanced; there was little or nothing to support the notion that application of state law in these categories would "prevent or significantly interfere" with the proper functioning of the banks' federal powers. Indeed, the OCC virtually adopted the OTS's concept of "field preemption."[342] Whether this sort of blunderbuss preemption was justified, in light of the OCC's weaker statutory foundation[343] and the Supreme Court's holding in *Barnett Bank*, was doubtful.[344]

In any event, by 2010 Congress concluded that both banking regulators had gone too far. Perhaps influenced by the spate of unbridled subprime and sometimes predatory loans that had contributed to the collapse of the housing and mortgage markets in 2007,[345] Congress, in the Dodd-Frank Act, elected to rein in the regulators' preemptive efforts.[346] It restated the *Barnett Bank* "prevents or significantly interferes" standard,

---

(N.J. 1999) (state law restricting lender from charging borrower for attorney review of documents).
* * *

[340] 69 Fed.Reg. 1904 (Jan. 13, 2004), amending 12 CFR § 7.4007–.4009 (non-real estate loans); 12 CFR § 34.3–.4 (real estate loans).

[341] 12 CFR § 34.4(a). See also Beneficial Nat'l Bank v. Anderson, 539 U.S. 1 U.S. (2003) (National Bank Act preempts state law usury claims against national banks). See Keith R. Fisher, Toward a Basal Tenth Amendment: A Riposte to National Bank Preemption of State Consumer Protection Laws, 29 Harv. J.L. & Pub. Pol'y 981 (2006); Mark A. Olthoff, National Bank Act Preemption in the Secondary Market, 123 Banking L.J. 401 (2006). As with the OTS, the OCC excluded from the preemption, "to the extent that they only incidentally affect the exercise of national banks' real estate lending powers," state laws governing contracts, torts, criminal law, homestead laws, rights to collect debts, acquisition and transfer of real property, taxation, and zoning. 12 CFR § 34.4(b). See Charter One Mortg. Corp. v. Condra, 847 N.E.2d 207 (Ind.App. 2006) (Indiana rule barring unauthorized practice of law was not preempted by the National Bank Act or 12 C.F.R. § 7.4002, even though it prevented national banks from charging document preparation fees for legal instruments prepared by non-attorneys).

[342] See Jared Elosta, Dynamic Federalism and Consumer Financial Protection: How the Dodd-Frank Act Changes the Preemption Debate, 89 N.C.L.Rev. 1273, 1280 (2011).

[343] See, e.g., Aguayo v. U.S. Bank, 653 F.3d 912 (9th Cir. 2011) ("The OTS. unlike the OCC, has explicit full field preemption.").

[344] See Watters v. Wachovia Bank, N.A., 550 U.S. 1, 22, 127 S.Ct. 1559, 1573 (2007) (Stevens, J., dissenting); Arthur E. Wilmarth Jr., The OCC's Preemption Rules Exceed the Agency's Authority and Present a Serious Threat to the Dual Banking System and Consumer Protection, 23 Ann. Rev. Banking & Fin. L. 225 (2004).

[345] See F. Paul Bland, Freedom from Abusive Preemption under Dodd-Frank, 49 Trial 18 (Dec. 2013).

[346] See Debra Lee Hovatter, Preemption Analysis under the National Bank Act: Then and Now, 67 Consumer Fin. L.Q. Rep. 5 (2013); Matthew Dyckman, Financial Regulatory Reform— The Dodd-Frank Act Rolls Back Federal Preemption, 64 Consumer Fin. L.Q. Rep. 129 (2010).

but it declared that determinations of preemption of "state consumer financial laws"[347] must now be made on the basis of "substantial evidence," and rendered on a case-by-case basis rather than by blanket regulation.[348]

Dodd-Frank limited the banking regulators' preemptive actions in several other ways. Preemption must be based on "substantial evidence" that the conflict meets the *Barnett Bank* standard.[349] If the regulator finds that law of another state has "substantively equivalent" terms as one that it is now preempting, it must first consult with the CFPB and take its views into consideration.[350] The OCC is also required to conduct a review of each preemption determination every five years, and to report to Congress on the outcome of these reviews.[351] Further, preemption determinations must now be "made by a court, or by regulation or order," rather than by informal letter rulings as had often been used in the past.[352] Finally, Dodd-Frank requires the OCC to publish, and update at least quarterly, a list of all of its preemption determinations.[353] One might have expected a wholesale revision by the OCC of its preemption regulation after Dodd-Frank went into effect, but in fact its revision made no changes in the listing of categories of states laws that were preempted; OCC took the position that Congress had no intent to force changes in this basic list.[354]

Two structural changes were also made to the banking regulators' preemptive authority by Dodd-Frank. First, the Supreme Court had previously held that the OCC had authority to preempt state law with respect to subsidiaries of national banks,[355] but under Dodd-Frank,

---

[347] A "state consumer financial law" is defined as one that "does not directly or indirectly discriminate against national banks and that directly and specifically regulates the manner, content, or terms and conditions of any financial transaction (as may be authorized for national banks to engage in), or any account related thereto, with respect to a consumer." 12 U.S.C.A. § 25b(a)(2). Thus, the banking regulators are free to preempt any state law that discriminates against federally-chartered institutions. In Cline v. Bank of America, N.A., 823 F. Supp.2d 387 (S.D.W.Va. 2011), the court found that a West Virginia statute designed to curb abusive debt collection practices was not a "state consumer financial law," since it did not regulate the original debt transaction.

[348] 12 U.S.C.A. § 25b(b)(3)(A). "Case by case" determination means that the regulators must make a determination "concerning the impact of a particular State consumer financial law on any national bank that is subject to" it.

[349] 12 U.S.C.A. § 25b(c).

[350] 12 U.S.C.A. § 25b(b)(3)(B).

[351] 12 U.S.C.A. § 25b(d).

[352] 12 U.S.C.A. § 25b(b)(1)(B).

[353] 12 U.S.C.A. § 25b(g).

[354] See OCC commentary to its final revised regulation, 76 Fed.Reg. 43549, 43557 (July 21, 2011): "The types and terms of laws that are set out in the 2004 preemption rules were based on the OCC's experience with the potential impact of such laws on national bank powers and operations. We have re-reviewed those rules in connection with this rulemaking to confirm that the specific types of laws cited in the rules are consistent with the standard for conflict preemption in the Supreme Court's *Barnett* decision." See Raymond Natter & Katie Wechsler, Dodd-Frank Act and National Bank Preemption: Much Ado About Nothing, 7 Va. L. & Bus. Rev. 301, 303 (2012) (asserting that Dodd-Frank's changes are "relatively minor").

[355] Watters v. Wachovia Bank, N.A., 550 U.S. 1 (2007).

subsidiaries and affiliates are entitled to no preemption at all.[356] Second, Congress completely eliminated the "field preemption" language of the Home Owners Loan Act, so that now federal savings associations are entitled to OTS preemption under exactly the same standards as are national banks under the OCC.[357]

The fact that Congress ratcheted up the procedures for preemption, but did so only with respect to "state consumer financial laws," is perplexing. What is now the preemption standard for state laws that are not "consumer financial laws?"[358] *Barnett Bank* is still in effect, and indeed seems to have received the imprimatur of Congress,[359] and its holding is not confined to "consumer financial laws." How the courts will respond when faced with attempted OCC preemption of such laws remains to be seen.[360]

H. ALTERNATIVE MORTGAGE INSTRUMENTS

In Section G of Chapter One of this book, we described and illustrated the operation of the traditional fixed-interest-rate, level-payment, fully-amortized mortgage loan. For many years, beginning during the New Deal of the 1930s, such loans constituted the great bulk of mortgage lending in the United States. See Adam J. Levitin & Susan M. Wachter, The Great Housing Bubble: What Went Wrong and How We Can Protect Ourselves in the Future (2020). But during the past 50 years or so a whole new set of mortgage instruments—"alternative mortgages"—has developed. This section will describe those instruments.

First, however, we need to identify the reasons alternative mortgage loans were created. One important reason was the dilemma of portfolio lenders, such as savings associations and the GSEs, that historically

---

[356] 12 U.S.C.A. § 25b(e).

[357] Dodd-Frank Act, Pub.L. 111–203 (2010), at § 1046, adding new § 6 to HOLA, stating: "Notwithstanding the authorities granted under sections 4 and 5, this Act does not occupy the field in any area of State law." Oddly, there is no mention at all of the National Credit Union Administration, the regulator of federal credit unions. Presumably it remains subject to the *Barnett Bank* standard, but without all of the additional restrictions to which OTS and OCC are now subject.

[358] See, e.g., Cline v. Bank of America, supra note 35.

[359] See, e.g., Baptista v. JPMorgan Chase Bank, N.A., 640 F.3d 1194 (11th Cir. 2011), applying *Barnett Bank* and concluding that there was an "irreconcilable conflict" between an OCC regulation expressly allowing banks to charge check-cashing fees and a Florida statute prohibiting such fees.

[360] See New Mexico v. Capital One Bank (USA) N.A., 980 F.Supp.2d 1314 (D.N.M. 2013) (state unfair trade practice laws prohibiting misrepresentation are not preempted except to the extent that they involve debt cancellation or suspension agreements, a field that OCC has expressly preempted); Sacco v. Bank of America, N.A., 2012 WL 6566681 (W.D.N.C. 2012) (not reported in F.Supp.2d) (OCC regulations preempted bank's "right to collect debts," but did not preempt state law governing abusive collection practices); Michael Bolos, The Application of Dodd-Frank's Dual Preemption Standard to State UDAP Laws, 14 U. Pa. J. Bus. L. 289 (2011), discussing preemption of state unfair and deceptive practices acts, and concluding that they are probably not "consumer financial laws."

"borrowed short and lent long." These lenders obtained short-term funds from savers or investors and loaned those funds as relatively long-term fixed-interest mortgage loans. That is, they engaged in "term intermediation." If short-term interest rates rose rapidly, the lenders' borrowing costs dramatically increased, while the interest yields on the lenders' portfolio of mortgages remained relatively constant. This risk was more than theoretical, as shown by the disastrous results for the thrift industry during the 1980–82 period of rapidly increasing interest rates. The perils of lending on long-term fixed-interest mortgages was starkly clear to the many lenders that did not survive that experience.

The obvious approach to this problem was to reduce the average term of the loan portfolio. One way for lenders to do this is to shift out of mortgage lending partially or entirely and to make other types of loans that, by their nature, have shorter terms. Both the Depository Institutions Deregulation and Monetary Control Act of 1980 and the Garn-St. Germain Depository Institutions Act of 1982 moved in this direction by authorizing thrift institutions to invest more of their assets in consumer and commercial loans, which tend to have shorter terms and higher interest rates than mortgage loans. However, this approach was fairly disastrous to the industry, in part because its management had no experience with this type of lending and made many bad loans.

The other major approach to reducing the risk of term intermediation is the main subject of this section of the book—the first and most important of the alternative mortgage instruments, the adjustable-rate mortgage loan ("ARM"). If interest rates on mortgage loans change when market rates change, the result is far more attractive to the institutions. In an ideal portfolio of this sort, the overall yield on the portfolio would always be precisely equal to the current market interest rate, so that the effective maturity of loans and of savings would match. In a rough way, this is the purpose for adjustable-rate mortgages, which mortgage lenders now widely offer.

Interest rates and mortgage affordability. If one assumes constant risks, maturities, and liquidities, mortgage interest rates are directly related to the inflation lenders anticipate will occur during the loan's term. This is reasonable because, if inflation occurs, lenders will receive repayment in devalued dollars. A 4 percent loan in a non-inflationary economy provides the same real return to the lender as a 14 percent loan in an economy with an inflation rate of 10 percent. From 1955–65, inflation averaged roughly 1.5% per year and mortgage interest rates averaged about 5.5%; both were relatively stable. This suggests that mortgage investors were demanding a real rate of return (after inflation) on the order of 4% and that interest rates above this level constituted an inflation premium. Other loan characteristics have changed since that era, so one should not take the 4% return figure as more than a rough estimate of the real rate lenders will demand today, but it is useful to bear in mind.

Most mortgage lenders will make loans only to those who "qualify" in terms of some standard ratio of housing expense to income. "Housing expense" generally includes the debt service on the mortgage, plus the annual property taxes, mortgage insurance and hazard insurance premiums, and any homeowners association dues or special assessments. Various lenders and secondary market investors have adopted different expense-to-income ratios, but they commonly range from about 28% to 33%. For simplicity's sake, ignore the taxes, insurance premiums, and other minor expenses and assume that the lender requires the mortgage payment-to-income ratio to be no more than 30%. This means that a family with a monthly income of $4,000 could not qualify for a loan with monthly payments exceeding $1,200. Even if the family were willing to make higher payments, the lender would simply refuse to make the loan.

The result is that rising interest rates tend to "ration" borrowers out of the market. The chart that follows shows the approximate principal amount a family with an income of $48,000 per year can qualify to borrow at various interest rates. It is based on a 30-year level-payment loan and a 30% payment-to-income ratio rule, so that the maximum monthly payment for principal and interest is $1,200.

Interest Rate	Principal Amount
6%	$200,000
8%	$163,500
10%	$136,700
12%	$116,700
14%	$101,300

Another way of looking at the problem is to examine how much income a family would need to qualify for, say, a $150,000 loan at various interest rates. The table below shows the answer, based on the same assumptions stated above.

Interest Rate	Monthly Payment	Annual Income Required
6%	$900	$36,000
8%	$1,100	$44,000
10%	$1,316	$52,640
12%	$1,543	$61,720
14%	$1,777	$71,080

The rationing effect of increasing interest rates is apparent. Ironically, many families' income will increase with inflation (or nearly as rapidly) over time if the lenders' expectations are correct. In a few years, a family that was clearly unqualified for a given loan may have increased its income sufficiently to pay the same loan with relative ease. However, because the payments are level, the family is unqualified in the only year that matters—the year in which they would like to borrow. They simply will not get the loan.

One might argue that if inflation and concomitant high interest rates are only temporary, the problem is not so bad. Unlike food, owner-occupied housing is a good whose consumption can be deferred. People can continue to rent, to live with relatives, and to double up in other ways. But high interest rates that persist over the long run indisputably have a harsh impact on large numbers of households.

The rationing effect of high interest rates leaves its mark on the supply side of the housing market as well. When rates rise and buyers cannot qualify, the effective demand for housing diminishes. Housing builders and sellers of existing housing units are often hard-hit. They find themselves with unsold properties on which mortgage interest and other expenses continue to accrue. Builders must lay off workers and cancel relationships with subcontractors and materials suppliers, and they may be forced to hold land that cannot be developed (and pay taxes and insurance costs on it) because the market demand has disappeared.

Since 1968, the nation's mortgage markets have undergone great changes that facilitate the easy flow of funds from the general capital markets into mortgage lending. These innovations in the secondary mortgage market and in mortgage securitizations have been strikingly successful in ameliorating the structural problems of housing finance. It is no longer common during periods of "tight money" for borrowers to find that local institutions simply have no lendable funds. But these institutional relationships do not solve the problem of affordability of high interest rates. So long as cycles of inflation and monetary stringency continue to occur, interest rates will continue to reach high levels from time to time. This explains the search for new forms of mortgage instruments that may soften the impact of high rates.

Affordability issues do not arise only because of high interest rates. During the first half of the 2000s, many regions of the nation experienced very rapid price appreciation in housing. Even though interest rates were very low, high prices made housing unaffordable for many families. Lenders adopted changes in the structure of their mortgage loans—in many cases, ill-advised and poorly designed changes—in order to address this issue.

We have now introduced two of the principal problems of housing finance—the difficulty lenders have in mediating between savers and borrowers in a rising-interest market, and the difficulty borrowers have in qualifying for loans when interest rates or housing prices are high. We are ready to turn to the innovations in mortgage loans that may help to resolve these problems. For most of the new mortgage forms (other than the ARM), we have provided only a brief description without extensive citations to the relevant federal regulations. However, agencies have authorized virtually all these forms. As you read about each of them, consider whether it is useful in protecting lenders from rate risk, making housing more affordable to borrowers, or both.

ARMs. ARMs are intended to deal with the lender's difficulties. They enable the lender to periodically modify the interest rate over the life of the loan as market rates change. Thus, the risk of rate fluctuations is shifted from the lender to the borrower. From the lender's viewpoint, the loan's rate of return will approximate the return on a series of short-term loans.

However, ARMs raise questions from the borrower's viewpoint. The most significant is whether the borrower will be able to pay higher rates in the future. The answer depends in part on how a rate increase will be implemented. There are at least three methods:

1. Monthly payments can be increased by an amount that fully amortizes the loan at the new, higher rate;

2. The loan maturity can be increased, but even very large increases in maturity can accommodate only small rate increases if the loan begins with a 30-year term; or

3. The increased interest can be capitalized (added to principal). This may result in "negative amortization," in which the loan balance increases, rather than decreases, each month.

Of course, combinations of these three methods are possible.

The federal financial regulatory agencies permit their regulated lenders to make ARM loans with relatively few limitations. However, the federal Truth in Lending Act requires that borrowers receive extensive disclosures relative to ARM mortgage loans. 12 C.F.R. § 226.19(b). These include the fact that the interest rate may increase over time, the index or formula that will determine the rate change, an explanation of the method employed, and an example showing what a change in the rate might look like and how it will affect the payment terms.

The following article describes the key features that a borrower should consider when evaluating an adjustable-rate mortgage loan.

JOHN E. JACOBS, EVERYTHING THE HOME OWNER'S COUNSEL WANTED TO KNOW ABOUT ADJUSTABLE RATE MORTGAGE LOANS
65 Mich. B.J. 156 (1986)

* * *

1. **Index.** A variety of Indexes may be used by lenders, which include: (i) U.S. Treasury security yields, (ii) long-term fixed rate mortgages, (iii) lender's cost of funds, or (iv) prime rate of the lender or a third party. The practitioner should advise his/her client on the relative merits of the various Indexes available. * * *

Generally, the Index will be the rate in effect on a certain date prior to the date upon which the interest rate changes. This date may be 30 to 45 days before the change date, thereby providing the lender with an adequate period of time to notify the borrower of the adjustment. Usually the promissory note provides that, if the Index is no longer available, the holder of the promissory note may choose a new Index, based upon comparable information.

The "change date" is the date upon which the interest begins to accrue at the new interest rate. The first installment, based on the new interest rate, will generally be due 30 days after the change date.

2. **Margin.** The Margin is the amount the lender adds to the Index in order to determine the interest rate. Generally, the Margin is the same amount throughout the term of the loan.

Lenders may, however, provide a Margin which is lower at the first adjustment than at subsequent adjustments. Most lenders charge a Margin between one and three percentage points. The existence of Interest Rate Caps, described below, may cause the Margin to be greater.

Promissory notes provide that the sum of the Margin plus the Index is either rounded to the "nearest one-eighth of one percent" or "up to the nearest one-eighth of one percent." The former clause will generally result in a lower interest rate.

3. **Initial Interest Rate.** The Initial Interest Rate is the rate charged during the first portion of the term of the loan, such as the first year. The Initial Interest Rate is generally one to three percentage points below the interest rate for fixed rate mortgage loans. It may also be less than the sum of the Margin plus the Index.

The Initial Interest Rate may be further reduced as the result of a "buy down." In this case, the home seller, builder or borrower pays a sum of money to the lender in order to reduce the Initial Interest Rate otherwise offered by the lender. The "bought down rate," however, may not be the rate applicable in calculating interest rate caps described below.

The lower Initial Interest Rate provides the lender with an ability to qualify the borrower for a loan for which the borrower may not otherwise be able to qualify. A low Initial Interest Rate is sometimes referred to as a "teaser" rate. Borrower's counsel should consult with the borrower as to whether the borrower's income will increase sufficiently to pay the increased installment payments after the Initial Interest Rate is no longer effective. * * *

4. **Adjustment Interval.** The Adjustment Interval is the period between changes in the interest rate. Most commonly, Adjustment Intervals are one, three or five years. A larger Adjustment Interval will generally result in a higher Initial Interest Rate. In addition, the Index may be tied to the Adjustment Interval. For example, if the Adjustment Interval is three years, the lender may require an Index of the yield on U.S. Treasury securities with a maturity of three years instead of one year. * * * [G]enerally, U.S. Treasury securities with a maturity of three years bear a higher interest rate than such securities with a maturity of one year.

5. **Interest Rate Caps.** An ARM may provide that the interest rate will not increase by more than a certain number of percentage points at each Adjustment Interval. Typically, the cap is one or two percentage points. Borrower's counsel should determine whether the cap applies to the initial adjustment of the interest rate. If the ARM has a teaser rate or the Initial Interest Rate has been bought down, the cap may not be applicable to the adjustment after this reduced interest rate is no longer applicable. The application of the cap to the first adjustment may avoid an increase in the monthly installment, which is substantially more than the increase in the borrower's income.

ARMs may also provide an interest rate cap over the life of the loan. The limitation may be expressed as a specified number of percentage points above the Initial Interest Rate or a specified rate of interest. The most common limitation is five percentage points above the Initial Interest Rate, assuming no teaser or bought down rate. Again, the practitioner should determine whether the cap is applied to the introductory interest rate or only after the first adjustment.

These caps result in limiting the rate of interest charged to the borrower. Therefore, the interest lost as a result of the cap is lost forever.

6. **Monthly Payment Cap.** The borrower may be given the option to limit the increase which would occur in the amount of the monthly installment as a result of the increase in the interest rate. Typically, the option will be to limit the increase in the monthly payment to 7–1/2% each year until the payment reaches the amount required to pay the loan in full over the remaining term at the current interest rate.

As opposed to the Interest Rate Cap, although the increase in the monthly payment is limited, interest continues to accrue at the new interest rate. Therefore, if the limited monthly payment is less than the amount of interest which accrues in the month, the accrued and unpaid portion of the interest will be added to the principal amount of the loan. This results in "negative amortization."

Such programs generally do not permit the principal balance of the loan to exceed a specified amount, often 125% of the original loan balance. If the principal balance would exceed the maximum amount, the monthly payment is then increased to the amount required to pay the then principal balance in full over the remaining term of the loan, at the interest rate currently in effect.

NOTES

1. *The yield curve.* Under normal economic conditions, and with all other variations held equal, a debt with a longer term to maturity will carry a higher interest rate than a debt of shorter maturity. The usual explanation of this phenomenon is that a lender that ties up its money for a longer term will, by doing so, ensure that it will miss out on any opportunities to reinvest the money at a higher interest if shorter-term rates move upward during the loan's term. Lenders demand compensation for this lost potential opportunity in the form of a higher rate on the loan being made.

One can make a graph showing interest rates as a function of loan maturity. Such a graph, called a "yield curve," appears below. Of course, it is important not to compare apples with oranges; a yield curve graph is meaningful only if all of the other characteristics of the debts on the graph are essentially similar. The graph below is based on U.S. Treasury debt instruments of various maturities. They meet our criteria of similarity; they carry virtually no credit risk, since it is assumed that the United States government will always pay its debts, and there is an active secondary market for all U.S. debt obligations, irrespective of their maturity.

Obviously, if lenders consider current rates to be abnormally high, so that there is an expectation that shorter-term rates will actually decline in the future, the yield curve will have a different shape, sloping downward to the right; this is called an "inverted yield curve." The period 1980–82, when interest rates were extremely high, was characterized by inverted yield curves. Economists typically view an inverted yield curve as an economic warning sign.

One implication of the normal yield curve is that ARMs generally carry lower interest rates than fixed-rate loans. The reason is that an ARM is economically equivalent to a series of shorter-term loans, each with its own interest rate that will approximate current market rates. (We say "approximate" because, if market rates change rapidly, the annual and lifetime rate caps on an ARM may prevent it from fully following the market rate changes.) Moreover, the frequency with which an ARM's interest can be adjusted has a strong impact on the initial rate. Thus, for example, an ARM which adjusts annually will, in normal economic times, have a lower initial interest rate that an ARM which adjusts every two years.

2. *Variations on ARMs.* It has become fairly common for lenders to provide a longer period of fixed interest before beginning to make rate adjustments. For example, the loan might have a fixed rate for 3, 5, or 7 years, and thereafter adjust annually. These loans would be known colloquially as 3/1, 5/1, and 7/1 hybrid ARMs. The longer the period during which the rate is fixed, the more the loan resembles a standard fixed-rate loan, and hence (assuming a normal yield curve), the higher the initial rate is likely to be.

Many indexes are used in constructing ARMs, but those mentioned below are the most popular:

- *Constant Maturity Treasury (CMT) indexes.* Each day the Treasury plots a yield curve of Treasury securities. This curve, which (as explained above) relates the yield on a security to its time to maturity, is based on the closing market bid yields on actively traded Treasury securities in the over-the-counter market. The information is gathered by the New York Federal Reserve Bank. These are not newly-issued securities, but rather those traded on the secondary market, and hence they may have a very wide range of remaining maturities. After the curve is created, the yield values are interpolated from the curve at fixed maturities of 1, 3 and 6 months and 1, 2, 3, 5, 7, 10, 20, and 30 years. This method provides a yield for a 10 year maturity, for example, even if no outstanding security traded on that date has exactly 10 years remaining to maturity. The most common ARM index is the 1-year CMT yield; about half of all ARMs use this index. Such ARMs usually adjust their rates annually.

- *Treasury Bill (T-Bill) indexes.* These indexes are based on the yields at the weekly auctions of new (original issue) debt securities by the Treasury. Monthly averages are then computed from the weekly auctions held during the previous month. The monthly 6-Month Treasury Bill index ("6-month T-Bill") is also a very commonly used index for ARMs, and such ARMs usually adjust every six months.

- *Twelve-month moving Treasury average (MTA) index.* This index is calculated by averaging the monthly yields of the 1-year CMT yield (see above) for the previous twelve months. Because it is a 12-month average, it tends to move more slowly and is less volatile that the CMT and T-Bill indexes mentioned above. For ARMs based on this index, the rate is usually adjusted every month and the monthly payment is adjusted either monthly or annually.

- *Eleventh District cost-of-funds (11th Dist. COFI) index.* A cost-of-funds index (COFI) is a weighted average of the interest rates paid by financial institutions to borrow money from their depositors, mainly on checking accounts, savings accounts, and certificates of deposit. This particular COFI is based on institutions that are members of the Eleventh Federal Home Loan Bank District, which includes California, Arizona, and Nevada. Because rates paid to depositors and savers tend to change relatively slowly, this index is less volatile than CMT and T-Bill indexes. On many loans based on this index, the rate is adjusted every month but the monthly payment is adjusted only once a year.

The Home Equity Conversion Mortgage (HECM)

The home equity conversion mortgage (HECM) is sometimes called a "reverse mortgage." It is designed to allow elderly or retired persons who have large equities in their home to borrow against the equity to help pay living expenses. In the simplest form, the lender makes monthly disbursements to the homeowner, and the outstanding balance on the loan increases to reflect both the disbursements and the accrued interest on those disbursements. When the balance reaches the maximum loan amount, the borrower has to repay the loan, which generally requires that the property be sold.

FHA introduced a HECM program in 1989; see 24 C.F.R. Part 206. While the program has been popular, significant concerns have also been raised about it, as the following excerpt suggests.

REVERSE MORTGAGES

Consumer Financial Protection Bureau
Report to Congress, June 2012[3]

For most Americans, their home is the single largest asset they own. In 2009, half of homeowners age 62 and older had at least 55 percent of their net worth tied up in home equity.[4] Home equity is accumulated over a life time of mortgage payments and house-price appreciation, but generally cannot be accessed without selling the home or taking out a loan. Reverse mortgages enable older homeowners to use that home equity to enjoy a more comfortable retirement without selling their home.

Reverse mortgages are not the only option for accessing home equity without selling the home, however. Traditional home equity loans and home equity lines of credit (HELOCs) are possibilities. Reverse mortgages offer a different set of benefits, costs, and risks to the borrower than home equity loans or HELOCs. Reverse mortgages generally are easier to qualify for than home equity loans or HELOCs, which require adequate income and credit scores. Reverse mortgages do not require monthly mortgage payments and offer several important financial protections, but they have higher costs. Home equity loans and HELOCs have required monthly payments and offer fewer financial protections for the borrower, but they have lower costs. * * *

Nearly all reverse mortgages today are insured by the Federal Housing Administration (FHA)a through its Home Equity Conversion Mortgage (HECM) program. The insurance guarantees that borrowers will be able to access their authorized loan funds in the future, subject to the terms of the loan, even if the loan balance exceeds the value of the home or

---

[3] Editors' Note: Footnotes have been omitted and some information has been updated to reflect current market trends.

[4] 2011 census data reveal that this has risen to more than two-thirds.

if the lender experiences financial difficulty. Lenders are guaranteed that they will be repaid in full when the home is sold, regardless of the loan balance or home value at repayment. Borrowers or their estates are not liable for loan balances that exceed the value of the home at repayment—FHA insurance covers this risk.

The original purpose envisioned for reverse mortgages was to convert home equity into cash that borrowers could use to help meet expenses in retirement. Borrowers could choose between an income stream for everyday expenses, a line of credit for major expenses (such as home repairs and medical expenses), or a combination of the two. It was anticipated that most, though not all, borrowers would use their loans to age in place, living in their current homes for the rest of their lives or at least until they needed skilled care. Upon the borrower's death, or upon leaving the home, the borrower or the estate would sell the home to repay the loan and would receive any remaining home equity.

Yet most of today's reverse mortgage borrowers do not use their loans to convert home equity into an income stream or a line of credit. Borrowers also do not typically live in their current homes until the end of their lives. Borrowers today are increasingly taking the full amount for which they qualify upfront as a lump sum. In many cases, borrowers are using that money to refinance an existing mortgage or other debt early in their retirement or even before reaching retirement. By refinancing with a reverse mortgage, these borrowers eliminate their monthly mortgage or debt payments, but the interest on the loan will chip away at their remaining home equity over time. In other cases, borrowers may be saving or investing the lump-sum proceeds, and may be earning less than they are paying in interest.* * *

KEY FINDINGS:

1. Reverse mortgages are complex products and difficult for consumers to understand.

    - Lessons learned from the traditional mortgage market do not always serve consumers well in the reverse mortgage market. The rising balance, falling equity nature of reverse mortgages is particularly difficult for consumers to grasp.

    - Recent innovation and policy changes have created more choices for consumers, including options with lower upfront costs. However, these changes have also increased the complexity of the choices and tradeoffs consumers have to make.

    - The tools—including federally required disclosures—available to consumers to help them understand prices and risks are insufficient to ensure that consumers are making good tradeoffs and decisions.

. . .

3. Product features, market dynamics, and industry practices also create risks for consumers.

    . . .

    ▪   Misleading advertising remains a problem in the industry and increases risks to consumers. This advertising contributes to consumer misperceptions about reverse mortgages, increasing the likelihood of poor consumer decision-making.

    ▪   Spouses of reverse mortgage borrowers who are not themselves named as co-borrowers are often unaware that they are at risk of losing their homes. If the borrowing spouse dies or needs to move, the non-borrowing spouse must sell the home or otherwise pay off the reverse mortgage at that time. Other family members (children, grandchildren, etc.) who live with reverse mortgage borrowers are also at risk of needing to find other living arrangements when the borrower dies or needs to move.

    ▪   The reverse mortgage market is increasingly dominated by small originators, most of which are not depository institutions. The changing economic and regulatory landscape faced by these small originators creates new risks for consumers.

4. Counseling, while designed to help consumers understand the risks associated with reverse mortgages, needs improvement in order to be able to meet these challenges.

    ▪   Reverse mortgages are inherently complicated, and the new array of product choices makes the counselor's job much more difficult. Counselors need improved methods to help consumers better understand the complex tradeoffs they face in deciding whether to get a reverse mortgage.

    ▪   Funding for housing counseling is under pressure, making access to high-quality counseling more difficult. Some counselors may frequently omit some of the required information or speed through the material.

    ▪   Some counseling agencies only receive payment if and when the reverse mortgage is closed (the counseling fee is paid with loan proceeds), which could undermine counselors' impartiality.

    ▪   Some borrowers may not take the counseling sessions seriously. Additional consumer awareness and education may be necessary.

    ▪   Counseling may be insufficient to counter the effects of misleading advertising, aggressive sales tactics, or questionable business practices. Stronger regulation, supervision of reverse mortgage companies, and enforcement of existing laws may also be necessary.

REVERSE MORTGAGES
Government Accountability Office
Report to Congressional Requestors, September 2019[5]

The vast majority of reverse mortgages are made under the Federal Housing Administration's (FHA) Home Equity Conversion Mortgage (HECM) program. In recent years, a growing percentage of HECMs insured by FHA have ended because borrowers defaulted on their loans. . .

Specific results for all major termination categories over the 5-year period [from 2014 to 2018] were as follows:

- Death. About 34 percent of terminations (approximately 87,000 loans) were due to the death of the borrower. Borrower deaths ranged from roughly 29 percent to 40 percent of annual terminations over the 5-year period.

- Default. About 15 percent of terminations (approximately 40,000 loans) were due to borrower defaults. . . . [T]his percentage varied widely by location and was highest in Michigan (36 percent) and lowest in the District of Columbia (1 percent). About 29,000 defaults were for noncompliance with occupancy or residency requirements, about 11,000 were for nonpayment of property charges, and about 200 were for not keeping the property in good repair. The borrowers of these loans likely lost their homes through foreclosure or a deed-in-lieu of foreclosure. However, it is possible that some of these borrowers would have ultimately lost their homes even if they had not taken out a HECM. For example, as noted in CFPB's 2012 report to Congress on reverse mortgages, some borrowers may have taken out a HECM to help pay off their traditional mortgage rather than as a way to pay for everyday expenses. In these cases, the money borrowers received from their HECMs may have helped them temporarily but may ultimately have been prolonging an unsustainable financial situation. In addition, some borrowers who did not meet occupancy or residency requirements may have permanently moved out of their homes—for example, to assisted living or nursing home facilities. Borrower defaults as a percentage of annual HECM terminations grew from 2 percent of terminations in fiscal year 2014 to 18 percent in fiscal year 2018. Noncompliance with occupancy requirements was the primary cause of

---

[5] Editors' Note: Footnotes have been omitted.

defaults each year, but unpaid property charges represented a growing share. From fiscal years 2014 through 2018, property charge defaults as a percentage of all defaults grew from 26 percent to 45 percent, and property charge defaults as a percentage of all terminations grew from less than 1 percent to 8 percent.

- Loan balance repaid. About 9 percent of terminations (approximately 23,000 loans) were due to the borrower repaying the loan balance. This category accounted for a declining share of terminations over the 5-year period, falling from 24 percent in fiscal year 2014 to 4 percent in 2018.

NOTE ON LESS FREQUENTLY USED ALTERNATIVE MORTGAGES

Lenders have developed a wide variety of alternative mortgages, though the availability of any particular type at a given time depends on market conditions. In addition to the alternative mortgages that we already have described, the following types are sometimes available:

The Price Level Adjusted Mortgage (PLAM). This mortgage format offers a different approach to the problem of mismatch between the maturities of a lender's loans and its funds sources. The PLAM is widely used in several other countries and presents an interesting alternative to the ARM. As we discussed earlier, mortgage interest rates reflect a component of real rate-of-return (perhaps 3% to 4%), plus an additional component for the lender's estimate of future inflation. In the PLAM, the lender charges only the real rate for interest, but the loan's outstanding principal balance is adjusted periodically (say, annually) to reflect changes in the nation's overall price levels. In the United States, the Consumer Price Index could be used for this purpose.

With a PLAM, payments are very low in the mortgage's early years, because they are based on the real interest rate of, say, 4%. If inflation occurs, however, payments will increase each year because the 4% rate will be applied to a higher outstanding balance. Note that *actual* inflation, rather than *expectations* about inflation, is relevant for the PLAM. For borrowers who believe that their income will increase, the PLAM might be quite attractive. See Michael S. Knoll, The Second Generation of Notes Indexed For Inflation, 39 Emory L.J. 499 (1990); Michael S. Knoll, Taxation, Negative Amortization and Affordable Mortgages, 53 Ohio St. L.J. 1341 (1992); Joel J. Goldberg, Note, Alternative Mortgage Instruments: Authorizing and Implementing Price Level Adjusted Mortgages, 16 U. Mich. J.L. Reform 115 (1982). For a review of other nations' experiences with the PLAM, see Harold Robinson, Readjustable Mortgages in an Inflationary Economy—A Study of the Israeli Experience, 5 J.L. & Econ. Dev. 169 (1970–1971).

PLAMs have occasionally been used on nonresidential mortgages in the United States. However, they make the most sense in a highly inflationary economy, and inflation has been relatively low in the U.S. in recent years, so there has been little interest in PLAMs. In Aztec Properties, Inc. v. Union Planters Nat'l Bank, 530 S.W.2d 756 (Tenn.1975), *cert. denied*, 425 U.S. 975, 96 S.Ct. 2175, 48 L.Ed.2d 799 (1976), the Tennessee Supreme Court held that the increases in principal under a PLAM were in reality interest, which triggered the usury statute. See Mildred B. Dodson, Note, Inflation and Indexing—Usury in Commercial Loans: *Aztec Properties, Inc. v. Union Planters National Bank*, 11 Tulsa L.J. 450 (1976).

The Shared Appreciation Mortgage (SAM). With this mortgage, a portion of the interest rate is payable only from increases in the mortgaged property's value. In effect, the lender holds an equity interest, as well as a security interest, in the real estate. For example, suppose a lender makes a 10-year loan with a 10 percent fixed interest rate and an additional 5 percent contingent rate. The borrower would make regular monthly payments based on the 10 percent rate. At the end of ten years or when the borrower sells the property, whichever occurs first, the 5 percent contingent interest is due. However, it is payable from only 40 percent of the property's increase in value since the loan was made.

If the property is sold, the selling price establishes its appreciated value. If it is not sold, it is appraised after ten years to determine its value. In calculating the net appreciation, the borrower receives credits for the property's original cost and for any improvements made during the loan term. If the borrower has not sold the property before the ten-year term expires, the lender may have to refinance it, including the accrued contingent interest, for a new 30-year term at the current fixed interest rate.

SAMs have been used in the United States mainly for commercial mortgage loans, but occasionally a lender offers SAM residential loans. See *generally* Anthony B. Sandersa & V. Carlos Slawson, Shared Appreciation Mortgages: Lessons from the UK, 14 J. Hous. Econ. 178 (Sept. 2005).

The Graduated Payment Mortgage (GPM). The graduated payment mortgage is designed to make housing more affordable. The interest rate is fixed for the life of the loan, but the payments increase, typically by X percent each year for the first Y years of the loan, and then remain constant for the remainder of the term. The result is heavier payments in the later years to compensate for the reduced payments in the early years of the loan. If the annual payment increase is not too steep, the borrower's income should have increased enough to cover it. Note, however, that the payment increases will occur even if the borrower's income diminishes or disappears.

FHA is authorized to insure GPM loans by Section 245 of the National Housing Act. Of the five FHA GPM plans, three allow mortgage payments to increase at a rate of 2.5 percent, 5 percent, or 7.5 percent each year for the first 5 years of the loan. In the other two plans, payments increase at a rate of 2 to 3 percent annually over a 10-year period. Beginning in the sixth year of the 5 year plans and in the eleventh year of the 10-year plans, payments stay the same for the remaining years of the mortgage. FHA plans that have a greater rate of increase over a longer period will have lower payments in the early years.

Part 3

Real Estate Development

■ ■ ■

PART 8

REAL ESTATE DEVELOPMENT

CHAPTER NINE

SUBDIVISIONS AND DETACHED HOUSE DEVELOPMENTS

■ ■ ■

This chapter is the first of two chapters that examine the legal aspects of specific types of real estate developments. This chapter covers subdivisions. The next chapter treats "common interest communities"—planned unit developments, condominiums, and cooperatives. Our objective is to provide a reasonably comprehensive picture of the legal issues relating to planning, financing, constructing, and marketing these kinds of developments and of the parties' legal rights when the developer does not meet its obligations. For the most part, we will not consider public controls over land use, such as zoning and subdivision regulations. These matters are highly complex and are frequently covered in separate law school courses with titles such as "land use planning law." We will also largely leave consideration of tax issues to your tax law courses.

A. OVERVIEW OF THE SUBDIVISION PROCESS

A land developer is a person who buys a relatively large tract of land and divides it into smaller parcels for resale. In most cases, the land's ultimate use (at least according to the developer's advertisements) will be residential, commercial, or recreational. Within this general characterization, we can identify three categories of developers:

1. *The remote developer's* land is usually rather far from any major urban area. Marketing efforts are often aimed toward persons who may wish to camp on their lots or to build smaller houses or cabins for weekend or summer use. The developer's sales force will often emphasize the subdivision's supposedly attractive investment opportunities and will cite figures predicting large capital value appreciation for the lots. The developer rarely builds any houses or cabins in this sort of development, and the other facilities it installs are often meager; paved roads, utility connections, waste disposal facilities, schools, and other parts of the infrastructure may be missing or promised for an indefinite future that never arrives.

2. *The suburban lot seller,* like the remote developer, does not build houses. But two factors distinguish this type of developer

from the sometimes-disreputable recreational lot seller. First, the land is located in the developing fringe of an urban area and, therefore, is desirable for immediate residential use. Most lot buyers plan to build homes in the near future. Second, the developer typically provides most or all of the normal public facilities required for a viable residential neighborhood, such as streets and sidewalks, street lighting, storm and sanitary sewers, utility connections, and sometimes parks or other recreational facilities. Many of these facilities are the developer's responsibility based on applicable city or county ordinances. In contrast, the remote developer usually operates in more remote jurisdictions that are not accustomed to major urban development and, therefore, do not require significant infrastructure improvements.

3. *The merchant builder* is probably the most familiar type of developer, because a large proportion of Americans live in homes these builders have constructed. Merchant builders usually operate in the same areas and provide the same range of facilities as the suburban lot seller, but they also build a house on each lot. The development may take the traditional form, with detached houses on quarter-acre to half-acre rectangular lots on rectilinear streets. Merchant builders increasingly have constructed curved streets and cul-de-sacs, semi-detached or attached houses, and relatively small private lots with larger common areas for children's play, swimming pools, and other recreational facilities. This newer format is often called a "planned unit development" ("PUD") or simply "planned development," but many of the legal issues it raises are similar to those of the more traditional grid-street subdivision.

The categories described above are not, of course, quite as neat as they seem. The distinction between remote developers and suburban lot sellers is sometimes hard to discern. Moreover, some suburban operators sell a portion of their lots without houses and build on the remainder. Even remote developers, in a few cases, sell finished houses on their lots. But, for the most part, i a particular developer can fairly easily be identified with one of these categories.

In this section, we will focus principally on merchant builders, but many of the legal problems raised by their operations are applicable to the other two categories of developers as well. We begin by presenting a general overview of the merchant builder's operations. We will examine a typical subdivision from initial land acquisition to final sale of completed houses. The following sections of this chapter will analyze in detail the legal issues raised by various phases of the developer's operations, such as construction financing.

Many developers are small businesspersons. The great majority probably build fewer than 50 houses per year. Although there has been some trend toward greater scale and concentration, it is by no means dominant. Perhaps the most salient fact about typical small builders is that they are very thinly capitalized. Even builders who have operated successfully for many years often operate with little equity capital. Builders prefer to employ borrowed money and to use as little of their own funds as possible. In the parlance of the industry, they are "highly leveraged" and prefer to come as close as possible to "mortgaging out," using no money of their own. These business practices put many small private land developers out of business in the 2008–2010 Great Recession At the time of this writing, the effect of the COVID-19 pandemic on the land development industry is uncertain, but initial signs point to significant demand for continued land development and suburban home construction, as dense urban apartment and condominium living becomes less appealing. In the post-2008 vacuum of small, private land developers, regional and national homebuilders have stepped in significantly more.

A sophisticated merchant builder's work begins well before it has identified any particular land for the subdivision. Because houses can be sold only where there are willing buyers, market research is necessary to demonstrate that homes of a particular design and price range can be sold in a given locality. Both construction and permanent lenders will be interested in this market data, but the developer must review it first to determine that going forward makes business sense.

Of course, many small builders do not perform or contract for formal market surveys. They rely instead on their own instincts and experience; they feel that they know what is selling and where. Indeed, in some metropolitan areas, housing demand appears to be so strong that market research seems superfluous. But housing demand is notoriously volatile, and even areas like these can become overbuilt, with unsold houses sitting for long periods of time in a saturated market. Market demand is also a function of interest rates and of the availability of financing. The builder's sales projections must be reviewed in the light of probable financial trends and buyers' ability to obtain mortgage loans at acceptable interest rates.

After determining market demand, the builder is ready to choose a specific site for the development. Sites for new subdivisions are typically in the developing urban fringe, although occasionally land may become available in already-urbanized areas as a result of urban renewal land clearance, the development of a "new town in town," or because a municipal, state, or the federal government makes land available that had previously been restricted to government use. In the usual suburban case, the land has been previously used for agriculture, although the developer does not always buy directly from the farmer. Often, land speculators will have purchased agricultural land that they anticipated would become desirable for subdivision in the near future, and the developer must then deal with them. In other cases, the developer is also a speculator and has decided that the market is ready for a subdivision on the land that it purchased some years earlier.

As the development process progresses, land prices increase. Land used for agricultural purposes may have a value of only a few thousand dollars per acre. A developer, however, will usually have to pay a substantial premium above that amount to acquire the land when it is ready for development. After the developer has obtained the necessary land use approvals, including any necessary rezoning, has invested in the necessary infrastructure, such as streets and sewers, and has paid the necessary fees for water, sewer, and other utility hookups and for local school, park, and other funds, the final market price of a finished lot will be many times its value as raw land. For this reason, if the developer does not already own the land, it often prefers reserving the right to buy with an option to purchase, rather than entering into a binding purchase agreement. With an option agreement, the developer can buy the land in the future if it decides to do so and will forfeit a relatively small amount of money if it decides not to exercise the option because the project turns out to be infeasible. In industry parlance, the developer does not own but "controls" the land under option to purchase agreements.

During the option period, the developer pursues a variety of matters more or less simultaneously, such as surveys, soil tests, and environmental investigations. The planning and engineering of the subdivision is a first concern, because both lenders and local governments will review the subdivision layout and design before giving their approvals. Additionally, in almost all cases, a local government agency must approve the subdivision. As part of this review and approval process, the developer prepares a subdivision plat, which is a map that shows the layout of streets, lots, easements, and other features of the subdivision. After the plat is approved, it is recorded with the county recorder or another appropriate government office and then provides the basis for legal descriptions of lots in the subdivision. If the developer has financed the land prior to recording the plat, the consent of the lender is required in order for the plat to have priority over the lender's mortgage and survive any foreclosure of that mortgage. In most jurisdictions, the plat also constitutes a dedication of the streets and other public facilities that it shows. Because the developer may not actually construct these facilities for some time, many local governments require the developer to escrow funds, post a bond or letter of credit from a commercial bank, or otherwise provide assurances that the improvements will be completed and that the developer will be financially responsible for their construction.

Before exercising the option, the developer also must attempt to obtain financing for the project. As described in the next section, the developer normally must arrange financing to acquire the land (purchase money land financing), to build the "horizontal improvements" for the project, such as streets, curbs, gutters, sewers, and other utilities (horizontal construction loan), and potentially to finance the new home construction (vertical construction loan). In addition to the loan costs, the developer usually is responsible for the fees of the attorneys, planners, and other professionals involved in the project, although it can sometimes persuade the original owner of the land to share the expenses. These loans are ultimately repaid by the sale of lots or homes to end users.

The developer will buy the land only after obtaining the necessary government approvals and arranging financing. Although these contingencies could have been included in a firm purchase agreement as preconditions to the developer's obligation to purchase the land, such a contract would be long and complex. Therefore, as described above, most developers prefer to use the option agreement. When all the necessary planning is completed and the government approvals have been obtained, the developer will exercise the option, thus creating a binding contract to purchase the land.

B. FINANCING THE PROJECT

1. PURCHASE MONEY LAND FINANCING

Developers rarely are willing or able to pay cash for the land to be developed. A cash purchase is feasible if the developer is willing to proceed very slowly; it can enter into option agreements with the owner that allow it to purchase a few lots at a time with the proceeds from sales of lots that it has previously developed. But a developer that wants to operate on a substantial scale must arrange credit to finance the land acquisition.

One possibility is to enter into a loan agreement with a single lender, such as a commercial bank or savings association, for enough funds to cover the entire project, including land acquisition, site development, and construction. Such loans are usually called "ADC" loans ("acquisition, development, and construction" loans). Although some lenders make them, the FDIC has warned that "ADC lending is a highly specialized field with inherent risks that must be managed and controlled to ensure that this activity remains profitable." FDIC Financial Institution Letter FIL–110–98 (Oct. 8, 1998). Because of this perception of risk, ADC loans tend to be made only to experienced and well-capitalized developers. The Office of the Comptroller of the Currency, the Board of Governors of the Federal Reserve System, and the Federal Deposit Insurance Corporation have promulgated a new rule that classifies many ADC loans as being "high volatility commercial real estate" loans and imposes new requirements on ADC lenders. The rule became effective on April 1, 2020. OCC Bulletin 2019–64

(Dec. 13, 2019). See William C. Handorf, Land Acquisition, Development and Construction Financing, Fall 2014 Real Estate Review 15.

Obtaining only a land acquisition loan from an institutional lender also can be difficult. Therefore, the developer often persuades the seller to extend credit for a large part of the land's purchase price. For the most common form of seller financing, the seller deeds the property to the developer, and the developer gives the seller a small down payment and a promissory note and purchase money mortgage on the property for the balance of the purchase price. Alternatively, the land can be sold by means of an installment contract pursuant to which the seller retains title to the land until the entire purchase price is paid. The developer adjusts the maturity of the purchase money obligation to reflect the development plans; the longer the construction time contemplated, the longer the maturity of the obligation.

Persuading the land seller to defer receipt of part of the purchase price often is possible because Internal Revenue Code § 453 permits sellers to spread the tax on the gain from the sale across the years in which the proceeds are actually received, rather than paying the entire tax in the year of sale. This treatment is available whether the sale is by installment contract or by deed with a note and mortgage back to the seller.

When completed homes are sold, the developer must be able to convey them free of the purchase money lien. Therefore, the loan documents usually include a partial release clause. Under this type of clause, the purchase money lien on a lot is released when the lot is sold and a specified fraction of the loan is paid to the lien holder. Alternatively, the land may be placed in a "subdivision trust" with a title company or other trustee who is instructed to convey each lot free of the purchase money lien when the portion of the loan attributable to that lot is paid to the lien holder. The developer may also reserve a right to prepay all or part of the land purchase obligation if more favorable interim financing becomes available.

2. CONSTRUCTION AND PERMANENT FINANCING

A construction loan is the usual source of funds for building the improvements on the land. The construction loan is a short-term loan that usually is secured by a mortgage or deed of trust on the property. The construction lender will take all the precautions normally associated with the acquisition of a mortgage lien. For example, the lender normally requires a title search and title insurance for the lender's construction mortgage, and the developer usually must be personally liable or provide a strong corporate parent guaranty for the debt if the nominal developing entity is a thinly-capitalized corporation or limited liability company. The construction loan is repaid as each improved lot is sold.

The most important construction lenders for commercial developments are commercial banks, insurance companies, and pension funds. Fannie Mae, Freddie Mac, and government agencies, such as the Federal Housing Administration, also are important construction lenders, but only for multi-family/apartment construction. Because these lenders almost always insist on first lien priority, the purchase money land lien and the lien for any site development loan normally must be refinanced and paid off by the construction loan, as construction lenders generally do not like subordinate creditors that could interfere with management of the loan. Sometimes, the construction lender may accept subordination of the purchase money mortgage to the construction mortgage. This subordination is best accomplished by language in the purchase money and site development loan security documents or in a separate agreement that the construction loan will have first priority. Subordination substantially increases the risk for the subordinated liens, a fact that the subordinated lienors may not fully appreciate.

From the construction lender's viewpoint, it is also important that a long-term permanent loan for a commercial development, such as a shopping mall, is available to pay off the entire construction loan when construction is complete. Unless the construction lender is very confident concerning the developer's solvency and the project's' marketability, it often requires the developer to obtain a permanent loan commitment as a condition to the construction loan being funded. For some types of construction lenders, an advance take-out commitment is a legal requirement. Sometimes, the construction lender also provides the permanent loan commitment. However, many large permanent lenders generally will not issue a permanent loan commitment until the construction is complete.

Another major concern of the construction lender is that the value of the improvements constructed with the loan proceeds at least equals those proceeds. Two common situations exist in which this expectation may not be fulfilled. First, the builder may "draw down" the construction funds but divert them to some use other than labor and materials on the construction site. For an unscrupulous builder, the funds' ultimate destination might be an offshore bank account. More frequently, the builder needs the money for other business purposes. For example, the builder may have another project that has run into financial difficulties and may hope to "bail it out" with the construction funds diverted from the present project.

Second, even if the developer is completely honest, the property's security value may be less than the amount of funds disbursed because of normal construction risks. During labor strikes, bad weather, and other delays, costs continue to accrue even though little or no work of value is being accomplished on the site. Similarly, material costs may rise substantially and unexpectedly. Although some kinds of hazards, such as fire, can be insured against, delays and some other types of risks are uninsurable. Therefore, a project into which one million dollars in construction loan funds have been poured very well may be worth only $800,000 or less.

If the builder becomes bankrupt, is unable to complete construction, or otherwise defaults on the construction loan, the construction lender may decide to foreclose and take title to the partially-completed property and hire another contractor or developer to complete the project. But this simply shifts to the construction lender all the risks that the builder could not manage, and most construction lenders have little desire to place themselves in that situation. On the contrary, the construction lender's principal goal is to have the builder successfully complete the project within the limits of the funds committed.

To achieve this goal, construction lenders have developed several techniques for insuring that the disbursed loan proceeds are used for improvements on the construction site. When the loan is made, the lender and builder execute a "construction loan agreement" that specifies the loan disbursement procedures and conditions. For a very complete and well-designed illustration, see Nelson, Whitman, Burkhart & Freyermuth, Real Estate Finance Law § 14:2 (6th ed. Practitioner Series 2014). See also Dianne S. Coscarelli, The Construction Loan Agreement: Six Provisions Important to Lender's Counsel, Prob. & Prop., Jan./Feb. 2001, at 30; Richard E. Strauss, Construction Financing: An Additional Dimension, 54 The Secured Lender, Nov./Dec. 1998, at 34. Various approaches are used by lenders in different areas of the nation, but the most common include the following:

1.   *Progress payments.* Under this approach, the lender advances funds as specific stages of construction are completed. For example, the lender might advance 1/7th of the funds when the excavation is completed and the foundation is poured, the next 1/7th when the exterior walls are framed, the next 1/7th when the roof is on, and so on. Monthly loan draws for work completed in the previous 30 days is also common.

2.   *The voucher system.* The lender may require the developer to pay the workers and suppliers directly and then to present those bills, marked "paid," to the lender for reimbursement. In principle, this assures the lender that the funds it disburses represent work already done on the property. However, the developer may be tempted to persuade or to coerce workers and suppliers to mark bills as being paid when they are not. This practice gives the developer some additional cash, but it violates the construction loan agreement and increases the lender's risk.

3. *Direct disbursements to workers and suppliers.* As a variant of the voucher system, the lender may require that the workers' and suppliers' bills be presented directly to it. The lender then pays them and debits the builder's construction loan account accordingly.

4. *Third party disbursing agents.* Rather than managing the construction loan itself, the lender may employ a third party, such as a title insurance company, a "construction control company," an escrow company, or some other independent entity, to make all disbursements to the workers and suppliers. The disbursing agent may be willing to guarantee that the funds have been disbursed only for work actually done on the project. The arrangement with the disbursing agent will be memorialized in a tri-party agreement between the lender, borrower, and disbursing agent.

5. *Inspections.* Lenders will often employ, at the borrower's expense, a construction inspector that regularly inspects the work completed on the project before each loan draw to make sure work is completed as represented in the loan draw request and is consistent with the project's plans and specifications.

No matter which approach the construction lender uses, it is likely to require that a certain fraction of the total cost, typically 5 to 10 percent, be "held back" until the construction on a particular house is completed and the local government issues a certificate of occupancy.

Construction loans do not always cover the entire cost of construction. Additionally, off-site improvements, such as storm and sanitary sewers and street paving, often must be constructed. The Lender will require a "balanced sources and uses" of funds, including off-site improvements, other "soft costs," and miscellaneous fees. Lenders also generally require that all borrower equity be invested in the project before any loan draws. To pay for these items, the builder may have to invest some of its own cash in the project. Lenders also often require the builder to post a cash deposit with the lender to provide assurance that the builder is sufficiently solvent to complete the project (with the equity spent on the project before any loan draws). Additionally, the lender may require the builder to post a payment and performance bond, which obligates the bonding company to complete the project within the agreed-upon budget if the builder cannot. However, bonds are somewhat uncommon because most small builders cannot qualify for them and because larger builders that can qualify are usually sufficiently solvent that a bond is thought to add little protection.

Both before and during construction, the construction lender takes a close interest in the plans and specifications for the project and for the off-site improvements. The lender frequently inspects the improvements to ensure that they are being completed in accordance with those plans and specifications. The construction lender is motivated by self-interest; if the development does not meet the specifications, the permanent lender may refuse to honor its loan commitment, and the construction lender may have a "white elephant" on its hands.

To provide additional protection, many construction lenders use "demand" notes, which allow the lender to require repayment of the note at any time and to foreclose if the builder is unable to comply. In the normal course of construction, the lender would not make such a demand. However, if the builder runs into serious difficulties, the lender can call the loan due, take over the project, and complete construction. This rarely occurs, but its threat can be an effective means of spurring the builder to more vigorous action.

For the reasons described above, construction lending is far more complex and burdensome than long-term lending, but it can also be more lucrative. Interest rates on construction loans are typically several percentage points higher than on permanent loans. Moreover, construction lenders use a variety of techniques for boosting the yields on these loans. "Loan fees" and "points" are often charged in addition to interest. The lender may also pay little or no interest on the funds that the builder is required to deposit with the lender to ensure financial responsibility.

When construction on a house in a subdivision is completed and a home buyer is found, the buyer obtains a purchase money loan and pays the purchase price to the builder. The builder, in turn, uses the purchase price to pay off a pro rata share of the construction loan, the purchase money land loan, and any site development loan, including accrued interest. The lenders then release their liens on the lot, which enables a clear conveyance of title. Sometimes, the release price is higher than a pro-rata share of the construction loan, as the lender wants "acceleration," such that the construction loan is repaid before the sale of every last lot.

A few decades ago, home developers often took a second mortgage from home buyers to reduce the down payment to a level that more people could afford. Because the developer usually needed cash and could not afford to hold second mortgages, it almost always sold this paper at a rather deep discount to some other lender. This practice has become less common for urban subdivision developers, but recreational developers still routinely provide financing for their customers by taking installment contracts or purchase-money mortgages and then usually selling or "discounting" them to finance companies or other investors.

The excerpt below illustrates in a concrete way some of the problems that can arise with construction lending. While it deals with an apartment project, rather than a subdivision, most of the issues are similar.

HENRY S. KESLER, CONSTRUCTION
LENDING RISKS AND RETURNS
Mortgage Banking, Jan. 1989, at 62

The Apartments at Purple Creek is an example of a construction lending project that involved many of the risks facing a construction lender. This was a $3,400,000 construction loan on a 96-unit garden apartment project in rural Evanston, Wyoming. Evanston was in the midst of the oil boom and had a housing shortage and prospects for continued expansion. The project had obtained a commitment for FHA-insured IRB (Industrial Revenue Bond) term financing sponsored by the city with a letter of credit enhancement from a major bank in a neighboring state.

The developers had only done one other apartment property. The partnership included a construction foreman who had worked for a successful apartment developer. To further simplify the construction, the project was a copy of a previously built apartment and was to be modular construction with pre-fabricated apartment units delivered to the site by a major home fabricator. The borrowers' net worth was modest and illiquid with the required cash equity being contributed from numerous limited partners, some closely related to the borrowers. A nine-month construction loan was approved and closed in December with substantial fees and course-of-construction, FHA inspections required.

The loan production officer was so optimistic that he failed to objectively present the borrowers' experience or financial status. Instead, the construction lender relied upon the existence of the FHA-insured take-out commitment to influence final approval. At loan closing, the loan officer casually approved the change of construction method from prefabricated, modular construction to onsite framing. Yet, no change was made to the construction budget. The loan was then turned over to the lender's construction loan administration division.

During an early inspection by the lender's independent architect not only was the construction method a surprise but the borrower/contractor had redesigned the project and was using unapproved plans.

Because of the lack of available skilled labor in this rural community and unusually severe weather conditions, construction costs skyrocketed. The borrower hid the cost increases from the lender until costs were out of control. Lien laws gave all laborers and suppliers priority over the construction loan. The foreman was diverting funds to his personal benefit and several subcontractors went bankrupt. The construction lender finally had to forcibly take control of the security pledged from the borrowers (their homes), and funded cost overruns by increasing the loan $700,000.

The project was ultimately completed nine months late. By that time, the Evanston economy had severely deteriorated and conventional financing would only support a $2,800,000 loan and the IRB could not be increased. Fortunately for the construction lender, the FHA commitment and the IRB had been extended but their funding prohibited any subordinate financing. As a result, the construction lender was forced to look only to the additional collateral pledged by the borrowers for satisfaction of a $700,000 loan increase. Thus, the lender ultimately experienced a loss in excess of $500,000.

This loan had it all: lack of thorough underwriting; undercapitalized inexperienced borrower/developers; multiple borrowers; underestimated costs; changes to the construction method; failure of subcontractors; fraudulent diversion of funds; loss of rental market; subsidized term financing; and the involvement of a supervising governmental agency. In addition, there was the poor judgment of the loan officer, the failure of early identification of the problems and lack of immediate control measures by the construction lender. Ultimately the letter-of-credit-issuing bank was required to fund to satisfy the bonds and also suffered a major loss.

NOTES ON CONSTRUCTION LENDER LIABILITY

1. *Liability for construction defects.* New home builders are now widely held liable for defects in design or construction on the basis of an implied warranty of habitability. Should such liability be imposed on a construction lender as well, if it reviewed and approved the defective plans and specifications or if it inspected the property and became aware of the defects? In many cases, the builder is judgment-proof or nearly so, while the lender is a "deep pocket." Most such claims against lenders have failed. See Skinner v. U.S. Bank Home Mortgage, 365 P.3d 398 (Idaho 2016) (lender did not owe borrowers fiduciary duty to inspect construction for their benefit); Craig R. Thorstenson, Comment, Mortgage Lender Liability to the Purchaser of New or Existing Homes, 1988 Ill.L.Rev. 191; Nelson, Whitman, Burkhart & Freyermuth, Real Estate Finance Law § 12.11 (6th ed.2015).

2. *Liability for hazardous waste contamination.* Consider a construction lender's potential liability for a violation of CERCLA (Comprehensive Environmental Response, Compensation and Liability Act of 1980, 42 U.S.C. §§ 9601–9675). Generally, the lender is protected if it meets the "All Appropriate Inquiries" standard that is set forth in CERCLA. But what is the liability of a construction lender that makes a loan for a residential subdivision on a site that was previously used for industrial purposes and is contaminated by industrial waste? Is the lender liable by virtue of its role in the construction process? At least one court has held that it is. Tanglewood East Homeowners v. Charles-Thomas, Inc., 849 F.2d 1568 (5th Cir.1988).

3. *Liability for discontinuance of loan funding.* During the 1980s, a great flurry of litigation involved what was loosely termed "lender liability." Most of the cases involved lines of credit granted to businesses or to farming operations. The loan documents provided for short-term loans (typically one

year). When the borrower's business began to falter or to fail, the lender refused to renew the line of credit. See, e.g., K.M.C. Co., Inc. v. Irving Trust Co., 757 F.2d 752 (6th Cir.1985); State Nat'l Bank v. Farah Mfg. Co., 678 S.W.2d 661 (Tex.App.1984). Borrowers usually asserted damages on the ground that the lender's termination of the credit line caused the business to fail or, at least, drove the nails into its coffin. They often based their claim on breach of a contractual duty of good faith and fair dealing, breach of a fiduciary relationship, tortious interference with contractual relations, or on the argument that the short-term credit agreement had been changed by the parties' course of conduct into a longer-term obligation to lend.

Nearly all these cases failed to establish liability. In the absence of highly improper or misleading statements by the lender, courts generally enforced the loan documents as written, permitted acceleration of the debt because it was in default or because the loan's term ended, and refused to find a continuing duty to lend. Nonetheless, lenders must be careful not to establish a "course of dealing" (e.g., frequently waiving loan covenants or requirements) where reversal of that accommodative pattern could be considered lender liability. See, e.g., Mitsui Manufacturers Bank v. Superior Court, 212 Cal.App.3d 726, 260 Cal.Rptr. 793 (1989); Batterman v. Wells Fargo Ag Credit Corp., 802 P.2d 1112 (Colo.App.1990); Lachenmaier v. First Bank Systems, Inc., 246 Mont. 26, 803 P.2d 614 (1990); Bloomfield v. Nebraska State Bank, 237 Neb. 89, 465 N.W.2d 144 (1991); Kathleen S. McLeroy, Note, Lender Liability and Discretionary Lending: Putting the Good Faith Performance Standard in Perspective, 46 Wash. & Lee L.Rev. 1067 (1989).

A few of these lender liability cases involved development or construction loans. For example, in Storek & Storek v. Citicorp Real Estate, Inc., 100 Cal.App.4th 44, 122 Cal.Rptr.2d 267 (2002), the developer argued that the construction lender had "set up" the developer for default on a loan to complete a partially-finished development. The construction loan agreement provided that a default existed if the loan was "out of balance" (i.e., if insufficient funds remained in the construction account to complete the project) when the lender knew that the loan was "out of balance" from the outset. The court held that, if the lender had reasonable evidence that the loan was out of balance, it could declare a default and foreclose regardless of its alleged bad motives.

However, if a lender cannot provide reasonable evidence of a default, it may indeed be liable for "calling" the loan. In Shaughnessy v. Mark Twain State Bank, 715 S.W.2d 944 (Mo.App.1986), Mark Twain State Bank gave a developer, Shaughnessy, a $50,000 line of credit to perform preliminary site development on a real estate project. The loan was secured by a deed of trust. After some funds were advanced and expended, the bank became dissatisfied with the project, refused to advance more funds, and "called" the loan. The developer sued for damages and prevailed. In rejecting the bank's defense, the court stated:

> Mark Twain argues that . . . three events of default occurred . . .: (1) the bank deemed itself insecure; (2) the bank determined that a

material adverse change had occurred in the financial condition of Shaughnessy; and (3) material falsehood in the loan application. Thus, Mark Twain argues that since one or more of these three conditions were met the note was in default and breach of the contract to lend occurred. We disagree.

These are factual issues. Mark Twain vigorously asserts that after it visited the Questover Canyon site, it discovered that things were not as it had thought. Thus, Mark Twain then could have considered itself insecure or that a materially adverse change had occurred, thus triggering default by Shaughnessy. However, Shaughnessy's evidence was that the bank never gave him any reason for cutting him off. Certainly had the bank felt it was insecure it would have articulated its reasons to Shaughnessy. It did not and therefore, we cannot say the trial court was clearly in error in finding no default occurred.

Mark Twain also claims that Shaughnessy defaulted by filing a materially false loan application. Mark Twain urges us to reverse based on the fact that Shaughnessy's 1978 income was $24,000 when in fact, according to his income tax return it was only $684.06. We disagree. First, the record shows that Shaughnessy's income from insurance sales in 1978 was not a crucial factor in the loan process as was Shaughnessy's equity in Questover Canyon and the prospect for payoff through sales. Secondly, there is no evidence that Mark Twain was aware of this discrepancy until after it refused to disburse.

The promissory note at issue in *Shaughnessy* was a demand note. That type of note provides that the lender can demand payment at any time. Section 1–309 of the Uniform Commercial Code deals with a similar yet distinct type of note. It specifies the circumstances under which a lender can accelerate a loan with a defined maturity date based on the lender's insecurity:

A term providing that one party or that party's successor in interest may accelerate payment or performance or require collateral or additional collateral . . . when the party "deems itself insecure," or words of similar import, means that the party has power to do so only if that party in good faith believes that the prospect of payment or performance is impaired. The burden of establishing lack of good faith is on the party against which the power has been exercised.

For the reasons cited above, lenders prefer clear, absolute, and unambiguous loan agreement conditions, such as liquidity covenants, minimum lot sales per quarter or year, and loan-in-balance covenant, the subjectivity to enforce such requirements is reduced.

3.   LOAN COMMITMENTS

Both construction and permanent loans are generally preceded by a loan commitment—a lender's written promise to make the loan when certain conditions are met. For example, in a permanent loan commitment in which the lender agrees to finance the purchase of an apartment building, the lender will condition the commitment on satisfactory completion of third-party due diligence reports (such as appraisal, environmental, and property condition reports), as these reports are typically not completed until shortly before loan closing. Before giving a commitment, the permanent lender usually reviews the available market research concerning the project and the plans and specifications for it. The commitment will be conditioned on the construction being completed in accordance with the plans and specifications.

Loan commitments made by major lenders on major projects, such as a life insurance company's permanent loan commitment on a multimillion-dollar shopping center, are usually lengthy (say, 20 to 30 pages), carefully negotiated, and well-drafted. On the other hand, commitments made by local lenders to local builders are often cursory and haphazard and give rise to numerous problems of interpretation. The following example of a construction loan commitment is somewhere in between.

EQUITY NATIONAL BANK

September 14, 2021

Mr. Edward Jones
1270 Sloan Street
Evergreen, Colorado 80439

    Re: Construction Loan

Dear Mr. Jones:

We are pleased to inform you that Equity National Bank ("Lender") has conditionally approved your application for a loan ("Loan") to construct a home on certain real estate located in Evergreen, Jefferson County, Colorado, and being more commonly known as "Longbourne" (the "Project"). The Loan and this Commitment are subject to the terms and conditions contained herein and the terms and conditions contained in the Standard Terms and Conditions attached hereto as Schedule "A" and made a part hereof (this commitment letter and the Standard Terms and Conditions being collectively referred to herein as the "Commitment").

1. **Identification of Borrower**:

Edward Jones, having a mailing address of 1270 Sloan Street, Evergreen, Colorado 80439 ("Borrower"). Borrower is/are [*choose one*]:

[x] a single adult individual over 18 years of age.

[ ] a married couple.

[ ] a _____ partnership.

[ ]   a _____ corporation.

[ ]   a _____ limited liability company.

[ ]   other: _____

2. **Loan Amount**:

The amount of the Loan shall be equal to the lesser of (a) Three Hundred Thousand and 00/100 Dollars ($300,000.00) and (b) [*choose applicable paragraph*]:

[ ]   Eighty percent (80%) of the lesser amount of the appraised value or the sales price of the Project, pursuant to an appraisal acceptable to Lender and otherwise satisfying the requirements of state and federal statutes and regulations.

[x]   Ninety percent (90%) of the purchase price of the Project provided that the Loan shall be modified to a permanent Loan upon completion of the Project.

3. **Loan Term**:

The Loan shall be due and payable on July 1, 2022 (the "Expiration Date"), without notice or demand.

4. **Interest Rate**:

The Loan shall be a variable rate loan. The outstanding principal balance of the Loan shall bear interest at a variable per annum rate equal to two percent (2%) above the prime rate of interest from time to time published in the Wall Street Journal. Interest shall be calculated on the basis of a three hundred sixty (360) day year applied to the actual number of days involved ("Applicable Interest Rate").

Default interest at a per annum rate equal to four percent (4%) above the then Applicable Interest Rate shall be applied under circumstances of default and situations in which Lender advances any monies on behalf of Borrower as more particularly described and provided in the Loan Documents.

5. **Payments**:

Interest only shall be due and payable, in arrears, each month during the Loan term, with payments commencing on the first day of the second month following the date of the Loan closing.

In any and all events, the Loan's entire unpaid principal balance, together with all accrued and unpaid interest thereon, shall be due and payable on the Expiration Date.

6. **Disbursements and Other Terms of Loan**:

Unless otherwise agreed in writing by Lender, the Loan shall be closed before construction commences on the Project. The Project shall be constructed in accordance with the proposal and other documentation submitted to Lender. Construction of the Project shall be completed on or before June 20, 2022 in strict accordance with the plans and specifications (the "Plans and Specifications"), construction contract, and cost breakdown approved in advance by Lender. Each request by Borrower for a disbursement of the Loan must be made pursuant to the procedures required from time to time by Lender.

Before Closing, Borrower shall deliver to Lender a detailed project budget and cost breakdown for the purchase of the real estate, if applicable, and the construction of the Project, including the extension of all utilities and the completion of all necessary landscaping. As soon as available, but in any event within five (5) days of execution, Borrower shall deliver to Lender copies of executed contracts from the general contractor that support the budget and cost breakdown, acceptable to Lender, and that specify the source of funds, if any, necessary to cover all costs in excess of the Loan. Unless waived by Lender, all construction contracts shall be fixed-price contracts containing no-lien provisions, shall be in recordable form, and shall otherwise comply with all applicable statutes.

Each request by Borrower for disbursement of proceeds from the Loan must (i) be made on Lender's form Request for Disbursement, executed by Borrower, and certified by an engineer or engineering firm acceptable to Lender but employed at the Borrower's expense, (ii) include such lien waivers as the Lender may require, all on forms and in substance satisfactory to Lender, and (iii) comply with all other conditions and requirements contained in the other Loan Documents. No disbursement shall be made on work requiring government inspections until all appropriate approvals have been obtained. Final disbursement of the Loan proceeds shall be made when construction has been fully completed, inspected, and approved by the inspecting architect, engineer, or appraiser. All construction draws must be supported by a title insurance endorsement that updates Lender's loan policy through the date of each requested disbursement and reflects a status of title satisfactory to Lender. All disbursements shall be made based on the percentage of work completed. Lender shall not be obligated to disburse more than the amounts listed as being funded by Lender on the Project budget and construction cost breakdown, nor shall Lender be obligated to fund any items not shown on the Project budget and construction cost breakdown.

The Project must be constructed in compliance with all ordinances, codes, statutes, and regulations applicable to the Project and in a professional manner in strict accordance with the Plans and Specifications. All construction work is subject to final inspection by Lender's representative, which inspection shall be for Lender's sole benefit and may not be relied on by Borrower.

7.   <u>Security</u>:

(a)   Borrower's obligations with respect to the Loan shall be secured
by:

<u>First Mortgage</u>. A first mortgage on the Project, together with a
security interest in all fixtures and equipment, now owned or
hereafter acquired and used or held for use in connection with the
construction, equipping, operation, or maintenance thereof.

(b)   In addition to (a) above, the Borrower's Loan obligations may, in
Lender's sole discretion, be secured by one or more of the following:

<u>Fixture Filing</u>. A separate fixture filing providing a lien on all
elements that are or may become fixtures to the Project;

<u>General Assignment</u>. An assignment of all Borrower's right, title,
and interest in and to the Plans and Specifications and all
construction contracts and subcontracts and contractor's,
subcontractor's, and supplier's warranties relating to the
construction, equipping, operation, or maintenance of the Project;

and any other additional security and/or instruments as may
be set forth elsewhere herein or otherwise required by Lender
and/or its counsel to fully and effectively secure Lender's
Loan and its priority in such security and the Project.

8.   <u>Unconditional Guaranty</u>:

Payment of the Loan and all obligations of Borrower shall be
unconditionally guaranteed by _____Not applicable_____
("Guarantor(s)"), in form and substance approved by Lender (the
"Guaranty(ies)"). Further, at Lender's sole discretion, the spouse of each
married Guarantor who is not otherwise a Guarantor of the Loan, may be
required to complete and deliver Lender's form Spousal Waiver, wherein
Guarantor's spouse waives and subjects his or her rights in jointly held
property to the rights of Lender under the Guaranty.

9.   <u>Loan Documents</u>:

The Loan shall be evidenced by this Commitment, a construction loan
agreement, a promissory note, a mortgage, and such other documents as
Lender may require, including such consents and other evidences of due
organization, authority, and/or power of Borrower and/or Guarantors, as
applicable, to enter into, deliver, and perform the obligations contemplated
by this Commitment and the other loan documents (collectively, the "Loan
Documents"). All instruments, documents, and other terms required in
connection with the Loan shall be in form and content satisfactory to
Lender and its counsel.

10. **Payment of Expenses**:

Borrower shall pay all costs incidental to the Loan, including, but not limited to, title insurance (including all updates of title required by Lender), survey charges, the cost of environmental inspections, appraisals, insurance premiums for all required insurance coverages, inspecting engineer's, architects', or appraiser fees, and any and all other incidental expenses of Lender, whether or not the Loan is closed, including Lender's reasonable attorneys' fees and costs incurred in connection with the review and documentation of the Loan or otherwise.

11. **Default**:

Any one or more of the following shall constitute an event of default: (a) failure to pay when due any principal or interest on the Loan or any other obligation or liability owed to Lender by Borrower; (b) failure to observe or perform any agreement or covenant contained in the Loan Documents; (c) breach of any warranty, representation, certification, or statement contained in the Loan Documents or in any certification or other agreement or document executed or delivered in connection with the Loan Documents, (d) death of any individual who is a Borrower or Guarantor; (e) assignment by Borrower or any guarantor for the benefit of its creditors; (f) appointment of a receiver or a trustee for Borrower or Guarantor or any of its assets; (g) the filing of a petition to adjudicate Borrower or Guarantor as bankrupt; (h) default by Borrower or Guarantor under any agreement with or undertaking to Lender whether or not related to the Loan; (i) Lender in good faith deems itself insecure; (j) any material adverse change in the financial, operating, or other condition of Borrower or Guarantor; or (k) Lender believes the prospect of payment or performance of the Loan is impaired.

The foregoing constitutes a list of the basic events of default and is not intended to be an exhaustive list. It shall be supplemented by such additional events of default as provided in the other Loan Documents.

After an event of default, at Lender's option and without further notice or demand to Borrower, the Loan shall become immediately due and payable. All rights and remedies of Lender herein specified and/or otherwise provided in the other Loan Documents, are cumulative and in addition to, not in limitation of, any rights and remedies that it may have by law or at equity.

12. **Commitment and Construction Loan Fee**:

(a) Borrower shall pay to Lender as a commitment fee in respect of the Loan the sum of One Thousand and 00/100 Dollars ($1,000.00). Such commitment fee shall be earned upon acceptance of this Commitment Letter and shall not be refunded even if the Loan is not approved. Lender shall apply the commitment fee to the construction loan fee charged by the Lender at the closing of the Loan.

(b) In consideration for the Loan, Borrower shall pay to Lender a construction loan fee of Three Thousand and 00/100 Dollars ($3,000.00), which shall be paid at the closing of the Loan.

13. **Other Conditions**:

In addition to all other terms, conditions, and requirements hereof, Borrower shall provide Lender before closing of the Loan evidence acceptable to Lender that Borrower has obtained a firm commitment for financing in amount sufficient to pay off the Loan at maturity (the "Take-Out Commitment"). In so doing, Borrower shall take all actions necessary and provide all information required by the terms of such Take-Out Commitment.

14. **Acceptance**:

This Commitment is not binding upon Lender unless an executed copy hereof is returned to the undersigned on or before September 21, 2021, together with the commitment fee provided in paragraph 12(a) above, which shall be paid to Lender in the form of a cashier's or certified check. In the event the Loan committed hereunder is not closed on or before October 9, 20121, this Commitment shall be null and void and have no further force or effect. Closing of the Loan is subject to the condition that, in Lender's sole discretion, there is no material deterioration of Borrower's or, if applicable, Guarantor's financial position, that Borrower has the power and financial capacity to repay all amounts owing or to be owed in connection with the Loan, and that all conditions have been satisfied, approvals have been obtained, and all documents, reports, surveys, and inspections are satisfactory to Lender. Any extension of this Commitment shall be made only with Lender's written approval.

15. **Inconsistencies**:

The terms and provisions of this Commitment and those contained in the other Loan Documents shall, to the fullest extent possible, be read and applied as supplementary to each other to fulfill the intents and purposes of the Loan Documents. Notwithstanding the foregoing, if any inconsistencies exist between the terms and conditions of this Commitment and any other Loan Document, the terms and conditions of this Commitment shall control and be binding.

Very truly yours,
EQUITY NATIONAL BANK

By: *Elizabeth Darcy*

Elizabeth Darcy
Its President

ACCEPTED AND AGREED to this _____ day of _____, 2021.

By: _____

Edward Jones

NOTES

1.   *Additional readings.* For a more detailed consideration of loan commitments, see John N. Oest, Negotiating the Loan Commitment: The Borrower's Perspective, 19 Bus. L. Today 61 (Jan./Feb. 2010); Susan G. Talley, Key Issues in Construction Lending (With Sample Forms), ALI-ABA Business Law Course Materials Journal, June 2007, at 15; George A. Nation, III, The *Clardy* Case: Lessons For Lenders Concerning Commitment Letters and Other Pre-loan Contracts, 114 Banking L.J. 347 (1997).

2.   *Representing Edward Jones.* Mr. Jones has asked you to review the commitment letter for him. Please advise him on the following issues:

(a)   Does the commitment letter obligate the bank to lend $300,000 to Mr. Jones? Does the letter obligate Mr. Jones to borrow the funds from Equity National Bank?

(b)   Under what circumstances can the bank refuse to make loan advances? What changes would you like to make?

(c)   If the construction costs more than anticipated, is the bank obligated to advance enough funds to complete construction?

(d)   Under what circumstances can the bank make the entire loan due and payable? Does Mr. Jones have the right to cure defaults? What changes would you like to make?

(e)   What other changes to the commitment letter would you recommend?

3.   *Term sheets.* Especially with large, institutional lenders and large real estate projects, loan commitment documents are uncommon. Covering all the possible scenarios under which the lender would be unwilling to close the loan would inflate and distort the loan commitment document beyond usefulness. These institutional lenders issue "term sheets" with disclaimer language similar to that that follows. Term sheets are typically vetted by loan and credit officers but can be issued more quickly than legally-binding loan commitments that require preparation by bank counsel and significant negotiation.

FOR   DISCUSSION   PURPOSES   ONLY—NOT   A COMMITMENT TO LEND

This Summary of Terms and Conditions is not intended to be and should not be construed as an offer, a commitment, nor agreement to lend, nor should it be construed as an attempt to establish all of the terms and conditions relating to the Facility. It is intended only to be indicative of certain terms and conditions around which credit approval may be sought, and if approved, how the loan documents might be structured, and shall not preclude negotiations within the general scope of these terms and conditions. No person or entity shall have any obligation to commence or thereafter continue any negotiations to enter into any definitive, binding agreement with respect to the Facility, and no person or entity should rely on an eventual formation of any agreement. Any party may freely enter into negotiations with any other person or entity, and nothing herein shall preclude any party from entering into a binding agreement with any other person or entity. The foregoing shall apply to this Summary of Terms and Conditions, as well as to any prior and subsequent communications between the Borrower and Lender with respect to the Facility, and only a definitive, written agreement, executed by both Borrower and Lender, shall be binding on Borrower and Lender with respect to the Facility. Borrower should retain a copy of this Summary of Terms and Conditions for its records.

4.   *Oral commitments.* The commitment above is written. Would it be enforceable if it had been given orally? See Coastland Corp. v. Third Nat'l Mortg. Co., 611 F.2d 969 (4th Cir.1979) (oral commitment enforceable). Compare Leeper v. Weintraub, 273 N.J.Super. 532, 642 A.2d 1032 (App.Div.1994); Ed Schory & Sons, Inc. v. Society Nat'l Bank, 75 Ohio St.3d 433, 662 N.E.2d 1074 (1996); Bridges v. Reliance Trust Co., 205 Ga.App. 400, 422 S.E.2d 277 (1992) (all holding that the Statute of Frauds barred enforcement). Of course, the wording of the particular Statute of Frauds is a critical factor. See Rhode Island Hospital Trust Nat'l Bank v. Varadian, 419 Mass. 841, 647 N.E.2d 1174 (1995) (the borrowers, who were sophisticated real estate developers, could not reasonably have understood the bank's promises to be a binding commitment).

5.   *Construction changes.* Construction projects rarely are built in exact accordance with the original plans and specifications. Changes result from materials shortages, unexpected conditions encountered in construction, shifts in market demand, and sometimes simply better ideas. If the builder and construction lender agree that a particular change is appropriate, is it necessary to get the permanent lender's approval? Is it reasonable for the permanent lender to insist upon a right to approve? See John P. McNearney & Jude J. Beller, Did Your Construction Lender Ask for That?, 18 Prob. & Prop. 58 (Nov./Dec. 2004).

6.   *Commitment fees.* A lender will usually charge a fee for a permanent loan commitment, especially if it includes a definite interest rate, because the lender is assuming the risk that market rates may increase. Typical charges are in the range of 0.5%–1% of the amount committed. Because construction loans normally are variable rate, the fee for that type of loan commitment is normally somewhat less.

7.   *Lender's retention of the fee.* If a developer pays a commitment fee but later obtains financing elsewhere, the lender that issued the commitment will

usually retain the fee. The commitment letter often expressly permits the lender to do so. Is this legally sound? Courts usually regard the fee as a form of reasonable liquidated damages. See Capital Holding Corp. v. Octagon Dev. Co., 757 S.W.2d 202 (Ky.App.1988); B.F. Saul Real Estate Inv. Trust v. McGovern, 683 S.W.2d 531 (Tex.App.1984). See also Annot., Enforceability of Provision in Loan Commitment Agreement Authorizing Lender to Charge Standby Fee, Commitment Fee, or Similar Deposit, 93 A.L.R.3d 1156.

8. *Specific performance of loan commitments.* If the lender reneges on the commitment, can the builder or house purchaser get specific performance? Courts usually say that promises to loan money are not specifically enforceable but that contracts to sell or purchase land are. Which type is a permanent loan commitment? A construction loan commitment? See Southampton Wholesale Food Terminal, Inc. v. Providence Produce Warehouse Co., 129 F.Supp. 663 (D.Mass.1955). To obtain specific performance, does the remedy at law have to be inadequate? Are there situations in which damages are an inadequate remedy for the permanent lender's refusal to honor its commitment? What is the proper measure of damages? See Higgins v. Arizona Sav. & Loan Ass'n, 85 Ariz. 6, 330 P.2d 504 (1958). Can the construction lender get damages or specific performance against the reneging permanent lender? See generally Robert Shadur, Avoiding Lender Liability at the Loan Commitment Stage, 6 Prac.Real Est.Law. 47 (No. 6, May 1990).

In a few cases, courts have granted specific performance against a lender. See Selective Builders, Inc. v. Hudson City Sav. Bank, 137 N.J.Super. 500, 349 A.2d 564 (Ch.Div.1975); First Nat'l State Bank of New Jersey v. Commonwealth Fed. Sav. & Loan Ass'n, 610 F.2d 164 (3d Cir.1979) (construction lender can enforce permanent lender's commitment). See Michael J. Mehr & Lawrence Kilgore, Enforcement of the Real Estate Loan Commitment: Improvement of the Borrower's Remedies, 24 Wayne L.Rev. 1011 (1978); Roger D. Groot, Specific Performance of Contracts to Provide Permanent Financing, 60 Cornell L.Rev. 718 (1975); Nelson, Whitman, Burkhart & Freyermuth, Real Estate Finance Law § 12.3 (6th ed.2015).

9. *Actions by lenders against borrowers.* If a loan applicant obtains a commitment but then refuses to borrow the funds (usually because it found a lower interest rate elsewhere), can the lender that issued the commitment recover damages for breach of contract? The answer depends on whether the commitment is a bilateral contract or merely gives the applicant an option to borrow. Every commitment should, of course, make this clear, but many do not. Compare Lincoln Nat'l Life Ins. Co. v. NCR Corp., 603 F.Supp. 1393 (N.D.Ind.1984) (contract bound borrower to draw down funds), with Capital Holding Corp. v. Octagon Dev. Co., 757 S.W.2d 202 (Ky.App.1988) (commitment did not bind borrower to draw funds). Often, the term "standby commitment" is a clue that the applicant has only an option, and not a duty, to take the loan.

Even if the commitment is bilateral and imposes a duty to borrow, the applicant who fails to do so does not always lose the commitment fee. In

Woodbridge Place Apts. v. Washington Square Capital, Inc., 965 F.2d 1429 (7th Cir.1992), the borrower's obligation to take the loan was subject to the condition that the subject apartment building reach 93% occupancy before the loan was to close. The building failed to do so. The court held that the borrower's refusal to draw the funds was due to a failure of the condition and was not a breach of the loan commitment. Hence, the court ordered the lender to refund the borrower's deposit. On the other hand, if the commitment had expressly made the deposit nonrefundable, the court would have reached the contrary result.

Even if the commitment imposes a duty to borrow, it seems settled that the lender cannot obtain a decree of specific performance against a loan applicant who refuses to borrow the funds. A recovery of damages, the remedy at law, is adequate. See City Centre One Assocs. v. Teachers Ins. & Annuity Ass'n, 656 F.Supp. 658 (D.Utah 1987).

10. *Conditions in commitments.* Permanent loan commitments are usually filled with conditions that must be met before the lender is obligated to fund the loan. Completion of the improvements is the most obvious example. Courts typically strictly enforce the conditions. If they are not met, the commitment expires, and, if the agreement so provides, the borrower loses the commitment fee. See, e.g., Johnson v. American Nat'l Ins. Co., 126 Ariz. 219, 613 P.2d 1275 (App.1980) (project not completed by commitment's expiration date); Mellon Bank v. Aetna Bus. Credit, Inc., 619 F.2d 1001 (3d Cir.1980) (permanent loan on office building project conditioned on borrower's solvency; borrower was insolvent). Cf. Hall v. W. L. Brady Inv., Inc., 684 S.W.2d 379 (Mo.App.1984) (substantial, but not perfect, completion of building satisfies requirements of permanent loan commitment). See Alvin L. Arnold, Checklist of Permanent Loan Commitment, 1 Real Estate Transactions: Structure and Analysis with Forms App. 5.3 (2013).

C. CONSTRUCTION LIEN PRIORITIES

Chapter Seven dealt with two important issues for construction lien priority—the optional vs. obligatory advance rule and mechanic's liens. This section covers some additional issues that are important for construction lending.

1. SUBORDINATION OF THE PURCHASE MONEY MORTGAGE

If the developer is to obtain a construction loan from an institutional lender, the lender usually requires a first mortgage or deed of trust to secure the loan. Some states statutorily require state-chartered banks and other financial institutions to obtain first liens on real estate loans. Even without a statutory requirement, lending institutions usually demand a first priority lien as a matter of policy. Frequently, the construction lender will require that the land purchase loan be paid off in full to eliminate potential problems in the event of a default on that loan. Otherwise, the construction lender will require that the relative priorities of the construction and purchase money mortgage be adjusted so that the construction mortgage is senior. While this adjustment is usually a simple task, it is essential because, without an explicit reversal of priorities, the law everywhere presumes that the purchase money mortgage is senior. See Cal.Civ.Code § 2898; Restatement (Third) of Property (Mortgages) § 7.2 (1997); Nelson, Whitman, Burkhart & Freyermuth, Real Estate Finance Law §§ 9.1–9.2 (6th ed.2015).

How is this reversal of priorities accomplished? If the developer has completed arrangements for the construction loan before acquiring the land, the purchase money mortgage can expressly provide that it is subordinate to the construction mortgage. The purchase money mortgage can incorporate the construction mortgage by reference or can include it as an attachment.

Another approach that is sometimes employed is to omit any reference in the mortgages to their relative priorities and instead to make certain that the documents are recorded in the following order: (1) deed from land seller to developer; (2) construction loan mortgage from developer to lender; and (3) purchase money mortgage from developer to land seller. To many actors in the real estate community, it seems obvious that the order of recording dictates the priority of the two mortgages, but this assumption is false. The typical recording statute provides: "All conveyances are void until recorded as against subsequent purchasers or creditors without notice and for valuable consideration [who record first]." (The last phrase is added in race-notice jurisdictions.) Hence, if all the parties know of one another's interest, as is usually the case, no one is "without notice," and it does not matter which mortgage is recorded first.

Courts sometimes treat the order of recording as representing the parties' intentions about priority and give effect to those intentions. See, e.g., BB & T of South Carolina v. Kidwell, 350 S.C. 382, 565 S.E.2d 316 (App.2002); Estate of Skvorak v. Security Union Title Ins. Co., 140 Idaho 16, 89 P.3d 856 (2004). But one cannot count on this result; the court may well (and quite properly) disregard the order of recording and base priority instead on the order that the mortgages were delivered and on the presumption of priority for purchase money mortgages. Hence, reliance on the order of recording to determine priority is a risky business. Express agreements stating the intended priority, signed by all affected parties, are far preferable. See Nelson, Whitman, Burkhart & Freyermuth, Real Estate Finance Law § 9.2 (6th ed.2015).

Suppose, however, that negotiations for the construction loan have not been completed before the developer takes title to the land. One possibility is for the developer to forbear from getting a subordination agreement from the land seller based on the assumption that the seller's self-interest will induce it to subordinate when a construction loan has been arranged. After all, if the seller does not subordinate, there will be no construction, no cash flow to the developer, and no payments to the land seller. Thus, perhaps the land seller can be expected to cooperate in subordinating to a reasonable construction loan when the time comes. The developer might even include language in the purchase money mortgage by which the land seller agrees to negotiate in good faith for subordination or words to that effect. Such language may be legally unenforceable as an "agreement to agree" but still worth having as a practical matter. But can you think of situations in which the land seller might have good economic reasons for refusal to cooperate?

For this reason, the developer might be quite reluctant to rely on the land seller's future good faith. As an alternative, the developer might insert language in the purchase money mortgage or in a side agreement that the land seller agrees to be subordinate to a construction loan to be made in the future, the elements of which may be spelled out with greater or lesser specificity. This is the so-called "automatic subordination"—that is, subordination to a loan that can't yet be precisely identified or described. From the land seller's viewpoint, such a subordination should set off flashing red lights. If the future construction loan proves to be unduly burdensome, the result may be a default by the developer and a foreclosure on the construction mortgage that wipes out the land seller's mortgage.

Should the law protect land sellers from entering into automatic subordination agreements that don't spell out the terms of the future loan specifically? Some courts have thought so. Consider the following description in Roskamp Manley Assocs., Inc. v. Davin Dev. & Inv. Corp., 184 Cal.App.3d 513, 519–20, 229 Cal.Rptr. 186, 189–90 (1986) of an important California Supreme Court case:

> In Handy v. Gordon, 65 Cal.2d 578, 55 Cal.Rptr. 769, 422 P.2d 329 [1967], defendant vendor agreed to sell land to plaintiff developer for $1,200,000 at 2 percent interest per year, payable in annual installments of $120,000, beginning three years after close of escrow, the balance due in ten years. Sellers agreed to subordinate their trust deed to other trust deeds securing construction loans. Terms of subordination were: loans in maximum amounts of $10,000 and $52,000 per lot, and maximum interest rate of 7 percent and 6.6 percent, to mature in not less than 6 and 35 years respectively. The contract did not specify the number of lots. Plaintiff sued for specific performance, and judgment on the pleadings for defendants was affirmed. The court stated: "Although the parties to a contract of sale containing a subordination clause may delegate to the vendee or third party lenders power to determine the details of subordinating loans, an

enforceable subordination clause must contain terms that will define and minimize the risk that the subordinating liens will impair or destroy the seller's security. [ ] Such terms may include limits on the use to which the proceeds may be put to insure that their use will improve the value of the land, maximum amounts so that the loans will not exceed the contemplated value of the improvements they finance, requirements that the loans do not exceed some specified percentage of the construction cost or value of the property as improved, specified amounts per square foot of construction, or other limits designed to protect the security. Without some such terms, however, the seller is forced to rely entirely on the buyer's good faith and ability as a developer to insure that he will not lose both his land and the purchase price. Even if we were to assume that a contract of sale contemplating subdivision by the vendee is sufficiently different from the usual land sale contract to take it out of the operation of the anti-deficiency legislation [ ], the personal liability alone of the vendee would not constitute sufficient protection to the vendor to permit specific performance." (*Id.*, at p. 581, 55 Cal.Rptr. 769, 422 P.2d 329.)

In *Handy*, the court found the contract did not afford defendants any additional protection since not all of the loan proceeds were to be used for construction, there was no assurance that the amounts of the loans would not exceed the value the improvements added to the security, and defendants were not assured that the total amount of the subordinating loans would be kept low enough to enable them to protect themselves by bidding on the property if the senior liens were foreclosed. (*Id.*, at p. 582, 55 Cal.Rptr. 769, 422 P.2d 329.) The court agreed with defendants, that as to them, the contract was not "just and reasonable" as a matter of law. (*Id.*, at p. 581, 55 Cal.Rptr. 769, 422 P.2d 329.)

While fairness is no doubt a good thing, there is by no means universal agreement that courts should impose it in automatic subordination cases. As Professor Patrick Randolph of the University of Missouri-Kansas City School of Law observed: "*Handy*, in fact, suggests that the court must be satisfied overall that the contract is fair, which of course means that no buyer, short of a lawsuit, can ever be confident that it has an enforceable subordination agreement."

Nonetheless, the reasoning in opinions like *Handy* has been highly influential, and courts in many cases have held subordination agreements to be unenforceable because of ambiguity or unfairness. Do you think that the following clauses should be enforceable?

(a) "Buyer to obtain loan in the amount of $63,500 from lending institution of their choice. Seller to carry $24,000 at 8.69% interest amortized over 30 years to balloon in 5 years. Seller may pay off Contract early without penalty." Linderkamp v. Hoffman, 562 N.W.2d 734 (N.D. 1997).

(b) "Twenty acres of said land are subordinated to the purchasers for immediate improvement, and such other tracts shall be subordinated to use as the occasion may arise." Grooms v. Williams, 227 Md. 165, 175 A.2d 575 (1961).

(c) "[Seller] agrees to carry 2nd Deed of Trust in the amount of $25,000 for 10 yrs., equal payments with 6% interest per annum." Hux v. Raben, 74 Ill.App.2d 214, 219 N.E.2d 770 (1966), aff'd, 38 Ill.2d 223, 230 N.E.2d 831 (1967).

(d) "[Seller agrees to subordinate] to any deed of trust that [buyer] might give to an FDIC insured lending institution." Stenehjem v. Kyn Jin Cho, 631 P.2d 482 (Alaska 1981).

(e) "[Seller] agrees to execute a deed of subordination upon the request of [buyer] in such amount as may be reasonably requested by the [buyer] so as to allow the [buyer] to procure a construction loan on the above-described real property." MCB Ltd. v. McGowan, 86 N.C.App. 607, 359 S.E.2d 50 (1987).

In all five cases, the court held that the agreement was unenforceable. However, other courts have enforced very similar subordination clauses. See, e.g., North Shore Realty Corp. v. Gallaher, 114 So.2d 634 (Fla.App.1959). See also Warren H. McNamara, Jr., Subordination Agreements as Viewed by Sellers, Purchasers, Construction Lenders, and Title Companies, 12 Real Est.L.J. 347 (1984).

The Restatement (Third) of Property (Mortgages) § 7.7 (1997) provides that if the subordination is to an interest to be created in the future, that interest must be described in the subordination "with reasonable specificity." According to comment b of that section:

> [R]easonable specificity requires at a minimum an identification of the new lender or the type of lender, an upper limit on the initial amount of that debt, and an upper limit on its interest rate. If the parties contemplate that the proceeds of the later mortgage will be used to improve the real estate, and that those improvements are part of the bargained-for security on which the subordinating mortgagee is relying, then reasonable specificity requires a statement requiring use of the subsequent loan proceeds for that purpose and a reasonable description of the improvements.

Compare Smith v. Martin, 124 N.C.App. 592, 478 S.E.2d 228 (N.C.App.1996) (subordination to a future mortgage must, at a minimum, state the loan's maximum amount and maximum interest rate). But see Wintroub v. Nationstar Mortgage LLC, 927 N.W.2d 19 (2019).

NOTES

1. *Interaction of subordination agreements and the optional advance doctrine.* What is the effect of a subordination agreement on the optional advance doctrine? In National Bank of Washington v. Equity Investors, 83 Wash.2d 435, 518 P.2d 1072 (1974), the construction lender was also competing with a group of subordinated land vendors. Their subordination agreement said "[the subordinator] does hereby unconditionally subordinate the lien of his mortgage * * * to the lien of the lender's mortgage * * * and all advances or charges made or accruing thereunder." The court held that this language subordinated the vendors to even the Bank's *optional* advances.

2. *Should mechanic's liens have priority over construction loans?* As we have seen, a construction lender that records its mortgage before any work is done and that administers the loan carefully, without reserving too much discretion, can maintain priority over subsequently-filed mechanic's liens in most states. However, as described in the treatise excerpt reprinted in the section on mechanic's liens, this may not work in Missouri and in a few other states; the mechanic's liens can be prior to the construction mortgage no matter what the lender does. Professor Ronald Mann surveyed a group of lenders and asked whether the Missouri rule discouraged them from making construction loans in Missouri:

> All had the same general response: they are willing to make loans in Missouri despite the lower priority, but they are more careful about risk there than they are in jurisdictions where they have a better priority position. That increased care is exactly what the system should seek because that increased attention to risk results in pricing that more accurately reflects the value of individual construction projects.

Ronald J. Mann, The First Shall Be Last: A Contextual Argument for Abandoning Temporal Rules of Lien Priority, 75 Tex.L.Rev. 11, 40 (1996). Professor Mann argued that construction lenders are far better positioned to control and manage construction risks than are individual contractors and suppliers and, therefore, that it is more efficient for the law to impose the primary risk of loss from defaulted projects on lenders. Do you agree? Adoption of his position would require a major restructuring of mechanic's lien statutes in most states.

3. *Waiver of judicial protection.* Can a land seller waive the type of protection given in *Handy*? Suppose the subordination clause describes in rather vague terms the first deed of trust loan to which the land seller is subordinating and then provides that this first deed of trust shall:

* * * constitute a lien or charge on said land prior and superior to the lien or charge of this deed of trust as to any and all loans or advances which shall be made under such hereafter executed deed of trust * * * and without regard to the application or use of the proceeds of such loan or advances insofar as the validity of this subordination is concerned.

See Weiss v. Brentwood Sav. & Loan Ass'n, 4 Cal.App.3d 738, 84 Cal.Rptr. 736 (1970); Schneider v. Ampliflo Corp., 148 Cal.App.3d 637, 196 Cal.Rptr. 172 (1983), in which the courts enforced similar language. Does this make sense? If the subordination is unfair because it is so vague, is it any more fair when the land seller admits in writing that she or he knows it is unfair?

4. *Remedies.* In *Handy* and in *Roskamp,* the developer wanted specific performance of the subordination agreement. Suppose the developer had sued the land seller for damages instead. Is there any reason that a vague or unfair subordination should be "more enforceable" at law than in equity?

If a court determines that a subordination clause is unenforceable under *Handy,* what is the result?

   (a) The seller is not obligated to convey the land?

   (b) The seller must convey the land but is entitled to cash?

   (c) The seller must convey the land and take back the agreed security instrument but has first priority?

See Gluskin v. Atlantic Sav. & Loan Ass'n, 32 Cal.App.3d 307, 108 Cal.Rptr. 318 (1973). Does it matter, in determining which remedy is appropriate, whether the subordination agreement was part of the contract of sale, of the mortgage or deed of trust, or in a separate document? Where would you put the agreement if you represented a California developer who insisted on having an automatic-type subordination?

5. *Statutory regulation of subordination clauses.* Cal.Civ.Code §§ 2953.1–.5 require that instruments that contain subordination agreements must call attention to them by prescribed legends in 10-point bold type. Failure to do so permits the clause to be declared void at the election of the person whose interest is subordinated. However, these provisions apply only when both the purchase money obligation and the maximum loan to which it may be subordinated do not exceed $25,000. How many such cases do you suppose there are?

An opposing approach is represented by Conn.Gen.Stat.Ann. § 49–31c, which provides that subordination to a future mortgage is valid "notwithstanding that [it] does not contain any of the terms or provisions of the future mortgage."

6. *Conditional subordination.* The protections that *Handy* requires in subordinations are really *conditions.* In effect, the subordinating party says: "I agree that my lien will become subordinate, but only if the lien that is gaining priority over mine satisfies certain specifications. Otherwise, I retain my

priority." If the condition isn't met, there's no subordination. No doubt exists that a court will uphold express conditions in a subordination agreement. See Bank v. Crumley, 699 S.W.2d 164 (Tenn.App.1985); Life Sav. & Loan Ass'n v. Bryant, 125 Ill.App.3d 1012, 81 Ill.Dec. 577, 467 N.E.2d 277 (1984); Riggs Nat'l Bank v. Wines, 59 Md.App. 219, 474 A.2d 1360 (1984); Hugh B. Lambe, Enforceability of Subordination Agreements, 19 Real Prop. Prob. & Tr.J. 631 (1984).

However, if the conditions are not met, a total denial of subordination may be inappropriate. Restatement (Third) of Property (Mortgages) § 7.7 comment c (1997) suggests that "in many cases in which the conditions are unsatisfied, justice can be done by imposing a *pro tanto* loss of priority to reflect the loss suffered by the subordinating mortgagee as a result of deviation from the conditions."

To illustrate, suppose Mortgagee1 agrees to subordinate to Mortgagee2's mortgage if the interest rate on Mortgagee2's loan is no higher than 10%. In fact, Mortgagee2 makes a loan to the borrower at 12%. Should Mortgagee2 get priority to the extent of the balance that would have been owing to it if the rate had been 10%, with Mortgagee1 having priority thereafter? Or can Mortgagee1 successfully argue that Mortgagee2 should lose priority entirely, because the higher interest rate made it more probable that the borrower would default?

The *pro tanto* approach suggested by the Restatement was not followed in Friarsgate, Inc. v. First Fed. Sav. & Loan Ass'n, 317 S.C. 452, 454 S.E.2d 901 (App.1995), in which the vendors agreed to subordinate on the condition that total future loans not exceed 75% of the fair market value of the lot and improvements. The future loans in fact exceeded 75%, and the court held that the subordination was completely ineffective.

7. *Implied conditions.* Suppose the mortgagee who has initial top priority enters into a subordination agreement but fails to include any protective conditions of the sort discussed in *Handy* and in *Roskamp*. Should a court imply reasonable conditions to protect the subordinating party? That is precisely what the California Court of Appeal did in Middlebrook-Anderson Co. v. Southwest Sav. & Loan Ass'n, 18 Cal.App.3d 1023, 1037, 96 Cal.Rptr. 338 (1971), discussed in Frederick D. Minnes, Note, Purchase Money Subordination Agreements in California: An Analysis of Conditional Subordination, 45 S.Cal.L.Rev. 1109 (1972). The court stated:

> An implied agreement in the instant case can and, in equity, should be spelled out from lender's alleged actual knowledge of the provisions of the seller's lien in general, and of the subordination therein in particular. In the superior position of a financial institution constantly engaged in professional construction lending, [the lender] had no reason to believe their trust deed conferred any lien to which the fee was subordinate other than to the extent of money spent for construction purposes. Its loan under the circumstances cannot be viewed other than as subject to the fair application of the construction funds. Accordingly, we conclude that

such lien as the trust deed might have conferred on the lender should not be advanced or preferred over the seller.

Accord Burkons v. Ticor Title Ins. Co., 168 Ariz. 345, 813 P.2d 710 (1991); Peoples Bank v. L & T Developers, Inc., 434 So.2d 699 (Miss.1983), noted 53 Miss.L.J. 691 (1983). In Ban-Co Inv. Co. v. Loveless, 22 Wash.App. 122, 587 P.2d 567 (1978), a land seller used a similar theory to support an action in damages against the developer.

Courts in many other cases have rejected the *Middlebrook* approach and refused to imply subordination conditions. See, e.g., Connecticut Bank & Trust Co. v. Carriage Lane Assocs., 219 Conn. 772, 595 A.2d 334 (1991); Home Sav. Ass'n v. State Bank of Woodstock, 763 F.Supp. 292 (N.D.Ill.1991). See generally Nelson, Whitman, Burkhart & Freyermuth, Real Estate Finance Law § 12.10 (6th ed.2015). The courts in these cases generally hold that the lender has no duty to junior lienors to use any particular care in ensuring that disbursements are used for construction, unless there are express conditions in the agreement, the junior lienor has been defrauded, or the lender and the developer colluded.

A few courts have held that construction lenders have an implied duty to use reasonable care in supervising disbursements to prevent diversion of the funds to other purposes. See Fikes v. First Federal Sav. & Loan Ass'n, 533 P.2d 251 (Alaska 1975); Cambridge Acceptance Corp. v. Hockstein, 102 N.J.Super. 435, 246 A.2d 138 (App.Div.1968). But this represents a small minority viewpoint. See Philip L. Bruner & Patrick J. O'Connor, Jr., Lender Liability in Construction Financing, Construction Briefings No. 2003–10; Annot., Construction Mortgagee-Lender's Duty to Protect Interest of Subordinated Purchase-Money Mortgagee, 13 A.L.R.5th 684.

8.   *What are "improvements"?* Under an express or implied clause that subordinates a mortgage only to advances "for improvements," what sorts of disbursements by the construction lender are included? Disbursements often do not pay directly for labor or materials on the site. Consider the following possibilities:

(a)   The lender makes an advance that it knows the developer will use to buy a new cabin cruiser.

(b)   The lender makes an advance that it believes will be used for construction. However, the lender's methods for verifying application of the funds are less rigorous than those of most construction lenders, and the developer diverts the funds to unrelated uses.

(c)   The facts are the same as in (b), except that the lender's methods are the same as those of most other lenders. Nonetheless, by fraud, forgery, or other artifice, the developer diverts the funds to unrelated uses.

(d)   The lender makes an "advance" to cover the "loan fee" on the construction loan by charging the developer's loan account with the fee but with no money changing hands. Does it matter whether the loan fee is 2% or 13%? What about an advance to cover the commitment fee on the permanent loan commitment?

(e) The lender makes an advance for attorney's fees, title insurance, and other closing costs in connection with the construction loan.

(f) Uninsured damage occurs to the improvements when the construction is partially completed. The lender advances additional funds, which the construction loan agreement does not require, to repair the damage.

Several cases deal with these issues, but little consistency exists among them. The court in Ban-Co Inv. Co. v. Loveless, 22 Wash.App. 122, 587 P.2d 567 (1978) held that the following were improper disbursements: (1) rent on the developer's ground lease; (2) payments for the developer's overhead and profit; and (3) payments to a general contractor that was working for the developer on another project. The last holding seems indisputable! See also Hyatt v. Maryland Fed. Sav. & Loan Ass'n, 42 Md.App. 623, 402 A.2d 118 (1979); G. Credit Co. v. Mid-West Land Dev., Inc., 207 Kan. 325, 485 P.2d 205 (1971). But the uncertainty concerning the meaning of "improvements" provides a strong incentive for the construction lender to require that the developer pay off the subordinate purchase money mortgage.

If you were drafting a subordination agreement, how would you define "construction"? What items are legitimate because they add permanent value to the land and, thus, do not increase the subordinated party's risk?

9. *Drafting subordinations.* Suppose you are representing a land vendor in a sale to a developer who wants subordination. What protective clauses would you try to insert? You might consider conditioning the subordination on some or all of the following:

(a) The construction lender's identity or type;

(b) The type of improvements to be constructed;

(c) The loan characteristics to which your client will subordinate;

(d) The requirement that loan funds be used for construction;

(e) A listing of the types of disbursements that will constitute payment for "construction;"

(f) The lender's method of disbursement;

(g) Your client's right to approve detailed plans and specifications;

(h) Procurement of a permanent loan commitment on terms that are satisfactory to your client;

(i) A requirement that the developer carry appropriate insurance;

(j) Your client's right to inspect the work progress and the developer's and lender's books; and

(k) Your client's rights to notice by the construction lender of any default on the loan and to cure within a reasonable time.

Of course, no substitute exists for the developer's integrity and experience. How could you help your client verify these qualities before signing a subordination agreement?

2. OTHER STATUTORY AND EQUITABLE LIENS

The stop notice (also called stop payment). If a construction lender uses sufficient care, it will usually be able to preserve the priority of its mortgage against mechanic's liens in most jurisdictions. This situation is highly unsatisfactory to mechanic's lien claimants because foreclosure of the construction mortgage will eliminate their liens and will leave them with only the tenuous hope that the foreclosure sale will generate some surplus proceeds. This hope is particularly tenuous because the construction lender usually is the only bidder at the sale, and it rarely will bid more than it is owed.

Recognizing the dilemma that mechanic's lienors face, several states have provided the stop notice as an alternative means of recovery for them. Under stop notice statutes, a mechanic's lienor (usually excepting the general contractor) may make a claim on any undisbursed construction funds in the hands of the lender and, under some statutes, of the borrower. This remedy is perhaps most fully developed in California, Cal.Civ.Code §§ 8500–60, but is also available in Alabama, Indiana, Mississippi, North Carolina, Rhode Island, Texas, and Washington. See Brewer Corp. v. Point Center Financial, Inc., 223 Cal. App. 4th 831 (2014); Roger Bernhardt, Construction Stop Notices vs. Construction Loan Assignments, Fall 2014 The Abstract 10.

Equitable lien on the land. Although an unpaid worker or materials supplier can generally file a mechanic's lien, the filing may be unavailing. For example, a construction mortgage that is recorded before work commenced on the project will have priority over mechanic's liens in most jurisdictions. Alternatively, the worker or supplier may have failed to file the required lien notice within the statutorily prescribed time or may have otherwise failed to comply with the lien statute. Finally, if the construction is on public land, it is exempt from mechanic's liens.

In these types of situations, a creative lawyer may try to rectify the thwarted lienor's problem by filing a suit that asserts an equitable lien against the land. As a practical matter, this sort of lien has little value unless a court will elevate its priority over that of the construction mortgage. But, far from giving priority to such a lien, a court might ordinarily be expected to hold that the mechanic's lien statute is the claimant's only remedy. See, e.g., Hill Behan Lumber Co. v. Marchese, 1 Ill.App.3d 789, 275 N.E.2d 451 (1971) ("We are unable to find any authority which would grant an equitable lien in a situation where it would have been appropriate to impose a mechanic's lien had there been compliance with the statute."); All State Plumbing, Inc. v. Mutual Security Life Ins. Co., 537 So.2d 598 (Fla.App.1988) (lien on land refused).

However, suppose there is evidence that the lien claimant (let's say, a framing subcontractor) had the following sort of conversation with the construction lender's loan officer before the construction mortgage was foreclosed:

Sub: We've been working on this project for several months now, but I have begun hearing rumors that the project is over-budget and may be foreclosed on.

Loan officer: I wouldn't be worried about that if I were you. The project is in good standing.

Sub: I would certainly want to know if the construction loan was in trouble. I don't want to keep working on the site if I'm not going to get paid. Can you assure me that I will get my money on this job?

Loan officer: Absolutely. Don't worry about a thing.

This conversation isn't entirely hypothetical. Consider the court's description of the facts in Rinker Materials Corp. v. Palmer First Nat'l Bank & Trust Co., 361 So.2d 156 (Fla.1978):

At one time or another, [the construction lender] assured all petitioners that there were sufficient funds in the loan account to complete the project; that they should continue to furnish labor and materials; that there was no need to file mechanic's liens; and that the bank would do everything it could to see that the subcontractors were paid, including the issuance of joint checks to the contractor and subcontractors if necessary. In reliance on the bank's statements, petitioners continued to furnish labor and materials.

Note that the loan officer in our little scene has a real dilemma. If the loan officer is candid and tells the subcontractor that the project is over-budget and that the lender is actively considering foreclosure, the sub probably will walk off the job, rather than throw good work after bad. That action by the sub would cause the other subs to walk off the job, too, which could virtually assure the project's failure and foreclosure. Obviously, the loan officer has no wish to hasten these events if there is any chance at all that the project can be saved. Candor obviously is contrary to the loan officer's self-interest. The temptation to lie, or at least to exaggerate the project's status, is strong.

Now assume that the construction loan mortgage for the project involved in the foregoing scenario is in fact foreclosed and that the mechanic's liens are subordinate to it. Can the subcontractor reasonably assert that the loan officer's statements were misleading or even fraudulent and that, as a result, the lender is estopped from denying that the mechanic's lien has priority over the mortgage? Such holdings are not uncommon. See Trout's Inv., Inc. v. Davis, 482 S.W.2d 510 (Mo.App.1972). A court accepted a similar argument in principle but rejected it for lack of evidence of such assurances in FDIC v. Key Biscayne Dev. Ass'n, 858 F.2d 670 (11th Cir.1988).

Alternatively, the subcontractor might argue that the misleading statements created an equitable lien that is senior to the mortgage. The subcontractor also can attempt to gain senior priority by arguing that the loan officer's statements amount to an oral or equitable subordination of the mortgage to the mechanic's liens. This approach was endorsed by the court in In re 200 Woodbury Realty Trust, 99 B.R. 184 (Bankr.D.N.H.1989), and was recognized in principle but rejected on the facts by the court in In re Commercial Inv., Ltd., 92 B.R. 488 (Bankr.D.N.M.1988).

But don't be too sanguine about the chances of a mechanic's lien claimant winning one of these cases. In *Rinker Materials Corp. v. Palmer First Nat'l Bank*, supra, the Florida Supreme Court held that "a party may successfully maintain a suit under the theory of equitable estoppel only where there is proof of fraud, misrepresentation, or other affirmative deception." Amazingly, it found that the statements described in the indented paragraph above did not meet this test: "The trial court in this case found that the bank's statements were neither fraudulent nor untrue." It denied the lien. Because the loan was indeed foreclosed and the mechanic's liens were wiped out, isn't it obvious that the statements were, at a minimum, misleading? Isn't the mechanic's lienor equally harmed by the statements whether they were made with conscious falsity or in perfect good faith? See also Curly Customs, Inc. v. Bank of Boston, 49 Mass.App.Ct. 197, 727 N.E.2d 1212 (2000) (requiring false or misleading representations by the lender).

Some theories have been suggested that might give unpaid workers and suppliers prime equitable liens without proof of the construction lender's fraudulent or false statements. One is unjust enrichment based on the notion that the lender has title to the improvements through foreclosure and that the contractor has not been paid for them. See generally Jeffrey Murray, Comment, Owner/Lender Liability to Unpaid Subcontractors, 29 Duq. L. Rev. 661 (1991); Nelson, Whitman, Burkhart & Freyermuth, Real Estate Finance Law § 12.6 (6th ed.2015). This theory makes considerable sense if the real estate is worth more than the construction lender's investment, so that it has received a windfall by foreclosing. Still, little judicial authority supports it. See, e.g., Bane-Nelson, Inc. v. Heritage Bank & Trust, 855 F.Supp. 280 (E.D.Wis.1994) (rejecting this theory under Wisconsin law).

Equitable lien on undisbursed construction funds. A second type of equitable lien might be asserted against the undisbursed funds remaining in the construction lender's loan account. This remedy is roughly analogous to a stop notice, except that it might be asserted in states with no stop notice statute or in cases in which the contractor has failed to satisfy the procedural requirements for a stop notice. It depends, of course, on the existence of undisbursed funds. If the construction project is already over-budget at the time of the foreclosure, as is often the case, there won't be any funds to assert the lien against.

The fundamental premise of a successful equitable lien against undisbursed funds is unjust enrichment. If the lender has foreclosed the construction mortgage and has acquired title to the project without spending the entire loan amount, it has gotten the project for less than its market value and has done so at the expense of the unpaid workers and suppliers.

A model case of this sort is Morgen-Oswood & Assocs. v. Continental Mortg. Investors, 323 So.2d 684 (Fla.App.1975), cert. dismissed, 342 So.2d 1100 (Fla.1977). Other examples include 1180 Raymond Urban Renewal, LLC v. 1180 Astro Urban Renewal Investors LLC, 2014 WL 9913181 (N.J. Super. Ct. App. Div. 2014) (unpublished); DeKalb County v. J & A Pipeline Co., Inc., 263 Ga. 645, 437 S.E.2d 327 (1993) (public project); Ten Hoeve Bros., Inc. v. City of Hartford, 1996 WL 285540 (Conn.Super. 1996) (not reported in A.2d) (public project); Twin City Constr. Co. v. ITT Indus. Credit Co., 358 N.W.2d 716 (Minn.App.1984). See generally Annot., Building and Construction Contracts: Contractor's Equitable Lien Upon Percentage of Funds Withheld by Contractee or Lender, 54 A.L.R.3d 848 (1974); George Lefcoe & Mark Schaffer, Construction Lending and the Equitable Lien, 40 S.Cal.L.Rev. 439 (1967). See also Emond Plumbing & Heating, Inc. v. BankNewport, 105 A.3d 85 (R.I. 2014).

Should it matter whether the contractor has completed the job? Can't the lender be unjustly enriched even if the contractor has not performed all its work or if the entire project is incomplete? Compare McBain v. Santa Clara Sav. & Loan Ass'n, 241 Cal.App.2d 829, 51 Cal.Rptr. 78 (1966)[1]

---

[1] The California cases imposing equitable liens are of only academic interest; a statute now limits all claims against construction loan funds to those permitted by stop notice. See Cal.Civil Code § 3264; Nibbi Bros., Inc. v. Brannan St. Investors, 205 Cal.App.3d 1415, 253 Cal.Rptr. 289 (1988). In contrast, the Washington Court of Appeals refused to read its state's stop notice statute as barring equitable liens. Town Concrete Pipe of Washington, Inc. v. Redford, 43 Wash.App. 493, 717 P.2d 1384 (1986).

(completion of project irrelevant) with Pioneer Plumbing Supply Co. v. Southwest Sav. & Loan Ass'n, 102 Ariz. 258, 428 P.2d 115 (1967); J. G. Plumbing Serv. Inc. v. Coastal Mortg. Co., 329 So.2d 393 (Fla.App.1976); Town Concrete Pipe of Washington, Inc. v. Redford, 43 Wash.App. 493, 717 P.2d 1384 (1986) (completion of project essential to lien). What does completion have to do with it? Isn't the issue whether the construction lender obtained excess value for its money while the workers and suppliers are unpaid?

Note that, unlike assertions of an equitable lien on the land, the existence of a misrepresentation by the construction lender to the mechanic's lien claimant is usually irrelevant when an equitable lien is asserted against undisbursed funds. *See* Emerald Designs, Inc. v. Citibank, 626 So.2d 1084 (Fla.App.1993); Swinerton & Walberg Co. v. Union Bank, 25 Cal.App.3d 259, 101 Cal.Rptr. 665 (1972).

The mechanic as a third party beneficiary. Suppose an unpaid worker or supplier can show that the construction lender did not follow the loan disbursement procedures in the construction loan agreement or procedures that are considered to be standard or prudent in the industry and that, as a result, the owner or prime contractor was able to divert the funds to other purposes. (There's an old joke about the developer who owns a beautiful boat named "First Draw" moored in the local marina.) Can the unpaid mechanic successfully argue that the construction lender owed it a duty to disburse the funds properly and, therefore, is liable to the mechanic up to the amount of the diverted funds?

In a few states, courts have held that the mechanic's liens have priority over the construction mortgage to the extent that the construction lender knowingly permitted diversion of construction funds to non-construction purposes. See Spickes Bros. Painting Contractors, Inc. v. Worthen Bank & Trust Co., N.A., 299 Ark. 79, 771 S.W.2d 258 (1989). But courts in most jurisdictions have refused to find that the lender has a duty to workers and suppliers to disburse the construction funds carefully. See, e.g., Peterson v. First Clayton Bank & Trust Co., 214 Ga.App. 94, 447 S.E.2d 63 (1994); Comet Dev. Corp. v. Prudential Ins. Co., 579 So.2d 355 (Fla.App.1991).

Alternatively, the mechanics might argue that they are third party beneficiaries of the construction loan agreement and can recover if the lender breaches it by using sloppy disbursement practices or by improperly refusing to disburse funds to pay them. Only rarely has a court accepted the third party beneficiary argument. See, e.g., United States v. Mill Ass'n, Inc., 480 F.Supp. 3 (E.D.N.Y.1978) (based on loan agreement's reference to state lien law). Courts in the great majority of cases hold that workers and suppliers are only incidental beneficiaries of the loan agreement and cannot enforce it. See, e.g., Van-Tex, Inc. v. Pierce, 703 F.2d 891 (5th Cir.1983); Silverdale Hotel Assocs. v. Lomas & Nettleton Co., 36 Wash.App.

762, 677 P.2d 773 (1984) (rejecting the third party beneficiary argument but awarding the unpaid contractor an equitable lien based on estoppel arising from the lender's assurances to the contractor that it would be paid).

To prevent a court from finding that mechanics can enforce the loan agreement as third party beneficiaries, lenders now usually insert language in the loan agreement that expressly disclaims intent to benefit workers or suppliers. Such language nearly always has the desired effect. *See* Howard Sav. Bank v. Lefcon Partn., 209 A.D.2d 473, 618 N.Y.S.2d 910 (1994). See generally Jeffrey Murray, Comment, Owner/Lender Liability to Unpaid Subcontractors, 29 Duq. L.Rev. 661 (1991); Nelson, Whitman, Burkhart & Freyermuth, Real Estate Finance Law § 12.6 (6th ed.2015); Robert K. Jordan, Construction Lender Liability to Third Parties, Prob. & Prop., Mar./Apr. 1991, at 45.

Continued funding of the over-budget project. Perhaps the most common form of optional advance occurs when the project has drawn down the full amount of the construction loan but is not yet complete. The lender clearly has no obligation to advance additional funds, see Kinner v. World Sav. & Loan Ass'n, 57 Cal.App.3d 724, 129 Cal.Rptr. 400 (1976), but it may reasonably believe that investing additional funds to complete the project is desirable and preferable to foreclosure from everyone's viewpoint. Can the lender plausibly argue that the additional advance is not optional because it is compelled by economic necessity and because all other courses of action are likely to produce much greater economic loss? Perhaps surprisingly, the additional advance may lose priority. See Percy Galbreath & Son, Inc. v. Watkins, 560 S.W.2d 239 (Ky.App.1977); Larry Skipworth, Should Construction Lenders Lose Out on Voluntary Advances If a Loan Turns Sour?, 5 Real Est.L.J. 221 (1977). In light of that possibility, what should the lender do before advancing the additional funds?

CHAPTER TEN

COMMON INTEREST OWNERSHIP

■ ■ ■

In this chapter we examine the financing and development of "common interest communities" such as condominiums, cooperatives, and planned communities. In many ways these developments are similar to detached-house subdivisions, for they involve the sale of individual units to purchasers, usually for use as personal residences. But common interest communities differ from conventional subdivisions in two important ways. The first difference might be termed "density," for these developments usually have a larger number of units packed into a smaller physical space than do subdivisions. They may take the form of town-house or row-house buildings, clustered but detached houses, or low-rise or high-rise multi-unit buildings. Often they will include some "common areas" (such as parks, pools, or other recreational facilities) which are open for all of the owners to use, perhaps as a way of compensating for the lack of large private yards associated with individual units. The second difference is the presence of some organized association of owners. This association may take one of several legal forms, and it may engage in numerous functions, but one of its purposes is nearly always the management of the common areas and the making and enforcement of rules and procedures for their use.

The growth in the development of common interest communities over the past four decades is staggering. According to the Community Associations Institute, in 1970, there were only 10,000 community associations in the United States, covering 701,000 residential units and housing a total of 2.1 million (about 1% of the population of the U.S.). By contrast, as of 2019, there were 27.2 million residential units in the United States governed by 351,000 community associations, housing a total of 73.9 million people. See Community Associations Institute, 2019–2020 U.S. National and State Statistical Review, https://foundation.caionline.org/wp-content/uploads/2020/08/2020StatsReview_Web.pdf. As most new residential development now occurs within common interest communities, these numbers will continue to grow for the foreseeable future. As a result, the modern real estate lawyer must have a firm grasp of the law governing the creation, financing, and governance of common interest communities.

This chapter begins with an introduction to the basic types of common interest developments—the condominium, the cooperative, and the planned community with a homeowners' association. This introduction will compare and contrast these forms of common interest developments, focusing upon the original legal framework upon which each developed while also highlighting recent law reform efforts to unify the law governing common interest development under the "common interest community" rubric. The chapter will then discuss a number of the practical and legal issues arising out of the creation, operation, and governance of common interest communities. As in the previous chapter on subdivisions, we have intentionally omitted any detailed discussion of local public land-use controls, such as zoning and subdivision ordinances. These are of great importance in higher-density developments, but because of their complexity must be left for coverage in a separate course.

A. TYPES OF COMMON INTEREST OWNERSHIP

1. CONDOMINIUMS

The condominium is a legal format for "unit ownership"—i.e., ownership of a specific portion of a larger parcel or structure. There is considerable interdependence among the unit owners in a condominium project, because they must usually be concerned with maintenance and management of "common areas" of the project. Although most condominiums are residential apartment buildings, it is possible to create an office building condominium (or even a campsite condominium in the woods!). Nevertheless, these materials will focus upon the housing condominium.

A condominium is created by the execution and recording of a "declaration." The declaration typically includes a legal description of the underlying land, a description of the anticipated improvements on the land (including both the housing units and any common facilities), and a statement identifying each unit owner's fraction of the rights and obligations associated with the common facilities. For each unit owner, this fraction establishes her ownership share of the common facilities, her obligation for the project's common expenses, and her proportionate voice and vote in managing the project. The declaration also commonly includes a set of covenants, conditions, and restrictions (CC&Rs) applicable to each unit. The CC&Rs establish both affirmative obligations binding on each unit owner (such as the obligation to pay assessments to fund the maintenance of common areas) and negative covenants and restrictions (such as limitations on the permitted use of units).

Much of the specific content of a declaration is established by a particular state's condominium statute. The first and most important function of this statute is to make clear that one can own a fee simple absolute interest in a housing unit even though it cannot be described purely by reference to boundaries on the surface of the earth. For example, if one owns a unit on the 10th floor of a high rise building, that ownership is essentially of air space. Of course, the statutes (even the most rudimentary ones) go far beyond this. For example, condominium statutes generally provide that the unit owners will own the common areas personally as tenants in common. In a condominium, the common areas are not only specific land areas such as the swimming pools and tennis courts; the applicable statute may well provide that all parts of the buildings except the portions within the interior walls of the individual units are deemed common areas. Under this view, common areas would include the exterior walls, roof, lobbies and hallways, and perhaps even some plumbing, heating, and electrical equipment.

The evolution of condominium acts. Section 234 of the National Housing Act, enacted in 1960, authorized the Federal Housing Administration (FHA) to insure mortgages on residential condominium units. Shortly thereafter, FHA drafted and promulgated a model state condominium statute based heavily on Puerto Rico's condominium statute. By 1968, all American states had adopted condominium statutes, and most of them were close copies of the FHA Model Act.

This "first generation" of condominium acts was both narrow in scope and very inflexible—and thus unsatisfactory in key respects for both developers and consumers. As development of a condominium proceeds, developers sometimes want to make changes to development plans, as dictated by marketing considerations. The first generation condominium acts, however, did not readily permit a developer to make such changes after recording the declaration. Likewise, during periods of economic difficulty, condominium projects under development may go into default, often to be taken over by the lender that has provided construction financing for the project. The first generation condominium acts did not adequately address the question of what happens to the developer's rights and obligations when a project is taken over by a successor such as the construction lender. Finally, first generation condominium acts were not "consumer friendly," and unsophisticated or uncounseled consumers often had difficulty adequately evaluating the nature of the rights they would obtain when purchasing a condominium unit.

These experiences led the Uniform Law Commission to draft the Uniform Condominium Act (UCA), first promulgated in 1977 and amended in 1980.[1] The UCA, which became the template for the "second generation" of condominium acts, was heavily influenced by contemporaneous revision of the existing condominium acts in Virginia and Florida. The UCA incorporated the concept of the "flexible condominium," making it possible for the declaration to provide clearly for the addition or removal of real

---

[1] In 2017, the Uniform Law Commission approved a set of technical and conforming amendments designed to conform the UCA to reflect amendments made to the Uniform Common Interest Ownership Act (UCIOA) in 1994, 2008, and 2014. UCIOA is discussed further in Section A4 infra.

estate from a condominium and the creation of additional units. The UCA also provided detailed provisions regarding the voluntary and involuntary transfer of the developer's rights, the extent of the developer's ability to control the unit owners' association during development, and the operation and governance of the unit owners' association (including the association's ability to impose liens for unpaid assessments). In exchange for this flexibility and certainty to the developer and the owners' association, the UCA also mandated more substantial consumer protections, including (among many others) mandatory and more thorough consumer disclosures, a fifteen-day "cooling off" period in which a purchaser may cancel a purchase agreement, statutory damages for failure to provide required disclosure, insurance requirements, and limitations upon the developer's ability to enter into contracts binding on the unit owners' association following completion of the project. For a more complete discussion of the UCA's consumer protection provisions, see David A. Thomas, The New Uniform Condominium Act, 64 A.B.A.J. 1370 (1978).

Condominium states based upon the UCA (or its corresponding provisions in the Uniform Common Interest Ownership Act) have been enacted in Alabama, Alaska, Arizona, Colorado, Connecticut, Delaware, Kentucky, Louisiana, Maine, Minnesota, Missouri, Nebraska, Nevada, New Mexico, North Carolina, Pennsylvania, Rhode Island, Texas, Vermont, Virginia, West Virginia, and Washington. For more detailed treatment of the UCA, see N. Walter Graff, Minnesota Uniform Condominium Act: The View of Developer's Counsel, 10 Wm. Mitchell L. Rev. 71 (1984); John B. Lundquist, Mixed Use Condominiums Under the Minnesota Uniform Condominium Act, 10 Wm. Mitchell L.Rev. 97 (1984); Kent H. Roberts, Uniform Condominium Act—New Flexibility for Developers, 40 J. Mo. Bar 177 (1984); William S. Ohlemeyer, Comment, The Uniform Condominium Act in Missouri, 49 Mo. L. Rev. 595 (1984).

After 1980, law reform organizations began working to integrate the law of condominiums with the laws governing other forms of common interest communities, including cooperatives and planned communities. This law reform effort has included both the Restatement (Third) of Property—Servitudes, approved by the American Law Institute in 2000, and the Uniform Common Interest Ownership Act (UCIOA), first promulgated by NCCUSL in 1982 and amended in 1994, 2008, and 2014. Both the Restatement of Servitudes and UCIOA are discussed further in Section A4 infra.

2. COOPERATIVES

Consumer and agricultural cooperatives are familiar to many Americans, especially in rural areas. In these organizations persons join together as buyers or sellers, creating a group which will have greater power in the marketplace than any of its individual members. If profits result from the enterprise, they are distributed to the cooperators (or "members") on an equitable basis.

Housing cooperatives serve a similar purpose, typically in densely populated urban areas (such as New York and Chicago) where land scarcity makes the construction of detached homes impossible or cost-prohibitive. A cooperative association is organized (typically in a not-for-profit form of business organization), and the cooperators are shareholders in this organization, which acquires and holds title to an apartment building or complex of buildings (the "project"). Each member is also a tenant of a particular apartment, with the cooperative organization as landlord. The member's lease is sometimes called a "proprietary lease," indicating that the member is in a sense an owner.

The cooperative organization must pay directly the various costs associated with the purchase and operation of the project. Typically the largest single monthly outlay is the debt service (payments of principal and interest) on the mortgage which covers the entire project. Other outlays of the cooperative organization include real estate taxes, maintenance and repairs, management and administrative expenses, insurance, and reserves for future replacements of items which may be expected to wear out over time. All of these charges are budgeted on a monthly basis and divided among the members in proportion to the shares of stock allocated to each apartment. Each member must pay her share of these charges as rent under the member's proprietary lease. However, the member may deduct the portion of those monthly payments attributable to mortgage interest and real estate taxes on the member's federal income tax return, provided that at least 80% of the gross income of the cooperative organization is derived from payments by tenant-shareholders. I.R.C. § 216.

There are certain hazards and limitations intrinsic in the nature of a housing cooperative. The presence of the blanket mortgage precludes the kind of flexible financing that would be possible if each apartment unit were considered a separate parcel of real estate. [Financing of individual cooperative units is discussed in more detail in Section B of this chapter.] Furthermore, the interdependence of the cooperative requires each member to place heavy reliance and trust on other members. If a member defaults on his monthly rent, the cooperative organization may dispossess the member through eviction and may foreclose on the member's ownership share of the organization. See, e.g., Village Green Mut. Homes, Inc. v. Randolph, 361 Md. 179, 760 A.2d 716 (2000). An occasional default is not too troublesome. However, if several members default at about the same time, perhaps as a result of adverse economic conditions, the organization risks going into default on the blanket mortgage, thus jeopardizing the interests of those members who are entirely current in their payments.

Nevertheless, there are significant reasons why a cooperative may be preferred over a condominium:

> Three of the strongest are the following: cooperative unit owners have a greater say in choosing their co-owners than do condominium unit owners; a cooperative corporation can raise money by borrowing against its assets, and usually at a good rate, whereas there is no convenient mechanism for condominium unit owners as a group to obtain funds for common purposes; and each cooperative unit owner, unlike his condominium counterpart in most instances, enjoys the extremely valuable benefit of limited liability that comes from operating in the corporate form. [Joel E. Miller, Congress Grants Co-op Limited and Uncertain Relief from General Utilities Repeal, 5 Tax Mgmt. Real Est.J. 15 (1989).]

Cooperative housing is quite popular in several areas of the United States. By far the largest concentration exists in New York City. Significant numbers of cooperatives also exist in Detroit, Minneapolis-St. Paul, and several other major cities, and occasionally rural housing cooperatives are found. Only a small percentage of the new housing projects developed in the United States each year are cooperatives, and their importance has been eclipsed in the past few years by the burgeoning development of condominiums.

In 1981, the Uniform Law Commission promulgated the Model Real Estate Cooperative Act (MRECA). Although enacted in Virginia, MRECA's relevance was diminished by the 1982 promulgation of the Uniform Common Interest Ownership Act (UCIOA), which subsumes condominiums, cooperatives, and planned communities under the broader "common interest community" rubric.

NOTE

Condominium or cooperative? Legal form and unit value. To what extent should the form of common interest ownership affect the value of an owner's unit investment? In a recent empirical study of the New York City residential market, Michael Schill, Ioan Voicu and Jonathan Miller concluded that the typical New York City condominium unit was more valuable than a comparable cooperative unit. This "condominium premium" varied, depending on the extent to which the cooperative owner was able to finance her purchase under the cooperative's rules and whether the cooperative was subject to a transfer fee covenant or "flip tax" (i.e., a fee payable to the cooperative association upon the approved resale of a cooperative unit). Where a cooperative apartment was subject to no financing restriction and no flip tax (the situation most comparable to the typical condominium unit), the condominium value premium was 13.4%. This premium decreased to 10.6% for cooperative units on which the unit owner could finance 60–79% of the purchase, and 8.8% for all cooperative units. However, for cooperatives in buildings that allow no financing by unit owners, the authors found no condominium premium at all; instead, in those situations, comparable condominium units were worth 25.4% less. What might explain these data?

[T]he existence of both cooperative and condominium buildings may be partly explained by the desire for social exclusivity. A landlord of a building catering to affluent tenants might seek to charge monopoly rents to tenants for the privilege of living in this type of unique environment. Collective ownership—through cooperative or condominium form—would provide a way to avoid this type of exploitation.

Indeed, our results showing that cooperative owners in buildings that prohibit mortgage financing enjoy a price premium relative to condominiums provides some support for this thesis. A large proportion (77.3 percent) of the apartment sales in buildings with rules prohibiting financing were also in the top quartile of cooperative apartment values. This suggests that affluent New Yorkers may be using the no-financing restriction to maintain an affluent living environment and that the benefits of social exclusiveness themselves generate value for these purchasers. . . .

. . . [The social exclusivity thesis] does not explain why the vast majority of cooperative apartments that serve nonaffluent households continue to exist. One possible reason concerns the transaction, or "switching" costs of moving from one form of ownership to the other. Liquidation of the corporation and distribution to share owners of interests in the real property could lead to a taxable event for the corporation as well as for its shareholders. Each shareholder would be required to contribute to the satisfaction of the blanket mortgage loan, renegotiate the terms of his or her individual cooperative share mortgage, and have new financing documents prepared and recorded. The new condominium association would also probably need to take steps to arrange financing for owners whose credit may have deteriorated between the time they took out their share mortgages and the time of conversion or who cannot qualify for the additional debt needed to pay off their shares of the underlying mortgage. A variety of other costs would be entailed, including fees for real estate consultants and attorneys, closing costs, and recording taxes. [The authors estimated these costs to be $31,000 per unit, or roughly 67% of the expected "condominium premium."]

Relatively high monetary transaction costs are compounded by . . . the "costs of collective decision making." The law and economics literature suggests that there are many barriers of a strategic nature to bargaining to an efficient outcome (in our case, the conversion), especially when the number of bargainers is greater than two. Given that a conversion involves tens or hundreds of people, it is easy to imagine them failing to reach an efficient outcome, even if the potential gains are very high.

This collective-action problem is likely to be particularly severe in urban communities where residents are not homogenous. It is highly likely that not all cooperative owners have similar time horizons or financial characteristics. For example, the members of households on a fixed income who wish to remain as occupants might prefer not to pay the high transaction costs of conversion for a speculative gain that would be realized only on sale. In addition, some households with bad credit might find themselves in a situation in which they are unable to qualify for a condominium unit loan.

The problem of collective action is exacerbated by statutory and contractual supermajority requirements. For example, New York State law requires that the owners of at least two-thirds of the shares must approve a proposed dissolution, and the bylaws of many cooperative corporations have thresholds as high as 80 percent. . . .

In the end, despite the premium typically associated with condominium status, it is much too early to sound the death knell for the cooperative apartment, at least in New York. While it is likely that new apartment buildings will be built as condominiums to take advantage of the economic benefits of this legal form, problems of collective action combined with inertia and substantial transaction costs suggest that at least for the foreseeable future the housing cooperative will remain a dominant feature of our nation's largest city.

Michael H. Schill, Ioan Voicu & Jonathan Miller, The Condominium Versus Cooperative Puzzle: An Empirical Analysis of Housing in New York City, 36 J. Leg. Stud. 275, 312–316 (2007).*

3. PLANNED COMMUNITIES

The "planned community" melds the concept of subdivision (introduced in Chapter Nine) with the concept of shared ownership of common facilities. The following materials discuss the evolution of the modern planned community, highlighting both its common law origins and the key structural differences between the planned community and condominiums or cooperatives.

---

*   Reprinted with the permission of The University of Chicago Press.

MICHAEL L. UTZ, COMMON INTEREST OWNERSHIP IN PENNSYLVANIA: AN EXAMINATION OF STATUTORY REFORM AND IMPLICATIONS FOR PRACTITIONERS

37 Duquesne L. Rev. 465, 468–477 (1999)*

The planned community with homeowners' association is second only to the condominium in popularity as a model for common interest ownership. In many areas of the country, the planned community with a homeowners' association is quickly becoming synonymous with suburban residential development. Unfortunately, courts, commentators, the American Law Institute ("ALI"), and even the [Uniform Law Commission] have been inconsistent in the use of terms to describe this model. However, it is not terminology but the method of common interest ownership that distinguishes the planned community from the condominium and the cooperative.

Unlike the condominium form of ownership, owners of individual units in a planned community do not own an undivided interest in common areas. Also, unlike the cooperative, all of the real estate is not owned by an entity separate and apart from the individual unit owners. Instead, ownership of common areas is typically vested in an incorporated homeowners' association, and residents retain fee simple ownership in their individual units. It is this unique legal structure that gives rise to the growing popularity of the planned community. . . .

The importance of the planned community cannot be overstated. The Urban Land Institute ("ULI") is credited with first describing the prototypical planned community in its landmark publication, The Homes Association Handbook.[49] The ULI describes how the basic model of the planned community evolved, tracing its origin to early seventeenth-century England.[51] Samuel Ruggles introduced the concept to the United States in 1831, when he developed Gramercy Park in Manhattan for which he used a trust arrangement whereby legal title to the park was vested in a trustee for the benefit of the surrounding owners. At the same time, the property owners of Louisburg Square in Boston drafted and recorded a land agreement to provide for maintenance of the park area in the center of the Square, thus becoming the first homeowners' association in the United States.[53]

---

* Reprinted with the permission of the Duquesne Law Review.

[49] Urban Land Institute, The Homes Association Handbook, Technical Bulletin 50 (1964) [hereinafter Homes Association Handbook].

[51] The ULI states "[the planned community] originated . . . when the Earl of Leicester built his London townhouse and laid out Leicester Square in front of it. By 1700 the Square was surrounded by buildings and, by 1743, the property owners had employed a legal device to assure the exclusive use and maintenance of this park." Homes Association Handbook, at 39.

[53] Id. Other early examples of this type of arrangement include Ocean Grove (New Jersey); Squirrel Island (Maine); and Delano Park (Maine). Id.

The first modern example of the typical suburban planned community to use covenants running with the land to enforce contractual arrangements between homeowners was Roland Park in Baltimore, which Edward H. Bouton developed in 1891. Another important development came with the development of Kensington in Great Neck, Long Island in 1909. This community helped establish the concept of automatic membership in a homeowners' association and concomitant assessments for maintenance of common areas, the obligation for which ran with the land. Kensington became the modern archetype of the planned community.

The planned community concept has proven exceptionally popular for many reasons. Homeowners overwhelmingly endorse the concept of shared ownership and association management of common areas.[58] Volunteer members who serve on boards of directors of homeowners' and condominium associations[59] also express satisfaction with the arrangement.[60] One of the reasons for the success of the planned community concept may be the feeling of community or belonging that this type of arrangement engenders. Although these concepts may be somewhat nebulous and certainly have different degrees of importance and meaning to different individuals, there is, nevertheless, empirical support for this proposition.[61]

This is not to suggest, however, that shared ownership coupled with community association management is an Edenic solution. Such problems as apathy, misunderstanding or deliberate disregard of covenants or community rules, failure to pay association fees, and interpersonal conflict among homeowners are all problems that associations face.[62] Notwithstanding these inherent shortcomings, the planned community managed by a homeowners' association continues to enjoy an unprecedented level of popularity and growth. The innate flexibility of this

---

[58] A recent survey conducted by the Research Foundation of the Community Associations Institute indicated that homeowners were satisfied with community association home ownership (common interest ownership coupled with a condominium association or homeowners' association). When asked the question whether "[homeowners] think that community association homeownership [sic] is a satisfactory housing choice," thirty percent agreed completely, fifty-two percent mostly agreed, and seven percent slightly agreed. . . .

[59] Both the condominium model and the planned community model of common interest ownership typically rely on residents voluntarily serving on a board of directors. In smaller communities, this board of directors assumes management functions, while in larger communities the board of directors may employ a professional management company.

[60] The Community Associations Institute asked board members whether "[s]erving on an association board of directors has been a good experience." Thirty-five of the respondents indicated that they completely agreed, forty-eight percent mostly agreed, and seven percent slightly agreed. . . .

[61] Id. When asked "[h]ow would you describe the level of community feeling in your development?" fifty-eight percent of residents indicated that their community was "friendly," and eight percent believed their community was "neighborly." . . .

[62] Id. Eighty percent of residents indicated that apathy or lack of interest was a problem, sixty-nine percent indicated that not understanding rules was a problem, thirty-four percent indicated that fiduciary irresponsibility was a problem, and thirty-two percent indicated that interpersonal conflict was a problem. . . .

arrangement may have contributed to its growing importance. Developers, home purchasers, city planners, and the zoning and land use legal community have long sought solutions that provide a greater degree of flexibility. . . .

Planned Communities and the Common Law

Although the condominium model of common interest ownership is largely a product of statutory law, . . . it was the common law that gave recognition to the planned community and controlled its operation and function. . . .

Under the common law, the developer created a common interest community by filing a declaration.[68] Once the developer established the common interest community, he or she typically provided for an association to manage the common property; however, if the declaration failed to establish the association, a majority of the lot or unit owners, the courts, or the local government had the ability to form an association to manage such common property. In addition to specific powers, the common law vested the common interest community with all powers reasonably necessary to carry out the management and enforcement of the servitude framework established by the declaration. Specific powers available to the association included the power to levy assessments, charge fees, and borrow money; manage, acquire, and improve common property; make rules and regulations for protection of lot or unit owners; and to enforce these provisions through the courts or via the imposition of fines, penalties, late fees, and withdrawal of privileges. The board did not, however, have the power to impose architectural restrictions either on the home itself or on landscaping. . . .

The common law also evolved to define certain duties owed by the common interest community to its members. In addition to the duties expressly stated in the governing documents, the common law imposed standards quite similar to those imposed on boards of directors under the laws pertaining to corporations. The association was required to meet an ordinary care standard, treat its members fairly, use its discretionary powers in a reasonable manner, and disclose to members information regarding association affairs. In any suit against the association, the member had the burden of proving both a breach of duty on the part of the association and actual or potential damage to the interests of the community. The common law placed similar duties on the individual members of the board of directors. Any breach of the foregoing duties

---

[68] The ALI defines declaration as "the recorded document or documents containing the servitudes that create and govern the common interest community." Restatement (Third) of the Law of Property: Servitudes § 6.2(5) (Tentative Draft No. 7, 1998). A servitude is "[a] charge or burden resting upon one estate for the benefit or advantage of another." Black's Law Dictionary 1370 (6th ed. 1990). Most declarations are called condominium declarations if the common interest community uses the condominium model or declaration of covenants, conditions, and restrictions ("CC&Rs") if the common interest model is the planned community.

usually did not subject the individual owners to joint and several liability; rather liability was limited to the individual owners [sic] proportionate share of association expenses.

The common law also addressed the issue of governance of common interest communities and required that it be a representative form of government with a board of directors entitled to exercise the powers given to the association in the governing documents or via judicial decision. Usually, each lot or unit owner was entitled to one vote absent an express provision to the contrary. In addition, the law gave members the right to attend board meetings and present their opinions on issues concerning the community.

Courts were also called upon to fashion a body of law concerning the relationship between the developer and the association. Typically, at the beginning of the development process, the developer formed and retained control over the association. At some point in the process, the developer ceded control to a duly elected board of directors. The common law imposed on the developer the duty to create the association and to turn over control of association affairs to the board of directors after a time sufficient to protect the interests of the developer. Once this formal change of control had taken place, the association gained the ability to treat as voidable many self-dealing contracts with the developer. Before the transfer of control, the developer owed certain duties to the association including the duties to use (1) reasonable care in managing common property, (2) ensure that association finances were handled responsibly, (3) enforce the servitude regime, including payment of assessments, and (4) to disclose certain matters to the association. The developer could not modify the declaration if such a modification would have a material effect on the character of the development or place an unfair burden on existing owners unless the declaration specifically put the unit or lot owners on notice that the developer retained such an ability to modify.

NOTES

1. *The Uniform Planned Community Act.* As market conditions created additional demand for planned communities, developers and law reformers sought to provide a more solid statutory foundation for the development of planned communities. In 1980, the Uniform Law Commission (ULC) promulgated the Uniform Planned Community Act (UPCA):

> UPCA not only codified the law of homeowner associations but also provided statutory enablement for a common-interest housing regime (defined in UPCA as a "planned community") in which title to all common areas (including hallways and other interior spaces in a high-rise building) could be held in the name of the governing association instead of being fragmented among its members.

Norman Geis, Beyond the Condominium: The Uniform Common-Interest Ownership Act, 17 Real Prop. Prob. & Trust J. 757, 758 (1982). As Geis noted, UPCA thus addressed a significant flaw in the early-generation condominium legislation, which had assumed that a condominium regime had to be operated by the unit owners acting collectively as an unincorporated association. Id.

UPCA has been enacted in North Carolina and Pennsylvania. However, as discussed in the next section, coverage of planned communities is now subsumed within the Uniform Common Interest Ownership Act, promulgated by the ULC in 1982 and subsequently amended in 1994, 2008, and 2014.

2. *Distinguishing planned communities and planned unit developments (PUDs).* It can be easy to confuse the term "planned community" with the "planned unit development" (or PUD). The planned community arises and is governed by virtue of private law; by contrast, PUD is a concept of zoning law. Most zoning schemes are based upon segregation of residential, commercial, and industrial uses, with the idea that commercial development cannot take place within a residential zone. However, a zoning ordinance can incorporate PUDs, in which a developer proposes a self-contained community within a particular zone. Zoning approval for a PUD permits a developer to build "mixed-use" developments that feature a combination of both high-and low-density residential and commercial development. With increasing concern that traditional zoning has exacerbated "urban sprawl," modern planners have manifested a renewed enthusiasm for PUDs as a means for municipalities to achieve "smart growth." For further background on PUDs, see Daniel R. Mandelker, Legislation for Planned Unit Developments and Master-Planned Communities, 40 Urb. Law. 419 (2008).

A PUD could (and often does) include one or more planned communities. For example, a PUD might include several different subdivisions of detached single-family homes (each governed by a separate homeowners' association and thus each a separate planned community), as well as several different condominium projects (each governed by a separate unit owners' association).

4. MODERN LAW REFORM: SYNTHESIZING COMMON INTEREST OWNERSHIP

The Uniform Common Interest Ownership Act. Because of the structural differences in the legal forms of condominiums, cooperatives, and planned communities, early-generation common interest ownership statutes tended to be form-specific. As discussed in the previous sections, the Uniform Law Commission (ULC) originally promulgated separate uniform acts for each type of development—the Uniform Condominium Act (UCA) (1977, amended in 1980), the Uniform Planned Community Act (UPCA) (1980), and the Model Real Estate Cooperative Act (MRECA) (1981). In preparing these separate acts, however, the drafters were cognizant of the fact that there existed a coherent and consistent set of rights and obligations that were shared by all common interest developments, regardless of their organizational form. In 1982, this led the

ULC to draft and promulgate the Uniform Common Interest Ownership Act (UCIOA), which was "based on the broad premise that all common-interest housing regimes have the same essential characteristics, and on the corollary notion that the various forms are differentiated from each other only by the scheme of ownership of the common elements and the units." Norman Geis, Beyond the Condominium: The Uniform Common-Interest Ownership Act, 17 Real Prop. Prob. & Trust J. 757, 759 (1982).

UCIOA incorporated the existing substantive provisions of its three predecessors, while creating the new defined term "common-interest community" which included the condominium, the cooperative, and the planned community:

> The defined term, common-interest community, expresses the central legal concept in UCIOA. The definition of this term provides a functional description of all regimes which are subject to the act and thereby establishes the outer reaches of the jurisdiction of the act. The wording of this key definition is deceptively simple:

> > "Common-Interest Community" means real estate with respect to which any person, by virtue of his ownership of a unit, is obligated to pay for real estate taxes, insurance premiums, maintenance or improvement of other real estate described in a declaration.

> The important components of this definition are: (1) there must exist a "unit" within the common-interest community (consisting of a physical portion of the real estate "designated for separate ownership or occupancy") whose owner must make the designated payments with respect to "other real estate described in a declaration;" and (2) those payments must be mandatory and not optional. These threshold requirements thus exclude from UCIOA any development where there is no division of the property into "units" and "other real estate" and any such development organized on a voluntary rather than compulsory membership basis. . . .

> Derived from the general definition of common-interest community are three subsidiary definitions which articulate the three different species into which all common-interest communities are divided: the "condominium," the "cooperative" and the "planned community." Each of these forms is differentiated from the other two by the manner in which title to the units and common elements comprising the real estate within the regime is divided between the managing association and its members.

Thus, "condominium" is defined as a common-interest community in which "portions of the real estate are designated for separate ownership and the remainder of the real estate is designated for common ownership solely by the owners of those portions." This definition is subject to the further proviso that "a common-interest community is not a condominium unless the undivided interest in the common elements are vested in the unit owners."

A "cooperative" is defined as a common-interest community in which "the real estate is owned by an association, each of whose members is entitled by virtue of his ownership interest in the association to exclusive possession of a unit." This definition is supplemented by a special refinement in the meaning of the term "unit" when that term is applied to a cooperative. Since the cooperative association holds legal title to both the units and common elements, it would be a misnomer to characterize each member as a "unit owner" of the cooperative real estate. Therefore, UCIOA provides that, in certain contexts, references to a cooperative "unit" will denote the legal interest in that unit rather than the parcel of real estate within the unit boundaries. This legal interest consists of the member's "right to possession of a unit under a proprietary lease coupled with the allocated interests of that unit." For this purpose, "allocated interests" is a defined term which means "the common expense liability and the ownership interest and votes in the association."

These interlocking definitions neatly and precisely describe the trilateral relationship between the members of a cooperative, the cooperative association, and the cooperative real estate. At the same time they allow all the provisions of UCIOA derived from UCA and UPCA relating to the ownership, conveyance and encumbrance of condominium and planned community units, to apply with equal force to cooperative units.

All other common-interest communities (i.e., those which do not fall within the statutory definitions of condominium or cooperative) are denominated "planned communities." Thus, "planned community" is a residual term which sweeps into the jurisdiction of UCIOA any regime falling within the generic definition of common-interest community which is neither a condominium nor a cooperative. Examples include a homeowner association regime which owns and administers the roads or recreational facilities in a planned unit development or cluster subdivision project, a "master association" which administers the inter-condominium facilities in a multi-condominium project, and any other form of multi-ownership development (containing "units" and "other real estate") administered by a mandatory-membership association that has the right to assess its members.

Geis, 17 Real Prop. Prob. & Trust J. at 759–761.* As Geis noted, this eliminated the need for UCIOA to repeat the provisions that were identical in its three predecessor acts, and provided states with flexibility in enactment. States without any common interest legislation could simply enact UCIOA, while the numerous states that had already adopted the UCA could transform their existing statute into UCIOA through amendments to key definitions and incorporation of selected provisions unique to cooperatives and planned communities.

UCIOA has been modestly successful in gaining adoptions. It has been enacted (with some modifications) in Alaska, Colorado, Connecticut, Delaware, Minnesota, Nevada, Vermont, Washington, and West Virginia. Although California did not adopt UCIOA, the Davis-Stirling Common Interest Development Act, enacted in 1985, is similar in purpose and scope. See West's Ann. Cal. Civ. Code §§ 4000–6150.

In 1994, the ULC substantially amended UCIOA, requiring additional consumer disclosures to purchasers, providing for greater developer flexibility as to future expansion or modification of the development, and giving greater power to owners associations in dealing with unruly and disruptive owners and their tenants. The ULC amended UCIOA again in 2008, most particularly incorporating a "homeowner bill of rights" (the Uniform Common Interest Owners Bill of Rights Act), which was prompted by concerns that developers or others in control of the decision-making apparatus of an association might abuse or take advantage of the rights of individual unit owners. Further amendments in 2014 focused solely upon issues associated with the priority of the association's lien for common expense assessments (to which we return in Section D of this chapter); an additional set of amendments is expected to be approved in July 2021.

The Restatement (Third) of Property—Servitudes. As you should recall from your Property course, the laws of easements and covenants (or promissory servitudes) arose as two distinct bodies of law. As a result, while easements and covenants serve similar purposes—facilitating and enhancing land use by tying rights and duties to ownership of land—laws governing easements and covenants developed independently and in ways that were not internally consistent. For example, while the holder of an easement in gross (such as a utility service easement) could continue to enforce that easement following a transfer of the servient estate, the common law held that a person holding the benefit of a covenant in gross could not do so following a transfer of the burdened land. Another example involves the "privity" requirement, which the common law applied to

---

* Reprinted with permission of Norman Geis. Copyright © 1982 by the author. All rights reserved.

efforts to enforce covenants against successors at law (in actions for damages), but did not apply in cases involving the enforcement of easements. By way of review, consider two neighboring landowners, Smith and Jones, who previously entered an agreement to limit their respective uses to residential purposes only. Further, assume that Jones later sold his land to Davis, who opened a bar on the land. Under the common law of covenants, Smith could not have recovered damages against Davis for breaching the agreement—even if the agreement had explicitly stated that it bound the successors of Smith and Jones—because no horizontal privity had existed between Smith and Jones at the time the easement was created. By contrast, if Jones had granted Smith an easement to cross Jones's parcel, the lack of horizontal privity between Jones and Smith would not have prevented Smith from crossing the land following its transfer from Jones to Davis.

Over the last half-century, courts and commentators began to question whether the common law rules of easements and covenants—as traditionally articulated in the original Restatement of Property in 1944—were ideally suited to modern land transfer and development patterns. These concerns became increasingly significant as more and more development began to occur in common interest developments, which (as discussed in the previous section) rely substantially upon the use of covenants as a means of land use control. These concerns ultimately led the ALI to undertake a new restatement of the law of easements and covenants. This effort, which occurred roughly contemporaneously with ULC's promulgation and later amendment of UCIOA, culminated in 2000 with the approval of the Restatement (Third) of Property—Servitudes.

The Restatement of Servitudes overtly attempts to modernize the law of easements and covenants in an integrated and coherent fashion under the rubric of "servitudes":

> [The Restatement's goal is] to present[ ] servitudes law as an integrated body of doctrine encompassing the rules applicable to profits, easements, and covenants. The draft reflects the modern analytical perception that all the servitude devices are functionally similar, and that for the most part they are, or should be, governed by the same rules. Only in the relatively few instances where there are real differences among the servitude devices are different rules justifiable. Treating all the servitude devices together, rather than dividing the subject into a division for each, not only avoids substantial repetition of identical rules, but also promotes thoughtful consideration of the reasons why different rules may be required. . . .

Restatement (Third) of Property—Servitudes, Tent. Draft No. 1 (April 5, 1989). Since its enactment, the new Restatement has proven increasingly influential in sparking substantial academic and practical commentary about the laws of easements and covenants.

In restating the laws governing owners associations, the Restatement takes an approach that is analytically similar to UCIOA, adopting the concept of the "common-interest community":

> A "common-interest community" is a real-estate development or neighborhood in which individually owned lots or units are burdened by a servitude that imposes an obligation that cannot be avoided by nonuse or withdrawal
>
> (1) to pay for the use of, or contribute to the maintenance of, property held or enjoyed in common by the individual owners, or
>
> (2) to pay dues or assessments to an association that provides services or facilities to the common property or to the individually owned property, or that enforces other servitudes burdening the property in the development or neighborhood. [Restatement (Third) of Property—Servitudes § 6.2(1) (2000).]

Like the comparable definition in UCIOA, this definition is inclusive of all of the traditional forms of common interest ownership. The Restatement also elaborates upon the powers and duties of a common-interest community as well as the relationship between the developer and the community (albeit in slightly less detail than UCIOA). In jurisdictions that have not adopted UCIOA, UCA, or some comparably detailed common interest ownership statute, the Restatement is likely to have increasing significance as a source for resolving disputes arising within common interest communities.

B. FINANCING OF PROJECTS AND UNITS

There is no special novelty in the financing of planned developments; in general, they are treated like other subdivisions, and both construction and permanent loans are made on them. The construction lender will often be willing to advance sufficient funds to cover most or all of the cost of the recreational facilities and other common area improvements as well as the construction of the units themselves.

While the same general types of financing arrangements are made for condominiums, lenders tend to be somewhat more cautious than with conventional subdivisions. Construction lenders virtually always require that a permanent loan commitment be obtained before construction commences. Many permanent lenders attempt to protect themselves against market failures by stipulating that no permanent loans will be made unless and until some specified portion of the units have been "pre-sold"—that is, the developer has signed agreements with buyers for them. Because of the pre-sale requirement, a condominium developer may launch its sales program at a very early stage, possibly even before construction begins.

With construction lending on condominiums, market surveys and other evidences of salability are of critical importance. The construction and permanent lenders will need to be satisfied with the documentation, including the declaration, bylaws, and any leases or other supporting instruments; reviewing these papers is commonly a rather massive task. Often the same institution will make both the construction and permanent loans, an arrangement which simplifies the review process. Under many statutes the condominium declaration can be recorded even before construction begins, but most construction lenders will not permit its filing until construction is nearly completed or at least until a high percentage of units has been sold. In this way, if sales are slow, the lender may require the developer to change the project to rental use, at which point the developer will not file a declaration of condominium status and will refund the deposits of the early unit buyers. The UCA compels delayed filing. UCA § 2–101 (1980) (declaration may not be recorded until all structural components and mechanical systems are substantially completed).

Permanent financing of condominium units. Institutional lenders generally may make permanent mortgage loans on condominium units on the same terms as loans on detached houses or other buildings. However, the permanent lender on a condominium unit must consider many factors which are unimportant or nonexistent in the financing of subdivision houses. Most of these factors are related to the importance of the owners association and the common areas to the success (and thus the future security value) of the project. While the discussion which follows concentrates on the permanent lender's concerns, construction lenders must also consider these factors, because construction lenders may be forced into a permanent lending role if the developer defaults on the construction loan or the permanent lender refuses to honor its loan commitment. Indeed, unit purchasers themselves should also consider these factors, although unit purchasers often lack the sophistication to realize the potential dangers.

Certain precautions are particularly significant to the permanent lender if it finances the sale of some units while other units or the common areas are still under construction or remain in the developer's hands. Obviously, the unit being financed should itself be completed. To ensure that the project will be successfully marketed as a condominium, many permanent lenders impose a "pre-sale requirement;" that is, they will refuse to close any loans until the developer has entered into binding sale contracts for some fixed percentage of the units. The permanent lender will also be legitimately concerned with the developer's financial ability to complete the project, and may wish to verify that sufficient funds remain in the construction loan account for this purpose.

The payment of assessments to the association for unsold units can also pose a problem. Many statutes make no distinction between sold and unsold units, and require that assessments be collected uniformly from all.[2] This approach seems unreasonable from the developer's viewpoint, because unoccupied units obviously contribute little or nothing to certain variable costs of the association's operations; for example, they supply no users for the swimming pool, tennis courts, or equestrian trails. However, many fixed costs are independent of the number of users. A fair resolution of this problem may require a somewhat smaller assessment for units still owned by the developer than for occupied units. While a two-level assessment system is not permitted under many statutes, the same result may be achieved if the developer pays a full assessment but is entitled to reimbursement of a portion from the other owners under a separate contract. Alternatively, the developer might pay the full assessment amounts and attempt to recover the outlays through higher sale prices for the later-sold units. In any event, the permanent lender should ascertain that the developer is obligated to pay a fair share of the costs of operating the association during the marketing period and has the financial strength to do so; a default might result in deteriorating physical facilities or a financially weakened or even insolvent association. The lender may even require a cash deposit or letter of credit from the developer to secure these payments.

The permanent lender must also be concerned with the developer's attempts to retain control over the association until most of the units have been sold. Developers often create two classes of stock, attached to unsold and sold units respectively, with the former having a greater voting power. For example, if the first class has three votes per share and the second only one vote per share, the developer can maintain effective control until the project is three-fourths sold. This degree of retention of control is probably reasonable to protect the developer against the enactment of rules or procedures that might make the project unattractive to some buyers and thus impair the developer's marketing program.[3] The permanent mortgagee, however, may refuse to lend if the period of developer control will extend past some given percentage of units transferred, and may also insist on the fixing of an outside date by which control must pass to the unit owners irrespective of the number of sales.

Virtually every important aspect of the association's ongoing functions concerns the permanent lender, because operational inadequacies may diminish the security value of the units. The lender will want a satisfactory answer to the following questions: Is membership in the association

---

[2] UCA § 3–115 requires that once any units have been assessed, all units (including those still owned by the developer) must be assessed under the same formula. Until that time, however, the developer is free to pay all common area expenses.

[3] A few statutes expressly limit the period of developer control; see, e.g., UCA § 3–103; West's Fla.Stat.Ann. §§ 718.301 (condominiums), 719.301 (cooperatives).

automatic? Has a lien for unpaid assessments been created by proper language in the declaration or master deed? Has the association established a reasonable budget, supported by adequate assessment amounts? Is the assessment delinquency rate reasonably low? Has the association established adequate reserves for repairs and replacements, with provision that they not be used except for specified items? Has the association hired a competent management firm (if the project is large enough to justify it)? Is the project subject to unreasonable management contracts or recreational facility leases? Is there provision for an independent annual audit of the association's books? Has the association arranged adequate blanket insurance for the common areas and exteriors of units, with provision for increased coverage to match inflation?

Many permanent lenders insist on certain types of protection in the condominium documentation. For example, the lender may want: notice from the association of default in assessments by any of its mortgagors; exemption (if the lender becomes the owner of a unit through foreclosure) from the usual clause giving the association a right of first refusal or other right to control the subsequent transfer of the unit, and from any restriction on leasing of units; notice of cancellation of any insurance policies on the project; the right to examine the association's books at reasonable times; notice of association meetings and the right to attend; notice of any substantial loss or damage to common areas; and the right to vote on, or even to veto, such major policy decisions as the hiring or firing of a management firm, amendments to the declaration or bylaws, expansion or contraction of the project, or use of hazard insurance proceeds other than for repairs.

Finally, the lender will often revise its usual mortgage and note forms to add special provisions relating to condominiums. These revisions will usually include covenants by the mortgagor to pay association assessments when due, to notify the lender of any delinquency notices received from the association, and to abide by all provisions of the condominium's declaration, bylaws, and rules. The documents may require that the mortgagor pay assessments to an escrow or impound account. The mortgagor may also be required to covenant not to vote in favor of major policy changes in the project without the mortgagee's consent. Failure of the association to maintain adequate insurance coverage may be made a condition of default, and the lender may reserve the right to pay delinquent assessments and to charge them against the mortgagor's loan balance.

Authority of lenders, insurers and investors. There is little controversy concerning the power of lenders to make permanent mortgage loans on condominium units. Both federally-chartered and state-chartered institutions are generally permitted to treat them as the equivalent of single-family houses, although the lending powers of state-chartered institutions are a matter of state law and some variations exist.

The Federal Housing Administration (FHA) insures permanent mortgages on condominium units under the same general terms and conditions as mortgages on detached houses.

The Department of Veterans Affairs (VA) was first given authority to guarantee loans on condominium units in 1970, but could do so only when at least one unit in the project had been insured by FHA. In 1975 this statutory limitation was dropped, and the VA now guarantees such loans regardless of prior FHA involvement.[4] VA imposes a number of requirements to protect its interests, including a seventy percent presale requirement (which may be reduced in special circumstances)[5] and limitations on reservations of rights by developers (such as the retention of a veto over the association after unit owners obtain majority control).[6] In addition, VA regards projects as unacceptable if they prohibit leasing of units, or impose a right of first refusal upon resale.[7] As with FHA, the terms of the VA loan guarantee are identical to those on detached houses.

Both Fannie Mae and Freddie Mac purchase permanent mortgage loans on condominium units. The two agencies have similar, but not identical, requirements; they are too numerous and complex to be set out in detail here, but generally deal with the issues and concerns discussed earlier in this section. The precise requirements depend on the nature of the project: primary residence, second home, or investor (rental) use. Among the matters covered by Fannie Mae and Freddie Mac rules are the following: the completion of common area improvements; the adequacy of reserves for repairs and replacements; the percentage of occupancy by year-round residents; the percentage of units pre-sold; the existence of reasonable provisions for transfer of control of the association from the developer to the residents; freedom for mortgagees from any rights of the association to restrict sales of units; and a power in the association to terminate management contracts by notice. This list is merely illustrative, and Fannie Mae and Freddie Mac consider many other matters as well.

Permanent financing of cooperative units. Traditionally the only permanent financing encumbering a cooperative project was its blanket mortgage. In most respects lenders have viewed blanket mortgages as similar to loans on rental apartment buildings, although they have been concerned to some extent with the governance, internal procedures, and financial stability of cooperative corporations. Permanent blanket mortgages (as well as construction loans) on cooperative projects can be

---

4   Veterans Housing Act of 1974, Pub.L. No. 93–569, § 3, 88 Stat. 1863 (presently codified at 38 U.S.C. §§ 3710–3714; statutory authorization for the guaranty of loans on condominium units appears at 38 U.S.C. § 3710(a)(6)).

5   38 C.F.R. § 36.4365(c).

6   38 C.F.R. § 36.4363(a).

7   38 C.F.R. § 36.4362(c)(6) (leasing restrictions). The disapproval of rights of first refusal applies only to projects established after December 1, 1976; see 38 C.F.R. § 36.4362(c)(5).

insured by FHA under section 213 of the National Housing Act.[8] Loan-to-value ratios may be as high as ninety-eight percent, a feature that makes section 213 more attractive than conventional loans, which are generally limited to eighty percent of value. While the time and complexity of FHA processing under section 213 reduce its usefulness, the program was for a time very active in those jurisdictions in which cooperatives are popular. FHA also insures cooperative blanket mortgages under National Housing Act sections 221(d)(3) and 221(d)(4), with 100 percent of replacement cost available under the d(3) program and 90% under d(4). Conventional blanket loans on co-ops are also widely available.

Beginning with the New York statute enacted in 1971,[9] many states have authorized institutional lenders to make loans, often called "share loans," on the security of individual cooperative units.[10] Prior to this development, lack of institutional financing was a major impediment to the financial success of cooperatives. Purchasers of units were obliged to pay cash, obtain personal loans from external sources, or negotiate installment contracts or promissory notes with unit sellers to cover the difference between the selling price of the unit and the unit's pro rata portion of the blanket mortgage.

Institutional financing of individual co-op units was given further impetus by section 4(b) of the Emergency Home Purchase Act of 1974, which added a new subsection (n) to section 203 of the National Housing Act, authorizing FHA to insure individual unit loans.[11] Under FHA's regulations, the loan must be secured by a first lien on the corporate stock certificate and the "occupancy certificate" or proprietary lease. The loan maturity is limited to thirty years, the remaining term of the blanket mortgage, or 75% of the remaining economic life of the building improvements, whichever is less.[12] The FHA regulations recognize that a unit purchaser is always taking, in effect, subject to the blanket mortgage; thus, a lien on the unit is economically analogous to a second mortgage.

---

[8]   12 U.S.C. § 1715e.

[9]   N.Y. McKinney's Bank. Law §§ 103(5) (banks), 235(8–a) (savings banks), 380(2–a) (savings and loan associations). These statutes have undergone a series of liberalizing amendments since their enactment in 1981. They now permit maturities and loan-to-value ratios as generous as on loans made to owner-occupants of single-family homes. See generally Charles A. Goldstein, Institutional Purchase Money Financing of Cooperative Apartments, 46 St. John's L.Rev. 632 (1972).

[10]   See, e.g., West's Ann. Cal. Fin. Code § 1494; Mass. Gen. Laws Ann. ch. 157B, § 13; Minn. Stat. Ann. § 47.20, subd. 3; N.J. Stat. Ann. § 17:2–6(d).

[11]   12 U.S.C. § 1709(n). See 24 C.F.R. § 203.43c(f). Initially, FHA could insure unit loans only in buildings that were subject to blanket mortgages insured by FHA under section 213, but this limitation was removed by § 419 of the Housing and Urban-Rural Recovery Act of 1983, Pub.L. No. 98–181, with respect to projects completed for more than one year. See 49 Fed.Reg. 40188 (Oct. 15, 1984).

[12]   24 C.F.R. § 203.43c(h)(4).

The regulations limit the share loan to no more than the normal FHA amount, less the unit's pro-rata share of the blanket mortgage.[13]

Several of the other major federal agencies involved in housing have followed FHA's example and included cooperative share loans in their programs. The Office of Comptroller of the Currency authorizes federally-chartered savings and loan associations to make share loans on the same basis as loans on detached housing.[14] The Veterans Administration authorizes share loans under its loan guaranty program, although it reserves the right to make project-by-project determinations of acceptability, rather than issuing detailed regulations specifying what loans will be approved.[15] Fannie Mae has a program for purchasing share loans originated by local lending institutions.[16] In the aggregate, these changes represent a vast increase in institutional borrowing opportunities over those available before the 1970s.

Creating and foreclosing share loan security interests. Despite the great expansion in institutional lending on cooperative apartments, there is still confusion as to the proper method for a lender to acquire, perfect, and foreclose on a security interest in the stock and proprietary lease that represent ownership of a co-op unit.[17] The problem stems from the fact that the cooperator holds two inseparable rights—a share of stock, which seems undeniably personal property, and a leasehold which may be viewed either as realty or personalty.[18] This dichotomy has proven troublesome in a variety of contexts: whether the federal securities laws govern cooperative apartment sales,[19] whether the usual rights and duties associated with

---

[13] See 24 C.F.R. § 203.43c(g).

[14] 12 C.F.R. § 560.30.

[15] See 38 C.F.R. § 36.4346.

[16] See Fannie Mae Selling Guide, B4–2.3–04: Loan Eligibility for Co-op Share Loans, available at https://www.fanniemae.com/content/guide/selling/b4/2.3/04.html#Co-op.20Share.20 Loan.20Eligibility.20Requirements.

[17] For an excellent review of New York law on these issues, see Robert E. Parella, Real Property, 1998–99 Survey of New York Law, 50 Syr. L. Rev. 863 (2000).

[18] The leasehold estate was traditionally regarded as a "chattel real," a species of personal property; see William B. Stoebuck & Dale A. Whitman, Property § 6.11 (3d ed. 2000).

[19] They do not; see United Housing Foundation, Inc. v. Forman, 421 U.S. 837, 95 S.Ct. 2051, 44 L.Ed.2d 621 (1975), rehearing denied, 423 U.S. 884, 96 S.Ct. 157, 46 L.Ed.2d 115 (1975).

landlord-tenant law apply,[20] and whether real estate or personal property concepts govern sales contracts[21] and distribution of decedents' estates.[22]

On the specific problem of perfection of a security interest in a cooperative apartment, the case law is helpful but not fully satisfactory. The New York courts approached the question by drawing an analogy to the cases that involve enforcement of sales contracts on cooperative apartments; those cases take the position that the principal rights of the cooperative tenant stem from the ownership of shares, and thus that the U.C.C. controls. This suggests that the U.C.C. should govern issues relating to security interests as well. The New York Court of Appeals adopted this view in 1977 in State Tax Commission v. Shor.[23] It held that, because the cooperative apartment was not realty, a creditor who obtained a judgment against an apartment owner would not thereby acquire an automatic lien on the apartment. In dictum, the *Shor* court asserted that a lender could perfect a security interest in the apartment merely by taking possession of the shares and the lease, in a manner analogous of the taking of a pledge of chattel paper or a promissory note. The share of stock was viewed as the primary indicium of ownership, with the lease being merely ancillary. Based upon the language of Article 9 in effect at the time of the case, the court concluded that the share certificate was an "instrument," that perfection of a security interest in the share certificate could be accomplished by possession, and that no filing of a financing statement would be necessary. Subsequent New York state and federal court decisions confirmed this view.[24]

---

[20] Compare Linden Hill No. 1 Cooperative Corp. v. Kleiner, 124 Misc.2d 1001, 478 N.Y.S.2d 519 (1984) (statute protecting tenant ownership of pets applies to cooperatives) and Suarez v. Rivercross Tenants' Corp., 107 Misc.2d 135, 438 N.Y.S.2d 164 (1981) (implied warranty of habitability for residential tenants applies to cooperatives) with Earl W. Jimerson Hous. Co. v. Butler, 97 Misc.2d 563, 412 N.Y.S.2d 560 (1978) (summary possession procedure, normally applicable to landlord-tenant relationship, does not apply to cooperatives).

[21] Compare Firth v. Lu, 103 Wash.App. 267, 12 P.3d 618 (2000) (sale of cooperative unit is a transfer of an interest in real property and is covered by the statute of frauds); Presten v. Sailer, 225 N.J.Super. 178, 542 A.2d 7 (1988) (same); and Moloney v. Weingarten, 118 A.D.2d 836, 500 N.Y.S.2d 320 (1986) (same) with Weiss v. Karch, 62 N.Y.2d 849, 850, 477 N.Y.S.2d 615, 615, 466 N.E.2d 155 (1984) (sale of cooperative apartment is analogous to a sale of securities, governed by Article 2 of the Uniform Commercial Code); Friedman v. Sommer, 63 N.Y.2d 788, 481 N.Y.S.2d 326, 471 N.E.2d 139 (1984) (same); and Silverman v. Alcoa Plaza Assocs., 37 A.D.2d 166, 323 N.Y.S.2d 39 (1971) (U.C.C. Article 2 governs, prohibiting forfeiture of purchaser's earnest money deposit). See also Star v. 308 Owners Corp., 130 Misc.2d 732, 497 N.Y.S.2d 282, 283 (1985) (building code enforceable against cooperative unit, as holder of interest in real estate); In re Carton, 4 B.R. 401, 403 (Bankr. D. Md. 1980) (under Maryland law, owner's interest in cooperative apartment is real estate for purposes of attachment of judgment lien).

[22] In re Jack's Estate, 126 Misc.2d 1060, 484 N.Y.S.2d 489 (1985) (cooperative apartment interest treated as personalty); In re Miller's Estate, 205 Misc. 770, 130 N.Y.S.2d 295 (1954) (same). See also In re Levenhar, 24 B.R. 331 (Bankr. E.D.N.Y. 1982) (cooperative apartment interest is personalty, and hence cannot be held in tenancy by the entirety).

[23] 43 N.Y.2d 151, 400 N.Y.S.2d 805, 371 N.E.2d 523 (1977).

[24] Superior Fin. Corp. v. Haskell, 556 F.Supp. 199 (S.D.N.Y. 1983) (upholding priority of lender's unfiled security interest in cooperative apartment, perfected by possession of documents,

Lenders outside New York may well be uncomfortable with these conclusions, which would no longer be appropriate in a transaction governed by revised Article 9 of the Uniform Commercial Code, which became effective in 2001. Under revised Article 9, the owner's rights in the cooperative entity, even if evidenced by a share certificate, are not an "instrument" under U.C.C. § 9–102(a)(47), because the certificate is not a "writing that evidences a right to the payment of a monetary obligation." Instead, these rights would be characterized either as a "general intangible" under U.C.C. § 9–102(a)(42) or a "security" governed by U.C.C. Article 8. A security interest in a general intangible must be perfected by the filing of a financing statement. U.C.C. § 9–310(a). A security interest in a certificated security can be perfected by delivery of the certificate under U.C.C. § 9–313(a).

Likewise, if the proprietary lease is viewed as the principal indicator of ownership and the share certificate is viewed as the ancillary item, then by its terms Article 9 would not apply to a security interest in the lease. See U.C.C. § 9–109(d)(11) (Article 9 does not apply to "the creation or transfer of an interest in or lien on real property, including a lease"). Thus, under this view, a security interest in the lease should be viewed as a real estate interest subject to perfection by recordation in the real property records. This view was followed in In re McGuinness.[25] Thus, to be certain that its interest in the proprietary lease is perfected, the lender may wish to obtain and record a real estate mortgage on the cooperator's leasehold estate, in addition to taking possession of the documents and filing a financing statement under Article 9.

A related question arises as to how a creditor can properly foreclose upon a security interest in a cooperative apartment. In FDIC v. Evans,[26] the secured lender, which had taken a possessory pledge of the shares and lease, conducted a nonjudicial sale to a bona fide purchaser, relying on Article 9's authorization to secured parties to dispose of collateral in a "commercially reasonable" manner. The court found this action proper, and rejected the argument of the preceding paragraph that a security interest in the proprietary lease is excluded from U.C.C. Article 9.[27] In another case, the New York Appellate Division indicated that a judicial foreclosure under

---

against a subsequently-filed federal tax lien); Brief v. 120 Owners Corp., 157 A.D.2d 515, 549 N.Y.S.2d 706 (1990) (same, as against all subsequent liens including federal tax liens).

[25]   139 B.R. 3 (Bankr. D. N.J. 1992).

[26]   No. 75–C–1947 (E.D.N.Y. Apr. 14, 1976), unreported. The opinion is reprinted in full in Patrick J. Rohan & Melvin A. Reskin, Cooperative Housing Law & Practice § 5A.12 (1984). See also Mehralian v. Riverview Tower Homeowners Ass'n, 464 N.W.2d 571 (Minn. Ct. App. 1990) (statute governing redemption following real estate mortgage foreclosure does not apply to foreclosure of stock in cooperative apartment).

[27]   The court also rejected an argument that the sale was a violation of Due Process because it was held without a prior hearing. This is consistent with the usual attitude of the courts in reviewing power-of-sale foreclosures of real estate mortgages.

Article 9 would also be proper.[28] But a Bankruptcy Court applying Illinois law disagreed, noting that the proprietary lease was real property, so that a collateral assignment of it was not within the scope of Article 9 and would have to be foreclosed as a real estate mortgage. The court conceded that Article 9 would control a foreclosure on shares of stock alone as collateral, but concluded that it would be improper to permit the severance of the lease and stock rights in a cooperative to subject the stock to Article 9.[29]

Because of the bifurcated nature of cooperative apartment ownership, questions of perfection and foreclosure of security interests are not easily answered within the framework of existing law. Clarifying legislation is badly needed, and has been enacted in two of the states where many cooperatives are located. A 1988 New York statute adopted the view of prior case law that cooperative apartments are personal property, but declared that security interests in them must be perfected by the filing of an Article 9 financing statement in the local government office in which real estate mortgages are recorded.[30] New York has likewise enacted special foreclosure procedures for foreclosing on cooperative interests; while Article 9 governs the foreclosure, New York has amended its version of Article 9 to require an additional pre-foreclosure notice at least 90 days prior to the foreclosure sale.[31] New Jersey took a different approach, but with much the same ultimate result; its statute treats cooperative units as a special type of real estate, with transfers of title and perfection of security interests accomplished through recordation in the county recorders' offices.[32] Such documents are recorded in the same way as real estate deeds and mortgages, and are also indexed in a master register maintained for each cooperative project.

---

[28]   Fundex Capital Corp. v. Reichard, 172 A.D.2d 420, 568 N.Y.S.2d 794 (1991) (foreclosure of security interest in stock and proprietary lease is governed by Article 9, which authorizes the secured party to "reduce his claim to judgment, foreclose or otherwise enforce the security interest by any available judicial procedure").

[29]   In re McNair, 90 B.R. 912 (Bankr. N.D. Ill. 1988). These problems are largely resolved if the cooperative is of the type in which each owner holds a fractional share in the project as a tenant in common. Such interests are readily mortgageable and may be foreclosed upon. See Future Fed. Sav. & Loan Ass'n v. Daunhauer, 687 S.W.2d 871 (Ky. Ct. App.1985).

[30]   N.Y. U.C.C. § 9–501(1)(c). New York has also amended its version of Article 9 to specify the particular content of a financing statement covering a cooperative unit, N.Y. U.C.C. § 9–502(a)(4), (e). Such a filing is effective for 50 years until terminated, without the need for periodic continuation statements. N.Y. U.C.C. § 9–515(h).

[31]   N.Y. U.C.C. § 9–611(f)(1). The statute dictates the form and content of this additional pre-foreclosure notice. N.Y. U.C.C. § 9–611(f)(2) to (5). Where a lender fails to comply with these requirements, a court can stay a nonjudicial sale of the cooperative unit under Article 9 until the lender does comply. See, e.g., Stern-Obstfeld v. Bank of America, 30 Misc. 3d 901, 915 N.Y.S.2d 456 (Sup. 2011). Finally, New York has also amended its version of Article 9 to permit "strict foreclosure" of a cooperative interest, which is the Article 9 analogue for a deed in lieu of foreclosure. N.Y. U.C.C. § 9–620(h).

[32]   N.J. Rev. Stat. § 46:8D–1 et seq. The statute has been construed to apply only to post-act cooperatives; see Drew Assocs. v. Travisano, 235 N.J.Super. 194, 561 A.2d 1177 (A.D.1989), aff'd in part, rev'd in part on other grounds, 122 N.J. 249, 584 A.2d 807 (1991). See also In re McGuinness, 139 B.R. 3 (Bankr. D. N.J. 1992), comparing pre-act law with the act.

This legislation has been extremely helpful in New York and New Jersey, but cooperatives in other states remain in a legally ambiguous position. An amendment to the U.C.C., adopted nationally, seems the best way to solve the problem, although no action on it has been taken at this writing.[33]

NOTES

1. *Foreclosure of cooperative unit and occupancy.* Keep in mind that the high bidder following the foreclosure of a cooperative unit has no guarantee of being able to occupy the unit. A sale of a cooperative unit is subject to the cooperative's governing documents, which typically require board approval of prospective purchasers.

2. *Mechanic's liens.* Mechanic's liens raise unique problems in condominiums. If a contractor performs work on an individual unit, there is no serious doubt that the lien for unpaid work attaches only to that unit. But suppose the work is performed on the common elements, either at the behest of the developer or the owners association. Many of the statutes explicitly disallow liens on the common elements; see UCA § 3–117(a); FHA Model Act § 9(a). Instead, the lien may attach to all affected units. Should this result follow even if the work was performed (or the lien attached) prior to the recording of the declaration? See Stevens Constr. Corp. v. Draper Hall, Inc., 73 Wis.2d 104, 242 N.W.2d 893 (1976). The acts often provide that each unit owner can satisfy and discharge the lien as to his or her unit by a pro rata payment; see UCA § 3–117(b); FHA Model Act § 9(b); 2 Nelson, Whitman, Burkhart & Freyermuth, Real Estate Finance Law § 13.3 (6th ed., Practitioner Series 2014); E.D. McGillicuddy Constr. Co., Inc. v. Knoll Recreation Ass'n, Inc., 31 Cal.App.3d 891, 107 Cal.Rptr. 899 (1973).

C. CONFLICTS BETWEEN DEVELOPER AND UNIT PURCHASERS

To a significant extent, the developer of a common interest community and the purchasers of units in that community have economic interests that converge. For example, it is in the best interest of the unit purchasers to have facilities, covenants, rules and regulations that will facilitate the orderly management of the community and thus help to preserve the value of each unit purchaser's investment. Likewise, if such facilities, covenants, rules and regulations exist, the developer should find it easier to sell units in the community.

Nevertheless, the interests of the developer and the unit purchasers are not identical. A developer's primary interest is in marketing units at a profit on its investment. As a result, the developer will want to retain the

---

[33] See Robert M. Zinman, Report on Condominium Communities to the Advisory Group on Real Estate Related Collateral, U.C.C. Article 9 Study Group.

flexibility to make changes to the community during the development and marketing phase if warranted by market conditions. For example, the developer of a condominium building originally planned for 250 units may wish to expand to 350 units if area demand for new condominium units is high. Such an expansion may come as an unwelcome or unexpected surprise, however, to early unit purchasers, who may feel that the larger community will devalue their units and create more stress upon shared facilities (e.g., more residents using the pool, clubhouse, or tennis courts).

In this section, we explore a variety of settings in which conflicts can arise between the developer and unit purchasers. One common conflict involves the extent to which a developer is subject to assessment for units that have not yet been built, or that are built but remain unsold. For example, suppose that Developer places a declaration upon 100 acres of land creating the Shady Acres Condominium, including 200 units (in 20 10-unit buildings), a pool and tennis courts, and parking. Developer built four of the buildings (40 units) along with the pool, tennis courts, and a portion of the parking, and sold all 40 units, but then ran out of financing. Must the owners of the 40 units bear all the cost of maintaining the pool and tennis courts, or must the Developer pay assessments on the 160 units that remain unbuilt? Can the declaration expressly relieve the Developer of the obligation to pay assessments on unbuilt or unsold units?

TARA MANATEE, INC. V. FAIRWAY GARDENS AT TARA CONDOMINIUM ASS'N, INC.

District Court of Appeal of Florida, Second District, 2003
870 So.2d 32

FULMER, JUDGE. Tara Manatee, Inc. (Developer) was the developer of a twenty-building, eighty-unit condominium project in Manatee County that is now operated by Fairway Gardens at Tara Condominium Association, Inc. (Association). Prior to turnover of control of the association, the Developer was operating under the developer guarantee provision of section 718.116(9)(a)(2), Florida Statutes (1995), which states in relevant part:

> A developer . . . who owns condominium units . . . may be excused from the payment of his share of the common expense which would have been assessed against those units during the period of time that he has guaranteed to each purchaser in the purchase contract, declaration, or prospectus . . . that the assessment for common expenses of the condominium imposed upon the unit owners would not increase over a stated dollar amount and has obligated himself to pay any amount of common expenses incurred during that period and not produced by the assessments at the guaranteed level receivable from other unit owners.

The premise of the developer guarantee provision is that a developer should be excused from paying assessments on its units during the initial sales phase when its units are typically unsold and, thus, not consuming services of the association. Joseph E. Adams, *Community Associations: 1998 Survey of Florida Law,* 23 Nova L.Rev. 65, 75 (1998). Otherwise, the developer would bear a disproportionate burden in the maintenance of the condominium. *Id.* However, the developer must guarantee that assessments against nondeveloper unit owners will not exceed a stated dollar amount and the developer must also agree to fund any deficit incurred in the operation of the condominium (including funding of reserves, unless properly waived) during the guarantee period. *Id.*

In this case, the Developer contended that there was no deficit at turnover. However, the Association contended that there was a deficit of $44,009 because the Developer failed to fund maintenance reserves for the units that had not yet been built. The Developer refused to pay the $44,009 and sought a declaratory judgment interpreting its obligations under the Declaration of Condominium and applicable statutes. The Association answered and filed a counterclaim seeking a money judgment for $44,009. Both parties filed motions for summary judgment. The trial court granted the Association's motion and entered a final judgment in the amount of $52,794.77, which represented the Association's claim for $44,009 plus prejudgment interest.

At the summary judgment hearing the Association argued that when the Declaration of Condominium was recorded the Developer became obligated to fund reserves for the maintenance of all eighty proposed units. In support, the Association first cited section 718.104(2), Florida Statutes (1995), which provides that "[u]pon the recording of the declaration . . . all units described in the declaration . . . as being located in or on the land then being submitted to condominium ownership shall come into existence, regardless of the state of completion of planned improvements in which the units may be located."

Next, the Association cited section 718.112(2)(f)(2), which contains a requirement that the annual budget of common expenses include reserve accounts for capital expenditures and deferred maintenance. The same subsection provides that "prior to turnover of control of an association . . . the developer may vote to waive the reserves or reduce the funding of reserves for the first 2 years." § 718.112(2)(f)(2). The Association argued that the Developer was obligated to fund maintenance reserves for all eighty units described in the declaration because the units came into existence when the declaration was recorded and the Developer did not vote to waive or reduce the reserves. Finally, the Association acknowledged that the condominium was being operated under a developer guarantee authorized by section 718.116(9)(a)(2) and asserted that the Developer's obligation under this provision included funding reserves for unbuilt units because maintenance reserves are a common expense incurred upon the recording of the declaration. And, if the Developer did not wish to fund these reserves, it should have built a phased condominium or should have voted to waive or reduce the reserves.

The Developer agreed that its unbuilt units came into existence when the declaration was recorded, and therefore, all proposed units were subject to assessments as they became due for the maintenance of common elements and built units. The Developer also agreed that as part of the developer guarantee it was obligated to ensure that reserves for constructed units and common elements such as the pool and roads were fully funded. However, with respect to reserves for deferred maintenance, the Developer argued that it was only obligated to fund reserves for the maintenance of constructed buildings and common elements.

On appeal, the Developer frames the issue as whether maintenance reserves for unbuilt units are an "incurred" common expense for which the Developer is liable under the developer guarantee provision. The determination of whether these reserves are an incurred common expense turns on a determination of what event triggers the requirement that they be funded. The trial court cited *Hyde Park Condominium Ass'n v. Estero Island Real Estate, Inc.*, 486 So.2d 1 (Fla. 2d DCA 1986), and concluded that the Developer became obligated to fund full reserves for all eighty units at the time the declaration was recorded because at that time "the eighty units came into existence." While we agree that the units came into legal existence upon the recording of the declaration, we do not agree that the obligation to fund deferred maintenance reserves for the unbuilt units also arose at that time.

In *Hyde Park*, the Hyde Park Condominium Association filed suit against the owners of Units D1–7 for failure to pay assessments for common expenses.... The owners denied responsibility for paying assessments because the property owned consisted of lots rather than constructed units. *Id.* The trial court found that lots 1–7 of Unit D were unimproved property and were not "units" subject to assessments. *Id.* This court reversed. *Id.* We noted that the Hyde Park Condominium declaration provided that all units were liable for a proportionate share of the common expenses in the same proportion as such units share in the common elements. *Id.* We concluded that the unimproved lots were units:

> Under the 1969 Act, condominium property includes land, all improvements, all improvements on the land, and all easements and rights with the condominium. § 711.03(9) [Fla. Stat. (1969)]. A "unit" is that part of the condominium property "which is *to be subject to private ownership*." § 711.03(13) (emphasis added). "Common elements" are defined as "portions of the condominium property *not included in the units*." § 711.03(4) (emphasis added).

Therefore, under the 1969 Act, the only type of private ownership available within a condominium is a "unit."

Id. Hyde Park stands for the proposition that all units, whether built or unbuilt, must share in assessments for common expenses of the condominium. For example, if only five units are constructed and sold in a fifty-unit condominium, assessments for the expense of maintaining the roads, landscaping, and common elements, such as a pool, would be levied against all fifty units and not just the five that were already constructed. *Hyde Park* does not stand for the proposition that deferred maintenance reserves for unbuilt units become an incurred common expense at the time a declaration is recorded and, therefore, does not support the trial court's order in this case.

We conclude that the requirement to fund reserves for deferred maintenance is not triggered by the recording of a declaration of condominium. We reach this conclusion by construing section 718.112(2)(f), which addresses what must be included in an annual budget, and more specifically subsection 718.112(2)(f)(2), which addresses reserve accounts. This subsection provides in part:

> In addition to annual operating expenses, the budget shall include reserve accounts for capital expenditures and deferred maintenance. These accounts shall include, but are not limited to, roof replacement, building painting, and pavement resurfacing, regardless of the amount of deferred maintenance expense or replacement cost, and for any other item for which the deferred maintenance expense or replacement cost exceeds $10,000. The amount to be reserved shall be computed by means of a formula which is based upon estimated remaining useful life and estimated replacement cost or deferred maintenance expense of each reserve item. The association may adjust replacement reserve assessments annually to take into account any changes in estimates or extension of the useful life of a reserve item caused by deferred maintenance. This subsection does not apply to budgets in which the members of an association have, by a majority vote at a duly called meeting of the association, determined for a fiscal year to provide no reserves or reserves less adequate than required by this subsection. However, prior to turnover of control of an association by a developer to unit owners other than a developer pursuant to § 718.301, the developer may vote to waive the reserves or reduce the funding of reserves for the first 2 years of the operation of the association, after which time reserves may only be waived or reduced upon the vote of a

majority of all nondeveloper voting interests voting in person or by limited proxy at a duly called meeting of the association. § 718.112(2)(f)(2).

We conclude that, based on the wording of this statute, a developer is not required to fund deferred maintenance reserves for unbuilt units. The formula prescribed to determine amounts to be reserved is based in part on the "remaining useful life" of each reserve item. The phrase "remaining useful life" suggests that the "useful life" of an improvement has already begun. The useful life of a unit in terms of maintenance does not commence until it is built because unbuilt units do not deteriorate and accrue maintenance needs. Furthermore, the provisions of section 718.112(2)(f)(2) whereby a developer may vote to waive or reduce the funding of reserves must be read to apply only to reserves that are required to be funded. We find no requirement to fund maintenance reserves for unbuilt units and, therefore, no waiver was necessary. . . .

NOTES

1. *Developer liability for assessments on unbuilt or unsold units.* Whether the owner of an unbuilt unit is liable for assessments (and in what amount) is a function of the declaration and any specific requirements set forth in the applicable statute. See, e.g., Aluminum Indus. Corp. v. Camelot Trails Condo. Corp., 535 N.W.2d 74 (Wis. Ct. App. 1995) (unbuilt unit subject to assessment unless declaration provides otherwise); Fox River Condo. Ass'n, Inc. v. Townhomes of River Place, 295 Wis. 2d 491 (Ct. App. 2006) (language of declaration did not impose assessment obligation on owners of unbuilt units); Palm Bay Towers Corp. v. Brooks, 466 So.2d 1071 (Fla. Ct. App. 1984) (terms of declaration do not overrule statutory obligation of developer to pay assessments on units it owns); UCA § 3–115(b), UCIOA § 3–115(b) (common expenses must be assessed against all units in accordance with allocations set in declaration); UCA § 2–107(a), UCIOA § 2–107(b) (developer may not allocated assessments among units in a fashion that discriminates in developer's favor); Alma Investments, Inc. v. Bahia Mar Co-owners Ass'n, 999 S.W.2d 820 (Tex. Ct. App. 1999) (provisions allowing developer to exempt certain units from paying assessment charges were void as against public policy).

Is there a meaningful difference between unsold units and unbuilt units? If assessments are based generally on the idea that those using common elements should pay for the maintenance of those elements, is it appropriate to hold the developer liable for assessments on unbuilt or "phantom" units? Why or why not? How does the Florida "guarantee" statute try to address this problem, and does it do so adequately? How else might a developer attempt to minimize its obligation for assessments on unbuilt or unsold units? Consider the following alternatives:

(a) *Amendment of declaration.* Often the declaration may permit its terms to be modified upon approval by a majority or supermajority of the unit owners. Returning to the hypothetical immediately prior to *Tara Manatee*, suppose that the declaration contains a provision allowing a majority of owners to modify the declaration, with voting determined by "one unit, one vote." Developer proposes to amend the declaration to relieve all Developer-owned units from assessments, and the amendment is approved when Developer (who owns the 160 unbuilt units) casts its votes in favor of the amendment. Should such an amendment enforceable? Why or why not? Investors Ltd. v. Sun Mountain Condo., 683 P.2d 891 (Idaho Ct. App. 1984) (developer/owner of unbuilt units was not "owner" entitled to vote on amendment seeking to add additional building to condominium); UCA § 2–107(a).

(b) *Annexation/phasing.* Now suppose that in the original declaration for Shady Acres Condominium, Developer only subjected the first 40 units, pool, tennis courts, and parking to the declaration, but that the declaration also provided: "Annexation by Developer. Developer shall have the unilateral privilege to subject all or any portions of real property owned by Developer to this Declaration." Developer plans to build the remaining 160 units in phases, as financing and market conditions permit, but as yet has not annexed the land on which those 160 units would be built. Would the Developer have any assessment liability for the unbuilt units?

2. *Funding of reserves.* Governing documents typically require the maintenance of a reserve fund for capital expenditures and deferred maintenance of common elements. If created and managed properly, a portion of the assessment against each unit is placed in a reserve account each assessment period, and these reserves are typically invested by the association until needed. This is sensible, as the cost of certain major repairs (e.g., replacing a condominium's roof) may well exceed the amount that an association could expect to raise through assessments in any one year. If the creation and funding of reserves is sensible, why did the court in *Tara Manatee* conclude that the developer was not obligated to pay reserves on unbuilt units?

3. *"Lowballing" of assessments.* Sometimes, a developer may subsidize the cost of maintaining common elements during development and marketing. This may permit the developer to establish artificially low assessments on unit purchasers, thereby enhancing the developer's ability to sell units. Of course, the piper must eventually be paid, and when the developer subsidies stop, assessment amounts may increase dramatically. Suppose that Smith purchases a home from such a developer, only to discover that when the developer stops subsidizing common expenses six months later, the association must triple its annual assessment amount. Should Smith be able to rescind the contract? Why or why not? What additional information, if any, would you like to discover before reaching a conclusion?

4. *Tardy completion of units and failure to complete common facilities.* Under all types of unit ownership plans, the developer often sells units prior to construction, or sells constructed units before completing common

recreational facilities. The buyers may rely on the developer's promise, oral or written, that completion will occur. Where the problem is failure to complete a unit, courts have held that if the developer does not finish the unit within a reasonable time of the agreed closing date, the buyer may rescind and recover the deposit. See, e.g., Daugherty v. Bruce Realty & Dev., 892 S.W.2d 332 (Mo. Ct. App. 1995); Reider v. P-48, Inc., 362 So.2d 105 (Fla. Ct. App. 1978). Should the same be true if the developer runs out of money and fails to complete common facilities? What protections can be devised for unit purchasers in this situation?

5. *Expansion of the project.* Suppose that the Developer of Village Green, a planned community expected to include 200 homes, is in the early stages of marketing. Early sales are very slow, due to market concerns that low- and moderate-income housing will be constructed on an adjoining parcel of land. In response, Developer acquires the adjoining parcel of land and announces plans to expand the planned community to incorporate this land. The new plans include the construction of a golf course, the maintenance of which would be subsidized through assessments, along with the construction of an additional 100 homes surrounding the golf course. Can Developer make such a change without the unanimous consent of all existing owners within the community?

First generation condominium acts (e.g., the FHA Model Act) did not satisfactorily address the extent to which the developer could expand the project after beginning construction and sales. This created great uncertainty, with some courts suggesting that expansion was improper absent unanimous approval of all unit owners. See Suprenant v. First Trade Union Sav. Bank, FSB, 666 N.E.2d 1026 (Mass. App. Ct. 1996). Second generation statutes such as UCA and UCIOA expressly permit a developer to amend or modify the declaration to permit expansion of a project, but this flexibility is not without limits. See, e.g., Restatement (Third) of Property—Servitudes § 6.21 ("A developer may not exercise a power to amend or modify the declaration in a way that would materially change the character of the development or the burdens on the existing community members unless the declaration fairly apprises purchasers that the power could be used for the kind of change proposed."). Should Developer be able to convert Village Green into a golf course community? What if Developer did not plan to build a golf course on the additional land, but only to add an additional 100 homes without adding any recreational facilities to the existing pool and four tennis courts? How specific must the declaration be before Developer should be able to make such changes? See UCIOA §§ 2–105, 2–110.

Court decisions have been solicitous of disappointed purchasers of condominium units, particularly where the purchase was made prior to completion of construction and where the developer made material changes to the project after the purchaser signed a contract. In such cases, courts have permitted the disappointed purchaser to rescind the contract. See, e.g., Barber v. Chalfonte Dev. Corp., 369 So.2d 983 (Fla. Ct. App. 1979) (changes in documents eliminating certain recreational facilities and imposing further restrictions on decoration of units); Aaronson v. Susi, 296 So.2d 508 (Fla. Ct. App. 1974) (developer converted part of the advertised recreational space into an additional apartment unit).

6. *Developer control of the association.* Developers frequently attempt to maintain control over the owners' association even after selling the majority of the units, either by retaining all powers of the association or by establishing voting rules that give disproportionate weight to the developer (e.g., unsold units retained by the developer have five times the votes of sold units) and thus allow the developer to "outvote" other owners within the association. This is motivated (at least in part) by fear that once the developer turns over control to the owners' association, the owners may make changes in the declaration or rules that would make it more difficult for the developer to market the remaining units. Such extensive developer control may prove very frustrating to unit purchasers when the developer and unit purchasers do not see eye-to-eye on matters of importance to the community residents.

Frequently, permanent lenders will refuse to make a mortgage loan on a project if the period of developer control will extend past some given percentage of units transferred, and may also insist on specifying a fixed date on which control will pass to the unit owners regardless of unit sales. At what point, even though still in the minority, should unit purchasers be entitled to some representation in the management of the condominium? See, e.g., Fla. Stat. Ann. § 718.301(1) (if unit purchasers other than developer own 15 percent or more of units, they are entitled to elect one-third of association board members; they are entitled to elect at least a majority if more than three years have passed since 50% of the units are sold, more than three months have passed since 90% of the units are sold, or seven years have passed since recording of the declaration); UCA § 3–103(d) (developer control of association terminates upon earliest of (1) 60 days after three-fourths of units are sold to purchasers other than developer; (2) two years after developer has ceased to offer units for sale in ordinary course; (3) two years after developer last exercised any right to add new units; or (4) developer's recording of an instrument voluntary surrendering control to the association).

Frequently, the struggle for control is not against the original developer, but against the developer's mortgagee who has acquired the developer's remaining units through foreclosure or a deed in lieu. To what extent should the mortgagee be treated as the "developer" for purposes of control? See McKnight v. Board of Directors, 32 Ohio St.3d 6, 512 N.E.2d 316 (1987). See 2 Nelson, Whitman, Burkhart & Freyermuth, Real Estate Finance Law § 13.3, at 366–367 (6th ed. Practitioner Series 2014).

7. *Rental of units by developer.* If unit sales are slow, the developer may decide to hold some units for rental purposes. Persons who have already purchased units may have strong objections to this practice, arguing that it produces a fundamental change in the character of the project. If the declaration gives the association clear authority to restrict or prohibit rentals, there seems no reason not to enforce the association's decisions. See, e.g., Le

Febvre v. Osterndorf, 87 Wis.2d 525, 275 N.W.2d 154 (Ct. App. 1979) (court enjoined developer from rental use of unsold units without permission of association's board of directors where permission was required under bylaws); Spratt v. Henderson Mill Condo. Ass'n, 224 Ga. App. 761, 481 S.E.2d 879 (1997) (where association had discretion to allow rental use, its decision to deny such use was upheld). Even if there is no authority for the association to control renting of units, a resolution of the association restricting rentals may be upheld anyway on the ground that it has a general authority to restrict use of the units. See Breezy Point Holiday Harbor Lodge-Beachside Apt. Owners' Ass'n v. B.P. Partn., 531 N.W.2d 917 (Minn. Ct. App. 1995).

8. *Defects in design and construction.* The same sort of protection given to buyers of detached houses for defects in design and construction is generally also extended to buyers of condominiums, cooperatives, and units in planned communities. See generally Chapter One, Section G supra. See, e.g., Jablonsky v. Klemm, 377 N.W.2d 560 (N.D. 1985); Rouse v. Glascam Builders, Inc., 101 Wash.2d 127, 677 P.2d 125 (1984); Gable v. Silver, 264 So.2d 418 (Fla. 1972). See generally Robert M. Diamond and Deborah K. Raines, Consumer Warranty Issues in the Sale of Residential Condominiums, 20 Real Prop. Prob. & Tr. J. 933 (1985); Mark D. Pearlstein, Developer Liability for Defects in Condominiums, 74 Ill. Bar. J. 18 (Sept. 1985); Comment, Caveat Venditor in Maryland Condominium Sales: Cases and Legislation Imposing Implied Warranties in Sales of Residential Condominiums, 14 U. Balt. L. Rev. 116 (1984); Annot., 50 A.L.R.3d 1071. The UCA contains express and implied warranty provisions similar to those of the ULTA; see UCA §§ 4–113 to 4–116.

9. *Condominiums and the Interstate Land Sales Full Disclosure Act.* In 1968, in response to perceptions of widespread fraud in the subdivision of vacant land and sale of lots to out-of-state purchasers for future development (i.e., the proverbial sales of "Florida swampland"), Congress enacted the Interstate Land Sales Full Disclosure Act (commonly referred to as ILSA). 15 U.S.C. § 1701 et seq. ILSA imposed upon developers stringent registration and disclosure requirements concerning the sale of subdivision "lots," and gave purchasers the ability to rescind purchase contracts for a period of two years if the developer failed to comply with these requirements.

In 1978, Congress added the term "condominium" to ILSA's "improved land" exclusion, see 15 U.S.C. § 1702(a)(2) (ILSA does not apply to "the sale or lease of any improved land on which there is a . . . condominium . . . building, or the sale or lease of land under a contract obligating the seller or lessor to erect such a building thereon within a period of two years"). Because condominium sale contracts often exculpate the developer from responsibility for delays in completing construction, federal courts began interpreting ILSA as applying to the sale of condominium units unless the condominium fell within one of ILSA's other exclusions. See, e.g., Cruz v. Leviev Fulton Club, LLC, 711 F.Supp.2d 329, 331 (S.D.N.Y. 2010) (citing cases); James L. Olivier, Beyond Consumer Protection: The Application of the Interstate Land Sales Full Disclosure Act to Condominium Sales, 37 U. Fla. L. Rev. 945 (1985).

During the recent recession, as condominium values plummeted in many markets, numerous condominium buyers (remorseful over the rapid decline in the value of the resale value of units they had contracted to purchase) began raising technical violations of ILSA's disclosure requirements in an attempt to escape liability on their purchase contracts. In response to pressure from developers, Congress finally reacted in 2014, amending ILSA to make clear that effective March 26, 2015, ILSA's registration and disclosure requirements will not apply to the sale or lease of a condominium unit.

Developer self-dealing. Suppose that shortly after purchasing and moving into a unit in Shady Acres Condominium, Smith learns two things that disturb him greatly. First, Smith learns that while Developer was still in control of the association, Developer entered into a contract with the association under which a related corporation (of which Developer is the sole shareholder) will manage the condominium for 25 years, at a property management fee that is 2% higher than that charged by comparable property managers. Second, Smith learns that the pool and tennis courts are not in fact owned by the unit owners, but by Developer, and are leased by Developer to the association for 99 years at a rental amount which, on an annual basis, is roughly equal to the fee simple value of the facilities! If Smith tries to mobilize the association to challenge the validity of these "sweetheart" contracts, should the law intervene to protect the owners, or are such deals the unavoidable consequence of freedom of contract?

While early decisions were unsympathetic to purchaser attacks on developer self-dealing, more recent decisions have allowed owners associations either to rescind sweetheart contracts or to recover from the developer for the benefit of the association unreasonable profits gained from such agreements. One good example of this judicial approach is Avila South Condo. Ass'n, Inc. v. Kappa Corp., 347 So.2d 599 (Fla. 1977). In that case a developer, while an officer and in control of the owners association, caused the association to enter into a 20-year lease to use recreational facilities owned by the developer's spouse. After unit owners took control of the association, they filed suit against the developer to recover for the association's benefit the difference between the rent reserved in the lease and the fair rental value of the facilities. The association claimed that the developer had a fiduciary obligation to it and had violated that duty. The Florida Supreme Court ruled that the complaint stated a cause of action.

State legislation has attempted to address the self-dealing problem. Florida legislation not only grants broad authority to the association to terminate leases and contracts entered into by the association while it was controlled by the developer, it also delineates certain minimum provisions that all such agreements must contain. West's Fla. Stat. Ann. §§ 718.302, 718.3025. See, e.g., Wash-Bowl Vending Co., Inc. v. No. 3 Condo. Ass'n,

Village Green, Inc., 485 So.2d 1307 (Fla. Ct. App. 1986) (laundry space lease); Tri-Properties, Inc. v. Moonspinner Condo. Ass'n, Inc., 447 So.2d 965 (Fla. Ct. App. 1984) (management contract). New Jersey has similar legislation. See N.J. Stat. Ann. § 46:8B–12.2. See also Va. Code § 55–79.74(C) (term of such a lease or contract cannot exceed two years and may be terminated by the association without penalty by 90 days written notice given no later than 60 days after expiration of developer control). UCA and UCIOA likewise provide robust protections against developer self-dealing. Following the end of the period of developer control of the association, the newly elected board may terminate without penalty any prior "management, maintenance, operations, or employment contract," any "lease of recreational or parking areas or facilities," or any contract or lease with the developer or an affiliate. See UCA § 3–105(a), UCIOA § 3–105(a). Query: if the new board can always cancel objectionable contracts or leases, is it possible that the original execution of those contracts or leases can be regarded as a breach of a fiduciary duty?

Recreational leases are commonly for very long terms, and developers often insert clauses which cause the rents to increase in accordance with the Consumer Price Index or some similar measure of inflation. The Florida statute prohibiting this device was upheld in Schlytter v. Baker, 580 F.2d 848 (5th Cir. 1978). See Fla. Stat. Ann. § 718.4015. See also Moonlit Waters Apts., Inc. v. Cauley, 666 So.2d 898 (Fla. 1996) (statute did not apply to a ground lease of land on which the entire project was constructed, as distinct from a lease of recreational facilities). Is there anything inherently unconscionable or offensive in such a clause? The same sort of device is very widely employed in long-term commercial leases.

Although regulation of real estate transactions is typically a matter of state law, it is not surprising that Congress has gotten involved in these issues given the volume of real estate marketed across state lines. In 1980, Congress adopted the Condominium and Cooperative Abuse Relief Act (CCARA), which addresses the above issues as well as other problems presented by the conversion of apartments to condominiums and cooperatives (and the concomitant displacement of tenants). See, e.g., 15 U.S.C. § 3607(a) (allowing termination of self-dealing management agreement without penalty within two years after developer control terminates or developer owns fewer than 25% of units, whichever occurs first, by vote of two-thirds of unit owners other than developer or affiliate); 15 U.S.C. § 3608(a) (association may obtain judicial determination that a self-dealing lease or portion thereof was unconscionable when made where lease term, including automatic renewals, exceeded 21 years and lease contained automatic rental increase); 15 U.S.C. § 3608(b) (setting forth circumstances under which self-dealing lease is presumptively unconscionable). CCARA does not apply to planned communities; is there a reason? Do the same potential abuses exist?

Is full disclosure the answer to self-dealing? Several of the "second-generation" statutes require extensive disclosure of documents (and summaries of them, as they are often too voluminous and technical for most unit purchasers). For example, UCA requires the distribution of a "public offering statement" by the developer, and gives buyers a right to cancel their purchaser contracts for 15 days after receiving it, UCA §§ 4–101 to 4–106. UCIOA contains comparable provisions. UCIOA §§ 4–101 to 4–108. Is any of this likely to be meaningful? If disclosure is to be compelled, is it better to disclose the original documents themselves, a summary-type of offering statement, or both? Should buyers be permitted to waive disclosure? What about buyers in industrial or commercial condominiums? Should disclosure rules apply to cooperatives and planned communities as well as condominiums?

Unit purchaser vs. lender disputes. Suppose that 100 buyers enter into pre-construction contracts for the purchase of a unit in the proposed Harbor View Condominiums, each making a $10,000 deposit. Partway through construction, the developer encounters unexpected cost overruns. The developer spends the accumulated purchasers' deposits, but still cannot complete construction. The developer then defaults on its construction loan, the lender forecloses its mortgage, and the lender acquires the partially completed project at the foreclosure sale. Have the buyers lost their deposits and/or the contractual rights to purchase their units, or can the buyers enforce their contracts against the lender?

STATE SAVINGS & LOAN ASS'N V. KAUAIAN DEVELOPMENT CO.

Supreme Court of Hawaii, 1968
50 Hawaii 540, 445 P.2d 109

LEVINSON, JUSTICE. . . . [The developer entered into pre-construction contracts of sale with a number of condominium unit purchasers. These contracts were unrecorded, but the construction lender, State Savings, had actual knowledge of them when it recorded its construction mortgage. Construction was completed, but sales were apparently slow and the developer defaulted on the construction loan. State Savings sought to foreclose on the property, including the interests of buyers under the pre-construction contracts.]

Except as modified by statute with respect to registered land, the proposition is well established that one who takes an interest in real property with knowledge of the existence of contracts of sale of other interests in the property is subject to the terms of the contracts, *Hurst v. Kukahi*, 25 Haw. 194 (1919). Furthermore, Hawaii recognizes the present transferability of interests in futuro which would have been invalid at common law, *Puukaiakea v. Hiaa*, 5 Haw. 484 (1885).

But the purchasers cite no authority, and we have found none, indicating that a contract for the sale of an interest in land and a building to be constructed on the land creates an equitable interest in the building superior to a mortgage securing a construction loan for the building. . . .

State Savings . . . contends that since the contracts were not specifically enforceable they did not convey an interest in real property. We recognize that equity courts generally refrain from issuing decrees which they cannot enforce, and that equity courts will not order acts requiring continuous supervision, such as construction of [a] building. But State Savings cites no authority which supports the conclusion that the inability, or refusal, of equity courts to grant a particular remedy indicates that no interest in real property has been conveyed. Recognition of an interest in real property does not necessarily depend on the availability of a specific remedy to protect such interests.

The question, then, is whether we ought to extend the protection equity historically has given to rights arising under an executory contract for the sale of land to interests of contract purchasers in a unit in a condominium to be built. Both parties agree that this case, and the issues involved in it, ought to be resolved in a manner which most effectively will implement the legislative desire to encourage the development of condominium projects in Hawaii. They disagree, obviously, as to the resolution which will best effectuate that purpose. The legislative enactment with which we are dealing in this case has profound social and economic overtones, not only in Hawaii but also in every densely populated area of the United States. Our construction of such legislation must be imaginative and progressive rather than restrictive.

We conclude that the overall objectives of [Hawaii's Horizontal Property Regimes Act, or H.P.R.A.] will best be effectuated by recognizing the rights of purchasers under the contracts as superior to those of a subsequent mortgagee receiving his mortgage with knowledge of those interests. First, equity courts long have recognized the basic unfairness of permitting a person to take an interest in property with knowledge that other interests, prior in time, exist, and permitting the subsequent interest to be free from those interests. As a general rule, a vendor can convey no more of an interest than he has at the time of the conveyance.

Second, and perhaps even more important, condominiums were developed as a method of ownership under which the individual purchaser's interest could be well protected. A significant part of the H.P.R.A. is devoted to ensuring that purchasers or potential purchasers will be well-informed of their rights and of the interests and liabilities they assume in purchasing a condominium unit. Obviously the purchasers cannot reasonably expect to receive their interests without paying for them or arranging for financing. Where an independent construction loan is necessary, it is a relatively small task to require the mortgagee to obtain subordination agreements from the purchasers as a condition of advancing the funds for construction. The burden cast upon the lending institution is light in comparison to the obvious virtue of this procedure in making clear to the unit purchaser his position. Undoubtedly this procedure would have been followed had State Savings hired an attorney to draw up the mortgage and advised him of the existing contracts of sale. It would be unconscionable for a lending institution to assume that it could ignore preexisting contract rights. The additional step of obtaining subordination agreements is consonant with the legislature's desire to protect the purchasers and to enable them to keep informed as to their rights and obligations. . . .

[Editors' Note: The court rejected the argument that the recording of the declaration prevented a mechanic's lien from attaching to the interests of the unit purchasers, holding that the unit purchasers took their interests subject to valid mechanic's and materialman's lien claims.]

GLENVIEW STATE BANK V. SHYMAN

Appellate Court of Illinois, First District, 1986
146 Ill.App.3d 136, 100 Ill.Dec. 13, 496 N.E.2d 1078

JUSTICE JIGANTI delivered the opinion of the court. This is an appeal by Glenview State Bank . . . from a trial court order finding that the interest of Leon Shyman . . . in condominium Unit A of Lakeshore Terrace has priority over two construction loan mortgages executed subsequent to the conveyance of Unit A, but recorded before the recordation of the deed as to Unit A. Whether the trial court erred in finding that Shyman's interest is free and clear of Glenview State Bank's claim of priority depends upon whether Glenview State Bank had notice of Shyman's interest at the time it executed the mortgages.

This action arose when Glenview State Bank filed a complaint to foreclose two mortgages on Lakeshore Terrace, Inc. Lakeshore Terrace was the mortgagor and the proceeds of the loan were to be used for the construction of the condominiums within the Lakeshore Terrace development. The mortgages were executed on March 28, 1981, and August 25, 1981, and were recorded on April 20, 1981, and August 31, 1981, respectively. In response to Glenview State Bank's complaint Shyman filed an answer and counterclaim in which he argued that Glenview State Bank had knowledge of his previously acquired interest in Unit A. This issue raised by the counterclaim was resolved by a bench trial.

At trial Shyman testified that in November of 1980 he signed a contract to purchase Unit R from Lakeshore Terrace. Thereafter Shyman was informed that Unit R was not available but that he could choose from one of the other condominium units. Shyman chose Unit A. However, that unit was also tentatively under agreement to be purchased. Nevertheless, Shyman testified that he and James Howard, president and developer of Lakeshore Terrace, orally agreed that if Unit A became available, and if Shyman contracted for Unit F and paid for Unit F, Shyman would be able to obtain Unit A. Although the parties entered into a contract for Unit F, no contract existed with respect to Unit A. It is important to note that the contract for Unit F contained a rider which provided that if the seller conveyed a unit prior to substantial completion, the title to that unit would be subject to the construction loan mortgage. This rider was also in the contracts used with regard to other units that had been sold before substantial completion.

In February of 1981 Shyman tendered the agreed-upon purchase price for Unit F and in return received a receipt which acknowledged the amount paid and recited that Units A through F could be selected at a later date. Soon thereafter Unit A was in fact conveyed to Shyman. The deed for Unit A was dated January 30, 1981, and was recorded on November 18, 1982, one year and three months after the mortgages. After the condominium unit was completed Shyman took possession of Unit A and began renting that unit.

With regard to the loans issued by Glenview State Bank, it was the opinion of Shyman's expert that because Glenview State Bank had knowledge that other condominium units had been presold the bank had inquiry notice of Shyman's interest in Unit A. Shyman argued that this inquiry notice would charge Glenview State Bank with notice of all facts that a diligent investigation or inquiry would have revealed and that in this case the investigation would have revealed Shyman's interest in Unit A. This also was the rationale underlying the trial court's decision. We disagree, however, that the evidence supports a finding that Glenview State Bank was put on notice of any prior interest in Unit A.

The contention in this case is that Glenview State Bank must be charged with inquiry notice of the prior unrecorded conveyance of Unit A. A person will be charged with notice when that person has knowledge of facts or circumstances that would cause a person of prudence to make further inquiry. If that person does not investigate further he or she will be charged with notice of any facts that may have been discovered by the inquiry. *Bryant v. Lakeside Galleries, Inc.* (1949), 402 Ill. 466, 478, 84 N.E.2d 412; *Burnex Oil Co. v. Floyd* (1969), 106 Ill.App.2d 16, 24, 245 N.E.2d 539.

In this case there was no documentation available to Glenview State Bank that would have placed it on notice that some interest in Unit A was affected. Although there were presale contracts pertaining to other units of Lakeshore Terrace of which Glenview State Bank had knowledge, no contract existed with regard to Unit A. Moreover, these other contracts made no reference to Unit A or to any fact that would have caused Glenview State Bank to inquire further into any potential interest in Unit A. On the contrary, these contracts would have caused one to believe that no further investigation was required as the rider specifically states that if the seller conveyed any of the units prior to substantial completion, as was done in this case, those units would be subject to the construction loan mortgages. We believe that Glenview State Bank had a right to rely on this provision and was under no duty to contact each presale purchaser to ascertain whether the terms of the contracts had been altered. To conclude otherwise would place an undue burden of inquiry on prospective purchasers and mortgagees. Consequently, we believe that the trial court's finding that Glenview State Bank had notice was against the manifest weight of the evidence and therefore must be reversed. . . .

For the foregoing reasons the order of the trial court declaring Shyman to be the owner in fee simple of Unit A free and clear of any claims of priority of Glenview State Bank as mortgagee is reversed. . . .

NOTES

1.   Kauaian *and* Shyman *compared.* Are *Kauaian* and *Shyman* consistent? Do you believe the appellate court in *Shyman* was correct to reverse the trial court's determination that the construction lender was on inquiry notice of the unit purchaser's interest? Do you suppose the *Kauaian* mortgagee had a greater degree of knowledge than its *Shyman* counterpart? See 2 Nelson, Whitman, Burkhart & Freyermuth, Real Estate Finance Law § 13.3 (6th ed., Practitioner Series 2014).

2.   *Use of subordination clauses in sales contracts.* In light of the *Kauaian* holding about priorities as between contract purchasers and construction lenders, would you advise construction lender-clients to insist that developers insert subordination clauses in their pre-construction sales contracts? How likely is it that the average unit buyer will understand the significance of the clause? How specific must the language of the clause be? Cf. Handy v. Gordon, 65 Cal.2d 578, 55 Cal.Rptr. 769, 422 P.2d 329 (1967), discussed in Chapter Nine, Section C, supra.

Consider the following subordination clause in a condominium purchase agreement:

> Purchaser agrees that the provisions of this Agreement are and shall be subject and subordinate to the lien of any mortgages heretofore or hereafter made and any payments or expenses already made or incurred or which hereafter may be made or incurred pursuant to the terms thereof . . . or to protect the security thereof, to the full extent, without the execution of any further legal documents by Purchaser.

Purchase Agreement for Seaview Estates Condominium ¶ 26(b), 1 Patrick J. Rohan & Melvin A. Reskin, Condominium Law and Practice—Forms, Appendix C-19. Does this pass the *Handy* test?

How do you think the *Shyman* court would have ruled if the construction mortgagee had conceded that it possessed the requisite knowledge and the purchaser had actually executed a purchase agreement on Unit A? Would it have used the subordination language in the agreement to find in favor of the construction lender? Would it have been justified in doing so? Why does the *Kauaian* court suggest that it would be unconscionable for a lending institution to assume that it can ignore pre-existing contract rights of unit purchasers, but that it is not unconscionable for mechanic's lienors to do so?

3. *Kauaian—subsequent history.* The *Kauaian* case returned to the Hawaii Supreme Court twelve years later. Construing the construction loan mortgage, which stated that it was "subject to" the condominium declaration, the court held that State Savings's priority was inferior to the equitable liens of the unit purchasers who signed their contracts after the construction mortgage was recorded as well as before. State Sav. & Loan Ass'n v. Kauaian Dev. Co., 62 Hawaii 188, 613 P.2d 1315 (1980).

4. *Washington approach.* The courts of Washington state have been unwilling to adopt the concept of equitable conversion in real estate sales contracts; see Ashford v. Reese, 132 Wash. 649, 233 P. 29 (1925). However, they have held, for purposes of the attachment of a judgment lien to the purchaser's interest, that it is indeed an "interest in real property." See Cascade Sec. Bank v. Butler, 88 Wash.2d 777, 567 P.2d 631 (1977). How should all of this affect priorities as between a construction loan deed of trust and an earlier purchaser's rights under a contract of sale? See Nelson v. Great Northwest Fed. Sav. & Loan Ass'n, 37 Wash.App. 316, 679 P.2d 953 (1984), holding the purchaser inferior despite the absence of any subordination language in the contract. The court simply held that the contract created no rights to the real estate.

5. *Post-closing foreclosure of construction mortgage.* Suppose the construction loan goes into default and foreclosure occurs after title to some units has passed to individual purchasers. Will their percentage interests in the common areas be protected from foreclosure? See FHA Model Act § 9. Even if so, can the lender foreclose on the percentage of the common areas attributable to unsold units? If it does, can the buyer at the foreclosure sale convert the unsold units into rental units? Can the buyer convert the recreational facilities to community-wide or even city-wide use? Must the buyer permit the owners' association to manage the recreational facilities? [Note that if the buyer has purchased enough unsold units, the buyer may well be able to control the association, and even to amend the bylaws if desired.] Can the purchasers of the early units guard against any of these eventualities?

6. *Escrow of earnest money.* A common method of protecting purchasers against loss of their earnest money deposits is to require the developer to hold them in escrow until construction is completed and the units are conveyed to their purchasers. This has long been an FHA requirement, and many "second-generation" statutes also require it. See, e.g., Fla. Stat. Ann. § 718.202; UCA § 4–110.

D. OPERATING THE COMMON INTEREST COMMUNITY

1. FINANCING COMMUNITY OPERATIONS

In the public sector, most municipalities depend on the ability to levy taxes and assessments against real estate as needed to fund public services and improvements. Common interest communities provide a private sector analogue; to be viable, common interest communities require efficient and enforceable assessment mechanisms sufficient to fund the maintenance of common facilities. Ever since the New York Court of Appeals upheld the enforcement of an assessment covenant in Neponsit Property Owners' Ass'n, Inc. v. Emigrant Indus. Sav. Bank, 278 N.Y. 248, 15 N.E.2d 793 (1938), the ability of a common interest community to provide for and collect assessments for common facilities has been well-accepted.

Accordingly, the declaration creating a common interest community typically establishes the initial and/or maximum amounts of assessments, procedures for increasing assessments or levying special assessments, the allocation of reserves for future capital needs, and mechanisms to facilitate the ability of the owners association to collect unpaid assessments. In the typical declaration, these mechanisms may include fines or the accrual of interest upon overdue assessments, as well as a lien in favor of the owners association on any assessed lot for which assessments remain unpaid. The foreclosure of such a lien, and the subsequent sale of the assessed parcel with the application of sale proceeds to satisfy the unpaid assessments, provides the association (at least theoretically) with the fiscal strength to satisfy its responsibilities to provide services and maintain common facilities.

Nevertheless, collection of unpaid assessments (particularly through foreclosure) presents owners associations with a number of practical and legal problems. The following case and notes address some of these problems, including: whether the association can foreclose its lien through private sale or must instead use judicial foreclosure; whether the sale is subject to standards of commercial reasonableness; how significant a default must exist before a foreclosure can proceed; and the priority of the association's lien vis-à-vis a mortgage lien against the assessed lot.

WILL V. MILL CONDOMINIUM OWNERS' ASSOCIATION

Supreme Court of Vermont, 2004
176 Vt. 380, 848 A.2d 336

AMESTOY, C.J. . . . Appellant owned a residential condominium unit at The Mill Condominiums in Ludlow, Vermont. After appellant failed to pay her condominium dues over a period of time, the officers of the Mill Condominium Owners' Association instructed attorney Martin Nitka to foreclose on the property. Attorney Nitka thereafter commenced a nonjudicial foreclosure pursuant to 27A V.S.A. § 3–116. Appellant had notice of the foreclosure sale and discussed the matter with attorney Nitka. She informed him that she would wire him the unpaid dues and asked him to postpone the sale scheduled for July 12, 2001, to a later time. Appellant's recollection of the discussion was that the sale would not take place if she wired the money to attorney Nitka's account by the close of the business day, July 16. According to attorney Nitka, he agreed to delay the sale only until July 13, but after the telephone conversation with appellant realized that he had other commitments, and moved the sale to July 16, 2001. At 10:00 a.m. on July 16, 2001, attorney Nitka proceeded with the auction of appellant's condominium. Appellant's wire transfer of funds sufficient to cover the dues, fees, and costs owed arrived at 11:00 a.m. By that time, the property had been sold to defendants Allen and Linda Seiple for $3510.10, the amount necessary to pay the delinquent dues, attorney's fees, and the costs of foreclosure. The trial court found that, at the time of the sale, attorney Nitka and the Seiples apparently believed that the unit was subject to a mortgage of $45,000. It was later determined that the mortgage had been earlier discharged. The trial court found that the fair market value of the condominium at the time of sale was approximately $70,000. Attorney Nitka delivered the deed to the Seiples on August 31, 2001.

In October 2001, appellant filed a complaint seeking a declaratory judgment setting aside the nonjudicial foreclosure. In December 2001, after trial, the court entered judgment for defendants on the record. . . .

[Appellant] claims that the condominium association and attorney Nitka breached their duties when they failed to maximize the sale price of the condominium. The trial court rejected this claim after concluding that there is no statutory requirement to conduct the sale in a commercially reasonable manner, and that neither the condominium association, nor Nitka, owed appellant a fiduciary duty. Nevertheless, appellant argues that 12 V.S.A. § 4532(g) imposes on the mortgagee an affirmative duty to conduct the nonjudicial sale in a commercially reasonable manner or in such a manner as to maximize the sales price of such property.

We note at the outset that although appellant has predicated her argument on theories of "fiduciary duty" and "commercial reasonableness," it is unnecessary to decide in the case the extent to which either theory might be applicable to a mortgagee utilizing the nonjudicial foreclosure procedures of 12 V.S.A. § 4352(g). Appellees' resort to the nonjudicial foreclosure statute arises not as a result of a mortgagor-mortgagee relationship—but rather because of the provisions of the Uniform Common Interest Ownership Act, 27A V.S.A. §§ 1–101–4–120 (UCIOA), which provides a statutory right to the Condominium Association to institute a nonjudicial foreclosure proceeding for nonpayment of condominium dues. Thus, the extent of the duty owed by the Condominium Association and its agent to the appellant is first established by discerning the obligations and rights of the parties under the Act.

The Association's commencement of a nonjudicial foreclosure was made pursuant to 27A V.S.A. § 3–116(i), which states, "The association's lien may be foreclosed pursuant to section 4531a of Title 12 in which case the association shall notify all the lienholders of the affected unit of its action."

The official comment to § 3–116 reveals the Legislature's intent to provide condominium associations with adequate mechanisms to collect unpaid dues while offering alternatives to the radical remedy of foreclosure. Thus, the comment notes that subsection (1) "makes clear that the association may have remedies short of foreclosure of its lien that can be used to collect unpaid assessments. The association, for example, might bring an action in debt or breach of contract against a recalcitrant unit owner rather than resorting to foreclosure." On the other hand, the Legislature reserves what it considers the more expeditious procedures for foreclosure on units belonging to a cooperative, since in these associations assessments are used to pay each unit's share of the common mortgage, and nonpayment may force the whole community into default. Thus, the statute allows for the treatment of units in cooperatives as personal property instead of realty, so that they can be foreclosed under the generally less expensive and faster procedure provided for under Article 9 of the Uniform Commercial Code (U.C.C.). The comment points out that condominium communities are generally not burdened by a substantial underlying mortgage and therefore,

> failure to pay assessments on time will have less serious consequences for the association than in the case of cooperatives. The section provides that the association lien in a condominium or planned community is to be foreclosed according to the rules generally applicable to real estate mortgages ... rather than setting out a special faster method of foreclosure in the statute. . . .

Although the rules "generally applicable to real estate mortgages" do not impose a commercial reasonableness standard on foreclosure sales, the UCIOA does provide for this additional layer of protection. Section 1–113 of the UCIOA states that "[e]very contract or duty governed by this title imposes an obligation of good faith on all parties in its performance or enforcement." The official comment explains:

> This section sets forth a basic principle running throughout this Act: in transactions involving common interest communities, good faith is required in the performance and enforcement of all agreements and duties. Good faith, as used in this Act, means

observance of two standards: "honesty in fact," and observance of reasonable standards of fair dealing. . . .

The U.C.C. and Uniform Simplification of Land Transfers Act sections alluded to in the official comment define and refer to the observance of "reasonable commercial standards of fair dealing in the trade." 9A V.S.A. § 2–103(1)(b) (U.C.C.). Hence, the official comment to § 1–113 expresses in unequivocal terms the Legislature's intent to import the commercial reasonableness standard into the UCIOA. . . .

The "commercial reasonableness" standard is well defined in Vermont. A secured party's disposition of collateral is governed by Part 6 of Article 9 of Vermont's Uniform Commercial Code. Title 9A, § 9–610(b) imposes a positive duty on the secured party to act in a commercially reasonable manner in every aspect of the disposition of collateral. 9A V.S.A. § 9–610(b). . . .

The commercial reasonableness of a sale must be determined on a case-by-case basis. *Fed. Fin. Co. v. Papadopoulos,* 168 Vt. 621, 623, 721 A.2d 501, 503 (1998) (mem.). The secured party bears the burden "to prove that the disposition of collateral was commercially reasonable." *Id.* . . .

The evidence in the record, however, does not support summary judgment under this standard; rather, it supports a finding that, as a matter of law, the sale did not conform with the requirements of good faith and commercial reasonableness set forth by § 1–113 of the UCIOA. First, the disparity between the condominium's sale price and its fair market value, although not dispositive, must be taken into account in the assessment of the reasonableness of the sale. See *Papadopoulos,* 168 Vt. at 623, 721 A.2d at 503. In this case the discrepancy suggests that no efforts were made to attain the best price for the unit. The trial court found the fair market value of the condominium to be "approximately $70,000." Although the court observed that attorney Nitka and the Seiples apparently thought that the property was subject to an undischarged $45,000 mortgage, the purchase price—even under such an assumption— was less than 15% of the value found by the trial court.

In addition, this Court has found that, in private sales, the seller's exclusive reliance on one bid may be a factor against a finding of reasonableness. *Id.* Although this was a public sale, it weighs against such a finding in this case as well, considering the alleged statement from Mr. Nitka to Mr. Seiple informing him that the minimum acceptable bid for this property would be $3510.50. Although there is no suggestion that this was done in bad faith, giving this information to the only bidder was certainly not a way to maximize the value of the collateral; rather, it was an assurance that the condominium would be sold for exactly that low amount.

Summary judgment is vacated, and the case remanded to the trial court for entry of judgment voiding foreclosure sale of appellant's condominium unit.

NOTES

1. *The scope of the assessment lien.* Under some first-generation legislation, it was often unclear that an association's lien could cover matters other than common expenses. See, e.g., FHA Model Act § 23; Elbadramany v. Oceans Seven Condo. Ass'n, Inc., 461 So.2d 1001 (Fla. Ct. App. 1984) (fine for parking boat in condominium parking lot could not be a lien because it was not a common expense). By contrast, the UCA and UCIOA expressly provide that the association's lien covers fees, charges, late charges, fines, and interest unless the declaration provides otherwise. UCA § 3–116, UCIOA § 3–116.

2. *Controversy over lien foreclosure.* There have been numerous stories in the popular media concerning alleged abuses of the lien foreclosure process. Most commonly, owners complained of foreclosures for relatively minor amounts, or for charges such as uncollected fines rather than the usual unpaid monthly assessments. See Gemma Giantosmasi, A Balancing Act: The Foreclosure Power of Homeowners' Associations, 72 Ford. L. Rev. 2503 (2004). In an attempt to respond to these concerns, the 2008 amendments to UCIOA articulated clearer limits on an association's ability to enforce its lien via foreclosure. First, the association may not begin a foreclosure unless the owner owes a sum equal to at least three months of regularly scheduled common expense assessments, the owner has failed to accept or comply with a payment plan offered by the association, and the association board has voted to commence foreclosure against the specific unit in question. UCIOA § 3–116(n). Second, nonjudicial foreclosure is permissible only when the unpaid sums include past due assessments; if the unpaid sums consist of fines or sums other than assessments, the association cannot foreclose without first obtaining a judgment for those sums and a judgment lien against the unit. UCIOA § 3–116(p). Finally, UCIOA now expressly resolves the interpretive question addressed in *Will*, requiring that any sale foreclosing an association's lien must be commercially reasonable in all respects, "including the method, advertising, time, place and terms." UCIOA § 3–116(q). These changes were inspired by similar limitations previously imposed by individual state legislatures. See, e.g., Ariz. Rev. Stat. Ann. § 33–1807(A) (requiring judicial process for enforcement as to fines and penalties); Cal. Civ. Code § 5720(b) (prohibiting association from foreclosing for unpaid assessment balance less than $1,800); Fla. Stat. Ann. § 720.305 (lien not available for fines less than $1,000).

An argument can be made that assessment liens are to owners associations what real estate tax liens are to government entities. Most tax lien foreclosure systems allow long redemption periods for delinquent taxpayers. Should such long periods be available to defaulting unit owners? Is it one thing to provide long redemption periods for delinquent real estate taxes (where the costs can be spread over the entire taxpaying public) and yet another to do so in common interest communities (where the shortfall may have to be borne by increased assessments on relatively few owners)?

3.   *Commercial reasonableness and advertisement.* As you learned in Chapter Six, mortgage law typically has not required a foreclosing mortgagee to conduct a commercially reasonable sale. As a result, foreclosure sales often involve little or no advertising beyond the legal notices required by most foreclosure statutes. The *Will* decision concluded that under Vermont's version of UCIOA, the association's duty of good faith and fair dealing effectively required the association to conduct its foreclosure sale in a commercially reasonable manner. Did the court inappropriately conflate "good faith" and "commercial reasonableness"?

As indicated in note 2, the 2014 amendments to UCIOA explicitly incorporate a requirement of commercial reasonableness for sales to enforce association liens. In the context of personal property foreclosure sales—for which Article 9 provides a comparable "commercial reasonableness" requirement in U.C.C. § 9–610(b)—courts have sometimes looked dimly upon a secured party that conducted a foreclosure sale involving minimal advertisement. For example, in Contrail Leasing Partners, Ltd. v. Consolidated Airways, Inc., 742 F.2d 1095 (7th Cir. 1984), the court held that a secured party that sold a corporate jet after publishing only one small advertisement failed to meet the "commercially reasonable" standard. The court suggested that the secured party's advertisement should have been more conspicuous and should have been placed in additional trade publications to expose the collateral to additional potential buyers.

Because the term "commercially reasonable" has long been incorporated within the U.C.C., to what extent should U.C.C. case law interpreting the term influence the evaluation of foreclosure sales involving association liens? What implications would this have for associations in collecting unpaid assessments? What advertisement or marketing should an association have to undertake prior to conducting a foreclosure sale?

4.   *Personal liability for assessments.* A unit owner has more to fear from an unpaid assessment than loss of his or her unit through foreclosure of the association lien. Each unit owner is also *personally liable* for assessments that are attributable to his or her period of ownership. See UCA § 3–116(f) and comment 3; UCIOA § 3–116(g) (2008). Moreover, where a unit is owned by more than one person, there often is joint and several liability for the assessment against the unit. See Chattahoochee Chase Condo. Ass'n v. Ruben, 221 Ga.App. 724, 472 S.E.2d 520 (1996) (unit owner with only a one percent interest in the unit held jointly and severally liable for the entire assessment against the unit). This personal liability can be discharged, however, if the unit owner goes through bankruptcy; this has proven to be a problem for some associations. See James L. Winokur, Critical Assessment: The Financial Role of Community Associations, 38 Santa Clara L. Rev. 1135 (1998).

5.   *Assessment lien priority vs. mortgage liens.* Under most first-generation condominium statutes, first mortgage liens on a unit have priority

over the association's lien for unpaid assessments against that unit. FHA Model Act § 23(a); Ariz. Rev. Stat. § 33–1807(B); N.Y. Real Prop. Law § 339z. Is this appropriate, given that liens for unpaid real estate taxes are senior to all mortgage liens? By contrast, both the UCA and UCIOA provide that an association's assessment lien has priority over an otherwise-prior mortgage on the assessed unit to the extent of unpaid assessments due during the six months immediately prior to the lien enforcement proceeding (and attorneys' fees and costs incurred by the association in foreclosing its lien). See UCA § 3–116; UCIOA § 3–116(b), (c). Professor Winokur explains the rationale for this approach:

> In addition to giving community associations a share—albeit a limited share—of the sale proceeds when residences in common interest communities are foreclosed, the more important consequence of limited "super-priority" for a portion of association assessment defaults may be in providing the association much needed leverage in getting the property more quickly into foreclosure, leading to purchase by a solvent owner (often the mortgagee), or by encouraging the senior mortgagee to pay assessments it might not technically be obligated to pay in order to gain control over the timing and mode of foreclosure. . . .

Winokur, supra note 4, at 1135. If the association forecloses its assessment lien, and the "first" mortgagee does not step forward and pay off the priority portion of the association's lien prior to the association's sale, does the sale extinguish the first mortgage lien? Does it matter whether the association foreclosed its lien in a judicial proceeding rather than a nonjudicial proceeding?

SFR INVESTMENTS POOL 1, LLC v. U.S. BANK, N.A.

Supreme Court of Nevada, 2014
130 Nev. 742, 334 P.3d 408

PICKERING, J. NRS 116.3116 gives a homeowners' association (HOA) a superpriority lien on an individual homeowner's property for up to nine months of unpaid HOA dues. With limited exceptions, this lien is "prior to all other liens and encumbrances" on the homeowner's property, even a first deed of trust recorded before the dues became delinquent. NRS 116.3116(2). We must decide whether this is a true priority lien such that its foreclosure extinguishes a first deed of trust on the property and, if so, whether it can be foreclosed nonjudicially. We answer both questions in the affirmative and therefore reverse. . . .

This dispute involves a residence located in a common-interest community known as Southern Highlands. The property was subject to Covenants, Conditions, and Restrictions (CC & Rs) recorded in 2000. In 2007 it was further encumbered by a note and deed of trust in favor of, via assignment, respondent U.S. Bank, N.A. By 2010, the former homeowners, who are not parties to this case, had fallen delinquent on their Southern

Highlands Community Association (SHHOA) dues and also defaulted on their obligations to U.S. Bank. Separately, SHHOA and U.S. Bank each initiated nonjudicial foreclosure proceedings.

Appellant SFR Investments Pool 1, LLC (SFR) purchased the property at the SHHOA's trustee's sale, which took place on September 5, 2012. SFR received and recorded a trustee's deed reciting compliance with all applicable notice requirements. In the meantime, the trustee's sale on U.S. Bank's deed of trust had been postponed to December 19, 2012. Days before then, SFR filed an action to quiet title and enjoin the sale. SFR alleged that the SHHOA trustee's deed extinguished U.S. Bank's deed of trust and vested clear title in SFR, leaving U.S. Bank nothing to foreclose.

. . . Ultimately, the district court denied SFR's motion for a preliminary injunction and granted U.S. Bank's countermotion to dismiss. It held that an HOA must proceed judicially to validly foreclose its superpriority lien. Since SHHOA foreclosed nonjudicially, the district court reasoned, U.S. Bank's first deed of trust survived the SHHOA trustee's sale and was senior to the trustee's deed SFR received. . . .

The HOA lien statute, NRS 116.3116, is a creature of the Uniform Common Interest Ownership Act of 1982, § 3–116, 7 U.L.A., part II 121–24 (2009) (amended 1994, 2008) (UCIOA), which Nevada adopted in 1991, 1991 Nev. Stat., ch. 245, § 1–128, at 535–79, and codified as NRS Chapter 116. . . .

NRS 116.3116(1) gives an HOA a lien on its homeowners' residences—the UCIOA calls them "units," see NRS 116.093—"for any construction penalty that is imposed against the unit's owner . . ., any assessment levied against that unit or any fines imposed against the unit's owner from the time the construction penalty, assessment or fine becomes due." NRS 116.3116(2) elevates the priority of the HOA lien over other liens. It states that the HOA's lien is "prior to all other liens and encumbrances on a unit" except for:

> (a) Liens and encumbrances recorded before the recordation of the declaration [creating the common-interest community] . . .;

> (b) A *first security interest on the unit recorded before the date on which the assessment sought to be enforced became delinquent* . . .; and

> (c) Liens for real estate taxes and other governmental assessments or charges against the unit or cooperative.

NRS 116.3116(2) (emphasis added). If subsection 2 ended there, a first deed of trust would have complete priority over an HOA lien. But it goes on to carve out a partial exception to subparagraph (2)(b)'s exception for first security interests:

The [HOA] lien is also prior to all security interests described in paragraph (b) to the extent of any [maintenance and nuisance-abatement] charges incurred by the association on a unit pursuant to NRS 116.310312 and *to the extent of the assessments for common expenses* [i.e., HOA dues] based on the periodic budget adopted by the association pursuant to NRS 116.3115 which would have become due in the absence of acceleration during the 9 months immediately preceding institution of an action to enforce the lien, unless federal regulations adopted by the Federal Home Loan Mortgage Corporation or the Federal National Mortgage Association require a shorter period of priority for the lien. . . . *This subsection does not affect* the priority of mechanics' or materialmen's liens, or *the priority of liens for other assessments made by the association.*

NRS 116.3116(2) (emphases added).

As to first deeds of trust, NRS 116.3116(2) thus splits an HOA lien into two pieces, a superpriority piece and a subpriority piece. The superpriority piece, consisting of the last nine months of unpaid HOA dues and maintenance and nuisance-abatement charges, is "prior to" a first deed of trust. The subpriority piece, consisting of all other HOA fees or assessments, is subordinate to a first deed of trust. . . .

U.S. Bank maintains that NRS 116.3116(2) merely creates a payment priority as between the HOA and the beneficiary of the first deed of trust. If so, then the dues and maintenance and nuisance-abatement piece of the HOA lien does not acquire superpriority status until the beneficiary of the first deed of trust forecloses, at which point, to obtain clear, insurable title, the foreclosure-sale buyer would have to pay off that piece of the HOA lien. But if the superpriority piece is a true priority lien, then it is senior to the first deed of trust. As such, it can be foreclosed and its foreclosure will extinguish the first deed of trust. See, e.g., Restatement (Third) of Prop.: Mortgages § 7.1 (1997) ("A valid foreclosure of a mortgage terminates all interests in the foreclosed real estate that are junior to the mortgage being foreclosed and whose holders are properly joined or notified under applicable law."). . . .

Textually, NRS 116.3116 supports the . . . view that it establishes a true priority lien. NRS 116.3116(2) does not speak in terms of payment priorities. It states that the HOA "lien . . . is *prior to*" other liens and encumbrances "except . . . [a] first security interest," then adds that, "The lien is *also prior to* [first] security interests" to the extent of nine months of unpaid HOA dues and maintenance and nuisance-abatement charges. *Ibid.* (emphases added). "Prior" refers to the lien, not payment or proceeds, and is used the same way in both sentences, a point the phrase "*also* prior to" drives home. And "priority lien" and "prior lien" mean the same thing, according to *Black's Law Dictionary* 1008 (9th ed.2009): "A lien that is superior to one or more other liens on the same property, usu. because it was perfected first."

The official comments to UCIOA § 3–116 confirm its text. Payment priority proponents insist that the statute cannot mean what it says because the result—a split lien, a piece of which has priority over a first deed of trust—is unprecedented. But the official comments to UCIOA § 3–116 forthrightly acknowledge that the split-lien approach represents a "significant departure from existing practice." 1982 UCIOA § 3–116 cmt. 1; 1994 & 2008 UCIOA § 3–116 cmt. 2. It is a specially devised mechanism designed to "strike[ ] an equitable balance between the need to enforce collection of unpaid assessments and the obvious necessity for protecting the priority of the security interests of lenders." *Id.* The comments continue: "As a practical matter, secured lenders will most likely pay the 6 [in Nevada, nine] months' assessments demanded by the association rather than having the association foreclose on the unit." *Id.* (emphasis added). If the superpriority piece of the HOA lien just established a payment priority, the reference to a first security holder paying off the superpriority piece of the lien to stave off foreclosure would make no sense.

"An official comment written by the drafters of a statute and available to a legislature before the statute is enacted has considerable weight as an aid to statutory construction." *Acierno v. Worthy Bros. Pipeline Corp.*, 656 A.2d 1085, 1090 (Del.1995). The comments to the 1982 UCIOA were available to the 1991 Legislature when it enacted NRS Chapter 116. Even though the comments emphasize that the split-lien approach is "[a] significant departure from existing practice," 1982 UCIOA § 3–116 cmt. 1, the Legislature enacted NRS 116.3116(2) with UCIOA § 3–116's superpriority provision intact. From this it follows that, however unconventional, the superpriority piece of the HOA lien carries true priority over a first deed of trust.

The Uniform Law Commission (ULC) has established a Joint Editorial Board for Uniform Real Property Acts (JEB), made up of members from the ULC; the ABA Section of Real Property, Probate and Trust Law; and the American College of Real Estate Lawyers, which "is responsible for monitoring all uniform real property acts," of which the UCIOA is one. The JEB's 2013 report entitled, The Six-Month "Limited Priority Lien" for Association Fees Under the Uniform Common Interest Ownership Act, also supports that § 3–116(b) establishes a true priority lien. Addressing the recent foreclosure crisis and the incentives the crisis created for first security holders to strategically delay foreclosure, this report canvasses the case law construing the UCIOA's superpriority lien. It endorses the decision in *Summerhill Village Homeowners Ass'n v. Roughley*, 289 P.3d 645, 647–48 (2012), which, addressing a statute using the same superpriority language as NRS 116.3116(2), holds that an HOA's judicial foreclosure of the superpriority piece of its lien extinguished the first deed of trust. JEB, The Six-Month "Limited Priority Lien," at 8–9. . . .

The comments liken the HOA lien to "other inchoate liens such as real estate taxes and mechanics liens." 1994 & 2008 UCIOA § 3–116 cmt. 1. An HOA's "sources of revenues are usually limited to common assessments." JEB, The Six-Month "Limited Priority Lien," at 4. This makes an HOA's ability to foreclose on the unpaid dues portion of its lien essential for common-interest communities. *Id.* at 1–2. Otherwise, when a homeowner walks away from the property and the first deed of trust holder delays foreclosure, the HOA has to "either increase the assessment burden on the remaining unit/parcel owners or reduce the services the association provides (e.g., by deferring maintenance on common amenities)." *Id.* at 5–6. To avoid having the community subsidize first security holders who delay foreclosure, whether strategically or for some other reason, UCIOA § 3–116 creates a true superpriority lien:

> A foreclosure sale of the association's lien (whether judicial or nonjudicial) is governed by the principles generally applicable to lien foreclosure sales, i.e., a foreclosure sale of a lien entitled to priority extinguishes that lien and any subordinate liens, transferring those liens to the sale proceeds. Nothing in the Uniform Laws establishes (or was intended to establish) a contrary result.

Id. at 9 (footnotes omitted).

U.S. Bank's final objection is that it makes little sense and is unfair to allow a relatively nominal lien—nine months of HOA dues—to extinguish a first deed of trust securing hundreds of thousands of dollars of debt. But as a junior lienholder, U.S. Bank could have paid off the SHHOA lien to avert loss of its security; it also could have established an escrow for SHHOA assessments to avoid having to use its own funds to pay delinquent dues. 1982 UCIOA § 3116 cmt. 1; 1994 & 2008 UCIOA § 3–116 cmt. 2. The inequity U.S. Bank decries is thus of its own making and not a reason to give NRS 116.3116(2) a singular reading at odds with its text and the interpretation given it by the authors and editors of the UCIOA. . . .

Since NRS 116.3116(2) establishes a true superpriority lien, the next question we must decide is whether the lien may be foreclosed nonjudicially or requires judicial foreclosure. NRS Chapter 116 answers this question directly: An HOA may foreclose its lien by nonjudicial foreclosure sale. Thus, NRS 116.3116(1) defines what an HOA lien covers, while NRS 116.31162(1) states that "in a planned community"—a "planned community" is any type of "common-interest community that is not a condominium or a cooperative," NRS 116.075—"the association may foreclose its lien by sale." To "foreclose [a] lien by sale" under NRS 116.31162(1) encompasses an HOAs conducting a nonjudicial foreclosure sale. This is evident from the remainder of NRS 116.31162, which speaks to the statutory notices of delinquency, default and election to sell required of a nonjudicial foreclosure sale, and the sections that follow, NRS 116.31163 through NRS 116.31168, all of which concern the mechanics and requirements of nonjudicial foreclosure sales of HOA liens. The only limits Chapter 116 places on HOA lien foreclosure sales appear in NRS 116.31162(5) and (6), which restrict foreclosure of HOA liens for certain fines and penalties and liens on homes in Nevada's foreclosure mediation program (FMP). Given this statutory text, we cannot agree with our dissenting colleagues that NRS Chapter 116 requires judicial foreclosure of the superpriority piece of an HOA lien but authorizes nonjudicial foreclosure of everything else.

Together, NRS 116.3116(1) and NRS 116.31162 provide for the nonjudicial foreclosure of the whole of an HOA's lien, not just the subpriority piece of it. U.S. Bank and our dissenting colleagues do not come to terms with NRS 116.31162. Instead, they focus on a single phrase in NRS 116.3116(2) which defines the superpriority piece of the lien as comprising "assessments for common expenses . . . which would have become due in the absence of acceleration during the 9 months immediately preceding *institution of an action to enforce the lien*." (Emphasis added.) Not acknowledging that NRS 116.3116(2) only discusses lien priority, not foreclosure methods, they maintain that the phrase "institution of an action to enforce the lien" suggests a civil action, a lawsuit brought in a court of law. But the phrase is not so narrow that it excludes nonjudicial foreclosure proceedings. *Black's Law Dictionary* 869 (9th ed.2009) defines "institution" as "[t]he commencement of something, *such as* a civil or criminal action." (Emphasis added.) As *Black's* recognizes, "foreclosure" proceedings are "instituted" and include both "judicial foreclosure" and "nonjudicial foreclosure" methods. *Id.* at 719 (defining "foreclosure," "judicial foreclosure," and "nonjudicial" or "power-of-sale foreclosure"). And in the context of foreclosures, "action" appears to be commonly used in connection with nonjudicial as well as judicial foreclosures. *See In re Bonner Mall P'ship*, 2 F.3d 899, 902 (9th Cir.1993) (referring to a bank "commenc[ing] a nonjudical foreclosure action"); *Santiago v. BAC Home Loans Servicing, L.P.*, 20 F.Supp.2d 585, 589 (W.D.Tex.2014) (holding an assignee to be "an appropriate party to initiate a nonjudicial foreclosure action against the Property"). . . .

U.S. Bank and the dissent argue that judicial foreclosure should be required as a matter of policy because of the safeguards it offers—notice and an opportunity to be heard, court supervision of the sale, judicial review of the amount of the lien comprising the superpriority piece, and a one-year redemption period. See NRS 40.430.463; NRS 21.190–.210. But this argument assumes that requiring the superpriority piece of an HOA lien to be judicially foreclosed will actually afford such protections without need of further amendment to Chapter 116, and this is far from clear. To allow nonjudicial foreclosure of the subpriority piece, which is where the dissent would draw the judicial v. nonjudicial foreclosure line, produces the same difficulties for the homeowners and junior lienholders that are cited as policy reasons for requiring judicial foreclosure of the superpriority piece of the lien; the only difference is the benefit that would inure to first security holders under the dissent's interpretation of Chapter 116. Surely, if the Legislature intended such an unusual distinction, it would have said so explicitly, but it did not.

We recognize that "there has been considerable publicity across the country regarding alleged abuse in the foreclosure process when unit owners fail to pay sums due" their HOA, prompting amendments to the UCIOA that "propose [ ] new and considerable restrictions on the foreclosure process as it applies to common interest communities." Prefatory Note to the 2008 Amendments to the UCIOA, 7 U.L.A., part IB, at 225 (2009). But the choice of foreclosure method for HOA liens is the Legislature's, and the Nevada Legislature has written NRS Chapter 116 to allow nonjudicial foreclosure of HOA liens, subject to the special notice requirements and protections handcrafted by the Legislature in NRS 116.31162 through NRS 116.31168. Countervailing policy arguments exist in favor of allowing nonjudicial foreclosure, including that judicial foreclosure takes longer to accomplish, thereby delaying the common-interest community's receipt of needed HOA funds. The consequences of such delays can be "devastating to the community and the remaining residents," who must either make up the dues deficiencies, arguably unjustly enriching the delaying lender, or abandon amenities and maintenance, thereby impairing the value of their homes. JEB, The Six-Month "Limited Priority Lien," at 4–5. If revisions to the foreclosure methods provided for in NRS Chapter 116 are appropriate, they are for the Legislature to craft, not this court. . . .

U.S. Bank last argues that, even if NRS 116.3116(2) allows nonjudicial foreclosure of a superpriority lien, the mortgage savings clause in the Southern Highlands CC & Rs subordinated SSHOA's superpriority lien to the first deed of trust. The mortgage savings clause states that "no lien created under this Article 9 [governing nonpayment of assessments], nor the enforcement of any provision of this Declaration shall defeat or render invalid the rights of the beneficiary under any Recorded first deed of trust encumbering a Unit, made in good faith and for value." It also states that "[t]he lien of the assessments, including interest and costs, shall be subordinate to the lien of any first Mortgage upon the Unit."

NRS 116.1104 defeats this argument. It states that Chapter 116's "provisions may not be varied by agreement, and rights conferred by it may not be waived . . . [e]xcept as *expressly* provided in" Chapter 116. (Emphasis added.) "Nothing in [NRS] 116.3116 expressly provides for a waiver of the

HOA's right to a priority position for the HOA's super priority lien." The mortgage savings clause thus does not affect NRS 116.3116(2)'s application in this case. . . .

NRS 116.3116(2) gives an HOA a true superpriority lien, proper foreclosure of which will extinguish a first deed of trust. Because Chapter 116 permits nonjudicial foreclosure of HOA liens, and because SFR's complaint alleges that proper notices were sent and received, we reverse the district court's order of dismissal. In view of this holding, we vacate the order denying preliminary injunctive relief and remand for further proceedings consistent with this opinion.

[The opinion of Gibbons, C.J., concurring in part and dissenting in part, is omitted.]

NOTES

1. *Considering the implications of* SFR Investments *and the UCIOA assessment lien superpriority.* Under the first-generation common interest statutes, the association's lien is entirely subordinate to the lien of a first mortgage on the unit or lot. As a policy matter, one might justify such an approach by arguing that (a) the first mortgage lien often secures purchase money credit that enabled the owner to acquire the unit or lot, and (b) without having the assurance of first priority, institutional lenders might be reluctant to extend mortgage credit on common interest units or lots. According full priority to the first mortgagee, however, creates a significant risk to the association in "down" markets. For example, suppose that Smith purchases a unit in Shady Acres Condominiums in 2006 for a price of $250,000, using the proceeds of a $225,000 mortgage loan from Bank. Three years later, as a result of the collapse in land values, Smith's unit declines in value to only $175,000, at which point Smith defaults on both the mortgage and the payment of association dues. In such a down market, Bank may choose to delay implementing a foreclosure of its mortgage. If Bank purchases the unit in a foreclosure sale, Bank becomes liable for assessments that accrue following its purchase (by contrast, Bank is not personally liable for assessments that accrue before it acquires title at foreclosure). The Bank may not wish to pay the cost of assessments for a period in which Bank is "stuck" with title to a unit that it cannot sell for an acceptable price in a down market. Instead, Bank might choose to delay the foreclosure, hoping that the market will recover.

But the Bank's ostensibly reasonable choice to delay foreclosure may be financially devastating for the association. If Smith is not paying his assessments, the association can theoretically foreclose its lien and have Smith's unit sold. But because Smith's unit is worth less than the balance owed to Bank, no buyer will be willing to pay anything to take the unit subject to Bank's mortgage lien! In a down market such as those experienced in the late 2000s and early 2010s, the association's ability to foreclose is an empty threat. As a result, associations are left with a dilemma—maintain the association's existing budget by increasing assessments on the nondefaulting unit owners, or cut the association's budget (and the common area maintenance funded by the budget).

By contrast, by giving the association a priority for six months of unpaid assessments, UCA and UCIOA preserve the association's leverage, even in a down market. If the association's lien has a true priority, and its sale would thus extinguish the otherwise-first mortgage lien, the association can now conduct a foreclosure of its lien with confidence that buyers (who would receive clear title at the sale) will be prepared to pay an amount sufficient to satisfy at least the priority portion of the unpaid assessment balance. See generally Stewart E. Sterk, Maintaining Condominiums and Homeowner Associations: How Much of a Priority?, 93 Ind. L.J. 807 (2018).

The result in *SFR Investments* is consistent with the weight of authority in states that have adopted UCA or UCIOA (or that provide an association lien with comparable limited priority). See, e.g., Summerhill Village Homeowner Ass'n v. Roughley, 289 P.3d 645 (Wash. Ct. App. 2012); Chase Plaza Condo. Ass'n, Inc. v. JPMorgan Chase Bank, N.A., 98 A.3d 166 (D.C. 2014); Twenty Eleven, LLC v. Botelho, 127 A.3d 897 (R.I. 2015). Is the result unduly harsh to U.S. Bank? Should U.S. Bank and other mortgage lenders refrain from making mortgage loans in UCIOA states, or charge increased interest rates on common interest unit loans? Look at paragraphs 3 and 4 of the Fannie/Freddie Uniform Instrument (Appendix). What might U.S. Bank have done differently to protect itself against the risks posed by the association's superpriority lien?

Note that U.S. Bank could have avoided the extinguishment of its lien by tendering payment to the association of an amount equal to the "priority" portion of the unpaid assessments (the amount for which the association's lien has priority). If U.S. Bank had done so prior to the association's foreclosure, the association could still have proceeded with the foreclosure (as its lien also secures the nonpriority portion of the unpaid assessments), but then the sale would have delivered title subject to U.S. Bank's mortgage lien. See, e.g., Bank of America, N.A. v. SFR Investments Pool 1, LLC, 134 Nev. 604, 427 P.3d 113 (2018).

2.   *2014 amendments to UCIOA § 3–116.* In 2014, the Uniform Law Commission made a number of amendments to UCIOA § 3–116. These amendments clarified that § 3–116 did in fact create a "true" lien priority (effectively codifying the result in *SFR Investments*). They also clarified that this priority existed regardless of the method by which the association foreclosed its lien (again, confirming the result in *SFR Investments*). Finally, the amendments would permit an association to use forcible entry and detainer to recover possession of the defaulting owner's unit. This would permit the association to rent the unit to another occupant pending the association's foreclosure (or to condition the defaulting owner's continued occupancy on payment of the assessments).

3.   *12 U.S.C. § 4617(j)(3) and the federal foreclosure bar.* At least in the 9th Circuit, the impact of the UCIOA association lien superpriority has been blunted by recent litigation over the impact of 12 U.S.C. § 4617. This section

governs the Federal Housing Finance Agency, which has functioned since 2008 as the conservator for Fannie Mae and Freddie Mac. In § 4617(j)(3), this statute provides that "No property of the Agency [FHFA] shall be subject to levy, attachment, garnishment, foreclosure, or sale without the consent of the Agency, nor shall any involuntary lien attach to the property of the Agency." What is the impact, if any, of this section on an association's foreclosure sale of its common expense assessment lien?

Imagine that Smith owned a condominium unit in Las Vegas, and is more than two years in arrears in payment of unit assessments. The association commences a foreclosure, and notifies Wells Fargo, which is servicing Smith's mortgage loan as an agent for Fannie Mae, which purchased the loan. Despite receiving notice of the sale, Wells Fargo does not tender payment of the priority portion of the association's lien. Instead, it allows the sale to proceed; at the sale, Investor purchases the unit for $10,500 (slightly more than the unpaid balance of Smith's unpaid assessments). Under the *SFR Investments* decision, the association's sale should extinguish Fannie Mae's mortgage lien. However, the FHFA argues that Fannie Mae's lien on the unit was "property of the Agency [the FHFA]" under 12 U.S.C. § 4617(j)(3), and thus that because the FHFA did not consent to the association's sale, the sale did not extinguish Fannie Mae's lien—notwithstanding the association's state law priority!

The FHFA's interpretation of § 4617(j)(3) is outrageous. Fannie and Freddie purchase their loans with notice of the priority that Nevada and other UCIOA states provide to association liens. Further, Fannie and Freddie's own servicing guidelines have long instructed their servicers (such as Wells Fargo) to pay condominium or HOA dues where necessary to protect the integrity of the mortgage lien. If Fannie or Freddie suffer a loss because Wells Fargo or another servicer failed to properly carry out its servicing duties, Fannie or Freddie could easily be made whole by the responsible servicer; using § 4617(j)(3) to challenge the validity/effect of the association's sale merely bails out servicers from facing the consequences of negligent servicing. As a policy matter, Fannie and Freddie should (like any other mortgage lender) take state law priority rules as it finds them.[34] See, e.g., R. Wilson Freyermuth & Dale A. Whitman, Can Associations Have Priority over Fannie or Freddie?, 29 Prob. & Prop. 27 (July/Aug. 2015).

Nevertheless, courts in the Ninth Circuit have accepted the FHFA's argument and have consistently concluded that 12 U.S.C. § 4617(j)(3) creates a "federal foreclosure bar" that prevents an association's foreclosure sale from invalidating a mortgage lien held by Fannie or Freddie, despite the association's clear statutory priority under state law. See, e.g., Berezovsky v. Moniz, 869 F.3d 923 (9th Cir. 2017). Does the federal foreclosure bar, or the lack of any consent procedure, call into question the constitutionality of

---

[34] To make matters worse, despite the fact that § 4617(j)(3) explicitly contemplates the possibility of FHFA consent, the FHFA has not established a consent procedure for an association to seek FHFA consent—even though the FHFA conservatorship has been going on for more than 13 years now—and the FHFA has represented that it will not grant consent to an association foreclosure sale.

§ 4617(j)(3) as applied to an association's lien or constitute a taking of the association's state law priority? Why or why not?

4.   *For what expenditures can members be assessed?* There is little doubt that an association can use assessments to fund customary maintenance and management expenses. See, e.g., Khan v. Alpine Haven Property Owners' Ass'n, Inc., 245 A.3d 1234 (Vt. 2020) (upholding assessment for road maintenance, trash service, streetlight expense and snow removal, without regard for whether lot owner actually used trash removal service); Telluride Lodge Ass'n v. Zoline, 707 P.2d 998 (Colo. Ct. App. 1985) (upholding assessment for a roof that was significantly different from the original). Note, however, that normally the association may assess unit owners only for maintenance and improvements on the common areas. Association funds may not be used, for example, to maintain individual units. See, e.g., Montgomery v. Columbia Knoll Condo. Council, 231 Va. 437, 344 S.E.2d 912 (1986) ($125,000 expenditure to replace all windows impermissible because windows were a part of individual units and not common areas).

What if the association's board decides to make some capital improvements in the common areas? For example, suppose that the board decides to spend $500 for new landscaping at the entrance to the community and $750,000 for an indoor pool and a gym with modern exercise equipment. Should these expenditures require a majority vote of the board, a majority vote of the owners themselves, or the unanimous vote of all owners? The answer may depend on both the statute and the declaration governing the community. See, e.g., San Antonio Villa Del Sol Homeowners Ass'n v. Miller, 761 S.W.2d 460 (Tex. Ct. App. 1988) (upholding $61,500 special assessment for plumbing as permitted capital improvement under condominium documents); Downey v. Jungle Den Villas Recreation Ass'n, Inc., 525 So.2d 438 (Fla. Ct. App. 1988) (association lacked authority to assess members for construction of pool absent unanimous vote where declaration did not permit approval by less-than-unanimous vote) Assessments for new recreational facilities are often controversial, because some owners may expect to make heavy use of them while others do not plan to use them at all.

Now consider a different scenario. Suppose that Shady Acres (a planned community) was created 40 years ago, with homes surrounding a lake owned by an owners association. Under the original declaration, membership in the owners association was voluntary; only members of the association paid assessments to maintain the lake, and nonmembers were not permitted to use the lake for boating, fishing, swimming, etc. Over time, however, the expenses of maintaining the lake and monitoring its use increased to the point that the board recommended that the association vote to impose mandatory assessments on all owners. If a majority of the owners vote to impose mandatory assessments, can such assessments be enforced against objecting owners?

EVERGREEN HIGHLANDS ASS'N V. WEST

Supreme Court of Colorado, 2003
73 P.3d 1

JUSTICE RICE. . . . Petitioner Evergreen Highlands Association, a Colorado non-profit corporation ("Association"), is the homeowner association for Evergreen Highlands Subdivision—Unit 4 ("Evergreen Highlands") in Jefferson County. The subdivision consists of sixty-three lots, associated roads, and a 22.3 acre park area which is open to use by all residents of the subdivision. The Association holds title to and maintains the park area, which contains hiking and equestrian trails, a barn and stables, a ball field, a fishing pond, and tennis courts. The park area is almost completely surrounded by private homeowners' lots, with no fence or other boundary separating the park area from the homes. Respondent Robert A. West owns one of the lots bordering directly on the park area, and has used the facilities there to play tennis, fish, and walk his dog.

Evergreen Highlands Subdivision was created and its plat filed in 1972. The plat indicated that the park area was to be conveyed to the homeowners association. Protective covenants for Evergreen Highlands were also filed in 1972, but did not require lot owners to be members of or pay dues to the Association. The Association, however, was incorporated in 1973 for the purposes of maintaining the common area and facilities, enforcing the covenants, paying taxes on the common area, and determining annual fees. The developer conveyed the park area to the Association in 1976. Between the years of 1976 and 1995, when the modification of the covenants at issue in this case occurred, the Association relied on voluntary assessments from lot owners to pay for maintenance of and improvements to the park area. Such expenses included property taxes, insurance for the park area and its structures, weed spraying, tennis court resurfacing, and barn and stable maintenance.

Article 13 of the original Evergreen Highlands covenants provides that a majority of lot owners may agree to modify the covenants, stating in relevant part as follows:

> [T]he owners of seventy-five percent of the lots which are subject to these covenants may release all or part of the land so restricted from any one or more of said restrictions, *or may change or modify any one or more of said restrictions*, by executing and acknowledging an appropriate agreement or agreements in writing for such purposes and filing the same in the Office of the County Clerk and Recorder of Jefferson County, Colorado.

Protective Covenants for Evergreen Highlands—Unit 4, art. 13 (Nov. 6, 1972) (emphasis added) (hereinafter "modification clause"). In 1995, pursuant to the modification clause, at least seventy-five percent of Evergreen Highlands' lot owners voted to add a new Article 16 to the covenants. This article required all lot owners to be members of and pay assessments to the Association, and permitted the Association to impose liens on the property of any owners who failed to pay their assessment. Assessments were set at fifty dollars per year per lot.

Respondent purchased his lot in 1986 when membership in the Association and payment of assessments was voluntary, a fact that Respondent contends positively influenced his decision to purchase in Evergreen Highlands. Respondent was not among the majority of homeowners who approved the 1995 amendment to the covenants, and he subsequently refused to pay his lot assessment. When the Association threatened to record a lien against his property, Respondent filed this lawsuit challenging the validity of the 1995 amendment. The Association counterclaimed for a declaratory judgment that it had the implied power to collect assessments from all lot owners in the subdivision, and accordingly sought damages from West for breach of the implied contract. The district court ruled in favor of the Association on the ground that the amendment was valid and binding; therefore, it never reached the merits of the Association's counterclaims.

The court of appeals reversed, finding that the terms "change or modify" as set forth in the modification clause of the covenants did not allow for the addition of a wholly new covenant, but only for modifications to the existing covenants. . . . The court of appeals did not address the issue of whether the Association had the implied power to collect assessments from lot owners, and therefore whether Respondent was in breach of an implied contract. We granted certiorari and now reverse and remand. . . .

[Editors' Note: We have omitted the portion of the court's opinion in which it held that the covenant had been properly modified under the terms of the modification provision.]

The Association additionally argues that, even in the absence of an express covenant imposing mandatory assessments, it has the implied power to collect assessments from its members. To this end, the Association brought a counterclaim against West for breach of an implied contract obligating him to pay a proportionate share for repair, upkeep, and maintenance of the common area. The Association now argues that, based on West's breach of the implied contract, it is entitled as a matter of law to collect the unpaid assessments from Respondent.

We agree. Our review of case law from other states, the Restatement of Property (Servitudes), and the declarations for Evergreen Highlands in effect when West purchased his property, as supported by our understanding of the purpose of the Colorado Common Interest Ownership Act ("CCIOA"), convinces us that such an implied power exists in these circumstances. We therefore hold that Evergreen Highlands is a common interest community by implication, and that the Association has the implied power to levy assessments against lot owners to provide for maintenance of and improvements to common areas of the subdivision.

This being a question of first impression in Colorado, we first examine case law from other jurisdictions and find it largely in concurrence with our holding. When faced with this issue, a substantial number of states have arrived at the conclusion that homeowner associations have the implied power to levy dues or assessments even in the absence of express authority. *See, e.g., Spinnler Point Colony Ass'n, Inc. v. Nash,* 689 A.2d 1026, 1028–29 (Pa.Commw.Ct.1997) (holding that where ownership in a residential community allows owners to utilize common areas, "there is an implied agreement to accept the proportionate costs for maintaining and repairing these facilities."); *Meadow Run & Mountain Lake Park Ass'n v. Berkel,* 409 Pa.Super. 637, 598 A.2d 1024, 1026 (1991) (same); *Seaview Ass'n of Fire Island, N.Y., Inc. v. Williams,* 69 N.Y.2d 987, 517 N.Y.S.2d 709, 510 N.E.2d 793, 794 (1987) (holding that when lot purchaser has knowledge that homeowners association provides facilities and services to community residents, purchase creates an implied-in-fact contract to pay a proportionate share of those facilities and services); *Perry v. Bridgetown Cmty. Ass'n, Inc.,* 486 So.2d 1230, 1234 (Miss.1986) ("A landowner who willfully purchases property subject to control of the association and derives benefits from membership in the association implies his consent to be charged assessments and dues common to all other members."). *But see Popponesset Beach Ass'n, Inc. v. Marchillo,* 39 Mass.App.Ct. 586, 658 N.E.2d 983, 987–88 (1996) (holding that where lot owner had no notice in his chain of title of assessments and had not used the common areas, there existed no implied-in-fact contract to pay past and future assessments).[7]

Reflecting this considerable body of law, the newest version of the Restatement of Property (Servitudes) provides that "a common-interest community has the power to raise the funds reasonably necessary to carry out its functions by levying assessments against the individually owned property in the community...." Restatement of Servitudes § 6.5(1)(a) (2000). In addition, as explained in a comment to that section, the power to levy assessments "will be implied if not expressly granted by the declaration or by statute." *Id.* at § 6.5 cmt. b; *see also* Wayne S. Hyatt, *Condominium and Homeowner Association Practice: Community Association Law* 36 (1981) ("The assessment is not equivalent to membership dues or some other discretionary charge.... As long as legitimate expenses are incurred, the individual member must bear his or her share.").

We find the Restatement and case law from other states persuasive in analyzing the issue before us today. In addition, these authorities are in harmony with the legislative purpose motivating the enactment of CCIOA.

---

[7]   We note that in contrast to *Marchillo,* testimony in this case showed that West had, in fact, availed himself of the benefits of the park area.

See, e.g., § 38–33.3–102(1)(b), 10 C.R.S. (2002) ("That the continuation of the economic prosperity of Colorado is dependent upon the strengthening of homeowner associations . . . through enhancing the financial stability of associations by increasing the association's powers to collect delinquent assessments"); § 38–33.3–102(1)(d) ("That it is the policy of this state to promote effective and efficient property management through defined operational requirements that preserve flexibility for such homeowner associations").

Respondent, however, argues that the implied power to mandate assessments can only be imputed to "common interest communities," which both CCIOA and the Restatement define as residential communities in which there exists a mandatory obligation or servitude imposed on individual owners to pay for common elements of the community. Respondent therefore contends that because the original covenants did not impose such a servitude, Evergreen Highlands is not a common interest community, and accordingly cannot have the implied power to levy assessments against its members pursuant to these authorities.

Respondent's argument, however, relies on the assumption that the servitude or obligation to pay which would have defined Evergreen Highlands as a common interest community was required to have been made express in the covenants or in his deed. This assumption is incorrect. CCIOA provides only that the obligation must arise from the "declarations," which are defined as "any recorded instruments however denominated, that create a common interest community, including any amendments to those instruments and also including, but not limited to, plats and maps." § 38–33.3–103(13), 10 C.R.S. (2002); *see also* Restatement of Servitudes § 6.2(5)(2000) (" 'Declaration' means the recorded document or documents containing the servitudes that create and govern the common-interest community.").

The declarations in effect for Evergreen Highlands in 1986 incorporated all documents recorded up to that date, and included not only: (1) the covenants, but also; (2) the 1972 plat, which noted that the park area would be conveyed to the homeowners association; (3) the 1973 Articles of Incorporation for the Association stating that the Association's purposes were to "own, acquire, build, operate, and maintain" the common area and facilities, to pay taxes on same, and to "determine annual membership or use fees"; and (4) the 1976 deed whereby the developer quit-claimed his ownership in the park area to the Association.

At the time Respondent purchased his lot in 1986, the Evergreen Highlands' declarations made clear that a homeowners association existed, it owned and maintained the park area, and it had the power to impose annual membership or use fees on lot owners. These declarations were sufficient to create a common interest community by implication. As explained by the Restatement:

> An implied obligation may . . . be found where the declaration expressly creates an association for the purpose of managing common property or enforcing use restrictions and design controls, but fails to include a mechanism for providing the funds necessary to carry out its functions. When such an implied obligation is established, the lots are a common-interest community within the meaning of this Chapter.

Restatement (Third) of Property: Servitudes § 6.2 cmt. a (2000); *see also id.* at illus. 2 (citing an example virtually identical to that of Evergreen Highlands and finding it a common interest community by judicial decree).

We accordingly adopt the position taken by the Restatement and many other states, and hold that the declarations for Evergreen Highlands were sufficient to create a common interest community by implication. The Association therefore has the implicit power to levy assessments against lot owners for the purpose of maintaining the common area of the subdivision. Respondent, as a lot owner, has an implied duty to pay his proportionate share of the cost of maintaining and operating the common area. We therefore remand the case to the court of appeals with orders to return it to the trial court to calculate Petitioner's damages in a manner consistent with this opinion. . . .

NOTE

Identifying the limits of the association's assessment power. Are you persuaded by the *West* court's analysis that a CIC has the implied power to levy assessments? Do you believe a reasonable purchaser in West's position would have appreciated the possibility of the future adoption of mandatory assessments? Would West's position be more reasonable if the declaration had not been amendable, and the association had been relying solely on its (alleged) implied power to impose mandatory assessments?

In considering this question, compare the situation in *West* with the hypothetical in note 4 prior to *West.* Suppose that Shady Acres originally did not have a pool or exercise gym. Suppose further that over 80% of the owners vote to approve the expenditure of funds, but Pushaw (one of the dissenting owners) files a lawsuit arguing that the association lacks the power to do this. Does the analysis in *West* suggest that the association would prevail? Why or why not? What additional information, if any, would you want to ascertain in making your judgment?

2. MANAGEMENT OF COMMUNITY
LIFE AND AFFAIRS

Common interest communities typically place a variety of contractual restrictions on owners within the community, as a means to protect community members from uses that might threaten their financial investment and/or their peaceful enjoyment of their units/lots. In this regard, common interest communities also resemble municipalities, which commonly use zoning and other police powers to regulate life within municipal boundaries. As common interest communities increasingly proliferate, disputes inevitably arise between neighbors over the extent to which the community should be able to control or prevent certain uses or activities within the community, either by direct limitations in the declaration itself or by rulemaking by the association board. When such disputes arise, what rule should courts play in interpreting and applying a community's declaration and rules? For example, would a residential-use-only covenant permit the community to prohibit a resident from operating a freelance website design business within her home, or from providing home-based day care for neighborhood children? To what extent can a community's declaration or rules prohibit an owner from transferring her interest, either by lease or outright fee transfer? To what extent do constitutional principles or public policy provide a basis for limiting a community's ability to enforce its declaration or rules? To what extent can an association, its board, or its members be held liable to individual members of the community harmed by an association or board decision? The following materials explore these and related questions.

SOUTHWIND HOMEOWNERS ASS'N V. BURDEN
Supreme Court of Nebraska, 2012
283 Neb. 522, 810 N.W.2d 714

HEAVICAN, C.J. David Burden and Wilai Burden provide childcare services in their home in Sarpy County, Nebraska. The Southwind Homeowners Association filed suit against the Burdens, alleging that the childcare services as provided violated several restrictive covenants applicable to the premises and asking that the Burdens be enjoined from providing those services. The district court found that the childcare services were in violation of several restrictive covenants and granted an injunction. The Burdens appeal. We affirm. . . .

The facts of this case are largely undisputed. The Burdens purchased the property in question, located in La Vista, Nebraska, on November 30, 2007. At the time of the purchase, a certified copy of various covenants, conditions, restrictions, and easements of the Southwind development was on file with the Sarpy County register of deeds. There is no dispute that the Burdens were given at least constructive notice of these covenants.

Moreover, the Burdens do not contend that they had no notice of the covenants.

As relevant, the covenants limit the use of the subject premises as follows:

1.   Each lot shall be used exclusively for single-family residential purposes . . . .

5.   . . . No business activities of any kind whatsoever shall be conducted on any Lot including home occupations as defined in the Zoning Code of the City of LaVista, Nebraska . . . .

6.   No obnoxious or offensive activity shall be carried on upon any Lot, nor shall anything be done thereon which may be, or may become, an annoyance or nuisance to the neighborhood, including, but not limited to, odors, dust, glare, sound, lighting, smoke, vibration, and radiation.

Apparently, since shortly after they purchased the residence, the Burdens have provided daytime childcare to between four and six children, ages 6 months to 10 years, Mondays through Saturdays from 6 a.m. to 6 p.m. Two of the children for whom they provide care are related to them. The Burdens charge a fee to provide this care. In 2008, the Burdens had a net income from childcare services of $2,625, and in 2009, the net income was $45. In 2010, the Burdens apparently earned less than $1,000. Wilai is licensed through the State of Nebraska to care for up to eight children full time and another two children part time.

Written notice was given to the Burdens on July 7, 2008, informing them that the use of the property as a daycare was in violation of the covenants. The Burdens continued to provide childcare services, and the Southwind Homeowners Association brought suit on September 17, 2010, asking that the court find the Burdens in violation of the covenants and enter an order enjoining the Burdens from continuing to operate the daycare.

On February 3, 2011, the Southwind Homeowners Association filed a motion for summary judgment. Following a hearing on March 25, that motion was granted on March 30. In granting the motion, the district court noted the language of the covenant prohibiting " 'business activities of any kind.' " The district court also rejected the Burdens' argument that they were authorized to provide childcare services on the premises by the Quality Child Care Act. [Neb. Rev. Stat. §§ 43–2061 to 43–2625.] The Burdens appeal. . . .

The issue presented by this case is whether the Burdens' conduct of providing childcare under these facts violated the restrictive covenants on their property.

Restrictive covenants are to be construed so as to give effect to the intentions of the parties at the time they agreed to the covenants. If the language is unambiguous, the covenant shall be enforced according to its plain language, and the covenant shall not be subject to rules of interpretation or construction. However, restrictive covenants are not favored in the law and, if ambiguous, should be construed in a manner which allows the maximum unrestricted use of the property. Where there has been a breach of a restrictive covenant, it is not necessary to prove that the injury will be irreparable in order to obtain injunctive relief.

While this court has not been presented with the issue of whether a home daycare is a violation of these types of restrictive covenants, this issue has been litigated in other jurisdictions. The prevailing weight of that authority suggests that the operation of a daycare is a violation of restrictive covenants allowing only single-family or residential use and/or prohibiting the operation of a trade or business.[9]

For example, in *Terrien v. Zwit*, [467 Mich. 56, 648 N.W.2d 602 (2002)], a Michigan Supreme Court case, the applicable covenants prohibited any use other than for "residential purposes" and further stated that "[n]o part . . . shall be used for any commercial, industrial, or business enterprises." The court held that the daycare in question violated these prohibitions. The court also rejected the defendants' contention that the operation of a family home daycare was a "favored use" and that thus, a covenant restricting that activity was in violation of public policy. In rejecting this argument, the court noted that assuming the operation of a daycare was part of Michigan's public policy, also part of public policy was a property holder's right to improve his or her property, including the adoption of covenants which would enhance the value of that property. The court stated that there were no "definite indications" in Michigan law of any public policy against such a covenant.

Other courts have also held that daycare facilities violated covenants similar to the ones at issue in this case. The Rhode Island Supreme Court, in *Martellini v. Little Angels Day Care, Inc.*, [847 A.2d 838 (R.I. 2004)] held that a covenant limiting the use of the property to "single family private residence purposes" was violated by the operation of a daycare. In that case, the court distinguished an earlier case, which held that allowing a group home was not a violation of a similar covenant. The court noted that

---

9   *Williams v. Tsiarkezos*, 272 A.2d 722 (Del.Ch.1970); *Chambers v. Gallaher*, 257 Ga. 795, 364 S.E.2d 576 (1988); *Lewis-Levett v. Day*, 875 N.E.2d 293 (Ind.App.2007); *Berry v. Hemlepp*, 460 S.W.2d 352 (Ky.App.1970); *Woodvale Condominium Trust v. Scheff*, 27 Mass.App. 530, 540 N.E.2d 206 (1989); *Terrien v. Zwit*, 467 Mich. 56, 648 N.W.2d 602 (2002); *Ginsberg v. Yeshiva of Far Rockaway*, 74 Misc.2d 391, 344 N.Y.S.2d 602 (1973); *Walton v. Carignan*, 103 N.C.App. 364, 407 S.E.2d 241 (1991); *Hill v. Lindner*, 769 N.W.2d 427 (N.D.2009); *Martellini v. Little Angels Day Care, Inc.*, 847 A.2d 838 (R.I.2004); *Metzner v. Wojdyla*, 125 Wash.2d 445, 886 P.2d 154 (1994). *But see, Shoaf v. Bland*, 208 Ga. 709, 69 S.E.2d 258 (1952); *Stewart v. Jackson*, 635 N.E.2d 186 (Ind.App.1994); *Beverly Island Ass'n v. Zinger*, 113 Mich.App. 322, 317 N.W.2d 611 (1982).

while residents of the group home were not a traditional family unit, the residents would operate as such, as distinguished from a daycare, which would be composed of several occupants that did not reside there or engage in the traditional family activities outside of the hours when they paid for care. The court also rejected the defendant's public policy argument.

The Burdens direct us to this court's decision in *Knudtson v. Trainor*, [216 Neb. 653, 345 N.W.2d 4 (1984)] and contend that that decision supports their position. We disagree. We held in *Knudtson* that the operation of a group home did not violate a covenant restricting the use of property to only a residential purpose. We read the term "residential" as meaning where people reside or dwell and distinguished it from use for commercial or business purposes. We noted that the home in question would continue to look like a single-family home and that people would continue to reside in it; thus, the use was in compliance with the covenant.

While it is true that the Burdens' home will continue to be a single-family residence, look like one, and have a family (the Burdens) living in it, the character of the home, for at least part of the day, will be different from any other single-family home. At least 5 days a week between the hours of 6 a.m. and 6 p.m., five children will become temporary residents. The amount of traffic will increase at child dropoff and pickup times and, to a lesser extent, between those times. This is compared to the group home in *Knudtson*, where the residence might not be used to house a traditional family, but nevertheless those residents will live together much in the same way that a traditional family would. We also note that in *Knudtson*, the only covenant at issue was one limiting the use to residential purposes, and not one explicitly prohibiting business or commercial activities.

The covenants in this case require that the property be used for a single-family dwelling only and expressly prohibit the operation of a business on the property. Where unambiguous, the terms of a restrictive covenant should be enforced by their terms. These terms are unambiguous; moreover, our conclusion is supported by the greater weight of case law. And no matter how the Burdens characterize the operation, the couple is running a daycare for profit (no matter how little profit it might generate) at their home. We conclude that this is a business purpose, which is prohibited by the covenants.

Because the terms are unambiguous and must therefore be enforced, the Burdens' arguments that the residential nature of the neighborhood is not impaired by their daycare are unavailing. The Southwind Homeowners Association need not prove irreparable damage in order to obtain an injunction and in turn enforce their covenants.

Finally, the Burdens' argument that public policy would prohibit the enforcement of these covenants is also unpersuasive. It is true that the Legislature has adopted legislation with respect to family home daycares like the one operated by the Burdens, including § 43–2616, which permits the establishment of a family home daycare in any "residential zone within the exercised zoning jurisdiction of any city or village."

But as the Burdens acknowledge, while the Quality Child Care Act "established a public policy in favor of permitting" family home daycares, § 43–2616 "does not specifically ban the enforcement of restrictive covenants prohibiting the establishment" of family home daycares. Thus, it would appear, as in *Terrien*, that there are no "definite indications" that covenants which would prohibit the operation of family home daycares would be against that public policy. . . .

NOTES

1. *The presumptive reasonableness of (unambiguous) covenants.* The *Southwind* court treats the covenant as presumptively reasonable and enforceable by the association against the Burdens without any showing of harm. The decision is consistent with the vast weight of authority that an unambiguous covenant is enforceable against unit/lot owners within the community unless it is inconsistent with the applicable common interest ownership statute, other legislation, or overriding public policy. See, e.g., Nahrstedt v. Lakeside Village Condo. Ass'n, 8 Cal.4th 361, 878 P.2d 1275, 33 Cal.Rptr.2d 63 (1994) (no-pet covenant contained in recorded condominium declaration is valid and may be enforced against unit owner without need for showing that unit owner's pet poses a specific or unique harm). See also Restatement (Third) of Property—Servitudes § 6.7 cmt. b (2000) (covenants in in recorded declaration constitute valid servitudes "unless illegal, unconstitutional, or against public policy." Restatement (Third) of Property—Servitudes § 6.7 cmt. b (2000).

On which portion of the covenants in *Southwind* does the court's judgment rest? Suppose that declaration had included Covenant 1, but not Covenant 5. Would the court have reached the same result (i.e., that the declaration unambiguously prohibited the Burdens' day care operation)?

The *Southwind* court notes the traditional rule that an ambiguous restrictive covenant should be construed narrowly, in favor of the "maximum unrestricted use." Is this crabbed approach appropriate in the common interest community setting? Consider the view expressed in the Restatement:

(1) A servitude should be interpreted to give effect to the intention of the parties ascertained from the language used in the instrument, or the circumstances surrounding creation of the servitude, and to carry out the purpose for which it was created.

(2) Unless the purpose for which the servitude is created violates public policy, and unless contrary to the intent of the parties, a servitude should be interpreted to avoid violating public policy. Among reasonable interpretations, that which is more consonant

with public policy should be preferred. [Restatement (Third) of Property—Servitudes § 4.1.]

This view "departs from the often expressed view that servitudes should be narrowly construed to favor the free use of land. It is based in the recognition that servitudes are widely used in modern land development and ordinarily play a valuable role in the utilization of land resources." Id. cmt. a. Under this approach, do you think the *Southwind* case is correctly decided? On what specific language in the declaration do you base your conclusion?

2.   *Amending the declaration*. Over time, residents in a community may conclude that a covenant in the declaration is suboptimal from a governance perspective. For example, the declaration of a condominium created in the 1960s almost certainly would not have restricted smoking within the building or within units. Today, with heightened awareness of the health risks associated with second-hand smoke, a new condominium declaration might well contain a covenant prohibiting smoking in common areas, and perhaps even within units.

Can the residents vote to modify or amend a declaration (either to liberalize it or make it more restrictive)? The answer depends on whether the declaration contains an amendment provision. If the declaration does not contain such a provision, any amendment to the covenants would require the unanimous consent of all unit/lot owners. As you can imagine, the unanimous consent of all unit/lot owners is highly unlikely.

For this reason, most declarations contain a provision allowing for amendments to the covenants by a defined majority or supermajority of the unit/lot owners. Even the use of such amendment provisions, however, has prompted litigation as to what constitutes an "amendment." For example, suppose that the original declaration did not restrict pet ownership, but allows an amendment to the covenants by a vote of 75% of the unit owners. After some pet-related incidents, 80% of the unit owners vote to amend the declaration to prohibit pets. Is this a proper and enforceable amendment?

A split of authority exists regarding such changes. Under the weight of traditional authority, most courts held that a provision in the declaration allowing the residents to "amend" or "change" a covenant permitted the residents to modify an existing covenant by the requisite majority or supermajority vote, but that the residents could not adopt a "new" covenant (i.e., one not contained in the original declaration) without unanimous consent. See, e.g., Boyles v. Hausmann, 246 Neb. 181, 517 N.W.2d 610 (1994); Caughlin Homeowners Ass'n v. Caughlin Club, 109 Nev. 264, 849 P.2d 310 (1993); Lakeland Prop. Owners Ass'n v. Larson, 121 Ill.App.3d 805, 77 Ill.Dec. 68, 459 N.E.2d 1164 (1984). By contrast, more recent decisions have held that a provision allowing the residents to "change or modify" the covenants by a defined majority or supermajority vote allows the addition of new and different covenants. See, e.g., Trustees of Clayton Terrace Subdivision v. 6 Clayton Terrace, LLC, 585 S.W.3d 269 (Mo. 2019) (amendment provision allowed nonunanimous addition of "one residence per lot" covenant); Evergreen

Highlands Ass'n v. West, 73 P.3d 1 (Colo. 2003) (amendment provision allowed nonunanimous imposition of mandatory assessment covenant to fund maintenance of common amenities).

3.   *The declaration vs. association governing board rules.* Many declarations also allow an association's governing board to promulgate "rules" governing the use of units/lots. Thus, for example, a condominium board might decide to enact a pet prohibition or pet regulations even though the declaration itself contained no pet restrictions. Would such rules be enforceable? Courts have traditionally subjected board-made rules to more searching scrutiny:

> We [have] differentiated use restrictions that are contained in the declaration or bylaws from those promulgated by board rule. The restrictions in the first category "are clothed in a very strong presumption of validity and will not be invalidated absent a showing that they are wholly arbitrary in their application, in violation of public policy, or that they abrogate some fundamental constitutional right. . . . '[R]easonableness' is not the appropriate test for such restrictions." However, when the board promulgates a rule restricting the use of property, the second category, "the board must affirmatively show the use it wishes to prohibit or restrict is 'antagonistic to the legitimate objectives of the condominium association.'" Thus, "[w]hen such a rule [use restriction] is adopted by the board alone or requires the board to exercise discretion, we will scrutinize the restriction and uphold it only if it is affirmatively shown to be reasonable in its purpose and application."

Board of Directors of 175 E. Delaware Place Homeowners Ass'n v. Hinojosa, 287 Ill.App.3d 886, 223 Ill.Dec. 222, 679 N.E.2d 407 (1997) (upholding a board-adopted rule that prohibited pets as "reasonable"). See also Restatement (Third) of Property—Servitudes § 6.7 cmt. b (2000) (board-promulgated rules must be "reasonable"). Why subject board-made rules to greater scrutiny that covenants in the declaration? In upholding the board no-pet rule, the *Hinojosa* court noted that

> The original purpose for promulgating the rule was due to an incident in which one dog killed another in the building. The Board had tried less restrictive measures to regulate dogs in the past. However, these measures did not cure or alleviate what the Board reasonably perceived to be potential and real problems. It should also be noted that when the no-dog rule was adopted, owners were allowed to retain existing dogs. The rule only prohibited additional and/or replacement dogs. [679 N.E. at 411.]

Do you agree with the conclusion in *Hinojosa* that a board-adopted "no pet" rule is reasonable? Suppose instead that the Board had adopted a rule banning smoking anywhere in the building, including inside individual units. Would that rule be reasonable? Should it matter whether the rules were adopted only after consideration by the board, or instead were ratified by a vote of association members? What if the state's condominium statute authorizes association bylaws to provide restrictions regarding the use of the units, which "may include other prohibitions on, or allowance of, smoking tobacco products"? Utah Code Ann. § 57–8–16(7)(b). See, e.g., Cara L. Thomas, Butt Out! Controlling Environmental Tobacco Smoke in Condominiums, Prob. & Prop. 15–16 (May/June 2008); David C. Drewes, Note, Putting the "Community" Back in Common Interest Communities: A Proposal for Participation-Enhancing Procedural Review, 101 Colum. L. Rev. 314 (2001) (suggesting judges should be more reluctant to find rules reasonable if adopted in a "hierarchical, exclusive process," so as to encourage boards to obtain broader participation of individual residents in rulemaking); Patrick A. Randolph, Changing the Rules: Should Courts Limit the Power of Common Interest Communities to Alter Unit Owners' Privileges in the Face of Vested Expectations?, 38 Santa Clara L.Rev. 1081 (1998) (suggesting factors court should consider in evaluating whether unit owner should be relieved from the impact of board rule).

In assessing the validity of a covenant amendment or a board rule, it is helpful to keep in mind the following issues:

(a) *Were applicable procedural requirements satisfied?* The failure to comply with notice and hearing requirements mandated by state statutes, or by the declaration or bylaws, may invalidate an amendment or board rule. See, e.g., Ridgely Condo. Ass'n, Inc. v. Smyrnioudis, 343 Md. 357, 681 A.2d 494 (1996) (bylaw amendment revoking right of commercial unit owners to have customers and clients use lobby was not merely a "use" restriction requiring a 2/3 vote of unit owners, but rather a restriction on an "interest in property" requiring consent of all unit owners).

(b) *Do the governing documents provide substantive authority for the rule or regulation?* Unless the governing statutes, declaration or bylaws authorize a board rule, it may be *ultra vires*. See, e.g., Carney v. Donley, 261 Ill.App.3d 1002, 199 Ill.Dec. 219, 633 N.E.2d 1015 (1994) (board lacks authority to authorize unit balcony extensions into common area); Makeever v. Lyle, 125 Ariz. 384, 609 P.2d 1084 (Ct. App. 1980) (board may not deprive an owner of his or her interest in common areas absent authorization by statute, the declaration or bylaws).

4. *Age and disability discrimination.* Age restrictions on condominium residency have proved to be a fertile source of litigation, especially restrictions on children and those under the age of majority. Prior to 1988, court decisions generally upheld such restrictions. Since 1988, however, discrimination against occupancy by children has been, in substantial degree, prohibited by the federal Fair Housing Act (FHA). The FHA makes it unlawful for most persons and entities engaged in residential real estate transactions to discriminate on the basis of "familial status," as well as on the previously forbidden grounds of race, color, religion, sex, handicap, or national origin. See 42 U.S.C. § 3605. "Familial status" is defined to mean families which include children under the age of 18. See 42 U.S.C. § 3602(k). See Martin v. Palm Beach Atlantic Ass'n, Inc., 696 So.2d 919 (Fla. Ct. App. 1997) (even though

rules prohibiting occupancy by children under the age of 12 were not enforced, their publication by the association was a violation of the FHA).

However, the FHA creates an exception for "housing for older persons" in which familial status discrimination is not prohibited. See 42 U.S.C. § 3607(b)(1). "Housing for older persons" includes housing which is "intended and operated for occupancy by at least one person 55 years of age or older per unit." This in turn means that at least 80% of the units are in fact occupied by at least one person over 55, and that the project has published and adheres to "policies and procedures which demonstrate an intent . . . to provide housing for persons 55 years of age or older." See 42 U.S.C. § 3607(b)(2)(C). HUD's regulations are found in 24 C.F.R. §§ 100.300 to 100.308. See also Jonathan I. Edelstein, Family Values: Prevention of Discrimination and the Housing for Older Persons Act of 1995, 52 U. Miami L. Rev. 947 (1998). Unless a common interest community can satisfy the "housing for older persons" exception, rules and regulations that prohibit residency by families containing persons under 18 will be unenforceable. See, e.g., Simovits v. Chanticleer Condo. Ass'n, 933 F.Supp. 1394 (N.D. Ill. 1996); Westwood Community Two Ass'n, Inc. v. Lewis, 687 So.2d 296 (Fla. Ct. App. 1997).

Note that the FHA also prohibits discrimination based on "handicap." Consider the implications of this Act for developers of common interest communities:

> Section 804 . . . states that discrimination includes "a refusal to make reasonable accommodations in rules, policies, practices, or services when such accommodations may be necessary to afford [a disabled person] equal opportunity to use and enjoy a dwelling. . . . The starting point for determining what constitutes a reasonable accommodation . . . is an understanding that the purpose of the law is to end the unnecessary exclusion of persons with handicaps from the American mainstream. The reasonable accommodation requirement does not entail, however, an obligation to do everything humanly possible to accommodate a disabled person; cost (to the defendant) and benefit (to the plaintiff) merit consideration as well. Similarly, the concept of necessity, at a minimum, must illustrate that the desired accommodation will affirmatively enhance a disabled person's quality of life by ameliorating the effects of the disability.

Gary A. Poliakoff, The Effect of the Fair Housing Act on Deed Restrictions and Rules and Regulations Within Common Interest Ownership Housing Communities, 17 Prob. & Prop. 36 (May/June 2003). One area where associations often must make accommodations is on the issue of service animals; obviously, an otherwise valid "no dog" rule could not be enforced against a blind resident whose mobility depended upon a seeing-eye dog. See, e.g., Rebecca J. Huss, No Pets Allowed: Housing Issues and Companion Animals, 11 Animal L. 69 (2005). Even though a "comfort" or "companion" animal is not a considered a "service" animal under the Americans with Disabilities Act, current HUD regulations contemplate the possibility that an emotional support pet that is not a "service" animal can still qualify as an "assistance animal" for which an association would have to provide reasonable accommodations. For further discussion, see Rebecca J. Huss, Pups, Paperwork, and Process: Confusion and Conflict Regarding Service and Assistance Animals Under Federal Law, 20 Nev. L.J. 785 (2020).

5. *Discipline and sanctions against cooperative members.* Theoretically, it should be easier to discipline a cooperative resident for violation of the rules or delinquencies in payment of assessments than in a condominium or planned community. Remember that each cooperator is "merely" a tenant, holding possession of the apartment under a proprietary lease. The cooperative board, then, may conclude that ordinary landlord-tenant remedies and rules apply, so that the association may remove the cooperator after some short period of statutory notice, with unlawful detainer available in the event the cooperator does not leave voluntarily.

The difficulty with landlord-tenant reasoning, of course, is that cooperators often have thousands of dollars in "equity" in their units, and the courts are not likely to approve forfeitures of such investments in a cavalier manner. In the context of rules violations, the courts nearly always refuse to terminate a proprietary lease unless the rule is reasonable and without first giving the tenant a generous grace period to come into compliance. See, e.g., Moss v. Elofsson, 194 Ill.App.3d 256, 141 Ill.Dec. 182, 550 N.E.2d 1228 (1990); 520 East 86th St., Inc. v. Leventritt, 127 Misc.2d 566, 486 N.Y.S.2d 854 (Civ. Ct. 1985); 40 West 67th Street v. Pullman, 100 N.Y.2d 147, 760 N.Y.S.2d 745, 790 N.E.2d 1174 (2003) (upholding termination of proprietary lease for outrageous violation of cooperative rules following properly-noticed hearing as provided in cooperative declaration); Patrick J. Rohan & Melvin A. Reskin, Cooperative Housing Law & Practice § 11.05[1]. An Arizona court completely rejected the landlord-tenant characterization and refused to permit the use of the forcible entry and detainer statute to evict a defaulting cooperator, instead characterizing the relationship as one "akin to that found in a deed of trust arrangement" under which the cooperator's interest "is clearly in the nature of an ownership or fee interest." Kadera v. Superior Court, 187 Ariz. 557, 931 P.2d 1067 (Ct. App. 1996).

6. *Is the association a "state actor" for federal or state constitutional purposes?* A city council ordinance must pass federal and state constitutional muster because such an ordinance constitutes "state action." Thus, severe First Amendment problems would arise if a city council prohibited the display of flags from apartment balconies. However, the First Amendment applies to government action to limit speech, not to private action. Thus, for example, a private employer can typically impose and enforce even content-based speech restrictions on its employees.

So suppose a community association board prohibits a unit owner from displaying an American flag from the balcony of his unit, or from displaying political yard signs. Is this state action in violation of the First Amendment, or private action free of constitutional constraints? Some academic commentators and many pro-homeowners advocates have argued strongly that the law should treat community associations as state actors subject to constitutional constraints. See, e.g., Weakland, Condominium Associations: Living Under the Due Process Shadow, 13 Pepp. L. Rev. 297 (1986). While an occasional decision has agreed, see, e.g., Gerber v. Longboat Harbour North Condo., Inc., 724 F.Supp. 884 (M.D. Fla. 1989), most courts have refused to treat community associations as state actors under either the U.S. Constitution or its state counterparts. See, e.g., Rosenberry, The Application of the Federal and State Constitutions to Condominiums, Cooperatives, and Planned Developments, 19 Real Prop., Prob. & Tr. L.J. 1 (1984); Natelson, Law of Property Owners Associations § 4.6.5 (1989).

In 2006, "community association as state actor" advocates were heartened by a temporary victory in a case involving Twin Rivers, a planned community of over 10,000 residents in East Windsor, New Jersey. The Twin Rivers Homeowners Association board adopted rules that restricted the posting of signs by residents, limiting residents to one sign per lawn and one per window and prohibiting the posting of signs on utility poles, trees, and other natural features within the community. The board also adopted policies with regard to the use of the Twin Rivers community room and with respect to the publication of the Association's monthly newspaper. Some number of unhappy residents established a committee that filed a lawsuit challenging the Association's policies as a violation of the guarantees of free speech and association protected by the New Jersey constitution. The trial court awarded summary judgment to the Association, but the intermediate appellate court reversed, concluding that the Association served quasi-municipal functions and thus its internal rules and regulations were subject to state constitutional standards. Committee for a Better Twin Rivers v. Twin Rivers Homeowners' Ass'n, 383 N.J. Super. 22, 890 A.2d 947 (2006). In its decision, the intermediate court relied on two prior New Jersey decisions, State v. Schmid, 84 N.J. 535, 423 A.2d 615 (1980) (which struck down a trespass conviction for distribution of political leaflets on the Princeton University campus) and New Jersey Coalition Against War in the Middle East v. J.M.B. Realty Corp., 138 N.J. 326, 650 A.2d 757 (1994), cert. denied, 516 U.S. 812 (1995) (which enjoined shopping center owner from absolutely excluding persons from distributing political leaflets).

In late 2007, the New Jersey Supreme Court unanimously reversed and reinstated the trial court's judgment. The Court held that the "nature, purposes, and primary use" of Twin Rivers's property was for private purposes, that the Association "had not invited the public to use its property," and that the Association had not unreasonably restricted the residents' free speech activities. The Court held that "[t]he Association's restrictions concerning the placement of the signs, the use of the community room, and access to its newspaper are reasonable 'concerning the time, place, and manner of' such restrictions" and thus did not infringe on the residents' state constitutional rights." Committee for a Better Twin Rivers v. Twin Rivers Homeowners' Ass'n, 192 N.J. 344, 929 A.2d 1060 (2007). The court also suggested that the interest of residents in free speech and assembly were adequately protected by the business judgment rule, public policy limitations on the enforceability of covenants, and the ability of the residents to influence community decisions through participation in community governance. If these protections are sufficient, under what circumstances might an association's conduct transgress constitutional limits?

7. *Statutory responses to intrusive association regulation.* Several states have enacted legislation that prevents homeowner and condominium associations from restricting the ability of their residents to display the American flag. Consider the following California statute:

> Except as required for the protection of the public health or safety, no governing document shall limit or prohibit, or be construed to limit or prohibit, the display of the flag of the United States by a member on or in the member's separate interest or within the member's exclusive use common area.

Cal. Civ. Code § 4705(a). See also Fla. Stat. Ann. § 720.304(2); Ariz. Rev. Stat. § 33–1261(A), (B).

Likewise, in the wake of the uproar following the California Supreme Court's decision in Nahrstedt v. Lakeside Village Condo. Ass'n, Inc., 8 Cal.4th 361, 33 Cal.Rptr.2d 63, 878 P.2d 1275 (1994) (enforcing as reasonable a no-pet restriction contained in the condominium declaration), the California legislature enacted Cal. Civ. Code § 4715(a), which provides that "[n]o governing documents shall prohibit the owner of a separate interest within a common interest development from keeping at least one pet within the common interest development, subject to reasonable rules and regulations of the association."

Return to *Southwind* and the court's conclusion that the covenants prohibited the Burdens' home-based day care. Consider the potential impact of the following Maryland legislation:

> (1)(i)   . . . [S]ubject to the provisions of paragraphs (2) and (3) of this subsection, a homeowners association may include in its declaration, bylaws, or recorded covenants and restrictions a provision expressly prohibiting the use of a residence as a family child care home or no-impact home-based business. . . .

> (2) A provision described under paragraph (1)(i) of this subsection . . . may not be enforced unless it is approved by a simple majority of the total eligible voters of the homeowners association, not including the developer, under the voting procedures contained in the declaration or bylaws of the homeowners association.

> (3) If a homeowners association includes in its declaration, bylaws, or recorded covenants and restrictions a provision [described in paragraph (1)(i)], it shall also include a provision stating that the prohibition may be eliminated and family child care homes or no-impact home-based businesses may be approved by a simple majority of the total eligible voters of the homeowners association under the

voting procedures contained in the declaration or bylaws of the homeowners association.

(4) If a homeowners association includes in its declaration, bylaws, or recorded covenants and restrictions a provision [described in paragraph (1)(i)], the prohibition may be eliminated and family child care or no-impact home-based business activities may be permitted by the approval of a simple majority of the total eligible voters of the homeowners association under the voting procedures contained in the declaration or bylaws of the homeowners association.

Md. Real Prop. Code § 11B–111.1(d). Would this statute have permitted the Burdens to operate their day care? What recourse would the Burdens have had under this statute that they did not have in *Southwind*?

8. *Restrictions on transfer.* In many common interest communities, the declaration or rules may contain restrictions upon a resident's ability to transfer her interest. Such restrictions may range from narrowly-tailored restrictions on leasing all the way up to complete prohibition on sale without the prior written consent of the association board. To what extent should an association be able to exercise control over a member's ability to transfer her interest in a unit or lot within the community?

AQUARIAN FOUNDATION, INC. V. SHOLOM HOUSE, INC.
District Court of Appeal of Florida, Third District, 1984
448 So.2d 1166

DANIEL S. PEARSON, JUDGE. All is not peaceful at the Sholom House Condominium. In disregard of a provision of the declaration of condominium requiring the written consent of the condominium association's board of directors to any sale, lease, assignment or transfer of a unit owner's interest, Bertha Albares, a member of the board of directors, sold her condominium unit to the Aquarian Foundation, Inc. without obtaining such consent. Eschewing its right to ratify the sale, the association, expressly empowered by the declaration to "arbitrarily, capriciously, or unreasonably" withhold its consent, sued to set aside the conveyance, to dispossess Aquarian, and to recover damages under a clause in the declaration which provides that:

In the event of a violation by the condominium [sic] by the unit owner of any of the covenants, restrictions and limitations, contained in this declaration, then in that event the fee simple title to the condominium parcel shall immediately revert to the association, subject to the association paying to said former unit owner, the fair appraised value thereof, at the time of reversion, to be determined as herein provided.

The trial court, after a non-jury trial, found that Albares had violated the declaration of condominium, thus triggering the reverter clause.

Accordingly, it entered a judgment for the association, declaring the conveyance to Aquarian null and void, ejecting Aquarian, and retaining jurisdiction to award damages, attorneys' fees and costs after a determination of the fair appraised value of the property. Aquarian appeals. We reverse.

The issue presented by this appeal is whether the power vested in the association to arbitrarily, capriciously, or unreasonably withhold its consent to transfer constitutes an unreasonable restraint on alienation, notwithstanding the above-quoted reverter clause which mandates that the association compensate the unit owner in the event, in this case, of a transfer of the unit in violation of the consent requirement.

It is well settled that increased controls and limitations upon the rights of unit owners to transfer their property are necessary concomitants of condominium living. *See Hidden Harbour Estates, Inc. v. Norman,* 309 So.2d 180 (Fla. 4th DCA 1975); *Holiday Out in America at St. Lucie, Inc. v. Bowes,* 285 So.2d 63 (Fla. 4th DCA 1973); *Chianese v. Culley,* 397 F.Supp. 1344 (S.D.Fla.1975). . . .

Accordingly, restrictions on a unit owner's right to transfer his property are recognized as a valid means of insuring the association's ability to control the composition of the condominium as a whole. . . .

However, despite the law's recognition of the particular desirability of restrictions on the right to transfer in the context of condominium living, such restrictions will be invalidated when found to violate some external public policy or constitutional right of the individual. *Hidden Harbour Estates, Inc. v. Basso,* 393 So.2d at 639–40. *See Pepe v. Whispering Sands Condominium Association, Inc.,* 351 So.2d 755 (Fla. 2d DCA 1977). Merely because a declaration of condominium is in the nature of a private compact and a *restriction* contained therein is not subject to the same reasonableness requirement as a restriction contained in a public regulation, *see White Egret Condominium, Inc. v. Franklin,* 379 So.2d 346, 350 (Fla.1979), where the restriction constitutes a restraint on alienation, condominium associations are not immune from the requirement that the *restraint* be reasonable. Thus, while a condominium association's board of directors has considerable latitude in withholding its consent to a unit owner's transfer, the resulting restraint on alienation must be reasonable. In this manner the balance between the right of the association to maintain its homogeneity and the right of the individual to alienate his property is struck.

The basic premise of the public policy rule against unreasonable restraints on alienation, *see* 7 *Thompson On Real Property,* § 3161 (1962); 31 C.J.S. *Estates* 8(b)(2) (1964), is that free alienability of property fosters economic growth and commercial development. *Davis v. Geyer,* 151 Fla. 362, 9 So.2d 727 (1942); *Seagate Condominium Association, Inc. v. Duffy,*

330 So.2d 484. Because "[t]he validity or invalidity of a restraint depends upon its long-term effect on the improvement and marketability of the property," *Iglehart v. Phillips,* 383 So.2d 610, 614 (Fla.1980), where the restraint, for whatever duration, does not impede the improvement of the property or its marketability, it is not illegal. Accordingly, where a restraint on alienation, no matter how absolute and encompassing, is conditioned upon the restrainer's obligation to purchase the property at the then fair market value, the restraint is valid.

The declaration of condominium in the present case permits the association to reject perpetually any unit owner's prospective purchaser for any or no reason. Such a provision, so obviously an absolute restraint on alienation, can be saved from invalidity only if the association has a corresponding obligation to purchase or procure a purchaser for the property from the unit owner at its fair market value. Otherwise stated, if, as here, the association is empowered to act arbitrarily, capriciously, and unreasonably in rejecting a unit owner's prospective purchaser, it must in turn be accountable to the unit owner by offering payment or a substitute market for the property. When this accountability exists, even an absolute and perpetual restraint on the unit owner's ability to select a purchaser is lawful. *See Chianese v. Culley,* 397 F.Supp. 1344 (notwithstanding association's right to approve any transfer except one to an existing unit owner, requirement that within sixty days association provide another purchaser or approve original purchaser creates a preemptive right in association and saves declaration of condominium from being an unlawful restraint on alienation).

The declaration of condominium involved in the instant case contains no language requiring the association to provide another purchaser, purchase the property from the unit owner, or, failing either of these, approve the proposed transfer. What it does contain is the reverter clause, which the association contends is the functional equivalent of a preemptive right and, as such, makes the restraint on alienation lawful.

In our view, the problem with the association's position is that the reverter clause imposes no obligation upon the association to compensate the unit owner within a reasonable time after the association withholds its consent to transfer, and the clause is not therefore the functional equivalent of a preemptive right. *Cf. Chianese v. Culley,* 397 F.Supp. 1344. Instead, the clause and the association's obligation do not come into effect until a violation of the restriction on an unapproved transfer occurs. . . .

The association's accountability to the unit owner is illusory. There is no reasonable likelihood that a potential purchaser, apprised by the condominium documents that the consent of the association is required and that a purchase without consent vitiates the sale, would be willing to acquire the property without the association's consent. Without a sale, there is no violation of the reverter clause. Without a violation of the reverter clause, the association has no obligation to pay the unit owner.

Effectively, then, the power of the association to arbitrarily, capriciously, and unreasonably withhold its consent to transfer prevents the activation of the reverter clause and eliminates the accountability of the association to the unit owner. Therefore, we conclude that the power of the association to arbitrarily, capriciously, and unreasonably withhold its consent to transfer is not saved by the reverter clause from being declared an invalid and unenforceable restraint on alienation. Accordingly, the judgment of the trial court is [r]eversed.

NOTES

1. *Restraints on alienation in the condominium setting.* For an excellent analysis of the competing policy concerns inherent in the application of restraints on alienation doctrine in the condominium setting, see Vincent DiLorenzo, Restraint on Alienation in a Condominium Context—An Evaluation and Theory for Decision Making, 24 Real Prop. Prob. & Tr. J. 403 (1989).

2. *Rights of first refusal.* Rights of first refusal (or "preemptive" rights) give the association the right to purchase the unit should the unit owner decide to sell it. Usually, the language of such a provision will give the association a fixed period of time to either meet the terms of an offer that the unit seller is otherwise willing to accept or to allow the proposed transfer. Such provisions normally are not deemed to be unreasonable restraints on alienation. See, e.g., Old Port Cove Holdings, Inc. v. Old Port Cove Condo. Ass'n One, Inc., 986 So.2d 1279 (Fla. 2008); Ritchey v. Villa Nueva Condo. Ass'n, 81 Cal.App.3d 688, 146 Cal.Rptr. 695 (1978). However, all courts require that the right be exercised reasonably. See, e.g., Lyons v. King, 397 So.2d 964 (Fla. Ct. App. 1981). Consequently, the use of the right to exclude purchasers on the basis of race, creed, gender, age, familial status or national origin will be deemed "unreasonable" and will often run afoul of federal or state statutes or local ordinances that prohibit discrimination in the sale of housing. See, e.g., Lippman v. Bridgecrest Estates I Unit Owners Ass'n, Inc., 991 S.W.2d 145 (Mo. Ct. App. 1998); Wolinsky v. Kadison, 114 Ill.App.3d 527, 70 Ill.Dec. 277, 449 N.E.2d 151 (1983); Olin L. Browder, Restraints on Alienation of Condominium Units (The Right of First Refusal), 1970 U. Ill. L.F. 231, 257–259 (1970).

Suppose that a condominium association amends its bylaws to provide that the development's 10 studio-size units can be sold only to owners of larger units. [Assume that the studio units were all initially sold to affluent buyers of larger units, who used them either for storage or as quarters for their servants.] If an owner of one of the studio units contracts to sell that unit to a current nonresident, should the court enforce the amended bylaw and enjoin the sale? Consider the following answer:

[It cannot] be said that the purpose of the restrictions of sale of studio units—to preserve the character of the Condominium—is unreasonable. Although the duration of the restriction appears to be unlimited on its face, the restriction can be modified at any time by a duly called meeting of the unit owners to further amend the bylaws.

Demchick v. 90 East End Ave. Condo., 18 A.D.3d 383, 384, 796 N.Y.S.2d 62, 63 (2005). Is this a satisfactory answer?

3. *Rights of first refusal and the rule against perpetuities.* The common law rule against perpetuities invalidates a contingent future interest in property that may vest more than 21 years after some life in being at the time the interest was created. A right of first refusal, if it is deemed a contingent future interest and is unlimited as to time, violates the rule because the owner of the burdened property could decide to sell (and the holder of the right decide to purchase) at any time in the future—potentially, after everyone alive at the time the right was created has died and an additional 21 years has passed. There is limited case authority invalidating such rights as a violation of the rule. See, e.g., Hensley-O'Neal v. Metropolitan Nat'l Bank, 297 S.W.3d 610 (Mo. Ct. App. 2009).

Nevertheless, many states have by statute exempted rights of first refusal from the rule, either generally or with particular reference to condominiums. Courts in other states have held that the rule against perpetuities does not apply to rights of first refusal, reasoning that the right is only a contractual one until exercised and thus is not a contingent future interest in property at the time of its creation. See, e.g., Old Port Cove Holdings, Inc. v. Old Port Cove Condo. Ass'n One, Inc., 986 So.2d 1279 (Fla. 2008). Likewise, most commentators and the Restatement agree that the rule should be inapplicable to such rights in the condominium context. See Olin L. Browder, Restraints on the Alienation of Condominium Units (The Right of First Refusal), 1970 U. Ill. L.F. 231, 248–256 (1970); Lawrence E. Allison, Comment, The Mississippi Condominium Act: An Analysis of Potential Problems, 44 Miss. L.J. 261 (1973); Restatement (Third) of Property—Servitudes § 3.3 (2000) (RAP does not apply to servitudes or powers to create servitudes).

4. *Restrictions on leasing.* It has become increasingly common for condominium documents to place significant restrictions on the unit owner's ability to lease her unit. For example, there may be a flat prohibition on the creation of all leaseholds. Alternatively, the prohibition may be effective only for a fixed time period, such as for 10 or 20 years. Why might an owners association find such restrictions desirable? What may happen to a condominium development where the majority of owners are absentee landlords?

Courts have shown support for such restrictions on leasehold creation. See Four Brothers Homes at Heartland Condo. II v. Gerbino, 262 A.D.2d 279, 691 N.Y.S.2d 114 (1999) (total prohibition on leasing units not an unreasonable restraint on alienation); Apple II Condo. Ass'n v. Worth Bank & Trust Co., 277 Ill.App.3d 345, 213 Ill.Dec. 463, 659 N.E.2d 93 (1995) (leasing prohibition in condominium declaration is presumed valid and will be upheld unless it can be shown that prohibition is arbitrary, contrary to public policy, or violates some fundamental constitutional right of unit owners); City of Oceanside v. McKenna, 215 Cal.App.3d 1420, 264 Cal.Rptr. 275 (1989) (a ten-year restriction on leasing condominium units in a publicly-financed project deemed reasonable and enforceable by injunctive relief); Cape May Harbor Village & Yacht Club Ass'n, Inc. v. Sbraga, 421 N.J. Super 56, 22 A.3d 158 (2011) (amendment to declaration prohibiting rental of homes to third parties held a reasonable restraint on alienation); Apple Valley Gardens Ass'n, Inc. v. MacHutta, 316 Wis.2d 85, 763 N.W.2d 126 (2009) (bylaw amendment prohibiting rental of condominium units did not conflict with declaration and was enforceable); Town Houses at Bonnet Shores Condo. Ass'n v. Langlois, 45 A.3d 577 (R.I. 2012) (third lease by unit owner during calendar year violated declaration prohibiting unit owner from leasing unit more than twice in a calendar year). Further, courts have held that the fact that an owner leased his home prior to the community's amendment of the declaration to restrict leasing did not mean that the owner had obtained a vested right to continue leasing his home following the amendment. See, e.g., Pasha v. Battle Creek Homeowners Ass'n, Inc., 350 Ga.App. 433, 829 S.E.2d 618 (2019).

Suppose that a condominium's declaration provides that any home may be conveyed or leased by its owner free of any restrictions provided that the owner is current in payment of its common expense assessments. Could the condominium board adopt a rule limiting short-term rentals? See, e.g., Olszewski v. Cannon Point Ass'n, Inc., 148 A.D.3d 1306, 49 N.Y.S.3d 571 (2017); Stobe v. 842–848 West Bradley Place Condo Ass'n, 48 N.E.3d 310 (Ill. Ct. App. 2016); Kiekel v. Four Colonies Homes Ass'n, 38 Kan.App.2d 102, 162 P.3d 57 (2007). Why or why not?

Professor Susan French has advocated declaration language providing that "the association shall not adopt rules that prohibit transfer of any lot or unit, or require consent of the association for transfer of any lot or unit, for any period greater than [two] months." Susan F. French, The Constitution of a Private Residential Government Should Include a Bill of Rights, 27 Wake Forest L.Rev. 345, 352 (1992). Do you agree? What concerns might justify placing this limitation upon an owners association? See also David E. Grassmick, Minding the Neighbor's Business: Just How Far Can Condominium Owners' Associations Go in Deciding Who Can Move Into the Building?, 2002 U. Ill. L. Rev. 185, 213.

5. *Other limitations on a unit owner's right to transfer.* Consider the following types of limitations on a unit owner's right to transfer her interest.

(a) *Restrictions on immediate resale or "flipping."* Suppose that Wells purchases a new condominium unit from the developer of a 250-unit project. The declaration provides:

> The original purchaser of any unit is prohibited from selling that unit for a period of two years following that purchase without the prior written consent of Developer. If Developer grants its consent to any

sale within such two-year period, Developer is entitled to receive 50% of any profit received by the original purchaser of the unit in the approved sale, after deduction of any real estate commissions and other necessary expenses of sale.

Six months later, Wells is transferred to another state and signs a contract to sell her unit to Lambert, without obtaining Developer's prior consent. Can Developer get an injunction to prevent the closing of the sale? If the sale closes, can Developer recover 50% of Wells's profit from the sale? How would you evaluate the reasonableness of this restriction, and what additional information (if any) do you think might be relevant to this evaluation?

(b) *Transfer fee covenants.* Suppose that the declaration imposes a covenant, binding upon the owner of each lot/unit (and their heirs, successors, and assigns), that specifies that the owner must pay a fee to the owners association upon a sale of the lot/unit equal to 1% of the sale price. Is there any problem enforcing such a covenant? In evaluating the reasonableness of this fee, is the fee qualitatively any different from a homeowners' association assessment?

Now suppose that the declaration imposes a comparable 1% resale fee, but specifies that the owner must pay the fee to *the developer* upon resale. Can this fee be upheld as reasonable? Why or why not? Compare Cal. Civ. Code § 1098.5 (yes, subject to statutory disclosure requirements) with Fla. Stat. Ann. § 689.28 and Mo. Rev. Stat. § 442.558 (no). Note that Federal Housing Finance Agency regulations now preclude Fannie Mae and Freddie Mac from purchasing mortgages on land subject to most "private" transfer fee covenants created after February 8, 2011. 12 C.F.R. §§ 1228.1 to 1228.4. Why should such private transfer fees be considered unreasonable? See, e.g., R. Wilson Freyermuth, Private Transfer Fee Covenants: Cleaning Up the Mess, 45 Real Prop. Tr. & Est. L.J. 419 (2010).

(c) *Restrictions on cooperative transfer.* In cooperatives, control over transfer frequently takes the form of an express prohibition on the member's alienation of her corporate shares and leasehold interest. While courts would deem such a direct restraint an unreasonable restraint on alienation in the context of a fee simple transfer of real estate, the assumption has been that the cooperative member's ownership interest is governed in this context by landlord-tenant law. Under the latter rules, courts generally uphold tenant covenants not to assign or sublease without the landlord's consent. Dale A. Whitman, Ann M. Burkhart, R. Wilson Freyermuth & Troy A. Rule, The Law of Property § 6.70 (4th ed. 2019).

Consequently, courts have afforded cooperative boards broad power to refuse consent to prospective transferees. See, e.g., Rossi v. Simms, 119 A.D.2d 137, 506 N.Y.S.2d 50 (1986); Patrick J. Rohan & Melvin A. Reskin, Cooperative Housing Law and Practice § 7.02[3]. Indeed, as one commentator has pointed out, "such individuals as Richard Nixon, Gloria Vanderbilt, Calvin Klein and Madonna have all been refused memberships in cooperatives." Stuart S. Moskowitz, Co-op Transfer Restrictions: Business Judgment, Board of

Discretion and Bankruptcy—Part II, 62 N.Y. State Bar J. 28, 31 (Dec. 1990). Importantly, however, the power to refuse consent is often limited by fair housing legislation and ordinances. For example, a New York statute prohibits a cooperative corporation from withholding "its consent to the sale or proposed sale of certificates of stock or other evidence of ownership of an interest in such corporation because of the race, creed, national origin, or sex of the purchaser." N.Y. McKinney's Civ. Rts. L. § 19–a(1). The federal Fair Housing Act will have the same effect.

Professor Rohan's observations regarding this power to refuse consent are informative:

> Even if the board acts in good faith, its ability to exercise broad discretion places the entire financial and social burden back on the outgoing unit owner, who, upon having his proffered buyer rejected, must now start the process of seeking an acceptable purchaser all over again. In recent years, this has worked an extreme hardship on unit sellers relocated to another city by their employers or whose units have become substantially devalued as a consequence of radical downturns in the co-op market. This evil is compounded by the fact that in most co-ops the cooperator has no right, or a very limited right, to lease out his unit to enable him to carry the unit pending its resale. This double blow to departing unit owners plays havoc with their finances and may impair their credit rating or even push them into insolvency.

Patrick J. Rohan, Preparing Community Associations for the Twenty-First Century: Anticipating the Legal Problems and Possible Solutions, 73 St. John's L. Rev. 3, 18 (1999). Recognizing this potential for abuse of a cooperator, courts may refuse to allow the enforcement of transfer restrictions to the extent that enforcement would work a forfeiture of the member's ownership interest. See, e.g., In re Bentley, 26 B.R. 69 (Bankr. S.D.N.Y. 1982).

Management of daily life within a common interest community depends upon the exercise of judgment by the association board (or some other authorized decision-making group). For example, many modern residential common interest developments are subject to covenants that prohibit lot owners from building a new home or modifying an existing one without obtaining prior approval of the building plans and specifications (either by the association board or an architectural control committee). An association board might have to make a decision between relying upon neighborhood residents to volunteer to mow grass or tend landscaping in common areas or to expend association funds to hire a private contractor to perform the job.

Our lived experience with the democratic process tells us that people of good will often disagree regarding how to govern or regulate life within the community. If a unit owner in a common interest development disagrees with a board's decision, should the law respond by deferring to the judgment as a product of the community's democratic process? Or should unit owners have recourse to judicial review—and, if so, what standard should govern that review?

LAMDEN v. LA JOLLA SHORES CLUBDOMINIUM HOMEOWNERS ASS'N

Supreme Court of California, 1999
21 Cal.4th 249, 87 Cal.Rptr.2d 237, 980 P.2d 940

WERDEGAR, J. . . . Plaintiff Gertrude M. Lamden owns a condominium unit in one of three buildings comprising the La Jolla Shores Clubdominium condominium development (Development). Over some years, the Board of Governors (Board) of defendant La Jolla Shores Clubdominium Homeowners Association (Association), an unincorporated community association, elected to spot treat (secondary treatment), rather than fumigate (primary treatment), for termites the building in which Lamden's unit is located (Building Three).

In the late 1980's, attempting to remedy water intrusion and mildew damage, the Association hired a contractor to renovate exterior siding on all three buildings in the Development. The contractor replaced the siding on the southern exposure of Building Three and removed damaged drywall and framing. Where the contractor encountered termites, a termite extermination company provided spot treatment and replaced damaged material.

Lamden remodeled the interior of her condominium in 1990. At that time, the Association's manager arranged for a termite extermination company to spot treat areas where Lamden had encountered termites.

The following year, both Lamden and the Association obtained termite inspection reports recommending fumigation, but the Association's Board decided against that approach. As the Court of Appeal explained, the Board based its decision not to fumigate on concerns about the cost of fumigation, logistical problems with temporarily relocating residents, concern that fumigation residue could affect residents' health and safety, awareness that upcoming walkway renovations would include replacement of damaged areas, pet moving expenses, anticipated breakage by the termite company, lost rental income and the likelihood that termite infestation would recur even if primary treatment were utilized. The Board decided to continue to rely on secondary treatment until a more widespread problem was demonstrated.

In 1991 and 1992, the Association engaged a company to repair water intrusion damage to four units in Building Three. The company removed siding in the balcony area, repaired and waterproofed the decks, and repaired joints between the decks and the walls of the units. The siding of the unit below Lamden's and one of its walls were repaired. Where termite infestation or damage became apparent during this project, spot treatment was applied and damaged material removed.

In 1993 and 1994, the Association commissioned major renovation of the Development's walkway system, underpinnings of which had suffered water and termite damage. The $1.6 million walkway project was monitored by a structural engineer and an on-site architect.

In 1994, Lamden brought this action for damages, an injunction and declaratory relief. She purported to state numerous causes of action based on the Association's refusal to fumigate for termites, naming as defendants certain individual members of the Board as well as the Association. Her amended complaint included claims sounding in breach of contract (viz., the governing Declaration of Restrictions [Declaration]), breach of fiduciary duty and negligence. She alleged that the Association, in opting for secondary over primary treatment, had breached Civil Code section 1364, subdivision (b)(1) and the Declaration in failing adequately to repair, replace and maintain the common areas of the Development. . . .

After both sides had presented evidence and argument, the trial court rendered findings related to the termite infestation affecting plaintiff's condominium unit, its causes, and the remedial steps taken by the Association. The trial court found there was "no question from all the evidence that Mrs. Lamden's unit . . . has had a serious problem with termites." In fact, the trial court found, "The evidence . . . was overwhelming that termites had been a problem over the past several years." The court concluded, however, that while "there may be active infestation" that would require "steps [to be] taken within the future years," there was no evidence that the condominium units were in imminent structural danger or "that these units are about to fall or something is about to happen."

The trial court also found that, "starting in the late '80's," the Association had arranged for "some work" addressing the termite problem to be done. Remedial and investigative work ordered by the Association included, according to the trial court, removal of siding to reveal the extent of damage, a "big project . . . in the early '90's," and an architect's report on building design factors. According to the court, the Board "did at one point seriously consider" primary treatment; "they got a bid for this fumigation, and there was discussion." The court found that the Board also considered possible problems entailed by fumigation, including relocation costs, lost rent, concerns about pets and plants, human health issues and eventual termite reinfestation.

As to the causes of the Development's termite infestation, the trial court concluded that "the key problem came about from you might say a poor design" and resulting "water intrusion." In short, the trial court stated, "the real culprit is not so much the Board, but it's the poor design and the water damage that is conducive to bringing the termites in."

As to the Association's actions, the trial court stated, "the Board did take appropriate action." The court noted the Board "did come up with a plan," viz., to engage a pest control service to "come out and [spot] treat [termite infestation] when it was found." The trial judge opined he might, "from a personal relations standpoint," have acted sooner or differently under the circumstances than did the Association, but nevertheless concluded "the Board did have a rational basis for their decision to reject fumigation, and do what they did." Ultimately, the court gave judgment for the Association, applying what it called a "business judgment test." Lamden appealed.

Citing *Frances T. v. Village Green Owners Association* (1986) 42 Cal.3d 490, 229 Cal.Rptr. 456, 723 P.2d 573 (*Frances T.*), the Court of Appeal agreed with Lamden that the trial court had applied the wrong standard of care in assessing the Association's actions. In the Court of Appeal's view, relevant statutes, the governing Declaration and principles of common law imposed on the Association an objective duty of reasonable care in repairing and maintaining the Development's common areas near Lamden's unit as occasioned by the presence of termites. The court also concluded that, had the trial court analyzed the Association's actions under an objective standard of reasonableness, an outcome more favorable to Lamden likely would have resulted. Accordingly, the Court of Appeal reversed the judgment of the trial court. . . .

The Association would have us decide this case through application of "the business judgment rule." As we have observed, that rule of judicial deference to corporate decisionmaking "exists in one form or another in every American jurisdiction." (*Frances T., supra,* 42 Cal.3d at p. 507, fn. 14, 229 Cal.Rptr. 456, 723 P.2d 573.)

"The common law business judgment rule has two components—one which immunizes [corporate] directors from personal liability if they act in accordance with its requirements, and another which insulates from court intervention those management decisions which are made by directors in good faith in what the directors believe is the organization's best interest." (*Lee v. Interinsurance Exchange* (1996) 50 Cal.App.4th 694, 714, 57 Cal.Rptr.2d 798) A hallmark of the business judgment rule is that, when the rule's requirements are met, a court will not substitute its judgment for that of the corporation's board of directors. . . . According to the Association, uniformly applying a business judgment standard in judicial review of community association board decisions would promote certainty, stability and predictability in common interest development governance. Plaintiff, on the other hand, contends general application of a business judgment standard to board decisions would undermine individual owners' ability, under Civil Code section 1354, to enforce, as equitable servitudes, the CC & R's in a common interest development's declaration. Stressing residents' interest in a stable and predictable living environment, as embodied in a given development's particular CC & R's, plaintiff encourages us to impose on community associations an objective standard of reasonableness in carrying out their duties under governing CC & R's or public policy. . . .

Our existing jurisprudence specifically addressing the governance of common interest developments is not voluminous. While we have not previously examined the question of what standard or test generally governs judicial review of decisions made by the board of directors of a community association, we have examined related questions.

Fifty years ago, in *Hannula v. Hacienda Homes* (1949) 34 Cal.2d 442, 211 P.2d 302, we held that the decision by the board of directors of a real estate development company to deny, under a restrictive covenant in a deed, the owner of a fractional part of a lot permission to build a dwelling thereon "must be a reasonable determination made in good faith." Sixteen years ago, we held that a condominium owners association is a "business establishment" within the meaning of the Unruh Civil Rights Act, section 51 of the Civil Code. (*O'Connor v. Village Green Owners Association* (1983) 33 Cal.3d 790, 796, 191 Cal.Rptr. 320, 662 P.2d 427.) And 10 years ago, in *Frances T., supra*, 42 Cal.3d 490, 229 Cal.Rptr. 456, 723 P.2d 573, we considered "whether a condominium owners association and the individual members of its board of directors may be held liable for injuries to a unit owner caused by third-party criminal conduct." (*Id.* at p. 495, 229 Cal.Rptr. 456, 723 P.2d 573.)

In *Frances T.*, a condominium owner who resided in her unit brought an action against the community association, a nonprofit corporation, and the individual members of its board of directors after she was raped and robbed in her dwelling. She alleged negligence, breach of contract and breach of fiduciary duty, based on the association's failure to install sufficient exterior lighting and its requiring her to remove additional lighting that she had installed herself. The trial court sustained the defendants' general demurrers to all three causes of action. (*Frances T., supra*, 42 Cal.3d at p. 495, 229 Cal.Rptr. 456, 723 P.2d 573.) We reversed. A community association, we concluded, may be held to a landlord's standard of care as to residents' safety in the common areas, and the plaintiff had alleged particularized facts stating a cause of action against both the association and the individual members of the board. The plaintiff failed, however, to state a cause of action for breach of contract, as neither the development's governing CC & R's nor the association's bylaws obligated the defendants to install additional lighting. The plaintiff failed likewise to state a cause of action for breach of fiduciary duties, as the defendants had fulfilled their duty to the plaintiff as a shareholder, and the plaintiff had alleged no facts to show that the association's board members had a fiduciary duty to serve as the condominium project's landlord. . . .

More recently, in *Nahrstedt v. Lakeside Village Condominium Assn.* (1994) 8 Cal.4th 361, 375, 33 Cal.Rptr.2d 63, 878 P.2d 1275 (*Nahrstedt*), we confronted the question, "When restrictions limiting the use of property within a common interest development satisfy the requirements of covenants running with the land or of equitable servitudes, what standard or test governs their enforceability?"

In *Nahrstedt*, an owner of a condominium unit who had three cats sued the community association, its officers and two of its employees for declaratory relief, seeking to prevent the defendants from enforcing against her a prohibition on keeping pets that was contained in the community association's recorded CC & R's. In resolving the dispute, we distilled from numerous authorities the principle that "[a]n equitable servitude will be enforced unless it violates public policy; it bears no rational relationship to the protection, preservation, operation or purpose of the affected land; or it otherwise imposes burdens on the affected land that are so disproportionate to the restriction's beneficial effects that the restriction should not be enforced." Applying this principle, and noting that a common interest development's recorded use restrictions are "enforceable equitable servitudes, unless unreasonable" (Civ.Code, § 1354, subd. (a)), we held that "such restrictions should be enforced unless they are wholly arbitrary, violate a fundamental public policy, or impose a burden on the use of affected land that far outweighs any benefit."

In deciding *Nahrstedt*, we noted that ownership of a unit in a common interest development ordinarily "entails mandatory membership in an owners association, which, through an elected board of directors, is empowered to enforce any use restrictions contained in the project's declaration or master deed and to enact new rules governing the use and occupancy of property within the project." "Because of its considerable power in managing and regulating a common interest development," we observed, "the governing board of an owners association must guard against the potential for the abuse of that power." We also noted that a community association's governing board's power to regulate "pertains to a 'wide spectrum of activities,' such as the volume of playing music, hours of social gatherings, use of patio furniture and barbecues, and rental of units."

We declared in *Nahrstedt* that, "when an association determines that a unit owner has violated a use restriction, the association must do so in good faith, not in an arbitrary or capricious manner, and its enforcement procedures must be fair and applied uniformly." Nevertheless, we stated, "Generally, courts will uphold decisions made by the governing board of an owners association so long as they represent good faith efforts to further the purposes of the common interest development, are consistent with the development's governing documents, and comply with public policy." . . .

[H]aving reviewed the record in this case, and in light of the foregoing authorities, we conclude that the Board's decision here to use secondary, rather than primary, treatment in addressing the Development's termite problem, a matter entrusted to its discretion under the Declaration and Civil Code section 1364, falls within [this pronouncement from] *Nahrstedt*. . . . Moreover, our deferring to the Board's discretion in this matter, which, as previously noted, is broadly conferred in the Development's CC & R's, is consistent with *Nahrstedt*'s holding that CC & R's "should be enforced unless they are wholly arbitrary, violate a fundamental public policy, or impose a burden on the use of affected land that far outweighs any benefit."

Here, the Board exercised discretion clearly within the scope of its authority under the Declaration and governing statutes to select among means for discharging its obligation to maintain and repair the Development's common areas occasioned by the presence of wood-destroying pests or organisms. The trial court found that the Board acted upon reasonable investigation, in good faith, and in a manner the Board believed was in the best interests of the Association and its members.

Contrary to the Court of Appeal, we conclude the trial court was correct to defer to the Board's decision. We hold that, where a duly constituted community association board, upon reasonable investigation, in good faith and with regard for the best interests of the community association and its members, exercises discretion within the scope of its authority under relevant statutes, covenants and restrictions to select among means for discharging an obligation to maintain and repair a development's common areas, courts should defer to the board's authority and presumed expertise. . . .

Plaintiff warns that judicial deference to the Board's decision in this case would not be appropriate, lest every community association be free to do as little or as much as it pleases in satisfying its obligations to its members. We do not agree. Our respecting the Association's discretion, under this Declaration, to choose among modes of termite treatment does not foreclose the possibility that more restrictive provisions relating to the same or other topics might be "otherwise provided in the declaration[s]" (Civ.Code, § 1364, subd. (b)(1)) of other common interest developments. As discussed, we have before us today a declaration constituting a general scheme for maintenance, protection and enhancement of value of the Development, one that entrusts to the Association the management, maintenance and preservation of the Development's common areas and confers on the Board the power and authority to maintain and repair those areas. Thus, the Association's obligation at issue in this case is broadly cast, plainly conferring on the Association the discretion to select, as it did, among available means for addressing the Development's termite infestation. Under the circumstances, our respecting that discretion obviously does not foreclose community association governance provisions that, within the bounds of the law, might more narrowly circumscribe association or board discretion. . . .

Finally, plaintiff contends a rule of judicial deference will insulate community association boards' decisions from judicial review. We disagree. As illustrated by *Fountain Valley Chateau Blanc Homeowner's Assn. v. Department of Veterans Affairs* (1998) 67 Cal.App.4th 743, 754–755, 79 Cal.Rptr.2d 248 (*Fountain Valley*), judicial oversight affords significant protection against overreaching by such boards.

In *Fountain Valley*, a homeowners association, threatening litigation against an elderly homeowner with Hodgkin's disease, gained access to the interior of his residence and demanded he remove a number of personal items, including books and papers not constituting "standard reading material," claiming the items posed a fire hazard. The homeowner settled the original complaint, but cross-complained for violation of privacy, trespass, negligence and breach of contract. The jury returned a verdict in his favor, finding specifically that the association had acted unreasonably. . . . [T]he Court of Appeal held that, in light of the operative facts found by the jury, it was "virtually impossible" to say the association had acted reasonably. The city fire department had found no fire hazard, and the association "did not have a good faith, albeit mistaken, belief in that danger." In the absence of such good faith belief, the court determined the jury's verdict must stand, thus impliedly finding no basis for judicial deference to the association's decision. . . .

Common sense suggests that judicial deference in such cases as this is appropriate, in view of the relative competence, over that of courts, possessed by owners and directors of common interest developments to make the detailed and peculiar economic decisions necessary in the maintenance of those developments. A deferential standard will, by minimizing the likelihood of unproductive litigation over their governing associations' discretionary economic decisions, foster stability, certainty and predictability in the governance and management of common interest developments. Beneficial corollaries include enhancement of the incentives for essential voluntary owner participation in common interest development governance and conservation of scarce judicial resources.

For the foregoing reasons, the judgment of the Court of Appeal is reversed.

NOTES

1. *The enforceability of assessments for community facilities/services and the quality of services provided.* Suppose that an owners association generally provides snow removal services, but fails to do so on two occasions during the year—and that as a result, several residents in a low-lying area of the development are unable to get to work. May those residents withhold some or all of their assessment payments? The majority view suggests that the answer is no; each landowner's assessment obligation is independent (*i.e.*, without regard to the association's performance of those services or her satisfaction with that performance). See, e.g., Kay v. Via Verde Homeowners Ass'n, Inc., 677 So.2d 337 (Fla. Ct. App. 1996) and Panther Lake Homeowner's Ass'n v. Juergensen, 76 Wash.App. 586, 887 P.2d 465 (1995) (denying offsets); but see Kirktown Homes Ass'n v. Arey, 812 S.W.2d 198 (Mo. Ct. App. 1991) (allowing offset). Some states protect association finances in this setting by statute. *See, e.g.*, Ga. Code Ann. § 44–3–80(d). Can you explain why the law should view the landowner's assessment obligation as independent? To what extent should the language of the declaration control this determination?

2. *Judicial review of association decisions.* Why was the court in *Lamden* willing to provide such strong deference to the Association's judgment as to how to address the termite infestation problem? Are you persuaded by the court's explanation? If you were representing Ms. Lamden, what facts (if true) might strengthen her case that the board's decision breached its duty to her as a unit owner?

3. TORT LIABILITY OF ASSOCIATIONS AND OWNERS

MARTINEZ V. WOODMAR IV CONDOMINIUMS HOMEOWNERS ASS'N, INC.

Supreme Court of Arizona In Banc, 1997
189 Ariz. 206, 941 P.2d 218

FELDMAN, JUSTICE. . . . Plaintiff was attending a graduation party at Defendant's 152-unit condominium complex. Plaintiff was a guest of the tenant of a unit owner. After fifteen minutes at the party, he and two other party-goers returned to the complex's parking lot to check on their cars. One of his friends found a group of local ruffians sitting in and on his car. A discussion ensued. As Plaintiff was running away from the altercation, he was shot in the back. The group scattered and no one has yet been apprehended and charged with the shooting.

From the descriptions given by Plaintiff and his friends, the live-in security officer for the complex recognized the group as a gang of young people from a neighboring complex that often would gather in the parking lot to sell drugs and participate in other unsavory activities. Usually, the security guard would disperse them when he saw them. However, because of budget constraints, Defendant employed only one guard, who patrolled

control over the land. In *Petolicchio v. Santa Cruz County Fair & Rodeo Ass'n*, we cited *Frances T. v. Village Green Owners Ass'n*, 42 Cal.3d 490, 229 Cal.Rptr. 456, 723 P.2d 573 (1986), for the proposition that in response to changed social conditions, courts may recognize a landowner's duty of reasonable care to protect against another's foreseeable criminal acts. 177 Ariz. 256, 261, 866 P.2d 1342, 1347 (1994). In *Frances T.*, the California court found a condominium association could be held liable as a landlord when it had actual knowledge of inadequate lighting and the hazardous condition it created, yet failed to remedy the condition that led to the plaintiff's rape and robbery. In the present case, the court of appeals noted *Frances T.* and stated: "Assuming without deciding that Woodmar acted like a landlord in controlling the complex common areas, it might have had some duty to protect an owner of a condominium unit or the owner's tenant." *Martinez*, 187 Ariz. at 409, 930 P.2d at 486. However, the court distinguished between a condominium owner and a social guest/licensee, holding any duty owed to a unit owner would not extend to Plaintiff. *Id.*

We believe this distinction is contrary to existing law when, as in this case, the danger causing the injury is located on property in the exclusive control of the landlord or condominium association. In Arizona, if there is no statute or case law on a particular subject, we have traditionally followed the Restatement of Laws. Restatement § 360 states:

> A possessor of land who leases a part thereof and retains in his own control any other part which the lessee is entitled to use as appurtenant to the part leased to him, is subject to liability to his lessee *and others lawfully upon the land with the consent of the lessee or a sublessee* for physical harm caused by a dangerous condition upon that part of the land retained in the lessor's control, if the lessor by the exercise of reasonable care could have discovered the condition and the unreasonable risk involved therein and could have made the condition safe.

(Emphasis added.) Restatement (Second) of Property § 17.3 contains an almost identical provision. With respect to common areas, § 360 was followed in *Dolezal v. Carbrey*, 161 Ariz. 365, 778 P.2d 1261 (App.1989) (landlord's duty of care extended to social guests of tenant). As was noted by Prosser & Keeton, landlord liability extends to areas where "the landlord has retained control over that aspect of the premises responsible for the injury." W. Page Keeton, et al., Prosser and Keeton on the Law of Torts § 63, at 442 (5th ed.1984).

We note Defendant in this case is not a lessor but a new type of possessor—a condominium association that has retained in its control common areas, such as the parking lot, that unit owners are entitled to use as appurtenant to their unit. We couple this with the introduction to Part Six of the Restatement (Second) of Property, which addresses the tort liability of landlords, stating: "In condominiums, the tort problem is the same as in any other case of the tort liability of the possessor of land to others."

The element of control, we believe, is essential to a finding of duty for the condominium association. Like a landlord who maintains control and liability for conditions in common areas, the condominium association controls all aspects of maintenance and security for the common areas and, most likely, forbids individual unit owners from taking on these chores. Thus, if the association owes no duty of care over the common areas of the property, no one does because no one else possesses the ability to cure defects in the common area. We do not believe the law recognizes such a lack of responsibility for safety. We therefore hold that with respect to common areas under its exclusive control, a condominium association has the same duties as a landlord. *Frances T.*, 229 Cal.Rptr. at 461, 723 P.2d at 578.

Thus, if we apply the rules of Restatement § 360 and Restatement (Second) of Property § 17.3, a condominium association has a duty not only to the unit owners and their tenants but also to those who are on the land with their consent and who will inevitably be expected to use common areas such as the parking lot. *See* Restatement § 360 cmt. d (the rule stated in § 360 applies to all common areas the lessee is expected to use, such as the yard). On this point, we believe the case law is quite clear and supports the Restatement view. Traditionally—Prosser & Keeton cites cases as early as 1880, *e.g., Looney v. McLean*, 129 Mass. 33 (1880)—common areas were considered under the control of the landlord, although open and necessary for use by tenants. This element of control creates an "affirmative obligation to exercise reasonable care to inspect and repair such parts of the premises for the protection of the lessee; and the duty extends also to members of the tenant's family, his employees, his invitees, his guests, and others on the land in the right of the tenant. . . ." Prosser & Keeton § 63, at 440. This, of course, is the duty enumerated in Restatement § 360. We hold that Defendant's duty with respect to the common areas, like that of a landlord, extends not only to the unit owners but also to those on the land with consent of the owners and their tenants.[6] . . .

The duty to maintain the safety of common areas applies not only to physical conditions on the land but, we believe, also to dangerous activities

---

[6] No other rule, we believe, makes sense. Suppose, for example, that a unit owner and his visiting brother were in the complex elevator and were injured when it malfunctioned because of the association's negligence in repair or maintenance. It would be a strange rule that would allow the injured unit owner to recover for his injuries while the brother, a guest equally expected and invited to use the elevator, could not. It would be possible, of course, to argue that the guest would recover if the defect were hidden but not if it were obvious. Could the association then escape responsibility simply by posting a sign stating "caution, elevator may malfunction"? We refuse to embrace such arcane and illogical distinctions. With respect to the common areas, the possessor— landlord or association—invites all tenants, owners and their guests, as users. See Restatement § 343.

on the land. See Restatement § 344; Restatement (Second) of Property § 17.3. Thus, the condominium association, like a landlord and certain other land possessors, has a duty to maintain the common areas it controls in a safe condition and protect both owners and their guests from dangerous conditions or activities.

The court of appeals noted the Restatement rule but stated that "given plaintiff's legal status [as a licensee], Woodmar only owed a duty to 'refrain from knowingly letting him run upon a hidden peril or wantonly or wilfully causing him harm.' " *Martinez*, 187 Ariz. at 410, 930 P.2d at 487. The court found the gang hanging out in the parking lot was not a hidden danger, stating the "transient harm created by third persons who commit crimes" is distinguishable from a dangerous physical condition that a landowner must make safe. *Id.* at 410, 930 P.2d at 487. Again, we disagree. *See Robertson v. Sixpence Inns*, 163 Ariz. 539, 544, 789 P.2d 1040,1045 (1990) (land possessor's duty encompasses reasonable care to protect from or warn of danger of criminal attacks); Restatement § 344. The duty to those using the common areas with consent of the association, its unit owners, and their tenants, includes the use of reasonable care to prevent harm from criminal intrusion. *See* Restatement (Second) of Property § 17.3 cmt. 1. . . .

It is well recognized at present that failure to provide adequate lighting, door locks, or other security measures may subject certain landowners to liability for harm caused by a criminal attack on persons to whom the owner owes a duty of care. . . . Restatement (Second) of Property § 17.3, illus. 18.

Logically, it cannot be otherwise. If one owes a duty of reasonable care to those on one's land with permission, then the circumstances will dictate what is reasonable to protect others from foreseeable and preventable danger. The category of danger neither creates nor eradicates duty; it only indicates what conduct may be reasonable to fulfill the duty. As Prosser & Keeton acknowledges, since 1970 courts have recognized the landlord's duty of care may include measures to protect others from criminal attacks, provided the attacks are reasonably foreseeable and preventable. Prosser & Keeton § 63, at 442–43 (citing *Kline v. 1500 Massachusetts Ave. Apartment Corp.*, 439 F.2d 477 (D.C.Cir.1970) (owner of urban multiple-unit apartment dwelling had duty of reasonable care to protect tenants from foreseeable criminal assaults)); *see also Robertson*, 163 Ariz. at 544, 789 P.2d at 1045 (duty to independent contractor foreseeably attacked by criminal); *Rosenbaum v. Security Pacific Corp.*, 43 Cal.App.4th 1084, 50 Cal.Rptr.2d 917 (1996); *Frances T.*, 229 Cal.Rptr. at 475–76, 723 P.2d at 593; *Doud v. Las Vegas Hilton Corp.*, 109 Nev. 1096, 864 P.2d 796, 798 (1993); *Berry Property Management, Inc. v. Bliskey*, 850 S.W.2d 644, 653 (Tex.App.1993).

Our case is the type in which courts are tempted to blur the concepts of duty and negligence. As we have previously indicated, we disapprove of attempts to equate the concepts of duty with specific details of conduct. *Markowitz v. Arizona Parks Bd.*, 146 Ariz. 352, 355, 706 P.2d 364, 367 (1985). Duty is an issue "of the relation between individuals which imposes upon one a legal obligation for the benefit of the other. . . ." *Id.* (quoting *Coburn v. City of Tucson*, 143 Ariz. 50, 52, 691 P.2d 1078, 1080 (1984)); Prosser & Keeton § 53, at 356. As the possessor of the common areas, Defendant had a relationship, similar to that of a landlord, with unit owners, their tenants, and persons on the land with consent and permission to use the common areas. That relationship required Defendant to use reasonable care to avoid causing the injury to those it permitted to use the property under its control. *Markowitz*, 146 Ariz. at 355, 706 P.2d at 367 (citing Restatement § 343 and quoting Prosser & Keeton § 61, at 419). The relationship between Defendant, its unit owners, and persons given permission to enter the common areas thus imposed an obligation on Defendant to take reasonable precautions for the latter's safety. The type of foreseeable danger did not dictate the existence of duty but only the nature and extent of the conduct necessary to fulfill the duty. The true issue on summary judgment in this case, therefore, was not the question of duty but rather the question of negligence. We turn, then, to the specific facts to determine whether the trial judge correctly granted summary judgment. . . .

In the response to the motion for summary judgment, there is evidence presented that Defendant knew of the incursion by gangs in the parking lot and other common areas of its property, knew the gangs engaged in drug dealing and other criminal activity, was warned by its own security guard of the need for 24-hour patrols, had hired a second guard for a short period but terminated him because of expense considerations, and knew a neighboring condominium complex had hired off-duty Phoenix police officers to patrol. We therefore hold there is sufficient evidence from which a jury could find the danger foreseeable and Defendant negligent.

On this record, also, we cannot say as a matter of law Defendant could not have taken reasonable measures that probably would have prevented the attack. It may be that increased security patrols, better fencing, calls for police control, or other measures might have prevented injury. This question of causation in fact is, of course, one especially for the jury. . . .

The record in this case provides sufficient evidence from which a jury could find negligence and causation. Accordingly, summary judgment was improper. Therefore, we vacate the court of appeals' opinion, reverse the trial court's grant of summary judgment, and remand to the trial court for proceedings consistent with this opinion. . . .

NOTES

1.   *Torts on the common areas.* What is the nature of the liability for torts occurring on common elements of a common interest community? Potential victims include the unit owners, their family members, invitees, and strangers. Negligent acts which cause injury may be committed by the same categories of persons, including (because they may be of particular importance) the officers, directors, or employees of the owners association. A matrix of possible litigation parties might look like this (with the plaintiff being the first-mentioned in each case):

Unit owner vs. association

Unit owner vs. other unit owners

Third parties vs. association

Third parties vs. unit owner or owners

We may be tempted to place great emphasis on whether the association is or is not incorporated, recalling that traditionally the shareholders of a corporation are not personally liable for its torts. In the condominium context, however, this conclusion is quite misleading; title to the common areas is with the individual members, who arguably have a legal duty to maintain "their" property in a reasonably safe condition—a duty which they cannot escape merely by employing an association (whether incorporated or not) to manage the property. In a cooperative, the insulation from liability may well have greater meaning, especially because the cooperative corporation holds legal title to real estate in which it may have substantial equity, a factor which diminishes the probability that a court will "pierce the corporate veil."

2.   *Liability of directors of association board.* If the association has tort liability with respect the common areas, what about its directors? In *Francis T.*, the plaintiff owned a unit in a condominium project in an area that had been subject to increased criminal activity. Concerned for her own safety, the plaintiff complained about inadequate exterior lighting on the units, and installed an exterior security light on her own unit. The board required her to remove the light on the ground that it violated the covenants governing the project. The night after the plaintiff removed the lighting, an intruder entered into the plaintiff's unit, where the plaintiff was raped and robbed. The plaintiff sued the individual directors of the association board, arguing that they breached a duty of care they owed to her by ordering her to remove the external lighting she had installed for her protection and by failing to provide adequate lighting within a reasonable period of time. The Supreme Court of California held:

> It is well settled that corporate directors cannot be held *vicariously* liable for the corporation's torts in which they do not participate. Their liability, if any, stems from their own tortious conduct, not from their status as directors or officers of the enterprise. . . .

To maintain a tort claim against a director in his or her personal capacity, a plaintiff must first show that the director specifically authorized, directed or participated in the allegedly tortious conduct; or that although they specifically knew or reasonably should have known that some hazardous condition or activity under their control could injure plaintiff, they negligently failed to take or order appropriate action to avoid the harm. The plaintiff must also allege and prove that an ordinarily prudent person, knowing what the director knew at that time, would not have acted similarly under the circumstances. . . .

Under the facts as alleged by plaintiff, the directors named as defendants had specific knowledge of a hazardous condition threatening physical injury to the residents, yet they failed to take any action to avoid the harm; moreover, the action they did take may have exacerbated the risk by causing plaintiff's unit to be without any lighting on the night she was attacked. Plaintiff has thus pled facts to support two theories of negligence, both of which state a cause of action under the standard stated above. . . .

Frances T. v. Village Green Owners Ass'n, 42 Cal.3d 490, 229 Cal.Rptr. 456, 723 P.2d 573 (1986) (citations omitted).

Many (if not most) condominium association officers and directors serve without compensation, unlike many of their corporate counterparts. In light of the language of *Frances T.,* would you be willing to serve on an association board or as an officer? California's statute insulates volunteer officers or directors of an association from acts or omissions liability in excess of insurance coverage for acts or omissions performed in good faith and within the scope of the officer's or director's duties if the act or omission was not "willful, wanton, or grossly negligent" and the association maintains liability coverage in the amount required by the statute ($500,000 in communities with 100 or fewer units and $1 million in communities with more than 100 units). Cal. Civ. Code § 5800. Would this statute allay your concerns about serving as an association officer or director? Does it go too far to protect volunteer officers or directors?

3.   *Necessity of insurance coverage.* The problems of adequately insuring a common interest community are extraordinarily complex. At a minimum, the following types of insurance are essential: (a) insurance against loss through fire and other casualties to both the common areas and the individual units; (b) liability insurance for wrongful acts imputed to both the association, its officers and directors and the occupants of the units; (c) insurance against casualty loss to personal property located in the units and in the common areas; (d) fidelity insurance to cover losses through dishonesty or defalcation by the association's officers, directors, and employees; (e) liability insurance for the association's officers and directors; (f) workman's compensation coverage for employees of the association; and (g) title insurance for the unit purchasers. See generally James M. Pedowitz, Condominium Unit Title Insurance, 73 St. John's L. Rev. 183 (1999); 1 Patrick J. Rohan & Melvin A. Reskin,

Condominium Law & Practice Ch. 11; Katharine Rosenberry & Clifford J. Treese, Purchasing Insurance for the Common Interest Community, 27 Wake Forest L. Rev. 397 (1992).

PEKELNAYA V. ALLYN

Supreme Court, New York, Appellate Division, First Department, 2005
25 A.D.3d 111, 808 N.Y.S.2d 590

TOM, J.P. The novel issue raised on this appeal is whether the proportionate interest in the common elements of a condominium held by the owners of the individual units subjects them to liability for injuries sustained by a third party as the result of a defective condition in a common element. . . .

Plaintiffs Aba and Michael Taratuta are father and son. Defendants are the individual owners of the 11 units comprising the Park 106 Condominium, located at 69 West 106th Street in Manhattan (collectively, the unit owners). While walking on the sidewalk, Aba and Michael Taratuta were struck and seriously injured by a section of chain-link fence, measuring approximately 4 feet by 5 feet, that fell from the roof of the condominium. The dislodged section was part of a security fence erected along the parapet wall of the roof to prevent access from adjoining buildings. It was installed prior to the time the condominium acquired the building and, thus, before the unit owners acquired their interest in the common elements upon taking possession of their respective apartments.

Michael Taratuta's injuries included traumatic brain injury, open comminuted skull fractures and multiple intracerebral hemorrhages and contusions, which rendered him severely and permanently disabled. His father sustained blunt head trauma and fractures of the vertebral column, among other injuries. Plaintiffs commenced a previous action against the condominium's board of managers on the theory that the board is responsible for the maintenance of common elements, including the rooftop security fence. Allegedly because damages will exceed the $2 million in insurance carried by the board, plaintiffs commenced this action against the unit owners. . . .

The unit owners hold title to their respective condominium apartments in fee simple absolute (Real Property Law § 339–e). The condominium declaration accords each unit an ownership interest of approximately 9% in the common elements, which comprises the unit owner's "common interest" (Real Property Law § 339–e[ii]). The roof of the premises is included in the common elements. However, it is designated a "limited" common element because its use is restricted to the owners of the fifth-floor apartments, defendants Hinojosa and Ragues, each of whom is allotted a 50% ownership interest in the limited common element. The provisions of the declaration notwithstanding, plaintiffs assert that "the 'access' to the roof is not exclusive to the owners of Units 5A and 5B since such units do not have 'direct and exclusive access from the interior of [their] respective units.' " Rather, all unit owners have the same access to the roof, which can only be reached by way of a common interior stairway leading to a common doorway at roof level. Thus, for purposes of this appeal, the unit owners are all in the same legal position.

The unit owners appeal from the denial of their motions for accelerated judgment dismissing the complaint and all cross claims against them (CPLR 3211; 3212). . . .

Supreme Court denied the motions, reasoning that Multiple Dwelling Law § 78 places the responsibility to maintain the premises in safe condition upon the "owner." Because the unit owners have not relinquished their collective ownership of the common elements, the court concluded that they are statutorily liable to plaintiffs.

On this appeal, the unit owners argue that the Condominium Act (Real Property Law § 339–d, *et seq.*) places the duty to maintain the common elements on the condominium's board of managers. They further contend that the court improperly applied the doctrine of res ipsa loquitur to subject them to liability.

Plaintiffs concede that the parapet-wall fence forms part of the common elements of the condominium. Plaintiffs also acknowledge that the board has the power and the duty to maintain the common elements. Nevertheless, plaintiffs contend that because of the part interest held by each individual unit owner in the condominium's common elements, Multiple Dwelling Law § 78 imposes upon them, as their collective owner, a nondelegable "duty to persons on its premises to maintain them in a reasonably safe condition.". . . Plaintiffs argue that statutory liability is abated only if an owner has parted with all possession and control of the premises. . . .

The issue to be decided on this appeal—whether liability should be imposed on the owners of individual condominium units for injuries to third persons resulting from a defect in a common element—is apparently a case of first impression. Plaintiffs note that, unlike some other jurisdictions, New York State has not provided for the allocation of responsibility for injury to third persons as the result of negligence in the maintenance and repair of common elements. . . .

[Plaintiffs contend] that Multiple Dwelling Law § 78 imposes liability on the unit owners by virtue of their ownership interest in the common elements. As previously noted, § 78 makes an "owner" responsible "for the safe maintenance of the building and its facilities". . . . The term "owner" is defined in Multiple Dwelling Law § 4(44) to "include the owner or owners of the freehold of the premises or lesser estate therein, a mortgagee or vendee in possession, assignee of rents, receiver, executor, trustee, lessee, agent, or any other person, firm or corporation, directly or indirectly in control of a dwelling." Plaintiffs argue that the unit owners, by virtue of their aggregate, respective minority ownership interests, are the "owner or owners" of the common elements. Alternatively, plaintiffs maintain that because the unit owners have surrendered less than complete ownership and control of the common elements to the board of managers, they cannot escape the liability imposed on owners by Multiple Dwelling Law § 78.

As this Court has stated, "The controlling tenet of statutory construction is that an act shall be given the effect intended by the Legislature (McKinney's Cons. Laws of NY, Book 1, Statutes § 92[a])" (*Thoreson v. Penthouse Intl.*, 179 A.D.2d 29, 33, 583 N.Y.S.2d 213, *affd.* 80 N.Y.2d 490, 591 N.Y.S.2d 978, 606 N.E.2d 1369). It is inconceivable that the Legislature intended the definition of the term "owner" contained in the Multiple Dwelling Law to apply to individual condominium unit owners because the Multiple Dwelling Law (L. 1929, ch. 713) preceded the enactment of the Condominium Act (L. 1964, ch. 82) by some 35 years.

Plaintiffs correctly note that the condominium form of ownership is purely a creature of statute. As a legislative enactment in derogation of the common law, the Condominium Act is subject to strict construction. . . . Plaintiffs do not point to any provision of the Condominium Act that imposes liability on a unit owner for injury caused by the defective condition of a common element; nor do they suggest that the common law recognizes liability based upon such a premise. Indeed, they concede that the Condominium Act does not address the apportionment of tort liability involving a common element.

The condominium being a creature of statute, the Legislature is the appropriate body to weigh the interest of an injured party in recovering damages against the interest of the individual unit owners in avoiding liability for the consequences of acts or omissions beyond their control. The failure of the Legislature to provide for liability in the absence of control by condominium unit owners over the maintenance and repair of the common elements precludes the courts from imposing responsibility by implication. Statutes which create such vicarious liability are narrowly construed. . . . "The Legislature is presumed to be aware of the law in existence at the time of an enactment and to have abrogated the common law only to the extent that the clear import of the language of the statute requires" (*B & F Bldg. Corp. v. Liebig*, 76 N.Y.2d 689, 693, 563 N.Y.S.2d 40, 564 N.E.2d 650). The condominium form of ownership being purely a creation of statute, in the absence of any provision in the Condominium Act holding the unit owners vicariously liable for the acts and omissions of the board of managers, it cannot be said that the Legislature intended to provide a means of recovery to an injured third person predicated solely upon the interest of the unit owners in the common elements.

Plaintiffs advance the argument that the unit owners should be held liable for the board's negligence in the maintenance of the common elements based upon a principal-agent relationship. Multiple Dwelling Law § 4(44) defines "owner" to include "any . . . person . . . directly or indirectly in control of a dwelling." Thus, plaintiffs suggest, the unit owners are responsible for maintenance and repairs to the common elements because the condominium board acts on their behalf.

While this argument is superficially plausible, it is unsupported by either common law, the Condominium Act or practical experience. Where, as here, the putative agent (the board of managers) is not a servant, vicarious liability will not be imposed on the principal (the unit owners, collectively). "Since an agent who is not a servant is not subject to any right of control by his employer over the details of his physical conduct, the responsibility ordinarily rests upon the agent alone, and the principal is not liable for the torts which [the agent] may commit" (Prosser and Keeton, Torts § 70, at 508).

Vicarious liability of a principal for an agent's negligence is predicated on "the general common law notion that one who is in a position to exercise some general control over the situation must exercise it or bear the loss" (*id.* § 69, at 500). In the extreme, where the principal's control is exclusive, liability may be imposed under the doctrine of res ipsa loquitur. . . .

Where control is lacking, however, liability is not imposed even when, in the context of a motion for summary judgment to dismiss the complaint, it is presumed that the putative principal's negligence can be established. . . .

It is clear that condominium common elements are solely under the control of the board of managers. The Condominium Act provides that the cost of materials and labor incurred in connection with the common elements is payable out of common charges (Real Property Law § 339–e), which "shall constitute trust funds for the purpose of paying the cost of such labor or materials performed or furnished at the express request or with the consent of the manager, managing agent or board of managers, and the same shall be expended first for such purpose before expending any part of the same for any other purpose" (Real Property Law § 339–*l*). Implicit in the statutory requirement that work on the common elements be performed "at the express request or with the consent of the . . . board of managers" is the recognition that the board exercises exclusive control over the common elements.

The control purportedly exercised by the unit owners, as collective principal, over the board of managers, as purported agent, is flatly contradicted by case law reflecting general experience with residential forms of common and cooperative ownership. A board of managers takes on the burden of managing the property for the benefit of the proprietary lessees. As one court observed, 'Every man may consider his home his castle and himself as the king thereof; nonetheless his sovereign fiat to use his property as he pleases must yield, at least in degree, where ownership is in common or cooperation with others. The benefits of condominium living demand no less' (*Matter of Levandusky v. One Fifth Ave. Apt. Corp.*, 75 N.Y.2d 530, 537, 554 N.Y.S.2d 807, 553 N.E.2d 1317).

The prerogative of a board of managers to conduct business as it sees fit is well established. If a condominium or cooperative board were the mere instrumentality of its constituent unit owners, as plaintiffs suggest, the Court of Appeals would not have been moved to note that "some check on its potential powers to regulate residents' conduct, life-style and property rights is necessary to protect individual residents from abusive exercise, notwithstanding that the residents have, to an extent, consented to be regulated and even selected their representatives" (*Levandusky,* 75 N.Y.2d at 537, 554 N.Y.S.2d 807, 553 N.E.2d 1317). However, judicial restraint of the board's powers is not permitted to abrogate "the purposes for which the residential community and its governing structure were formed: protection of the interest of the entire community of residents in an environment managed by the board for the common benefit" (*id.*). Under the applicable standard of review afforded by the business judgment rule, so long as a managing board acts without discriminatory intent, actions taken "in furtherance of a legitimate purpose of the cooperative or condominium . . . will generally be upheld" (*Levandusky*).

The realities of cooperative and condominium governance simply do not comport with plaintiffs' attribution of control to the unit owners based on the board's designation as their agent. Since the unit owners have no control over, or direct responsibility for, the common elements and neither statutory nor common law renders an individual condominium unit owner liable for injuries sustained as the result of defects in the common elements, the unit owners are not liable for plaintiffs' damages. . . . As this Court stated in *Aarons v. 401 Hotel,* 12 A.D.3d 293, 293–294, 785 N.Y.S.2d 73, "An undivided interest in the common elements, including the land, does not equate with a proprietary interest in the portion of the building where the accident occurred sufficient to impose liability."

Plaintiffs further argue that the unit owners should be held liable as a matter of policy to afford a means of recovery to a person injured by a defect in the common elements. They note that unlike the cooperative form of ownership, in which the corporation is the owner of the premises and thus provides a source of payment for damages in excess of insurance coverage, the condominium is owned by the unit owners. Therefore, if the condominium's board of managers does not carry insurance against injury to third persons, the effect is to render the condominium judgment proof under circumstances such as these.

While the concern voiced by plaintiffs is sound, it is not material to the matter before us. Here, the condominium board has obtained substantial insurance coverage. Plaintiffs' grievance is not that the amount of liability insurance is inconsequential but that it will be insufficient to cover their damages. Be that as it may, the law only affords a means of recovery; it does not guarantee that the defendant will have sufficient resources to provide full compensation for any and all losses sustained. The situation confronting plaintiffs in this regard is no different than that faced by a plaintiff who is severely injured by a motorist carrying only the minimum liability insurance required by the Vehicle and Traffic Law.

We note that the Condominium Act, while setting forth minimum insurance requirements for property damage (Real Property Law § 339-bb), makes no provision for minimum liability coverage. Defendant . . . points out that California Civil Code § 1365.9(b)(2)(A) requires a condominium to obtain minimum liability insurance in the amount of $2 million if it contains 100 or fewer units. This is precisely the amount of liability coverage obtained by the board of managers in this case. Thus, the board cannot be faulted for unreasonably disregarding the interests of third parties who might sustain injury as the result of the condition of the premises. Nor can it be said that the board failed to exercise good faith in deciding the appropriate amount of liability coverage or that its decision was not the product of honest judgment in furtherance of a legitimate purpose of the condominium.

Whether a judgment awarding damages for personal injury sustained as the result of the defective condition of the common elements of a condominium should be enforceable against the individual dwelling units and whether the board of managers of a condominium should be required to carry a minimum amount of general liability insurance, and the amount of such coverage, are matters appropriately addressed by the Legislature. Balancing the resulting public benefit against the financial impact upon the individual condominium unit owners and the infringement upon the discretion of the board of managers to exercise its business judgment involves competing policy considerations that are within the particular province of the legislative branch of government. We urge legislation to require a condominium to obtain a minimum amount of liability insurance coverage in such amount as may be deemed adequate to protect the public. . . .

NOTES

1. *An alternative judicial solution.* The Texas Supreme Court took another approach to the question of unit owner liability for torts on the common areas:

> We hold . . . that because of the limited control afforded a unit owner by the statutory condominium regime, the creation of a regime effects a reallocation of tort liability. The liability of a condominium co-owner is limited to his *pro rata* interest in the regime as a whole, where such liability arises from those areas held in tenancy-in-common.

Dutcher v. Owens, 647 S.W.2d 948 (Tex.1983). To what extent would the Texas approach have helped the unit owners in *Pekelnaya?*

2. *Legislative approaches.* A significant number of states have attempted to resolve legislatively the question of unit owner liability for torts arising out of the common areas. The most common approach is reflected in the UCA, under which, "an action alleging a wrong done by the association must be brought against the association and not against any unit owner." UCA § 3–111. Under UCA § 3–117, a money judgment against the association constitutes "a lien in favor of the judgment lienholder against all of the units in the condominium at the time at which the judgment is entered." However, the owner of an affected unit may redeem the unit from the lien of the judgment by paying to the lienholder an amount equal to the owner's pro rata share of the judgment; once the owner pays this amount, the judgment lienholder must deliver a release of the lien covering that unit. UCA § 3–117(c).

In California, an important appellate case, Ruoff v. Harbor Creek Community Ass'n, 10 Cal.App.4th 1624, 13 Cal.Rptr.2d 755 (1992), endorsed a joint and several liability approach to unit owner liability. In response, California enacted 1995 legislation that provided civil liability protection to individual unit owners if the owners association maintains insurance coverage for the association's general liability of "at least two million dollars if the common interest development consists of 100 or fewer separate interests" or "at least three million dollars if the common interest development consists of more than 100 separate interests." Cal. Civ. Code § 5805. Presumably, if the association fails to carry the requisite insurance, there is joint and several liability for unit owners. See Jerry C.M. Orten & John H. Zacharia, Allocation of Damages for Tort Liability in Common Interest Communities, 31 Real Prop. Prob & Tr. J. 647 (1997).

E. CONVERSION OF RENTAL HOUSING TO CONDOMINIUMS AND COOPERATIVES

Sometimes a developer seeking a new project will convert an existing apartment building into a condominium (or, less commonly, a cooperative) rather than undertake construction of a new project. There are a number of reasons the developer may prefer conversion; these may include:

- *Initial cost.* The developer may find it cheaper to buy and renovate an existing building than to undertake new construction.

- *Location.* An existing apartment building may occupy a desirable location that is preferable to sites available for new construction.

- *Aesthetic concerns.* An existing building may have architectural or design features that cannot be reproduced in new construction, or at least not without significant expense.

- *Legal constraints.* The developer of a newly-constructed condominium would typically hold warranty liability to the purchaser; by contrast, conversion of an existing building may only require a disclosure of the property's condition and may carry no warranty. Likewise, while new construction requires strict adherence to current building codes, renovation of existing buildings may not. From a cost perspective, these lesser constraints may mean that conversion is more profitable for the developer than new construction, and converted units may in some cases be more affordable to unit purchasers than newly-constructed units.

- *Relative profitability of rental vs. sale markets.* During a long and sustained period of low mortgage interest rates, homeownership becomes more affordable and it becomes easier for consumers to shift from rental to ownership. In a market with increasing demand for homeownership and decreasing demand for tenancies, owners of apartments may conclude that they can earn a greater return by converting and selling the units than by continuing to operate them as apartments. The relative profitability of conversion can also be accentuated by state and local tax policy, particularly in jurisdictions where real property tax assessment rates are higher for rental real property than for owner-occupied property.

The first significant wave of conversions began in the 1970s, and it presented two basic problems. The first was that first-generation common interest ownership statutes did not adequately address or regulate the conversion process and the rights of existing tenants in that process. The second was a perception that conversion displaced existing lower-income tenants and resulted in a reduction in the stock of affordable housing. See, e.g., Kathryn B. Richards, Note, The Illinois Condominium Property Act: An Analysis of Legislative Efforts to Improve Tenants' Rights in the Condominium Conversion Process, 57 DePaul L. Rev. 829, 832–834 (2008) (noting that conversion had resulted in a net loss of rental units in Chicago market).

As these concerns struck the public consciousness, state and local governments began responding through regulatory legislation designed to limit condominium conversions or their negative impacts.

JENNIFER SILVER AND CATHY SHREVE, CONDOMINIUM CONVERSION CONTROLS

An Information Bulletin of the Community and Economic
Development Task Force of the Urban Consortium, 1979

Because of the relative newness of both the conversion phenomenon and the legislative responses developed in reaction to it there is an absence of case law dealing directly with conversion legality issues at the local level. A 1976 National Institute of Municipal Law Officers Report suggests that court decisions related to rent control legislation are the most analogous, and discussed four legal issues raised in relation to rent control, and applicable to conversion control legislation. The first is whether restrictions on the use of private property are a valid exercise of municipal police power in housing situations which threaten the public health, safety or welfare. With respect to rent control provisions, courts have consistently upheld the right to regulate rents under certain housing market conditions which constitute an emergency situation. Generally, emergencies have been found when there is a low or zero vacancy rate,[6] or exorbitant increases in rents[7] or when there is an imbalance in the housing market caused by abnormal events.[8] It should not be assumed, however, that regulations adopted in some areas will be valid in others, since the circumstances which define legitimate use of police power vary with local circumstances and conditions. It is likely, however, that in areas which already have rent control legislation on the books, condominium conversion restrictions are likely to be more easily accepted.

A second legal issue common to both rent control and conversion control is whether these kinds of regulations result in a taking of private property without just compensation, or an "unconstitutional taking" which violates due process of law. Generally, courts have held that these types of regulations fall within municipalities' legitimate police power, the exercise of which does not require compensation. In one case, it was held that "a prohibition simply upon the use of property for purposes that are declared, by valid legislation, to be injurious to health, morals or safety of the community cannot . . . be deemed a taking . . . of property for the public

---

[6]   Albigese v. Jersey City, 127 N.J.Super. 101, 316 A.2d 483 (1974).

[7]   Birkenfeld v. City of Berkeley, 49 Cal.App.3d 464, 122 Cal.Rptr. 891 (1975).

[8]   Edgar A. Levy Leasing Co. v. Siegel, 258 U.S. 242, 42 S.Ct. 289, 66 L.Ed. 595 (1922); Chastleton Corp. v. Sinclair, 264 U.S. 543, 44 S.Ct. 405, 68 L.Ed. 841 (1924).

benefit."[9] Overall, case law has upheld the notion that property owners do not have a right to the most beneficial use of their property, and that restrictions which limit profitability are valid, when they are in the interest of the public welfare.

A third legal issue is whether rent control or conversion restrictions on private property violate the Equal Protection Clause of the Fourteenth Amendment because they discriminate against certain classes of owners. Again, in rent control decisions courts have given municipalities fairly broad latitude in defining restrictions, and have found that equal protection is not violated as long as some reasonable or rational basis exists for the restrictions in question. In one particular case, courts upheld the validity of rent control restrictions which affect certain classes of property owners more than others with the following language:

> Regulatory need in a particular field may appear to the legislative mind in different dimensions and proportions, as more acute in one area than in another. Consequently, the reform may proceed one step at a time, addressing itself to the aspects of the problem which seems the most pressing.[10]

A fourth legal issue is whether local conversion regulations conflict in any way with existing state condominium statutes. If locally adopted restrictions have the effect of circumscribing or prohibiting what is expressly permitted by State Law, they may be struck down.

Overall, there is ample precedent in case law to support the validity of municipal regulations restricting condominium conversions, provided that:

- the laws are adopted as a valid exercise of police power in a clearly defined emergency housing situation in the interest of public welfare;

- the nature of the restrictions is not so onerous or confiscatory as to constitute a taking of private property without just compensation;

- the basis for the restrictions is rational in relation to the specific objective of the regulatory legislation;

- the restrictions do not conflict with existing state statutes.

---

[9] Goldblatt v. Hempstead, 369 U.S. 590, 593, 82 S.Ct. 987, 989, 8 L.Ed.2d 130 (1962), quoting from Mugler v. Kansas, 123 U.S. 623, 8 S.Ct. 273, 31 L.Ed. 205 (1887).

[10] Albigese v. Jersey City, supra. [Editors' Note: The conclusion in the text was reinforced by Pennell v. City of San Jose, 485 U.S. 1, 108 S.Ct. 849, 99 L.Ed.2d 1 (1988), in which the U.S. Supreme Court held that a provision in a rent control ordinance that allowed a hearing officer to consider tenant hardship in fixing a reasonable rent violated neither due process nor equal protection provisions of the United States Constitution. The Court also concluded that it was premature to consider whether the provision created a "taking" of private property without just compensation. See also Yee v. City of Escondido, 503 U.S. 519, 112 S.Ct. 1522, 118 L.Ed.2d 153 (1992) (upholding mobile home rent control physical taking claim).]

NOTES

1.   *Tenant displacement and federal inaction.* Despite widespread concern regarding the extent to which conversion activity produces tenant displacement, Congress has never enacted federal legislation addressing or regulating conversions. In fact, Section 606 of the Condominium and Cooperative Abuse Relief Act of 1980 provided that while "[i]t is the sense of the Congress that . . .[tenants] are entitled to adequate notice of the pending conversion and to receive the first opportunity to purchase units in the converted projects," Congress concluded that "it is the responsibility of state and local governments to provide for such notice and opportunity to purchase" and thus "[left] this responsibility to state and local governments to be carried out." 15 U.S.C. § 3605.

2.   *Uniform Condominium Act.* The UCA contains two sections dealing with conversion issues. Section 4–106 requires the converter to provide additional information in the public offering statements, including an engineering report on structural, mechanical, and electrical systems, the converter's estimate of the useful life of these items (or a statement that no representations in that respect are made), and a list of outstanding code violations and the estimated cost of curing them. Section 4–112 deals with protection of existing tenants. It gives them a right to 120 days written notice before they must vacate their apartments. For 60 days after receiving this notice, they have the right of first refusal to purchase their units at the public offering price. Following the tenant's 60-day period, the converter may not sell a unit on more favorable terms to an outsider within the following 180 days.

3.   *State legislation.* Many states have enacted conversion legislation that is more sweeping and restrictive than the UCA. Increasingly, legislation has focused on protecting elderly and disabled tenants who become involved in the conversion process. See, e.g., Mo. Rev. Stat. § 448.4–112(3) (limiting a converter's right to evict low-and moderate-income elderly and the disabled for up to 15 years if state Housing Development Commission money is available for "acquisition, planning, rehabilitation or other expenses" in connection with the conversion). Consider the far-reaching and restrictive nature of the New York statute:

> No eviction proceedings will be commenced at any time against non-purchasing tenants for failure to purchase or any other reason applicable to expiration of tenancy; provided that such proceedings may be commenced for non-payment of rent, illegal use or occupancy of the premises, refusal of reasonable access to the owner or a similar breach by the non-purchasing tenant of his obligations to the owner of the dwelling unit or the shares allocated thereto; and provided further that an owner of a unit or of the shares allocated thereto may not commence an action to recover possession of a dwelling unit from a non-purchasing tenant on the grounds that he seeks the dwelling unit for the use and occupancy of himself or his family.

N.Y. Gen. Bus. Law § 352–eeee(2)(c)(ii).

4. *Local ordinances and preemption challenges.* Municipalities have often enacted conversion ordinances designed to regulate or restrict conversions within the local market. For example, Chapter 11A of the Montgomery County (Md.) Code provides that both the County and its Housing Opportunities Commission have a right of first refusal to purchase a multi-family apartment building containing more than ten rental units that is being sold for the purpose of conversion to a condominium. See, e.g., Kevin L. Shepherd, Maryland Purchase and Sale Issues for Buyers, Prac. Real Est. Law., Vol. 33, No. 1 (Jan. 2017). Both Denver and San Francisco have ordinances that create rights of first refusal to purchase apartment buildings to preserve affordable housing. See, e.g., Denver Rev. Mun. Code ch. 27, art. III, § 27–47(g) (2019); San. Fran. Admin. Code ch. 60, § 60.8 (2019). Does a public right of first refusal provide meaningful protection for affordable housing? What happens if the city lacks the necessary funds to exercise the right? See generally Peter Damrosch, Note, Public Rights of First Refusal, 129 Yale L.J. 812 (2020) (discussing the merits and shortcomings of such rights).

Developers have frequently challenged municipal conversion ordinances on the ground that state laws addressing conversion preempt local ordinances. These challenges have met with mixed success, depending on the language and scope of the state's conversion legislation. For example, a city ordinance that imposes a moratorium on conversion may be held to conflict with state legislation that authorizes conversion but merely requires notice to tenants as a condition precedent. Where a state has enacted a comprehensive set of protections for tenants in a conversion building, a court may hold that the state legislature has "occupied the field" so as to prohibit municipal conversion limitations of any kind. See, e.g., Claridge House One, Inc. v. Borough of Verona, 490 F.Supp. 706 (D. N.J. 1980), aff'd, 633 F.2d 209 (3d Cir. 1980) (one year local moratorium preempted by comprehensive state regulatory scheme). Sometimes a city or county may simply lack power under its state constitution or statutes to enact the conversion regulation. See Greater Boston Real Estate Bd. v. City of Boston, 397 Mass. 870, 494 N.E.2d 1301 (1986) (city lacked authority under rent control enabling statute to enact condominium and cooperative conversion ordinance); Bannerman v. City of Fall River, 391 Mass. 328, 461 N.E.2d 793 (1984) (ordinance permitting conversion only with approval of housing conversion board held to violate constitutional provision prohibiting cities from enacting a private or civil law governing civil relationships except as an incident to exercise of an independent municipal power). For further background on municipal authority, see generally Sandra M. Stevenson, Understanding Local Government §§ 2.2 to 2.5 (2d. ed. 2009).

5. *The tenancy in common as a device for avoiding conversion restrictions.* In some cities, owners of rental buildings stymied by local conversion ordinances have chosen to eschew the conversion route entirely. Instead, they sell tenancy in common interests in the building to would-be unit purchasers. As part of this transaction, the purchaser receives the right to occupy a particular apartment. The purchaser, in turn, is able to finance the purchase by giving a mortgage on his or her undivided interest in the building.

[For a description of such an arrangement, referred to in California as a "community apartment" or a "deed plan," see Adler v. Elphick, 184 Cal.App.3d 642, 229 Cal.Rptr. 254 (1986).] In San Francisco, this practice led the city council to enact an ordinance extending its regulation of condo conversions to the tenancy in common approach, prohibiting exclusive occupancy agreements between the co-tenants. The ordinance was successfully challenged by building owners on privacy and state preemption grounds. Tom v. City & County of San Francisco, 120 Cal.App.4th 674, 16 Cal.Rptr.3d 13 (2004).

6. *Conversion from cooperative to condominium.* Starting in the 1990s, some cooperatives began to convert to condominium status. See, e.g., Richard Siegler, The Feasibility of Co-op to Condo Conversion, N.Y. Law J., March 5, 1997 p.3. This trend was driven by several factors. The first is the perception that condominium units were selling for significantly more than their coop counterparts. See, e.g., Michael H. Schill, Ioan Voicu & Jonathan Miller, The Condominium v. Cooperative Puzzle: An Empirical Analysis of Housing in New York City, 36 J.Leg.Stud. 275, 312 (2007) (finding 8.8 percent premium). The second factor is the problem of transferability. As we noted earlier, cooperative associations wield more substantial control over an owner's ability to sell or rent a unit than do most condominium associations. While the cooperative's ability to control transfer may be reassuring to those who purchase an apartment with the intent to stay for a long period, the control reduces the pool of potential buyers and makes sale more difficult for those attempting to sell. In New York City, in particular, there have been frequent press articles about what are perceived to be arbitrary and capricious refusals of boards to approve coop transfers. For a useful checklist of the steps necessary in the cooperative-to-condominium conversion, see Stuart M. Saft, Financing Coop-to-Condo Conversion, 16 Real Est. Fin. J. 45 (2001).

7. *Conversion literature.* There has been an enormous output of law review work on the conversion topic. See, e.g., Leighton J. Hyde, Rethinking *Roth*: Why the Florida Legislature Should Empower Local Governments to Regulate Condominium Conversions, 42 Stetson L. Rev. 751 (2013); Julie D. Lawton, Tenant Purchase as a Means of Creating and Preserving Affordable Homeownership, 20 Georgetown J. on Poverty L. & Pol'y 55 (2012); Sarah Comeau, Judicial Sponsored Gentrification of the District of Columbia: The Tenant Opportunity to Purchase Act, 19 Amer. U.J. Gender Soc. Pol'y & L. 401 (2011); Aaron O'Toole & Benita Jones, Tenant Purchase Laws as a Tool for Affordable Housing Preservation: The D.C. Experience, 18 J. Affordable Hous. & Comm. Dev. L. 367 (Summer 2009); Kathryn B. Richards, Note, The Illinois Condominium Property Act: An Analysis of Legislative Efforts to Improve Tenants' Rights in the Condominium Conversion Process, 57 DePaul L. Rev. 829 (2008); Douglas E. Chabot, Note, Casting New Light on a Continuing Problem: Reconsidering the Scope and Protections Offered by Massachusetts's Condominium Conversion Regulations, 42 Suffolk U.L. Rev. 101 (2008); Jonathan Feldman, Regulating Condominium Conversions: The Constitutionality of Tenant Approval Provisions, 21 Urb. L. 85 (1989); Bernard V. Keenan, Condominium Conversion of Residential Rental Units: A Proposal

for State Regulation and a Model Act, 20 U. Mich. J.L. Ref. 639 (1987); David James Burge, Statutory Protection Against Condominium Conversions for North Carolina Residential Tenants, 62 N.C. L. Rev. 1346 (1984).

F. VACATION AND RESORT PROJECTS

Many of us would like to own an interest in an apartment unit at an attractive vacation spot, but few of us have the means to make this possible. Further, most of us would not want to carry the costs of owning such a unit 52 weeks each year merely to enjoy it for a few weeks (or weekends) in our busy schedules. One solution to this problem is "time-sharing" or "interval ownership." These phrases indicate that the "owner" owns only the right to possess the unit for a specified period of time each year—say, from June 1 to June 14. If the interval is two weeks in length, there may be 24 other owners, each of which also has an assigned time slot, making a total of 50 weeks of use each year. [The two remaining weeks may be reserved for cleaning and refurbishing by the management.] Obviously, the purchase of a two-week time interval is much less costly than the purchase of the entire unit. Time-share units are often sold for as little as a few thousand dollars, although in places where recreational activities are seasonal (such as skiing), the price may vary quite widely with the time of year in which the interval is placed.

The following excerpt provides useful insight on the origins and evolution of the time-share concept, and the ensuing notes highlight some of the legal issues associated with time-sharing.

ARTHUR O. SPAULDING, JR. & KAREN D. DENNISON, TIME SHARE TODAY—WILL IT WORK FOR YOUR PROJECT?
Prac. Real Est. Law., Vol. 35, No. 4, 43–45 (July 2019)

Time sharing, as a concept, was conceived in Europe in the 1960s, where it was originally presented as a contractual lodging arrangement featuring the right to make reservations in multiple properties owned by the offeror or even third parties. Ironically, viewed with hindsight, that lodging concept looks surprisingly like the new poster-child of today's time share industry, vacation clubs.

Time sharing first appeared in the United States in the mid to late 1970s. In its early iterations, many time share projects were failed condominiums. Developers of such projects saw time sharing as a panacea for their woes. These time share offerings involved a fixed-unit, fixed-time format, whereby undivided fractional interests in a condominium were offered to multiple owners at a fraction of the cost of whole ownership and provided an owner the right to occupy "his or her" unit each year, on a recurring basis, during the same time period. In the late 1970s, a Seattle-based company, Vacation Internationale, adopted the European model and created the first U.S. vacation club, selling memberships in the club that carried with them rights of use and occupancy for lodging accommodations that company owned or leased. . . .

In the parlance of the time share industry, the first of the two approaches just described is referred to as "deeded ownership" (time share estates, where the time share interest is coupled with an interest in real estate) and the second is referred to as "right to use" (time share interests not coupled with an interest in real estate). Historically, in the deeded ownership model, developers and their lawyers relied on traditional notions of real property development and sale, founded on the principle that buyers in this Country were more accepting of a product that was, essentially, an interest in land. This deeded ownership was one that:

- Could be conveyed by real estate purchase and sales documents;

- Could be transferred by deed;

- Could be seller-financed like conventional real estate, using a seller carry-back note and mortgage.

By the early 1980s, transient lodging facilities such as small hotels and motels, and apartment buildings, were being sold on a deeded ownership basis; but, in lieu of undivided 1/51st interests in specified condominiums, the offering might also involve undivided interests in the entirety of a building (known as "UDIs"). As an example, and in light of the potential difficulty of converting a hotel building into a condominium project, if a hotel property containing 50 rooms were to be time shared on a deeded interest basis using 51 weeks per room, the interests sold would be undivided 1/2550th interests in the whole building, rather than an undivided 1/51st interest in a particular unit.

To the extent that there were regulatory issues or concerns, they were issues and concerns with which real estate developers were familiar. As sales of these products took off in the early 1980s, regulators took a significant interest in adapting their real estate laws and regulations to include time shares as a regulated product. During the 1980s, laws specifically addressing the time share industry were enacted.

In the early days of the time share industry in the United States, most of the developers of time share projects were independent entrepreneurs. It wasn't until later in the 1980s that the success of the product caught the attention of the hotel companies. When those hospitality companies perceived that they could enhance their balance sheets by selling the equivalence of hotel suites "in advance" to up to 50 buyers (or more) per room, the economics of the business persuaded companies like Marriott, Hilton, Hyatt, Wyndham and Disney to jump into the time share market in a major way.

The entry of the hotel companies into the time share business coincided with a movement towards the offering of time shares with more and more flexible features. The fixed-unit, fixed-week product morphed into "floating-unit", "floating-week" interests, often with use rights exercisable only in alternating years.

Another feature of the early time share programs was the inherent limitation of owners having to take a one week vacation at the same project year after year. In many early programs, the owners were locked into the property in which they owned their deeded interest. To address the potential desire of time share owners to vacation elsewhere, two companies were formed to provide a vehicle to channel these desires into a business. These were the so-called time share exchange companies, Resort Condominiums International (RCI) and Interval International (II).

As the time share industry matured in the United States during the 1990s, the business began to see consolidation. The major hotel companies came to dominate the landscape, and their products were coupled with their loyalty programs in ways that were unimaginable in the early 1980s. The independent, single-site time share developer became the exception rather than the norm. The very presence of the hotel companies as the leaders of the industry lent credence to the time share industry like never before. The industry's trade association, the American Resort Development Association (ARDA) became a vocal and effective lobbying advocate for the business. The industry had evolved into a three tiered industry, with the major hotel companies occupying the top tier, time share companies unassociated with hotel products but offering multiple resorts occupying the second tier, and "one-off" developers occupying the bottom tier. The resort products involved not only conventional time share projects, but also ultra-luxury products, such as the Ritz Carlton Club.

By the end of the 1990s, the perceived demand by the marketplace for more and more flexible products ushered in the "vacation club" era. Companies whose offerings were previously of the deeded ownership variety sought to shift into the offering of non-deeded, right-to-use club memberships, where the time share owners association (the "Association") either owned the real estate used and enjoyed by the members, or title to the real estate was held in a trust for the benefit of the HOA and the members. Although vacation clubs could be "single site" projects, most of the vacation club programs were designed to consist of multiple locations, and internal exchange mechanisms were developed to allow "members" of the vacation club to reserve units in different locations within the club. Thus, the vacation clubs took on the image of the exchange companies, at least as far as their own resorts were concerned, while still maintaining the affiliation arrangements with an exchange company to allow the members to "exchange" out of their club and into properties operated by another developer or organization. In addition, the hotel companies operating in the time share business also made it possible for their club members to "exchange" their time share use rights (usually expressed as "points") into their branded loyalty programs, enabling a member to vacation at a hotel operating within the brand's system. . . .

. . . [O]ne of the economic linchpins of the time share business model was the extremely profitable nature of the time share sale financing. A developer often made more money from the hypothecation of the time share notes and purchase contracts than the developer made from the sale of the time share interests themselves. In addition, the major time share development companies, including both the first-tier companies such as the hotel companies and the larger second tier companies, found a ready market for the securitization of time share paper in the late 1990s and the 2000s up until the Great Recession. The arbitrage involved between the consumer paper interest rates (in the mid-teens) and the end-buyer rates (in the stabilized upper single digits) made for attractive returns to the developer hypothecators.

In recent years, the time share industry has continued its path to consolidation. The over-supply of inventory built through the 2000s into the Great Recession, coupled with the limited availability of securitization financing during the Great Recession, caused the major time share players not only to retrench, but precipitated the spin-offs of the time share divisions of the hotel companies into free-standing entities no longer a part of the operating hotel companies. This was in part the result of the continuing demand being made by shareholders in the publicly-traded hotel company sector for earnings, and the drag on earnings posed by the continuing need by the time share companies to invest new capital to create new inventory. In order to avoid the over-commitment of capital for inventory acquisition, the time share companies now prefer arrangements denominated "fee for services" programs, whereby the time share company agrees to license the use of its name to an independent third-party developer/property owner, and to conduct a sales and marketing program for the developer/property owner using inventory owned or built by the third party developer/owner without ever acquiring that inventory itself. Further, as financing for some time share companies dried up after 2008, a number of the second tier companies were acquired and absorbed by the first-tier companies, leaving the industry dominated by first-tier companies.

NOTES

1. *What interest does the time-share owner have?* There are four approaches for creating a time-share interest. To begin, there are two different techniques to the "deeded ownership" approach noted in the excerpt. One involves a "time span estate," under which the buyer of a unit receives a combination of an undivided present interest in a fee simple in the unit (held

as a tenant in common with other time-share owners of the unit), the exclusive right to possession and occupancy of that unit during a regularly recurring period, and an undivided interest in fee simple of the common areas of the project. The "regularly recurring period" (e.g., the third week in July) could be delineated in the deed itself, or more likely in an agreement among all owners in the project identifying each owner's specific period of occupancy. See Daniel T. Engle, Comment, Legal Challenges to Time Sharing Ownership, 45 Mo. L. Rev. 423, 426–27 (1980). By contrast, the other technique involves an "interval estate." The purchaser of an interval estate receives a defeasible estate for the time period during which the purchaser is entitled to occupy the unit, subject to a shifting executory interest which passes to the "next" owner at the end of the interval period, as well as an undivided interest in fee simple in the common areas of the project. Id. at 426.

A third method of creating a time-share interest is simply to convey a fee simple estate which is described as giving possession for a specified period each year. Such estates are not included in the traditional corpus of estates in land recognized by the common law, and for this reason, many attorneys are reluctant to take this approach. At least one state, however, specifically recognizes this approach by statute. See Utah Code Ann. § 57–8–6. A fourth approach (the "right to use" approach described in the excerpt) encompasses a variety of non-fee ownership concepts, such as licenses, leases and club memberships.

2. *State legislation.* Many states have enacted time-sharing legislation. A significant number of these statutes are comprehensive in scope. See, e.g., Fla. Stat. Ann. §§ 721.01 to 721.32; Haw. Rev. Stat. Ann. §§ 514E–1 to 514E–31; Tenn. Code Ann. §§ 66–32–101 to 66–32–139; S.C. Code §§ 27–32–10 to 27–32–250; Neb. Rev. Stat. §§ 76–1701 to 76–1741; Va. Code §§ 55–360 to 55–365.1. Two model timeshare acts served as the impetus and guide for much of this legislation. In 1980, the ULC promulgated the Model Real Estate Time-Share Act (MRETSA), which parallels the UCA and extends much of UCA's consumer protection provisions to time-share purchasers. States that have adopted MRETSA or its substantial equivalent include Louisiana, Maryland and Rhode Island. See La. Stat. Ann. §§ 9–1131.1 to 9–1131.30; Md. Code Real Prop. §§ 11A–101 to 11A–129; R.I. Gen. Laws §§ 34–41–1.01 to 34–41–5.07.

The National TimeSharing Council of the American Land Development Association and the National Association of Real Estate License Law Officials jointly drafted a Model Timeshare Act. This Act is less complex and detailed than MRETSA and affords developers greater flexibility in structuring their documents. Several states patterned their legislation in whole or in part on the Model Timeshare Act, including Florida, Hawaii, Tennessee, Nebraska and Virginia.

Law review commentary on time-sharing and the foregoing legislation is substantial. See, e.g., Elizabeth A. Cameron & Salina Maxwell, Protecting Consumers: The Contractual and Real Estate Issues Involving Timeshares, Quartershares, and Fractional Ownerships, 37 Real Est. L.J. 278 (2009); David

A. Bowen, Note, Timeshare Ownership: Regulation and Common Sense, 18 Loy. Cons. L. Rev. 459 (2006); Robert E. Dady & Robert S. Freedman, To Deed or Not to Deed: That Is the Timeshare Question, 15 Prob. & Prop. 49 (March/April 2001); Mary Lou Savage, Colin M. Lancaster & Nicholas C. Bougopoulos, Time Share Regulation: The Wisconsin Model, 77 Marq. L. Rev. 719 (1994); Cynthia J. Bart, From the Legislatures: The New Mexico Time Share Act, 16 Real Est. L.J. 181 (1987); Robert M. Kessler, Note, The North Carolina Time Share Act, 62 N.C. L. Rev. 1356 (1984); Joseph M. Meier, Note, Timesharing: Oregon's Legislation, 20 Willamette L. Rev. 283 (1984); Ellen R. Peirce & Richard A. Mann, Time-Share Interests in Real Estate: A Critical Evaluation of the Regulatory Environment, 59 Notre Dame L. Rev. 9 (1983).

3. *Time-sharing legal issues.* A number of legal questions exist with respect to time-sharing. They are discussed in the law review comments cited above and will be mentioned only briefly here. They are more acute in the case of plans which make the owners of a given unit tenants in common.

(a) Can a federal tax lien (or other type of lien under state law) against one owner be asserted against the entire unit, jeopardizing the rights of the other owners?

(b) Can the interest of one of the owners of a unit be levied upon to satisfy judgments for torts committed in the common areas or in a unit by another owner, or for damage to the unit itself which injures the enjoyment of another owner?

(c) Is the agreement of the owners of a given unit not to seek partition of that unit an enforceable agreement?

(d) To what extent do covenants not to partition, to share expenses, etc., run with the land and bind future owners?

4. *The partition problem.* Where the time-share owner is a tenant in common with other weekly owners, serious partition problems arise. Typically tenants in common have a right to partition. This could give enormous leverage and potential for mischief to the owner of a single week. Consequently, many time-share declarations prohibit such partition actions. Should such language be enforceable? What if the time-share documents are silent as to this issue? Consider the following North Carolina statute:

> When a time share is owned by two or more persons as tenants in common or as joint tenants either may seek a partition by sale of that interest but no purchaser of a time share may maintain an action for partition by sale or in kind of the unit in which such time share is held.

N.C. Gen. Stat. § 93A–43. For similar statutes, see, e.g., Nev. Rev. Stat. Ann. § 119A.500; N.M. Stat. Ann. § 47–11–3.

5. *The time-share as an "executory contract."* Under each of the first three time-share ownership methods described earlier, the purchaser receives some type of fee interest. Consequently, her ownership is not jeopardized by

subsequent developer bankruptcy. However, where the ownership falls into the fourth category, developer bankruptcy in the past has sometimes proved to be fatal to the time-share owner. To the extent that the purchaser's ownership right was characterized as merely contractual and executory, it was capable of being terminated by a bankruptcy trustee who asserted the power to avoid executory contracts under section 365 of the Bankruptcy Code. See Sombrero Reef Club, Inc. v. Allman, 18 B.R. 612 (Bankr. S.D. Fla. 1982); Mark C. Eriks, Note, Treatment of Time-Share Interests Under the Bankruptcy Code, 59 Ind.L.J. 223 (1984). In response to this problem, Congress in 1984 amended section 365 to give such time-share purchasers essentially the same protection in developer bankruptcy as is afforded an installment land contract vendee when her vendor goes into bankruptcy. 11 U.S.C. § 365(i).

6.   *Governance of a time-share development.* In a sense, time-sharing is inconsistent with the "miniature democracy" concept of the condominium owners association. The owners of a given unit may be scattered over a number of states or even countries, and only a small fraction of them will be in residence in the condominium project at any given time. Their ability to organize and to exchange information and views is obviously very limited. The professional management (usually affiliated with the developer) occupies a position of far greater power than in a project designed for year-around residence. In many cases the owners are asked to give their proxies to the management, and most presumably do so. The MRETSA attempts to encourage owner participation by providing for initiative, referendum, and recall so that owners can institute major policy changes in the project's operation. Is this sort of effort likely to be successful? See Stephen G. Johnakin, Self-Governance in Timeshare Projects: Mail-Order Democracy, 19 Real Prop. Prob. & Tr. J. 705 (1984).

7.   *The regular/time-share condominium "hybrid."* Occasionally a developer will create a condominium project that consists partially of "normal" condominium units and partially of time-share units. Usually the developer did not plan to create this arrangement at the outset. Rather, it typically arises out of an attempt to salvage a traditional condominium development that has not sold well. For example, a developer may have sold only 40–50% of the units and may decide to sell the balance as time-shares. Does this arrangement pose special problems for owners of the regular units? Should time-share owners also be concerned? How should voting and governance be allocated between the two types of owners? Should there be two owners associations? For a good example of how these latter issues can be the source of significant conflict, see Lake Arrowhead Chalets Timeshare Owners Ass'n v. Lake Arrowhead Chalets Owners Ass'n, 51 Cal.App.4th 1403, 59 Cal.Rptr.2d 875 (1996) (by-law amendment that permitted time-share owners to elect only 3 out of 7 directors disadvantaged that class of members, and was ineffective under applicable corporation code because it was not approved by the members of that class); Surrey Condo. Ass'n, Inc. v. Webb, 163 S.W.3d 531, 536 (Mo. Ct. App. 2005) (declaration did not permit association to assessment that included reserve

fund charge for refurbishing time-share units against owner whose unit was not time-shared and who thus received no benefit from such charges).

From the developer's perspective, the failure of the original documents in a "regular" condominium development to authorize the subsequent conversion of unsold units to time share status can sometimes pose an insurmountable hurdle to such a conversion. See, e.g., Colo. Rev. Stat. 38–33–111(1) ("No time share estates shall be created with respect to any condominium unit except pursuant to provisions in the project instruments expressly permitting the creation of such estates."). Thus, a prudent developer who wants to retain the option to convert some or all of the units to time share status should include such an authorization in the original project documents.

Another form of hybrid is the condominium hotel: a real estate project that presents itself to the world as a traditional hotel, but in which some of its rooms or units are actually condominium units owned by individuals. For further discussion, see Alvin L. Arnold, 2 Real Estate Transactions: Structure and Analysis § 16:214.

8. *Real estate interests as securities.* With time-share and hybrid projects of the type noted above, it is often the case that the documentation may allow a unit owner to place their unit into a "rental pool." The manager of the project can make units in the pool available for temporary occupancy, with unit owners entitled to receive the net revenues generated by the temporary occupancy of their units. This may permit a unit owner in a hybrid project to defray a portion of their ownership costs (and for this reason, the availability of a rental pool may be a key selling point for the developer of such a hybrid project).

These arrangements raise the question whether the developer of such projects should be considered as selling "securities" and thus should be subject to federal and state securities laws. The subject is an important one, although the detailed consequences of classification of an offering as a security are far beyond the scope of this book. In general, several results follow. The offering may become subject to the rather onerous registration requirements of the Securities Act of 1933 or to similar state laws in some jurisdictions. In some states, a state agency may exercise even more direct supervision over the offering, requiring that it be found "fair, just, and reasonable" or in compliance with some similar standard before it can be sold. Further, the Securities Exchange Act of 1934 may raise problems for the offeror; the sales people may need to be licensed by the SEC, the offeror may be subject to certain record-keeping requirements, and may be limited by law in the ability to offer financing for the units. Finally, the stringent antifraud provisions of federal and some state securities acts may subject the offeror to a much stronger probability of liability for misstatements or half-truths than would be the case under common law fraud rules. The result is that real estate developers are exceedingly reluctant to have their offerings considered securities.

Under SEC v. W.J. Howey Co., 328 U.S. 293, 66 S.Ct. 1100, 90 L.Ed. 1244 (1946), a security exists where there is "a contract, transaction or scheme whereby a person invests his money in a common enterprise and is led to expect profits solely from the efforts of the promoter or a third party, it being immaterial whether the shares in the enterprise are evidenced by formal certificates or by nominal interests in the physical assets employed in the enterprise." Thus, if the property is to be rented out to others full-time, and the developer or an affiliate will be involved in managing or renting it, then a security is being offered under the *Howey* test. Thus limited partnership interests, or even tenancies in common, in rental apartment buildings and commercial properties are quite obviously securities if there is some centralized management (as is nearly always the case). But property which the purchaser can occupy personally certainly is not a security in most cases. It would be quite a surprise if the courts began to hold that the typical suburban homebuilder was actually selling securities! The matter might be thought a bit more debatable in the case of cooperatives, since a co-operative buyer does receive a share of stock (an instrument traditionally associated with the concept of a security). But in United Housing Foundation, Inc. v. Forman, 421 U.S. 837, 95 S.Ct. 2051, 44 L.Ed.2d 621 (1975), the Supreme Court rejected such an argument. It held that a security was an "investment contract," and that no such contract was involved when a cooperative unit was sold.

Thus, the extremes of characterization are clear. If one purchases solely for one's own use and occupancy, there is no security, while if one purchases for the purpose of making money through the efforts of others, a security is being sold. Between these poles, however, many intermediate situations exist, the resolution of which is beyond the focus of this book. For further discussion, see, e.g., Alexander D. Selig, A Practitioner's Guide to When Real Estate Becomes a Security, 9 Elon L. Rev. 391 (2017); Timi A. Hallem & Jason T. Taketa, Treatment of Condominium Hotels as Securities after *Salameh*, 36 L.A. Law. 11 (Jan. 2014); Alvin Robert Thorup, TIC or Treat: How Tenant-in-Common Real Estate Sales Can Avoid the Reach of the Securities Laws, 34 Real Est. L.J. 422 (2006); James McGuire & Daniel Brown, Are Condo Hotels Subject to SEC Regulations?, 20 N.Y. Real Est. L. Rep. (Feb. 2006), at 1; Elena Marty-Nelson, When Is a Real Estate Interest a "Security"?, 17 Prac. Real Est. Law. 7 (May 2001); Kenneth P. Krohn, Fractional Ownership and Timeshare Programs: Are They Subject to the Securities Act of 1933 and Securities Exchange Act of 1934?, 54 Bus. Law. 1181 (1999); Edward T. DeSilva, Comment, *Hocking v. Dubois*: Applying the Securities Laws to Condominium Resales, 58 Ford. L. Rev. 1121 (1990); Peter A. MacLaren, Note, Profits in Paradise: When Resort Condominiums Qualify as Investment Contracts, 19 Golden Gate U.L. Rev. 177 (1989).

APPENDIX

LAND FINANCING FORMS

■ ■ ■

1. FANNIE MAE/FREDDIE MAC MULTISTATE FIXED RATE NOTE—SINGLE FAMILY

This Note, together with the Fannie Mae/Freddie Mac Uniform Mortgage and Deed of Trust Instruments, also reproduced in this Appendix, constitute the core of the most pervasively used single family residential financing document package. Because use of these documents is required for secondary market purchase by Fannie Mae and Freddie Mac, they have established a nationwide norm on numerous substantive issues, many of which are considered elsewhere in this volume.

NOTE

_____, ____   _____   _____
     [Date]   [City]   [State]

_____
                    [Property Address]

1. BORROWER'S PROMISE TO PAY

In return for a loan that I have received, I promise to pay U.S. $_____ (this amount is called "Principal"), plus interest, to the order of the Lender. The Lender is _____. I will make all payments under this Note in the form of cash, check or money order.

I understand that the Lender may transfer this Note. The Lender or anyone who takes this Note by transfer and who is entitled to receive payments under this Note is called the "Note Holder."

2. INTEREST

Interest will be charged on unpaid principal until the full amount of Principal has been paid. I will pay interest at a yearly rate of _____%.

The interest rate required by this Section 2 is the rate I will pay both before and after any default described in Section 6(B) of this Note.

3. PAYMENTS

(A) Time and Place of Payments

I will pay principal and interest by making a payment every month.

I will make my monthly payment on the _____ day of each month beginning on _____, _____. I will make these payments every month until I have paid all of the principal and interest and any other charges described below that I may owe under this Note. Each monthly payment will be applied as of its scheduled due date and will be applied to interest before Principal. If, on _____, 20_____, I still owe amounts under this Note, I will pay those amounts in full on that date, which is called the "Maturity Date."

I will make my monthly payments at _____ or at a different place if required by the Note Holder.

(B) Amount of Monthly Payments

My monthly payment will be in the amount of U.S. $_____.

4.   BORROWER'S RIGHT TO PREPAY

I have the right to make payments of Principal at any time before they are due. A payment of Principal only is known as a "Prepayment." When I make a Prepayment, I will tell the Note Holder in writing that I am doing so. I may not designate a payment as a Prepayment if I have not made all the monthly payments due under the Note.

I may make a full Prepayment or partial Prepayments without paying a Prepayment charge. The Note Holder will use my Prepayments to reduce the amount of Principal that I owe under this Note. However, the Note Holder may apply my Prepayment to the accrued and unpaid interest on the Prepayment amount, before applying my Prepayment to reduce the Principal amount of the Note. If I make a partial Prepayment, there will be no changes in the due date or in the amount of my monthly payment unless the Note Holder agrees in writing to those changes.

5.   LOAN CHARGES

If a law, which applies to this loan and which sets maximum loan charges, is finally interpreted so that the interest or other loan charges collected or to be collected in connection with this loan exceed the permitted limits, then: (a) any such loan charge shall be reduced by the amount necessary to reduce the charge to the permitted limit; and (b) any sums already collected from me which exceeded permitted limits will be refunded to me. The Note Holder may choose to make this refund by reducing the Principal I owe under this Note or by making a direct payment to me. If a refund reduces Principal, the reduction will be treated as a partial Prepayment.

6.   BORROWER'S FAILURE TO PAY AS REQUIRED

(A) Late Charge for Overdue Payments

If the Note Holder has not received the full amount of any monthly payment by the end of _____ calendar days after the date it is due, I will pay a late charge to the Note Holder. The amount of the charge will be _____% of my overdue payment of principal and interest. I will pay this late charge promptly but only once on each late payment.

(B) Default

If I do not pay the full amount of each monthly payment on the date it is due, I will be in default.

(C) Notice of Default

If I am in default, the Note Holder may send me a written notice telling me that if I do not pay the overdue amount by a certain date, the Note Holder may require me to pay immediately the full amount of Principal which has not been paid and all the interest that I owe on that amount. That date must be at least 30 days after the date on which the notice is mailed to me or delivered by other means.

(D) No Waiver By Note Holder

Even if, at a time when I am in default, the Note Holder does not require me to pay immediately in full as described above, the Note Holder will still have the right to do so if I am in default at a later time.

(E) Payment of Note Holder's Costs and Expenses

If the Note Holder has required me to pay immediately in full as described above, the Note Holder will have the right to be paid back by me for all of its costs and expenses in enforcing this Note to the extent not prohibited by applicable law. Those expenses include, for example, reasonable attorneys' fees.

7. GIVING OF NOTICES

Unless applicable law requires a different method, any notice that must be given to me under this Note will be given by delivering it or by mailing it by first class mail to me at the Property Address above or at a different address if I give the Note Holder a notice of my different address.

Any notice that must be given to the Note Holder under this Note will be given by delivering it or by mailing it by first class mail to the Note Holder at the address stated in Section 3(A) above or at a different address if I am given a notice of that different address.

8. OBLIGATIONS OF PERSONS UNDER THIS NOTE

If more than one person signs this Note, each person is fully and personally obligated to keep all of the promises made in this Note, including the promise to pay the full amount owed. Any person who is a guarantor, surety or endorser of this Note is also obligated to do these things. Any person who takes over these obligations, including the obligations of a guarantor, surety or endorser of this Note, is also obligated to keep all of the promises made in this Note. The Note Holder may enforce its rights under this Note against each person individually or against all of us together. This means that any one of us may be required to pay all of the amounts owed under this Note.

9. WAIVERS

I and any other person who has obligations under this Note waive the rights of Presentment and Notice of Dishonor. "Presentment" means the right to require the Note Holder to demand payment of amounts due. "Notice of Dishonor" means the right to require the Note Holder to give notice to other persons that amounts due have not been paid.

10. UNIFORM SECURED NOTE

This Note is a uniform instrument with limited variations in some jurisdictions. In addition to the protections given to the Note Holder under this Note, a Mortgage, Deed of Trust, or Security Deed (the "Security Instrument"), dated the same date as this Note, protects the Note Holder from possible losses which might result if I do not keep the promises which I make in this Note. That Security Instrument describes how and under what conditions I may be required to make immediate payment in full of all amounts I owe under this Note. Some of those conditions are described as follows:

If all or any part of the Property or any Interest in the Property is sold or transferred (or if Borrower is not a natural person and a beneficial interest in Borrower is sold or transferred) without Lender's prior written consent, Lender may require immediate payment in full of all sums secured by this Security Instrument. However, this option shall not be exercised by Lender if such exercise is prohibited by Applicable Law.

If Lender exercises this option, Lender shall give Borrower notice of acceleration. The notice shall provide a period of not less than 30 days from the date the notice is given in accordance with Section 15 within which Borrower must pay all sums secured by this Security Instrument. If Borrower fails to pay these sums prior to the expiration of this period, Lender may invoke any remedies permitted by this Security Instrument without further notice or demand on Borrower.

Witness the Hand(s) and Seal(s) of the Undersigned.

_____

_____
(Seal)
-Borrower

_____ (Seal)
-Borrower

_____ (Seal)
-Borrower

[Sign Original Only]

2. FANNIE MAE/FREDDIE MAC ADJUSTABLE RATE NOTE

The drafter of a mortgage note with an adjustable interest rate provision must address a variety of issues. A major factor is the *index* itself. Another is the *frequency* of rate adjustment. In practice, these two factors are often tied together. For example, if the index is the rate on three-year U.S. Treasury securities, the adjustment frequency will typically be every three years. In addition, the documents may or may not have an *interest rate cap*—a limit above which the rate will not be raised, regardless of the movement of the index rate. Similarly, a *payment cap* may be imposed, so that monthly payments will not exceed a given amount, notwithstanding index rate fluctuations.

The particular form presented here, prepared by Fannie Mae and Freddie Mac, adopts a "one-year index"—that is, the weekly average yield of U.S. Treasury securities, adjusted to a constant maturity of one year. The reader is cautioned that transactions which employ different parameters than these will require considerable redrafting or the adoption of different Fannie Mae and Freddie Mac forms if such are available to fit the transaction.

ADJUSTABLE RATE NOTE

(One-Year Treasury Index-Rate Caps)

THIS NOTE PROVIDES FOR A CHANGE IN MY FIXED INTEREST RATE TO AN ADJUSTABLE INTEREST RATE. THIS NOTE LIMITS THE AMOUNT MY ADJUSTABLE INTEREST RATE CAN CHANGE AT ANY ONE TIME AND THE MAXIMUM RATE I MUST PAY.

_____, ____   _____   _____
        [Date]   [City]   [State]

_____
[Property Address]

1. BORROWER'S PROMISE TO PAY

In return for a loan that I have received, I promise to pay U.S. $_____ (this amount is called "Principal"), plus interest, to the order of Lender. Lender is _____. I will make all payments under this Note in the form of cash, check or money order.

I understand that Lender may transfer this Note. Lender or anyone who takes this Note by transfer and who is entitled to receive payments under this Note is called the "Note Holder."

2. INTEREST

Interest will be charged on unpaid principal until the full amount of Principal has been paid. I will pay interest at a yearly rate of _____%. The interest rate I will pay may change in accordance with Section 4 of this Note.

The interest rate required by this Section 2 and Section 4 of this Note is the rate I will pay both before and after any default described in Section 7(B) of this Note.

3. PAYMENTS

(A) Time and Place of Payments

I will pay principal and interest by making a payment every month.

I will make my monthly payments on the first day of each month beginning on _____, ____. I will make these payments every month until I have paid all of the principal and interest and any other charges described below that I may owe under this Note. Each monthly payment will be applied as of its scheduled due date and will be applied to interest before Principal. If, on _____, ____, I still owe amounts under this Note, I will pay those amounts in full on that date, which is called the "Maturity Date."

I will make my monthly payments at _____ or at a different place if required by the Note Holder.

(B) Amount of My Initial Monthly Payments

Each of my initial monthly payments will be in the amount of U.S. $_____. This amount may change.

(C) Monthly Payment Changes

Changes in my monthly payment will reflect changes in the unpaid principal of my loan and in the interest rate that I must pay. The Note Holder will determine my new interest rate and the changed amount of my monthly payment in accordance with Section 4 of this Note.

4.   ADJUSTABLE INTEREST RATE AND MONTHLY PAYMENT CHANGES

(A) Change Dates

The initial fixed interest rate I will pay will change to an adjustable interest rate on the first day of _____, ____, and the adjustable interest rate I will pay may change on that day every 12th month thereafter. The date on which my initial fixed interest rate changes to an adjustable interest rate, and each date on which my adjustable interest rate could change, is called a "Change Date."

(B) The Index

Beginning with the first Change Date, my adjustable interest rate will be based on an Index that is calculated and provided to the general public by an administrator (the "Administrator"). The "Index" is the weekly average yield on United States Treasury securities adjusted to a constant maturity of one year, as made available by the Board of Governors of the Federal Reserve System. The most recent Index value available as of the date 45 days before each Change Date is called the "Current Index," provided that if the Current Index is less than zero, then the Current Index will be deemed to be zero for purposes of calculating my interest rate.

If the Index is no longer available, it will be replaced in accordance with Section 4(G) below.

(C) Calculation of Changes

Before each Change Date, the Note Holder will calculate my new interest rate by adding _____ percentage points (_____%) (the "Margin") to the Current Index. The Margin may change if the Index is replaced by the Note Holder in accordance with Section 4(G)(2) below. The Note Holder will then round the result of the Margin plus the Current Index to the nearest one-eighth of one percentage point (0.125%). Subject to the limits stated in Section 4(D) below, this rounded amount will be my new interest rate until the next Change Date.

The Note Holder will then determine the amount of the monthly payment that would be sufficient to repay the unpaid principal that I am expected to owe at the Change Date in full on the Maturity Date at my new interest rate in substantially equal payments. The result of this calculation will be the new amount of my monthly payment.

(D) Limits on Interest Rate Changes

The interest rate I am required to pay at the first Change Date will not be greater than _____% or less than _____%. Thereafter, my adjustable interest rate will never be increased or decreased on any single Change Date by more than two percentage points from the rate of interest I have been paying for the preceding 12 months. My interest rate will never be greater than _____% or less than _____%.

(E) Effective Date of Changes

My new interest rate will become effective on each Change Date. I will pay the amount of my new monthly payment beginning on the first monthly payment date after the Change Date until the amount of my monthly payment changes again.

(F) Notice of Changes

The Note Holder will deliver or mail to me a notice of any changes in my initial fixed interest rate to an adjustable interest rate and of any changes in my adjustable interest rate before the effective date of any change. The notice will include the amount of my monthly payment, any information required by law to be given to me and also the title and telephone number of a person who will answer any question I may have regarding the notice.

(G) Replacement Index and Replacement Margin

The Index is deemed to be no longer available and will be replaced if any of the following events (each, a "Replacement Event") occur: (i) the Administrator has permanently or indefinitely stopped providing the Index to the general public; or (ii) the Administrator or its regulator issues an official public statement that the Index is no longer reliable or representative.

If a Replacement Event occurs, the Note Holder will select a new index (the "Replacement Index") and may also select a new margin (the "Replacement Margin"), as follows:

(1) If a replacement index has been selected or recommended for use in consumer products, including residential adjustable-rate mortgages, by the Board of Governors of the Federal Reserve System, the Federal Reserve Bank of New York, or a committee endorsed or convened by the Board of Governors of the Federal Reserve System or the Federal Reserve Bank of New York at the time of a Replacement Event, the Note Holder will select that index as the Replacement Index.

(2) If a replacement index has not been selected or recommended for use in consumer products under Section (G)(1) at the time of a Replacement Event, the Note Holder will make a reasonable, good faith effort to select a Replacement Index and a Replacement Margin that, when added together, the Note Holder reasonably expects will minimize any change in the cost of the loan, taking into account the historical performance of the Index and the Replacement Index.

The Replacement Index and Replacement Margin, if any, will be operative immediately upon a Replacement Event and will be used to determine my interest rate and monthly payments on Change Dates that are more than 45 days after a Replacement Event. The Index and Margin could be replaced more than once during the term of my Note, but only if another Replacement Event occurs. After a Replacement Event, all references to the "Index" and "Margin" will be deemed to be references to the "Replacement Index" and "Replacement Margin."

The Note Holder will also give me notice of my Replacement Index and Replacement Margin, if any, and such other information required by applicable law and regulation.

5. BORROWER'S RIGHT TO PREPAY

I have the right to make payments of Principal at any time before they are due. A payment of Principal only is known as a "Prepayment." When I make a Prepayment, I will tell the Note Holder in writing that I am doing so. I may not designate a payment as a Prepayment if I have not made all the monthly payments due under this Note.

I may make a full Prepayment or partial Prepayments without paying any Prepayment charge. The Note Holder will use my Prepayments to reduce the amount of Principal that I owe under this Note. However, the Note Holder may apply my Prepayment to the accrued and unpaid interest on the Prepayment amount before applying my Prepayment to reduce the Principal amount of this Note. If I make a partial Prepayment, there will be no changes in the due dates of my monthly payments unless the Note Holder agrees in writing to those changes. My partial Prepayment may reduce the amount of my monthly payments after the first Change Date following my partial Prepayment. However, any reduction due to my partial Prepayment may be offset by an interest rate increase.

6. LOAN CHARGES

If a law, which applies to this loan and which sets maximum loan charges, is finally interpreted so that the interest or other loan charges collected or to be collected in connection with this loan exceed the permitted limits, then: (a) any such loan charge shall be reduced by the amount necessary to reduce the charge to the permitted limit; and (b) any sums already collected from me that exceeded permitted limits will be refunded to me. The Note Holder may choose to make this refund by reducing the Principal I owe under this Note or by making a direct payment to me. If a refund reduces Principal, the reduction will be treated as a partial Prepayment.

7. BORROWER'S FAILURE TO PAY AS REQUIRED

(A) Late Charges for Overdue Payments

If the Note Holder has not received the full amount of any monthly payment by the end of _____ calendar days after the date it is due,

I will pay a late charge to the Note Holder. The amount of the charge will be _____% of my overdue payment of principal and interest. I will pay this late charge promptly but only once on each late payment.

(B) Default

If I do not pay the full amount of each monthly payment on the date it is due, I will be in default.

(C) Notice of Default

If I am in default, the Note Holder may send me a written notice telling me that if I do not pay the overdue amount by a certain date, the Note Holder may require me to pay immediately the full amount of Principal that has not been paid and all the interest that I owe on that amount. That date must be at least 30 days after the date on which the notice is mailed to me or delivered by other means.

(D) No Waiver By Note Holder

Even if, at a time when I am in default, the Note Holder does not require me to pay immediately in full as described above, the Note Holder will still have the right to do so if I am in default at a later time.

(E) Payment of Note Holder's Costs and Expenses

If the Note Holder has required me to pay immediately in full as described above, the Note Holder will have the right to be paid back by me for all of its costs and expenses in enforcing this Note to the extent not prohibited by applicable law. Those expenses include, for example, reasonable attorneys' fees.

8. GIVING OF NOTICES

Unless applicable law requires a different method, any notice that must be given to me under this Note will be given by delivering it or by mailing it by first class mail to me at the Property Address above or at a different address if I give the Note Holder a notice of my different address.

Unless the Note Holder requires a different method, any notice that must be given to the Note Holder under this Note will be given by mailing it by first class mail to the Note Holder at the address stated in Section 3(A) above or at a different address if I am given a notice of that different address.

9. OBLIGATIONS OF PERSONS UNDER THIS NOTE

If more than one person signs this Note, each person is fully and personally obligated to keep all of the promises made in this Note, including the promise to pay the full amount owed. Any person who is a guarantor, surety or endorser of this Note is also obligated to do these things. Any person who takes over these obligations, including the obligations of a guarantor, surety or endorser of this Note, is also obligated to keep all of the promises made in this Note. The Note Holder may enforce its rights under this Note against each person individually or against all of us together. This means that any one of us may be required to pay all of the amounts owed under this Note.

10. WAIVERS

I and any other person who has obligations under this Note waive the rights of Presentment and Notice of Dishonor. "Presentment" means the right to require the Note Holder to demand payment of amounts due. "Notice of Dishonor" means the right to require the Note Holder to give notice to other persons that amounts due have not been paid.

11. UNIFORM SECURED NOTE

This Note is a uniform instrument with limited variations in some jurisdictions. In addition to the protections given to the Note Holder under this Note, a Mortgage, Deed of Trust, or Security Deed (the "Security Instrument"), dated the same date as this Note, protects the Note Holder from possible losses that might result if I do not keep the promises that I make in this Note. That Security Instrument describes how and under what conditions I may be required to make immediate payment in full of all amounts I owe under this Note. Some of those conditions read as follows:

(A) Until my initial fixed interest rate changes to an adjustable interest rate under the terms stated in Section 4 above, Uniform Covenant 18 of the Security Instrument shall read as follows:

Transfer of the Property or a Beneficial Interest in Borrower. As used in this Section 18, "Interest in the Property" means any legal or beneficial interest in the Property, including, but not limited to, those beneficial interests transferred in a bond for deed, contract for deed, installment sales contract or escrow agreement, the intent of which is the transfer of title by Borrower at a future date to a purchaser.

If all or any part of the Property or any Interest in the Property is sold or transferred (or if Borrower is not a natural person and a beneficial interest in Borrower is sold or transferred) without Lender's prior written consent, Lender may require immediate payment in full of all sums secured by this Security Instrument. However, this option shall not be exercised by Lender if such exercise is prohibited by Applicable Law.

If Lender exercises this option, Lender shall give Borrower notice of acceleration. The notice shall provide a period of not less than 30 days from the date the notice is given in accordance with Section 15 within which Borrower must pay all sums secured by this Security Instrument. If Borrower fails to pay these sums prior to the expiration of this period, Lender may invoke any remedies permitted by this Security Instrument without further notice or demand on Borrower.

(B) When my initial fixed interest rate changes to an adjustable interest rate under the terms stated in Section 4 above, Uniform Covenant 18 of the Security Instrument described in Section 11(A) above shall then cease to be in effect, and Uniform Covenant 18 of the Security Instrument shall instead read as follows:

Transfer of the Property or a Beneficial Interest in Borrower. As used in this Section 18, "Interest in the Property" means any legal or beneficial interest in the Property, including, but not limited to, those beneficial interests transferred in a bond for deed, contract for deed, installment sales contract or escrow agreement, the intent of which is the transfer of title by Borrower at a future date to a purchaser.

If all or any part of the Property or any Interest in the Property is sold or transferred (or if Borrower is not a natural person and a beneficial interest in Borrower is sold or transferred) without Lender's prior written consent, Lender may require immediate payment in full of all sums secured by this Security Instrument. However, this option shall not be exercised by Lender if such exercise is prohibited by Applicable Law. Lender also shall not exercise this option if: (a) Borrower causes to be submitted to Lender information required by Lender to evaluate the intended transferee as if a new loan were being made to the transferee; and (b) Lender reasonably determines that Lender's security will not be impaired by the loan assumption and that the risk of a breach of any covenant or agreement in this Security Instrument is acceptable to Lender.

To the extent permitted by Applicable Law, Lender may charge a reasonable fee as a condition to Lender's consent to the loan assumption. Lender also may require the transferee to sign an assumption agreement that is acceptable to Lender and that obligates the transferee to keep all the promises and agreements made in the Note and in this Security Instrument. Borrower will continue to be obligated under the Note and this Security Instrument unless Lender releases Borrower in writing.

If Lender exercises the option to require immediate payment in full, Lender shall give Borrower notice of acceleration. The notice shall provide a period of not less than 30 days from the date the notice is given in accordance with Section 15 within which Borrower must pay all sums secured by this Security Instrument. If Borrower fails to pay these sums prior to the expiration of this period, Lender may invoke any remedies permitted by this Security Instrument without further notice or demand on Borrower.

WITNESS THE HAND(S) AND SEAL(S) OF THE UNDERSIGNED.

_____(Seal)
-Borrower

                                     _____(Seal)
                                     -Borrower

                                     _____(Seal)
                                     -Borrower

3. FANNIE MAE/FREDDIE MAC UNIFORM MORTGAGE—DEED OF TRUST COVENANTS—SINGLE FAMILY

    Fannie Mae and Freddie Mac have prepared a uniform mortgage or deed of trust (whichever is locally customary) for each U.S. state. The Uniform Covenants (clauses 1 through 21) reproduced below are contained in all Fannie Mae/Freddie Mac single-family mortgages and deeds of trust, and serve to foster national uniformity on a variety of significant substantive mortgage law issues. We also include here an introductory "Definitions" section that defines the terms used in the Uniform Covenants. The Fannie Mae/Freddie Mac forms also include non-uniform covenants for each state to take into account local real estate security formats, substantive law requirements, and foreclosure methods. The Uniform Covenants as reprinted here were last revised in January, 2001. The non-uniform covenants in several states have been revised more recently to reflect changes in state law.

DEFINITIONS

Words used in multiple sections of this document are defined below and other words are defined in Sections 3, 11, 13, 18, 20, and 21. Certain rules regarding the usage of words used in this document are also provided in Section 16.

(A) "Security Instrument" means this document, which is dated _____, _____, together with all Riders to this document.

(B) "Borrower" is _____. Borrower is the trustor under this Security Instrument.

(C) "Lender" is _____. Lender is a _____ organized and existing under the laws of _____. Lender's address is _____. Lender is the beneficiary under this Security Instrument.

(D) "Trustee" is _____.

(E) "Note" means the promissory note signed by Borrower and dated _____, _____. The Note states that Borrower owes Lender _____ Dollars (U.S. $_____) plus interest. Borrower has promised to pay this debt in regular Periodic Payments and to pay the debt in full not later than _____.

(F) "Property" means the property that is described below under the heading "Transfer of Rights in the Property."

(G) "Loan" means the debt evidenced by the Note, plus interest, any prepayment charges and late charges due under the Note, and all sums due under this Security Instrument, plus interest.

(H) "Riders" means all Riders to this Security Instrument that are executed by Borrower. The following Riders are to be executed by Borrower [check box as applicable]:

- ☐ Adjustable Rate Rider
- ☐ Balloon Rider
- ☐ 1–4 Family Rider
- ☐ Condominium Rider
- ☐ Planned Unit Development Rider
- ☐ Biweekly Payment Rider
- ☐ Second Home Rider
- ☐ Other(s) [specify] _____

(I) "Applicable Law" means all controlling applicable federal, state and local statutes, regulations, ordinances and administrative rules and orders (that have the effect of law) as well as all applicable final, non-appealable judicial opinions.

(J) "Community Association Dues, Fees, and Assessments" means all dues, fees, assessments and other charges that are imposed on Borrower or the Property by a condominium association, homeowners association or similar organization.

(K) "Electronic Funds Transfer" means any transfer of funds, other than a transaction originated by check, draft, or similar paper instrument, which is initiated through an electronic terminal, telephonic instrument, computer, or magnetic tape so as to order, instruct, or authorize a financial institution to debit or credit an account. Such term includes, but is not limited to, point-of-sale transfers, automated teller machine transactions, transfers initiated by telephone, wire transfers, and automated clearinghouse transfers.

(L) "Escrow Items" means those items that are described in Section 3.

(M) "Miscellaneous Proceeds" means any compensation, settlement, award of damages, or proceeds paid by any third party (other than insurance proceeds paid under the coverages described in Section 5) for: (i) damage to, or destruction of, the Property; (ii) condemnation or other taking of all or any part of the Property; (iii) conveyance in lieu of condemnation; or (iv) misrepresentations of, or omissions as to, the value and/or condition of the Property.

(N) "Mortgage Insurance" means insurance protecting Lender against the nonpayment of, or default on, the Loan.

(O) "Periodic Payment" means the regularly scheduled amount due for (i) principal and interest under the Note, plus (ii) any amounts under Section 3 of this Security Instrument.

(P) "RESPA" means the Real Estate Settlement Procedures Act (12 U.S.C. § 2601 et seq.) and its implementing regulation, Regulation X (24 C.F.R. Part 3500), as they might be amended from time to time, or any additional or successor legislation or regulation that governs the same subject matter. As used in this Security Instrument, "RESPA" refers to all requirements and restrictions that are imposed in regard to a "federally related mortgage loan" even if the Loan does not qualify as a "federally related mortgage loan" under RESPA.

(Q) "Successor in Interest of Borrower" means any party that has taken title to the Property, whether or not that party has assumed Borrower's obligations under the Note and/or this Security Instrument.

TRANSFER OF RIGHTS IN THE PROPERTY. This Security Instrument secures to Lender: (i) the repayment of the Loan, and all renewals, extensions, and modifications of the Note; and (ii) the performance of Borrower's covenants and agreements under this Security Instrument and the Note. For this purpose, Borrower irrevocably grants and conveys to Trustee, in trust, with power of sale, the following described property located in [Type of Recording Jurisdiction] of [Name of Recording Jurisdiction]:

[Legal description]

which currently has the address of: [Street, City, State, Zip] ("Property Address").

TOGETHER WITH all the improvements now or hereafter erected on the property, and all easements, appurtenances, and fixtures now or hereafter a part of the property. All replacements and additions shall also be covered by this Security Instrument. All of the foregoing is referred to in this Security Instrument as the "Property."

BORROWER COVENANTS that Borrower is lawfully seised of the estate hereby conveyed and has the right to grant and convey the Property and that the Property is unencumbered, except for encumbrances of record. Borrower warrants and will defend generally the title to the Property against all claims and demands, subject to any encumbrances of record.

THIS SECURITY INSTRUMENT combines uniform covenants for national use and non-uniform covenants with limited variations by jurisdiction to constitute a uniform security instrument covering real property.

UNIFORM COVENANTS. Borrower and Lender covenant and agree as follows:

1. Payment of Principal, Interest, Escrow Items, Prepayment Charges, and Late Charges. Borrower shall pay when due the principal of, and interest on, the debt evidenced by the Note and any prepayment charges and late charges due under the Note. Borrower shall also pay funds for Escrow Items pursuant to Section 3. Payments due under the Note and this Security Instrument shall be made in U.S. currency. However, if any check or other instrument received by Lender as payment under the Note or this Security Instrument is returned to Lender unpaid, Lender may require that any or all subsequent payments due under the Note and this Security Instrument be made in one or more of the following forms, as selected by Lender: (a) cash; (b) money order; (c) certified check, bank check, treasurer's check or cashier's check, provided any such check is drawn upon an institution whose deposits are insured by a federal agency, instrumentality, or entity; or (d) Electronic Funds Transfer.

Payments are deemed received by Lender when received at the location designated in the Note or at such other location as may be designated by Lender in accordance with the notice provisions in Section 15. Lender may return any payment or partial payment if the payment or partial payments are insufficient to bring the Loan current. Lender may accept any payment or partial payment insufficient to bring the Loan current, without waiver of any rights hereunder or prejudice to its rights to refuse such payment or partial payments in the future, but Lender is not obligated to apply such payments at the time such payments are accepted. If each Periodic Payment is applied as of its scheduled due date, then Lender need not pay interest on unapplied funds. Lender may hold such unapplied funds until Borrower makes payment to bring the Loan current. If Borrower does not do so within a reasonable period of time, Lender shall either apply such funds or return them to Borrower. If not applied earlier, such funds will be applied to the outstanding principal balance under the Note immediately prior to foreclosure. No offset or claim which Borrower might have now or in the future against Lender shall relieve Borrower from making payments due under the Note and this Security Instrument or performing the covenants and agreements secured by this Security Instrument.

2. Application of Payments or Proceeds. Except as otherwise described in this Section 2, all payments accepted and applied by Lender shall be applied in the following order of priority: (a) interest due under the Note; (b) principal due under the Note; (c) amounts due under Section 3. Such payments shall be applied to each Periodic Payment in the order in which it became due. Any remaining amounts shall be applied first to late charges, second to any other amounts due under this Security Instrument, and then to reduce the principal balance of the Note.

If Lender receives a payment from Borrower for a delinquent Periodic Payment which includes a sufficient amount to pay any late charge due, the payment may be applied to the delinquent payment and the late charge. If more than one Periodic Payment is outstanding, Lender may apply any payment received from Borrower to the repayment of the Periodic Payments if, and to the extent that, each payment can be paid in full. To the extent that any excess exists after the payment is applied to the full payment of one or more Periodic Payments, such excess may be applied to any late charges due. Voluntary prepayments shall be applied first to any prepayment charges and then as described in the Note.

Any application of payments, insurance proceeds, or Miscellaneous Proceeds to principal due under the Note shall not extend or postpone the due date, or change the amount, of the Periodic Payments.

3. Funds for Escrow Items. Borrower shall pay to Lender on the day Periodic Payments are due under the Note, until the Note is paid in full, a sum (the "Funds") to provide for payment of amounts due for: (a) taxes and assessments and other items which can attain priority over this Security Instrument as a lien or encumbrance on the Property; (b) leasehold payments or ground rents on the Property, if any; (c) premiums for any and all insurance required by Lender under Section 5; and (d) Mortgage Insurance premiums, if any, or any sums payable by Borrower to Lender in lieu of the payment of Mortgage Insurance premiums in accordance with the provisions of Section 10. These items are called "Escrow Items." At origination or at any time during the term of the Loan, Lender may require that Community Association Dues, Fees, and Assessments, if any, be escrowed by Borrower, and such dues, fees and assessments shall be an Escrow Item. Borrower shall promptly furnish to Lender all notices of amounts to be paid under this Section. Borrower shall pay Lender the Funds for Escrow Items unless Lender waives Borrower's obligation to pay the Funds for any or all Escrow Items. Lender may waive Borrower's obligation to pay to Lender Funds for any or all Escrow Items at any time. Any such waiver may only be in writing. In the event of such waiver, Borrower shall pay directly, when and where payable, the amounts due for any Escrow Items for which payment of Funds has been waived by Lender and, if Lender requires, shall furnish to Lender receipts evidencing such payment within such time period as Lender may require. Borrower's obligation to make such payments and to provide receipts shall for all purposes be deemed to be a covenant and agreement contained in this Security Instrument, as the phrase "covenant and agreement" is used in Section 9. If Borrower is obligated to pay Escrow Items directly, pursuant to a waiver, and Borrower fails to pay the amount due for an Escrow Item, Lender may exercise its rights under Section 9 and pay such amount and Borrower shall then be obligated under Section 9 to repay to Lender any such amount. Lender may revoke the waiver as to any or all Escrow Items at any time by a notice given in accordance with Section 15 and, upon such revocation, Borrower shall pay to Lender all Funds, and in such amounts, that are then required under this Section 3.

Lender may, at any time, collect and hold Funds in an amount (a) sufficient to permit Lender to apply the Funds at the time specified under RESPA, and (b) not to exceed the maximum amount a lender can require under RESPA. Lender shall estimate the amount of Funds due on the basis of current data and reasonable estimates of expenditures of future Escrow Items or otherwise in accordance with Applicable Law.

The Funds shall be held in an institution whose deposits are insured by a federal agency, instrumentality, or entity (including Lender, if Lender is an institution whose deposits are so insured) or in any Federal Home Loan Bank. Lender shall apply the Funds to pay the Escrow Items no later than the time specified under RESPA. Lender shall not charge Borrower for holding and applying the Funds, annually analyzing the escrow account, or verifying the Escrow Items, unless Lender pays Borrower interest on the Funds and Applicable Law permits Lender to make such a charge. Unless an agreement is made in writing or Applicable Law requires interest to be paid on the Funds, Lender shall not be required to pay Borrower any interest or earnings on the Funds. Borrower and Lender can agree in writing, however, that interest shall be paid on the Funds. Lender shall give to Borrower, without charge, an annual accounting of the Funds as required by RESPA.

If there is a surplus of Funds held in escrow, as defined under RESPA, Lender shall account to Borrower for the excess funds in accordance with RESPA. If there is a shortage of Funds held in escrow, as defined under RESPA, Lender shall notify Borrower as required by RESPA, and Borrower shall pay to Lender the amount necessary to make up the shortage in accordance with RESPA, but in no more than 12 monthly payments. If there is a deficiency of Funds held in escrow, as defined under RESPA, Lender shall notify Borrower as required by RESPA, and Borrower shall pay to Lender the amount necessary to make up the deficiency in accordance with RESPA, but in no more than 12 monthly payments.

Upon payment in full of all sums secured by this Security Instrument, Lender shall promptly refund to Borrower any Funds held by Lender.

4. **Charges; Liens.** Borrower shall pay all taxes, assessments, charges, fines, and impositions attributable to the Property which can attain priority over this Security Instrument, leasehold payments or ground rents on the Property, if any, and Community Association Dues, Fees, and Assessments, if any. To the extent that these items are Escrow Items, Borrower shall pay them in the manner provided in Section 3.

Borrower shall promptly discharge any lien which has priority over this Security Instrument unless Borrower: (a) agrees in writing to the payment of the obligation secured by the lien in a manner acceptable to Lender, but only so long as Borrower is performing such agreement; (b) contests the lien in good faith by, or defends against enforcement of the lien in, legal proceedings which in Lender's opinion operate to prevent the enforcement of the lien while those proceedings are pending, but only until such proceedings are concluded; or (c) secures from the holder of the lien an agreement satisfactory to Lender subordinating the lien to this Security Instrument. If Lender determines that any part of the Property is subject to a lien which can attain priority over this Security Instrument, Lender may give Borrower a notice identifying the lien. Within 10 days of the date on which that notice is given, Borrower shall satisfy the lien or take one or more of the actions set forth above in this Section 4.

Lender may require Borrower to pay a one-time charge for a real estate tax verification and/or reporting service used by Lender in connection with this Loan.

5. Property Insurance. Borrower shall keep the improvements now existing or hereafter erected on the Property insured against loss by fire, hazards included within the term "extended coverage," and any other hazards including, but not limited to, earthquakes and floods, for which Lender requires insurance. This insurance shall be maintained in the amounts (including deductible levels) and for the periods that Lender requires. What Lender requires pursuant to the preceding sentences can change during the term of the Loan. The insurance carrier providing the insurance shall be chosen by Borrower subject to Lender's right to disapprove Borrower's choice, which right shall not be exercised unreasonably. Lender may require Borrower to pay, in connection with this Loan, either: (a) a one-time charge for flood zone determination, certification and tracking services; or (b) a one-time charge for flood zone determination and certification services and subsequent charges each time remappings or similar changes occur which reasonably might affect such determination or certification. Borrower shall also be responsible for the payment of any fees imposed by the Federal Emergency Management Agency in connection with the review of any flood zone determination resulting from an objection by Borrower.

If Borrower fails to maintain any of the coverages described above, Lender may obtain insurance coverage, at Lender's option and Borrower's expense. Lender is under no obligation to purchase any particular type or amount of coverage. Therefore, such coverage shall cover Lender, but might or might not protect Borrower, Borrower's equity in the Property, or the contents of the Property, against any risk, hazard or liability and might provide greater or lesser coverage than was previously in effect. Borrower acknowledges that the cost of the insurance coverage so obtained might significantly exceed the cost of insurance that Borrower could have obtained. Any amounts disbursed by Lender under this Section 5 shall become additional debt of Borrower secured by this Security Instrument. These amounts shall bear interest at the Note rate from the date of disbursement and shall be payable, with such interest, upon notice from Lender to Borrower requesting payment.

All insurance policies required by Lender and renewals of such policies shall be subject to Lender's right to disapprove such policies, shall include a standard mortgage clause, and shall name Lender as mortgagee and/or as an additional loss payee and Borrower further agrees to generally assign rights to insurance proceeds to the holder of the Note up to the amount of the outstanding loan balance. Lender shall have the right to hold the policies and renewal certificates. If Lender requires, Borrower shall promptly give to Lender all receipts of paid premiums and renewal notices. If Borrower obtains any form of insurance coverage, not otherwise required by Lender, for damage to, or destruction of, the Property, such policy shall include a standard mortgage clause and shall name Lender as mortgagee and/or as an additional loss payee and Borrower further agrees to generally assign rights to insurance proceeds to the holder of the Note up to the amount of the outstanding loan balance.

In the event of loss, Borrower shall give prompt notice to the insurance carrier and Lender. Lender may make proof of loss if not made promptly by Borrower. Unless Lender and Borrower otherwise agree in writing, any insurance proceeds, whether or not the underlying insurance was required by Lender, shall be applied to restoration or repair of the Property, if the restoration or repair is economically feasible and Lender's security is not lessened. During such repair and restoration period, Lender shall have the right to hold such insurance proceeds until Lender has had an opportunity to inspect such Property to ensure the work has been completed to Lender's satisfaction, provided that such inspection shall be undertaken promptly. Lender may disburse proceeds for the repairs and restoration in a single payment or in a series of progress payments as the work is completed. Unless an agreement is made in writing or Applicable Law requires interest to be paid on such insurance proceeds, Lender shall not be required to pay Borrower any interest or earnings on such proceeds. Fees for public adjusters, or other third parties, retained by Borrower shall not be paid out of the insurance proceeds and shall be the sole obligation of Borrower. If the restoration or repair is not economically feasible or Lender's security would be lessened, the insurance proceeds shall be applied to the sums secured by this Security Instrument, whether or not then due, with the excess, if any, paid to Borrower. Such insurance proceeds shall be applied in the order provided for in Section 2.

If Borrower abandons the Property, Lender may file, negotiate and settle any available insurance claim and related matters. If Borrower does not respond within 30 days to a notice from Lender that the insurance carrier has offered to settle a claim, then Lender may negotiate and settle the claim. The 30-day period will begin when the notice is given. In either event, or if Lender acquires the Property under Section 22 or otherwise, Borrower hereby assigns to Lender (a) Borrower's rights to any insurance proceeds in an amount not to exceed the amounts unpaid under the Note or this Security Instrument, and (b) any other of Borrower's rights (other than the right to any refund of unearned premiums paid by Borrower) under all insurance policies covering the Property, insofar as such rights are applicable to the coverage of the Property. Lender may use the insurance proceeds either to repair or restore the Property or to pay amounts unpaid under the Note or this Security Instrument, whether or not then due.

6. Occupancy. Borrower shall occupy, establish, and use the Property as Borrower's principal residence within 60 days after the execution of this Security Instrument and shall continue to occupy the Property as Borrower's principal residence for at least one year after the date of occupancy, unless Lender otherwise agrees in writing, which consent shall not be unreasonably withheld, or unless extenuating circumstances exist which are beyond Borrower's control.

7. Preservation, Maintenance and Protection of the Property; Inspections. Borrower shall not destroy, damage or impair the Property, allow the Property to deteriorate or commit waste on the Property. Whether or not Borrower is residing in the Property, Borrower shall maintain the Property in order to prevent the Property from deteriorating or decreasing in value due to its condition. Unless it is determined pursuant to Section 5 that repair or restoration is not economically feasible, Borrower shall promptly repair the Property if damaged to avoid further deterioration or damage. If insurance or condemnation proceeds are paid in connection with damage to, or the taking of, the Property, Borrower shall be responsible for repairing or restoring the Property only if Lender has released proceeds for such purposes. Lender may disburse proceeds for the repairs and restoration in a single payment or in a series of progress payments as the work is completed. If the insurance or condemnation proceeds are not sufficient to repair or restore the Property, Borrower is not relieved of Borrower's obligation for the completion of such repair or restoration.

Lender or its agent may make reasonable entries upon and inspections of the Property. If it has reasonable cause, Lender may inspect the interior of the improvements on the Property. Lender shall give Borrower notice at the time of or prior to such an interior inspection specifying such reasonable cause.

8. Borrower's Loan Application. Borrower shall be in default if, during the Loan application process, Borrower or any persons or entities acting at the direction of Borrower or with Borrower's knowledge or consent gave materially false, misleading, or inaccurate information or statements to Lender (or failed to provide Lender with material information) in connection with the Loan. Material representations include, but are not limited to, representations concerning Borrower's occupancy of the Property as Borrower's principal residence.

9.   Protection of Lender's Interest in the Property and Rights Under this Security Instrument. If (a) Borrower fails to perform the covenants and agreements contained in this Security Instrument, (b) there is a legal proceeding that might significantly affect Lender's interest in the Property and/or rights under this Security Instrument (such as a proceeding in bankruptcy, probate, for condemnation or forfeiture, for enforcement of a lien which may attain priority over this Security Instrument or to enforce laws or regulations), or (c) Borrower has abandoned the Property, then Lender may do and pay for whatever is reasonable or appropriate to protect Lender's interest in the Property and rights under this Security Instrument, including protecting and/or assessing the value of the Property, and securing and/or repairing the Property. Lender's actions can include, but are not limited to: (a) paying any sums secured by a lien which has priority over this Security Instrument; (b) appearing in court; and (c) paying reasonable attorneys' fees to protect its interest in the Property and/or rights under this Security Instrument, including its secured position in a bankruptcy proceeding. Securing the Property includes, but is not limited to, entering the Property to make repairs, change locks, replace or board up doors and windows, drain water from pipes, eliminate building or other code violations or dangerous conditions, and have utilities turned on or off. Although Lender may take action under this Section 9, Lender does not have to do so and is not under any duty or obligation to do so. It is agreed that Lender incurs no liability for not taking any or all actions authorized under this Section 9.

Any amounts disbursed by Lender under this Section 9 shall become additional debt of Borrower secured by this Security Instrument. These amounts shall bear interest at the Note rate from the date of disbursement and shall be payable, with such interest, upon notice from Lender to Borrower requesting payment.

If this Security Instrument is on a leasehold, Borrower shall comply with all the provisions of the lease. If Borrower acquires fee title to the Property, the leasehold and the fee title shall not merge unless Lender agrees to the merger in writing.

10.   Mortgage Insurance. If Lender required Mortgage Insurance as a condition of making the Loan, Borrower shall pay the premiums required to maintain the Mortgage Insurance in effect. If, for any reason, the Mortgage Insurance coverage required by Lender ceases to be available from the mortgage insurer that previously provided such insurance and Borrower was required to make separately designated payments toward the premiums for Mortgage Insurance, Borrower shall pay the premiums required to obtain coverage substantially equivalent to the Mortgage Insurance previously in effect, at a cost substantially equivalent to the cost to Borrower of the Mortgage Insurance previously in effect, from an alternate mortgage insurer selected by Lender.

If substantially equivalent Mortgage Insurance coverage is not available, Borrower shall continue to pay to Lender the amount of the separately designated payments that were due when the insurance coverage ceased to be in effect. Lender will accept, use and retain these payments as a non-refundable loss reserve in lieu of Mortgage Insurance. Such loss reserve shall be non-refundable, notwithstanding the fact that the Loan is ultimately paid in full, and Lender shall not be required to pay Borrower any interest or earnings on such loss reserve. Lender can no longer require loss reserve payments if Mortgage Insurance coverage (in the amount and for the period that Lender requires) provided by an insurer selected by Lender again becomes available, is obtained, and Lender requires separately designated payments toward the premiums for Mortgage Insurance. If Lender required Mortgage Insurance as a condition of making the Loan and Borrower was required to make separately designated payments toward the premiums for Mortgage Insurance, Borrower shall pay the premiums required to maintain Mortgage Insurance in effect, or to provide a non-refundable loss reserve, until Lender's requirement for Mortgage Insurance ends in accordance with any written agreement between Borrower and Lender providing for such termination or until termination is required by Applicable Law. Nothing in this Section 10 affects Borrower's obligation to pay interest at the rate provided in the Note.

Mortgage Insurance reimburses Lender (or any entity that purchases the Note) for certain losses it may incur if Borrower does not repay the Loan as agreed. Borrower is not a party to the Mortgage Insurance.

Mortgage insurers evaluate their total risk on all such insurance in force from time to time, and may enter into agreements with other parties that share or modify their risk, or reduce losses. These agreements are on terms and conditions that are satisfactory to the mortgage insurer and the other party (or parties) to these agreements. These agreements may require the mortgage insurer to make payments using any source of funds that the mortgage insurer may have available (which may include funds obtained from Mortgage Insurance premiums).

As a result of these agreements, Lender, any purchaser of the Note, another insurer, any reinsurer, any other entity, or any affiliate of any of the foregoing, may receive (directly or indirectly) amounts that derive from (or might be characterized as) a portion of Borrower's payments for Mortgage Insurance, in exchange for sharing or modifying the mortgage insurer's risk, or reducing losses. If such agreement provides that an affiliate of Lender takes a share of the insurer's risk in exchange for a share of the premiums paid to the insurer, the arrangement is often termed "captive reinsurance." Further:

(a) Any such agreements will not affect the amounts that Borrower has agreed to pay for Mortgage Insurance, or any other terms of the Loan. Such agreements will not increase the amount Borrower will owe for Mortgage Insurance, and they will not entitle Borrower to any refund.

(b) Any such agreements will not affect the rights Borrower has—if any—with respect to the Mortgage Insurance under the Homeowners Protection Act of 1998 or any other law. These rights may include the right to receive certain disclosures, to request and obtain cancellation of the Mortgage Insurance, to have the Mortgage Insurance terminated automatically, and/or to receive a refund of any Mortgage Insurance premiums that were unearned at the time of such cancellation or termination.

11. Assignment of Miscellaneous Proceeds; Forfeiture. All Miscellaneous Proceeds are hereby assigned to and shall be paid to Lender.

If the Property is damaged, such Miscellaneous Proceeds shall be applied to restoration or repair of the Property, if the restoration or repair is economically feasible and Lender's security is not lessened. During such repair and restoration period, Lender shall have the right to hold such Miscellaneous Proceeds until Lender has had an opportunity to inspect such Property to ensure the work has been completed to Lender's satisfaction, provided that such inspection shall be undertaken promptly. Lender may pay for the repairs and restoration in a single disbursement or in a series of progress payments as the work is completed. Unless an agreement is made in writing or Applicable Law requires interest to be paid on such Miscellaneous Proceeds, Lender shall not be required to pay Borrower any interest or earnings on such Miscellaneous Proceeds. If the restoration or repair is not economically feasible or Lender's security would be lessened, the Miscellaneous Proceeds shall be applied to the sums secured by this Security Instrument, whether or not then due, with the excess, if any, paid to Borrower. Such Miscellaneous Proceeds shall be applied in the order provided for in Section 2.

In the event of a total taking, destruction, or loss in value of the Property, the Miscellaneous Proceeds shall be applied to the sums secured by this Security Instrument, whether or not then due, with the excess, if any, paid to Borrower.

In the event of a partial taking, destruction, or loss in value of the Property in which the fair market value of the Property immediately before the partial taking, destruction, or loss in value is equal to or greater than the amount of the sums secured by this Security Instrument immediately before the partial taking, destruction, or loss in value, unless Borrower and Lender otherwise agree in writing, the sums secured by this Security Instrument shall be reduced by the amount of the Miscellaneous Proceeds multiplied by the following fraction: (a) the total amount of the sums secured immediately before the partial taking, destruction, or loss in value divided by (b) the fair market value of the Property immediately before the partial taking, destruction, or loss in value. Any balance shall be paid to Borrower.

In the event of a partial taking, destruction, or loss in value of the Property in which the fair market value of the Property immediately before the partial taking, destruction, or loss in value is less than the amount of the sums secured immediately before the partial taking, destruction, or loss in value, unless Borrower and Lender otherwise agree in writing, the Miscellaneous Proceeds shall be applied to the sums secured by this Security Instrument whether or not the sums are then due.

If the Property is abandoned by Borrower, or if, after notice by Lender to Borrower that the Opposing Party (as defined in the next sentence) offers to make an award to settle a claim for damages, Borrower fails to respond to Lender within 30 days after the date the notice is given, Lender is authorized to collect and apply the Miscellaneous Proceeds either to restoration or repair of the Property or to the sums secured by this Security Instrument, whether or not then due. "Opposing Party" means the third party that owes Borrower Miscellaneous Proceeds or the party against whom Borrower has a right of action in regard to Miscellaneous Proceeds.

Borrower shall be in default if any action or proceeding, whether civil or criminal, is begun that, in Lender's judgment, could result in forfeiture of the Property or other material impairment of Lender's interest in the Property or rights under this Security Instrument. Borrower can cure such a default and, if acceleration has occurred, reinstate as provided in Section 19, by causing the action or proceeding to be dismissed with a ruling that, in Lender's judgment, precludes forfeiture of the Property or other material impairment of Lender's interest in the Property or rights under this Security Instrument. The proceeds of any award or claim for damages that are attributable to the impairment of Lender's interest in the Property are hereby assigned and shall be paid to Lender.

All Miscellaneous Proceeds that are not applied to restoration or repair of the Property shall be applied in the order provided for in Section 2.

12. Borrower Not Released; Forbearance By Lender Not a Waiver. Extension of the time for payment or modification of amortization of the sums secured by this Security Instrument granted by Lender to Borrower or any Successor in Interest of Borrower shall not operate to release the liability of Borrower or any Successors in Interest of Borrower. Lender shall not be required to commence proceedings against any Successor in Interest of Borrower or to refuse to extend time for payment or otherwise modify amortization of the sums secured by this Security Instrument by reason of any demand made by the original Borrower or any Successors in Interest of Borrower. Any forbearance by Lender in exercising any right or remedy including, without limitation, Lender's acceptance of payments from third persons, entities or Successors in Interest of Borrower or in amounts less than the amount then due, shall not be a waiver of or preclude the exercise of any right or remedy.

13. Joint and Several Liability; Co-signers; Successors and Assigns Bound. Borrower covenants and agrees that Borrower's obligations and liability shall be joint and several. However, any Borrower who co-signs this Security Instrument but does not execute the Note (a "co-signer"): (a) is co-signing this Security Instrument only to mortgage, grant and convey the co-signer's interest in the Property under the terms of this Security Instrument; (b) is not personally obligated to pay the sums secured by this Security Instrument; and (c) agrees that Lender and any other Borrower can agree to extend, modify, forbear or make any accommodations with regard to the terms of this Security Instrument or the Note without the co-signer's consent.

Subject to the provisions of Section 18, any Successor in Interest of Borrower who assumes Borrower's obligations under this Security Instrument in writing, and is approved by Lender, shall obtain all of Borrower's rights and benefits under this Security Instrument. Borrower shall not be released from Borrower's obligations and liability under this Security Instrument unless Lender agrees to such release in writing. The covenants and agreements of this Security Instrument shall bind (except as provided in Section 20) and benefit the successors and assigns of Lender.

14. Loan Charges. Lender may charge Borrower fees for services performed in connection with Borrower's default, for the purpose of protecting Lender's interest in the Property and rights under this Security Instrument, including, but not limited to, attorneys' fees, property inspection and valuation fees. In regard to any other fees, the absence of express authority in this Security Instrument to charge a specific fee to Borrower shall not be construed as a prohibition on the charging of such fee. Lender may not charge fees that are expressly prohibited by this Security Instrument or by Applicable Law.

If the Loan is subject to a law which sets maximum loan charges, and that law is finally interpreted so that the interest or other loan charges collected or to be collected in connection with the Loan exceed the permitted limits, then: (a) any such loan charge shall be reduced by the amount necessary to reduce the charge to the permitted limit; and (b) any sums already collected from Borrower which exceeded permitted limits will be refunded to Borrower. Lender may choose to make this refund by reducing the principal owed under the Note or by making a direct payment to Borrower. If a refund reduces principal, the reduction will be treated as a partial prepayment without any prepayment charge (whether or not a prepayment charge is provided for under the Note). Borrower's acceptance of any such refund made by direct payment to Borrower will constitute a waiver of any right of action Borrower might have arising out of such overcharge.

15. Notices. All notices given by Borrower or Lender in connection with this Security Instrument must be in writing. Any notice to Borrower in connection with this Security Instrument shall be deemed to have been given to Borrower when mailed by first class mail or when actually delivered to Borrower's notice address if sent by other means. Notice to any one Borrower shall constitute notice to all Borrowers unless Applicable Law expressly requires otherwise. The notice address shall be the Property Address unless Borrower has designated a substitute notice address by notice to Lender. Borrower shall promptly notify Lender of Borrower's change of address. If Lender specifies a procedure for reporting Borrower's change of address, then Borrower shall only report a change of address through that specified procedure. There may be only one designated notice address under this Security Instrument at any one time. Any notice to Lender shall be given by delivering it or by mailing it by first class mail to Lender's address stated herein unless Lender has designated another address by notice to Borrower. Any notice in connection with this Security Instrument shall not be deemed to have been given to Lender until actually received by Lender. If any notice required by this Security Instrument is also required under Applicable Law, the Applicable Law requirement will satisfy the corresponding requirement under this Security Instrument.

16. Governing Law; Severability; Rules of Construction. This Security Instrument shall be governed by federal law and the law of the jurisdiction in which the Property is located. All rights and obligations contained in this Security Instrument are subject to any requirements and limitations of Applicable Law. Applicable Law might explicitly or implicitly allow the parties to agree by contract or it might be silent, but such silence shall not be construed as a prohibition against agreement by contract. In the event that any provision or clause of this Security Instrument or the Note conflicts with Applicable Law, such conflict shall not affect other provisions of this Security Instrument or the Note which can be given effect without the conflicting provision.

As used in this Security Instrument: (a) words of the masculine gender shall mean and include corresponding neuter words or words of the feminine gender; (b) words in the singular shall mean and include the plural and vice versa; and (c) the word "may" gives sole discretion without any obligation to take any action.

17. Borrower's Copy. Borrower shall be given one copy of the Note and of this Security Instrument.

18. Transfer of the Property or a Beneficial Interest in Borrower. As used in this Section 18, "Interest in the Property" means any legal or beneficial interest in the Property, including, but not limited to, those beneficial interests transferred in a bond for deed, contract for deed, installment sales contract or escrow agreement, the intent of which is the transfer of title by Borrower at a future date to a purchaser.

If all or any part of the Property or any Interest in the Property is sold or transferred (or if Borrower is not a natural person and a beneficial interest in Borrower is sold or transferred) without Lender's prior written consent, Lender may require immediate payment in full of all sums secured by this Security Instrument. However, this option shall not be exercised by Lender if such exercise is prohibited by Applicable Law.

If Lender exercises this option, Lender shall give Borrower notice of acceleration. The notice shall provide a period of not less than 30 days from the date the notice is given in accordance with Section 15 within which Borrower must pay all sums secured by this Security Instrument. If Borrower fails to pay these sums prior to the expiration of this period, Lender may invoke any remedies permitted by this Security Instrument without further notice or demand on Borrower.

19. Borrower's Right to Reinstate After Acceleration. If Borrower meets certain conditions, Borrower shall have the right to have enforcement of this Security Instrument discontinued at any time prior to the earliest of: (a) five days before sale of the Property pursuant to any power of sale contained in this Security Instrument; (b) such other period as Applicable Law might specify for the termination of Borrower's right to reinstate; or (c) entry of a judgment enforcing this Security Instrument. Those conditions are that Borrower: (a) pays Lender all sums which then would be due under this Security Instrument and the Note as if no acceleration had occurred; (b) cures any default of any other covenants or agreements; (c) pays all expenses incurred in enforcing this Security Instrument, including, but not limited to, reasonable attorneys' fees, property inspection and valuation fees, and other fees incurred for the purpose of protecting Lender's interest in the Property and rights under this Security Instrument; and (d) takes such action as Lender may reasonably require to assure that Lender's interest in the Property and rights under this Security Instrument, and Borrower's obligation to pay the sums secured by this Security Instrument, shall continue unchanged. Lender may require that Borrower pay such reinstatement sums and expenses in one or more of the following forms, as selected by Lender: (a) cash; (b) money order; (c) certified check, bank check, treasurer's check or cashier's check, provided any such check is drawn upon an institution whose deposits are insured by a federal agency, instrumentality or entity; or (d) Electronic Funds Transfer. Upon reinstatement by Borrower, this Security Instrument and obligations secured hereby shall remain fully effective as if no acceleration had occurred. However, this right to reinstate shall not apply in the case of acceleration under Section 18.

20. Sale of Note; Change of Loan Servicer; Notice of Grievance. The Note or a partial interest in the Note (together with this Security Instrument) can be sold one or more times without prior notice to Borrower. A sale might result in a change in the entity (known as the "Loan Servicer") that collects Periodic Payments due under the Note and this Security Instrument and performs other mortgage loan servicing obligations under the Note, this Security Instrument, and Applicable Law. There also might be one or more changes of the Loan Servicer unrelated to a sale of the Note. If there is a change of the Loan Servicer, Borrower will be given written notice of the change which will state the name and address of the new Loan Servicer, the address to which payments should be made and any other information RESPA requires in connection with a notice of transfer of servicing. If the Note is sold and thereafter the Loan is serviced by a Loan Servicer other than the purchaser of the Note, the mortgage loan servicing obligations to Borrower will remain with the Loan Servicer or be transferred to a successor Loan Servicer and are not assumed by the Note purchaser unless otherwise provided by the Note purchaser.

Neither Borrower nor Lender may commence, join, or be joined to any judicial action (as either an individual litigant or the member of a class) that arises from the other party's actions pursuant to this Security Instrument or that alleges that the other party has breached any provision of, or any duty owed by reason of, this Security Instrument, until such Borrower or Lender has notified the other party (with such notice given in compliance with the requirements of Section 15) of such alleged breach and afforded the other party hereto a reasonable period after the giving of such notice to take corrective action. If Applicable Law provides a time period which must elapse before certain action can be taken, that time period will be deemed to be reasonable for purposes of this paragraph. The notice of acceleration and opportunity to cure given to Borrower pursuant to Section 22 and the notice of acceleration given to Borrower pursuant to Section 18 shall be deemed to satisfy the notice and opportunity to take corrective action provisions of this Section 20.

21. Hazardous Substances. As used in this Section 21: (a) "Hazardous Substances" are those substances defined as toxic or hazardous substances, pollutants, or wastes by Environmental Law and the following substances: gasoline, kerosene, other flammable or toxic petroleum products, toxic pesticides and herbicides, volatile solvents, materials containing asbestos or formaldehyde, and radioactive materials; (b) "Environmental Law" means federal laws and laws of the jurisdiction where the Property is located that relate to health, safety or environmental protection; (c) "Environmental Cleanup" includes any response action, remedial action, or removal action, as defined in Environmental Law; and (d) an "Environmental Condition" means a condition that can cause, contribute to, or otherwise trigger an Environmental Cleanup.

Borrower shall not cause or permit the presence, use, disposal, storage, or release of any Hazardous Substances, or threaten to release any Hazardous Substances, on or in the Property. Borrower shall not do, nor allow anyone else to do, anything affecting the Property (a) that is in violation of any Environmental Law, (b) which creates an Environmental Condition, or (c) which, due to the presence, use, or release of a Hazardous Substance, creates a condition that adversely affects the value of the Property. The preceding two sentences shall not apply to the presence, use, or storage on the Property of small quantities of Hazardous Substances that are generally recognized to be appropriate to normal residential uses and to maintenance of the Property (including, but not limited to, hazardous substances in consumer products).

Borrower shall promptly give Lender written notice of (a) any investigation, claim, demand, lawsuit or other action by any governmental or regulatory agency or private party involving the Property and any Hazardous Substance or Environmental Law of which Borrower has actual knowledge, (b) any Environmental Condition, including but not limited to, any spilling, leaking, discharge, release or threat of release of any Hazardous Substance, and (c) any condition caused by the presence, use or release of a Hazardous Substance which adversely affects the value of the Property. If Borrower learns, or is notified by any governmental or regulatory authority, or any private party, that any removal or other remediation of any Hazardous Substance affecting the Property is necessary, Borrower shall promptly take all necessary remedial actions in accordance with Environmental Law. Nothing herein shall create any obligation on Lender for an Environmental Cleanup.

[Here non-Uniform Covenants applicable
to a particular state are inserted.]

4. FANNIE MAE/FREDDIE MAC MORTGAGE—SINGLE FAMILY—KANSAS

Kansas, like such other states as Florida, Illinois, Iowa, and New York, uses the mortgage as the predominant financing device and permits only foreclosure by judicial action. Consequently, the Kansas form makes no reference to a non-judicial foreclosure.

MORTGAGE

[Here insert definitions from Form 3, supra.]

TRANSFER OF RIGHTS IN THE PROPERTY. This Security Instrument secures to Lender: (i) the repayment of the Loan, and all renewals, extensions and modifications of the Note; and (ii) the performance of Borrower's covenants and agreements under this Security Instrument and the Note. For this purpose, Borrower mortgages and warrants to Lender and Lender's successors and assigns the following described property located in the [Type of Recording Jurisdiction] of [Name of Recording Jurisdiction]:

[Legal description]

which currently has the address of [Street, City], Kansas [Zip Code] ("Property Address"):

TOGETHER WITH all the improvements now or hereafter erected on the property, and all easements, appurtenances, and fixtures now or hereafter a part of the property. All replacements and additions shall also be covered by this Security Instrument. All of the foregoing is referred to in this Security Instrument as the "Property."

BORROWER COVENANTS that Borrower is lawfully seised of the estate hereby conveyed and has the right to mortgage, grant and convey the Property and that the Property is unencumbered, except for encumbrances of record. Borrower warrants and will defend generally the title to the Property against all claims and demands, subject to any encumbrances of record.

THIS SECURITY INSTRUMENT combines uniform covenants for national use and non-uniform covenants with limited variations by jurisdiction to constitute a uniform security instrument covering real property.

UNIFORM COVENANTS. Borrower and Lender covenant and agree as follows:

[Uniform Covenants appear here. See Form 3, supra.]

NON-UNIFORM COVENANTS. Borrower and Lender further covenant and agree as follows:

22. Acceleration; Remedies. Lender shall give notice to Borrower prior to acceleration following Borrower's breach of any covenant or agreement in this Security Instrument (but not prior to acceleration under Section 18 unless Applicable Law provides otherwise). The notice shall specify: (a) the default; (b) the action required to cure the default; (c) a date, not less than 30 days from the date the notice is given to Borrower, by which the default must be cured; and (d) that failure to cure the default on or before the date specified in the notice may result in acceleration of the sums secured by this Security Instrument, foreclosure by judicial proceeding and sale of the Property. The notice shall further inform Borrower of the right to reinstate after acceleration and the right to assert in the foreclosure proceeding the non-existence of a default or any other defense of Borrower to acceleration and foreclosure. If the default is not cured on or before the date specified in the notice, Lender at its option may require immediate payment in full of all sums secured by this Security Instrument without further demand and may foreclose this Security Instrument by judicial proceeding. Lender shall be entitled to collect all expenses incurred in pursuing the remedies provided in this Section 22, including, but not limited to, costs of title evidence.

Lender shall be entitled to collect all reasonable expenses incurred in pursuing the remedies provided in this Section 22, including, but not limited to, reasonable attorneys' fees, to the extent allowed by Applicable Law.

23. Release. Upon payment of all sums secured by this Security Instrument, Lender shall release this Security Instrument. Lender may charge Borrower a fee for releasing this Security Instrument, but only if the fee is paid to a third party for services rendered and the charging of the fee is permitted under Applicable Law.

24. Waiver of Redemption. Borrower waives all rights of redemption to the extent allowed by law.

BY SIGNING BELOW, Borrower accepts and agrees to the terms and covenants contained in this Security Instrument and in any Rider executed by Borrower and recorded with it.

Witnesses:_____(Seal)
      _____Borrower
      _____(Seal)
      _____Borrower

5. FANNIE MAE/FREDDIE MAC MORTGAGE WITH POWER OF SALE—SINGLE FAMILY—MINNESOTA

Minnesota uses a mortgage with power of sale as the most common land financing device. Minn.Stat.Ann. § 580.01 et seq. While judicial foreclosure is, of course, permissible, foreclosure is almost always by power of sale, or, as it is referred to locally, by "advertisement." The power of sale is exercised by the sheriff. see Minn.Stat.Ann. § 580.06.

MORTGAGE

[Here insert definitions from Form 3, supra.]

TRANSFER OF RIGHTS IN THE PROPERTY. This Security Instrument secures to Lender: (i) the repayment of the Loan, and all renewals, extensions and modifications of the Note; and (ii) the performance of Borrower's covenants and agreements under this Security Instrument and the Note. For this purpose, Borrower does hereby mortgage, grant and convey to Lender and Lender's successors and assigns, with power of sale, the following described property located in the [Type of Recording Jurisdiction] of [Name of Recording Jurisdiction]:

[Legal description]

which currently has the address of [Street, City], Minnesota [Zip Code] ("Property Address"):

TOGETHER WITH all the improvements now or hereafter erected on the property, and all easements, appurtenances, and fixtures now or hereafter a part of the property. All replacements and additions shall also be covered by this Security Instrument. All of the foregoing is referred to in this Security Instrument as the "Property."

BORROWER COVENANTS that Borrower is lawfully seised of the estate hereby conveyed and has the right to mortgage, grant and convey the Property and that the Property is unencumbered, except for encumbrances of record. Borrower warrants and will defend generally the title to the Property against all claims and demands, subject to any encumbrances of record.

THIS SECURITY INSTRUMENT combines uniform covenants for national use and non-uniform covenants with limited variations by jurisdiction to constitute a uniform security instrument covering real property.

UNIFORM COVENANTS. Borrower and Lender covenant and agree as follows:

[Uniform Covenants appear here, See Form 3, supra.]

NON-UNIFORM COVENANTS. Borrower and Lender further covenant and agree as follows:

22. Acceleration; Remedies. Lender shall give notice to Borrower by certified mail to the address of the Property or another address designated by Borrower prior to acceleration following Borrower's breach of any covenant or agreement in this Security Instrument (but not prior to acceleration under Section 18 unless Applicable Law provides otherwise). The notice shall specify: (a) the default; (b) the action required to cure the default; (c) a date, not less than 30 days from the date the notice is given to Borrower, by which the default must be cured; and (d) that failure to cure the default on or before the date specified in the notice may result in acceleration of the sums secured by this Security Instrument and sale of the Property. The notice shall further inform Borrower of the right to reinstate after acceleration and the right to bring a court action to assert the non-existence of a default or any other defense of Borrower to acceleration and sale. If the default is not cured on or before the date specified in the notice, Lender at its option may require immediate payment in full of all sums secured by this Security Instrument without further demand and may invoke the power of sale and any other remedies permitted by Applicable Law. Lender shall be entitled to collect all expenses incurred in pursuing the remedies provided in this Section 22, including, but not limited to, reasonable attorneys' fees.

If Lender invokes the power of sale, Lender shall cause a copy of a notice of sale to be served upon any person in possession of the Property. Lender shall publish a notice of sale, and the Property shall be sold at public auction in the manner prescribed by Applicable Law. Lender or its designee may purchase the Property at any sale. The proceeds of the sale shall be applied in the following order: (a) to all expenses of the sale, including, but not limited to, reasonable attorneys' fees; (b) to all sums secured by this Security Instrument; and (c) any excess to the person or persons legally entitled to it.

23. Release. Upon payment of all sums secured by this Security Instrument, Lender shall discharge this Security Instrument. Borrower shall pay any recordation costs. Lender may charge Borrower a fee for releasing this Security Instrument, but only if the fee is paid to a third party for services rendered and the charging of the fee is permitted under Applicable Law.

24. Waiver of Homestead. Borrower waives all right of homestead exemption in the Property.

25. Interest on Advances. The interest rate on advances made by Lender under this Security Instrument shall not exceed the maximum rate allowed by Applicable Law.

BY SIGNING BELOW, Borrower accepts and agrees to the terms and covenants contained in this Security Instrument and in any Rider executed by Borrower and recorded with it.

Witnesses:_____(Seal)
_____Borrower
_____(Seal)
_____Borrower

6. FANNIE MAE/FREDDIE MAC DEED OF TRUST—SINGLE FAMILY—CALIFORNIA

California, like many Western and Midwestern states, uses the deed of trust with power of sale as the predominant land financing instrument. While deeds of trust differ from mortgages in certain minor respects, most substantive mortgage law is applicable to them. Mortgages seldom are used in such states because they can be foreclosed only by judicial action.

DEED OF TRUST

[Here insert definitions from Form 3, supra.]

TRANSFER OF RIGHTS IN THE PROPERTY. This Security Instrument secures to Lender: (i) the repayment of the Loan, and all renewals, extensions and modifications of the Note; and (ii) the performance of Borrower's covenants and agreements under this Security Instrument and the Note. For this purpose, Borrower irrevocably grants and conveys to Trustee, in trust, with power of sale, the following described property located in the [Type of Recording Jurisdiction] of [Name of Recording Jurisdiction]:

[Legal description]

which currently has the address of [Street, City], California [Zip Code] ("Property Address"):

TOGETHER WITH all the improvements now or hereafter erected on the property, and all easements, appurtenances, and fixtures now or hereafter a part of the property. All replacements and additions shall also be covered by this Security Instrument. All of the foregoing is referred to in this Security Instrument as the "Property."

BORROWER COVENANTS that Borrower is lawfully seised of the estate hereby conveyed and has the right to grant and convey the Property and that the Property is unencumbered, except for encumbrances of record. Borrower warrants and will defend generally the title to the Property against all claims and demands, subject to any encumbrances of record.

THIS SECURITY INSTRUMENT combines uniform covenants for national use and non-uniform covenants with limited variations by jurisdiction to constitute a uniform security instrument covering real property.

UNIFORM COVENANTS. Borrower and Lender covenant and agree as follows:

[Uniform covenants appear here. See Form 3, supra.]

NON-UNIFORM COVENANTS. Borrower and Lender further covenant and agree as follows:

22. Acceleration; Remedies. Lender shall give notice to Borrower prior to acceleration following Borrower's breach of any covenant or agreement in this Security Instrument (but not prior to acceleration under Section 18 unless Applicable Law provides otherwise). The notice shall specify: (a) the default; (b) the action required to cure the default; (c) a date, not less than 30 days from the date the notice is given to Borrower, by which the default must be cured; and (d) that failure to cure the default on or before the date specified in the notice may result in acceleration of the sums secured by this Security Instrument and sale of the Property. The notice shall further inform Borrower of the right to reinstate after acceleration and the right to bring a court action to assert the non-existence of a default or any other defense of Borrower to acceleration and sale. If the default is not cured on or before the date specified in the notice, Lender at its option may require immediate payment in full of all sums secured by this Security Instrument without further demand and may invoke the power of sale and any other remedies permitted by Applicable Law. Lender shall be entitled to collect all expenses incurred in pursuing the remedies provided in this Section 22, including, but not limited to, reasonable attorneys' fees and costs of title evidence.

If Lender invokes the power of sale, Lender shall execute or cause Trustee to execute a written notice of the occurrence of an event of default and of Lender's election to cause the Property to be sold. Trustee shall cause this notice to be recorded in each county in which any part of the Property is located. Lender or Trustee shall mail copies of the notice as prescribed by Applicable Law to Borrower and to the other persons prescribed by Applicable Law. Trustee shall give public notice of sale to the persons and in the manner prescribed by Applicable Law. After the time required by Applicable Law, Trustee, without demand on Borrower, shall sell the Property at public auction to the highest bidder at the time and place and under the terms designated in the notice of sale in one or more parcels and in any order Trustee determines. Trustee may postpone sale of all or any parcel of the Property by public announcement at the time and place of any previously scheduled sale. Lender or its designee may purchase the Property at any sale.

Trustee shall deliver to the purchaser Trustee's deed conveying the Property without any covenant or warranty, expressed or implied. The recitals in the Trustee's deed shall be prima facie evidence of the truth of the statements made therein. Trustee shall apply the proceeds of the sale in the following order: (a) to all expenses of the sale, including, but not limited to, reasonable Trustee's and attorneys' fees; (b) to all sums secured by this Security Instrument; and (c) any excess to the person or persons legally entitled to it.

23. Reconveyance. Upon payment of all sums secured by this Security Instrument, Lender shall request Trustee to reconvey the Property and shall surrender this Security Instrument and all notes evidencing debt secured by this Security Instrument to Trustee. Trustee shall reconvey the Property without warranty to the person or persons legally entitled to it. Lender may charge such person or persons a reasonable fee for reconveying the Property, but only if the fee is paid to a third party (such as the Trustee) for services rendered and the charging of the fee is permitted under Applicable Law. If the fee charged does not exceed the fee set by Applicable Law, the fee is conclusively presumed to be reasonable.

24. Substitute Trustee. Lender, at its option, may from time to time appoint a successor trustee to any Trustee appointed hereunder by an instrument executed and acknowledged by Lender and recorded in the office of the Recorder of the county in which the Property is located. The instrument shall contain the name of the original Lender, Trustee and Borrower, the book and page where this Security Instrument is recorded and the name and address of the successor trustee. Without conveyance of the Property, the successor trustee shall succeed to all the title, powers and duties conferred upon the Trustee herein and by Applicable Law. This procedure for substitution of trustee shall govern to the exclusion of all other provisions for substitution.

25. Statement of Obligation Fee. Lender may collect a fee not to exceed the maximum amount permitted by Applicable Law for furnishing the statement of obligation as provided by Section 2943 of the Civil Code of California.

BY SIGNING BELOW, Borrower accepts and agrees to the terms and covenants contained in this Security Instrument and in any Rider executed by Borrower and recorded with it.

Witnesses:_____(Seal)
          _____Borrower
          _____(Seal)
          _____Borrower

7. FANNIE MAE/FREDDIE MAC MULTISTATE 1–4 FAMILY RIDER

Rather confusingly, Fannie Mae and Freddie Mac define the term "single-family mortgage" to include mortgages on one-to-four unit residential properties. This rider is normally required for multi-unit rental properties.

1–4 FAMILY RIDER
(Assignment of Rents)

THIS 1–4 FAMILY RIDER is made this _____ day of _____, _____, and is incorporated into and shall be deemed to amend and supplement the Mortgage, Deed of Trust, or Security Deed (the "Security Instrument") of the same date given by the undersigned (the "Borrower") to secure Borrower's Note to _____ _____ (the "Lender") of the same date and covering the Property described in the Security Instrument and located at:

_____

[Property Address]

1–4 FAMILY COVENANTS. In addition to the covenants and agreements made in the Security Instrument, Borrower and Lender further covenant and agree as follows:

A. **ADDITIONAL PROPERTY SUBJECT TO THE SECURITY INSTRUMENT.** In addition to the Property described in Security Instrument, the following items now or hereafter attached to the Property to the extent they are fixtures are added to the Property description, and shall also constitute the Property covered by the Security Instrument: building materials, appliances and goods of every nature whatsoever now or hereafter located in, on, or used, or intended to be used in connection with the Property, including, but not limited to, those for the purposes of supplying or distributing heating, cooling, electricity, gas, water, air and light, fire prevention and extinguishing apparatus, security and access control apparatus, plumbing, bath tubs, water heaters, water closets, sinks, ranges, stoves, refrigerators, dishwashers, disposals, washers, dryers, awnings, storm windows, storm doors, screens, blinds, shades, curtains and curtain rods, attached mirrors, cabinets, paneling and attached floor coverings, all of which, including replacements and additions thereto, shall be deemed to be and remain a part of the Property covered by the Security Instrument. All of the foregoing together with the Property described in the Security Instrument (or the leasehold estate if the Security Instrument is on a leasehold) are referred to in this 1–4 Family Rider and the Security Instrument as the "Property."

B. **USE OF PROPERTY; COMPLIANCE WITH LAW.** Borrower shall not seek, agree to or make a change in the use of the Property or its zoning classification, unless Lender has agreed in writing to the change. Borrower shall comply with all laws, ordinances, regulations and requirements of any governmental body applicable to the Property.

C. **SUBORDINATE LIENS.** Except as permitted by federal law, Borrower shall not allow any lien inferior to the Security Instrument to be perfected against the Property without Lender's prior written permission.

D. **RENT LOSS INSURANCE.** Borrower shall maintain insurance against rent loss in addition to the other hazards for which insurance is required by Section 5.

E. **"BORROWER'S RIGHT TO REINSTATE" DELETED.** Section 19 is deleted.

F. **BORROWER'S OCCUPANCY.** Unless Lender and Borrower otherwise agree in writing, Section 6 concerning Borrower's occupancy of the Property is deleted.

G. **ASSIGNMENT OF LEASES.** Upon Lender's request after default, Borrower shall assign to Lender all leases of the Property and all security deposits made in connection with leases of the Property. Upon the assignment, Lender shall have the right to modify, extend or terminate the existing leases and to execute new leases, in Lender's sole discretion. As used in this paragraph G, the word "lease" shall mean "sublease" if the Security Instrument is on a leasehold.

H. **ASSIGNMENT OF RENTS; APPOINTMENT OF RECEIVER; LENDER IN POSSESSION.** Borrower absolutely and unconditionally assigns and transfers to Lender all the rents and revenues ("Rents") of the Property, regardless of to whom the Rents of the Property are payable. Borrower authorizes Lender or Lender's agents to collect the Rents, and agrees that each tenant of the Property shall pay the Rents to Lender or Lender's agents. However, Borrower shall receive the Rents until (i) Lender has given Borrower notice of default pursuant to Section 22 of the Security Instrument and (ii) Lender has given notice to the tenant(s) that the Rents are to be paid to Lender or Lender's agent. This assignment of Rents constitutes an absolute assignment and not an assignment for additional security only.

If Lender gives notice of default to Borrower: (i) all Rents received by Borrower shall be held by Borrower as trustee for the benefit of Lender only, to be applied to the sums secured by the Security Instrument; (ii) Lender shall be entitled to collect and receive all of the Rents of the Property; (iii) Borrower agrees that each tenant of the Property shall pay all Rents due and unpaid to Lender or Lender's agents upon Lender's written demand to the tenant; (iv) unless applicable law provides otherwise, all Rents collected by Lender or Lender's agents shall be applied first to the costs of taking control of and managing the Property and collecting the Rents, including, but not limited to, attorney's fees, receiver's fees, premiums on receiver's bonds, repair and maintenance costs, insurance premiums, taxes, assessments and other charges on the Property, and then to the sums secured by the Security Instrument; (v) Lender, Lender's agents or any judicially appointed receiver shall be liable to account for only those Rents actually received; and (vi) Lender shall be entitled to have a receiver appointed to take possession of and manage the Property and collect the Rents and profits derived from the

Property without any showing as to the inadequacy of the Property as security.

If the Rents of the Property are not sufficient to cover the costs of taking control of and managing the Property and of collecting the Rents any funds expended by Lender for such purposes shall become indebtedness of Borrower to Lender secured by the Security Instrument pursuant to Section 9.

Borrower represents and warrants that Borrower has not executed any prior assignment of the Rents and has not performed, and will not perform, any act that would prevent Lender from exercising its rights under this paragraph.

Lender, or Lender's agents or a judicially appointed receiver, shall not be required to enter upon, take control of or maintain the Property before or after giving notice of default to Borrower. However, Lender, or Lender's agents or a judicially appointed receiver, may do so at any time when a default occurs. Any application of Rents shall not cure or waive any default or invalidate any other right or remedy of Lender. This assignment of Rents of the Property shall terminate when all the sums secured by the Security Instrument are paid in full.

I. **CROSS-DEFAULT PROVISION.** Borrower's default or breach under any note or agreement in which Lender has an interest shall be a breach under the Security Instrument and Lender may invoke any of the remedies permitted by the Security Instrument.

BY SIGNING BELOW, Borrower accepts and agrees to the terms and covenants contained in this 1–4 Family Rider.

_____(Seal)
-Borrower
_____(Seal)
-Borrower

8. FANNIE MAE/FREDDIE MAC CONDOMINIUM RIDER

Permanent mortgage loans on condominium units are usually made on much the same terms as loans on detached residential real estate. However, the condominium mortgage addresses a variety of concerns that are unimportant or nonexistent in more traditional financing contexts. Most of these concerns relate to the importance of the owners association and the common areas to the long term success of the project and, thus, to the security value of the units themselves. See Chapter 10 supra. The Condominium Rider reflects an attempt to deal with many of these special problems. A separate rider is also required in connection with planned unit development mortgage loans. Because it is virtually identical to the

Condominium Rider, we chose not to include it in this volume. See Fannie Mae/Freddie Mac Multistate PUD Rider Single Family—Form 3150.

CONDOMINIUM RIDER

THIS CONDOMINIUM RIDER is made this _____ day of _____, _____, and is incorporated into and shall be deemed to amend and supplement the Mortgage, Deed of Trust, or Security Deed (the "Security Instrument") of the same date given by the undersigned (the "Borrower") to secure Borrower's Note to _____ (the "Lender") of the same date and covering the Property described in the Security Instrument and located at:

_____

[Property Address]

The Property includes a unit in, together with an undivided interest in the common elements of, a condominium project known as:

_____

[Name of Condominium Project]

(the "Condominium Project"). If the owners association or other entity which acts for the Condominium Project (the "Owners Association") holds title to property for the benefit or use of its members or shareholders, the Property also includes Borrower's interest in the Owners Association and the uses, proceeds and benefits of Borrower's interest.

CONDOMINIUM COVENANTS. In addition to the covenants and agreements made in the Security Instrument, Borrower and Lender further covenant and agree as follows:

- A. **Condominium Obligations**. Borrower shall perform all of Borrower's obligations under the Condominium Project's Constituent Documents. The "Constituent Documents" are the: (i) Declaration or any other document which creates the Condominium Project; (ii) by-laws; (iii) code of regulations; and (iv) other equivalent documents. Borrower shall promptly pay, when due, all dues and assessments imposed pursuant to the Constituent Documents.

- B. **Property Insurance**. So long as the Owners Association maintains, with a generally accepted insurance carrier, a "master" or "blanket" policy on the Condominium Project which is satisfactory to Lender and which provides insurance coverage in the amounts (including deductible levels), for the periods, and against loss by fire, hazards included within the term "extended coverage," and any other hazards, including, but not limited to, earthquakes and floods, from which Lender requires insurance, then: (i) Lender waives the provision in Section 3 for the Periodic

Payment to Lender of the yearly premium installments for property insurance on the Property; and (ii) Borrower's obligation under Section 5 to maintain property insurance coverage on the Property is deemed satisfied to the extent that the required coverage is provided by the Owners Association policy.

What Lender requires as a condition of this waiver can change during the term of the loan.

Borrower shall give Lender prompt notice of any lapse in required property insurance coverage provided by the master or blanket policy.

In the event of a distribution of property insurance proceeds in lieu of restoration or repair following a loss to the Property, whether to the unit or to common elements, any proceeds payable to Borrower are hereby assigned and shall be paid to Lender for application to the sums secured by the Security Instrument, whether or not then due, with the excess, if any, paid to Borrower.

C. **Public Liability Insurance**. Borrower shall take such actions as may be reasonable to insure that the Owners Association maintains a public liability insurance policy acceptable in form, amount, and extent of coverage to Lender.

D. **Condemnation**. The proceeds of any award or claim for damages, direct or consequential, payable to Borrower in connection with any condemnation or other taking of all or any part of the Property, whether of the unit or of the common elements, or for any conveyance in lieu of condemnation, are hereby assigned and shall be paid to Lender. Such proceeds shall be applied by Lender to the sums secured by the Security Instrument as provided in Section 11.

E. **Lender's Prior Consent**. Borrower shall not, except after notice to Lender and with Lender's prior written consent, either partition or subdivide the Property or consent to: (i) the abandonment or termination of the Condominium Project, except for abandonment or termination required by law in the case of substantial destruction by fire or other casualty or in the case of a taking by condemnation or eminent domain; (ii) any amendment to any provision of the Constituent Documents if the provision is for the express benefit of Lender; (iii) termination of professional management and assumption of self-management of the Owners Association; or (iv) any action which would have the effect of rendering the public liability insurance coverage maintained by the Owners Association unacceptable to Lender.

F. Remedies. If Borrower does not pay condominium dues and assessments when due, then Lender may pay them. Any amounts disbursed by Lender under this paragraph F shall become additional debt of Borrower secured by the Security Instrument. Unless Borrower and Lender agree to other terms of payment, these amounts shall bear interest from the date of disbursement at the Note rate and shall be payable, with interest, upon notice from Lender to Borrower requesting payment.

BY SIGNING BELOW, Borrower accepts and agrees to the terms and covenants contained in this Condominium Rider.

_____(Seal)
-Borrower
_____(Seal)
-Borrower

9. FANNIE MAE/FREDDIE MAC SECOND HOME RIDER

Before April 2019, Fannie Mae and Freddie Mac guidelines indicated that owners could not rent a second home if it was encumbered by a mortgage held by Fannie Mae or Freddie Mac. These guidelines were amended to clarify that a second home can be rented, subject to certain conditions that are spelled out in this rider.

SECOND HOME RIDER

THIS SECOND HOME RIDER is made this _____ day of _____, _____, and is incorporated into and shall be deemed to amend and supplement the Mortgage, Deed of Trust, or Security Deed (the "Security Instrument") of the same date given by the undersigned (the "Borrower," whether there are one or more persons undersigned) to secure Borrower's Note to _____

_____
(the "Lender") of the same date and covering the Property described in the Security Instrument (the "Property"), which is located at:

_____

[Property Address]

In addition to the covenants and agreements made in the Security Instrument, Borrower and Lender further covenant and agree that Sections 6 and 8 of the Security Instrument are deleted and are replaced by the following:

6. Occupancy. Borrower will occupy and use the Property as Borrower's second home. Borrower will maintain exclusive control over the occupancy of the Property, including short-term rentals, and will not subject the Property to any timesharing or other shared ownership arrangement or to any rental pool or agreement that requires Borrower either to rent the Property or give a management firm or any other person or entity any control over the occupancy or use of the Property. Borrower will keep the Property available primarily as a residence for Borrower's personal use and enjoyment for at least one year after the date of this Second Home Rider, unless Lender otherwise agrees in writing, which consent shall not be unreasonably withheld, or unless extenuating circumstances exist which are beyond Borrower's control.

8. Borrower's Loan Application. Borrower shall be in default if, during the Loan application process, Borrower or any persons or entities acting at the direction of Borrower or with Borrower's knowledge or consent gave materially false, misleading, or inaccurate information or statements to Lender (or failed to provide Lender with material information) in connection with the Loan. Material representations include, but are not limited to, representations concerning Borrower's occupancy of the Property as Borrower's second home.

BY SIGNING BELOW, Borrower accepts and agrees to the terms and covenants contained in this Second Home Rider.

_____(Seal)

-Borrower
_____(Seal)

-Borrower

10. CONTRACT FOR DEED—INDIVIDUAL SELLER— MINNESOTA

Although Minnesota authorizes nonjudicial foreclosure of mortgages containing a power of sale, installment land contracts (contracts for deed) are frequently used in vendor financing settings. A major reason for this use is to avoid statutory redemption rights that mortgagors and junior lienors enjoy after power of sale foreclosure in Minnesota. See Minn.Stat.Ann. §§ 580.23 & 530.24. The forfeiture clause is enforceable by complying with Minn.Stat.Ann. § 559.21. The following contract for deed form (30.1.1) is part of a compilation published pursuant to Minn.Stat.Ann. § 507.09.

Form 30.1.1 (2011)

DATE: _____

(month/day/year)

THIS CONTRACT FOR DEED (the "Contract") is made on the above date by _____ (insert name and marital status of each Seller) _____ ("Seller"), And _____ (insert name of each Purchaser)

_____, ("Purchaser"). (*Check box if* ❑ *joint tenancy.*)

Seller and Purchaser agree to the following terms:

1.   Property Description. Seller hereby sells and Purchaser hereby buys real property in _____ County, Minnesota, described as follows:

_____

Check here if all or part of the described real property is Registered (Torrens)
❑

together with all hereditaments and appurtenances belonging thereto (the "Property"). Unless otherwise specified, Seller hereby delivers possession of the Property to Purchaser on the date hereof.

Check applicable box:

❑   The Seller certifies that the Seller does not know of any wells on the described real property.

❑   A well disclosure certificate accompanies this document or has been electronically filed. (If electronically filed, insert WDC number:) _____

❑   I am familiar with the property described in this instrument and I certify that the status and number of wells on the described real property have not changed since the last previously filed well disclosure certificate.

2.   Title. Seller warrants that title to the Property is, on the date of this Contract, subject only to the following exceptions:

  (a) Covenants, conditions, restrictions (without effective forfeiture provisions) and declarations of record, if any;

  (b) Reservation of minerals or mineral rights by the State of Minnesota, if any;

  (c) Utility and drainage easements which do not interfere with present improvements;

  (d) Applicable laws, ordinances, and regulations;

  (e) The lien of real estate taxes and installments of special assessments which are payable by Purchaser pursuant to paragraph 6 of this Contract; and

  (f) The following liens or encumbrances:

3.   Delivery of Deed and Evidence of Title. Upon Purchaser's full performance of this Contract, Seller shall:

  (a) Execute, acknowledge, and deliver to Purchaser a _____ Deed, in recordable form, conveying marketable title to the Property to Purchaser, subject only to the following exceptions:

    (i)   Those exceptions referred to in paragraph 2(a), (b), (c), (d), and (e) of this Contract;

    (ii) Liens, encumbrances, adverse claims or other matters which Purchaser has created, suffered or permitted to accrue after the date of this Contract; and

    (iii) The following liens or encumbrances:

  (b) Deliver to Purchaser the abstract of title to the Property, without further extension, to the extent required by the purchase agreement (if any) between Seller and Purchaser.

4. Purchase Price. Purchaser shall pay to Seller at _____ the sum of _____ Dollars ($ _____), as and for the purchase price (the "Purchase Price") for the Property, payable as follows:

5. Prepayment. Unless otherwise provided in this Contract, Purchaser shall have the right to fully or partially prepay this Contract at any time without penalty. Any partial prepayment shall be applied first to payment of amounts then due under this Contract, including unpaid accrued interest, and the balance shall be applied to the principal installments to be paid in the inverse order of their maturity. Partial prepayment shall not postpone the due date of the installments to be paid pursuant to this Contract or change the amount of such installments.

6. Real Estate Taxes and Assessments. Real estate taxes and installments of special assessments which are due and payable in the year in which this Contract is dated shall be paid as follows:

    Purchaser shall pay, before penalty accrues, all real estate taxes and installments of special assessments assessed against the Property which are due and payable in all subsequent years. Seller warrants that the real estate taxes and installments of special assessments which were due and payable in the years preceding the year in which this Contract is dated are paid in full. If the Property is subject to a recorded declaration providing for assessments to be levied against the Property by any owners' association, Purchaser shall promptly pay, when due, all assessments imposed by the owners' association or other governing body as required by the provisions of the declaration or other related documents.

7. Property Insurance.

    (a) Insured Risks and Amounts. Purchaser shall keep all buildings, improvements, and fixtures now or later located on or a part of the Property insured against loss by fire, lightning and such other perils as are included in a standard "all-risk" endorsement, and against loss or damage by all other risks and hazards covered by a standard extended coverage insurance policy, including, without limitation, vandalism, malicious mischief, burglary, theft and, if applicable, steam boiler explosion. Such insurance shall be in an amount no less than the full replacement cost of the buildings, improvements, and fixtures, without deduction for physical depreciation. If any of the buildings, improvements, or fixtures are located in a federally designated flood prone area, and if flood insurance is available for that area, Purchaser shall procure and maintain flood insurance in amounts reasonably satisfactory to Seller.

(b) Other Terms. The insurance policy shall contain a loss payable clause in favor of Seller which provides that Seller's right to recover under the insurance shall not be impaired by any acts or omissions of Purchaser or Seller, and that Seller shall otherwise be afforded all rights and privileges customarily provided a mortgagee under the so-called standard mortgage clause.

(c) Notice of Damage. In the event of damage to the Property by fire or other casualty, Purchaser shall promptly give notice of such damage to Seller and the insurance company.

8. Damage to the Property.

(a) Application of Insurance Proceeds. If the Property is damaged by fire or other casualty, the insurance proceeds paid on account of such damage shall be applied to payment of the amounts payable by Purchaser under this Contract, even if such amounts are not then due to be paid, unless Purchaser makes a permitted election described in the next paragraph. Such amounts shall be first applied to unpaid accrued interest and next to the installments to be paid as provided in this Contract in the inverse order of their maturity. Such payment shall not postpone the due date of the installments to be paid pursuant to this Contract or change the amount of such installments. The balance of insurance proceeds, if any, shall be the property of Purchaser.

(b) Purchaser's Election to Rebuild. If Purchaser is not in default under this Contract, or after curing any such default, and if the mortgagees in any prior mortgages and sellers in any prior contracts for deed do not require otherwise, Purchaser may elect to have that portion of such insurance proceeds necessary to repair, replace, or restore the damaged Property (the "Repairs") deposited in escrow with a bank or title insurance company qualified to do business in the State of Minnesota, or such other party as may be mutually agreeable to Seller and Purchaser. The election may only be made by written notice to Seller within sixty (60) days after the damage occurs. Also, the election will only be permitted if the plans and specifications and contracts for the Repairs are approved by Seller, which approval Seller shall not unreasonably withhold or delay. If such a permitted election is made by Purchaser, Seller and Purchaser shall jointly deposit, when paid, such insurance proceeds into such escrow. If such insurance proceeds are insufficient for the Repairs, Purchaser shall, before the commencement of the Repairs, deposit into such escrow sufficient additional money to insure the full payment for the Repairs. Even if the insurance proceeds are unavailable or are insufficient to pay the cost of the Repairs, Purchaser shall at all times be responsible to pay the full cost of the Repairs. All escrowed funds shall be disbursed by the escrowee in accordance with generally accepted sound construction disbursement procedures. The costs incurred or to be incurred on account of such escrow shall be deposited by Purchaser into such escrow before the commencement of the Repairs. Purchaser shall complete the Repairs as soon as reasonably possible and in a good and workmanlike manner, and in any event the Repairs shall be completed by Purchaser within one (1) year after the damage occurs. If, following the completion of and payment for the Repairs, there remains any undisbursed escrow funds, such funds shall be applied to payment of the amounts payable by Purchaser under this Contract in accordance with paragraph 8(a) above.

(c) Owners' Association. If the Property is subject to a recorded declaration, so long as the owners' association maintains a master or blanket policy of insurance against fire, extended coverage perils and such other hazards and in such amount as are required by this Contract, then: (i) Purchaser's obligation in the Contract to maintain hazard insurance coverage on the Property is satisfied; (ii) the provisions of paragraph 8(a) of this Contract regarding application of insurance proceeds shall be superseded by the provisions of the declaration or other related documents; and (iii) in the event of a distribution of insurance proceeds in lieu of restoration or repair following an insured casualty loss to the Property, any such proceeds payable to Purchaser are hereby assigned and shall be paid to Seller for application to the sum secured by this Contract, with the excess, if any, paid to Purchaser.

9. Injury or Damage Occurring on the Property.

(a) Liability. Seller shall be free from liability and claims for damages by reason of injuries occurring on or after the date of this Contract to any person or persons or property while on or about the Property. Purchaser shall defend and indemnify Seller from all liability, loss, cost, and obligations, including reasonable attorneys' fees, on account of or arising out of any such injuries. However, Purchaser shall have no liability or obligation to Seller for such injuries which are caused by the negligence or intentional wrongful acts or omissions of Seller.

(b) Liability Insurance. Purchaser shall, at Purchaser's own expense, procure and maintain liability insurance against claims for bodily injury, death and property damage occurring on or about the Property in amounts reasonably satisfactory to Seller and naming Seller as an additional insured.

10. Insurance Generally. The insurance which Purchaser is required to procure and maintain pursuant to paragraphs 7 and 9 of this Contract shall be issued by an insurance company or companies licensed to do business in the State of Minnesota and acceptable to Seller. The insurance shall be maintained by Purchaser at all times while any amount remains unpaid under this Contract. The insurance policies shall provide for not less than ten (10) days written notice to Seller before cancellation, non-renewal, termination or change in coverage, and Purchaser shall deliver to Seller a duplicate original or certificate of such insurance policy or policies.

11. Condemnation. If all or any part of the Property is taken in condemnation proceedings instituted under power of eminent domain or is conveyed in lieu thereof under threat of condemnation, the money paid pursuant to such condemnation or conveyance in lieu thereof shall be applied to payment of the amounts payable by Purchaser under this Contract, even if such amounts are not then due to be paid. Such amounts shall be applied in the same manner as a prepayment as provided in paragraph 5 of this Contract. Such payments shall not postpone the due date of the installments to be paid pursuant to this Contract or change the amount of such installments. The balance, if any, shall be the property of Purchaser.

12. Waste, Repair, and Liens. Purchaser shall not remove or demolish any buildings, improvements, or fixtures now or later located on or a part of the Property, nor shall Purchaser commit or allow waste of the Property. Purchaser shall maintain the Property in good condition and repair. Purchaser shall not create or permit to accrue liens or adverse claims against the Property which constitute a lien or claim against Seller's interest in the Property. Purchaser shall pay to Seller all amounts, costs and expenses, including reasonable attorneys' fees, incurred by Seller to remove any such liens or adverse claims.

13. Compliance with Laws. Except for matters which Seller has created, suffered, or permitted to exist prior to the date of this Contract, Purchaser shall comply or cause compliance with all laws and regulations of any governmental authority which affect the Property or the manner of using or operating the same, and with all restrictive covenants, if any, affecting title to the Property or the use thereof.

14. Recording of Contract; Deed Tax. Purchaser shall, at Purchaser's expense, record this Contract in the Office of the County Recorder or Registrar of Titles in the county in which the Property is located within four (4) months after the date hereof. Purchaser shall pay any penalty imposed under Minn. Stat. 507.235 for failure to timely record the Contract. Seller shall, upon Purchaser's full performance of this Contract, pay the deed tax due upon the recording of the deed to be delivered by Seller.

15. Notice of Assignment. If either Seller or Purchaser assigns its interest in the Property, the assigning party shall promptly furnish a copy of such assignment to the non-assigning party.

16. Protection of Interests. If Purchaser fails to pay any sum of money required under the terms of this Contract or fails to perform any of the Purchaser's obligations as set forth in this Contract, Seller may, at Seller's option, pay the same or cause the same to be performed, or both, and the amounts so paid by Seller and the cost of such performance shall be payable at once, with interest at the rate stated in paragraph 4 of this Contract, as an additional amount due Seller under this Contract. If there now exists, or if Seller hereafter creates, suffers or permits to accrue, any mortgage, contract for deed, lien or encumbrance against the Property which is not herein expressly assumed by Purchaser, and provided Purchaser is not in default under this Contract, Seller shall timely pay all amounts due thereon, and if Seller fails to do so, Purchaser may, at Purchaser's option, pay any such delinquent amounts or take any actions reasonably necessary to cure defaults thereunder and deduct the amounts so paid together with interest at the rate provided in this Contract from the payments next coming due under this Contract.

17. Defaults and Remedies. The time of performance by Purchaser of the terms of this Contract is an essential part of this Contract. If Purchaser fails to timely perform any term of this Contract, Seller may, at Seller's option, elect to declare this Contract cancelled and terminated by notice to Purchaser in accordance with applicable law or elect any other remedy available at law or in equity. If Seller elects to terminate this Contract, all right, title, and interest acquired under this Contract by Purchaser shall then cease and terminate, and all improvements made upon the Property and all payments made by Purchaser pursuant to this Contract (including escrow payments, if any) shall belong to Seller as liquidated damages for breach of this Contract. Neither the extension of the time for payment of any sum of money to be paid hereunder nor any waiver by Seller of Seller's rights to declare this Contract forfeited by reason of any breach shall in any manner affect Seller's right to cancel this Contract because of defaults subsequently occurring, and no extension of time shall be valid unless agreed to in writing. After service of notice of default and failure to cure such default within the period allowed by law, Purchaser shall, upon demand, surrender possession of the Property to Seller, but Purchaser shall be entitled to possession of the Property until the expiration of such period. Failure by Seller to exercise one or more remedies available under this paragraph 17 shall not constitute a waiver of the right to exercise such remedy or remedies thereafter.

18. Binding Effect. The terms of this Contract shall run with the land and bind the parties hereto and the successors in interest.

19. Headings. Headings of the paragraphs of this Contract are for convenience only and do not define, limit, or construe the contents of such paragraphs.

20. Additional Terms: Check here if ❏ an addendum to this Contract containing additional terms and conditions is attached hereto.

INDEX

References are to Pages